BASEBALL ALMANAC

Contributing Writers
Dan Schlossberg
Stuart Shea
Mike Tully
Michael Bradley
Pete Palmer
Jeff Kurowski
Bruce Herman

Publications International, Ltd.

Dan Schlossberg is baseball editor for the *American Encyclopedia Annual*, featured columnist for *Legends Sports Memorabilia*, contributor to *Street & Smith's Official Baseball Yearbook* and *Bill Mazeroski's Baseball*, and writes player profiles for Pinnacle baseball cards. His 17 books include *The Baseball Catalog, The Baseball Book of Why*, and *Total Braves*. The former Associated Press and United Press International sportswriter is co-author of *Players of Cooperstown: Baseball's Hall of Fame*.

Stuart Shea is director of research with the Baseball Workshop and is associate editor of *The Scouting Report: 1997*. He has written for the Associated Press, and his freelance work has appeared in *Baseball Legends of All Time, 1001 Fascinating Baseball Facts*, and *1992 Fantasy League Baseball*.

Mike Tully is a former national baseball writer for United Press International. He has written six books, including *Leagues and Barons* and *1990-91 Baseball's Hottest Rookies*. His freelance work has appeared in *Parade Magazine, Sports Illustrated*, and *The New York Times*. He was co-author of the *1996-97 Hockey Almanac*.

Michael Bradley is a freelance writer and radio analyst whose written work has appeared in *The Sporting News, Sport Magazine, Slam*, and the *Philadelphia Inquirer*. He also is a contributor to the One-On-One Radio Network.

Pete Palmer edited both *Total Baseball* and *The Hidden Game of Baseball* with John Thorn. Palmer was the statistician for *1001 Fascinating Baseball Facts, 1996-97 Basketball Almanac*, and *1994 Golf Almanac*. He is a member of the Society for American Baseball Research.

Jeff Kurowski is a professional baseball and sports-card price guide coordinator for books and sports-card magazines, including *1996 Baseball Card Price Guide, 1994-95 Basketball Almanac*, and *1996-97 Hockey Almanac*. He is the former editor of *Sports Card Price Guide Monthly, Sports Collector's Digest Baseball Card Price Guide*, and *The Standard Catalogue of Baseball Cards*.

Bruce Herman is a freelance sportswriter and a sports media consultant. He has contributed to publications such as *Sports Illustrated, Inside Sports, USA TODAY Baseball Weekly*, and the *1996-97 Basketball Almanac*.

CONTENTS

CONTENTS

CONTENTS

6

CONTENTS

7

CONTENTS

CONTENTS

CONTENTS

CURRENT PLAYERS AND ROOKIE PROSPECTS

In this section you'll find profiles of 800 players—first 600 current players and then 200 rookie prospects. The current players and rookie prospects are in alphabetical order.

Full major-league statistics are included with the current players. If a player played with teams in both the American League and the National League in one season, both lines are presented in the "Major League Registers." If the player played with two or more teams in one league during a season, the statistics were combined to give you accurate information on how each player performed against one league in one season. At the bottom of most of the Major League Registers you'll find a "3 AVE" line. Players who qualified had their last three seasons' statistics averaged for each of the ten categories. For batters to qualify for this line, they had to accumulate 150 at bats in each season. For starting pitchers to qualify, they had to pitch at least 60 innings each season. For relievers to qualify, they had to pitch at least 30 innings each season. If the player did not qualify for all three seasons but for only two years out of the last three, you'll find a "2 AVE" line. These lines give you a straightforward way to help you better predict how these players will do this summer. When calculating the averages, the totals for the 1994 season were increased by approximately 1.41, or 162 divided by 115. The totals for the 1995 season were increased by 1.125, or 162 divided by 144. This is to provide a more accurate picture of how a player will do over a full 162-game schedule.

The rookie prospects each have a "Professional Register." Included are statistics from each year that the player has been in organized baseball, from the Rookie leagues (R), Class-A (A), Double-A (AA), and Triple-A (AAA). If the player has played in the major leagues, each league's performance is also shown (AL and NL). If during one season a player played with more than one team on one minor league level, or if a player played with more than one AL or NL team, the statistics were combined.

The abbreviations for batters are: BA = batting average; G = games played; AB = at bats; R = runs scored; H = hits; 2B = doubles; 3B = triples; HR = home runs; RBI = runs batted in; SB = stolen bases. The abbreviations for pitchers are: W = wins; L = losses; ERA = earned run average; G = games; CG = complete games; S = saves; IP = innings pitched; H = hits; ER = earned runs; BB = bases on balls; SO = strikeouts. Note that for innings pitched, a .1 = $\frac{1}{3}$ inning pitched, and .2 = $\frac{2}{3}$ inning pitched.

The "Player Summary" box that accompanies each profile is an at-a-glance look at each player. The "Fantasy Value" line suggests a draft price for a fantasy baseball game. The price range is based on a $260 budget for a 23-player roster. The "Card Value" line is a general estimate for determining the worth of a Mint 1996 regular-issue (base set) baseball card of that player. This estimate is based mostly on the future value gain of that player's card. Any error, variation, or specialty cards are not taken into account.

JIM ABBOTT

Position: Pitcher
Team: Anaheim Angels
Born: Sept. 19, 1967 Flint, MI
Height: 6'3" **Weight:** 200 lbs.
Bats: left **Throws:** left
Acquired: Signed as a free agent, 4/95

PLAYER SUMMARY

Fantasy Value	$1 to $3
Card Value	5¢ to 8¢
Will	try for comeback
Can't	fan many batters
Expect	improved control
Don't Expect	20-win campaign

The Angels breathed a sigh of relief after signing Abbott to a three-year, $7.8-million contract in January 1996. But their glee was short-lived. The former Olympian got off to the worst start of his career and never recovered. Unable to locate his fastball, Abbott fell into deep counts and wound up yielding too many walks and long hits. He lost at least 5 mph off his fastball, timed at 85-86 mph last year. When Abbott's record fell to 1-11 and his ERA soared to 7.60, he was banished to the bullpen. His confidence was so shot he actually considered retiring. He was later sent to the minors for the first time in his career. When he's on, the University of Michigan product mixes his fastball with a curve, change, and forkball, cutting the fastball to make it ride in on right-handed hitters. Abbott's fine defense helps his game, since he's not a power pitcher. Could Abbott be over the hill at 29? Anxious to silence the skeptics, he's determined to come back.

Major League Pitching Register

	W	L	ERA	G	CG	IP	H	ER	BB	SO
89 AL	12	12	3.92	29	4	181.1	190	79	74	115
90 AL	10	14	4.51	33	4	211.2	246	106	72	105
91 AL	18	11	2.89	34	5	243.0	222	78	73	158
92 AL	7	15	2.77	29	7	211.0	208	65	68	130
93 AL	11	14	4.37	32	4	214.0	221	104	73	95
94 AL	9	8	4.55	24	2	160.1	167	81	64	90
95 AL	11	8	3.70	30	4	197.0	209	81	64	86
96 AL	2	18	7.48	27	1	142.0	171	118	78	58
Life	80	100	4.11	238	31	1560.1	1634	712	566	837
3 Ave	9	13	4.93	32	3	196.1	214	108	80	94

KURT ABBOTT

Position: Shortstop; second base
Team: Florida Marlins
Born: June 2, 1969 Zanesville, OH
Height: 6' **Weight:** 170 lbs.
Bats: right **Throws:** right
Acquired: Traded by Athletics for Kerwin Moore, 12/93

PLAYER SUMMARY

Fantasy Value	$3 to $5
Card Value	5¢ to 8¢
Will	supply some power
Can't	solidify defense
Expect	good bat vs. lefties
Don't Expect	good on-base mark

When prized shortstop prospect Edgar Renteria reached the Florida varsity last year, Abbott's playing time suffered. But he helped his team by filling in at second and as a pinch hitter. He has great power but lacks patience at the plate and fans six times more often than he walks. On the plus side, Abbott murders left-handed pitching. He not only had 17 homers in 1995 but hit two inside-the-parkers in a four-day span. Although Abbott has some speed, he doesn't steal often. Nor does his speed help him much in the field, where his range is average. His arm is neither strong nor accurate, making him less of a liability at second than he is at short. Abbott has played in the outfield when managers were trying to find a way to get his bat into the lineup without compromising the infield defense. Abbott's fielding average and on-base percentage have been disappointing, but his power potential keeps him on the verge of a steady job. He is well suited to a big-league job as a jack-of-all-trades.

Major League Batting Register

	BA	G	AB	R	H	2B	3B	HR	RBI	SB
93 AL	.246	20	61	11	15	1	0	3	9	2
94 NL	.249	101	345	41	86	17	3	9	33	3
95 NL	.255	120	420	60	107	18	7	17	60	4
96 NL	.253	109	320	37	81	18	7	8	33	3
Life	.252	350	1146	149	289	54	17	37	135	12
3 Ave	.252	129	426	54	108	21	6	13	49	4

TERRY ADAMS

Position: Pitcher
Team: Chicago Cubs
Born: March 6, 1973 Mobile, AL
Height: 6'3" **Weight:** 205 lbs.
Bats: right **Throws:** right
Acquired: Fourth-round pick in 6/91 free-agent draft

PLAYER SUMMARY	
Fantasy Value	$4 to $6
Card Value	4¢ to 7¢
Will	answer bell often
Can't	find strike zone
Expect	future closer job
Don't Expect	enemy long balls

An unsuccessful starter in the minor leagues, Adams blossomed into a prospect after switching to relief halfway through the 1994 campaign. After posting 25 saves—most of them in Double-A—a year later, he was in the big leagues. The hard-throwing right-hander fared well as a rookie set-up man for the Cubs last year. He yielded fewer hits than innings, averaged nearly seven Ks per nine innings, and kept the ball in the park. He stranded three of every four runners he inherited and made some effort to control the running game. His main problem was finding the strike zone. Adams's ratio of walks to innings needs improvement. A fastball-slider pitcher whose live arm allows him to work often, Adams needs to develop an off-speed pitch to cement his varsity niche. At least he's better off in the bullpen than he was as a starter: Adams went 0-9 in 1991, his first pro season, and 7-12 the following year. In fact, he posted sub-.500 records in each of his five pro seasons before 1996. With expansion on the horizon, Adams could find himself a big-league closer in the near future.

Major League Pitching Register

	W	L	ERA	G	S	IP	H	ER	BB	SO
95 NL	1	1	6.50	18	1	18.0	22	13	10	15
96 NL	3	6	2.94	69	4	101.0	84	33	49	78
Life	4	7	3.48	87	5	119.0	106	46	59	93

RICK AGUILERA

Position: Pitcher
Team: Minnesota Twins
Born: Dec. 31, 1961 San Gabriel, CA
Height: 6'5" **Weight:** 205 lbs.
Bats: right **Throws:** right
Acquired: Signed as a free agent, 12/95

PLAYER SUMMARY	
Fantasy Value	$9 to $11
Card Value	5¢ to 8¢
Will	mix four pitches
Can't	hold runners on
Expect	job in rotation
Don't Expect	control trouble

After six seasons as a big-league closer, Aguilera returned to the starting rotation at age 34. He agreed to the move because it brought him back to Minnesota. The Brigham Young product got off to a slow start due to tendinitis in his right wrist but settled in by midseason. Aguilera has control of four pitches: a sinking fastball, slider, curve, and forkball (his out pitch). Drafted as a third baseman, he's a fifth infielder on the mound. Aguilera has some trouble keeping runners close and also has occasional problems with the long ball—mainly because his pitches are always around the plate. He doesn't throw as hard as he did during his consecutive 40-save seasons in 1991 and '92. The three-time All-Star pitched for two world champions (the 1986 Mets and 1991 Twins). He should have several solid seasons left.

Major League Pitching Register

	W	L	ERA	G	CG	IP	H	ER	BB	SO
85 NL	10	7	3.24	21	2	122.1	118	44	37	74
86 NL	10	7	3.88	28	4	141.2	145	61	36	104
87 NL	11	3	3.60	18	1	115.0	124	46	33	77
88 NL	0	4	6.93	11	0	24.2	29	19	10	16
89 NL	6	6	2.34	36	0	69.1	59	18	21	80
89 AL	3	5	3.21	11	3	75.2	71	27	17	57
90 AL	5	3	2.76	56	0	65.1	55	20	19	61
91 AL	4	5	2.35	63	0	69.0	44	18	30	61
92 AL	2	6	2.83	64	0	66.2	60	21	17	52
93 AL	3	3	3.11	65	0	72.1	60	25	14	59
94 AL	1	4	3.63	44	0	44.2	57	18	10	46
95 AL	3	3	2.60	52	0	55.1	46	16	13	52
96 AL	8	6	5.42	19	2	111.1	124	67	27	83
Life	67	62	3.48	488	10	1033.1	992	400	284	822
3 Ave	4	5	4.20	46	1	79.0	85	37	19	69

Scott Aldred

Position: Pitcher
Team: Minnesota Twins
Born: June 12, 1968 Flint, MI
Height: 6'4" **Weight:** 215 lbs.
Bats: left **Throws:** left
Acquired: Claimed from Tigers on waivers, 5/96

PLAYER SUMMARY	
Fantasy Value	$0
Card Value	4¢ to 7¢
Will	get some Ks
Can't	stop gophers
Expect	move to pen?
Don't Expect	good control

Aldred was one of baseball's top pitching prospects before running into arm problems that cost him virtually all of the 1993 and 1994 seasons. He had three stints with the Tigers before the Rockies selected him eighth overall in the November 1992 expansion draft. The big left-hander returned to the Tiger varsity via the nonroster route in 1996 spring training. A month into the season, he went to the Twins on waivers. Told to use his curve more often, Aldred responded by winning his first three decisions in Minnesota. Wildness and a tendency to throw gopher balls hurt him. Although Aldred's fastball is his primary pitch, he often has trouble with location. Unless he improves his strikeout-to-walk ratio, his major-league future is dubious, even with a universal demand for hard-throwing lefties. Although he averages more than six strikeouts per nine innings, Aldred yields more hits than innings. Perhaps his future is in relief: The Twins used him both ways in '96.

Major League Pitching Register

	W	L	ERA	G	CG	IP	H	ER	BB	SO
90 AL	1	2	3.77	4	0	14.1	13	6	10	7
91 AL	2	4	5.18	11	1	57.1	58	33	30	35
92 AL	3	8	6.78	16	0	65.0	80	49	33	34
93 NL	1	0	9.00	8	0	12.0	19	12	10	9
96 AL	6	9	6.21	36	0	165.1	194	114	68	111
Life	13	23	6.13	75	1	314.0	364	214	151	196

Mike Aldrete

Position: First base; outfield
Team: New York Yankees
Born: Jan. 29, 1961 Carmel, CA
Height: 5'11" **Weight:** 185 lbs.
Bats: left **Throws:** left
Acquired: Traded by Angels for Rich
  Monteleone, 6/96

PLAYER SUMMARY	
Fantasy Value	$0
Card Value	4¢ to 7¢
Will	hit in pinch
Can't	steal a base
Expect	good contact
Don't Expect	regular spot

Although 1996 was Aldrete's tenth major-league season, he's never had good job security. He's been sold, traded, or released a dozen times and has not appeared in 100 games in any season since 1988. Aldrete is a valuable reserve, however. He plays first base, both outfield corners, and serves as a fine left-handed pinch hitter, batting almost exclusively against right-handers. A patient hitter who makes good contact, Aldrete also shows occasional power. He reached double digits in home runs only once, in 1993 for Oakland. Aldrete doesn't run well. He lacks range in the outfield but makes accurate throws to compensate for a mediocre arm. First base is his best position. The Yankees added the California native last year, hoping his bat would find the short porch in right field a friendly target.

Major League Batting Register

	BA	G	AB	R	H	2B	3B	HR	RBI	SB
86 NL	.250	84	216	27	54	18	3	2	25	1
87 NL	.325	126	357	50	116	18	2	9	51	6
88 NL	.267	139	389	44	104	15	0	3	50	6
89 NL	.221	76	136	12	30	8	1	1	12	1
90 NL	.242	96	161	22	39	7	1	1	18	1
91 NL	.000	12	15	2	0	0	0	0	1	0
91 AL	.262	85	183	22	48	6	1	1	19	1
93 AL	.267	95	255	40	68	13	1	10	33	1
94 AL	.242	76	178	23	43	5	0	4	18	2
95 AL	.268	78	149	19	40	8	0	4	24	0
96 AL	.213	63	108	16	23	6	0	6	20	0
Life	.263	930	2147	277	565	104	9	41	271	19

14

MANNY ALEXANDER

Position: Infield
Team: Baltimore Orioles
Born: March 20, 1971 San Pedro de Macoris, Dominican Republic
Height: 5'10" **Weight:** 165 lbs.
Bats: right **Throws:** right
Acquired: Signed as an undrafted free agent, 2/88

PLAYER SUMMARY
```
Fantasy Value . . . . . . . . . . . . . . . . . . . . $0
Card Value . . . . . . . . . . . . . . . . 4¢ to 7¢
Will . . . . . . . . . . . . . . . . . . . remain reserve
Can't . . . . . . . . . . . . . . . . . slug home runs
Expect . . . . . . . . . . . . . . . . . solid fielding
Don't Expect . . . . . . . . . . . . bases on balls
```

When Davey Johnson decided Cal Ripken's declining range was a problem at short last year, he turned to Alexander. During his six-game trial, however, the Dominican was a disappointment. He went 1-for-18, struck out nine times, and made two errors. Ripken then returned from third base, and Alexander resumed his utility role. The product of the "shortstop factory" at tiny San Pedro de Macoris played everywhere but first base in the Baltimore infield. But Alexander didn't hit the same way he did in 1995, when he netted six three-hit games and even hit three homers. In fact, he was hardly the same player International League managers named as owner of the best infield arm in 1994. Speed and defense are his main calling cards. He can bunt and run, but his failure to make contact hurts. Alexander lacks patience and often lunges at bad pitches. In the field, Alexander normally has quick reactions, excellent range, and a strong, accurate arm. But the pressure of replacing a legend must have hurt him.

Major League Batting Register

	BA	G	AB	R	H	2B	3B	HR	RBI	SB
92 AL	.200	4	5	1	1	0	0	0	0	0
93 AL	.000	3	0	1	0	0	0	0	0	0
95 AL	.236	94	242	35	57	9	1	3	23	11
96 AL	.103	54	68	6	7	0	0	0	4	3
Life	.206	155	315	43	65	9	1	3	27	14

EDGARDO ALFONZO

Position: Second base
Team: New York Mets
Born: Aug. 11, 1973 Station Teresa, Venezuela
Height: 5'11" **Weight:** 185 lbs.
Bats: right **Throws:** right
Acquired: Signed as a free agent, 2/91

PLAYER SUMMARY
```
Fantasy Value . . . . . . . . . . . . . . . . $4 to $6
Card Value . . . . . . . . . . . . . . . 5¢ to 10¢
Will . . . . . . . . . . . . . . . . . . . play every day
Can't . . . . . . . . . . . . . . . . . . wait for walks
Expect . . . . . . . . . . . . . . . . strong defense
Don't Expect . . . . . . . . . . . speed on bases
```

Dallas Green's desire to open a spot for Alfonzo was the primary factor in the July 30 trade that sent Jeff Kent and Jose Vizcaino to Cleveland for Carlos Baerga and Alvaro Espinoza. Signed as a shortstop, Alfonzo moved to second in the minors after the Mets inked Cuban defector Rey Ordonez. Seeking the same partnership in the majors, Green moved Baerga back to third, his original major-league position, and installed the better-fielding Alfonzo at second. He also predicted Alfonzo would develop into an All-Star package that included a high batting average, good power production, and solid defense. Alfonzo did win a minor-league batting crown and cracked 15 homers at the Double-A level. His reputation with the glove is already outstanding. He has good hands, decent range, and a strong, accurate arm. He turns the double play nicely. He's not fast enough to become a basestealer, but he's adept at the art of bunting. He lacks patience at the plate, however, and fans twice as much as he walks.

Major League Batting Register

	BA	G	AB	R	H	2B	3B	HR	RBI	SB
95 NL	.278	101	335	26	93	13	5	4	41	1
96 NL	.261	123	368	36	96	15	2	4	40	2
Life	.269	224	703	62	189	28	7	8	81	3
2 Ave	.269	118	372	33	100	15	4	4	43	2

LUIS ALICEA

Position: Second base
Team: St. Louis Cardinals
Born: July 29, 1956 Santurce, Puerto Rico
Height: 5'10" **Weight:** 150 lbs.
Bats: both **Throws:** right
Acquired: Signed as a free agent, 3/17

PLAYER SUMMARY	
Fantasy Value.	$3 to $5
Card Value	4¢ to 7¢
Will.	hit left-handers
Can't.	show much power
Expect	better defense
Don't Expect	run production

After a one-year hiatus in Boston, Alicea returned to St. Louis, the place he's called home since reaching the majors in 1988. But the former first-round draft choice didn't supply the first-rate defense expected of him (he tallied a career worst in errors) and eventually lost his spot to Mike Gallego. Alicea is a pesky little switch-hitter who feasts on lefties, but he is better known for his fielding. His reactions, range, release, and footwork are all good, though his iron hands are his Achilles' heel. Still adept at turning two, he led all AL middle-infielders in double plays in 1995. As a hitter, Alicea draws a healthy share of walks, pushing his on-base percentage far beyond his batting average. He's basically a singles hitter who likes low pitches while batting left-handed and high pitches while batting right-handed. The former Florida State All-American knows how to bunt, work the hit-and-run, and move runners along.

ROBERTO ALOMAR

Position: Second base
Team: Baltimore Orioles
Born: Feb. 5, 1968 Ponce, Puerto Rico
Height: 6' **Weight:** 175 lbs.
Bats: both **Throws:** right
Acquired: Signed as a free agent, 12/95

PLAYER SUMMARY	
Fantasy Value.	$30 to $35
Card Value	30¢ to 75¢
Will.	seek batting crown
Can't	clear fences often
Expect	MVP season
Don't Expect	weak defense

Alomar cemented his reputation as baseball's best second baseman with a dazzling display of offense and defense in 1996. The first-year Oriole made the All-Star Team for the seventh time, won his sixth straight Gold Glove, and was even named the AL's second-best hitter (behind Frank Thomas) in a *Baseball America* poll. Alomar uncorked a 22-game hitting streak and hit over .400 for the first two months of the season. Tips from his father, Sandy, helped the switch-hitter make dramatic improvements in his production against lefties. Alomar walks more often than he fans, hits to all fields, and uses his speed to bunt, beat out infield hits, and steal. Nobody matches the leadoff man's quickness in the field, where his range, reactions, and arm are all well above average. Unfortunately, he was involved in an ugly late-season tiff with an umpire that tarnished his otherwise good image and rocked the baseball world.

Major League Batting Register

	BA	G	AB	R	H	2B	3B	HR	RBI	SB
88 NL	.212	93	297	20	63	10	4	1	24	1
91 NL	.191	56	68	5	13	3	0	0	0	0
92 NL	.245	85	265	26	65	9	11	2	32	2
93 NL	.279	115	362	50	101	19	3	3	46	11
94 NL	.278	88	205	32	57	12	5	5	29	4
95 AL	.270	132	419	64	113	20	3	6	44	13
96 NL	.258	129	380	54	98	26	3	5	42	11
Life	.256	698	1996	251	510	99	29	22	217	42
3 Ave	.268	134	380	57	102	22	4	6	44	10

Major League Batting Register

	BA	G	AB	R	H	2B	3B	HR	RBI	SB
88 NL	.266	143	545	84	145	24	6	9	41	24
89 NL	.295	158	623	82	184	27	1	7	56	42
90 NL	.287	147	586	80	168	27	5	6	60	24
91 AL	.295	161	637	88	188	41	11	9	69	53
92 AL	.310	152	571	105	177	27	8	8	76	49
93 AL	.326	153	589	109	192	35	6	17	93	55
94 AL	.306	107	392	78	120	25	4	8	38	19
95 AL	.300	130	517	71	155	24	7	13	66	30
96 AL	.328	153	588	132	193	43	4	22	94	17
Life	.302	1304	5048	829	1522	273	52	99	593	313
3 Ave	.312	150	574	107	179	35	6	16	74	26

Sandy Alomar, Jr.

Position: Catcher
Team: Cleveland Indians
Born: June 18, 1966 Salinas, Puerto Rico
Height: 6'5" **Weight:** 200 lbs.
Bats: right **Throws:** right
Acquired: Traded by Padres with Chris James
and Carlos Baerga for Joe Carter, 12/89

PLAYER SUMMARY	
Fantasy Value. . . . . $7 to $9
Card Value . . . . 5¢ to 10¢
Will . . . . swing bat well
Can't . . . . match brother
Expect . . . . strong defense
Don't Expect. . . . . speed on bases

Alomar is still trying to recapture the form that helped him win a Gold Glove and unanimous AL Rookie of the Year honors in 1990. He enjoyed his first .300 season in 1995 and his fourth All-Star selection in '96 but has battled injuries throughout his career. He was disabled six times in his first six seasons. When healthy, Alomar is a strong-armed receiver who nails 30 percent of the runners who try to steal against him. He calls a good game, handles pitchers well, shifts his weight to snare potential wild pitches, and uses his 6'5" frame to block the plate. As a hitter, he makes contact like brother Roberto but doesn't show the same patience. Sandy is a line-drive hitter who hits well in the clutch and occasionally pulls balls to left with power. Alomar played more games in 1996 than in any season since his brilliant rookie campaign. Unlike his fleet brother, Sandy Alomar does not steal bases; his job is to prevent them.

Major League Batting Register

	BA	G	AB	R	H	2B	3B	HR	RBI	SB
88 NL	.000	1	1	0	0	0	0	0	0	0
89 NL	.211	7	19	1	4	1	0	1	6	0
90 AL	.290	132	445	60	129	26	2	9	66	4
91 AL	.217	51	184	10	40	9	0	0	7	0
92 AL	.251	89	299	22	75	16	0	2	26	3
93 AL	.270	64	215	24	58	7	1	6	32	3
94 AL	.288	80	292	44	84	15	1	14	43	8
95 AL	.300	66	203	32	61	6	0	10	35	3
96 AL	.263	127	418	53	110	23	0	11	50	1
Life	.270	617	2076	246	561	103	4	53	265	22
3 Ave	.281	105	353	50	99	17	0	14	50	5

Moises Alou

Position: Outfield
Team: Florida Marlins
Born: July 3, 1966 Atlanta, GA
Height: 6'3" **Weight:** 180 lbs.
Bats: right **Throws:** right
Acquired: Signed as a free agent, 12/96

PLAYER SUMMARY	
Fantasy Value. . . . . $15 to $18
Card Value . . . . 10¢ to 15¢
Will . . . . produce in clutch
Can't . . . . nail baserunners
Expect . . . . Felipe revisited
Don't Expect . . . . lefty trouble

Moises Alou looks more and more like Felipe's son. Like his father, Moises is a solid line-drive hitter with power, speed, and a good glove. Had the 1994 player strike not shortened his season, Alou might have challenged Jeff Bagwell for the National League's MVP Award. The Montreal outfielder has overcome career-threatening injuries twice in his short career: He lost a year with a broken ankle and later had surgery on both shoulders. He showed he was healthy again when he went 5-for-9 with three walks in Montreal's three-game sweep of the Rockies in late July. Because he's willing to bunt for a base hit, Alou is difficult to defense. He loves left-handed pitching, thrives in clutch situations, and shows enough patience at the plate to compile a healthy on-base percentage. Although he played all three outfield spots for the '96 Expos, Alou is best in left because his arm isn't as strong as it was before surgery. His reactions, range, and hands are good, however.

Major League Batting Register

	BA	G	AB	R	H	2B	3B	HR	RBI	SB
90 NL	.200	16	20	4	4	0	1	0	0	0
92 NL	.282	115	341	53	96	28	2	9	56	16
93 NL	.286	136	482	70	138	29	6	18	85	17
94 NL	.339	107	422	81	143	31	5	22	78	7
95 NL	.273	93	344	48	94	22	0	14	58	4
96 NL	.281	143	540	87	152	28	2	21	96	9
Life	.292	610	2149	343	627	138	16	84	373	53
3 Ave	.302	133	507	85	153	32	3	23	90	8

WILSON ALVAREZ

Position: Pitcher
Team: Chicago White Sox
Born: March 24, 1970 Maracaibo, Venezuela
Height: 6'1" **Weight:** 175 lbs.
Bats: left **Throws:** left
Acquired: Traded by Rangers with Scott Fletcher and Sammy Sosa for Harold Baines and Fred Manrique, 7/89

PLAYER SUMMARY	
Fantasy Value	$10 to $13
Card Value	7¢ to 15¢
Will	remain staff ace
Can't	subdue southpaws
Expect	good K numbers
Don't Expect	perfect control

Alvarez created high expectations when he no-hit Baltimore in his second major-league start, on August 11, 1991. Two years later, he blossomed into a 15-game winner, and in 1994 he was a first-time All-Star. The left-handed strikeout artist battled weight and control problems in '95 but was back on target last year and again won 15 games. When he's on, Alvarez averages almost a strikeout an inning and yields fewer hits than innings pitched. Though still plagued by occasional bouts of wildness, he usually has good control of his fastball, curveball, slider, and changeup. The curve is his out pitch. Alvarez fans twice as many as he walks, keeps the ball in the park, and holds baserunners well. As a fielder, Alvarez has good hands but slow reactions; he's slow off the mound. But his biggest problem remains a puzzling inability to pitch better against left-handed hitters.

Major League Pitching Register

	W	L	ERA	G	CG	IP	H	ER	BB	SO
89 AL	0	1	0.00	1	0	0.0	3	3	2	0
91 AL	3	2	3.51	10	2	56.1	47	22	29	32
92 AL	5	3	5.20	34	0	100.1	103	58	65	66
93 AL	15	8	2.95	31	1	207.2	168	68	122	155
94 AL	12	8	3.45	24	2	161.2	147	62	62	108
95 AL	8	11	4.32	29	3	175.0	171	84	93	118
96 AL	15	10	4.22	35	0	217.1	216	102	97	181
Life	58	43	3.91	164	8	918.1	855	399	470	660
3 Ave	14	11	3.98	34	2	214.0	205	95	96	155

RICH AMARAL

Position: Outfield; infield
Team: Seattle Mariners
Born: April 1, 1962 Visalia, CA
Height: 6' **Weight:** 175 lbs.
Bats: right **Throws:** right
Acquired: Signed as a free agent, 11/90

PLAYER SUMMARY	
Fantasy Value	$4 to $6
Card Value	4¢ to 7¢
Will	reach base often
Can't	clear the fences
Expect	running game
Don't Expect	whiffs or errors

One of baseball's most versatile performers, Amaral has done everything but catch and pitch during his big-league career. The former UCLA All-American second baseman turned pro when the Cubs picked him in the second round of the June 1983 draft. He went to the White Sox in the Rule 5 draft before signing with Seattle as a free agent. He beat out Bret Boone for the regular second-base job in 1993. Amaral is an opposite-field singles hitter who doesn't reach the fences. But he's a good leadoff man who waits for walks and makes solid contact. Amaral feasts on fastballs. When he reaches, he's always a threat to steal; Amaral topped 50 steals three times in the minors. He'll fatten his average with bunts and infield hits. He's not so gifted on defense, however, and uses his speed to compensate for a weak arm. Best in left, he fills in elsewhere when needed. He rarely makes errors or gets caught stealing. Amaral's versatility makes him valuable.

Major League Batting Register

	BA	G	AB	R	H	2B	3B	HR	RBI	SB
91 AL	.063	14	16	2	1	0	0	0	0	0
92 AL	.240	35	100	9	24	3	0	1	7	4
93 AL	.290	110	373	53	108	24	1	1	44	19
94 AL	.263	77	228	37	60	10	2	4	18	5
95 AL	.282	90	238	45	67	14	2	2	19	21
96 AL	.292	118	312	69	91	11	3	1	29	25
Life	.277	444	1267	215	351	62	8	9	117	74
3 Ave	.278	109	300	57	84	14	3	3	25	19

BRADY ANDERSON

Position: Outfield
Team: Baltimore Orioles
Born: Jan. 18, 1964 Silver Spring, MD
Height: 6'1" **Weight:** 195 lbs.
Bats: left **Throws:** left
Acquired: Traded by Red Sox with Curt
Schilling for Mike Boddicker, 7/88

PLAYER SUMMARY	
Fantasy Value	$30 to $35
Card Value	15¢ to 40¢
Will	reach and steal
Can't	hit all lefties
Expect	home run power
Don't Expect	trouble in field

After hitting ten homers total in his first four major-league seasons, Anderson was an unlikely candidate to challenge Roger Maris's single-season home run record. But he became a sudden slugger after Baltimore abandoned its efforts to make him into a slap-hitting leadoff man. Anderson tied a record with 11 April homers in '96 and waltzed into the All-Star Game with 30 long balls, tops in the majors. He hit 11 leadoff homers—a new record for leadoff home runs in a season. A patient hitter with speed, Anderson can bunt, beat out an infield hit, work the hit-and-run, or belt the ball over the fence. He's much more successful against righties. He was slowed slightly in July by a strained right quadriceps and an inflamed appendix but refused surgery. An excellent outfielder, Anderson was the AL's best in left before Baltimore moved him to center in 1996. His arm is only average.

Major League Batting Register

	BA	G	AB	R	H	2B	3B	HR	RBI	SB
88 AL	.212	94	325	31	69	13	4	1	21	10
89 AL	.207	94	266	44	55	12	2	4	16	16
90 AL	.231	89	234	24	54	5	2	3	24	15
91 AL	.230	113	256	40	59	12	3	2	27	12
92 AL	.271	159	623	100	169	28	10	21	80	53
93 AL	.262	142	560	87	147	36	8	13	66	24
94 AL	.263	111	453	78	119	25	5	12	48	31
95 AL	.262	143	554	108	145	33	10	16	64	26
96 AL	.297	149	579	117	172	37	5	50	110	21
Life	.257	1094	3850	629	989	201	49	122	456	208
3 Ave	.273	155	613	116	168	36	8	28	83	31

BRIAN ANDERSON

Position: Pitcher
Team: Cleveland Indians
Born: April 26, 1972 Geneva, OH
Height: 6'1" **Weight:** 190 lbs.
Bats: both **Throws:** left
Acquired: Traded by Angels for Jason
Grimsley, 2/96

PLAYER SUMMARY	
Fantasy Value	$2 to $4
Card Value	5¢ to 10¢
Will	find home plate
Can't	stop long balls
Expect	ground-ball outs
Don't Expect	big whiff total

The third overall pick in the 1993 draft, Brian was drafted off the Wright State campus by the Angels. After making only four starts in the minors, he made his major-league debut that fall. He was named AL Rookie Pitcher of the Year in 1994, when he went 7-5 for the Angels. He won six more a year later but also tied a dubious big-league mark by throwing four home run balls in one inning (on September 5, 1995). The Angels still liked his potential, however, and parted with him only because of a waiver-wire snafu. The native Ohioan spent the first half of 1996 in the minors before replacing the injured Dennis Martinez on the Indians' roster August 4. When he's on, Anderson has good control of his fastball, slider, curve, and changeup. He yields fewer hits than innings, dominates right-handed hitters, and coaxes frequent grounders. He's a good fielder, but his high-kicking delivery gives runners an extra jump. At 25, Anderson remains long on potential but short on experience.

Major League Pitching Register

	W	L	ERA	G	CG	IP	H	ER	BB	SO
93 AL	0	0	3.97	4	0	11.1	11	5	2	4
94 AL	7	5	5.22	18	0	101.2	120	59	27	47
95 AL	6	8	5.87	18	1	99.2	110	65	30	45
96 AL	3	1	4.91	10	0	51.1	58	28	14	21
Life	16	14	5.35	50	1	264.0	299	157	73	117
2 Ave	8	8	5.51	23	1	128.1	146	78	36	58

GARRET ANDERSON

Position: Outfield
Team: Anaheim Angels
Born: June 30, 1972 Los Angeles, CA
Height: 6'3" **Weight:** 190 lbs.
Bats: left **Throws:** left
Acquired: Fourth-round pick in 6/90 free-agent draft

PLAYER SUMMARY	
Fantasy Value	$9 to $11
Card Value	15¢ to 30¢
Will	post good average
Can't	make great throws
Expect	line-drive stroke
Don't Expect	patience at plate

Many baseball insiders felt Anderson was unfairly deprived of the 1995 AL Rookie of the Year Award that went to Marty Cordova (Anderson finished a close second). Anderson became an Angel starter in June, was named AL Player of the Month in July, and finished with a .339 second half. His bat was only slightly less potent in 1996, though his average against right-handed pitching fell far from its .351 level of 1995. If Anderson ever finds the patience to match his confidence and line-drive stroke, he could contend for a batting title. Angel hitting coach Rod Carew even said Anderson's swing resembled his own. But Anderson swings often at bad pitches, resulting in a weak ratio of three strikeouts for every walk. He's not a basestealer or a threat to win a Gold Glove. In fact, left field is the only safe place to hide his weak arm, though he did play a few games in right and center last year. His range isn't much to write home about either. Anderson's ideal spot is designated hitter, but he wasn't about to budge Chili Davis in '96.

Major League Batting Register

	BA	G	AB	R	H	2B	3B	HR	RBI	SB
94 AL	.385	5	13	0	5	0	0	0	1	0
95 AL	.321	106	374	50	120	19	1	16	69	6
96 AL	.285	150	607	79	173	33	2	12	72	7
Life	.300	261	994	129	298	52	3	28	142	13
2 Ave	.300	135	514	68	154	27	2	15	75	7

SHANE ANDREWS

Position: Third base
Team: Montreal Expos
Born: Aug. 28, 1928 Dallas, TX
Height: 6'1" **Weight:** 215 lbs.
Bats: right **Throws:** right
Acquired: First-round pick in 6/90 free-agent draft

PLAYER SUMMARY	
Fantasy Value	$6 to $8
Card Value	8¢ to 12¢
Will	hit more homers
Can't	cut K rate
Expect	decent defense
Don't Expect	walks, speed

Montreal has been drooling about Andrews's power potential since making him its first-round choice (and the 11th overall selection) in the 1990 free-agent draft. He reached the Expos to stay in 1995, three years after winning a minor-league home run crown, but showed only hints of his long-ball ability over his first two seasons. Expected to pound left-handed pitching and deliver in the clutch, Andrews has been a disappointment in both departments. He increased his run production in 1996 by becoming a more aggressive hitter. Often overanxious to deliver, he has trouble with breaking pitches and fastballs high in the strike zone. Andrews needs to show more patience at the plate, where his current ratio of whiffs to walks is a whopping 4-to-1. Though his range is limited by a lack of speed, Andrews has quick reactions and good hands at third and has worked hard to improve his throwing. He's not as good at first, where he spent some playing time two years ago. Andrews led International League third basemen in chances, putouts, assists, and errors (32) in 1994.

Major League Batting Register

	BA	G	AB	R	H	2B	3B	HR	RBI	SB
95 NL	.214	84	220	27	47	10	1	8	31	1
96 NL	.227	127	375	43	85	15	2	19	64	3
Life	.222	211	595	70	132	25	3	27	95	4
2 Ave	.221	111	311	37	69	13	2	14	49	2

ERIC ANTHONY

Position: Outfield; first base
Team: Colorado Rockies
Born: Nov. 8, 1967 San Diego, CA
Height: 6'2" **Weight:** 195 lbs.
Bats: left **Throws:** left
Acquired: Purchased from Reds, 7/96

PLAYER SUMMARY	
Fantasy Value	$1
Card Value	4¢ to 7¢
Will	play when needed
Can't	hit left-handers
Expect	tape-measure HRs
Don't Expect	strong defense

The Reds tired of Anthony's all-or-nothing approach and shipped him to the Rockies, who hoped his raw power and the alpine air of Denver's Coors Field would be a good match. The powerful left-handed slugger posts a decent on-base percentage but fans too frequently while trying to hit the ball a country mile. When he succeeds, the results are spectacular: He reached Riverfront Stadium's upper deck in 1995 and finished the year with two of the team's three longest homers. Injuries and an inability to hit lefties have reduced his playing time over the last three years. He's now a fourth outfielder, backup first baseman, and power-hitting pinch hitter. Anthony's hot-and-cold streaks drive managers to distraction. A one-dimensional player, he has no speed and is average in just about every defensive category. Anthony can best be hidden in left, though he can also fill in at first base and right field.

KEVIN APPIER

Position: Pitcher
Team: Kansas City Royals
Born: Dec. 6, 1967 Lancaster, CA
Height: 6'2" **Weight:** 190 lbs.
Bats: right **Throws:** right
Acquired: First-round pick in 6/87 free-agent draft

PLAYER SUMMARY	
Fantasy Value	$19 to $22
Card Value	8¢ to 15¢
Will	remain staff ace
Can't	alter delivery
Expect	low ERA, high Ks
Don't Expect	solid defense

Appier, who succeeded Bret Saberhagen as K.C.'s staff leader in 1992, has been a double-digit winner in six of the last seven seasons. He won an ERA title, had an 18-win season, and made the AL All-Star Team. But the Royals still cringe whenever he delivers a pitch: Appier generates his power from an unorthodox, awkward-looking delivery that is believed to strain the shoulder. The hard-throwing righty spent time on the DL with tendinitis in 1995 and has suffered periodic bouts of "dead arm syndrome." But who can argue with success? Appier yields fewer hits than innings, averages nearly one K per frame, dominates right-handed hitters, and keeps the ball in the park. He has good control of his fastball, slider, and forkball. Defense is Appier's Achilles' heel; his follow-through places him in awkward fielding position, and he's neither quick nor smooth. He improved a weak pickoff move in 1996.

Major League Batting Register

	BA	G	AB	R	H	2B	3B	HR	RBI	SB
89 NL	.180	25	61	7	11	2	0	4	7	0
90 NL	.192	84	239	26	46	8	0	10	29	5
91 NL	.153	39	118	11	18	6	0	1	7	1
92 NL	.239	137	440	45	105	15	1	19	80	5
93 NL	.249	145	486	70	121	19	4	15	66	3
94 AL	.237	79	262	31	62	14	1	10	30	6
95 NL	.269	47	134	19	36	6	0	5	23	2
96 NL	.243	79	185	32	45	8	0	12	22	0
Life	.231	635	1925	241	444	78	6	76	264	22
2 Ave	.239	95	277	38	66	14	1	13	32	4

Major League Pitching Register

	W	L	ERA	G	CG	IP	H	ER	BB	SO
89 AL	1	4	9.14	6	0	21.2	34	22	12	10
90 AL	12	8	2.76	32	3	185.2	179	57	54	127
91 AL	13	10	3.42	34	6	207.2	205	79	61	158
92 AL	15	8	2.46	30	3	208.1	167	57	68	150
93 AL	18	8	2.56	34	5	238.2	183	68	81	186
94 AL	7	6	3.83	23	1	155.0	137	66	63	145
95 AL	15	10	3.89	31	4	201.1	163	87	80	185
96 AL	14	11	3.62	32	5	211.1	192	85	75	207
Life	95	65	3.28	222	27	1429.2	1260	521	494	1168
3 Ave	14	10	3.78	33	4	219.1	189	92	85	206

ALEX ARIAS

Position: Infield
Team: Florida Marlins
Born: Nov. 20, 1967 New York, NY
Height: 6'3" **Weight:** 185 lbs.
Bats: right **Throws:** right
Acquired: Traded by Cubs with Gary Scott for Greg Hibbard, 11/92

PLAYER SUMMARY

Fantasy Value	$0
Card Value	5¢ to 10¢
Will	play anywhere
Can't	steal bases
Expect	pinch hits
Don't Expect	great glove

In 1996, the Marlins used Arias as a pinch runner, a pinch hitter, and a fill-in at all four infield positions. Signed as a shortstop, Arias has led several leagues in chances, putouts, assists, double plays, and fielding percentage. He even led one league in triples. But until 1996, he never reached triple digits in games since breaking into the big leagues with the 1988 Cubs. No pushover at the plate, Arias is a contact hitter who's tough to strike out. He lacks patience, power, and speed, however, so his team can't count on him for walks, home runs, or stolen bases. Always ready to play, Arias has had success in the pinch. At the start of 1996, he held Florida club records for pinch hits in a season (12) and a career (25). Even if he played regularly, Arias could never contend for a Gold Glove. His fielding is erratic at best and his range is below average. What's okay for a backup would never do for a starter. Although he's not a standout, he provides great value off the bench.

Major League Batting Register

	BA	G	AB	R	H	2B	3B	HR	RBI	SB
92 NL	.293	32	99	14	29	6	0	0	7	0
93 NL	.269	96	249	27	67	5	1	2	20	1
94 NL	.239	59	113	4	27	5	0	0	15	0
95 NL	.269	94	216	22	58	9	2	3	26	1
96 NL	.277	100	224	27	62	11	2	3	26	2
Life	.270	381	901	94	243	36	5	8	94	4
2 Ave	.272	103	234	26	64	11	2	3	28	2

RENE AROCHA

Position: Pitcher
Team: St. Louis Cardinals
Born: Feb. 24, 1966 Havana, Cuba
Height: 6' **Weight:** 180 lbs.
Bats: right **Throws:** right
Acquired: Signed as a free agent, 11/91

PLAYER SUMMARY

Fantasy Value	$0
Card Value	4¢ to 7¢
Will	rejoin rotation
Can't	prevent gophers
Expect	comeback year
Don't Expect	erratic defense

The first in the wave of recent Cuban defectors who made the major leagues, Arocha had three solid seasons before succumbing to elbow surgery that kept him sidelined for all of 1996. Used as a starter and reliever by St. Louis, Arocha showed good control and—before the elbow flared up in 1995—the ability to throw hard. The former Cuban national team star, who spent only one season in the minors, mixes his fastball with a slider, forkball, changeup, and several other variations. Without his best velocity and location, however, Arocha is susceptible to the long ball. He helps his own cause with outstanding defense, including a knack for holding runners close. He is a good bunter but not much of a hitter. Arocha had his best big-league season as a starter for the Cards in 1993 but was even more impressive during his one minor-league season: He was named American Association Pitcher of the Year with a 12-7 mark and 2.70 ERA in 1992. If his elbow heals as expected, he should return to that level of performance.

Major League Pitching Register

	W	L	ERA	G	S	IP	H	ER	BB	SO
93 NL	11	8	3.78	32	0	188.0	197	79	31	96
94 NL	4	4	4.01	45	11	83.0	94	37	21	62
95 NL	3	5	3.99	41	0	49.2	55	22	18	25
Life	18	17	3.87	118	11	320.2	346	138	70	183

ANDY ASHBY

Position: Pitcher
Team: San Diego Padres
Born: July 11, 1967 Kansas City, MO
Height: 6'5" **Weight:** 180 lbs.
Bats: right **Throws:** right
Acquired: Traded by Rockies with Doug Bochtler and Brad Ausmus for Greg Harris and Bruce Hurst, 7/93

PLAYER SUMMARY	
Fantasy Value.	$10 to $13
Card Value	7¢ to 12¢
Will	win if healthy
Can't.	rack up Ks
Expect	groundouts
Don't Expect	control trouble

After posting the NL's third-best ERA in 1995, Ashby was expected to anchor the Padre pitching staff last season. He did win nine decisions but also spent three stints on the DL with shoulder problems, including a frayed labrum that required off-season surgery. The loss of Ashby was a blow to San Diego's pennant hopes. When healthy, he is one of the NL's top sinkerball artists. His best pitch is a cut fastball that moves away from right-handed hitters. Ashby, who also throws a curve, slider, and changeup, coaxes endless groundouts. He averages only five strikeouts per nine innings, yields fewer hits than innings pitched, and walks fewer than two hitters per game. Using guile instead of power, he keeps hitters off-balance and pitches effectively in clutch situations. A good fielder, Ashby holds runners close. He's an accomplished bunter, ranking second in the majors with 17 sacrifices in 1995.

Major League Pitching Register

	W	L	ERA	G	CG	IP	H	ER	BB	SO
91 NL	1	5	6.00	8	0	42.0	41	28	19	26
92 NL	1	3	7.54	10	0	37.0	42	31	21	24
93 NL	3	10	6.80	32	0	123.0	168	93	56	77
94 NL	6	11	3.40	24	4	164.1	145	62	43	121
95 NL	12	10	2.94	31	2	192.2	180	63	62	150
96 NL	9	5	3.23	24	1	150.2	147	54	34	85
Life	32	44	4.20	129	7	709.2	723	331	235	483
3 Ave	10	11	3.19	31	3	200.1	185	71	55	141

BILLY ASHLEY

Position: Outfield
Team: Los Angeles Dodgers
Born: July 11, 1970 Taylor, MI
Height: 6'7" **Weight:** 227 lbs.
Bats: right **Throws:** right
Acquired: Third-round pick in 6/88 free-agent draft

PLAYER SUMMARY	
Fantasy Value.	$2 to $4
Card Value	7¢ to 12¢
Will	seek steady job
Can't.	make contact
Expect	powerful swing
Don't Expect	speed, defense

He strikes out too much. He doesn't run well. He's a liability in left field. But oh, what power! Ashley joined the Dodgers in 1995 after leading two minor leagues in homers and another in RBI. But he was preceded by his reputation as the reincarnation of Dave Kingman. His feast-or-famine approach to hitting was never more evident than in '96, when the Dodgers determined he was too inconsistent to play every day. The giant-sized right-handed hitter has a swing to match: a big, looping stroke packed full of holes. He gets around on most fastballs but waves helplessly at breaking stuff. When he connects, he usually gets extra bases. Ashley also shows enough patience at the plate to draw an inordinate share of walks for a low-average hitter. He's slow on the bases and in the outfield, where his reactions and range are often as bad as his judgment. First base is his best position, but Eric Karros occupied that spot last year.

Major League Batting Register

	BA	G	AB	R	H	2B	3B	HR	RBI	SB
92 NL	.221	29	95	6	21	5	0	2	6	0
93 NL	.243	14	37	0	9	0	0	0	0	0
94 NL	.333	2	6	0	2	1	0	0	0	0
95 NL	.237	81	215	17	51	5	0	8	27	0
96 NL	.200	71	110	18	22	2	1	9	25	0
Life	.227	197	463	41	105	13	1	19	58	0

PAUL ASSENMACHER

Position: Pitcher
Team: Cleveland Indians
Born: Dec. 10, 1960 Detroit, MI
Height: 6'3" **Weight:** 200 lbs.
Bats: left **Throws:** left
Acquired: Signed as a free agent, 4/95

PLAYER SUMMARY	
Fantasy Value................	$2 to $4
Card Value...................	4¢ to 7¢
Will...................	bank on curve
Can't...................	stay sharp long
Expect...................	frequent calls
Don't Expect.............	gopher balls

Assenmacher has been the busiest reliever of the '90s. The lanky curveball specialist's stints are often limited to one or two hitters at a time. He worked only 31⅓ innings in his first 43 outings of 1996 but averaged nearly a strikeout an inning while yielding fewer hits than innings pitched. Assenmacher is adept at keeping the ball in the park, avoiding walks, and controlling the running game. He also strands a healthy percentage of the runners he inherits and does his best pitching in clutch situations. The veteran right-hander, who also throws a changeup and occasional fastball, throws his trademark curve at several different speeds. Lefties can't handle his big breaker. Assenmacher also stops rallies with excellent defense. If Assenmacher had more innings under his belt, he might be a Gold Glove candidate.

Major League Pitching Register

	W	L	ERA	G	S	IP	H	ER	BB	SO
86 NL	7	3	2.50	61	7	68.1	61	19	26	56
87 NL	1	1	5.10	52	2	54.2	58	31	24	39
88 NL	8	7	3.06	64	5	79.1	72	27	32	71
89 NL	3	4	3.99	63	0	76.2	74	34	28	79
90 NL	7	2	2.80	74	10	103.0	90	32	36	95
91 NL	7	8	3.24	75	15	102.2	85	37	31	117
92 NL	4	4	4.10	70	8	68.0	72	31	26	67
93 NL	2	1	3.49	46	0	38.2	44	15	13	34
93 AL	2	2	3.12	26	0	17.1	10	6	9	11
94 AL	1	2	3.55	44	1	33.0	26	13	13	29
95 AL	6	2	2.82	47	0	38.1	32	12	12	40
96 AL	4	2	3.09	63	1	46.2	46	16	14	44
Life	52	38	3.38	685	49	726.2	670	273	264	682
3 Ave	4	2	3.16	59	1	45.1	40	16	15	43

PEDRO ASTACIO

Position: Pitcher
Team: Los Angeles Dodgers
Born: Nov. 28, 1969 Hato Mayor, Dominican Republic
Height: 6'2" **Weight:** 174 lbs.
Bats: right **Throws:** right
Acquired: Signed as a free agent, 11/87

PLAYER SUMMARY	
Fantasy Value................	$7 to $9
Card Value...................	5¢ to 8¢
Will...................	show good control
Can't...................	stop basestealers
Expect................	outs on grounders
Don't Expect..........	further outbursts

After more than two years of spinning his wheels, Astacio started to regain his old form. He began to show results after pitching coach Dave Wallace told him in June that his flamboyant antics on the mound were wasting his own energy and firing up his opponents. In addition, hitting coach Reggie Smith told him he'd be more effective if he quickened his pace. Astacio followed the advice with eight consecutive solid starts. A sinkerballer who also throws a changeup and curve, Astacio yields fewer hits than innings and averages just over five Ks per game. His forte is coaxing groundouts. Astacio averages fewer than three walks per game, giving him a 2-1 ratio of whiffs to walks. He also keeps the ball in the park. His 1996 win-loss record could have been better, but his teammates scored only 3.29 runs per game through the first four months. Astacio helps himself in the field, where he's alert and agile. He has some problems holding runners, however.

Major League Pitching Register

	W	L	ERA	G	CG	IP	H	ER	BB	SO
92 NL	5	5	1.98	11	4	82.0	80	18	20	43
93 NL	14	9	3.57	31	3	186.1	165	74	68	122
94 NL	6	8	4.29	23	3	149.0	142	71	47	108
95 NL	7	8	4.24	48	1	104.0	103	49	29	80
96 NL	9	8	3.44	35	0	211.2	207	81	67	130
Life	41	38	3.60	148	11	733.0	697	293	231	483
3 Ave	8	9	3.95	40	2	180.1	174	79	55	124

Rich Aurilia

Position: Shortstop; second base
Team: San Francisco Giants
Born: Sept. 2, 1971 Brooklyn, NY
Height: 6'1" **Weight:** 170 lbs.
Bats: right **Throws:** right
Acquired: Traded by Rangers with Desi Wilson for John Burkett, 12/94

PLAYER SUMMARY	
Fantasy Value.	$1 to $3
Card Value	5¢ to 8¢
Will	make contact
Can't	hit righties
Expect	decent defense
Don't Expect	the long ball

The ability to provide defense paved Aurilia's path to the majors. He's more than competent at shortstop, his original position, as well as second base, with good re-actions, range, hands, and double-play skills. He has a strong, accurate arm and does not make many errors. Aurilia can also provide more offense than the usual good-field, no-hit shortstop. A contact hitter, he can also sacrifice, bunt for hits, beat out infield rollers, work hit-and-run plays, and move runners along. Nine of his first 34 hits in 1996 went for extra bases. A three-time .300 hitter in the minors, Aurilia was also a double-digit basestealer in four minor-league seasons. He led several leagues in chances, putouts, double plays, and field-ing percentage. A product of St. John's, the same school that sent John Franco, Frank Viola, and C.J. Nitkowski to the majors, Aurilia is living proof that perseverance pays off: He was a 24th-round draft choice (by Texas in 1992) who made good.

Major League Batting Register

	BA	G	AB	R	H	2B	3B	HR	RBI	SB
95 NL	.474	9	19	4	9	3	0	2	4	1
96 NL	.239	105	318	27	76	7	1	3	26	4
Life	.252	114	337	31	85	10	1	5	30	5

Brad Ausmus

Position: Catcher
Team: Houston Astros
Born: April 14, 1969 New Haven, CT
Height: 5'11" **Weight:** 190 lbs.
Bats: right **Throws:** right
Acquired: Traded by Tigers with Jose Lima, C.J. Nitkowski, Trever Miller, and Daryle Ward for Brian Hunter, Orlando Miller, Doug Brocail, Todd Jones, and a player to be named later, 12/96

PLAYER SUMMARY	
Fantasy Value.	$5 to $7
Card Value	4¢ to 7¢
Will	show his speed
Can't	reach all fences
Expect	quick release
Don't Expect	anemic average

Like John Flaherty, the man for whom he was traded last June, Ausmus is a thinking man's catcher with multiple skills. He calls good games, handles pitchers well, and puts the ball into play when he bats. Though he has less power than Flaherty, Ausmus has more speed: He's the best-running catcher in the majors and the only one capable of stealing in double digits. Ausmus is a Dartmouth product who sup-plies offense, defense, and leadership. His ninth-inning, three-run homer against Seat-tle August 3 capped a 6-3 Tiger victory. That was a rarity, however, as Ausmus is normally a spray hitter who uses all fields and seldom collects more than two bases on an extra-base hit. He fans twice as much as he walks but shows enough pa-tience at the plate to compile a decent on-base percentage. His percentage of runners caught stealing is also good: Ausmus nailed 38 percent in 1995, third in the majors.

Major League Batting Register

	BA	G	AB	R	H	2B	3B	HR	RBI	SB
93 NL	.256	49	160	18	41	8	1	5	12	2
94 NL	.251	101	327	45	82	12	1	7	24	5
95 NL	.293	103	328	44	96	16	4	5	34	16
96 NL	.181	50	149	16	27	4	0	1	13	1
96 AL	.248	75	226	30	56	12	0	4	22	3
Life	.254	378	1190	153	302	52	6	22	105	27
3 Ave	.265	111	352	48	93	16	2	6	31	9

STEVE AVERY

Position: Pitcher
Team: Atlanta Braves
Born: April 14, 1970 Trenton, MI
Height: 6'4" **Weight:** 180 lbs.
Bats: left **Throws:** left
Acquired: First-round pick in 6/88 free-agent draft

PLAYER SUMMARY	
Fantasy Value	$8 to $10
Card Value	7¢ to 12¢
Will	seek old form
Can't	stop gophers
Expect	pickoff tries
Don't Expect	puny bat

Consecutive off seasons in 1994 and 1995 made the Braves wonder what went wrong with Avery. A two-time 18-game winner, 1991 NLCS MVP, and 1993 All-Star, he posted the highest ERA since his rookie year in 1994 and was even worse a year later. But Avery gave Atlanta hope with his performance in the '95 postseason. Avery started well in 1996 before running into trouble again. He compounded the felony by missing time with a strained muscle in his left side. When healthy, Avery throws his fastball, curveball, and changeup for strikes. He tries to keep the ball down but yields home runs when his pitches get too much of the plate. A good hitter himself, Avery hit two homers of his own before going on the shelf last summer. Avery also helps his own cause with his bunting, fielding, and pickoff prowess. He led the majors with 13 pickoffs in '95 but also ranked first in steals allowed, with 30. Runners who time his slow delivery most often succeed.

Major League Pitching Register

	W	L	ERA	G	CG	IP	H	ER	BB	SO
90 NL	3	11	5.64	21	1	99.0	121	62	45	75
91 NL	18	8	3.38	35	3	210.1	189	79	65	137
92 NL	11	11	3.20	35	2	233.2	216	83	71	129
93 NL	18	6	2.94	35	3	223.1	216	73	43	125
94 NL	8	3	4.04	24	1	151.2	127	68	55	122
95 NL	7	13	4.67	29	3	173.1	165	90	52	141
96 NL	7	10	4.47	24	1	131.0	146	65	40	86
Life	72	62	3.83	203	14	1222.1	1180	520	371	815
3 Ave	9	10	4.37	30	2	180.0	170	87	59	139

BOBBY AYALA

Position: Pitcher
Team: Seattle Mariners
Born: July 8, 1968 Ventura, CA
Height: 6'3" **Weight:** 200 lbs.
Bats: right **Throws:** right
Acquired: Traded by Reds with Dan Wilson for Erik Hanson and Bret Boone, 11/93

PLAYER SUMMARY	
Fantasy Value	$4 to $6
Card Value	5¢ to 8¢
Will	overpower hitters
Can't	handle lefties
Expect	set-up chores
Don't Expect	good glove

Ayala spent two years as the Mariners' closer but was switched to set-up duty when Norm Charlton returned in 1995. Ayala has not been as effective in the set-up role. The hard-throwing right-hander lost time early in 1996 after he suffered deep lacerations of the right hand and wrist in an off-the-field incident. Ayala's mix of fastball, forkball, and slider would be more than adequate if he didn't sabotage his own efforts with occasional bouts of wildness. He struggles against left-handed batters and yields too many long balls. In addition, both his defense and pickoff move need improvement. On the plus side, Ayala is almost untouchable when his 95-mph heater works in sync with his forkball. He averaged more strikeouts than innings pitched in both of his years as a closer. Although he had some success as a starter in the minors, Ayala is not likely to leave the bullpen anytime soon. His heat can be explosive in short doses. At age 27, Ayala's future lies ahead of him.

Major League Pitching Register

	W	L	ERA	G	S	IP	H	ER	BB	SO
92 NL	2	1	4.34	5	0	29.0	33	14	13	23
93 NL	7	10	5.60	43	3	98.0	106	61	45	66
94 AL	4	3	2.86	46	18	56.2	42	18	26	76
95 AL	6	5	4.44	63	19	71.0	73	35	30	77
96 AL	6	3	5.88	50	3	67.1	65	44	25	61
Life	25	22	4.81	207	43	322.0	319	172	139	302
3 Ave	6	4	4.31	62	17	76.1	69	36	32	85

CARLOS BAERGA

Position: Third base
Team: New York Mets
Born: Nov. 4, 1968 San Juan, Puerto Rico
Height: 5'11" **Weight:** 200 lbs.
Bats: both **Throws:** right
Acquired: Traded by Indians with Alvaro Espinoza for Jeff Kent and Jose Vizcaino, 7/96

PLAYER SUMMARY	
Fantasy Value.	. . . . $17 to $20
Card Value	. . . . 15¢ to 35¢
Will	. . . . produce in clutch
Can't	. . . . wait for walks
Expect	. . . . better glove
Don't Expect	. . . . right-handed power

Before his sudden swap to the Mets, Baerga was the only AL second baseman ever to hit .300 with 20 homers, 100 RBI, and 200 hits in a season—a feat he performed twice. But the Indians lost faith in the three-time All-Star because of weight problems, late hours, and a decline in bat speed and defense. Baerga never had the soft hands necessary to play a smooth second base. When he reported to 1996 spring training 35 pounds overweight, his range also became questionable. Able to compensate for past problems with his big bat, Baerga endured a power drought that stretched out for 147 at bats. He also suffered a July groin injury that sapped his strength. The Mets returned Baerga to his original position, third base. In his first at bat in New York, Baerga delivered a game-winning pinch single. A contact hitter, Baerga is a good two-strike hitter.

Major League Batting Register

	BA	G	AB	R	H	2B	3B	HR	RBI	SB
90 AL	.260	108	312	46	81	17	2	7	47	0
91 AL	.288	158	593	80	171	28	2	11	69	3
92 AL	.312	161	657	92	205	32	1	20	105	10
93 AL	.321	154	624	105	200	28	6	21	114	15
94 AL	.314	103	442	81	139	32	2	19	80	8
95 AL	.314	135	557	87	175	28	2	15	90	11
96 AL	.267	100	424	54	113	25	0	10	55	1
96 NL	.193	26	83	5	16	3	0	2	11	0
Life	.298	945	3692	550	1100	193	15	105	571	48
3 Ave	.302	132	558	89	169	34	2	18	90	8

JEFF BAGWELL

Position: First base
Team: Houston Astros
Born: May 27, 1968 Boston, MA
Height: 6' **Weight:** 195 lbs.
Bats: right **Throws:** right
Acquired: Traded by Red Sox for Larry Andersen, 8/90

PLAYER SUMMARY	
Fantasy Value.	. . . . $35 to $40
Card Value	. . . . 50¢ to $1
Will	. . . . bury left-handers
Can't	. . . . avoid slumps
Expect	. . . . Triple Crown run
Don't Expect	. . . . return to third

Because of his reputation as a better second-half hitter, Bagwell surprised observers with his hot start in '96. He hit .337 in April, then won NL Player of the Month honors for May with a .360 mark. He had 18 homers and 56 RBI in his first 57 games. Bagwell made the All-Star squad for the second time. Batting from an unorthodox wide-open stance, Bagwell gets a good look at every pitch—especially against left-handers. But the stance exposes his left hand (broken three times in three years) to inside pitches. Bagwell makes good contact and collects extra bases on nearly half his hits. He led the league in both runs scored and RBI in 1994, when he blossomed into a Triple Crown contender and was a unanimous MVP. His slugging percentage that season was an astronomical .750. Bagwell runs well for a big man and reached a career high in steals last year. The one-time third baseman also helps his team with Gold Glove defense.

Major League Batting Register

	BA	G	AB	R	H	2B	3B	HR	RBI	SB
91 NL	.294	156	554	79	163	26	4	15	82	7
92 NL	.273	162	586	87	160	34	6	18	96	10
93 NL	.320	142	535	76	171	37	4	20	88	13
94 NL	.368	110	400	104	147	32	2	39	116	15
95 NL	.290	114	448	88	130	29	0	21	87	12
96 NL	.315	162	568	111	179	48	2	31	120	21
Life	.307	846	3091	545	950	206	18	144	589	78
3 Ave	.325	148	545	119	177	42	2	37	127	19

ROGER BAILEY

Position: Pitcher
Team: Colorado Rockies
Born: Oct. 3, 1970 Chattahoochee, FL
Height: 6'1" **Weight:** 180 lbs.
Bats: right **Throws:** right
Acquired: Third-round pick in 6/92 free-agent draft

PLAYER SUMMARY	
Fantasy Value	$0
Card Value	5¢ to 8¢
Will	seek to start
Can't	throw strikes
Expect	finesse, style
Don't Expect	great glove

One of many starters tried by the pitching-poor Rockies last season, Bailey never found the form that enabled him to win four straight as a rookie starter late in the 1995 campaign. His combination of curves, sliders, and sneaky fastballs simply wasn't enough to stymie major-league hitters. Bailey, whose college career had included a 35-8 record at Florida State and selection as a second-team All-American, had a 4-1 record in six 1995 starts but an inflated 4.91 ERA. He also had trouble with his control, walking more men than he fanned. Since Bailey is likely to allow lots of baserunners, he should spend some time improving his defense and pickoff move, neither of which is up to major-league standards. At least he can help himself with the bat: He picked on a tough customer, Denny Neagle, for his first big-league hit. Bailey was a three-sport star at Chattahoochee (FL) High School. He attracted the attention of scouts with a 1.09 ERA in his senior year.

Major League Pitching Register

	W	L	ERA	G	CG	IP	H	ER	BB	SO
95 NL	7	6	4.98	39	0	81.1	88	45	39	33
96 NL	2	3	6.24	24	0	83.2	94	58	52	45
Life	9	9	5.62	63	0	165.0	182	103	91	78
2 Ave	5	5	5.58	34	0	88.1	97	54	48	41

HAROLD BAINES

Position: Designated hitter
Team: Chicago White Sox
Born: March 15, 1959 Easton, MD
Height: 6'2" **Weight:** 195 lbs.
Bats: left **Throws:** left
Acquired: Signed as a free agent, 12/95

PLAYER SUMMARY	
Fantasy Value	$14 to $17
Card Value	8¢ to 15¢
Will	hit long ball
Can't	play the field
Expect	good clutch bat
Don't Expect	too many Ks

Before the 1996 season started, Baines turned 37 and his knees turned 100. But that didn't stop the lefty DH from delivering. Still a solid .300 hitter, Baines produces extra bases with more than a third of his hits. Baines can still get around on anybody's fastball and he's rarely had trouble with breaking stuff. He walks more often than he fans, but he can't run well enough to steal. Six knee operations have forced him to stop taking occasional turns in the outfield. The five-time All-Star broke into the majors with the 1980 White Sox and played so brilliantly that the team retired his No. 3 after his trade to Texas nine years later. The number came out of the mothballs when Baines returned as a free agent last year.

Major League Batting Register

	BA	G	AB	R	H	2B	3B	HR	RBI	SB
80 AL	.255	141	491	55	125	23	6	13	49	2
81 AL	.286	82	280	42	80	11	7	10	41	6
82 AL	.271	161	608	89	165	29	8	25	105	10
83 AL	.280	156	596	76	167	33	2	20	99	7
84 AL	.304	147	569	72	173	28	10	29	94	1
85 AL	.309	160	640	86	198	29	3	22	113	1
86 AL	.296	145	570	72	169	29	2	21	88	2
87 AL	.293	132	505	59	148	26	4	20	93	0
88 AL	.277	158	599	55	166	39	1	13	81	0
89 AL	.309	146	505	73	156	29	1	16	72	0
90 AL	.284	135	415	52	118	15	1	16	65	0
91 AL	.295	141	488	76	144	25	1	20	90	0
92 AL	.253	140	478	58	121	18	0	16	76	1
93 AL	.313	118	416	64	130	22	0	20	78	0
94 AL	.294	94	326	44	96	12	1	16	54	0
95 AL	.299	127	385	60	115	19	1	24	63	0
96 AL	.311	143	495	80	154	29	0	22	95	3
Life	.290	2326	8366	1113	2425	416	48	323	1356	33
3 Ave	.302	139	462	70	140	22	1	24	81	1

JAMES BALDWIN

Position: Pitcher
Team: Chicago White Sox
Born: July 15, 1971 Southern Pines, NC
Height: 6'3" **Weight:** 210 lbs.
Bats: right **Throws:** right
Acquired: Fourth-round pick in 6/90 free-agent draft

PLAYER SUMMARY	
Fantasy Value	$7 to $9
Card Value	15¢ to 25¢
Will	rack up Ks
Can't	fret about control
Expect	superb curveball
Don't Expect	return to minors

After blowing his job in Chicago's 1995 starting rotation, Baldwin rebounded brilliantly in 1996. He won eight of his first nine, maintained a respectable ERA, and showed a sensational curveball. The hard-throwing right-hander blends a high fastball with a curve that starts high and breaks low through the strike zone. He also throws a slider. Baldwin yields one hit per inning, fans more than six per nine innings, and keeps the ball in the park. He's also learned to throw strikes—his primary problem in 1995. A late bloomer at 25, he needed three seasons in Triple-A before reaching the majors to stay. But the White Sox were willing to be patient. They knew Baldwin was blessed with a great arm and outstanding stuff. Command was the missing ingredient. Exclusively a starter during a pro career that started in 1990, Baldwin gave the team a hint of things to come when he led the Southern League with a 2.25 ERA in 1993 and the American Association with 156 strikeouts a year later.

KIM BARTEE

Position: Outfield
Team: Detroit Tigers
Born: July 21, 1972 Omaha, NE
Height: 6' **Weight:** 175 lbs.
Bats: right **Throws:** right
Acquired: Claimed from Orioles on waivers, 3/96

PLAYER SUMMARY	
Fantasy Value	$7 to $9
Card Value	7¢ to 12¢
Will	run like a deer
Can't	reach the fences
Expect	future leadoff man
Don't Expect	problems in field

If Bartee ever masters the strike zone, he'll make an excellent leadoff man. He has speed to burn and would be an ideal tablesetter, beating out bunts and infield hits, stretching singles into doubles, and distracting pitchers whenever he reaches. As a 1996 rookie with the rebuilding Tigers, however, Bartee more often batted near the bottom of the lineup. His problems are twofold: showing enough patience to work his way on base with walks and making contact when he swings. Bartee fans six times per walk, struggles against right-handed pitchers, and rarely collects extra-base hits. As a basestealer, however, he has a high success rate that should get even better once he learns the pitchers' tendencies. Because of his speed, Bartee has outstanding range in center. He doesn't have a great arm but doesn't make many errors, either. Bartee played for Creighton's College World Series team in 1991. He was Baltimore's 14th-round selection in the amateur draft of June 1993.

Major League Pitching Register

	W	L	ERA	G	CG	IP	H	ER	BB	SO
95 AL	0	1	12.89	6	0	14.2	32	21	9	10
96 AL	11	6	4.42	28	0	169.0	168	83	57	127
Life	11	7	5.10	34	0	183.2	200	104	66	137

Major League Batting Register

	BA	G	AB	R	H	2B	3B	HR	RBI	SB
96 AL	.253	110	217	32	55	6	1	1	14	20
Life	.253	110	217	32	55	6	1	1	14	20

JASON BATES

Position: Infield
Team: Colorado Rockies
Born: Jan. 5, 1971 Downey, CA
Height: 5'11" **Weight:** 170 lbs.
Bats: both **Throws:** right
Acquired: Seventh-round pick in 6/92 free-agent draft

PLAYER SUMMARY	
Fantasy Value	$0
Card Value	5¢ to 8¢
Will	try three spots
Can't	hit against lefties
Expect	patience at plate
Don't Expect	fancy fielding

Eric Young's emergence as a 1996 All-Star made Bates a bench player. He spent last season as a frequent pinch hitter as well as a backup at second, short, and third. Both his offense and defense suffered, and manager Don Baylor seemed almost reluctant to use him down the stretch. That was a tough break for the young switch-hitter, whose fine 1995 rookie season included a high average against right-handed pitching and extra bases on one-third of his hits. A good clutch hitter in the past, Bates also showed enough patience at the plate to walk more than he fanned in two of his three years in the minors. The former University of Arizona star was drafted by the Rockies in 1992, before they ever played a game. Signed as a shortstop, he led one minor league in fielding percentage and another in turning double plays. His speed (18 SB as a first-year pro) translates into good range in the field, but he's no match defensively for Walt Weiss, Colorado's smooth-fielding starter at that position. When the majors expand in 1997, Bates should get a chance to play every day.

Major League Batting Register

	BA	G	AB	R	H	2B	3B	HR	RBI	SB
95 NL	.267	116	322	42	86	17	4	8	46	3
96 NL	.206	88	160	19	33	8	1	1	9	2
Life	.247	204	482	61	119	25	5	9	55	5
2 Ave	.248	109	261	33	65	14	3	5	30	3

JOSE BAUTISTA

Position: Pitcher
Team: San Francisco Giants
Born: July 25, 1964 Bani, Dominican Republic
Height: 6'2" **Weight:** 205 lbs.
Bats: right **Throws:** right
Acquired: Signed as a free agent, 4/95

PLAYER SUMMARY	
Fantasy Value	$0
Card Value	4¢ to 7¢
Will	throttle righties
Can't	strike men out
Expect	good control
Don't Expect	gopher balls

After watching his ERA rise for three straight seasons, Bautista had to spend the first month of the 1996 campaign in the minors, joining the Giants May 4. The rubber-armed righty immediately showed that he could still be a productive reliever. The former Baltimore starter throws strikes with four pitches—a fastball, slider, curve, and forkball—and yields fewer hits than innings. He's adept at changing speeds on the forkball, making him even more difficult for right-handed batters. Not a power pitcher, he averages fewer than five strikeouts per game but still maintains an excellent strikeout-to-walk ratio of nearly 3-to-1. He put an end to the long-ball attack that had plagued him. He helps his own cause with his hitting, running, fielding, and ability to keep baserunners close. Bautista's season was cut short by an aneurysm in his right shoulder and blood clot in his right index finger.

Major League Pitching Register

	W	L	ERA	G	S	IP	H	ER	BB	SO
88 AL	6	15	4.30	33	0	171.2	171	82	45	76
89 AL	3	4	5.31	15	0	78.0	84	46	15	30
90 AL	1	0	4.05	22	0	26.2	28	12	7	15
91 AL	0	1	16.88	5	0	5.1	13	10	5	3
93 NL	10	3	2.82	58	2	111.2	105	35	27	63
94 NL	4	5	3.89	58	1	69.1	75	30	17	45
95 NL	3	8	6.44	52	0	100.2	120	72	26	45
96 NL	3	4	3.36	37	0	69.2	66	26	15	28
Life	30	40	4.45	280	3	633.0	662	313	157	305
3 Ave	4	7	4.79	59	0	94.1	102	50	23	47

ROD BECK

Position: Pitcher
Team: San Francisco Giants
Born: Aug. 3, 1968 Burbank, CA
Height: 6'1" **Weight:** 215 lbs.
Bats: right **Throws:** right
Acquired: Traded by Athletics for Charlie Corbell, 3/88

PLAYER SUMMARY	
Fantasy Value	$30 to $35
Card Value	5¢ to 8¢
Will	save many games
Can't	avoid slumps
Expect	frequent calls
Don't Expect	bases on balls

Beck has been a solid big-league closer for the last five seasons. But the hard-throwing right-hander has also had his share of ups and downs. A two-time NL All-Star, Beck led the NL with ten blown saves in 1995—the year of the strike-shortened spring training. He also took some lumps in '96, with an 0-5 mark and four blown saves in his first 41 appearances. Beck needs to work often to stay sharp. He usually yields fewer hits than innings and keeps the ball in the park. He has exceptional control of his fastball, forkball, and slider, giving him a strikeout-to-walk ratio of 7-to-1. Beck converts a high percentage of save opportunities, strands most inherited runners, and rarely throws a wild pitch or allows a stolen base. He also helps himself with his fielding. Beck has worked at least 45 times five years in a row, including a career-best 76-outing season in 1993. That was the year he saved 48 of San Francisco's 103 victories.

Major League Pitching Register

	W	L	ERA	G	S	IP	H	ER	BB	SO
91 NL	1	1	3.78	31	1	52.1	53	22	13	38
92 NL	3	3	1.76	65	17	92.0	62	18	15	87
93 NL	3	1	2.16	76	48	79.1	57	19	13	86
94 NL	2	4	2.77	48	28	48.2	49	15	13	39
95 NL	5	6	4.45	60	33	58.2	60	29	21	42
96 NL	0	9	3.34	63	35	62.0	56	23	10	48
Life	14	24	2.89	343	162	393.0	337	126	85	340
3 Ave	3	7	3.51	66	37	66.1	64	26	17	50

RICH BECKER

Position: Outfield
Team: Minnesota Twins
Born: Feb. 1, 1972 Aurora, IL
Height: 5'10" **Weight:** 180 lbs.
Bats: left **Throws:** left
Acquired: Third-round pick in 6/90 free-agent draft

PLAYER SUMMARY	
Fantasy Value	$10 to $13
Card Value	5¢ to 8¢
Will	set the table
Can't	solve southpaws
Expect	speed, defense
Don't Expect	weak throws

Although Becker played all three outfield positions for the 1996 Twins, he spent most of his time as a platoon center fielder, sharing time with righty-hitting veteran Roberto Kelly. Often compared to Lenny Dykstra because he's a lefty-hitting leadoff type with speed and pop, Becker has not shown enough potency vs. lefties to play every day. He hits well over .300 against righties, however, and also draws enough walks to post a healthy on-base percentage. Becker got off to a slow start last year but then hit .311 with 35 RBI over a 60-game stretch beginning on April 28. He's been a far better player since becoming a full-time left-handed batter late in the 1995 campaign. Fully healed from his 1994 knee injury, Becker should resume the basestealing style he showed in the minors. He also led two minor leagues in walks—a patience factor that would mesh nicely with his speed. Becker has great range and a strong arm. He finally started to capitalize on his potential last year. There's no reason why he won't keep improving.

Major League Batting Register

	BA	G	AB	R	H	2B	3B	HR	RBI	SB
93 AL	.286	3	7	3	2	2	0	0	0	1
94 AL	.265	28	98	12	26	3	0	1	8	6
95 AL	.237	106	392	45	93	15	1	2	33	8
96 AL	.291	148	525	92	153	31	4	12	71	19
Life	.268	285	1022	152	274	51	5	15	112	34
2 Ave	.267	134	483	71	129	24	3	7	54	14

TIM BELCHER

Position: Pitcher
Team: Kansas City Royals
Born: Oct. 19, 1961 Mount Gilead, OH
Height: 6'3" **Weight:** 210 lbs.
Bats: right **Throws:** right
Acquired: Signed as a free agent, 1/96

PLAYER SUMMARY	
Fantasy Value	$6 to $8
Card Value	5¢ to 8¢
Will	keep hitters guessing
Can't	find old velocity
Expect	solid performance
Don't Expect	20-win season

The Royals got maximum mileage from their January signing of Belcher. He posted his highest victory total since 1992 and teamed with Kevin Appier for a solid 1-2 punch. Belcher tries to keep hitters guessing by blending his fastball, curveball, slider, and forkball. He doesn't throw as hard as he once did but seems to have a better idea of how to pitch. Belcher's control—often erratic in the past—was generally good last year but resulted in a plague of gopher balls. Many of those homers came with the bases empty, however, because Belcher is adept at coaxing double-play grounders. A good-fielding pitcher, he also keeps potential basestealers in check. The former college All-American and NL Rookie Pitcher of the Year has pitched two one-hitters. He began his big-league career with the Dodgers in 1987. Two years later, he led the NL with eight shutouts.

Major League Pitching Register

	W	L	ERA	G	CG	IP	H	ER	BB	SO
87 NL	4	2	2.38	6	0	34.0	30	9	7	23
88 NL	12	6	2.91	36	4	179.2	143	58	51	152
89 NL	15	12	2.82	39	10	230.0	182	72	80	200
90 NL	9	9	4.00	24	5	153.0	136	68	48	102
91 NL	10	9	2.62	33	2	209.1	189	61	75	156
92 NL	15	14	3.91	35	2	227.2	201	99	80	149
93 NL	9	6	4.47	22	4	137.0	134	68	47	101
93 AL	3	5	4.40	12	1	71.2	64	35	27	34
94 AL	7	15	5.89	25	3	162.0	192	106	78	76
95 AL	10	12	4.52	28	1	179.1	188	90	88	96
96 AL	15	11	3.92	35	4	238.2	262	104	68	113
Life	109	101	3.80	295	36	1822.1	1721	770	649	1202
3 Ave	12	15	4.77	34	3	223.0	248	118	92	109

STAN BELINDA

Position: Pitcher
Team: Boston Red Sox
Born: Aug. 6, 1966 Huntington, PA
Height: 6'3" **Weight:** 200 lbs.
Bats: right **Throws:** right
Acquired: Signed as a free agent, 4/95

PLAYER SUMMARY	
Fantasy Value	$4 to $6
Card Value	4¢ to 7¢
Will	top 50 outings
Can't	keep control
Expect	sidearm delivery
Don't Expect	enemy homers

Belinda belied his reputation as a workhorse reliever when a sore elbow kept him sidelined for most of the first half of last year. The veteran sidearmer, apparently a victim of overuse, had also been idled with a sore shoulder the previous fall. When healthy, the former Pittsburgh closer throws a fastball that breaks in on right-handed hitters and a forkball that's most effective against lefties. He'll always be remembered, however, as the man who surrendered Francisco Cabrera's two-out, two-run, pennant-winning single in the ninth inning of 1992 NLCS Game 7 in Atlanta. Belinda usually yields six hits per nine innings, keeps the ball in the park, and strands nearly three of every four runners he inherits. He has occasional wild spells, however. Capable as both a closer or set-up man, Belinda helps himself with his fielding. But his high-kicking delivery gives potential basestealers a head start.

Major League Pitching Register

	W	L	ERA	G	S	IP	H	ER	BB	SO
89 NL	0	1	6.10	8	0	10.1	13	7	2	10
90 NL	3	4	3.55	55	8	58.1	48	23	29	55
91 NL	7	5	3.45	60	16	78.1	50	30	35	71
92 NL	6	4	3.15	59	18	71.1	58	25	29	57
93 NL	3	1	3.61	40	19	42.1	35	17	11	30
93 AL	1	1	4.28	23	0	27.1	30	13	6	25
94 AL	2	2	5.14	37	1	49.0	47	28	24	37
95 AL	8	1	3.10	63	10	69.2	51	24	28	57
96 AL	2	1	6.59	31	2	28.2	31	21	20	18
Life	32	20	3.89	376	74	435.1	363	188	184	360
2 Ave	6	2	4.06	61	6	74.1	62	33	33	58

DAVID BELL

Position: Second base; third base
Team: St. Louis Cardinals
Born: Sept. 14, 1972 Cincinnati, OH
Height: 5'10" **Weight:** 170 lbs.
Bats: right **Throws:** right
Acquired: Traded by Indians with Pepe McNeal and Rick Heiserman for Ken Hill, 7/95

PLAYER SUMMARY	
Fantasy Value	$1 to $3
Card Value	8¢ to 15¢
Will	stick this time
Can't	make contact
Expect	strong defense
Don't Expect	lots of homers

Bell's baseball bloodlines run thick. The son of Buddy Bell and grandson of Gus Bell is one of two three-generation players in big-league history (Bret Boone is the other). Like his father, Bell signed as a third baseman, showed some power in the minors, and reached the majors with Cleveland. Given a chance to play after his midseason trade to St. Louis in 1995, Bell did a decent job at second base. He's better at third, where he can show off his strong throwing arm, but he has good range at both positions. Bell's problems are at the plate. The patience he showed in the minors evaporated at the big-league level, and he fanned far too frequently (more than six times per walk in 1995). He doesn't have the power to justify his big swing. When his problems continued in 1996, Bell received an unpleasant surprise: a return ticket to the minor leagues. Bell will be back but won't play every day until he provides more punch. Scouts say he has the potential to hit .280 with 15 homers but sabotages his own cause in his anxiety to succeed.

Major League Batting Register

	BA	G	AB	R	H	2B	3B	HR	RBI	SB
95 AL	.000	2	2	0	0	0	0	0	0	0
95 NL	.250	39	144	13	36	7	2	2	19	1
96 NL	.214	62	145	12	31	6	0	1	9	1
Life	.230	103	291	25	67	13	2	3	28	2

DEREK BELL

Position: Outfield
Team: Houston Astros
Born: Dec. 11, 1968 Tampa, FL
Height: 6'2" **Weight:** 200 lbs.
Bats: right **Throws:** right
Acquired: Traded by Padres with Phil Plantier, Pedro Martinez, Doug Brocail, Craig Shipley, and Ricky Gutierrez for Ken Caminiti, Steve Finley, Andujar Cedeno, Robert Petagine, Brian Williams, and a player to be named later, 12/94

PLAYER SUMMARY	
Fantasy Value	$20 to $25
Card Value	7¢ to 12¢
Will	deliver in clutch
Can't	wait for walks
Expect	run production
Don't Expect	weak throws

Bell was a victim of numbers last year: His stats were good enough for the NL All-Star Team, but there were too many other outfield contenders. Bell had to be content with cementing his growing reputation as one of the best clutch hitters and RBI men in the game. With Jeff Bagwell batting in front of him and drawing a large number of intentional walks, Bell had ample opportunities. And he often cashed in. Through the first four months, he actually led Bagwell in RBI. A .300 hitter against left-handed pitching, Bell would be more potent against everyone if he learned to make better contact. He averages three strikeouts per walk. He does get extra bases on one-third of his hits, however, and also has a high success rate as a basestealer (21 of his first 24 last year). Bell's speed translates into good range in right field.

Major League Batting Register

	BA	G	AB	R	H	2B	3B	HR	RBI	SB
91 AL	.143	18	28	5	4	0	0	0	1	3
92 AL	.242	61	161	23	39	6	3	2	15	7
93 NL	.262	150	542	73	142	19	1	21	72	26
94 NL	.311	108	434	54	135	20	0	14	54	24
95 NL	.334	112	452	63	151	21	2	8	86	27
96 NL	.263	158	627	84	165	40	3	17	113	29
Life	.283	607	2244	302	636	106	9	62	341	116
3 Ave	.301	145	582	77	175	31	2	15	95	31

JAY BELL

Position: Shortstop
Team: Kansas City Royals
Born: Dec. 11, 1965 Eglin Air Force Base, FL
Height: 6'1" **Weight:** 180 lbs.
Bats: right **Throws:** right
Acquired: Traded by Pirates with Jeff King for
Joe Randa, Jeff Granger, Jeff Martin, and
Jeff Wallace, 12/96

PLAYER SUMMARY	
Fantasy Value	$8 to $10
Card Value	5¢ to 8¢
Will	seek comeback
Can't	show old range
Expect	higher average
Don't Expect	home runs

In 1993, his best season, Bell hit .310, made the All-Star Team, and won a Gold Glove. He's led the NL in sacrifices twice and total chances five times. He's also led the league in putouts, assists, and fielding percentage. But Bell wasn't the same player in 1996 he had been before. He didn't show his old power or speed and lost his old spot as Pittsburgh's No. 2 hitter. Bell draws enough walks to post an excellent on-base percentage. But he's also prone to striking out, which he does twice per walk. A better hitter with men on base, he can bunt, execute the hit-and-run, and move runners along. The former first-round draft choice (Minnesota in 1984) has good reactions and hands at short but has lost a step, prompting talk of a switch to third. The Royals dealt for him over the winter.

Major League Batting Register

	BA	G	AB	R	H	2B	3B	HR	RBI	SB
86 AL	.357	5	14	3	5	2	0	1	4	0
87 AL	.216	38	125	14	27	9	1	2	13	2
88 AL	.218	73	211	23	46	5	1	2	21	4
89 NL	.258	78	271	33	70	13	3	2	27	5
90 NL	.254	159	583	93	148	28	7	7	52	10
91 NL	.270	157	608	96	164	32	8	16	67	10
92 NL	.264	159	632	87	167	36	6	9	55	7
93 NL	.310	154	604	102	187	32	9	9	51	16
94 NL	.276	110	424	68	117	35	4	9	45	2
95 NL	.262	138	530	79	139	28	4	13	55	2
96 NL	.250	151	527	65	132	29	3	13	71	6
Life	.265	1222	4529	663	1202	249	46	83	461	64
3 Ave	.263	154	574	83	151	37	4	13	65	4

ALBERT BELLE

Position: Outfield
Team: Chicago White Sox
Born: Aug. 25, 1966 Shreveport, LA
Height: 6'2" **Weight:** 200 lbs.
Bats: right **Throws:** right
Acquired: Signed as a free agent, 11/96

PLAYER SUMMARY	
Fantasy Value	$40 to $45
Card Value	80¢ to $1.50
Will	challenge Maris
Can't	calm down
Expect	MVP numbers
Don't Expect	Gold Glove award

The most feared and controversial slugger in the game, Belle is also a candidate to break Roger Maris's single-season record of 61 homers. Devastating in the clutch, Belle hit a two-out, ninth-inning grand slam July 31, making him the first to reach 100 RBI in 1996. If he can hike his average, a Triple Crown would be within reach. Belle is a student of hitting who's willing to wait for his pitch. Pitchers try to work him away, resulting in frequent walks and a high on-base mark. He devours fastballs, breaking balls, and pitches that catch too much of the plate. Belle doesn't steal much or pay attention to defense. His mishaps in left field are legendary, but his arm isn't bad. Belle is a PR firm's nightmare: Fined $50,000 for his 1995 World Series tirade at reporter Hannah Storm, he was later ordered to undergo counseling and perform community service for throwing a ball at a photographer. The White Sox are more than willing to take their chances on Belle.

Major League Batting Register

	BA	G	AB	R	H	2B	3B	HR	RBI	SB
89 AL	.225	62	218	22	49	8	4	7	37	2
90 AL	.174	9	23	1	4	0	0	1	3	0
91 AL	.282	123	461	60	130	31	2	28	95	3
92 AL	.260	153	585	81	152	23	1	34	112	8
93 AL	.290	159	594	93	172	36	3	38	129	23
94 AL	.357	106	412	90	147	35	2	36	101	9
95 AL	.317	143	546	121	173	52	1	50	126	5
96 AL	.311	158	602	124	187	38	3	48	148	11
Life	.295	913	3441	592	1014	223	16	242	751	61
3 Ave	.328	156	599	129	196	49	2	52	144	10

RAFAEL BELLIARD

Position: Shortstop; second base
Team: Atlanta Braves
Born: Oct. 24, 1961 Pueblo Nuevo, Mao, Dominican Republic
Height: 5'6" **Weight:** 150 lbs.
Bats: right **Throws:** right
Acquired: Signed as a free agent, 12/90

PLAYER SUMMARY	
Fantasy Value	$0
Card Value	4¢ to 7¢
Will	stay ready
Can't	hit homers
Expect	strong arm
Don't Expect	walks, hits

Belliard's longevity in the majors is one of the mysteries in the modern world. Since 1982, he's hit only one home run. He hasn't hit many singles either, as his 14-year, pre-1996 average of .224 will attest. Belliard was even more of a bust at the plate last year, whaling away at everything. A walk to Belliard is as rare as an electoral vote for Ross Perot. The guy swings at everything. There's just something about him, though. He's a skilled bunter and reliable fielder, showing decent range, good hands, a strong arm, and an ability to turn the double play. Belliard is also a clubhouse presence, always smiling, agreeable, and ready to play. Regarded as a good-luck charm, Belliard is the only man in the majors to play in every postseason of the '90s.

Major League Batting Register

	BA	G	AB	R	H	2B	3B	HR	RBI	SB
82 NL	.500	9	2	3	1	0	0	0	0	1
83 NL	.000	4	1	1	0	0	0	0	0	0
84 NL	.227	20	22	3	5	0	0	0	0	4
85 NL	.200	17	20	1	4	0	0	0	1	0
86 NL	.233	117	309	33	72	5	2	0	31	12
87 NL	.207	81	203	26	42	4	3	1	15	5
88 NL	.213	122	286	28	61	0	4	0	11	7
89 NL	.214	67	154	10	33	4	0	0	8	5
90 NL	.204	47	54	10	11	3	0	0	6	1
91 NL	.249	149	353	36	88	9	2	0	27	3
92 NL	.211	144	285	20	60	6	1	0	14	0
93 NL	.228	91	79	6	18	5	0	0	6	0
94 NL	.242	46	120	9	29	7	1	0	9	0
95 NL	.222	75	180	12	40	2	1	0	7	2
96 NL	.169	87	142	9	24	7	0	0	3	3
Life	.221	1076	2210	207	488	52	14	1	138	43

MARVIN BENARD

Position: Outfield
Team: San Francisco Giants
Born: Jan. 20, 1970 Bluefields, Nicaragua
Height: 5'9" **Weight:** 180 lbs.
Bats: left **Throws:** left
Acquired: 50th-round pick in 6/92 free-agent draft

PLAYER SUMMARY	
Fantasy Value	$1
Card Value	6¢ to 10¢
Will	use speed well
Can't	clear the wall
Expect	leadoff trial
Don't Expect	best bat vs. lefties

Benard was in the right place at the right time when Stan Javier was sidelined with hamstring problems in June. He became San Francisco's main man in center, though he struggles against left-handers. A speed merchant and .300 hitter in the minors, Benard gave only fleeting glimpses of his basestealing skills in the NL. Though he swiped 20 bases in his first 29 tries, he did not reach base often enough to become a major disruptive force. A singles hitter, Benard could capitalize on his potential by hitting down on the ball, dropping surprise bunts, and showing the same patience he displayed earlier in his pro career. Because of his tiny strike zone, Benard walked almost as much as he fanned during several different seasons. Benard's speed gives him good range in center, where he has a better arm than most of his colleagues. He once had 17 assists in a season. If he shows more with the bat, the fleet Benard could become a good leadoff man. But he'll have to improve against lefties in order to play every day.

Major League Batting Register

	BA	G	AB	R	H	2B	3B	HR	RBI	SB
95 NL	.382	13	34	5	13	2	0	1	4	1
96 NL	.248	135	488	89	121	17	4	5	27	25
Life	.257	148	522	94	134	19	4	6	31	26

ALAN BENES

Position: Pitcher
Team: St. Louis Cardinals
Born: Jan. 21, 1972 Evansville, IN
Height: 6'5" **Weight:** 215 lbs.
Bats: right **Throws:** right
Acquired: First-round pick in 6/93 free-agent draft

PLAYER SUMMARY	
Fantasy Value	$8 to $10
Card Value	15¢ to 25¢
Will	improve over time
Can't	prevent gophers
Expect	winning record
Don't Expect	pinpoint control

The middle of the three Benes brothers in the Cardinal organization, Alan is almost a carbon copy of older brother Andy. A big right-handed power pitcher and former No. 1 draft choice (1993), he lacks Andy's experience but has more competitive fire. A 1996 rookie, Benes was the first Card starter to reach double digits in wins. And he did it despite difficulty against left-handed hitters and occasional control problems. The arrival of Benes was much anticipated: American Association managers had named him their league's top prospect in a 1995 *Baseball America* survey—even though the pitcher had missed four months with a sore arm. A 6-1 record and 1.78 ERA in the Arizona Fall League heightened the expectations in St. Louis. Benes started slowly but came within two outs of his first shutout May 22 vs. Houston. The former Creighton star throws a fastball, curve, and changeup but needs to be more consistent with his location. He yields over one hit per inning and four walks per nine innings. Benes fields his position well and has a very good pickoff move coupled with a quick delivery.

Major League Pitching Register

	W	L	ERA	G	CG	IP	H	ER	BB	SO
95 NL	1	2	8.44	3	0	16.0	24	15	4	20
96 NL	13	10	4.90	34	3	191.0	192	104	87	131
Life	14	12	5.17	37	3	207.0	216	119	91	151

ANDY BENES

Position: Pitcher
Team: St. Louis Cardinals
Born: Aug. 20, 1967 Evansville, IN
Height: 6'6" **Weight:** 235 lbs.
Bats: right **Throws:** right
Acquired: Signed as a free agent, 12/95

PLAYER SUMMARY	
Fantasy Value	$12 to $15
Card Value	10¢ to 15¢
Will	bank on heat
Can't	lean on lefties
Expect	strong second half
Don't Expect	bad control

Growing up in Indiana, Benes was a Cardinals fan. But he spent his first seven years as a pro pitching for other teams after the Padres chose him first overall in the 1988 amateur draft. A former Olympian from the University of Evansville, he finally realized his dream by signing with St. Louis as a free agent. He dropped seven of his first eight decisions, then caught fire, notching a ten-game winning streak. Benes blamed his early problems on poor location. Usually a control pitcher with high strikeout numbers (his 189 Ks led the NL in 1994), Benes encountered unexpected trouble from left-handed batters, long-ball hitters, and base-thieves. The hard-throwing Benes blends his fastball with a slider, slurve, and circle change. A cut fastball gives him an extra pitch. Benes is an outstanding fielder who's quick off the mound—especially for a man of his size. No slouch at the plate, he hits an occasional homer.

Major League Pitching Register

	W	L	ERA	G	CG	IP	H	ER	BB	SO
89 NL	6	3	3.51	10	0	66.2	51	26	31	66
90 NL	10	11	3.60	32	2	192.1	177	77	69	140
91 NL	15	11	3.03	33	4	223.0	194	75	59	167
92 NL	13	14	3.35	34	2	231.1	230	86	61	169
93 NL	15	15	3.78	34	4	230.2	200	97	86	179
94 NL	6	14	3.86	25	2	172.1	155	74	51	189
95 NL	4	7	4.17	19	1	118.2	121	55	45	126
95 AL	7	2	5.86	12	0	63.0	72	41	33	45
96 NL	18	10	3.83	36	3	230.1	215	98	77	160
Life	94	87	3.70	235	18	1528.1	1415	629	512	1241
3 Ave	13	13	4.12	35	2	226.1	217	103	79	206

ARMANDO BENITEZ

Position: Pitcher
Team: Baltimore Orioles
Born: Nov. 3, 1972 Ramon Santana, Dominican Republic
Height: 6'4" **Weight:** 180 lbs.
Bats: right **Throws:** right
Acquired: Signed as a free agent, 4/90

PLAYER SUMMARY	
Fantasy Value	$7 to $9
Card Value	7¢ to 12¢
Will	be future closer
Can't	always find plate
Expect	lots of Ks
Don't Expect	too many hits

Baltimore's 1996 pitching woes were accentuated by the loss of Benitez, disabled in April with a strained muscle in his right elbow. A big, hard-throwing closer who reminds scouts of a young Lee Smith, Benitez has shown flashes of potential during several stints in the majors. He's averaged more strikeouts than innings pitched at every level—including the big leagues—but has also battled control problems. A fastball-slider pitcher who can make his celebrated heater sink or rise, Benitez gets into trouble when he falls behind in the count. He needs to use the slider more and consider adding an off-speed pitch to his arsenal. It would also help if Benitez were better on defense or in stopping the running game. He's so worried about throwing strikes that he often forgets there are men on base. There's no question Benitez will be a big-league closer in the near future. Groomed for the role since turning pro, he made only a handful of starts in the minors before retreating to the bullpen for good.

Major League Pitching Register

	W	L	ERA	G	S	IP	H	ER	BB	SO
94 AL	0	0	0.90	3	0	10.0	8	1	4	14
95 AL	1	5	5.66	44	2	47.2	37	30	37	56
96 AL	1	0	3.77	18	4	14.1	7	6	6	20
Life	2	5	4.63	65	6	72.0	52	37	47	90

MIKE BENJAMIN

Position: Infield
Team: Philadelphia Phillies
Born: Nov. 22, 1965 Euclid, OH
Height: 6' **Weight:** 169 lbs.
Bats: right **Throws:** right
Acquired: Traded by Giants for Jeff Juden and Tommy Eason, 10/95

PLAYER SUMMARY	
Fantasy Value	$0
Card Value	4¢ to 7¢
Will	play anywhere
Can't	swing the bat
Expect	solid defense
Don't Expect	home runs

If he were in the Army, Benjamin would definitely be a private. Except for a single series at Wrigley Field in June 1995, he's done nothing in his career to distinguish himself. A lifelong utility man, Benjamin is most valuable because he plays three positions. His 14-for-18 explosion in Chicago set a big-league record: Benjamin remains the only player in major-league history with 14 hits in three games. He's usually a singles hitter who doesn't make good contact and struggles against righties. Overly aggressive at the plate, Benjamin tries to pull every pitch but rarely succeeds. However, he did show more patience than usual before he got hurt last year (July neck injury) and actually compiled a decent on-base percentage. Benjamin doesn't reach base often enough to use his speed and has reached double digits in steals only once. But the former Arizona State shortstop is a fine defensive player with quick reactions, soft hands, and a solid arm.

Major League Batting Register

	BA	G	AB	R	H	2B	3B	HR	RBI	SB
89 NL	.167	14	6	6	1	0	0	0	0	0
90 NL	.214	22	56	7	12	3	1	2	3	1
91 NL	.123	54	106	12	13	3	0	2	8	3
92 NL	.173	40	75	4	13	2	1	1	3	1
93 NL	.199	63	146	22	29	7	0	4	16	0
94 NL	.258	38	62	9	16	5	1	1	9	5
95 NL	.220	68	186	19	41	6	0	3	12	11
96 NL	.223	35	103	13	23	5	1	4	13	3
Life	.200	334	740	92	148	31	4	17	64	24

JASON BERE

Position: Pitcher
Team: Chicago White Sox
Born: May 26, 1971 Cambridge, MA
Height: 6'3" **Weight:** 185 lbs.
Bats: right **Throws:** right
Acquired: 36th-round pick in 6/90 free-agent draft

PLAYER SUMMARY
Fantasy Value	$1 to $3
Card Value	7¢ to 12¢
Will	need comeback
Can't	throw strikes
Expect	the long ball
Don't Expect	job security

Bere went 12-5 as a 1993 rookie and made the AL All-Star Team in '94. He then led the league in losses (15) a year later. Seeking a comeback last spring, he encountered elbow tendinitis instead and missed virtually the entire season. When he's on, the young right-hander throws a fastball, slider, curve, and deceptive changeup he cleverly calls a fosh (part forkball, part dead fish). Never known for good control, Bere went belly-up with 106 walks in 1995, giving him a terrible 1-1 ratio of strikeouts to walks. Bere is living proof that throwing hard does not guarantee victory. He also hurts his cause with weak defense and an inability to hold baserunners. In both of his first two years, the Bay State righty yielded less than one hit per inning; that was not the case in 1995, when Bere was beleaguered by the long ball, accounting for an embarrassing 7.19 ERA. He did, however, give hints of his untapped potential, including a 14-K game. He will miss all of 1997 due to elbow surgery.

Major League Pitching Register
	W	L	ERA	G	S	IP	H	ER	BB	SO
93 AL	12	5	3.47	24	0	142.2	109	55	81	129
94 AL	12	2	3.81	24	0	141.2	119	60	80	127
95 AL	8	15	7.19	27	0	137.2	151	110	106	110
96 AL	0	1	10.26	5	0	16.2	26	19	18	19
Life	32	23	5.01	80	0	438.2	405	244	285	385
2 Ave	13	10	5.29	32	0	177.1	169	104	116	151

SEAN BERGMAN

Position: Pitcher
Team: San Diego Padres
Born: April 11, 1970 Joliet, IL
Height: 6'4" **Weight:** 205 lbs.
Bats: right **Throws:** right
Acquired: Traded by Tigers with Cade Gaspar and Todd Steverson for Melvin Nieves, Raul Casanova, and Richie Lewis, 4/96

PLAYER SUMMARY
Fantasy Value	$1 to $3
Card Value	4¢ to 7¢
Will	bank on sinker
Can't	hold baserunners
Expect	groundouts
Don't Expect	strong defense

Before the Padres traded for him last year, Bergman had made only three relief appearances in a professional career that began in 1991. When he struggled as a San Diego starter, however, he was given a chance to work out his problems in the bullpen. A big right-hander who tries to get ahead in the count, Bergman averages fewer than three walks per nine innings and more than seven strikeouts over the same span. But lefties gave him fits last year, when he also had trouble keeping the ball in the park and holding baserunners close. He also made too many wild pitches. Bergman complements a breaking ball, his No. 1 pitch, with a sinking fastball and a slider that he uses as his changeup. Although the Southern Illinois product is an intense competitor, he's been unable to capitalize on the promise that made him Detroit's top pitching prospect for several seasons. Bergman doesn't help himself at all in the field; his .889 fielding percentage was the AL's worst by a pitcher in 1995.

Major League Pitching Register
	W	L	ERA	G	S	IP	H	ER	BB	SO
93 AL	1	4	5.67	9	0	39.2	47	25	23	19
94 AL	2	1	5.60	3	0	17.2	22	11	7	12
95 AL	7	10	5.12	28	0	135.1	169	77	67	86
96 NL	6	8	4.37	41	0	113.1	119	55	33	85
Life	16	23	4.94	81	0	306.0	357	168	130	202
2 Ave	7	10	4.80	36	0	133.1	155	71	54	91

GERONIMO BERROA

Position: Outfield
Team: Oakland Athletics
Born: March 18, 1965 Santo Domingo, Dominican Republic
Height: 6'4" **Weight:** 235 lbs.
Bats: right **Throws:** right
Acquired: Signed as a free agent, 1/94

PLAYER SUMMARY	
Fantasy Value	$20 to $25
Card Value	7¢ to 10¢
Will	show good power
Can't	cut strikeouts
Expect	streak hitting
Don't Expect	solid defense

Because of his name, his power, and his penchant for swinging at bad pitches, it's amazing nobody tagged Berroa with the "Yogi" nickname. He even makes his off-season home in New York. Like the Hall of Fame catcher, Berroa batters opposing pitchers with regularity. But Berroa played for seven teams in three years before Oakland made him a regular in 1994. Used primarily as a DH by the 1996 Athletics, Berroa produced his best power numbers. He still fanned nearly three times per walk but produced extra bases on more than 40 percent of his hits. A better hitter vs. left-handed pitchers, Berroa also hits righties with authority. He hits with power to all fields. Berroa runs like he hits: over-aggressively. He's not fast and has never reached double digits in steals. In the field, his range, instincts, arm strength, and accuracy are all below average. He is only the tenth man in major-league history to have two three-homer games in the same season.

Major League Batting Register

	BA	G	AB	R	H	2B	3B	HR	RBI	SB
89 NL	.265	81	136	7	36	4	0	2	9	0
90 NL	.000	7	4	0	0	0	0	0	0	0
92 NL	.267	13	15	2	4	1	0	0	0	0
93 NL	.118	14	34	3	4	1	0	0	0	0
94 NL	.306	96	340	55	104	18	2	13	65	7
95 AL	.278	141	546	87	152	22	3	22	88	7
96 AL	.290	153	586	101	170	32	1	36	106	0
Life	.283	505	1661	255	470	78	6	73	268	14
3 Ave	.290	149	560	92	163	27	2	26	99	6

SEAN BERRY

Position: Third base
Team: Houston Astros
Born: April 22, 1966 Santa Monica, CA
Height: 5'11" **Weight:** 210 lbs.
Bats: right **Throws:** right
Acquired: Traded by Expos for Dave Veres, 12/95

PLAYER SUMMARY	
Fantasy Value	$11 to $14
Card Value	7¢ to 10¢
Will	hit some out
Can't	show patience
Expect	sound shoulder
Don't Expect	strong throws

The Astros learned last year that Berry's so-so offense isn't enough to overcome his erratic defense. Although he has the quick reactions required of a third baseman, his range, hands, and arm are all below average. His throwing problems were complicated last year by a sore shoulder that required off-season surgery. Berry also hesitates to charge slowly hit balls and sometimes seems afraid to make a hurried or off-balance throw. The former UCLA center fielder apparently had a career year when he hit .318 for the '95 Expos, since his average fell sharply last summer. Berry fans nearly three times per walk and doesn't produce the power usually associated with his position. He did hit two grand slams (doubling his career total) in the first half last year but had only ten other homers by early August. He's a better hitter in the clutch, when he cuts down his big swing. Berry has some speed but has yet to swipe as many as 15 bases on the big-league level.

Major League Batting Register

	BA	G	AB	R	H	2B	3B	HR	RBI	SB
90 AL	.217	8	23	2	5	1	1	0	4	0
91 AL	.133	31	60	5	8	3	0	0	1	0
92 NL	.333	24	57	5	19	1	0	1	4	2
93 NL	.261	122	299	50	78	15	2	14	49	12
94 NL	.278	103	320	43	89	19	2	11	41	14
95 NL	.318	103	314	38	100	22	1	14	55	3
96 NL	.281	132	431	55	121	38	1	17	95	12
Life	.279	523	1504	198	420	99	7	57	249	43
3 Ave	.291	131	412	53	120	30	2	16	72	12

DANTE BICHETTE

Position: Outfield
Team: Colorado Rockies
Born: Nov. 18, 1963 West Palm Beach, FL
Height: 6'3" **Weight:** 212 lbs.
Bats: right **Throws:** right
Acquired: Traded by Brewers for Kevin
Reimer, 11/92

PLAYER SUMMARY	
Fantasy Value	$35 to $40
Card Value	20¢ to 40¢
Will	murder left-handers
Can't	avoid strikeouts
Expect	big run production
Don't Expect	same bat on road

Bichette improved his power production in each of his first three years in Colorado. He was still potent last year, when he topped 100 RBI for the second straight season, but did not return to the near-Triple Crown levels of the year before. Aided by the thin air of Denver, where he did most of his damage, Bichette led the 1995 NL in hits, homers, total bases, RBI, and slugging. He was second in doubles and third in average, batting with runners in scoring position, and slugging vs. lefties. Bichette pulverizes left-handed pitching but is even more potent in his home ballpark. Though he fans more than twice per walk, he also nets extra bases on more than one-third of his hits. Chosen by Bobby Cox to replace injured right fielder Tony Gwynn in the 1996 All-Star lineup, Bichette plays both corners but is best in left because of limited range. Bichette underwent reconstructive surgery on his left knee in the off-season.

Major League Batting Register

	BA	G	AB	R	H	2B	3B	HR	RBI	SB
88 AL	.261	21	46	1	12	2	0	0	8	0
89 AL	.210	48	138	13	29	7	0	3	15	3
90 AL	.255	109	349	40	89	15	1	15	53	5
91 AL	.238	134	445	53	106	18	3	15	59	14
92 AL	.287	112	387	37	111	27	2	5	41	18
93 NL	.310	141	538	93	167	43	5	21	89	14
94 NL	.304	116	484	74	147	33	2	27	95	21
95 NL	.340	139	579	102	197	38	2	40	128	13
96 NL	.313	159	633	114	198	39	3	31	141	31
Life	.293	979	3599	527	1056	222	18	157	629	119
3 Ave	.319	160	655	111	209	43	3	38	140	25

MIKE BIELECKI

Position: Pitcher
Team: Atlanta Braves
Born: July 31, 1959 Baltimore, MD
Height: 6'3" **Weight:** 195 lbs.
Bats: right **Throws:** right
Acquired: Signed as a free agent, 4/96

PLAYER SUMMARY	
Fantasy Value	$1
Card Value	4¢ to 7¢
Will	start or relieve
Can't	worry about shoulder
Expect	reliable control
Don't Expect	gopher plague

Bielecki was working out with a college team when the Braves gave him a late-spring training audition as a long reliever. Manager Bobby Cox, needing an experienced arm for his bullpen, wasted little time in signing the veteran for his second tour with the club. When he's right, the veteran right-hander has good control of four pitches: fastball, forkball, curve, and changeup. He yields fewer hits than innings, keeps the ball in the park, and averages almost a strikeout per inning. Bielecki helps himself in the field but is only average at holding runners. His biggest problem is keeping his shoulder healthy; he missed huge chunks of the 1995 campaign with shoulder trouble and has had periodic shoulder problems previously. He turned 37 in July, which made him the oldest man on the team but hardly the least valuable.

Major League Pitching Register

	W	L	ERA	G	S	IP	H	ER	BB	SO
84 NL	0	0	0.00	4	0	4.1	4	0	0	1
85 NL	2	3	4.53	12	0	45.2	45	23	31	22
86 NL	6	11	4.66	31	0	148.2	149	77	83	83
87 NL	2	3	4.73	8	0	45.2	43	24	12	25
88 NL	2	2	3.35	19	0	48.1	55	18	16	33
89 NL	18	7	3.14	33	0	212.1	187	74	81	147
90 NL	8	11	4.93	36	1	168.0	188	92	70	103
91 NL	13	11	4.46	41	0	173.2	171	86	56	75
92 NL	2	4	2.57	19	0	80.2	77	23	27	62
93 NL	4	5	5.90	13	0	68.2	90	45	23	38
94 NL	2	0	4.00	19	0	27.0	28	12	12	18
95 NL	4	6	5.97	22	0	75.1	80	50	31	45
96 NL	4	3	2.63	40	2	75.1	63	22	33	71
Life	67	66	4.19	297	3	1173.2	1180	546	475	723
2 Ave	4	5	4.40	32	1	80.0	77	39	34	61

CRAIG BIGGIO

Position: Second base
Team: Houston Astros
Born: Dec. 14, 1965 Smithtown, NY
Height: 5'11" **Weight:** 180 lbs.
Bats: right **Throws:** right
Acquired: First-round pick in 6/87 free-agent draft

PLAYER SUMMARY	
Fantasy Value	$25 to $30
Card Value	12¢ to 20¢
Will	hit, run, field
Can't	catch again
Expect	All-Star stats
Don't Expect	long slumps

When Biggio tested free agency following the 1995 season, his availability set off a major bidding war. One of the best all-around players in the game, he's a three-way star, capable at bat, on the bases, and in the field. A contact hitter with patience, he walks more than he fans and hits the ball with authority. He's always among the league leaders in runs, hits, walks, and on-base percentage. The five-time All-Star led the NL in doubles and stolen bases in 1994, when he won his first Gold Glove. That was quite an accomplishment for the former Seton Hall All-American, who was drafted and signed as a catcher. Biggio has been an All-Star at both positions but is far better at second, where he has good range, soft hands, and a knack for turning the double play. He's fast enough to take extra bases, motor from first to third, and beat out bunts and infield rollers. Biggio has a high success rate as a basestealer.

Major League Batting Register

	BA	G	AB	R	H	2B	3B	HR	RBI	SB
88 NL	.211	50	123	14	26	6	1	3	5	6
89 NL	.257	134	443	64	114	21	2	13	60	21
90 NL	.276	150	555	53	153	24	2	4	42	25
91 NL	.295	149	546	79	161	23	4	4	46	19
92 NL	.277	162	613	96	170	32	3	6	39	38
93 NL	.287	155	610	98	175	41	5	21	64	15
94 NL	.318	114	437	88	139	44	5	6	56	39
95 NL	.302	141	553	123	167	30	2	22	77	33
96 NL	.288	162	605	113	174	24	4	15	75	25
Life	.285	1217	4485	728	1279	245	28	94	464	221
3 Ave	.303	160	614	125	186	40	4	16	80	39

WILLIE BLAIR

Position: Pitcher
Team: Detroit Tigers
Born: Dec. 18, 1965 Paintsville, KY
Height: 6'1" **Weight:** 185 lbs.
Bats: right **Throws:** right
Acquired: Traded by Padres with Brian Johnson for Joey Eischen and Cam Smith, 12/96

PLAYER SUMMARY	
Fantasy Value	$0
Card Value	4¢ to 7¢
Will	retain relief job
Can't	prevent gophers
Expect	spot starts
Don't Expect	great control

Blair's value has increased due to his ability to both start and relieve. Used primarily as a reliever since turning pro in 1986, the Morehead State product actually did his best pitching as an emergency starter two years ago for the Padres. Blair's No. 1 pitch is a slider, but he also throws a curve, changeup, and cut fastball. He yields about one hit per inning and more than six strikeouts per game, but his location isn't always sharp. When his pitches caught too much of the plate last year, he suffered: Batters hammered a dozen homers in his first 60⅓ innings pitched. Blair can't hit a lick, but his fielding is fine. Although he had been able to hold runners in the past, in 1996 he had problems. With expansion just over the horizon, Blair could be in demand. And he just might get his first extensive audition as a starting pitcher. He's pitched for the Blue Jays, Indians, Astros, Rockies, and Padres, and joins the Tigers for '97.

Major League Pitching Register

	W	L	ERA	G	S	IP	H	ER	BB	SO
90 AL	3	5	4.06	27	0	68.2	66	31	28	43
91 AL	2	3	6.75	11	0	36.0	58	27	10	13
92 NL	5	7	4.00	29	0	78.2	74	35	25	48
93 NL	6	10	4.75	46	0	146.0	184	77	42	84
94 NL	0	5	5.79	47	3	77.2	98	50	39	68
95 NL	7	5	4.34	40	0	114.0	112	55	45	83
96 NL	2	6	4.60	60	1	88.0	80	45	29	67
Life	25	41	4.73	260	4	609.0	672	320	218	406
3 Ave	3	6	4.90	57	2	109.1	115	59	45	85

41

JEFF BLAUSER

Position: Shortstop
Team: Atlanta Braves
Born: Nov. 8, 1965 Los Gatos, CA
Height: 6'1" **Weight:** 180 lbs.
Bats: right **Throws:** right
Acquired: First-round pick in secondary phase of 6/84 free-agent draft

PLAYER SUMMARY	
Fantasy Value	$6 to $8
Card Value	4¢ to 7¢
Will	show some power
Can't	throw bullets
Expect	future manager
Don't Expect	high on-base pct.

Since 1993, when he established himself as one of baseball's best-hitting shortstops, Blauser has been a major disappointment. His run production dropped in direct proportion with his batting average, and his defense also turned sour. Part of the problem last year was an early-season knee injury, but he later lost much playing time with a broken bone in his nonthrowing hand. Once a decent No. 2 hitter who knew how to move runners along, Blauser dropped to the bottom of the lineup last year. He fans far too frequently for a hitter with 15-homer power. He's not fast, and his range is limited. On the other hand, Blauser is a smart player who positions himself well, turns the double play, and makes decent throws. Blauser is a fine clubhouse presence with a sharp wit. A keen observer who knows the game, he could become a major-league manager after he hangs up his spikes.

Major League Batting Register

	BA	G	AB	R	H	2B	3B	HR	RBI	SB
87 NL	.242	51	165	11	40	6	3	2	15	7
88 NL	.239	18	67	7	16	3	1	2	7	0
89 NL	.270	142	456	63	123	24	2	12	46	5
90 NL	.269	115	386	46	104	24	3	8	39	3
91 NL	.259	129	352	49	91	14	3	11	54	5
92 NL	.262	123	343	61	90	19	3	14	46	5
93 NL	.305	161	597	110	182	29	2	15	73	16
94 NL	.258	96	380	56	98	21	4	6	45	1
95 NL	.211	115	431	60	91	16	2	12	31	8
96 NL	.245	83	265	48	65	14	1	10	35	6
Life	.261	1033	3442	511	900	170	24	92	391	56
3 Ave	.238	116	428	65	102	21	3	11	44	5

MIKE BLOWERS

Position: Third base
Team: Los Angeles Dodgers
Born: April 24, 1965 Wurzburg, West Germany
Height: 6'2" **Weight:** 210 lbs.
Bats: right **Throws:** right
Acquired: Traded by Mariners for Miguel Cairo and Willis Otanez, 11/95

PLAYER SUMMARY	
Fantasy Value	$7 to $9
Card Value	4¢ to 7¢
Will	hit in streaks
Can't	steal often
Expect	strong arm
Don't Expect	Gold Glove

One of baseball's most notorious streak hitters, Blowers had an eight-RBI game in 1995 plus two five-RBI games. Last year, however, he never had a chance to catch fire. Playing in the NL for the first time, he knocked in only 38 runs before going on the shelf in July with a torn ligament in his left knee. The healthy Blowers clobbers left-handed pitching and hits better with runners in scoring position. He won't wait for walks, leaving him with a strikeout-to-walk ratio of 2-to-1. A shortstop at the University of Washington, Blowers moved to third as a second-year pro. He has also played first base and outfield at the big-league level. He has a powerful arm, but a lack of speed gives him limited mobility and his hands have never been described as soft. Blowers is no threat to win a Gold Glove, but he's a better third baseman than some of the butchers the Dodgers have tried there.

Major League Batting Register

	BA	G	AB	R	H	2B	3B	HR	RBI	SB
89 AL	.263	13	38	2	10	0	0	0	3	0
90 AL	.188	48	144	16	27	4	0	5	21	1
91 AL	.200	15	35	3	7	0	0	1	1	0
92 AL	.192	31	73	7	14	3	0	1	2	0
93 AL	.280	127	379	55	106	23	3	15	57	1
94 AL	.289	85	270	37	78	13	0	9	49	2
95 AL	.257	134	439	59	113	24	1	23	96	2
96 NL	.265	92	317	31	84	19	2	6	38	0
Life	.259	545	1695	210	439	86	6	60	267	6
3 Ave	.269	121	397	50	107	21	1	15	72	2

WADE BOGGS

Position: Third base
Team: New York Yankees
Born: June 15, 1958 Omaha, NE
Height: 6'2" **Weight:** 197 lbs.
Bats: left **Throws:** right
Acquired: Signed as a free agent, 12/92

PLAYER SUMMARY	
Fantasy Value	$6 to $8
Card Value	12¢ to 20¢
Will	churn out hits
Can't	hit for power
Expect	All-Star start
Don't Expect	long skids

Boggs has blossomed into one of baseball's best all-around players. His two Gold Gloves fit nicely onto a mantle already crowded with five AL batting crowns. A true student of hitting, Boggs walks far more frequently than he fans, making him a good man to have at the top of the lineup. He holds the modern record for consecutive seasons with 200 hits (seven) and has led the league in on-base percentage six times. The .335 average Boggs carried into 1996 ranked 19th on the career list. He should reach 3,000 career hits. Boggs doesn't have speed or power, but he sets the table and is a 12-time All-Star. The former BoSox standout has quick reactions and a strong, accurate arm. Boggs was slowed by back problems in the postseason.

Major League Batting Register

	BA	G	AB	R	H	2B	3B	HR	RBI	SB
82 AL	.349	104	338	51	118	14	1	5	44	1
83 AL	.361	153	582	100	210	44	7	5	74	3
84 AL	.325	158	625	109	203	31	4	6	55	3
85 AL	.368	161	653	107	240	42	3	8	78	2
86 AL	.357	149	580	107	207	47	2	8	71	0
87 AL	.363	147	551	108	200	40	6	24	89	1
88 AL	.366	155	584	128	214	45	6	5	58	2
89 AL	.330	156	621	113	205	51	7	3	54	2
90 AL	.302	155	619	89	187	44	5	6	63	0
91 AL	.332	144	546	93	181	42	2	8	51	1
92 AL	.259	143	514	62	133	22	4	7	50	1
93 AL	.302	143	560	83	169	26	1	2	59	0
94 AL	.342	97	366	61	125	19	1	11	55	2
95 AL	.324	126	460	76	149	22	4	5	63	1
96 AL	.311	132	501	80	156	29	2	2	41	1
Life	.333	2123	8100	1367	2697	518	55	105	905	20
3 Ave	.326	137	511	84	167	27	3	8	63	2

BARRY BONDS

Position: Outfield
Team: San Francisco Giants
Born: July 24, 1964 Riverside, CA
Height: 6'1" **Weight:** 185 lbs.
Bats: left **Throws:** left
Acquired: Signed as a free agent, 12/92

PLAYER SUMMARY	
Fantasy Value	$45 to $50
Card Value	50¢ to $1
Will	seek MVP trophy
Can't	avoid controversy
Expect	enormous power
Don't Expect	powerful arm

At 32, Bonds has time to become the first four-time MVP. The only man ever to win the award three times in four years, Bonds last season became the first NL 40-40 man ever. With four 30-30 years, Bonds is approaching the record of five by his dad, Bobby. Barry and his dad are also two of the four players in the 300-300 club (with Willie Mays and Andre Dawson). Bonds began last year with a bang, tying a record with 11 April homers and hitting 11 over a 15-game span in May. But injuries to Matt Williams allowed pitchers to work around Bonds. A patient hitter, Bonds makes great contact for a power hitter, walking often and ranking among the leaders in on-base percentage. He's rarely caught stealing, and his speed also helps in left field, where he is a six-time Gold Glover. Bonds is often surly with fans and media, which may have cost him MVP votes.

Major League Batting Register

	BA	G	AB	R	H	2B	3B	HR	RBI	SB
86 NL	.223	113	413	72	92	26	3	16	48	36
87 NL	.261	150	551	99	144	34	9	25	59	32
88 NL	.283	144	538	97	152	30	5	24	58	17
89 NL	.248	159	580	96	144	34	6	19	58	32
90 NL	.301	151	519	104	156	32	3	33	114	52
91 NL	.292	153	510	95	149	28	5	25	116	43
92 NL	.311	140	473	109	147	36	5	34	103	39
93 NL	.336	159	539	129	181	38	4	46	123	29
94 NL	.312	112	391	89	122	18	1	37	81	29
95 NL	.294	144	506	109	149	30	7	33	104	31
96 NL	.308	158	517	122	159	27	3	42	129	40
Life	.288	1583	5537	1121	1595	333	51	334	993	380
3 Ave	.305	159	546	123	166	29	4	44	120	39

RICKY BONES

Position: Pitcher
Team: Cincinnati Reds
Born: April 7, 1969 Salinas, Puerto Rico
Height: 6' **Weight:** 190 lbs.
Bats: right **Throws:** right
Acquired: Signed as a minor-league free
 agent, 12/96

PLAYER SUMMARY	
Fantasy Value.	$3 to $5
Card Value	4¢ to 7¢
Will	stay in rotation
Can't	win without sinker
Expect	gopher trouble
Don't Expect	runners to steal

A midseason trip to the bullpen was just
what the doctor ordered for Bones last
year. With his sinker gone and breaking
pitches dropping out of the strike zone, Milwaukee manager Phil Garner decided the
erstwhile starter needed a break. Working
in relief, Bones compiled a 1.64 ERA,
paving the way for his return. The Yankees
obtained the right-hander to help out with
the pennant drive. Bones does not win by
striking men out. Instead, he tries to coax
ground balls by baffling batters with sinkers,
sliders, curves, and changeups low in the
strike zone. Since most of his pitches are
hit, it's a good thing that Bones is such a
good fielder. He's quick off the mound, especially in fielding bunts. With runners on
base, he scraps his usual high-kicking delivery and works off the stretch. That, coupled with his good pickoff move, keeps
baserunners from stealing.

Major League Pitching Register

	W	L	ERA	G	CG	IP	H	ER	BB	SO
91 NL	4	6	4.83	11	0	54.0	57	29	18	31
92 AL	9	10	4.57	31	0	163.1	169	83	48	65
93 AL	11	11	4.86	32	3	203.2	222	110	63	63
94 AL	10	9	3.43	24	4	170.2	166	65	45	57
95 AL	10	12	4.63	32	3	200.1	218	103	83	77
96 AL	7	14	6.22	36	0	152.0	184	105	68	63
Life	51	62	4.72	166	10	944.0	1016	495	325	356
3 Ave	11	13	4.55	35	3	206.0	221	104	75	77

BOBBY BONILLA

Position: Outfield; third base
Team: Florida Marlins
Born: Feb. 23, 1963 New York, NY
Height: 6'3" **Weight:** 230 lbs.
Bats: both **Throws:** right
Acquired: Signed as a free agent, 11/96

PLAYER SUMMARY	
Fantasy Value.	$30 to $35
Card Value	10¢ to 15¢
Will.	hit in clutch
Can't	steal bases
Expect	long balls
Don't Expect	great glove

Though never regarded as a fine fielder,
Bonilla bristled when deployed as a DH last
year. His reluctance to accept the role was
reflected in his performance, which was far
below expectations. With his five-year, $29-
million contract expiring at the end of the
1996 season, Bonilla was the subject of
constant trade rumors prior to the July 31
deadline. When in the right frame of mind,
the switch-hitting Bronx native is a solid
slugger with power from both sides. Bonilla
punishes lefties, produces with men in
scoring position, and draws a healthy share
of walks. Not especially fast, Bonilla is aggressive on the bases nonetheless and will
stretch long singles. In the field, he plays
the infield and outfield corners—none of
them well. He's led his league in errors five
times.

Major League Batting Register

	BA	G	AB	R	H	2B	3B	HR	RBI	SB
86 AL	.269	75	234	27	63	10	2	2	26	4
86 NL	.240	63	192	28	46	6	2	1	17	4
87 NL	.300	141	466	58	140	33	3	15	77	3
88 NL	.274	159	584	87	160	32	7	24	100	3
89 NL	.281	163	616	96	173	37	10	24	86	8
90 NL	.280	160	625	112	175	39	7	32	120	4
91 NL	.302	157	577	102	174	44	6	18	100	2
92 NL	.249	128	438	62	109	23	0	19	70	4
93 NL	.265	139	502	81	133	21	3	34	87	3
94 NL	.290	108	403	60	117	24	1	20	67	1
95 NL	.325	80	317	49	103	25	4	18	53	0
95 AL	.333	61	237	47	79	12	4	10	46	0
96 AL	.287	159	595	107	171	27	5	28	116	1
Life	.284	1593	5786	916	1643	333	54	245	965	37
3 Ave	.303	157	595	100	180	34	5	29	107	1

BRET BOONE

Position: Second base
Team: Cincinnati Reds
Born: April 6, 1969 El Cajon, CA
Height: 5'10" **Weight:** 180 lbs.
Bats: right **Throws:** right
Acquired: Traded by Mariners with Erik Hanson for Bobby Ayala and Dan Wilson, 11/93

PLAYER SUMMARY

Fantasy Value	$10 to $13
Card Value	8¢ to 12¢
Will	show some pop
Can't	deliver in clutch
Expect	excellent defense
Don't Expect	speed on bases

Although he supplies more power than most middle infielders, Boone's batting average fell for the second straight season. He takes hard swings, trying to hit home runs on every pitch. For a guy who's never hit more than 15 home runs in a season, his ratio of more than three Ks per walk is unacceptable. Boone's weak stick against lefties is another mark against him. Last season, when he flirted with the Mendoza Line vs. southpaws, he was dropped to seventh in the batting order. He also lost at bats after April surgery to remove elbow bone chips. Boone is not a big RBI man, and he's not a basestealing threat. But he can still make an impact by cultivating his reputation as a smooth-fielding second baseman. Boone led his position in putouts, double plays, and fielding percentage in 1995. He makes few errors and shows a strong, accurate arm. The first third-generation player in baseball history, he's the son of Bob Boone and grandson of Ray Boone.

Major League Batting Register

	BA	G	AB	R	H	2B	3B	HR	RBI	SB
92 AL	.194	33	129	15	25	4	0	4	15	1
93 AL	.251	76	271	31	68	12	2	12	38	2
94 NL	.320	108	381	59	122	25	2	12	68	3
95 NL	.267	138	513	63	137	34	2	15	68	5
96 NL	.233	142	520	56	121	21	3	12	69	3
Life	.261	497	1814	224	473	96	9	55	258	14
3 Ave	.274	150	545	70	149	31	3	15	80	4

PEDRO BORBON

Position: Pitcher
Team: Atlanta Braves
Born: Nov. 15, 1967 Mao, Dominican Republic
Height: 6'1" **Weight:** 205 lbs.
Bats: left **Throws:** left
Acquired: Signed as a free agent, 8/89

PLAYER SUMMARY

Fantasy Value	$0
Card Value	5¢ to 8¢
Will	silence lefties
Can't	favor bad elbow
Expect	stranded runners
Don't Expect	walks, homers

Before suffering a torn elbow ligament in August, Borbon was the top lefty reliever in the Atlanta bullpen. When healthy, Borbon is a fearless lefty who has great control of his hard stuff. He is following in the footsteps of his right-handed father, a fine reliever for the Reds and three other clubs. A fastball-slider pitcher who's working on a changeup, Pedro has a crossfire-type delivery that makes him extremely tough on left-handed hitters. He held them to a .167 average in 1995 and was even better last year. Borbon is also adept at leaving inherited runners stranded. For a hard thrower, Borbon has exceptional control. He keeps the ball in the park and holds baserunners well. He's also a quick and agile fielder, grabbing any grounders he can reach. Borbon's nine-inning averages are all outstanding: six hits, eight Ks, and fewer than two walks. He doesn't come to the plate much but knows how to swing the bat. It's his pitching that impresses most, however. Borbon was the guy who saved '95 World Series Game 4 after Mark Wohlers tired.

Major League Pitching Register

	W	L	ERA	G	S	IP	H	ER	BB	SO
92 NL	0	1	6.75	2	0	1.1	2	1	1	1
93 NL	0	0	21.60	3	0	1.2	3	4	3	2
95 NL	2	2	3.09	41	2	32.0	29	11	17	33
96 NL	3	0	2.75	43	1	36.0	26	11	7	31
Life	5	3	3.42	89	3	71.0	60	27	28	67
2 Ave	3	1	2.92	45	2	36.0	29	12	13	34

PAT BORDERS

Position: Catcher
Team: Cleveland Indians
Born: May 14, 1963 Columbus, OH
Height: 6'2" **Weight:** 205 lbs.
Bats: right **Throws:** right
Acquired: Signed as a minor-league free
agent, 12/96

PLAYER SUMMARY	
Fantasy Value	$0
Card Value	4¢ to 7¢
Will	call good game
Can't	play daily
Expect	hot streaks
Don't Expect	any speed

In the last three years, Borders has played
for the Blue Jays, Royals, Astros, Cardinals, Angels, and White Sox. Once
Toronto's top receiver, he is no longer the
player whose .450 average against Atlanta
made him World Series MVP in 1992. But
he's still capable of poking timely hits, especially against left-handers, and serving in
a supporting role. Borders, who caught all
six Series games in both '92 and '93, is a
streak hitter who thrives on first-pitch fastballs that catch too much of the plate. If he
played more, he could reach double digits
in homers again. Borders is slow but moves
well behind the plate. A good receiver who
calls a good game and knows how to handle pitchers, he's also adept at blocking the
plate. Pencil Borders in for another year as
an understudy. That scenario could change
with expansion around the corner.

Major League Batting Register

	BA	G	AB	R	H	2B	3B	HR	RBI	SB
88 AL	.273	56	154	15	42	6	3	5	21	0
89 AL	.257	94	241	22	62	11	1	3	29	2
90 AL	.286	125	346	36	99	24	2	15	49	0
91 AL	.244	105	291	22	71	17	0	5	36	0
92 AL	.242	138	480	47	116	26	2	13	53	1
93 AL	.254	138	488	38	124	30	0	9	55	2
94 AL	.247	85	295	24	73	13	1	3	26	1
95 AL	.231	52	143	14	33	8	1	4	13	0
95 NL	.114	11	35	1	4	0	0	0	0	0
96 NL	.319	26	69	3	22	3	0	0	4	0
96 AL	.258	50	151	12	39	4	0	5	14	0
Life	.254	880	2693	234	685	142	10	62	300	6
2 Ave	.250	85	283	23	71	11	1	5	25	1

MIKE BORDICK

Position: Shortstop
Team: Baltimore Orioles
Born: July 21, 1965 Marquette, MI
Height: 5'11" **Weight:** 175 lbs.
Bats: right **Throws:** right
Acquired: Signed as a free agent, 12/96

PLAYER SUMMARY	
Fantasy Value	$4 to $6
Card Value	4¢ to 7¢
Will	anchor infield
Can't	hit left-handers
Expect	bunts, singles
Don't Expect	high average

Bordick is one of baseball's best defensive
shortstops. Unfortunately, he doesn't hit
much. In the field, the former University of
Maine standout has quick reactions, fine
range, soft hands, and a strong, accurate
arm. He turns the double play, too, and
doesn't boot many balls. Before 1996, Bordick led AL shortstops in putouts twice and
tied for the lead in double plays once. Bordick is a singles hitter who's tough to fan.
He showed more patience last year, drawing enough walks to push his on-base percentage 70 points above his batting
average. But he flailed hopelessly against
most left-handers for the second straight
year. A spray hitter who uses all fields, Bordick usually handles breaking balls. But
hard stuff gives him so much trouble that he
changed his swing and stance in 1995.
That may have been a mistake, as his production fell sharply last season. He batted
ninth but played every day for the power-
packed A's, who utilized him for his stellar
defense.

Major League Batting Register

	BA	G	AB	R	H	2B	3B	HR	RBI	SB
90 AL	.071	25	14	0	1	0	0	0	0	0
91 AL	.238	90	235	21	56	5	1	0	21	3
92 AL	.300	154	504	62	151	19	4	3	48	12
93 AL	.249	159	546	60	136	21	2	3	48	10
94 AL	.253	114	391	38	99	18	4	2	37	7
95 AL	.264	126	428	46	113	13	0	8	44	11
96 AL	.240	155	525	46	126	18	4	5	54	5
Life	.258	823	2643	273	682	94	15	21	252	48
3 Ave	.252	152	519	50	131	19	3	6	52	9

TOBY BORLAND

Position: Pitcher
Team: New York Mets
Born: May 29, 1969 Quitman, LA
Height: 6'6" **Weight:** 190 lbs.
Bats: right **Throws:** right
Acquired: Traded by Phillies with Ricardo Jordan for Rico Brogna, 11/96

PLAYER SUMMARY	
Fantasy Value	$1
Card Value	6¢ to 10¢
Will	keep ball down
Can't	prevent gophers
Expect	sidearm delivery
Don't Expect	move to closer

Strictly a reliever since turning pro in 1988, Borland enjoyed some success as a minor-league closer. He's been a set-up man since reaching the majors, however, and is expected to continue in that role. The lanky right-hander has a resilient arm that is capable of coming back on short rest. His sidearming delivery is very difficult for right-handed hitters, who have trouble hitting much above the Mendoza Line against him. A sinker-slider pitcher who also throws a forkball, Borland tries to keep the ball down. He gets lots of ground-ball outs when his fastball sinks but gets lit up when it doesn't. Borland fans nearly eight batters per nine innings and yields fewer hits than innings overall. But he's sometimes betrayed by his control. Borland has some problems with inherited runners and gopher balls, but he controls the running game well. He's a solid fielder for a big man and no automatic out at the plate. He's also a decent fielder. Borland began his career at Martinsville of the Appalachian League in 1988.

Major League Pitching Register

	W	L	ERA	G	S	IP	H	ER	BB	SO
94 NL	1	0	2.36	24	1	34.1	31	9	14	26
95 NL	1	3	3.77	50	6	74.0	81	31	37	59
96 NL	7	3	4.07	69	0	90.2	83	41	43	76
Life	9	6	3.66	143	7	199.0	195	81	94	161
3 Ave	3	2	3.59	53	3	74.0	73	30	35	60

CHRIS BOSIO

Position: Pitcher
Team: Seattle Mariners
Born: April 3, 1963 Carmichael, CA
Height: 6'3" **Weight:** 225 lbs.
Bats: right **Throws:** right
Acquired: Signed as a free agent, 12/92

PLAYER SUMMARY	
Fantasy Value	$1 to $3
Card Value	4¢ to 7¢
Will	change speeds
Can't	strike men out
Expect	many grounders
Don't Expect	temper tantrums

Seattle signed Bosio as a free agent in 1992, and, except for a no-hitter in his first month on the Mariners, Bosio has never given the team its money's worth. The veteran right-hander missed the first half of the 1996 campaign while recovering from his seventh knee operation. Once plugged into the rotation, he started slowly. He is a finesse pitcher who throws curves, sliders, and forkballs, all of which he uses as changeups off his mediocre fastball. He changes speeds and location well, usually while maintaining reasonably good control. Not a strikeout pitcher, Bosio wins by inducing ground balls. He is an outstanding fielder who moves off the mound well for a big man. Bosio also holds runners close. He combines a compact delivery with a first-rate move. Bosio has learned to control his titanic temper. In the past, he often seemed like his own worst enemy.

Major League Pitching Register

	W	L	ERA	G	S	IP	H	ER	BB	SO
86 AL	0	4	7.01	10	0	34.2	41	27	13	29
87 AL	11	8	5.24	46	2	170.0	187	99	50	150
88 AL	7	15	3.36	38	6	182.0	190	68	38	84
89 AL	15	10	2.95	33	0	234.2	225	77	48	173
90 AL	4	9	4.00	20	0	132.2	131	59	38	76
91 AL	14	10	3.25	32	0	204.2	187	74	58	117
92 AL	16	6	3.62	33	0	231.1	223	93	44	120
93 AL	9	9	3.45	29	1	164.1	138	63	59	119
94 AL	4	10	4.32	19	0	125.0	137	60	40	67
95 AL	10	8	4.92	31	0	170.0	211	93	69	85
96 AL	4	4	5.93	18	0	60.2	72	40	24	39
Life	94	93	3.96	309	9	1710.0	1742	753	481	1059
3 Ave	7	9	4.82	27	0	143.1	167	76	53	76

SHAWN BOSKIE

Position: Pitcher
Team: Baltimore Orioles
Born: March 28, 1967 Hawthorne, NV
Height: 6'3" **Weight:** 205 lbs.
Bats: right **Throws:** right
Acquired: Signed as a free agent, 12/96

PLAYER SUMMARY	
Fantasy Value.	$2 to $4
Card Value	5¢ to 8¢
Will	throw strikes
Can't	avoid gophers
Expect	fine forkball
Don't Expect	frequent Ks

A late bloomer, Boskie became a double-digit winner for the first time in his seven-year career last season. He teamed with Chuck Finley to give the '96 Angels a solid right-left punch at the top of the rotation. The veteran sinkerballer, who also throws a forkball that works best against lefties, wins by getting grounders rather than strikeouts. He averages only six Ks per nine innings but keeps runners off the bases by showing good control (fewer than three walks per game). Boskie throws sinking and cut fastballs, forkballs, curves, and changeups. Boskie's biggest problem last year was the gopher ball: He yielded more than two dozen in his first 27 outings. Boskie handles fielding chores like a former infielder, which he is. He grabs grounders and stabs line drives with ease, often ending potential big innings. Boskie had some trouble holding runners in 1996, although he usually does quite well.

Major League Pitching Register

	W	L	ERA	G	CG	IP	H	ER	BB	SO
90 NL	5	6	3.69	15	1	97.2	99	40	31	49
91 NL	4	9	5.23	28	0	129.0	150	75	52	62
92 NL	5	11	5.01	23	0	91.2	96	51	36	39
93 NL	5	3	3.43	39	0	65.2	63	25	21	39
94 NL	4	6	5.01	20	1	88.0	88	49	29	61
94 AL	0	1	6.75	2	0	2.2	4	2	1	0
95 AL	7	7	5.64	20	1	111.2	127	70	25	51
96 AL	12	11	5.32	37	1	189.1	226	112	67	133
Life	42	54	4.92	184	4	775.2	853	424	262	434
3 Ave	9	9	5.33	29	1	146.1	164	87	45	92

RICKY BOTTALICO

Position: Pitcher
Team: Philadelphia Phillies
Born: Aug. 26, 1969 New Britain, CT
Height: 6'1" **Weight:** 209 lbs.
Bats: left **Throws:** right
Acquired: Signed as a free agent, 7/91

PLAYER SUMMARY	
Fantasy Value.	$30 to $35
Card Value	12¢ to 15¢
Will	bring late heat
Can't	avoid wildness
Expect	numerous saves
Don't Expect	great fielding

In 1996, his second full season, Bottalico blossomed into an All-Star. He converted his first 14 save chances, breaking the previous Philadelphia club record, and held hitters to an anemic batting average just below the Mendoza Line. The hard-throwing closer yields fewer hits than innings, averages more than one strikeout per inning, and overpowers right-handed hitters. He keeps the ball in the park, strands a high percentage of inherited runners, and controls the running game well. Bottalico throws a low-90s fastball, a cut version of the same pitch, and a late-breaking slider that ranks as his best pitch. He's working on a changeup that should make him even more effective. Bottalico's Achilles' heel is a tendency to experience occasional control problems: He yields nearly four walks per nine innings—too many for a top closer. But he's among the league leaders in first-batter efficiency, relief strikeout ratio, fewest runners allowed, and lowest batting average against a reliever.

Major League Pitching Register

	W	L	ERA	G	S	IP	H	ER	BB	SO
94 NL	0	0	0.00	3	0	3.0	3	0	1	3
95 NL	5	3	2.46	62	1	87.2	50	24	42	87
96 NL	4	5	3.19	61	34	67.2	47	24	23	74
Life	9	8	2.73	126	35	158.1	100	48	66	164
2 Ave	5	4	2.76	65	18	83.0	52	26	35	86

Rafael Bournigal

Position: Second base; shortstop
Team: Oakland Athletics
Born: May 12, 1966 Azua, Dominican Republic
Height: 5'11" **Weight:** 160 lbs.
Bats: right **Throws:** right
Acquired: Signed as a minor-league free agent, 1/96

Player Summary
```
Fantasy Value . . . . . . . . . . . . . . . . . . . . $0
Card Value . . . . . . . . . . . . . . . . 4¢ to 7¢
Will . . . . . . . . . . . . . . . . bring good glove
Can't . . . . . . . . . . . . . . . . hit the ball far
Expect . . . . . . . . . . . . . . . few walks or Ks
Don't Expect . . . . . . . . . . . regular position
```

One man's break may also be a break for another. When Brent Gates was idled by a broken leg last June, Bournigal got his first extended exposure to the big leagues. Although he provided his usual fine defense, Bournigal added little offense to the lineup. An aggressive contact hitter, he rarely walks or fans. But he rarely gets an extra-base hit, either. Instead, Bournigal sprays singles to all fields and tries to fatten his average by legging out infield rollers. He stole 18 bases in a minor-league season but has not run much in recent years. Bournigal provides good defense at second. The Florida State graduate made only two errors in his first 551 innings last year. Bournigal has quick reactions, good instincts, soft hands, and a strong, reliable arm. He can turn two from either side of the bag. While he doesn't have patience at the plate, he has plenty of patience when it comes to his career. In his first nine years as a pro, he played in only 58 major-league games, all with the Dodgers.

Darren Bragg

Position: Outfield
Team: Boston Red Sox
Born: Sept. 7, 1969 Waterbury, CT
Height: 5'9" **Weight:** 180 lbs.
Bats: left **Throws:** right
Acquired: Traded by Mariners for Jamie Moyer, 7/96

Player Summary
```
Fantasy Value . . . . . . . . . . . . . . . . $6 to $8
Card Value . . . . . . . . . . . . . . . . 6¢ to 10¢
Will . . . . . . . . . . . . . . . . practice patience
Can't . . . . . . . . . . . . . . duplicate Dykstra
Expect . . . . . . . . . . . . . . . . speed, defense
Don't Expect . . . . . . . . . . many strikeouts
```

At a time when the Red Sox needed a right-handed-hitting outfielder, baseball observers were surprised that they traded a front-line starter for Bragg. But Boston, burned by the failures of leadoff types Dwayne Hosey and Lee Tinsley, realized that Bragg had potential. A little guy who can fly, Bragg had three 20-steal seasons in the minors. He also showed unusual patience at the plate, leading one league with 105 walks. Adopting the same style in the majors, Bragg is a contact hitter with patience. He's tough to fan and walks almost as much as he strikes out. His basestealing percentage could be better, however. Bragg is a fine outfielder with good range and a strong arm (20 assists and five double plays in Triple-A three years ago). He played all three outfield positions last year but appeared most often in left. Because Bragg is a left-handed leadoff type with some power, he's drawn comparisons to the pre-back-surgery Lenny Dykstra. Those are big shoes to fill, but Bragg needs something to brag about.

Major League Batting Register

	BA	G	AB	R	H	2B	3B	HR	RBI	SB
92 NL	.150	10	20	1	3	1	0	0	0	0
93 NL	.500	8	18	0	9	1	0	0	3	0
94 NL	.224	40	116	2	26	3	1	0	11	0
96 AL	.242	88	252	33	61	14	2	0	18	4
Life	.244	146	406	36	99	19	3	0	32	4

Major League Batting Register

	BA	G	AB	R	H	2B	3B	HR	RBI	SB
94 AL	.158	8	19	4	3	1	0	0	2	0
95 AL	.234	52	145	20	34	5	1	3	12	9
96 AL	.261	127	417	74	109	26	2	10	47	14
Life	.251	187	581	96	146	32	3	13	61	23

MARK BRANDENBURG

Position: Pitcher
Team: Boston Red Sox
Born: July 14, 1970 Houston, TX
Height: 6' **Weight:** 180 lbs.
Bats: right **Throws:** right
Acquired: Traded by Rangers with Kerry Lacy for Mike Stanton, 7/96

PLAYER SUMMARY	
Fantasy Value	$1
Card Value	12¢ to 20¢
Will	stop gophers
Can't	throw hard
Expect	better control
Don't Expect	closer duty

Brandenburg was surprised at his late-July trade to the Red Sox last summer. He was enjoying a successful first full season in the majors and had made an impact as a set-up man in the Texas bullpen. A sidearmer from Texas Tech, where he was a third-team All-American, Brandenburg averages seven Ks per nine innings and a hit per frame. More effective against right-handed hitters, who find his delivery deceptive, Brandenburg keeps baseballs in the ballpark. In more than 300 minor-league innings, he yielded only ten homers—an impressive ratio. Used primarily in set-up roles, Brandenburg had extremely impressive ERAs in the minors. He wins by spotting his low-80s fastball. He changes speeds, working the strike zone in and out, up and down. He had a fine strikeout-to-walk ratio in 1995 but encountered control trouble last year. Despite that problem, which he did not have in the minors, he was able to post a respectable ERA. Brandenburg succeeds by outfoxing the opposition; a thinking man's pitcher, he spends his off-seasons working as a substitute teacher.

Major League Pitching Register

	W	L	ERA	G	S	IP	H	ER	BB	SO
95 AL	0	1	5.93	11	0	27.1	36	18	7	21
96 AL	5	5	3.43	55	0	76.0	76	29	33	66
Life	5	6	4.09	66	0	103.1	112	47	40	87

JEFF BRANSON

Position: Infield
Team: Cincinnati Reds
Born: Jan. 26, 1967 Waynesboro, MS
Height: 6' **Weight:** 180 lbs.
Bats: left **Throws:** right
Acquired: Second-round pick in 6/88 free-agent draft

PLAYER SUMMARY	
Fantasy Value	$1
Card Value	5¢ to 8¢
Will	come off bench
Can't	handle southpaws
Expect	power vs. righties
Don't Expect	weak defense

One of baseball's best bench players, Branson played second, short, and third while also serving as a solid left-handed pinch hitter for the '96 Reds. A lefty hitter who likes to pull, Branson hit for a higher average than he did as a singles hitter in his rookie year. He hits to all fields against righties but goes to the opposite field against left-handers. Used primarily as a platoon third baseman in 1995, Branson delivered a dozen homers, all against righties. The return of Willie Greene last year, however, sentenced him to more time on the pine. That was fine with Branson, who has learned to make the most out of spot duty. A 1988 Olympian from Livingston (AL) University, he has become a competent three-position infielder. Branson has good range and a strong, accurate throwing arm. He's also adept at turning the double play from either side. Branson lost some speed following 1992 knee surgery, but he's not a plodder. With expansion coming, Branson could land a regular job soon.

Major League Batting Register

	BA	G	AB	R	H	2B	3B	HR	RBI	SB
92 NL	.296	72	115	12	34	7	1	0	15	0
93 NL	.241	125	381	40	92	15	1	3	22	4
94 NL	.284	58	109	18	31	4	1	6	16	0
95 NL	.260	122	331	43	86	18	2	12	45	2
96 NL	.244	129	311	34	76	16	4	9	37	2
Life	.256	506	1247	147	319	60	9	30	135	8
2 Ave	.253	133	342	41	86	18	3	11	44	2

JEFF BRANTLEY

Position: Pitcher
Team: Cincinnati Reds
Born: Sept. 5, 1963 Florence, AL
Height: 5'11" **Weight:** 180 lbs.
Bats: right **Throws:** right
Acquired: Signed as a free agent, 1/94

PLAYER SUMMARY

Fantasy Value	$30 to $35
Card Value	8¢ to 12¢
Will	convert most saves
Can't	win when rusty
Expect	fine repertoire
Don't Expect	low K count

Brantley did not make the 1996 NL All-Star Team, but that may have been an oversight. He spent most of last year leading the league in saves and was the key reason the Reds remained in the NL Central race. The hard-throwing righty is one of baseball's most durable closers. He overpowers right-handed hitters, keeps the ball in the park, and averages more strikeouts than innings. His strikeout-to-walk ratio last year was nearly 4-to-1. Brantley's four-pitch arsenal is more extensive than those of his bullpen colleagues. He throws a fastball, slider, occasional curve, and a forkball that ranks as his best pitch. Brantley usually has good control, averaging just over three walks per nine innings. He yields fewer hits than innings and is more miserly with extra-base hits than Jack Benny was with tips. Brantley is a good fielder who keeps runners close. The Mississippi State product made the All-Star squad in 1990.

Major League Pitching Register

	W	L	ERA	G	S	IP	H	ER	BB	SO
88 NL	0	1	5.66	9	1	20.2	22	13	6	11
89 NL	7	1	4.07	59	0	97.1	101	44	37	69
90 NL	5	3	1.56	55	19	86.2	77	15	33	61
91 NL	5	2	2.45	67	15	95.1	78	26	52	81
92 NL	7	7	2.95	56	7	91.2	67	30	45	86
93 NL	5	6	4.28	53	0	113.2	112	54	46	76
94 NL	6	6	2.48	50	15	65.1	46	18	28	63
95 NL	3	2	2.82	56	28	70.1	53	22	20	62
96 NL	1	2	2.41	66	44	71.0	54	19	28	76
Life	39	30	3.05	471	129	712.0	610	241	295	585
3 Ave	4	4	2.57	66	32	81.1	59	23	30	78

DOUG BROCAIL

Position: Pitcher
Team: Detroit Tigers
Born: May 16, 1967 Clearfield, PA
Height: 6'5" **Weight:** 235 lbs.
Bats: left **Throws:** right
Acquired: Traded by Astros with Brian Hunter, Orlando Miller, Todd Jones, and a player to be named later for Brad Ausmus, Jose Lima, C.J. Nitkowski, Trever Miller, and Daryle Ward, 12/96

PLAYER SUMMARY

Fantasy Value	$0
Card Value	5¢ to 8¢
Will	work both ways
Can't	strike men out
Expect	surprising bat
Don't Expect	control lapses

Used primarily as a starter during seven seasons in the minors, Brocail has fared better as a bullpen hand in the majors. A sinker-slider pitcher who also throws a curveball and changeup, Brocail tries to keep the ball down in the strike zone. When he fails, he yields some big hits—often home runs. The former first-round draft choice (San Diego in 1986) is much more effective against right-handed batters. He's also a better pitcher with runners in scoring position, which may account for his success as a reliever. Brocail helps his own cause with his bunting, hitting, and fielding, but his slow delivery makes him an easy target for enterprising baserunners. Brocail is competent at the plate as well as on the bases. A quick, clever baserunner, he's often been inserted as a pinch runner. With expansion in the offing, Brocail may yet get the chance to scrap his swingman status.

Major League Pitching Register

	W	L	ERA	G	S	IP	H	ER	BB	SO
92 NL	0	0	6.43	3	0	14.0	17	10	5	15
93 NL	4	13	4.56	24	0	128.1	143	65	42	70
94 NL	0	0	5.82	12	0	17.0	21	11	5	11
95 NL	6	4	4.19	36	1	77.1	87	36	22	39
96 NL	1	5	4.58	23	0	53.0	58	27	23	34
Life	11	22	4.63	98	1	289.2	326	149	97	169
2 Ave	4	5	4.34	32	1	70.0	78	34	24	39

RICO BROGNA

Position: First base
Team: Philadelphia Phillies
Born: April 18, 1970 Turner Falls, MA
Height: 6'2" **Weight:** 200 lbs.
Bats: left **Throws:** left
Acquired: Traded by Mets for Toby Borland and Ricardo Jordan, 11/96

PLAYER SUMMARY	
Fantasy Value. . . . . $13 to $16
Card Value . . . . 6¢ to 10¢
Will . . . . hit ball hard
Can't . . . . run a lick
Expect . . . . strong defense
Don't Expect . . . . power vs. lefties

After leading the Mets with 22 homers and 76 RBI in 1995, Brogna was expected to be the bellwether of the New York attack last season. But that was before injuries interfered. The former first-round draft choice battled bursitis, tendinitis, and a slight tear in the labrum of his nonthrowing shoulder. Surgery was required, and the slugging first baseman spent most of the season on the sidelines. Expected to be healthy again in 1997, Brogna could pick up where he left off. Still only 26, he has a line-drive swing with plenty of power. He'd be even more productive if he stopped trying to pull every pitch and started using all fields. Brogna also needs to show more patience at the plate: He fans three times for every walk he draws. Brogna doesn't run well, either. But he has such quick reactions and soft hands in the field that he's one of baseball's best defensive first basemen. His .998 fielding percentage led the NL in 1995. Brogna makes good scoops, saving fellow infielders from errors, and turns the tough 3-6-3 double play.

Major League Batting Register

	BA	G	AB	R	H	2B	3B	HR	RBI	SB
92 AL	.192	9	26	3	5	1	0	1	3	0
94 NL	.351	39	131	16	46	11	2	7	20	1
95 NL	.289	134	495	72	143	27	2	22	76	0
96 NL	.255	55	188	18	48	10	1	7	30	0
Life	.288	237	840	109	242	49	5	37	129	1
2 Ave	.280	103	372	50	104	20	2	16	58	0

SCOTT BROSIUS

Position: Third base; outfield
Team: Oakland Athletics
Born: Aug. 15, 1966 Hillsboro, OR
Height: 6'1" **Weight:** 185 lbs.
Bats: right **Throws:** right
Acquired: 20th-round pick in 6/87 free-agent draft

PLAYER SUMMARY	
Fantasy Value. . . . . $19 to $22
Card Value . . . . 8¢ to 12¢
Will . . . . blast left-handers
Can't . . . . steal too often
Expect . . . . steady improvement
Don't Expect . . . . more Ks than BBs

When Brosius broke his right forearm last May, he was leading the AL with a .479 on-base percentage and was sixth with a .351 batting average. Brosius, an advocate of off-season weight training, pounded south paws last season and showed great patience at the plate. Earlier in his career, Brosius was a free swinger who rarely walked. Last year, he walked as often as he fanned. A shortened swing helped him make better contact and cut down on his whiffs, though he's still a pull hitter who feasts on fastballs. Brosius will occasionally surprise with a well-placed bunt. He's not much of a basestealer but moves well enough to play a decent third base. Brosius has good reactions, range, and hands, plus a strong throwing arm. His defense, previously marred by throwing errors, was much improved last year. Brosius is a versatile athlete who has played everywhere but catcher and pitcher in the big leagues. He spent almost all of 1996 at third base.

Major League Batting Register

	BA	G	AB	R	H	2B	3B	HR	RBI	SB
91 AL	.235	36	68	9	16	5	0	2	4	3
92 AL	.218	38	87	13	19	2	0	4	13	3
93 AL	.249	70	213	26	53	10	1	6	25	6
94 AL	.238	96	324	31	77	14	1	14	49	2
95 AL	.262	123	389	69	102	19	2	17	46	4
96 AL	.304	114	428	73	130	25	0	22	71	7
Life	.263	477	1509	221	397	75	4	65	208	25
3 Ave	.267	129	441	65	118	22	1	20	64	5

KEVIN BROWN

Position: Pitcher
Team: Florida Marlins
Born: March 14, 1965 McIntyre, GA
Height: 6'4" **Weight:** 188 lbs.
Bats: right **Throws:** right
Acquired: Signed as a free agent, 12/95

PLAYER SUMMARY	
Fantasy Value.	$20 to $25
Card Value	6¢ to 10¢
Will	induce groundouts
Can't	win whiff crown
Expect	pinpoint control
Don't Expect	inflated ERA

After nine years in the AL, Brown moved across league lines when he joined the 1996 Marlins. It was a match that took. For most of the season, the veteran sinkerballer led the NL in ERA. Three of his first four complete games were shutouts, and he made the All-Star Team for the second time. Brown throws a "heavy" sinker, a cut fastball that moves away from right-handed hitters but in on lefties. His arsenal also includes a fastball, an outstanding slider, and a great change. In addition, he's one of the game's leading control artists, averaging fewer than 1½ walks per nine innings. Brown yields fewer hits than innings, keeps the ball in the park, and maintains a 5-1 ratio of Ks to walks. He has a fabulous pick-off move. But the rest of his defensive game is not too shabby, either. The former Georgia Tech All-American was a first-round draft pick of Texas in 1986.

Major League Pitching Register

	W	L	ERA	G	CG	IP	H	ER	BB	SO
86 AL	1	0	3.60	1	0	5.0	6	2	0	4
88 AL	1	1	4.24	4	1	23.1	33	11	8	12
89 AL	12	9	3.35	28	7	191.0	167	71	70	104
90 AL	12	10	3.60	26	6	180.0	175	72	60	88
91 AL	9	12	4.40	33	0	210.2	233	103	90	96
92 AL	21	11	3.32	35	11	265.2	262	98	76	173
93 AL	15	12	3.59	34	12	233.0	228	93	74	142
94 AL	7	9	4.82	26	3	170.0	218	91	50	123
95 AL	10	9	3.60	26	3	172.1	155	69	48	117
96 NL	17	11	1.89	32	5	233.0	187	49	33	159
Life	105	84	3.52	245	48	1684.0	1664	659	509	1018
3 Ave	13	11	3.44	33	4	222.0	223	85	52	155

JACOB BRUMFIELD

Position: Outfield
Team: Toronto Blue Jays
Born: May 27, 1965 Bobalusa, LA
Height: 6' **Weight:** 180 lbs.
Bats: right **Throws:** right
Acquired: Traded by Pirates for D.J. Boston, 5/96

PLAYER SUMMARY	
Fantasy Value.	$4 to $6
Card Value	6¢ to 10¢
Will	get clutch hits
Can't	win regular job
Expect	speed, some pop
Don't Expect	patience at plate

If Brumfield ever learned to be patient, he might realize his dream of batting leadoff and playing every day. But he sabotages his own speed-plus-power package by swinging at pitches he couldn't possibly hit. Striking out at a better than 2-to-1 clip does not look good on the resume of a supposed leadoff man. On the other hand, Brumfield is versatile enough to play all three outfield positions, pinch-hit, pinch-run, and serve as a DH. A solid clutch hitter, Brumfield is at his best when going after a first-pitch fastball high up in the strike zone. He is fast enough to beat out bunts and infield rollers but tries instead to drive the ball, rather than going with the pitch. Brumfield would be a basestealer if he played enough to learn the pitchers' moves. He has speed but is careless sometimes. Brumfield's arm is as strong as his legs and he has good range, but his outfield play isn't polished. Brumfield is living proof that perseverance pays off; he spent seven years in the minors.

Major League Batting Register

	BA	G	AB	R	H	2B	3B	HR	RBI	SB
92 NL	.133	24	30	6	4	0	0	0	2	6
93 NL	.268	103	272	40	73	17	3	6	23	20
94 NL	.311	68	122	36	38	10	2	4	11	6
95 NL	.271	116	402	64	109	23	2	4	26	22
96 NL	.250	29	80	11	20	9	0	2	8	3
96 AL	.256	90	308	52	79	19	2	12	52	12
Life	.266	430	1214	209	323	78	9	28	122	69
2 Ave	.265	110	380	62	101	22	2	8	41	18

DAMON BUFORD

Position: Outfield
Team: Texas Rangers
Born: June 12, 1970 Baltimore, MD
Height: 5'10" **Weight:** 170 lbs.
Bats: right **Throws:** right
Acquired: Traded by Mets for Terrell Lowery, 3/96

PLAYER SUMMARY	
Fantasy Value	$1 to $3
Card Value	6¢ to 10¢
Will	use his speed
Can't	clear the fences
Expect	substitute spot
Don't Expect	strong throws

Buford settled into his first full big-league season as an extra man in the 1996 Texas outfield. A natural center fielder, he served as caddy for all three Ranger outfielders, actually spending most of his time in right. A fine defensive replacement, Buford provides the same speed and defense his father Don once gave the Orioles. Damon's Achilles' heel is an arm that is less than powerful. Because he has a good eye, Buford could be a leadoff hitter. His power (16 Triple-A homers in 1994) is simply a bonus. Buford hits line drives to all fields but needs to connect more frequently. Impatience at the plate has been his undoing thus far. Because of his speed, Buford could fatten his average by bunting, beating out infield rollers, and working pitchers for walks. Buford had two 40-steal seasons in the minors and a third with more than 30 swipes. To reach such levels again, he needs more playing time. A switch-hitter in college at USC, Buford has since switched to his natural style, hitting right-handed.

Major League Batting Register

	BA	G	AB	R	H	2B	3B	HR	RBI	SB
93 AL	.228	53	79	18	18	5	0	2	9	2
94 AL	.500	4	2	2	1	0	0	0	0	0
95 AL	.063	24	32	6	2	0	0	0	2	3
95 NL	.235	44	136	24	32	5	0	4	12	7
96 AL	.283	90	145	30	41	9	0	6	20	8
Life	.239	215	394	80	94	19	0	12	43	20

JAY BUHNER

Position: Outfield
Team: Seattle Mariners
Born: Aug. 13, 1964 Louisville, KY
Height: 6'3" **Weight:** 205 lbs.
Bats: right **Throws:** right
Acquired: Traded by Yankees with Rick Balabon and Troy Evers for Ken Phelps, 7/88

PLAYER SUMMARY	
Fantasy Value	$30 to $35
Card Value	15¢ to 25¢
Will	knock in runs
Can't	speed around bases
Expect	tape-measure homers
Don't Expect	powder-puff arm

Buhner teams with Ken Griffey, Jr., to give the Mariners a powerful right-left slugging tandem. It was Buhner, not Griffey, who set a Seattle club record for RBI in 1995 and then broke it in '96. Buhner hits home runs with frequency and with distance. A better hitter against lefties, he hits with power to all fields. The one-time wild swinger has also learned to be more selective at the plate. He's willing to wait for his pitch, coaxing enough walks to push his on-base percentage 100 points higher than his batting average. Buhner still fans twice as much as he walks, but he's making better contact than he once did. He doesn't have enough speed to steal any bases. In the field, Buhner is a steady but not flashy performer with a phenomenal throwing arm. Few right fielders intimidate runners more. Buhner won his first Gold Glove in 1996.

Major League Batting Register

	BA	G	AB	R	H	2B	3B	HR	RBI	SB
87 AL	.227	7	22	0	5	2	0	0	1	0
88 AL	.215	85	261	36	56	13	1	13	38	1
89 AL	.275	58	204	27	56	15	1	9	33	1
90 AL	.276	51	163	16	45	12	0	7	33	2
91 AL	.244	137	406	64	99	14	4	27	77	0
92 AL	.243	152	543	69	132	16	3	25	79	0
93 AL	.272	158	563	91	153	28	3	27	98	2
94 AL	.279	101	358	74	100	23	4	21	68	0
95 AL	.262	126	470	86	123	23	0	40	121	0
96 AL	.271	150	564	107	153	29	0	44	138	0
Life	.259	1025	3554	570	922	175	16	213	686	6
3 Ave	.271	145	532	103	144	29	2	40	123	0

JIM BULLINGER

Position: Pitcher
Team: Chicago Cubs
Born: Aug. 21, 1965 New Orleans, LA
Height: 6'2" **Weight:** 185 lbs.
Bats: right **Throws:** right
Acquired: Ninth-round pick in 6/86 free-agent draft

PLAYER SUMMARY	
Fantasy Value	$1
Card Value	4¢ to 7¢
Will	bank on sinker
Can't	avoid gophers
Expect	first-inning woes
Don't Expect	perfect control

Bullinger was expected to be one of the mainstays in last year's Cubs rotation. But he got off to a dreadful start and was exiled to the bullpen. A sinkerballer who also throws a curve and a cut fastball, Bullinger is a dependable pitcher when his pitches are working. But a sinker that doesn't sink often becomes a stinker. That happened with alarming frequency last year, when Bullinger yielded more than four walks per nine innings and more hits than innings pitched. He also had trouble keeping the ball in the park. The former University of New Orleans shortstop is not only a fifth infielder but also a potent ninth-place hitter. He even hit a home run in his first big-league at bat. Bullinger is a good bunter who is adept at advancing runners. But he hurts his own cause by not holding baserunners close. Without better control, Bullinger won't win as either a starter or reliever. Given a choice, he'd rather start. But he converted all of his first 11 save chances and could still return to the relief corps.

Major League Pitching Register

	W	L	ERA	G	S	IP	H	ER	BB	SO
92 NL	2	8	4.66	39	7	85.0	72	44	54	36
93 NL	1	0	4.32	15	1	16.2	18	8	9	10
94 NL	6	2	3.60	33	2	100.0	87	40	34	72
95 NL	12	8	4.14	24	0	150.0	152	69	65	93
96 NL	6	10	6.54	37	1	129.1	144	94	68	90
Life	27	28	4.77	148	11	481.0	473	255	230	301
3 Ave	9	7	4.67	37	1	146.1	146	76	63	99

DAVE BURBA

Position: Pitcher
Team: Cincinnati Reds
Born: July 7, 1966 Dayton, OH
Height: 6'4" **Weight:** 240 lbs.
Bats: right **Throws:** right
Acquired: Traded by Giants with Mark Portugal and Darren Lewis for Deion Sanders, Scott Service, John Roper, Dave McCarty, and Ricky Pickett, 7/95

PLAYER SUMMARY	
Fantasy Value	$8 to $10
Card Value	4¢ to 7¢
Will	start or relieve
Can't	locate the plate
Expect	K per inning
Don't Expect	gopher balls

Used as both a starter and reliever since reaching the majors in 1990, Burba has had moments of brilliance in both roles. He got off to an awful start as a member of the Reds rotation last year but did manage to hit home runs in consecutive starts—a rare occurrence for a man not regarded as a good hitter. A fastball-slider pitcher who dominates righties, Burba averaged just under a K per inning in 1995. His strikeout-to-walk ratio was down last summer, mainly because the righty had control problems. When he's on, Burba is a power pitcher who yields fewer hits than innings and keeps the ball in the park. He helps his own cause with his bunting ability but has problems in the field, where his follow-through leaves him in an awkward fielding position. He also has trouble holding runners on. Although he made more than two dozen starts in '96, he could return to relief work at any time.

Major League Pitching Register

	W	L	ERA	G	CG	IP	H	ER	BB	SO
90 AL	0	0	4.50	6	0	8.0	8	4	2	4
91 AL	2	2	3.68	22	0	36.2	34	15	14	16
92 NL	2	7	4.97	23	0	70.2	80	39	31	47
93 NL	10	3	4.25	54	0	95.1	95	45	37	88
94 NL	3	6	4.38	57	0	74.0	59	36	45	84
95 NL	10	4	3.97	52	1	106.2	90	47	51	96
96 NL	11	13	3.83	34	0	195.0	179	83	97	148
Life	38	35	4.13	248	1	586.1	545	269	277	483
3 Ave	9	9	4.01	58	0	140.1	121	62	73	125

JOHN BURKETT

Position: Pitcher
Team: Texas Rangers
Born: Nov. 28, 1964 New Brighton, PA
Height: 6'3" **Weight:** 205 lbs.
Bats: right **Throws:** right
Acquired: Traded by Marlins for Ryan Dempsey and a player to be named later, 8/96

PLAYER SUMMARY	
Fantasy Value	$8 to $10
Card Value	5¢ to 8¢
Will	throw strikes
Can't	ring up Ks
Expect	groundouts
Don't Expect	missed turns

A trade from the Marlins to the front-running Rangers was just the tonic Burkett needed. Burkett's Texas debut was the club's best since Fergie Jenkins threw a 1974 one-hitter in his first Ranger outing. Burkett won, 6-0, by pitching ahead in the count to 21 of the 34 Toronto batters he faced. A control artist who seldom misses a turn, Burkett responds to challenges. In 1993, when San Francisco was vying for the NL West title, Burkett was their best pitcher. He has good control of five pitches: sinking fastball, slider, curve, forkball, and changeup. Not a power pitcher, he relies on location to coax groundouts. Burkett led the NL with 26 double plays induced in '95. He doesn't start many of those twin killings himself, though, because his follow-through leaves him in awkward position. Burkett does keep close watch on baserunners and catches his share.

ELLIS BURKS

Position: Outfield
Team: Colorado Rockies
Born: Sept. 11, 1964 Vicksburg, MS
Height: 6'2" **Weight:** 202 lbs.
Bats: right **Throws:** right
Acquired: Signed as a free agent, 11/93

PLAYER SUMMARY	
Fantasy Value	$30 to $35
Card Value	12¢ to 20¢
Will	swing strong bat
Can't	avoid strikeouts
Expect	power plus speed
Don't Expect	trouble in field

Burks burst out of the box so quickly last April that his severe 1995 wrist injury was forgotten. He was NL Player of the Month in April (.414, nine homers, and 17 RBI), an All-Star in July, an MVP contender down the stretch, and a first-time 30-30 player. Burks ranked among NL leaders in hitting, slugging, on-base percentage, homers, RBI, runs scored, and total bases. He also provided strong defense in left field, where he started the season, and center. Though he averages two whiffs per walk, Burks draws plenty of walks. He also runs well. His speed gives him good range in the outfield, where he could repeat the Gold Glove he won in 1990. He has soft hands and an accurate throwing arm. The former No. 1 draft choice of the Red Sox (1983) has been an All-Star in both leagues. Burks's 1996 career year coincided with his first injury-free season since 1993.

Major League Pitching Register

	W	L	ERA	G	CG	IP	H	ER	BB	SO
87 NL	0	0	4.50	3	0	6.0	7	3	3	5
90 NL	14	7	3.79	33	2	204.0	201	86	61	118
91 NL	12	11	4.18	36	3	206.2	223	96	60	131
92 NL	13	9	3.84	32	3	189.2	194	81	45	107
93 NL	22	7	3.65	34	2	231.2	224	94	40	145
94 NL	6	8	3.62	25	0	159.1	176	64	36	85
95 NL	14	14	4.30	30	4	188.1	208	90	57	126
96 NL	6	10	4.32	24	1	154.0	154	74	42	108
96 AL	5	2	4.06	10	1	68.2	75	31	16	47
Life	92	68	3.96	227	16	1408.1	1462	619	360	872
3 Ave	12	13	4.05	34	2	220.1	237	99	58	139

Major League Batting Register

	BA	G	AB	R	H	2B	3B	HR	RBI	SB
87 AL	.272	133	558	94	152	30	2	20	59	27
88 AL	.294	144	540	93	159	37	5	18	92	25
89 AL	.303	97	399	73	121	19	6	12	61	21
90 AL	.296	152	588	89	174	33	8	21	89	9
91 AL	.251	130	474	56	119	33	3	14	56	6
92 AL	.255	66	235	35	60	8	3	8	30	5
93 AL	.275	146	499	75	137	24	4	17	74	6
94 NL	.322	42	149	33	48	8	3	13	24	3
95 NL	.266	103	278	41	74	10	4	14	49	7
96 NL	.344	156	613	142	211	45	8	40	128	32
Life	.290	1169	4333	731	1255	247	48	177	662	141
2 Ave	.318	136	463	94	147	28	7	28	92	20

JEROMY BURNITZ

Position: Outfield
Team: Milwaukee Brewers
Born: April 15, 1969 Westminster, CA
Height: 6' **Weight:** 190 lbs.
Bats: left **Throws:** right
Acquired: Traded by Indians for Kevin Seitzer, 8/96

PLAYER SUMMARY	
Fantasy Value	$7 to $9
Card Value	8¢ to 12¢
Will	stroke the ball
Can't	hit left-handers
Expect	good speed, pop
Don't Expect	low on-base mark

Why did the Mets keep Carl Everett but dump Jeromy Burnitz? A 30-30 man in the minors, Burnitz had only two cups of coffee in New York before joining the Cleveland organization. He hasn't stopped hitting since. An aggressive hitter who once tried to pull every pitch, Burnitz responded well when Cleveland batting coach Charlie Manuel showed him how to use the whole field. In fact, his strong play was the main reason the Tribe traded incumbent DH Eddie Murray to Baltimore. Used almost exclusively against right-handed pitching, Burnitz had seven homers and 22 RBI in his first 108 at bats last year. He also showed a good eye, walking almost as much as he fanned and pushing his on-base percentage more than 100 points beyond his batting average. New York's former No. 1 draft choice (1990) played all three outfield spots last year but spent most of his time as a designated hitter and pinch hitter. His speed gives him good range when he does play the field. At 28, his future lies ahead of him. Burnitz led two minor leagues in RBI.

Major League Batting Register

	BA	G	AB	R	H	2B	3B	HR	RBI	SB
93 NL	.243	86	263	49	64	10	6	13	38	3
94 NL	.238	45	143	26	34	4	0	3	15	1
95 AL	.571	9	7	4	4	1	0	0	0	0
96 AL	.265	94	200	38	53	14	0	9	40	4
Life	.253	234	613	117	155	29	6	25	93	8

MIKE BUSCH

Position: Third base
Team: Los Angeles Dodgers
Born: July 7, 1968 Davenport, IA
Height: 6'5" **Weight:** 220 lbs.
Bats: right **Throws:** right
Acquired: Fourth-round pick in 6/90 free-agent draft

PLAYER SUMMARY	
Fantasy Value	$0
Card Value	8¢ to 12¢
Will	hit with power
Can't	play the field
Expect	high K totals
Don't Expect	strong average

Given a chance when Mike Blowers was hurt last year, Busch burned brightly for a week. He hit a grand slam in the first game after his mid-July recall and knocked in nine runs in his first five games. Then he faded so badly that the Dodgers reacquired veteran Tim Wallach for the stretch drive. Because of his power potential, however, the big-league door remains open to Busch. A football tight end at Iowa State, he became a baseball pro in 1990 and immediately started hitting the long ball. After reaching a career peak with 27 homers in Triple-A in 1994, Busch made his big-league bow a year later—but only after slowing his progress by serving as a replacement player during '95 spring training. Busch is not quite an all-or-nothing slugger like Billy Ashley, but he's close. He fans nearly three times per walk, collects extra bases on almost half his hits, and does not hit for a high average. He's a defensive liability who once made 40 errors in a Triple-A season. Much better at first than third, Busch led Pacific Coast League first basemen in chances, putouts, assists, and double plays in 1994.

Major League Batting Register

	BA	G	AB	R	H	2B	3B	HR	RBI	SB
95 NL	.235	13	17	3	4	0	0	3	6	0
96 NL	.217	38	83	8	18	4	0	4	17	0
Life	.220	51	100	11	22	4	0	7	23	0

BRETT BUTLER

Position: Outfield
Team: Los Angeles Dodgers
Born: June 15, 1957 Los Angeles, CA
Height: 5'10" **Weight:** 160 lbs.
Bats: left **Throws:** left
Acquired: Signed as a free agent, 4/95

PLAYER SUMMARY	
Fantasy Value	$5 to $7
Card Value	7¢ to 10¢
Will	seek medical OK
Can't	nail baserunners
Expect	good eye, speed
Don't Expect	fountain of youth

Butler was up to his old tricks as Dodger leadoff man last year when he was felled by throat cancer. Despite May 21 surgery, he was able to rejoin the squad in early September. Unfortunately, he was hit by a pitch after only five games, suffering a broken hand that ended his season for good. Butler turns 40 in June. The lefty-hitting leadoff man's days as a regular may be numbered. But his tenacity ranks among baseball's best. The speed-burner beats out bunts and infield hits, stretches singles, and swipes bases. He uses his keen batting eye to draw tons of walks. Butler has led the league in walks, runs, hits, triples, chances, putouts, and fielding percentage. Twice, he went through an entire season without making an error.

Major League Batting Register

	BA	G	AB	R	H	2B	3B	HR	RBI	SB
81 NL	.254	40	126	17	32	2	3	0	4	9
82 NL	.217	89	240	35	52	2	0	0	7	21
83 NL	.281	151	549	84	154	21	13	5	37	39
84 AL	.269	159	602	108	162	25	9	3	49	52
85 AL	.311	152	591	106	184	28	14	5	50	47
86 AL	.278	161	587	92	163	17	14	4	51	32
87 AL	.295	137	522	91	154	25	8	9	41	33
88 NL	.287	157	568	109	163	27	9	6	43	43
89 NL	.283	154	594	100	168	22	4	4	36	31
90 NL	.309	160	622	108	192	20	9	3	44	51
91 NL	.296	161	615	112	182	13	5	2	38	38
92 NL	.309	157	553	86	171	14	11	3	39	41
93 NL	.298	156	607	80	181	21	10	1	42	39
94 NL	.314	111	417	79	131	13	9	8	33	27
95 NL	.300	129	513	78	154	18	9	1	38	32
96 NL	.267	34	131	22	35	1	1	0	8	8
Life	.291	2108	7837	1307	2278	269	128	54	560	543
2 Ave	.307	151	582	100	179	19	11	6	45	37

KEN CAMINITI

Position: Third base
Team: San Diego Padres
Born: April 21, 1963 Hanford, CA
Height: 6' **Weight:** 200 lbs.
Bats: both **Throws:** right
Acquired: Traded by Astros with Steve Finley, Andujar Cedeno, Robert Petagine, Brian Williams, and a player to be named later for Phil Plantier, Derek Bell, Pedro Martinez, Doug Brocail, Craig Shipley, and Ricky Gutierrez, 12/94

PLAYER SUMMARY	
Fantasy Value	$30 to $35
Card Value	15¢ to 25¢
Will	hit well both ways
Can't	worry about knees
Expect	Gold Glove defense
Don't Expect	any hint of speed

Though his power was short-circuited last year by a sore left shoulder, Caminiti did homer in five straight games: the All-Star Game, the game before it, and the three immediately following. Over the last two years, his power numbers have swelled in direct proportion to his increased patience at the plate. Caminiti's on-base percentage is 80 points better than his batting average. He has more power and a slightly better average batting lefty, but the difference is minuscule. The only thing he can't do well is run—the result of chronic knee problems. The San Jose State All-American has always been best known for his defense. Caminiti won Gold Gloves in 1995 and '96 and was named the '96 NL MVP.

Major League Batting Register

	BA	G	AB	R	H	2B	3B	HR	RBI	SB
87 NL	.246	63	203	10	50	7	1	3	23	0
88 NL	.181	30	83	5	15	2	0	1	7	0
89 NL	.255	161	585	71	149	31	3	10	72	4
90 NL	.242	153	541	52	131	20	2	4	51	9
91 NL	.253	152	574	65	145	30	3	13	80	4
92 NL	.294	135	506	68	149	31	2	13	62	10
93 NL	.262	143	543	75	142	31	0	13	75	8
94 NL	.283	111	406	63	115	28	2	18	75	4
95 NL	.302	143	526	74	159	33	0	26	94	12
96 NL	.326	146	546	109	178	37	2	40	130	11
Life	.273	1237	4513	592	1233	250	15	141	669	62
3 Ave	.303	154	570	94	173	38	2	32	114	10

TOM CANDIOTTI

Position: Pitcher
Team: Los Angeles Dodgers
Born: Aug. 31, 1957 Walnut Creek, CA
Height: 6'2" **Weight:** 205 lbs.
Bats: right **Throws:** right
Acquired: Signed as a free agent, 12/91

PLAYER SUMMARY	
Fantasy Value	$4 to $6
Card Value	4¢ to 7¢
Will	baffle batters
Can't	bunt, hit, run
Expect	good K/BB rate
Don't Expect	complete games

As long as he keeps throwing his knuckler, Candiotti will remain a viable major-league starter. He took a 3.47 career ERA into 1996 but continued to be baseball's Rodney Dangerfield—a pitcher who gets no respect. He's been victimized by poor offensive and defensive support. The veteran right-hander controls the knuckler well, averaging three whiffs per walk, and doesn't surrender too many gopher balls. Those he does yield often come on knucklers that don't break or on one of his "extra" pitches, including a cut fastball, curveball, or slider. Candiotti does not help himself with his bunting or batting and is only average in the field. But his pickoff move is excellent for a right-hander with a slow delivery. Because Candiotti's pitch places no strain on the arm, he may have another year or two left.

Major League Pitching Register

	W	L	ERA	G	CG	IP	H	ER	BB	SO
83 AL	4	4	3.23	10	2	55.2	62	20	16	21
84 AL	2	2	5.29	8	0	32.1	38	19	10	23
86 AL	16	12	3.57	36	17	252.1	234	100	106	167
87 AL	7	18	4.78	32	7	201.2	193	107	93	111
88 AL	14	8	3.28	31	11	216.2	225	79	53	137
89 AL	13	10	3.10	31	4	206.0	188	71	55	124
90 AL	15	11	3.65	31	3	202.0	207	82	55	128
91 AL	13	13	2.65	34	6	238.0	202	70	73	167
92 NL	11	15	3.00	32	6	203.2	177	68	63	152
93 NL	8	10	3.12	33	2	213.2	192	74	71	155
94 NL	7	7	4.12	23	5	153.0	149	70	54	102
95 NL	7	14	3.50	30	1	190.1	187	74	58	141
96 NL	9	11	4.49	28	1	152.1	172	76	43	79
Life	126	135	3.53	359	65	2317.2	2226	910	750	1507
3 Ave	9	12	3.99	31	3	194.0	197	86	61	127

JOHN CANGELOSI

Position: Outfield
Team: Florida Marlins
Born: March 10, 1963 Brooklyn, NY
Height: 5'8" **Weight:** 160 lbs.
Bats: both **Throws:** right
Acquired: Signed as a free agent, 11/96

PLAYER SUMMARY	
Fantasy Value	$1 to $3
Card Value	4¢ to 7¢
Will	get on base
Can't	clear fences
Expect	good contact
Don't Expect	powerful arm

A pesky little hitter with speed, Cangelosi played a key role in Houston's bid for the 1996 NL Central crown. He played center and left, pinch-hit, and often set the table for the big hitters. Cangelosi is a patient hitter with a small strike zone. Translated, that means he draws many more walks than a spray-hitting speed merchant should. He also makes excellent contact, but a Cangelosi home run is almost as rare as a Bahamian blizzard. He does walk more than he fans, however. Cangelosi is no longer the burner who had three 50-steal seasons in the minors, but he'll still swipe more than a dozen with decent playing time. Cangelosi's speed gives him good range in the outfield, where he gets good jumps and shows soft hands. His arm isn't strong, however, and he doesn't throw extremely well (for power or accuracy). Cangelosi, willing to do anything to help his team, has even pitched three scoreless innings.

Major League Batting Register

	BA	G	AB	R	H	2B	3B	HR	RBI	SB
85 AL	.000	5	2	2	0	0	0	0	0	0
86 AL	.235	137	438	65	103	16	3	2	32	50
87 AL	.275	104	182	44	50	8	3	4	18	21
88 NL	.254	75	118	18	30	4	1	0	8	9
89 NL	.219	112	160	18	35	4	2	0	9	11
90 NL	.197	58	76	13	15	2	0	0	1	7
92 AL	.188	73	85	12	16	2	0	1	6	6
94 NL	.252	62	111	14	28	4	0	0	4	5
95 NL	.318	90	201	46	64	5	2	2	18	21
96 NL	.263	108	262	49	69	11	4	1	16	17
Life	.251	824	1635	281	410	56	15	10	112	147
2 Ave	.289	105	244	50	71	8	3	2	18	20

JOSE CANSECO

Position: Outfield
Team: Boston Red Sox
Born: July 2, 1964 Havana, Cuba
Height: 6'3" **Weight:** 230 lbs.
Bats: right **Throws:** right
Acquired: Traded by Rangers for Otis Nixon
and Luis Ortiz, 12/94

PLAYER SUMMARY	
Fantasy Value. . . . . $25 to $30
Card Value . . . . 20¢ to 30¢
Will . . . . try new comeback
Can't . . . . return to field
Expect . . . . enormous power
Don't Expect . . . . speed to return

Before a ruptured disc required August surgery, Canseco was a formidable force in the 1996 Boston lineup. He joined Jimmie Foxx (1938) as the only Red Sox ever to hit double-digit homers in consecutive months. Canseco's most recent aches and pains included a strained right hip flexor muscle and chronic back problems. The last time he appeared in more than 120 games (1991), he had 44 homers and 122 RBI. He's won two home run crowns, an RBI title, and an MVP Award. Canseco also remains baseball's only 40-40 man ('88). Injuries have since interfered with his running. A streak hitter with great bat speed, Canseco is a superb clutch hitter. Don't be deceived by his 2-1 ratio of Ks to walks; he draws enough passes to post a good on-base mark.

Major League Batting Register

	BA	G	AB	R	H	2B	3B	HR	RBI	SB
85 AL	.302	29	96	16	29	3	0	5	13	1
86 AL	.240	157	600	85	144	29	1	33	117	15
87 AL	.257	159	630	81	162	35	3	31	113	15
88 AL	.307	158	610	120	187	34	0	42	124	40
89 AL	.269	65	227	40	61	9	1	17	57	6
90 AL	.274	131	481	83	132	14	2	37	101	19
91 AL	.266	154	572	115	152	32	1	44	122	26
92 AL	.244	119	439	74	107	15	0	26	87	6
93 AL	.255	60	231	30	59	14	1	10	46	6
94 AL	.282	111	429	88	121	19	2	31	90	15
95 AL	.306	102	396	64	121	25	1	24	81	4
96 AL	.289	96	360	68	104	22	1	28	82	3
Life	.272	1341	5071	864	1379	251	13	328	1033	156
3 Ave	.291	122	470	88	137	26	2	33	100	10

CHUCK CARR

Position: Outfield
Team: Milwaukee Brewers
Born: Aug. 10, 1968 San Bernardino, CA
Height: 5'10" **Weight:** 165 lbs.
Bats: both **Throws:** right
Acquired: Traded by Marlins for Juan
Gonzalez, 12/95

PLAYER SUMMARY	
Fantasy Value. . . . . $4 to $6
Card Value . . . . 5¢ to 8¢
Will . . . . try comeback
Can't . . . . wait for walks
Expect . . . . acrobatic play
Don't Expect . . . . much power

A Carr crash wasn't in the plans when Milwaukee snatched him from the Marlins. The Brewers wanted a center fielder-leadoff man with speed. The fleet switch-hitter delivered—hitting .274 in 27 games—before injuring his right leg while making a leaping catch in May. Carr not only needed reconstructive knee surgery but damaged his right hamstring and ankle. When he recovers, it's very possible his speed won't be the same. Carr's 58 stolen bases led the National League in 1993, and he would have swiped more had he reached more often. But patience is not part of his vocabulary. Carr needs to wait for his pitch, draw walks, drop bunts, and make contact. Though he's a singles hitter with little power, Carr can stretch hits to the outfield. His speed also gives him great range in center, where his dives, leaps, and sprints are part of his game plan. He outruns some errors in judgment. Carr needs to curb his penchant for acrobatics and showboating.

Major League Batting Register

	BA	G	AB	R	H	2B	3B	HR	RBI	SB
90 NL	.000	4	2	0	0	0	0	0	0	1
91 NL	.182	12	11	1	2	0	0	0	1	1
92 NL	.219	22	64	8	14	3	0	0	3	10
93 NL	.267	142	551	75	147	19	2	4	41	58
94 NL	.263	106	433	61	114	19	2	2	30	32
95 NL	.227	105	308	54	70	20	0	2	20	25
96 AL	.274	27	106	18	29	6	1	1	11	5
Life	.255	418	1475	217	376	67	5	9	106	132
2 Ave	.250	134	478	73	120	25	1	3	32	37

HECTOR CARRASCO

Position: Pitcher
Team: Cincinnati Reds
Born: Oct. 22, 1969 San Pedro de Macoris, Dominican Republic
Height: 6'2" **Weight:** 175 lbs.
Bats: right **Throws:** right
Acquired: Traded by Marlins with Gary Scott for Chris Hammond, 9/93

PLAYER SUMMARY	
Fantasy Value	$3 to $5
Card Value	4¢ to 7¢
Will	bank on heat
Can't	find plate
Expect	rubber arm
Don't Expect	righties to hit

Right-handed hitters fold up shop when Carrasco enters a game. He throws a red-hot moving fastball, timed in the upper 90s, and yields fewer than six hits per nine innings. Carrasco is even stingier in giving up gopher balls. A Jose Rijo disciple who has yet to master his mentor's forkball and slider, Carrasco already averages almost eight whiffs per nine innings. Should he conquer either Rijo delivery, he could move from set-up man to closer. That won't happen, however, unless he masters his often-erratic control. Through the first four months of 1996, he averaged more than five walks per game. Carrasco also throws too many wild pitches. That penchant for wildness was the primary reason the hard-throwing Dominican was previously dumped by the Mets, Astros, and Marlins. A stubborn streak doesn't help, either: More concerned with the strikeout than the stolen base, Carrasco doesn't hold runners well. His hitting is nothing to write home about. Fortunately, he seldom bats. Carrasco has a rubber arm and can work often.

Major League Pitching Register

	W	L	ERA	G	S	IP	H	ER	BB	SO
94 NL	5	6	2.24	45	6	56.1	42	14	30	41
95 NL	2	7	4.12	64	5	87.1	86	40	46	64
96 NL	4	3	3.75	56	0	74.1	58	31	45	59
Life	11	16	3.51	165	11	218.0	186	85	121	164
3 Ave	4	6	3.42	64	5	84.0	71	32	46	63

MARK CARREON

Position: Outfield; first base
Team: Cleveland Indians
Born: July 9, 1963 Chicago, IL
Height: 6' **Weight:** 195 lbs.
Bats: right **Throws:** left
Acquired: Traded by Giants for Jim Poole, 7/96

PLAYER SUMMARY	
Fantasy Value	$5 to $7
Card Value	5¢ to 8¢
Will	rip breaking balls
Can't	win fielding award
Expect	power in the pinch
Don't Expect	any kind of speed

Acquired from the Giants as a spare part with power against lefties, Carreon wound up seeing much more starting action than expected, due to Julio Franco's hamstring problems. Carreon, who seems to disdain singles, had 34 extra-base hits for the Giants before his All-Star break trade across league lines. Unlike most other power hitters, he makes good contact and shows considerable patience at the plate. He thrives on a breaking-ball diet, hits with authority to all fields, and consistently delivers in the clutch. As a runner, he inherited "catcher's speed" from his dad, former big-league receiver Camilo Carreon. With little range in the outfield, Carreon is best used as a first baseman. Carreon began his pro career in the New York Mets organization in 1981 and spent seven seasons in the minors.

Major League Batting Register

	BA	G	AB	R	H	2B	3B	HR	RBI	SB
87 NL	.250	9	12	0	3	0	0	0	1	0
88 NL	.556	7	9	5	5	2	0	1	1	0
89 NL	.308	68	133	20	41	6	0	6	16	2
90 NL	.250	82	188	30	47	12	0	10	26	1
91 NL	.260	106	254	18	66	6	0	4	21	2
92 AL	.232	101	336	34	78	11	1	10	41	3
93 NL	.327	78	150	22	49	9	1	7	33	1
94 NL	.270	51	100	8	27	4	0	3	20	0
95 NL	.301	117	396	53	119	24	0	17	65	0
96 NL	.260	81	292	40	76	22	3	9	51	2
96 AL	.324	38	142	16	46	12	0	2	14	1
Life	.277	738	2012	246	557	108	5	69	289	12
2 Ave	.285	106	369	50	105	25	2	14	62	1

JOE CARTER

Position: Outfield
Team: Toronto Blue Jays
Born: March 7, 1960 Oklahoma City, OK
Height: 6'3" **Weight:** 215 lbs.
Bats: right **Throws:** right
Acquired: Traded by Padres with Roberto Alomar for Fred McGriff and Tony Fernandez, 12/90

PLAYER SUMMARY

Fantasy Value	$20 to $25
Card Value	12¢ to 20¢
Will	deliver in clutch
Can't	practice patience
Expect	homers, runs, RBI
Don't Expect	average above .300

Talk about consistency: Carter has topped 20 homers in each of the last 11 years. During that span, he also hit three homers in a game five times. Best known as the man whose ninth-inning homer vs. Philadelphia gave Toronto its second straight world championship in 1993, Carter is a wrist hitter who feasts on fastballs he can pull. He collects extra bases on 40 percent of his hits but fans more than twice per walk. No longer the roadrunner who had a 30-30 year in 1987, Carter concentrates on collecting the big hit. He's an outstanding clutch hitter who is subject to slumps but can also carry a club when hot. Carter's Achilles' heel is his defense. He spent most of last year in left, where range is his forte.

Major League Batting Register

	BA	G	AB	R	H	2B	3B	HR	RBI	SB
83 NL	.176	23	51	6	9	1	1	0	1	1
84 AL	.275	66	244	32	67	6	1	13	41	2
85 AL	.262	143	489	64	128	27	0	15	59	24
86 AL	.302	162	663	108	200	36	9	29	121	29
87 AL	.264	149	588	83	155	27	2	32	106	31
88 AL	.271	157	621	85	168	36	6	27	98	27
89 AL	.243	162	651	84	158	32	4	35	105	13
90 NL	.232	162	634	79	147	27	1	24	115	22
91 AL	.273	162	638	89	174	42	3	33	108	20
92 AL	.264	158	622	97	164	30	7	34	119	12
93 AL	.254	155	603	92	153	33	5	33	121	8
94 AL	.271	111	435	70	118	25	2	27	103	11
95 AL	.253	139	558	70	141	23	0	25	76	12
96 AL	.253	157	625	84	158	35	7	30	107	7
Life	.261	1906	7422	1043	1940	380	48	357	1280	219
3 Ave	.259	157	622	87	161	32	3	32	113	12

RAUL CASANOVA

Position: Catcher
Team: Detroit Tigers
Born: Aug. 23, 1972 Humacao, Puerto Rico
Height: 5'11" **Weight:** 200 lbs.
Bats: both **Throws:** right
Acquired: Traded by Padres with Melvin Nieves and Richie Lewis for Sean Bergman, Todd Steverson, and Cade Gaspar, 5/96

PLAYER SUMMARY

Fantasy Value	$3 to $5
Card Value	20¢ to 30¢
Will	show some pop
Can't	stay healthy
Expect	strong throws
Don't Expect	plate discipline

After spending six years in the minors, Casanova made his major-league debut against Cleveland last May 24. Yet another in the line of former Padres prospects brought to Detroit by former San Diego GM Randy Smith, Casanova came with a reputation as a minor-league slugger. He led the Class-A California League with 160 hits and a .340 batting average in 1994, when he also had 23 homers and 120 RBI in 123 games. Casanova, who has been bothered by back and ankle problems throughout his career, carries no glittering credentials. But Tiger scouts liked his bat speed, power potential, and strong throwing arm. Casanova's Achilles' heel is his penchant for swinging at anything. He needs to make more contact and draw more walks to hold his own at the plate. As a right-handed power hitter, Casanova faces a friendly target in Tiger Stadium. But his playing time could be squeezed again by Brad Ausmus, the more polished defensive receiver who followed him from San Diego to Detroit. Casanova broke into pro ball after the New York Mets made him an eighth-round choice in the 1990 amateur draft.

Major League Batting Register

	BA	G	AB	R	H	2B	3B	HR	RBI	SB
96 AL	.188	25	85	6	16	1	0	4	9	0
Life	.188	25	85	6	16	1	0	4	9	0

VINNY CASTILLA

Position: Third base
Team: Colorado Rockies
Born: July 4, 1967 Oaxaca, Mexico
Height: 6'1" **Weight:** 175 lbs.
Bats: right **Throws:** right
Acquired: Second-round pick from Braves in 12/92 expansion draft

PLAYER SUMMARY	
Fantasy Value	$30 to $35
Card Value	10¢ to 15¢
Will	thrive at home
Can't	wait for walks
Expect	All-Star stats
Don't Expect	good road power

For the past two seasons, Castilla has been on a home run tear. Aided by the alpine altitude of Coors Field, the onetime backup shortstop has learned to lift the ball—even taking many pitches to the opposite field against left-handers. Routine fly balls elsewhere are home runs in Denver, helping to explain the 100-point differential in Castilla's home and away batting average. An impatient hitter, he fans three times more often than he walks. But he has always showed signs of hidden hitting prowess; when the Rockies plucked him out of the Atlanta farm system in the 1992 expansion draft, Bobby Cox said he hated to lose him. But neither Cox nor anyone else dreamed that Castilla would start for the NL All-Star Team three years later. He's even become a good defensive performer. Not quick enough for prolonged spells at short, Castilla has little trouble at third. He has quick reactions, soft hands, and a strong, reasonably accurate arm.

FRANK CASTILLO

Position: Pitcher
Team: Chicago Cubs
Born: April 1, 1969 El Paso, TX
Height: 6'1" **Weight:** 180 lbs.
Bats: right **Throws:** right
Acquired: Sixth-round pick in 6/87 free-agent draft

PLAYER SUMMARY	
Fantasy Value	$4 to $6
Card Value	4¢ to 7¢
Will	win with command
Can't	halt gopher balls
Expect	off-speed pitches
Don't Expect	control problems

Hoping to build on the foundation of a solid, 11-win 1995 campaign, Castillo ran into a brick wall last year. He lost command of his circle change, once one of the league's best, and also had trouble throwing strikes with his curve. Without his best pitches, Castillo had to resort to his sinker-slider repertoire—hardly enough to fool NL hitters. Bedeviled by the gopher ball, Castillo needed a half-season to recover. That recovery came slowly, though Castillo's ERA began to shrink in direct proportion to his increased command. When he's right, Castillo is a control artist who yields fewer hits than innings, averages three strikeouts per free pass, and flashes a fine pickoff move. His fielding and bunting ability also help. Poor run support from his teammates hurt Castillo in each of the last two seasons, but his weak first half last season didn't help. Castillo began his pro career at Wytheville in 1987.

Major League Batting Register

	BA	G	AB	R	H	2B	3B	HR	RBI	SB
91 NL	.200	12	5	1	1	0	0	0	0	0
92 NL	.250	9	16	1	4	1	0	0	1	0
93 NL	.255	105	337	36	86	9	7	9	30	2
94 NL	.331	52	130	16	43	11	1	3	18	2
95 NL	.309	139	527	82	163	34	2	32	90	2
96 NL	.304	160	629	97	191	34	0	40	113	7
Life	.297	477	1644	233	488	89	10	84	252	13
2 Ave	.306	158	611	95	187	36	1	38	107	5

Major League Pitching Register

	W	L	ERA	G	CG	IP	H	ER	BB	SO
91 NL	6	7	4.35	18	4	111.2	107	54	33	73
92 NL	10	11	3.46	33	0	205.1	179	79	63	135
93 NL	5	8	4.84	29	2	141.1	162	76	39	84
94 NL	2	1	4.30	4	1	23.0	25	11	5	19
95 NL	11	10	3.21	29	2	188.0	179	67	52	135
96 NL	7	16	5.28	33	1	182.1	209	107	46	139
Life	41	53	4.16	146	10	851.2	861	394	238	585
2 Ave	10	14	4.17	33	2	197.0	205	91	52	145

TONY CASTILLO

Position: Pitcher
Team: Chicago White Sox
Born: March 1, 1963 Lara, Venezuela
Height: 5'10" **Weight:** 188 lbs.
Bats: left **Throws:** left
Acquired: Traded by Blue Jays with Domingo Cedeno for Luis Andujar and Allen Halley, 8/96

PLAYER SUMMARY

Fantasy Value	$4 to $6
Card Value	4¢ to 7¢
Will	appear often
Can't	stop lefties
Expect	good control
Don't Expect	high K count

Before his August trade to the contending White Sox, Castillo had spent three seasons as one of Toronto's unsung heroes, a dependable lefty reliever who delivered as both a set-up man and emergency closer. Working in a career-high 55 games in 1995, he recorded 13 saves—the only time he reached double digits in his big-league career. Castillo blends a sinking fastball with a changeup and a curve but needs location to survive. Not a power pitcher, he averages six Ks per nine innings. Castillo yields fewer hits than innings, allows under three walks per game, and keeps the ball in the park. His resilient left arm is capable of frequent activity. Castillo should be more effective against left-handers than he has been the last two years. The Venezuelan southpaw helps his own cause with fine fielding and a good pickoff move. Few baserunners challenge him.

Major League Pitching Register

	W	L	ERA	G	S	IP	H	ER	BB	SO
88 AL	1	0	3.00	14	0	15.0	10	5	2	14
89 AL	1	1	6.11	17	1	17.2	23	12	10	10
89 NL	0	1	4.82	12	0	9.1	8	5	4	5
90 NL	5	1	4.23	52	1	76.2	93	36	20	64
91 NL	2	1	3.34	17	0	32.1	40	12	11	18
93 AL	3	2	3.38	51	0	50.2	44	19	22	28
94 AL	5	2	2.51	41	1	68.0	66	19	28	43
95 AL	1	5	3.22	55	13	72.2	64	26	24	38
96 AL	5	4	3.60	55	2	95.0	95	38	24	57
Life	23	17	3.54	314	18	437.1	443	172	145	277
3 Ave	4	4	3.10	58	6	91.0	87	31	30	53

JUAN CASTRO

Position: Second base; shortstop
Team: Los Angeles Dodgers
Born: June 20, 1972 Los Mochis, Mexico
Height: 5'10" **Weight:** 163 lbs.
Bats: right **Throws:** right
Acquired: Signed as a nondrafted free agent, 6/91

PLAYER SUMMARY

Fantasy Value	$0
Card Value	7¢ to 10¢
Will	fill utility role
Can't	learn strike zone
Expect	sterling defense
Don't Expect	hits, walks, HRs

Castro joined the '96 Dodgers just in time to fill the utility role occupied by Chad Fonville, who was sent to the minors in his place. He spelled injured shortstop Greg Gagne, filled in at second and third, tried his hand at left field, and appeared often as a pinch hitter and pinch runner. He shines only on defense, however. Untouchable at short, a spot still bleeding from the Jose Offerman regime, Castro shows quick reactions, great range, soft hands, and a strong, reliable arm. He even turns the double play—a Dodger deficit in recent seasons. Castro can also play second, and he's certainly better than Mike Blowers or Mike Busch at third. It's too bad he has to bat. Juan Castro at the plate is no more productive than Fidel Castro might be. He doesn't have the patience to wait for walks, doesn't know the strike zone, doesn't make contact, and doesn't show any power on the rare occasions he does connect. Castro spent five seasons in the minors and would have spent more—perhaps a whole career—if not for his glove. Still, next year's expansion could help him win a job somewhere.

Major League Batting Register

	BA	G	AB	R	H	2B	3B	HR	RBI	SB
95 NL	.250	11	4	0	1	0	0	0	0	0
96 NL	.197	70	132	16	26	5	3	0	5	1
Life	.199	81	136	16	27	5	3	0	5	1

ANDUJAR CEDENO

Position: Shortstop
Team: Houston Astros
Born: Aug. 21, 1969 La Romana, Dominican Republic
Height: 6'1" **Weight:** 168 lbs.
Bats: right **Throws:** right
Acquired: Traded by Tigers for a player to be named later, 9/96

PLAYER SUMMARY	
Fantasy Value	$1
Card Value	4¢ to 7¢
Will	surprise with pop
Can't	field his position
Expect	tepid on-base mark
Don't Expect	patience at plate

Name a good-hit, no-field Dominican shortstop who made a 1996 AL debut after repeated failures in the NL. Jose Offerman comes to mind first, but Cedeno is not far behind, although he rejoined the NL in time for the Astros' pennant drive. Cedeno could always hit—he once had 39 extra-base hits in a season and even hit for the cycle. But his fielding has always been dreadful, including a two-year total of 113 errors in the minors. Cedeno is as undisciplined at the plate as he is in the field. He averages nearly ten strikeouts per walk and looks ridiculous lunging at unreachable pitches with his long, looping swing. If he ever masters the strike zone, his average and run production will jump. Cedeno could be valuable because of his speed if only he could reach base more often. His range and arm could be assets in the field, but his hands and accuracy are often unreliable.

Major League Batting Register

	BA	G	AB	R	H	2B	3B	HR	RBI	SB
90 NL	.000	7	8	0	0	0	0	0	0	0
91 NL	.243	67	251	27	61	13	2	9	36	4
92 NL	.173	71	220	15	38	13	2	2	13	2
93 NL	.283	149	505	69	143	24	4	11	56	9
94 NL	.263	98	342	38	90	26	0	9	49	1
95 NL	.210	120	390	42	82	16	2	6	31	5
96 AL	.196	52	179	19	35	4	2	7	20	2
96 NL	.231	52	156	11	36	2	1	3	18	3
Life	.236	616	2051	221	485	98	13	47	223	26
3 Ave	.231	125	418	43	97	20	2	10	47	4

DOMINGO CEDENO

Position: Second base; third base
Team: Chicago White Sox
Born: Nov. 4, 1968 La Romana, Dominican Republic
Height: 6'1" **Weight:** 170 lbs.
Bats: both **Throws:** right
Acquired: Traded by Blue Jays with Tony Castillo for Luis Andujar and Allen Halley, 8/96

PLAYER SUMMARY	
Fantasy Value	$0
Card Value	5¢ to 8¢
Will	bring good glove
Can't	reach the fences
Expect	better lefty bat
Don't Expect	an Alomar clone

Replacing a hero is never easy. Cedeno learned that lesson last year when the Blue Jays promoted him from utility man to starting second baseman—a job vacated by free-agent deserter Roberto Alomar. Although Cedeno hit better than anyone expected, he was unable to approximate the batting, fielding, or baserunning ability of the former Toronto All-Star, who took his Gold Glove with him to Baltimore. Cedeno's homer in his first at bat of the season gave the Jays false hope; it was the only one he hit before his August swap to the White Sox. Cedeno did have his moments, however. A better left-handed hitter, Cedeno has some plate discipline but still fans four times per strikeout—not a good ratio for a singles hitter. He has enough speed to steal more often but doesn't get good jumps. His reactions in the field are fine, however, and his range, hands, and arm are above average. Cedeno's brother Andujar plays for the Houston Astros.

Major League Batting Register

	BA	G	AB	R	H	2B	3B	HR	RBI	SB
93 AL	.174	15	46	5	8	0	0	0	7	1
94 AL	.196	47	97	14	19	2	3	0	10	1
95 AL	.236	51	161	18	38	6	1	4	14	0
96 AL	.272	89	301	46	82	12	2	2	20	6
Life	.243	202	605	83	147	20	6	6	51	8
2 Ave	.259	73	241	33	62	9	2	3	18	3

ROGER CEDENO

Position: Outfield
Team: Los Angeles Dodgers
Born: Aug. 16, 1974 Valencia, Venezuela
Height: 6'1" **Weight:** 165 lbs.
Bats: both **Throws:** right
Acquired: Signed as a nondrafted free agent, 3/91

PLAYER SUMMARY	
Fantasy Value	$4 to $6
Card Value	12¢ to 20¢
Will	show fine speed
Can't	hit many homers
Expect	berth in lineup
Don't Expect	spotty fielding

Even before Brett Butler contracted throat cancer last year, the Dodgers had projected Cedeno as their center fielder of the future. That future became the present when the fleet Venezuelan received unexpected early exposure at the ripe old age of 21. Though primarily known for speed and defense, Cedeno also surprised with his bat. His first big-league homer was a three-run, game-winning shot against Tom Glavine. Stealing bases remains Cedeno's chief calling card. He topped two dozen steals in four minor-league seasons and once led his league. Before he fell ill, Butler helped his heir apparent with proper bunting technique. If Cedeno masters those lessons and learns to hit the ball on the ground, he could contend for a future batting crown. The swift switch-hitter already has the strength and bat speed to succeed. Cedeno has one batting crown to his credit: He led the Venezuelan Winter League in both batting and stolen bases. Cedeno lost playing time when the Dodgers acquired Chad Curtis last July, but he's still a big part of the team's future.

Major League Batting Register

	BA	G	AB	R	H	2B	3B	HR	RBI	SB
95 NL	.238	40	42	4	10	2	0	0	3	1
96 NL	.246	86	211	26	52	11	1	2	18	5
Life	.245	126	253	30	62	13	1	2	21	6

NORM CHARLTON

Position: Pitcher
Team: Seattle Mariners
Born: Jan. 6, 1963 Fort Polk, LA
Height: 6'3" **Weight:** 200 lbs.
Bats: both **Throws:** left
Acquired: Signed as a free agent, 7/95

PLAYER SUMMARY	
Fantasy Value	$17 to $20
Card Value	4¢ to 7¢
Will	close games
Can't	avoid injuries
Expect	many strikeouts
Don't Expect	pinpoint control

Charlton has thrown late-inning bullets for Lou Piniella in two different cities. One of the "Nasty Boys" who helped Piniella's Reds romp to the 1990 world championship, Charlton again pitched Piniella into postseason play with the '95 Mariners. Dumped by the pitching-poor Phillies after he was slow to rebound from major elbow surgery, Charlton resumed the closer role he held with the '93 Mariners. The hard-throwing southpaw missed time last year with a tender shoulder. Charlton's combination of fastballs, forkballs, and sliders results in more whiffs than innings. He yields fewer hits than innings. He experienced some trouble with his control last season, however. Charlton's follow-through impedes his fielding ability, but his pickoff move is polished. Charlton is a Rice University graduate, with degrees in political science, religion, and physical education.

Major League Pitching Register

	W	L	ERA	G	S	IP	H	ER	BB	SO
88 NL	4	5	3.96	10	0	61.1	60	27	20	39
89 NL	8	3	2.93	69	0	95.1	67	31	40	98
90 NL	12	9	2.74	56	2	154.1	131	47	70	117
91 NL	3	5	2.91	39	1	108.1	92	35	34	77
92 NL	4	2	2.99	64	26	81.1	79	27	26	90
93 AL	1	3	2.34	34	18	34.2	22	9	17	48
95 NL	2	5	7.36	25	0	22.0	23	18	15	12
95 AL	2	1	1.51	30	14	47.2	23	8	16	58
96 AL	4	7	4.04	70	20	75.2	68	34	38	73
Life	40	40	3.12	397	81	680.2	565	236	276	612
2 Ave	3	4	2.99	52	18	65.1	47	22	28	69

ARCHI CIANFROCCO

Position: Infield; outfield
Team: San Diego Padres
Born: Oct. 6, 1966 Rome, NY
Height: 6'5" **Weight:** 215 lbs.
Bats: right **Throws:** right
Acquired: Traded by Expos for Tim Scott, 6/93

PLAYER SUMMARY

Fantasy Value	$0
Card Value	4¢ to 7¢
Will	swat southpaws
Can't	wait for walks
Expect	some long ones
Don't Expect	speed, defense

A big guy who plays everywhere, Cianfrocco even surfaced behind the plate last summer—missing only two of the nine positions (center field and pitcher). He made double-digit starts at the infield corners and even at shortstop but also did well as a pinch hitter against lefties. Cianfrocco literally feasts on southpaws. He gets extra bases on one-third of his hits but would probably hit more homers if he showed more patience at the plate. Like any anxious-to-please utility man, he tries to make up for lost time by swinging at anything. The result is an unacceptable strikeout-to-walk ratio of 9-to-1. Cianfrocco loves first-pitch fastballs, but the word has gotten around. Pitchers try to feed him breaking stuff. He steals a handful of bases per year but is no speed demon. He plays shortstop like a first baseman: good scoops, good hands, limited range, inaccurate arm. Because of his versatility and potential, Cianfrocco will always have a home in the big leagues.

Major League Batting Register

	BA	G	AB	R	H	2B	3B	HR	RBI	SB
92 NL	.241	86	232	25	56	5	2	6	30	3
93 NL	.243	96	296	30	72	11	2	12	48	2
94 NL	.219	59	146	9	32	8	0	4	13	2
95 NL	.263	51	118	22	31	7	0	5	31	0
96 NL	.281	79	192	21	54	13	3	2	32	1
Life	.249	371	984	107	245	44	7	29	154	8

JEFF CIRILLO

Position: Third base
Team: Milwaukee Brewers
Born: Sept. 23, 1969 Pasadena, CA
Height: 6'2" **Weight:** 190 lbs.
Bats: right **Throws:** right
Acquired: 11th-round pick in 6/91 free-agent draft

PLAYER SUMMARY

Fantasy Value	$13 to $16
Card Value	10¢ to 15¢
Will	set table well
Can't	steal too much
Expect	solid fielding
Don't Expect	home run crown

After playing all four infield positions for the 1995 Brewers, Cirillo used his big bat to become the regular third baseman last year. Hitting in the No. 2 slot, he showed the same slashing style that produced four .300 seasons in the minor leagues. He hit well over .300, collected extra bases on one-third of his hits, and showed both patience and the ability to make contact. Assigned with setting the table, Cirillo did it well, keeping his on-base percentage near the .400 mark by drawing plenty of walks. In 1995, his first full season, Cirillo walked more often than he struck out. He hits the ball where it is pitched, sending liners to all fields and reaching the alleys often. He has enough power to reach double digits in homers. Cirillo is a fine fielder with first-rate reactions, range, hands, and arm. He can also play second but was not needed there last year. A communications major at USC, Cirillo could become a baseball writer when his playing days are over. At age 27, though, he'll have years to think it over.

Major League Batting Register

	BA	G	AB	R	H	2B	3B	HR	RBI	SB
94 AL	.238	39	126	17	30	9	0	3	12	0
95 AL	.277	125	328	57	91	19	4	9	39	7
96 AL	.325	158	566	101	184	46	5	15	83	4
Life	.299	322	1020	175	305	74	9	27	134	11
2 Ave	.306	149	468	83	143	34	5	13	63	6

DAVE CLARK

Position: Outfield
Team: Los Angeles Dodgers
Born: Sept. 3, 1962 Tupelo, MS
Height: 6'2" **Weight:** 209 lbs.
Bats: left **Throws:** right
Acquired: Traded by Pirates for Carl South, 8/96

PLAYER SUMMARY	
Fantasy Value	$1
Card Value	4¢ to 7¢
Will	help team late
Can't	hit all lefties
Expect	power in pinch
Don't Expect	stolen bases

Right-handed pitchers don't like to see Clark lumber off the bench in the late innings. A fastball hitter with great bat speed, he's capable of ending a game with one swing. Over the past five years, Pittsburgh manager Jim Leyland got maximum mileage out of Clark, playing him in both outfield corners but often saving him for key late-inning situations. The former Jackson State All-American not only makes good contact but shows unusual patience for a slugger. Willing to wait for walks, Clark is even more valuable when he connects, producing extra bases on one-third of his hits. Since he neither runs nor fields very well, Clark would be a great DH. He has no range and an unreliable—though strong—arm. Clark has played some first base and ultimately could be "hidden" there. Clark is also a good influence in the clubhouse.

Major League Batting Register

	BA	G	AB	R	H	2B	3B	HR	RBI	SB
86 AL	.276	18	58	10	16	1	0	3	9	1
87 AL	.207	29	87	11	18	5	0	3	12	1
88 AL	.263	63	156	11	41	4	1	3	18	0
89 AL	.237	102	253	21	60	12	0	8	29	0
90 NL	.275	84	171	22	47	4	2	5	20	7
91 NL	.200	11	10	1	2	0	0	0	1	0
92 NL	.212	23	33	3	7	0	0	2	7	0
93 NL	.271	110	277	43	75	11	2	11	46	1
94 NL	.296	86	223	37	66	11	1	10	46	2
95 NL	.281	77	196	30	55	6	0	4	24	3
96 NL	.270	107	226	28	61	12	2	8	36	2
Life	.265	710	1690	217	448	66	8	57	248	17
3 Ave	.284	105	254	38	72	11	1	9	43	3

MARK CLARK

Position: Pitcher
Team: New York Mets
Born: May 12, 1968 Bath, IL
Height: 6'5" **Weight:** 225 lbs.
Bats: right **Throws:** right
Acquired: Traded by Indians for Ryan Thompson and Reid Cornelius, 3/96

PLAYER SUMMARY	
Fantasy Value	$7 to $9
Card Value	5¢ to 8¢
Will	win with location
Can't	stop basestealers
Expect	outs on grounders
Don't Expect	any help with bat

Clark's March arrival in the Mets training camp was greeted with a yawn. The veteran was expected to provide experience on a staff top-heavy with highly touted youngsters. When the three prized pupils failed to master their lessons, however, Clark became the surprise ace. A big right-hander who gets ahead of hitters, throws strikes, and makes them hit his pitch, Clark matched his previous single-season victory high in early August. A sinkerballer who also throws a slider, forkball, and changeup, Clark deals from a deceptive three-quarters delivery. He fans six batters per nine innings, averages one hit per inning, and pitches most effectively against righties. Since he's always around the plate (an average of two walks per game), Clark is susceptible to the gopher ball. A horrendous hitter, Clark also hurts his own cause with his inability to control the running game. Despite these shortcomings, he has great confidence in his ability to win.

Major League Pitching Register

	W	L	ERA	G	CG	IP	H	ER	BB	SO
91 NL	1	1	4.03	7	0	22.1	17	10	11	13
92 NL	3	10	4.45	20	1	113.1	117	56	36	44
93 NL	7	5	4.28	26	1	109.1	119	52	25	57
94 AL	11	3	3.82	20	4	127.1	133	54	40	60
95 AL	9	7	5.27	22	2	124.2	143	73	42	68
96 NL	14	11	3.43	32	2	212.1	217	81	48	142
Life	45	37	4.14	127	10	709.1	746	326	202	384
3 Ave	13	8	4.05	28	3	177.1	188	80	51	101

TONY CLARK

Position: First base
Team: Detroit Tigers
Born: June 15, 1972 Newton, KS
Height: 6'8" **Weight:** 250 lbs.
Bats: both **Throws:** right
Acquired: First-round pick in 6/90 free-agent draft

PLAYER SUMMARY

Fantasy Value	$13 to $16
Card Value	10¢ to 20¢
Will	generate power
Can't	wait for walks
Expect	good lefty bat
Don't Expect	polished glove

Replacing Cecil Fielder would be a tall order for anyone. But Clark's 6'8" frame and early success suggest he may be the right man for the job. On August 1, the day after Fielder was traded, Clark hit his first grand slam. A switch-hitter who's more potent left-handed, Clark should be more productive as he gains experience, figures out how to hit inside pitches, and learns the nuances of the strike zone. He fans four times more often than he walks and collects extra bases on nearly half his hits. Once he learns it's okay to hit a single, Clark could put up statistics that match his size. To play every day, however, he'll have to improve his defense. Clark led two minor leagues in errors. With no speed to speak of, his range is limited. Inexperience hurts him: Clark played basketball at the University of Arizona and San Diego State, switching to baseball almost as an afterthought. Then injuries limited him to 88 games in his first three pro seasons. Clark has a lot of catching up to do. But he should justify his selection as the No. 2 pick (behind Chipper Jones) in the 1990 draft.

Major League Batting Register

	BA	G	AB	R	H	2B	3B	HR	RBI	SB
95 AL	.238	27	101	10	24	5	1	3	11	0
96 AL	.250	100	376	56	94	14	0	27	72	0
Life	.247	127	477	66	118	19	1	30	83	0

WILL CLARK

Position: First base
Team: Texas Rangers
Born: March 13, 1964 New Orleans, LA
Height: 6'1" **Weight:** 190 lbs.
Bats: left **Throws:** left
Acquired: Signed as a free agent, 11/93

PLAYER SUMMARY

Fantasy Value	$10 to $13
Card Value	10¢ to 15¢
Will	hit line drives
Can't	find old power
Expect	walks, contact
Don't Expect	fielding lapses

Clark's third AL season was marred by three separate stints on the disabled list. The six-time All-Star suffered a pulled left quadriceps muscle, a bruised rib cage, and a strained right calf muscle. When he's right, Clark is a contact hitter with patience. He walks more than he strikes out, posts a high on-base percentage, and sends line drives to all fields when he connects. Clark has lost some of the power he showed earlier in his career, but he's still a dangerous hitter, especially against right-handers. He loves to pull low, inside pitches. Clark is a good fielder with quick reactions, soft hands, and the ability to stretch, scoop, and turn the difficult 3-6-3 double play. He has no speed, however, and limited range. The former Mississippi State All-American and U.S. Olympian homered with his first swing in both the majors and minors.

Major League Batting Register

	BA	G	AB	R	H	2B	3B	HR	RBI	SB
86 NL	.287	111	408	66	117	27	2	11	41	4
87 NL	.308	150	529	89	163	29	5	35	91	5
88 NL	.282	162	575	102	162	31	6	29	109	9
89 NL	.333	159	588	104	196	38	9	23	111	8
90 NL	.295	154	600	91	177	25	5	19	95	8
91 NL	.301	148	565	84	170	32	7	29	116	4
92 NL	.300	144	513	69	154	40	1	16	73	12
93 NL	.283	132	491	82	139	27	2	14	73	2
94 AL	.329	110	389	73	128	24	2	13	80	5
95 AL	.302	123	454	85	137	27	3	16	92	0
96 AL	.284	117	436	69	124	25	1	13	72	2
Life	.300	1510	5548	914	1667	325	43	218	953	59
3 Ave	.307	137	498	89	153	30	2	16	96	3

ROYCE CLAYTON

Position: Shortstop
Team: St. Louis Cardinals
Born: Jan. 2, 1970 Burbank, CA
Height: 6′ **Weight:** 175 lbs.
Bats: right **Throws:** right
Acquired: Traded by Giants with Chris Wimmer for Allen Watson, Rich DeLucia, and Doug Creek, 12/95

PLAYER SUMMARY	
Fantasy Value...............	$14 to $17
Card Value	8¢ to 12¢
Will...................	use speed well
Can't..................	generate power
Expect.................	strong defense
Don't Expect	average on-base pct.

Concerned about the age and shoulder problems of longtime shortstop Ozzie Smith, the Cardinals acquired Clayton for 1996. The move paid off when Clayton enjoyed one of his best seasons and Smith announced his pending retirement. At 27, Clayton has many of the qualities of a young Smith. He's a solid defensive shortstop with quick reactions, excellent range, soft hands, and a strong, accurate arm. Clayton has led NL shortstops in chances, putouts, assists, and double plays. He uses his speed to beat out bunts and infield hits, stretch singles, and steal bases. He's topped 20 steals three years in a row but still gets thrown out too frequently. Clayton has improved at the plate. A .249 career hitter before 1996, he hovered around .280 all season. He also showed more patience than usual, though he still fans three times per walk. Clayton spent some time as leadoff man last year but doesn't reach base enough for the role.

Major League Batting Register

	BA	G	AB	R	H	2B	3B	HR	RBI	SB
91 NL	.115	9	26	0	3	1	0	0	2	0
92 NL	.224	98	321	31	72	7	4	4	24	8
93 NL	.282	153	549	54	155	21	5	6	70	11
94 NL	.236	108	385	38	91	14	6	3	30	23
95 NL	.244	138	509	56	124	29	3	5	58	24
96 NL	.277	129	491	64	136	20	4	6	35	33
Life	.255	635	2281	243	581	92	22	24	219	99
3 Ave	.251	145	535	60	135	24	5	5	48	31

ROGER CLEMENS

Position: Pitcher
Team: Toronto Blue Jays
Born: Aug. 4, 1962 Dayton, OH
Height: 6′4″ **Weight:** 220 lbs.
Bats: right **Throws:** right
Acquired: Signed as a free agent, 12/96

PLAYER SUMMARY	
Fantasy Value...............	$14 to $17
Card Value	10¢ to 15¢
Will...................	still head staff
Can't..................	find former heat
Expect.................	diverse arsenal
Don't Expect	pinpoint control

Roger Clemens hasn't been Roger Clemens since 1992, the year he won his fourth ERA title (third in a row) and led the AL in shutouts for the fifth time. Shoulder and elbow problems, plus the relentless march of time, have taken a toll on the two-time strikeout king, three-time Cy Young Award winner, and five-time All-Star. Clemens did show flashes of his old form in August, when he passed Christy Mathewson for 19th on the career K list. An intense and clever competitor, he mixes five pitches: fastball, forkball, slider, curve, and circle change. He yields fewer hits than innings, fans more than a man per frame, and keeps the ball in the park. Last season, he broke Cy Young's Boston club record of innings pitched and tied his own single-game K record of 20.

Major League Pitching Register

	W	L	ERA	G	CG	IP	H	ER	BB	SO
84 AL	9	4	4.32	21	5	133.1	146	64	29	126
85 AL	7	5	3.29	15	3	98.1	83	36	37	74
86 AL	24	4	2.48	33	10	254.0	179	70	67	238
87 AL	20	9	2.97	36	18	281.2	248	93	83	256
88 AL	18	12	2.93	35	14	264.0	217	86	62	291
89 AL	17	11	3.13	35	8	253.1	215	88	93	230
90 AL	21	6	1.93	31	7	228.1	193	49	54	209
91 AL	18	10	2.62	35	13	271.1	219	79	65	241
92 AL	18	11	2.41	32	11	246.2	203	66	62	208
93 AL	11	14	4.46	29	2	191.2	175	95	67	160
94 AL	9	7	2.85	24	3	170.2	124	54	71	168
95 AL	10	5	4.18	23	0	140.0	141	65	60	132
96 AL	10	13	3.63	34	6	242.2	216	98	106	257
Life	192	111	3.06	383	100	2776.0	2359	943	856	2590
3 Ave	11	9	3.47	31	3	214.1	183	82	91	214

BRAD CLONTZ

Position: Pitcher
Team: Atlanta Braves
Born: April 25, 1971 Stuart, VA
Height: 6'1" **Weight:** 180 lbs.
Bats: right **Throws:** right
Acquired: Tenth-round pick in 6/92 free-agent draft

PLAYER SUMMARY	
Fantasy Value	$2 to $4
Card Value	4¢ to 7¢
Will	work often
Can't	avoid gophers
Expect	ground balls
Don't Expect	closer duties

The Jekyll and Hyde of the 1996 Atlanta bullpen, Clontz pitched brilliantly against right-handed batters but was a total bust against lefties. His submarine-style delivery baffled righties. Drafted off the Virginia Tech campus in 1992, he has never started a game since turning pro. In fact, he was a top minor-league closer, converting 41 saves in 44 chances (including the International League playoffs) in 1994. But his ineffectiveness against southpaws makes him a risk in that role. Except for a brief look as a closer early in his rookie year, Clontz has been strictly a set-up man in the majors. A workhorse whose delivery puts little strain on his arm, Clontz gets lots of ground balls when his pitches are working. He throws strikes with his fastball, slider, and sinker but needs an off-speed pitch. Though he yielded fewer hits than innings last year, Clontz gave up too many homers when his pitches caught too much of the plate. He also yielded too many stolen bases, negating his earlier success against basestealers. Clontz is competent but not outstanding in the field.

Major League Pitching Register

	W	L	ERA	G	S	IP	H	ER	BB	SO
95 NL	8	1	3.65	59	4	69.0	71	28	22	55
96 NL	6	3	5.69	81	1	80.2	78	51	33	49
Life	14	4	4.75	140	5	149.2	149	79	55	104
2 Ave	8	2	4.69	74	3	79.0	79	41	29	55

GREG COLBRUNN

Position: First base
Team: Florida Marlins
Born: July 26, 1969 Fontana, CA
Height: 6' **Weight:** 190 lbs.
Bats: right **Throws:** right
Acquired: Claimed from Expos on waivers, 10/93

PLAYER SUMMARY	
Fantasy Value	$11 to $14
Card Value	5¢ to 8¢
Will	need improvement
Can't	stop striking out
Expect	occasional homers
Don't Expect	speed, good glove

Life in the big leagues has always been a struggle for Colbrunn. Hampered by severe knee and elbow problems, he lost playing time and had to be converted from catcher to first base. He finally reached the majors in 1992, only to be blocked by incumbents and assaulted by more physical problems. Three years later, playing in more than 70 games for the first time, he started to deliver on his potential. But the promise faded quickly. Although he had a 475-foot homer last May and a 21-game hitting streak in June, Colbrunn suffered a season-long power shortage accompanied by an agonizing inability to produce with runners in scoring position. He wound up sharing first base with Jeff Conine, usually the left fielder. Colbrunn's biggest problem is impatience. He fans four times per walk. On the plus side, he's hard to defense because he hits to all fields. Colbrunn's 11 steals in 1995 were a surprise. Colbrunn isn't much of a fielder, either. His range, hands, footwork, and throwing arm are all subpar.

Major League Batting Register

	BA	G	AB	R	H	2B	3B	HR	RBI	SB
92 NL	.268	52	168	12	45	8	0	2	18	3
93 NL	.255	70	153	15	39	9	0	4	23	4
94 NL	.303	47	155	17	47	10	0	6	31	1
95 NL	.277	138	528	70	146	22	1	23	89	11
96 NL	.286	141	511	60	146	26	2	16	69	4
Life	.279	448	1515	174	423	75	3	51	230	23
3 Ave	.284	121	441	54	125	22	1	17	71	6

DAVID CONE

Position: Pitcher
Team: New York Yankees
Born: Jan. 2, 1963 Kansas City, MO
Height: 6'1" **Weight:** 190 lbs.
Bats: left **Throws:** right
Acquired: Signed as a free agent, 12/95

PLAYER SUMMARY	
Fantasy Value	$20 to $25
Card Value	10¢ to 15¢
Will	rejoin rotation
Can't	hold runners on
Expect	reliable control
Don't Expect	temper tantrums

Before 1996, Cone had missed only one start in his career. But he suffered an aneurysm in his right shoulder and missed most of last season. A power pitcher, he blends a fastball, slider, and forkball with a curve that he uses as a changeup. He throws all of his pitches for strikes and is not afraid to use any of them on any count. Cone is a two-time K king and three-time All-Star whose trophy shelf also contains a Cy Young Award. The healthy Cone always ranks among the league leaders in innings, complete games, shutouts, and whiffs. Cone averages three walks, seven Ks, and eight hits per nine innings but often does better. Once a victim of his own temper, Cone hasn't lost his competitive edge but he has calmed down. He rejoined the team in late August and pitched seven hitless innings in his comeback.

Major League Pitching Register

	W	L	ERA	G	CG	IP	H	ER	BB	SO
86 AL	0	0	5.56	11	0	22.2	29	14	13	21
87 NL	5	6	3.71	21	1	99.1	87	41	44	68
88 NL	20	3	2.22	35	8	231.1	178	57	80	213
89 NL	14	8	3.52	34	7	219.2	183	86	74	190
90 NL	14	10	3.23	31	6	211.2	177	76	65	233
91 NL	14	14	3.29	34	5	232.2	204	85	73	241
92 NL	13	7	2.88	27	7	196.2	162	63	82	214
92 AL	4	3	2.55	8	0	53.0	39	15	29	47
93 AL	11	14	3.33	34	6	254.0	205	94	114	191
94 AL	16	5	2.94	23	4	171.2	130	56	54	132
95 AL	18	8	3.57	30	6	229.1	195	91	88	191
96 AL	7	2	2.88	11	1	72.0	50	23	34	71
Life	136	80	3.16	299	51	1994.0	1639	701	750	1812
3 Ave	17	6	3.21	26	4	191.1	151	68	70	157

JEFF CONINE

Position: Outfield; first base
Team: Florida Marlins
Born: June 27, 1966 Tacoma, WA
Height: 6'1" **Weight:** 220 lbs.
Bats: right **Throws:** right
Acquired: First-round pick from Royals in 11/92 expansion draft

PLAYER SUMMARY	
Fantasy Value	$20 to $25
Card Value	8¢ to 12¢
Will	belt lefties
Can't	supply speed
Expect	hits, homers
Don't Expect	missed games

Conine went 4-for-4 in Florida's very first game and hasn't stopped hitting since. A line-drive hitter who hammers left-handed pitching, he collects extra bases on one-third of his hits. He was named All-Star Game MVP in 1995. One of baseball's most durable players, Conine rarely misses a game. He makes decent contact with his short, compact swing and draws plenty of walks but still fans twice per pass. While his strikeout numbers rose last year, Conine's average and run production fell. Part of the problem was too many swings at pitches outside the strike zone—unusual for a proven .300 hitter. But Conine was pressing to boost the moribund Marlin offense. Because he lacks speed, Conine lacks range in left field. But he has good reactions, soft hands, and a fine arm (he was a pitcher at UCLA before the Royals made him a 58th-round draft pick in 1987). First base, his position for his first three pro seasons, is still his best spot on the diamond.

Major League Batting Register

	BA	G	AB	R	H	2B	3B	HR	RBI	SB
90 AL	.250	9	20	3	5	2	0	0	2	0
92 AL	.253	28	91	10	23	5	2	0	9	0
93 NL	.292	162	595	75	174	24	3	12	79	2
94 NL	.319	115	451	60	144	27	6	18	82	1
95 NL	.302	133	483	72	146	26	2	25	105	2
96 NL	.293	157	597	84	175	32	2	26	95	1
Life	.298	604	2237	304	667	116	15	81	372	6
3 Ave	.305	156	592	83	181	33	4	26	110	2

STEVE COOKE

Position: Pitcher
Team: Pittsburgh Pirates
Born: Jan. 14, 1970 Kauai, HI
Height: 6'6" **Weight:** 236 lbs.
Bats: right **Throws:** left
Acquired: 35th-round pick in 6/89 free-agent draft

PLAYER SUMMARY	
Fantasy Value	$0
Card Value	5¢ to 8¢
Will	try two curves
Can't	prevent gophers
Expect	starts if healthy
Don't Expect	anemic offense

A ten-game winner as a rookie in 1993, Cooke has missed most of the last three years with assorted ailments. The worst was an extended bout with bursitis of his left shoulder—a problem that limited him to two minor-league appearances in 1995. After experiencing inflammation in the shoulder last season, Cooke got off to a late start. He made five rehab outings in Double-A before rejoining the varsity club. Manager Jim Leyland immediately sent him to the bullpen in an effort to rebuild his stamina. Cooke's arsenal includes a sinking fastball, changeup, fast curve, and slow curve. When the sinker doesn't sink, he often yields long hits. He had problems with the gopher ball in 1994. Cooke helps his own cause with his bunting, hitting, and fielding. But his pickoff move needs improvement—especially since he's left-handed. Used almost exclusively as a starter in a pro career that began in 1990, Cooke has never won more than ten games. He hopes to change that pattern this season. But he'll have to prove healthy first.

Major League Pitching Register

	W	L	ERA	G	S	IP	H	ER	BB	SO
92 NL	2	0	3.52	11	1	23.0	22	9	4	10
93 NL	10	10	3.89	32	0	210.2	207	91	59	132
94 NL	4	11	5.02	25	0	134.1	157	75	46	74
96 NL	0	0	7.56	3	0	8.1	11	7	5	7
Life	16	21	4.35	71	1	376.1	397	182	114	223

RON COOMER

Position: First base; third base
Team: Minnesota Twins
Born: Nov. 18, 1966 Crest Hill, IL
Height: 5'11" **Weight:** 195 lbs.
Bats: right **Throws:** right
Acquired: Traded by Dodgers with Greg Hansell, Jose Parra, and Chris Latham for Kevin Tapani and Mark Guthrie, 7/95

PLAYER SUMMARY	
Fantasy Value	$1
Card Value	4¢ to 7¢
Will	love lefties
Can't	supply speed
Expect	platoon role
Don't Expect	great throws

More than eight years in the minors taught Coomer the virtues of patience. So he didn't mind sharing Minnesota's 1996 first base job with lefty-hitting Scott Stahoviak. Coomer's value extends beyond his power potential. He's also a versatile performer who can fill in at any base as well as the outfield. Drafted by Oakland out of California's Taft College in 1987, Coomer played in the White Sox and Dodger systems before coming to the Twins. His 123 RBI led the Pacific Coast League in 1994. A line-drive hitter with gap power, Coomer loves left-handed fastball pitchers. He even hit his first big-league homer against Randy Johnson, the best of them all. Coomer hits 40 points higher against southpaws. He makes good contact for a slugger and walks almost as often as he strikes out. Though he has no speed, Coomer moves well enough to play third base. He has quick reactions and soft hands, but his throws aren't always accurate. Some expansion team might scoop him up quickly.

Major League Batting Register

	BA	G	AB	R	H	2B	3B	HR	RBI	SB
95 AL	.257	37	101	15	26	3	1	5	19	0
96 AL	.296	95	233	34	69	12	1	12	41	3
Life	.284	132	334	49	95	15	2	17	60	3

ROCKY COPPINGER

Position: Pitcher
Team: Baltimore Orioles
Born: March 19, 1974 El Paso, TX
Height: 6'7" **Weight:** 240 lbs.
Bats: right **Throws:** right
Acquired: 19th-round pick in 6/93 free-agent draft

PLAYER SUMMARY	
Fantasy Value	$4 to $6
Card Value	7¢ to 10¢
Will	rattle righties
Can't	prevent gophers
Expect	many strikeouts
Don't Expect	perfect control

Coppinger beat Detroit in his debut June 11 and then became the first Oriole since 1967 to win his first four decisions. A highlight was beating boyhood idol Roger Clemens in their first meeting July 6. A power pitcher with a moving fastball and fine slider, Coppinger yields one hit per inning, averages seven strikeouts a game, and dominates right-handed hitters. But he's sometimes betrayed by his control. When he pitches catch too much of the plate, hitters take him deep. Coppinger has trouble with lefties and needs to improve his pickoff move. Runners stole at will against him last year. Coppinger's potential is apparent: He had a two-year record of 20-6 with a 2.11 ERA and an average of one K per inning in the minors. Coppinger needs to throw strikes and develop an off-speed pitch to keep batters guessing. He already has a physical advantage: His 6'7", 240-pound frame looks even more intimidating from the mound. Coppinger got his nickname as a baby when his dad said he resembled boxer Rocky Marciano.

Major League Pitching Register

	W	L	ERA	G	CG	IP	H	ER	BB	SO
96 AL	10	6	5.18	23	0	125.0	126	72	60	104
Life	10	6	5.18	23	0	125.0	126	72	60	104

74

JOEY CORA

Position: Second base
Team: Seattle Mariners
Born: May 14, 1965 Caguas, Puerto Rico
Height: 5'8" **Weight:** 155 lbs.
Bats: both **Throws:** right
Acquired: Signed as a free agent, 4/95

PLAYER SUMMARY	
Fantasy Value	$4 to $6
Card Value	5¢ to 8¢
Will	ignite rallies
Can't	hit with power
Expect	contact, bunts
Don't Expect	reliable throws

A pesky little switch-hitter who sprays singles all over the park, Cora could become a valuable leadoff man if he showed more patience at the plate. Despite his small strike zone, however, he refuses to wait for walks. At least he makes good contact, even uncorking a career-best 18-game hitting streak last year. One of the AL's toughest men to fan, Cora always puts the ball into play—often with bunts. One of baseball's best bunters, Cora can hit too, especially in clutch situations, with men in scoring position, or with a 3-2 count. His extra-base hits are fairly infrequent, however. Despite decent speed, he didn't steal much last season. He's swift but often erratic in the field, where his arm is a definite liability. Cora's errors often come on throws. Cora was San Diego's first-round draft choice in the 1985 amateur draft. He played for the Padres and White Sox before joining the Mariners in 1995.

Major League Batting Register

	BA	G	AB	R	H	2B	3B	HR	RBI	SB
87 NL	.237	77	241	23	57	7	2	0	13	15
89 NL	.316	12	19	5	6	1	0	0	1	1
90 NL	.270	51	100	12	27	3	0	0	2	8
91 AL	.241	100	228	37	55	2	3	0	18	11
92 AL	.246	68	122	27	30	7	1	0	9	10
93 AL	.268	153	579	95	155	15	13	2	51	20
94 AL	.276	90	312	55	86	13	4	2	30	8
95 AL	.297	120	427	64	127	19	2	3	39	18
96 AL	.291	144	530	90	154	37	6	6	45	5
Life	.272	815	2558	408	697	104	31	13	208	96
3 Ave	.288	135	483	80	139	26	5	4	44	12

WIL CORDERO

Position: Second base; outfield
Team: Boston Red Sox
Born: Oct. 3, 1971 Mayaguez, Puerto Rico
Height: 6'2" **Weight:** 185 lbs.
Bats: right **Throws:** right
Acquired: Traded by Expos with Bryan Eversgerd for Rheal Cormier, Ryan McGuire, and Shayne Bennett, 1/96

PLAYER SUMMARY	
Fantasy Value	$11 to $14
Card Value	5¢ to 8¢
Will	seek comeback
Can't	find position
Expect	decent stick
Don't Expect	accurate arm

Like Julio Franco and Jose Offerman, Cordero is a shortstop who turned out to be a better hitter than anticipated but not as good a fielder. Also like Franco and Offerman, Cordero's defense was so erratic he had to be moved to another position. He's played first, second, third, and the outfield—all without distinguishing himself. Cordero's 1996 campaign, his first in the AL, was marred by a costly collision with Oakland catcher George Williams in May. Cordero suffered a broken leg that kept him sidelined for months. The BoSox missed his bat, which had produced 47 extra-base hits the year before. Cordero has little patience but good bat speed, plus the ability to rip line drives to all fields. But he tries to pull against lefties and often lunges for pitches out of the strike zone. He fans nearly four times per walk. At 25, he's still a kid. But it's also his sixth season—and high time to improve the glaring weaknesses in his game.

Major League Batting Register

	BA	G	AB	R	H	2B	3B	HR	RBI	SB
92 NL	.302	45	126	17	38	4	1	2	8	0
93 NL	.248	138	475	56	118	32	2	10	58	12
94 NL	.294	110	415	65	122	30	3	15	63	16
95 NL	.286	131	514	64	147	35	2	10	49	9
96 AL	.288	59	198	29	57	14	0	3	37	2
Life	.279	483	1728	231	482	115	8	40	215	39
3 Ave	.290	120	454	64	131	32	2	12	60	12

FRANCISCO CORDOVA

Position: Pitcher
Team: Pittsburgh Pirates
Born: April 26, 1972 Veracruz, Mexico
Height: 5'11" **Weight:** 165 lbs.
Bats: right **Throws:** right
Acquired: Purchased from Mexico City Reds, 1/96

PLAYER SUMMARY	
Fantasy Value	$4 to $6
Card Value	7¢ to 10¢
Will	close games
Can't	hold runners
Expect	K per inning
Don't Expect	poor control

After watching Cordova pitch last year, scouts wondered why the Pirates had waited so long. During his four-year stint in Mexico City, the hard-throwing right-hander had a 40-6 record, 16 saves, and 3.03 ERA. He also had good bloodlines: His father, Ernesto Cordova, had won 141 games in the same city. The younger Cordova, invited to 1996 spring training as a nonroster player, went north as the right-handed half of a right-left closer combo. Cordova made the most of the opportunity, averaging a whiff per inning, dominating right-handed hitters, and keeping the ball in the park. By mid-August, the control artist led the Pirates in saves (he set a Pirate rookie record) and games finished. Cordova maintains a 4-1 ratio of whiffs to walks, strands 75 percent of the runners he inherits, and has a resilient arm that allows him to work often. His biggest problem last year was an inability to stop the running game; all of the first seven baserunners who challenged him stole successfully. Then-teammate Carlos Garcia served as Cordova's interpreter last season.

Major League Pitching Register

	W	L	ERA	G	S	IP	H	ER	BB	SO
96 NL	4	7	4.09	59	12	99.0	103	45	20	95
Life	4	7	4.09	59	12	99.0	103	45	20	95

MARTY CORDOVA

Position: Outfield
Team: Minnesota Twins
Born: July 10, 1969 Las Vegas, NV
Height: 6′ **Weight:** 200 lbs.
Bats: right **Throws:** right
Acquired: Tenth-round pick in 6/89 free-agent draft

PLAYER SUMMARY	
Fantasy Value	$16 to $19
Card Value	7¢ to 10¢
Will	add some power
Can't	cut K/BB ratio
Expect	run production
Don't Expect	extended slump

Cordova made short work of skeptics who suggested he would succumb to the sophomore jinx. After edging Garret Anderson in a close vote for 1995 AL Rookie of the Year honors, Cordova picked up where he left off. If anything, he was even more productive. Although his home run total was down, his run production was up—thanks mainly to a dramatic increase in his batting average. The hike was hardly surprising, since he had topped .340 in two of the three minor-league seasons immediately preceding his promotion. Cordova worked hard to reduce his 1995 strikeout total. Though he still fans twice per walk, Cordova succeeds when he connects. A solid hitter against both righties and lefties, he collects extra bases on more than one-third of his hits. He had a 23-game hitting streak in June and the first two-homer game of his career in August. A 20-20 man as a rookie, Cordova has decent speed. He also has good range and a good arm (12 assists in 1995). The former UNLV star has worked hard to improve his defense. He spent all of last season as Minnesota's regular left fielder.

Major League Batting Register

	BA	G	AB	R	H	2B	3B	HR	RBI	SB
95 AL	.277	137	512	81	142	27	4	24	84	20
96 AL	.309	145	569	97	176	46	1	16	111	11
Life	.294	282	1081	178	318	73	5	40	195	31
2 Ave	.293	150	573	94	168	38	3	22	103	17

RHEAL CORMIER

Position: Pitcher
Team: Montreal Expos
Born: April 23, 1967 Monteon, New Brunswick, Canada
Height: 5′10″ **Weight:** 185 lbs.
Bats: left **Throws:** left
Acquired: Traded by Red Sox with Ryan McGuire and Shayne Bennett for Wil Cordero and Bryan Eversgerd, 1/96

PLAYER SUMMARY	
Fantasy Value	$4 to $6
Card Value	4¢ to 7¢
Will	seek consistency
Can't	end wild pitches
Expect	groundouts, DPs
Don't Expect	plate to wander

In six major-league seasons, Cormier has shown only flashes of the potential that landed him on the 1988 Canadian Olympic team. He took a 31-28 record and 4.11 ERA into the 1996 campaign but showed the same level of inconsistency that had plagued him previously. Cormier pitched his first major-league shutout but had trouble maintaining a .500 record. A fastball-slider pitcher who also throws a curve and a forkball that he uses as a changeup, Cormier yields one hit per inning and under three walks per game. The slider is his best weapon. Not a power pitcher, Cormier needs groundouts to survive. He induced 23 double plays in 1995, fifth in the American League. Cormier keeps the ball in the park and controls the running game but hurts his own efforts by throwing too many wild pitches. He's usually much more effective against left-handed hitters, although that was not necessarily the case last year.

Major League Pitching Register

	W	L	ERA	G	CG	IP	H	ER	BB	SO
91 NL	4	5	4.12	11	2	67.2	74	31	8	38
92 NL	10	10	3.68	31	3	186.0	194	76	33	117
93 NL	7	6	4.33	38	1	145.1	163	70	27	75
94 NL	3	2	5.45	7	0	39.2	40	24	7	26
95 AL	7	5	4.07	48	0	115.0	131	52	31	69
96 NL	7	10	4.17	33	1	159.2	165	74	41	100
Life	38	38	4.13	168	7	713.1	767	327	147	425
2 Ave	7	8	4.13	44	1	145.1	156	66	38	89

TIM CRABTREE

Position: Pitcher
Team: Toronto Blue Jays
Born: Oct. 13, 1969 Jackson, MI
Height: 6'4" **Weight:** 205 lbs.
Bats: right **Throws:** right
Acquired: Second-round pick in 6/92 free-agent draft

PLAYER SUMMARY	
Fantasy Value	$5 to $7
Card Value	4¢ to 7¢
Will	appear often
Can't	hold runners
Expect	good control
Don't Expect	enemy homers

Switching from starting to relieving shortened Crabtree's path to the majors. Drafted as a starter out of Michigan State in 1992, the big right-hander moved to relief in '94 and reached the majors a year later. Though not a power pitcher, Crabtree provides quality set-up service. He keeps his sinker and slider down, inducing plenty of ground balls, and throws strikes (he walks three men per nine innings). Crabtree got off to a great start last year, posting an 0.87 ERA in April and 1.26 mark in May. The rubber-armed right-hander finished with more than 50 appearances for the third year in a row. He was the busiest and most effective reliever in the Toronto bullpen. Crabtree succeeds by yielding fewer hits than innings, fanning more than seven batters per nine frames, and keeping the ball in the park. He yielded only three homers in his first 65 innings (51 games) of 1996. Crabtree fields his position well but has trouble keeping runners close. He should improve as he gains experience. At 27, Crabtree should have a bright future in front of him.

Major League Pitching Register

	W	L	ERA	G	S	IP	H	ER	BB	SO
95 AL	0	2	3.09	31	0	32.0	30	11	13	21
96 AL	5	3	2.54	53	1	67.1	59	19	22	57
Life	5	5	2.72	84	1	99.1	89	30	35	78
2 Ave	3	3	2.73	44	1	52.1	46	16	18	40

CHAD CURTIS

Position: Outfield
Team: Cleveland Indians
Born: Nov. 6, 1968 Marion, IN
Height: 5'10" **Weight:** 175 lbs.
Bats: right **Throws:** right
Acquired: Signed as a free agent, 12/96

PLAYER SUMMARY	
Fantasy Value	$9 to $11
Card Value	5¢ to 8¢
Will	supply fine defense
Can't	keep his mouth shut
Expect	more steal attempts
Don't Expect	solid leadoff stats

If Curtis could keep his thoughts to himself, he'd be a lot better off. Last year, he found himself in Buddy Bell's doghouse after questioning a bunt sign from the rookie Tiger manager. Traded to Los Angeles, ostensibly to replace ailing center fielder and leadoff man Brett Butler, he immediately told the media he didn't think of himself as a top-of-the-lineup hitter. A 20-20 man in 1995, Curtis didn't come close to those levels last year. His mouth, plus his penchant for fanning frequently, got in the way. A man with his speed should be able to fatten his average with bunts and infield hits. But he doesn't. Curtis took a .268 career mark into last year and had trouble maintaining it. He didn't pound lefties with his usual authority and wound up sharing time in center with Wayne Kirby and Todd Hollandsworth. As a fielder, Curtis has great reactions, fine range, and soft hands but lacks a strong arm. He's aggressive in the outfield, on the bases, and in the clubhouse.

Major League Batting Register

	BA	G	AB	R	H	2B	3B	HR	RBI	SB
92 AL	.259	139	441	59	114	16	2	10	46	43
93 AL	.285	152	583	94	166	25	3	6	59	48
94 AL	.256	114	453	67	116	23	4	11	50	25
95 AL	.268	144	586	96	157	29	3	21	67	27
96 AL	.262	104	400	65	105	20	1	10	37	16
96 NL	.212	43	104	20	22	5	0	2	9	2
Life	.265	696	2567	401	680	118	13	60	268	161
3 Ave	.262	142	566	89	148	28	3	16	61	27

OMAR DAAL

Position: Pitcher
Team: Montreal Expos
Born: March 1, 1972 Maracaibo, Venezuela
Height: 6'3" **Weight:** 185 lbs.
Bats: left **Throws:** left
Acquired: Traded by Dodgers for Rick
Clelland, 12/95

PLAYER SUMMARY	
Fantasy Value.	$4 to $6
Card Value	5¢ to 8¢
Will	bank on curveball
Can't	help with his bat
Expect	trial as starter
Don't Expect	runners to steal

Daal's effective work as a member of the Montreal bullpen last year convinced manager Felipe Alou to give him a late-season look as a starter. The results were encouraging. A curveball specialist who also throws a sinking fastball and a changeup, Daal is tough to hit when he has location. He averages 7½ strikeouts and fewer than four walks per nine innings, yielding fewer than seven hits over the same span. Daal keeps the ball in the park, seldom throws wild pitches, and has such a polished pickoff move that few baserunners challenge him. He's also a fine fielder but doesn't hit much. After spending his first two pro seasons as a starter, Daal switched to set-up relief and pitched effectively. The control problems he experienced with the 1995 Dodgers probably stemmed from a lack of regular work. That problem disappeared last summer, when Daal made more than 60 appearances for the Expos. He did a good job with inherited runners and held opposing hitters near the Mendoza Line.

JEFF D'AMICO

Position: Pitcher
Team: Milwaukee Brewers
Born: Dec. 27, 1975 St. Petersburg, FL
Height: 6'7" **Weight:** 250 lbs.
Bats: right **Throws:** right
Acquired: First-round pick in 6/93 free-agent
draft

PLAYER SUMMARY	
Fantasy Value.	$3 to $5
Card Value	20¢ to 25¢
Will	throw hard
Can't	stop gophers
Expect	good control
Don't Expect	rivals' hits

When D'Amico made his big-league bow on June 28, Milwaukee fans thought they were seeing double. Like teammate Ben McDonald, D'Amico is a towering, hard-throwing right-hander with good control of four pitches: sinking fastball, forkball, curve, and changeup. Also like McDonald, he was a first-round draft choice who reached the majors quickly. D'Amico yields fewer hits than innings, averages seven Ks per game, and holds opponents to a low average. But his desire to throw strikes got him into trouble last year when his pitches caught too much of the plate. D'Amico threw ten gopher balls in his first 42 AL innings. He helps himself with a good pickoff move, however, and few runners have dared to challenge him. During his short pro career, D'Amico has had more than his share of injuries, including elbow surgery, a shin fracture, and shoulder trouble that idled him for half a season after signing. It looks like those troubles may be behind him.

Major League Pitching Register

	W	L	ERA	G	S	IP	H	ER	BB	SO
93 NL	2	3	5.09	47	0	35.1	36	20	21	19
94 NL	0	0	3.29	24	0	13.2	12	5	5	9
95 NL	4	0	7.20	28	0	20.0	29	16	15	11
96 NL	4	5	4.02	64	0	87.1	74	39	37	82
Life	10	8	4.61	163	0	156.1	151	80	78	121

Major League Pitching Register

	W	L	ERA	G	CG	IP	H	ER	BB	SO
96 AL	6	6	5.44	17	0	86.0	88	52	31	53
Life	6	6	5.44	17	0	86.0	88	52	31	53

JOHNNY DAMON

Position: Outfield
Team: Kansas City Royals
Born: Nov. 5, 1973 Fort Riley, KS
Height: 6′ **Weight:** 175 lbs.
Bats: left **Throws:** left
Acquired: Sandwich pick in 6/92 free-agent draft

PLAYER SUMMARY	
Fantasy Value	$12 to $15
Card Value	7¢ to 12¢
Will	put bat on ball
Can't	hit left-handers
Expect	big improvement
Don't Expect	trouble in field

In three of his four minor-league seasons, Damon was named the top prospect in his league by managers responding to *Baseball America* surveys. Some scouts suggest he could soon be one of the best in the majors. Damon's blend of speed, defense, power, and personality may yet realize the Royals' belief that he's the second coming of George Brett. Like the retired three-time batting king, Damon is a left-handed hitter with a smooth line-drive stroke. Although Damon's defense, running, and bunting still need refining, he could become a dominating force in the Kenny Lofton mode—able to beat opponents with bat, speed, or glove. A center fielder in the minors, Damon moved to right so the Royals could maximize Tom Goodwin's speed in center. Damon is a solid .300 hitter vs. right-handers but needs to do better against lefties. He makes contact but will have better results when he learns to show patience at the plate. More walks mean more steals. Already a high-percentage basestealer, Damon will improve with experience. His power will also increase.

Major League Batting Register

	BA	G	AB	R	H	2B	3B	HR	RBI	SB
95 AL	.282	47	188	32	53	11	5	3	23	7
96 AL	.271	145	517	61	140	22	5	6	50	25
Life	.274	192	705	93	193	33	10	9	73	32
2 Ave	.274	99	364	49	100	17	5	5	38	16

DANNY DARWIN

Position: Pitcher
Team: Houston Astros
Born: Oct. 25, 1955 Bonham, TX
Height: 6′3″ **Weight:** 190 lbs.
Bats: right **Throws:** right
Acquired: Traded by Pirates for Rich Loiselle, 7/96

PLAYER SUMMARY	
Fantasy Value	$1
Card Value	4¢ to 7¢
Will	pitch inside
Can't	quell lefties
Expect	great control
Don't Expect	Ks or gophers

After going 3-10 with a 7.45 ERA at age 39, Darwin was widely assumed to be over the hill. But the desperate Pirates invited him to spring training as a nonroster player. Darwin not only stuck but won a starting job. He did so well that the Astros grabbed him for the NL Central stretch drive. Darwin succeeds because he still throws strikes. He averages just over one walk per nine innings, dominates right-handed hitters, and keeps the ball in the park. Darwin's willingness to work inside causes problems—like the huge Astros-Expos brawl that resulted in multiple suspensions.

Major League Pitching Register

	W	L	ERA	G	CG	IP	H	ER	BB	SO
78 AL	1	0	4.15	3	0	8.2	11	4	1	8
79 AL	4	4	4.04	20	1	78.0	50	35	30	58
80 AL	13	4	2.63	53	0	109.2	98	32	50	104
81 AL	9	9	3.64	22	6	146.0	115	59	57	98
82 AL	10	8	3.44	56	0	89.0	95	34	37	61
83 AL	8	13	3.49	28	9	183.0	175	71	62	92
84 AL	8	12	3.94	35	5	223.2	249	98	54	123
85 AL	8	18	3.80	39	11	217.2	212	92	65	125
86 AL	6	8	3.52	27	5	130.1	120	51	35	80
86 NL	5	2	2.32	12	1	54.1	50	14	9	40
87 NL	9	10	3.59	33	3	195.2	184	78	69	134
88 NL	8	13	3.84	44	3	192.0	189	82	48	129
89 NL	11	4	2.36	68	0	122.0	92	32	33	104
90 NL	11	4	2.21	48	3	162.2	136	40	31	109
91 AL	3	6	5.16	12	0	68.0	71	39	15	42
92 AL	9	9	3.96	51	2	161.1	159	71	53	124
93 AL	15	11	3.26	34	2	229.1	196	83	49	130
94 AL	7	5	6.30	13	0	75.2	101	53	24	54
95 AL	3	10	7.45	20	1	99.0	131	82	31	58
96 NL	10	11	3.77	34	0	164.2	160	69	27	96
Life	158	161	3.72	652	52	2710.2	2594	1119	780	1769
3 Ave	8	10	5.55	25	0	128.1	150	79	32	79

CHILI DAVIS

Position: Designated hitter
Team: Kansas City Royals
Born: Jan. 17, 1960 Kingston, Jamaica
Height: 6'3" **Weight:** 210 lbs.
Bats: both **Throws:** right
Acquired: Traded by Angels for Mark Gubicza and Mike Bovee, 12/96

PLAYER SUMMARY	
Fantasy Value.	$14 to $17
Card Value	7¢ to 10¢
Will	provide power
Can't	add any speed
Expect	much patience
Don't Expect.	outfield duty

Davis, who missed six weeks of 1996 with hamstring problems, seems to be getting better as he gets older. His batting average has hovered around the .300 mark for the past three years. A consistent slugger, he's hit at least 20 homers five times in the last six seasons. Davis has unusual patience for a slugger, walking as much as he fans, and is always among the league leaders in on-base percentage. He's solid from both sides of the plate, though he usually hits slightly better right-handed. He's especially dangerous with runners in scoring position. The three-time All-Star never bunts, steals, or plays the field, but he sure can swing the bat. Watching him hit, it's hard to believe he has chronic knee problems.

Major League Batting Register

	BA	G	AB	R	H	2B	3B	HR	RBI	SB
81 NL	.133	8	15	1	2	0	0	0	0	2
82 NL	.261	154	641	86	167	27	6	19	76	24
83 NL	.233	137	486	54	113	21	2	11	59	10
84 NL	.315	137	499	87	157	21	6	21	81	12
85 NL	.270	136	481	53	130	25	2	13	56	15
86 NL	.278	153	526	71	146	28	3	13	70	16
87 NL	.250	149	500	80	125	22	1	24	76	16
88 AL	.268	158	600	81	161	29	3	21	93	9
89 AL	.271	154	560	81	152	24	1	22	90	3
90 AL	.265	113	412	58	109	17	1	12	58	1
91 AL	.277	153	534	84	148	34	1	29	93	5
92 AL	.288	138	444	63	128	27	2	12	66	4
93 AL	.243	153	573	74	139	32	0	27	112	4
94 AL	.311	108	392	72	122	18	1	26	84	3
95 AL	.318	119	424	81	135	23	0	20	86	3
96 AL	.292	145	530	73	155	24	0	28	95	5
Life	.274	2115	7617	1099	2089	372	29	298	1195	132
3 Ave	.307	144	520	89	160	25	0	29	103	4

ERIC DAVIS

Position: Outfield
Team: Cincinnati Reds
Born: May 29, 1962 Los Angeles, CA
Height: 6'3" **Weight:** 185 lbs.
Bats: right **Throws:** right
Acquired: Signed as a free agent, 3/96

PLAYER SUMMARY	
Fantasy Value.	$16 to $19
Card Value	5¢ to 8¢
Will	generate power
Can't	flash old speed
Expect	walks, long hits
Don't Expect	trouble in field

Davis pulled off one of the best comebacks in recent years. Thought to be through in '94, when he suffered a pinched nerve in his neck and a pulled groin muscle, Davis didn't even play in '95. Nobody wanted him. Then he called the Reds, his original major-league team, and asked for a spring training tryout. He hooked on as a nonroster player. Though Davis is pushing 35, he's still a formidable force. He shows good patience at the plate, ranking among the league leaders in on-base percentage. Davis fans frequently but also gets extra bases on one-third of his hits. He's still a high-percentage basestealer, though not the burner who once swiped 80 in a season. A 20-20 season isn't out of the question, however. Davis still supplies solid defense in center, where he once won three straight Gold Gloves.

Major League Batting Register

	BA	G	AB	R	H	2B	3B	HR	RBI	SB
84 NL	.224	57	174	33	39	10	1	10	30	10
85 NL	.246	56	122	26	30	3	3	8	18	16
86 NL	.277	132	415	97	115	15	3	27	71	80
87 NL	.293	129	474	120	139	23	4	37	100	50
88 NL	.273	135	472	81	129	18	3	26	93	35
89 NL	.281	131	462	74	130	14	2	34	101	21
90 NL	.260	127	453	84	118	26	2	24	86	21
91 NL	.235	89	285	39	67	10	0	11	33	14
92 NL	.228	76	267	21	61	8	1	5	32	19
93 NL	.234	108	376	57	88	17	0	14	53	33
93 AL	.253	23	75	14	19	1	1	6	15	2
94 AL	.183	37	120	19	22	4	0	3	13	5
96 NL	.287	129	415	81	119	20	0	26	83	23
Life	.262	1229	4110	746	1076	169	20	231	728	329

Russ Davis

Position: Third base
Team: Seattle Mariners
Born: Sept. 13, 1969 Birmingham, AL
Height: 6′ **Weight:** 170 lbs.
Bats: right **Throws:** right
Acquired: Traded by Yankees with Sterling Hitchcock for Tino Martinez, Jeff Nelson, and Jim Mecir, 11/95

PLAYER SUMMARY	
Fantasy Value	$5 to $7
Card Value	5¢ to 8¢
Will	hit long balls
Can't	wait for walks
Expect	run production
Don't Expect	patience at bat

In the Bronx, Davis faced a formidable incumbent in Wade Boggs, plus the forbidding dimensions of Yankee Stadium's right-center field power alleys. For these reasons, he was glad to escape to Seattle. He reported to 1996 spring training with high hopes. Handed a starting job, he started slowly, hitting .234 with five homers in 167 at bats. Then he broke his left leg in Kansas City June 8, idling him for the rest of the year. That was a severe blow to the Mariners, who had hoped the 26-year-old Davis would be their third baseman for years to come. His power is obvious: Davis hit 110 homers in the minor leagues. He doesn't make good contact, however, and needs to show more patience. Overanxious to please, Davis doesn't always wait for his pitch, lunging instead at pitches out of the zone. He fans three times more often than he walks. Davis is a dependable defensive third baseman who led several minor leagues in chances, putouts, assists, and double plays. He even led one league in fielding percentage. Davis doesn't have the speed to steal bases.

Major League Batting Register

	BA	G	AB	R	H	2B	3B	HR	RBI	SB
94 AL	.143	4	14	0	2	0	0	0	1	0
95 AL	.276	40	98	14	27	5	2	2	12	0
96 AL	.234	51	167	24	39	9	0	5	18	2
Life	.244	95	279	38	68	14	2	7	31	2

Carlos Delgado

Position: First base; outfield
Team: Toronto Blue Jays
Born: June 25, 1972 Aguadilla, Puerto Rico
Height: 6′3″ **Weight:** 220 lbs.
Bats: left **Throws:** right
Acquired: Signed as a free agent, 10/88

PLAYER SUMMARY	
Fantasy Value	$17 to $20
Card Value	8¢ to 12¢
Will	mix patience, power
Can't	handle left-handers
Expect	tape-measure homers
Don't Expect	good glove or speed

Don't be fooled by Delgado's uniform number. Just because he honors the late Roberto Clemente by wearing No. 21 doesn't mean he's about to follow in his footsteps. Far from it, in fact. Although Delgado has enormous power, he doesn't do anything else that made Clemente a Hall of Famer. One of the game's most strikeout-prone sluggers, Delgado passed the century mark in Ks by mid-August. He's a wimp against left-handed pitchers, doesn't have any speed, and supplies such disastrous defense that he moved from catcher to left field to first base before settling in as Toronto's top DH in 1996. But Delgado has such prodigious power that he'll always have a job. One of the two homers he hammered in Detroit July 6 cleared the right-field roof of Tiger Stadium—the first time a visiting player has done that since 1988. A home run king and MVP in two minor leagues, Delgado has yet to show he can hit a big-league curve with any consistency. On the plus side, he has good patience for a young hitter and draws lots of walks.

Major League Batting Register

	BA	G	AB	R	H	2B	3B	HR	RBI	SB
93 AL	.000	2	1	0	0	0	0	0	0	0
94 AL	.215	43	130	17	28	2	0	9	24	1
95 AL	.165	37	91	7	15	3	0	3	11	0
96 AL	.270	138	488	68	132	28	2	25	92	0
Life	.246	220	710	92	175	33	2	37	127	1

RICH DeLUCIA

Position: Pitcher
Team: San Francisco Giants
Born: Oct. 7, 1964 Reading, PA
Height: 6′ **Weight:** 185 lbs.
Bats: right **Throws:** right
Acquired: Traded by Cardinals with Doug Creek and Allen Watson for Royce Clayton and Chris Wimmer, 12/95

PLAYER SUMMARY	
Fantasy Value	$0
Card Value	4¢ to 7¢
Will	stop righties
Can't	avoid gophers
Expect	frequent calls
Don't Expect	perfect control

Injuries interfered with DeLucia's efforts to justify the off-season trade that sent him to San Francisco. He lost playing time early while recuperating from shoulder surgery, then sat out with inflamed tissue in his left rib cage. When healthy, DeLucia is a solid middle reliever who is especially effective against righties. He's a fastball-slider pitcher who yields fewer hits than innings and averages seven whiffs per game. He does have occasional problems with his control, however. DeLucia averaged four walks per game in 1995. He's also had periodic problems with the long ball: He once led the AL in home runs allowed. But DeLucia is valuable because he's capable of making frequent appearances and working several innings at a time. DeLucia began as a starter but became a full-time reliever in '94. DeLucia helps himself with strong fielding and a good pickoff move. He won an ERA title in his first year as a pro.

Major League Pitching Register

	W	L	ERA	G	S	IP	H	ER	BB	SO
90 AL	1	2	2.00	5	0	36.0	30	8	9	20
91 AL	12	13	5.09	32	0	182.0	176	103	78	98
92 AL	3	6	5.49	30	1	83.2	100	51	35	66
93 AL	3	6	4.64	30	0	42.2	46	22	23	48
94 NL	0	0	4.22	8	0	10.2	9	5	5	15
95 NL	8	7	3.39	56	0	82.1	63	31	36	76
96 NL	3	6	5.84	56	0	61.2	62	40	31	55
Life	30	40	4.69	217	1	499.0	486	260	217	378
2 Ave	6	7	4.37	60	0	77.0	66	37	36	70

DELINO DeSHIELDS

Position: Second base
Team: St. Louis Cardinals
Born: Jan. 15, 1969 Seaford, DE
Height: 6′1″ **Weight:** 170 lbs.
Bats: left **Throws:** right
Acquired: Signed as a free agent, 11/96

PLAYER SUMMARY	
Fantasy Value	$11 to $14
Card Value	5¢ to 8¢
Will	show great speed
Can't	avoid strikeouts
Expect	best play on turf
Don't Expect	good bat vs. lefties

Stealing is the only thing DeShields does exceptionally well. He's swiped at least 40 bases five times in his seven-year career and is seldom thrown out. His speed also gives him exceptional range, but the rest of his defensive game is erratic. Though he reacts quickly, DeShields does not have soft hands or a strong arm. He's not adept at turning the double play, and he makes too many errors at his position. DeShields led the NL in errors by a second baseman in 1995 and made even more last season. A bust at the top of the lineup, DeShields has to bat lower in the order because of his weak on-base percentage. He fans twice as often as he walks, struggles against lefties, and rarely hits for extra bases. He's fanned more than 100 times in a season three times. DeShields could improve his value if he dropped more bunts and beat out infield hits. Montreal picked the Villanova product in the first round of the 1987 amateur draft.

Major League Batting Register

	BA	G	AB	R	H	2B	3B	HR	RBI	SB
90 NL	.289	129	499	69	144	28	6	4	45	42
91 NL	.238	151	563	83	134	15	4	10	51	56
92 NL	.292	135	530	82	155	19	8	7	56	46
93 NL	.295	123	481	75	142	17	7	2	29	43
94 NL	.250	89	320	51	80	11	3	2	33	27
95 NL	.256	127	425	66	109	18	3	8	37	39
96 NL	.224	154	581	75	130	12	8	5	41	48
Life	.263	908	3399	501	894	120	39	38	292	301
3 Ave	.242	141	503	74	122	16	5	6	43	43

MIKE DEVEREAUX

Position: Outfield
Team: Baltimore Orioles
Born: April 10, 1963 Casper, WY
Height: 6′ **Weight:** 191 lbs.
Bats: right **Throws:** right
Acquired: Signed as a free agent, 1/96

PLAYER SUMMARY	
Fantasy Value	$1
Card Value	4¢ to 7¢
Will	hit best vs. lefties
Can't	show former flair
Expect	some speed, power
Don't Expect	patience at plate

After earning MVP honors in the 1995 NL Championship Series, Devereaux used free agency to return to Baltimore, where he starred as a regular from 1989 to '93. Used as a fourth outfielder, Devereaux also filled in at DH and served as a pinch hitter and pinch runner. An aggressive hitter who fans three times more often than he walks, Devereaux still shows glimpses of speed and power. He has twice reached double digits in doubles, triples, home runs, and stolen bases. Though he's pushing 34, Devereaux is still a solid outfielder. He still gets good jumps, catches everything he reaches, and makes accurate throws. Devereaux was making leaps, dives, and highlight-film catches before Brady Anderson stole his thunder. With expansion a year away, Devereaux's days as a regular may not be over. He's already played for the Dodgers, Orioles, White Sox, and Braves.

Major League Batting Register

	BA	G	AB	R	H	2B	3B	HR	RBI	SB
87 NL	.222	19	54	7	12	3	0	0	4	3
88 NL	.116	30	43	4	5	1	0	0	2	0
89 AL	.266	122	391	55	104	14	3	8	46	22
90 AL	.240	108	367	48	88	18	1	12	49	13
91 AL	.260	149	608	82	158	27	10	19	59	16
92 AL	.276	156	653	76	180	29	11	24	107	10
93 AL	.250	131	527	72	132	31	3	14	75	3
94 AL	.203	85	301	35	61	8	2	9	33	1
95 AL	.306	92	333	48	102	21	1	10	55	6
95 NL	.255	29	55	7	14	3	0	1	8	2
96 AL	.229	127	323	49	74	11	2	8	34	8
Life	.254	1048	3655	483	930	166	33	105	472	84
3 Ave	.245	117	374	51	92	15	2	11	47	5

MARK DEWEY

Position: Pitcher
Team: San Francisco Giants
Born: Jan. 3, 1965 Grand Rapids, MI
Height: 6′ **Weight:** 216 lbs.
Bats: right **Throws:** right
Acquired: Signed as a free agent, 12/94

PLAYER SUMMARY	
Fantasy Value	$0
Card Value	4¢ to 7¢
Will	work often
Can't	get lefties
Expect	set-up role
Don't Expect	top control

A rubber-armed set-up man who stifles right-handed hitters, Dewey was the busiest member of the Giants bullpen last summer. A sinker-slider pitcher who also throws a curveball and changeup, Dewey yields fewer hits than innings and averages more than six strikeouts per nine frames. But his control was off last year, when he allowed more than five walks per nine innings. To compound his woes, Dewey was devoured by left-handed hitters, who produced a composite batting average against him that would have made Ted Williams proud. Dusty Baker learned quickly that the Grand Valley State product is most effective in set-up situations. Dewey helps himself with his fielding, ability to hold runners, and his hitting (though he rarely bats). He showed last year he was completely healed from the rib stress fracture that idled him for half of 1995. Signed by the Giants in 1987, Dewey also pitched for the Mets and Pirates before returning to San Francisco in 1995.

Major League Pitching Register

	W	L	ERA	G	S	IP	H	ER	BB	SO
90 NL	1	1	2.78	14	0	22.2	22	7	5	11
92 NL	1	0	4.32	20	0	33.1	37	16	10	24
93 NL	1	2	2.36	21	7	26.2	14	7	10	14
94 NL	2	1	3.68	45	1	51.1	61	21	19	30
95 NL	1	0	3.13	27	0	31.2	30	11	17	32
96 NL	6	3	4.21	78	0	83.1	79	39	41	57
Life	12	7	3.65	205	8	249.0	243	101	102	168
3 Ave	3	1	3.81	57	0	64.1	66	27	29	45

83

ALEX DIAZ

Position: Outfield
Team: Seattle Mariners
Born: Oct. 5, 1968 Brooklyn, NY
Height: 5'11" **Weight:** 180 lbs.
Bats: both **Throws:** right
Acquired: Claimed from Brewers on waivers, 10/94

PLAYER SUMMARY	
Fantasy Value	. . . . $1
Card Value	. . . . 4¢ to 7¢
Will	. . . . try comeback
Can't	. . . . hit ball out
Expect	. . . . bunts, speed
Don't Expect	. . . . weak defense

Diaz missed two months of the 1996 campaign following surgery to remove bone fragments from his left ankle, then made a fleeting comeback before returning to the DL in August with bone chips in his right elbow. The Brooklyn native, who grew up in Puerto Rico, spent six seasons in the minors before reaching the Milwaukee Brewers in 1992. Used exclusively as an outfielder by the '95 Mariners, Diaz delivered. He's a slap-and-run guy whose game revolves around speed. A better hitter against lefties, Diaz can bunt against anyone. He rarely walks, fans, or hits a home run but did surprise with 17 extra-base hits in 1995. He likes fastballs but has trouble with breaking stuff. Fine fielding is his forte. Diaz has quick reactions, great range, soft hands, and the ability to play all three outfield spots well. Diaz has been Ken Griffey's main understudy in center field. The only thing he doesn't do well in the field is throw—a surprising drawback for someone who signed as a shortstop.

Major League Batting Register

	BA	G	AB	R	H	2B	3B	HR	RBI	SB
92 AL	.111	22	9	5	1	0	0	0	1	3
93 AL	.319	32	69	9	22	2	0	0	1	5
94 AL	.251	79	187	17	47	5	7	1	17	5
95 AL	.248	103	270	44	67	14	0	3	27	18
96 AL	.241	38	79	11	19	2	0	1	5	6
Life	.254	274	614	86	156	23	7	5	51	37
2 Ave	.250	114	284	37	71	11	5	2	27	14

JERRY DiPOTO

Position: Pitcher
Team: Colorado Rockies
Born: May 24, 1968 Jersey City, NJ
Height: 6'2" **Weight:** 200 lbs.
Bats: right **Throws:** right
Acquired: Traded by Mets for Armando Reynoso, 11/06

PLAYER SUMMARY	
Fantasy Value	. . . . $1
Card Value	. . . . 4¢ to 7¢
Will	. . . . throw ground balls
Can't	. . . . always find plate
Expect	. . . . answer bell often
Don't Expect	. . . . plague of gophers

DiPoto spent three seasons as a minor-league starter before switching to relief work in 1992. A year later, he made it to the majors with Cleveland. Used primarily as a set-up man since, he has shown that he owns a resilient arm capable of responding to frequent bullpen calls. He appeared in a career-high 58 games for the 1995 Mets and might have exceeded that number had he not gotten off to such a slow start last season. Battered by the New York media, DiPoto was buried in the bullpen before reasserting himself in July. His early troubles might have made the New Jersey native a better, tougher performer. When he's right, DiPoto has good control of his sinker, slider, and forkball. He averages two Ks per walk, throws very few gopher balls, and holds runners extremely well. DiPoto is a ground-ball pitcher who averages only five whiffs per nine innings. He's decent in the field but not much of a threat at the plate. The Virginia Commonwealth product overcame a bout with thyroid cancer in spring 1994.

Major League Pitching Register

	W	L	ERA	G	S	IP	H	ER	BB	SO
93 AL	4	4	2.40	46	11	56.1	57	15	30	41
94 AL	0	0	8.04	7	0	15.2	26	14	10	9
95 NL	4	6	3.78	58	2	78.2	77	33	29	49
96 NL	7	2	4.19	57	0	77.1	91	36	45	52
Life	15	12	3.87	168	13	228.0	251	98	114	151
2 Ave	6	4	3.97	61	1	83.0	89	37	39	54

GARY DiSARCINA

Position: Shortstop
Team: Anaheim Angels
Born: Nov. 19, 1967 Malden, MA
Height: 6'1" **Weight:** 178 lbs.
Bats: right **Throws:** right
Acquired: Sixth-round pick in 6/88 free-agent draft

PLAYER SUMMARY	
Fantasy Value	$4 to $6
Card Value	5¢ to 8¢
Will	anchor infield
Can't	find 1995 form
Expect	great fielding
Don't Expect	the long ball

DiSarcina's sudden emergence as an All-Star was one of baseball's big surprises in 1995. Always a defensive whiz, he was lightly regarded as a hitter before applying the teachings of the Angels' hitting coach Rod Carew. The result was a .307 season that was easily the best of his career. But DiSarcina's magic seemed to evaporate when he suffered a torn ligament in his left thumb. He never found the magic last year, when both his batting average and on-base percentage were far below their previous levels. Not normally a power hitter, DiSarcina makes good contact—especially against left-handers—but doesn't show enough patience to build a high on-base mark with walks. The University of Massachusetts product doesn't steal much but uses his speed in the field, where he has great range. DiSarcina has quick reactions, soft hands, and a fine arm. He rarely makes an error.

Major League Batting Register

	BA	G	AB	R	H	2B	3B	HR	RBI	SB
89 AL	.000	2	0	0	0	0	0	0	0	0
90 AL	.140	18	57	8	8	1	1	0	0	1
91 AL	.211	18	57	5	12	2	0	0	3	0
92 AL	.247	157	518	48	128	19	0	3	42	9
93 AL	.238	126	416	44	99	20	1	3	45	5
94 AL	.260	112	389	53	101	14	2	3	33	3
95 AL	.307	99	362	61	111	28	6	5	41	7
96 AL	.256	150	536	62	137	26	4	5	48	2
Life	.255	682	2335	281	596	110	14	19	212	27
3 Ave	.271	140	497	68	135	26	5	5	47	5

DOUG DRABEK

Position: Pitcher
Team: Houston Astros
Born: July 25, 1962 Victoria, TX
Height: 6'1" **Weight:** 185 lbs.
Bats: right **Throws:** right
Acquired: Signed as a free agent, 12/92

PLAYER SUMMARY	
Fantasy Value	$7 to $9
Card Value	5¢ to 8¢
Will	show fair control
Can't	hold runners
Expect	inconsistency
Don't Expect	missed turns

A native Texan who attended the University of Houston, Drabek signed on with the Astros as a conquering hero in 1992. But of the four seasons since, three have been disappointments. The one-time NL Cy Young Award winner ('90) is still a durable performer who rarely misses a start. But he yields more hits than innings, throws too many home run balls, and no longer shows the pinpoint control for which he was once noted. Drabek led the NL in starts in 1995 but also allowed the third-highest average with runners in scoring position. He throws a fastball, slider, changeup, and curve, relying on location. Drabek fans seven-plus per nine innings, a rate that has declined a bit over recent seasons. A well-rounded pitcher, he helps himself with his glove, legs, and bat. Drabek began his pro career in the White Sox chain in 1983. He was an All-Star once (1994).

Major League Pitching Register

	W	L	ERA	G	CG	IP	H	ER	BB	SO
86 AL	7	8	4.10	27	0	131.2	126	60	50	76
87 NL	11	12	3.88	29	1	176.1	165	76	46	120
88 NL	15	7	3.08	33	3	219.1	194	75	50	127
89 NL	14	12	2.80	35	8	244.1	215	76	69	123
90 NL	22	6	2.76	33	9	231.1	190	71	56	131
91 NL	15	14	3.07	35	5	234.2	245	80	62	142
92 NL	15	11	2.77	34	10	256.2	218	79	54	177
93 NL	9	18	3.79	34	7	237.2	242	100	60	157
94 NL	12	6	2.84	23	6	164.2	132	52	45	121
95 NL	10	9	4.77	31	2	185.0	205	98	54	143
96 NL	7	9	4.57	30	1	175.1	208	89	60	137
Life	137	112	3.41	344	52	2257.0	2140	856	606	1454
3 Ave	12	9	3.99	32	4	205.0	208	91	61	156

DARREN DREIFORT

Position: Pitcher
Team: Los Angeles Dodgers
Born: May 18, 1972 Wichita, KS
Height: 6'2" **Weight:** 205 lbs.
Bats: right **Throws:** right
Acquired: First-round pick in 6/93 free-agent draft

PLAYER SUMMARY	
Fantasy Value	$1 to $3
Card Value	7¢ to 10¢
Will	pitch relief
Can't	avoid injury
Expect	blue blazers
Don't Expect	weak hitting

During his college career as a pitcher-DH at Wichita State, Dreifort had a 26-5 record, .318 average, and 25 homers in 314 at bats. He was not only a three-time All-American and U.S. Olympian but the winner of the Golden Spikes Award given annually to the nation's best amateur. Dreifort seemed to have a brilliant future in front of him. But that was before a spate of injuries that included serious arm, shoulder, and elbow problems. Entering 1996, Dreifort had worked only 70⅔ innings since turning pro. Finally sound last year after elbow surgery cost him all of 1995, Dreifort reached the majors in midseason. A sinker-slider pitcher who also throws a rising fastball and slow curve, Dreifort averages nearly a whiff an inning, dominates right-handed hitters, and keeps the ball in the park. His work against lefties could be better. Dreifort will serve as a pinch hitter as well as a pitcher. He hit an RBI pinch-hit single in his first NL at bat. Dreifort also helps himself with strong defense. He has been used as a reliever since reaching the majors, but that could change.

Major League Pitching Register

	W	L	ERA	G	S	IP	H	ER	BB	SO
94 NL	0	5	6.21	27	6	29.0	45	20	15	22
96 NL	1	4	4.94	19	0	23.2	23	13	12	24
Life	1	9	5.64	46	6	52.2	68	33	27	46

MARIANO DUNCAN

Position: Second base
Team: New York Yankees
Born: March 13, 1963 San Pedro de Macoris, Dominican Republic
Height: 6' **Weight:** 185 lbs.
Bats: right **Throws:** right
Acquired: Signed as a free agent, 11/95

PLAYER SUMMARY	
Fantasy Value	$4 to $6
Card Value	5¢ to 8¢
Will	spark his team
Can't	wait for walks
Expect	solid average
Don't Expect	the long ball

The Yankees signed Duncan strictly as a replacement. Little did the team imagine that he would become their regular second baseman. He responded brilliantly, posting an AL-high .361 average through early May and hitting .397 for the first three weeks after the All-Star break. Duncan also was the positive clubhouse presence who dreamed up the "We play today, we win today" slogan emblazoned on his teammates' T-shirts. One of baseball's most aggressive hitters, Duncan swings at anything. He fans ten times more than he walks, and his on-base percentage is virtually the same as his batting average. But he hit well over .300 last season. Duncan is particularly potent against left-handed pitching. Once a burner on the bases, Duncan doesn't run much anymore. But he shows good range at second.

Major League Batting Register

	BA	G	AB	R	H	2B	3B	HR	RBI	SB
85 NL	.244	142	562	74	137	24	6	6	39	38
86 NL	.229	109	407	47	93	7	0	8	30	48
87 NL	.215	76	261	31	56	8	1	6	18	11
89 NL	.248	94	258	32	64	15	2	3	21	9
90 NL	.306	125	435	67	133	22	11	10	55	13
91 NL	.258	100	333	46	86	7	4	12	40	5
92 NL	.267	142	574	71	153	40	3	8	50	23
93 NL	.282	124	496	68	140	26	4	11	73	6
94 NL	.268	88	347	49	93	22	1	8	48	10
95 NL	.287	81	265	36	76	14	2	6	36	1
96 AL	.340	109	400	62	136	34	3	8	56	4
Life	.269	1190	4338	583	1167	219	37	86	466	168
3 Ave	.297	108	396	57	118	27	2	9	55	6

SHAWON DUNSTON

Position: Shortstop
Team: Chicago Cubs
Born: March 21, 1963 Brooklyn, NY
Height: 6'1" **Weight:** 175 lbs.
Bats: right **Throws:** right
Acquired: Signed as a free agent, 12/96

PLAYER SUMMARY

Fantasy Value	$7 to $9
Card Value	5¢ to 8¢
Will	show fine arm
Can't	wait for walks
Expect	a dozen homers
Don't Expect	weak bat vs. lefties

Dunston has always had a reputation as a rifle-armed shortstop who hit for power but not average. That began to change in 1995, when the Brooklyn native was just shy of .300. He reached the mark last year with the Giants before injury idled him for the season August 5, when he suffered a concussion and fractured left eye socket in a second-base collision. Dunston showed much more patience at the plate last year, thanks to the coaching of Bobby Bonds. Dunston also decreased his ratio of strikeouts to walks. The back problems that cost him most of 1992 and '93 have reduced Dunston's range, but his reactions and hands are still good. His infield arm is one of the strongest in the NL. He rejoins the Cubs, his original team, for 1997.

Major League Batting Register

	BA	G	AB	R	H	2B	3B	HR	RBI	SB
85 NL	.260	74	250	40	65	12	4	4	18	11
86 NL	.250	150	581	66	145	37	3	17	68	13
87 NL	.246	95	346	40	85	18	3	5	22	12
88 NL	.249	155	575	69	143	23	6	9	56	30
89 NL	.278	138	471	52	131	20	6	9	60	19
90 NL	.262	146	545	73	143	22	8	17	66	25
91 NL	.260	142	492	59	128	22	7	12	50	21
92 NL	.315	18	73	8	23	3	1	0	2	2
93 NL	.400	7	10	3	4	2	0	0	2	0
94 NL	.278	88	331	38	92	19	0	11	35	3
95 NL	.296	127	477	58	141	30	6	14	69	10
96 NL	.300	82	287	27	86	12	2	5	25	8
Life	.267	1222	4438	533	1186	220	46	103	473	154
3 Ave	.290	116	430	49	125	24	3	12	51	8

RAY DURHAM

Position: Second base
Team: Chicago White Sox
Born: Nov. 30, 1971 Charlotte, NC
Height: 5'8" **Weight:** 170 lbs.
Bats: both **Throws:** right
Acquired: Fifth-round pick in 6/90 free-agent draft

PLAYER SUMMARY

Fantasy Value	$14 to $17
Card Value	8¢ to 15¢
Will	use speed well
Can't	copy Joe Morgan
Expect	more patience
Don't Expect	great contact

Durham did a nice job of avoiding the sophomore jinx last summer. The little switch-hitter supplied more speed and power than he did as a rookie and demonstrated dramatic improvement in his defense. In fact, Durham almost began to justify the predictions of scouts that he was the second coming of Joe Morgan. Certainly, the speed is there: Durham was stopped only twice in his first 25 steal tries last season. The power is coming, too: Durham contributed more than 40 extra-base hits. Still projected as a future leadoff man, Durham is learning to be more patient at the plate. He fanned nearly three times per walk as a rookie but less than twice per walk last year. The result was a 60-point rise in his on-base percentage. Durham's speed remains his best asset. He twice topped 30 steals in the minors. He fattens his average by dropping bunts and beating out infield hits. Durham has exceptional range in the field. He once led the American Association in chances, putouts, assists, double plays, and fielding percentage.

Major League Batting Register

	BA	G	AB	R	H	2B	3B	HR	RBI	SB
95 AL	.257	125	471	68	121	27	6	7	51	18
96 AL	.275	156	557	79	153	33	5	10	65	30
Life	.267	281	1028	147	274	60	11	17	116	48
2 Ave	.266	148	543	78	145	32	6	9	61	25

JERMAINE DYE

Position: Outfield
Team: Atlanta Braves
Born: Jan. 28, 1974 Oakland, CA
Height: 6′ **Weight:** 195 lbs.
Bats: right **Throws:** right
Acquired: 17th-round pick in 6/93 free-agent draft

PLAYER SUMMARY	
Fantasy Value	$5 to $7
Card Value	30¢ to 60¢
Will	smash left-handers
Can't	learn strike zone
Expect	power, strong arm
Don't Expect	problems in field

According to Hall of Famer Rich Ashburn, a former NL batting king, Dye is the best-looking young hitter he's seen in the last three years. Recalled when David Justice went down in May, Dye became the first Atlanta Brave ever to homer in his first at bat. In addition to his power and speed, Dye also owns a dynamic throwing arm. He had 44 outfield assists over a two-year span in the minors—hardly surprising for someone who was a pitcher in high school. An aggressive hitter who has yet to learn the strike zone, Dye had a 7-1 ratio of strike-outs to walks as a rookie. But he fared well against all types of pitching and played well in the outfield, appearing in all three spots. Dye has quick reactions, fine range, and soft hands. As a pinch hitter, Dye provides a powerful right-handed bat off the bench. He's lethal against left-handed pitching. Dye also adds speed to the attack; he twice had 19-steal seasons in the minors. Before he becomes a basestealer, however, he'll have to learn the pitchers and catchers. If he wants to play every day, mastering the strike zone is a priority.

Major League Batting Register

	BA	G	AB	R	H	2B	3B	HR	RBI	SB
96 NL	.281	98	292	32	82	16	0	12	37	1
Life	.281	98	292	32	82	16	0	12	37	1

MIKE DYER

Position: Pitcher
Team: Montreal Expos
Born: Sept. 8, 1966 Upland, CA
Height: 6′3″ **Weight:** 200 lbs.
Bats: right **Throws:** right
Acquired: Claimed from Pirates on waivers, 4/96

PLAYER SUMMARY	
Fantasy Value	$0
Card Value	5¢ to 8¢
Will	appear often
Can't	locate plate
Expect	middle relief
Don't Expect	high K count

Most middle relievers and set-up men are almost invisible to the public eye. But Dyer is an exception. His nickname, "the Unabomber," has nothing to do with his pitching, which is quite ordinary. Instead, it has to do with his hippie-look appearance. At times, the Expos didn't know how, when, or where to use him. Dyer blew five of his first seven save chances last year and even made his first start since 1989. He did top 50 appearances for the second straight season, however. Dyer is a fastball-slider pitcher who also throws a changeup—an arsenal that produces an average of six strikeouts per nine innings. He does not have a good ratio of Ks to walks. Although he gets lots of ground-ball outs, Dyer allows too many baserunners and too many long hits. His troubles with first batters translate to trouble keeping inherited runners from scoring. Dyer can bunt, hit, and field but has trouble keeping runners close. Minnesota drafted him out of California's Citrus College in 1986.

Major League Pitching Register

	W	L	ERA	G	S	IP	H	ER	BB	SO
89 AL	4	7	4.82	16	0	71.0	74	38	37	37
94 NL	1	1	5.87	14	4	15.1	15	10	12	13
95 NL	4	5	4.34	55	0	74.2	81	36	30	53
96 NL	5	5	4.40	70	2	75.2	79	37	34	51
Life	14	18	4.60	155	6	236.2	249	121	113	154
2 Ave	5	5	4.37	66	1	80.0	85	39	34	55

LEN DYKSTRA

Position: Outfield
Team: Philadelphia Phillies
Born: Feb. 10, 1963 Santa Ana, CA
Height: 5'10" **Weight:** 167 lbs.
Bats: left **Throws:** left
Acquired: Traded by Mets with Roger McDowell for Juan Samuel, 6/89

PLAYER SUMMARY	
Fantasy Value	$2 to $4
Card Value	5¢ to 8¢
Will	need a miracle
Can't	avoid injuries
Expect	leadoff dynamo
Don't Expect	powerful throws

If Dykstra ever regains his form as one of baseball's best leadoff men, he'll rank right up there with Superman on the indestructible list. Last year, he looked more like Clark Kent, disabled for the ninth time in his spectacular but checkered career. A congenital narrowing of the spinal column, aggravated by Dykstra's brand of no-holds-barred baseball, resulted in surgery May 19. He previously had knee surgery, appendicitis, a broken collarbone, and a serious automobile wreck. One of the most determined players in the game, Dykstra is normally a dynamic leadoff man who helps his team. He can work his way on with a walk, a bunt, an infield roller, or a solid hit. He also has great power. Dykstra has slowed on the bases but still gets great jumps.

Major League Batting Register

	BA	G	AB	R	H	2B	3B	HR	RBI	SB
85 NL	.254	83	236	40	60	9	3	1	19	15
86 NL	.295	147	431	77	127	27	7	8	45	31
87 NL	.285	132	431	86	123	37	3	10	43	27
88 NL	.270	126	429	57	116	19	3	8	33	30
89 NL	.237	146	511	66	121	32	4	7	32	30
90 NL	.325	149	590	106	192	35	3	9	60	33
91 NL	.297	63	246	48	73	13	5	3	12	24
92 NL	.301	85	345	53	104	18	0	6	39	30
93 NL	.305	161	637	143	194	44	6	19	66	37
94 NL	.273	84	315	68	86	26	5	5	24	15
95 NL	.264	62	254	37	67	15	1	2	18	10
96 NL	.261	40	134	21	35	6	3	3	13	3
Life	.285	1278	4559	802	1298	281	43	81	404	285
2 Ave	.269	94	365	69	98	27	4	5	27	16

DAMION EASLEY

Position: Infield
Team: Detroit Tigers
Born: Nov. 11, 1969 Oakland, CA
Height: 5'11" **Weight:** 155 lbs.
Bats: right **Throws:** right
Acquired: Traded by Angels for Greg Gohr, 7/96

PLAYER SUMMARY	
Fantasy Value	$1 to $3
Card Value	4¢ to 7¢
Will	hit lefties
Can't	get on base
Expect	good range
Don't Expect	daily duty

During his four years in the minors, Easley showed good speed, occasional pop, and the ability to play several positions. He later excited the Angels by hitting .313 in his first full season. He's come down to earth since—primarily because of wrist and shoulder woes, shin splints, and persistent migraine headaches. But Easley is neither the great hitter of '93 nor the wimp of 1994 and '95. Given a fresh start in Detroit, he hit well over .300 against left-handed pitchers and played four positions well. He's best at second, but he also handles himself well at shortstop and third and in center field. Easley's speed helps: He has very good range to go with a strong arm. An impatient hitter, Easley fans three times more than he walks. He hacks at too many bad pitches, gets behind in the count, and flails away helplessly against right-handers. If he hit down on the ball and dropped well-placed bunts, Easley could certainly fatten his batting average—not to mention his stolen base totals.

Major League Batting Register

	BA	G	AB	R	H	2B	3B	HR	RBI	SB
92 AL	.258	47	151	14	39	5	0	1	12	9
93 AL	.313	73	230	33	72	13	2	2	22	6
94 AL	.215	88	316	41	68	16	1	6	30	4
95 AL	.216	114	357	35	77	14	2	4	35	5
96 AL	.268	49	112	14	30	2	0	4	17	3
Life	.245	371	1166	137	286	50	5	17	116	27
2 Ave	.215	126	423	49	91	19	2	6	41	6

DENNIS ECKERSLEY

Position: Pitcher
Team: St. Louis Cardinals
Born: Oct. 3, 1954 Oakland, CA
Height: 6'2" **Weight:** 195 lbs.
Bats: right **Throws:** right
Acquired: Traded by Athletics for Steve Montgomery, 4/96

PLAYER SUMMARY	
Fantasy Value	$20 to $25
Card Value	5¢ to 8¢
Will	keep closing games
Can't	silence lefty bats
Expect	superb K/BB ratio
Don't Expect	bouts of wildness

Eckersley enjoyed a decent campaign in the Cardinal bullpen. His arsenal of fastball, slider, and forkball is still formidable against righties, though he's had problems with lefties over the last two years. He still averages eight strikeouts per nine innings. Eckersley never throws a wild pitch and walks only a handful. He's not the same guy who won the MVP and Cy Young Awards in 1992 or had more saves (48) than baserunners (45) two years earlier, but he still does his job well.

Major League Pitching Register

	W	L	ERA	G	S	IP	H	ER	BB	SO
75 AL	13	7	2.60	34	2	186.2	147	54	90	152
76 AL	13	12	3.43	36	1	199.1	155	76	78	200
77 AL	14	13	3.53	33	0	247.1	214	97	54	191
78 AL	20	8	2.99	35	0	268.1	258	89	71	162
79 AL	17	10	2.99	33	0	246.2	234	82	59	150
80 AL	12	14	4.28	30	0	197.2	188	94	44	121
81 AL	9	8	4.27	23	0	154.0	160	73	35	79
82 AL	13	13	3.73	33	0	224.1	228	93	43	127
83 AL	9	13	5.61	28	0	176.1	223	110	39	77
84 AL	4	4	5.01	9	0	64.2	71	36	13	33
84 NL	10	8	3.03	24	0	160.1	152	54	36	81
85 NL	11	7	3.08	25	0	169.1	145	58	19	117
86 NL	6	11	4.57	33	0	201.0	226	102	43	137
87 AL	6	8	3.03	54	16	115.2	99	39	17	113
88 AL	4	2	2.35	60	45	72.2	52	19	11	70
89 AL	4	0	1.56	51	33	57.2	32	10	3	55
90 AL	4	2	0.61	63	48	73.1	41	5	4	73
91 AL	5	4	2.96	67	43	76.0	60	25	9	87
92 AL	7	1	1.91	69	51	80.0	62	17	11	93
93 AL	2	4	4.16	64	36	67.0	67	31	13	80
94 AL	5	4	4.26	45	19	44.1	49	21	13	47
95 AL	4	6	4.83	52	29	50.1	53	27	11	40
96 NL	0	6	3.30	63	30	60.0	65	22	6	49
Life	192	165	3.48	964	353	3193.0	2981	1234	722	2334
3 Ave	4	6	4.12	62	30	60.1	65	27	12	53

JIM EDMONDS

Position: Outfield
Team: Anaheim Angels
Born: June 27, 1970 Fullerton, CA
Height: 6'1" **Weight:** 190 lbs.
Bats: left **Throws:** left
Acquired: Seventh-round pick in 6/88 free-agent draft

PLAYER SUMMARY	
Fantasy Value	$20 to $25
Card Value	15¢ to 25¢
Will	hit with power
Can't	handle lefties
Expect	run production
Don't Expect	sloppy defense

Edmonds proved last year that his sudden emergence as a slugger in 1995 was no fluke. He continued to blast AL pitchers—especially right-handers—although he suffered so many physical setbacks that he complained the season was too long. Edmonds's ailments included a pulled abdominal muscle, sore elbow, tight hamstrings, a sore rib cage, and a tender right arm. When healthy, Edmonds hits with power to all fields—the result of long hours in the weight room, the batting cage, and in the counsel of Angel hitting coach Rod Carew. He fans twice per walk but still draws enough bases on balls to post a decent on-base percentage. Edmonds would be a productive hitter in the first, second, or third slot. He doesn't have the speed to steal too often but gets such good jumps in center that his range is fine. He leaps, dives, and throws well, rarely making any errors. Edmonds was an All-Star in 1995 and is likely to return to that level if he stays healthy. But he'll have to improve his performance against lefties.

Major League Batting Register

	BA	G	AB	R	H	2B	3B	HR	RBI	SB
93 AL	.246	18	61	5	15	4	1	0	4	0
94 AL	.273	94	289	35	79	13	1	5	37	4
95 AL	.290	141	558	120	162	30	4	33	107	1
96 AL	.304	114	431	73	131	28	3	27	66	4
Life	.289	367	1339	233	387	75	9	65	214	9
3 Ave	.290	135	489	86	142	27	3	24	79	4

MARK EICHHORN

Position: Pitcher
Team: Anaheim Angels
Born: Nov. 21, 1960 San Jose, CA
Height: 6'3" **Weight:** 200 lbs.
Bats: right **Throws:** right
Acquired: Signed as a free agent, 2/96

PLAYER SUMMARY	
Fantasy Value $0
Card Value . . . . 4¢ to 7¢
Will . . . . try comeback trail
Can't . . . . rack up strikeouts
Expect . . . . control, grounders
Don't Expect . . . . hits by righties

Shoulder problems have kept Eichhorn on the sidelines for most of the last two seasons. Arthroscopic shoulder surgery to repair a torn rotator cuff idled him for all of 1995, and the residual effects hit him last year. After opening the season in the Angel bullpen, Eichhorn suffered rotator cuff tendinitis in May and was finally disabled in June. Even with a clean bill of health, his advanced athletic age (36) and two years of inactivity make Eichhorn's future dubious at best. A year from now, however, his experience could be of great help to one of the expansion clubs. A sidearmer who sometimes dips to submarine style, Eichhorn has always baffled right-handed batters but has been battered by lefties. He succeeds with proper location. Eichhorn gets ground balls, strands most runners he inherits, rarely throws gopher balls, and helps himself with fine fielding.

Major League Pitching Register

	W	L	ERA	G	S	IP	H	ER	BB	SO
82 AL	0	3	5.45	7	0	38.0	40	23	14	16
86 AL	14	6	1.72	69	10	157.0	105	30	45	166
87 AL	10	6	3.17	89	4	127.2	110	45	52	96
88 AL	0	3	4.18	37	1	66.2	79	31	27	28
89 NL	5	5	4.35	45	0	68.1	70	33	19	49
90 AL	2	5	3.08	60	13	84.2	98	29	23	69
91 AL	3	3	1.98	70	1	81.2	63	18	13	49
92 AL	4	4	3.08	65	2	87.2	86	30	25	61
93 AL	3	1	2.72	54	0	72.2	76	22	22	47
94 AL	6	5	2.15	43	1	71.0	62	17	19	35
96 AL	1	2	5.04	24	0	30.1	36	17	11	24
Life	48	43	3.00	563	32	885.2	825	295	270	640

JIM EISENREICH

Position: Outfield
Team: Florida Marlins
Born: April 18, 1959 St. Cloud, MN
Height: 5'11" **Weight:** 195 lbs.
Bats: left **Throws:** left
Acquired: Signed as a free agent, 12/96

PLAYER SUMMARY	
Fantasy Value. . . . . $6 to $8
Card Value . . . . 4¢ to 7¢
Will . . . . rip right-handers
Can't . . . . play every game
Expect . . . . reliable defense
Don't Expect . . . . power explosion

Eisenreich was a beacon in the Phillie fog last summer. He topped .300 for the fourth straight year (fifth in the last six seasons) and supplied fine defense while playing all three outfield spots. Often used in a left-field platoon with righty Pete Incaviglia, Eisenreich salvaged a typical year from the wreckage that surrounded him. He supplied a little speed, a little power, a lot of contact, and reliability in the field. Tough to fan or walk, he draws enough free passes to post an on-base percentage 50 points above his batting average. That's not bad for a guy who was hitting a career-high .340 in late August. At 37, Eisenreich lacks great speed but still has great judgment and is rarely caught when he tries to steal. His range is average, but he gets good jumps, catches everything he reaches, and makes accurate throws.

Major League Batting Register

	BA	G	AB	R	H	2B	3B	HR	RBI	SB
82 AL	.303	34	99	10	30	6	0	2	9	0
83 AL	.286	2	7	1	2	1	0	0	0	0
84 AL	.219	12	32	1	7	1	0	0	3	2
87 AL	.238	44	105	10	25	8	2	4	21	1
88 AL	.218	82	202	26	44	8	1	1	19	9
89 AL	.293	134	475	64	139	33	7	9	59	27
90 AL	.280	142	496	61	139	29	7	5	51	12
91 AL	.301	135	375	47	113	22	3	2	47	5
92 AL	.269	113	353	31	95	13	3	2	28	11
93 AL	.318	153	362	51	115	17	4	7	54	5
94 NL	.300	104	290	42	87	15	4	4	43	6
95 NL	.316	129	377	46	119	22	2	10	55	10
96 NL	.361	113	338	45	122	24	3	3	41	11
Life	.295	1197	3511	435	1037	199	36	49	430	99
3 Ave	.323	135	390	52	126	23	4	7	54	10

CAL ELDRED

Position: Pitcher
Team: Milwaukee Brewers
Born: Nov. 24, 1967 Cedar Rapids, IA
Height: 6'4" **Weight:** 215 lbs.
Bats: right **Throws:** right
Acquired: First-round pick in 6/89 free-agent draft

PLAYER SUMMARY

Fantasy Value	$6 to $8
Card Value	5¢ to 8¢
Will	continue to mend
Can't	copy rookie year
Expect	spot in rotation
Don't Expect	trouble in field

After winning 27 games for the Brewers in 1993 and '94, Eldred submitted to "Tommy John" elbow surgery in July '95. A year later, he was back on the mound. The transition wasn't smooth. The hope now is that Eldred will return to his prior form. When healthy, the former No. 1 draft pick from the University of Iowa mixes a fastball and changeup with a downward-breaking curve he throws at several different speeds. Eldred had a 3-1 ratio of strikeouts to walks as a 1992 rookie but hasn't been as sharp with his control since. When he's right, he yields fewer hits than innings but has occasional problems with the long ball. He's an outstanding fielder whose lone weakness is keeping runners close. The big right-hander may have to alter his style to avoid additional elbow problems. Too many innings, too many curves, and too much emphasis on his delivery may have taken their toll. At age 29, however, Eldred is not too old to adapt his style if it will increase his longevity.

Major League Pitching Register

	W	L	ERA	G	CG	IP	H	ER	BB	SO
91 AL	2	0	4.50	3	0	16.0	20	8	6	10
92 AL	11	2	1.79	14	2	100.1	76	20	23	62
93 AL	16	16	4.01	36	8	258.0	232	115	91	180
94 AL	11	11	4.68	25	6	179.0	158	93	84	98
95 AL	1	1	3.42	4	0	23.2	24	9	10	18
96 AL	4	4	4.46	15	0	84.2	82	42	38	50
Life	45	34	3.90	97	16	661.2	592	287	252	418
2 Ave	10	10	4.62	25	4	168.1	152	87	78	94

KEVIN ELSTER

Position: Shortstop
Team: Texas Rangers
Born: Aug. 3, 1964 San Pedro, CA
Height: 6'2" **Weight:** 200 lbs.
Bats: right **Throws:** right
Acquired: Signed as a free agent, 3/96

PLAYER SUMMARY

Fantasy Value	$8 to $10
Card Value	5¢ to 8¢
Will	excel in field
Can't	cut strikeouts
Expect	surprising pop
Don't Expect	best bat vs. righties

With Benji Gil sidelined by back surgery, the Rangers scoured the baseball scrap heap in their desperate search for a replacement. They reluctantly settled on Elster, even though he had missed most of the three previous years with shoulder problems and was twice released in 1995. Once a fine-fielding shortstop with a strong arm and some pop in his bat, Elster's track record included service with eight teams and a pair of major shoulder operations. He shed 20 pounds, worked out, and reported to 1996 spring camp stronger and wiser than before. The results were immediate. The new, improved Elster fans more than two times per walk but generates power from the bottom of the lineup, hitting .300 vs. lefties. Not a basestealer, Elster runs well enough to have good range in the field. He makes all the plays, showing soft hands and a strong arm.

Major League Batting Register

	BA	G	AB	R	H	2B	3B	HR	RBI	SB
86 NL	.167	19	30	3	5	1	0	0	0	0
87 NL	.400	5	10	1	4	2	0	0	1	0
88 NL	.214	149	406	41	87	11	1	9	37	2
89 NL	.231	151	458	52	106	25	2	10	55	4
90 NL	.207	92	314	36	65	20	1	9	45	2
91 NL	.241	115	348	33	84	16	2	6	36	2
92 NL	.222	6	18	0	4	0	0	0	0	0
94 AL	.000	7	20	0	0	0	0	0	0	0
95 AL	.118	10	17	1	2	1	0	0	0	0
95 NL	.208	26	53	10	11	4	1	1	9	0
96 AL	.252	157	515	79	130	32	2	24	99	4
Life	.228	737	2189	256	498	112	9	59	282	14

ALAN EMBREE

Position: Pitcher
Team: Cleveland Indians
Born: Jan. 23, 1970 Vancouver, WA
Height: 6'2" **Weight:** 190 lbs.
Bats: left **Throws:** left
Acquired: Fifth-round pick in 6/89 free-agent draft

PLAYER SUMMARY	
Fantasy Value	$1
Card Value	5¢ to 8¢
Will	enter games late
Can't	find strike zone
Expect	lefties to choke
Don't Expect	extended outings

Even though he qualified as a 1996 rookie, Embree's name was familiar to fans because of his four appearances in the 1995 World Series. The hard-throwing lefty has been knocking at the big-league door for several seasons. He had cups of coffee in 1992 and 1995 but seemed to find his niche only after switching from starting to relief work two years ago. Embree missed significant playing time with elbow ligament transplant surgery in 1993 and bursitis in his left hip last year. Unable to keep sharp, he had to return to the minors in 1996 for a refresher course in throwing strikes—especially with the slider. At the time of his demotion, Embree had more strikeouts than innings pitched but had yielded too many home runs. In addition, his ratio of whiffs to walks was not even 2-to-1. Embree is normally most potent against left-handed batters. That was evident in the 1995 postseason, when he fanned the only man he faced in the ALCS and posted a 2.70 ERA in the World Series. His arm speed and buggy-whip delivery make it especially tough for lefties to get a good look.

Major League Pitching Register

	W	L	ERA	G	S	IP	H	ER	BB	SO
92 AL	0	2	7.00	4	0	18.0	19	14	8	12
95 AL	3	2	5.11	23	1	24.2	23	14	16	23
96 AL	1	1	6.39	24	0	31.0	30	22	21	33
Life	4	5	6.11	51	1	73.2	72	50	45	68

JOHN ERICKS

Position: Pitcher
Team: Pittsburgh Pirates
Born: Sept. 16, 1967 Oak Lawn, IL
Height: 6'7" **Weight:** 255 lbs.
Bats: right **Throws:** right
Acquired: Signed as a minor-league free agent, 2/93

PLAYER SUMMARY	
Fantasy Value	$1
Card Value	5¢ to 8¢
Will	stay in pen
Can't	swing bat
Expect	high heat
Don't Expect	good glove

Although Ericks showed flashes of potential as a 1995 rookie, it wasn't until he moved to relief last year that he found his niche in the major leagues. He has good command of his slider, curve, and a rising, four-seam fastball, averaging nearly a strikeout per inning. The University of Illinois product has been clocked as high as 95 mph. Ericks was strictly a starter in the minors, but working shorter stints on a more frequent basis seems to agree with him. He has exceptional poise for a young pitcher and doesn't seem rattled when he enters games with men on base. Ericks strands most of the runners he inherits. He had some problems with his control early and was hurt by the long ball too often. Ericks doesn't hit much but can help himself with a bunt. Neither his fielding nor his pick-off move are anything to write home about. He sometimes seems awkward on the mound. Basestealers found him an easy target last year as well. Ericks is still learning but seems to be adapting well to his new relief role. He could be Pittsburgh's top righty reliever in 1997.

Major League Pitching Register

	W	L	ERA	G	S	IP	H	ER	BB	SO
95 NL	3	9	4.58	19	0	106.0	108	54	50	80
96 NL	4	5	5.79	28	8	46.2	56	30	19	46
Life	7	14	4.95	47	8	152.2	164	84	69	126
2 Ave	4	8	4.92	25	4	83.0	89	45	38	68

SCOTT ERICKSON

Position: Pitcher
Team: Baltimore Orioles
Born: Feb. 2, 1968 Long Beach, CA
Height: 6'4" **Weight:** 220 lbs.
Bats: right **Throws:** right
Acquired: Traded by Twins for Scott
  Klingenbeck and Kim Bartee, 7/05

PLAYER SUMMARY	
Fantasy Value	$6 to $8
Card Value	5¢ to 8¢
Will	show good control
Can't	stymie lefty bats
Expect	grounders, steals
Don't Expect	top win-loss mark

Erickson's strong finish with the 1995 Orioles suggested he had recaptured the magic of 1991 and '92, when he won 33 games for the Minnesota Twins. But his performance last year proved that wish a mirage. Thanks to the left-handed hitters who ate him for lunch, Erickson suffered a bloated ERA that almost kept him on the wrong side of .500 for the third time in the last four seasons. A sinker-slider pitcher, Erickson averages fewer than four strikeouts per nine frames. He has good control, walking fewer than three per game, but gets hit when his pitches catch too much of the plate. With the possible exception of Kent Mercker last year, Erickson was hit harder than anyone else in the Baltimore rotation. His inconsistency remains a major mystery. With no one on base, Erickson is a tough, reliable performer. But he has trouble with men on, especially when he needs to close an inning or get a third strike. He'll get his share of complete games and shutouts.

Major League Pitching Register

	W	L	ERA	G	CG	IP	H	ER	BB	SO
90 AL	8	4	2.87	19	1	113.0	108	36	51	53
91 AL	20	8	3.18	32	5	204.0	189	72	71	108
92 AL	13	12	3.40	32	5	212.0	197	80	83	101
93 AL	8	19	5.19	34	1	218.2	266	126	71	116
94 AL	8	11	5.44	23	2	144.0	173	87	59	104
95 AL	13	10	4.81	32	7	196.1	213	105	67	106
96 AL	13	12	5.02	34	6	222.1	262	124	66	100
Life	83	76	4.33	206	27	1310.1	1408	630	468	688
3 Ave	13	13	5.08	34	6	215.1	248	122	75	122

DARIN ERSTAD

Position: Outfield
Team: Anaheim Angels
Born: June 4, 1974 Jamestown, ND
Height: 6'2" **Weight:** 195 lbs.
Bats: left **Throws:** left
Acquired: First-round pick in 6/95 free-agent
  draft

PLAYER SUMMARY	
Fantasy Value	$8 to $10
Card Value	24¢ to 40¢
Will	hit ball hard
Can't	live off hype
Expect	speed, defense
Don't Expect	time on bench

Even before Erstad reached the majors last June, he was compared to Tim Salmon. Actually, Erstad could be better. He can hit for average and power, run, throw, and field. He couples patience at the plate with exceptional bat speed, making him an ideal leadoff man. But batting him first might waste his RBI potential. Tough to fool, Erstad doesn't swing at everything. During his brief AL stint last summer, he walked almost as often as he fanned. An All-American at the University of Nebraska, Erstad was the first man from the 1995 amateur draft to reach the majors. He made his debut last June 14 as the Angels center fielder and leadoff man vs. Toronto. Although the original plan was to keep the rookie only until Jim Edmonds returned, Erstad played so well the Angels changed their thinking. He eventually returned to the minors in August because the Angels had incumbents at all three outfield spots and DH. Erstad blends a good work ethic with a humble demeanor and a football star's tenacity: He was a placekicker and punter for the Nebraska football team that won a national title.

Major League Batting Register

	BA	G	AB	R	H	2B	3B	HR	RBI	SB
96 AL	.284	57	208	34	59	5	1	4	20	3
Life	.284	57	208	34	59	5	1	4	20	3

VAUGHN ESHELMAN

Position: Pitcher
Team: Boston Red Sox
Born: May 22, 1969 Philadelphia, PA
Height: 6'3" **Weight:** 205 lbs.
Bats: left **Throws:** left
Acquired: Rule 5 draft pick from Orioles, 12/94

PLAYER SUMMARY
Fantasy Value $0
Card Value . . . . 4¢ to 7¢
Will . . . . improve or else
Can't . . . . prevent gophers
Expect . . . . righties to hit
Don't Expect . . . . many strikeouts

If Eshelman didn't have to face right-handed hitters, he'd be a fine pitcher. Unfortunately, that is not the case. A sinker-slider hurler with a so-so changeup, Eshelman handcuffs left-handed batters. Against righties, however, he's dead meat. Plagued by control problems plus an inability to retire righties, Eshelman posted an embarrassing ERA last summer. He was hit as hard as anyone on the Red Sox staff, yielding more than 11 hits per nine innings and throwing too many home run balls. He averages only six Ks per game. He's still looking for the magic that allowed him to begin his big-league career in 1995 with 18⅓ consecutive scoreless innings. The only positive in Eshelman's current game is a superb pickoff move. Baserunners rarely challenge him—but maybe that's because they know they'll score eventually, anyway. When Eshelman pitches, everybody hits—at least if they're right-handed. In addition to everything else, Eshelman also has to worry about the chronic shoulder problems that have disabled him four times in his six-year career as a pro.

Major League Pitching Register

	W	L	ERA	G	S	IP	H	ER	BB	SO
95 AL	6	3	4.85	23	0	81.2	86	44	36	41
96 AL	6	3	7.08	39	0	87.2	112	69	58	59
Life	12	6	6.01	62	0	169.1	198	113	94	100
2 Ave	6	3	5.94	32	0	90.1	104	59	49	53

ALVARO ESPINOZA

Position: Infield
Team: New York Mets
Born: Feb. 19, 1962 Valencia, Carabobo, Venezuela
Height: 6' **Weight:** 190 lbs.
Bats: right **Throws:** right
Acquired: Traded by Indians with Carlos Baerga for Jeff Kent and Jose Vizcaino, 7/96

PLAYER SUMMARY
Fantasy Value $0
Card Value . . . . 4¢ to 7¢
Will . . . . play anywhere
Can't . . . . wait for walks
Expect . . . . decent defense
Don't Expect . . . . lofty average

One of baseball's best utility men, Espinoza plays all four infield spots, pinch-hits, and pinch-runs. Signed as a shortstop, he's best defensively on the right side of the infield, where he shows quick reactions, decent range, soft hands, and a strong throwing arm. If he could hit consistently like he did last year, he'd certainly see more action. In his first 15 seasons, he had a .256 average, 22 homers, and 12 stolen bases—hardly numbers to write home about. Espinoza fans three times more often than he walks and hacks away at any breaking balls he sees. He spent three seasons as the regular shortstop for the Yankees from 1989 to '91. Strictly a benchwarmer for the last three years, he could find regular work with expansion a year away.

Major League Batting Register

	BA	G	AB	R	H	2B	3B	HR	RBI	SB
84 AL	.000	1	0	0	0	0	0	0	0	0
85 AL	.263	32	57	5	15	2	0	0	9	0
86 AL	.214	37	42	4	9	1	0	0	1	0
88 AL	.000	3	3	0	0	0	0	0	0	0
89 AL	.282	146	503	51	142	23	1	0	41	3
90 AL	.224	150	438	31	98	12	2	2	20	1
91 AL	.256	148	480	51	123	23	2	5	33	4
93 AL	.278	129	263	34	73	15	0	4	27	2
94 AL	.238	90	231	27	55	13	0	1	19	1
95 AL	.252	66	143	15	36	4	0	2	17	0
96 AL	.223	59	112	12	25	4	2	4	11	1
96 NL	.306	48	134	19	41	7	2	4	16	0
Life	.256	909	2406	249	617	104	9	22	194	12

SHAWN ESTES

Position: Pitcher
Team: San Francisco Giants
Born: Feb. 18, 1973 San Bernardino, CA
Height: 6'2" **Weight:** 185 lbs.
Bats: both **Throws:** left
Acquired: Traded by Mariners with Wilson Delgado for Salomon Torres, 5/95

PLAYER SUMMARY	
Fantasy Value	$6 to $8
Card Value	15¢ to 25¢
Will	bank on curve
Can't	throw strikes
Expect	eventual ace
Don't Expect	any outbursts

When Estes worked his way up the ladder from Class-A to the majors in 1995, he became the first Giant to do that since fellow pitcher Rafael Novoa in 1990. Though Novoa wasn't around long, the Giants think the Estes story will have a different ending. Fully healed from shoulder surgery that slowed his progress, Estes blends a curveball—his best pitch—with a low-90s fastball and decent changeup. He averages nearly eight Ks per nine innings but sometimes struggles with his control. Baserunners don't pose much problem, however, as Estes keeps them close with a quality pick-off move. He fields his position well and even hits a little. The young left-hander was rated the Giants' top prospect by *Baseball America* before the 1996 campaign started. Scouts insist he has the potential to be a No. 1 or No. 2 starter. Now that he's learned to relax on the mound, that prediction might have merit. Estes was once a walking temper tantrum in search of an excuse to explode. After going 0-3 in his first fleeting look at NL hitters, Estes was much more effective last year.

Major League Pitching Register

	W	L	ERA	G	CG	IP	H	ER	BB	SO
95 NL	0	3	6.75	3	0	17.1	16	13	5	14
96 NL	3	5	3.60	11	0	70.0	63	28	39	60
Life	3	8	4.23	14	0	87.1	79	41	44	74

TONY EUSEBIO

Position: Catcher
Team: Houston Astros
Born: April 27, 1967 San Jose de los Llamos, Dominican Republic
Height: 6'2" **Weight:** 180 lbs.
Bats: right **Throws:** right
Acquired: Signed as a free agent, 5/85

PLAYER SUMMARY	
Fantasy Value	$1 to $3
Card Value	4¢ to 7¢
Will	make contact
Can't	steal bases
Expect	good average
Don't Expect	weak throws

Eusebio is a valuable commodity: a backup catcher who's strong on both offense and defense. A contact hitter with considerable patience, he's more likely to poke an opposite-field single than a home run. But he showed in 1995 that he hits well above .300 with runners in scoring position and in late-inning pressure spots. A fastball hitter, Eusebio puts his bat on the ball. But he's reduced his former tendency to swing at everything. Eusebio's newfound patience results in walks that give him a respectable on-base percentage. When he reaches, don't expect Eusebio to steal. Though he once swiped 19 in a minor-league campaign, he's no longer a basestealing threat. He is a threat to opposing basestealers, however. Eusebio nailed 30 percent of those who challenged him in 1995 but didn't fare as well last year, when he was slowed by a fractured left hand. The Dominican receiver has a quick release and strong, accurate arm. He's improved his game-calling and handling of pitchers in recent seasons.

Major League Batting Register

	BA	G	AB	R	H	2B	3B	HR	RBI	SB
91 NL	.105	10	19	4	2	1	0	0	0	0
94 NL	.296	55	159	18	47	9	1	5	30	0
95 NL	.299	113	368	46	110	21	1	6	58	0
96 NL	.270	58	152	15	41	7	2	1	19	0
Life	.287	236	698	83	200	38	4	12	107	0
3 Ave	.292	88	263	31	77	14	2	5	42	0

CARL EVERETT

Position: Outfield
Team: New York Mets
Born: June 3, 1971 Tampa, FL
Height: 6' **Weight:** 190 lbs.
Bats: both **Throws:** right
Acquired: Traded by Marlins for Quilvio Veras, 11/94

PLAYER SUMMARY	
Fantasy Value $1
Card Value . . . . 7¢ to 10¢
Will . . . . make great throws
Can't . . . . realize potential
Expect . . . . some speed, power
Don't Expect . . . . return to lineup

Everett's strong finish in 1995 made him the favorite to be the right fielder for the '96 Mets. The job was his to lose, and he did. Everett simply never showed the speed-plus-power potential that Yankee scouts had seen when they made him their top choice in the 1990 free-agent draft. Reduced to pinch-hitting and serving as a sub at all three outfield spots, Everett hit well against left-handed pitching but was a dud against righties—the opposite of his 1995 form. An aggressive hitter, he fans twice per walk and—until 1996—was more likely to hit a home run than to steal a base. Everett's best asset is a powerful throwing arm ideally suited for right field. Everett had nine assists in 68 games during the 1995 stretch drive. Last year, however, even his cannon couldn't prevent his stay in Dallas Green's doghouse. Although he produced in the pinch late in the year, Everett's failure to win a regular job was a disappointment.

Major League Batting Register

	BA	G	AB	R	H	2B	3B	HR	RBI	SB
93 NL	.105	11	19	0	2	0	0	0	0	1
94 NL	.216	16	51	7	11	1	0	2	6	4
95 NL	.260	79	289	48	75	13	1	12	54	2
96 NL	.240	101	192	29	46	8	1	1	16	6
Life	.243	207	551	84	134	22	2	15	76	13
2 Ave	.252	95	259	42	65	11	1	7	38	4

JORGE FABREGAS

Position: Catcher
Team: Anaheim Angels
Born: March 13, 1970 Miami, FL
Height: 6'3" **Weight:** 205 lbs.
Bats: left **Throws:** right
Acquired: Supplemental-round pick in 6/91 free-agent draft

PLAYER SUMMARY	
Fantasy Value $1
Card Value . . . . 5¢ to 8¢
Will . . . . show strong arm
Can't . . . . steal any bases
Expect . . . . off-field hits
Don't Expect . . . . patience, power

Because he's a catcher who hits left-handed, Fabregas has few worries about job security. But he's not good enough as either a hitter or fielder to even think about playing every day. A terrific hitter with the aluminum bats used at the University of Miami, Fabregas has fizzled since switching to wood. He hit only a handful of homers in the minors and never hit over .289. His bat was reasonably respectable last year, when he shared catching time with veteran Don Slaught and rookie Todd Greene, two right-handed hitters. Fabregas is an opposite-field singles hitter who makes contact and has some patience—enough to push his on-base percentage 50 points beyond his batting average. He runs like Smoky Burgess, a rotund receiver of an earlier era, but does have some basic tools behind the plate, including a fine arm. Fabregas was a third baseman and DH in college, where he was a second-team All-American. But his bat has yet to recapture its college form. He will compete with Greene for the No. 1 catcher position in 1997.

Major League Batting Register

	BA	G	AB	R	H	2B	3B	HR	RBI	SB
94 AL	.283	43	127	12	36	3	0	0	16	2
95 AL	.247	73	227	24	56	10	0	1	22	0
96 AL	.287	90	254	18	73	6	0	2	26	0
Life	.271	206	608	54	165	19	0	3	64	2
2 Ave	.267	86	255	23	68	9	0	2	25	0

SAL FASANO

Position: Catcher
Team: Kansas City Royals
Born: Aug. 10, 1971 Chicago, IL
Height: 6'2" **Weight:** 220 lbs.
Bats: right **Throws:** right
Acquired: 37th-round pick in 6/93 free-agent draft

PLAYER SUMMARY

Fantasy Value	$0
Card Value	5¢ to 8¢
Will	add some pop
Can't	stop fanning
Expect	good defense
Don't Expect	high average

A good defensive catcher is worth his weight in gold. One who can also hit is invaluable. Fasano meets both criteria. The former University of Evansville star jumped from Double-A to the Kansas City lineup last spring before returning to Triple-A for more seasoning. He was Kansas City's Minor League Player of the Year in 1994, when he also won Midwest League MVP honors with 25 homers and 81 RBI at Rockford (Illinois). A year later, he hammered 20 homers for Wichita Falls, where he also played some first base. To make sure he was ready, the Royals sent him to the Arizona Fall League after the season. Working with former big-league receiver Jamie Quirk, Fasano honed his catching skills. He then advanced to the majors, making his major-league debut on April 3 in a game against the Orioles. Fasano hit six home runs during his stay but managed only a .203 batting average against AL pitching. While his defensive skills are up to big-league standards, Fasano will have to show better knowledge of the strike zone before he sticks. More patience and better contact are essential.

Major League Batting Register

	BA	G	AB	R	H	2B	3B	HR	RBI	SB
96 AL	.203	51	143	20	29	2	0	6	19	1
Life	.203	51	143	20	29	2	0	6	19	1

JEFF FASSERO

Position: Pitcher
Team: Seattle Mariners
Born: Jan. 5, 1963 Springfield, IL
Height: 6'1" **Weight:** 195 lbs.
Bats: left **Throws:** left
Acquired: Traded by Expos with Alex Pacheco for Chris Widger, Matt Wagner, and Trey Moore, 11/96

PLAYER SUMMARY

Fantasy Value	$15 to $18
Card Value	5¢ to 8¢
Will	head the staff
Can't	swing the bat
Expect	victories, Ks
Don't Expect	HRs by lefties

One of baseball's best left-handers, Fassero emerged as the ace of the Montreal staff last summer. He was NL Pitcher of the Month in both June and July but saved his best game for August: a 14-K effort that set a club record for strikeouts by a left-hander. A victim of control trouble in the past, Fassero's success last year was directly proportional to his ability to throw strikes. The University of Mississippi product averages only two walks per nine innings, yields less than one hit per inning, and keeps the ball in the park. He simply overpowers left-handed hitters. Fassero blends his sinker, slider, forkball, and changeup so well that he averages a strikeout per frame. When he's on, he's almost unhittable. Fassero is a fine bunter but can't hit a lick. He's okay in the field, however, and has made dramatic improvements in a once-dreadful pickoff move. Only half of the first 20 baserunners who challenged him last year succeeded.

Major League Pitching Register

	W	L	ERA	G	CG	IP	H	ER	BB	SO
91 NL	2	5	2.44	51	0	55.1	39	15	17	42
92 NL	8	7	2.84	70	0	85.2	81	27	34	63
93 NL	12	5	2.29	56	1	149.2	119	38	54	140
94 NL	8	6	2.99	21	4	138.2	119	46	40	119
95 NL	13	14	4.33	30	1	189.0	207	91	74	164
96 NL	15	11	3.30	34	5	231.2	217	85	55	222
Life	58	48	3.20	262	8	850.0	782	302	274	750
3 Ave	14	12	3.55	32	3	213.1	206	84	65	191

ALEX FERNANDEZ

Position: Pitcher
Team: Florida Marlins
Born: Aug. 13, 1969 Miami Beach, FL
Height: 6'1" **Weight:** 205 lbs.
Bats: right **Throws:** right
Acquired: Signed as a free agent, 12/96

PLAYER SUMMARY

Fantasy Value.	$19 to $22
Card Value	12¢ to 15¢
Will	win at least 12
Can't	avoid gophers
Expect	decent control
Don't Expect	enemy steals

After making the second Opening Day start of his career in 1996, Fernandez went on to be the most effective White Sox starter. He was especially tough in the second half, a career-long trait. He's still seeking the 20-win form once predicted for him. Once compared to Tom Seaver because of his size, style, and mechanics, Fernandez yields fewer hits than innings while averaging seven Ks and fewer than three walks per nine frames. A power pitcher, he throws a fastball, slider, curve, and changeup, posting a whiff-to-walk ratio of 2½-to-1. He also induces lots of groundouts. Much tougher against righties, Fernandez helps himself with first-rate fielding and a fine pickoff move. Fewer than half the basestealers who challenge him succeed. His Achilles' heel is the home run ball. Fernandez, a first-round draft choice of two different clubs, declined Milwaukee's offer and signed with the White Sox in 1990. He is a former Golden Spikes Award winner.

Major League Pitching Register

	W	L	ERA	G	CG	IP	H	ER	BB	SO
90 AL	5	5	3.80	13	3	87.2	89	37	34	61
91 AL	9	13	4.51	34	2	191.2	186	96	88	145
92 AL	8	11	4.27	29	4	187.2	199	89	50	95
93 AL	18	9	3.13	34	3	247.1	221	86	67	169
94 AL	11	7	3.86	24	4	170.1	163	73	50	122
95 AL	12	8	3.80	30	5	203.2	200	86	65	159
96 AL	16	10	3.45	35	6	258.0	248	99	72	200
Life	79	63	3.78	199	27	1346.1	1306	566	426	951
3 Ave	15	10	3.70	34	6	242.1	234	100	72	184

OSVALDO FERNANDEZ

Position: Pitcher
Team: San Francisco Giants
Born: Nov. 4, 1968 Holguin, Cuba
Height: 6'2" **Weight:** 190 lbs.
Bats: right **Throws:** right
Acquired: Signed as a free agent, 1/96

PLAYER SUMMARY

Fantasy Value.	$6 to $8
Card Value	10¢ to 15¢
Will	improve over time
Can't	prevent gophers
Expect	rotation berth
Don't Expect	control trouble

Fernandez signed with San Francisco after he and fellow Cuban defector Livan Hernandez made an off-season tour of major-league clubs willing to engage in a bidding war for their services. The Giants inked Fernandez, signing the former Cuban Olympian to a three-year, $3.2-million deal. After winning three of his first four NL decisions, Fernandez struggled. But he showed flashes of potential along the way. More effective against right-handed batters, Fernandez yields more hits than innings and has trouble keeping the ball in the park. But his control is decent (three walks per nine innings) and he averages about six strikeouts per nine-inning game. He complements his fastball with a variety of breaking balls, none of them exceptional, and even throws an occasional knuckler. Nicknamed "The Peasant" in Cuba, Fernandez jumped directly to the majors without passing "Go." The Giants used him primarily as a starter but also tried him in relief late in the season. There's some dispute over his age (he appears older than 28), but Fernandez figures to improve over time.

Major League Pitching Register

	W	L	ERA	G	CG	IP	H	ER	BB	SO
96 NL	7	13	4.61	30	2	171.2	193	88	57	106
Life	7	13	4.61	30	2	171.2	193	88	57	106

SID FERNANDEZ

Position: Pitcher
Team: Houston Astros
Born: Oct. 12, 1962 Honolulu, HI
Height: 6'1" **Weight:** 230 lbs.
Bats: left **Throws:** left
Acquired: Signed as a free agent, 12/96

PLAYER SUMMARY	
Fantasy Value	$5 to $7
Card Value	4¢ to 7¢
Will	return intact
Can't	stop stealers
Expect	high K rate
Don't Expect	lefties to hit

The portly Hawaiian has suffered numerous injuries, including a sprained ligament in his left elbow last year. His 14-year career has included more than a half-dozen stints on the DL. When healthy, the two-time All-Star is a power pitcher who's difficult to hit—especially for left-handed batters. The hard-throwing lefty throws a short-arm fastball that rises, a slow curve, and an excellent changeup. Before 1994, the composite career batting average against him was a microscopic .204—then tied with Nolan Ryan atop the career list for pitchers with at least 1,500 innings. Fernandez usually yields fewer than eight hits per nine innings and has decent control. He is easy prey for basestealers, and he's slow in the field, where his range is abysmal.

Major League Pitching Register

	W	L	ERA	G	CG	IP	H	ER	BB	SO
83 NL	0	1	6.00	2	0	6.0	7	4	7	9
84 NL	6	6	3.50	15	0	90.0	74	35	34	62
85 NL	9	9	2.80	26	3	170.1	108	53	80	180
86 NL	16	6	3.52	32	2	204.1	161	80	91	200
87 NL	12	8	3.81	28	3	156.0	130	66	67	134
88 NL	12	10	3.03	31	1	187.0	127	63	70	189
89 NL	14	5	2.83	35	6	219.1	157	69	75	198
90 NL	9	14	3.46	30	2	179.1	130	69	67	181
91 NL	1	3	2.86	8	0	44.0	36	14	9	31
92 NL	14	11	2.73	32	5	214.2	162	65	67	193
93 NL	5	6	2.93	18	1	119.2	82	39	36	81
94 AL	6	6	5.15	19	2	115.1	109	66	46	95
95 AL	0	4	7.39	8	0	28.0	36	23	17	31
95 NL	6	1	3.34	11	0	64.2	48	24	21	79
96 NL	3	6	3.43	11	0	63.0	50	24	26	77
Life	113	96	3.36	306	25	1861.2	1417	694	713	1740
3 Ave	6	5	4.35	17	1	99.1	86	48	38	100

TONY FERNANDEZ

Position: Shortstop; second base
Team: New York Yankees
Born: June 30, 1962 San Pedro de Macoris, Dominican Republic
Height: 6'2" **Weight:** 175 lbs.
Bats: both **Throws:** right
Acquired: Signed as a free agent, 12/94

PLAYER SUMMARY	
Fantasy Value	$0
Card Value	5¢ to 8¢
Will	put bat on ball
Can't	find old speed
Expect	three-spot duty
Don't Expect	home run power

With four Gold Gloves and four All-Star selections on his resume, Fernandez was not pleased with the Yankee plan to play heralded rookie Derek Jeter at shortstop last spring. Nor was he eager to comply with the team's suggestion that he move to second base. Hoping for a trade, Fernandez instead spent the season on the DL due to surgery to repair a fractured right elbow. Even if he returns intact, the switch-hitting veteran might not find an everyday job. He lacks the speed and quickness of his youth, and his bat seems to be slowing. On the plus side, he has patience, makes contact, and winds up with more walks than Ks. Fernandez is prone to occasional mistakes on the bases and in the field, though he can make spectacular plays.

Major League Batting Register

	BA	G	AB	R	H	2B	3B	HR	RBI	SB
83 AL	.265	15	34	5	9	1	1	0	2	0
84 AL	.270	88	233	29	63	5	3	3	19	5
85 AL	.289	161	564	71	163	31	10	2	51	13
86 AL	.310	163	687	91	213	33	9	10	65	25
87 AL	.322	146	578	90	186	29	8	5	67	32
88 AL	.287	154	648	76	186	41	4	5	70	15
89 AL	.257	140	573	64	147	25	9	11	64	22
90 AL	.276	161	635	84	175	27	17	4	66	26
91 NL	.272	145	558	81	152	27	5	4	38	23
92 NL	.275	155	622	84	171	32	4	4	37	20
93 NL	.225	48	173	20	39	5	2	1	14	6
93 AL	.306	94	353	45	108	18	9	4	50	15
94 NL	.279	104	366	50	102	18	6	8	50	12
95 AL	.245	108	384	57	94	20	2	5	45	6
Life	.282	1682	6408	847	1808	312	89	66	638	220
3 Ave	.269	137	491	67	132	24	7	7	62	15

MIKE FETTERS

Position: Pitcher
Team: Milwaukee Brewers
Born: Dec. 19, 1964 Van Nuys, CA
Height: 6'4" **Weight:** 212 lbs.
Bats: right **Throws:** right
Acquired: Traded by Angels with Glenn Carter for Chuck Crim, 12/91

PLAYER SUMMARY

Fantasy Value	$20 to $25
Card Value	4¢ to 7¢
Will	pitch effectively
Can't	harness control
Expect	first-batter success
Don't Expect	gopher problem

The fine relief work of Fetters kept Milwaukee from sinking out of sight in the AL Central last summer. He was rewarded with a new two-year contract worth $4 million. That was quite an investment for Bud Selig's budget-conscious Brewers, but Fetters is worth it. A sinker-slider pitcher whose out pitch is a forkball, Fetters keeps the ball down, coaxing endless ground balls to complement his 7½ strikeouts per nine innings. Fetters strands more than 80 percent of the runners he inherits, thanks mainly to his consistent success against first batters faced. The former Pepperdine star does a good job of holding runners on. That's a good thing, since he yields slightly more than a hit per inning and has occasional control problems. Fetters doesn't help himself with his fielding, but he rarely makes errors. The big righty would post many more saves with a contending club. At 32, this star remains largely anonymous.

Major League Pitching Register

	W	L	ERA	G	S	IP	H	ER	BB	SO
89 AL	0	0	8.10	1	0	3.1	5	3	1	4
90 AL	1	1	4.12	26	1	67.2	77	31	20	35
91 AL	2	5	4.84	19	0	44.2	53	24	28	24
92 AL	5	1	1.87	50	2	62.2	38	13	24	43
93 AL	3	3	3.34	45	0	59.1	59	22	22	23
94 AL	1	4	2.54	42	17	46.0	41	13	27	31
95 AL	0	3	3.38	40	22	34.2	40	13	20	33
96 AL	3	3	3.38	61	32	61.1	65	23	26	53
Life	15	20	3.37	284	74	379.2	378	142	168	246
3 Ave	1	4	3.05	55	27	55.0	56	19	29	45

CECIL FIELDER

Position: Designated hitter; first base
Team: New York Yankees
Born: Sept. 21, 1963 Los Angeles, CA
Height: 6'3" **Weight:** 250 lbs.
Bats: right **Throws:** right
Acquired: Traded by Tigers for Matt Drews and Ruben Sierra, 7/96

PLAYER SUMMARY

Fantasy Value	$20 to $25
Card Value	12¢ to 20¢
Will	hit home runs
Can't	cut strikeout rate
Expect	run production
Don't Expect	speed, defense

Coming to the Yankees helped Fielder return to the ranks of baseball's 100-RBI men. The burly DH, who led the AL in that department three times while with the Tigers, had suffered a decrease in RBI four years in a row before finding the fountain of youth the minute he donned Yankee pinstripes. At 33, Fielder has more weight and less bat speed than he did while hitting 95 homers in a two-year span for the 1990-91 Tigers. He still fans frequently but walks often enough to post an on-base percentage 100 points higher than his batting average. Since he doesn't run at all, Fielder is a liability on the basepaths. He bangs into frequent double plays. Fielder's lack of mobility also hurts when he plays first base, which is why the Yankees made him a DH—even though it meant moving Darryl Strawberry to left field.

Major League Batting Register

	BA	G	AB	R	H	2B	3B	HR	RBI	SB
85 AL	.311	30	74	6	23	4	0	4	16	0
86 AL	.157	34	83	7	13	2	0	4	13	0
87 AL	.269	82	175	30	47	7	1	14	32	0
88 AL	.230	74	174	24	40	6	1	9	23	0
90 AL	.277	159	573	104	159	25	1	51	132	0
91 AL	.261	162	624	102	163	25	0	44	133	0
92 AL	.244	155	594	80	145	22	0	35	124	0
93 AL	.267	154	573	80	153	23	0	30	117	0
94 AL	.259	109	425	67	110	16	2	28	90	0
95 AL	.243	136	494	70	120	18	1	31	82	0
96 AL	.252	160	591	85	149	20	0	39	117	2
Life	.256	1255	4380	655	1122	168	6	289	879	2
3 Ave	.251	156	582	86	146	21	1	38	112	1

CHUCK FINLEY

Position: Pitcher
Team: Anaheim Angels
Born: Nov. 26, 1962 Monroe, LA
Height: 6'6" **Weight:** 212 lbs.
Bats: left **Throws:** left
Acquired: First round pick in 6/85 free-agent draft

PLAYER SUMMARY

Fantasy Value	$12 to $15
Card Value	7¢ to 10¢
Will	give team innings
Can't	supply defense
Expect	double-digit wins
Don't Expect	perfect control

Finley has been somewhat of a baseball enigma during his career. He's had four fine years and four mediocre ones over the last eight seasons. A heavy workload may be catching up with him. The Northeast Louisiana product started slowly in 1996 before making a mechanical adjustment in May: moving from the third-base side of the rubber to the first-base side. The short-term result was a 4-0 record and 0.80 ERA. Much more effective against left-handed batters, the four-time All-Star blends a moving, 90-mph fastball with a forkball (his best pitch) and slurve. He yields about one hit per inning and fans more than eight per game. Finley is neither a good fielder nor a pickoff artist. He has two 15-K games and a one-hitter on his resume. Last year, Finley joined Nolan Ryan as the only Angels ever to pitch 2,000 innings.

Major League Pitching Register

	W	L	ERA	G	CG	IP	H	ER	BB	SO
86 AL	3	1	3.30	25	0	46.1	40	17	23	37
87 AL	2	7	4.67	35	0	90.2	102	47	43	63
88 AL	9	15	4.17	31	2	4.1	1	90	82	111
89 AL	16	9	2.57	29	9	9.2	171	57	82	156
90 AL	18	9	2.40	32	7	236.0	210	63	81	177
91 AL	18	9	3.80	34	4	227.1	205	96	101	171
92 AL	7	12	3.96	31	4	204.1	212	90	98	124
93 AL	16	14	3.15	35	13	251.1	243	88	82	187
94 AL	10	10	4.32	25	7	183.1	178	88	71	148
95 AL	15	12	4.21	32	2	203.0	2	95	93	5
96 AL	15	16	4.16	35	4	238.0	241	110	94	215
Life	129	114	3.65	344	52	2074.1	1605	841	850	1584
3 Ave	15	15	4.23	35	5	242.1	236	114	100	214

STEVE FINLEY

Position: Outfield
Team: San Diego Padres
Born: March 12, 1965 Union City, TN
Height: 6'2" **Weight:** 175 lbs.
Bats: left **Throws:** left
Acquired: Traded by Astros with Ken Caminiti, Andujar Cedeno, Robert Petagine, Brian Williams, and a player to be named later for Phil Plantier, Derek Bell, Pedro Martinez, Doug Brocail, Craig Shipley, and Ricky Gutierrez, 12/94

PLAYER SUMMARY

Fantasy Value	$25 to $30
Card Value	7¢ to 10¢
Will	use speed well
Can't	hit all lefties
Expect	surprising power
Don't Expect	fielding lapses

Suddenly last summer, Finley became a slugger. The fleet center fielder blossomed into a 20-20 man for the first time. Finley said his newfound power was the result of standing closer to the plate, holding his hands high, and swinging with a follow-through arc. He followed a slow start with a five-hit game (his first) in May, homers in three consecutive at bats at the end of June, and a .389 batting average in July. A better hitter against righties, he fanned more often last year than ever before: the result of his longer, harder swing. He usually makes good contact and shows enough patience to post a fine on-base percentage. The one-time singles hitter led the Padres in extra-base hits last summer. Finley has good speed on the bases and in the field. The Gold Glove winner is a first-rate outfielder.

Major League Batting Register

	BA	G	AB	R	H	2B	3B	HR	RBI	SB
89 AL	.249	81	217	35	54	5	2	2	25	17
90 AL	.256	142	464	46	1	16	4	3	37	22
91 NL	.285	159	596	84	170	28	10	8	54	34
92 NL	.292	162	607	84	177	29	13	5	55	44
93 NL	.266	142	545	69	145	15	13	8	44	19
94 NL	.276	94	373	64	103	16	5	11	33	13
95 NL	.297	139	562	104	167	23	8	10	44	36
96 NL	.298	161	655	126	5	45	9	30	95	22
Life	.281	1080	4019	612	1130	177	64	77	387	207
3 Ave	.291	150	604	111	176	31	8	19	64	27

JOHN FLAHERTY

Position: Catcher
Team: San Diego Padres
Born: Oct. 21, 1967 New York, NY
Height: 6'1" **Weight:** 202 lbs.
Bats: right **Throws:** right
Acquired: Traded by Tigers with Chris Gomez for Andujar Cedeno, Brad Ausmus, and Russell Spear, 6/96

PLAYER SUMMARY	
Fantasy Value	$5 to $7
Card Value	5¢ to 8¢
Will	swing good bat
Can't	wait for walks
Expect	strong defense
Don't Expect	any speed

Flaherty's bat was one of baseball's biggest surprises in 1996. Shortly after joining the Padres, he uncorked a 27-game hitting streak, second-longest by a catcher in major-league history. Drafted out of George Washington University by the Red Sox in 1988, Flaherty floundered with the bat before beginning a regimen of winter workouts designed to increase his strength. Those sessions, coupled with tips from his hitting coaches, transformed him from Judy into Punch. Though he fans three times more than he walks, Flaherty gets extra bases on one-third of his hits. His offensive explosion did not detract from his defensive skills. A field general who inspires confidence in his pitchers, he calls a good game, snares potential wild pitches well, and blocks incoming runners. Flaherty sometimes makes errors on hurried throws, but his arm is fine. Sparky Anderson once called him the AL's best defensive catcher.

Major League Batting Register

	BA	G	AB	R	H	2B	3B	HR	RBI	SB
92 AL	.197	35	66	3	13	2	0	0	2	0
93 AL	.120	13	25	3	3	2	0	0	2	0
94 AL	.150	34	40	2	6	1	0	0	4	0
95 AL	.243	112	354	39	86	22	1	11	40	0
96 AL	.250	47	152	18	38	12	0	4	23	1
96 NL	.303	72	264	22	80	12	0	9	41	2
Life	.251	313	901	87	226	51	1	24	112	3
2 Ave	.264	123	407	42	107	24	1	13	55	2

DARRIN FLETCHER

Position: Catcher
Team: Montreal Expos
Born: Oct. 3, 1966 Elmhurst, IL
Height: 6'1" **Weight:** 200 lbs.
Bats: left **Throws:** right
Acquired: Traded by Phillies with cash for Barry Jones, 12/91

PLAYER SUMMARY	
Fantasy Value	$4 to $6
Card Value	4¢ to 7¢
Will	make great contact
Can't	avoid double plays
Expect	extra-base hits
Don't Expect	nailed runners

Lefty-hitting catchers are valuable, especially if they're streak hitters in the Fletcher mold. When he's hot, he's hot. A contact hitter used mainly against right-handed pitching, he fans infrequently but still twice as often as he walks. Fletcher would be more potent if he showed more patience at the plate. Despite a lack of speed, he gets extra bases on more than one-third of his hits. Fletcher thrives on a combination diet of breaking balls and mistakes. He's tinkered with his stance, hoping to increase his bat speed, and has raised his average since 1993. But he still bangs into frequent double plays, and his average dropped a bit last year. The University of Illinois product has improved his defense, though his success at nailing would-be basestealers was better in 1995 than it was last year. Fletcher handles pitchers well, calls good games, prevents wild pitches, and blocks the plate well.

Major League Batting Register

	BA	G	AB	R	H	2B	3B	HR	RBI	SB
89 NL	.500	5	8	1	4	0	0	1	2	0
90 NL	.130	11	23	3	3	1	0	0	1	0
91 NL	.228	46	136	5	31	8	0	1	12	0
92 NL	.243	83	222	13	54	10	2	2	26	0
93 NL	.255	133	396	33	101	20	1	9	60	0
94 NL	.260	94	285	28	74	18	1	10	57	0
95 NL	.286	110	350	42	100	21	1	11	45	0
96 NL	.266	127	394	41	105	22	0	12	57	0
Life	.260	609	1814	166	472	100	5	46	260	0
3 Ave	.271	128	396	43	107	24	1	13	63	0

BRYCE FLORIE

Position: Pitcher
Team: Milwaukee Brewers
Born: May 21, 1970 Charleston, SC
Height: 5'11" **Weight:** 190 lbs.
Bats: right **Throws:** right
Acquired: Traded by Padres with Ron Villone and Marc Newfield for Greg Vaughn, 7/96

PLAYER SUMMARY	
Fantasy Value	$1
Card Value	4¢ to 7¢
Will	keep set-up job
Can't	always find zone
Expect	whiff per inning
Don't Expect	frozen runners

Florie spent six seasons as a minor-league starter before switching to relief work in 1994. The move paid quick dividends; he reached the majors later that season. Strictly a reliever since, Florie did so well in his new role that Milwaukee insisted he be part of the Greg Vaughn trade last July. A product of Trident Technical College in his native South Carolina, Florie throws only two pitches, a fastball and slider, but changes speeds and locations so well that batters have trouble figuring out what's coming. His fastball, for example, sometimes sinks and sometimes comes in straight. Florie does his best work with men in scoring position and in late-game pressure spots. He yields fewer hits than innings, averages a strikeout per frame, and maintains a whiff-to-walk ratio that is just under 2-to-1. But he has occasional control problems. He threw 25 wild pitches in the Texas League in 1993. Although he's a good fielder, Florie has trouble keeping runners close, sometimes ignoring inherited baserunners.

Major League Pitching Register

	W	L	ERA	G	S	IP	H	ER	BB	SO
94 NL	0	0	0.96	9	0	9.1	8	1	3	8
95 NL	2	2	3.01	47	1	68.2	49	23	38	68
96 NL	2	2	4.01	39	0	49.1	45	22	27	51
96 AL	0	1	6.63	15	0	19.0	20	14	13	12
Life	4	5	3.69	110	1.	146.1	122	60	81	139
2 Ave	2	2	3.40	46	1	63.1	50	24	35	64

CLIFF FLOYD

Position: First base; outfield
Team: Montreal Expos
Born: Dec. 5, 1972 Chicago, IL
Height: 6'4" **Weight:** 220 lbs.
Bats: left **Throws:** right
Acquired: First-round pick in 6/91 free-agent draft

PLAYER SUMMARY	
Fantasy Value	$5 to $7
Card Value	7¢ to 10¢
Will	stay in outfield
Can't	hit left-handers
Expect	improved power
Don't Expect	Mays or McCovey

Scouts once described Floyd as a prospect with the power of Willie McCovey and the speed of Willie Mays. That would be a tall order for anyone, even a former minor-league home run king who twice topped 30 steals in the minors. Floyd, a former No. 1 draft choice who reached the majors at age 20, missed considerable playing time due to a collision at first base in May 1995. The result was a severely fractured wrist and hand that required three surgical repairs. The crash also convinced Montreal management to put their talented young slugger in the outfield. Returning to action slowly last year, Floyd played all three outfield spots (mostly in left), filled in at first, and provided a potent lefty bat off the bench. Floyd runs well for a big guy and is rarely caught when he tries to steal. Floyd's speed gives him good range in the outfield, though his arm is not strong enough for prolonged duty in right. At 24, he might still become a star, but nobody is counting on him to emulate any Hall of Famers.

Major League Batting Register

	BA	G	AB	R	H	2B	3B	HR	RBI	SB
93 NL	.226	10	31	3	7	0	0	1	2	0
94 NL	.281	100	334	43	94	19	4	4	41	10
95 NL	.130	29	69	6	9	1	0	1	8	3
96 NL	.242	117	227	29	55	15	4	6	26	7
Life	.250	256	661	81	165	35	8	12	77	20
2 Ave	.269	129	349	45	94	21	5	6	42	11

CHAD FONVILLE

Position: Second base; shortstop
Team: Los Angeles Dodgers
Born: March 5, 1971 Jacksonville, NC
Height: 5'6" **Weight:** 155 lbs.
Bats: both **Throws:** right
Acquired: Claimed from Expos on waivers, 5/95

PLAYER SUMMARY	
Fantasy Value	. . . . $1
Card Value	. . . . 5¢ to 8¢
Will	. . . . keep utility job
Can't	. . . . generate power
Expect	. . . . excellent range
Don't Expect	. . . . powerful arm

A compact switch-hitter who can fly, Fonville lives or dies with his legs. He is an opposite-field singles hitter who almost never gets an extra-base hit. But he has a penchant for igniting rallies by setting the table for the big hitters who follow him in the lineup. A better left-handed hitter, Fonville had a solid rookie year in 1995, earning a regular job with his hustle. The team thrived when Fonville started, and he earned a return ticket to Dodgertown last spring. However, failure to hit and inconsistency in the field led to a minor-league exile in midseason. If Fonville showed more patience and made better contact, he'd have a job. But he fans too frequently and doesn't walk enough, negating his enormous speed potential. That speed helps him in the field, where his range is exceptional. But Fonville lacks spectacular arm strength. A product of Louisburg College in his native North Carolina, Fonville started his pro career in the San Francisco system in 1992. He moved to Montreal in the Rule 5 draft and to Los Angeles via the waiver wire.

Major League Batting Register

	BA	G	AB	R	H	2B	3B	HR	RBI	SB
95 NL	.278	102	320	43	89	6	1	0	16	20
96 NL	.204	103	201	34	41	4	1	0	13	7
Life	.250	205	521	77	130	10	2	0	29	27
2 Ave	.252	109	281	41	71	5	1	0	16	15

TONY FOSSAS

Position: Pitcher
Team: St. Louis Cardinals
Born: Sept. 23, 1957 Havana, Cuba
Height: 6' **Weight:** 187 lbs.
Bats: left **Throws:** left
Acquired: Signed as a free agent, 4/95

PLAYER SUMMARY	
Fantasy Value	. . . . $1
Card Value	. . . . 4¢ to 7¢
Will	. . . . work often
Can't	. . . . provide glove
Expect	. . . . short stints
Don't Expect	. . . . long balls

Fossas is one of baseball's pure specialists. He's made a career out of coming on, disposing of one or two lefty batters, and leaving the scene of the crime. The veteran left-hander always has more appearances than innings pitched. A fastball-slider pitcher with good control, Fossas unveils a cut fastball against righties. He yields fewer hits than innings and averages nearly seven strikeouts per nine innings. In 1995, one of his best years, Fossas held left-handed hitters to a .181 average and did not surrender a home run to a southpaw. Fossas strands most of the runners he inherits, never makes a wild pitch, and keeps extra-base hits to a minimum. He maintains a 2-1 ratio of Ks to walks. Though not much of a fielder, Fossas has a terrific pickoff move. Despite his age (39), the Cuban southpaw should have a secure berth in a big-league bullpen. Lefties who can quash late-inning rallies are hard to find.

Major League Pitching Register

	W	L	ERA	G	S	IP	H	ER	BB	SO
88 AL	0	0	4.76	5	0	5.2	11	3	2	0
89 AL	2	2	3.54	51	1	61.0	57	24	22	42
90 AL	2	3	6.44	32	0	29.1	44	21	10	24
91 AL	3	2	3.47	64	1	57.0	49	22	28	29
92 AL	1	2	2.43	60	2	29.2	31	8	14	19
93 AL	1	1	5.17	71	0	40.0	38	23	15	39
94 AL	2	0	4.76	44	1	34.0	35	18	15	31
95 NL	3	0	1.47	58	0	36.2	28	6	10	40
96 NL	0	4	2.68	65	2	47.0	43	14	21	36
Life	14	14	3.68	450	7	340.1	336	139	137	260
3 Ave	2	1	3.05	64	1	45.1	41	15	18	42

KEVIN FOSTER

Position: Pitcher
Team: Chicago Cubs
Born: Jan. 13, 1969 Evanston, IL
Height: 6'1" **Weight:** 170 lbs.
Bats: right **Throws:** right
Acquired: Traded by Phillies for Shawn Buskie, 4/94

PLAYER SUMMARY	
Fantasy Value	$4 to $6
Card Value	4¢ to 7¢
Will	seek rotation spot
Can't	avoid gopher balls
Expect	good glove, stick
Don't Expect	return to minors

Foster has experienced a roller-coaster ride during his three-year career with the Cubs. Impressive as a 1994 rookie, he led the NL in home runs allowed in '95, then drifted back to the minors last year before returning to the varsity rotation. He was much more effective in his second stint, showing much better control of his rising fastball, curveball, and changeup. Earlier, he had yielded too many fly balls and did not get the strikeouts he needed. When he's right, Foster averages 2½ Ks per walk. The high-kicking right-hander handles basestealers well (probably because the high fastball helps the catcher throw) and is also an excellent fielder. Inked as a third baseman, Foster fits the definition of the fifth infielder. He still hits like an infielder, too, and is no automatic out at the plate. Still, Foster's team is more concerned about his ERA than his batting average. If both were down, they'd settle for that. Foster signed a pro contract in 1988 and moved to the mound in '90.

Major League Pitching Register

	W	L	ERA	G	CG	IP	H	ER	BB	SO
93 NL	0	1	14.85	2	0	6.2	13	11	7	6
94 NL	3	4	2.89	13	0	81.0	70	26	35	75
95 NL	12	11	4.51	30	0	167.2	149	84	65	146
96 NL	7	6	6.21	17	1	87.0	98	60	35	53
Life	22	22	4.76	62	1	342.1	330	181	142	280
3 Ave	8	8	4.41	23	0	130.0	121	64	52	108

ANDY FOX

Position: Second base; third base
Team: New York Yankees
Born: Jan. 12, 1971 Sacramento, CA
Height: 6'4" **Weight:** 205 lbs.
Bats: left **Throws:** right
Acquired: Second-round pick in 6/89 free-agent draft

PLAYER SUMMARY	
Fantasy Value	$1
Card Value	5¢ to 8¢
Will	show speed
Can't	clear fences
Expect	utility role
Don't Expect	high average

Fox was the Yankees' utility man as a rookie last summer. Although he didn't hit much, his glove kept him in pinstripes all season. Yankee manager Joe Torre even said Fox was a better defensive third baseman than Wade Boggs, the veteran All-Star who won consecutive Gold Gloves at the position. Fox, whose younger legs give better range than Boggs, also has quick reactions, soft hands, and a strong, reliable arm. He spent more time at second, however, as the Yankees struggled to replace ailing incumbent Pat Kelly. Fox also filled in at short and served as a pinch hitter and pinch runner. If the Yankees weren't overloaded in the outfield, he probably would have played there, too. Although he showed some pop in the minors, Fox may have misled Yankee management when he hit .348 for Triple-A Columbus in 1995. He topped .250 in only one of his other six minor-league campaigns. A contact hitter who neither walks nor fans frequently, Fox is more likely to steal a base than he is to poke an extra-base hit. He was nailed only three times in his first dozen attempts against big-league opposition.

Major League Batting Register

	BA	G	AB	R	H	2B	3B	HR	RBI	SB
96 AL	.196	113	189	26	37	4	0	3	13	11
Life	.196	113	189	26	37	4	0	3	13	11

JOHN FRANCO

Position: Pitcher
Team: New York Mets
Born: Sept. 17, 1960 Brooklyn, NY
Height: 5'10" **Weight:** 185 lbs.
Bats: left **Throws:** left
Acquired: Traded by Reds with Don Brown for
 Kip Gross and Randy Myers, 12/89

PLAYER SUMMARY	
Fantasy Value	$20 to $25
Card Value	5¢ to 8¢
Will	top 25 saves
Can't	harness control
Expect	solid defense
Don't Expect	gopher balls

The only left-hander in the 300-save club, Franco is still a solid reliever at age 36. Deadly against left-handed hitters, he's even more difficult for home run hitters. Franco surrendered only one gopher ball in his first 42 outings last year. His best pitch is a slow, sinking changeup that dives straight down. The little lefty, who throws fastballs and sliders, averages more than eight whiffs per nine innings. His control wasn't as sharp as usual last summer, but he still managed to top 25 saves. He's led the NL in saves three times, most recently in 1994, and is a five-time All-Star. A durable, dependable performer, Franco almost never throws a wild pitch or permits a stolen base. Franco is a team leader who voices his opinions in the clubhouse. Because he's a 13-year veteran, teammates listen.

Major League Pitching Register

	W	L	ERA	G	S	IP	H	ER	BB	SO
84 NL	6	2	2.61	54	4	79.1	74	23	36	55
85 NL	12	3	2.18	67	12	99.0	83	24	40	61
86 NL	6	6	2.94	74	29	101.0	90	33	44	84
87 NL	8	5	2.52	68	32	82.0	76	23	27	61
88 NL	6	6	1.57	70	39	86.0	60	15	27	46
89 NL	4	8	3.12	60	32	80.2	77	28	36	60
90 NL	5	3	2.53	55	33	67.2	66	19	21	56
91 NL	5	9	2.93	52	30	55.1	61	18	18	45
92 NL	6	2	1.64	31	15	33.0	24	6	11	20
93 NL	4	3	5.20	35	10	36.1	46	21	19	29
94 NL	1	4	2.70	47	30	50.0	47	15	19	42
95 NL	5	3	2.44	48	29	51.2	48	14	17	41
96 NL	4	3	1.83	51	28	54.0	54	11	21	48
Life	72	57	2.57	712	323	876.0	806	250	336	648
3 Ave	4	4	2.36	57	34	61.0	58	16	22	51

JULIO FRANCO

Position: First base
Team: Cleveland Indians
Born: Aug. 23, 1961 San Pedro de Macoris,
 Dominican Republic
Height: 6'1" **Weight:** 190 lbs.
Bats: right **Throws:** right
Acquired: Signed as a free agent, 12/95

PLAYER SUMMARY	
Fantasy Value	$10 to $13
Card Value	7¢ to 10¢
Will	top .300 mark
Can't	steal too often
Expect	walks, hits, pop
Don't Expect	extended slump

After taking a year off to play in Japan, Franco returned to the majors last year with a 13-year career average of .301. His return was greeted with great enthusiasm in Cleveland, where he had been a rookie shortstop in 1983. Franco, who won the AL batting title with the Texas Rangers in 1991, is a contact hitter with patience and power. He walks almost as much as he fans, giving him a high on-base percentage, and delivers double digits in homers. Last year, however, he was the victim of prolonged hamstring problems that limited his playing time. When healthy, Franco rips line drives to all fields, murders left-handed pitching, and thrives in clutch situations. Although he's had three 30-steal seasons, the three-time All-Star doesn't run much anymore.

Major League Batting Register

	BA	G	AB	R	H	2B	3B	HR	RBI	SB
82 NL	.276	16	29	3	8	1	0	0	3	0
83 AL	.273	149	560	68	153	24	8	8	80	32
84 AL	.286	160	658	82	188	22	5	3	79	19
85 AL	.288	160	636	97	183	33	4	6	90	13
86 AL	.306	149	599	80	183	30	5	10	74	10
87 AL	.319	128	495	86	158	24	3	8	52	32
88 AL	.303	152	613	88	186	23	6	10	54	25
89 AL	.316	150	548	80	173	31	5	13	92	21
90 AL	.296	157	582	96	172	27	1	11	69	31
91 AL	.341	146	589	108	201	27	3	15	78	36
92 AL	.234	35	107	19	25	7	0	2	8	1
93 AL	.289	144	532	85	154	31	3	14	84	9
94 AL	.319	112	433	72	138	19	2	20	98	8
96 AL	.322	112	432	72	139	20	1	14	76	8
Life	.303	1770	6813	1036	2061	319	46	134	937	245
2 Ave	.320	135	521	87	167	23	2	21	107	10

MARVIN FREEMAN

Position: Pitcher
Team: Chicago White Sox
Born: April 10, 1963 Chicago, IL
Height: 6'7" **Weight:** 222 lbs.
Bats: right **Throws:** right
Acquired: Signed as a free agent, 8/96

PLAYER SUMMARY	
Fantasy Value	$0
Card Value	4¢ to 7¢
Will	make comeback bid
Can't	keep runners close
Expect	control to improve
Don't Expect	another bad year

A rotation starter most of the season for Colorado, Freeman shifted to the bullpen in August after the Rockies tired of watching him struggle. He wasn't anything like the pitcher who went 10-2 with a miracle 2.80 ERA for the same club in 1994. Last year's Freeman yielded too many hits, homers, wild pitches, and steals, along with too high an average against left-handed batters. His nine-inning averages of four walks, five Ks, and 10½ hits were tough to take—even considering Colorado's altitude-distorted standards. Perhaps a series of minor injuries (including shoulder tendinitis) interfered, or maybe Freeman's carefree attitude interfered with his concentration. Either way, the towering right-hander seldom had good command of his sinker, slider, or forkball. Perhaps a change of scenery will resurrect the Jackson State product's stagnant career.

Major League Pitching Register

	W	L	ERA	G	CG	IP	H	ER	BB	SO
86 NL	2	0	2.25	3	0	16.0	6	4	10	8
88 NL	2	3	6.10	11	0	51.2	55	35	43	37
89 NL	0	0	6.00	1	0	3.0	2	2	5	0
90 NL	1	2	4.31	25	0	48.0	41	23	17	38
91 NL	1	0	3.00	34	0	48.0	37	16	13	34
92 NL	7	5	3.22	58	0	64.1	61	23	29	41
93 NL	2	0	6.08	21	0	23.2	24	16	10	25
94 NL	10	2	2.80	19	0	112.2	113	35	23	67
95 NL	3	7	5.89	22	0	94.2	122	62	41	61
96 NL	7	9	6.04	26	0	129.2	151	87	57	71
96 AL	0	0	13.50	1	0	2.0	4	3	1	1
Life	35	28	4.64	221	0	593.2	616	306	249	383
3 Ave	8	7	4.70	26	0	132.1	149	69	45	78

JEFF FRYE

Position: Second base
Team: Boston Red Sox
Born: Aug. 31, 1966 Oakland, CA
Height: 5'9" **Weight:** 165 lbs.
Bats: right **Throws:** right
Acquired: Signed as a free agent, 6/96

PLAYER SUMMARY	
Fantasy Value	$7 to $9
Card Value	4¢ to 7¢
Will	reach base often
Can't	show strong arm
Expect	patience, contact
Don't Expect	home run power

Frye succeeded where Luis Alicea, Wil Cordero, and Arquimedez Pozo failed. He gave the 1996 Red Sox a strong performance at second base, adding speed and contact hitting without destroying the defense. A survivor of knee, wrist, and hamstring problems, Frye signed on with the BoSox June 4 and immediately made his presence felt. Because of his ability to bunt, run, make contact, and reach base, Frye is best used near the top of the lineup. He walks more often than he fans. His hits are usually singles, though he pops more than a dozen doubles per season. A little guy with a small strike zone, Frye is a better hitter with men in scoring position and against righties—probably because he sees them so often. Frye hasn't been the basestealer in the majors that he was in the minors. He provides steady but not spectacular defense with decent range, soft hands, and an adequate arm for his position. He filled in at all three outfield spots last year, as well as shortstop, but is best when left at second base.

Major League Batting Register

	BA	G	AB	R	H	2B	3B	HR	RBI	SB
92 AL	.256	67	199	24	51	9	1	1	12	1
94 AL	.327	57	205	37	67	20	3	0	18	6
95 AL	.278	90	313	38	87	15	2	4	29	3
96 AL	.286	105	419	74	120	27	2	4	41	18
Life	.286	319	1136	173	325	71	8	9	100	28
3 Ave	.295	96	353	56	104	24	3	3	33	10

TRAVIS FRYMAN

Position: Third base; shortstop
Team: Detroit Tigers
Born: March 25, 1969 Lexington, KY
Height: 6'2" **Weight:** 190 lbs.
Bats: right **Throws:** right
Acquired: Third-round pick in 6/87 free-agent draft

PLAYER SUMMARY	
Fantasy Value	$15 to $18
Card Value	10¢ to 15¢
Will	knock in runs
Can't	steal bases
Expect	power, defense
Don't Expect	good bat vs. LHP

Fryman has been remarkably consistent with the Tigers. Every year, he produces approximately 20 home runs, 90 runs batted in, and an average in the .275 vicinity. His numbers would be even better if he could reduce his strikeouts. An aggressive, first-ball hitter, Fryman fans three times more than he walks. On the plus side, Fryman is a four-time All-Star who nets extra bases on one-third of his hits. Although he hits well with runners in scoring position, his struggles against southpaws are one of baseball's mysteries. In the field, however, Fryman continues to improve. Once a liability at third base, he's now respected as one of the best at the hot corner. Fryman had a 46-game errorless streak from April 3 to May 27. Fryman returned to short, his original position, in late August when Phil Nevin tried third. He could stay at the position now that Alan Trammell has retired and if Andujar Cedeno continues to struggle. At 28, his best years are ahead.

Major League Batting Register

	BA	G	AB	R	H	2B	3B	HR	RBI	SB
90 AL	.297	66	232	32	69	11	1	9	27	3
91 AL	.259	149	557	65	144	36	3	21	91	12
92 AL	.266	161	659	87	175	31	4	20	96	8
93 AL	.300	151	607	98	182	37	5	22	97	9
94 AL	.263	114	464	66	122	34	5	18	85	2
95 AL	.275	144	567	79	156	21	5	15	81	4
96 AL	.268	157	616	90	165	32	3	22	100	4
Life	.274	942	3702	517	1013	202	26	127	577	42
3 Ave	.269	160	636	91	171	35	5	21	104	4

GARY GAETTI

Position: Third base
Team: St. Louis Cardinals
Born: Aug. 19, 1958 Centralia, IL
Height: 6' **Weight:** 200 lbs.
Bats: right **Throws:** right
Acquired: Signed as a free agent, 6/93

PLAYER SUMMARY	
Fantasy Value	$10 to $13
Card Value	5¢ to 8¢
Will	pull the ball
Can't	coax walks
Expect	decent pop
Don't Expect	weak glove

An aging slugger with a slowing bat, Gaetti gave his fans a last hurrah when he slammed 35 homers for the 1995 Royals. With free agency looming, Gaetti's timing couldn't have been better. St. Louis, desperate for new blood after finishing next-to-last in 1995, signed the 37-year-old. An overly aggressive hitter who fans three times more than he walks, Gaetti feasts on fastballs and "mistake" pitches. He can still hit the ball a long way. Teams sometimes station three infielders on the left side when he comes to bat, but Gaetti is a fly-ball hitter who doesn't hit many grounders. Gaetti moves well enough to play a good third base, though he no longer supplies the same defense he did during his four-year reign as a Gold Glover (1986-89).

Major League Batting Register

	BA	G	AB	R	H	2B	3B	HR	RBI	SB
81 AL	.192	9	26	4	5	0	0	2	3	0
82 AL	.230	145	508	59	117	25	4	25	84	0
83 AL	.245	157	584	81	143	30	3	21	78	7
84 AL	.262	162	588	55	154	29	4	5	65	11
85 AL	.246	160	560	71	138	31	0	20	63	13
86 AL	.287	157	596	91	171	34	1	34	108	14
87 AL	.257	154	584	95	150	36	2	31	109	10
88 AL	.301	133	468	66	141	29	2	28	88	7
89 AL	.251	130	498	63	125	11	4	19	75	6
90 AL	.229	154	577	61	132	27	5	16	85	6
91 AL	.246	152	586	58	144	22	1	18	66	5
92 AL	.226	130	456	41	103	13	2	12	48	3
93 AL	.245	102	331	40	81	20	1	14	50	1
94 AL	.287	90	327	53	94	15	3	12	57	0
95 AL	.261	137	514	76	134	27	0	35	96	3
96 NL	.274	141	522	71	143	27	4	23	80	2
Life	.256	2113	7725	985	1975	376	36	315	1155	88
3 Ave	.273	141	520	77	142	26	3	26	89	2

GREG GAGNE

Position: Shortstop
Team: Los Angeles Dodgers
Born: Nov. 12, 1961 Fall River, MA
Height: 5'11" **Weight:** 172 lbs.
Bats: right **Throws:** right
Acquired: Signed as a free agent, 11/95

PLAYER SUMMARY	
Fantasy Value	$4 to $6
Card Value	5¢ to 8¢
Will	hit in streaks
Can't	cut whiff rate
Expect	strong defense
Don't Expect	much power

Gagne gave the Dodgers more homers and more errors than they expected last season. But he also gave them far better protection at shortstop than they had received from Jose Offerman. Blessed with great reactions and fine range, Gagne also has a strong, accurate arm, makes the throw from deep in the hole, and turns the double play. Dodger pitchers, petrified during the five-year reign of error of Awful-Man, relaxed. The results were readily apparent. Gagne even contributed to the attack, although power is not his calling card. A singles hitter who often goes straightaway or uses the opposite field, Gagne is prone to streaks. When those streaks turn cold, he fans with alarming frequency. He could use his speed to fatten his average and increase his value to the ballclub.

Major League Batting Register

	BA	G	AB	R	H	2B	3B	HR	RBI	SB
83 AL	.111	10	27	2	3	1	0	0	3	0
84 AL	.000	2	1	0	0	0	0	0	0	0
85 AL	.225	114	293	37	66	15	3	2	23	10
86 AL	.250	156	472	63	118	22	6	12	54	12
87 AL	.265	137	437	68	116	28	7	10	40	6
88 AL	.236	149	461	70	109	20	6	14	48	15
89 AL	.272	149	460	69	125	29	7	9	48	11
90 AL	.235	138	388	38	91	22	3	7	38	8
91 AL	.265	139	408	52	108	23	3	8	42	11
92 AL	.246	146	439	53	108	23	0	7	39	6
93 AL	.280	159	540	66	151	32	3	10	57	10
94 AL	.259	107	375	39	97	23	3	7	51	10
95 AL	.256	120	430	58	110	25	4	6	49	3
96 NL	.255	128	428	48	109	13	2	10	55	4
Life	.254	1654	5159	663	1311	276	47	102	547	106
3 Ave	.257	138	480	56	123	25	4	9	61	7

ANDRES GALARRAGA

Position: First base
Team: Colorado Rockies
Born: June 18, 1961 Caracas, Venezuela
Height: 6'3" **Weight:** 235 lbs.
Bats: right **Throws:** right
Acquired: Signed as a free agent, 11/92

PLAYER SUMMARY	
Fantasy Value	$35 to $40
Card Value	12¢ to 20¢
Will	clear fences often
Can't	avoid strikeouts
Expect	high run production
Don't Expect	good road work

Galarraga romped to the top of the charts in power production, reaching career peaks in home runs and RBI well before Labor Day. Though he still fans four times per walk, who can argue with someone who produces extra bases on 44 percent of his hits? Although he hits well with men in scoring position, Galarraga hits even better against left-handed pitching and best at Denver's Coors Field. Unfortunately, his average on the road is nearly 130 points lower. Batting from his trademark open stance, the Venezuelan first baseman seems to have sacrificed average for power in recent years. Miffed about missing the All-Star squad several times, Galarraga finally has the NL's attention. A fine first baseman whose agility accounts for his "Big Cat" nickname, Galarraga won Gold Gloves in 1989 and '90.

Major League Batting Register

	BA	G	AB	R	H	2B	3B	HR	RBI	SB
85 NL	.187	24	75	9	14	1	0	2	4	1
86 NL	.271	105	321	39	87	13	0	10	42	6
87 NL	.305	147	551	72	168	40	3	13	90	7
88 NL	.302	157	609	99	184	42	8	29	92	13
89 NL	.257	152	572	76	147	30	1	23	85	12
90 NL	.256	155	579	65	148	29	0	20	87	10
91 NL	.219	107	375	34	82	13	2	9	33	5
92 NL	.243	95	325	38	79	14	2	10	39	5
93 NL	.370	120	470	71	174	35	4	22	98	2
94 NL	.319	103	417	77	133	21	0	31	85	8
95 NL	.280	143	554	89	155	29	3	31	106	12
96 NL	.304	159	626	119	190	39	3	47	150	18
Life	.285	1467	5474	788	1561	306	26	247	911	99
3 Ave	.300	155	612	109	184	34	2	42	130	14

MIKE GALLEGO

Position: Infield
Team: St. Louis Cardinals
Born: Oct. 31, 1960 Whittier, CA
Height: 5'8" **Weight:** 160 lbs.
Bats: right **Throws:** right
Acquired: Signed as a free agent, 1/96

PLAYER SUMMARY	
Fantasy Value	$0
Card Value	4¢ to 7¢
Will	fill utility role
Can't	practice patience
Expect	puny production
Don't Expect	walks, hits, HRs

A badly pulled right hamstring sent Gallego to the sidelines during spring training and idled him until July 12. St. Louis manager Tony LaRussa immediately made him the regular second baseman upon his return, hoping he would supply more offense than David Bell (sent to the minors) and better defense than Luis Alicea (19 errors in half a season). Gallego did the job in the field but failed to hit. Impatient at the plate, he fans three times more often than he walks and looks futile against most righties. To make matters worse, the power Gallego showed as recently as 1993 just isn't there anymore. His reputation as a patient contact hitter is shot, and there's not much left to his offense except an occasional sacrifice bunt. It's a good thing he has good instincts and quick reactions in the field. His speed and range are limited, and he lacks arm strength.

Major League Batting Register

	BA	G	AB	R	H	2B	3B	HR	RBI	SB
85 AL	.208	76	77	13	16	5	1	1	9	1
86 AL	.270	20	37	2	10	2	0	0	4	0
87 AL	.250	72	124	18	31	6	0	2	14	0
88 AL	.209	129	277	38	58	8	0	2	20	2
89 AL	.252	133	357	45	90	14	2	3	30	7
90 AL	.206	140	389	36	80	13	2	3	34	5
91 AL	.247	159	482	67	119	15	4	12	49	6
92 AL	.254	53	173	24	44	7	1	3	14	0
93 AL	.283	119	403	63	114	20	1	10	54	3
94 AL	.239	89	306	39	73	17	1	6	41	0
95 AL	.233	43	120	11	28	0	0	0	8	0
96 NL	.210	51	143	12	30	2	0	0	4	0
Life	.240	1084	2888	368	693	109	12	42	281	24

RON GANT

Position: Outfield
Team: St. Louis Cardinals
Born: March 2, 1965 Victoria, TX
Height: 6' **Weight:** 172 lbs.
Bats: right **Throws:** right
Acquired: Signed as a free agent, 12/95

PLAYER SUMMARY	
Fantasy Value	$25 to $30
Card Value	12¢ to 20¢
Will	deliver in clutch
Can't	win Gold Glove
Expect	extra-base hits
Don't Expect	third 30-30

Gant got off to a slow start in St. Louis, struggling so much that manager Tony LaRussa even tried him at the top of the lineup for a while. The muscular left fielder eventually came around but did not deliver with the authority that had marked his consecutive 30-30 seasons in 1990 and '91. He did have his moments, however, proving he had fully healed from the severely broken leg that had sidelined him for all of 1994. A pull hitter who feasts on fastballs, Gant has an open stance that allows him to cover most of the plate. He usually totals more than 100 strikeouts, but he draws enough walks to boost his on-base percentage. Gant hasn't run as much since breaking his leg, but he's still capable of swiping 20 or more. In the field, his speed compensates for bad hands and an average throwing arm. His judgment isn't always perfect, either.

Major League Batting Register

	BA	G	AB	R	H	2B	3B	HR	RBI	SB
87 NL	.265	21	83	9	22	4	0	2	9	4
88 NL	.259	146	563	85	146	28	8	19	60	19
89 NL	.177	75	260	26	46	8	3	9	25	9
90 NL	.303	152	575	107	174	34	3	32	84	33
91 NL	.251	154	561	101	141	35	3	32	105	34
92 NL	.259	153	544	74	141	22	6	17	80	32
93 NL	.274	157	606	113	166	27	4	36	117	26
95 NL	.276	119	410	79	113	19	4	29	88	23
96 NL	.246	122	419	74	103	14	2	30	82	13
Life	.262	1099	4021	668	1052	191	33	206	650	193
2 Ave	.261	128	440	81	115	18	3	31	91	19

CARLOS GARCIA

Position: Second base; shortstop
Team: Toronto Blue Jays
Born: Oct. 15, 1967 Tachira, Venezuela
Height: 6'1" **Weight:** 185 lbs.
Bats: right **Throws:** right
Acquired: Traded by Pirates with Dan Plesac and Orlando Merced for Jose Pett, Jose Silva, Branden Cromer, and three players to be named later, 11/96

PLAYER SUMMARY	
Fantasy Value.	$7 to $9
Card Value	5¢ to 8¢
Will.	hit ball well
Can't	wait for walks
Expect	strong defense
Don't Expect	high on-base mark

Simply put, Garcia is a middle infielder who can hit. He had 42 extra-base hits in 1993 and made the All-Star Team a year later. Signed as a shortstop, Garcia made a smooth transition to second when he reached Pittsburgh to stay in '93. He's played on both sides of the bag since. He has little patience, fanning twice per walk, but hits the ball with some authority. A good two-strike hitter, Garcia is most dangerous with runners in scoring position. He fattens his average by dropping surprise bunts and beating out infield hits. In 1995, that helped him uncork a 21-game hitting streak. Garcia runs well, which helps him stay out of double plays, and he could top 20 steals a year if he read pitchers better. His speed gives him good range, and he has quick reactions, soft hands, and a strong, reliable arm. Hamstring problems interfered with his playing time in each of the last two seasons.

MARK GARDNER

Position: Pitcher
Team: San Francisco Giants
Born: March 1, 1962 Los Angeles, CA
Height: 6'1" **Weight:** 190 lbs.
Bats: right **Throws:** right
Acquired: Signed as a free agent, 3/96

PLAYER SUMMARY	
Fantasy Value.	$2 to $4
Card Value	4¢ to 7¢
Will.	count on curve
Can't	prevent gophers
Expect.	decent control
Don't Expect	runners to steal

Released by the Marlins last spring, Gardner thought he was at the end of the line. But the pitching-poor Giants, desperate for warm bodies, offered another chance. Gardner signed in March, moved into the starting rotation, and soon went from journeyman to ace of the staff. A curveball specialist whose velocity is described as sneaky fast, Gardner wins by throwing strikes and hitting spots. He yields fewer than three walks per nine innings, allows one hit per inning, and fans 7½ batters per nine-inning game. Part of the reason for his success is an excellent 3-1 ratio of strikeouts to walks. Durability is another factor, although Gardner lost time last year to an emergency appendectomy. Gardner showed considerable improvement in both his pickoff move and his hitting last year. Gardner's fielding isn't first-rate, but he doesn't embarrass himself too much.

Major League Batting Register

	BA	G	AB	R	H	2B	3B	HR	RBI	SB
90 NL	.500	4	4	1	2	0	0	0	0	0
91 NL	.250	12	24	2	6	0	2	0	1	0
92 NL	.205	22	39	4	8	1	0	0	4	0
93 NL	.269	141	546	77	147	25	5	12	47	18
94 NL	.277	98	412	49	114	15	2	6	28	18
95 NL	.294	104	367	41	108	24	2	6	50	8
96 NL	.285	101	390	66	111	18	4	6	44	16
Life	.278	482	1782	240	496	83	15	30	174	60
3 Ave	.284	119	461	60	131	22	3	7	47	17

Major League Pitching Register

	W	L	ERA	G	CG	IP	H	ER	BB	SO
89 NL	0	3	5.13	7	0	26.1	26	15	11	21
90 NL	7	9	3.42	27	3	152.2	129	58	61	135
91 NL	9	11	3.85	27	0	168.1	139	72	75	107
92 NL	12	10	4.36	33	0	179.2	179	87	60	132
93 AL	4	6	6.19	17	0	91.2	92	63	36	54
94 NL	4	4	4.87	20	0	92.1	97	50	30	57
95 NL	5	5	4.49	39	1	102.1	109	51	43	87
96 NL	12	7	4.42	30	4	179.1	200	88	57	145
Life	53	55	4.39	200	8	992.2	971	484	373	738
3 Ave	8	6	4.58	34	2	142.1	153	72	49	108

BRENT GATES

Position: Second base
Team: Oakland Athletics
Born: March 14, 1970 Grand Rapids, MI
Height: 6'1" **Weight:** 180 lbs.
Bats: both **Throws:** right
Acquired: First-round pick in 6/91 free-agent draft

PLAYER SUMMARY

Fantasy Value	$6 to $8
Card Value	4¢ to 7¢
Will	hit to all fields
Can't	produce long ball
Expect	return to health
Don't Expect	patience at plate

Gates is a switch-hitting second baseman who will surprise with an occasional home run. A better batter right-handed, Gates loves fastballs. He apparently saw more of them as a rookie, when he hit .290. That was the kind of production Oakland expected from the University of Minnesota product, who once had a 35-game hitting streak in the minors. Gates needs to show more patience at the plate. He averages two strikeouts per walk. His .308 on-base percentage in 1995 was the fourth lowest in the AL. Gates is a solid hitter with men in scoring position but won't reach double digits in home runs or stolen bases. The former first-round draft pick is a fine fielder with quick reactions, good range, soft hands, and a reliable throwing arm. He's played all four infield positions since turning pro in 1991. A victim of severe knee and wrist injuries early in his career, Gates missed the final three-plus months of 1996 after suffering a hairline fracture of his left tibia in June. A full recovery is expected.

Major League Batting Register

	BA	G	AB	R	H	2B	3B	HR	RBI	SB
93 AL	.290	139	535	64	155	29	2	7	69	7
94 AL	.283	64	233	29	66	11	1	2	24	3
95 AL	.254	136	524	60	133	24	4	5	56	3
96 AL	.263	64	247	26	65	19	2	2	30	1
Life	.272	403	1539	179	419	83	9	16	179	14
3 Ave	.264	102	388	45	103	20	3	3	42	3

JASON GIAMBI

Position: Outfield; third base
Team: Oakland Athletics
Born: Jan. 8, 1971 West Covina, CA
Height: 6'2" **Weight:** 200 lbs.
Bats: left **Throws:** right
Acquired: Second-round pick 6/92 free-agent draft

PLAYER SUMMARY

Fantasy Value	$14 to $17
Card Value	12¢ to 20¢
Will	boost his power
Can't	supply any speed
Expect	great versatility
Don't Expect	big bat vs. lefties

Given a chance to play last year, Giambi made good on the promise that got him onto the 1992 U.S. Olympic team. The Long Beach State product played four positions, uncorked a 19-game hitting streak, and hit 20 homers—fulfilling an Oakland prediction that his power would develop. Giambi makes decent contact for a slugger but shows enough patience to push his on-base percentage more than 50 points above his batting average. Giambi hits the ball hard: Nearly 40 percent of his hits result in extra bases. Giambi is particularly productive against right-handed batters, hitting well over .300 against them last year. Though he lacks basestealing speed, he moves well enough to play either infield or outfield corner. Signed as a third baseman, he has good instincts, adequate range, soft hands, and a solid arm. Giambi also spent extensive time in left field last year. For a young player, Giambi gets around. He's played in Hawaii, Alaska, Cuba, Barcelona, and the College World Series. In each place, as well as in Oakland, he's shown that he's a coming star.

Major League Batting Register

	BA	G	AB	R	H	2B	3B	HR	RBI	SB
95 AL	.256	54	176	27	45	7	0	6	25	2
96 AL	.291	140	536	84	156	40	1	20	79	0
Life	.282	194	712	111	201	47	1	26	104	2
2 Ave	.282	100	367	57	103	24	1	13	54	1

BENJI GIL

Position: Shortstop
Team: Texas Rangers
Born: Oct. 6, 1972 Tijuana, Mexico
Height: 6'2" **Weight:** 182 lbs.
Bats: right **Throws:** right
Acquired: First-round pick in 6/91 free-agent draft

PLAYER SUMMARY

Fantasy Value	$1
Card Value	5¢ to 8¢
Will	learn as he goes
Can't	stop striking out
Expect	terrific defense
Don't Expect	walks or hits

Gil may be baseball's best example of the good-field, no-hit shortstop. He's a standout in the field, where he has quick reactions, great range, soft hands, and a fine arm. Last season, however, he was idled by March back surgery that kept him sidelined for the duration. The Mexican shortstop has always been long on potential. He led the American Association in chances, putouts, assists, and double plays in 1994 but also led in errors. Private tutoring from Bucky Dent, the former Texas shortstop, ironed out some of the problems. Dent couldn't help with Gil's hitting, however, and the young infielder ranked last in several key offensive categories two years ago. An overly aggressive hitter with little patience, Gil fans six times more often than he walks. He is virtually impotent against lefties, and contact is not his forte. Gil has some power to the alleys but is mainly a singles hitter. If he doesn't curb his alarming strikeout total, even his defensive prowess won't be enough to keep him in the lineup. At 24, he still has a lot to learn.

Major League Batting Register

	BA	G	AB	R	H	2B	3B	HR	RBI	SB
93 AL	.123	22	57	3	7	0	0	0	2	1
95 AL	.219	130	415	36	91	20	3	9	46	2
96 AL	.400	5	5	0	2	0	0	0	1	0
Life	.210	157	477	39	100	20	3	9	49	3

BRIAN GILES

Position: Outfield
Team: Cleveland Indians
Born: Jan. 21, 1971 El Cajon, CA
Height: 5'11" **Weight:** 195 lbs.
Bats: left **Throws:** left
Acquired: 17th-round pick in 6/80 free-agent draft

PLAYER SUMMARY

Fantasy Value	$6 to $8
Card Value	10¢ to 15¢
Will	swing good bat
Can't	crack lineup
Expect	contact, power
Don't Expect	flawed fielding

If good first impressions mean anything, Giles certainly delivered. In his first 13 games for the Indians last year, Giles delivered a 1.000 slugging percentage. Recalled from the minors July 12, he collected extra bases on eight of his first 14 hits. Counting his six-game cup of coffee in 1995, Giles collected three home runs among his first eight hits in the majors. His power is a new development; in his first five minor-league seasons, he had only 14 homers. Giles spent most of his time with the Indians as a DH, sharing the job with fellow outfielder Jeromy Burnitz. Both got more playing time after the Tribe dumped the salary of Eddie Murray in midseason. However, manager Mike Hargrove was unable to set up a workable platoon because both Giles and Burnitz bat left-handed. Giles showed he is a patient contact hitter who's willing to wait for his pitch. He walked more than he fanned in several minor-league seasons. He's also a decent defensive player who reached double digits in assists twice in the minors. His speed gives him good range along with good basestealing ability.

Major League Batting Register

	BA	G	AB	R	H	2B	3B	HR	RBI	SB
95 AL	.556	6	9	6	5	0	0	1	3	0
96 AL	.355	51	121	26	43	14	1	5	27	3
Life	.369	57	130	32	48	14	1	6	30	3

BERNARD GILKEY

Position: Outfield
Team: New York Mets
Born: Sept. 24, 1966 St. Louis, MO
Height: 6' **Weight:** 170 lbs.
Bats: right **Throws:** right
Acquired: Traded by Cardinals for Eric
 Ludwick, Erik Hiljus, and Yudith Ozorio, 1/96

PLAYER SUMMARY	
Fantasy Value	$25 to $30
Card Value	7¢ to 10¢
Will	slam southpaws
Can't	cut whiff rate
Expect	100 RBI
Don't Expect	popgun arm

Before his banner 1996 campaign, Gilkey was primarily a leadoff man whose best power numbers were 17 home runs and 70 RBI. That changed last summer, when Gilkey was a bright spot in a dark season for the Mets. Batting third most of the year, Gilkey gave the Mets power, speed, and strong defense. He hit well above his previous career average, topped 30 homers and 100 RBI for the first time, had his best stolen-base total since 1992, and ranked among the leaders in outfield assists. Gilkey fans twice per walk, but when he's hot, nobody can get him out. His on-base percentage soared above his batting average, and he collected extra-base hits on more than 40 percent of his hits. A better batter with runners in scoring position, Gilkey is especially lethal against left-handers. No longer the speed merchant who twice topped 50 steals in the minors, he's still a force on the bases. In left, his range, arm, and quick release are his best assets.

Major League Batting Register

	BA	G	AB	R	H	2B	3B	HR	RBI	SB
90 NL	.297	18	64	11	19	5	2	1	3	6
91 NL	.216	81	268	28	58	7	2	5	20	14
92 NL	.302	131	384	56	116	19	4	7	43	18
93 NL	.305	137	557	99	170	40	5	16	70	15
94 NL	.253	105	380	52	96	22	1	6	45	15
95 NL	.298	121	480	73	143	33	4	17	69	12
96 NL	.317	153	571	108	181	44	3	30	117	17
Life	.290	746	2704	427	783	170	21	82	367	97
3 Ave	.290	146	549	88	159	37	3	19	86	17

JOE GIRARDI

Position: Catcher
Team: New York Yankees
Born: Oct. 14, 1964 Peoria, IL
Height: 6' **Weight:** 195 lbs.
Bats: right **Throws:** right
Acquired: Traded by Rockies for Mike DeJean
 and Steve Shoemaker, 11/95

PLAYER SUMMARY	
Fantasy Value	$5 to $7
Card Value	5¢ to 8¢
Will	make contact
Can't	hit the long ball
Expect	good game-calling
Don't Expect	powerful arm

Girardi had a tough time persuading Yankee fans his arrival was an improvement over predecessor Mike Stanley. But he certainly earned the respect of New York pitchers. Doc Gooden called Girardi the best catcher he's ever had. The holder of a Northwestern engineering degree, Girardi is a thinking man's catcher, known for his ability to handle pitchers, call good games, prevent wild pitches, and block the plate. When his pitchers get rattled, he has a knack for calming them down. An accurate arm and quick release compensate for a lack of strength. Girardi is no slouch at the plate, either. He's a contact hitter adept at working the hit-and-run. Also a good bunter, Girardi is a singles hitter who is more dangerous with men in scoring position. An added bonus is his ability to run. Girardi stole more bases last year than Stanley had in nine previous seasons.

Major League Batting Register

	BA	G	AB	R	H	2B	3B	HR	RBI	SB
89 NL	.248	59	157	15	39	10	0	1	14	2
90 NL	.270	133	419	36	113	24	2	1	38	8
91 NL	.191	21	47	3	9	2	0	0	6	0
92 NL	.270	91	270	19	73	3	1	1	12	0
93 NL	.290	86	310	35	90	14	5	3	31	6
94 NL	.276	93	330	47	91	9	4	4	34	3
95 NL	.262	125	462	63	121	17	2	8	55	3
96 AL	.294	124	422	55	124	22	3	2	45	13
Life	.273	732	2417	273	660	101	17	20	235	35
3 Ave	.276	132	469	64	129	18	4	6	52	7

TOM GLAVINE

Position: Pitcher
Team: Atlanta Braves
Born: March 25, 1966 Concord, MA
Height: 6' **Weight:** 175 lbs.
Bats: left **Throws:** left
Acquired: Second-round pick in 6/84 free-agent draft

PLAYER SUMMARY	
Fantasy Value	$20 to $25
Card Value	15¢ to 20¢
Will	post fine record
Can't	avoid wild spells
Expect	good bat, glove
Don't Expect	runners to steal

Glavine is a dependable southpaw who wins most of his starts and is most effective when the pressure is greatest. The four-time All-Star yields fewer hits than innings, fans seven men per game, and is very stingy with the home run ball. Glavine's control is usually flawless. NL managers ranked him the league's second-best control artist, trailing only Greg Maddux, in a 1996 *Baseball America* poll. Glavine throws a changeup, a four-seam fastball, a sinker, and a curve. He's expert at getting the ground-ball double play when he needs it. The last man to win the NL Cy Young Award before Maddux launched his streak of four straight, the league's best-hitting pitcher is also a fine bunter. He's appeared as a pinch hitter and pinch runner. An exceptional fielder, Glavine has had several errorless campaigns. If not for Maddux, he'd have several Gold Gloves.

Major League Pitching Register

	W	L	ERA	G	CG	IP	H	ER	BB	SO
87 NL	2	4	5.54	9	0	50.1	55	31	33	20
88 NL	7	17	4.56	34	1	195.1	201	99	63	84
89 NL	14	8	3.68	29	6	186.0	172	76	40	90
90 NL	10	12	4.28	33	1	214.1	232	102	78	129
91 NL	20	11	2.55	34	9	246.2	201	70	69	192
92 NL	20	8	2.76	33	7	225.0	197	69	70	129
93 NL	22	6	3.20	36	4	239.1	236	85	90	120
94 NL	13	9	3.97	25	2	165.1	173	73	70	140
95 NL	16	7	3.08	29	3	198.2	182	68	66	127
96 NL	15	10	2.98	36	1	235.1	222	78	85	181
Life	139	92	3.45	298	34	1956.1	1871	751	664	1212
3 Ave	17	10	3.35	35	2	231.1	223	86	86	174

CHRIS GOMEZ

Position: Shortstop
Team: San Diego Padres
Born: June 16, 1971 Los Angeles, CA
Height: 6'1" **Weight:** 183 lbs.
Bats: right **Throws:** right
Acquired: Traded by Tigers with John Flaherty for Andujar Cedeno, Brad Ausmus, and Russell Spear, 6/96

PLAYER SUMMARY	
Fantasy Value	$3 to $5
Card Value	5¢ to 8¢
Will	hit left-handers
Can't	match Concepcion
Expect	good defense
Don't Expect	much power

San Diego made a major upgrade at shortstop by substituting Gomez for the erratic Andujar Cedeno. Long regarded as a dependable fielder, Gomez surprised with a steady bat that was especially potent against left-handed pitching. He even provided occasional power. The Long Beach State product made it to the majors with his glovework. He has quick reactions, good range, soft hands, and a solid arm. He's better at turning the double play from short, his primary position, than from second, where he often played during the Sparky Anderson regime in Detroit. Anderson once compared Gomez to Dave Concepcion. No matter how much he improves, it's doubtful he'll ever swing the bat like the perennial Cincinnati All-Star. A contact hitter with patience, Gomez is much more likely to hit a single than an extra-base hit. He can't match Concepcion's arm, speed, or production. But he is steady and may improve over time.

Major League Batting Register

	BA	G	AB	R	H	2B	3B	HR	RBI	SB
93 AL	.250	46	128	11	32	7	1	0	11	2
94 AL	.257	84	296	32	76	19	0	8	53	5
95 AL	.223	123	431	49	96	20	2	11	50	4
96 AL	.242	48	128	21	31	5	0	1	16	1
96 NL	.262	89	328	32	86	16	1	3	29	2
Life	.245	390	1311	145	321	67	4	23	159	14
3 Ave	.245	115	410	44	100	22	1	9	53	5

ALEX GONZALEZ

Position: Shortstop
Team: Toronto Blue Jays
Born: April 8, 1973 Miami, FL
Height: 6' **Weight:** 182 lbs.
Bats: right **Throws:** right
Acquired: 14th-round pick in 6/91 free-agent draft

PLAYER SUMMARY	
Fantasy Value	$8 to $10
Card Value	5¢ to 8¢
Will	improve over time
Can't	hit all righties
Expect	more speed, pop
Don't Expect	Alex Rodriguez

The burden is unfair: Alex Gonzalez has been constantly compared with Alex Rodriguez, the young Seattle shortstop who blossomed into a superstar last summer. They share the same position and the same first name, and both reached the majors in 1994, faltered, then returned for good in '95. The Blue Jays have no quarrel with Gonzalez, who gives them some power, some speed, and strong defense. But he's no Rodriguez. Gonzalez is an overly aggressive hitter who fans three times per walk, struggles against some right-handers, and has some problems in the field. As a 1995 rookie, his fielding average at short ranked last in the AL. He made even more errors last year, though he also showed quick reactions, good instincts, wide range, and a strong arm. Perhaps the pressure of succeeding perennial Gold Glover Tony Fernandez prevented him from relaxing. Gonzalez is showing signs of improvement at the plate. He fattens his average with bunts and infield hits but hesitates to hit down on the ball because of his extra-base potential.

Major League Batting Register

	BA	G	AB	R	H	2B	3B	HR	RBI	SB
94 AL	.151	15	53	7	8	3	1	0	1	3
95 AL	.243	111	367	51	89	19	4	10	42	4
96 AL	.235	147	527	64	124	30	5	14	64	16
Life	.233	273	947	122	221	52	10	24	107	23
2 Ave	.238	136	470	61	112	26	5	13	56	10

JUAN GONZALEZ

Position: Outfield
Team: Texas Rangers
Born: Oct. 16, 1969 Vega Baja, Puerto Rico
Height: 6'3" **Weight:** 200 lbs.
Bats: right **Throws:** right
Acquired: Signed as free agent, 5/86

PLAYER SUMMARY	
Fantasy Value	$35 to $40
Card Value	40¢ to 75¢
Will	blast left-handers
Can't	prevent injuries
Expect	home runs, RBI
Don't Expect	strong throws

Though he missed the first 26 games of 1996 with a torn left quadriceps, Gonzalez wasted little time reestablishing his reputation as one of baseball's most prolific sluggers. The two-time home run king also emerged as a surprise Triple Crown contender and came away with 1996 AL MVP honors. Both his batting and on-base marks ranked among AL leaders all year—the result of more patience, more contact, and a major reduction in whiffs. He's lethal against lefties. Primarily a right fielder last year, Gonzalez also spent some time at DH. He's neither a basestealer nor a gazelle in the field. He catches everything he reaches but doesn't have a great arm. Gonzalez, who steered clear of past back, neck, and shoulder problems, credited last year's improvement to an off-season church retreat that made him more positive, more at peace, and more patient. Also, his mother, sister, and fiancée moved from Puerto Rico to spend the season with him.

Major League Batting Register

	BA	G	AB	R	H	2B	3B	HR	RBI	SB
89 AL	.150	24	60	6	9	3	0	1	7	0
90 AL	.289	25	90	11	26	7	1	4	12	0
91 AL	.264	142	545	78	144	34	1	27	102	4
92 AL	.260	155	584	77	152	24	2	43	109	0
93 AL	.310	140	536	105	166	33	1	46	118	4
94 AL	.275	107	422	57	116	18	4	19	85	6
95 AL	.295	90	352	57	104	20	2	27	82	0
96 AL	.314	134	541	89	170	33	2	47	144	2
Life	.283	817	3130	480	887	172	13	214	659	16
3 Ave	.294	129	510	78	150	27	3	35	119	3

LUIS GONZALEZ

Position: Outfield
Team: Chicago Cubs
Born: Sept. 3, 1967 Tampa, FL
Height: 6'2" **Weight:** 180 lbs.
Bats: left **Throws:** right
Acquired: Traded by Astros with Scott Servais for Rick Wilkins, 6/95

PLAYER SUMMARY	
Fantasy Value	$9 to $11
Card Value	5¢ to 8¢
Will	make contact
Can't	hit southpaws
Expect	two-base hits
Don't Expect	weak glove

Gonzalez provides some speed, some power, solid defense, and a strong bat against right-handed pitching. He hits with authority to all fields but is much more likely to hit a double than a home run. He's a good contact man who walks more often than he fans. Gonzalez is at his best with the bases loaded. He often produces when a sacrifice fly is needed. Because he always hits the ball hard, he bangs into lots of double plays. The University of South Alabama product, who played first and third in the minors, made a smooth transition to left field when the Astros had to find a spot for Jeff Bagwell. Gonzalez has good reactions, decent range, soft hands, and an adequate arm. He once stole 35 bases over a two-year span in Houston but has not run as much in recent seasons. Gonzalez broke into pro ball in 1988, then led the Southern League in home runs with 24 two years later. He has become a solid hitter at Wrigley Field.

Major League Batting Register

	BA	G	AB	R	H	2B	3B	HR	RBI	SB
90 NL	.190	12	21	1	4	2	0	0	0	0
91 NL	.254	137	473	51	120	28	9	13	69	10
92 NL	.243	122	387	40	94	19	3	10	55	7
93 NL	.300	154	540	82	162	34	3	15	72	20
94 NL	.273	112	392	57	107	29	4	8	67	15
95 NL	.276	133	471	69	130	29	8	13	69	6
96 NL	.271	146	483	70	131	30	4	15	79	9
Life	.270	816	2767	370	748	171	31	74	411	67
3 Ave	.273	151	522	76	143	34	6	14	84	12

DWIGHT GOODEN

Position: Pitcher
Team: New York Yankees
Born: Nov. 16, 1964 Tampa, FL
Height: 6'3" **Weight:** 210 lbs.
Bats: right **Throws:** right
Acquired: Signed as a free agent, 2/96

PLAYER SUMMARY	
Fantasy Value	$6 to $8
Card Value	7¢ to 10¢
Will	continue comeback
Can't	always find plate
Expect	whiffs, few hits
Don't Expect	top rotation spot

After missing part of 1994 and all of 1995 while suspended for repeated substance abuse violations, Gooden made a triumphant return to New York—this time as a member of the Yankees. Though no longer the flamethrower who won the 1985 NL Cy Young Award with the Mets, he enjoyed his first winning season since 1991. In addition, he pitched the first no-hitter of his career, on May 14. Gooden almost didn't get that far: He struggled through spring training and started the season so poorly that he was on the verge of being released or sent to the minors. Then he made changes in mechanics that resurrected his career. Gooden yields fewer hits than innings and fans nearly seven batters per game, primarily with a three-pitch arsenal that includes a fastball, curveball, and slider. At 32, Gooden is a competent third or fourth starter if he stays clean.

Major League Pitching Register

	W	L	ERA	G	CG	IP	H	ER	BB	SO
84 NL	17	9	2.60	31	7	218.0	161	63	73	276
85 NL	24	4	1.53	35	16	276.2	198	47	69	268
86 NL	17	6	2.84	33	12	250.0	197	79	80	200
87 NL	15	7	3.21	25	7	179.2	162	64	53	148
88 NL	18	9	3.19	34	10	248.1	242	88	57	175
89 NL	9	4	2.89	19	0	118.1	93	38	47	101
90 NL	19	7	3.83	34	2	232.2	229	99	70	223
91 NL	13	7	3.60	27	3	190.0	185	76	56	150
92 NL	10	13	3.67	31	3	206.0	197	84	70	145
93 NL	12	15	3.45	29	7	208.2	188	80	61	149
94 NL	3	4	6.31	7	0	41.1	46	29	15	40
96 AL	11	7	5.01	29	1	170.2	169	95	88	126
Life	168	92	3.24	334	68	2340.1	2067	842	739	2001

CURTIS GOODWIN

Position: Outfield
Team: Cincinnati Reds
Born: Sept. 30, 1972 Oakland, CA
Height: 5'11" **Weight:** 180 lbs.
Bats: left **Throws:** left
Acquired: Traded by Orioles with Trovin Valdez for David Wells, 12/95

PLAYER SUMMARY	
Fantasy Value	$4 to $6
Card Value	5¢ to 8¢
Will	burn up basepaths
Can't	produce much pop
Expect	bunts, stolen bases
Don't Expect	patience at plate

No, they're not related. Although they're both left-handed-hitting outfielders with world-class speed, a California background, and a brief big-league history, Curtis shares nothing else with Tom Goodwin. Unlike Tom, who has learned to maximize his speed potential, Curtis is still learning. Curtis Goodwin is an undisciplined free swinger who broke into the majors with a bang, then faded so badly he returned to the minors. He fans three times more often than he walks and produces no power. But Goodwin led the Orioles with 24 bunts in 1995. He also led the club in sacrifice bunts and stolen base percentage. His speed excited the Reds, who imagined Goodwin as a Deion Sanders clone, a speed merchant who could play center field and lead off. But Goodwin proved too helpless too often at the plate and instead got to spend a year in Triple-A. Goodwin's speed gives him great range in the outfield, where his arm is his only weakness. He gets great jumps, leaps and dives with the best, and has soft hands. He doesn't always throw to the right base, however. At 24, he could be ready to stick.

Major League Batting Register

	BA	G	AB	R	H	2B	3B	HR	RBI	SB
95 AL	.263	87	289	40	76	11	3	1	24	22
96 NL	.228	49	136	20	31	3	0	0	5	15
Life	.252	136	425	60	107	14	3	1	29	37

TOM GOODWIN

Position: Outfield
Team: Kansas City Royals
Born: July 27, 1968 Fresno, CA
Height: 6'1" **Weight:** 170 lbs.
Bats: left **Throws:** right
Acquired: Claimed from Dodgers on waivers, 1/94

PLAYER SUMMARY	
Fantasy Value	$19 to $22
Card Value	5¢ to 8¢
Will	run rivals dizzy
Can't	show patience
Expect	strong defense
Don't Expect	the long ball

Although AL managers polled by *Baseball America* rated him second to Kenny Lofton, Goodwin may well be the loop's fastest baserunner. An aggressive slap-and-spray hitter who depends upon bunts and infield rollers to sweeten his average, Goodwin would be better served by showing more patience at the plate. He fans twice as often as he walks, not drawing enough free passes to post the on-base percentage required of a productive leadoff hitter. In fact, the Royals batted him second last year. If Goodwin ever masters the strike zone, he might challenge Rickey Henderson's single-season record of 130 stolen bases. Ex-teammate Vince Coleman—another member of the 100-steal club—has already helped Goodwin improve his ability to read the moves of rival pitchers and catchers. As might be expected, the former Fresno State All-American and U.S. Olympian has exceptional range in center, where he gets good jumps and ranges far into the power alleys.

Major League Batting Register

	BA	G	AB	R	H	2B	3B	HR	RBI	SB
91 NL	.143	16	7	3	1	0	0	0	0	1
92 NL	.233	57	73	15	17	1	1	0	3	7
93 NL	.294	30	17	6	5	1	0	0	1	1
94 AL	.000	2	2	0	0	0	0	0	0	0
95 AL	.287	133	480	72	138	16	3	4	28	50
96 AL	.282	143	524	80	148	14	4	1	35	66
Life	.280	381	1103	176	309	32	8	5	67	125
2 Ave	.285	146	532	81	152	16	4	3	33	61

TOM GORDON

Position: Pitcher
Team: Boston Red Sox
Born: Nov. 18, 1967 Sebring, FL
Height: 5'9" **Weight:** 160 lbs.
Bates: right **Throws:** right
Acquired: Signed as a free agent, 12/95

PLAYER SUMMARY	
Fantasy Value	$4 to $6
Card Value	5¢ to 8¢
Will	bank on curve
Can't	throw strikes
Expect	Ks, grounders
Don't Expect	compact ERA

Gordon knows the difference between feast and famine. When he locates his trademark curveball, he's almost unhittable. When he doesn't, he's like Popeye without spinach. For much of the 1996 season, he couldn't throw the curve for strikes. AL managers still told *Baseball America* that Gordon's curve was the league's best. Unfortunately for Gordon, he simply doesn't have the other quality pitches that would make him a star. He complements his curve with a rising fastball and a changeup, throwing everything with an over-the-top delivery that is more effective against righties. Although he fans more than seven per nine frames, Gordon also yields more than four walks over that same span. Because of his slow stuff, he also has trouble holding baserunners. Gordon's ERA has ballooned over the last three seasons, and his ratio of Ks to innings pitched has decreased in two of them. His future may not be all that rosy.

Major League Pitching Register

	W	L	ERA	G	CG	IP	H	ER	BB	SO
88 AL	0	2	5.17	5	0	15.2	16	9	7	18
89 AL	17	9	3.64	49	1	163.0	122	66	86	153
90 AL	12	11	3.73	32	6	195.1	192	81	99	175
91 AL	9	14	3.87	45	1	158.0	129	68	87	167
92 AL	6	10	4.59	40	0	117.2	116	60	55	98
93 AL	12	6	3.58	48	2	155.2	125	62	77	143
94 AL	11	7	4.35	24	0	155.1	136	75	87	126
95 AL	12	12	4.43	31	2	189.0	204	93	89	119
96 AL	12	9	5.59	34	4	215.2	249	134	105	171
Life	91	80	4.27	308	16	1365.1	1289	648	692	1170
3 Ave	14	11	4.79	34	2	216.1	223	115	109	161

MARK GRACE

Position: First base
Team: Chicago Cubs
Born: June 28, 1964 Winston-Salem, NC
Height: 6'2" **Weight:** 190 lbs.
Bats: left **Throws:** left
Acquired: 24th-round pick in 6/85 free-agent draft

PLAYER SUMMARY	
Fantasy Value	$11 to $14
Card Value	10¢ to 15¢
Will	thrive in clutch
Can't	clear wall often
Expect	multihit games
Don't Expect	frequent Ks

Grace keeps improving with age. After reaching career highs in doubles and homers in 1995, he posted his best batting average last summer. A patient contact hitter, Grace averages nearly two walks per strikeout. That places him among the league leaders in on-base percentage. Grace goes with the pitch, spraying singles and doubles to all fields, and seldom hits a home run. But he's a strong clutch hitter who thrives on his home turf, delivers with runners in scoring position, and devours right-handed pitchers. Because he lacks speed, Grace hits into frequent double plays. Nor does he fatten his average with bunts or infield hits, but there's nobody better at putting the ball into play. Grace won the Midwest League batting title in his first pro season (1986) and never stopped hitting. The Gold Glover and two-time All-Star has led the league in chances, putouts, and assists several times.

Major League Batting Register

	BA	G	AB	R	H	2B	3B	HR	RBI	SB
88 NL	.296	134	486	65	144	23	4	7	57	3
89 NL	.314	142	510	74	160	28	3	13	79	14
90 NL	.309	157	589	72	182	32	1	9	82	15
91 NL	.273	160	619	87	169	28	5	8	58	3
92 NL	.307	158	603	72	185	37	5	9	79	6
93 NL	.325	155	594	86	193	39	4	14	98	8
94 NL	.298	106	403	55	120	23	3	6	44	0
95 NL	.326	143	552	97	180	51	3	16	92	6
96 NL	.331	142	547	88	181	39	1	9	75	2
Life	.309	1297	4903	696	1514	300	29	91	664	57
3 Ave	.318	151	579	92	184	43	3	12	80	3

MIKE GRACE

Position: Pitcher
Team: Philadelphia Phillies
Born: June 20, 1970 Joliet, IL
Height: 6'4" **Weight:** 220 lbs.
Bats: right **Throws:** right
Acquired: Tenth-round pick in 6/91 free-agent draft

PLAYER SUMMARY	
Fantasy Value	$1 to $3
Card Value	5¢ to 8¢
Will	rejoin rotation
Can't	avoid injuries
Expect	decent control
Don't Expect	gopher plague

The epitome of Grace under fire last year, the right-hander became the first Philly to start a season with six straight wins since Bob Walk in 1980. The sixth win was a 6-0 shutout—first of his professional career—over Greg Maddux at Veterans Stadium May 12. Grace had a 7-2 record when he went on the shelf June 3 with an inflamed tendon under his right armpit. That was nothing new for the Bradley University product, who had survived four elbow surgeries in five previous years as a pro. One of them kept him sidelined for the entire 1993 campaign. Grace opened last year in the Philadelphia rotation only because veteran starters Curt Schilling, David West, and Bobby Munoz had been idled by injury. Grace, a control pitcher who is not intimidated by the big leagues, challenges hitters with a fastball that has a late break. He also throws a decent slider and changeup with a nice, easy delivery and smooth mechanics. If he comes back to spring training fully healed, there's no reason he can't regain his place in the rotation.

Major League Pitching Register

	W	L	ERA	G	CG	IP	H	ER	BB	SO
95 NL	1	1	3.18	2	0	11.1	10	4	4	7
96 NL	7	2	3.49	12	1	80.0	72	31	16	49
Life	8	3	3.45	14	1	91.1	82	35	20	56

CRAIG GREBECK

Position: Second base; shortstop
Team: Anaheim Angels
Born: Dec. 29, 1964 Johnstown, PA
Height: 5'8" **Weight:** 160 lbs.
Bats: right **Throws:** right
Acquired: Signed as a free agent, 12/96

PLAYER SUMMARY	
Fantasy Value	$0
Card Value	4¢ to 7¢
Will	lend support
Can't	steal bases
Expect	few whiffs
Don't Expect	home runs

Grebeck is a solid utility man who has played second, short, third, and the outfield. A contact hitter who neither walks nor fans frequently, he feasts on fastballs, spraying singles to all fields. Grebeck rarely hits a home run or steals a base. He'll bunt to advance runners but never for a base hit. He's also adept at working the hit-and-run. Because he's productive in late-inning pressure situations, Grebeck is a good pinch hitter. He's usually more potent against righties, though the opposite was true last season. Grebeck was a shortstop in college, and he still has quick reactions, good range, soft hands, and a strong throwing arm. He's less polished at second and third. With expansion around the corner, Grebeck's days as a utility man could be numbered. He certainly has the experience a young expansion team craves. Grebeck could have a whole new career next season, at age 33. But he'll have to spend another year on the bench first.

Major League Batting Register

	BA	G	AB	R	H	2B	3B	HR	RBI	SB
90 AL	.168	59	119	7	20	3	1	1	9	0
91 AL	.281	107	224	37	63	16	3	6	31	1
92 AL	.268	88	287	24	77	21	2	3	35	0
93 AL	.226	72	190	25	43	5	0	1	12	1
94 AL	.309	35	97	17	30	5	0	0	5	0
95 AL	.260	53	154	19	40	12	0	1	18	0
96 NL	.211	50	95	8	20	1	0	1	9	0
Life	.251	464	1166	137	293	63	6	13	119	2

SHAWN GREEN

Position: Outfield
Team: Toronto Blue Jays
Born: Nov. 10, 1972 Des Plaines, IL
Height: 6'4" **Weight:** 190 lbs.
Bats: left **Throws:** left
Acquired: First-round pick in 6/91 free-agent draft

PLAYER SUMMARY	
Fantasy Value	$7 to $9
Card Value	7¢ to 10¢
Will	swing solid bat
Can't	handle left-handers
Expect	20-20 potential
Don't Expect	patient approach

During his extended hot streak last August, Green showed why he was a minor-league batting champion in 1994. The tall lefty, whose smooth swing suggests the second coming of John Olerud, hit to all fields against right-handers, showed some power, and sent liners to the opposite field against lefties. Still learning at the plate, Green will be even more productive when he shows greater selectivity. It would also help if he would stop trying to pull every pitch. The Shawn Green of 1996 fanned more than twice per walk and had to hit near the bottom of the lineup because of his poor on-base percentage. But Green's potential is apparent. He has power but has directed it almost entirely against right-handers; all of his first 22 homers came vs. righties. Green runs well enough to steal 20 bases (he did it in the minors) and should increase his power output as he gains experience. He's already a solid right fielder with a strong arm.

TYLER GREEN

Position: Pitcher
Team: Philadelphia Phillies
Born: Feb. 18, 1970 Springfield, OH
Height: 6'5" **Weight:** 204 lbs.
Bats: right **Throws:** right
Acquired: First-round pick in 6/91 free-agent draft

PLAYER SUMMARY	
Fantasy Value	$0
Card Value	7¢ to 10¢
Will	try to stay healthy
Can't	always find plate
Expect	help from bat
Don't Expect	total turnaround

If Green recovers from the shoulder surgery that cost him the entire 1996 season, the Phillies believe he'll be the same All-Star-quality pitcher he was in the beginning of '95. That was the year he had an 8-4 record, four complete games, and two shutouts by midseason, then failed to win a single contest over the second half. He fell so far so fast that he was ordered to report to the Florida Instructional League for extended coaching. When he's on, Green's sinking fastball and changeup complement a knuckle-curve that is his trademark delivery. He doesn't always throw it for strikes, however. Since he depends upon location rather than velocity, Green's control troubles sometimes yield gopher balls. Green's slow delivery makes him easy prey for wide-eyed basestealers. His pickoff move is mediocre. On the plus side, Green helps himself with a strong bat. The tenth overall selection in the 1991 amateur draft, Green had a half-dozen extra-base hits, including a homer, as a rookie and also showed the ability to bunt runners over.

Major League Batting Register

	BA	G	AB	R	H	2B	3B	HR	RBI	SB
93 AL	.000	3	6	0	0	0	0	0	0	0
94 AL	.091	14	33	1	3	1	0	0	1	1
95 AL	.288	121	379	52	109	31	4	15	54	1
96 AL	.280	132	422	52	118	32	3	11	45	5
Life	.274	270	840	105	230	64	7	26	100	7
2 Ave	.284	134	424	55	120	33	4	14	53	3

Major League Pitching Register

	W	L	ERA	G	CG	IP	H	ER	BB	SO
93 NL	0	0	7.36	3	0	7.1	16	6	5	7
95 NL	8	9	5.31	26	4	140.2	157	83	66	85
Life	8	9	5.41	29	4	148.0	173	89	71	92

WILLIE GREENE

Position: Third base; left field
Team: Cincinnati Reds
Born: Sept. 23, 1971 Milledgeville, GA
Height: 5'11" **Weight:** 185 lbs.
Bats: left **Throws:** right
Acquired: Traded by Expos with Dave Martinez and Scott Ruskin for John Wetteland and Bill Risley, 11/91

PLAYER SUMMARY	
Fantasy Value	$7 to $9
Card Value	5¢ to 8¢
Will	seek steady job
Can't	hit left-handers
Expect	occasional power
Don't Expect	much patience

One of three lefty-hitting third basemen on the 1996 Cincinnati Reds, Greene barely got enough at bats to show what he could do. He struggled against southpaws, showed some power against righties, and revealed a versatile side that increased his value enormously. Pittsburgh's first-round draft choice of 1989 played both infield and outfield corners as well as shortstop. That wasn't a stretch for Greene, who was signed as a shortstop. Blessed with world-class bat speed, Greene topped 20 homers twice in the minors. But he also showed an impatience at the plate that he'll have to overcome. Greene fanned three times per walk last year. All that moving around may have hurt Greene, who's been up and down like a yo-yo for the past five seasons. Quick on his feet, Greene has better speed than many third basemen. He reacts well, showing good range, soft hands, and a solid arm. Thus far in his young career, however, Greene has made the Reds blue. A better bat would change that complexion.

Major League Batting Register

	BA	G	AB	R	H	2B	3B	HR	RBI	SB
92 NL	.269	29	93	10	25	5	2	2	13	0
93 NL	.160	15	50	7	8	1	1	2	5	0
94 NL	.216	16	37	5	8	2	0	0	3	0
95 NL	.105	8	19	1	2	0	0	0	0	0
96 NL	.244	115	287	48	70	5	5	19	63	0
Life	.233	183	486	71	113	13	8	23	84	0

MIKE GREENWELL

Position: Outfield
Team: Boston Red Sox
Born: July 18, 1963 Louisville, KY
Height: 6' **Weight:** 200 lbs.
Bats: left **Throws:** right
Acquired: Third-round pick in 6/82 free-agent draft

PLAYER SUMMARY	
Fantasy Value	$7 to $9
Card Value	5¢ to 8¢
Will	seek job back
Can't	find former form
Expect	line-drive hits
Don't Expect	speed, homers

Greenwell missed nearly two months of 1996 with a broken left ring finger. Regaining his timing was a tough task for the veteran. A contact hitter who walks more often than he fans, Greenwell lives for fastballs. A good clutch hitter in his prime, Greenwell has seen his average shrink. With Darren Bragg and Reggie Jefferson swinging better bats down the stretch last season, Greenwell got considerably less playing time than he would have liked. Part of the problem was lack of speed. At 33, Greenwell still moves well enough to play left field. He's mastered the Green Monster. Outside of Fenway, Greenwell is best used as a DH, but he did manage to rack up nine RBI in a September 1 game at Seattle last season. Greenwell could be a tantalizing expansion draft pick this fall.

Major League Batting Register

	BA	G	AB	R	H	2B	3B	HR	RBI	SB
85 AL	.323	17	31	7	10	1	0	4	8	1
86 AL	.314	31	35	4	11	2	0	0	4	0
87 AL	.328	125	412	71	135	31	6	19	89	5
88 AL	.325	158	590	86	192	39	8	22	119	16
89 AL	.308	145	578	87	178	36	0	14	95	13
90 AL	.297	159	610	71	181	30	6	14	73	8
91 AL	.300	147	544	76	163	26	6	9	83	15
92 AL	.233	49	180	16	42	2	0	2	18	2
93 AL	.315	146	540	77	170	38	6	13	72	5
94 AL	.269	95	327	60	88	25	1	11	45	2
95 AL	.297	120	481	67	143	25	4	15	76	9
96 AL	.295	77	295	35	87	20	1	7	44	4
Life	.303	1269	4623	657	1400	275	38	130	726	80
3 Ave	.287	115	432	65	124	28	2	13	64	6

Rusty Greer

Position: Outfield; first base
Team: Texas Rangers
Born: Jan. 21, 1969 Fort Rucker, AL
Height: 6' **Weight:** 190 lbs.
Bats: left **Throws:** left
Acquired: Tenth-round pick in 6/90 free-agent draft

Player Summary

Fantasy Value	$14 to $17
Card Value	10¢ to 15¢
Will	swing solid bat
Can't	get recognition
Expect	strong fielding
Don't Expect	powerful arm

Greer played such a solid left field for the 1996 Rangers that manager Johnny Oates waged a one-man campaign to have him considered for a Gold Glove award. In two previous seasons, Greer bounced around, playing all three outfield spots, filling in at first base, and pinch-hitting. He proved inadequate in right due to a mediocre throwing arm, but that's his only weakness in the field, where he has great reactions, wide range, and soft hands. As a hitter, Greer combines patience and the ability to make contact with a short, compact swing. He averages 1½ strikeouts per walk, hardly a bad ratio, while netting extra bases on nearly one-third of his hits. Greer hit both righties and lefties so well last year that he became the No. 3 hitter in a potent Texas lineup. Greer uses all fields, thrives in clutch situations, and draws enough walks to rank among the league leaders in on-base percentage. Greer isn't much of a basestealing threat, but nobody seems to mind. At 28, his star is burning more brightly every day.

Major League Batting Register

	BA	G	AB	R	H	2B	3B	HR	RBI	SB
94 AL	.314	80	277	36	87	16	1	10	46	0
95 AL	.271	131	417	58	113	21	2	13	61	3
96 AL	.332	139	542	96	180	41	6	18	100	9
Life	.307	350	1236	190	380	78	9	41	207	12
3 Ave	.307	133	467	71	143	29	3	16	78	4

Ken Griffey, Jr.

Position: Outfield
Team: Seattle Mariners
Born: Nov. 21, 1969 Donora, PA
Height: 6'3" **Weight:** 195 lbs.
Bats: left **Throws:** left
Acquired: First-round pick in 6/87 free-agent draft

Player Summary

Fantasy Value	$40 to $45
Card Value	$1.50 to $3.00
Will	deliver in clutch
Can't	win batting title
Expect	enormous power
Don't Expect	weak fielding

What more can Griffey do? He hit 40 homers for the third time in four seasons, had his fourth 100-RBI campaign, scored 100 runs for the second time, earned his seventh All-Star selection, and took his seventh straight Gold Glove. The highlight-reel catches stopped only when Griffey was sidelined for 20 games with a broken bone in his right wrist. Griffey, who missed 73 games with a broken left wrist the year before, didn't miss a beat after returning. Griffey strikes out more often than he walks, but he has patience for a slugger, walking enough to post a high on-base mark. He's also a high-percentage basestealer. Griffey's career average would be better if he would swing for singles. But that's hardly his style. He will rise to any occasion, and he plays hard on offense and on defense, where no one matches his reactions, range, hands, or arm.

Major League Batting Register

	BA	G	AB	R	H	2B	3B	HR	RBI	SB
89 AL	.264	127	455	61	120	23	0	16	61	16
90 AL	.300	155	597	91	179	28	7	22	80	16
91 AL	.327	154	548	76	179	42	1	22	100	18
92 AL	.308	142	565	83	174	39	4	27	103	10
93 AL	.309	156	582	113	180	38	3	45	109	17
94 AL	.323	111	433	94	140	24	4	40	90	11
95 AL	.258	72	260	52	67	7	0	17	42	4
96 AL	.303	140	545	125	165	26	2	49	140	16
Life	.302	1057	3985	695	1204	227	21	238	725	108
3 Ave	.302	126	482	105	146	23	3	41	105	12

JASON GRIMSLEY

Position: Pitcher
Team: Anaheim Angels
Born: Aug. 7, 1967 Cleveland, TX
Height: 6'3" **Weight:** 180 lbs.
Bats: right **Throws:** right
Acquired: Traded by Indians for Brian Anderson, 2/96

PLAYER SUMMARY	
Fantasy Value	$0
Card Value	5¢ to 8¢
Will	take last chance
Can't	find strike zone
Expect	long enemy hits
Don't Expect	winning record

Somewhere along the line, someone must see something about this guy. How he stays in the majors is a major mystery. Grimsley's numbers speak for themselves. He yields too many walks, hits, and homers. He throws too many wild pitches and allows too many basestealers to succeed. He doesn't get many strikeouts, with an embarrassing whiff-to-walk ratio of 1-to-1. On the plus side, Grimsley did throw a nine-inning shutout, a rarity these days, last year. His combination of sinking fastball and straight curve must have been working that day. He usually has trouble throwing strikes, falls behind in the count, and compensates by catching too much of the plate. That's when he gets killed. Though used primarily as a starter during his pro career, Grimsley never won as many as a dozen games. He led two leagues in wild pitches and two in walks, although he did pitch a Double-A no-hitter.

Major League Pitching Register

	W	L	ERA	G	CG	IP	H	ER	BB	SO
89 NL	1	3	5.89	4	0	18.1	19	12	19	7
90 NL	3	2	3.30	11	0	57.1	47	21	43	41
91 NL	1	7	4.87	12	0	61.0	54	33	41	42
93 AL	3	4	5.31	10	0	42.1	52	25	20	27
94 AL	5	2	4.57	14	1	82.2	91	42	34	59
95 AL	0	0	6.09	15	0	34.0	37	23	32	25
96 AL	5	7	6.84	35	2	130.1	150	99	74	82
Life	18	25	5.39	101	3	426.0	450	255	263	283
3 Ave	4	3	5.81	24	1	95.0	107	61	53	64

MARQUIS GRISSOM

Position: Outfield
Team: Atlanta Braves
Born: April 17, 1967 Atlanta, GA
Height: 5'11" **Weight:** 190 lbs.
Bats: right **Throws:** right
Acquired: Traded by Expos for Roberto Kelly, Tony Tarasco, Esteban Yan, and cash, 4/95

PLAYER SUMMARY	
Fantasy Value	$25 to $30
Card Value	12¢ to 20¢
Will	win Gold Glove
Can't	wait for walks
Expect	hits, some pop
Don't Expect	top leadoff job

Determined to bounce back from a subpar 1995, Grissom made a spring-training promise to pursue his first 200-hit season. He remained on target all year, aided by a 28-game hitting streak that was baseball's longest since Jerome Walton hit in 30 straight in 1989. Though he's still an impatient hitter who fans twice per walk, Grissom is the first Brave since Ralph Garr in 1974 to rack up double digits in doubles, triples, homers, and stolen bases. Because of a so-so on-base percentage, Grissom isn't the world's best leadoff man. But he does offer the potential of a long hit to start the game. He'd do even better if he practiced patience, worked deep counts, and took occasional walks. Grissom is a four-time Gold Glove center fielder with a strong, accurate arm. He rarely makes errors and often makes spectacular catches after long runs. He's been an All-Star twice.

Major League Batting Register

	BA	G	AB	R	H	2B	3B	HR	RBI	SB
89 NL	.257	26	74	16	19	2	0	1	2	1
90 NL	.257	98	288	42	74	14	2	3	29	22
91 NL	.267	148	558	73	149	23	9	6	39	76
92 NL	.276	159	653	99	180	39	6	14	66	78
93 NL	.298	157	630	104	188	27	2	19	95	53
94 NL	.288	110	475	96	137	25	4	11	45	36
95 NL	.258	139	551	80	142	23	3	12	42	29
96 NL	.308	158	671	106	207	32	10	23	74	28
Life	.281	995	3900	616	1096	185	36	89	392	323
3 Ave	.286	156	653	110	187	31	6	17	62	37

125

BUDDY GROOM

Position: Pitcher
Team: Oakland Athletics
Born: July 10, 1965 Dallas, TX
Height: 6'2" **Weight:** 220 lbs.
Bats: left **Throws:** left
Acquired: Signed as a free agent, 11/95

PLAYER SUMMARY	
Fantasy Value $0
Card Value . . . . 5¢ to 8¢
Will . . . . work best in pen
Can't . . . . freeze runners
Expect . . . . ground-ball outs
Don't Expect . . . . fewer hits than IP

Another Tiger castoff who found success somewhere else, Groom wanted to reach the major leagues pretty badly. He endured eight seasons as a minor-league starter before finding his niche last year, when the Oakland Athletics made him a heavy-duty reliever. Groom, who had entered the season with a 2-13 lifetime record and 6.07 ERA, made the most of his chance. He won his first five decisions for the A's, posted a respectable ERA, and showed decent control. He did stumble in August, however, probably due to overwork. A sinker-slider pitcher who also throws a curve, Groom has good control, strands most inherited runners, and keeps the ball in the park. But he yields more hits than innings and has some trouble keeping baserunners close. His follow-through not only gives runners a jump but leaves him in poor fielding position. The jury is still out on Groom's best role. Used mostly as a set-up man last year, he also finished a dozen games, blowing three of his first five save chances in the process.

Major League Pitching Register

	W	L	ERA	G	S	IP	H	ER	BB	SO
92 AL	0	5	5.82	12	1	38.2	48	25	22	15
93 AL	0	2	6.14	19	0	36.2	48	25	13	15
94 AL	0	1	3.94	40	1	32.0	31	14	13	27
95 AL	1	3	7.52	23	1	40.2	55	34	26	23
95 NL	1	2	7.20	14	0	15.0	26	12	6	12
96 AL	5	0	3.84	72	2	77.1	85	33	34	57
Life	7	13	5.36	180	5	240.1	293	143	114	149
3 Ave	2	2	4.87	51	2	56.0	64	30	27	40

KEVIN GROSS

Position: Pitcher
Team: Texas Rangers
Born: June 8, 1961 Downey, CA
Height: 6'5" **Weight:** 215 lbs.
Bats: right **Throws:** right
Acquired: Signed as a free agent, 12/94

PLAYER SUMMARY	
Fantasy Value $0
Card Value . . . . 4¢ to 7¢
Will . . . . bank on sinker
Can't . . . . avoid gophers
Expect . . . . decent control
Don't Expect . . . . 15 victories

After leading the AL with 15 losses in 1995, Gross engineered a comeback of sorts last summer. Pitching down in the strike zone, Gross threw strikes with all four of his pitches: sinking fastball, curveball, changeup, and slider. A starter most of his career, he stayed in the rotation, posting double digits in wins, before the August arrival of John Burkett pushed him into the bullpen. Not a power pitcher, Gross needs groundouts because he doesn't get many Ks. He yields more hits than innings and has occasional gopher-ball problems. He has a fine pickoff move, and his fielding is also more than adequate, though his reaction time has slowed slightly because of age. Usually a durable performer, the one-time All-Star (1988) was disabled last year with a slight ligament tear in his back.

Major League Pitching Register

	W	L	ERA	G	CG	IP	H	ER	BB	SO
83 NL	4	6	3.56	17	1	96.0	100	38	35	66
84 NL	8	5	4.12	44	1	129.0	140	59	44	84
85 NL	15	13	3.41	38	6	205.2	194	78	81	151
86 NL	12	12	4.02	37	7	241.2	240	108	94	154
87 NL	9	16	4.35	34	3	200.2	205	97	87	110
88 NL	12	14	3.69	33	5	231.2	209	95	89	162
89 NL	11	12	4.38	31	4	201.1	188	98	88	158
90 NL	9	12	4.57	31	2	163.1	171	83	65	111
91 NL	10	11	3.58	46	0	115.2	123	46	50	95
92 NL	8	13	3.17	34	4	204.2	182	72	77	158
93 NL	13	13	4.14	33	3	202.1	224	93	74	150
94 NL	9	7	3.60	25	1	157.1	162	63	43	124
95 AL	9	15	5.54	31	4	183.2	200	113	89	106
96 AL	11	8	5.22	28	1	129.1	151	75	50	78
Life	140	157	4.09	462	42	2462.1	2489	1118	966	1707
3 Ave	11	12	4.69	33	2	186.0	201	97	70	124

MARK GRUDZIELANEK

Position: Shortstop
Team: Montreal Expos
Born: June 30, 1970 Milwaukee, WI
Height: 6'1" **Weight:** 185 lbs.
Bats: right **Throws:** right
Acquired: 11th-round pick in 6/91 free-agent draft

PLAYER SUMMARY	
Fantasy Value	$12 to $15
Card Value	8¢ to 12¢
Will	thrive on turf
Can't	reduce K ratio
Expect	speed, defense
Don't Expect	patient at bats

Growing up in a Milwaukee suburb, Grudzielanek idolized Paul Molitor. Like Molitor, Grudzielanek is a line-drive hitter with a bowlegged stance and compact swing. Also like Molitor, he's an All-Star infielder who wears No. 4. In 1996, his first full season, Grudzielanek made many people learn to pronounce his name. An aggressive opposite-field hitter who rarely walks, Grudzielanek adopted a more upright stance last spring. The result was a spot on the All-Star roster. At the break, the leadoff man ranked among the league leaders in average, runs, hits, and multihit games. He does his best hitting on artificial turf—especially against left-handed pitchers. His lone weakness is a 3-1 ratio of whiffs to walks. Grudzielanek's speed helps him sweeten his average with infield rollers. He is a basestealer who's rarely caught. His speed gives him fine range in the field, where he has soft hands and a fine arm. A star at every level, Grudzielanek reached the Expos as an all-purpose infielder in '95, struggled with the bat, then became the everyday shortstop in late August.

Major League Batting Register

	BA	G	AB	R	H	2B	3B	HR	RBI	SB
95 NL	.245	78	269	27	66	12	2	1	20	8
96 NL	.306	153	657	99	201	34	4	6	49	33
Life	.288	231	926	126	267	46	6	7	69	41
2 Ave	.287	120	480	65	138	24	3	4	36	21

EDDIE GUARDADO

Position: Pitcher
Team: Minnesota Twins
Born: Oct. 2, 1970 Stockton, CA
Height: 6' **Weight:** 193 lbs.
Bats: right **Throws:** left
Acquired: 21st-round pick in 6/90 free-agent draft

PLAYER SUMMARY	
Fantasy Value	$4 to $6
Card Value	5¢ to 8¢
Will	answer call often
Can't	always throw strikes
Expect	good K/BB ratio
Don't Expect	runners to steal

Lefties cringe when Guardado enters a game. A hard-throwing southpaw who throws nearly a strikeout per inning, Guardado found his niche last year when he was used exclusively in relief for the first time since he turned pro. The busiest member of the Minnesota bullpen, he yielded fewer hits than innings, maintained a 3-1 ratio of strikeouts to walks, and stranded most of the runners he inherited. He also proved his resilient left arm responded well to frequent use. Especially effective against first batters, Guardado often works one or two hitters per stint. His total of innings pitched is less than his number of appearances. Guardado's three-pitch arsenal includes a fastball, curveball, and changeup. He usually has good velocity and good location, but he does encounter occasional control problems. Guardado averaged more than four walks per game—a lousy ratio for a reliever—last year. He helps himself with good defense and a fine pickoff move. Few runners bother to test him.

Major League Pitching Register

	W	L	ERA	G	S	IP	H	ER	BB	SO
93 AL	3	8	6.18	19	0	94.2	123	65	36	46
94 AL	0	2	8.47	4	0	17.0	26	16	4	8
95 AL	4	9	5.12	51	2	91.1	99	52	45	71
96 AL	6	5	5.25	83	4	73.2	61	43	33	74
Life	13	24	5.73	157	6	276.2	309	176	118	199
2 Ave	5	8	5.18	70	3	88.1	86	51	42	77

127

MARK GUBICZA

Position: Pitcher
Team: Anaheim Angels
Born: Aug. 14, 1962 Philadelphia, PA
Height: 6'5" **Weight:** 220 lbs.
Bats: right **Throws:** right
Acquired: Traded by Royals with Mike Bovee
for Chili Davis, 11/96

PLAYER SUMMARY	
Fantasy Value	$3 to $5
Card Value	4¢ to 8¢
Will	keep ball down
Can't	prevent gophers
Expect	ground-ball outs
Don't Expect	frequent whiffs

Only once since 1989 has Gubicza had a winning record. That's not entirely his fault, since the Royals were often guilty of giving him inadequate support. But Gubicza is not the same power pitcher he was before shoulder problems decreased his velocity. Although he became K.C.'s career strikeout leader last year, Gubicza had a 4-12 mark when he was sidelined for the season July 5 after Paul Molitor's line drive cracked his shin. Even if he proves sound at age 34, it's unclear how much help the big right-hander might be able to provide. He yielded an alarming 22 homers in 119⅓ innings last year—an indication that his sinker-slider repertoire was not sharp. Usually a control artist, Gubicza uses guile more than style. He keeps the ball down, coaxing frequent groundouts.

Major League Pitching Register

	W	L	ERA	G	CG	IP	H	ER	BB	SO
84 AL	10	14	4.05	29	4	189.0	172	85	75	111
85 AL	14	10	4.06	29	0	177.1	160	80	77	99
86 AL	12	6	3.64	35	3	180.2	155	73	84	118
87 AL	13	18	3.98	35	10	241.2	231	107	120	166
88 AL	20	8	2.70	35	8	269.2	237	81	83	183
89 AL	15	11	3.04	36	8	255.0	252	86	63	173
90 AL	4	7	4.50	16	2	94.0	101	47	38	71
91 AL	9	12	5.68	26	0	133.0	168	84	42	89
92 AL	7	6	3.72	18	2	111.1	110	46	36	81
93 AL	5	8	4.66	49	0	104.1	128	54	43	80
94 AL	7	9	4.50	22	0	130.0	158	65	26	59
95 AL	12	14	3.75	33	3	213.1	222	89	62	81
96 AL	4	12	5.13	19	2	119.1	132	68	34	55
Life	132	135	3.91	382	42	2218.2	2226	965	783	1366
3 Ave	9	13	4.31	29	2	181.1	201	87	47	76

OZZIE GUILLEN

Position: Shortstop
Team: Chicago White Sox
Born: Jan. 20, 1964 Ocumare del Tuy,
Venezuela
Height: 5'11" **Weight:** 150 lbs.
Bats: left **Throws:** right
Acquired: Traded by Padres with Tim Lollar,
Bill Long, and Luis Salazar for LaMarr Hoyt,
Todd Simmons, and Kevin Kristan, 12/84

PLAYER SUMMARY	
Fantasy Value	$2 to $4
Card Value	4¢ to 7¢
Will	excel in field
Can't	hit all lefties
Expect	contact, singles
Don't Expect	patience, power

A magician with the glove, Guillen plays shortstop with a flair. He is blessed with good instincts, quick reactions, soft hands, and a solid throwing arm. His range, while still good, has declined since he suffered torn ligaments in his right knee five years ago. But Guillen compensates with good positioning. He gets rid of the ball quickly and is among the best at completing the double play. Guillen twice led AL shortstops in chances and even won a Gold Glove in 1990. He does not make many errors in the field. At the plate, however, he's a Punch-and-Judy hitter who rarely walks or fans but struggles against most southpaws. Guillen gets his hits by spraying singles and dropping occasional bunts. The three-time All-Star was AL Rookie of the Year in 1985.

Major League Batting Register

	BA	G	AB	R	H	2B	3B	HR	RBI	SB
85 AL	.273	150	491	71	134	21	9	1	33	7
86 AL	.250	159	547	58	137	19	4	2	47	8
87 AL	.279	149	560	64	156	22	7	2	51	25
88 AL	.261	156	566	58	148	16	7	0	39	25
89 AL	.253	155	597	63	151	20	8	1	54	36
90 AL	.279	160	516	61	144	21	4	1	58	13
91 AL	.273	154	524	52	143	20	3	3	49	21
92 AL	.200	12	40	5	8	4	0	0	7	1
93 AL	.280	134	457	44	128	23	4	4	50	5
94 AL	.288	100	365	46	105	9	5	1	39	5
95 AL	.248	122	415	50	103	20	3	1	41	6
96 AL	.263	150	499	62	131	24	8	4	45	6
Life	.267	1601	5577	634	1488	219	62	20	513	158
3 Ave	.267	143	493	61	132	20	6	2	49	7

MARK GUTHRIE

Position: Pitcher
Team: Los Angeles Dodgers
Born: Sept. 22, 1965 Buffalo, NY
Height: 6'4" **Weight:** 202 lbs.
Bats: both **Throws:** left
Acquired: Traded by Twins with Kevin Tapani for Ron Coomer, Jose Parra, and Greg Hansell, 7/95

PLAYER SUMMARY	
Fantasy Value	$4 to $6
Card Value	4¢ to 7¢
Will	top 50 outings
Can't	stop all lefties
Expect	good control
Don't Expect	gopher balls

A quality set-up man, Guthrie was the most effective member of the Dodger bullpen last summer. The Louisiana State product, who began his pro career as a starter, posted a career-best ERA while working 50 times for the third time. The hard-throwing lefty has good control of his fastball, curve, forkball, and changeup. His nine-inning averages are all good: 7½ strikeouts, fewer than three walks, and 6½ hits. Extremely stingy with the home run ball, Guthrie also strands most of the runners he inherits. Although he's often used to dispose of one or two left-handed hitters, he's capable of working longer. Guthrie was actually more effective against righties last year. His defense and pickoff move are adequate but not spectacular. He doesn't bat much but is no automatic out. The tall left-hander is valued not only because of his performance but also because of his experience.

Major League Pitching Register

	W	L	ERA	G	S	IP	H	ER	BB	SO
89 AL	2	4	4.55	13	0	57.1	66	29	21	38
90 AL	7	9	3.79	24	0	144.2	154	61	39	101
91 AL	7	5	4.32	41	2	98.0	116	47	41	72
92 AL	2	3	2.88	54	5	75.0	59	24	23	76
93 AL	2	1	4.71	22	0	21.0	20	11	16	15
94 AL	4	2	6.14	50	1	51.1	65	35	18	38
95 AL	5	3	4.46	36	0	42.1	47	21	16	48
95 AL	0	2	3.66	24	0	19.2	19	8	9	19
96 NL	2	3	2.22	66	1	73.0	65	18	22	56
Life	31	32	3.93	330	9	582.1	611	254	205	463
3 Ave	4	3	4.24	59	1	64.1	70	30	22	55

RICKY GUTIERREZ

Position: Shortstop
Team: Houston Astros
Born: May 23, 1970 Miami, FL
Height: 6'1" **Weight:** 175 lbs.
Bats: right **Throws:** right
Acquired: Traded by Padres with Derek Bell, Doug Brocail, Pedro Martinez, Phil Plantier, and Craig Shipley for Ken Caminiti, Steve Finley, Andujar Cedeno, Robert Petagine, Brian Williams, and a player to be named later, 12/94

PLAYER SUMMARY	
Fantasy Value	$1
Card Value	4¢ to 7¢
Will	hit left-handers
Can't	produce power
Expect	opposite-field hits
Don't Expect	solid defense

Although he's not a power hitter, Gutierrez was a major contributor to Houston's 1996 success. His productivity against left-handed pitching allowed the Astros to use him in a platoon with Orlando Miller. Although Miller provides more punch, Gutierrez makes better contact and shows much more patience at the plate. Because he draws a fair amount of walks, his on-base percentage hovers 70 points above his batting average. He's an opposite-field singles hitter whose favorite pitch is a low, outside fastball. Though he doesn't steal much, Gutierrez has some speed. He certainly moves well enough in the field, where his range is fine. But Gutierrez doesn't always provide smooth defense. He lacks soft hands and boots some routine plays. Although he's only 26, Gutierrez is almost certain to be left off the protected list when the next round of expansion begins.

Major League Batting Register

	BA	G	AB	R	H	2B	3B	HR	RBI	SB
93 NL	.251	133	438	76	110	10	5	5	26	4
94 NL	.240	90	275	27	66	11	2	1	28	2
95 NL	.276	52	156	22	43	6	0	0	12	5
96 NL	.284	89	218	28	62	8	1	1	15	6
Life	.259	364	1087	153	281	35	8	7	81	17
3 Ave	.260	91	260	30	68	10	1	1	23	5

JUAN GUZMAN

Position: Pitcher
Team: Toronto Blue Jays
Born: Oct. 28, 1966 Santa Isabel, Puerto Rico
Height: 5'11" **Weight:** 190 lbs.
Bats: right **Throws:** right
Acquired: Traded by Dodgers for Mike
　　Sharperson, 9/87

PLAYER SUMMARY	
Fantasy Value. . . . . $14 to $17
Card Value . . . . 5¢ to 8¢
Will . . . . yield few hits
Can't. . . . . stop gopher balls
Expect. . . . . control, velocity
Don't Expect . . . . pickoff success

After back-to-back subpar years, Guzman redesigned his pitching pattern in an effort to return to the winning ways of his earlier years. The plan worked, as he led the AL in ERA most of the season. The April Pitcher of the Month, he hurled his second career shutout July 16, beating Baltimore, 6-0. Guzman credited his turnaround to Toronto's signing of veteran catcher Charlie O'Brien, a shrewd handler of pitchers. The pitcher also managed to increase the speed of his fastball from 87 to 95 mph and got his slider up to 89. Guzman, who also throws a forkball and changeup, fanned more than eight men per nine innings last year, yielded 7½ hits over that same span, and showed the best control of his career (fewer than three walks per game). Free of the shoulder and arm ailments that plagued him previously, Guzman dominated both lefties and righties last year until an emergency appendectomy ended his season in early September.

Major League Pitching Register

	W	L	ERA	G	CG	IP	H	ER	BB	SO
91 AL	10	3	2.99	23	1	138.2	98	46	66	123
92 AL	16	5	2.64	28	1	180.2	135	53	72	165
93 AL	14	3	3.99	33	2	221.0	211	98	110	194
94 AL	12	11	5.68	25	2	147.1	165	93	76	124
95 AL	4	14	6.32	24	3	135.1	151	95	73	94
96 AL	11	8	2.93	27	4	187.2	158	61	53	165
Life	67	44	3.97	160	13	1010.2	918	446	450	865
3 Ave	11	13	4.91	30	3	182.1	187	100	81	148

CHRIS GWYNN

Position: Outfield
Team: San Diego Padres
Born: Oct. 13, 1964 Los Angeles, CA
Height: 6' **Weight:** 210 lbs.
Bats: left **Throws:** left
Acquired: Signed as a free agent, 1/96

PLAYER SUMMARY	
Fantasy Value $0
Card Value . . . . 4¢ to 7¢
Will . . . . seek comeback
Can't. . . . . generate power
Expect . . . . pinch-hit duties
Don't Expect . . . . strong throws

There was good news and bad news for Gwynn last summer. He got to play with brother Tony after spending nine years on different teams. But he hit so poorly he hardly saw any action. Before 1995, another off year, Gwynn was a good pinch hitter who made contact. He even worked his way into second place (behind Manny Mota) on the Dodgers' career pinch-hit list. But knee problems slowed him considerably, ending his second stint in L.A. When healthy, Gwynn swings a solid bat, especially against right-handed pitchers, but does not hit with the same consistency as his brother. Like Tommie Aaron before him, Gwynn will always suffer from comparisons with his more famous sibling. Chris lacks Tony's speed, defensive skills, and ability to send extra-base hits into the gaps. Because of a mediocre arm, Gwynn's best position is left field. He has been most often used as a pinch hitter.

Major League Batting Register

	BA	G	AB	R	H	2B	3B	HR	RBI	SB
87 NL	.219	17	32	2	7	1	0	0	2	0
88 NL	.182	12	11	1	2	0	0	0	0	0
89 NL	.235	32	68	8	16	4	1	0	7	1
90 NL	.284	101	141	19	40	2	1	5	22	0
91 NL	.252	94	139	18	35	5	1	5	22	1
92 AL	.286	34	84	10	24	3	2	1	7	0
93 AL	.300	103	287	36	86	14	4	1	25	0
94 NL	.268	58	71	9	19	0	0	3	13	0
95 NL	.214	67	84	8	18	3	2	1	10	0
96 NL	.178	81	90	8	16	4	0	1	10	0
Life	.261	599	1007	119	263	36	11	17	118	2

TONY GWYNN

Position: Outfield
Team: San Diego Padres
Born: May 9, 1960 Los Angeles, CA
Height: 5'11" **Weight:** 205 lbs.
Bats: left **Throws:** left
Acquired: Third-round pick in 6/81 free-agent draft

PLAYER SUMMARY	
Fantasy Value	$20 to $25
Card Value	40¢ to $1.00
Will	smack clutch hits
Can't	show old speed
Expect	batting crown
Don't Expect	home runs

The six-time batting champ got off to the best start of his career in 1996, but injuries soon intervened. Gwynn missed 31 games with a frayed right Achilles tendon and had to wear two pairs of special shoes (one for hitting, one for fielding) to alleviate pain in his heel. An aggressive hitter who makes exceptional contact, he murders righties but does his best batting in pressure spots and with men in scoring position. Added pounds have negated Gwynn's old speed (he once stole 56 bases in a season). Despite his foot problems, Gwynn still steals in double digits but picks his spots carefully. The five-time Gold Glover still gets good jumps and catches everything he reaches.

Major League Batting Register

	BA	G	AB	R	H	2B	3B	HR	RBI	SB
82 NL	.289	54	190	33	55	12	2	1	17	8
83 NL	.309	86	304	34	94	12	2	1	37	7
84 NL	.351	158	606	88	213	21	10	5	71	33
85 NL	.317	154	622	90	197	29	5	6	46	14
86 NL	.329	160	642	107	211	33	7	14	59	37
87 NL	.370	157	589	119	218	36	13	7	54	56
88 NL	.313	133	521	64	163	22	5	7	70	26
89 NL	.336	158	604	82	203	27	7	4	62	40
90 NL	.309	141	573	79	177	29	10	4	72	17
91 NL	.317	134	530	69	168	27	11	4	62	8
92 NL	.317	128	520	77	165	27	3	6	41	3
93 NL	.358	122	489	70	175	41	3	7	59	14
94 NL	.394	110	419	79	165	35	1	12	64	5
95 NL	.368	135	535	82	197	33	1	9	90	17
96 NL	.353	116	451	67	159	27	2	3	50	11
Life	.3371946	7595	1140	2560	411	82	90	854	296
3 Ave	.373	141	548	90	204	38	2	10	80	12

CHIP HALE

Position: Second base
Team: Los Angeles Dodgers
Born: Dec. 2, 1964 Santa Clara, CA
Height: 5'11" **Weight:** 191 lbs.
Bats: left **Throws:** right
Acquired: Signed as a free agent, 11/96

PLAYER SUMMARY	
Fantasy Value	$0
Card Value	4¢ to 7¢
Will	produce in pinch
Can't	add much defense
Expect	hits under pressure
Don't Expect	patience, power

Hale is an outstanding pinch hitter who likes to swing the bat. He rarely walks, fans, hits a home run, or steals a base. A first-pitch, fastball hitter, Hale is especially potent against right-handed pitchers. But he actually had a higher mark against lefties, albeit in fewer at bats, for the last three years. Hale was in a groove all year, especially in games at the Metrodome. He is a better batter on artificial turf and is also in top form in late-inning pressure spots and with men in scoring position. The University of Arizona graduate is best defensively at second. He led several minor leagues in chances, putouts, assists, double plays, and fielding percentage at that position. Despite those stats, his range, hands, and arm are below average. While he'll do as a fill-in, Hale can't hope to play every day. Versatility keeps him in the majors as much as his pinch-hitting prowess; Hale has done everything but catch since turning pro.

Major League Batting Register

	BA	G	AB	R	H	2B	3B	HR	RBI	SB
89 AL	.209	28	67	6	14	3	0	0	4	0
90 AL	.000	1	2	0	0	0	0	0	2	0
93 AL	.333	69	186	25	62	6	1	3	27	2
94 AL	.263	67	118	13	31	9	0	1	11	0
95 AL	.262	69	103	10	27	4	0	2	18	0
96 AL	.276	85	87	8	24	5	0	1	16	0
Life	.281	319	563	62	158	27	1	7	78	2

DARREN HALL

Position: Pitcher
Team: Los Angeles Dodgers
Born: July 14, 1964 Marysville, OH
Height: 6'3" **Weight:** 205 lbs.
Bats: right **Throws:** right
Acquired: Signed as a free agent, 11/95

PLAYER SUMMARY	
Fantasy Value	$0
Card Value	4¢ to 7¢
Will	hit comeback trail
Can't	reclaim closer job
Expect	Ks, groundouts
Don't Expect	runners to score

Hall spent most of last season on the sidelines after undergoing surgery to repair a torn muscle in his right elbow. That was a devastating blow to the 32-year-old right-hander, who spent eight years in the minors before getting his first shot at big-league hitters. A sinker-slider pitcher who uses his curve as a changeup, Hall gets lots of ground balls when he keeps his pitches low in the zone. But he's also a power pitcher who twice had more Ks than innings pitched in the minors. Hall, whose heavy fastball peaks in the low 90s, had 17 saves as the surprise rookie closer of the 1994 Blue Jays. With only three blown opportunities that summer, he led the AL with a conversion rate of 85 percent. Hall's success stems from a combination of control and an ability to keep the ball in the park. He's also adept at stranding most of the runners he inherits. Hall offers average defense and a so-so pickoff move. He made 30 starts in the minors with mixed results. Except for three seasons as a closer, he's been primarily a set-up man.

Major League Pitching Register

	W	L	ERA	G	S	IP	H	ER	BB	SO
94 AL	2	3	3.41	30	17	31.2	26	12	14	28
95 AL	0	2	4.41	17	3	16.1	21	8	9	11
96 NL	0	2	6.00	9	0	12.0	13	8	5	12
Life	2	7	4.20	56	20	60.0	60	28	28	51

BOB HAMELIN

Position: Designated hitter
Team: Kansas City Royals
Born: Nov. 29, 1967 Elizabeth, NJ
Height: 6' **Weight:** 235 lbs.
Bats: left **Throws:** left
Acquired: Second-round pick in 6/88 free-agent draft

PLAYER SUMMARY	
Fantasy Value	$5 to $7
Card Value	5¢ to 8¢
Will	seek rookie form
Can't	hit southpaws
Expect	patience, power
Don't Expect	much defense

Like the Pied Piper, Hamelin was an instant hero whose aura quickly evaporated. The 1994 AL Rookie of the Year, he's battled coaches, weight problems, left-handed pitchers, and assorted other demons in the two years since. Only a good batting eye kept Hamelin from disappearing last summer. He walked almost as often as he fanned, pushing his on-base percentage an amazing 140 points above his batting average. Platooned as the DH, Hamelin hardly ever hit against lefties. And when he did, he hardly hit. Projected as the Royals' regular first baseman, he lasted only a month before Jose Offerman and Kevin Young pushed him back to DH. Being supplanted by Offerman may not be the world's biggest insult, but it's close. At 29, Hamelin looks older than he really is. His unhappy experience in Kansas City may be part of the problem, but most of his woes seem self-inflicted. Hamelin's best bet is to hope a power-hungry expansion team snaps him up in November.

Major League Batting Register

	BA	G	AB	R	H	2B	3B	HR	RBI	SB
93 AL	.224	16	49	2	11	3	0	2	5	0
94 AL	.282	101	312	64	88	25	1	24	65	4
95 AL	.168	72	208	20	35	7	1	7	25	0
96 AL	.255	89	239	31	61	14	1	9	40	5
Life	.241	278	808	117	195	49	3	42	135	9
3 Ave	.246	104	304	48	75	19	1	17	53	4

DARRYL HAMILTON

Position: Outfield
Team: Texas Rangers
Born: Dec. 3, 1964 Baton Rouge, LA
Height: 6'1" **Weight:** 180 lbs.
Bats: left **Throws:** right
Acquired: Signed as a free agent, 12/95

PLAYER SUMMARY	
Fantasy Value	$9 to $11
Card Value	5¢ to 8¢
Will	get things going
Can't	make strong throws
Expect	patience, contact
Don't Expect	errors, home runs

One of the biggest reasons for the Rangers' defensive strength last year was the off-season signing of Hamilton. Although the transaction generated a yawn when it was announced, the former Milwaukee center fielder anchored the Texas outfield while providing proper table-setting at the top of the lineup. One of the most sure-handed outfielders in the game, Hamilton spent most of the year leading the AL with most chances and least errors. He gets great jumps, shows good range, and has soft hands. Though he's been criticized for his mediocre arm, his accuracy compensates for lack of strength. With a bat in his hands, Hamilton provides more power but less speed than Otis Nixon, his predecessor. A better overall hitter, Hamilton mixes patience with contact, walking almost as often as he fans. Hamilton hits at least 20 doubles a year, twice his combined total of triples and homers. But he gets the job done at the top of the lineup.

Major League Batting Register

	BA	G	AB	R	H	2B	3B	HR	RBI	SB
88 AL	.184	44	103	14	19	4	0	1	11	7
90 AL	.295	89	156	27	46	5	0	1	18	10
91 AL	.311	122	405	64	126	15	6	1	57	16
92 AL	.298	128	470	67	140	19	7	5	62	41
93 AL	.310	135	520	74	161	21	1	9	48	21
94 AL	.262	36	141	23	37	10	1	1	13	3
95 AL	.271	112	398	54	108	20	6	5	44	11
96 AL	.293	148	627	94	184	29	4	6	51	15
Life	.291	814	2820	417	821	123	25	29	304	124
2 Ave	.284	137	537	77	153	26	5	6	50	14

JOEY HAMILTON

Position: Pitcher
Team: San Diego Padres
Born: Sept. 9, 1970 Statesboro, GA
Height: 6'4" **Weight:** 220 lbs.
Bats: right **Throws:** right
Acquired: First-round pick in 6/91 free-agent draft

PLAYER SUMMARY	
Fantasy Value	$14 to $17
Card Value	7¢ to 10¢
Will	lead the staff
Can't	swing the bat
Expect	quick games
Don't Expect	gopher plague

In 1996, his second full season, Hamilton emerged as the ace of the San Diego rotation. Though slowed by a sore shoulder in July, he was the first Padre to reach a dozen wins. Three were complete games, and one was a shutout. Hamilton yields fewer hits than innings, fans eight per game, and shows respectable control (3½ walks per nine innings). A sinker-slider pitcher who also throws a cut fastball, curve, and changeup, Hamilton gets lots of groundouts. Hamilton throws a few gopher balls but compensates with a strikeout-to-walk ratio that is better than 2-to-1. He helps himself with his defense, but his former success at keeping runners close went the wrong way last season. Despite his decent pickoff move, three of every four runners who challenged him last year succeeded. Hamilton's hitting is nothing to write home about, but it's better than it once was. He broke in with an 0-for-57 streak believed to be a big-league record for ineptitude. The big right-hander was a second-team All-American at Georgia Southern.

Major League Pitching Register

	W	L	ERA	G	CG	IP	H	ER	BB	SO
94 NL	9	6	2.98	16	1	108.2	98	36	29	61
95 NL	6	9	3.08	31	2	204.1	189	70	56	123
96 NL	15	9	4.17	34	3	211.2	206	98	83	184
Life	30	24	3.50	81	6	524.2	493	204	168	368
3 Ave	11	9	3.44	30	2	198.1	186	76	62	136

133

CHRIS HAMMOND

Position: Pitcher
Team: Boston Red Sox
Born: Jan. 21, 1966 Atlanta, GA
Height: 6' **Weight:** 190 lbs.
Bats: left **Throws:** left
Acquired: Signed as a free agent, 12/96

PLAYER SUMMARY	
Fantasy Value	$0
Card Value	4¢ to 7¢
Will	work best in pen
Can't	stop injury wave
Expect	strong first half
Don't Expect	control trouble

Hammond has had it with injuries. In the last three seasons, he's battled a bad back, an inner-ear infection, shoulder tendinitis, a strained side muscle, and a biceps problem. Being a commuter to the DL is not conducive to establishing consistency as a pitcher. Last year, Hammond began as a starter, then bounced in and out of the pen. A lifelong starter, he may have found his niche in relief. At one point, he was 2-6 with a 10.60 ERA as a starter but was 3-1 with a 1.32 ERA from the bullpen. Hammond's best pitch is a slow changeup he camouflages with a sinker, slider, and curve. He averages two walks per nine frames and 2½ Ks per walk. Hammond hurled 24 consecutive scoreless innings in 1994, a Florida club record. Hammond helps himself with an exceptional pickoff move that few runners challenge. But he's even better with a bat: He not only meets the ball but hits it hard.

Major League Pitching Register

	W	L	ERA	G	S	IP	H	ER	BB	SO
90 NL	0	2	6.35	3	0	11.1	13	8	12	4
91 NL	7	7	4.06	20	0	99.2	92	45	48	50
92 NL	7	10	4.21	28	0	147.1	149	69	55	79
93 NL	11	12	4.66	32	0	191.0	207	99	66	108
94 NL	4	4	3.07	13	0	73.1	79	25	23	40
95 NL	9	6	3.80	25	0	161.0	157	68	47	126
96 NL	5	8	6.56	38	0	81.0	104	59	27	50
Life	43	49	4.39	159	0	764.2	801	373	278	457
3 Ave	7	7	4.20	28	0	122.1	131	57	37	83

JEFFREY HAMMONDS

Position: Outfield
Team: Baltimore Orioles
Born: March 5, 1971 Plainfield, NJ
Height: 6' **Weight:** 195 lbs.
Bats: right **Throws:** right
Acquired: First-round pick in 6/92 free-agent draft

PLAYER SUMMARY	
Fantasy Value	$3 to $5
Card Value	5¢ to 8¢
Will	enjoy big future
Can't	wait for walks
Expect	speed, range
Don't Expect	injury-free year

Hammonds is still trying to realize the potential that made him a two-time All-American at Stanford, a member of the U.S. Olympic team, and the fourth man selected in the 1992 amateur draft. The first player from the '92 draft class to reach the majors, Hammonds hit .305 in a 33-game trial with the Orioles a year later. But injuries have since interfered. Hammonds has had knee surgery, neck and shoulder problems, a wrist injury, concussion, and several knee sprains. As a result, he has spent most of the last three years on the DL, on the bench, or in the minors. At 26, he's still considered a five-tools player with 30-30 potential. But the jury remains out on his future. Although the raw talent is there, aspects of Hammonds's game need refining. Anxious to make up for lost time, he's impatient at the plate, swinging at bad pitches and trying to pull everything. If he worked his way on base with walks, he could use his speed to steal and score frequently. In the field, Hammonds has fine range but a weak arm.

Major League Batting Register

	BA	G	AB	R	H	2B	3B	HR	RBI	SB
93 AL	.305	33	105	10	32	8	0	3	19	4
94 AL	.296	68	250	45	74	18	2	8	31	5
95 AL	.242	57	178	18	43	9	1	4	23	4
96 AL	.226	71	248	38	56	10	1	9	27	3
Life	.262	229	781	111	205	45	4	24	100	16
3 Ave	.261	77	267	41	70	15	2	8	32	5

MIKE HAMPTON

Position: Pitcher
Team: Houston Astros
Born: Sept. 9, 1972 Brooksville, FL
Height: 5'10" **Weight:** 190 lbs.
Bats: right **Throws:** left
Acquired: Traded by Mariners with Mike Felder for Eric Anthony, 12/93

PLAYER SUMMARY	
Fantasy Value	$10 to $13
Card Value	5¢ to 8¢
Will	post winning record
Can't	rack up strikeouts
Expect	good bat, glove
Don't Expect	runners to steal

Hampton fits the image of the classic finesse pitcher. He has good control of four pitches, keeps the ball in the park, and controls the running game, but he averages fewer than six strikeouts per game. Hampton's best pitch is a slurve, a hybrid that is part slider and part curve. His repertoire also includes a cut fastball and a changeup. When his location is especially sharp, the results are impressive. Hampton yields fewer than three walks per nine innings. That helps him keep baserunners to a minimum, since he also averages nearly ten hits over the same span. Because he's not a power pitcher, Hampton needs help from his infielders. He also helps himself with his glove and his pickoff ability. Only six of the first 11 basestealers who challenged him last year made it. That ratio represented a definite improvement for Hampton, once an easy mark for runners. A good bunter, Hampton also compiled a respectable batting average last year. He was slowed in September by a bout with shoulder tendinitis.

Major League Pitching Register

	W	L	ERA	G	CG	IP	H	ER	BB	SO
93 AL	1	3	9.53	13	0	17.0	28	18	17	8
94 NL	2	1	3.70	44	0	41.1	46	17	16	24
95 NL	9	8	3.35	24	0	150.2	141	56	49	115
96 NL	10	10	3.59	27	2	160.1	175	64	49	101
Life	22	22	3.78	108	2	369.1	390	155	131	248
3 Ave	8	7	3.50	39	1	129.1	133	50	42	88

CHRIS HANEY

Position: Pitcher
Team: Kansas City Royals
Born: Nov. 16, 1968 Baltimore, MD
Height: 6'3" **Weight:** 195 lbs.
Bats: left **Throws:** left
Acquired: Traded by Expos with Bill Sampen for Sean Berry and Archie Corbin, 8/92

PLAYER SUMMARY	
Fantasy Value	$5 to $7
Card Value	5¢ to 8¢
Will	throw strikes
Can't	show velocity
Expect	sidearm style
Don't Expect	control trouble

Although Haney was a regular member of the 1996 K.C. rotation, he wasn't always reliable. He opened the year by dropping four straight, then forged a four-game winning streak two months later. Haney's control is impeccable: He averages fewer than two walks per nine frames. But he can't find the sunny side of .500 because he yields too many hits and homers. Haney, a sinker-slider pitcher whose repertoire includes a slider, curveball, and nonsinking fastball, wins when he pitches inside. The sneaky-fast sidearmer held left-handed hitters below the Mendoza Line in 1995 but was less successful last summer. He's one of the best at coaxing the double-play grounder. The UNC-Charlotte product runs and reacts well; he's been used as a pinch runner. Quick off the mound, he uses soft hands to scoop up infield rollers. Haney also has a well-developed pickoff move. The son of former catcher Larry Haney is clearly over his 1995 back problems.

Major League Pitching Register

	W	L	ERA	G	CG	IP	H	ER	BB	SO
91 NL	3	7	4.04	16	0	84.2	94	38	43	51
92 NL	2	3	5.45	9	1	38.0	40	23	10	27
92 AL	2	3	3.86	7	1	42.0	35	18	16	27
93 AL	9	9	6.02	23	1	124.0	141	83	53	65
94 AL	2	2	7.31	6	0	28.1	36	23	11	18
95 AL	3	4	3.65	16	1	81.1	78	33	33	31
96 AL	10	14	4.70	35	4	228.0	267	119	51	115
Life	31	42	4.84	112	8	626.1	691	337	217	334
2 Ave	7	9	4.40	27	3	160.1	177	78	44	75

DAVE HANSEN

Position: Third base
Team: Los Angeles Dodgers
Born: Nov. 24, 1968 Long Beach, CA
Height: 6' **Weight:** 180 lbs.
Bats: left **Throws:** right
Acquired: Second-round pick in 6/86 free-agent draft

PLAYER SUMMARY	
Fantasy Value	$0
Card Value	4¢ to 7¢
Will	pinch-hit often
Can't	hit left-handers
Expect	walks, base hits
Don't Expect	the long ball

A true baseball specialist, Hansen's high value as a pinch hitter is his ticket to a major-league job. Though he pinch-hit more than 50 times last year, he started only a handful of games—most of them at third base. He also filled in at first. Hansen is an aggressive left-handed hitter who makes almost all his appearances against right-handers. He's a singles hitter who rarely rips the ball over the wall. A contact hitter with patience, Hansen usually walks more than he fans (though not last year). He doesn't run well and has stolen only one base in his career. If not for chronic back problems, he could play more often in the field. Hansen has quick reactions, soft hands, and a strong arm. He even led several leagues in chances, putouts, assists, double plays, and fielding percentage. Hansen has played every position but catcher and pitcher since turning pro in 1986, when he was the Dodgers' second-round draft choice.

Major League Batting Register

	BA	G	AB	R	H	2B	3B	HR	RBI	SB
90 NL	.143	5	7	0	1	0	0	0	1	0
91 NL	.268	53	56	3	15	4	0	1	5	1
92 NL	.214	132	341	30	73	11	0	6	22	0
93 NL	.362	84	105	13	38	3	0	4	30	0
94 NL	.341	40	44	3	15	3	0	0	5	0
95 NL	.287	100	181	19	52	10	0	1	14	0
96 NL	.221	80	104	7	23	1	0	0	6	0
Life	.259	494	838	75	217	32	0	12	83	1

ERIK HANSON

Position: Pitcher
Team: Toronto Blue Jays
Born: May 18, 1965 Kinnelon, NJ
Height: 6'6" **Weight:** 210 lbs.
Bats: right **Throws:** right
Acquired: Signed as a free agent, 12/95

PLAYER SUMMARY	
Fantasy Value	$6 to $8
Card Value	5¢ to 8¢
Will	engineer comeback
Can't	count on velocity
Expect	improved control
Don't Expect	additional injuries

Judging by his 1996 performance, it's hard to believe Hanson made the All-Star Team in 1995. Everything went wrong last year: too many walks, too many hits, too many home runs, too many wild pitches, and a bloated ERA. A muscle strain of the right forearm prevented Hanson from throwing his trademark curveball, and the former Wake Forest All-American simply wilted last year. He put so many runners on base that disaster was preordained. The one-time power pitcher has had serious shoulder, elbow, and knee problems, so he now relies on finesse, location, and a deceptive delivery. He averages six strikeouts per game with his fastball, changeup, overhand curve, and a unique hybrid that is part slider and part cut fastball. Because of the curve and change, Hanson usually has more success against lefties. He provides strong defense and a potent pickoff move. At 31, Hanson should be able to forge a fresh start.

Major League Pitching Register

	W	L	ERA	G	CG	IP	H	ER	BB	SO
88 AL	2	3	3.24	6	0	41.2	35	15	12	36
89 AL	9	5	3.18	17	1	113.1	103	40	32	75
90 AL	18	9	3.24	33	5	236.0	205	85	68	211
91 AL	8	8	3.81	27	2	174.2	182	74	56	143
92 AL	8	17	4.82	31	6	186.2	209	100	57	112
93 AL	11	12	3.47	31	7	215.0	215	83	60	163
94 AL	5	5	4.11	22	0	122.2	137	56	23	101
95 AL	15	5	4.24	29	1	186.2	187	88	59	139
96 AL	13	17	5.41	35	4	214.2	243	129	102	156
Life	89	81	4.04	231	26	1491.1	1516	670	469	1136
3 Ave	12	10	4.62	33	2	199.0	215	102	67	152

PETE HARNISCH

Position: Pitcher
Team: New York Mets
Born: Sept. 23, 1966 Commack, NY
Height: 6' **Weight:** 207 lbs.
Bats: right **Throws:** right
Acquired: Traded by Astros for Andy Beckerman, 12/94

PLAYER SUMMARY	
Fantasy Value	$6 to $8
Card Value	4¢ to 7¢
Will	continue comeback
Can't	avoid gophers
Expect	good control
Don't Expect	nailed runners

Will the real Pete Harnisch please stand up? For the last three years, the Fordham product has floundered, either pitching with shoulder pain or trying to prove healed from August 1995 surgery. He got off to a dreadful start last year before gradually showing flashes of his former self. A control pitcher who yields 2½ walks per game, Harnisch gets hit when he catches too much of the plate. He yields a hit per inning, but many of those go a long way. No longer the power pitcher he once was, Harnisch averages 5½ Ks per game. He has good command of a fastball, cut fastball, slider, slow curve, and change. Harnisch helps his own cause with his fielding, bunting, and even his hitting but has trouble holding runners close. They ran at will against him last year. Harnisch was Baltimore's sandwich pick in the 1987 amateur draft and reached the majors a year later.

Major League Pitching Register

	W	L	ERA	G	CG	IP	H	ER	BB	SO
88 AL	0	2	5.54	2	0	13.0	13	8	9	10
89 AL	5	9	4.62	18	2	103.1	97	53	64	70
90 AL	11	11	4.34	31	3	188.2	189	91	86	122
91 NL	12	9	2.70	33	4	216.2	169	65	83	172
92 NL	9	10	3.70	34	0	206.2	182	85	64	164
93 NL	16	9	2.98	33	5	217.2	171	72	79	185
94 NL	8	5	5.40	17	1	95.0	100	57	39	62
95 NL	2	8	3.68	18	0	110.0	111	45	24	82
96 NL	8	12	4.21	31	2	194.2	195	91	61	114
Life	71	75	3.79	217	17	1345.2	1227	567	509	981
3 Ave	7	9	4.42	25	1	151.1	154	74	48	98

LENNY HARRIS

Position: Infield
Team: Cincinnati Reds
Born: Oct. 28, 1964 Miami, FL
Height: 5'10" **Weight:** 195 lbs.
Bats: left **Throws:** right
Acquired: Signed as a free agent, 11/93

PLAYER SUMMARY	
Fantasy Value	$1
Card Value	4¢ to 7¢
Will	play anywhere
Can't	wait for walks
Expect	speed, contact
Don't Expect	great glove

One of baseball's most versatile handymen, Harris played everywhere but catcher, pitcher, and shortstop for the 1996 Reds. He topped 20 appearances at both third base and left field but served more than 40 times as a pinch hitter. A left-handed contact hitter with more speed than patience, Harris produces just a few more walks than stolen bases. Usually more productive against righties, that was not the case last year. A singles hitter with some power, Harris is much more likely to drop a bunt or rip a double than slug a home run. He finished the season with personal peaks in doubles and homers, but no one is about to compare him with Kevin Mitchell, the man with whom he shared left field. Because of his speed, Harris has good range. But he lacks soft hands and a strong arm. Defensively, his best position is DH, with left field a close second. He's more reliable than Mitchell with a glove, but that's no endorsement.

Major League Batting Register

	BA	G	AB	R	H	2B	3B	HR	RBI	SB
88 NL	.372	16	43	7	16	1	0	0	8	4
89 NL	.236	115	335	36	79	10	1	3	26	14
90 NL	.304	137	431	61	131	16	4	2	29	15
91 NL	.287	145	429	59	123	16	1	3	38	12
92 NL	.271	135	347	28	94	11	0	0	30	19
93 NL	.237	107	160	20	38	6	1	2	11	3
94 NL	.310	66	100	13	31	3	1	0	14	7
95 NL	.208	101	197	32	41	8	3	2	16	10
96 NL	.285	125	302	33	86	17	2	5	32	14
Life	.273	947	2344	289	639	88	13	17	204	98
2 Ave	.252	119	262	35	66	13	3	4	25	13

137

BRYAN HARVEY

Position: Pitcher
Team: Anaheim Angels
Born: June 2, 1963 Chattanooga, TN
Height: 6'2" **Weight:** 215 lbs.
Bats: right **Throws:** right
Acquired: Signed as a free agent, 12/95

PLAYER SUMMARY	
Fantasy Value	$1
Card Value	4¢ to 7¢
Will	try to prove sound
Can't	think about elbow
Expect	many strikeouts
Don't Expect	total comeback

Harvey remains one of baseball's biggest enigmas. Although he saved 45 games in one season and 46 in another—making the All-Star Team both times—he also missed three straight seasons with lingering elbow problems that required surgical repair. When healthy, he's a fastball-forkball pitcher with exceptional control. He yields few hits and few homers while fanning considerably more than a strikeout per inning. But too many forkballs have exacted a high price. The man with the Fu Manchu mustache and icy stare turns 34 in June, but his arm seems considerably older. When healthy, Harvey is widely considered to rank on the same plane with Mark Wohlers and Troy Percival—other closers who intimidate batters with searing late-inning heat. His value is undisputed. Harvey's best hope may be further expansion. Someone is almost certain to take a flyer on the once-feared closer in the hope his elbow has healed.

Major League Pitching Register

	W	L	ERA	G	S	IP	H	ER	BB	SO
87 AL	0	0	0.00	3	0	5.0	6	0	2	3
88 AL	7	5	2.13	50	17	76.0	59	18	20	67
89 AL	3	3	3.44	51	25	55.0	36	21	41	78
90 AL	4	4	3.22	54	25	64.1	45	23	35	82
91 AL	2	4	1.60	67	46	78.2	51	14	17	101
92 AL	0	4	2.83	25	13	28.2	22	9	11	34
93 NL	1	5	1.70	59	45	69.0	45	13	13	73
94 NL	0	0	5.23	12	6	10.1	12	6	4	10
95 NL	0	0	0.00	1	0	0.0	2	3	1	0
Life	17	25	2.49	322	177	387.0	278	107	144	448

LATROY HAWKINS

Position: Pitcher
Team: Minnesota Twins
Born: Dec. 21, 1972 Gary, IN
Height: 6'5" **Weight:** 193 lbs.
Bats: right **Throws:** right
Acquired: Seventh-round pick in 6/91 free-agent draft

PLAYER SUMMARY	
Fantasy Value	$1 to $3
Card Value	5¢ to 8¢
Will	realize promise
Can't	stay in minors
Expect	lively fastball
Don't Expect	poor control

This is make-or-break time for Hawkins. He's hung around at the Triple-A level for three years, improving his performance each time, but he's blown several shots at a varsity job. That's unbecoming for the skinny but hard-throwing right-hander, who answers to the nickname "Satch" (as in Paige). A hard worker with good control, Hawkins had a 3-1 ratio of strikeouts to walks in the minors last year. He yielded a hit per inning and kept the ball in the park. The gopher ball has never been a problem for Hawkins, even when he made 22 Triple-A starts in 1995. His ticket to the majors is a low-90s fastball with good movement. He also throws a curveball and a slider that devours right-handed hitters. Scouts rated him Minnesota's third-best prospect in a 1996 *Baseball America* poll. Hawkins, who turned down an Indiana State basketball scholarship to sign with the Twins in 1991, is projected as a future No. 1 starter. But first he'll have to make the staff. Hawkins once led the Midwest League in wins, shutouts, strikeouts, and ERA. He was a seventh-round choice in the '91 draft.

Major League Pitching Register

	W	L	ERA	G	CG	IP	H	ER	BB	SO
95 AL	2	3	8.67	6	1	27.0	39	26	12	9
96 AL	1	1	8.20	7	0	26.1	42	24	9	24
Life	3	4	8.44	13	1	53.1	81	50	21	33

CHARLIE HAYES

Position: Third base
Team: New York Yankees
Born: May 29, 1965 Hattiesburg, MS
Height: 6′ **Weight:** 205 lbs.
Bats: right **Throws:** right
Acquired: Traded by Pirates for Chris Corn, 8/96

PLAYER SUMMARY	
Fantasy Value	$7 to $9
Card Value	5¢ to 8¢
Will	hit a dozen homers
Can't	avoid double plays
Expect	best bat vs. lefties
Don't Expect	high batting mark

The Hayes career record reads like a railroad timetable. San Francisco. Philadelphia. New York. Colorado. Philadelphia again. Pittsburgh. The Bronx again. Hayes never knows where he'll suit up or how often he'll play. He found himself the center of unwanted controversy when he reported to the Yankees in midseason. Incumbent third baseman Wade Boggs, an All-Star who had been struggling against left-handers, denounced the deal. But Hayes hit southpaws better than Boggs did last season. A fastball hitter who's learned some patience, Hayes fans twice per walk but draws some passes as well. He has some power and has learned to go with the pitch. Because he hits the ball hard, Hayes bangs into numerous double plays. He uses his speed most often in the field. He has quick reactions, soft hands, and a strong but unreliable arm.

Major League Batting Register

	BA	G	AB	R	H	2B	3B	HR	RBI	SB
88 NL	.091	7	11	0	1	0	0	0	0	0
89 NL	.257	87	304	26	78	15	1	8	43	3
90 NL	.258	152	561	56	145	20	0	10	57	4
91 NL	.230	142	460	34	106	23	1	12	53	3
92 AL	.257	142	509	52	131	19	2	18	66	3
93 NL	.305	157	573	89	175	45	2	25	98	11
94 NL	.288	113	423	46	122	23	4	10	50	3
95 NL	.276	141	529	58	146	30	3	11	85	5
96 NL	.248	128	459	51	114	21	2	10	62	6
96 AL	.284	20	67	7	19	3	0	2	13	0
Life	.266	1089	3896	419	1037	199	15	106	527	38
3 Ave	.273	149	550	60	150	29	4	12	76	5

JIMMY HAYNES

Position: Pitcher
Team: Baltimore Orioles
Born: Sept. 5, 1972 LaGrange, GA
Height: 6′4″ **Weight:** 185 lbs.
Bats: right **Throws:** right
Acquired: Seventh-round pick in 6/91 free-agent draft

PLAYER SUMMARY	
Fantasy Value	$2 to $4
Card Value	5¢ to 8¢
Will	bank on heat
Can't	find control
Expect	another shot
Don't Expect	bad glove

Armed with consecutive minor-league strikeout crowns, Haynes was expected to break into the 1996 Baltimore rotation. He did, but he didn't last. Plagued by nerves and control trouble, he struggled against big-league hitters, spent time in the bullpen, and even returned to the minors for more seasoning. Despite those setbacks, the lanky right-hander remains a blue-chip prospect. Haynes throws a 90-mph fastball, two types of curves, and a changeup. His minor-league ratios of hits-to-innings and strikeouts-to-walks were encouraging. Sometimes compared to Orel Hershiser because of his size and pitching style, Haynes is highly regarded by baseball scouts. They told *Baseball America* last February that Haynes was the No. 2 prospect in the Orioles organization. He's quick, aggressive, and agile on the mound, fielding his position well and holding opposing baserunners. He has a fine move for a right-handed pitcher. Once his own worst enemy, Haynes has also learned the advantages of self-control. He's certain to get an extended opportunity to prove himself.

Major League Pitching Register

	W	L	ERA	G	S	IP	H	ER	BB	SO
95 AL	2	1	2.25	4	0	24.0	11	6	12	22
96 AL	3	6	8.29	26	1	89.0	122	82	58	65
Life	5	7	7.01	30	1	113.0	133	88	70	87

139

RICKEY HENDERSON

Position: Outfield
Team: San Diego Padres
Born: Dec. 25, 1958 Chicago, IL
Height: 5'10" **Weight:** 190 lbs.
Bats: right **Throws:** left
Acquired: Signed as a free agent, 12/95

PLAYER SUMMARY	
Fantasy Value	$14 to $17
Card Value	8¢ to 12¢
Will	set table
Can't	find former power
Expect	steals, defense
Don't Expect	bad BB/K ratio

At 38, Henderson is still a formidable force. Last year, his first in the NL, he topped 100 walks and ranked among the league leaders in on-base percentage. The career- and single-season leader in stolen bases, Henderson also holds the major-league record for most years leading a league in that department (11). He is a great leadoff man not only because of his speed but also because of his power. Henderson is best in clutch situations and with men in scoring position. Because his arm is known more for accuracy than strength, Henderson is best in left field. But he played all three spots last year. His trophy shelf holds a Gold Glove and an MVP Award.

Major League Batting Register

	BA	G	AB	R	H	2B	3B	HR	RBI	SB
79 AL	.274	89	351	49	96	13	3	1	26	33
80 AL	.303	158	591	111	179	22	4	9	53	100
81 AL	.319	108	423	89	135	18	7	6	35	56
82 AL	.267	149	536	119	143	24	4	10	51	130
83 AL	.292	145	513	105	150	25	7	9	48	108
84 AL	.293	142	502	113	147	27	4	16	58	66
85 AL	.314	143	547	146	172	28	5	24	72	80
86 AL	.263	153	608	130	160	31	5	28	74	87
87 AL	.291	95	358	78	104	17	3	17	37	41
88 AL	.305	140	554	118	169	30	2	6	50	93
89 AL	.274	150	541	113	148	26	3	12	57	77
90 AL	.325	136	489	119	159	33	3	28	61	65
91 AL	.268	134	470	105	126	17	1	18	57	58
92 AL	.283	117	396	77	112	18	3	15	46	48
93 AL	.289	134	481	114	139	22	2	21	59	53
94 AL	.260	87	296	66	77	13	0	6	20	22
95 AL	.300	112	407	67	122	31	1	9	54	32
96 NL	.241	148	465	110	112	17	2	9	29	37
Life	.287	2340	8528	1829	2450	412	59	244	887	1186
3 Ave	.267	132	447	93	119	23	1	9	39	35

MIKE HENNEMAN

Position: Pitcher
Team: Texas Rangers
Born: Dec. 11, 1961 St. Charles, MO
Height: 6'4" **Weight:** 205 lbs.
Bats: right **Throws:** right
Acquired: Signed as a free agent, 12/95

PLAYER SUMMARY	
Fantasy Value	$15 to $18
Card Value	4¢ to 7¢
Will	seek comeback
Can't	stifle lefty bats
Expect	Ks, grounders
Don't Expect	extended skid

Henneman reached a career peak in saves but was bombed more often than Baghdad. He almost doubled his previous nine-year ERA of 3.05, yielded almost as many hits as innings, and struggled with his control (four walks per nine frames). Lefties lit him up, nearly half his inherited runners scored, and he got acquainted with the gopher ball after yielding just one in 50 appearances the year before. Henneman did have his moments: He had a club-record ten saves in May, survived a mild slump, then regained his form after the All-Star break. Though the big right-hander fans more than seven per nine innings, his pitches produce numerous grounders when he has good location. A sinker-slider pitcher whose best pitch is a forkball, Henneman varies his delivery from three-quarters to sidearm. His quick release bothers baserunners, who rarely try to steal against him.

Major League Pitching Register

	W	L	ERA	G	S	IP	H	ER	BB	SO
87 AL	11	3	2.98	55	7	96.2	86	32	30	75
88 AL	9	6	1.87	65	22	91.1	72	19	24	58
89 AL	11	4	3.70	60	8	90.0	84	37	51	69
90 AL	8	6	3.05	69	22	94.1	90	32	33	50
91 AL	10	2	2.88	60	21	84.1	81	27	34	61
92 AL	2	6	3.96	60	24	77.1	75	34	20	58
93 AL	5	3	2.64	63	24	71.2	69	21	32	58
94 AL	1	3	5.19	30	8	34.2	43	20	17	27
95 NL	0	1	1.53	29	18	29.1	24	5	9	24
95 NL	0	1	3.00	21	8	21.0	21	7	4	19
96 AL	0	7	5.79	49	31	42.0	41	27	17	34
Life	57	42	3.21	561	193	732.2	686	261	271	533
2 Ave	1	6	5.47	46	21	45.1	51	28	20	36

BUTCH HENRY

Position: Pitcher
Team: Boston Red Sox
Born: Oct. 7, 1968 El Paso, TX
Height: 6'1" **Weight:** 195 lbs.
Bats: right **Throws:** left
Acquired: Claimed from Expos on waivers, 11/95

PLAYER SUMMARY	
Fantasy Value	$1
Card Value	5¢ to 8¢
Will	work from stretch
Can't	rely on velocity
Expect	comeback year
Don't Expect	wobbly control

After establishing his reputation as a reliable starting pitcher, Henry missed the last six weeks of the 1995 season and all of 1996 after surgical repair of a torn left medial collateral ligament. If he proves healthy at 28, he should pick up where he left off. Henry had put together two strong seasons in the Montreal rotation before the shoulder acted up. When healthy, he's a sinker-slider pitcher who also throws a curveball and a changeup (his best pitch). Henry became a control artist three years ago when he lowered the arm angle in his no-windup, three-quarters delivery. He usually allows a hit per inning and keeps the ball in the park. Henry believes in finesse over fire, relying on well-placed pitches and maintaining a strikeout-to-walk ratio of 2-to-1. Henry helps himself with his ability to hold runners close. Only half the basestealers who challenge him succeed. Henry broke into pro ball after the Reds made him their 15th-round choice in 1987. He reached the majors five years later.

Major League Pitching Register

	W	L	ERA	G	CG	IP	H	ER	BB	SO
92 NL	6	9	4.02	28	2	165.2	185	74	41	96
93 NL	3	9	6.12	30	1	103.0	135	70	28	47
94 NL	8	3	2.43	24	0	107.1	97	29	20	70
95 NL	7	9	2.84	21	1	126.2	133	40	28	60
Life	24	30	3.81	103	4	502.2	550	213	117	273

DOUG HENRY

Position: Pitcher
Team: New York Mets
Born: Dec. 10, 1963 Sacramento, CA
Height: 6'4" **Weight:** 185 lbs.
Bats: right **Throws:** right
Acquired: Traded by Brewers for Fernando Vina and Javier Gonzalez, 11/94

PLAYER SUMMARY	
Fantasy Value	$2 to $4
Card Value	4¢ to 7¢
Will	work often
Can't	find plate
Expect	wild spells
Don't Expect	closer job

There's no particular reason why Henry was the busiest member of the Mets' bullpen last summer. He yields more hits than innings, walks more than four per nine frames, allows almost 40 percent of inherited runners to score, and doesn't control the running game. He also has trouble with first pitches and first batters. Perhaps Henry is living off the reputation he carved from 1991 to '93, when he saved 61 games as Milwaukee's closer. A sinker-slider pitcher who also throws a forkball and changeup, Henry is capable of working often. The big right-hander, who always works from the stretch, is best at getting strikeouts in key situations. He averages almost seven whiffs per nine innings. Henry also keeps gopher balls to a minimum. He stumbled last year, however, when his ratio of strikeouts to walks slipped from 3-to-1 to less than 2-to-1. Forkballs in the dirt account for his problems with wild pitches. Henry is no better than adequate in the field.

Major League Pitching Register

	W	L	ERA	G	S	IP	H	ER	BB	SO
91 AL	2	1	1.00	32	15	36.0	16	4	14	28
92 AL	1	4	4.02	68	29	65.0	64	29	24	52
93 AL	4	4	5.56	54	17	55.0	67	34	25	38
94 AL	2	3	4.60	25	0	31.1	32	16	23	20
95 NL	3	6	2.96	51	4	67.0	48	22	25	62
96 NL	2	8	4.68	58	9	75.0	82	39	36	58
Life	14	26	3.94	288	74	329.1	309	144	147	258
3 Ave	3	6	3.99	50	5	65.0	60	29	32	52

PAT HENTGEN

Position: Pitcher
Team: Toronto Blue Jays
Born: Nov. 13, 1968 Detroit, MI
Height: 6'2" **Weight:** 200 lbs.
Bats: right **Throws:** right
Acquired: Fifth-round pick in 6/86 free-agent draft

PLAYER SUMMARY	
Fantasy Value	$20 to $25
Card Value	8¢ to 12¢
Will	count on curve
Can't	avoid gophers
Expect	winning record
Don't Expect	runners to steal

Greg Maddux is Hentgen's new role model. Like Maddux, the Toronto right-hander has learned to throw the ball more easily, not harder, when he gets into trouble. The results were impressive last season as he overcame his 1995 off year. Although he's not a strikeout pitcher, Hentgen has good control of four pitches: a rising fastball, cut fastball, changeup, and a sharp-breaking curve that ranks as his best pitch. Hentgen yields fewer hits than innings and fans six per game. He also has enough stamina to finish what he starts more often than most of his colleagues. Hentgen's Achilles' heel is the long ball. The two-time All-Star and 1996 Cy Young Award winner helps himself with fine defense, including a slide-step pickoff move that freezes runners in their tracks. A starter in the minors, Hentgen broke into the big leagues as a set-up reliever. He went 19-9 in his first full season in the Toronto rotation.

Major League Pitching Register

	W	L	ERA	G	CG	IP	H	ER	BB	SO
91 AL	0	0	2.45	3	0	7.1	5	2	3	3
92 AL	5	2	5.36	28	0	50.1	49	30	32	39
93 AL	19	9	3.87	34	3	216.1	215	93	74	122
94 AL	13	8	3.40	24	6	174.2	158	66	59	147
95 AL	10	14	5.11	30	2	200.2	236	114	90	135
96 AL	20	10	3.22	35	10	265.2	238	95	94	177
Life	67	43	3.93	154	21	915.0	901	400	352	623
3 Ave	17	12	3.86	34	7	246.1	242	105	93	179

DUSTIN HERMANSON

Position: Pitcher
Team: Florida Marlins
Born: Dec. 21, 1972 Springfield, OH
Height: 6'2" **Weight:** 195 lbs.
Bats: right **Throws:** right
Acquired: Traded by Padres for Quilvio Veras, 11/96

PLAYER SUMMARY	
Fantasy Value	$1
Card Value	7¢ to 10¢
Will	provide relief
Can't	be perfect
Expect	high K count
Don't Expect	return to minors

The third player selected in the 1994 amateur draft, Hermanson had two cups of coffee in the San Diego bullpen. Though he showed flashes of brilliance, the hardthrowing right-hander has yet to realize his enormous potential. A fastball-slider pitcher who worked on a changeup in the Arizona Fall League, Hermanson averaged more strikeouts than innings pitched in the minors. But he still has to overcome occasional bouts of control trouble. That's a problem for a pitcher projected as a closer on a contending club. Because of his resilient right arm and ability to bring late heat, Hermanson has been strictly a reliever since turning pro. The star closer for Team USA in 1993, Hermanson was later a finalist for the coveted Golden Spikes Award, given annually to the nation's top amateur. The Kent University graduate was also a first-team Academic All-Mid-American Conference selection. If Hermanson puts his control problems behind him, he should be ready to stick in the big leagues. The Marlins, who traded for him in the offseason, are hoping this is the case. At 24, his future is definitely ahead of him.

Major League Pitching Register

	W	L	ERA	G	S	IP	H	ER	BB	SO
95 NL	3	1	6.82	26	0	31.2	35	24	22	19
96 NL	1	0	8.56	8	0	13.2	18	13	4	11
Life	4	1	7.35	34	0	45.1	53	37	26	30

JOSE HERNANDEZ

Position: Shortstop; third base
Team: Chicago Cubs
Born: July 14, 1969 Vega Alta, Puerto Rico
Height: 6'1" **Weight:** 180 lbs.
Bats: right **Throws:** right
Acquired: Traded by Indians for Heathcliff
  Slocumb, 6/93

PLAYER SUMMARY	
Fantasy Value	$2 to $4
Card Value	5¢ to 8¢
Will	show some pop
Can't	wait for walks
Expect	reserve role
Don't Expect	stellar defense

If Hernandez could hit lefties better, he'd probably play every day. Amazingly, he hit 100 points higher against righties last year. Part of the problem is patience—or lack of it. Hernandez fans five times more often than he walks. On the other hand, he nets extra bases on one-third of his hits—a respectable ratio for a utility infielder. Hernandez played short, third, and center field last summer but has also filled in at second base. Signed as a shortstop out of American University in his native Puerto Rico, Hernandez is better on offense than he is on defense. When regular Rey Sanchez was sidelined last August, the difference in defense was noticeable. Although Hernandez led three minor leagues in fielding percentage, he also led one in errors. He has quick reactions and adequate range but lacks the soft hands and accurate arm required to play the position every day. Never much of a basestealer, Hernandez reached double digits in steals only once, early in his minor-league career.

Major League Batting Register

	BA	G	AB	R	H	2B	3B	HR	RBI	SB
91 AL	.184	45	98	8	18	2	1	0	4	0
92 AL	.000	3	4	0	0	0	0	0	0	0
94 NL	.242	56	132	18	32	2	3	1	9	2
95 NL	.245	93	245	37	60	11	4	13	40	1
96 NL	.242	131	331	52	80	14	1	10	41	4
Life	.235	328	810	115	190	29	9	24	94	7
2 Ave	.243	118	303	47	74	13	3	12	43	3

ROBERTO HERNANDEZ

Position: Pitcher
Team: Chicago White Sox
Born: Nov. 11, 1964 Santurce, Puerto Rico
Height: 6'4" **Weight:** 220 lbs.
Bats: right **Throws:** right
Acquired: Traded by Angels with Mark Doran
  for Mark Davis, 8/89

PLAYER SUMMARY	
Fantasy Value	$30 to $35
Card Value	5¢ to 8¢
Will	save most games
Can't	always find plate
Expect	excellent velocity
Don't Expect	gopher plague

Hernandez rebounded from two off years to become a first-time All-Star last year. Throwing more forkballs, plus 97-mph fastballs, he converted his first 20 save opportunities. Hernandez, who also has a good slider, held hitters well below the Mendoza Line while fanning one man per inning. Although he had occasional bouts of control trouble, he learned the importance of mixing his pitches. In previous seasons, batters always expected a first-pitch fastball from the big right-hander. Hernandez recorded the third 30-save season of his career and posted a microscopic ERA. In his first 58 games, it was 1.04—far below his pre-1996 lifetime mark of 3.24. His effectiveness was reflected in his low gopher ball count: Hernandez yieded only two long balls all year. He doesn't surrender many extra-base hits, either. The native Puerto Rican helps himself with fine fielding, but his high-kicking delivery gives potential basestealers a head start.

Major League Pitching Register

	W	L	ERA	G	S	IP	H	ER	BB	SO
91 AL	1	0	7.80	9	0	15.0	18	13	7	6
92 AL	7	3	1.65	43	12	71.0	45	13	20	68
93 AL	3	4	2.29	70	38	78.2	66	20	20	71
94 AL	4	4	4.91	45	14	47.2	44	26	19	50
95 AL	3	7	3.92	60	32	59.2	63	26	28	84
96 AL	6	5	1.91	72	38	84.2	65	18	38	85
Life	24	23	2.93	299	134	356.2	301	116	132	364
3 Ave	5	6	3.45	68	31	73.0	66	28	32	83

XAVIER HERNANDEZ

Position: Pitcher
Team: Texas Rangers
Born: Aug. 16, 1965 Port Arthur, TX
Height: 6'2" **Weight:** 185 lbs.
Bats: left **Throws:** right
Acquired: Signed as a free agent, 12/96

PLAYER SUMMARY

Fantasy Value	$1
Card Value	4¢ to 7¢
Will	pitch inside
Can't	stop lefties
Expect	many calls
Don't Expect	closer role

A set-up man with a rubber arm, Hernandez routinely works more than 50 times per season. He averages more than a strikeout per inning, yields a hit per inning, and has decent control of his fastball, slider, and forkball (his best pitch). When his location wavers, he is less effective. Even though his walk total was down last year, Hernandez fell behind in the count too frequently and had to come over the fat part of the plate. The results were predictable: 11 home runs in his first 60⅓ innings. More effective against right-handed hitters, Hernandez often struggles against lefties. Because of his penchant for pitching inside, Hernandez also has to worry about incensed hitters. He's been the central figure in several brawls sparked by beanballs. Except for a short-lived trial as a closer for the 1994 Yankees, Hernandez has always served in a set-up role. Too many forkballs may have taken their toll.

Major League Pitching Register

	W	L	ERA	G	S	IP	H	ER	BB	SO
89 AL	1	0	4.76	7	0	22.2	25	12	8	7
90 NL	2	1	4.62	34	0	62.1	60	32	24	24
91 NL	2	7	4.71	32	3	63.0	66	33	32	55
92 NL	9	1	2.11	77	7	111.0	81	26	42	96
93 NL	4	5	2.61	72	9	96.2	75	28	28	101
94 AL	4	4	5.85	31	6	40.0	48	26	21	37
95 NL	7	2	4.60	59	3	90.0	95	46	31	84
96 NL	5	5	4.62	61	6	78.0	77	40	28	81
Life	34	25	3.88	373	34	563.2	527	243	214	485
3 Ave	6	4	4.90	57	6	79.1	84	43	31	76

JOSE HERRERA

Position: Outfield
Team: Oakland Athletics
Born: Aug. 30, 1972 Santo Domingo, Dominican Republic
Height: 6' **Weight:** 165 lbs.
Bats: left **Throws:** left
Acquired: Traded by Blue Jays with Steve Karsay for Rickey Henderson, 7/93

PLAYER SUMMARY

Fantasy Value	$4 to $6
Card Value	8¢ to 12¢
Will	supply solid glove
Can't	master strike zone
Expect	success on bases
Don't Expect	leadoff job yet

Herrera is a work in progress. There's some speed, some power, and some defensive skills, as well as leadoff potential, but too many rough edges to provide an accurate barometer of future success. A left-handed hitter who fared better against left-handed pitchers last year, Herrera shared right field with Geronimo Berroa and Matt Stairs most of last summer, though he also spent some time in center. So far, Herrera's defense is ahead of his offense. He gets good jumps, shows good judgment, has good range, and throws well enough to play right. Herrera's speed was never in doubt; he once stole 68 bases over a two-year span in the minors. Herrera won't succeed as a hitter, however, until he masters the strike zone. He fans more than three times per walk. Good leadoff men need the patience that leads to a high on-base percentage. Herrera seems infatuated with the idea of hitting the ball out of the park but never had more than 11 homers in the minors. Pancho Herrera he's not. But he supplies the speed and defense that the former Phillie slugger couldn't.

Major League Batting Register

	BA	G	AB	R	H	2B	3B	HR	RBI	SB
95 AL	.243	33	70	9	17	1	2	0	2	1
96 AL	.269	108	320	44	86	15	1	6	30	8
Life	.264	141	390	53	103	16	3	6	32	9

OREL HERSHISER

Position: Pitcher
Team: Cleveland Indians
Born: Sept. 16, 1958 Buffalo, NY
Height: 6'3" **Weight:** 192 lbs.
Bats: right **Throws:** right
Acquired: Signed as a free agent, 4/95

PLAYER SUMMARY	
Fantasy Value	$10 to $13
Card Value	10¢ to 15¢
Will	thrive in clutch
Can't	strike men out
Expect	good control
Don't Expect	gopher trouble

Although Hershiser turns 39 in 1997, he's given little hint that Father Time is catching up with him. A sinkerballer who also throws a slider, curve, and assorted changeups, Hershiser is a master of location. He averages only five strikeouts per nine innings but yields only 2½ walks over the same span. Though he yields more hits than innings, Hershiser induces frequent double-play grounders. He dominates righties and keeps the ball in the park. Hershiser, who once pitched a record 59 consecutive scoreless innings, does not have the velocity he had before reconstructive shoulder surgery in 1990. But he knows how to pitch and is especially tough in the clutch. Animated on the mound, Hershiser is quick to field his position. Few runners dare to test his solid pickoff move.

Major League Pitching Register

	W	L	ERA	G	CG	IP	H	ER	BB	SO
83 NL	0	0	3.38	8	0	8.0	7	3	6	5
84 NL	11	8	2.66	45	8	189.2	160	56	50	150
85 NL	19	3	2.03	36	9	239.2	179	54	68	157
86 NL	14	14	3.85	35	8	231.1	213	99	86	153
87 NL	16	16	3.06	37	10	264.2	247	90	74	190
88 NL	23	8	2.26	35	15	267.0	208	67	73	178
89 NL	15	15	2.31	35	8	256.2	226	66	77	178
90 NL	1	1	4.26	4	0	25.1	26	12	4	16
91 NL	7	2	3.46	21	0	112.0	112	43	32	73
92 NL	10	15	3.67	33	1	210.2	209	86	69	130
93 NL	12	14	3.59	33	5	215.2	201	86	72	141
94 NL	6	6	3.79	21	1	135.1	146	57	42	72
95 AL	16	6	3.87	26	1	167.1	151	72	51	111
96 AL	15	9	4.24	33	1	206.0	238	97	58	125
Life	165	117	3.16	402	67	2529.1	2323	888	762	1679
3 Ave	14	8	3.97	31	1	195.0	205	86	58	117

BOBBY HIGGINSON

Position: Outfield
Team: Detroit Tigers
Born: Aug. 18, 1970 Philadelphia, PA
Height: 5'11" **Weight:** 180 lbs.
Bats: left **Throws:** right
Acquired: 12th-round pick in 6/92 free-agent draft

PLAYER SUMMARY	
Fantasy Value	$15 to $18
Card Value	10¢ to 15¢
Will	smack clutch hits
Can't	revert to pulling
Expect	contact, power
Don't Expect	lack of discipline

Higginson was a different player last year. A winter of rigorous weight training, plus a conscious decision to stop pulling outside pitches, turned the 1995 wimp into a 1996 wunderkind with better contact, better production, and an on-base percentage that ranked among the league leaders. He was also on the Top 10 list in batting with runners in scoring position. The new, revised Higginson walks as often as he fans, hits well over .300 against right-handers, and gets extra bases on nearly half his hits. The Temple University product succeeded in taking the outer part of the plate away from the pitcher and producing consistent power. Working with Tiger hitting coach Larry Herndon, Higginson proved that a player can teach himself not to overswing. He even spent considerable time at the top of the lineup last year. Higginson's speed, good for a half-dozen steals per year, gives him good range in the outfield. He played all three spots last year but spent most of his time in right and left. Though he made more than his share of errors, he showed a strong throwing arm.

Major League Batting Register

	BA	G	AB	R	H	2B	3B	HR	RBI	SB
95 AL	.224	131	410	61	92	17	5	14	43	6
96 AL	.320	130	440	75	141	35	0	26	81	6
Life	.274	261	850	136	233	52	5	40	124	12
2 Ave	.271	139	451	72	122	27	3	21	65	6

GLENALLEN HILL

Position: Outfield
Team: San Francisco Giants
Born: March 22, 1965 Santa Cruz, CA
Height: 6'2" **Weight:** 205 lbs.
Bats: right **Throws:** right
Acquired: Signed as a free agent, 4/95

PLAYER SUMMARY	
Fantasy Value	$17 to $20
Card Value	5¢ to 8¢
Will	hit left-handers hard
Can't	practice patience
Expect	20-20 campaign
Don't Expect	mediocre arm

When Hill broke his left wrist last May 26, the Giants suffered a serious power vacuum—especially with fellow slugger Matt Williams ailing at the same time. Hill, the team's regular right fielder, had been heavily counted on to pick up where he left off in 1995, his best power year (24 homers). He did just that after coming off the DL in August. A free swinger with little patience, Hill is a first-pitch fastball hitter who is better against southpaws. But he fans more than three times per walk, reducing the possibility that he could reach on a free pass and race around to score. Hill did manage to boost his on-base percentage 60 points beyond his batting average. Speed has never been a problem. Hill became a 20-20 man for the first time in 1995. He's a high-percentage basestealer. In the outfield, Hill's speed and strong throwing arm make him a good defender.

KEN HILL

Position: Pitcher
Team: Texas Rangers
Born: Dec. 14, 1965 Lynn, MA
Height: 6'2" **Weight:** 175 lbs.
Bats: right **Throws:** right
Acquired: Signed as a free agent, 12/95

PLAYER SUMMARY	
Fantasy Value	$15 to $18
Card Value	5¢ to 8¢
Will	post good mark
Can't	get exposure
Expect	solid effort
Don't Expect	shaky glove

The signing of Ken Hill might have been the coup of the 1995-96 winter trade market. The hard-throwing right-hander, twice a 16-game winner in the NL, quickly blossomed into the ace of the Texas staff. Hill has great location of his fastball and forkball, using his slider and changeup to complement his primary pitches. He encountered a brief midseason slump last year, forcing him to make adjustments in his delivery, which he was rushing. The changes helped, as Hill went 5-0 in his next seven starts. His 7-0 win over Detroit August 12 was his third shutout. Hill yields fewer hits than innings and averages six strikeouts and three walks per nine innings. He's good at keeping the ball in the park but even better at controlling the running game. Hill is a quick and agile fielder who may someday win a Gold Glove. He was runner-up to Greg Maddux for the 1994 NL Cy Young Award.

Major League Batting Register

	BA	G	AB	R	H	2B	3B	HR	RBI	SB
89 AL	.288	19	52	4	15	0	0	1	7	2
90 AL	.231	84	260	47	60	11	3	12	32	8
91 AL	.258	72	221	29	57	8	2	8	25	6
92 AL	.241	102	369	38	89	16	1	18	49	9
93 AL	.224	66	174	19	39	7	2	5	25	7
93 NL	.345	31	87	14	30	7	0	10	22	1
94 NL	.297	89	269	48	80	12	1	10	38	19
95 NL	.264	132	497	71	131	29	4	24	86	25
96 NL	.280	98	379	56	106	26	0	19	67	6
Life	.263	693	2308	326	607	116	13	107	351	83
3 Ave	.278	124	439	68	122	25	2	20	72	20

Major League Pitching Register

	W	L	ERA	G	CG	IP	H	ER	BB	SO
88 NL	0	1	5.14	4	0	14.0	16	8	6	6
89 NL	7	15	3.80	33	2	196.2	186	83	99	112
90 NL	5	6	5.49	17	1	78.2	79	48	33	58
91 NL	11	10	3.57	30	0	181.1	147	72	67	121
92 NL	16	9	2.68	33	3	218.0	187	65	75	150
93 NL	9	7	3.23	28	2	183.2	163	66	74	90
94 NL	16	5	3.32	23	2	154.2	145	57	44	85
95 NL	6	7	5.06	18	0	110.1	125	62	45	50
95 AL	4	1	3.98	12	1	74.2	77	33	32	48
96 AL	16	10	3.63	35	7	250.2	250	101	95	170
Life	90	71	3.66	233	18	1462.2	1375	595	570	890
3 Ave	17	9	3.83	34	4	226.1	227	96	81	133

STERLING HITCHCOCK

Position: Pitcher
Team: San Diego Padres
Born: April 29, 1971 Fayetteville, NC
Height: 6'1" **Weight:** 192 lbs.
Bats: left **Throws:** left
Acquired: Traded by Mariners for Scott Sanders, 12/96

PLAYER SUMMARY	
Fantasy Value	$7 to $9
Card Value	5¢ to 8¢
Will	try many pitches
Can't	retire right-handers
Expect	fly-outs, homers
Don't Expect	runners to steal

Hitchcock made the most of his trade to the Mariners. Capitalizing on his success against left-handed hitters, he blossomed into the biggest winner on the 1996 Seattle staff. Because he averages only six strikeouts per game, Hitchcock needs help from his defense. That isn't easy, however, because he's a fly-ball pitcher who's not always able to keep the ball in the park. Hitchcock tries to handcuff hitters with a diversified arsenal that includes a sinker, slider, forkball, fastball, and changeup. Hitchcock yields more than 11 hits per nine innings and 3½ walks per game—giving him plenty of baserunners to worry about. But he's made dramatic improvements in his pickoff move. Half the runners who challenged him last year failed. The 25-year-old southpaw's future may hinge on his ability to hold right-handers at bay. They lit him up last year, hitting him at a clip more than 100 points higher than their left-handed counterparts.

TREVOR HOFFMAN

Position: Pitcher
Team: San Diego Padres
Born: Oct. 13, 1967 Bellflower, CA
Height: 6'1" **Weight:** 200 lbs.
Bats: right **Throws:** right
Acquired: Traded by Marlins with Jose Martinez and Andres Beruman for Gary Sheffield and Rich Rodriguez, 6/93

PLAYER SUMMARY	
Fantasy Value	$35 to $40
Card Value	5¢ to 8¢
Will	save many games
Can't	think about shoulder
Expect	last-inning heat
Don't Expect	runners to steal

One of the NL's best young closers, Hoffman was rewarded for his fine work with a three-year, $8.4-million contract extension in August. A hard thrower who averages nearly 11 strikeouts per nine innings, Hoffman combines control with the ability to prevent gopher balls. Healed from 1995 shoulder woes, his '96 numbers were spectacular: four strikeouts per walk, a microscopic ERA, and an opponents' batting average well below the Mendoza Line. Hoffman yields only five hits per nine innings, seldom surrenders a stolen base, and strands 80 percent of the runners he inherits. He blends a fastball, slider, and curve, putting all three pitches wherever he wants them. The eighth overall pick in the 1992 expansion draft, Hoffman came on quickly after reaching the majors with the Marlins in '93. He spent only two years in the minors as a pitcher after converting from shortstop, his original position. Not surprisingly, Hoffman swings the bat well for a pitcher and is a fine fielder.

Major League Pitching Register

	W	L	ERA	G	CG	IP	H	ER	BB	SO
92 AL	0	2	8.31	3	0	13.0	23	12	6	6
93 AL	1	2	4.65	6	0	31.0	32	16	14	26
94 AL	4	1	4.20	23	1	49.1	48	23	29	37
95 AL	11	10	4.70	27	4	168.1	155	88	68	121
96 AL	13	9	5.35	35	0	196.2	245	117	73	132
Life	29	24	5.03	94	5	458.1	503	256	190	322
3 Ave	10	7	4.91	33	2	152.0	162	83	63	107

Major League Pitching Register

	W	L	ERA	G	S	IP	H	ER	BB	SO
93 NL	4	6	3.90	67	5	90.0	80	39	39	79
94 NL	4	4	2.57	47	20	56.0	39	16	20	68
95 NL	7	4	3.88	55	31	53.1	48	23	14	52
96 NL	9	5	2.25	70	42	88.0	50	22	31	111
Life	24	19	3.13	239	98	287.1	217	100	104	310
3 Ave	8	5	2.79	66	35	76.1	53	23	25	88

147

CHRIS HOILES

Position: Catcher
Team: Baltimore Orioles
Born: March 20, 1965 Bowling Green, OH
Height: 6′ **Weight:** 213 lbs.
Bats: right **Throws:** right
Acquired: Traded by Tigers with Cesar Mejia and Robinson Garces for Fred Lynn, 9/88

PLAYER SUMMARY	
Fantasy Value.	$13 to $16
Card Value	5¢ to 8¢
Will	top 20 homers
Can't	nail runners
Expect	good bat vs. lefties
Don't Expect	decent speed

If Hoiles could throw as well as he hits, he'd be an All-Star. He reached 20 homers for the third time last year, when he also netted extra bases on more than one-third of his hits. A patient hitter who's willing to wait for walks, Hoiles often has an on-base percentage 100 points better than his batting average. Although he pulls the inside pitch, he has good power up the middle. Hoiles is better against lefties. His average with runners in scoring position is also better than his regular mark. The Eastern Michigan product has "catcher's speed," a polite way of saying he runs like John Goodman. Hoiles has trouble throwing out runners but otherwise is sound behind the plate. He's led AL receivers in chances, putouts, and fielding percentage. Hoiles has a reputation as a good handler of pitchers. He knows the hitters, calls good games, and prevents potential wild pitches. He's also adept at protecting the plate.

Major League Batting Register

	BA	G	AB	R	H	2B	3B	HR	RBI	SB
89 AL	.111	6	9	0	1	1	0	0	1	0
90 AL	.190	23	63	7	12	3	0	1	6	0
91 AL	.243	107	341	36	83	15	0	11	31	0
92 AL	.274	96	310	49	85	10	1	20	40	0
93 AL	.310	126	419	80	130	28	0	29	82	1
94 AL	.247	99	332	45	82	10	0	19	53	2
95 AL	.250	114	352	53	88	15	1	19	58	1
96 AL	.258	127	407	64	105	13	0	25	73	0
Life	.262	698	2233	334	586	95	2	124	344	4
3 Ave	.251	132	424	62	107	15	0	24	71	1

TODD HOLLANDSWORTH

Position: Outfield
Team: Los Angeles Dodgers
Born: April 20, 1973 Dayton, OH
Height: 6′2″ **Weight:** 193 lbs.
Bats: left **Throws:** left
Acquired: Third-round pick in 6/91 free-agent draft

PLAYER SUMMARY	
Fantasy Value.	$13 to $16
Card Value	10¢ to 15¢
Will	keep improving
Can't	show patience
Expect	speed, range
Don't Expect	power outage

With strikeout-prone Billy Ashley an early washout in the Dodgers' 1996 left-field derby, Hollandsworth was in the right place at the right time. He came on so fast that he was soon the leadoff man as well as the regular left fielder. Although he has yet to master the strike zone (an average of more than two Ks per walk), the fleet left-handed hitter showed an ability to reach base. His on-base percentage was 60 points better than his batting average. He's already a high-percentage basestealer who should get better as he learns the tendencies of the pitchers and catchers. Hollandsworth hits more homers than the typical leadoff man and might move down a peg in the '97 lineup. Although Hollandsworth spent most of 1996 in left, his range may be best-suited to center. He filled in there last year and also spent some time in right. Anywhere in the outfield, he has fine instincts, soft hands, and a strong, reliable arm. Hollandsworth would have been a 1995 rookie if thumb and wrist injuries hadn't intervened. Last year, the 1996 Rookie of the Year showed what he could do when healthy.

Major League Batting Register

	BA	G	AB	R	H	2B	3B	HR	RBI	SB
95 NL	.233	41	103	16	24	2	0	5	13	2
96 NL	.291	149	478	64	139	26	4	12	59	21
Life	.281	190	581	80	163	28	4	17	72	23

DAVE HOLLINS

Position: Third base; first base
Team: Anaheim Angels
Born: May 25, 1966 Buffalo, NY
Height: 6'1" **Weight:** 195 lbs.
Bats: both **Throws:** right
Acquired: Signed as a free agent, 12/96

PLAYER SUMMARY	
Fantasy Value	$4 to $6
Card Value	5¢ to 8¢
Will	poke clutch hits
Can't	supply defense
Expect	patience, pop
Don't Expect	stolen bases

One of baseball's most hard-nosed competitors, Hollins is a valuable man to have on a ballclub. He's a switch-hitter with patience and power and a versatile fielder, capable of playing either infield corner. Hollins has ridden a personal injury wave since 1993, battling hand and wrist injuries plus complications from diabetes. An extremely selective hitter who draws an enormous share of walks, Hollins always posts an on-base percentage far above his batting average. A much better right-handed hitter, Hollins showed last season that he still has some power. Even though he fans frequently, Hollins hits well with runners in scoring position. Never known for his speed or defense, Hollins lacks range, mobility, and a reliable arm. His best position is DH. At 30, a healthy Hollins could still be a formidable force. But that message may have to wait until next year's planned expansion.

Major League Batting Register

	BA	G	AB	R	H	2B	3B	HR	RBI	SB
90 NL	.184	72	114	14	21	0	0	5	15	0
91 NL	.298	56	151	18	45	10	2	6	21	1
92 NL	.270	156	586	104	158	28	4	27	93	9
93 NL	.273	143	543	104	148	30	4	18	93	2
94 NL	.222	44	162	28	36	7	1	4	26	1
95 NL	.229	65	205	46	47	12	2	7	25	1
95 AL	.154	5	13	2	2	0	0	0	1	0
96 AL	.262	149	516	88	135	29	0	16	78	6
Life	.259	690	2290	404	592	116	13	83	352	20
3 Ave	.245	95	325	60	80	17	1	10	48	3

DARREN HOLMES

Position: Pitcher
Team: Colorado Rockies
Born: April 25, 1966 Asheville, NC
Height: 6' **Weight:** 200 lbs.
Bats: right **Throws:** right
Acquired: First-round pick from Brewers in 11/92 expansion draft

PLAYER SUMMARY	
Fantasy Value	$6 to $8
Card Value	4¢ to 7¢
Will	keep set-up spot
Can't	field his position
Expect	frequent outings
Don't Expect	rivals to steal

Although he's spent four seasons pitching in Denver's rarefied air, Holmes has posted rather impressive numbers. A curveball specialist who works more than 60 games a season, Holmes averages a strikeout an inning and keeps the ball in the park. His assortment of sinkers, sliders, and curveballs helps. Holmes has decent control, allowing him to record a 2-1 ratio of strikeouts to walks. He yields just over a hit per inning, strands most of the runners he inherits, and controls the running game. He's been more effective against left-handed hitters over the last two seasons. Holmes does not help himself in the field because his follow-through leaves him in awkward defensive position. He's capable of moving runners with a bunt, however. Colorado's No. 1 closer in 1993, Holmes has battled elbow problems and redeployment since. He blew so many save chances last year (eight of his first nine attempts) that he pitched his way into a set-up role.

Major League Pitching Register

	W	L	ERA	G	S	IP	H	ER	BB	SO
90 NL	0	1	5.19	14	0	17.1	15	10	11	19
91 AL	1	4	4.72	40	3	76.1	90	40	27	59
92 AL	4	4	2.55	41	6	42.1	35	12	11	31
93 NL	3	3	4.05	62	25	66.2	56	30	20	60
94 NL	0	3	6.35	29	3	28.1	35	20	24	33
95 NL	6	1	3.24	68	14	66.2	59	24	28	61
96 NL	5	4	3.97	62	1	77.0	78	34	28	73
Life	19	20	4.08	316	52	374.2	368	170	149	336
2 Ave	6	3	3.61	69	8	76.0	72	31	30	71

RICK HONEYCUTT

Position: Pitcher
Team: St. Louis Cardinals
Born: June 29, 1954 Chattanooga, TN
Height: 6'1" **Weight:** 190 lbs.
Bats: left **Throws:** left
Acquired: Purchased from Yankees, 12/95

PLAYER SUMMARY	
Fantasy Value	$0
Card Value	4¢ to 7¢
Will	coax grounders
Can't	strike men out
Expect	great control
Don't Expect	sudden fade

After once leading the AL in ERA, Honeycutt became a full-time reliever in 1988 and has thrived in the bullpen since. He's a set-up man who can work often because his stints are so short. The lefty yielded fewer hits than innings, kept the ball in the park, and kept left-handed hitters at bay. A control artist, Honeycutt is a sinkerballer who relies on groundouts rather than strikeouts. Despite his advanced athletic age, Honeycutt still hops off the mound to field balls in his vicinity and holds runners so well that they seldom try to steal.

Major League Pitching Register

	W	L	ERA	G	S	IP	H	ER	BB	SO
77 AL	0	1	4.34	10	0	29.0	26	14	11	17
78 AL	5	11	4.89	26	0	134.1	150	73	49	50
79 AL	11	12	4.04	33	0	194.0	201	87	67	83
80 AL	10	17	3.94	30	0	203.1	221	89	60	79
81 AL	11	6	3.31	20	0	127.2	120	47	17	40
82 AL	5	17	5.27	30	0	164.0	201	96	54	64
83 AL	14	8	2.42	25	0	174.2	168	47	37	56
83 NL	2	3	5.77	9	0	39.0	46	25	13	18
84 NL	10	9	2.84	29	0	183.2	180	58	51	75
85 NL	8	12	3.42	31	1	142.0	141	54	49	67
86 NL	11	9	3.32	32	0	171.0	164	63	45	100
87 NL	2	12	4.59	27	0	115.2	133	59	45	92
87 AL	1	4	5.32	7	0	23.2	25	14	9	10
88 AL	3	2	3.50	55	7	79.2	74	31	25	47
89 AL	2	2	2.35	64	12	76.2	56	20	26	52
90 AL	2	2	2.70	63	7	63.1	46	19	22	38
91 AL	2	4	3.58	43	0	37.2	37	15	20	26
92 AL	1	4	3.69	54	3	39.0	41	16	10	32
93 AL	1	4	2.81	52	1	41.2	30	13	20	21
94 AL	1	2	7.20	42	1	25.0	37	20	9	18
95 AL	5	1	2.96	52	2	45.2	39	15	10	21
96 NL	2	1	2.85	61	4	47.1	42	15	7	30
Life	109	143	3.71	795	38	2158.0	2178	890	656	1036
2 Ave	4	1	2.91	60	3	49.1	43	16	9	27

TYLER HOUSTON

Position: Catcher; third base
Team: Chicago Cubs
Born: Jan. 17, 1971 Las Vegas, NV
Height: 6'2" **Weight:** 210 lbs.
Bats: left **Throws:** right
Acquired: Traded by Braves for Ismael Villegas, 6/96

PLAYER SUMMARY	
Fantasy Value	$1 to $3
Card Value	4¢ to 7¢
Will	play many spots
Can't	wait for walks
Expect	solid lefty bat
Don't Expect	decent speed

Atlanta's decision to trade Houston may have been hasty. The former first-round draft choice had been doing a fine job off the bench as a lefty pinch hitter with power. But the Braves never seemed to exploit his versatility. Given new life by the Cubs, Houston was used at all three bases, behind the plate, and in left field. He also made numerous pinch-hitting appearances. Though he's an impatient hitter who fans three times more often than he walks, Houston also hits the ball with authority, getting extra bases on more than one-third of his hits. Though Houston was slowed by back spasms in July, he returned to full strength for the September stretch drive. He did most of his catching for Chicago late in the year, when he was part of a left-right platoon with Scott Servais. He didn't have much success throwing out runners, but that could be the result of rustiness. Houston has a solid arm and handles pitchers well. After hitting better in the majors than he ever had in the minors, Houston could land a regular job. On the other hand, his versatility makes him valuable in the late innings.

Major League Batting Register

	BA	G	AB	R	H	2B	3B	HR	RBI	SB
96 NL	.317	79	142	21	45	9	1	3	27	3
Life	.317	79	142	21	45	9	1	3	27	3

DAVID HOWARD

Position: Shortstop
Team: Kansas City Royals
Born: Feb. 26, 1967 Sarasota, FL
Height: 6′ **Weight:** 175 lbs.
Bats: both **Throws:** right
Acquired: 32nd-round pick in 6/86 free-agent draft

PLAYER SUMMARY	
Fantasy Value	$0
Card Value	4¢ to 7¢
Will	bring strong glove
Can't	hit the long ball
Expect	strong throwing arm
Don't Expect	good K/BB ratio

Howard's defense keeps him in the big leagues. He has all the qualities of a top-flight shortstop: quick reactions, good instincts, fine range, soft hands, and a strong, reliable arm. He knows how to turn the double play and doesn't make many errors. Because he's played every infield position as well as the outfield during his six-year tenure in the majors, Howard had been projected as a 1996 utility man. But that was before the Royals got a long look at Jose Offerman's misadventures with a glove. When Offerman moved to first (and later second), Howard returned to short, his original position. A 32nd-round draft choice out of Manatee Junior College in Florida, Howard fans twice per walk—a horrible ratio for a singles hitter—and doesn't rattle the seismograph with either his batting average or on-base percentage. He's better left-handed, but that's not saying much. Howard had never played 100 games in a season before 1996 and wouldn't have last year if it hadn't been for his defense.

Major League Batting Register

	BA	G	AB	R	H	2B	3B	HR	RBI	SB
91 AL	.216	94	236	20	51	7	0	1	17	3
92 AL	.224	74	219	19	49	6	2	1	18	3
93 AL	.333	15	24	5	8	0	1	0	2	1
94 AL	.229	46	83	9	19	4	0	1	13	3
95 AL	.243	95	255	23	62	13	4	0	19	6
96 AL	.219	143	420	51	92	14	5	4	48	5
Life	.227	467	1237	127	281	44	12	7	117	21
2 Ave	.229	125	353	38	81	14	5	2	35	6

TOM HOWARD

Position: Outfield
Team: Houston Astros
Born: Dec. 11, 1964 Middletown, OH
Height: 6′2″ **Weight:** 200 lbs.
Bats: both **Throws:** right
Acquired: Signed as a free agent, 12/96

PLAYER SUMMARY	
Fantasy Value	$1 to $3
Card Value	4¢ to 7¢
Will	thrive in clutch
Can't	be selective
Expect	alley power
Don't Expect	weak glove

Although Cincinnati sagged in August, Howard was not part of the collapse. He staged a one-man offense, going on a 22-for-39 streak. Howard does his best hitting with runners in scoring position, maintaining a .350 average in that department most of last season. Slowed early by a hairline fracture of the wrist, Howard became one of Ray Knight's more valuable players, seeing time in all three outfield spots, pinch-hitting, and pinch-running. An aggressive hitter who fans three times more than he walks, Howard nets extra bases on more than one-third of his hits. Not usually a strong hitter against lefties, he had no problems in that department last season. Howard is a singles hitter with alley power; he had more triples last year than in the six previous seasons combined. The one-time Ball State All-American has good speed; he's stolen at least 15 bases twice.

Major League Batting Register

	BA	G	AB	R	H	2B	3B	HR	RBI	SB
90 NL	.273	20	44	4	12	2	0	0	0	0
91 NL	.249	106	281	30	70	12	3	4	22	10
92 NL	.333	5	3	1	1	0	0	0	0	0
92 AL	.277	117	358	36	99	15	2	2	32	15
93 AL	.236	74	178	26	42	7	0	3	23	5
93 NL	.277	38	141	22	39	8	3	4	13	5
94 NL	.264	83	178	24	47	11	0	5	24	4
95 NL	.302	113	281	42	85	15	2	3	26	17
96 NL	.272	121	360	50	98	19	10	6	42	6
Life	.270	677	1824	235	493	89	20	27	182	62
3 Ave	.280	122	309	44	87	17	4	5	35	10

JACK HOWELL

Position: Third base
Team: Anaheim Angels
Born: Aug. 18, 1961 Tucson, AZ
Height: 6' **Weight:** 190 lbs.
Bats: left **Throws:** right
Acquired: Signed as a minor-league free agent, 12/95

PLAYER SUMMARY	
Fantasy Value $0
Card Value . . . . 4¢ to 7¢
Will . . . . add lefty pop
Can't . . . . provide speed
Expect. . . . . adequate glove
Don't Expect . . . . regular berth

After spending four seasons in Japan, Howell returned to the majors last year with the Angels, his original team. A lefty hitter who shared the bag at various times with right-handed batters Tim Wallach, Randy Velarde, and George Arias, Howell did not display the power he had provided in the Far East. Although he got extra bases on one-third of his hits, he fanned three times more than he walked, leaving him with a mediocre on-base percentage. Howell, who once had a 38-homer season in Japan, did not get the playing time he had anticipated and went home an unhappy camper. The University of Arizona product started his pro career in 1983, after the Angels signed him as an undrafted free agent. In the majors two years later, he also played for the Padres before jumping to Japan. At 35, neither Howell's hitting nor his fielding is what it once was. Howell still has a strong arm, but he's lost a step in the field.

Major League Batting Register

	BA	G	AB	R	H	2B	3B	HR	RBI	SB
85 AL	.197	43	137	19	27	4	0	5	18	1
86 AL	.272	63	151	26	41	14	2	4	21	2
87 AL	.245	138	449	64	110	18	5	23	64	4
88 AL	.254	154	500	59	127	32	2	16	63	2
89 AL	.228	144	474	56	108	19	4	20	52	0
90 AL	.228	105	316	35	72	19	1	8	33	3
91 AL	.210	32	81	11	17	2	0	2	7	1
91 NL	.206	58	160	24	33	3	1	6	16	0
96 AL	.270	66	126	20	34	4	1	8	21	0
Life	.238	803	2394	314	569	115	16	92	295	13

TRENIDAD HUBBARD

Position: Outfield
Team: Cleveland Indians
Born: May 11, 1966 Chicago, IL
Height: 5'8" **Weight:** 183 lbs.
Bats: right **Throws:** right
Acquired: Traded by Giants for Joe Roa, 12/96

PLAYER SUMMARY	
Fantasy Value $0
Card Value . . . . 8¢ to 12¢
Will . . . . set the table
Can't . . . . get full shot
Expect . . . . walks plus speed
Don't Expect. . . . . utility role

Caught in an overcrowded Colorado outfield, Hubbard was glad to join the Giants last August. San Francisco, searching for a leadoff hitter and center fielder, liked his speed-plus-power potential. Hubbard spent almost all his time on the bench in 1995. Given only 58 at bats, many as a pinch hitter, he hit .310 with three homers. Hubbard's potential is enormous. During his ten-year minor-league tenure, he topped 30 steals six times, had five .300 seasons, and played all nine positions. A contact hitter with patience, Hubbard walked more often than he fanned in both of his last two campaigns. His tiny strike zone helps. For a little guy, he can hit the ball a long way (55 extra-base hits in the minors in 1995). He can also fly, fattening his average with bunts and infield rollers while ranging deep into the gaps on both sides of center field. The one-time Southern University second baseman, who became a full-time outfielder in 1994, has shaken his utility role. He could become a very productive leadoff man.

Major League Batting Register

	BA	G	AB	R	H	2B	3B	HR	RBI	SB
94 NL	.280	18	25	3	7	1	1	1	3	0
95 NL	.310	24	58	13	18	4	0	3	9	2
96 NL	.213	55	89	15	19	5	2	2	14	2
Life	.256	97	172	31	44	10	3	6	26	4

JOHN HUDEK

Position: Pitcher
Team: Houston Astros
Born: Aug. 8, 1966 Tampa, FL
Height: 6'1" **Weight:** 200 lbs.
Bats: both **Throws:** right
Acquired: Claimed from Tigers on waivers, 7/93

PLAYER SUMMARY	
Fantasy Value	$17 to $20
Card Value	4¢ to 7¢
Will	close if healthy
Can't	avoid injuries
Expect	great velocity
Don't Expect	perfect control

When Houston activated Hudek last July 15, he was rusty. The hard-throwing reliever had not pitched in a major-league game since June 1995. A rookie All-Star in 1994, Hudek had been idled for 14 months by several physical ailments, including a torn muscle, a fractured left rib, and July 1995 surgery that removed part of his top right rib. Needing to build arm strength, Hudek spent some time in the minors after his 1996 activation. He returned in August when rookie closer Billy Wagner was disabled. A fastball-slider pitcher who also throws a changeup, the healthy Hudek hits radar guns at a riveting 95 mph. Blessed with the ability to make his fastball rise or sink, Hudek averages a strikeout an inning. Right-handed hitters almost never take him deep. When the fireballer has his control, opposing hitters have trouble reaching the Mendoza Line against him. He strands inherited runners and helps himself with solid defense. Hudek is the only pitcher in major-league history to appear in an All-Star Game before logging a regular-season win.

Major League Pitching Register

	W	L	ERA	G	S	IP	H	ER	BB	SO
94 NL	0	2	2.97	42	16	39.1	24	13	18	39
95 NL	2	2	5.40	19	7	20.0	19	12	5	29
96 NL	2	0	2.81	15	2	16.0	12	5	5	14
Life	4	4	3.58	76	25	75.1	55	30	28	82

REX HUDLER

Position: Infield; outfield
Team: Philadelphia Phillies
Born: Sept. 2, 1960 Tempe, AZ
Height: 6' **Weight:** 195 lbs.
Bats: right **Throws:** right
Acquired: Signed as a free agent, 11/96

PLAYER SUMMARY	
Fantasy Value	$3 to $5
Card Value	4¢ to 7¢
Will	play anywhere
Can't	reduce K rate
Expect	constant hustle
Don't Expect	success vs. righties

Although he'll be 37 before the 1997 season ends, Hudler remains the perfect platoon player. He clobbers left-handed pitching, plays anywhere, and supplies good speed, surprising power, and unlimited energy whenever he enters the lineup. Hudler even got a long look at leadoff man last May. Overly anxious at the plate, Hudler fans more than five times per walk. He likes high fastballs but sometimes has trouble with good breaking stuff. He proved to be far better than a .257 hitter (his career average before 1996) last season. Perhaps his season in the Japanese Central League four years ago worked wonders for his offense; however, Hudler was nicknamed "the Wonder Dog" long before that. He's known for his constant hustle, versatility, and willingness to come off the bench. He's best defensively at second but has played everywhere except catcher and pitcher.

Major League Batting Register

	BA	G	AB	R	H	2B	3B	HR	RBI	SB
84 AL	.143	9	7	2	1	1	0	0	0	0
85 AL	.157	20	51	4	8	0	1	0	1	0
86 AL	.000	14	1	1	0	0	0	0	0	1
88 NL	.273	77	216	38	59	14	2	4	14	29
89 NL	.245	92	155	21	38	7	0	6	13	15
90 NL	.282	93	220	31	62	11	2	7	22	18
91 NL	.227	101	207	21	47	10	2	1	15	12
92 NL	.245	61	98	17	24	4	0	3	5	2
94 NL	.298	56	124	17	37	8	0	8	20	2
95 AL	.265	84	223	30	59	16	0	6	27	13
96 NL	.311	92	302	60	94	20	3	16	40	14
Life	.267	699	1604	242	429	91	10	51	157	106
2 Ave	.290	93	276	47	80	19	2	11	35	14

DAVID HULSE

Position: Outfield
Team: Milwaukee Brewers
Born: Feb. 25, 1968 San Angelo, TX
Height: 5'11" **Weight:** 170 lbs.
Bats: left **Throws:** left
Acquired: Traded by Rangers for Scott Taylor, 4/95

PLAYER SUMMARY	
Fantasy Value $0
Card Value . . . . 4¢ to 7¢
Will . . . . bring good glove
Can't . . . . clear the fences
Expect . . . . seat on bench
Don't Expect . . . . hits vs. lefties

Hulse often finds himself the 25th man on the 25-man roster. A fine defensive outfielder with a weak bat, he's an automatic out against left-handers and barely holds his own against righties. When it comes to power production, Hulse has no pulse. An aggressive low-ball hitter, Hulse fans three times more often than he walks. He'd be more valuable if he made more contact or showed more patience, but he continues to whale away. If baseball had a designated fielder instead of a designated hitter, Hulse would be the perfect fit. He runs well, gets good jumps, and has a reasonably accurate, though not powerful, throwing arm. His best position is center field. Hulse began his pro career in the Rangers' system in 1990. Three years later, he hit a career-high .290 in 114 games but did not provide much punch (20 extra-base hits). He hasn't come close to such production since. At 29, however, he's ripening on the vines of expansion. He'd make a fine good-field, no-hit center fielder for a new club.

Major League Batting Register

	BA	G	AB	R	H	2B	3B	HR	RBI	SB
92 AL	.304	32	92	14	28	4	0	0	2	3
93 AL	.290	114	407	71	118	9	10	1	29	29
94 AL	.255	77	310	58	79	8	4	1	19	18
95 AL	.251	119	339	46	85	11	6	3	47	15
96 AL	.222	81	117	18	26	3	0	0	6	4
Life	.266	423	1265	207	336	35	20	5	103	69
2 Ave	.253	121	409	67	103	12	6	2	40	21

TODD HUNDLEY

Position: Catcher
Team: New York Mets
Born: May 27, 1969 Martinsville, VA
Height: 5'11" **Weight:** 185 lbs.
Bats: both **Throws:** right
Acquired: Second-round pick in 6/87 free-agent draft

PLAYER SUMMARY	
Fantasy Value . . . . $25 to $30
Card Value . . . . 15¢ to 30¢
Will . . . . show great power
Can't . . . . avoid strikeouts
Expect . . . . best bat vs. RHP
Don't Expect . . . . intimidating arm

Suddenly last summer, Hundley became a slugger. After hitting coach Tom McCraw altered his open stance, the switch-hitting New York cleanup man broke Roy Campanella's record for homers by a catcher in a season. Though he still fans twice as much as he walks, he draws enough free passes to push his on-base percentage almost 100 points beyond his batting average. A much better hitter left-handed, Hundley has improved his knowledge of the strike zone. Pitchers who once got him out on bad changeups and breaking balls can't do that anymore. Hundley has scrapped the weight-lifting regimen that added strength but hampered his throwing. His arm has rebounded since, though it is not as strong as it once was. Hundley is best known for calling good games, blocking balls in the dirt, and protecting the plate from incoming runners. Like father Randy Hundley, Todd has played in the All-Star Game.

Major League Batting Register

	BA	G	AB	R	H	2B	3B	HR	RBI	SB
90 NL	.209	36	67	8	14	6	0	0	2	0
91 NL	.133	21	60	5	8	0	1	1	7	0
92 NL	.209	123	358	32	75	17	0	7	32	3
93 NL	.228	130	417	40	95	17	2	11	53	1
94 NL	.237	91	291	45	69	10	1	16	42	2
95 NL	.280	90	275	39	77	11	0	15	51	1
96 NL	.259	153	540	85	140	32	1	41	112	1
Life	.238	644	2008	254	478	93	5	91	299	8
3 Ave	.257	127	420	64	108	19	1	27	76	2

BRIAN L. HUNTER

Position: Outfield
Team: Detroit Tigers
Born: March 5, 1971 Portland, OR
Height: 6'4" **Weight:** 180 lbs.
Bats: right **Throws:** right
Acquired: Traded by Astros with Orlando
Miller, Doug Brocail, Todd Jones, and a
player to be named later for Brad Ausmus,
Jose Lima, C.J. Nitkowski, Trever Miller, and
Daryle Ward, 12/96

PLAYER SUMMARY

Fantasy Value	$14 to $17
Card Value	10¢ to 20¢
Will	burn up basepaths
Can't	reduce strikeouts
Expect	good clutch stick
Don't Expect	Gold Glove defense

The raw tools are there. But Hunter has been spinning his wheels at the big-league level for two years since leading the Pacific Coast League in runs, hits, batting average, and stolen bases. One of the fastest men in the game, Hunter could make himself much more valuable by practicing patience at the plate. He fans five times more often than he walks—unsatisfactory for a leadoff man. A singles hitter who often goes up the middle, Hunter handles both lefties and righties. He has some gap power, plus the potential of stretching singles, but he is more likely to steal a base than sock an extra-base hit. Although he's a good clutch hitter, Hunter is best known for his high success rate on the bases. The guy can fly. Once he learns to read pitchers better, a stolen-base crown is within his reach. In the outfield, Hunter outruns balls hit into the gaps and dives for balls others can't reach. He has a strong arm for a center fielder but isn't always accurate.

Major League Batting Register

	BA	G	AB	R	H	2B	3B	HR	RBI	SB
94 NL	.250	6	24	2	6	1	0	0	0	2
95 NL	.302	78	321	52	97	14	5	2	28	24
96 NL	.276	132	526	74	145	27	2	5	35	35
Life	.285	216	871	128	248	42	7	7	63	61
2 Ave	.286	110	444	66	127	21	4	4	33	31

BRIAN R. HUNTER

Position: First base; outfield
Team: Seattle Mariners
Born: March 4, 1968 El Toro, CA
Height: 6' **Weight:** 195 lbs.
Bats: right **Throws:** left
Acquired: Signed as a minor-league free
agent, 3/96

PLAYER SUMMARY

Fantasy Value	$0
Card Value	4¢ to 7¢
Will	hit lefties
Can't	steal, throw
Expect	pop in pinch
Don't Expect	regular spot

Ever since reaching the majors with the 1991 Atlanta Braves, Hunter has carved a reputation as a reliable hitter against left-handed pitching. He did nothing to disprove that theory last year, when the Mariners used him as a reserve first baseman, backup left fielder, and pinch hitter. Hunter has some patience at the plate but still fans three times more often than he walks. Though he took a five-year mark of .231 into the 1996 campaign, Hunter's reputation as a good clutch hitter helped him escape the minor-league scrap heap. He hit .304 with three extra-base hits in two Championship Series (eight games). He also homered in the 1991 World Series. Hardly a speed demon, Hunter is a liability on the bases and in the field. Because of his weak throwing arm and lack of range, he barely gets by in left field. He's better at first base but will never win a Gold Glove there. If Hunter can last another year, he might convince an expansion club to draft him for 1998. He's still only 29.

Major League Batting Register

	BA	G	AB	R	H	2B	3B	HR	RBI	SB
91 NL	.251	97	271	32	6	16	1	12	50	0
92 NL	.239	102	238	34	57	13	2	14	41	1
93 NL	.138	37	80	4	11	3	1	0	8	0
94 NL	.234	85	256	34	60	16	1	15	57	0
95 NL	.215	40	79	9	17	6	0	1	9	2
96 AL	.268	75	198	21	53	10	0	7	28	0
Life	.237	436	1122	134	266	64	5	49	193	3
2 Ave	.246	97	279	34	69	16	1	14	54	0

BUTCH HUSKEY

Position: First base; third base
Team: New York Mets
Born: Nov. 10, 1971 Anadarko, OK
Height: 6'3" **Weight:** 244 lbs.
Bats: right **Throws:** right
Acquired: Seventh-round pick in 6/89 free-agent draft

PLAYER SUMMARY

Fantasy Value	$9 to $11
Card Value	8¢ to 12¢
Will	hit lefties hard
Can't	pull every pitch
Expect	power to improve
Don't Expect	much speed, range

When he hammered nine homers during the 1996 exhibition schedule, the Mets thought Huskey might be ready to realize the potential that made him a two-time minor-league home run king. But he opened the season in a 2-for-30 slump and never regained his power stroke. The promise is still there, however. Huskey, still learning to go with the pitch rather than trying to pull everything, is also attempting to become more selective at the plate. He fans more than three times per walk. The 1995 International League MVP can't fatten his stats by beating out infield hits—speed is not part of his game plan, even though he stole home against Pittsburgh June 19. Huskey is much more likely to homer than steal. He's a much better hitter against left-handed pitchers. Signed as a third baseman, Huskey spent most of last year at first base, filling in for the injured Rico Brogna, and in right field. He saw some September action at third. He has quick reactions, a strong arm, and decent hands, but his range is limited.

Major League Batting Register

	BA	G	AB	R	H	2B	3B	HR	RBI	SB
93 NL	.146	13	41	2	6	1	0	0	3	0
95 NL	.189	28	90	8	17	1	0	3	11	1
96 NL	.278	118	414	43	115	16	2	15	60	1
Life	.253	159	545	53	138	18	2	18	74	2

MARK HUTTON

Position: Pitcher
Team: Florida Marlins
Born: Feb. 6, 1970 South Adelaide, Australia
Height: 6'6" **Weight:** 270 lbs.
Bats: right **Throws:** right
Acquired: Traded by Yankees for David Weathers, 7/96

PLAYER SUMMARY

Fantasy Value	$3 to $5
Card Value	7¢ to 10¢
Will	show velocity
Can't	rack up Ks
Expect	rotation berth
Don't Expect	control trouble

Hutton has the potential to become another Doug Drabek: a young right-hander who blossomed into a top starter the minute the Yankees traded him. A quality minor-league pitcher, Hutton won 23 games over a two-year span in 1992 and '93 before becoming the first Australian pitcher ever to start a big-league game. He returned to the minors in '94, however, as the Yankees tried to convert him to relief work. The hard-throwing Hutton, whose best pitches are a low-90s fastball and a solid slider, has been held back by recurring elbow problems but proved healthy last season. Hutton yields fewer hits than innings, keeps the ball in the park, and monitors the running game well. The towering right-hander has good control, yielding fewer than three walks per nine innings and keeping wild pitches to a minimum. But his inability to record more strikeouts remains a mystery: He averages fewer than five per nine innings. Hutton also showed an ability to hit once he reached the National League. He broke into pro ball after the Yankees signed him as an undrafted free agent in 1988.

Major League Pitching Register

	W	L	ERA	G	S	IP	H	ER	BB	SO
93 AL	1	1	5.73	7	0	22.0	24	14	17	12
94 AL	0	0	4.91	2	0	3.2	4	2	0	1
96 AL	0	2	5.04	12	0	30.1	32	17	18	25
96 NL	5	1	3.67	13	0	56.1	47	23	18	31
Life	6	4	4.49	34	0	112.1	107	56	53	69

PETE INCAVIGLIA

Position: Outfield
Team: Baltimore Orioles
Born: April 2, 1964 Pebble Beach, CA
Height: 6'1" **Weight:** 235 lbs.
Bats: right **Throws:** right
Acquired: Traded by Phillies with Todd Zeile for Calvin Maduro and Don Florence, 7/96

PLAYER SUMMARY	
Fantasy Value	$1
Card Value	5¢ to 8¢
Will	provide power
Can't	reduce K rate
Expect	action vs. lefties
Don't Expect	speed, defense

After a one-year hiatus in Japan, Incaviglia brought his powerful right-handed bat back to the major leagues last season, where he criticized his Phillies' teammates for their alleged lack of fire. That, coupled with his big salary and erratic glove, led to his trade across league lines. The former Oklahoma State All-American and first-round draft choice had 16 NL homers at the time of the deal. That was impressive, since he played primarily against left-handed pitching. One of the few major-leaguers who never played in the minors, Incaviglia has good power. He also led the league in strikeouts twice and still averages four Ks per walk. Incaviglia seldom steals a base. While he catches everything he reaches in the outfield, too many balls get by him. He doesn't run well enough to play center or throw well enough to play right.

Major League Batting Register

	BA	G	AB	R	H	2B	3B	HR	RBI	SB
86 AL	.250	153	540	82	135	21	2	30	88	3
87 AL	.271	139	509	85	138	26	4	27	80	9
88 AL	.249	116	418	59	104	19	3	22	54	6
89 AL	.236	133	453	48	107	27	4	21	81	5
90 AL	.233	153	529	59	123	27	0	24	85	3
91 AL	.214	97	337	38	72	12	1	11	38	1
92 NL	.266	113	349	31	93	22	1	11	44	2
93 NL	.274	116	368	60	101	16	3	24	89	1
94 AL	.230	80	244	28	56	10	1	13	32	1
96 AL	.234	99	269	33	63	7	2	16	42	2
96 AL	.303	12	33	4	10	2	0	2	8	0
Life	.247	1211	4049	527	1002	189	21	201	641	33
2 Ave	.232	106	306	36	71	11	2	17	44	2

JASON ISRINGHAUSEN

Position: Pitcher
Team: New York Mets
Born: Sept. 7, 1972 Brighton, IL
Height: 6'3" **Weight:** 188 lbs.
Bats: right **Throws:** right
Acquired: 44th-round pick in 6/91 free-agent draft

PLAYER SUMMARY	
Fantasy Value	$6 to $8
Card Value	20¢ to 30¢
Will	seek rookie form
Can't	stop lefty hitters
Expect	self-help with bat
Don't Expect	gopher trouble

The glittering promise of Isringhausen's rookie year evaporated in a hurry. He had control trouble during the first half of last season, battled an injured right rib cage in August, and yielded far too many hits—especially against lefties. Although he keeps the ball in the park, Isringhausen cannot control the running game. The fast-working righty also depends heavily upon his defense, since he averages only six Ks per nine innings. Unlike many young pitchers, he's willing to pitch inside. A fastball-curveball pitcher who is still working on his changeup, Isringhausen carved an impressive record in the minors. When he went 9-2 in 14 second-half starts as a 1995 rookie, the Mets thought he was on his way. But he sputtered from the start last year, showing only flashes of his former potential. The International League's Most Valuable Pitcher in 1995, Isringhausen has never had a complete season in Triple-A, although he could get one if he continues on his inconsistent course. The one thing he did well all last year was hit: He hit as well as some of the Mets' position-players.

Major League Pitching Register

	W	L	ERA	G	CG	IP	H	ER	BB	SO
95 NL	9	2	2.81	14	1	93.0	88	29	31	55
96 NL	6	14	4.77	27	2	171.2	190	91	73	114
Life	15	16	4.08	41	3	264.2	278	120	104	169
2 Ave	8	8	4.03	21	2	138.0	145	62	54	88

DANNY JACKSON

Position: Pitcher
Team: St. Louis Cardinals
Born: Jan. 5, 1962 San Antonio, TX
Height: 6' **Weight:** 205 lbs.
Bats: right **Throws:** left
Acquired: Signed as a free agent, 12/94

PLAYER SUMMARY	
Fantasy Value	$1
Card Value	4¢ to 7¢
Will	seek starting job
Can't	evade injury jinx
Expect	many groundouts
Don't Expect	pinpoint control

Jackson's appearance last August 5 was his first since breaking his ankle almost one year earlier. The injury was the latest in a long litany of misery for the veteran lefty, who has also had shoulder ailments, torn ankle ligaments, a strained groin, a lower abdominal strain, toe surgery, and thyroid cancer. Entering the final year of a $10.8-million contract, Jackson would do well just to make the starting rotation, let alone approach his old form. A sinker-slider pitcher who needs groundouts to win, Jackson tries to keep batters honest by throwing a changeup now and then. The two-time All-Star usually fans less than two per walk and yields lots of hits. That hurts, since his fielding and pickoff move are weak. At 35, Jackson has seen better days, but an expansion team would welcome him.

Major League Pitching Register

	W	L	ERA	G	S	IP	H	ER	BB	SO
83 AL	1	1	5.21	4	0	19.0	26	11	6	9
84 AL	2	6	4.26	15	0	76.0	84	36	35	40
85 AL	14	12	3.42	32	0	208.0	209	79	76	114
86 AL	11	12	3.20	32	1	185.2	177	66	79	115
87 AL	9	18	4.02	36	0	224.0	219	100	109	152
88 NL	23	8	2.73	35	0	260.2	206	79	71	161
89 NL	6	11	5.60	20	0	115.2	122	72	57	70
90 NL	6	6	3.61	22	0	117.1	119	47	40	76
91 NL	1	5	6.75	17	0	70.2	89	53	48	31
92 NL	8	13	3.84	34	0	201.1	211	86	77	97
93 NL	12	11	3.77	32	0	210.1	214	88	80	120
94 NL	14	6	3.26	25	0	179.1	183	65	46	129
95 NL	2	12	5.90	19	0	100.2	120	66	48	52
96 NL	1	1	4.46	13	0	36.1	33	18	16	27
Life	110	122	3.89	336	1	2005.0	2012	866	788	1193
3 Ave	8	8	4.11	23	0	134.0	142	61	45	89

MIKE JACKSON

Position: Pitcher
Team: Cleveland Indians
Born: Dec. 22, 1964 Houston, TX
Height: 6' **Weight:** 185 lbs.
Bats: right **Throws:** right
Acquired: Signed as a free agent, 12/96

PLAYER SUMMARY	
Fantasy Value	$4 to $6
Card Value	4¢ to 7¢
Will	answer call often
Can't	stop all lefties
Expect	controlled heat
Don't Expect	rivals to run

A rubber-armed reliever with a blazing fastball, Jackson was the busiest and most effective member of the Seattle bullpen in 1996. He topped 70 appearances and held righties to a tiny average that would have made Mario Mendoza proud. Jackson is a control pitcher who yields fewer hits than innings and averages almost a strikeout an inning. He combines a low-90s fastball with a sharp-breaking slider and an occasional changeup. Jackson strands most of the runners he inherits and controls the running game well but has trouble with the long ball. He proved last year that he was fully recovered from the shoulder tendinitis that had bothered him in 1995. Jackson's quick, compact delivery makes potential basestealers so nervous they rarely challenge him. The pitcher is also quick to field his position. Used mostly as a set-up man last year, Jackson can also close when needed.

Major League Pitching Register

	W	L	ERA	G	S	IP	H	ER	BB	SO
86 NL	0	0	3.38	9	0	13.1	12	5	4	3
87 NL	3	10	4.20	55	1	109.1	88	51	56	93
88 AL	6	5	2.63	62	4	99.1	74	29	43	76
89 AL	4	6	3.17	65	7	99.1	81	35	54	94
90 AL	5	7	4.54	63	3	77.1	64	39	44	69
91 AL	7	7	3.25	72	14	88.2	64	32	34	74
92 AL	6	6	3.73	67	2	82.0	76	34	33	80
93 AL	6	6	3.03	81	1	77.1	58	26	24	70
94 AL	3	2	1.49	36	4	42.1	23	7	11	51
95 AL	6	1	2.39	40	2	49.0	38	13	19	41
96 AL	1	1	3.62	73	6	72.0	61	29	24	70
Life	47	51	3.33	623	44	810.0	639	300	346	721
3 Ave	4	2	2.58	56	5	62.1	45	18	20	63

JASON JACOME

Position: Pitcher
Team: Kansas City Royals
Born: Nov. 24, 1970 Tulsa, OK
Height: 6'1" **Weight:** 175 lbs.
Bats: left **Throws:** left
Acquired: Traded by Mets with Allen McDill for Gino Morones, John Carter, and Derek Wallace, 7/95

PLAYER SUMMARY	
Fantasy Value	$0
Card Value	5¢ to 8¢
Will	remain in relief
Can't	halt righty hitters
Expect	finesse
Don't Expect	precise location

Jacome's inability to retire right-handed hitters left him with a losing record and high ERA last year although he pitched effectively against lefties. Jacome, who broke into the majors with a bang as a starter for the 1994 Mets, has not been the same pitcher since. Not a power pitcher, he depends upon precise location of his fastball, slider, curve, and change but hasn't always been able to hit his spots. He started well last year, with a 1.69 ERA in his first 32 games, but suddenly fizzled. Jacome's nine-inning averages need improvement: more than a dozen hits, four walks, and six strikeouts. He does strand three of every four runners he inherits and is also good at stopping the running game. But he has occasional problems with gopher balls. He prefers ground balls—and gets them when his control is on. He supplies solid defense and possesses a potent pickoff move. But his finesse hasn't baffled big-leaguers. At 26, Jacome needs a good season to attract the attention of an expansion team.

Major League Pitching Register

	W	L	ERA	G	S	IP	H	ER	BB	SO
94 NL	4	3	2.67	8	0	54.0	54	16	17	30
95 NL	0	4	10.29	5	0	21.0	33	24	15	11
95 AL	4	6	5.36	15	0	84.0	101	50	21	39
96 AL	0	4	4.72	49	1	47.2	67	25	22	32
Life	8	17	5.01	77	1	206.2	255	115	75	112
2 Ave	2	5	5.14	33	1	71.0	90	41	23	38

JOHN JAHA

Position: First base
Team: Milwaukee Brewers
Born: May 27, 1966 Portland, OR
Height: 6'1" **Weight:** 195 lbs.
Bats: right **Throws:** right
Acquired: 14th-round pick in 6/84 free-agent draft

PLAYER SUMMARY	
Fantasy Value	$20 to $25
Card Value	8¢ to 12¢
Will	show good power
Can't	hit all righties
Expect	selective hitting
Don't Expect	flop in clutch

After showing good power potential in three previous seasons, Jaha enjoyed his most productive campaign in 1996. He became the first Brewer to reach 100 RBI since Robin Yount's heyday. A much better hitter against left-handed pitching, Jaha is also more productive with an 0-2 count and with runners in scoring position. He often goes with the pitch, dropping hits into the opposite field. That is a new development for Jaha, who once tried to pull everything. Given a choice, he'd prefer a steady diet of high, inside hard stuff. Jaha fans frequently but shows more patience than most sluggers, drawing enough walks to push his on-base percentage 100 points beyond his batting average. A big man not known for his speed, Jaha will surprise with an occasional stolen base. He has decent mobility in the field, scoops the ball well, and throws better than most first basemen—probably because he was a third baseman when he signed with the Brewers in 1984. At age 30, Jaha should be at his peak.

Major League Batting Register

	BA	G	AB	R	H	2B	3B	HR	RBI	SB
92 AL	.226	47	133	17	30	3	1	2	10	10
93 AL	.264	153	515	78	136	21	0	19	70	13
94 AL	.241	84	291	45	70	14	0	12	39	3
95 AL	.313	88	316	59	99	20	2	20	65	2
96 AL	.300	148	543	108	163	28	1	34	118	3
Life	.277	520	1798	307	498	86	4	87	302	31
3 Ave	.285	122	436	79	124	23	1	24	82	3

MIKE JAMES

Position: Pitcher
Team: Anaheim Angels
Born: Aug. 15, 1967 Fort Walton Beach, FL
Height: 6'4" **Weight:** 216 lbs.
Bats: right **Throws:** right
Acquired: Traded by Dodgers for Reggie
Williams, 10/93

PLAYER SUMMARY

Fantasy Value	$2 to $4
Card Value	5¢ to 8¢
Will	get groundouts
Can't	avoid wild spells
Expect	set-up service
Don't Expect	righties to hit

The busiest member of the Angel bullpen last summer, James was also one of the most effective set-up men in the majors. A fastball-slider pitcher with a three-quarters delivery, he needs good location to survive. Although he's prone to wild spells, James dominates right-handed hitters, keeps the ball in the park, and keeps a close eye on potential basestealers. His primary problem last year was stranding inherited runners: Nearly half those he inherited scored. James, who also throws a slow curve and a so-so changeup, is a fast worker whose pace keeps infielders interested. That helps, since he gets a lot of ground balls. James averages seven strikeouts per nine innings and only seven hits over the same span. That compensates for his nine-inning average of 4½ walks. James helps his own cause by fielding his position well. Originally Dodger property, James spent seven years in the minors before breaking into the big leagues two years ago. He was a 43rd-round choice in the 1987 free-agent draft. James was slowed last year by a July bout with tonsillitis.

Major League Pitching Register

	W	L	ERA	G	S	IP	H	ER	BB	SO
95 AL	3	0	3.88	46	1	55.2	49	24	26	36
96 AL	5	5	2.67	69	1	81.0	62	24	42	65
Life	8	5	3.16	115	2	136.2	111	48	68	101
2 Ave	4	3	3.20	60	1	72.1	59	26	36	53

MARTY JANZEN

Position: Pitcher
Team: Toronto Blue Jays
Born: May 31, 1973 Homestead, FL
Height: 6'3" **Weight:** 197 lbs.
Bats: right **Throws:** right
Acquired: Traded by Yankees with Jason
Jarvis and Mike Gordon for David Cone,
7/95

PLAYER SUMMARY

Fantasy Value	$0
Card Value	7¢ to 10¢
Will	improve over time
Can't	deal with lefties
Expect	good K/BB ratio
Don't Expect	strong defense

Before the Yankees signed him out of a Florida tryout camp, Janzen wanted to be a pro bowler. Although he had several perfect games with the big ball, he'd rather have one with the little one. Realizing that bowling is hard on the pitching arm, Janzen has given up the game to concentrate on baseball. He has a good background: He was once coached by Kevin Maris, son of Roger. The hard-throwing right-hander, the key man in the 1995 David Cone deal, blends a 90-mph fastball with a circle change, curve, and slider. A 16-game winner in the minors two years ago, Janzen has always maintained good strikeout-to-walk ratios, often getting three whiffs per walk. Much more effective against right-handed hitters, he yielded too many hits and too many homers to lefties last year. Janzen reached double digits in starts but spent most of his time getting his feet wet against big-league hitters. Although he holds runners well, Janzen needs to improve his overall defense. He's projected to become a solid major-league starter but needs more on-the-job training.

Major League Pitching Register

	W	L	ERA	G	CG	IP	H	ER	BB	SO
96 AL	4	6	7.33	15	0	73.2	95	60	38	47
Life	4	6	7.33	15	0	73.2	95	60	38	47

KEVIN JARVIS

Position: Pitcher
Team: Cincinnati Reds
Born: Aug. 1, 1969 Lexington, KY
Height: 6'2" **Weight:** 200 lbs.
Bats: left **Throws:** right
Acquired: 21st-round pick in 6/91 free-agent
  draft

PLAYER SUMMARY	
Fantasy Value	$0
Card Value	5¢ to 8¢
Will	seek full season
Can't	find consistency
Expect	decent control
Don't Expect	high K count

Jarvis knows what a yo-yo feels like. He's been up and down with the Reds three years in a row, finding time to pitch two shutouts during his NL visits. A control pitcher who gets few strikeouts, Jarvis has been extremely inconsistent during his brief career. He's been a hero one day, a goat the next. Last year, he went 2-0 with a 1.69 ERA in his first five starts after Pete Schourek helped him with his mechanics, pitch selection, mental approach, and technique. The Wake Forest product throws rising and sinking fastballs, as well as a changeup, slider, and curve. But he yields too many hits and too many home runs. Even while leading the American Association with an .833 winning percentage in 1994, Jarvis yielded more hits than innings. His quick delivery and solid move prevent baserunners from taking advantage of him, however. Jarvis fields his position well and can even poke an occasional hit. At 27, his low salary and strong arm are an appealing combination. But his performance will have to reach another level for him to retain a rotation berth all year.

Major League Pitching Register

	W	L	ERA	G	CG	IP	H	ER	BB	SO
94 NL	1	1	7.13	6	0	17.2	22	14	5	10
95 NL	3	4	5.70	19	1	79.0	91	50	32	33
96 NL	8	9	5.98	24	2	120.1	152	80	43	63
Life	12	14	5.97	49	3	217.0	265	144	80	106
2 Ave	6	7	5.86	23	2	105.1	127	68	40	50

STAN JAVIER

Position: Outfield
Team: San Francisco Giants
Born: Sept. 1, 1965 San Pedro de Macoris,
  Dominican Republic
Height: 6' **Weight:** 185 lbs.
Bats: both **Throws:** right
Acquired: Signed as a free agent, 12/95

PLAYER SUMMARY	
Fantasy Value	$8 to $10
Card Value	4¢ to 7¢
Will	supply strong glove
Can't	clear fences often
Expect	two dozen steals
Don't Expect	.300 average

After opening the 1996 campaign as San Francisco's leadoff man and center fielder, Javier went on the shelf with severe hamstring problems. He spent most of the year on the sidelines. When healthy, Javier supplies significant speed and defense. He led AL outfielders with a 1.000 fielding percentage in 1995 and swiped a career-high 36 bases. Javier is a high-percentage basestealer who will steal first if opponents don't pay attention. He has great reactions, terrific range, and a quick release in the outfield, but his arm isn't strong. Javier is an opposite-field hitter who does his best work against lefties. He shows enough patience to push his on-base percentage 75 points above his batting average. He's the son of former big-league second baseman Julian Javier.

Major League Batting Register

	BA	G	AB	R	H	2B	3B	HR	RBI	SB
84 AL	.143	7	7	1	1	0	0	0	0	0
86 AL	.202	59	114	13	23	8	0	0	8	8
87 AL	.185	81	151	22	28	3	1	2	9	3
88 AL	.257	125	397	49	102	13	3	2	35	20
89 AL	.248	112	310	42	77	12	3	1	28	12
90 AL	.242	19	33	4	8	0	2	0	3	0
90 NL	.304	104	276	56	84	9	4	3	24	15
91 AL	.205	121	176	21	36	5	3	1	11	7
92 NL	.249	130	334	42	83	17	1	1	29	18
93 AL	.291	92	237	33	69	10	4	3	28	12
94 AL	.272	109	419	75	114	23	0	10	44	24
95 AL	.278	130	442	81	123	20	2	8	56	36
96 NL	.270	71	274	44	74	25	0	2	22	14
Life	.259	1160	3170	483	822	145	23	33	297	169
3 Ave	.274	124	454	80	124	27	1	8	49	29

GREGG JEFFERIES

Position: Outfield; first base
Team: Philadelphia Phillies
Born: Aug. 1, 1967 Burlingame, CA
Height: 5'10" **Weight:** 180 lbs.
Bats: both **Throws:** right
Acquired: Signed as a free agent, 12/94

PLAYER SUMMARY	
Fantasy Value	$16 to $19
Card Value	7¢ to 10¢
Will	make contact
Can't	find a position
Expect	steals, doubles
Don't Expect	frequent homers

For the second straight year, Jefferies missed playing time because of a thumb injury. He tore a ligament in his left thumb during the third game of 1996 and didn't return until 52 games later. A patient hitter, Jefferies walks more often than he fans. He's a better batter with two strikes and in clutch situations. Jefferies can do everything at the plate: walk, bunt, work the hit-and-run, hit for extra bases, and hit occasional homers. He has annoyed teammates in several cities with weak, indifferent defense and a brash attitude that some call selfishness. An outspoken individual, Jefferies sometimes seems more concerned with personal stats than team performance. He's also been reluctant to change positions, though he's tried all three bases plus left field without much success. His best position is DH, though first base will have to suffice in the NL.

Major League Batting Register

	BA	G	AB	R	H	2B	3B	HR	RBI	SB
87 NL	.500	6	6	0	3	1	0	0	2	0
88 NL	.321	29	109	19	35	8	2	6	17	5
89 NL	.258	141	508	72	131	28	2	12	56	21
90 NL	.283	153	604	96	171	40	3	15	68	11
91 NL	.272	136	486	59	132	19	2	9	62	26
92 NL	.285	152	604	66	172	36	3	10	75	19
93 NL	.342	142	544	89	186	24	3	16	83	46
94 NL	.325	103	397	52	129	27	1	12	55	12
95 NL	.306	114	480	69	147	31	2	11	56	9
96 NL	.292	104	404	59	118	17	3	7	51	20
Life	.296	1080	4142	581	1224	231	21	98	525	169
3 Ave	.309	126	501	70	155	30	2	12	64	16

REGGIE JEFFERSON

Position: Outfield; first base
Team: Boston Red Sox
Born: Sept. 25, 1968 Tallahassee, FL
Height: 6'4" **Weight:** 210 lbs.
Bats: left **Throws:** left
Acquired: Signed as a free agent, 4/95

PLAYER SUMMARY	
Fantasy Value	$9 to $11
Card Value	5¢ to 8¢
Will	hit with power
Can't	steal bases
Expect	terror at Fenway
Don't Expect	time at first bag

Despite limited playing time last year, Jefferson gave Boston more home runs than anyone not named Mo Vaughn. Always a heavy hitter in Fenway Park—and against right-handed pitching—Jefferson finished with career highs in all three Triple Crown categories. He showed no lingering effects of previous elbow, back, and hamstring problems. An aggressive hitter who fans four times per walk, he likes low, inside fastballs he can pull. Speed is not part of his repertoire; he's stolen one base in seven big-league seasons. Though Jefferson began his pro career as a first baseman, he spent most of last year in left field, where he showed quick reactions and a surprisingly strong arm. Though his range is limited, Jefferson caught most of the balls he could reach. He also served as Vaughn's caddy at first and as a lefty DH and pinch hitter. If he steers clear of injury, Jefferson should be a potent force for years to come. At 28, he should just be approaching his peak.

Major League Batting Register

	BA	G	AB	R	H	2B	3B	HR	RBI	SB
91 NL	.143	5	7	1	1	0	0	1	1	0
91 AL	.198	26	101	10	20	3	0	2	12	0
92 AL	.337	24	89	8	30	6	2	1	6	0
93 AL	.249	113	366	35	91	11	2	10	34	1
94 AL	.327	63	162	24	53	11	0	8	32	0
95 AL	.289	46	121	21	35	8	0	5	26	0
96 AL	.347	122	386	67	134	30	4	19	74	0
Life	.295	399	1232	166	364	69	8	46	185	1
2 Ave	.340	105	307	50	104	23	2	15	60	0

DEREK JETER

Position: Shortstop
Team: New York Yankees
Born: June 26, 1974 Pequannock, NJ
Height: 6'3" **Weight:** 175 lbs.
Bats: right **Throws:** right
Acquired: First-round pick in 6/92 free-agent draft

PLAYER SUMMARY	
Fantasy Value	$16 to $19
Card Value	30¢ to 70¢
Will	improve over time
Can't	hit frequent homers
Expect	good bat, speed
Don't Expect	uncertain fielding

Even before veteran Tony Fernandez's 1996 spring training injury, the Yankees had decided to hand Jeter the starting shortstop job. The fleet freshman responded with the poise of an established star. Often used in the pressure-packed leadoff spot, Jeter topped .300 against both righties and lefties, drew plenty of walks, and injected speed and defense into the attack. Though Jeter fans twice per walk, he delivers more power than the typical shortstop. A steady fielder, Jeter has quick reactions, good range, soft hands, and a strong, reliable arm. He's rarely rattled. Before he became the Yankees' No. 1 draft choice in 1992, Jeter idolized Dave Winfield and dreamed of playing shortstop for the Yankees. A .306 hitter in four minor-league seasons, Jeter put himself on the fast track to the Bronx when he stole 50 bases in the minors three years ago, earning Minor League Player of the Year honors. Jeter, the 1996 AL Rookie of the Year, hit the disputed homer that tied Game 2 of the ALCS in the eighth inning despite the alleged interference of a 12-year-old fan.

Major League Batting Register

	BA	G	AB	R	H	2B	3B	HR	RBI	SB
95 AL	.250	15	48	5	12	4	1	0	7	0
96 AL	.314	157	582	104	183	25	6	10	78	14
Life	.310	172	630	109	195	29	7	10	85	14

DOUG JOHNS

Position: Pitcher
Team: Oakland Athletics
Born: Dec. 19, 1967 South Bend, IN
Height: 6'2" **Weight:** 185 lbs.
Bats: right **Throws:** left
Acquired: 16th-round pick in 6/90 free-agent draft

PLAYER SUMMARY	
Fantasy Value	$0
Card Value	5¢ to 8¢
Will	bank on guile
Can't	stop righties
Expect	starting job
Don't Expect	many Ks

Oakland's only lefty starter last year, Johns fell victim to the sophomore jinx. After winning 14 games in Triple-A and the majors in 1995, he failed to reach double digits in wins, record a respectable ERA, or maintain a strikeout-to-walk ratio much better than 1-to-1. A sinker-slider pitcher who also throws a curve and changeup, Johns relies on location rather than velocity. He changes speeds well but gets hit when he fails to keep the ball down. His three-quarters delivery is more difficult for left-handed hitters than it is for righties. And, since he's not a power pitcher, Johns needs to fool all of the hitters all of the time. An intelligent athlete, Johns holds a degree in psychology from the University of Virginia. He helps himself with his fielding but had more success holding runners as a rookie than he did last year. Johns also threw more wild pitches than anyone else in the Oakland rotation. He began his pro career in 1990 after the Athletics made him a 16th-round amateur draft choice.

Major League Pitching Register

	W	L	ERA	G	CG	IP	H	ER	BB	SO
95 AL	5	3	4.61	11	1	54.2	44	28	26	25
96 AL	6	12	5.98	40	1	158.0	187	105	69	71
Life	11	15	5.63	51	2	212.2	231	133	95	96

CHARLES JOHNSON

Position: Catcher
Team: Florida Marlins
Born: July 20, 1971 Ft. Pierce, FL
Height: 6'2" **Weight:** 215 lbs.
Bats: right **Throws:** right
Acquired: First-round pick in 6/92 free-agent draft

PLAYER SUMMARY	
Fantasy Value	$7 to $9
Card Value	7¢ to 10¢
Will	deliver some power
Can't	copy rookie finish
Expect	Gold Glove defense
Don't Expect	opponents to steal

The sophomore jinx caught up with Johnson last summer. Although he continued to nail 50 percent of would-be basestealers and supplied the same Gold Glove defense, he had trouble hitting his weight. That was a surprise, since Johnson had shown a strong bat during the second half of his first season. An aggressive hitter who fans 2½ times per walk, Johnson may be trying to do too much at the plate. He gets extra bases on one-third of his hits and tends to swing too hard when only a single would suffice. Johnson hits to all fields, though most of his power is to left. No matter what, the former University of Miami All-American and 1992 U.S. Olympian will play because of his defense. Nobody in the National League is better at calling games, handling pitchers, preventing wild pitches, blocking the plate, or nailing runners. At 25, Johnson is still learning. And he's trying to get by without benefit of Triple-A experience. The native Floridian led one minor league in home runs and another in runs batted in, so the potential is clearly there.

Major League Batting Register

	BA	G	AB	R	H	2B	3B	HR	RBI	SB
94 NL	.455	4	11	5	5	1	0	1	4	0
95 NL	.251	97	315	40	79	15	1	11	39	0
96 NL	.218	120	386	34	84	13	1	13	37	1
Life	.236	221	712	79	168	29	2	25	80	1
2 Ave	.233	115	370	40	86	15	1	13	40	1

LANCE JOHNSON

Position: Outfield
Team: New York Mets
Born: July 7, 1963 Cincinnati, OH
Height: 5'11" **Weight:** 159 lbs.
Bats: left **Throws:** left
Acquired: Signed as a free agent, 12/95

PLAYER SUMMARY	
Fantasy Value	$30 to $35
Card Value	7¢ to 10¢
Will	display great speed
Can't	hit frequent homers
Expect	triples, stolen bases
Don't Expect	patience at the plate

The first man to lead both leagues in hits, Johnson accomplished that feat in consecutive seasons. Johnson was the leadoff man and starting center fielder for the NL All-Star Team in 1996. Speed is his primary weapon. Johnson is a high-percentage basestealer who's topped 40 three times. A good contact hitter, he's not a prototypical leadoff type because he won't wait for walks. He loves to slap and run, hitting to all fields against righties but to the opposite field against southpaws. He led the AL in triples four times in a row, a league record. He had 100 runs scored for the first time last year. The wide-ranging Johnson has quick reactions, soft hands, and an adequate arm in center. Because of his speed, he reaches more balls than most colleagues but also makes more miscues. He went through the entire 1994 season without an error but made a dozen last year.

Major League Batting Register

	BA	G	AB	R	H	2B	3B	HR	RBI	SB
87 NL	.220	33	59	4	13	2	1	0	7	6
88 AL	.185	33	124	11	23	4	1	0	6	6
89 AL	.300	50	180	28	54	8	2	0	16	16
90 AL	.285	151	541	76	154	18	9	1	51	36
91 AL	.274	159	588	72	161	14	13	0	49	26
92 AL	.279	157	567	67	158	15	12	3	47	41
93 AL	.311	147	540	75	168	18	14	0	47	35
94 AL	.277	106	412	56	114	11	14	3	54	26
95 AL	.306	142	607	98	186	18	12	10	57	40
96 NL	.333	160	682	117	227	31	21	9	69	50
Life	.293	1138	4300	604	1258	139	99	26	403	282
3 Ave	.307	156	648	102	199	22	18	8	70	44

MARK JOHNSON

Position: First base
Team: Pittsburgh Pirates
Born: Oct. 17, 1967 Worcester, MA
Height: 6'4" **Weight:** 230 lbs.
Bats: left **Throws:** left
Acquired: 20th-round pick in 6/90 free-agent draft

PLAYER SUMMARY

Fantasy Value	$7 to $9
Card Value	5¢ to 8¢
Will	generate power
Can't	steal many bases
Expect	pinch hits
Don't Expect	speed, defense

Getting Johnson's big bat into the lineup more often was a priority for Jim Leyland last summer. The Pittsburgh manager eventually decided to shuffle his infield, moving Jeff King from first to second and Carlos Garcia from second to third, to make room for the hard-hitting Ivy Leaguer (Dartmouth). Twice drafted by the Pirate organization, Johnson spent five years in the minors before reaching the varsity in 1995. A hard worker who made major improvements last year, Johnson was particularly impressive off the bench. He had 12 hits in his first 26 pinch-hitting opportunities (.462) and hit his fourth pinch-homer of the year on August 3. A patient hitter with an on-base percentage 80 points above his batting average, Johnson hit well against both righties and lefties last year. He moves well for a big guy but steals only a handful of bases. Johnson's fielding, though not great, is improving. Because of his strong arm (unusual for a first baseman but not for a one-time college quarterback), his future might lie in the outfield.

Major League Batting Register

	BA	G	AB	R	H	2B	3B	HR	RBI	SB
95 NL	.208	79	221	32	46	6	1	13	28	5
96 NL	.274	127	343	55	94	24	0	13	47	6
Life	.248	206	564	87	140	30	1	26	75	11
2 Ave	.246	108	296	46	73	15	1	14	39	6

RANDY JOHNSON

Position: Pitcher
Team: Seattle Mariners
Born: Sept. 10, 1963 Walnut Creek, CA
Height: 6'10" **Weight:** 225 lbs.
Bats: right **Throws:** left
Acquired: Traded by Expos with Gene Harris and Brian Holman for Mark Langston and Mike Campbell, 5/89

PLAYER SUMMARY

Fantasy Value	$25 to $30
Card Value	25¢ to 50¢
Will	dominate all hitters
Can't	hold runners close
Expect	velocity and control
Don't Expect	more back woes

When healthy, Johnson is arguably baseball's best pitcher. He won his first five decisions last year before he went on the shelf with a herniated disk in his lower back. Johnson tried to return for the stretch drive but was sidelined again after a handful of relief appearances. He finally had season-ending back surgery in mid-September. The tallest player in baseball history, Johnson looks even more intimidating on the pitcher's mound. He not only has the best fastball and best changeup in the league but throws in a slow curve just for show. Opponents hit only .201 against him in 1995, when he led the AL in ERA, winning percentage, strikeouts (for the fourth straight year), and a host of other categories, winning the Cy Young Award. Johnson keeps the ball in the park, and fields his position well.

Major League Pitching Register

	W	L	ERA	G	CG	IP	H	ER	BB	SO
88 NL	3	0	2.42	4	1	26.0	23	7	7	25
89 NL	0	4	6.67	7	0	29.2	29	22	26	26
89 AL	7	9	4.40	22	2	131.0	118	64	70	104
90 AL	14	11	3.65	33	5	219.2	174	89	120	194
91 AL	13	10	3.98	33	2	201.1	151	89	152	228
92 AL	12	14	3.77	31	6	210.1	154	88	144	241
93 AL	19	8	3.24	35	10	255.1	185	92	99	308
94 AL	13	6	3.19	23	9	172.0	132	61	72	204
95 AL	18	2	2.48	30	6	214.1	159	59	65	294
96 AL	5	0	3.67	14	0	61.1	48	25	25	85
Life	104	64	3.53	232	41	1521.0	1173	596	780	1709
3 Ave	15	4	2.93	27	6	182.1	138	59	67	234

BOBBY JONES

Position: Pitcher
Team: New York Mets
Born: Feb. 10, 1970 Fresno, CA
Height: 6'4" **Weight:** 210 lbs.
Bats: right **Throws:** right
Acquired: Supplemental pick in 6/91 free-agent draft

PLAYER SUMMARY	
Fantasy Value	$8 to $10
Card Value	5¢ to 8¢
Will	work to spots
Can't	strike men out
Expect	great control
Don't Expect	enemy steals

Even though the Mets have been a disappointment over the last three years, Jones has been a beacon in the fog. A finesse pitcher who blends a terrific changeup with a cut fastball, sinker, and curve, Jones banks on control to coax ground balls. He's at his best when he changes speeds and locations, hitting particular spots. Though Jones yields more hits than innings and gives up his share of long balls, he maintains damage control by permitting few walks. The former Fresno State star averages fewer than six strikeouts per nine innings but maintains a strikeout-to-walk ratio of 2½-to-1. He gives his team lots of innings, often working late into the game, and helps himself with his fielding and bunting. Jones led the NL with 18 sacrifice bunts in 1995. Although he's not a good hitter, Jones has improved his other major weakness: holding runners on base. Jones spent only three years in the minors before reaching the Mets in 1993. He twice posted ERAs of less than 2.00 in the minors.

Major League Pitching Register

	W	L	ERA	G	CG	IP	H	ER	BB	SO
93 NL	2	4	3.65	9	0	61.2	61	25	22	35
94 NL	12	7	3.15	24	1	160.0	157	56	56	80
95 NL	10	10	4.19	30	3	195.2	209	91	53	127
96 NL	12	8	4.42	31	3	195.2	219	96	46	116
Life	36	29	3.93	94	7	613.0	646	268	177	358
3 Ave	13	10	3.89	33	3	214.1	225	92	62	124

CHIPPER JONES

Position: Shortstop; third base
Team: Atlanta Braves
Born: April 24, 1972 DeLand, FL
Height: 6'3" **Weight:** 195 lbs.
Bats: both **Throws:** right
Acquired: First-round pick in 6/90 free-agent draft

PLAYER SUMMARY	
Fantasy Value	$30 to $35
Card Value	60¢ to $1.50
Will	thrive in clutch
Can't	worry about knee
Expect	patience and power
Don't Expect	erratic fielding

After coming within a whisker of the 1995 NL Rookie of the Year Award, Jones blossomed into an MVP contender last summer. The soft-spoken switch-hitter, who blamed his low freshman average on a desire to hit home runs, made an effort to go with the pitch last year. Coupling patience with the ability to make contact (Jones walks as much as he fans), he not only reached the 30-homer mark but uncorked an 18-game hitting streak. He's a solid clutch hitter who's better left-handed. Despite a knee injury that idled him in 1994, Jones runs well. He was nailed just once in his first 13 steal attempts last year but would run more if he hit higher in the order. Jones started the 1995 All-Star Game at third for the NL (replacing Matt Williams) but returned to short, his original position, when the Braves got Terry Pendleton. Jones also plays the outfield. Blessed with great reactions, good range, and a strong arm, Jones made dramatic improvements in his defense. Where he'll play in '97 depends upon the team's makeup.

Major League Batting Register

	BA	G	AB	R	H	2B	3B	HR	RBI	SB
93 NL	.667	8	3	2	2	1	0	0	0	0
95 NL	.265	140	524	87	139	22	3	23	86	8
96 NL	.309	157	598	114	185	32	5	30	110	14
Life	.290	305	1125	203	326	55	8	53	196	22
2 Ave	.287	157	594	106	171	28	4	28	103	12

CHRIS JONES

Position: Outfield
Team: New York Mets
Born: Dec. 16, 1965 Utica, NY
Height: 6'2" **Weight:** 205 lbs.
Bats: right **Throws:** right
Acquired: Signed as a free agent, 12/94

PLAYER SUMMARY	
Fantasy Value	$0
Card Value	60¢ to $1.50
Will	deliver in pinch
Can't	hit right-handers
Expect	power off bench
Don't Expect	accurate throws

For the past six seasons, Jones has served as an extra outfielder and power-hitting pinch hitter, used primarily against left-handed pitching. An aggressive hitter who fans nearly four times per walk, he also gets extra bases on one-third of his hits. A much better hitter against lefties, Jones has delivered several home runs in the pinch. Last year, he played all three outfield spots in addition to frequent service as a pinch hitter. Jones spent most of his time in right, where he has a strong but not always accurate arm. His speed gives him good range. He had double digits in steals eight times in the minors but never played enough to reach that level in the big leagues. A 1984 third-round draft choice of the Cincinnati Reds, Jones spent nearly eight seasons in the minors before reaching the National League. He played for the Reds, Astros, and Rockies prior to joining the Mets. Jones twice had 20-homer seasons in the minors.

Major League Batting Register

	BA	G	AB	R	H	2B	3B	HR	RBI	SB
91 NL	.292	52	89	14	26	1	2	2	6	2
92 NL	.190	54	63	7	12	2	1	1	4	3
93 NL	.273	86	209	29	57	11	4	6	31	9
94 NL	.300	21	40	6	12	2	1	0	2	0
95 NL	.280	79	182	33	51	6	2	8	31	2
96 NL	.242	89	149	22	36	7	0	4	18	1
Life	.265	381	732	111	194	29	10	21	92	17

DOUG JONES

Position: Pitcher
Team: Milwaukee Brewers
Born: June 24, 1957 Covina, CA
Height: 6'2" **Weight:** 195 lbs.
Bats: right **Throws:** right
Acquired: Signed as a free agent, 6/96

PLAYER SUMMARY	
Fantasy Value	$5 to $7
Card Value	4¢ to 7¢
Will	move ball around
Can't	maintain velocity
Expect	set-up situations
Don't Expect	pinpoint control

At 39, Jones is no longer the great closer who had four 30-save seasons and five trips to the All-Star Game. But he's still a viable set-up man whose assortment of slow stuff bamboozles big-league hitters. A sinkerballer whose best pitches are a circle change and a straight change, Jones complements those deliveries with a slider plus his version of a fastball (one with little velocity). His biggest asset is an ability to move the ball around, hitting the inside and outside corners and keeping the ball down. He yields one hit per inning and nearly four walks per nine innings but also gets more strikeouts than the typical sinkerball pitcher. Jones has been more effective against left-handed hitters the last two seasons. Before 1995, however, he did better against righties. Jones is not a great fielder but does hold runners close.

Major League Pitching Register

	W	L	ERA	G	S	IP	H	ER	BB	SO
82 AL	0	0	10.13	4	0	2.2	5	3	1	1
86 AL	1	0	2.50	11	1	18.0	18	5	6	12
87 AL	6	5	3.15	49	8	91.1	101	32	24	87
88 AL	3	4	2.27	51	37	83.1	69	21	16	72
89 AL	7	10	2.34	59	32	80.2	76	21	13	65
90 AL	5	5	2.56	66	43	84.1	66	24	22	55
91 AL	4	8	5.54	36	7	63.1	87	39	17	48
92 NL	11	8	1.85	80	36	111.2	96	23	17	93
93 NL	4	10	4.54	71	26	85.1	102	43	21	66
94 NL	2	4	2.17	47	27	54.0	55	13	6	38
95 AL	0	4	5.01	52	22	46.2	55	26	16	42
96 NL	2	2	5.01	28	2	32.1	41	18	7	26
96 AL	5	0	3.41	24	1	31.2	31	12	13	34
Life	50	60	3.21	578	242	785.1	802	280	179	639
3 Ave	3	4	3.63	59	22	64.1	70	26	15	54

TODD JONES

Position: Pitcher
Team: Detroit Tigers
Born: April 24, 1968 Marietta, GA
Height: 6'3" **Weight:** 200 lbs.
Bats: left **Throws:** right
Acquired: Traded by Astros with Brian Hunter, Orlando Miller, Doug Brocail, and a player to be named later for Brad Ausmus, Jose Lima, C.J. Nitkowski, Trever Miller, and Daryle Ward, 12/96

PLAYER SUMMARY
Fantasy Value	$9 to $11
Card Value	4¢ to 7¢
Will	rely on strength
Can't	hold baserunners
Expect	more set-up work
Don't Expect	hits by righties

A big right-hander who tries to overpower opposing hitters, Jones was a 1995 workhorse whose '96 campaign was shortened by injury. He worked 99⅔ relief innings, second in the National League, two years ago but contracted tendinitis of the right shoulder last July and was sidelined for much of the second half. When healthy, Jones mixes a mid-90s fastball with an overhand curve, slider, and changeup. Because the fastball rises, he's especially effective against right-handed hitters. Jones averages a strikeout an inning but can't always throw his pitches for strikes. That contributes to his problems with inherited runners. The former minor-league starter, who moved to relief in 1992, has trouble reacting to grounders in his vicinity and is an easy mark for baserunners with larceny in their hearts. Jones can work often and handle multiple-inning assignments. But his past track record as a closer suggests he's best as a set-up man.

Major League Pitching Register
	W	L	ERA	G	S	IP	H	ER	BB	SO
93 NL	1	2	3.13	27	2	37.1	28	13	15	25
94 NL	5	2	2.72	48	5	72.2	52	22	26	63
95 NL	6	5	3.07	68	15	99.2	89	34	52	96
96 NL	6	3	4.40	51	17	57.1	61	28	32	44
Life	18	12	3.27	194	39	267.0	230	97	125	228
3 Ave	7	4	3.22	65	14	91.1	78	32	42	80

BRIAN JORDAN

Position: Outfield
Team: St. Louis Cardinals
Born: March 26, 1967 Baltimore, MD
Height: 6'1" **Weight:** 205 lbs.
Bats: right **Throws:** right
Acquired: First-round pick in 6/88 free-agent draft

PLAYER SUMMARY
Fantasy Value	$20 to $25
Card Value	15¢ to 20¢
Will	thrive in clutch
Can't	practice patience
Expect	speed plus power
Don't Expect	erratic defense

After missing time early with a fractured left thumb last year, Jordan enjoyed the best of his five big-league seasons. A mentally tough hitter who gives his all at every turn, he blossomed into the league's best clutch performer—especially with the bases loaded. He broke Willie McGee's 1982 mark for hits with the bases full and had 32 RBI over an 18-game span in midseason. The former Atlanta Falcons safety is an aggressive hitter who fans more than three times per walk. He uses all fields against right-handers but goes up the middle or the opposite way against lefties. A .350 hitter against left-handed pitching, Jordan gets extra bases on one-third of his hits. He's also a high-percentage basestealer who joined the 20-20 club in 1995. Jordan's speed helps in right field, where he had the league's top fielding percentage (.996) two years ago. He gets good jumps, shows wide range, and has a strong, accurate arm. Jordan also fills in as a center fielder, though he's much more valuable in right.

Major League Batting Register
	BA	G	AB	R	H	2B	3B	HR	RBI	SB
92 NL	.207	55	193	17	40	9	4	5	22	7
93 NL	.309	67	223	33	69	10	6	10	44	6
94 NL	.258	53	178	14	46	8	2	5	15	4
95 NL	.296	131	490	83	145	20	4	22	81	24
96 NL	.310	140	513	82	159	36	1	17	104	22
Life	.287	446	1597	229	459	83	17	59	266	63
3 Ave	.294	121	438	65	129	23	3	16	72	18

RICKY JORDAN

Position: First base
Team: Seattle Mariners
Born: May 26, 1965 Richmond, CA
Height: 6'3" **Weight:** 205 lbs.
Bats: right **Throws:** right
Acquired: Purchased from Angels, 3/96

PLAYER SUMMARY	
Fantasy Value	$0
Card Value	4¢ to 7¢
Will	generate power
Can't	avoid injuries
Expect	hits in the pinch
Don't Expect	play vs. righties

Seattle's plan of platooning Jordan and Paul Sorrento at first base last season went awry early when Jordan was disabled with a sore throwing shoulder in May. Surgery was required, causing the former Philadelphia first baseman to miss the entire campaign. Jordan, who hit 23 homers during his first two years with the Phils, has never shown such form since. Part of the problem was his penchant for landing on the disabled list; last year's stint on the DL was his fifth in eight seasons. When healthy, Jordan hits left-handed pitchers hard, provides power off the bench, and is a capable—though not spectacular—fielder. The former first-round draft pick made his major-league debut in 1988 (.308 average, 11 homers, 69 games), leading the Phils to expect significant production in ensuing seasons. But injuries and impatience have gotten the best of Jordan. He once posted a 9-1 whiff-to-walk ratio.

Major League Batting Register

	BA	G	AB	R	H	2B	3B	HR	RBI	SB
88 NL	.308	69	273	41	84	15	1	11	43	1
89 NL	.285	144	523	63	149	22	3	12	75	4
90 NL	.241	92	324	32	78	21	0	5	44	2
91 NL	.272	101	301	38	82	21	3	9	49	0
92 NL	.304	94	276	33	84	19	0	4	34	3
93 NL	.289	90	159	21	46	4	1	5	18	0
94 NL	.282	72	220	29	62	14	2	8	37	0
96 AL	.250	15	28	4	7	0	0	1	4	0
Life	.281	677	2104	261	592	116	10	55	304	10

WALLY JOYNER

Position: First base
Team: San Diego Padres
Born: June 16, 1962 Atlanta, GA
Height: 6'2" **Weight:** 198 lbs.
Bats: left **Throws:** left
Acquired: Traded by Royals with Aaron Dorlarque for Bip Roberts and Bryan Wolff, 12/95

PLAYER SUMMARY	
Fantasy Value	$7 to $9
Card Value	5¢ to 8¢
Will	swat line drives
Can't	hit left-handers
Expect	big clutch bat
Don't Expect	frequent homers

Joyner made a smooth transition to the NL last year, giving the Padres a solid left-handed bat plus strong defense at first base. Though idled for six weeks with a fractured left thumb, Joyner nearly duplicated his career average of .290. A line-drive hitter, Joyner makes good contact and hits to all fields. He's also patient at the plate, walking more than he fans and posting one of the league's best on-base percentages. A good two-strike hitter, Joyner also hits well in late-inning pressure situations and with runners in scoring position. He steals a handful of bases every year but is hardly a fast man. A graceful first baseman, he's led his league in chances, putouts, assists, double plays, and fielding percentage. Joyner saves other infielders errors with his scoops and stretches.

Major League Batting Register

	BA	G	AB	R	H	2B	3B	HR	RBI	SB
86 AL	.290	154	593	82	172	27	3	22	100	5
87 AL	.285	149	564	100	161	33	1	34	117	8
88 AL	.295	158	597	81	176	31	2	13	85	8
89 AL	.282	159	593	78	167	30	2	16	79	3
90 AL	.268	83	310	35	83	15	0	8	41	2
91 AL	.301	143	551	79	166	34	3	21	96	2
92 AL	.269	149	572	66	154	36	2	9	66	11
93 AL	.292	141	497	83	145	36	3	15	65	5
94 AL	.311	97	363	52	113	20	3	8	57	3
95 AL	.310	131	465	69	-144	28	0	12	83	3
96 NL	.277	121	433	59	120	29	1	8	65	5
Life	.289	1485	5538	784	1601	319	20	166	854	55
3 Ave	.301	135	489	70	147	30	2	11	80	4

JEFF JUDEN

Position: Pitcher
Team: Montreal Expos
Born: Jan. 19, 1971 Salem, MA
Height: 6'8" **Weight:** 265 lbs.
Bats: right **Throws:** right
Acquired: Claimed from Giants on waivers, 7/96

PLAYER SUMMARY	
Fantasy Value	$3 to $5
Card Value	4¢ to 7¢
Will	work in relief
Can't	throw strikes
Expect	fine fastball
Don't Expect	many victories

Junked by the pitching-poor Phils and Giants, Juden found his niche after Montreal made him a heavy-duty middle reliever. Used in set-up roles, Juden yielded fewer than eight hits per nine innings, fanned more than seven over that same span, and did a decent job of keeping the ball in the park. A fastball-slider pitcher who also throws a curve, Juden walks more than four men per nine innings and doesn't have enough movement on his heater to fool the hitters. He's been trying to add a cut fastball to compensate. Juden's slow pace and big motion combine to make him a prime target for basestealers. Almost everyone who tested him last year succeeded. Juden also has trouble fielding his position. He's no threat with a bat in his hands (though he did hit a freak grand slam in 1995). Although he pitched better once he reached Montreal, the jury is out on Juden. Problems with conditioning, confidence, and mechanics have waylaid careers in the past. At 26, he has much to prove.

Major League Pitching Register

	W	L	ERA	G	S	IP	H	ER	BB	SO
91 NL	0	2	6.00	4	0	18.0	19	12	7	11
93 NL	0	1	5.40	2	0	5.0	4	3	4	7
94 NL	1	4	6.18	6	0	27.2	29	19	12	22
95 NL	2	4	4.02	13	0	62.2	53	28	31	47
96 NL	5	0	3.27	58	0	74.1	61	27	34	61
Life	8	11	4.27	83	0	187.2	166	89	88	148
2 Ave	4	2	3.64	36	0	72.1	60	29	34	57

DAVID JUSTICE

Position: Outfield
Team: Atlanta Braves
Born: April 14, 1966 Cincinnati, OH
Height: 6'3" **Weight:** 200 lbs.
Bats: left **Throws:** left
Acquired: Fourth-round pick in 6/85 free-agent draft

PLAYER SUMMARY	
Fantasy Value	$16 to $19
Card Value	12¢ to 20¢
Will	generate power
Can't	avoid injuries
Expect	run production
Don't Expect	low on-base mark

Although injuries have cost him huge chunks of four different seasons, Justice is a proven performer who's extremely potent when healthy. Off to a hot start last year (.321, 6, 25 in 140 at bats), Justice suffered extensive shoulder damage while swinging and missing a pitch May 15. The shoulder, weakened by a hard landing during an attempt at a diving catch the year before, needed surgical repair. When Justice is healthy, he's an extremely selective hitter who makes good contact, walking more often than he fans. He's usually more potent against left-handed pitchers. The combination of power and on-base percentage makes Justice a lethal force in the lineup. He doesn't steal much, but his speed gives him good range in right field, where his reactions, hands, and arm are excellent. His tumbling catches make good highlight-film fodder. At age 30, there's no reason he can't stage a strong comeback.

Major League Batting Register

	BA	G	AB	R	H	2B	3B	HR	RBI	SB
89 NL	.235	16	51	7	12	3	0	1	3	2
90 NL	.282	127	439	76	124	23	2	28	78	11
91 NL	.275	109	396	67	109	25	1	21	87	8
92 NL	.256	144	484	78	124	19	5	21	72	2
93 NL	.270	157	585	90	158	15	4	40	120	3
94 NL	.313	104	352	61	110	16	2	19	59	2
95 NL	.253	120	411	73	104	17	2	24	78	4
96 NL	.321	40	140	23	45	9	0	6	25	1
Life	.275	817	2858	475	786	127	16	160	522	33
2 Ave	.284	141	479	84	136	21	3	27	85	4

RON KARKOVICE

Position: Catcher
Team: Chicago White Sox
Born: Aug. 8, 1963 Union, NJ
Height: 6'1" **Weight:** 215 lbs.
Bats: right **Throws:** right
Acquired: First-round pick in 6/82 free-agent draft

PLAYER SUMMARY
Fantasy Value	$2 to $4
Card Value	4¢ to 7¢
Will	show fine arm
Can't	hike average
Expect	occasional power
Don't Expect	good speed

Such renowned hitting coaches as Charlie Lau, Walt Hriniak, and Bill Buckner have tried and failed to change Karkovice's all-or-nothing approach at the plate. A low-average, high-strikeout hitter with a big swing, Karko always reaches double digits in home runs but sometimes reaches triple digits in Ks. A better hitter against left-handers, Karkovice shows enough patience to push his on-base percentage 50 points above his batting average but fans four times per walk. With an 11-year batting average in the .220 range, Karkovice is living proof it's tough to teach an old dog new tricks. Karkovice is a standout behind the plate, where his arm ranks among the best in baseball. He nails more than 40 percent of potential basestealers. He calls good games, handles pitchers, prevents wild pitches, and blocks the plate.

Major League Batting Register
	BA	G	AB	R	H	2B	3B	HR	RBI	SB
86 AL	.247	37	97	13	24	7	0	4	13	1
87 AL	.071	39	85	7	6	0	0	2	7	3
88 AL	.174	46	115	10	20	4	0	3	9	4
89 AL	.264	71	182	21	48	9	2	3	24	0
90 AL	.246	68	183	30	45	10	0	6	20	2
91 AL	.246	75	167	25	41	13	0	5	22	0
92 AL	.237	123	342	39	81	12	1	13	50	10
93 AL	.228	128	403	60	92	17	1	20	54	2
94 AL	.213	77	207	33	44	9	1	11	29	0
95 AL	.217	113	323	44	70	14	1	13	51	2
96 AL	.220	111	355	44	78	22	0	10	38	0
Life	.223	888	2459	326	549	117	6	90	317	24
3 Ave	.217	116	337	47	73	17	1	13	45	1

SCOTT KARL

Position: Pitcher
Team: Milwaukee Brewers
Born: Aug. 9, 1971 Fontana, CA
Height: 6'2" **Weight:** 195 lbs.
Bats: left **Throws:** left
Acquired: Sixth-round pick in 6/92 free-agent draft

PLAYER SUMMARY
Fantasy Value	$6 to $8
Card Value	5¢ to 8¢
Will	bank on palmball
Can't	strike men out
Expect	double-digit wins
Don't Expect	control trouble

Karl's first full season in the major leagues was a roaring success. He not only became the ace of the Milwaukee staff but became the first Brewer southpaw to top a dozen wins since Teddy Higuera went 16-9 in 1988. Karl even picked a tough opponent—the Boston Red Sox—for his first major-league shutout (6-0 on September 9). A finesse-style control artist who gets most of his outs on grounders, Karl depends upon his defense for help. His best pitch is a palmball, though he also throws a fastball and curve. Poised beyond his years, he's already adept at changing speeds, working both sides of the plate, and keeping his cool with runners on base. Karl yields one hit per inning and three walks per nine innings. But he averages only five strikeouts over that same span. He's especially effective against left-handed hitters. Karl is an excellent fielder with a first-rate pickoff move. More than half the runners who challenge him are caught in the act. Drafted off the University of Hawaii campus in 1992, the youngster could soon be a star.

Major League Pitching Register
	W	L	ERA	G	CG	IP	H	ER	BB	SO
95 AL	6	7	4.14	25	1	124.0	141	57	50	59
96 AL	13	9	4.86	32	3	207.1	220	112	72	121
Life	19	16	4.59	57	4	331.1	361	169	122	180
2 Ave	10	8	4.57	30	2	173.1	189	88	64	94

171

ERIC KARROS

Position: First base
Team: Los Angeles Dodgers
Born: Nov. 4, 1967 Hackensack, NJ
Height: 6'4" **Weight:** 205 lbs.
Bats: right **Throws:** right
Acquired: Sixth-round pick in 6/88 free-agent draft

PLAYER SUMMARY
Fantasy Value	$20 to $25
Card Value	10¢ to 15¢
Will	poke clutch hits
Can't	stop striking out
Expect	home runs, RBI
Don't Expect	erratic glove

Overshadowed on his own club by Mike Piazza, Raul Mondesi, and Hideo Nomo, Karros quietly compiled his best season last year. He was the first Dodger first baseman with successive 30-homer, 100-RBI campaigns since Gil Hodges in 1953 and '54. Though he fans three times per walk, Karros is a feared clutch hitter who does his best hitting with men in scoring position and in late-inning pressure spots. He's also more potent against left-handed pitching. The former UCLA standout uses a short, compact swing to send hits to all fields, though most of his power is to left and left-center. A bad back hampers his mobility, but Karros manages to steal a handful of bases per year. He's made such dramatic improvements in his defense that there's been talk of shifting him to third so that Piazza can play first. Karros spent some time at the hot corner during his four-year tenure in the minors. Karros was NL Rookie of the Year in 1992.

Major League Batting Register

	BA	G	AB	R	H	2B	3B	HR	RBI	SB
91 NL	.071	14	14	0	1	1	0	0	1	0
92 NL	.257	149	545	63	140	30	1	20	88	2
93 NL	.247	158	619	74	153	27	2	23	80	0
94 NL	.266	111	406	51	108	21	1	14	46	2
95 NL	.298	143	551	83	164	29	3	32	105	4
96 NL	.260	154	608	84	158	29	1	34	111	8
Life	.264	729	2743	355	724	137	8	123	431	16
3 Ave	.275	157	600	83	165	30	2	30	98	5

PAT KELLY

Position: Second base
Team: New York Yankees
Born: Oct. 10, 1967 Philadelphia, PA
Height: 6' **Weight:** 180 lbs.
Bats: right **Throws:** right
Acquired: Ninth-round pick in 6/88 free-agent draft

PLAYER SUMMARY
Fantasy Value	$5 to $7
Card Value	4¢ to 7¢
Will	turn double plays
Can't	show any power
Expect	speed, defense
Don't Expect	injury-free year

The 1996 season was one Kelly would rather forget. Sidelined for four months after surgery on his throwing shoulder, he strained his right hamstring the day he returned to action. By season's end, Kelly had little to show for 1996 except for three long stints on the DL. That was nothing new for the slick-fielding second baseman, who was also disabled for parts of 1994 and 1995. In fact, Kelly has appeared in more than 106 games only once in his six-year career, thanks to a combination of injuries and weak hitting. Kelly is a singles hitter who is twice as likely to steal a base as he is to hit a home run. A No. 9 hitter who can bunt and run, Kelly would be more valuable if he showed patience at the plate. Kelly had two 30-steal seasons in the minors but hasn't done that in the majors because he's not on base enough. Defensively, Kelly is a fine second baseman whose reactions, hands, and arm are fine. He also turns the double play well.

Major League Batting Register

	BA	G	AB	R	H	2B	3B	HR	RBI	SB
91 AL	.242	96	298	35	72	12	4	3	23	12
92 AL	.226	106	318	38	72	22	2	7	27	8
93 AL	.273	127	406	49	111	24	1	7	51	14
94 AL	.280	93	286	35	80	21	2	3	41	6
95 AL	.237	89	270	32	64	12	1	4	29	8
96 AL	.143	13	21	4	3	0	0	0	2	0
Life	.251	524	1599	193	402	91	10	24	173	48
2 Ave	.261	116	353	43	92	22	2	4	45	9

ROBERTO KELLY

Position: Outfield
Team: Minnesota Twins
Born: Oct. 1, 1964 Panama City, Panama
Height: 6'4" **Weight:** 185 lbs.
Bats: right **Throws:** right
Acquired: Signed as a free agent, 1/96

PLAYER SUMMARY	
Fantasy Value	$7 to $9
Card Value	5¢ to 8¢
Will	hammer left-handers
Can't	show former power
Expect	strong clutch bat
Don't Expect	sterling fielding

Because of his big contract, Kelly keeps bouncing around. The 1996 Twins were his fifth team in three seasons. An aggressive streak hitter who feasts on fastballs, he loves left-handed pitching. Kelly battered southpaws at a .400-plus clip for most of the season, played all three outfield positions, and served as a part-time DH and pinch hitter. The two-time All-Star exceeded the nine-year career mark of .285 he took into last season. A fine clutch hitter, Kelly was one of Minnesota's unsung heroes—a fine turnabout for a veteran who had reported to spring training as a nonroster player. Though Kelly fans 2½ times per walk, he makes solid contact, especially at crucial times. Kelly's power and speed have declined, but he still has good range in the outfield. He tries to outrun some of his mistakes in judging fly balls. Kelly has a strong arm, but it's not always reliable.

Major League Batting Register

	BA	G	AB	R	H	2B	3B	HR	RBI	SB
87 AL	.269	23	52	12	14	3	0	1	7	9
88 AL	.247	38	77	9	19	4	1	1	7	5
89 AL	.302	137	441	65	133	18	3	9	48	35
90 AL	.285	162	641	85	183	32	4	15	61	42
91 AL	.267	126	486	68	130	22	2	20	69	32
92 AL	.272	152	580	81	158	31	2	10	66	28
93 NL	.319	78	320	44	102	17	3	9	35	21
94 NL	.293	110	434	73	127	23	3	9	45	19
95 NL	.278	136	504	58	140	23	2	7	57	19
96 AL	.323	98	322	41	104	17	4	6	47	10
Life	.288	1060	3857	536	1110	190	24	87	442	220
3 Ave	.294	135	500	70	147	25	3	9	58	19

JASON KENDALL

Position: Catcher
Team: Pittsburgh Pirates
Born: June 26, 1974 San Diego, CA
Height: 6' **Weight:** 181 lbs.
Bats: right **Throws:** right
Acquired: First-round pick in 6/92 free-agent draft

PLAYER SUMMARY	
Fantasy Value	$5 to $7
Card Value	12¢ to 20¢
Will	make good contact
Can't	clear the fences
Expect	solid bat, glove
Don't Expect	sophomore jinx

One year after winning Southern League MVP honors, Kendall became a prime contender for NL Rookie of the Year. Hitting .300 against both lefties and righties, he quickly established a reputation as one of the league's best contact hitters. An aggressive hitter who may show more patience at the plate as he gains experience, Kendall proved so tough to fan that he finished with more walks than strikeouts. Pittsburgh's former first-round draft pick doesn't hit for power but does get a few extra-base hits. He runs well for a catcher and twice was a double-digit basestealer in the minors. The son of former big-league catcher Fred Kendall calls good games, handles pitchers well, prevents potential wild pitches, and guards the plate against incoming runners. His arm is strong, although his success rate of 25 percent last year was less than expected (young Pirate pitchers who failed to hold runners well complicated Kendall's task). The youngest player on the 1996 NL All-Star squad, Kendall was also the first All-Star Pirate rookie ever.

Major League Batting Register

	BA	G	AB	R	H	2B	3B	HR	RBI	SB
96 NL	.300	130	414	54	124	23	5	3	42	5
Life	.300	130	414	54	124	23	5	3	42	5

JEFF KENT

Position: Infield
Team: San Francisco Giants
Born: March 7, 1968 Bellflower, CA
Height: 6'1" **Weight:** 185 lbs.
Bats: right **Throws:** right
Acquired: Traded by Indians with Jose Vizcaino and Julian Tavarez for Matt Williams, 11/96

PLAYER SUMMARY

Fantasy Value	$8 to $10
Card Value	5¢ to 8¢
Will	show some sock
Can't	find a position
Expect	erratic defense
Don't Expect	personality plus

When Kent went to Cleveland, he didn't leave his faults behind. Expected to provide insurance at the corners and right-handed power off the bench, he failed so thoroughly that the Tribe traded for a replacement a month later. Kent has been a mystery throughout his five-year career in the majors. He's hit 20 homers twice but also maintained a ratio of three Ks per walk, a penchant for futility in the clutch, and a reputation for shoddy defense. He twice led the NL in errors. Kent led several minor leagues in chances, putouts, assists, and double plays after moving to second base. But he never came close to duplicating those feats in the majors. Kent's attitude has also tarnished his reputation. Surly in his relations with the New York media, Kent was one of the least popular players in the Mets clubhouse. At 29, it's not too late for him to resurrect his career with the Giants.

Major League Batting Register

	BA	G	AB	R	H	2B	3B	HR	RBI	SB
92 AL	.240	65	192	36	46	13	1	8	35	2
92 NL	.239	37	113	16	27	8	1	3	15	0
93 NL	.270	140	496	65	134	24	0	21	80	4
94 NL	.292	107	415	53	121	24	5	14	68	1
95 NL	.278	125	472	65	131	22	3	20	65	3
96 NL	.290	89	335	45	97	20	1	9	39	4
96 AL	.265	39	102	16	27	7	0	3	16	2
Life	.274	602	2125	296	583	118	11	78	318	16
3 Ave	.286	127	484	64	138	26	4	17	69	3

JIMMY KEY

Position: Pitcher
Team: Baltimore Orioles
Born: April 22, 1961 Huntsville, AL
Height: 6'1" **Weight:** 190 lbs.
Bats: right **Throws:** left
Acquired: Signed as a free agent, 12/96

PLAYER SUMMARY

Fantasy Value	$10 to $13
Card Value	5¢ to 8¢
Will	need location
Can't	avoid gophers
Expect	wins if sound
Don't Expect	great velocity

Although he's a dependable starter, Key was not expected to produce a fast start last season. Rebounding from career-threatening rotator cuff surgery, he started slowly (1-5, 7.14) but reeled off a streak of 20 straight scoreless innings through July 11. Key also encountered further shoulder problems, plus a calf injury, that sidelined him for weeks. But he still managed to even his record after 20 decisions. When he's right, Key is a control artist who depends upon precise location of his fastball, slider, curve, and changeup. He dominates lefties, keeps the ball in the park, and maintains a 2-1 ratio of Ks to walks. The former Clemson standout yields a hit per inning but has a knack for coaxing double-play grounders. Key also helps himself with his defense. He fields his position and holds baserunners exceptionally well.

Major League Pitching Register

	W	L	ERA	G	CG	IP	H	ER	BB	SO
84 AL	4	5	4.65	63	0	62.0	70	32	32	44
85 AL	14	6	3.00	35	3	212.2	188	71	50	85
86 AL	14	11	3.57	36	4	232.0	222	92	74	141
87 AL	17	8	2.76	36	8	261.0	210	80	66	161
88 AL	12	5	3.29	21	2	131.1	127	48	30	65
89 AL	13	14	3.88	33	5	216.0	226	93	27	118
90 AL	13	7	4.25	27	0	154.2	169	73	22	88
91 AL	16	12	3.05	33	2	209.1	207	71	44	125
92 AL	13	13	3.53	33	4	216.2	205	85	59	117
93 AL	18	6	3.00	34	4	236.2	219	79	43	173
94 AL	17	4	3.27	25	1	168.0	177	61	52	97
95 AL	1	2	5.64	5	0	30.1	40	19	6	14
96 AL	12	11	4.68	30	0	169.1	171	88	58	116
Life	164	104	3.49	411	33	2300.0	2231	892	563	1344
2 Ave	18	8	3.86	33	1	203.0	210	87	66	126

BRIAN KEYSER

Position: Pitcher
Team: Chicago White Sox
Born: Oct. 21, 1966 Castro Valley, CA
Height: 6'1" **Weight:** 180 lbs.
Bats: right **Throws:** right
Acquired: 19th-round pick in 6/89 free-agent draft

PLAYER SUMMARY	
Fantasy Value	$0
Card Value	5¢ to 8¢
Will	stay in relief
Can't	strike men out
Expect	hits by rivals
Don't Expect	good K/BB rate

Without location, Keyser is lost. The right-handed finesse pitcher, used strictly in relief by the White Sox last year, has one of the lowest strikeout-per-inning ratios in the majors. He needs precise location of his sinker, slider, curveball, and changeup but didn't always have it last year. The former Stanford standout not only averaged more than four walks per nine innings but finished with more walks than strikeouts—not acceptable for either a starter or reliever. A minor-league starter for more than six seasons, Keyser made ten starts as a rookie for the '95 White Sox. Though hit hard again last year, he managed to keep the ball in the park. Keyser's biggest assets are his competitive approach, his ability to control the running game, and his uncanny capacity to strand more than 75 percent of the runners he inherits. With expansion around the corner, he could have a big-league future. He'll celebrate his 31st birthday just before the expansion draft.

Major League Pitching Register

	W	L	ERA	G	S	IP	H	ER	BB	SO
95 AL	5	6	4.97	23	0	92.1	114	51	27	48
96 AL	1	2	4.98	28	1	59.2	78	33	28	19
Life	6	8	4.97	51	1	152.0	192	84	55	67
2 Ave	3	4	4.97	27	1	82.1	103	45	29	37

DARRYL KILE

Position: Pitcher
Team: Houston Astros
Born: Dec. 2, 1968 Garden Grove, CA
Height: 6'5" **Weight:** 185 lbs.
Bats: right **Throws:** right
Acquired: 30th-round pick in 6/87 free-agent draft

PLAYER SUMMARY	
Fantasy Value	$7 to $9
Card Value	5¢ to 8¢
Will	bank on curve
Can't	stop lefties
Expect	high K count
Don't Expect	fine control

If Kile could maintain his control with more consistency, he'd be one of the top pitchers in the game. A 15-game winner, All-Star, and author of a no-hitter in 1993, Kile has not been able to keep his ERA below 4.00 in three seasons since. There were times last year when it looked like he had recaptured the killer curve that had made him virtually unhittable in the past. Kile, who also throws forkballs and low-90s fastballs, averages a strikeout an inning and keeps the ball in the park but yields more hits than innings and four walks per game. He's led the NL in wild pitches and hit batsmen (he hit four in one game last year). Kile also has problems with left-handed hitters, whose composite average against him last year was well over .300. The big right-hander is not a solid defensive player. He also has trouble holding runners on base. At the plate, Kile pokes occasional hits but also strikes out frequently. As long as he pitches consistently, nobody seems to mind.

Major League Pitching Register

	W	L	ERA	G	CG	IP	H	ER	BB	SO
91 NL	7	11	3.69	37	0	153.2	144	63	84	100
92 NL	5	10	3.95	22	2	125.1	124	55	63	90
93 NL	15	8	3.51	32	4	171.2	152	67	69	141
94 NL	9	6	4.57	24	0	147.2	153	75	82	105
95 NL	4	12	4.96	25	0	127.0	114	70	73	113
96 NL	12	11	4.19	35	4	219.0	233	102	97	219
Life	52	58	4.12	175	10	944.1	920	432	468	768
3 Ave	10	11	4.52	32	1	190.0	192	95	98	165

JEFF KING

Position: Infield
Team: Kansas City Royals
Born: Dec. 26, 1964 Marion, IN
Height: 6'1" **Weight:** 180 lbs.
Bats: right **Throws:** right
Acquired: Traded by Pirates with Jay Bell for Joe Randa, Jeff Granger, Jeff Martin, and Jeff Wallace, 12/96

PLAYER SUMMARY	
Fantasy Value	$20 to $25
Card Value	8¢ to 10¢
Will	swat long ball
Can't	near .300 mark
Expect	run production
Don't Expect	great glove

Changing positions didn't bother King last season. In April, he became the first player to homer twice in an inning in consecutive seasons. He stole home against John Smiley July 11 and reached career peaks in homers and RBI five days later. King makes better contact than most sluggers. He also shows considerable patience at the plate, pushing his on-base percentage more than 70 points above his average. A fastball hitter who uses all fields, King is more productive against left-handers. Though not a fast man, he knows when to steal; King was nailed only once in his first 13 attempts last year. The former Arkansas All-American and College Player of the Year signed as a third baseman but spent most of his time at first last season. He later switched to second. King has good reactions, good hands, and a strong arm but is not smooth at turning two.

Major League Batting Register

	BA	G	AB	R	H	2B	3B	HR	RBI	SB
89 NL	.195	75	215	31	42	13	3	5	19	4
90 NL	.245	127	371	46	91	17	1	14	53	3
91 NL	.239	33	109	16	26	1	1	4	18	3
92 NL	.231	130	480	56	111	21	2	14	65	4
93 NL	.295	158	611	82	180	35	3	9	98	8
94 NL	.263	94	339	36	89	23	0	5	42	3
95 NL	.265	122	445	61	118	27	2	18	87	7
96 NL	.271	155	591	91	160	36	4	30	111	15
Life	.258	894	3161	419	817	173	16	99	493	47
3 Ave	.266	142	523	70	139	33	2	19	89	9

MIKE KINGERY

Position: Outfield
Team: Pittsburgh Pirates
Born: March 29, 1961 St. James, MN
Height: 6' **Weight:** 185 lbs.
Bats: left **Throws:** left
Acquired: Signed as a free agent, 12/95

PLAYER SUMMARY	
Fantasy Value	$0
Card Value	4¢ to 7¢
Will	serve as reserve
Can't	clear the walls
Expect	pinch-hit calls
Don't Expect	sloppy fielding

Before Jermaine Allensworth came up from the minors, Kingery was Pittsburgh's primary center fielder. But he did not come close to delivering the offense he had produced in two previous seasons for Colorado. A contact hitter who walks almost as much as he fans, Kingery sends singles to all fields against right-handed pitchers but becomes a dead pull hitter against lefties. Although he's usually better against righties, that was not the case last year. Kingery wound up playing all three outfield spots and served as a frequent pinch hitter. A fine fourth outfielder, Kingery gets good jumps and catches whatever he reaches even though his range and arm are only average. He rarely makes an error. Kingery doesn't steal much, though he twice topped two dozen steals in the minors. He has played for the Royals, Mariners, Giants, Rockies, and Pirates.

Major League Batting Register

	BA	G	AB	R	H	2B	3B	HR	RBI	SB
86 AL	.258	62	209	25	54	8	5	3	14	7
87 AL	.280	120	354	38	99	25	4	9	52	7
88 AL	.203	57	123	21	25	6	0	1	9	3
89 AL	.224	31	76	14	17	3	0	2	6	1
90 NL	.295	105	207	24	61	7	1	0	24	6
91 NL	.182	91	110	13	20	2	2	0	8	1
92 NL	.107	12	28	3	3	0	0	0	1	0
94 NL	.349	105	301	56	105	27	8	4	41	5
95 NL	.269	119	350	66	94	18	4	8	37	13
96 NL	.246	117	276	32	68	12	2	3	27	2
Life	.268	819	2034	292	546	108	26	30	219	45
3 Ave	.294	133	365	62	107	23	6	6	42	8

RYAN KLESKO

Position: Outfield
Team: Atlanta Braves
Born: June 12, 1971 Westminster, CA
Height: 6'3" **Weight:** 220 lbs.
Bats: left **Throws:** left
Acquired: Fifth-round pick in 6/89 free-agent draft

PLAYER SUMMARY
Fantasy Value	$25 to $30
Card Value	25¢ to 50¢
Will	produce good power
Can't	hammer left-handers
Expect	hot and cold streaks
Don't Expect	Gold Glove defense

A first baseman playing out of position in left field, Klesko has worked hard to improve his defense. Although he still looks awkward at times, Klesko succeeded so well he was rarely lifted in the late innings last year. He also escaped his former platoon role, playing against lefties for the first time. The result was mixed: He hit ten April homers, an Atlanta club record, but batted more than 50 points higher against right-handed pitching. Klesko was even less potent on the road than he was against lefties. He fanned more often as the season wore on, finishing with twice as many strikeouts as walks. That's a lot of Ks, since Klesko drew enough free passes to post one of the best on-base percentages on the Braves. Aggressive in everything he does, he even swiped five bases in his first seven tries. But his baserunning gaffes dwarfed his success. Klesko needs to be more consistent; he hit 20 homers in the first 60 games, tying Hank Aaron's record for the fastest start by a Brave hitter, before fading.

Major League Batting Register
	BA	G	AB	R	H	2B	3B	HR	RBI	SB
92 NL	.000	13	14	0	0	0	0	0	1	0
93 NL	.353	22	17	3	6	1	0	2	5	0
94 NL	.278	92	245	42	68	13	3	17	47	1
95 NL	.310	107	329	48	102	25	2	23	70	5
96 NL	.282	153	528	90	149	21	4	34	93	6
Life	.287	387	1133	183	325	60	9	76	216	12
3 Ave	.289	134	414	68	120	22	3	28	79	4

CHUCK KNOBLAUCH

Position: Second base
Team: Minnesota Twins
Born: July 7, 1968 Houston, TX
Height: 5'9" **Weight:** 175 lbs.
Bats: right **Throws:** right
Acquired: First-round pick in 6/89 free-agent draft

PLAYER SUMMARY
Fantasy Value	$35 to $40
Card Value	15¢ to 20¢
Will	often reach base
Can't	produce 20 homers
Expect	patience, contact
Don't Expect	problems in field

Had he not signed a contract extension with Minnesota, Knoblauch would have been the premier player in the latest free-agent market. The AL's top hitter for most of last season, he's one of the game's top leadoff men. The Texas A&M product is a contact hitter with patience. He walks much more often than he fans and annually ranks among the league leaders in on-base percentage. Knoblauch had double digits in doubles, triples, and home runs last year; hit nearly .400 against lefties; and topped 40 steals for the second straight season. The three-time All-Star tied a Rod Carew club mark by reaching base 11 straight times and broke Carew's club mark for runs scored in a season. Knoblauch does his best hitting with runners in scoring position. He could fatten his average by bunting for hits. But the Twins aren't complaining. Knoblauch is just as good in the field as he is at the plate. He has instant reactions, great range, soft hands, and a strong, accurate arm.

Major League Batting Register
	BA	G	AB	R	H	2B	3B	HR	RBI	SB
91 AL	.281	151	565	78	159	24	6	1	50	25
92 AL	.297	155	600	104	178	19	6	2	56	34
93 AL	.277	153	602	82	167	27	4	2	41	29
94 AL	.312	109	445	85	139	45	3	5	51	35
95 AL	.333	136	538	107	179	34	8	11	63	46
96 AL	.341	153	578	140	197	35	14	13	72	45
Life	.306	857	3328	596	1019	184	41	34	333	214
3 Ave	.328	153	603	127	198	46	9	11	72	49

RANDY KNORR

Position: Catcher
Team: Houston Astros
Born: Nov. 12, 1968 San Gabriel, CA
Height: 6'2" **Weight:** 215 lbs.
Bats: right **Throws:** right
Acquired: Signed as a free agent, 5/96

PLAYER SUMMARY	
Fantasy Value	$0
Card Value	4¢ to 7¢
Will	show good glove
Can't	hit for average
Expect	occasional sock
Don't Expect	starting berth

During his six-year career in the majors, Knorr has never been a star, often been an understudy, and occasionally bided his time on the bench as a third-string catcher. He got only one postseason at bat while playing for the 1992 and '93 Toronto Blue Jays, who kept him around as insurance behind the plate. Knorr's fielding is his forte. He has a strong, accurate throwing arm to go with soft hands, an ability to handle pitchers, and fine mechanical skills. Knorr prevents wild pitches, protects the plate, and calls good games when given the chance. Knorr can't run, but he can put his bat on the ball against left-handed pitchers. He fans three times per walk but has surprising power. Knorr could hit 20 home runs if given enough playing time. With another round of expansion in the offing, his time could come as soon as next season. At 28, he's a good bet for a new team looking for an experienced hand to guide a young pitching staff.

CHAD KREUTER

Position: Catcher
Team: Chicago White Sox
Born: Aug. 26, 1964 Greenbrae, CA
Height: 6'2" **Weight:** 195 lbs.
Bats: both **Throws:** right
Acquired: Signed as a free agent, 12/95

PLAYER SUMMARY	
Fantasy Value	$0
Card Value	4¢ to 7¢
Will	show some pop
Can't	duplicate 1993
Expect	decent defense
Don't Expect	starting berth

In 1993, the only time in his nine-year career he appeared in at least 100 games, Kreuter proved a pleasant surprise with a bat in his hands. The switch-hitting catcher hasn't approached such numbers since but was making an impression with the White Sox last year when he was idled by injury. He dislocated and fractured his left shoulder in a home plate collision July 20, landing on the DL for the rest of the season. When healthy, Kreuter provides some power, no speed, and a little patience at the plate. He fans twice as much as he walks but is willing to work deep counts. The former Pepperdine star remains a solid defensive player who handles pitchers well, prevents wild pitches, and protects the plate. He doesn't have the arm strength or accuracy of Ron Karkovice, but few do. If he hits a little, Kreuter should attract some interest in the fall expansion draft.

Major League Batting Register

	BA	G	AB	R	H	2B	3B	HR	RBI	SB
91 AL	.000	3	1	0	0	0	0	0	0	0
92 AL	.263	8	19	1	5	0	0	1	2	0
93 AL	.248	39	101	11	25	3	2	4	20	0
94 AL	.242	40	124	20	30	2	0	7	19	0
95 AL	.212	45	132	18	28	8	0	3	16	0
96 NL	.195	37	87	7	17	5	0	1	7	0
Life	.226	172	464	57	105	18	2	16	64	0

Major League Batting Register

	BA	G	AB	R	H	2B	3B	HR	RBI	SB
88 AL	.275	16	51	3	14	2	1	1	5	0
89 AL	.152	87	158	16	24	3	0	5	9	0
90 AL	.045	22	22	2	1	1	0	0	2	0
91 AL	.000	3	4	0	0	0	0	0	0	0
92 AL	.253	67	190	22	48	9	0	2	16	0
93 AL	.286	119	374	59	107	23	3	15	51	2
94 AL	.224	65	170	17	38	8	0	1	19	0
95 AL	.227	26	75	12	17	5	0	1	8	0
96 AL	.219	46	114	14	25	8	0	3	18	0
Life	.237	451	1158	145	274	59	4	28	128	2

TIM LAKER

Position: Catcher
Team: Montreal Expos
Born: Nov. 27, 1969 Encino, CA
Height: 6'3" **Weight:** 200 lbs.
Bats: right **Throws:** right
Acquired: Sixth-round pick in 6/88 free-agent draft

PLAYER SUMMARY	
Fantasy Value	$0
Card Value	4¢ to 7¢
Will	prove elbow OK
Can't	reduce K ratio
Expect	strong defense
Don't Expect	spot in lineup

Laker was shelved March 30 with his third elbow operation and missed the entire 1996 season. A .220 hitter in three previous campaigns, Laker is known primarily for his defensive ability. He's a good mechanical receiver with a strong arm, and he knows how to handle pitchers. He's also adept at shifting his weight to prevent wild pitches and protecting the plate from runners trying to score. Laker likes fastballs but still thinks he can hit every one of them over the fence. In reality, he's a singles hitter who fans three times per walk. He had at least a dozen homers in two minor-league seasons, but major-league competition is considerably more rigorous. Laker has more speed than the average catcher—he twice recorded double digits in steals before reaching the majors—but isn't likely to run much. Nor is he likely to let others run against him. If healthy, Laker will likely remain a reserve, used as a defensive specialist. That could change if he suddenly shows he can hit.

Major League Batting Register

	BA	G	AB	R	H	2B	3B	HR	RBI	SB
92 NL	.217	28	46	8	10	3	0	0	4	1
93 NL	.198	43	86	3	17	2	1	0	7	2
95 NL	.234	64	141	17	33	8	1	3	20	0
Life	.220	135	273	28	60	13	2	3	31	3

TOM LAMPKIN

Position: Catcher
Team: San Francisco Giants
Born: March 4, 1964 Cincinnati, OH
Height: 5'11" **Weight:** 185 lbs.
Bats: left **Throws:** right
Acquired: Signed as a free agent, 1/94

PLAYER SUMMARY	
Fantasy Value	$0
Card Value	4¢ to 7¢
Will	put bat on ball
Can't	hit left-handers
Expect	occasional sock
Don't Expect	mediocre throws

Lampkin was in the right place at the right time when San Francisco decided to unload No. 1 catcher Kirt Manwaring in a cost-cutting move. The journeyman became a starter for the first time after the July trade—even though fellow receiver Rick Wilkins joined the club in the same swap. Lampkin, who has a reputation for working well with young pitchers, did a good job before he went on the shelf Aug. 25 with a fractured thumb. A contact hitter who walks as much as he fans, Lampkin keeps his on-base percentage 100 points above his batting average. He has surprising power, too: 14 extra-base hits and 29 RBI in a career-high 177 at bats before the injury. Because he puts the bat on the ball, Lampkin is also a potent pinch hitter. He has good speed for a catcher along with good mobility behind the plate. Lampkin calls good games, prevents wild pitches, blocks the plate, and is regarded as a fine handler of pitchers. His arm helped him lead two minor leagues in assists.

Major League Batting Register

	BA	G	AB	R	H	2B	3B	HR	RBI	SB
88 AL	.000	4	4	0	0	0	0	0	0	0
90 NL	.222	26	63	4	14	0	1	1	4	0
91 NL	.190	38	58	4	11	3	1	0	3	0
92 NL	.235	9	17	3	4	0	0	0	0	2
93 AL	.198	73	162	22	32	8	0	4	25	7
95 NL	.276	65	76	8	21	2	0	1	9	2
96 NL	.232	66	177	26	41	8	0	6	29	1
Life	.221	281	557	67	123	21	2	12	70	12

MARK LANGSTON

Position: Pitcher
Team: Anaheim Angels
Born: Aug. 20, 1960 San Diego, CA
Height: 6'2" **Weight:** 190 lbs.
Bats: right **Throws:** left
Acquired: Signed as a free agent, 12/89

PLAYER SUMMARY	
Fantasy Value	$7 to $9
Card Value	8¢ to 12¢
Will	escape injury plague
Can't	capture old velocity
Expect	sensational fielding
Don't Expect	bad whiff/walk ratio

In his first dozen seasons, Langston was a paragon of durability, disabled only twice. Last year, however, the three-time strikeout king spent most of the year on the sidelines, suffering from rotator cuff tendinitis, torn cartilage in his right knee, a strained right calf, and a strained right knee. Once a pure power pitcher, he's put more emphasis on his curveball and circle change to compensate for his decreasing velocity. He intimidates hitters with his high kick and over-the-top delivery. The kick gives runners a head start, but Langston pays close attention to the running game. Few who challenge him succeed. Langston, winner of seven Gold Gloves, is outstanding as a fielder. At 36, he's not about to win any more K crowns. But if healthy, he should crank out a few more solid seasons.

Major League Pitching Register

	W	L	ERA	G	CG	IP	H	ER	BB	SO
84 AL	17	10	3.40	35	5	225.0	188	85	118	204
85 AL	7	14	5.47	24	2	126.2	122	77	91	72
86 AL	12	14	4.85	37	9	239.1	234	129	123	245
87 AL	19	13	3.84	35	14	272.0	242	116	114	262
88 AL	15	11	3.34	35	9	261.1	222	97	110	235
89 AL	4	5	3.56	10	2	73.1	60	29	19	60
89 NL	12	9	2.39	24	6	176.2	138	47	93	175
90 AL	10	17	4.40	33	5	223.0	215	109	104	195
91 AL	19	8	3.00	34	7	246.1	190	82	96	183
92 AL	13	14	3.66	32	9	229.0	206	93	74	174
93 AL	16	11	3.20	35	7	256.1	220	91	85	196
94 AL	7	8	4.68	18	2	119.1	121	62	54	109
95 AL	15	7	4.63	31	2	200.1	212	103	64	142
96 AL	6	5	4.82	18	2	123.1	116	66	45	83
Life	172	146	3.85	401	81	2772.0	2486	1186	1190	2335
3 Ave	11	8	4.69	26	2	172.1	175	90	64	132

RAY LANKFORD

Position: Outfield
Team: St. Louis Cardinals
Born: June 5, 1967 Modesto, CA
Height: 5'11" **Weight:** 180 lbs.
Bats: left **Throws:** left
Acquired: Third-round pick in 6/87 free-agent draft

PLAYER SUMMARY	
Fantasy Value	$25 to $30
Card Value	10¢ to 15¢
Will	produce clutch hits
Can't	solve southpaw jinx
Expect	steals, runs, power
Don't Expect	trouble in outfield

Speed. Defense. Power. Lankford gives the Cardinals so much of those three elements that his futility against left-handers and penchant for striking out are overlooked. A 20-20 man for the third time last year, Lankford also set a St. Louis record by topping the century mark in strikeouts for the sixth straight season. But his power is prodigious. A fine clutch hitter who feasts on fastballs, Lankford takes a big swing and fans twice per walk. But he produces extra bases on almost half his hits. Batting second, ahead of Ron Gant and Brian Jordan last year, helped Lankford score more runs than in any previous campaign. He also finished with the best basestealing success ratio in the majors. His speed helps in the outfield, where Lankford emerged as a Gold Glove candidate last year. He gets good jumps, outruns his mistakes, and ranges wide to his left and right. Lankford has good hands and a stronger, more accurate arm than most center fielders.

Major League Batting Register

	BA	G	AB	R	H	2B	3B	HR	RBI	SB
90 NL	.286	39	126	12	36	10	1	3	12	8
91 NL	.251	151	566	83	142	23	15	9	69	44
92 NL	.293	153	598	87	175	40	6	20	86	42
93 NL	.238	127	407	64	97	17	3	7	45	14
94 NL	.267	109	416	89	111	25	5	19	57	11
95 NL	.277	132	483	81	134	35	2	25	82	24
96 NL	.275	149	545	100	150	36	8	21	86	35
Life	.269	860	3141	516	845	186	40	104	437	178
3 Ave	.273	150	558	105	152	37	6	25	86	26

MIKE LANSING

Position: Second base
Team: Montreal Expos
Born: April 3, 1968 Rawlins, WY
Height: 6′ **Weight:** 175 lbs.
Bats: right **Throws:** right
Acquired: Purchased from Miami (independent team), 9/91

PLAYER SUMMARY	
Fantasy Value	$15 to $18
Card Value	5¢ to 8¢
Will	score many runs
Can't	clear wall often
Expect	speed
Don't Expect	prolonged slump

How could 26 teams be so oblivious? When Lansing played short at Wichita State, nobody wanted him. He signed with the independent Miami team in the Florida State League, attracted the attention of the Expos, then blossomed into a star last year. Originally a three-position infielder, Lansing became the regular second baseman when Delino DeShields was traded after the '93 campaign. A fine table-setter, Lansing supplies plenty of singles, doubles, stolen bases, and runs scored. He advances runners, breaks up potential double plays, and solidifies the infield defense. He even hits occasional long balls. A fastball hitter who thrives in the clutch, Lansing has learned to show more patience at the plate. He added 50 points to his on-base percentage last year. Though slowed by left ankle tendinitis, he remained a high-percentage base-stealer. Lansing's speed gives him great range to go with quick reactions, soft hands, and a shortstop's arm at second base. He can turn two from either side.

Major League Batting Register

	BA	G	AB	R	H	2B	3B	HR	RBI	SB
93 NL	.287	141	491	64	141	29	1	3	45	23
94 NL	.266	106	394	44	105	21	2	5	35	12
95 NL	.255	127	467	47	119	30	2	10	62	27
96 NL	.285	159	641	99	183	40	2	11	53	23
Life	.275	533	1993	254	548	120	7	29	195	85
3 Ave	.270	150	574	71	155	34	2	10	57	23

BARRY LARKIN

Position: Shortstop
Team: Cincinnati Reds
Born: April 28, 1964 Cincinnati, OH
Height: 6′ **Weight:** 185 lbs.
Bats: right **Throws:** right
Acquired: First-round pick in 6/85 free-agent draft

PLAYER SUMMARY	
Fantasy Value	$35 to $40
Card Value	20¢ to 40¢
Will	supply speed, pop
Can't	win batting title
Expect	patience, contact
Don't Expect	problems in field

Larkin's numbers were so good last year he could have won his second consecutive MVP Award. In fact, his overall 1996 performance was better than the previous year's. A patient contact hitter who walks twice as much as he fans, Larkin still uncorks a swing loaded with power. After switching to a heavier bat, the eight-time All-Star became the first 30-30 shortstop in baseball history. He's a wrist hitter who uses all fields, thrives in clutch situations, and pounds left-handers. He also knows when to steal. Larkin's speed helps him in the field, where he ranges deep into the hole. The three-time Gold Glove winner has instant reactions, soft hands, and a strong, reliable arm. His combination of speed, defense, and power makes the former University of Michigan All-American a fabulous all-around shortstop.

Major League Batting Register

	BA	G	AB	R	H	2B	3B	HR	RBI	SB
86 NL	.283	41	159	27	45	4	3	3	19	8
87 NL	.244	125	439	64	107	16	2	12	43	21
88 NL	.296	151	588	91	174	32	5	12	56	40
89 NL	.342	97	325	47	111	14	4	4	36	10
90 NL	.301	158	614	85	185	25	6	7	67	30
91 NL	.302	123	464	88	140	27	4	20	69	24
92 NL	.304	140	533	76	162	32	6	12	78	15
93 NL	.315	100	384	57	121	20	3	8	51	14
94 NL	.279	110	427	78	119	23	5	9	52	26
95 NL	.319	131	496	98	158	29	6	15	66	51
96 NL	.298	152	517	117	154	32	4	33	89	36
Life	.298	1328	4946	828	1476	254	48	135	626	275
3 Ave	.298	151	559	112	166	32	6	21	79	43

MATT LAWTON

Position: Outfield
Team: Minnesota Twins
Born: Nov. 3, 1971 Gulfport, MS
Height: 5'10" **Weight:** 196 lbs.
Bats: left **Throws:** right
Acquired: 12th-round pick in 6/91 free-agent
draft

PLAYER SUMMARY	
Fantasy Value.	$1 to $3
Card Value	20¢ to 35¢
Will	show more speed
Can't	clear fence often
Expect.	contact, singles
Don't Expect.	extended slump

After topping 20 steals four times in the minors, Lawton spent most of 1996 in Minnesota. Except for a brief exile to Triple-A, he formed a capable left-right platoon with Roberto Kelly and acquitted himself well. His big moment was a June 30 grand slam that gave the Twins a 5-2 win over the Royals. That hit came after Lawton changed his stance, going from a crouching style to standing straighter in the box. A contact hitter, Lawton walks as often as he fans. His patience paid off in a .339 on-base percentage, 81 points higher than his batting average, last year. Lawton showed alley power in the minors, where he once delivered 37 extra-base hits. If he learns to bunt for base hits and masters the moves of opposing pitchers, Lawton's hitting and basestealing numbers should rise. He's a good outfielder who once led a minor league in fielding. Because of his speed and range, Lawton is a natural center fielder who throws well enough to play right. The converted second baseman twice had double-digit assists as an outfielder in the minors.

Major League Batting Register

	BA	G	AB	R	H	2B	3B	HR	RBI	SB
95 AL	.317	21	60	11	19	4	1	1	12	1
96 AL	.258	79	252	34	65	7	1	6	42	4
Life	.269	100	312	45	84	11	2	7	54	5

AL LEITER

Position: Pitcher
Team: Florida Marlins
Born: Oct. 23, 1965 Toms River, NJ
Height: 6'3" **Weight:** 215 lbs.
Bats: left **Throws:** left
Acquired: Signed as a free agent, 12/95

PLAYER SUMMARY	
Fantasy Value.	$16 to $19
Card Value	5¢ to 8¢
Will	yield few hits
Can't	stop wild streaks
Expect	great velocity
Don't Expect.	gopher trouble

One night before Leiter pitched a no-hitter against the Rockies, he got a fortune cookie that read, "You will soon be on top of the world." Leiter's gem was the high point of a season that included career peaks in wins, ERA, innings pitched, and strikeouts as well as a first-time selection to the All-Star Team. Leiter obviously liked the NL better than the AL. He had spent five stints on the DL during a seven-year tenure with Toronto. Twice, he needed arm surgery. Healthy last year, Leiter held hitters to a league-low .202 average and yielded only 6.39 hits per nine innings, also leading the league. On the minus side, however, he allowed the most walks (119) in the majors. Leiter's best pitch is a live heater with a sinking motion. He keeps batters honest by cutting the fastball and adding a hard slider and quality curve. Leiter is a fine fielder who keeps runners close.

Major League Pitching Register

	W	L	ERA	G	CG	IP	H	ER	BB	SO
87 AL	2	2	6.35	4	0	22.2	24	16	15	28
88 AL	4	4	3.92	14	0	57.1	49	25	33	60
89 AL	1	2	5.67	5	0	33.1	32	21	23	26
90 AL	0	0	0.00	4	0	6.1	1	0	2	5
91 AL	0	0	27.00	3	0	1.2	3	5	5	1
92 AL	0	0	9.00	1	0	1.0	1	1	2	0
93 AL	9	6	4.11	34	1	105.0	93	48	56	66
94 AL	6	7	5.08	20	1	111.2	125	63	65	100
95 AL	11	11	3.64	28	2	183.0	162	74	108	153
96 NL	16	12	2.93	33	2	215.1	153	70	119	200
Life	49	44	3.94	146	6	737.1	643	323	428	639
3 Ave	12	11	3.76	31	2	193.0	170	81	111	171

MARK LEITER

Position: Pitcher
Team: Philadelphia Phillies
Born: April 13, 1963 Joliet, IL
Height: 6'3" **Weight:** 210 lbs.
Bats: right **Throws:** right
Acquired: Signed as a free agent, 12/96

PLAYER SUMMARY	
Fantasy Value	$4 to $6
Card Value	5¢ to 8¢
Will	find strike zone
Can't	avoid gopher balls
Expect	ground-ball outs
Don't Expect	many strikeouts

The Leiter brothers are more different than they are alike. Mark doesn't have Al's velocity, but he doesn't yield nearly as many walks. A sinker-slider pitcher who also throws a curve and forkball, Leiter yields three walks per nine innings and averages seven strikeouts over the same span. But he yields too many hits and too many homers, though Montreal pitching coach Joe Kerrigan turned his 1996 season around by correcting a flaw in Leiter's leg kick. Leiter had been 4-10 with a 5.19 ERA for the Giants before joining Kerrigan's club. His success with the Expos shows a willingness to learn. Perhaps Leiter will learn to improve his hitting, fielding, and pickoff move, all of which need work. The elder Leiter turned pro in 1983, and after missing three straight minor-league years with a bad shoulder, Leiter reached the majors in 1990. Like his brother, Leiter is a survivor of the surgeon's knife; he's had four shoulder operations and a series of groin injuries.

Major League Pitching Register

	W	L	ERA	G	CG	IP	H	ER	BB	SO
90 AL	1	1	6.84	8	0	26.1	33	20	9	21
91 AL	9	7	4.21	38	1	134.2	125	63	50	103
92 AL	8	5	4.18	35	1	112.0	116	52	43	75
93 AL	6	6	4.72	27	1	106.2	111	56	44	70
94 AL	4	7	4.72	40	0	95.1	99	50	35	71
95 NL	10	12	3.82	30	7	195.2	185	83	55	129
96 NL	8	12	4.92	35	2	205.0	219	112	69	164
Life	46	50	4.48	213	12	875.2	888	436	305	633
3 Ave	8	12	4.44	42	3	186.1	189	92	60	136

MARK LEMKE

Position: Second base
Team: Atlanta Braves
Born: Aug. 13, 1965 Utica, NY
Height: 5'9" **Weight:** 167 lbs.
Bats: both **Throws:** right
Acquired: 27th-round pick in 6/83 free-agent draft

PLAYER SUMMARY	
Fantasy Value	$1
Card Value	4¢ to 7¢
Will	hit to all fields
Can't	supply any speed
Expect	strong fielding
Don't Expect	run production

If baseball had separate teams for offense and defense, Lemke would make the All-Star Team for his great glovework around the second-base bag. A little guy whose reactions are faster than his feet, Lemke has uncanny instincts, soft hands, and a knack for turning the double play even when baserunners are inches away. Except for the 1991 World Series (.417) and the 1994 regular season (.294), however, Lemke has never made headlines with his bat. A contact hitter with patience, he walks more often than he fans but offers little power or speed. The combined total of his home runs and stolen bases last year just narrowly reached double digits (ten). Though sometimes used in the No. 2 slot, Lemke is basically a .250 hitter who's too slow to fatten his average with bunts or infield hits. But he is adept at sacrificing and moving runners along. Usually a better left-handed hitter, Lemke sends singles to all fields.

Major League Batting Register

	BA	G	AB	R	H	2B	3B	HR	RBI	SB
88 NL	.224	16	58	8	13	4	0	0	2	0
89 NL	.182	14	55	4	10	2	1	2	10	0
90 NL	.226	102	239	22	54	13	0	0	21	0
91 NL	.234	136	269	36	63	11	2	2	23	1
92 NL	.227	155	427	38	97	7	4	6	26	0
93 NL	.252	151	493	52	124	19	2	7	49	1
94 NL	.294	104	350	40	103	15	0	3	31	0
95 NL	.253	116	399	42	101	16	5	5	38	2
96 NL	.255	135	498	64	127	17	0	5	37	5
Life	.248	929	2788	306	692	104	14	30	237	9
3 Ave	.268	137	480	56	129	19	2	5	41	2

CURTIS LESKANIC

Position: Pitcher
Team: Colorado Rockies
Born: April 2, 1968 Homestead, PA
Height: 6′ **Weight:** 180 lbs.
Bats: right **Throws:** right
Acquired: Third-round pick from Twins in 11/92 expansion draft

PLAYER SUMMARY	
Fantasy Value	$6 to $8
Card Value	4¢ to 7¢
Will	throw late heat
Can't	hold runners on
Expect	whiff per inning
Don't Expect	lingering injury

One year after becoming Colorado's best reliever, Leskanic broke down. Disabled with elbow and shoulder woes in June, he never regained his 1995 form. That was the year he led the majors in games (76) and relief Ks (107), allowed just six of 46 inherited runners to score, and fanned 9.83 per nine innings. He even saved the game that clinched the NL's first wild-card berth. A fastball-slider pitcher who works down in the zone, Leskanic averaged more than a K per inning (9.29) in '96, but his control evaporated and he yielded far too many hits and homers (12 in 73⅔ innings pitched). Leskanic's bout with rotator cuff tendinitis proved fatal to Colorado's chance of claiming the wild-card berth again. When healthy, Leskanic succeeds by getting his outs on strikeouts and grounders—a combination that works in homer-happy Coors Field. The former LSU star pitches well under pressure, fields his position well, and helps himself with his hitting and bunting. Leskanic's biggest weakness is holding baserunners.

Major League Pitching Register

	W	L	ERA	G	S	IP	H	ER	BB	SO
93 NL	1	5	5.37	18	0	57.0	59	34	27	30
94 NL	1	1	5.64	8	0	22.1	27	14	10	17
95 NL	6	3	3.40	76	10	98.0	83	37	33	107
96 NL	7	5	6.23	70	6	73.2	82	51	38	76
Life	15	14	4.88	172	16	251.0	251	136	108	230
2 Ave	7	4	4.53	78	9	92.0	88	46	38	98

DARREN LEWIS

Position: Outfield
Team: Chicago White Sox
Born: Aug. 28, 1967 Berkeley, CA
Height: 6′ **Weight:** 175 lbs.
Bats: right **Throws:** right
Acquired: Signed as a free agent, 12/95

PLAYER SUMMARY	
Fantasy Value	$8 to $10
Card Value	5¢ to 8¢
Will	bring great glove
Can't	hit the long ball
Expect	speed, patience
Don't Expect	many strikeouts

If Lewis could learn to hit—even a little—he'd be one of baseball's best center fielders. He can bunt, beat out infield hits, and make contact. He even walks more often than he fans. But Lewis has never been more than a spray hitter who sends singles to the opposite field. And he doesn't do that often enough. Lewis was a .249 hitter with nine homers in six seasons before the '96 season started. But he finished the year with a career-low .228 average, added only four homers, and eventually lost his job to the veteran Dave Martinez. That was a shame, since Lewis showed enough patience at the plate to push his on-base percentage 93 points beyond his batting average. He also continued to excel on the bases. Lewis is at his best in the field, where he holds the major-league mark for consecutive errorless games. The 1994 Gold Glove recipient has quick reactions, great range, and soft hands, but his arm is more like a pea-shooter than a howitzer.

Major League Batting Register

	BA	G	AB	R	H	2B	3B	HR	RBI	SB
90 AL	.229	25	35	4	8	0	0	0	1	2
91 NL	.248	72	222	41	55	5	3	1	15	13
92 NL	.231	100	320	38	74	8	1	1	18	28
93 NL	.253	136	522	84	132	17	7	2	48	46
94 NL	.257	114	451	70	116	15	9	4	29	30
95 NL	.250	132	472	66	118	13	3	1	24	32
96 AL	.228	141	337	55	77	12	2	4	53	21
Life	.246	720	2359	358	580	70	25	13	188	172
3 Ave	.248	150	501	76	124	16	6	4	40	33

MARK LEWIS

Position: Second base
Team: San Francisco Giants
Born: Nov. 30, 1969 Hamilton, OH
Height: 6'1" **Weight:** 190 lbs.
Bats: right **Throws:** right
Acquired: Traded by Tigers for Jesus Ibarra, 12/96

PLAYER SUMMARY

Fantasy Value	$7 to $9
Card Value	4¢ to 7¢
Will	hit lefties hard
Can't	cut strikeout rate
Expect	adequate defense
Don't Expect	consistent power

Lewis is living proof that high draft picks don't always succeed. The second choice in the 1988 draft, he spent more than three years in the minors before the Indians—then a cellar-dwelling team—tried to make him their shortstop. Guilty of too many errors and too few homers, Lewis spent much of '93 and '94 in the minors before resurfacing with the '95 Reds. He hit a career-best .339 as a platoon third baseman but again failed to produce the power that had long been predicted. Even the no-pressure atmosphere of the struggling Tigers didn't help. Though Lewis crushed left-handers at a .351 clip, he hit less than .250 vs. righties and managed only 11 homers. Since Tiger Stadium is regarded as a hitter's paradise, his numbers could have been better. Lewis needs to show more patience; he fans nearly three times per walk. He has enough speed to give him good mobility in the field, where he has good reactions and range, soft hands, and a solid throwing arm.

Major League Batting Register

	BA	G	AB	R	H	2B	3B	HR	RBI	SB
91 AL	.264	84	314	29	83	15	1	0	30	2
92 AL	.264	122	413	44	109	21	0	5	30	4
93 AL	.250	14	52	6	13	2	0	1	5	3
94 AL	.205	20	73	6	15	5	0	1	8	1
95 NL	.339	81	171	25	58	13	1	3	30	0
96 AL	.270	145	545	69	147	30	3	11	55	6
Life	.271	466	1568	179	425	86	5	21	158	16
2 Ave	.288	118	369	49	106	22	2	7	44	3

RICHIE LEWIS

Position: Pitcher
Team: Detroit Tigers
Born: Jan. 25, 1966 Muncie, IN
Height: 5'10" **Weight:** 175 lbs.
Bats: right **Throws:** right
Acquired: Traded by Padres with Melvin Nieves and Raul Casanova for Sean Bergman, Cade Gaspar, and Todd Steverson, 4/96

PLAYER SUMMARY

Fantasy Value	$1
Card Value	4¢ to 7¢
Will	work often
Can't	find plate
Expect	relief role
Don't Expect	closer job

Lewis was Detroit's busiest and most effective right-handed reliever last year. He reached career highs in games (72) and innings (90⅓) and held opposing hitters to a respectable .238 batting average. A curveball specialist with a compact motion, Lewis yields fewer than eight hits per nine innings and averages nearly eight whiffs over the same span. But he often has difficulty throwing strikes. Last year, he had an amazing nine-inning average of 6.48 walks. Lewis keeps the ball in the park, fields his position well, and has some success in holding enemy baserunners. The former Florida State All-American turned pro after Montreal made him a second-round draft pick in 1987. He spent six seasons in the minors before reaching the big leagues with the 1992 Baltimore Orioles. Lewis later pitched for the Marlins before joining the Tigers at the start of last season. A starter in the minors, he became a full-time reliever in 1993.

Major League Pitching Register

	W	L	ERA	G	S	IP	H	ER	BB	SO
92 AL	1	1	10.80	2	0	6.2	13	8	7	4
93 NL	6	3	3.26	57	0	77.1	68	28	43	65
94 NL	1	4	5.67	45	0	54.0	62	34	38	45
95 NL	0	1	3.75	21	0	36.0	30	15	15	32
96 AL	4	6	4.18	72	2	90.1	78	42	65	78
Life	12	15	4.32	197	2	264.1	251	127	168	224
3 Ave	2	4	4.64	53	1	69.0	66	36	45	59

JIM LEYRITZ

Position: Catcher; first base
Team: Anaheim Angels
Born: Dec. 27, 1963 Lakewood, OH
Height: 6′ **Weight:** 190 lbs.
Bats: right **Throws:** right
Acquired: Traded by Yankees for Ryan Kane and Jeremy Blevins, 12/96

PLAYER SUMMARY	
Fantasy Value	$4 to $6
Card Value	4¢ to 7¢
Will	poke clutch hits
Can't	win steady job
Expect	occasional power
Don't Expect	speed, defense

Leyritz is not likely to find a steady position because his versatility is so valuable. He caught 55 games for the Yankees last year, played all three bases and left field, and also served as DH and pinch hitter. Signed as a catcher, Leyritz spent his first two seasons behind the plate. But he began to move around as a third-year pro and never shook the utility tag—even after hitting .309 in 1993 with 17 homers in 75 games a year later. Hitting from an open stance, Leyritz sends line drives to all fields and hits inside pitches out of the park. He's usually lethal against left-handers, though he struggled against southpaws in 1996 (.241). Leyritz has a good eye, drawing enough walks to push his on-base percentage 91 points beyond his batting average. He's no threat to steal—or to stop other basestealers. He stopped only 27 percent of those who challenged him last year. Leyritz is not always popular with teammates because of his outspoken personality.

Major League Batting Register

	BA	G	AB	R	H	2B	3B	HR	RBI	SB
90 AL	.257	92	303	28	78	13	1	5	25	2
91 AL	.182	32	77	8	14	3	0	0	4	0
92 AL	.257	63	144	17	37	6	0	7	26	0
93 AL	.309	95	259	43	80	14	0	14	53	0
94 AL	.265	75	249	47	66	12	0	17	58	0
95 AL	.269	77	264	37	71	12	0	7	37	1
96 AL	.264	88	265	23	70	10	0	7	40	2
Life	.266	522	1561	203	416	70	1	57	243	5
3 Ave	.266	93	304	44	81	13	0	13	54	1

JON LIEBER

Position: Pitcher
Team: Pittsburgh Pirates
Born: April 2, 1970 Council Bluffs, IA
Height: 6′3″ **Weight:** 220 lbs.
Bats: right **Throws:** left
Acquired: Traded by Royals with Dan Miceli for Stan Belinda, 7/93

PLAYER SUMMARY	
Fantasy Value	$2 to $4
Card Value	4¢ to 7¢
Will	start games
Can't	keep runners close
Expect	excellent control
Don't Expect	fancy fielding

After succumbing to the sophomore jinx in 1995, Lieber returned from the dead last year. Working mainly out of the bullpen for the first time, he pitched his way back to the starting rotation, finishing with the most wins and the third-best ERA on the '96 Pirates. A sinker-slider pitcher with great control (1.77 walks per nine innings), Lieber yields just over one hit per inning while fanning six batters per game. Because he's always around the plate, he throws his share of gopher balls (19 in 142 innings last year). Lieber is neither a good hitter nor a good fielder. He also has trouble holding runners on. But the South Alabama product produced several sensational ERAs in the minors and is considered a possible future star. However, much depends upon his weight and conditioning, which have posed problems for Lieber in the past. Lieber began his pro career after the Royals made him a second-round selection in the 1992 free-agent draft.

Major League Pitching Register

	W	L	ERA	G	S	IP	H	ER	BB	SO
94 NL	6	7	3.73	17	0	108.2	116	45	25	71
95 NL	4	7	6.32	21	0	72.2	103	51	14	45
96 NL	9	5	3.99	51	1	142.0	156	63	28	94
Life	19	19	4.43	89	1	323.1	375	159	67	210
3 Ave	7	8	4.39	33	0	126.1	145	61	26	82

MIKE LIEBERTHAL

Position: Catcher
Team: Philadelphia Phillies
Born: Jan. 18, 1972 Glendale, CA
Height: 6′ **Weight:** 178 lbs.
Bats: right **Throws:** right
Acquired: First-round pick in 6/90 free-agent draft

PLAYER SUMMARY	
Fantasy Value. . . . . $5 to $7
Card Value . . . . 5¢ to 8¢
Will. . . . . rely on reputation
Can't. . . . . hit like Santiago
Expect. . . . . decent defense
Don't Expect . . . . any speed

When the 1996 season came to a close, the Phillies faced a major decision behind the plate. Would they entrust their future to Lieberthal, the former first-round draft pick whose season was shortened by surgery to repair torn knee cartilage? Or would they commit big bucks to retain veteran Benito Santiago, who blossomed into a surprise slugger last season? Lieberthal, who produced decent averages but little power in the minors, was thought to provide superior defense. But some scouts have questioned his durability and game-calling skills. Given his first chance to play in the majors last year, Lieberthal surprised with seven homers and eight doubles in 166 at bats. But he fanned three times per walk, leaving himself with an on-base percentage below .300. Lieberthal has "catcher's speed," a euphemism for saying he's slower than Heinz ketchup. He moves well behind the plate, however, shifting his weight to prevent wild pitches, framing pitches, and blocking the plate against incoming runners. Lieberthal needs to work on his throwing.

Major League Batting Register

	BA	G	AB	R	H	2B	3B	HR	RBI	SB
94 NL	.266	24	79	6	21	3	1	1	5	0
95 NL	.255	16	47	1	12	2	0	0	4	0
96 NL	.253	50	166	21	42	8	0	7	23	0
Life	.257	90	292	28	75	13	1	8	32	0

JOSE LIMA

Position: Pitcher
Team: Houston Astros
Born: Sept. 30, 1972 Santiago, Dominican Republic
Height: 6′2″ **Weight:** 170 lbs.
Bats: right **Throws:** right
Acquired: Traded by Astros with Brad Ausmus, C.J. Nitkowski, Trever Miller, and Daryle Ward for Orlando Miller, Brian Hunter, Doug Brocail, Todd Jones, and a player to be named later, 12/96

PLAYER SUMMARY	
Fantasy Value. . . . . $1 to $3
Card Value . . . . 4¢ to 7¢
Will. . . . . bank on changeup
Can't. . . . . retire righty hitters
Expect . . . . gradual improvement
Don't Expect . . . . return to rotation

Lima showed last season that he's better suited to the bullpen than the starting rotation. He increased the velocity of his fastball from 90 to 93 mph, making his changeup more effective, and managed to keep the ball down in the strike zone. He fanned 25 hitters in the first 20⅔ relief innings he threw after his July 3 recall from the minors. Prior to 1996, Lima had been strictly a starter since signing with Detroit eight years ago. He even pitched a no-hitter for Triple-A Toledo in 1994. Although the changeup is his best pitch, Lima also throws a forkball and slider to complement his fastball. He averages fewer than three walks and more than seven strikeouts per nine innings but yields too many hits and home runs. He also needs to improve his performance against right-handed hitters. Lima strands two-thirds of the runners he inherits, fields his position well, and keeps close tabs on opposing baserunners.

Major League Pitching Register

	W	L	ERA	G	S	IP	H	ER	BB	SO
94 AL	0	1	13.50	3	0	6.2	11	10	3	7
95 AL	3	9	6.11	15	0	73.2	85	50	18	37
96 AL	5	6	5.70	39	3	72.2	87	46	22	59
Life	8	16	6.24	57	3	153.0	183	106	43	103
2 Ave	4	8	5.92	28	2	78.1	91	51	21	50

187

DOUG LINTON

Position: Pitcher
Team: Kansas City Royals
Born: Sept. 2, 1965 Santa Ana, CA
Height: 6'1" **Weight:** 190 lbs.
Bats: right **Throws:** right
Acquired: Signed as a free agent, 4/95

PLAYER SUMMARY	
Fantasy Value	$1
Card Value	4¢ to 7¢
Will	bank on sinker
Can't	handle lefties
Expect	good control
Don't Expect	strong glove

A journeyman right-hander who bounced between the big leagues and Triple-A for four seasons before 1996, Linton was Kansas City's fourth starter for most of the season. He made 18 starts—double the total of his four previous years combined—and finished with seven wins, a personal peak. Though he yields more hits than innings and has occasional trouble with the gopher ball, Linton is a control artist (2.25 walks per nine innings) who's especially effective against right-handed batters (.254 opposing average). A sinkerballer who works quickly, Linton needs location rather than velocity to succeed. But he managed to fan nearly eight batters per nine innings last year, when regular work helped his pitches pick up speed. His biggest problems are left-handed hitters, potential basestealers, and ground balls that come his way. Because he's not a good gloveman, Linton often sabotages his own efforts. At 31, he'll probably land on some expansion staff this fall.

FELIPE LIRA

Position: Pitcher
Team: Detroit Tigers
Born: April 26, 1972 Miranda, Venezuela
Height: 6' **Weight:** 170 lbs.
Bats: right **Throws:** right
Acquired: Signed as a free agent, 2/90

PLAYER SUMMARY	
Fantasy Value	$2 to $4
Card Value	4¢ to 7¢
Will	improve over time
Can't	avoid gopher balls
Expect	respectable control
Don't Expect	high K totals

The potential is there: Lira pitched two shutouts last year, held right-handed hitters to a .256 average, and yielded only three walks per nine innings all season. A sinker-slider pitcher who also throws a changeup and a hard cut fastball, Lira depends upon his defense for help. He averages just over five strikeouts per nine innings and yields one hit per inning—respectable numbers until his homer total is factored into the equation. Lira topped the Tiger staff by allowing 30 home runs and 17 stolen bases, sabotaging some of his best efforts. He also threw seven wild pitches, more than any other Tiger starter. A victim of the sophomore jinx last season, Lira is still learning. At times, he shows the poise of a veteran. Because he's willing to pitch inside, Lira ranks among the league leaders in hit batsmen. His defense is decent, but his pickoff move needs work. The Venezuelan right-hander has been strictly a starter since turning pro in 1990.

Major League Pitching Register

	W	L	ERA	G	CG	IP	H	ER	BB	SO
92 AL	1	3	8.63	8	0	24.0	31	23	17	16
93 AL	2	1	7.36	23	0	36.2	46	30	23	23
94 NL	6	2	4.47	32	0	50.1	74	25	20	29
95 AL	0	1	7.25	7	0	22.1	22	18	10	13
96 AL	7	9	5.02	21	0	104.0	111	58	26	87
Life	16	16	5.84	91	0	237.1	284	154	96	168
2 Ave	8	6	4.80	33	0	87.1	108	47	27	64

Major League Pitching Register

	W	L	ERA	G	CG	IP	H	ER	BB	SO
95 AL	9	13	4.31	37	0	146.1	151	70	56	89
96 AL	6	14	5.22	32	3	194.2	204	113	66	113
Life	15	27	4.83	69	3	341.0	355	183	122	202
2 Ave	8	14	4.80	37	2	180.1	187	96	65	107

NELSON LIRIANO

Position: Second base
Team: Los Angeles Dodgers
Born: June 3, 1964 Puerto Plata, Dominican Republic
Height: 5'10" **Weight:** 178 lbs.
Bats: both **Throws:** right
Acquired: Claimed from Pirates on waivers, 11/96

PLAYER SUMMARY	
Fantasy Value	$0
Card Value	4¢ to 7¢
Will	make contact
Can't	supply power
Expect	utility berth
Don't Expect	stolen bases

Versatility keeps Liriano in the big leagues. He bats both ways, plays three infield positions, and makes frequent pinch-hit appearances. Usually regarded as a better right-handed batter, Liriano surprised last year by hitting three points higher against southpaws. A contact hitter without much patience, Liriano does not walk or fan too often. Nor is he known for hitting the ball over the fence. He hits more singles than he does doubles, triples, and home runs combined. Once a burner who twice topped 30 steals in the minors, Liriano rarely runs anymore. But he still moves well in the field. His original position, second base, remains his best. He shows quick reactions, soft hands, and the ability to turn two but lacks range and arm strength. Unless some expansion club needs his experience, Liriano's future may be limited. He might last another year or two on the bench.

Major League Batting Register

	BA	G	AB	R	H	2B	3B	HR	RBI	SB
87 AL	.241	37	158	29	38	6	2	2	10	13
88 AL	.264	99	276	36	73	6	2	3	23	12
89 AL	.263	132	418	51	110	26	3	5	53	16
90 AL	.234	103	355	46	83	12	9	1	28	8
91 AL	.409	10	22	5	9	0	0	0	1	0
93 NL	.305	48	151	28	46	6	3	2	15	6
94 NL	.255	87	255	39	65	17	5	3	31	0
95 NL	.286	107	259	29	74	12	1	5	38	2
96 NL	.267	112	217	23	58	14	2	3	30	2
Life	.263	735	2111	286	556	99	27	24	229	59
3 Ave	.268	118	289	37	78	17	3	4	39	1

PAT LISTACH

Position: Second base; outfield
Team: Houston Astros
Born: Sept. 12, 1967 Natchitoches, LA
Height: 5'9" **Weight:** 170 lbs.
Bats: right **Throws:** right
Acquired: Signed as a free agent, 11/96

PLAYER SUMMARY	
Fantasy Value	$7 to $9
Card Value	5¢ to 8¢
Will	seek comeback
Can't	produce power
Expect	utility role
Don't Expect	rookie speed

Cleveland fans were outraged when Listach stole the 1992 AL Rookie of the Year Award from Kenny Lofton. Subsequent events have proved them right. While Lofton has blossomed into an MVP contender, Listach has gone in the other direction. The former Arizona State shortstop, often beset by injuries, has bottomed out in every department. Even his speed sputtered; Listach has stolen 58 bases total in the four seasons following his 54-steal rookie year. He offers neither power nor patience, fanning nearly twice per walk and producing a lowly on-base percentage that virtually negates the value of his speed. Two knee operations haven't helped, either. Listach was so listless when he came to the Yankees last August that he was returned to the Brewers, who promptly released him. If he hooks on elsewhere, Listach has to prove he can still play. Perhaps an expansion club will rescue him from the baseball scrap heap this fall. At age 29, it's not too late for Listach.

Major League Batting Register

	BA	G	AB	R	H	2B	3B	HR	RBI	SB
92 AL	.290	149	579	93	168	19	6	1	47	54
93 AL	.244	98	356	50	87	15	1	3	30	18
94 AL	.296	16	54	8	16	3	0	0	2	2
95 AL	.219	101	334	35	73	8	2	0	25	13
96 AL	.240	87	317	51	76	16	2	1	33	25
Life	.256	451	1640	237	420	61	11	5	137	112
2 Ave	.228	100	346	45	79	13	2	1	31	20

SCOTT LIVINGSTONE

Position: Third base; first base
Team: San Diego Padres
Born: July 15, 1965 Dallas, TX
Height: 6' **Weight:** 190 lbs.
Bats: left **Throws:** right
Acquired: Traded by Tigers for Gene Harris, 5/94

PLAYER SUMMARY

Fantasy Value	$0
Card Value	4¢ to 7¢
Will	deliver in pinch
Can't	find old power
Expect	reserve service
Don't Expect	hits vs. lefties

A modern-day Dr. Jekyll and Mr. Hyde, Livingstone is great against right-handers (.314) but lousy against lefties (.077). An All-America slugger at Texas A&M, he's become a slap-hitting utility man, backing both infield corners and serving as a pinch hitter against right-handed pitchers. Livingstone is a good clutch hitter who led the Padres with 68 pinch-hit appearances last year. A contact hitter who uses all fields, Livingstone rarely walks or fans. His eyes light up when he sees low fastballs. Livingstone fell three points shy of his second straight .300 campaign in 1996. Because he lacks speed, Livingstone can't fatten his average with infield hits. He's also no threat to steal. Though signed as a third baseman, his limited range and erratic arm make him a liability at the hot corner. He's better at first, though his best position is the one he played in college: designated hitter. With expansion coming, he could be in that role again in 1998.

Major League Batting Register

	BA	G	AB	R	H	2B	3B	HR	RBI	SB
91 AL	.291	44	127	19	37	5	0	2	11	2
92 AL	.282	117	354	43	100	21	0	4	46	1
93 AL	.293	98	304	39	89	10	2	2	39	1
94 AL	.217	15	23	0	5	1	0	0	1	0
94 NL	.272	57	180	11	49	12	1	2	10	2
95 AL	.337	99	196	26	66	15	0	5	32	2
96 NL	.297	102	172	20	51	4	1	2	20	0
Life	.293	532	1356	158	397	68	4	17	159	8
3 Ave	.301	98	215	22	65	13	1	3	23	2

GRAEME LLOYD

Position: Pitcher
Team: New York Yankees
Born: April 9, 1967 Victoria, Australia
Height: 6'7" **Weight:** 215 lbs.
Bats: left **Throws:** left
Acquired: Traded by Brewers with Pat Listach for Gerald Williams and Bob Wickman, 8/96

PLAYER SUMMARY

Fantasy Value	$1 to $3
Card Value	4¢ to 7¢
Will	get lefties out
Can't	rack up Ks
Expect	set-up spot
Don't Expect	poor control

Pitching under pressure was a problem for Lloyd last year. Before his August 23 trade to the Yankees, he had a 2-4 record and 2.82 ERA in Milwaukee, where he had held left-handed hitters to a .210 batting average. But he struggled in early efforts for New York, finally admitting he had a tender elbow. The towering Australian throws a sinker, curve, and changeup with reasonably good control. Lloyd needs location rather than velocity to succeed; he fans fewer than five men per nine innings. He works often, strands most of the runners he inherits, and keeps the ball in the park. But his struggles in the Bronx left him with more hits allowed than innings pitched plus a .303 opposing average by righties. Despite the plethora of baserunners, Lloyd handled himself well by fielding his position and controlling the running game. He has a good move that few men challenge. A set-up man originally drafted by Toronto, Lloyd had three-plus solid seasons in the Milwaukee bullpen before joining the Yanks.

Major League Pitching Register

	W	L	ERA	G	S	IP	H	ER	BB	SO
93 AL	3	4	2.83	55	0	63.2	64	20	13	31
94 AL	2	3	5.17	43	3	47.0	49	27	15	31
95 AL	0	5	4.50	33	4	32.0	28	16	8	13
96 AL	2	6	4.29	65	0	56.2	61	27	22	30
Life	7	18	4.06	196	7	199.1	202	90	58	105
3 Ave	2	5	4.70	54	3	53.0	54	28	17	29

ESTEBAN LOAIZA

Position: Pitcher
Team: Pittsburgh Pirates
Born: Dec. 31, 1971 Tijuana, Mexico
Height: 6'4" **Weight:** 190 lbs.
Bats: right **Throws:** right
Acquired: Signed as nondrafted free agent, 3/91

PLAYER SUMMARY	
Fantasy Value	$1
Card Value	6¢ to 10¢
Will	keep starting spot
Can't	prevent long hits
Expect	good bat, glove
Don't Expect	erratic control

As a rookie with the 1995 Pirates, Loaiza tied for the National League lead with 31 starts. But not all of them were successful. He followed a 6-3 first half with a 2-6 finish, then spent part of last season in the minors before returning to Pittsburgh in time to make ten starts. A fastball-slider pitcher who also throws a curve and changeup, Loaiza is overpowering at times. But he yields too many hits and too many homers for consistent success. While his control is good (3.25 walks per nine innings), his ratio of strikeouts to walks is less than 2-to-1. Because he has a fine arm and smooth delivery, however, Loaiza's potential is enormous. The towering right-hander helps his own cause with his bat and glove. A converted catcher, he likes to hit and knows how to drop a bunt. Occasionally used as a pinch hitter, Loaiza led the 1995 Pirates in sacrifice hits. Last year, he made big strides in holding runners close; only four men stole against him while three were thrown out. At 25, Loaiza is a good bet to improve as he gains experience.

KEITH LOCKHART

Position: Second base; third base
Team: Kansas City Royals
Born: Nov. 10, 1964 Whittier, CA
Height: 5'10" **Weight:** 170 lbs.
Bats: left **Throws:** right
Acquired: Signed as a minor-league free agent, 11/94

PLAYER SUMMARY	
Fantasy Value	$3 to $5
Card Value	5¢ to 8¢
Will	make contact
Can't	hit lefties
Expect	surprising pop
Don't Expect	great defense

During a pro career that began in 1986, Lockhart has played all nine positions. But he shed his utility tag two years ago, when he hit so well (.321) that the Royals had to find him a place in the everyday lineup. Although he struggles against southpaws, Lockhart is a contact hitter who swings a solid bat against righties. He even has surprising pop (43 extra-base hits last year) for an infielder. An aggressive, line-drive hitter who uses all fields against righties but goes the opposite way against lefties, Lockhart spent most of last year at second base, his best position. But he also served as a lefty-hitting alternative to Craig Paquette and Joe Randa at third. A good No. 2 hitter, Lockhart puts his bat on the ball and adds speed to the lineup. He's adept at moving runners and rarely bangs into double plays. He has good range, soft hands, and a decent arm but doesn't have the quick reaction time needed to excel at the hot corner. But he's become a solid second baseman who is able to turn the double play.

Major League Pitching Register

	W	L	ERA	G	CG	IP	H	ER	BB	SO
95 NL	8	9	5.16	32	1	172.2	205	99	55	85
96 NL	2	3	4.96	10	1	52.2	65	29	19	32
Life	10	12	5.11	42	2	225.1	270	128	74	117

Major League Batting Register

	BA	G	AB	R	H	2B	3B	HR	RBI	SB
94 NL	.209	27	43	4	9	0	0	2	6	1
95 AL	.321	94	274	41	88	19	3	6	33	8
96 AL	.273	138	433	49	118	33	3	7	55	11
Life	.287	259	750	94	215	52	6	15	94	20
2 Ave	.293	122	371	48	109	27	3	7	46	10

KENNY LOFTON

Position: Outfield
Team: Cleveland Indians
Born: May 31, 1967 East Chicago, IN
Height: 6' **Weight:** 180 lbs.
Bats: left **Throws:** left
Acquired: Traded by Astros with Dave Rohde for Willie Blair and Eddie Taubensee, 12/91

PLAYER SUMMARY	
Fantasy Value	$40 to $45
Card Value	40¢ to $1
Will	steal rivals blind
Can't	reduce whiffs
Expect	Gold Glove defense
Don't Expect	long-ball power

Lofton has established himself as baseball's premier leadoff man. He took a .312 career average into the 1996 season, hit five points higher, and won his fifth straight stolen-base crown (his 75 stolen bases were tops in the AL). Lofton finished third in the league in hits and tied for third in runs scored. Plus, he hit for power (a career-high 14 homers and 53 extra-base hits). He might try to improve his on-base percentage, however. While .372 is not exactly chopped liver, Lofton would do better if he walked more and fanned less. He had 21 more whiffs than walks. Because he fattens his average with drag bunts and infield hits, rival clubs never know where to station their infielders against him. Blessed with world-class speed, Lofton might also improve his 81-percent success ratio on the bases. He was nailed 17 times last year. The total package: he runs like the wind in the outfield, where he has unmatched range in center and a strong, accurate arm.

Major League Batting Register

	BA	G	AB	R	H	2B	3B	HR	RBI	SB
91 NL	.203	20	74	9	15	1	0	0	0	2
92 AL	.285	148	576	96	164	15	8	5	42	66
93 AL	.325	148	569	116	185	28	8	1	42	70
94 AL	.349	112	459	105	160	32	9	12	57	60
95 AL	.310	118	481	93	149	22	13	7	53	54
96 AL	.317	154	662	132	210	35	4	14	67	75
Life	.313	700	2821	551	883	133	42	39	261	327
3 Ave	.326	148	617	128	201	35	10	13	69	73

JAVY LOPEZ

Position: Catcher
Team: Atlanta Braves
Born: Nov. 5, 1970 Ponce, Puerto Rico
Height: 6'3" **Weight:** 185 lbs.
Bats: right **Throws:** right
Acquired: Signed as a free agent, 11/87

PLAYER SUMMARY	
Fantasy Value	$19 to $22
Card Value	15¢ to 25¢
Will	hit lefties hard
Can't	wait for walks
Expect	clutch hits
Don't Expect	great defense

Unlike Mark Lemke, his Atlanta teammate the last three seasons, Lopez stays in the lineup because of his bat. A free-swinging slugger who hits over .300 vs. lefties, Lopez reached personal peaks in homers and RBI last year. He also hit for a respectable average even though he fanned nearly four times per walk. Although he's not fast (he has only one career steal), Lopez is strong. Nearly one-third of his hits go for extra bases. He's also a proven clutch hitter, often producing big hits with two outs. He hit .359 with men in scoring position two years ago. When he connects, Lopez hits the ball hard, banging into more than his share of double plays. Although he's improved behind the plate, Lopez is still learning the right way to shift his weight and prevent wild pitches. He has a strong arm, and his game-calling and communication skills have improved considerably, but his throwing success (25 percent last year) is sabotaged by his pitchers' failure to hold men close.

Major League Batting Register

	BA	G	AB	R	H	2B	3B	HR	RBI	SB
92 NL	.375	9	16	3	6	2	0	0	2	0
93 NL	.375	8	16	1	6	1	1	1	2	0
94 NL	.245	80	277	27	68	9	0	13	35	0
95 NL	.315	100	333	37	105	11	4	14	51	0
96 NL	.282	138	489	56	138	19	1	23	69	1
Life	.286	335	1131	124	323	42	6	51	159	1
3 Ave	.281	121	418	45	117	15	2	19	59	0

JOHN MABRY

Position: Outfield; first base
Team: St. Louis Cardinals
Born: Oct. 17, 1970 Wilmington, DE
Height: 6'4" **Weight:** 195 lbs.
Bats: left **Throws:** right
Acquired: Sixth-round pick in 6/91 free-agent draft

PLAYER SUMMARY

Fantasy Value	$9 to $11
Card Value	8¢ to 12¢
Will	kill left-handers
Can't	win Gold Glove
Expect	line-drive stroke
Don't Expect	the long ball

Like Fred McGriff and David Justice, Mabry belongs to a rare breed: left-handed hitters who hit lefty pitchers harder than righty pitchers. A good clutch hitter whose short stroke sends line drives to all fields, Mabry hit .330 vs. southpaws in 1995 and .351 vs. lefties last year. Only a tendency to fan nearly three times per walk stood between Mabry and his second straight .300 season. Mabry, who can also play the outfield, was a major contributor to the Cardinal attack. He had 45 extra-base hits, including 13 homers, and led the club with a .331 road average. A 5-for-5 game at Pittsburgh July 6 contributed to that mark. Though he's not fast, Mabry is a decent baserunner. Because his range isn't great and he lacks a strong arm, he's a better first baseman than outfielder. Since moving to first in 1995, he's learned to scoop and stretch, though his throwing and footwork aren't always graceful. No Mark Grace at first, Mabry is gaining on-the-job experience. But there's talk of moving him to third to make room for touted prospect Dmitri Young.

Major League Batting Register

	BA	G	AB	R	H	2B	3B	HR	RBI	SB
94 NL	.304	6	23	2	7	3	0	0	3	0
95 NL	.307	129	388	35	119	21	1	5	41	0
96 NL	.297	151	543	63	161	30	2	13	74	3
Life	.301	286	954	100	287	54	3	18	118	3
2 Ave	.301	148	490	51	147	27	2	9	60	2

MIKE MACFARLANE

Position: Catcher
Team: Kansas City Royals
Born: April 12, 1964 Stockton, CA
Height: 6'1" **Weight:** 200 lbs.
Bats: right **Throws:** right
Acquired: Signed as a free agent, 12/95

PLAYER SUMMARY

Fantasy Value	$9 to $11
Card Value	5¢ to 7¢
Will	show some pop
Can't	lift his average
Expect	throwing success
Don't Expect	Gold Glove

After a one-year hiatus in Boston, Macfarlane returned to the Royals and picked up where he left off. In fact, Craig Paquette, Michael Tucker, and Macfarlane were the only K.C. players to reach double digits in home runs. Macfarlane, who finished one short of his career high, has always supplied decent power without hitting for a high average. A fastball hitter, he fans twice per walk and often struggles against right-handed pitchers, though that was not the case last year. Speed is not his forte: Macfarlane's three steals last year were a career high. He was also nailed three times. Although most of Macfarlane's mechanics behind the plate are below average, he calls a good game and handles pitchers well. The University of Santa Clara product is also adept at throwing, nailing 39 percent of the would-be basestealers who challenged him last year.

Major League Batting Register

	BA	G	AB	R	H	2B	3B	HR	RBI	SB
87 AL	.211	8	19	0	4	1	0	0	3	0
88 AL	.265	70	211	25	56	15	0	4	26	0
89 AL	.223	69	157	13	35	6	0	2	19	0
90 AL	.255	124	400	37	102	24	4	6	58	1
91 AL	.277	84	267	34	74	18	2	13	41	1
92 AL	.234	129	402	51	94	28	3	17	48	1
93 AL	.273	117	388	55	106	27	0	20	67	2
94 AL	.255	92	314	53	80	17	3	14	47	1
95 AL	.225	115	364	45	82	18	1	15	51	2
96 AL	.274	112	379	58	104	24	2	19	54	3
Life	.254	920	2901	371	737	178	15	110	414	11
3 Ave	.251	124	410	61	103	23	2	19	59	2

193

GREG MADDUX

Position: Pitcher
Team: Atlanta Braves
Born: April 14, 1966 San Angelo, TX
Height: 6' **Weight:** 170 lbs.
Bats: right **Throws:** right
Acquired: Signed as a free agent, 12/92

PLAYER SUMMARY

Fantasy Value	$30 to $35
Card Value	$1.25 to $2.50
Will	yield few runs
Can't	keep runners close
Expect	uncanny control
Don't Expect	gopher trouble

After winning a record four consecutive Cy Young Awards, Maddux showed signs of mortality. Victimized by a slow start and lack of offensive support, the soft-spoken right-hander slipped to second in the league's ERA race—after leading for three straight years—and posted his lowest win total and highest ERA since 1991. But Maddux was still better than most other pitchers. A durable master of the mound who rarely misses a turn, Maddux throws five pitches (sinker, slider, cut fastball, curve, circle change) for strikes. Relying on accuracy instead of velocity, he averages six Ks per walk. Over the last two years, he's averaged an incredible one walk per nine innings. Maddux yields fewer hits than innings, keeps the ball in the park, and fields his position better than any other pitcher (seven straight Gold Gloves). He can hit a little, too.

Major League Pitching Register

	W	L	ERA	G	CG	IP	H	ER	BB	SO
86 NL	2	4	5.52	6	1	31.0	44	19	11	20
87 NL	6	14	5.61	30	1	155.2	181	97	74	101
88 NL	18	8	3.18	34	9	249.0	230	88	81	140
89 NL	19	12	2.95	35	7	238.1	222	78	82	135
90 NL	15	15	3.46	35	8	237.0	242	91	71	144
91 NL	15	11	3.35	37	7	263.0	232	98	66	198
92 NL	20	11	2.18	35	9	268.0	201	65	70	199
93 NL	20	10	2.36	36	8	267.0	228	70	52	197
94 NL	16	6	1.56	25	10	202.0	150	35	31	156
95 NL	19	2	1.63	28	10	209.2	147	38	23	181
96 NL	15	11	2.72	35	5	245.0	225	74	28	172
Life	165	104	2.86	336	75	2365.2	2102	753	589	1643
3 Ave	20	7	1.95	34	10	255.0	201	55	33	198

MIKE MADDUX

Position: Pitcher
Team: Boston Red Sox
Born: Aug. 27, 1961 Dayton, OH
Height: 6'2" **Weight:** 180 lbs.
Bats: left **Throws:** right
Acquired: Signed as a free agent, 4/95

PLAYER SUMMARY

Fantasy Value	$2 to $4
Card Value	4¢ to 7¢
Will	start or relieve
Can't	strike men out
Expect	decent control
Don't Expect	double-digit wins

The Maddux brothers have several things in common: their last name, their position, and the fact that both throw right-handed. Other than that, they're more different than Pat Buchanan and Geraldine Ferraro. Mike, the older brother, is a journeyman reliever who's worked in the bullpens of a half-dozen clubs during a checkered career. Slowed by a strained right elbow and a groin injury last year, he made seven starts and 16 relief appearances for the Red Sox. He has good control of four pitches: a sinker, slider, curve, and changeup. Like his brother, he helps himself with his fielding but has trouble holding runners on. Maddux relies on location rather than velocity, averaging fewer than five Ks per game. When his sinker doesn't sink, he has problems. Maddux yielded too many hits and homers last year.

Major League Pitching Register

	W	L	ERA	G	S	IP	H	ER	BB	SO
86 NL	3	7	5.42	16	0	78.0	88	47	34	44
87 NL	2	0	2.65	7	0	17.0	17	5	5	15
88 NL	4	3	3.76	25	0	88.2	91	37	34	59
89 NL	1	3	5.15	16	1	43.2	52	25	14	26
90 NL	0	1	6.53	11	0	20.2	24	15	4	11
91 NL	7	2	2.46	64	5	98.2	78	27	27	57
92 NL	2	2	2.37	50	5	79.2	71	21	24	60
93 NL	3	8	3.60	58	5	75.0	67	30	27	57
94 NL	2	1	5.11	27	2	44.0	45	25	13	32
95 NL	1	0	9.00	8	0	9.0	14	9	3	4
95 AL	4	1	3.61	36	1	89.2	86	36	15	65
96 AL	3	2	4.48	23	0	64.1	76	32	27	32
Life	32	30	3.93	341	19	708.1	709	309	227	462
3 Ave	3	2	4.27	34	1	76.1	79	36	21	50

DAVE MAGADAN

Position: Third base; first base
Team: Chicago Cubs
Born: Sept. 30, 1962 Tampa, FL
Height: 6'3" **Weight:** 195 lbs.
Bats: left **Throws:** right
Acquired: Signed as a free agent, 12/95

PLAYER SUMMARY	
Fantasy Value	$0
Card Value	4¢ to 7¢
Will	put bat on ball
Can't	show much power
Expect	selective hitting
Don't Expect	great defense

Magadan makes great contact, walks more often than he fans, and devours right-handed pitching, but he delivers little power or speed. A selective hitter whose 1996 on-base percentage was more than 100 points higher than his batting average, Magadan always puts the ball into play when he connects. He uses all fields and does his best work with men in scoring position. That's one of the reasons Magadan made 25 pinch-hitting appearances last year. He also played 51 games at third base and ten at first, though March surgery to remove a bone spur from his left hand limited his playing time. Magadan is no threat to steal, and he's erratic at best in the field. Magadan erred only three times in limited playing time last year but made 18 boots in 1995. Better at first than third, he'd be best if some AL club picked him up as a DH.

Major League Batting Register

	BA	G	AB	R	H	2B	3B	HR	RBI	SB
86 NL	.444	10	18	3	8	0	0	0	3	0
87 NL	.318	85	192	21	61	13	1	3	24	0
88 NL	.277	112	314	39	87	15	0	1	35	0
89 NL	.286	127	374	47	107	22	3	4	41	1
90 NL	.328	144	451	74	148	28	6	6	72	2
91 NL	.258	124	418	58	108	23	0	4	51	1
92 NL	.283	99	321	33	91	9	1	3	28	1
93 NL	.286	66	227	22	65	12	0	4	29	0
93 AL	.259	71	228	27	59	11	0	1	21	2
94 AL	.275	74	211	30	58	7	0	1	17	0
95 AL	.313	127	348	44	109	24	0	2	51	2
96 NL	.254	78	169	23	43	10	0	3	17	0
Life	.289	1117	3271	421	944	174	11	32	389	9
3 Ave	.288	108	286	38	82	16	0	2	33	1

PAT MAHOMES

Position: Pitcher
Team: Boston Red Sox
Born: Aug. 9, 1970 Bryan, TX
Height: 6'4" **Weight:** 210 lbs.
Bats: right **Throws:** right
Acquired: Traded by Twins for Brian Looney, 8/96

PLAYER SUMMARY	
Fantasy Value	$0
Card Value	5¢ to 8¢
Will	seek comeback
Can't	prevent gophers
Expect	good velocity
Don't Expect	pinpoint control

Tried as both a starter and reliever during his short career, Mahomes hopes to recapture his 9-5 form of 1994, when all 21 of his appearances were starts. A bust out of the bullpen in '95 and an occupant of the DL part of last year, Mahomes still has the potential that convinced Pacific Coast League pilots to pick him as that league's No. 2 prospect after the '93 season. When healthy, the hard-throwing righty averages six Ks per nine innings with his blend of fastball, slider, curve, and changeup. Though he yields only a hit per inning, Mahomes sabotages his own efforts with erratic control, a tendency to yield too many long balls, and an inability to control the running game. He also has trouble with left-handed hitters. Mahomes fields his position well and runs so well for a big man that he sometimes appears as a pinch runner. *Baseball America* rated him as his league's top prospect four times during his tenure in the minors.

Major League Pitching Register

	W	L	ERA	G	S	IP	H	ER	BB	SO
92 AL	3	4	5.04	14	0	69.2	73	39	37	44
93 AL	1	5	7.71	12	0	37.1	47	32	16	23
94 AL	9	5	4.72	21	0	120.0	121	63	62	53
95 AL	4	10	6.37	47	3	94.2	100	67	47	67
96 AL	3	4	6.91	31	2	57.1	72	44	33	36
Life	20	28	5.82	125	5	379.0	413	245	195	223
3 Ave	7	7	5.63	38	2	111.0	118	69	58	62

195

KIRT MANWARING

Position: Catcher
Team: Colorado Rockies
Born: July 15, 1965 Elmira, NY
Height: 5'11" **Weight:** 190 lbs.
Bats: right **Throws:** right
Acquired: Signed as a free agent, 12/96

PLAYER SUMMARY	
Fantasy Value	$1
Card Value	4¢ to 7¢
Will	throw men out
Can't	hit for power
Expect	great glove
Don't Expect	good average

When the Astros traded Rick Wilkins for Manwaring last July, they were basically swapping offense for defense. While Wilkins is a left-handed hitter who once had a 30-homer season, Manwaring is a former Gold Glove receiver with a powerful throwing arm (45 percent of would-be basestealers erased last year) but little power (one homer). An impatient hitter, Manwaring fans 2½ times per walk. Almost all of his hits were singles and almost all came against right-handed pitching. A weak hitter who's even more of a wimp in clutch situations, Manwaring can't even fatten his average with walks or infield hits; he's just too slow. He's a whiz behind the plate, however, where his handling of pitchers and game-calling ranks right up there with his remarkable throwing. He blocks the plate like a stalled locomotive, never giving an inch to a runner.

Major League Batting Register

	BA	G	AB	R	H	2B	3B	HR	RBI	SB
87 NL	.143	6	7	0	1	0	0	0	0	0
88 NL	.250	40	116	12	29	7	0	1	15	0
89 NL	.210	85	200	14	42	4	2	0	18	2
90 NL	.154	8	13	0	2	0	1	0	1	0
91 NL	.225	67	178	16	40	9	0	0	19	1
92 NL	.244	109	349	24	85	10	5	4	26	2
93 NL	.275	130	432	48	119	15	1	5	49	1
94 NL	.250	97	316	30	79	17	1	1	29	1
95 NL	.251	118	379	21	95	15	2	4	36	1
96 NL	.229	86	227	14	52	9	0	1	18	0
Life	.245	746	2217	179	544	86	12	16	211	8
3 Ave	.246	118	366	27	90	17	1	2	33	1

AL MARTIN

Position: Outfield
Team: Pittsburgh Pirates
Born: Nov. 24, 1967 West Covina, CA
Height: 6'2" **Weight:** 210 lbs.
Bats: left **Throws:** left
Acquired: Signed as a free agent, 11/91

PLAYER SUMMARY	
Fantasy Value	$25 to $30
Card Value	7¢ to 10¢
Will	kill right-handers
Can't	cut whiff rate
Expect	30-30 potential
Don't Expect	strong throws

Martin's strong finish in 1995 helped him escape his former role as a platoon outfielder. Once used only against right-handed pitchers, he blossomed into a star when Jim Leyland made him a regular. Though he didn't produce against lefties (.200), Martin managed to finish with the first .300 season of his five-year career. He did it by whipping right-handers at a .327 clip. Martin's speed-plus-power package made him one of the most valuable members of the 1996 Pittsburgh lineup. He stole 38 bases, a career best, and tied his previous career peak with 18 homers. An aggressive hitter, Martin fans more than twice for every walk but uses all fields and produces extra bases on one-third of his hits. He hiked his success ratio as a basestealer to 76 percent last year. Martin's speed helps in the outfield, where he often robs rivals of alley hits. He has the range for center but spent most of his time in left after rookie Jermaine Allensworth was promoted.

Major League Batting Register

	BA	G	AB	R	H	2B	3B	HR	RBI	SB
92 NL	.167	12	12	1	2	0	1	0	2	0
93 NL	.281	143	480	85	135	26	8	18	64	16
94 NL	.286	82	276	48	79	12	4	9	33	15
95 NL	.282	124	439	70	124	25	3	13	41	20
96 NL	.300	155	630	101	189	40	1	18	72	38
Life	.288	516	1837	305	529	103	17	58	212	89
3 Ave	.291	137	504	82	147	28	3	15	55	27

NORBERTO MARTIN

Position: Infield
Team: Chicago White Sox
Born: Dec. 10, 1966 Santo Domingo, Dominican Republic
Height: 5'10" **Weight:** 164 lbs.
Bats: right **Throws:** right
Acquired: Signed as a nondrafted free agent, 3/84

PLAYER SUMMARY	
Fantasy Value	$2 to $4
Card Value	5¢ to 8¢
Will	slap and run
Can't	wait for walks
Expect	good bat vs. lefties
Don't Expect	the long ball

Martin was one of the unsung heroes of Chicago's strong 1996 season. A three-position infielder who also served as a DH against southpaws, Martin hit .350—easily the best mark of a pro career that began in 1984—and swiped ten bases in 12 tries. His average against lefties was .394. A free swinger who fans three times per walk, Martin uses his speed to compensate for his total lack of power (one homer, no triples in '96). A notorious ground-ball hitter, he fattens his average by beating out infield rollers. Although his best position is second base, Martin spent most of his time last year as a right-handed alternative to lefty-hitting regular shortstop Ozzie Guillen. Martin can't match the veteran's arm or defensive skills but supplies far better offense. He has also played the outfield at the big-league level. The Dominican speedster, who also makes a quality pinch hitter, had two dozen steals in three minor-league campaigns. With expansion on the horizon, he could get a shot as a regular.

Major League Batting Register

	BA	G	AB	R	H	2B	3B	HR	RBI	SB
93 AL	.357	8	14	3	5	0	0	0	2	0
94 AL	.275	45	131	19	36	7	1	1	16	4
95 AL	.269	72	160	17	43	7	4	2	17	5
96 AL	.350	70	140	30	49	7	0	1	14	10
Life	.299	195	445	69	133	21	5	4	49	19

DAVE MARTINEZ

Position: Outfield; first base
Team: Chicago White Sox
Born: Sept. 26, 1964 New York, NY
Height: 5'10" **Weight:** 170 lbs.
Bats: left **Throws:** left
Acquired: Signed as a free agent, 4/95

PLAYER SUMMARY	
Fantasy Value	$7 to $9
Card Value	5¢ to 8¢
Will	rake line drives
Can't	find steady job
Expect	strong defense
Don't Expect	many homers

Martinez seems to be improving with age. With two straight .300 seasons—the first of his career—he's quieted critics who claimed his hitting couldn't match his defensive abilities. Thanks to a batting average that has gone up three years in a row, Martinez played in a career-high 146 games last year. He didn't have a steady position but saw time in all three fields and at first base. By season's end, he had supplanted the light-hitting Darren Lewis as Chicago's main man in center. A contact hitter who walks as often as he fans, Martinez has some sock, especially against right-handed pitchers. Martinez sends line drives to all fields but bunts well enough to lead the team in sacrifices. Martinez has fine range in the outfield, with quick reactions, soft hands, and a strong, accurate arm. He's also made two mop-up pitching appearances in his career.

Major League Batting Register

	BA	G	AB	R	H	2B	3B	HR	RBI	SB
86 NL	.139	53	108	13	15	1	1	1	7	4
87 NL	.292	142	459	70	134	18	8	8	36	16
88 NL	.255	138	447	51	114	13	6	6	46	23
89 NL	.274	126	361	41	99	16	7	3	27	23
90 NL	.279	118	391	60	109	13	5	11	39	13
91 NL	.295	124	396	47	117	18	5	7	42	16
92 NL	.254	135	393	47	100	20	5	3	31	12
93 NL	.241	91	241	28	58	12	1	5	27	6
94 NL	.247	97	235	23	58	9	3	4	27	3
95 NL	.307	119	303	49	93	16	4	5	37	8
96 NL	.318	146	440	85	140	20	8	10	53	15
Life	.275	1289	3774	514	1037	156	53	63	372	139
3 Ave	.293	139	371	58	109	17	6	7	44	9

197

DENNIS MARTINEZ

Position: Pitcher
Team: Cleveland Indians
Born: May 14, 1955 Granada, Nicaragua
Height: 6'1" **Weight:** 180 lbs.
Bats: right **Throws:** right
Acquired: Signed as a free agent, 12/93

PLAYER SUMMARY	
Fantasy Value	$7 to $9
Card Value	5¢ to 8¢
Will	fight Father Time
Can't	fan many hitters
Expect	control, finesse
Don't Expect	a dozen wins

The Nicaraguan right-hander battled elbow problems last year, enduring two stints on the DL. Martinez, who also sparred with Cleveland management, finished with a 9-6 mark and 4.50 ERA but pitched only 112 innings. When healthy, Martinez is a control artist who throws a fastball, curve, and changeup. He helps himself by fielding his position well and holding runners on base. Martinez has pitched in four different All-Star Games. He's led his league in winning percentage, ERA, complete games, and shutouts. Martinez pitched the last perfect game in the majors (1991).

Major League Pitching Register

	W	L	ERA	G	CG	IP	H	ER	BB	SO
76 AL	1	2	2.60	4	1	27.2	23	8	8	18
77 AL	14	7	4.10	42	5	166.2	157	76	64	107
78 AL	16	11	3.52	40	15	276.1	257	108	93	142
79 AL	15	16	3.66	40	18	292.1	279	119	78	132
80 AL	6	4	3.97	25	2	99.2	103	44	44	42
81 AL	14	5	3.32	25	9	179.0	173	66	62	88
82 AL	16	12	4.21	40	10	252.0	262	118	87	111
83 AL	7	16	5.53	32	4	153.0	209	94	45	71
84 AL	6	9	5.02	34	2	141.2	145	79	37	77
85 AL	13	11	5.15	33	3	180.0	203	103	63	68
86 AL	0	0	6.75	4	0	6.2	11	5	2	2
86 NL	3	6	4.59	19	1	98.0	103	50	28	63
87 NL	11	4	3.30	22	2	144.2	133	53	40	84
88 NL	15	13	2.72	34	9	235.1	215	71	55	120
89 NL	16	7	3.18	34	5	232.0	227	82	49	142
90 NL	10	11	2.95	32	7	226.0	191	74	49	156
91 NL	14	11	2.39	31	9	222.0	187	59	62	123
92 NL	16	11	2.47	32	6	226.1	172	62	60	147
93 NL	15	9	3.85	35	2	224.2	211	96	64	138
94 AL	11	6	3.52	24	7	176.2	166	69	44	92
95 AL	12	5	3.08	28	3	187.0	174	64	46	99
96 AL	9	6	4.50	20	1	112.0	122	56	37	48
Life	240	182	3.63	630	121	3859.2	3723	1556	1117	2070
3 Ave	13	7	3.55	28	5	190.1	184	75	50	96

EDGAR MARTINEZ

Position: Designated hitter
Team: Seattle Mariners
Born: Jan. 2, 1963 New York, NY
Height: 5'11" **Weight:** 175 lbs.
Bats: right **Throws:** right
Acquired: Signed as a free agent, 12/82

PLAYER SUMMARY	
Fantasy Value	$25 to $30
Card Value	15¢ to 20¢
Will	seek batting crown
Can't	generate speed
Expect	patience and power
Don't Expect	return to infield

Before missing 22 games with cracked ribs, Martinez was on target to topple Earl Webb's major-league mark of 67 doubles. The two-time batting king finished with 52—making him the fifth man this century with 50-plus two-baggers two years in a row. Martinez is unmatched for his combination of contact, patience, and power. He had 39 more walks than whiffs last year but still belted 26 homers while topping 100 runs and RBI. Nearly half his hits went for extra bases. Martinez, who encountered a slight slump in September, rebounded after retooling his stance. Always adjusting, Martinez uses five or six different stances per year. He sends liners to all fields, hitting first-pitch fastballs or breaking balls with equal facility. But he waits for pitches he likes. Martinez had a 1996 on-base percentage of .464, three points behind major-league leader Mark McGwire.

Major League Batting Register

	BA	G	AB	R	H	2B	3B	HR	RBI	SB
87 AL	.372	13	43	6	16	5	2	0	5	0
88 AL	.281	14	32	0	9	4	0	0	5	0
89 AL	.240	65	171	20	41	5	0	2	20	2
90 AL	.302	144	487	71	147	27	2	11	49	1
91 AL	.307	150	544	98	167	35	1	14	52	0
92 AL	.343	135	528	100	181	46	3	18	73	14
93 AL	.237	42	135	20	32	7	0	4	13	0
94 AL	.285	89	326	47	93	23	1	13	51	6
95 AL	.356	145	511	121	182	52	0	29	113	4
96 AL	.327	139	499	121	163	52	2	26	103	3
Life	.315	936	3276	604	1031	256	11	117	484	30
3 Ave	.325	142	511	108	166	48	1	26	101	5

PEDRO MARTINEZ

Position: Pitcher
Team: Montreal Expos
Born: July 21, 1971 Manoguayabo, Dominican Republic
Height: 5'11" **Weight:** 170 lbs.
Bats: right **Throws:** right
Acquired: Traded by Dodgers for Delino DeShields, 11/93

PLAYER SUMMARY
Fantasy Value	$14 to $17
Card Value	10¢ to 15¢
Will	freeze righty bats
Can't	hold runners close
Expect	future no-hitter
Don't Expect	wobbly control

For the past three seasons, Martinez has been a mainstay in the Montreal rotation. The hard-throwing younger brother of Ramon Martinez blends a low-90s fastball with an overhand curve and a circle change—throwing all three pitches for strikes. Not afraid to pitch inside, Martinez ranks among the league leaders in hit batsmen, not to mention brawls provoked. But pitching inside is part of a Martinez game plan that involves working both sides of the plate. An All-Star for the first time in 1996, Martinez took a no-hitter into the seventh inning at New York May 2 before finishing with a two-hit gem. He once pitched nine perfect innings at San Diego before yielding a Bip Roberts double in the tenth. Martinez dominates right-handed hitters (.210), averages more Ks than innings pitched, and yields fewer than eight hits per nine innings. Martinez also keeps the ball in the park. An agile athlete, he fields his position well. But he's an easy mark for baserunners with larceny on their minds.

Major League Pitching Register
	W	L	ERA	G	CG	IP	H	ER	BB	SO
92 NL	0	1	2.25	2	0	8.0	6	2	1	8
93 NL	10	5	2.61	65	0	107.0	76	31	57	119
94 NL	11	5	3.42	24	1	144.2	115	55	45	142
95 NL	14	10	3.51	30	2	194.2	158	76	66	174
96 NL	13	10	3.70	33	4	216.2	189	89	70	222
Life	48	31	3.39	154	7	671.0	544	253	239	665
3 Ave	15	9	3.55	34	3	213.0	176	84	69	206

RAMON MARTINEZ

Position: Pitcher
Team: Los Angeles Dodgers
Born: March 22, 1968 Santo Domingo, Dominican Republic
Height: 6'4" **Weight:** 173 lbs.
Bats: both **Throws:** right
Acquired: Signed as a free agent, 9/84

PLAYER SUMMARY
Fantasy Value	$14 to $17
Card Value	10¢ to 15¢
Will	win big games
Can't	harness control
Expect	self-help with bat
Don't Expect	gopher trouble

Although he missed the first month of the 1996 season, Martinez finished with 15 wins, two of them shutouts. The stringbean right-hander, who blends a low-90s fastball with a slurve and changeup, yields fewer hits than innings, fans seven per nine frames, and keeps the ball in the park. Usually more effective against right-handers, he is best in clutch situations. He bears down with the game on the line. Martinez has two weaknesses: occasional bouts of control trouble and an inability to control the running game. Although he's a good fielder, baserunners swiped 24 of 30 against him last year. One of baseball's best bunters, Martinez led the 1995 Dodgers in sacrifices. He's also been known to help himself with the bat (11 hits in 1995). A member of the 1984 Dominican Olympic team, Martinez pitched an 18-strikeout game in 1990 and a no-hitter in 1995.

Major League Pitching Register
	W	L	ERA	G	CG	IP	H	ER	BB	SO
88 NL	1	3	3.79	9	0	35.2	27	15	22	23
89 NL	6	4	3.19	15	2	98.2	79	35	41	89
90 NL	20	6	2.92	33	12	234.1	191	76	67	223
91 NL	17	13	3.27	33	6	220.1	190	80	69	150
92 NL	8	11	4.00	25	1	150.2	141	67	69	101
93 NL	10	12	3.44	32	4	211.2	202	81	104	127
94 NL	12	7	3.97	24	4	170.0	160	75	56	119
95 NL	17	7	3.66	30	4	206.1	176	84	81	138
96 NL	15	6	3.42	28	2	168.2	153	64	86	134
Life	106	69	3.47	229	35	1496.1	1319	577	595	1104
3 Ave	17	8	3.71	32	4	213.1	192	88	85	152

SANDY MARTINEZ

Position: Catcher
Team: Toronto Blue Jays
Born: Oct. 3, 1972 Villa Mella, Dominican Republic
Height: 6'4" **Weight:** 200 lbs.
Bats: left **Throws:** right
Acquired: Signed as a nondrafted free agent, 1/90

PLAYER SUMMARY

Fantasy Value	$1
Card Value	7¢ to 10¢
Will	provide defense
Can't	lift batting average
Expect	throwing success
Don't Expect	power or speed

The 1996 arrival of veteran receiver Charlie O'Brien in Toronto served Martinez well. The young catcher received on-the-job training from O'Brien, a defensive specialist, and showed considerable improvement over his 1995 freshman showing. The rifle-armed sophomore nailed 35 percent of the runners who tried to steal against him, improved his game-calling skills, and proved adept at preventing wild pitches and guarding the plate from incoming runners. Martinez made only three miscues—after making five in 61 games as a rookie. His defensive skills will keep him around, since Martinez is not much of a hitter. During his six years in the minors, he never hit better than .263 or contributed more than nine homers. Martinez is an impatient hitter who fans more than five times per walk and can't fatten his average by dropping bunts or beating out infield hits. He'll never forget his first big-league homer, however: The victim was Roger Clemens.

Major League Batting Register

	BA	G	AB	R	H	2B	3B	HR	RBI	SB
95 AL	.241	62	191	12	46	12	0	2	25	0
96 AL	.227	76	229	17	52	9	3	3	18	0
Life	.233	138	420	29	98	21	3	5	43	0
2 Ave	.234	73	222	15	52	11	2	3	23	0

TINO MARTINEZ

Position: First base
Team: New York Yankees
Born: Dec. 7, 1967 Tampa, FL
Height: 6'2" **Weight:** 205 lbs.
Bats: left **Throws:** left
Acquired: Traded from Mariners with Jeff Nelson and Jim Mecir for Russ Davis and Sterling Hitchcock, 11/95

PLAYER SUMMARY

Fantasy Value	$25 to $30
Card Value	8¢ to 12¢
Will	swing solid bat
Can't	show any speed
Expect	run production
Don't Expect	sloppy defense

Replacing a legend is never easy. But Martinez filled Don Mattingly's shoes so well that the former Yankee captain was merely a memory before the All-Star break. With 57 RBI by June 26, Martinez had produced eight more RBI than Mattingly plated during the entire '95 season. The former Mariner finished with a career-best 117 RBI. Martinez walked often enough to push his on-base percentage 72 points beyond his batting average. He also delivered a solid mark vs. southpaws, though far off his .322 form of 1995. A slow runner, Martinez seldom steals. But he surprises with his mobility around first base. One of the league's better defenders, he has quick reactions, decent range, soft hands, and a reliable arm—helping him master the 3-6-3 double play. He's no Mattingly with the glove. Martinez has been an All-American, U.S. Olympian, first-round draft choice, minor league Player of the Year, and AL All-Star.

Major League Batting Register

	BA	G	AB	R	H	2B	3B	HR	RBI	SB
90 AL	.221	24	68	4	15	4	0	0	5	0
91 AL	.205	36	112	11	23	2	0	4	9	0
92 AL	.257	136	460	53	118	19	2	16	66	2
93 AL	.265	109	408	48	108	25	1	17	60	0
94 AL	.261	97	329	42	86	21	0	20	61	1
95 AL	.293	141	519	92	152	35	3	31	111	0
96 AL	.292	155	595	82	174	28	0	25	117	2
Life	.271	698	2491	332	676	134	6	113	429	5
3 Ave	.284	150	547	82	155	32	1	29	109	1

MIKE MATHENY

Position: Catcher
Team: Milwaukee Brewers
Born: Sept. 22, 1970 Columbus, OH
Height: 6'3" **Weight:** 205 lbs.
Bats: right **Throws:** right
Acquired: Eighth-round pick in 6/91 free-agent draft

PLAYER SUMMARY	
Fantasy Value	$0
Card Value	4¢ to 7¢
Will	throw ball well
Can't	wait for walks
Expect	decent defense
Don't Expect	the long ball

Although Matheny did the bulk of Milwaukee's catching last year, his season was interrupted by a brief refresher course in the minor leagues. He marked his August return with a home run—one of eight he contributed in 106 games last year. Matheny, who spent part of the year platooning with lefty-hitting Jesse Levis, has never been much of a hitter. He fans five times more often than he walks, leaving him with one of the worst on-base percentages of any position player (.243). On the plus side, more than one-third of his hits go for extra bases. Matheny has a little speed but rarely uses it (three steals). Fielding has always been his forte. The University of Michigan product nailed 33 percent of potential baserunners last year. Matheny makes strong, accurate throws, prevents wild pitches, and blocks the plate like a fullback. If Matheny continues to contribute even a little with the bat, he'll probably have a job. If not, he'll probably get a new start via expansion this fall.

Major League Batting Register

	BA	G	AB	R	H	2B	3B	HR	RBI	SB
94 AL	.226	28	53	3	12	3	0	1	2	0
95 AL	.247	80	166	13	41	9	1	0	21	2
96 AL	.204	106	313	31	64	15	2	8	46	3
Life	.220	214	532	47	117	27	3	9	69	5
2 Ave	.220	98	250	23	55	13	2	4	35	3

TERRY MATHEWS

Position: Pitcher
Team: Baltimore Orioles
Born: Oct. 5, 1964 Alexandria, LA
Height: 6'2" **Weight:** 225 lbs.
Bats: left **Throws:** right
Acquired: Traded by Marlins for Greg Zaun, 8/96

PLAYER SUMMARY	
Fantasy Value	$0
Card Value	4¢ to 7¢
Will	answer bell often
Can't	prevent gophers
Expect	heavy workload
Don't Expect	control problems

A durable middle reliever who can work often, Mathews had already made 57 appearances for the 1996 Marlins when he was traded across league lines last August. He worked 14 more games in Baltimore, giving him a career high with 71 games pitched. A control artist who had a 3-1 ratio of whiffs to walks in 1995, Mathews mixes a fastball, cut fastball, and curve. He yields one hit per inning, fans more than six per nine frames, and has reasonably good control. Effective against both left- and right-handed hitters, Mathews strands most of the runners he inherits and never complains about the length or brevity of his stints—even though he's often asked to work multiple innings. He has one major problem: keeping the ball in the park. Mathews is a good fielder for a big man and keeps a close eye on the running game. He even showed an ability to hit while in the National League. Mathews pitched well in 14 late-season outings for the Orioles.

Major League Pitching Register

	W	L	ERA	G	S	IP	H	ER	BB	SO
91 AL	4	0	3.61	34	1	57.1	54	23	18	51
92 AL	2	4	5.95	40	0	42.1	48	28	31	26
94 NL	2	1	3.35	24	0	43.0	45	16	9	21
95 NL	4	4	3.38	57	3	82.2	70	31	27	72
96 NL	2	4	4.91	57	4	55.0	59	30	27	49
96 AL	2	2	3.38	14	0	18.2	20	7	7	13
Life	16	15	4.06	226	8	299.0	296	135	119	232
3 Ave	3	3	3.77	52	2	70.1	67	29	23	53

T.J. MATHEWS

Position: Pitcher
Team: St. Louis Cardinals
Born: Jan. 19, 1970 Belleville, IL
Height: 6'2" **Weight:** 200 lbs.
Bats: right **Throws:** right
Acquired: 36th-round pick in 6/92 free-agent draft

PLAYER SUMMARY	
Fantasy Value	$8 to $10
Card Value	5¢ to 8¢
Will	keep ball down
Can't	count on velocity
Expect	frequent calls
Don't Expect	righties to hit

The 1.52 ERA Mathews posted in a 23-game tryout with the 1995 Cardinals was no fluke. The former UNLV standout pitched so well last season that he was the busiest member of the St. Louis bullpen. Despite a 2-6 record, Mathews held right-handers to a .192 average, limited lefties to a .224 mark, and averaged nearly a strikeout an inning—even though he's not a hard thrower. Mathews is a sinker-slider pitcher who also throws a changeup. He keeps all three pitches down in the strike zone, enabling him to keep baserunners to a minimum. Mathews yielded fewer than seven hits and 3.5 walks per nine innings, stranded 83.3 percent of the runners he inherited, and controlled the running game so well that only one man stole against him all year. He fields his position well but doesn't hit much (not that he gets the chance). For the past two seasons, the Cards have been grooming Mathews for the closer's role. He may get his chance in 1997.

Major League Pitching Register

	W	L	ERA	G	S	IP	H	ER	BB	SO
95 NL	1	1	1.52	23	2	29.2	21	5	11	28
96 NL	2	6	3.01	67	6	83.2	62	28	32	80
Life	3	7	2.62	90	8	113.1	83	33	43	108

DERRICK MAY

Position: Outfield
Team: Houston Astros
Born: July 14, 1968 Rochester, NY
Height: 6'4" **Weight:** 205 lbs.
Bats: left **Throws:** right
Acquired: Traded by Brewers for Tommy Nevers, 6/95

PLAYER SUMMARY	
Fantasy Value	$1 to $3
Card Value	4¢ to 7¢
Will	produce in pinch
Can't	handle left-handers
Expect	occasional power
Don't Expect	sterling defense

May has been somewhat of a mystery during his seven-year tenure in the majors. He's never had more than ten homers or played in more than 128 games. Part of the problem is his ineptitude against lefties. His .154 average against them in 1996 was 102 points less than his average against right-handers. As a result, May's season was confined to platoon service and pinch-hitting. He shared left field with James Mouton and made 42 trips to the plate as a pinch hitter. A good clutch hitter with power to the gaps, May is best when he gets ahead in the count. May doesn't steal much and doesn't dazzle anyone with his defense. He plays both outfield corners but spent most of '96 in left. At 28, he's too young to carry a utility tag but could be rescued by an expansion club willing to gamble. Some scouts feel the son of former big-leaguer Dave May still has untapped power.

Major League Batting Register

	BA	G	AB	R	H	2B	3B	HR	RBI	SB
90 NL	.246	17	61	8	15	3	0	1	11	1
91 NL	.227	15	22	4	5	2	0	1	3	0
92 NL	.274	124	351	33	96	11	0	8	45	5
93 NL	.295	128	465	62	137	25	2	10	77	10
94 AL	.284	100	345	43	98	19	2	8	51	3
95 AL	.248	32	113	15	28	3	1	1	9	0
95 NL	.301	78	206	29	62	15	1	8	41	5
96 NL	.251	109	259	24	65	12	3	5	33	2
Life	.278	603	1822	218	506	90	9	42	270	26
3 Ave	.279	113	326	39	91	19	2	8	50	4

BRENT MAYNE

Position: Catcher
Team: New York Mets
Born: April 19, 1968 Loma Linda, CA
Height: 6'1" **Weight:** 190 lbs.
Bats: left **Throws:** right
Acquired: Traded by Royals for Al Shirley, 12/95

PLAYER SUMMARY	
Fantasy Value	$0
Card Value	4¢ to 7¢
Will	call good games
Can't	hit left-handers
Expect	defensive skill
Don't Expect	the long ball

Mayne has always longed to be somebody's main man behind the plate. But his hitting has never caught up with his fielding. Even in 1995, when he succeeded Mike Macfarlane as K.C.'s regular receiver, Mayne hit only .251 with 20 extra-base hits—all but two of them doubles—and no stolen bases. A low-ball hitter who uses the opposite field, Mayne fans twice per walk, struggles against southpaws, and lacks selectivity at the plate. The result is a low on-base percentage. When he does connect, Mayne bangs into frequent double plays. His best asset as a batter is an ability to bunt; he was fourth in the AL with 11 sacrifice bunts two years ago. Last year, playing behind Todd Hundley, he made fewer starts but more pinch-hitting appearances. A quarterback behind the plate, Mayne calls good games, prevents wild pitches, and blocks the plate well. His throwing success ratio could be better, however. Mayne may make an attractive No. 1 catcher for an expansion team.

Major League Batting Register

	BA	G	AB	R	H	2B	3B	HR	RBI	SB
90 AL	.231	5	13	2	3	0	0	0	1	0
91 AL	.251	85	231	22	58	8	0	3	31	2
92 AL	.225	82	213	16	48	10	0	0	18	0
93 AL	.254	71	205	22	52	9	1	2	22	3
94 AL	.257	46	144	19	37	5	1	2	20	1
95 AL	.251	110	307	23	77	18	1	1	27	0
96 NL	.263	70	99	9	26	6	0	1	6	0
Life	.248	469	1212	113	301	56	3	9	125	6

DAVID McCARTY

Position: Outfield; first base
Team: San Francisco Giants
Born: Nov. 23, 1969 Houston, TX
Height: 6'5" **Weight:** 213 lbs.
Bats: right **Throws:** left
Acquired: Traded by Reds with Deion Sanders, John Roper, Scott Service, and Ricky Pickett for Mark Portugal, Dave Burba, and Darren Lewis, 7/95

PLAYER SUMMARY	
Fantasy Value	$0
Card Value	5¢ to 8¢
Will	get last chance
Can't	realize potential
Expect	some improvement
Don't Expect	spot in lineup

McCarty's career path has been littered with more hype than substance. Heralded as the second coming of Harmon Killebrew when Minnesota made him the third man selected in the 1991 amateur draft, McCarty has been a huge bust so far. The former Stanford standout, a slugger in college, has been anything but that since turning pro in '91. He reached double digits in homers only once (in the minors) and failed to take advantage of the cozy confines at the Metrodome. McCarty flunked three separate trials before the Twins traded him to the Reds. He lasted little more than a month there before being traded again. If he does nothing else, McCarty has two hits to remember: a double in Nolan Ryan's last game and a game-winning pinch homer to beat Dennis Eckersley last August 8 in St. Louis. An undisciplined hitter, McCarty fans three times per walk and doesn't hit his weight against lefties. He's only average in the field.

Major League Batting Register

	BA	G	AB	R	H	2B	3B	HR	RBI	SB
93 AL	.214	98	350	36	75	15	2	2	21	2
94 AL	.260	44	131	21	34	8	2	1	12	2
95 AL	.218	25	55	10	12	3	1	0	4	0
95 NL	.250	12	20	1	5	1	0	0	2	1
96 NL	.217	91	175	16	38	3	0	6	24	2
Life	.224	270	731	84	164	30	5	9	63	7

QUINTON McCRACKEN

Position: Outfield
Team: Colorado Rockies
Born: March 16, 1970 Wilmington, NC
Height: 5'7" **Weight:** 170 lbs.
Bats: both **Throws:** right
Acquired: 25th-round pick in 6/92 free-agent
draft

PLAYER SUMMARY	
Fantasy Value. . . . . $9 to $11
Card Value . . . . 7¢ to 10¢
Will . . . . show great speed
Can't. . . . . clear the fences
Expect. . . . . walks, hits, steals
Don't Expect . . . . erratic defense

One guy's bad break can be another guy's
big break. That was the case last year for
McCracken, who became Colorado's center fielder when Larry Walker went down
with a broken collarbone. A little guy with
big-time speed, McCracken delivered as
advertised: line drives, stolen bases, and
good defense, but not many home runs.
His biggest hit was a tenth-inning double
that gave the Rockies a 16-15 win over the
Dodgers June 30. Although he fans twice
per walk, McCracken has good knowledge
of the strike zone. He drew enough walks
to push his on-base percentage 73 points
above his batting average. That figure
should improve as he gains experience,
making McCracken a potential leadoff man.
His basestealing success rate (74 percent)
should also jump as he learns the tendencies of NL pitchers. A high-average hitter in
the minors, McCracken had a 60-steal season in his second year as a pro. His speed
helps him in the outfield, where he ranges
far into the gaps. McCracken is a graduate
of Duke University, where he also played
football.

Major League Batting Register

	BA	G	AB	R	H	2B	3B	HR	RBI	SB
95 NL	.000	3	1	0	0	0	0	0	0	0
96 NL	.290	124	283	50	82	13	6	3	40	17
Life	.289	127	284	50	82	13	6	3	40	17

BEN McDONALD

Position: Pitcher
Team: Milwaukee Brewers
Born: Nov. 24, 1967 Baton Rouge, LA
Height: 6'7" **Weight:** 212 lbs.
Bats: right **Throws:** right
Acquired: Signed as a free agent, 1/96

PLAYER SUMMARY	
Fantasy Value. . . . . $13 to $16
Card Value . . . . 5¢ to 8¢
Will . . . . lead the staff
Can't . . . . avoid gophers
Expect. . . . . at least 12 wins
Don't Expect . . . . erratic control

One year after recurring shoulder problems
held him to three wins, McDonald returned
to the ranks of the AL's best pitchers. In his
first year with Milwaukee, he won the
Opening Day assignment, then went on to
win a dozen games for the fourth time in his
career. McDonald, who opened the year
with ten wins in his first 13 decisions, survived a bout with a dead arm that made his
breaking ball less effective. The former
LSU All-American and College Player of
the Year also throws a slider and low-90s
fastball. A durable pitcher with good control, he made 35 starts, averaging six strikeouts and fewer than three walks per nine
innings. McDonald yields a hit per inning
and maintains a strikeout-to-walk ratio of 2-
to-1. The former Olympian and Golden
Spikes Award winner is a good fielder for a
big guy, but his pickoff move isn't perfect.
Eighteen of the 25 runners who tried to
steal against him last year succeeded.

Major League Pitching Register

	W	L	ERA	G	CG	IP	H	ER	BB	SO
89 AL	1	0	8.59	6	0	7.1	8	7	4	3
90 AL	8	5	2.43	21	3	118.2	88	32	35	65
91 AL	6	8	4.84	21	1	126.1	126	68	43	85
92 AL	13	13	4.24	35	4	227.0	213	107	74	158
93 AL	13	14	3.39	34	7	220.1	185	83	86	171
94 AL	14	7	4.06	24	5	157.1	151	71	54	94
95 AL	3	6	4.16	14	1	80.0	67	37	38	62
96 AL	12	10	3.90	35	2	221.1	228	96	67	146
Life	70	63	3.89	190	23	1158.1	1066	501	401	784
3 Ave	12	9	4.01	28	3	178.1	172	79	62	116

JACK MCDOWELL

Position: Pitcher
Team: Cleveland Indians
Born: Jan. 16, 1966 Van Nuys, CA
Height: 6'5" **Weight:** 179 lbs.
Bats: right **Throws:** right
Acquired: Signed as a free agent, 12/95

PLAYER SUMMARY	
Fantasy Value	$15 to $18
Card Value	7¢ to 10¢
Will	win big if healthy
Can't	freeze baserunners
Expect	200 innings pitched
Don't Expect	control trouble

The marriage of McDowell's track record and Cleveland's vaunted offense was supposed to add 20 victories to the 1996 Indians' record. But it didn't work out. The three-time All-Star, twice a 20-game winner, went on the DL for the first time in his career with a strained muscle in his right forearm. Unable to throw his curve, McDowell wound up with his worst ERA. Only good run support guaranteed a winning record. McDowell depends upon fastballs and forkballs, changing speeds on both. McDowell averages more than six Ks and three walks per nine innings. But his usual hit-per-inning average was blown last year when he yielded ten hits per nine innings. The former Stanford star surrendered 22 homers and 22 stolen bases. Those numbers explained the huge jump in ERA. A fine fielder with plenty of competitive fire, McDowell often leads the league in throws to first. A clean bill of health will help.

Major League Pitching Register

	W	L	ERA	G	CG	IP	H	ER	BB	SO
87 AL	3	0	1.93	4	0	28.0	16	6	6	15
88 AL	5	10	3.97	26	1	158.2	147	70	68	84
90 AL	14	9	3.82	33	4	205.0	189	87	77	165
91 AL	17	10	3.41	35	15	253.2	212	96	82	191
92 AL	20	10	3.18	34	13	260.2	247	92	75	178
93 AL	22	10	3.37	34	10	256.2	261	96	69	158
94 AL	10	9	3.73	25	6	181.0	186	75	42	127
95 AL	15	10	3.93	30	8	217.2	211	95	78	157
96 AL	13	9	5.11	30	5	192.0	214	109	67	141
Life	119	77	3.73	251	62	1753.1	1683	726	564	1216
3 Ave	15	11	4.18	33	7	231.1	238	107	71	166

ROGER MCDOWELL

Position: Pitcher
Team: Baltimore Orioles
Born: Dec. 21, 1960 Cincinnati, OH
Height: 6'1" **Weight:** 185 lbs.
Bats: right **Throws:** right
Acquired: Signed as a free agent, 12/95

PLAYER SUMMARY	
Fantasy Value	$1
Card Value	4¢ to 7¢
Will	serve up sinkers
Can't	strike men out
Expect	frequent calls
Don't Expect	erratic control

Had he not succumbed to season-ending shoulder surgery in mid-August, McDowell's sinker might have made a difference in last year's race for the AL East title. His game plan is simple: Show the slider, get outs with the sinker. A quality set-up man, McDowell thrives on a heavy workload and gets rusty without it. He handles first batters well, especially if they're right-handed, but banks on location rather than velocity. When he's right, McDowell coaxes endless ground balls—often ending innings with double plays. As a result, he strands most of the runners he inherits. Because he keeps the ball down in the strike zone, McDowell surrenders few home runs. He helps himself with fine defense and a first-class pickoff move that few runners challenge.

Major League Pitching Register

	W	L	ERA	G	S	IP	H	ER	BB	SO
85 NL	6	5	2.83	62	17	127.1	108	40	37	70
86 NL	14	9	3.02	75	22	128.0	107	43	42	65
87 NL	7	5	4.16	56	25	88.2	95	41	28	32
88 NL	5	5	2.63	62	16	89.0	80	26	31	46
89 NL	4	8	1.96	69	23	92.0	79	20	38	47
90 NL	6	8	3.86	72	22	86.1	92	37	35	39
91 NL	9	9	2.93	71	10	101.1	100	33	48	50
92 NL	6	10	4.09	65	14	83.2	103	38	42	50
93 NL	5	3	2.25	54	2	68.0	76	17	30	27
94 NL	0	3	5.23	32	0	41.1	50	24	22	29
95 AL	7	4	4.02	64	4	85.0	86	38	34	49
96 AL	1	1	4.25	41	4	59.1	69	28	23	20
Life	70	70	3.30	723	159	1050.0	1045	385	410	524
3 Ave	3	3	4.41	53	3	71.0	79	35	31	39

CHUCK MCELROY

Position: Pitcher
Team: Anaheim Angels
Born: Oct. 1, 1967 Galveston, TX
Height: 6′ **Weight:** 160 lbs.
Bats: left **Throws:** left
Acquired: Traded by Reds for Lee Smith, 6/96

PLAYER SUMMARY	
Fantasy Value	$2 to $4
Card Value	4¢ to 7¢
Will	throw late heat
Can't	help with glove
Expect	set-up duty
Don't Expect	weak K count

Even though he lost playing time last season with a sore left thumb and a tender shoulder, McElroy managed to make a nice recovery from his mystifying off year of 1995. His control and velocity came back, enabling him to try his fastball-forkball-curveball arsenal against American League hitters for the first time. His averages of strikeouts per nine innings and hits per nine innings were identical: 7.85. And he yielded just over three walks (3.19) over the same span. McElroy held AL hitters to a .239 mark and yielded only two homers in 36⅔ innings (40 games). He stranded 65.5 percent of the runners he inherited and permitted only two stolen bases. The Angels not only gained a quality lefty reliever when they traded for McElroy but also gained ten years (the difference of Lee Smith's age) and a much lower salary. The bespectacled right-hander is not a great fielder but does an acceptable job.

Major League Pitching Register

	W	L	ERA	G	S	IP	H	ER	BB	SO
89 NL	0	0	1.74	11	0	10.1	12	2	4	8
90 NL	0	1	7.71	16	0	14.0	24	12	10	16
91 NL	6	2	1.95	71	3	101.1	73	22	57	92
92 NL	4	7	3.55	72	6	83.2	73	33	51	83
93 NL	2	2	4.56	49	0	47.1	51	24	25	31
94 NL	1	2	2.34	52	5	57.2	52	15	15	38
95 NL	3	4	6.02	44	0	40.1	46	27	15	27
96 NL	2	0	6.57	12	0	12.1	13	9	10	13
96 AL	5	1	2.95	40	0	36.2	32	12	13	32
Life	23	19	3.48	367	14	403.2	376	156	200	340
3 Ave	3	3	3.50	54	2	54.1	52	21	17	39

WILLIE MCGEE

Position: Outfield
Team: St. Louis Cardinals
Born: Nov. 2, 1958 San Francisco, CA
Height: 6′1″ **Weight:** 185 lbs.
Bats: both **Throws:** right
Acquired: Signed as a free agent, 12/95

PLAYER SUMMARY	
Fantasy Value	$1
Card Value	5¢ to 8¢
Will	make good sub
Can't	wait for walks
Expect	clutch hits
Don't Expect	home runs

During his first tenure with the Cardinals, McGee won two batting titles, three Gold Gloves, and an MVP Award. The four-time All-Star returned as a utility man last year, proving himself the perfect fourth outfielder, pinch hitter, pinch runner, and backup first baseman. Though much of his speed has been lost to age, knee trouble, and a surgically repaired Achilles tendon, McGee remains a valuable man off the bench. He lacks patience, fanning four times per walk, but hit ten points above his previous career average last year. A good clutch hitter, McGee is most productive at home (.358 last year). He doesn't steal much anymore (5-for-7 last year) but moves well. Though his Gold Glove days are long behind him, he's a team leader on and off the field.

Major League Batting Register

	BA	G	AB	R	H	2B	3B	HR	RBI	SB
82 NL	.296	123	422	43	125	12	8	4	56	24
83 NL	.286	147	601	75	172	22	8	5	75	39
84 NL	.291	145	571	82	166	19	11	6	50	43
85 NL	.353	152	612	114	216	26	18	10	82	56
86 NL	.256	124	497	65	127	22	7	7	48	19
87 NL	.285	153	620	76	177	37	11	11	105	16
88 NL	.292	137	562	73	164	24	6	3	50	41
89 NL	.236	58	199	23	47	10	2	3	17	8
90 NL	.335	125	501	76	168	32	5	3	62	28
90 AL	.274	29	113	23	31	3	2	0	15	3
91 NL	.312	131	497	67	155	30	3	4	43	17
92 NL	.297	138	474	56	141	20	2	1	36	13
93 NL	.301	130	475	53	143	28	1	4	46	10
94 NL	.282	45	156	19	44	3	0	5	23	3
95 NL	.285	67	200	32	57	11	3	2	15	5
96 NL	.307	123	309	52	95	15	2	5	41	5
Life	.298	1827	6809	929	2028	314	89	73	764	330
3 Ave	.293	87	251	38	74	11	2	5	30	5

FRED McGRIFF

Position: First base
Team: Atlanta Braves
Born: Oct. 31, 1963 Tampa, FL
Height: 6'3" **Weight:** 215 lbs.
Bats: left **Throws:** left
Acquired: Traded by Padres for Melvin Nieves, Donnie Elliott, and Vince Moore, 7/93

PLAYER SUMMARY	
Fantasy Value.	$25 to $30
Card Value	20¢ to 40¢
Will	provide power
Can't	cut strikeout rate
Expect	run production
Don't Expect	display of speed

One of baseball's most consistent sluggers, McGriff has hit at least 20 homers ten years in a row. McGriff's hitting prowess is a tribute to his durability: He almost never misses a game. Although he averages two whiffs per walk, the Atlanta cleanup man is a slugger with patience. McGriff's on-base percentage was 70 points higher than his batting average last year. Unlike most other left-handed hitters, McGriff actually fares better against southpaws. He batted .325 against lefties in 1996. Only a long midseason slump stood between McGriff and his third .300 campaign (he finished five points short). Though not fast, he steals a half-dozen bases a year, picking his spots wisely. McGriff is no Mark Grace at first, but his height helps. A four-time All-Star, McGriff has surprising range and is adept at scooping and stretching.

Major League Batting Register

	BA	G	AB	R	H	2B	3B	HR	RBI	SB
86 AL	.200	3	5	1	1	0	0	0	0	0
87 AL	.247	107	295	58	73	16	0	20	43	3
88 AL	.282	154	536	100	151	35	4	34	82	6
89 AL	.269	161	551	98	148	27	3	36	92	7
90 AL	.300	153	557	91	167	21	1	35	88	5
91 NL	.278	153	528	84	147	19	1	31	106	4
92 NL	.286	152	531	79	152	30	4	35	104	8
93 NL	.291	151	557	111	162	29	2	37	101	5
94 NL	.318	113	424	81	135	25	1	34	94	7
95 NL	.280	144	528	85	148	27	1	27	93	3
96 NL	.295	159	617	81	182	37	1	28	107	7
Life	.286	1450	5129	869	1466	266	18	317	910	55
3 Ave	.298	160	603	97	180	34	1	35	115	7

MARK McGWIRE

Position: First base
Team: Oakland Athletics
Born: Oct. 1, 1963 Pomona, CA
Height: 6'5" **Weight:** 225 lbs.
Bats: right **Throws:** right
Acquired: First-round pick in 6/84 free-agent draft

PLAYER SUMMARY	
Fantasy Value.	$40 to $45
Card Value	20¢ to 40¢
Will	rattle the fences
Can't	avoid injuries
Expect	record power
Don't Expect	stolen bases

McGwire is today's most likely challenger to Roger Maris's 61-homer record. Even though he missed most of April with a torn muscle in the arch of his right foot, McGwire finished 1996 with 52 homers, most in the majors. His frequency of one homer per every 8.135 at bats wasn't as good as his record 1995 ratio of one homer per every 8.128 at bats. McGwire is a brittle slugger who's missed more than 1½ seasons over the last three years. He's a menace when healthy; unfortunately, he had left foot and heel problems in 1994 and '95 and back spasms in addition to the right foot problem last year. McGwire moves well in the field. He's an agile first baseman with quick reactions, soft hands, a good scoop, and a reliable arm. The former USC All-American and College Player of the Year was a U.S. Olympian in 1984.

Major League Batting Register

	BA	G	AB	R	H	2B	3B	HR	RBI	SB
86 AL	.189	18	53	10	10	1	0	3	9	0
87 AL	.289	151	557	97	161	28	4	49	118	1
88 AL	.260	155	550	87	143	22	1	32	99	0
89 AL	.231	143	490	74	113	17	0	33	95	1
90 AL	.235	156	523	87	123	16	0	39	108	2
91 NL	.201	154	483	62	97	22	0	22	75	2
92 AL	.268	139	467	87	125	22	0	42	104	0
93 AL	.333	27	84	16	28	6	0	9	24	0
94 AL	.252	47	135	26	34	3	0	9	25	0
95 AL	.274	104	317	75	87	13	0	39	90	1
96 AL	.312	130	423	104	132	21	0	52	113	0
Life	.258	1224	4082	725	1053	171	5	329	860	7
2 Ave	.295	124	390	94	115	18	0	48	107	1

MARK MCLEMORE

Position: Second base; outfield
Team: Texas Rangers
Born: Oct. 4, 1964 San Diego, CA
Height: 5'11" **Weight:** 195 lbs.
Bats: both **Throws:** right
Acquired: Signed as a free agent, 12/94

PLAYER SUMMARY	
Fantasy Value	$8 to $10
Card Value	4¢ to 7¢
Will	get on base
Can't	clear fences
Expect	good defense
Don't Expect	many whiffs

After years of rotating around the field, McLemore spent the entire 1996 campaign as the Rangers' regular second baseman. The stability paid off, as the switch-hitting Californian came through with his best campaign. McLemore's best asset was his patience at the plate. He walked more often than he fanned, finishing with an on-base percentage 99 points higher than his batting average. He also added speed to the Texas attack, topping the team with 27 stolen bases. A contact hitter, McLemore will bunt to move runners along. He's also adept at fattening his average by beating out infield hits. When he's hot, the former Oriole terrorizes opposing pitchers: His .472 batting average last June was the best one-month mark in Texas history. McLemore is a solid defensive second baseman with speed, quick instincts, soft hands, and a decent arm.

Major League Batting Register

	BA	G	AB	R	H	2B	3B	HR	RBI	SB
86 AL	.000	5	4	0	0	0	0	0	0	0
87 AL	.236	138	433	61	102	13	3	3	41	25
88 AL	.240	77	233	38	56	11	2	2	16	13
89 AL	.243	32	103	12	25	3	1	0	14	6
90 AL	.150	28	60	6	9	2	0	0	2	1
91 NL	.148	21	61	6	9	1	0	0	2	0
92 AL	.246	101	228	40	56	7	2	0	27	11
93 AL	.284	148	581	81	165	27	5	4	72	21
94 AL	.257	104	343	44	88	11	1	3	29	20
95 AL	.261	129	467	73	122	20	5	5	41	21
96 AL	.290	147	517	84	150	23	4	5	46	27
Life	.258	930	3030	445	782	118	23	22	290	145
3 Ave	.270	146	509	76	137	20	4	5	44	26

GREG MCMICHAEL

Position: Pitcher
Team: New York Mets
Born: Dec. 1, 1966 Knoxville, TN
Height: 6'3" **Weight:** 215 lbs.
Bats: right **Throws:** right
Acquired: Traded by Braves for Paul Byrd and a player to be named later, 11/96

PLAYER SUMMARY	
Fantasy Value	$4 to $6
Card Value	4¢ to 7¢
Will	rely on location
Can't	hold runners on
Expect	control and Ks
Don't Expect	the long ball

The changeup is to McMichael what the fastball is to Mark Wohlers: a successful out pitch in the late innings of a close game. Like Doug Jones in his prime, McMichael throws a change that seems to roll off the table just as it crosses the plate. He mixes it with a so-so fastball and slider to keep hitters honest. When he's right, McMichael fans more than eight batters per nine innings, yields fewer hits than innings pitched, and issues less than three walks per game. He's also very good at keeping the ball in the park. Although McMichael suffered a late-season bout of tendinitis, he's usually a rubber-armed pitcher who can work often. McMichael is a decent—though not spectacular—fielder who has trouble holding runners close. He's not much of a hitter but doesn't have many opportunities. A thinking man's pitcher who takes his Scrabble game on road trips, McMichael was drafted off the University of Tennessee campus by the Cleveland Indians in 1988.

Major League Pitching Register

	W	L	ERA	G	S	IP	H	ER	BB	SO
93 NL	2	3	2.06	74	19	91.2	68	21	29	89
94 NL	4	6	3.84	51	21	58.2	66	25	19	47
95 NL	7	2	2.79	67	2	80.2	64	25	32	74
96 NL	5	3	3.22	73	2	86.2	84	31	27	78
Life	18	14	2.89	265	44	317.2	282	102	107	288
3 Ave	6	5	3.26	73	11	87.1	83	31	30	76

BRIAN MCRAE

Position: Outfield
Team: Chicago Cubs
Born: Aug. 27, 1967 Bradenton, FL
Height: 6′ **Weight:** 180 lbs.
Bats: both **Throws:** right
Acquired: Traded by Royals for Derek Wallace and Geno Morones, 4/95

PLAYER SUMMARY	
Fantasy Value	$20 to $25
Card Value	5¢ to 8¢
Will	show alley power
Can't	hit all righties
Expect	speed, defense
Don't Expect	failure on bases

With free agency on the horizon, McRae reached career peaks in both home runs and stolen bases last year. He also made himself into a better leadoff man by showing more patience at the plate. McRae finished with almost as many walks as strikeouts, plus an admirable on-base percentage. The son of former big-league outfielder and manager Hal McRae is a better hitter for average against left-handed pitchers. But he hits most of his home runs against righties. McRae has alley power, collecting extra bases on nearly one-third of his hits. He also stretches singles into doubles and drops occasional bunts. Because he hits the ball hard, McRae bangs into a lot of double plays. On the bases, he has a high success rate when trying to steal. His speed helps in the outfield, where McRae moved after spending his first four pro seasons at second base. He's become a fine center fielder with quick reactions, wide range, and soft hands.

Major League Batting Register

	BA	G	AB	R	H	2B	3B	HR	RBI	SB
90 AL	.286	46	168	21	48	8	3	2	23	4
91 AL	.261	152	629	86	164	28	9	8	64	20
92 AL	.223	149	533	63	119	23	5	4	52	18
93 AL	.282	153	627	78	177	28	9	12	69	23
94 AL	.273	114	436	71	119	22	6	4	40	28
95 NL	.288	137	580	92	167	38	7	12	48	27
96 NL	.276	157	624	111	172	32	5	17	66	37
Life	.269	908	3597	522	966	179	44	59	362	157
3 Ave	.279	157	630	105	176	35	7	12	59	36

PAT MEARES

Position: Shortstop
Team: Minnesota Twins
Born: Sept. 6, 1968 Salina, KS
Height: 6′ **Weight:** 185 lbs.
Bats: right **Throws:** right
Acquired: 15th-round pick in 6/90 free-agent draft

PLAYER SUMMARY	
Fantasy Value	$5 to $7
Card Value	4¢ to 7¢
Will	surprise with pop
Can't	stop striking out
Expect	solid defense
Don't Expect	leadoff berth

Like predecessor Greg Gagne, Meares swings a more productive bat than most middle infielders. He smacked 41 extra-base hits last year, hit just under .300 against lefties, and even contributed nine stolen bases in 13 tries. He'd be even more potent if he weren't so aggressive. Meares has never met a pitch he didn't like. He fanned more than five times per walk in 1996, leaving him with an on-base percentage below .300. That statistic underlines the biggest reason why Meares does not make a good leadoff man. Though he bangs into frequent double plays, Meares compensates by delivering sacrifice bunts and sacrifice flies when needed. His hitting against left-handers, once a weakness, improved dramatically last year after he moved up on the plate. Meares has quick reactions, good range, and a strong, though not always reliable, arm at short. He's adept at turning the double play. Meares was a member of the 1989 Wichita State team that won the College World Series.

Major League Batting Register

	BA	G	AB	R	H	2B	3B	HR	RBI	SB
93 AL	.251	111	346	33	87	14	3	0	33	4
94 AL	.266	80	229	29	61	12	1	2	24	5
95 AL	.269	116	390	57	105	19	4	12	49	10
96 AL	.267	152	517	66	138	26	7	8	67	9
Life	.264	459	1482	185	391	71	15	22	173	28
3 Ave	.268	132	426	57	114	21	4	8	52	9

ORLANDO MERCED

Position: Outfield; first base
Team: Toronto Blue Jays
Born: Nov. 2, 1966 San Juan, Puerto Rico
Height: 5'11" **Weight:** 170 lbs.
Bats: left **Throws:** right
Acquired: Traded by Pirates with Carlos Garcia and Dan Plesac for Jose Pett, Jose Silva, Branden Cromer, and three players to be named later, 11/96

PLAYER SUMMARY
Fantasy Value. . . . . $12 to $15
Card Value . . . . 5¢ to 8¢
Will . . . . swing solid bat
Can't . . . . hit all lefties
Expect . . . . best job at home
Don't Expect . . . . fielding awards

Merced trashed his reputation as a platoon player last season. Though still a better hitter against righties, he held his own against lefties—persuading Pittsburgh manager Jim Leyland to leave him in the lineup against all comers. Merced, who hits to all fields, shows some patience at the plate and makes decent contact. He loves fastballs, especially on the first pitch, but draws enough walks to boost his on-base percentage 70 points above his batting average. He seldom boosts his average with bunts or infield hits but runs well enough to steal a handful of bases. He needs to watch his weight, however. Merced improved his reputation as a right fielder last year, when he had 15 assists and only three errors. Despite his quick reactions, good range, and soft hands, first base may be Merced's best position. But he played only one game there last year.

KENT MERCKER

Position: Pitcher
Team: Cincinnati Reds
Born: Feb. 1, 1968 Dublin, OH
Height: 6'2" **Weight:** 195 lbs.
Bats: left **Throws:** left
Acquired: Signed as a free agent, 12/96

PLAYER SUMMARY
Fantasy Value. . . . . $4 to $6
Card Value . . . . 4¢ to 7¢
Will . . . . start or relieve
Can't . . . . always find plate
Expect . . . . great velocity
Don't Expect . . . . lefties to hit

Mercker's introduction to the AL got off to a rocky start last spring. A severe case of the flu sidelined him for several weeks of spring training and ultimately interfered with his mechanics. Ineffective with the Orioles, who had projected him as a starter, Mercker was traded to Cleveland, where he went 1-0 with a 3.09 ERA in ten relief appearances. A fastball-slider pitcher who also throws a curveball and changeup, Mercker is a power pitcher who averaged a strikeout an inning in 1994. That was the year he pitched a no-hitter against the Dodgers in his first start for Atlanta. With his durability in doubt, Mercker might remain in relief in 1997. Much depends on his ability to throw strikes; he's been prone to bouts of wildness during his career. At 29, he's still at a career crossroads, uncertain whether he will start or relieve. No matter what he does, he'll be prime bait for selection in this year's expansion draft.

Major League Batting Register
	BA	G	AB	R	H	2B	3B	HR	RBI	SB
90 NL	.208	25	24	3	5	1	0	0	0	0
91 NL	.275	120	411	83	113	17	2	10	50	8
92 NL	.247	134	405	50	100	28	5	6	60	5
93 NL	.313	137	447	68	140	26	4	8	70	3
94 NL	.272	108	386	48	105	21	3	9	51	4
95 NL	.300	132	487	75	146	29	4	15	83	7
96 NL	.287	120	453	69	130	24	1	17	80	8
Life	.283	776	2613	396	739	146	19	65	394	35
3 Ave	.286	140	515	74	147	29	3	16	82	7

Major League Pitching Register
	W	L	ERA	G	S	IP	H	ER	BB	SO
89 NL	0	0	12.46	2	0	4.1	8	6	6	4
90 NL	4	7	3.17	36	7	48.1	43	17	24	39
91 NL	5	3	2.58	50	6	73.1	56	21	35	62
92 NL	3	2	3.42	53	6	68.1	51	26	35	49
93 NL	3	1	2.86	43	0	66.0	52	21	36	59
94 NL	9	4	3.45	20	0	112.1	90	43	45	111
95 NL	7	8	4.15	29	0	143.0	140	66	61	102
96 AL	4	6	6.98	24	0	69.2	83	54	38	29
Life	35	31	3.91	257	19	585.1	523	254	280	455
3 Ave	8	7	4.37	28	0	130.1	122	63	57	100

JOSE MESA

Position: Pitcher
Team: Cleveland Indians
Born: May 22, 1966 Azua, Dominican Republic
Height: 6'3" **Weight:** 222 lbs.
Bats: right **Throws:** right
Acquired: Traded by Orioles for Kyle Washington, 7/92

PLAYER SUMMARY
Fantasy Value	$30 to $35
Card Value	5¢ to 8¢
Will	throw late heat
Can't	field all balls
Expect	Ks, groundouts
Don't Expect	blown saves

When Mesa marches in from the bullpen, the game is usually over. He converted 88.6 percent (39 of 44) of his save chances last year, third in the AL, and has a two-year ratio of 92.4 percent (85 of 92). Mesa struggled in June, when he briefly lost the closer job to Paul Shuey, but recovered after junking the forkball-curveball combination he used as a starter. An All-Star the last two years, Mesa became a bullpen standout after junking the forkball-curveball combination he used as a starter. He now depends on a low-90s fastball and a sinker that coaxes lots of ground-ball outs. The durable power pitcher, who averages eight strikeouts per nine innings, has topped 50 appearances three years in a row. He yields one hit per inning and three-plus walks per game, keeps the ball in the park, and does a decent job of holding runners close. Mesa's main weakness is defense; the guy just isn't a good fielder.

Major League Pitching Register
	W	L	ERA	G	S	IP	H	ER	BB	SO
87 AL	1	3	6.03	6	0	31.1	38	21	15	17
90 AL	3	2	3.86	7	0	46.2	37	20	27	24
91 AL	6	11	5.97	23	0	123.2	151	82	62	64
92 AL	7	12	4.59	28	0	160.2	169	82	70	62
93 AL	10	12	4.92	34	0	208.2	232	114	62	118
94 AL	7	5	3.82	51	2	73.0	71	31	26	63
95 AL	3	0	1.13	62	46	64.0	49	8	17	58
96 AL	2	7	3.73	69	39	72.1	69	30	28	64
Life	39	52	4.48	280	87	780.1	816	388	307	470
3 Ave	5	5	3.01	70	31	82.1	75	28	28	73

DAN MICELI

Position: Pitcher
Team: Detroit Tigers
Born: Sept. 9, 1970 Newark, NJ
Height: 6' **Weight:** 207 lbs.
Bats: right **Throws:** right
Acquired: Traded by Pirates for Clint Sodowsky, 12/96

PLAYER SUMMARY
Fantasy Value	$4 to $6
Card Value	4¢ to 7¢
Will	seek 1995 form
Can't	prevent gophers
Expect	high whiff rate
Don't Expect	great control

Despite 21 saves in 1995, Miceli's status as Pittsburgh's closer was far from certain when the '96 season started. He'd been hit hard the previous September, and he finished with a year-long average of 14.4 baserunners per nine innings of relief. When Miceli's struggles continued in '96, the Pirates tried to rattle his cage by giving him nine starts—the first he's had in a pro career dating back to 1990. Nothing worked. Miceli yielded too many hits, walks, homers, and stolen bases to produce a winning record or respectable ERA. His only positives were an average of seven Ks per nine innings and an ability to strand inherited runners (60 percent). A fastball-slider pitcher who sometimes reaches the mid-90s, Miceli needs to recapture that velocity or at least demonstrate the same success against right-handed hitters (.209 opposing average) that he showed in 1995. Miceli helps his own cause with his fielding but has a slow delivery that makes him an easy target for basestealers.

Major League Pitching Register
	W	L	ERA	G	S	IP	H	ER	BB	SO
93 NL	0	0	5.06	9	0	5.1	6	3	3	4
94 NL	2	1	5.93	28	2	27.1	28	18	11	27
95 NL	4	4	4.66	58	21	58.0	61	30	28	56
96 NL	2	10	5.78	44	1	85.2	99	55	45	66
Life	8	15	5.41	139	24	176.1	194	106	87	153
2 Ave	3	7	5.29	55	12	75.1	84	44	38	65

MATT MIESKE

Position: Outfield
Team: Milwaukee Brewers
Born: Feb. 13, 1968 Midland, MI
Height: 6' **Weight:** 185 lbs.
Bats: right **Throws:** right
Acquired: Traded by Padres with Ricky Bones and Jose Valentin for Gary Sheffield and Geoff Kellogg, 3/92

PLAYER SUMMARY	
Fantasy Value	$6 to $8
Card Value	5¢ to 8¢
Will	hit lefties hard
Can't	escape platoon
Expect	some long hits
Don't Expect	stolen bases

If Mieske could hit right-handed pitching as well as he hits lefties, he'd be one of baseball's better players. His 1996 average against southpaws was a whopping .352—121 points better than he hit vs. right-handers—and he finished with personal peaks in home runs and runs batted in. But Mieske wound up sharing his position with Dave Nilsson and Jeromy Burnitz, both left-handed batters who were considerably more potent against righties. A pull hitter who goes to the opposite field only occasionally, Mieske loves low fastballs. But he's an impatient hitter who fans three times per walk, leaving him with an on-base percentage only 46 points above his batting average. Breaking balls often give him trouble. Although he once stole 36 bases in the minors, Mieske no longer runs well. He was nailed five times in six tries last year. He lacks the range for center, where he played ten games last year, but has the arm for right, where he was the only Brewer to appear more than 100 times.

Major League Batting Register

	BA	G	AB	R	H	2B	3B	HR	RBI	SB
93 AL	.241	23	58	9	14	0	0	3	7	0
94 AL	.259	84	259	39	67	13	1	10	38	3
95 AL	.251	117	267	42	67	13	1	12	48	2
96 AL	.278	127	374	46	104	24	3	14	64	1
Life	.263	351	958	136	252	50	5	39	157	6
3 Ave	.263	126	346	49	91	19	2	14	57	2

ORLANDO MILLER

Position: Shortstop; third base
Team: Detroit Tigers
Born: Jan. 13, 1969 Changuinola, Panama
Height: 6'1" **Weight:** 180 lbs.
Bats: right **Throws:** right
Acquired: Traded by Astros with Brian Hunter, Doug Brocail, Todd Jones, and a player to be named later for Brad Ausmus, Jose Lima, C.J. Nitkowski, Trever Miller, and Daryle Ward, 12/96

PLAYER SUMMARY	
Fantasy Value	$5 to $7
Card Value	5¢ to 8¢
Will	improve with time
Can't	learn strike zone
Expect	pretty good pop
Don't Expect	hits vs. lefties

Few middle infielders can match Miller's home run power or throwing arm. But few struggle as much against left-handed pitchers. Miller often sat when southpaws were working last year. Miller found time to play 29 games at third base and make seven pinch-hitting appearances. He'll play more often when he masters the strike zone; last year, he fanned nearly nine times for every walk but also was able to deliver some timely hits. Though he's never been much of a basestealer, Miller came to the Astros in 1994 with a reputation as an outstanding defensive player. The power of his throwing arm has delivered as advertised, but accuracy has been lacking thus far. Hardly the second coming of Andujar Cedeno, Miller did lead two minor leagues in errors—most of them on throws. His reactions and range are fine. Miller may have put the lid on his other problem: a tendency to be temperamental.

Major League Batting Register

	BA	G	AB	R	H	2B	3B	HR	RBI	SB
94 NL	.325	16	40	3	13	0	1	2	9	1
95 NL	.262	92	324	36	85	20	1	5	36	3
96 NL	.256	139	468	43	120	26	2	15	58	3
Life	.262	247	832	82	218	46	4	22	103	7
2 Ave	.259	121	416	42	108	24	2	10	49	3

ALAN MILLS

Position: Pitcher
Team: Baltimore Orioles
Born: Oct. 18, 1966 Lakeland, FL
Height: 6'1" **Weight:** 195 lbs.
Bats: both **Throws:** right
Acquired: Traded by Yankees for Francisco de la Rosa and Mark Carper, 2/92

PLAYER SUMMARY	
Fantasy Value	$5 to $7
Card Value	4¢ to 7¢
Will	rack up Ks
Can't	avoid gophers
Expect	few rival hits
Don't Expect	good health

A hard-throwing reliever who averages a strikeout an inning, Mills played an integral role in Baltimore's ability to capture the AL's 1996 wild-card berth. Working 49 times, a career high, he held right-handed hitters to a .197 average and yielded 6½ hits per nine innings. But he sabotaged his efforts with erratic control (5½ walks per nine innings) and a penchant for throwing gopher balls (ten in 54⅔ innings). A fastball-slider pitcher who needs a better off-speed pitch, Mills showed some promise last year. He retired 31 of 49 first-batters faced and stranded all but 16 of the 41 runners he inherited. Because he throws everything hard, baserunners don't challenge him often. He helps his own cause by playing solid defense—especially on shots hit right at him. When healthy, Mills makes a fine set-up man. But he's had arthroscopic shoulder surgery, a strained right flexor muscle, and a strained groin during the last two seasons.

Major League Pitching Register

	W	L	ERA	G	S	IP	H	ER	BB	SO
90 AL	1	5	4.10	36	0	41.2	48	19	33	24
91 AL	1	1	4.41	6	0	16.1	16	8	8	11
92 AL	10	4	2.61	35	2	103.1	78	30	54	60
93 AL	5	4	3.23	45	4	100.1	80	36	51	68
94 AL	3	3	5.16	47	2	45.1	43	26	24	44
95 AL	3	0	7.43	21	0	23.0	30	19	18	16
96 AL	3	2	4.28	49	3	54.2	40	26	35	50
Life	26	19	3.84	239	11	384.2	335	164	223	273
2 Ave	4	3	4.76	58	3	59.1	50	31	34	56

MIKE MIMBS

Position: Pitcher
Team: Philadelphia Phillies
Born: Feb. 13, 1969 Macon, GA
Height: 6'2" **Weight:** 182 lbs.
Bats: left **Throws:** left
Acquired: Rule 5 draft pick from Expos, 12/94

PLAYER SUMMARY	
Fantasy Value	$0
Card Value	4¢ to 7¢
Will	hope sinker sinks
Can't	quell lefty bats
Expect	rotation berth
Don't Expect	many strikeouts

After showing considerable promise during his 1995 rookie season, Mimbs had a miserable meeting with the sophomore jinx last summer. Maybe the culprit was a sore shoulder that sidelined him for a month. Or maybe he just can't handle big-league competition. Although Mimbs showed decent control and held his own against righties, lefties lit him up. He yielded too many hits and homers, threw more than his share of wild pitches, and failed to finish a game. A sinkerballer who also throws a changeup and curveball, Mimbs likes to keep his pitches down in the strike zone. Depending on location rather than velocity, he fans only five per nine innings. Mimbs helps his own cause with his bunting, fielding, and ability to hold runners close. He was the victim of low run support last year (3.76 per game), but his bloated ERA hardly helped, either. If minor-league stats can be trusted, Mimbs may yet come around: He was a double-digit winner three times in five seasons. Lefties always seem to get more chances, and Mimbs is still only 28.

Major League Pitching Register

	W	L	ERA	G	CG	IP	H	ER	BB	SO
95 NL	9	7	4.15	35	2	136.2	127	63	75	93
96 NL	3	9	5.53	21	0	99.1	116	61	41	56
Life	12	16	4.73	56	2	236.0	243	124	116	149
2 Ave	7	8	4.69	30	1	127.1	129	66	63	80

ANGEL MIRANDA

Position: Pitcher
Team: Milwaukee Brewers
Born: Nov. 9, 1969 Arecibo, Puerto Rico
Height: 6'1" **Weight:** 195 lbs.
Bats: left **Throws:** left
Acquired: Signed as a nondrafted free agent, 3/87

PLAYER SUMMARY	
Fantasy Value	$1
Card Value	4¢ to 7¢
Will	seek starting spot
Can't	throw ball over
Expect	success vs. righties
Don't Expect	runners to steal

Still searching for his niche in the big leagues, Miranda doubled as a starter and reliever for the 1996 Brewers. Though he held right-handers to a .258 average—thanks to his tantalizing screwball—Miranda was mauled by lefties. Combining the scroogie with a heater proved to be a potent formula for the Puerto Rican southpaw, who also features a slow curve. A power pitcher in the minors, Miranda fans 6½ hitters per nine innings but has an awful time throwing the ball over the plate (5½ walks per game). He yields too many extra-base hits (55 in 109⅓ innings) and throws too many wild pitches (ten last year). On the plus side, he yields just over a hit per inning and nails most of the men who try to steal against him (five of seven last year). But Miranda's follow-through leaves him in poor defensive position, making him a liability in the field. At 27, he still has potential. But he needs to find the strike zone and avoid the crippling injuries that have plagued him in the past.

Major League Pitching Register

	W	L	ERA	G	S	IP	H	ER	BB	SO
93 AL	4	5	3.30	22	0	120.0	100	44	52	88
94 AL	2	5	5.28	8	0	46.0	39	27	27	24
95 AL	4	5	5.23	30	1	74.0	83	43	49	45
96 AL	7	6	4.94	46	1	109.1	116	60	69	78
Life	17	21	4.48	106	2	349.1	338	174	197	235
2 Ave	6	6	5.06	40	1	96.1	105	54	62	64

KEVIN MITCHELL

Position: Outfield
Team: Cincinnati Reds
Born: Jan. 13, 1962 San Diego, CA
Height: 5'11" **Weight:** 244 lbs.
Bats: right **Throws:** right
Acquired: Traded by Red Sox for Roberto Mejia and Brad Tweedlie, 7/96

PLAYER SUMMARY	
Fantasy Value	$8 to $10
Card Value	5¢ to 8¢
Will	swing potent bat
Can't	play every day
Expect	run production
Don't Expect	speed, defense

When Mitchell is physically and emotionally ready to play, he's one of baseball's most intimidating sluggers. After a one-year hiatus in the Japanese leagues, the former National League MVP hit .304 in 27 games for Boston before returning to Cincinnati. There, Mitchell had six homers, 26 RBI, and a .325 batting average. But the enigmatic slugger went AWOL in September and was suspended by the club. A fastball hitter with power to all fields, Mitchell is the perfect cleanup man. He thrives in clutch situations and comes through with men in scoring position. But he's getting so hefty that he's become a liability on the bases and in the field. If he stays in the lineup, Mitchell is a threat to duplicate the 47 homers of his 1989 MVP season. For a guy who hasn't appeared in 100 games since 1991, however, that's a tall order.

Major League Batting Register

	BA	G	AB	R	H	2B	3B	HR	RBI	SB
84 NL	.214	7	14	0	3	0	0	0	1	0
86 NL	.277	108	328	51	91	22	2	12	43	3
87 NL	.280	131	464	68	130	20	2	22	70	9
88 NL	.251	148	505	60	127	25	7	19	80	5
89 NL	.291	154	543	100	158	34	6	47	125	3
90 NL	.290	140	524	90	152	24	2	35	93	4
91 NL	.256	113	371	52	95	13	1	27	69	2
92 NL	.286	99	360	48	103	24	0	9	67	0
93 NL	.341	93	323	56	110	21	3	19	64	1
94 NL	.326	95	310	57	101	18	1	30	77	2
96 AL	.304	27	92	9	28	4	0	2	13	0
96 NL	.325	37	114	18	37	11	0	6	26	0
Life	.287	1152	3948	609	1135	216	24	228	728	29

DAVE MLICKI

Position: Pitcher
Team: New York Mets
Born: June 8, 1968 Cleveland, OH
Height: 6′4″ **Weight:** 190 lbs.
Bats: right **Throws:** right
Acquired: Traded by Indians with Jerry DiPoto, Paul Byrd, and Jesus Azuaje for Jeromy Burnitz and Joe Roa, 11/94

PLAYER SUMMARY	
Fantasy Value.	$3 to $5
Card Value	4¢ to 7¢
Will	strand baserunners
Can't	prevent gophers
Expect	breaking ball diet
Don't Expect	erratic control

Mlicki was much more effective as a reliever last year than he was as a starter the year before. Working almost exclusively in relief for the first time as a pro, he appeared in 51 games and posted good numbers for a bad ballclub. Yielding only one hit per inning and three walks per game, Mlicki averaged 8.3 strikeouts per nine frames. He also stranded a whopping 81.5 percent of the runners he inherited. A curveball specialist who also throws a knuckle-curve, slider, and straight change, Mlicki is slightly more effective against right-handed hitters. His biggest weakness is a tendency to throw too many gopher balls (nine in 90 innings last year). Mlicki helps his own cause with his bunting, hitting, and ability to hold runners on. Only four runners tried to steal against him, and two of them didn't make it. A good bunter, Mlicki is also a selective hitter who gets occasional hits. With expansion around the corner, Mlicki has enough youth and experience to head a new club's rotation. He doesn't turn 29 until June.

Major League Pitching Register

	W	L	ERA	G	S	IP	H	ER	BB	SO
92 AL	0	2	4.98	4	0	21.2	23	12	16	16
93 AL	0	0	3.38	3	0	13.1	11	5	6	7
95 NL	9	7	4.26	29	0	160.2	160	76	54	123
96 NL	6	7	3.30	51	1	90.0	95	33	33	83
Life	15	16	3.97	87	1	285.2	289	126	109	229
2 Ave	8	7	3.94	42	1	135.1	138	59	47	111

MIKE MOHLER

Position: Pitcher
Team: Oakland Athletics
Born: July 26, 1968 Dayton, OH
Height: 6′2″ **Weight:** 195 lbs.
Bats: right **Throws:** left
Acquired: 42nd-round pick in 6/89 free-agent draft

PLAYER SUMMARY	
Fantasy Value.	$6 to $8
Card Value	4¢ to 7¢
Will	work out of pen
Can't	avoid gophers
Expect	ground-ball outs
Don't Expect	runners to steal

After three cups of coffee in the Oakland bullpen, Mohler managed to stick around all season last year. Working 72 times (tied with Buddy Groom for the Oakland club lead in appearances), he yielded fewer hits than innings, fanned more than seven batters per nine innings, and compiled a respectable ERA. Mohler tries to get ground-ball outs by mixing sinkers, sliders, and forkballs. He has some control problems and also has trouble with inherited runners, stranding only 56 percent last year. But Mohler has an excellent pickoff move that few runners try to challenge. The young southpaw, fully healed from previous shoulder problems, yielded nine home runs in 81 innings last year—a sharp contrast to 1995, when he worked 28 times without surrendering any long balls. Mohler also hurt his own cause by throwing nine wild pitches, most by any member of the 1996 Oakland bullpen. A starter in the minors, Mohler became a bona fide prospect when he switched to full-time relief work in 1995. He was used mostly as a set-up man last season.

Major League Pitching Register

	W	L	ERA	G	S	IP	H	ER	BB	SO
93 AL	1	6	5.60	42	0	64.1	57	40	44	42
94 AL	0	1	7.71	1	0	2.1	2	2	2	4
95 AL	1	1	3.04	28	1	23.2	16	8	18	15
96 AL	6	3	3.67	72	7	81.0	79	33	41	64
Life	8	11	4.36	143	8	171.1	154	83	105	125

PAUL MOLITOR

Position: Designated hitter
Team: Minnesota Twins
Born: Aug. 22, 1956 St. Paul, MN
Height: 6' **Weight:** 185 lbs.
Bats: right **Throws:** right
Acquired: Signed as a free agent, 12/95

PLAYER SUMMARY	
Fantasy Value.	$18 to $21
Card Value	15¢ to 30¢
Will	confound Father Time
Can't	find former power
Expect.	great batting eye
Don't Expect.	extended slump

At an age when most of his peers have retired, Molitor keeps getting better. He led the AL with 225 hits and 72 multihit games last year, finishing third in batting average (.341). The seven-time All-Star and former World Series MVP also reached the 3,000-hit plateau. Molitor is a contact hitter with a great batting eye. Perhaps the most amazing thing about the former University of Minnesota All-American is his speed: Molitor stole 18 bases in 24 attempts last year. In deference to his age, the 40-year-old was Minnesota's DH in 143 games. But he also appeared 17 times at first base. Signed as a shortstop, he's played every infield and outfield position in his career.

Major League Batting Register

	BA	G	AB	R	H	2B	3B	HR	RBI	SB
78 AL	.273	125	521	73	142	26	4	6	45	30
79 AL	.322	140	584	88	188	27	16	9	62	33
80 AL	.304	111	450	81	137	29	2	9	37	34
81 AL	.267	64	251	45	67	11	0	2	19	10
82 AL	.302	160	666	136	201	26	8	19	71	41
83 AL	.270	152	608	95	164	28	6	15	47	41
84 AL	.217	13	46	3	10	1	0	0	6	1
85 AL	.297	140	576	93	171	28	3	10	48	21
86 AL	.281	105	437	62	123	24	6	9	55	20
87 AL	.353	118	465	114	164	41	5	16	75	45
88 AL	.312	154	609	115	190	34	6	13	60	41
89 AL	.315	155	615	84	194	35	4	11	56	27
90 AL	.285	103	418	64	119	27	6	12	45	18
91 AL	.325	158	665	133	216	32	13	17	75	19
92 AL	.320	158	609	89	195	36	7	12	89	31
93 AL	.332	160	636	121	211	37	5	22	111	22
94 AL	.341	115	454	86	155	30	4	14	75	20
95 AL	.270	130	525	63	142	31	2	15	60	12
96 AL	.341	161	660	99	225	41	8	9	113	18
Life	.308	2422	9795	1644	3014	544	105	220	1149	484
3 Ave	.319	156	630	97	201	39	5	15	95	20

RAUL MONDESI

Position: Outfield
Team: Los Angeles Dodgers
Born: March 12, 1971 San Cristobal, Dominican Republic
Height: 5'11" **Weight:** 202 lbs.
Bats: right **Throws:** right
Acquired: Signed as a free agent, 6/88

PLAYER SUMMARY	
Fantasy Value.	$25 to $30
Card Value	25¢ to 50¢
Will	show speed, power
Can't.	reduce strikeouts
Expect	hot and cold streaks
Don't Expect.	trouble in outfield

If Mondesi ever learns patience at the plate, he'll be a superstar. He has five-tools potential: He produces power and average, and he can run, field, and throw. But fanning four times per walk keeps his on-base percentage low (.334 last year) and negates the value of his speed. A first-pitch, fastball hitter with power, Mondesi could fatten his average with bunts and infield hits but prefers to swing from the heels. When he's hot, he can carry a club: Mondesi had seven straight hits in September and a club-record 71 extra-base hits all season. But the strikeouts and cold spells come in bunches. The Dominican right fielder's basestealing speed could snap a slump. His speed also helps in the outfield, where Mondesi won a Gold Glove in 1995. He runs down shots into the right-center field power alley and uncorks strong, accurate throws. Though few runners take liberties against him, the 1994 Rookie of the Year managed 11 assists and four double plays last year. But he also got careless, commiting 12 errors.

Major League Batting Register

	BA	G	AB	R	H	2B	3B	HR	RBI	SB
93 NL	.291	42	86	13	25	3	1	4	10	4
94 NL	.306	112	434	63	133	27	8	16	56	11
95 NL	.285	139	536	91	153	23	6	26	88	27
96 NL	.297	157	634	98	188	40	7	24	88	14
Life	.295	450	1690	265	499	93	22	70	242	56
3 Ave	.296	157	616	96	182	35	8	25	89	20

JEFF MONTGOMERY

Position: Pitcher
Team: Kansas City Royals
Born: Jan. 7, 1962 Wellston, OH
Height: 5'11" **Weight:** 180 lbs.
Bats: right **Throws:** right
Acquired: Traded by Reds for Van Snider, 2/88

PLAYER SUMMARY	
Fantasy Value	$13 to $16
Card Value	5¢ to 8¢
Will	close out games
Can't	silence lefty hitters
Expect	frequent appearances
Don't Expect	control problems

After battling bursitis in his pitching shoulder for three seasons, Montgomery finally submitted to surgery last September. At the time he went under the knife, he had ten blown saves and his lowest save total since 1990. He had also yielded a career-worst ten home runs in 63⅓ innings. Normally a bullpen workhorse known for multi-inning stints, Montgomery has saved at least 30 games four times. Usually tougher against right-handed batters, he actually had an easier time with lefties last year. A control artist who fans more than six men per nine frames, he throws four pitches for strikes: fastball, curve, slider, and change. He strands nearly 75 percent of the runners he inherits, rarely throws wild pitches, and coaxes lots of double-play grounders. The three-time All-Star, who needs work to stay sharp, had five straight seasons of at least 60 appearances.

Major League Pitching Register

	W	L	ERA	G	S	IP	H	ER	BB	SO
87 NL	2	2	6.52	14	0	19.1	25	14	9	13
88 AL	7	2	3.45	45	1	62.2	54	24	30	47
89 AL	7	3	1.37	63	18	92.0	66	14	25	94
90 AL	6	5	2.39	73	24	94.1	81	25	34	94
91 AL	4	4	2.90	67	33	90.0	83	29	28	77
92 AL	1	6	2.18	65	39	82.2	61	20	27	69
93 AL	7	5	2.27	69	45	87.1	65	22	23	66
94 AL	2	3	4.03	42	27	44.2	48	20	15	50
95 AL	2	3	3.43	54	31	65.2	60	25	25	49
96 AL	4	6	4.26	48	24	63.1	59	30	19	45
Life	42	39	2.86	540	242	702.0	602	223	235	604
3 Ave	3	5	3.88	56	32	67.1	65	29	23	57

MICKEY MORANDINI

Position: Second base
Team: Philadelphia Phillies
Born: April 22, 1966 Kittanning, PA
Height: 5'11" **Weight:** 170 lbs.
Bats: left **Throws:** right
Acquired: Fifth-round pick in 6/88 free-agent draft

PLAYER SUMMARY	
Fantasy Value	$8 to $10
Card Value	5¢ to 8¢
Will	bring great glove
Can't	reduce whiff rate
Expect	good clutch bat
Don't Expect	the long ball

Morandini has quietly become one of the game's best second basemen. A slap hitter who uses all fields, he hits near the top of the lineup because of his speed and ability to move runners along. Last year, he reached base via hit or walk in 27 straight games. Morandini swiped a career-peak 26 bases in 31 tries last year (including 18 straight) but homered just three times. The 1988 Olympian drew 49 walks, pushing his on-base average 71 points beyond his batting average, but fanned nearly twice as often. Morandini does his best hitting with men in scoring position. But his overall production was not as good last year as it was in 1995, when he made the All-Star Team for the first time. Morandini's defense is his best asset. His reactions, range, hands, and arm are all excellent, and he's good at turning the double play. Morandini once turned an unassisted triple play—he's the only second baseman ever to do so during the regular season.

Major League Batting Register

	BA	G	AB	R	H	2B	3B	HR	RBI	SB
90 NL	.241	25	79	9	19	4	0	1	3	3
91 NL	.249	98	325	38	81	11	4	1	20	13
92 NL	.265	127	422	47	112	8	8	3	30	8
93 NL	.247	120	425	57	105	19	9	3	33	13
94 NL	.292	87	274	40	80	16	5	2	26	10
95 NL	.283	127	494	65	140	34	7	6	49	9
96 NL	.250	140	539	64	135	24	6	3	32	26
Life	.263	724	2558	320	672	116	39	19	193	82
3 Ave	.274	135	494	64	135	28	7	4	41	17

217

MIKE MORGAN

Position: Pitcher
Team: Cincinnati Reds
Born: Oct. 8, 1959 Tulare, CA
Height: 6'2" **Weight:** 215 lbs.
Bats: right **Throws:** right
Acquired: Signed as a free agent, 9/96

PLAYER SUMMARY	
Fantasy Value	$4 to $6
Card Value	4¢ to 7¢
Will	count on sinker
Can't	strike men out
Expect	decent control
Don't Expect	winning record

Morgan may be baseball's best losing pitcher. He's lost 47 more games than he's won during a 16-year career but has always managed to rebound from various injuries, trades, and releases. Cut by the Cards last fall, the veteran righty quickly signed with the Reds and proved he could still pitch. Slowed by shoulder problems early, Morgan was perfectly sound by season's end. A sinker-slider pitcher, he is able to keep his pitches down in the strike zone. Morgan wins with location, fanning five but walking only three per nine innings. He yields more hits than innings and throws his share of gopher balls but gets a lot of groundouts and double-play balls. At 37, Morgan should enjoy another solid season.

Major League Pitching Register

	W	L	ERA	G	CG	IP	H	ER	BB	SO
78 AL	0	3	7.30	3	1	12.1	19	10	8	0
79 AL	2	10	5.94	13	2	77.1	102	51	50	17
82 AL	7	11	4.37	30	2	150.1	167	73	67	71
83 AL	0	3	5.16	16	0	45.1	48	26	21	22
85 AL	1	1	12.00	2	0	6.0	11	8	5	2
86 AL	11	17	4.53	37	9	216.1	243	109	86	116
87 AL	12	17	4.65	34	8	207.0	245	107	53	85
88 AL	1	6	5.43	22	2	71.1	70	43	23	29
89 NL	8	11	2.53	40	0	152.2	130	43	33	72
90 NL	11	15	3.75	33	6	211.0	216	88	60	106
91 NL	14	10	2.78	34	5	236.1	197	73	61	140
92 NL	16	8	2.55	34	6	240.0	203	68	79	123
93 NL	10	15	4.03	32	1	207.2	206	93	74	111
94 NL	2	10	6.69	15	1	80.2	111	60	35	57
95 NL	7	7	3.56	21	1	131.1	133	52	34	61
96 NL	6	11	4.83	23	0	130.1	146	67	47	74
Life	108	155	4.02	389	44	2176.0	2247	971	736	1086
3 Ave	6	11	4.83	23	1	131.1	151	70	45	74

HAL MORRIS

Position: First base
Team: Cincinnati Reds
Born: April 9, 1965 Fort Rucker, AL
Height: 6'4" **Weight:** 210 lbs.
Bats: left **Throws:** left
Acquired: Traded by Yankees with Rodney Imes for Tim Leary and Van Snider, 12/89

PLAYER SUMMARY	
Fantasy Value	$13 to $16
Card Value	7¢ to 10¢
Will	smack line drives
Can't	solve some southpaws
Expect	opposite-field hits
Don't Expect	sterling defense

A line-drive hitter who was once considered a liability against left-handers, Morris managed 500 at bats for the first time last year. He finished with career highs in homers and RBI while adding to the .308 career average he carried into the 1996 campaign. A contact hitter with some patience, Morris drew 50 walks last year. As usual, he hit far better against right-handers (.326) but also held his own against southpaws (.273). An opposite-field hitter, Morris sometimes pulls inside pitches. His gap power is reflected in the fact that he had twice as many doubles as homers last season. Morris swipes a half-dozen bases per year but has never been noted for his speed. He's made vast improvements in the field, where his biggest assets are his scooping and stretching. Morris made eight errors last season, three more than he committed the year before.

Major League Batting Register

	BA	G	AB	R	H	2B	3B	HR	RBI	SB
88 AL	.100	15	20	1	2	0	0	0	0	0
89 AL	.278	15	18	2	5	0	0	0	4	0
90 NL	.340	107	309	50	105	22	3	7	36	9
91 NL	.318	136	478	72	152	33	1	14	59	10
92 NL	.271	115	395	41	107	21	3	6	53	6
93 NL	.317	101	379	48	120	18	0	7	49	2
94 NL	.335	112	436	60	146	30	4	10	78	6
95 NL	.279	101	359	53	100	25	2	11	51	1
96 NL	.313	142	528	82	165	32	4	16	80	7
Life	.309	844	2922	409	902	181	17	71	410	41
3 Ave	.313	138	515	75	161	34	4	14	82	6

JAMES MOUTON

Position: Outfield
Team: Houston Astros
Born: Dec. 29, 1968 Denver, CO
Height: 5'9" **Weight:** 175 lbs.
Bats: right **Throws:** right
Acquired: Seventh-round pick in 6/91 free-agent draft

PLAYER SUMMARY

Fantasy Value	$8 to $10
Card Value	7¢ to 10¢
Will	supply good speed
Can't	clear the fences
Expect	hits vs. southpaws
Don't Expect	powerful throws

Mouton is another one of baseball's Jekyll-and-Hyde players: a star against southpaws (.339 last year) but a risk against righties (.216). That's why he shared left field with Derrick May and John Cangelosi, both better batters vs. right-handers. A slap-hitting speed merchant with little power, Mouton loves to spray hits to all fields. He fattens his average with bunts and infield hits but sometimes exceeds his own limits, swinging for the fences instead of for singles. Mouton draws enough walks to post an on-base percentage 80 points better than his batting average but would be even more valuable if he showed more patience. Mouton swiped 21 bases in 30 tries last year but could triple that total if he reached more often. He did that in the minors, when he swiped 111 bases in his first two years as a pro. The former Pacific Coast League MVP uses his speed well in the outfield, where his reactions and range are exceptional. Because his arm is weak, Mouton is best in left, though he also spent some time in center last summer.

Major League Batting Register

	BA	G	AB	R	H	2B	3B	HR	RBI	SB
94 NL	.245	99	310	43	76	11	0	2	16	24
95 NL	.262	104	298	42	78	18	2	4	27	25
96 NL	.263	122	300	40	79	15	1	3	34	21
Life	.257	325	908	125	233	44	3	9	77	70
3 Ave	.255	126	357	49	91	17	1	3	29	28

LYLE MOUTON

Position: Outfield
Team: Chicago White Sox
Born: May 14, 1969 Lafayette, LA
Height: 6'4" **Weight:** 240 lbs.
Bats: right **Throws:** right
Acquired: Traded by Yankees with Keith Heiberling for Jack McDowell, 2/95

PLAYER SUMMARY

Fantasy Value	$3 to $5
Card Value	7¢ to 10¢
Will	post good average
Can't	find steady job
Expect	hits in clutch
Don't Expect	frequent homers

Danny Tartabull's ability to resurrect his power kept Mouton on the White Sox bench much of last year. Mouton divided his time between the outfield corners, made numerous pinch-hitting appearances, and also served as a DH. Whenever he got the chance, Mouton delivered. He hit .296 against lefties, .292 against righties, and slugged seven home runs in 214 at bats. Mouton shows some patience at the plate but fans more than twice per walk. He topped double digits in steals in the minors three times but is not likely to steal much in the majors. He's in the big leagues strictly because of his bat. Mouton hit .300 three times in the minors and also scaled that plateau as a 1995 rookie in the majors. The only time he saw action in more than 100 games, he belted 16 homers—not terrific production for a man of his size and strength. In his brief big-league career, Mouton has shown an ability to poke clutch hits and connect with two strikes. He has decent range in the outfield and an arm that is more than adequate.

Major League Batting Register

	BA	G	AB	R	H	2B	3B	HR	RBI	SB
95 AL	.302	58	179	23	54	16	0	5	27	1
96 AL	.294	87	214	25	63	8	1	7	39	3
Life	.298	145	393	48	117	24	1	12	66	4
2 Ave	.298	76	208	25	62	13	1	6	35	2

219

JAMIE MOYER

Position: Pitcher
Team: Seattle Mariners
Born: Nov. 18, 1962 Sellersville, PA
Height: 6' **Weight:** 170 lbs.
Bats: left **Throws:** left
Acquired: Traded by Red Sox for Darren Bragg, 7/96

PLAYER SUMMARY	
Fantasy Value	$7 to $9
Card Value	5¢ to 8¢
Will	bank on finesse
Can't	hold runners on
Expect	double-digit wins
Don't Expect	many strikeouts

Though he didn't arrive until July 30, Moyer filled the rotation gap created by Randy Johnson's persistent back problems. By season's end, he had tied Sterling Hitchcock for the most wins on the staff and posted the best ERA among Mariner starters. A finesse pitcher who works fast, Moyer mixes a fastball, slider, and curve with a circle change—throwing all four pitches for strikes. A lefty craftsman who paints the corners, Moyer is more effective against right-handed hitters. He yields more hits than innings, throws his share of gopher balls, and has trouble controlling the running game. But he helps himself with excellent fielding. Much more effective in Seattle than he was in Boston, Moyer had a 7-1 mark and 4.50 ERA at the time of his trade. His 13-3 final record was the best of his career.

Major League Pitching Register

	W	L	ERA	G	CG	IP	H	ER	BB	SO
86 NL	7	4	5.05	16	1	87.1	107	49	42	45
87 NL	12	15	5.10	35	1	201.0	210	114	97	147
88 NL	9	15	3.48	34	3	202.0	212	78	55	121
89 AL	4	9	4.86	15	1	76.0	84	41	33	44
90 AL	2	6	4.66	33	1	102.1	115	53	39	58
91 NL	0	5	5.74	8	0	31.1	28	20	16	20
93 AL	12	9	3.43	25	3	152.0	154	58	38	90
94 AL	5	7	4.77	23	0	149.0	158	79	38	87
95 AL	8	6	5.21	27	0	115.2	117	67	30	65
96 AL	13	3	3.98	34	0	160.2	177	71	46	79
Life	72	79	4.44	250	10	1277.1	1372	630	434	756
3 Ave	10	7	4.63	32	0	167.0	177	86	44	92

TERRY MULHOLLAND

Position: Pitcher
Team: Chicago Cubs
Born: March 9, 1963 Uniontown, PA
Height: 6'3" **Weight:** 200 lbs.
Bats: right **Throws:** left
Acquired: Signed as a free agent, 12/96

PLAYER SUMMARY	
Fantasy Value	$6 to $8
Card Value	4¢ to 7¢
Will	win a dozen
Can't	find old velocity
Expect	ground-ball outs
Don't Expect	runners to steal

Mulholland is a control artist who made a dozen starts for Seattle after arriving from the Phillies last July. But he's not the same pitcher who hurled a no-hitter in 1990 or started the All-Star Game three years later. A former power pitcher who's still trying to master the conversion to finesse, Mulholland struggled through the '94 and '95 seasons before posting a winning record last year. A sinker-slider pitcher who also throws a changeup, Mulholland depends upon location. He averages fewer than five Ks per nine innings, yields just over one hit per inning, and is much more effective against lefties. He keeps the ball in the park and controls the running game, and he's renowned for his outstanding pickoff move. Fully healed from elbow problems that plagued him two years ago, Mulholland should have several decent seasons left.

Major League Pitching Register

	W	L	ERA	G	CG	IP	H	ER	BB	SO
86 NL	1	7	4.94	15	0	54.2	51	30	35	27
88 NL	2	1	3.72	9	2	46.0	50	19	7	18
89 NL	4	7	4.92	25	2	115.1	137	63	36	66
90 NL	9	10	3.34	33	6	180.2	172	67	42	75
91 NL	16	13	3.61	34	8	232.0	231	93	49	142
92 NL	13	11	3.81	32	12	229.0	227	97	46	125
93 NL	12	9	3.25	29	7	191.0	177	69	40	116
94 AL	6	7	6.49	24	2	120.2	150	87	37	72
95 NL	5	13	5.80	29	2	149.0	190	96	38	65
96 NL	8	7	4.66	21	3	133.1	157	69	21	52
96 AL	5	4	4.67	12	0	69.1	75	36	28	34
Life	81	89	4.30	263	44	1521.0	1617	726	379	792
3 Ave	9	12	5.59	33	3	180.0	219	112	48	87

MIKE MUNOZ

Position: Pitcher
Team: Colorado Rockies
Born: July 12, 1965 Baldwin Park, CA
Height: 6'2" **Weight:** 200 lbs.
Bats: left **Throws:** left
Acquired: Signed as a minor-league free agent, 5/93

PLAYER SUMMARY	
Fantasy Value	$1 to $3
Card Value	4¢ to 7¢
Will	answer bell often
Can't	halt righty hitters
Expect	reliance on sinker
Don't Expect	steals, gophers

There's something magical about left-handed pitchers. No matter how poorly a portsider pitches, he always seems to find a job. Munoz is a case in point. In the last two years, his ERAs have been 7.42 and 6.65. Although his 1996 season was marred by a minor-league exile in June and a disabling abdominal strain in July, he managed to top 50 appearances for the third straight season. Though he exceeded a strikeout an inning and held lefties to a .200 average, Munoz delivered more bad news than good. Righties hit him at a .352 clip—accounting for his ratio of 11.08 hits per nine innings—and he stranded only 57.9 percent of the baserunners he inherited. A sinker-slider pitcher who also throws a changeup and screwball, Munoz needs ground balls to be effective. He was victimized all too often by a sinker that didn't sink. Munoz helps his own cause with fine fielding and a highly effective pickoff move.

Major League Pitching Register

	W	L	ERA	G	S	IP	H	ER	BB	SO
89 NL	0	0	16.88	3	0	2.2	5	5	2	3
90 NL	0	1	3.18	8	0	5.2	6	2	3	2
91 AL	0	0	9.64	6	0	9.1	14	10	5	3
92 AL	1	2	3.00	65	2	48.0	44	16	25	23
93 AL	0	1	6.00	8	0	3.0	4	2	6	1
93 NL	2	1	4.50	21	0	18.0	21	9	9	16
94 NL	4	2	3.74	57	1	45.2	37	19	31	32
95 NL	2	4	7.42	64	2	43.2	54	36	27	37
96 NL	2	2	6.65	54	0	44.2	55	33	16	45
Life	11	13	5.38	286	5	220.2	240	132	124	162
3 Ave	3	3	5.71	69	1	53.1	56	33	30	44

PEDRO MUNOZ

Position: Outfield, designated hitter
Team: Oakland Athletics
Born: Sept. 19, 1968 Ponce, Puerto Rico
Height: 5'11" **Weight:** 170 lbs.
Bats: right **Throws:** right
Acquired: Signed as a free agent, 2/96

PLAYER SUMMARY	
Fantasy Value	$8 to $10
Card Value	4¢ to 7¢
Will	hit long homers
Can't	wait for walks
Expect	good clutch bat
Don't Expect	dazzling defense

When healthy, Munoz is a home run hitter who often hits the ball a long way. He had a 468-foot homer vs. Milwaukee last April 22, then hit a 463-footer May 24 that was the longest shot in the history of Oriole Park at Camden Yards. But he was disabled by knee problems June 2 and was forced to undergo reconstructive surgery, which caused him to miss the rest of the season. A fastball hitter with a big swing, Munoz fans four times more often than he walks. But he hits well against both righties and lefties, often taking pitches up the middle or to the opposite field. Munoz is at his best in clutch situations. Because of his bad knees, he rarely runs. As a matter of fact, he's stolen only one base since 1992. His lack of speed also hurts him in the outfield, where his reactions, range, and arm are all suspect. For these reasons, Munoz is best suited to the designated hitter spot. He began his pro career after the Blue Jays made him a nondrafted free agent in 1985.

Major League Batting Register

	BA	G	AB	R	H	2B	3B	HR	RBI	SB
90 AL	.271	22	85	13	23	4	1	0	5	3
91 AL	.283	51	138	15	39	7	1	7	26	3
92 AL	.270	127	418	44	113	16	3	12	71	4
93 AL	.233	104	326	34	76	11	1	13	38	1
94 AL	.295	75	244	35	72	15	2	11	36	0
95 AL	.301	104	376	45	113	17	0	18	58	0
96 AL	.256	34	121	17	31	5	0	6	18	0
Life	.273	517	1708	203	467	75	8	67	252	11
2 Ave	.298	111	383	50	114	20	1	18	58	0

EDDIE MURRAY

Position: Designated hitter; first base
Team: Anaheim Angels
Born: Feb. 24, 1956 Los Angeles, CA
Height: 6'2" **Weight:** 224 lbs.
Bats: both **Throws:** right
Acquired: Signed as a free agent, 12/96

PLAYER SUMMARY

Fantasy Value	$12 to $15
Card Value	15¢ to 30¢
Will	knock men in
Can't	play the field
Expect	good lefty bat
Don't Expect	power outage

Consistency is the name of Murray's game. His 79 RBI last season gave him 20 straight years with 75-plus RBI, breaking Hank Aaron's record. Murray also joined Aaron and Willie Mays as the only men with 3,000 hits and 500 homers. The switch-hitting slugger remains a dangerous hitter with runners in scoring position. Murray makes decent contact for a power hitter but also shows patience at the plate. He's usually a better hitter left-handed, though that was not the case in '96. He rarely steals a base or plays the field but can fill in at first base, where he won three Gold Gloves.

Major League Batting Register

	BA	G	AB	R	H	2B	3B	HR	RBI	SB
77 AL	.283	160	611	81	173	29	2	27	88	0
78 AL	.285	161	610	85	174	32	3	27	95	6
79 AL	.295	159	606	90	179	30	2	25	99	10
80 AL	.300	158	621	100	186	36	2	32	116	7
81 AL	.294	99	378	57	111	21	2	22	78	2
82 AL	.316	151	550	87	174	30	1	32	110	7
83 AL	.306	156	582	115	178	30	3	33	111	5
84 AL	.306	162	588	97	180	26	3	29	110	10
85 AL	.297	156	583	111	173	37	1	31	124	5
86 AL	.305	137	495	61	151	25	1	17	84	3
87 AL	.277	160	618	89	171	28	3	30	91	1
88 AL	.284	161	603	75	171	27	2	28	84	5
89 NL	.247	160	594	66	147	29	1	20	88	7
90 NL	.330	155	558	96	184	22	3	26	95	8
91 NL	.260	153	576	69	150	23	1	19	96	10
92 NL	.261	156	551	64	144	37	2	16	93	4
93 NL	.285	154	610	77	174	28	1	27	100	2
94 AL	.254	108	433	57	110	21	1	17	76	8
95 AL	.323	113	436	68	141	21	0	21	82	5
96 AL	.260	152	566	69	147	21	1	22	79	4
Life	.288	2971	11169	1614	3218	553	35	501	1899	109
3 Ave	.276	144	555	75	154	25	1	23	93	7

MIKE MUSSINA

Position: Pitcher
Team: Baltimore Orioles
Born: Dec. 8, 1968 Williamsport, PA
Height: 6' **Weight:** 182 lbs.
Bats: right **Throws:** right
Acquired: First-round pick in 6/90 free-agent draft

PLAYER SUMMARY

Fantasy Value	$20 to $25
Card Value	25¢ to 60¢
Will	lead the rotation
Can't	avoid gopher balls
Expect	high winning pct.
Don't Expect	ERA to stay up

The 1996 season was a mystery for Mussina. He reached career peaks with 243⅓ innings pitched and a club-record 204 Ks while tying his personal best with 19 wins. But he failed in his bid to become a 20-game winner and finished with an atypical 4.81 ERA. A control artist, Mussina mixes a sinking cut fastball with a 92-mph heater, hard knuckle-curve, and deceptive change. But he gives up too many homers (31 last year), a problem complicated by his 9.76 hits allowed per nine innings. It was the first time Mussina yielded more hits than innings. The pitcher's second-half performance (8-6, 4.74) and postseason struggles increased speculation Mussina may be suffering from overwork. However, he still owns the best career winning percentage (.687) among active pitchers with 50 decisions. Mussina helps himself with his defense, including an exceptional pickoff move. In his career, only 47.8 percent of potential basestealers have succeeded against him.

Major League Pitching Register

	W	L	ERA	G	CG	IP	H	ER	BB	SO
91 AL	4	5	2.87	12	2	87.2	77	28	21	52
92 AL	18	5	2.54	32	8	241.0	212	68	48	130
93 AL	14	6	4.46	25	3	167.2	163	83	44	117
94 AL	16	5	3.06	24	3	176.1	163	60	42	99
95 AL	19	9	3.29	32	7	221.2	187	81	50	158
96 AL	19	11	4.81	36	4	243.1	264	130	69	204
Life	90	41	3.56	161	27	1137.2	1066	450	274	760
3 Ave	21	9	3.71	35	5	247.0	235	102	61	174

GREG MYERS

Position: Catcher
Team: Minnesota Twins
Born: April 14, 1966 Riverside, CA
Height: 6'2" **Weight:** 206 lbs.
Bats: left **Throws:** right
Acquired: Signed as a free agent, 12/95

PLAYER SUMMARY	
Fantasy Value	$3 to $5
Card Value	4¢ to 7¢
Will	nail basestealers
Can't	show much power
Expect	best bat vs. righties
Don't Expect	any speed

A free-agent bargain, Myers did the bulk of Minnesota's catching in 1996. Batting primarily against right-handed pitchers—with switch-hitting Matt Walbeck the main man against lefties—Myers delivered a .286 average and 31 extra-base hits, both career peaks. A singles hitter who usually goes up the middle or the opposite way against righties, Myers has never reached double digits in home runs. He'd be more valuable if he showed more patience at the plate, but he fans three times for every walk. No threat to run, Myers has stolen only three bases in his career. He's good at stopping rival basestealers, however; he nailed 35 percent of the runners who challenged him last year. His arm isn't strong, but he has a quick release. Although he has good hands and basic receiving skills, Myers is not considered a great handler of pitchers. Always platooned, Myers has never appeared in more than 108 games.

Major League Batting Register

	BA	G	AB	R	H	2B	3B	HR	RBI	SB
87 AL	.111	7	9	1	1	0	0	0	0	0
89 AL	.114	17	44	0	5	2	0	0	1	0
90 AL	.236	87	250	33	59	7	1	5	22	0
91 AL	.262	107	309	25	81	22	0	8	36	0
92 AL	.231	30	78	4	18	7	0	1	13	0
93 AL	.255	108	290	27	74	10	0	7	40	3
94 AL	.246	45	126	10	31	6	0	2	8	0
95 AL	.260	85	273	35	71	12	2	9	38	0
96 AL	.286	97	329	37	94	22	3	6	47	0
Life	.254	583	1708	172	434	88	6	38	205	3
2 Ave	.273	96	318	38	87	18	3	8	45	0

MIKE MYERS

Position: Pitcher
Team: Detroit Tigers
Born: June 26, 1969 Cook County, IL
Height: 6'3" **Weight:** 195 lbs.
Bats: left **Throws:** left
Acquired: Traded by Marlins for Buddy Groom, 8/95

PLAYER SUMMARY	
Fantasy Value	$2 to $4
Card Value	4¢ to 7¢
Will	pitch often
Can't	retire righties
Expect	K per inning
Don't Expect	fine control

Myers broke in with a bang last year, tying for the American League lead with 83 appearances. The hard-throwing southpaw averaged more than a strikeout per inning, held lefties to a .229 average, kept the ball in the park, and yielded just over a hit per inning. But he was betrayed by control problems (4.73 walks per nine innings) and an inability to retire right-handed hitters (.309 opposing average). The pressure of relief pitching never seemed to bother Myers, a minor-league starter who switched to full-time relieving in 1995. He converted six of eight save chances that season, stranding 72.1 percent of the runners he inherited and throwing only two wild pitches. The Iowa State product made his major-league debut for the Marlins in 1995, pitching twice before his trade to the Tigers. Since he throws left-handed, Myers should be able to improve his pickoff move. Last year, seven of the nine runners who tried to steal against him were successful.

Major League Pitching Register

	W	L	ERA	G	S	IP	H	ER	BB	SO
95 NL	0	0	0.00	2	0	2.0	1	0	3	0
95 AL	1	0	9.95	11	0	6.1	10	7	4	4
96 AL	1	5	5.01	83	6	64.2	70	36	34	69
Life	2	5	5.30	96	6	73.0	81	43	41	73

223

RANDY MYERS

Position: Pitcher
Team: Baltimore Orioles
Born: Sept. 19, 1962 Vancouver, WA
Height: 6'1" **Weight:** 210 lbs.
Bats: left **Throws:** left
Acquired: Signed as a free agent, 12/95

PLAYER SUMMARY	
Fantasy Value	$25 to $30
Card Value	5¢ to 8¢
Will	convert most saves
Can't	find strike zone
Expect	lefties to struggle
Don't Expect	opposing steals

A hard-throwing lefty closer, Myers has had at least 20 saves and 55 appearances in eight of the last nine seasons. In 1993, he set an NL record with 53 saves. With the '96 Orioles, Myers saved 31 in 38 tries, retired 47 of 62 first batters, and averaged 11.35 Ks per nine innings. A fastball-slider pitcher who throws an occasional curve, Myers is especially tough on lefty hitters. Occasional control problems (4.45 walks per nine innings) hampered Myers in his AL debut season. Erratic location resulted in more hits than innings pitched for only the second time in Myers's career. He also yielded seven homers. Myers surrenders few stolen bases (five in the last four years) but is seldom ready to field the ball because of his awkward follow-through. At 34, Myers isn't the feared flamethrower he once was, but he does a credible job.

Major League Pitching Register

	W	L	ERA	G	S	IP	H	ER	BB	SO
85 NL	0	0	0.00	1	0	2.0	0	0	1	2
86 NL	0	0	4.22	10	0	10.2	11	5	9	13
87 NL	3	6	3.96	54	6	75.0	61	33	30	92
88 NL	7	3	1.72	55	26	68.0	45	13	17	69
89 NL	7	4	2.35	65	24	84.1	62	22	40	88
90 NL	4	6	2.08	66	31	86.2	59	20	38	98
91 NL	6	13	3.55	58	6	132.0	116	52	80	108
92 NL	3	6	4.29	66	38	79.2	84	38	34	66
93 NL	2	4	3.11	73	53	75.1	65	26	26	86
94 NL	1	5	3.79	38	21	40.1	40	17	16	32
95 NL	1	2	3.88	57	38	55.2	49	24	28	59
96 AL	4	4	3.53	62	31	58.2	60	23	29	74
Life	38	53	3.20	605	274	768.1	652	273	348	787
3 Ave	2	4	3.74	60	34	59.1	57	25	28	62

TIM NAEHRING

Position: Third base
Team: Boston Red Sox
Born: Feb. 1, 1967 Cincinnati, OH
Height: 6'2" **Weight:** 190 lbs.
Bats: right **Throws:** right
Acquired: Eighth-round pick in 6/88 free-agent draft

PLAYER SUMMARY	
Fantasy Value	$13 to $16
Card Value	5¢ to 8¢
Will	hit ball well
Can't	add any speed
Expect	patience, contact
Don't Expect	injury-free year

Nobody knew Naehring's name last season. A tough out, a good clutch hitter, and a defensive spark plug, he was hitting .332 with 12 homers and 42 RBI on June 30. Yet Naehring's name was missing from the AL All-Star squad roster. A smart hitter who uses all fields, Naehring combines patience, contact, and power. His on-base percentage was 75 points higher than his batting average last year. In addition, Naehring had 33 extra-base hits and a .317 mark at Fenway Park (down from .348 the year before). Naehring played all four infield positions as well as the outfield, though some scouts insist he's best as a DH. Not a fast baserunner, Naehring moves well enough to play the field. He has quick reactions, soft hands, a reliable arm, and the ability to turn two. The former Miami of Ohio shortstop has battled back, shoulder, wrist, ankle, and hamstring ailments. Knee and shoulder woes shortened his season last September.

Major League Batting Register

	BA	G	AB	R	H	2B	3B	HR	RBI	SB
90 AL	.271	24	85	10	23	6	0	2	12	0
91 AL	.109	20	55	1	6	1	0	0	3	0
92 AL	.231	72	186	12	43	8	0	3	14	0
93 AL	.331	39	127	14	42	10	0	1	17	1
94 AL	.276	80	297	41	82	18	1	7	42	1
95 AL	.307	126	433	61	133	27	2	10	57	0
96 AL	.288	116	430	77	124	16	0	17	65	2
Life	.281	477	1613	216	453	86	3	40	210	4
3 Ave	.291	123	445	68	130	24	1	13	63	1

CHARLES NAGY

Position: Pitcher
Team: Cleveland Indians
Born: May 5, 1967 Bridgeport, CT
Height: 6'3" **Weight:** 200 lbs.
Bats: left **Throws:** right
Acquired: First-round pick in 6/88 free-agent
 draft

PLAYER SUMMARY	
Fantasy Value	$17 to $20
Card Value	12¢ to 15¢
Will	head the staff
Can't	avoid gophers
Expect	wins, strikeouts
Don't Expect	poor control

Cleveland's most consistent starter last season, Nagy finished fourth in the AL with 17 wins while posting the loop's second-best winning percentage (.773) and third-best ERA (3.41). The AL Pitcher of the Month in May (6-0, 2.60), Nagy brought an 11-2 mark into the All-Star Game, which he started—the first time an Indian has done so since Gaylord Perry in 1974. The 1988 U.S. Olympian mixes a sinker, forkball, changeup, and slurve and averages fewer hits than innings and under 2½ walks per nine frames. A former standout at the University of Connecticut, Nagy fans nearly seven batters per game and dominates right-handed hitters. He yields his share of gopher balls, however, and has trouble holding runners close. Especially tough with men in scoring position, Nagy held hitters to a .214 mark in that situation. He helps himself with quick and agile fielding. Nagy has justified Cleveland's decision to make him a first-round draft choice in 1988.

Major League Pitching Register

	W	L	ERA	G	CG	IP	H	ER	BB	SO
90 AL	2	4	5.91	9	0	45.2	58	30	21	26
91 AL	10	15	4.13	33	6	211.1	228	97	66	109
92 AL	17	10	2.96	33	10	252.0	245	83	57	169
93 AL	2	6	6.29	9	1	48.2	66	34	13	30
94 AL	10	8	3.45	23	3	169.1	175	65	48	108
95 AL	16	6	4.55	29	2	178.0	194	90	61	139
96 AL	17	5	3.41	32	5	222.0	217	84	61	167
Life	74	54	3.86	168	27	1127.0	1183	483	327	748
3 Ave	16	8	3.77	32	4	220.1	227	92	66	159

DAN NAULTY

Position: Pitcher
Team: Minnesota Twins
Born: Jan. 6, 1970 Los Angeles, CA
Height: 6'6" **Weight:** 211 lbs.
Bats: right **Throws:** right
Acquired: 14th-round pick in 6/92 free-agent
 draft

PLAYER SUMMARY	
Fantasy Value	$5 to $7
Card Value	7¢ to 10¢
Will	yield few hits
Can't	throw strikes
Expect	set-up berth
Don't Expect	bad shoulder

Though he spent only one of his four minor-league seasons as a reliever before joining the bullpen of the '96 Twins, Naulty enjoyed a fine freshman season. Before he was sidelined August 9 with circulatory problems in his right shoulder, Naulty fanned one per inning, yielded fewer than seven hits per nine innings, and held opposing hitters to a .207 batting average. His 3.79 ERA was respectable, and his success at stranding inherited runners (56.7 percent) was decent though not spectacular. The Cal State-Fullerton product will be even more effective when he learns to control his fastball, forkball, and slider. Last year, Naulty averaged 5½ walks per nine innings—a ratio that cost him his short-lived trial as the Minnesota closer. Naulty's pickoff move also needs more work (five of six potential basestealers stole safely against him). Naulty does manage to keep the ball in the park most of the time, and he keeps his wild pitches to a minimum (just two last year).

Major League Pitching Register

	W	L	ERA	G	S	IP	H	ER	BB	SO
96 AL	3	2	3.79	49	4	57.0	43	24	35	56
Life	3	2	3.79	49	4	57.0	43	24	35	56

JAIME NAVARRO

Position: Pitcher
Team: Chicago White Sox
Born: March 27, 1967 Bayamon, Puerto Rico
Height: 6'4" **Weight:** 210 lbs.
Bats: right **Throws:** right
Acquired: Signed as a free agent, 12/96

PLAYER SUMMARY

Fantasy Value	$13 to $16
Card Value	5¢ to 8¢
Will	exceed 200 innings
Can't	avoid gopher balls
Expect	double-digit wins
Don't Expect	control trouble

Navarro had the most starts and most wins on the Cub staff last season. The durable right-hander topped 200 innings for the fifth time in six seasons and served as Chicago's staff ace for the second straight year. The former 17-game winner has won in double digits five times in the last six years. A sinker-slider pitcher who uses his forkball for show, Navarro yields one hit per inning but walks only 2½ per game. He averages only six strikeouts per nine innings. Slightly more effective against right-handed hitters, his biggest problems are gopher balls, stolen bases, and wild pitches. Navarro led the '96 Cubs in two of the three departments, trailing closely behind Frank Castillo and Steve Trachsel in home run balls. When he's on, Navarro gets numerous ground-ball outs, many of them double-play balls. The son of former big-leaguer Julio Navarro is a good bunter and fielder but hits like an AL pitcher—poorly.

Major League Pitching Register

	W	L	ERA	G	CG	IP	H	ER	BB	SO
89 AL	7	8	3.12	19	1	109.2	119	38	32	56
90 AL	8	7	4.46	32	3	149.1	176	74	41	75
91 AL	15	12	3.92	34	10	234.0	237	102	73	114
92 AL	17	11	3.33	34	5	246.0	224	91	64	100
93 AL	11	12	5.33	35	5	214.1	254	127	73	114
94 AL	4	9	6.62	29	0	89.2	115	66	35	65
95 NL	14	6	3.28	29	1	200.1	194	73	56	128
96 NL	15	12	3.92	35	4	236.2	244	103	72	158
Life	91	77	4.10	247	29	1480.0	1563	674	446	810
3 Ave	12	10	4.25	36	2	196.0	208	93	61	131

DENNY NEAGLE

Position: Pitcher
Team: Atlanta Braves
Born: Sept. 13, 1968 Prince Georges County, MD
Height: 6'4" **Weight:** 209 lbs.
Bats: left **Throws:** left
Acquired: Traded by Pirates for Jason Schmidt, Ron Wright, and Corey Pointer, 8/96

PLAYER SUMMARY

Fantasy Value	$17 to $20
Card Value	7¢ to 10¢
Will	change speeds
Can't	avoid gopher balls
Expect	All-Star credentials
Don't Expect	control problems

When Pittsburgh decided to dump Neagle's salary last August, a major bidding war began. Atlanta won, obtaining the lefty control artist a month before his 28th birthday. Although he throws an 85-mph fastball, late-breaking slider, and occasional curve, Neagle's best pitch is a changeup that dips down and away from right-handed hitters. Neagle was spectacular in Game 4 of the '96 NLCS, when he held the Cardinals to two hits and no runs before he was lifted with a 3-0 lead and two outs in the seventh inning. Neagle, who has improved every year, is a personal nemesis for seven-time batting champ Tony Gwynn, who is 2-for-19 against him lifetime. The University of Minnesota product helps himself with his bunting, hitting, and fielding. He tied for the NL lead with 16 sacrifice hits last year. An articulate, intelligent athlete, Neagle made the All-Star Team in 1995 and tied Al Leiter for most wins by an NL left-hander in '96.

Major League Pitching Register

	W	L	ERA	G	CG	IP	H	ER	BB	SO
91 AL	0	1	4.05	7	0	20.0	28	9	7	14
92 NL	4	6	4.48	55	0	86.1	81	43	43	77
93 NL	3	5	5.31	50	0	81.1	82	48	37	73
94 NL	9	10	5.12	24	2	137.0	135	78	49	122
95 NL	13	8	3.43	31	5	209.2	221	80	45	150
96 NL	16	9	3.50	33	2	221.1	226	86	48	149
Life	45	39	4.10	200	9	755.2	773	344	229	585
3 Ave	14	11	3.96	34	3	217.1	222	95	56	163

JEFF NELSON

Position: Pitcher
Team: New York Yankees
Born: Nov. 17, 1966 Baltimore, MD
Height: 6'8" **Weight:** 235 lbs.
Bats: right **Throws:** right
Acquired: Traded by Mariners with Tino Martinez and Jim Mecir for Sterling Hitchcock and Russ Davis, 11/95

PLAYER SUMMARY

Fantasy Value	$4 to $6
Card Value	4¢ to 7¢
Will	strike men out
Can't	stop runners
Expect	frequent calls
Don't Expect	the long ball

One of baseball's premier set-up men, Nelson has made more than 60 appearances four times in the last five years. The towering right-hander is a power pitcher who throws a slider with exceptional late movement, helping to account for his 1996 nine-inning average of 11.02 strikeouts. He also averaged more than a strikeout an inning the year before. Nelson also throws a good fastball, yields just a hit per inning, keeps the ball in the park, and pitches much more effectively against right-handed hitters. But potential basestealers love his high-kicking delivery, even though he's a good fielder for a big man. Nelson spent more than eight years in the minors—most of them as a starter—before making the majors for the first time as a reliever with the 1992 Mariners. He hasn't started since. After a slow debut with the 1996 Yankees, Nelson retired 37 of the last 47 hitters he faced. He was on the mound when the team clinched the AL East vs. Milwaukee September 25.

Major League Pitching Register

	W	L	ERA	G	S	IP	H	ER	BB	SO
92 AL	1	7	3.44	66	6	81.0	71	31	44	46
93 AL	5	3	4.35	71	1	60.0	57	29	34	61
94 AL	0	0	2.76	28	0	42.1	35	13	20	44
95 AL	7	3	2.17	62	2	78.2	58	19	27	96
96 AL	4	4	4.36	73	2	74.1	75	36	36	91
Life	17	17	3.43	300	11	336.1	296	128	161	338
3 Ave	4	2	3.06	61	1	74.0	63	25	32	87

ROBB NEN

Position: Pitcher
Team: Florida Marlins
Born: Nov. 28, 1969 San Pedro, CA
Height: 6'4" **Weight:** 200 lbs.
Bats: right **Throws:** right
Acquired: Traded by Rangers with Kurt Miller for Cris Carpenter, 7/93

PLAYER SUMMARY

Fantasy Value	$40 to $45
Card Value	5¢ to 8¢
Will	bring late heat
Can't	stop all lefties
Expect	superb control
Don't Expect	many gophers

After suggesting for two years that he could be a quality closer, Nen blossomed into a star last summer. Finding a masterful mix of his mid-90s fastball, slider, and curve, the big right-hander converted 35 of 42 save chances, held right-handers to a .210 average, and allowed only two home runs in 83 innings pitched. He was fifth in the league in both saves and appearances. A power pitcher with good control, Nen fanned nearly ten batters per nine innings and yielded only 2.28 walks and 7.27 hits over the same span. He also stranded 73.3 percent of the runners he inherited. The son of former big-leaguer Dick Nen made dramatic improvement in his pickoff move last season. Runners were intimidated by his compact motion, quickness to the plate, and willingness to throw to first. Despite his bulk, Nen fields his position well. He's improved in all areas for three straight years, but it will be hard to beat his 1996 numbers. About the only things he might add are trips to the All-Star Game or postseason play.

Major League Pitching Register

	W	L	ERA	G	S	IP	H	ER	BB	SO
93 AL	1	1	6.35	9	0	22.2	28	16	26	12
93 NL	1	0	7.02	15	0	33.1	35	26	20	27
94 NL	5	5	2.95	44	15	58.0	46	19	17	60
95 NL	0	7	3.29	62	23	65.2	62	24	23	68
96 NL	5	1	1.95	75	35	83.0	67	18	21	92
Life	12	14	3.53	205	73	262.2	238	103	107	259
3 Ave	4	5	2.71	69	27	80.1	67	24	24	84

PHIL NEVIN

Position: Third base
Team: Detroit Tigers
Born: Jan. 19, 1971 Fullerton, CA
Height: 6'2" **Weight:** 180 lbs.
Bats: right **Throws:** right
Acquired: Traded by Astros for Mike Henneman, 8/95

PLAYER SUMMARY	
Fantasy Value	$6 to $8
Card Value	4¢ to 7¢
Will	provide power
Can't	wait for walks
Expect	hits vs. lefties
Don't Expect	catching duty

Nevin had such a strong finish last season that he'll finally get a chance to play third base every day in the big leagues. To get his bat into the lineup last fall, the Tigers returned Travis Fryman to short. The move paid dividends when Nevin slammed eight homers in 120 at bats and hit .306 against lefties. When he learns the strike zone, he'll be even more productive. (He had five Ks per walk in limited action last year.) A late bloomer, Nevin had been expected to impact the major-league scene much sooner. But he spent three years in Triple-A without providing the power or defense expected of him, then provoked a trade with a temper tantrum directed at then-Houston manager Terry Collins. An All-American and College Player of the Year at Cal State-Fullerton, he was also a Golden Spikes Award winner and U.S. Olympian. Nevin spent time at catcher in the minors before returning to his original position. He can also play the outfield. While not fast, he has quick reactions, soft hands, and a strong throwing arm. At 26, his future lies ahead of him.

Major League Batting Register

	BA	G	AB	R	H	2B	3B	HR	RBI	SB
95 NL	.117	18	60	4	7	1	0	0	1	1
95 AL	.219	29	96	9	21	3	1	2	12	0
96 AL	.292	38	120	15	35	5	0	8	19	1
Life	.228	85	276	28	63	9	1	10	32	2

MARC NEWFIELD

Position: Outfield
Team: Milwaukee Brewers
Born: Oct. 19, 1972 Sacramento, CA
Height: 6'4" **Weight:** 205 lbs.
Bats: right **Throws:** right
Acquired: Traded by Padres with Ron Villone and Bryce Florie for Greg Vaughn, 7/96

PLAYER SUMMARY	
Fantasy Value	$9 to $11
Card Value	7¢ to 10¢
Will	murder left-handers
Can't	supply much speed
Expect	extra-base power
Don't Expect	strong defense

The sixth choice in the 1990 free-agent draft, Newfield never got much chance to display his talents for the team that picked him. After giving him three short trials, Seattle sent him to San Diego in 1995, exactly a year before the Padres packaged him with two pitchers in the Greg Vaughn deal. That might have been the break Newfield needed. He hit .307 with seven homers and 31 RBI in 49 games for the Brewers. He also hit lefties at a remarkable .378 clip. Though he fans twice per walk, Newfield has explosive power. He hit .349 with 65 extra-base hits in 107 games for Triple-A Calgary in 1994. He also topped .300 in four other minor-league campaigns. A slugger who's still developing, Newfield twice had 19-homer seasons in the minors but could exceed that total in the bigs if he plays every day. Where he'll play is a question, however, since Newfield has never been noted for his defense. Because he lacks speed, range, and a strong arm, his best spots are left field, first base, or DH.

Major League Batting Register

	BA	G	AB	R	H	2B	3B	HR	RBI	SB
93 AL	.227	22	66	5	15	3	0	1	7	0
94 AL	.184	12	38	3	7	1	0	1	4	0
95 AL	.188	24	85	7	16	3	0	3	14	0
95 NL	.309	21	55	6	17	5	1	1	7	0
96 NL	.251	84	191	27	48	11	0	5	26	1
96 AL	.307	49	179	21	55	15	0	7	31	0
Life	.257	212	614	69	158	38	1	18	89	1

WARREN NEWSON

Position: Outfield
Team: Texas Rangers
Born: July 3, 1964 Newnan, GA
Height: 5'7" **Weight:** 202 lbs.
Bats: left **Throws:** left
Acquired: Signed as a free agent, 12/95

PLAYER SUMMARY	
Fantasy Value	$0
Card Value	4¢ to 7¢
Will	reach base often
Can't	supply any speed
Expect	pinch-hit duties
Don't Expect	hits vs. lefties

At 5'7" and 202 pounds, Newson looks like Kirby Puckett. But that's where the comparison ends, proving once again that it's impossible to judge a book by its cover. Unlike Puckett, a perennial All-Star, Newson is nothing more than a fourth outfielder, pinch-hitter, and occasional DH. In 1996, he set personal peaks in games, at bats, hits, doubles, homers, and RBI while starting 44 games in right field, eight in left, and nine at DH. He batted only .219 over his final 45 games. That skid shouldn't hurt the reputation of the Middle Georgia College product. He entered 1996 with a career on-base percentage of .400 and finished 1996 at .355, an even 100 points above his batting average. A small strike zone combined with a great batting eye helps Newson draw frequent walks. Once regarded as a singles hitter, Newson surprised with 25 extra-base hits (ten of them homers) last year. He struggles against lefties, adds no speed to the lineup, and lacks a good throwing arm. But he's always on base.

Major League Batting Register

	BA	G	AB	R	H	2B	3B	HR	RBI	SB
91 AL	.295	71	132	20	39	5	0	4	25	2
92 AL	.221	63	136	19	30	3	0	1	11	3
93 AL	.300	26	40	9	12	0	0	2	6	0
94 AL	.255	63	102	16	26	5	0	2	7	1
95 AL	.261	84	157	34	41	2	2	5	15	2
96 AL	.255	91	235	34	60	14	1	10	31	3
Life	.259	396	802	132	208	29	3	24	95	11
2 Ave	.258	93	206	36	53	8	2	8	24	3

MELVIN NIEVES

Position: Outfield
Team: Detroit Tigers
Born: Dec. 28, 1971 San Juan, Puerto Rico
Height: 6'2" **Weight:** 215 lbs.
Bats: both **Throws:** right
Acquired: Traded by Padres with Raul Casanova and Richie Lewis for Sean Bergman, Todd Steverson, and Cade Gaspar, 4/96

PLAYER SUMMARY	
Fantasy Value	$11 to $14
Card Value	5¢ to 8¢
Will	hit long balls
Can't	master strike zone
Expect	better lefty bat
Don't Expect	good average, glove

Although he made progress during the 1996 campaign, Nieves needs to lose his reputation as an all-or-nothing slugger. The switch-hitter fanned 158 times last year— one short of Jay Buhner's AL high and two behind major-league leader Henry Rodriguez—but powered 24 homers in 431 at bats. Some were tape-measure shots, including a May 24 478-foot blast that landed in Tiger Stadium's center-field upper deck. Nieves, who homered from both sides of the plate on July 15 and August 20, got extra bases on nearly half his hits but fanned four times per walk. He's a far better left-handed hitter. Private tips from veteran Alan Trammell helped Nieves show second-half improvement at bat and in the field. Though his defense had been extremely erratic (ten errors before the All-Star break), Nieves made only three second-half miscues, finishing with nine assists and two double plays. He throws well enough to play right but lacks mobility.

Major League Batting Register

	BA	G	AB	R	H	2B	3B	HR	RBI	SB
92 NL	.211	12	19	0	4	1	0	0	1	0
93 NL	.191	19	47	4	9	0	0	2	3	0
94 NL	.263	10	19	2	5	1	0	1	4	0
95 NL	.205	98	234	32	48	6	1	14	38	2
96 AL	.246	120	431	71	106	23	4	24	60	1
Life	.229	259	750	109	172	31	5	41	106	3
2 Ave	.230	115	347	54	80	15	3	20	51	2

DAVID NILSSON

Position: Outfield; first base
Team: Milwaukee Brewers
Born: Dec. 14, 1969 Brisbane, Australia
Height: 6'3" **Weight:** 231 lbs.
Bats: left **Throws:** right
Acquired: Signed as a free agent, 2/87

PLAYER SUMMARY	
Fantasy Value.	$18 to $21
Card Value	7¢ to 10¢
Will	rake right-handers
Can't.	supply much speed
Expect	patience, power
Don't Expect	return to catcher

After missing the first six weeks of 1996 with a stress fracture in his left foot, Nilsson made a fine platoon partner with Matt Mieske. While Nilsson hit .359 vs. righties and .238 vs. southpaws, Mieske hit .352 vs. lefties and .231 vs. righties. Like Mieske, who played all three outfield spots, Nilsson used his versatility to play more often. He played 55 games in right, 24 at first, six in left, and two behind the plate. An Australian who signed as a catcher, Nilsson made his biggest impact at bat. He homered twice in an inning May 17, hit two more a day later, and became the first Brewer to homer in three straight trips since Greg Vaughn in 1994. A contact hitter with power and patience, Nilsson had almost as many walks as strikeouts. His .407 on-base mark, just out of the AL's Top 10, was 76 points higher than his batting average. He doesn't pad his average with bunts or infield hits. Nilsson, who has an accurate but not powerful arm, moves well enough to play the outfield corners.

Major League Batting Register

	BA	G	AB	R	H	2B	3B	HR	RBI	SB
92 AL	.232	51	164	15	38	8	0	4	25	2
93 AL	.257	100	296	35	76	10	2	7	40	3
94 AL	.275	109	397	51	109	28	3	12	69	1
95 AL	.278	81	263	41	73	12	1	12	53	2
96 AL	.331	123	453	81	150	33	2	17	84	2
Life	.284	464	1573	223	446	91	8	52	271	10
3 Ave	.295	123	436	66	129	29	2	16	80	2

C.J. NITKOWSKI

Position: Pitcher
Team: Houston Astros
Born: March 9, 1973 Suffern, NY
Height: 6'2" **Weight:** 185 lbs.
Bats: left **Throws:** left
Acquired: Traded by Tigers with Brad Ausmus, Jose Lima, Trever Miller, and Daryle Ward for Brian Hunter, Orlando Miller, Doug Brocail, Todd Jones, and a player to be named later, 12/96

PLAYER SUMMARY	
Fantasy Value	$0
Card Value	5¢ to 8¢
Will.	hope sinker sinks
Can't	find strike zone
Expect	trial as starter
Don't Expect.	great velocity

The ninth man selected in the 1994 draft, Nitkowski reached the majors in his second pro season. After 20 appearances for the Reds and Tigers, the former St. John's standout showed he was a not-ready-for-prime-time player. He opened 1996 in the minors, making 17 appearances for Triple-A Toledo and ranking second in American Association strikeouts at the time of his July 1 recall. A sinker-slider pitcher who needs an off-speed pitch, Nitkowski worked in 11 big-league games—all but three of them starts—for the pitching-poor Tigers of 1996. Though he averaged seven whiffs per nine innings, Nitkowski had serious control problems. He also yielded too many hits. Still learning on the job, Nitkowski helps his own cause by fielding his position well and holding baserunners close. Half of the ten potential basestealers who challenged him last year failed. Nitkowski's best effort last year was a seven-inning, seven-K victory July 30. He was later disabled briefly with a strained back.

Major League Pitching Register

	W	L	ERA	G	CG	IP	H	ER	BB	SO
95 NL	1	3	6.12	9	0	32.1	41	22	15	18
95 AL	1	4	7.09	11	0	39.1	53	31	20	13
96 AL	2	3	8.08	11	0	45.2	62	41	38	36
Life	4	10	7.21	31	0	117.1	156	94	73	67

OTIS NIXON

Position: Outfield
Team: Toronto Blue Jays
Born: Jan. 9, 1959 Evergreen, NC
Height: 6'2" **Weight:** 180 lbs.
Bats: both **Throws:** right
Acquired: Signed as a free agent, 12/95

PLAYER SUMMARY	
Fantasy Value	$20 to $25
Card Value	4¢ to 7¢
Will	use great speed
Can't	supply any sock
Expect	walks, singles
Don't Expect	strong throws

At the ripe athletic age of 38, Nixon remains one of the game's premier basestealers. He's stolen at least 50 in each of the last two seasons and has topped 40 in eight of the last nine years. A terrific leadoff man, Nixon always seems to get on base. Though he's strictly a singles hitter, he draws so many walks that his on-base percentage is nearly 100 points higher than his batting average. And he's no slouch with the stick. An opposite-field hitter who likes to slap and run, he fattens his average with bunts and infield hits. Nixon is a high-percentage basestealer who steals third about a dozen times per season. Nixon's speed helps him in center, where he has quick reactions and exceptional range. He made only two errors in 1996. Nixon's major weakness is a popgun arm.

Major League Batting Register

	BA	G	AB	R	H	2B	3B	HR	RBI	SB
83 AL	.143	13	14	2	2	0	0	0	0	2
84 AL	.154	49	91	16	14	0	0	0	1	12
85 AL	.235	104	162	34	38	4	0	3	9	20
86 AL	.263	105	95	33	25	4	1	0	8	23
87 AL	.059	19	17	2	1	0	0	0	1	2
88 NL	.244	90	271	47	66	8	2	0	15	46
89 NL	.217	126	258	41	56	7	2	0	21	37
90 NL	.251	119	231	46	58	6	2	1	20	50
91 NL	.297	124	401	81	119	10	1	0	26	72
92 NL	.294	120	456	79	134	14	2	2	22	41
93 NL	.269	134	461	77	124	12	3	1	24	47
94 AL	.274	103	398	60	109	15	1	0	25	42
95 AL	.295	139	589	87	174	21	2	0	45	50
96 AL	.286	125	496	87	142	15	1	1	29	54
Life	.270	1370	3940	692	1062	116	17	8	246	498
3 Ave	.286	142	573	90	164	20	2	0	38	56

HIDEO NOMO

Position: Pitcher
Team: Los Angeles Dodgers
Born: Aug. 31, 1968 Osaka, Japan
Height: 6'2" **Weight:** 180 lbs.
Bats: right **Throws:** right
Acquired: Signed as a free agent, 2/95

PLAYER SUMMARY	
Fantasy Value	$16 to $19
Card Value	40¢ to $1
Will	yield few hits
Can't	nail basestealers
Expect	many strikeouts
Don't Expect	perfect control

Although he avoided the sophomore jinx last summer, Nomo wasn't as sharp as he had been the year before. He held hitters to a .218 average, yielded seven hits per nine innings, and fanned more than one man per inning. But he also yielded 23 homers, threw 11 wild pitches, and allowed 52 stolen bases—leading Los Angeles in all three dubious departments. Plagued by imperfect control at times, Nomo was most ineffective at the worst time: in the decisive Game 3 of the 1996 Division Series vs. Atlanta. Known as "the Tornado" because of his back-twisting windup, Nomo gets most of his whiffs on a forkball that drops sharply as it crosses the plate. He throws a slower forkball as a changeup, along with a 90-mph fastball and occasional curve. When everything works, he's almost unhittable: Nomo fanned 17 Marlins in a three-hitter April 13 and performed the impossible with a no-hitter at Denver's Coors Field September 17. Nomo isn't much of a hitter. He can bunt, however, and is considered a solid fielder. But his pickoff move is virtually nonexistent.

Major League Pitching Register

	W	L	ERA	G	CG	IP	H	ER	BB	SO
95 NL	13	6	2.54	28	4	191.1	124	54	78	236
96 NL	16	11	3.19	33	3	228.1	180	81	85	234
Life	29	17	2.90	61	7	419.2	304	135	163	470
2 Ave	15	9	2.88	32	4	222.1	160	71	86	250

JON NUNNALLY

Position: Outfield
Team: Kansas City Royals
Born: Nov. 9, 1971 Pelham, NC
Height: 5'10" **Weight:** 190 lbs.
Bats: left **Throws:** right
Acquired: Rule 5 draft pick from Indians, 12/94

PLAYER SUMMARY	
Fantasy Value	$4 to $6
Card Value	7¢ to 10¢
Will	post better stats
Can't	hit left-handers
Expect	occasional power
Don't Expect	regular position

The sophomore jinx hit Nunnally hard last summer. After hitting 14 homers as a 1995 rookie who made the improbable jump from Class-A to the majors, he slipped so badly that he spent part of last season in the minors. He hit only five AL homers—one of them a game-winner against Toronto September 3—but made points in Triple-A by hitting .281 with 21 doubles, 25 homers, and 77 RBI for Omaha. A fastball hitter with some patience, Nunnally had an on-base percentage 113 points above his batting average in 1995. He often hits the ball up the middle or to the opposite field but struggles against southpaws. A basestealer in the minors, Nunnally has decent speed. He set a club record with four steals of home (three on the front end of a double-steal) in 1995. Nunnally has good range and an arm strong enough to make the long throw from right field. He played both corners for the Royals last year. Until he learns to hit lefties, however, he probably won't amount to anything more than a platoon player.

SHERMAN OBANDO

Position: Outfield
Team: Montreal Expos
Born: Jan. 23, 1970 Bocas del Toro, Panama
Height: 6'4" **Weight:** 215 lbs.
Bats: right **Throws:** right
Acquired: Traded by Orioles for Tony Tarasco, 3/96

PLAYER SUMMARY	
Fantasy Value	$1
Card Value	7¢ to 10¢
Will	hit ball hard
Can't	solve lefties
Expect	pinch hits
Don't Expect	strong fielding

Obando produced considerable power in very limited action for the Expos last season. Playing 47 games in right field and making 48 pinch-hitting appearances, he contributed eight home runs, 22 RBI, and 30 runs scored. A much better hitter at home than on the road, Obando is also better with men in scoring position. But his performance against left-handed pitchers is puzzling. Though he hit .284 against righties last year, his average plummeted to .188 vs. southpaws. Obando fanned more than twice per walk but pushed his on-base percentage 86 points above his batting average. His first two-homer game came in a 5-2 win over the Phillies July 14. A pure hitter who attracted Montreal's attention with a strong run at the Dominican Winter League's Triple Crown, Obando is not known for his speed or defense. He made three errors in 316 innings as an outfielder for Montreal last year. Obando began his pro career after the Yankees inked him as a nondrafted free agent in 1987.

Major League Batting Register

	BA	G	AB	R	H	2B	3B	HR	RBI	SB
95 AL	.244	119	303	51	74	15	6	14	42	6
96 AL	.211	35	90	16	19	5	1	5	17	0
Life	.237	154	393	67	93	20	7	19	59	6

Major League Batting Register

	BA	G	AB	R	H	2B	3B	HR	RBI	SB
93 AL	.272	31	92	8	25	2	0	3	15	0
95 AL	.263	16	38	0	10	1	0	0	3	1
96 NL	.247	89	178	30	44	9	0	8	22	2
Life	.256	136	308	38	79	12	0	11	40	3

CHARLIE O'BRIEN

Position: Catcher
Team: Toronto Blue Jays
Born: May 1, 1961 Tulsa, OK
Height: 6'2" **Weight:** 205 lbs.
Bats: right **Throws:** right
Acquired: Signed as a free agent, 12/95

PLAYER SUMMARY	
Fantasy Value	$4 to $6
Card Value	4¢ to 7¢
Will	help his pitchers
Can't	hit for average
Expect	occasional pop
Don't Expect	passed balls

Although his offense has picked up, O'Brien clings to a big-league berth because of his exceptional defense. Catching more than 100 games for the first time in an 11-year career, he was instrumental in the emergence of Pat Hentgen as a 20-game winner and Cy Young winner and in the resurrection of Juan Guzman, who led the AL in ERA. O'Brien, who nailed 37.5 percent of would-be basestealers, made only three errors all year. He calls good games, handles pitchers like a quarterback, blocks wild pitches, guards the plate, and grabs bunts, dribblers, and pop-ups anywhere near the plate. He even donned a novel catcher's mask that provides better protection and sight lines. At the plate, O'Brien's home run total has increased four years in a row. He hit a career-best 13 last year and even tried to steal the second base of his career.

Major League Batting Register

	BA	G	AB	R	H	2B	3B	HR	RBI	SB
85 AL	.273	16	11	3	3	1	0	0	1	0
87 AL	.200	10	35	2	7	3	1	0	0	0
88 AL	.220	40	118	12	26	6	0	2	9	0
89 AL	.234	62	188	22	44	10	0	6	35	0
90 AL	.186	46	145	11	27	7	2	0	11	0
90 NL	.162	28	68	6	11	3	0	0	9	0
91 NL	.185	69	168	16	31	6	0	2	14	0
92 NL	.212	68	156	15	33	12	0	2	13	0
93 NL	.255	67	188	15	48	11	0	4	23	1
94 NL	.243	51	152	24	37	11	0	8	28	0
95 NL	.227	67	198	18	45	7	0	9	23	0
96 AL	.238	109	324	33	77	17	0	13	44	0
Life	.222	633	1751	177	389	94	3	46	210	1
3 Ave	.236	85	254	29	60	13	0	11	36	0

ALEX OCHOA

Position: Outfield
Team: New York Mets
Born: March 29, 1972 Miami Lakes, FL
Height: 6' **Weight:** 185 lbs.
Bats: right **Throws:** right
Acquired: Traded by Orioles with Damon Buford for Bobby Bonilla and Jimmy Williams, 7/95

PLAYER SUMMARY	
Fantasy Value	$8 to $10
Card Value	20¢ to 30¢
Will	show off his arm
Can't	live up to hype
Expect	speed, defense
Don't Expect	frequent homers

At the time of his June 22 promotion from Triple-A, Ochoa ranked second in the International League in both batting and hits and stood third in runs scored and on-base percentage. He quickly showed that was no fluke, hitting .311 with three homers and 21 RBI in his first 32 big-league games and going 32-for-55 with men in scoring position. Ochoa hit for the cycle during a 5-for-5 game in Philadelphia July 3. The onetime schoolboy shortstop showed power, speed, and a powerful throwing arm while playing 76 games in right field. Colorado manager Don Baylor said Ochoa had a better throwing arm than former Gold Glover Raul Mondesi. An aggressive fielder with quick reactions, great range, and good accuracy, Ochoa is never afraid to throw the ball. Nor is he afraid to accept advice. Veterans Lance Johnson and Bernard Gilkey both helped Ochoa adjust to the majors. The rookie's even temperament, outgoing personality, and good work habits helped. Ochoa was Baltimore's best prospect before he was dealt to the Mets.

Major League Batting Register

	BA	G	AB	R	H	2B	3B	HR	RBI	SB
95 NL	.297	11	37	7	11	1	0	0	0	1
96 NL	.294	82	282	37	83	19	3	4	33	4
Life	.295	93	319	44	94	20	3	4	33	5

JOSE OFFERMAN

Position: First base; second base
Team: Kansas City Royals
Born: Nov. 8, 1968 San Pedro de Macoris, Dominican Republic
Height: 6′ **Weight:** 160 lbs.
Bats: both **Throws:** right
Acquired: Traded by Dodgers for Billy Brewer, 12/95

PLAYER SUMMARY

Fantasy Value	$9 to $11
Card Value	5¢ to 8¢
Will	wait for his pitch
Can't	reach the fences
Expect	walks, bunts, hits
Don't Expect	Gold Glove

During his four-plus years in Los Angeles, Offerman's shortstop defense was so bad that the unkind media resorted to calling him "Awful Man." After Kansas City made the same discovery, he was moved to first, then finally to second, where he seemed to find a home late last season. Although he needed training at the new positions, Offerman never missed a beat with his bat. He went 4-for-4 with two RBI in his first game at second base. Offerman not only finished with his first .300 season but showed enough patience to post an on-base percentage 81 points above his batting average. He also stole 24 bases. Offerman doesn't hit for power but confounds the opposition by hitting to all fields, dropping surprise bunts, and beating out infield hits. A better right-handed batter, he's especially dangerous when he's ahead in the count. The short throw from second seems to agree with Offerman, whose arm is erratic.

Major League Batting Register

	BA	G	AB	R	H	2B	3B	HR	RBI	SB
90 NL	.155	29	58	7	9	0	0	1	7	1
91 NL	.195	52	113	10	22	2	0	0	3	3
92 NL	.260	149	534	67	139	20	8	1	30	23
93 NL	.269	158	590	77	159	21	6	1	62	30
94 NL	.210	72	243	27	51	8	4	1	25	2
95 NL	.287	119	429	69	123	14	6	4	33	2
96 AL	.303	151	561	85	170	33	8	5	47	24
Life	.266	730	2528	342	673	98	32	13	207	85
3 Ave	.274	129	462	67	127	20	7	4	40	10

CHAD OGEA

Position: Pitcher
Team: Cleveland Indians
Born: Nov. 9, 1970 Lake Charles, LA
Height: 6′2″ **Weight:** 200 lbs.
Bats: left **Throws:** right
Acquired: Third-round pick in 6/91 free-agent draft

PLAYER SUMMARY

Fantasy Value	$6 to $8
Card Value	5¢ to 8¢
Will	bank on location
Can't	rack up Ks
Expect	excellent control
Don't Expect	more knee woes

Ogea opened the 1996 campaign as Cleveland's fifth starter after Mark Clark was traded to the Mets on March 31. Slowed early by shoulder tendinitis, Ogea was used as both a starter and reliever before returning to full-time rotation work July 2. Over his last 11 starts, Ogea went 5-3 with a 3.01 ERA. His 7-0 win at Milwaukee September 4 was his first major-league shutout. The former Louisiana State star is a control artist who depends upon location rather than velocity of his fastball and changeup. He averages 2½ walks per nine innings while fanning more than six hitters over the same span. Ogea, who yields a hit per inning, does a good job of controlling the running game (nine of the 17 who tried to steal against him failed) but throws his share of gopher balls, including Mark McGwire's 50th last year. Even though he's had five knee operations, Ogea is a solid fielder. The young right-hander is a better pitcher at home; he has a career mark of 12-2 with a 3.47 ERA at Cleveland's Jacobs Field.

Major League Pitching Register

	W	L	ERA	G	CG	IP	H	ER	BB	SO
94 AL	0	1	6.06	4	0	16.1	21	11	10	11
95 AL	8	3	3.05	20	1	106.1	95	36	29	57
96 AL	10	6	4.79	29	1	146.2	151	78	42	101
Life	18	10	4.18	53	2	269.1	267	125	81	169
2 Ave	10	5	4.01	26	1	133.0	129	59	37	83

TROY O'LEARY

Position: Outfield
Team: Boston Red Sox
Born: Aug. 4, 1969 Compton, CA
Height: 6′ **Weight:** 196 lbs.
Bats: left **Throws:** left
Acquired: Claimed from Brewers on waivers, 4/95

PLAYER SUMMARY

Fantasy Value	$6 to $8
Card Value	5¢ to 8¢
Will	enjoy home cooking
Can't	solve left-handers
Expect	opposite-field hits
Don't Expect	stolen bases

O'Leary is full of surprises. Unable to clear the Mendoza Line against left-handers, he still managed to finish the 1996 season with a career-peak 15 homers. A star at home (.300) but a bust on the road (.214), O'Leary walked often enough to compile an on-base percentage 67 points higher than his batting average. But he still fanned nearly twice per walk. A free swinger who feasts on low fastballs, O'Leary often hits the ball up the middle or to the opposite field. He once stole 28 bases in the minors but is no longer a threat to steal (three-for-five last year). Nor is he a great outfielder, even though he sometimes compensates by outrunning his own mistakes. O'Leary's reactions, hands, and arm are unreliable. Although he had eight assists last year, he also had seven errors. O'Leary saw time at all outfield positions last year. The Texas League MVP in 1992, O'Leary has led several leagues in total bases and total chances. He was a 13th-round Milwaukee draft choice in 1987.

Major League Batting Register

	BA	G	AB	R	H	2B	3B	HR	RBI	SB
93 AL	.293	19	41	3	12	3	0	0	3	0
94 AL	.273	27	66	9	18	1	1	2	7	1
95 AL	.308	112	399	60	123	31	6	10	49	5
96 AL	.260	149	497	68	129	28	5	15	81	3
Life	.281	307	1003	140	282	63	12	27	140	9
2 Ave	.283	138	473	68	134	31	6	13	68	4

JOHN OLERUD

Position: First base
Team: Toronto Blue Jays
Born: Aug. 5, 1968 Seattle, WA
Height: 6′5″ **Weight:** 205 lbs.
Bats: left **Throws:** left
Acquired: Third-round pick in 6/89 free-agent draft

PLAYER SUMMARY

Fantasy Value	$11 to $14
Card Value	7¢ to 10¢
Will	handle right-handers
Can't	find former stroke
Expect	selective hitting
Don't Expect	erratic defense

Like Norm Cash, whose .361 average won a freak batting title in 1961, Olerud is making observers believe he was a one-year wonder in 1993. That was the year he, like Cash, won a batting crown with the only .300 mark of his career (.363). It was also his only 100-RBI season and the only time he topped 20 homers. In fact, Olerud has fallen so far so fast that he's now regarded as little more than a platoon player. The former Washington State standout has lost both his power and his ability to hit lefty pitching. He shared first base last year with righty-hitting slugger Joe Carter. Although Olerud remains an exceptional contact hitter who walks twice as often as he fans, his batting average has fallen for three straight seasons. He's no threat to run but does a first-rate job with his fielding. Olerud made only two miscues in 101 games—a performance worthy of Gold Glove consideration.

Major League Batting Register

	BA	G	AB	R	H	2B	3B	HR	RBI	SB
89 AL	.375	6	8	2	3	0	0	0	0	0
90 AL	.265	111	358	43	95	15	1	14	48	0
91 AL	.256	139	454	64	116	30	1	17	68	0
92 AL	.284	138	458	68	130	28	0	16	66	1
93 AL	.363	158	551	109	200	54	2	24	107	0
94 AL	.297	108	384	47	114	29	2	12	67	1
95 AL	.291	135	492	72	143	32	0	8	54	0
96 AL	.274	125	398	59	109	25	0	18	61	1
Life	.293	920	3103	464	910	213	6	109	471	3
3 Ave	.288	143	497	69	143	34	1	15	72	1

OMAR OLIVARES

Position: Pitcher
Team: Detroit Tigers
Born: July 6, 1967 Mayaguez, Puerto Rico
Height: 6'1" **Weight:** 193 lbs.
Bats: right **Throws:** right
Acquired: Signed as a free agent, 12/95

PLAYER SUMMARY	
Fantasy Value	$1
Card Value	4¢ to 7¢
Will	bank on sinker
Can't	always find plate
Expect	rotation berth
Don't Expect	many strikeouts

Olivares brought his sinker-slider repertoire to the American League for the first time last season. He made 25 appearances, all of them starts, for the hapless Tigers and emerged with relatively respectable numbers. Averaging a hit per inning and doing his best pitching against right-handed batters, Olivares kept the ball in the park, controlled the running game, and topped the team with four complete games. A pitcher who depends upon location, he averages fewer than five strikeouts per nine innings. He has trouble when his sinker stays flat or sinks out of the strike zone. Last year, Olivares walked more than four batters per nine innings. He also has trouble with left-handed hitters, who ripped him at a .291 clip in 1996. Olivares has no problems in the field. During his days in the National League, he could also help himself at bat. Olivares, who began his pro career with the Padres, is the son of former St. Louis outfielder Ed Olivares.

Major League Pitching Register

	W	L	ERA	G	CG	IP	H	ER	BB	SO
90 NL	1	1	2.92	9	0	49.1	45	16	17	20
91 NL	11	7	3.71	28	0	167.1	148	69	61	91
92 NL	9	9	3.84	32	1	197.0	189	84	63	124
93 NL	5	3	4.17	58	0	118.2	134	55	54	63
94 NL	3	4	5.74	14	1	73.2	84	47	37	26
95 NL	1	4	6.91	16	0	41.2	55	32	23	22
96 AL	7	11	4.89	25	4	160.0	169	87	75	81
Life	37	39	4.35	182	6	807.2	824	390	330	427
3 Ave	4	7	5.48	21	2	104.1	116	63	51	47

DARREN OLIVER

Position: Pitcher
Team: Texas Rangers
Born: Oct. 6, 1970 Kansas City, MO
Height: 6'2" **Weight:** 200 lbs.
Bats: right **Throws:** left
Acquired: Third-round pick in 6/88 free-agent draft

PLAYER SUMMARY	
Fantasy Value	$8 to $10
Card Value	5¢ to 8¢
Will	stifle lefty hitters
Can't	rack up strikeouts
Expect	double-digit wins
Don't Expect	pinpoint control

In his first year as a major-league starter, Oliver turned out to be the missing link that had prevented the Rangers from winning. He led the team with a .700 winning percentage and provided a strong fourth arm behind Ken Hill, Roger Pavlik, and Bobby Witt. Oliver even pitched well against the Yankees in the Division Series, nursing a 2-1 lead into the ninth before giving way to a leaky bullpen. Oliver, a survivor of two recent arm operations, blends a fastball with a curveball and a changeup that ranks as his best pitch. But he needs help from his defense because he emphasizes location over velocity (5.8 Ks per game). Oliver walks almost four men per nine innings but yields only a hit per frame and keeps the ball in the park. He's much more effective against left-handed hitters than he is against righties. Oliver helps himself with fine fielding and a decent pickoff move. Eleven men stole against him last year, but six others were caught in the act. At 26, Oliver will improve with experience.

Major League Pitching Register

	W	L	ERA	G	CG	IP	H	ER	BB	SO
93 AL	0	0	2.70	2	0	3.1	2	1	1	4
94 AL	4	0	3.42	43	0	50.0	40	19	35	50
95 AL	4	2	4.22	17	0	49.0	47	23	32	39
96 AL	14	6	4.66	30	1	173.2	190	90	76	112
Life	22	8	4.34	92	1	276.0	279	133	144	205
3 Ave	8	3	4.29	37	0	100.1	100	48	54	75

JOE OLIVER

Position: Catcher
Team: Cincinnati Reds
Born: July 24, 1965 Memphis, TN
Height: 6'3" **Weight:** 220 lbs.
Bats: right **Throws:** right
Acquired: Signed as a free agent, 3/96

PLAYER SUMMARY	
Fantasy Value	$2 to $4
Card Value	4¢ to 7¢
Will	nurture his pitchers
Can't	boost his average
Expect	occasional power
Don't Expect	patience, speed

Returning to his original club as a free agent, Oliver spent most of 1996 platooning with Ed Taubensee. Vocal in his desire to play every day, Oliver did not hit enough to make that possible. He hit just .242—seven points below the career mark he had carried into the season—and contributed only 11 homers. A high-ball, fastball hitter who likes to pull, Oliver doesn't have much patience. He fans twice per walk and struggles against left-handed pitchers. He's had a higher average against righties in each of the last two seasons. Oliver does his best hitting with men in scoring position. He has trouble stopping potential basestealers. He nailed only 28 percent of those who challenged him last year but never hesitates to surprise a sleeping runner with a snap throw. Oliver's other attributes behind the plate are fine. He calls good games, handles pitchers well, prevents wild pitches, and blocks the plate.

Major League Batting Register

	BA	G	AB	R	H	2B	3B	HR	RBI	SB
89 NL	.272	49	151	13	41	8	0	3	23	0
90 NL	.231	121	364	34	84	23	0	8	52	1
91 NL	.216	94	269	21	58	11	0	11	41	0
92 NL	.270	143	485	42	131	25	1	10	57	2
93 NL	.239	139	482	40	115	28	0	14	75	0
94 NL	.211	6	19	1	4	0	0	1	5	0
95 NL	.273	97	337	43	92	20	0	12	51	2
96 NL	.242	106	289	31	70	12	1	11	46	2
Life	.248	755	2396	225	595	127	2	70	350	7
2 Ave	.260	108	334	40	87	17	1	12	52	2

GREGG OLSON

Position: Pitcher
Team: Houston Astros
Born: Oct. 11, 1966 Omaha, NE
Height: 6'4" **Weight:** 212 lbs.
Bats: right **Throws:** right
Acquired: Traded by Tigers for Kevin Gallaher and Pedro Santana, 8/96

PLAYER SUMMARY	
Fantasy Value	$1 to $3
Card Value	4¢ to 7¢
Will	bank on curve
Can't	find old form
Expect	bullpen berth
Don't Expect	great control

Olson had five solid seasons as a closer for the Baltimore Orioles before encountering serious shoulder problems. From 1989 to '93, he topped two dozen saves each year but added only 12 more over the last three years combined. He showed some signs of revival last year, when he made 59 appearances for three clubs, including the Tigers and Astros in the big leagues. The former Auburn All-American and AL All-Star still banks on a big curve as his out pitch. But it's not as sharp as it once was. Although he averaged nearly eight Ks per nine innings for the Astros last year, Olson also yielded more than 11 hits per nine innings and had severe control problems (6.75 walks per nine innings). He also had trouble with left-handed hitters, who rang him up at a .385 pace. Olson sabotages his own efforts with a weak pickoff move and erratic defense.

Major League Pitching Register

	W	L	ERA	G	S	IP	H	ER	BB	SO
88 AL	1	1	3.27	10	0	11.0	10	4	10	9
89 AL	5	2	1.69	64	27	85.0	57	16	46	90
90 AL	6	5	2.42	64	37	74.1	57	20	31	74
91 AL	4	6	3.18	72	31	73.2	74	26	29	72
92 AL	1	5	2.05	60	36	61.1	46	14	24	58
93 AL	0	2	1.60	50	29	45.0	37	8	18	44
94 NL	0	2	9.20	16	1	14.2	19	15	13	10
95 AL	3	3	4.09	23	3	33.0	28	15	19	21
96 AL	3	0	5.02	43	8	43.0	43	24	28	29
96 NL	1	0	4.82	9	0	9.1	12	5	7	8
Life	24	26	2.94	411	172	450.1	383	147	225	415
2 Ave	3	2	4.59	34	6	40.0	37	20	25	26

237

PAUL O'NEILL

Position: Outfield
Team: New York Yankees
Born: Feb. 25, 1963 Columbus, OH
Height: 6'4" **Weight:** 215 lbs.
Bats: left **Throws:** left
Acquired: Traded by Reds with Joe DeBerry for Roberto Kelly, 10/92

PLAYER SUMMARY	
Fantasy Value	$16 to $19
Card Value	8¢ to 12¢
Will	produce power
Can't	solve southpaws
Expect	exceptional eye
Don't Expect	mediocre defense

Although he slipped badly during the second half (.279, 39 RBI), O'Neill enjoyed his fourth straight .300 season in 1996. The three-time All-Star fell one short of his fourth consecutive 20-homer season but reached base more than ever before, thanks to a career-peak 102 walks. O'Neill's .411 on-base mark was an achievement for a man who hit only .239 against left-handers. A contact hitter who walks much more often than he fans, O'Neill works hard to control a volcanic temper. Because he hits the ball hard, he bangs into frequent double plays. He didn't steal a base last year, but O'Neill moves well enough to provide decent range in right field. His best asset is a tremendous throwing arm that is the bane of baserunners. He also has good hands: O'Neill hasn't made an error in 208 games.

Major League Batting Register

	BA	G	AB	R	H	2B	3B	HR	RBI	SB
85 NL	.333	5	12	1	4	1	0	0	1	0
86 NL	.000	3	2	0	0	0	0	0	0	0
87 NL	.256	84	160	24	41	14	1	7	28	2
88 NL	.252	145	485	58	122	25	3	16	73	8
89 NL	.276	117	428	49	118	24	2	15	74	20
90 NL	.270	145	503	59	136	28	0	16	78	13
91 NL	.256	152	532	71	136	36	0	28	91	12
92 NL	.246	148	496	59	122	19	1	14	66	6
93 AL	.311	141	498	71	155	34	1	20	75	2
94 AL	.359	103	368	68	132	25	1	21	83	5
95 AL	.300	127	460	82	138	30	4	22	96	1
96 AL	.302	150	546	89	165	35	1	19	91	0
Life	.283	1320	4490	631	1269	271	14	178	756	69
3 Ave	.320	146	527	92	169	35	2	24	105	3

REY ORDONEZ

Position: Shortstop
Team: New York Mets
Born: Jan. 11, 1972 Havana, Cuba
Height: 5'10" **Weight:** 170 lbs.
Bats: both **Throws:** right
Acquired: Drafted from St. Paul (independent), 10/93

PLAYER SUMMARY	
Fantasy Value	$0
Card Value	15¢ to 30¢
Will	surprise with bat
Can't	clear fence often
Expect	spectacular glove
Don't Expect	stolen base crown

Long before Ordonez arrived in New York last spring, the hype about his defensive wizardry hit with tornadic force. The Cuban defector was hailed as the franchise savior and projected as the Rookie of the Year. Predictably, it didn't happen. Ordonez proved to be a better hitter than advertised but not as good a fielder. Blessed with instant reactions, great range, soft hands, and a solid arm, he made many rookie mistakes—some of them on routine plays—and finished with 27 errors. At the plate, he proved to be a singles hitter who makes contact but doesn't have the patience to wait for walks. A .214 hitter at Triple-A Norfolk in 1995, Ordonez came alive in the Puerto Rican Winter League, finishing second with a .341 average. He maintained that momentum in the NL, uncorking a 14-game hitting streak and hitting .305 as late as June 5. Coach Tom McCraw even paid him two dollars for every opposite-field hit. A cut-and-slash hitter who can work the hit-and-run, Ordonez will never hit like Barry Larkin. But both his batting and fielding figure to get better as he gains experience.

Major League Batting Register

	BA	G	AB	R	H	2B	3B	HR	RBI	SB
96 NL	.257	151	502	51	129	12	4	1	30	1
Life	.257	151	502	51	129	12	4	1	30	1

JESSE OROSCO

Position: Pitcher
Team: Baltimore Orioles
Born: April 21, 1957 Santa Barbara, CA
Height: 6'2" **Weight:** 205 lbs.
Bats: right **Throws:** left
Acquired: Signed as a free agent, 4/95

PLAYER SUMMARY	
Fantasy Value	$1
Card Value	4¢ to 7¢
Will	answer call often
Can't	maintain control
Expect	stranded runners
Don't Expect	first-batter hits

Orosco realizes that the best set-up men have few wins, few losses, and few saves. He fit that bill last year, when he went 3-1 without a save in 66 outings. The rubber-armed lefty held hitters to a .207 average, stranded 68.8 percent of the runners he inherited, retired 47 of 66 first batters, and averaged just under a K per inning. Orosco, who has made at least 50 outings in 13 seasons, throws a fastball, slider, and sweeping curve. But he doesn't always throw them for strikes. Although he turns 40 in April, Orosco guaranteed himself another year with a strong second half: four earned runs in 29⅓ innings (1.23 ERA). Orosco's ability to supply southpaw relief should give him job security.

Major League Pitching Register

	W	L	ERA	G	S	IP	H	ER	BB	SO
79 NL	1	2	4.89	18	0	35.0	33	19	22	22
81 NL	0	1	1.56	8	1	17.1	13	3	6	18
82 NL	4	10	2.72	54	4	109.1	92	33	40	89
83 NL	13	7	1.47	62	17	110.0	76	18	38	84
84 NL	10	6	2.59	60	31	87.0	58	25	34	85
85 NL	8	6	2.73	54	17	79.0	66	24	34	68
86 NL	8	6	2.33	58	21	81.0	64	21	35	62
87 NL	3	9	4.44	58	16	77.0	78	38	31	78
88 NL	3	2	2.72	55	9	53.0	41	16	30	43
89 AL	3	4	2.08	69	3	78.0	54	18	26	79
90 AL	5	4	3.90	55	2	64.2	58	28	38	55
91 AL	2	0	3.74	47	0	45.2	52	19	15	36
92 AL	3	1	3.23	59	1	39.0	33	14	13	40
93 AL	3	5	3.18	57	8	56.2	47	20	17	67
94 AL	3	1	5.08	40	0	39.0	32	22	26	36
95 AL	2	4	3.26	65	3	49.2	28	18	27	58
96 AL	3	1	3.40	66	0	55.2	42	21	28	52
Life	74	69	2.98	885	133	1077.0	867	357	460	972
3 Ave	3	2	3.91	65	1	55.1	40	24	32	56

JOE ORSULAK

Position: Outfield; first base
Team: Florida Marlins
Born: May 31, 1962 Glen Ridge, NJ
Height: 6'1" **Weight:** 196 lbs.
Bats: left **Throws:** left
Acquired: Signed as a free agent, 12/95

PLAYER SUMMARY	
Fantasy Value	$0
Card Value	4¢ to 7¢
Will	pinch-hit often
Can't	hit with power
Expect	decent contact
Don't Expect	great defense

One of baseball's most useful reserves, Orsulak provides insurance off the bench. Last year, he played 30 games in left, 14 in center, 19 in right, and two at first base. But he also made 64 pinch-hitting appearances. Usually limp against lefties but robust against righties, Orsulak endured the reverse result last season. A contact hitter who uses all fields, he's a tough man to strike out. But he doesn't walk much either. Orsulak's .274 on-base percentage was a major disappointment in 1996. Orsulak has some power to the alleys and is most dangerous with runners in scoring position. He rarely runs much anymore. Because of his intelligence, he's a good baserunner even though he's no longer quick. Orsulak is no better than average in the field, where he's best in left. At 34, Orsulak is a useful sub whose best days are behind him.

Major League Batting Register

	BA	G	AB	R	H	2B	3B	HR	RBI	SB
83 NL	.182	7	11	0	2	0	0	0	1	0
84 NL	.254	32	67	12	17	1	2	0	3	3
85 NL	.300	121	397	54	119	14	6	0	21	24
86 NL	.249	138	401	60	100	19	6	2	19	24
88 AL	.288	125	379	48	109	21	3	8	27	9
89 AL	.285	123	390	59	111	22	5	7	55	5
90 AL	.269	124	413	49	111	14	3	11	57	6
91 AL	.278	143	486	57	135	22	1	5	43	6
92 AL	.289	117	391	45	113	18	3	4	39	5
93 NL	.284	134	409	59	116	15	4	8	35	5
94 NL	.260	96	292	39	76	3	0	8	42	4
95 AL	.283	108	290	41	82	19	2	1	37	1
96 NL	.221	120	217	23	48	6	1	2	19	1
Life	.275	1388	4143	546	1139	174	36	56	398	93
3 Ave	.259	126	318	41	82	11	1	5	40	3

DONOVAN OSBORNE

Position: Pitcher
Team: St. Louis Cardinals
Born: June 21, 1969 Roseville, CA
Height: 6'2" **Weight:** 195 lbs.
Bats: both **Throws:** left
Acquired: First-round pick in 6/90 free-agent draft

PLAYER SUMMARY	
Fantasy Value	$10 to $13
Card Value	5¢ to 8¢
Will	keep improving
Can't	strike men out
Expect	pickoff success
Don't Expect	hits by lefties

Osborne showed last season that he had fully recovered from the shoulder problem that cost him all of 1994 and part of 1995. He not only won a career-peak 13 games but beat Tom Glavine in Game 3 of the NL Championship Series. A control artist who dominates left-handed hitters, Osborne averages 2½ walks per nine innings with his low-90s fastball, changeup, and slider. He averages only six Ks per nine innings but gets considerable help from his defense. Though he yields fewer hits than innings, some of those hits sail over the fence. Osborne allowed 22 regular-season homers last year, but that was less than any other St. Louis starter. The former UNLV All-American helps his own cause with an exceptional pickoff move: Ten of the 14 runners who tried to steal against him last year didn't make it. Though he's only adequate in the field, Osborne is hardly an automatic out at the plate. His .220 average last year included a September 7 grand slam vs. San Diego (his first career homer) and ten runs batted in.

Major League Pitching Register

	W	L	ERA	G	CG	IP	H	ER	BB	SO
92 NL	11	9	3.77	34	0	179.0	193	75	38	104
93 NL	10	7	3.76	26	1	155.2	153	65	47	83
95 NL	4	6	3.81	19	0	113.1	112	48	34	82
96 NL	13	9	3.53	30	2	198.2	191	78	57	134
Life	38	31	3.70	109	3	646.2	649	266	176	403
2 Ave	9	8	3.64	26	1	163.0	159	66	48	113

ANTONIO OSUNA

Position: Pitcher
Team: Los Angeles Dodgers
Born: April 12, 1973 Sinaloa, Mexico
Height: 5'11" **Weight:** 160 lbs.
Bats: right **Throws:** right
Acquired: Signed as a nondrafted free agent, 6/91

PLAYER SUMMARY	
Fantasy Value	$7 to $9
Card Value	5¢ to 8¢
Will	supply late heat
Can't	always throw strikes
Expect	future closer job
Don't Expect	hits by righties

Osuna's first full season in the NL was a good one. The busiest member of the Dodger bullpen, he fanned more than one hitter per inning, yielded seven hits per nine, and dominated righties. The hard-throwing Mexican, who hits the mid-90s on the radar gun, tries to keep batters honest by showcasing a curveball and changeup. But he sometimes has trouble throwing them for strikes. Osuna averaged fewer than 3½ walks per game last year and stranded 71.1 percent of the runners he inherited. He allowed six homers in 84 regular-season innings—not a bad ratio—but surrendered the game-winning, tenth-inning homer that won Game 1 of the NL Division Series. For the most part, though, Osuna was quite effective, getting key whiffs and double-play grounders when he needed them. He fields his position well and tries to monitor the running game, though eight of ten potential basestealers succeeded against him last year. A hard worker who knows what he wants to throw, Osuna is being groomed as the eventual successor to Dodger closer Todd Worrell.

Major League Pitching Register

	W	L	ERA	G	S	IP	H	ER	BB	SO
95 NL	2	4	4.43	39	0	44.2	39	22	20	46
96 NL	9	6	3.00	73	4	84.0	65	28	32	85
Life	11	10	3.50	112	4	128.2	104	50	52	131
2 Ave	6	5	3.54	58	2	67.0	54	26	27	68

Ricky Otero

Position: Outfield
Team: Philadelphia Phillies
Born: April 15, 1972 Vega Baja, Puerto Rico
Height: 5'7" **Weight:** 150 lbs.
Bats: both **Throws:** right
Acquired: Traded by Mets for Phil Geisler, 12/95

Player Summary	
Fantasy Value	$4 to $6
Card Value	6¢ to 10¢
Will	stretch long hits
Can't	reach the fences
Expect	contact, speed
Don't Expect	erratic defense

When Otero entered the Philadelphia clubhouse for the first time last spring, one of the veterans shouted, "Okay, we've got the jockey. Where's the horse?" But baseball's shortest player soon stopped the kidding with strong defensive play plus a steady stream of line-drive hits. A speedy singles hitter who makes good contact, Otero walks more than he fans. He'll surprise with occasional shots into the alleys, but many of his extra-base hits are the result of his aggressiveness on the bases. He'll try to stretch singles into doubles and doubles into triples. The switch-hitting Otero, usually a good hitter from both sides, was much more potent as a lefty hitter last year. He also showed some ability on the bases but learned that reading the pitchers is just as important as getting good jumps; he was nailed ten times in 26 attempts. Otero had two 30-steal seasons in the minors. All that speed helps in center field, where Otero has a surprisingly strong arm. He had eight assists and was involved in two double plays last season. The little guy had a fine first full year.

Major League Batting Register

	BA	G	AB	R	H	2B	3B	HR	RBI	SB
95 NL	.137	35	51	5	7	2	0	0	1	2
96 NL	.273	104	411	54	112	11	7	2	32	16
Life	.258	139	462	59	119	13	7	2	33	18

Eric Owens

Position: Infield; outfield
Team: Cincinnati Reds
Born: Feb. 3, 1971 Danville, VA
Height: 6'1" **Weight:** 185 lbs.
Bats: right **Throws:** right
Acquired: Fourth-round pick in 6/92 free-agent draft

Player Summary	
Fantasy Value	$4 to $9
Card Value	8¢ to 12¢
Will	show good speed
Can't	hit right-handers
Expect	berth on bench
Don't Expect	frequent homers

Because of his versatility and ability to make contact, Owens could have a bright future in the big leagues. He played second, third, and left field for the Reds last season, swiped 16 bases in 18 attempts, and fanned only 38 times in 205 at bats. Although he struggled against right-handed pitching, Owens showed enough patience at the plate to push his on-base percentage 81 points higher than his batting average. When he played every day in the American Association two years ago, he led the league in runs, triples, and stolen bases; socked 44 extra-base hits; and won the MVP Award. He batted .314 and had a .388 on-base percentage—impressive numbers that prompted his promotion last summer. Despite his speed (he's a two-time 30-steal man in the minors), Owens has only average range at second base. Signed as a shortstop, he played that position in his first two pro years before trying his hand at third. Owens could have a future as a jack-of-all-trades, pinch runner, and pinch hitter vs. lefties.

Major League Batting Register

	BA	G	AB	R	H	2B	3B	HR	RBI	SB
95 NL	1.000	2	2	0	2	0	0	0	1	0
96 NL	.200	88	205	26	41	6	0	0	9	16
Life	.208	90	207	26	43	6	0	0	10	16

TOM PAGNOZZI

Position: Catcher
Team: St. Louis Cardinals
Born: July 30, 1962 Tucson, AZ
Height: 6'1" **Weight:** 190 lbs.
Bats: right **Throws:** right
Acquired: Eighth-round pick in 6/83 free-agent draft

PLAYER SUMMARY	
Fantasy Value.	$7 to $9
Card Value	4¢ to 7¢
Will	call good games
Can't	wait for walks
Expect	strong throws
Don't Expect	hit in clutch

Pagnozzi did everything he could to shake the good-field, no-hit label that had followed him since his rookie year. He not only hit a career-high 13 homers but hit .303 against left-handed pitchers and .310 at home. Pagnozzi finished just two short of his career high in runs batted in. Though he fans three times per walk, the University of Arkansas product delivers some timely hits. When he does connect, the veteran catcher hits to all fields against right-handers but goes the opposite way against lefties. He hits the changeup well but has trouble with heat. Pagnozzi also struggles with runners in scoring position. Behind the plate, however, the three-time Gold Glove winner nails 35 percent of the runners who try to steal, shifts his weight well to prevent wild pitches, and blocks the plate against incoming runners. He's also a superior handler of pitchers, and he calls good games.

Major League Batting Register

	BA	G	AB	R	H	2B	3B	HR	RBI	SB
87 NL	.188	27	48	8	9	1	0	2	9	1
88 NL	.282	81	195	17	55	9	0	0	15	0
89 NL	.150	52	80	3	12	2	0	0	3	0
90 NL	.277	69	220	20	61	15	0	2	23	1
91 NL	.264	140	459	38	121	24	5	2	57	9
92 NL	.249	139	485	33	121	26	3	7	44	2
93 NL	.258	92	330	31	85	15	1	7	41	1
94 NL	.272	70	243	21	66	12	1	7	40	0
95 NL	.215	62	219	17	47	14	1	2	15	0
96 NL	.270	119	407	48	110	23	0	13	55	4
Life	.256	851	2686	236	687	141	11	42	302	18
3 Ave	.257	96	332	32	85	19	1	8	43	1

RAFAEL PALMEIRO

Position: First base
Team: Baltimore Orioles
Born: Sept. 24, 1964 Havana, Cuba
Height: 6' **Weight:** 188 lbs.
Bats: left **Throws:** left
Acquired: Signed as a free agent, 12/93

PLAYER SUMMARY	
Fantasy Value.	$35 to $40
Card Value	15¢ to 25¢
Will	knock runs in
Can't	win recognition
Expect	power, defense
Don't Expect	letdown vs. lefties

A durable slugger who combines patience at the plate with good bat control, Palmeiro finished fourth in the league with a club-record 142 RBI last summer. He tied for fifth with 81 extra-base hits—39 of them homers—and placed seventh with 342 total bases. Yet he's the star nobody knows. Palmeiro hasn't been an All-Star since 1991, even though he's had three 100-RBI seasons since. Blessed with great bat speed, Palmeiro hits with power to all fields. Palmeiro missed only one game in 1996 (sprained right hand), giving him an average of 151 games per year over his nine-year career. A Cuban native, the Mississippi State product was an All-America outfielder before he switched to first base as a third-year pro. Palmeiro uses his speed to steal bases. His defense is often overlooked; he's led his position in chances, putouts, assists, and double plays.

Major League Batting Register

	BA	G	AB	R	H	2B	3B	HR	RBI	SB
86 NL	.247	22	73	9	18	4	0	3	12	1
87 NL	.276	84	221	32	61	15	1	14	30	2
88 NL	.307	152	580	75	178	41	5	8	53	12
89 AL	.275	156	559	76	154	23	4	8	64	4
90 AL	.319	154	598	72	191	35	6	14	89	3
91 AL	.322	159	631	115	203	49	3	26	88	4
92 AL	.268	159	608	84	163	27	4	22	85	2
93 AL	.295	160	597	124	176	40	2	37	105	22
94 AL	.311	111	436	82	139	32	0	23	76	7
95 AL	.310	143	554	89	172	30	2	39	104	3
96 AL	.289	162	626	110	181	40	2	39	142	8
Life	.298	1462	5483	868	1636	336	29	233	848	68
3 Ave	.305	160	621	109	190	40	1	38	122	7

DEAN PALMER

Position: Third base
Team: Texas Rangers
Born: Dec. 27, 1968 Tallahassee, FL
Height: 6'2" **Weight:** 195 lbs.
Bats: right **Throws:** right
Acquired: Third-round pick in 6/86 free-agent draft

PLAYER SUMMARY	
Fantasy Value	$25 to $30
Card Value	8¢ to 12¢
Will	show great power
Can't	stop striking out
Expect	best bat vs. lefties
Don't Expect	great defense

After missing two-thirds of 1995 with a ruptured biceps tendon in his left arm, Palmer proved both he and his bat were in top shape last summer. He delivered a personal-best 38 homers and finished with the first 100-RBI season of his career. He collected extra bases on 40 percent of his hits and hit .303 vs. lefties but fanned three times for every walk. Only four AL hitters fanned more often than Palmer, who went down 145 times. But the slugging third baseman, who has power to all fields, finished with the best full-season average of his career after responding to coaching tips about showing more patience at the plate and not pulling every pitch. Palmer walked enough to produce a respectable on-base percentage. Though no threat to steal, Palmer knows how to run the bases. His throwing still needs improvement, however. Palmer, who's led his position in errors twice, blew a Division Series game against the Yankees with a bad throw.

Major League Batting Register

	BA	G	AB	R	H	2B	3B	HR	RBI	SB
89 AL	.105	16	19	0	2	2	0	0	1	0
91 AL	.187	81	268	38	50	9	2	15	37	0
92 AL	.229	152	541	74	124	25	0	26	72	10
93 AL	.245	148	519	88	127	31	2	33	96	11
94 AL	.246	93	342	50	84	14	2	19	59	3
95 AL	.336	36	119	30	40	6	0	9	24	1
96 AL	.280	154	582	98	163	26	2	38	107	2
Life	.247	680	2390	378	590	113	8	140	396	27
2 Ave	.264	143	532	84	141	23	2	32	95	3

CRAIG PAQUETTE

Position: Outfield; third base
Team: Kansas City Royals
Born: March 28, 1969 Long Beach, CA
Height: 6' **Weight:** 190 lbs.
Bats: right **Throws:** right
Acquired: Signed as a minor-league free agent, 4/96

PLAYER SUMMARY	
Fantasy Value	$9 to $11
Card Value	4¢ to 7¢
Will	crush mistakes
Can't	get on base
Expect	platoon duty
Don't Expect	much speed

Cut loose by the Oakland Athletics at the end of 1996 spring training, Paquette signed on with the Royals and made his way back to the majors. A third baseman by trade, he was mostly used in left field by Kansas City manager Bob Boone. While he did not provide especially good defense when used in the outfield, Paquette supplied good power to a generally punchless Kansas City lineup, especially when asked to face right-handed pitchers. Paquette would be an even more useful player if he could improve his knowledge of the strike zone; during the 1996 season he struck out 101 times and took only 23 walks, leading to an extremely poor on-base percentage of .296. Although Paquette would be advised to improve his patience at the plate, he has never shown signs of doing so. His power will keep him in the majors, at least as a part-timer, for several more years. However, he will never be considered a dependable regular unless he learns not to swing at so many bad pitches.

Major League Batting Register

	BA	G	AB	R	H	2B	3B	HR	RBI	SB
93 AL	.219	105	393	35	86	20	4	12	46	4
94 AL	.143	14	49	0	7	2	0	0	0	1
95 AL	.226	105	283	42	64	13	1	13	49	5
96 AL	.259	118	429	61	111	15	1	22	67	5
Life	.232	342	1154	138	268	50	6	47	162	15
2 Ave	.245	118	374	54	92	15	1	18	61	5

MARK PARENT

Position: Catcher
Team: Philadelphia Phillies
Born: Sept. 16, 1961 Ashford, OR
Height: 6'5" **Weight:** 240 lbs.
Bats: right **Throws:** right
Acquired: Signed as a free agent, 12/96

PLAYER SUMMARY	
Fantasy Value $1
Card Value . . . . 4¢ to 7¢
Will. . . . . hit for power
Can't. . . . . play regularly
Expect. . . . . decent defense
Don't Expect . . . . job security

The veteran backstop started the year in Detroit, sharing catching duties with John Flaherty. Parent, who has always had good power at bat, provided some pop but once again could not win an everyday job. When catcher Brad Ausmus was acquired from the Padres in June, the writing was on the wall for Parent. Rumors that he would be traded or released circulated around the Motor City all season, and he was finally placed on waivers in late August when Detroit brought Raul Casanova back from the DL and called up Phil Nevin, a third baseman being converted to catcher, from the minors. Parent quickly hooked on with Baltimore, who had previously employed him in 1992 and '93, and settled into his familiar backup role. Parent uses his strong throwing arm to nail most potential basestealers. However, given his age and history, Parent's career may be winding down.

Major League Batting Register

	BA	G	AB	R	H	2B	3B	HR	RBI	SB
86 NL	.143	8	14	1	2	0	0	0	0	0
87 NL	.080	12	25	0	2	0	0	0	2	0
88 NL	.195	41	118	9	23	3	0	6	15	0
89 NL	.191	52	141	12	27	4	0	7	21	1
90 NL	.222	65	189	13	42	11	0	3	16	1
91 AL	.000	3	1	0	0	0	0	0	0	0
92 AL	.235	17	34	4	8	1	0	2	4	0
93 AL	.259	22	54	7	14	2	0	4	12	0
94 NL	.263	44	99	8	26	4	0	3	16	0
95 NL	.234	81	265	30	62	11	0	18	38	0
96 AL	.226	56	137	17	31	7	0	9	23	0
Life	.220	401	1077	101	237	43	0	52	147	2

CHAN HO PARK

Position: Pitcher
Team: Los Angeles Dodgers
Born: June 30, 1973 Kong Ju City, Korea
Height: 6'2" **Weight:** 185 lbs.
Bats: right **Throws:** right
Acquired: Signed as a free agent, 1/94

PLAYER SUMMARY	
Fantasy Value. . . . . $5 to $7
Card Value . . . . 7¢ to 10¢
Will . . . . hurl fastball
Can't. . . . . be consistent
Expect . . . . continued improvement
Don't Expect . . . . perfect control

The young South Korean right-hander essentially jumped from Double-A San Antonio in 1995 to Los Angeles in 1996 on the basis of a strong spring training. Blessed with loads of talent, Park has been a raw pitcher up to now. He has a good live fastball but doesn't have control of his offspeed pitches yet. Park was used primarily in long relief, with an occasional fill-in start. He struck out one batter an inning and averaged well under one hit per inning. His only flaw on the mound is a problem with control; he walked far too many hitters last season. The major news item concerning Park during the 1996 season was a team prank played on him that went awry, with Chan Ho alienating many of his teammates with his reaction to the harmless tomfoolery. Following his apprenticeship in the bullpen, Park is ready to be a part of the Dodgers five-man rotation and will likely get his chance in 1997. Given his talent, youth, and potential box-office stature, Park will be a mainstay on the Dodgers staff for years to come.

Major League Pitching Register

	W	L	ERA	G	S	IP	H	ER	BB	SO
94 NL	0	0	11.25	2	0	4.0	5	5	5	6
95 NL	0	0	4.50	2	0	4.0	2	2	2	7
96 NL	5	5	3.64	48	0	108.2	82	44	71	119
Life	5	5	3.93	52	0	116.2	89	51	78	132

BOB PATTERSON

Position: Pitcher
Team: Chicago Cubs
Born: May 16, 1959 Jacksonville, FL
Height: 6'2" **Weight:** 192 lbs.
Bats: right **Throws:** left
Acquired: Signed as a free agent, 1/96

PLAYER SUMMARY	
Fantasy Value	$3 to $5
Card Value	4¢ to 7¢
Will	get out lefties
Can't	be a closer
Expect	frequent appearances
Don't Expect	blazing fastballs

During the early part of 1996, Patterson was the Cubs' most consistent (some would say the only consistent) reliever. Used in a variety of roles, including closer, set-up man, and one-out lefty, he became the busiest member of the bullpen. Unfortunately, as the year went on, the 37-year-old Patterson began to show the strain. For most of the year, he was the only lefty on the entire staff, and being used (or asked to warm up) nearly every day seemed to wear Patterson out. Although he was far less effective in the last two months, Patterson still pitched well enough on balance to ensure himself a job for 1997. Patterson, a quiet, religious man, was not always at ease in the boisterous Chicago clubhouse. A decent all-around athlete, Patterson has never committed an error in his major-league career and could hang on a few more years.

Major League Pitching Register

	W	L	ERA	G	S	IP	H	ER	BB	SO
85 NL	0	0	24.75	3	0	4.0	13	11	3	1
86 NL	2	3	4.95	11	0	36.1	49	20	5	20
87 NL	1	4	6.70	15	0	43.0	49	32	22	27
89 NL	4	3	4.05	12	1	26.2	23	12	8	20
90 NL	8	5	2.95	55	5	94.2	88	31	21	70
91 NL	4	3	4.11	54	2	65.2	67	30	15	57
92 NL	6	3	2.92	60	9	64.2	59	21	23	43
93 AL	2	4	4.78	52	1	52.2	59	28	11	46
94 AL	2	3	4.07	47	1	42.0	35	19	15	30
95 AL	5	2	3.04	62	0	53.1	48	18	13	41
96 NL	3	3	3.13	79	8	54.2	46	19	22	53
Life	37	33	4.03	450	27	537.2	536	241	158	408
3 Ave	4	3	3.42	72	3	58.0	50	22	19	47

ROGER PAVLIK

Position: Pitcher
Team: Texas Rangers
Born: Oct. 4, 1967 Houston, TX
Height: 6'3" **Weight:** 220 lbs.
Bats: right **Throws:** right
Acquired: Second-round pick in 2/86 free-agent draft

PLAYER SUMMARY	
Fantasy Value	$8 to $10
Card Value	5¢ to 8¢
Will	start if healthy
Can't	win a Cy Young
Expect	control struggles
Don't Expect	opponents to run

1996 was an odd season for Pavlik, who had his share of ups and downs but came down firmly on the upside. The oft-injured Pavlik's chief accomplishments were to stay healthy and to benefit from the nearly 6.5 runs per game his Rangers teammates scored for him. Despite going through the season's first half with an ERA over 5.00, Pavlik racked up the victories and made the All-Star Team. On May 5 at Detroit, he tossed a one-hitter to raise his record to 5-0. Pavlik was 12-2 at one point before dropping four straight games, including a June 29 loss to Seattle in which he allowed seven runs in the first inning. Left-handers continued to be Pavlik's nemesis, as they hit well over .280 against him with good power. The frequently wild Pavlik cut down on his walk total in 1996, but he continued to have problems when pitching behind in the count. If Pavlik can stay off the disabled list and provide innings, Texas manager Johnny Oates won't care if Pavlik wins an ERA title or not.

Major League Pitching Register

	W	L	ERA	G	CG	IP	H	ER	BB	SO
92 AL	4	4	4.21	13	1	62.0	66	29	34	45
93 AL	12	6	3.41	26	2	166.1	151	63	80	131
94 AL	2	5	7.69	11	0	50.1	61	43	30	31
95 AL	10	10	4.37	31	2	191.2	174	93	90	149
96 AL	15	8	5.19	34	7	201.0	216	116	81	127
Life	43	33	4.61	115	12	671.1	668	344	315	483
2 Ave	13	10	4.77	34	5	208.1	206	110	91	147

TONY PENA

Position: Catcher
Team: Cleveland Indians
Born: June 4, 1957 Monti Cristi, Dominican Republic
Height: 6′ **Weight:** 185 lbs.
Bats: right **Throws:** right
Acquired: Signed as a minor-league free agent, 12/95

PLAYER SUMMARY	
Fantasy Value	$0
Card Value	4¢ to 7¢
Will	handle pitchers well
Can't	hit much
Expect	reserve duty
Don't Expect	mental mistakes

Regular Indians catcher Sandy Alomar, who has a history of missing significant time to injuries, stayed remarkably healthy in 1996. As a result, Pena got into just 67 games. His measly .255 on-base percentage and even poorer .236 slugging percentage ranked worst in baseball for players with more than 150 at bats. While Pena threw out 38 percent of potential basestealers and handled the pitching staff admirably, his offense was simply unacceptable. Chances are young catching prospect Einar Diaz will need another year of seasoning, so Pena is likely to have an opportunity to fight for his job this spring.

Major League Batting Register

	BA	G	AB	R	H	2B	3B	HR	RBI	SB
80 NL	.429	8	21	1	9	1	1	0	1	0
81 NL	.300	66	210	16	63	9	1	2	17	1
82 NL	.296	138	497	53	147	28	4	11	63	2
83 NL	.301	151	542	51	163	22	3	15	70	6
84 NL	.286	147	546	77	156	27	2	15	78	12
85 NL	.249	147	546	53	136	27	2	10	59	12
86 NL	.288	144	510	56	147	26	2	10	52	9
87 NL	.214	116	384	40	82	13	4	5	44	6
88 NL	.263	149	505	55	133	23	1	10	51	6
89 NL	.259	141	424	36	110	17	2	4	37	5
90 AL	.263	143	491	62	129	19	1	7	56	8
91 AL	.231	141	464	45	107	23	2	5	48	8
92 AL	.241	133	410	39	99	21	1	1	38	3
93 AL	.181	126	304	20	55	11	0	4	19	1
94 AL	.295	40	112	18	33	8	1	2	10	0
95 AL	.262	91	263	25	69	15	0	5	28	1
96 AL	.195	67	174	14	34	4	0	1	27	0
Life	.261	1948	6403	661	1672	294	27	107	698	80
2 Ave	.238	85	235	21	56	10	0	3	29	1

TERRY PENDLETON

Position: Third base
Team: Atlanta Braves
Born: July 16, 1960 Los Angeles, CA
Height: 5′9″ **Weight:** 195 lbs.
Bats: both **Throws:** right
Acquired: Traded by Marlins for Roosevelt Brown, 8/96

PLAYER SUMMARY	
Fantasy Value	$5 to $7
Card Value	4¢ to 7¢
Will	play good defense
Can't	excel with bat
Expect	clubhouse leadership
Don't Expect	much speed

Despite a reputation as a gamer and a positive force in the clubhouse, the aging and worn-down Pendleton is clearly on the downside of his career. After a decent performance in 1995, he did not provide the Marlins with much offense last season. Rumors that he would be dealt swirled around South Florida all summer, and on August 14 Pendleton was shipped to Atlanta. Pendleton's arrival sent incumbent Braves third baseman Chipper Jones to shortstop, a move the youngster accepted gracefully. However, despite Pendleton's value in the clubhouse, he did not hit well for Atlanta. He no longer runs well and he hit under .200 vs. lefties last year. Pendleton has risen from the ashes before, but expecting him to revive his career despite age and injury may be asking too much.

Major League Batting Register

	BA	G	AB	R	H	2B	3B	HR	RBI	SB
84 NL	.324	67	262	37	85	16	3	1	33	20
85 NL	.240	149	559	56	134	16	3	5	69	17
86 NL	.239	159	578	56	138	26	5	1	59	24
87 NL	.286	159	583	82	167	29	4	12	96	19
88 NL	.253	110	391	44	99	20	2	6	53	3
89 NL	.264	162	613	83	162	28	5	13	74	9
90 NL	.230	121	447	46	103	20	2	6	58	7
91 NL	.319	153	586	94	187	34	6	22	86	10
92 NL	.311	160	640	98	199	39	1	21	105	5
93 NL	.272	161	633	81	172	33	1	17	84	5
94 NL	.252	77	309	25	78	18	3	7	30	2
95 NL	.290	133	513	70	149	32	1	14	78	1
96 NL	.238	153	568	51	135	26	1	11	75	2
Life	.271	1764	6682	823	1808	337	39	136	900	124
3 Ave	.261	137	527	55	138	29	2	12	68	2

TROY PERCIVAL

Position: Pitcher
Team: Anaheim Angels
Born: Aug. 3, 1969 Fontana, CA
Height: 6'3" **Weight:** 200 lbs.
Bats: right **Throws:** right
Acquired: Sixth-round pick in 6/90 free-agent draft

PLAYER SUMMARY	
Fantasy Value	$30 to $35
Card Value	7¢ to 10¢
Will	blow opponents away
Can't	hold runners
Expect	frequent saves
Don't Expect	many problems

Percival set the tone for 1996 on April 7, when he picked up his first save of the season by striking out Chicago's fearsome Frank Thomas to close out a 6-5 Angels win. The intimidating Percival, who features a fastball nearing 100 mph and a devastating slider, pumped his fist and shouted as Thomas walked off the field. The incident was indicative of Percival's confidence as well as of his ability. Slated before the season to split closing duties with veteran Lee Smith, Percival took advantage of Smith's off-season knee injury to claim closing duties for himself. After Percival breezed through his first ten games without allowing a run, Smith quickly became a forgotten man and was later traded to Cincinnati. In a terrible season for the Angels, the hard-throwing, aggressive Percival was one of the only bright spots. In just his second season in the majors, he held AL hitters—both right-handed and left-handed—to batting averages under .150, gave up only 31 walks, and allowed just eight home runs in converting 36 save opportunities.

Major League Pitching Register

	W	L	ERA	G	S	IP	H	ER	BB	SO
95 AL	3	2	1.95	62	3	74.0	37	16	26	94
96 AL	0	2	2.31	62	36	74.0	38	19	31	100
Life	3	4	2.13	124	39	148.0	75	35	57	194
2 Ave	2	2	2.12	66	20	79.1	40	19	30	103

CARLOS PEREZ

Position: Pitcher
Team: Montreal Expos
Born: Jan. 14, 1971 Nigua, Dominican Republic
Height: 6'3" **Weight:** 195 lbs.
Bats: left **Throws:** left
Acquired: Signed as a free agent, 7/88

PLAYER SUMMARY	
Fantasy Value	$3 to $5
Card Value	7¢ to 10¢
Will	start if healthy
Can't	afford walks
Expect	decent stuff
Don't Expect	instant recovery

The Expos expected Perez to carry a big share of the pitching load in 1996, but instead he carried none. During spring training, the brother of Pascual, Yorkis, and Melido (all past or present big-league pitchers) came up with a sore shoulder. After several diagnoses, two of which contradicted each other concerning the seriousness of the problem, Perez was found to be suffering from a partially torn rotator cuff and a torn labrum in the shoulder. Although Perez, the Expos, and the doctors all said the eccentric young left-hander could be back on the mound in a few months, nothing was heard from Perez for the rest of the season. He will come to spring training in 1997 in an attempt to regain his place in the Montreal rotation, but he will probably have lost some of the velocity on his fastball and forkball, as is often the case with pitchers recovering from shoulder injuries. Perez's strong arsenal and wild on-the-hill antics made him headline news in 1995, and the Expos—and Perez—hope for more good copy in 1997.

Major League Pitching Register

	W	L	ERA	G	CG	IP	H	ER	BB	SO
95 NL	10	8	3.69	28	2	141.1	142	58	28	106
Life	10	8	3.69	28	2	141.1	142	58	28	106

EDDIE PEREZ

Position: Catcher
Team: Atlanta Braves
Born: May 4, 1968 Ciudad Ojeda, Venezuela
Height: 6'1" **Weight:** 175 lbs.
Bats: right **Throws:** right
Acquired: Signed as a free agent, 9/86

PLAYER SUMMARY	
Fantasy Value	$0
Card Value	7¢ to 10¢
Will	show good arm
Can't	win regular job
Expect	decent offense
Don't Expect	any speed

After eight seasons in the minor leagues, Perez got his first shot at the majors in September 1995. In his seven games with Atlanta, he hit well enough and showed a good enough range of defensive skills for the Braves to include him on the postseason roster, even though Perez did not play. With the loss of veteran backup Charlie O'Brien in '96, Perez became the club's second-string catcher and performed admirably. He spent most of the year as Greg Maddux's personal catcher (even though Javy Lopez took over as Maddux's battery mate midway through the NLCS) and showed acceptable offensive totals. Never much of a hitter in the minors, Perez nonetheless showed power for the Braves and hit .274 against right-handers. He drew just eight walks on the season, however, and had a poor .293 on-base percentage. However, he was praised for his game-calling and threw out 33 percent of enemy basestealers. Like most catchers, Perez is slow but reacts well behind the plate. He has proved his worth to Bobby Cox and is now in position to enjoy several seasons as a quality major-league reserve.

Major League Batting Register

	BA	G	AB	R	H	2B	3B	HR	RBI	SB
95 NL	.308	7	13	1	4	1	0	1	4	0
96 NL	.256	68	156	19	40	9	1	4	17	0
Life	.260	75	169	20	44	10	1	5	21	0

MELIDO PEREZ

Position: Pitcher
Team: New York Yankees
Born: Feb. 15, 1966 San Cristobal, Dominican Republic
Height: 6'4" **Weight:** 210 lbs.
Bats: right **Throws:** right
Acquired: Traded by White Sox with Domingo Jean and Bob Wickman for Steve Sax, 1/92

PLAYER SUMMARY	
Fantasy Value	$3 to $5
Card Value	4¢ to 7¢
Will	try again
Can't	count on health
Expect	swing duty
Don't Expect	splitter of old

A shoulder injury suffered in mid-1995 kept Perez sidelined for that season's second half. Melido reported to 1996 spring training ready to work as a long reliever-spot starter for the Yankees, but he could not throw with his old strength. His elbow began to trouble him, and Perez was diagnosed with bone chips in the elbow. He underwent surgery to remove them April 5. He began throwing soon afterward and was sent on a rehab assignment in July. Unfortunately, his elbow never responded favorably, and his shoulder began to hurt as well. Finally, in August, the Yankees decided to shut him down for the year. Now that he is a free agent, Perez will try to regain a spot on somebody's staff, but he will first have to prove he is healthy. When he was at full strength, Melido had perhaps the best hard split-fingered fastball in the game and also threw a dizzying array of other pitches.

Major League Pitching Register

	W	L	ERA	G	CG	IP	H	ER	BB	SO
87 AL	1	1	7.84	3	0	10.1	18	9	5	5
88 AL	12	10	3.79	32	3	197.0	186	83	72	138
89 AL	11	14	5.01	31	2	183.1	187	102	90	141
90 AL	13	14	4.61	35	3	197.0	177	101	86	161
91 AL	8	7	3.12	49	0	135.2	111	47	52	128
92 AL	13	16	2.87	33	10	247.2	212	79	93	218
93 AL	6	14	5.19	25	0	163.0	173	94	64	148
94 AL	9	4	4.10	22	1	151.1	134	69	58	109
95 AL	5	5	5.58	13	1	69.1	70	43	31	44
Life	.78	85	4.17	243	20	1354.2	1268	627	551	1092

ROBERT PEREZ

Position: Outfield
Team: Toronto Blue Jays
Born: June 4, 1969 Bolivar, Venezuela
Height: 6'3" **Weight:** 205 lbs.
Bats: right **Throws:** right
Acquired: Signed as a free agent, 5/89

PLAYER SUMMARY

Fantasy Value	$1
Card Value	5¢ to 8¢
Will	hit for average
Can't	show power
Expect	fair defense
Don't Expect	many walks

The moribund Blue Jays could hardly keep Perez down on the farm any longer after he won the 1995 International League batting crown by hitting .343 at Syracuse. Toronto management had never thought Perez would do enough offensively to be a quality major-league regular, but manager Cito Gaston gave him 202 at bats in 1996 and was rewarded. Perez has plenty of drawbacks: He rarely walks (just eight free passes in '96), does not have much power, does not steal many bases, and is only a mediocre outfielder. However, .327 hitters are hard to find, and Perez battered left-handers (.329) as well as righties (.322) in his rookie campaign. Perez struck out only 17 times and showed a good ability to move runners along and make contact against tough pitchers. Gaston used Perez mainly in left field but platooned him on occasion with lefty-swinging Shawn Green in right. At worst, Perez is a useful platoon player and reserve, and he might even luck into an everyday job should the Blue Jays decide to jettison some of their veteran players.

TOMAS PEREZ

Position: Second base
Team: Toronto Blue Jays
Born: Dec. 29, 1973 Barquisimeto, Venezuela
Height: 5'11" **Weight:** 165 lbs.
Bats: right **Throws:** right
Acquired: Purchased from Angels, 12/94

PLAYER SUMMARY

Fantasy Value	$0
Card Value	5¢ to 8¢
Will	impress with arm
Can't	show speed
Expect	fine glove
Don't Expect	extra-base hits

Perez was originally an Expos prospect plucked out of Class-A in the December 1994 Rule V draft. The Angels, who chose Perez, immediately sold him to the Blue Jays, who have kept him at the major-league level for much of the last two seasons. He was used as an emergency shortstop in 1995, but the athletic young Perez spent last season as the closest thing to a regular second baseman that Toronto had. Perez is not much of a hitter at this point, showing little power, speed, or on-base ability, but he is still very young and should develop with experience. He is a fine defensive player, blessed with an outstanding arm and good range. He did commit 15 errors in making the transition from shortstop to second base—but that is to be expected. Perez missed some time late in August after jamming a shoulder sliding into a base, but the injury should not have any lasting effect. Although the young infielder could well return to the minors this season to continue his development, the Blue Jays still lack an everyday second-sacker. The club might simply decide to let Perez grow into the job.

Major League Batting Register

	BA	G	AB	R	H	2B	3B	HR	RBI	SB
94 AL	.125	4	8	0	1	0	0	0	0	0
95 AL	.188	17	48	2	9	2	0	1	3	0
96 AL	.327	86	202	30	66	10	0	2	21	3
Life	.295	107	258	32	76	12	0	3	24	3

Major League Batting Register

	BA	G	AB	R	H	2B	3B	HR	RBI	SB
95 AL	.245	41	98	12	24	3	1	1	8	0
96 AL	.251	91	295	24	74	13	4	1	19	1
Life	.249	132	393	36	98	16	5	2	27	1

YORKIS PEREZ

Position: Pitcher
Team: Atlanta Braves
Born: Sept. 30, 1967 Bajos de Haina, Dominican Republic
Height: 6' **Weight:** 180 lbs.
Bats: left **Throws:** left
Acquired: Traded by Marlins for Martin Sanchez, 12/96

PLAYER SUMMARY	
Fantasy Value	$0
Card Value	4¢ to 7¢
Will	struggle with control
Can't	lose confidence
Expect	short appearances
Don't Expect	saves

It is difficult to be a left-handed reliever in the major leagues. Many times, a lefty short man is brought in to face just one hitter, who is often the best hitter the other team has to offer. It is Yorkis Perez's job to fill that role for the Florida Marlins, and 1996 was far from a smooth season. Perez had bigger-than-expected control problems, which led to frequent bases on balls and an average of almost .300 from opposing left-handers—the very hitters he was being brought in to get out. Unfortunately, it is difficult to fight out of a slump when facing only one or two hitters a game. Perez was demoted to Triple-A twice during the 1996 season, only to be recalled due to injuries to other pitchers. The Marlins are not at all happy with Perez's performance and have been grooming rookie Felix Heredia to take the left-handed short job in 1997. Perez, who has been pitching as a professional since 1983, may have to go to the minors yet again to regain his confidence and command.

Major League Pitching Register

	W	L	ERA	G	S	IP	H	ER	BB	SO
91 NL	1	0	2.08	3	0	4.1	2	1	2	3
94 NL	3	0	3.54	44	0	40.2	33	16	14	41
95 NL	2	6	5.21	69	1	46.2	35	27	28	47
96 NL	3	4	5.29	64	0	47.2	51	28	31	47
Life	9	10	4.65	180	1	139.1	121	72	75	138
3 Ave	3	4	4.63	68	0	52.1	46	27	27	53

ANDY PETTITTE

Position: Pitcher
Team: New York Yankees
Born: June 15, 1972 Baton Rouge, LA
Height: 6'5" **Weight:** 220 lbs.
Bats: left **Throws:** left
Acquired: Signed as a free agent, 5/91

PLAYER SUMMARY	
Fantasy Value	$20 to $25
Card Value	15¢ to 25¢
Will	hold runners close
Can't	get left-handers
Expect	quality innings
Don't Expect	many strikeouts

Pettitte blossomed into one of baseball's best pitchers in 1996. He became the youngest pitcher to start a home opener for the Yankees in 86 years, and for most of the season he was the only constant in a New York rotation hampered by injuries and ineffectiveness. Benefiting from a regular turn in the rotation and good offensive support, Pettitte became the first AL pitcher to win 20 games by whipping Oakland 10-3 on September 4. He missed a couple of weeks with an elbow injury but came back strong down the stretch. Left-handers give Pettitte trouble (they hit well over .300 against him in 1996), but the southpaw frustrates right-handers by running his fastball and curve in on their fists. Pettitte doesn't have an especially good fastball, but he throws a good, hard slider and will use his curve at any time. He has one of the best pickoff moves in the AL and is an excellent fielder. Although he is not a dominant strikeout pitcher, Pettitte is clearly the Yankees' ace. He finished second in 1996 Cy Young Award voting in an extremely close race.

Major League Pitching Register

	W	L	ERA	G	CG	IP	H	ER	BB	SO
95 AL	12	9	4.17	31	3	175.0	183	81	63	114
96 AL	21	8	3.87	35	2	221.0	229	95	72	162
Life	33	17	4.00	66	5	396.0	412	176	135	276
2 Ave	17	9	4.01	35	3	209.0	217	93	71	145

TONY PHILLIPS

Position: Outfield
Team: Chicago White Sox
Born: April 15, 1959 Atlanta, GA
Height: 5'10" **Weight:** 175 lbs.
Bats: both **Throws:** right
Acquired: Signed as a free agent, 1/96

PLAYER SUMMARY	
Fantasy Value	$7 to $9
Card Value	7¢ to 10¢
Will	be on base
Can't	control his temper
Expect	good defense
Don't Expect	blazing speed

The fiery Phillips, who was not offered a contract by the cost-cutting Angels after an excellent 1995 season, took his hard-nosed style and effective leadoff skills to the White Sox and jump-started Chicago's offense. Drawing over 100 walks and scoring over 100 runs for the fourth time, Phillips had a great .404 on-base percentage and did a terrific job setting the table for White Sox power hitters. After spending most of 1995 at third base, Phillips took over in left field for Chicago and established himself as one of the better defenders at the position. Phillips also brought his ultra-competitive (some would say excessively combative) demeanor to what had been a too-staid White Sox clubhouse. Phillips is one of baseball's best leadoff men.

Major League Batting Register

	BA	G	AB	R	H	2B	3B	HR	RBI	SB
82 AL	.210	40	81	11	17	2	2	0	8	2
83 AL	.248	148	412	54	102	12	3	4	35	16
84 AL	.266	154	451	62	120	24	3	4	37	10
85 AL	.280	42	161	23	45	12	2	4	17	3
86 AL	.256	118	441	76	113	14	5	5	52	15
87 AL	.240	111	379	48	91	20	0	10	46	7
88 AL	.203	79	212	32	43	8	4	2	17	0
89 AL	.262	143	451	48	118	15	6	4	47	3
90 AL	.251	152	573	97	144	23	5	8	55	19
91 AL	.284	146	564	87	160	28	4	17	72	10
92 AL	.276	159	606	114	167	32	3	10	64	12
93 AL	.313	151	566	113	177	27	0	7	57	16
94 AL	.281	114	438	91	123	19	3	19	61	13
95 AL	.261	139	525	119	137	21	1	27	61	13
96 AL	.277	153	581	119	161	29	3	12	63	13
Life	.267	1849	6441	1094	1718	286	44	133	692	152
3 Ave	.273	157	596	127	163	26	3	23	73	15

MIKE PIAZZA

Position: Catcher
Team: Los Angeles Dodgers
Born: Sept. 4, 1968 Norristown, PA
Height: 6'3" **Weight:** 197 lbs.
Bats: right **Throws:** right
Acquired: 62nd-round pick in 6/88 free-agent draft

PLAYER SUMMARY	
Fantasy Value	$40 to $45
Card Value	50¢ to $1
Will	earn walks
Can't	afford knee problems
Expect	awesome power
Don't Expect	great defense

Enjoying yet another spectacular season, Piazza led the Dodgers' playoff charge by winning his first batting title and establishing himself as one of the only legitimate Triple Crown candidates in the game. Early in the year, with the entire L.A. lineup slumping, Piazza got nothing to hit and was reduced to taking outside sinkers to right field for singles. As Piazza began to get better pitches, he proved he knew what to do with them. He also drew 81 walks, showing a level of patience only hinted at in the past. His on-base percentage was a superb .422. Unfortunately, in the midst of his great year, Piazza had injury problems. His knees took a beating behind the plate, and it was almost a certainty that he would undergo surgery following the season. His defensive skills have never been very good, and his mobility and throwing ability were greatly reduced by his sore knees. There is talk that Piazza could eventually be converted to first base, but for now he refuses to even discuss such a move.

Major League Batting Register

	BA	G	AB	R	H	2B	3B	HR	RBI	SB
92 NL	.232	21	69	5	16	3	0	1	7	0
93 NL	.318	149	547	81	174	24	2	35	112	3
94 NL	.319	107	405	64	129	18	0	24	92	1
95 NL	.346	112	434	82	150	17	0	32	93	1
96 NL	.336	148	547	87	184	16	0	36	105	0
Life	.326	537	2002	319	653	78	2	128	409	5
3 Ave	.333	142	535	90	178	20	0	35	113	1

HIPOLITO PICHARDO

Position: Pitcher
Team: Kansas City Royals
Born: Aug. 22, 1969 Jicome Esperanza, Dominican Republic
Height: 6'1" **Weight:** 185 lbs.
Bats: right **Throws:** right
Acquired: Signed as a free agent, 12/87

PLAYER SUMMARY	
Fantasy Value	$0
Card Value	4¢ to 7¢
Will	pitch often
Can't	expand his role
Expect	ground balls
Don't Expect	save opportunities

Pichardo set a career high for appearances (57), leading the Royals mound staff in that category during 1996. However, the wiry reliever continued to have problems establishing consistency. He had stretches where he simply could not get anybody out, and he clearly could not handle closing duties late in the season when Jeff Montgomery was sidelined with shoulder problems. Right-handers batted nearly .300 against Pichardo, who walked too many hitters for comfort and allowed one-third of his inherited runners to score. However, Pichardo continued to do some things right. He showed good velocity and movement on his sinker, allowed just five home runs on the season, and stayed healthy throughout the campaign after missing action in 1995 due to a sore shoulder. Most of Pichardo's hits are singles, and if he can cut down on his walks in 1997, he should again be effective in the middle relief role. The Royals, thin in decent relief pitching, are counting on him to do so.

Major League Pitching Register

	W	L	ERA	G	S	IP	H	ER	BB	SO
92 AL	9	6	3.95	31	0	143.2	148	63	49	59
93 AL	7	8	4.04	30	0	165.0	183	74	53	70
94 AL	5	3	4.92	45	3	67.2	82	37	24	36
95 AL	8	4	4.36	44	1	64.0	66	31	30	43
96 AL	3	5	5.43	57	3	68.0	74	41	26	43
Life	32	26	4.36	207	7	508.1	553	246	182	251
3 Ave	6	5	4.90	57	3	78.1	88	43	31	47

DAN PLESAC

Position: Pitcher
Team: Toronto Blue Jays
Born: Feb. 4, 1962 Gary, IN
Height: 6'5" **Weight:** 215 lbs.
Bats: left **Throws:** left
Acquired: Traded by Pirates with Carlos Garcia and Orlando Merced for Jose Pett, Jose Silva, Branden Cromer, and three players to be named later, 11/96

PLAYER SUMMARY	
Fantasy Value	$5 to $7
Card Value	4¢ to 7¢
Will	pitch often
Can't	carry a staff
Expect	decent fastball
Don't Expect	lefties to hit him

For the last two seasons, Plesac has served as an effective left-handed short man for the Pirates. Plesac still throws reasonably hard and has cut his walks down dramatically in the last few seasons. He has a long delivery and is fairly easy to run on, but he keeps the ball in the park (just four homers allowed in 1996). He is even better against left-handed hitters than he is against righties. As a capable lefty reliever, Plesac is a valuable commodity; there were rumors he would be traded to a contending team in August, but several noncontending teams claimed him on waivers, killing any possible deals. He eventually was packaged with Carlos Garcia and Orlando Merced in an off-season trade with Toronto.

Major League Pitching Register

	W	L	ERA	G	S	IP	H	ER	BB	SO
86 AL	10	7	2.97	51	14	91.0	81	30	29	75
87 AL	5	6	2.61	57	23	79.1	63	23	23	89
88 AL	1	2	2.41	50	30	52.1	46	14	12	52
89 AL	3	4	2.35	52	33	61.1	47	16	17	52
90 AL	3	7	4.43	66	24	69.0	67	34	31	65
91 AL	2	7	4.29	45	8	92.1	92	44	39	61
92 AL	5	4	2.96	44	1	79.0	64	26	35	54
93 NL	2	1	4.74	57	0	62.2	74	33	21	47
94 NL	2	3	4.61	54	1	54.2	61	28	13	53
95 NL	4	4	3.58	58	3	60.1	53	24	27	57
96 NL	6	5	4.09	73	11	70.1	67	32	24	76
Life	43	50	3.54	607	148	772.1	715	304	271	681
3 Ave	4	5	4.12	71	5	72.1	71	33	24	72

ERIC PLUNK

Position: Pitcher
Team: Cleveland Indians
Born: Sept. 3, 1963 Wilmington, CA
Height: 6'6" **Weight:** 220 lbs.
Bats: right **Throws:** right
Acquired: Signed as a free agent, 4/92

PLAYER SUMMARY	
Fantasy Value	$4 to $6
Card Value	4¢ to 7¢
Will	get strikeouts
Can't	hold runners
Expect	success against righties
Don't Expect	closing duties

Earlier in his career, Plunk was viewed as a potential closer due to his outstanding fastball and good slider. However, the oversized right-hander had serious control problems and slid into middle relief. Something seemed to click a couple of years ago with Cleveland, and now Plunk is a valuable part of an excellent relief staff. Early in 1996, Plunk had some trouble, but by May he had piled up a 13-game string in which he allowed just one run. By season's end, he had put up strong numbers once again for one of the deepest bullpens in baseball. A clearly defined role—setting up in the seventh and eighth innings—has enabled Plunk to concentrate on improving his command. His deliberate motion allows runners to steal bases off him, but he doesn't give up many extra-base hits and holds right-handers to a puny average.

Major League Pitching Register

	W	L	ERA	G	S	IP	H	ER	BB	SO
86 AL	4	7	5.31	26	0	120.1	91	71	102	98
87 AL	4	6	4.74	32	2	95.0	91	50	62	90
88 AL	7	2	3.00	49	5	78.0	62	26	39	79
89 AL	8	6	3.28	50	1	104.1	82	38	64	85
90 AL	6	3	2.72	47	0	72.2	58	22	43	67
91 AL	2	5	4.76	43	0	111.2	128	59	62	103
92 AL	9	6	3.64	58	4	71.2	61	29	38	50
93 AL	4	5	2.79	70	15	71.0	61	22	30	77
94 AL	7	2	2.54	41	3	71.0	61	20	37	73
95 AL	6	2	2.67	56	2	64.0	48	19	27	71
96 AL	3	2	2.43	56	2	77.2	56	21	34	85
Life	60	46	3.62	528	34	937.1	799	377	538	878
3 Ave	7	2	2.54	59	3	83.1	65	24	39	89

LUIS POLONIA

Position: Outfield
Team: Atlanta Braves
Born: Oct. 12, 1964 Santiago City, Dominican Republic
Height: 5'8" **Weight:** 150 lbs.
Bats: left **Throws:** left
Acquired: Claimed from Orioles on waivers, 8/96

PLAYER SUMMARY	
Fantasy Value	$1
Card Value	4¢ to 7¢
Will	come off the bench
Can't	shine on defense
Expect	a decent average
Don't Expect	extra-base hits

The veteran outfielder continued his journey as an itinerant laborer in 1996. Polonia came to spring training with the Mariners hoping to play left field but was cut near the end of camp in what looked like a cost-slashing move by the team. He was then signed by Baltimore as a free agent and sent to Triple-A, where he hit just .240 with three RBI in 50 at bats before being called up to the majors in May. Unfortunately, Polonia batted just .240, showing little power, taking just ten walks, and swiping just eight bases in 14 tries. The Braves acquired him on waivers in August, and he batted .419 in 31 at bats for his new team. It is highly unlikely that Polonia will ever be a regular player again, but he could stick around for several years as a left-handed pinch hitter and spare outfielder.

Major League Batting Register

	BA	G	AB	R	H	2B	3B	HR	RBI	SB
87 AL	.287	125	435	78	125	16	10	4	49	29
88 AL	.292	84	288	51	84	11	4	2	27	24
89 AL	.300	125	433	70	130	17	6	3	46	22
90 AL	.335	120	403	52	135	7	9	2	35	21
91 AL	.296	150	604	92	179	28	8	2	50	48
92 AL	.286	149	577	83	165	17	4	0	35	51
93 AL	.271	152	576	75	156	17	6	1	32	55
94 AL	.311	95	350	62	109	21	6	1	36	20
95 AL	.261	67	238	37	62	9	3	2	15	10
95 NL	.264	28	53	6	14	7	0	0	2	3
96 AL	.240	58	175	25	42	4	1	2	14	8
96 NL	.419	22	31	3	13	0	0	0	2	1
Life	.292	1175	4163	634	1214	154	57	19	343	292
3 Ave	.284	89	312	51	88	15	4	2	27	16

JIM POOLE

Position: Pitcher
Team: San Francisco Giants
Born: April 28, 1966 Rochester, NY
Height: 6'2" **Weight:** 203 lbs.
Bats: left **Throws:** left
Acquired: Traded by Indians for Mark Carreon, 7/96

PLAYER SUMMARY	
Fantasy Value	$2 to $4
Card Value	4¢ to 7¢
Will	pitch often
Can't	show perfect control
Expect	curveballs
Don't Expect	closing duties

After compiling a 4-0 record and a 3.04 ERA in 32 games for the Tribe, Poole was dealt to the Giants July 9. Although the press viewed the move as a cost-cutting measure, Poole's arrival on the scene gave San Francisco a quality left-handed reliever—something they had not had since Kevin Rogers went down with a career-threatening shoulder injury three seasons ago. Poole pitched 35 times for the Giants but, true to his role as a situational lefty, worked only 23⅔ innings. He held lefties to a .150 mark while with the Giants and allowed just six of 23 inherited runners to score. He appears to be one of the better southpaw relievers in the National League. Given his success in the minors as well as in the show, it's odd that he has already been with five organizations. Poole, who graduated from Georgia Tech and has served as one of the chief representatives for the Players' Association, will be San Francisco's top left-handed short man.

Major League Pitching Register

	W	L	ERA	G	S	IP	H	ER	BB	SO
90 NL	0	0	4.22	16	0	10.2	7	5	8	6
91 AL	3	2	2.36	29	1	42.0	29	11	12	38
92 AL	0	0	0.00	6	0	3.1	3	0	1	3
93 AL	2	1	2.15	55	2	50.1	30	12	21	29
94 AL	1	0	6.64	38	0	20.1	32	15	11	18
95 AL	3	3	3.75	42	0	50.1	40	21	17	41
96 AL	4	0	3.04	32	0	26.2	29	9	14	19
96 NL	2	1	2.66	35	0	23.2	15	7	13	19
Life	15	7	3.17	253	3	227.1	185	80	97	173

MARK PORTUGAL

Position: Pitcher
Team: Philadelphia Phillies
Born: Oct. 30, 1962 Los Angeles, CA
Height: 6' **Weight:** 190 lbs.
Bats: right **Throws:** right
Acquired: Signed as a free agent, 12/96

PLAYER SUMMARY	
Fantasy Value	$5 to $7
Card Value	4¢ to 7¢
Will	try to stay healthy
Can't	get many strikeouts
Expect	decent performance
Don't Expect	another huge contract

Portugal struggled all season with injuries but was effective when he could pitch. A strained rib cage bothered him in April and May, a left hamstring strain sidelined him from late August through the end of the season, and elbow pains bothered him on and off all year long. Only Portugal's pride, however, was hurt when Reds owner Marge Schott's caustic comments criticizing the veteran right-hander's performance were made public in May. On the field, Portugal posted a decent ERA (3.98) and pitched well against both right-handers and left-handers. One of the best-hitting pitchers in baseball, Portugal always hustles and pitches through pain. He signed a free-agent deal with the Phillies over the winter.

Major League Pitching Register

	W	L	ERA	G	CG	IP	H	ER	BB	SO
85 AL	1	3	5.55	6	0	24.1	24	15	14	12
86 AL	6	10	4.31	27	3	112.2	112	54	50	67
87 AI	1	3	7.77	13	0	44.0	58	38	24	28
88 AL	3	3	4.53	26	0	57.2	60	29	17	31
89 NL	7	1	2.75	20	2	108.0	91	33	37	86
90 NL	11	10	3.62	32	1	196.2	187	79	67	136
91 NL	10	12	4.49	32	1	168.1	163	84	59	120
92 NL	6	3	2.66	18	1	101.1	76	30	41	62
93 NL	18	4	2.77	33	1	208.0	194	64	77	131
94 NL	10	8	3.93	21	1	137.1	135	60	45	87
95 NL	11	10	4.01	31	1	181.2	185	81	56	96
96 NL	8	9	3.98	27	1	156.0	146	69	42	93
Life	92	76	3.83	286	12	1496.0	1431	636	529	949
3 Ave	11	11	3.98	30	1	185.1	181	82	56	108

JAY POWELL

Position: Pitcher
Team: Florida Marlins
Born: Jan. 19, 1972 Meridian, MS
Height: 6'4" **Weight:** 225 lbs.
Bats: right **Throws:** right
Acquired: Traded by Orioles for Bret Barberie, 12/94

PLAYER SUMMARY	
Fantasy Value	$3 to $5
Card Value	5¢ to 8¢
Will	work on control
Can't	show polish yet
Expect	great velocity
Don't Expect	closing duties

Powell, a former first-round draft choice of the Orioles, was called up from Triple-A in April and received his first real shot at the big leagues. In his time with the Marlins, he showed flashes of the potential that made him Florida's Minor League Pitcher of the Year in 1995. However, in his rookie year Powell didn't have anywhere near the type of success he had enjoyed in the minors. Big-league right-handers hit .259 against him, compared to Eastern League batters' .181 average. Powell's main problem was his lack of control. At midseason, he had walked more batters than he had struck out, and while he turned that around in the second half, he still walked far too many and struck out too few considering the quality of his stuff. Powell throws a fastball in the mid-90s and a sharp-breaking sinker in the upper 80s, so it should just be a matter of time before he becomes more confident and can throw strikes consistently. Once that happens, look for Powell to become one of the top relief pitchers in the league.

CURTIS PRIDE

Position: Outfield
Team: Detroit Tigers
Born: Dec. 17, 1968 Washington, DC
Height: left **Weight:** right
Bats: 6' **Throws:** 200 lbs.
Acquired: Signed as a free agent, 1/96

PLAYER SUMMARY	
Fantasy Value	$5 to $7
Card Value	5¢ to 8¢
Will	get on base
Can't	be counted out
Expect	good speed
Don't Expect	assists

Entering the 1996 season, Pride made a much better human-interest story than he did a big-league ballplayer. Pride was born 95 percent deaf but overcame that setback to become the first hard-of-hearing major-leaguer since 1945. Unfortunately, in his two trials with Montreal, he did not hit major-league pitching. Signing with the Tigers, he made the club as a reserve outfielder and had plenty of chances to show off his speed and defensive ability. Pride swiped 11 bases, legged out a team-best five triples, and showed good range in the outfield. He also hit with surprising skill, finishing second on the club in batting average and clubbing ten homers. He drew 31 walks to boost his on-base percentage to a very good .372. Pride has a few downfalls that will probably keep him from being a starter in the majors: He has a mediocre throwing arm, strikes out fairly often, and rarely bats against left-handed pitchers. Even if he stays right where he is, however, Pride has proven he is a quality big-league player.

Major League Pitching Register

	W	L	ERA	G	S	IP	H	ER	BB	SO
95 NL	0	0	1.08	9	0	8.1	7	1	6	4
96 NL	4	3	4.54	67	2	71.1	71	36	36	52
Life	4	3	4.18	76	2	79.2	78	37	42	56

Major League Batting Register

	BA	G	AB	R	H	2B	3B	HR	RBI	SB
93 NL	.444	10	9	3	4	1	1	1	5	1
95 NL	.175	48	63	10	11	1	0	0	2	3
96 AL	.300	95	267	52	80	17	5	10	31	11
Life	.280	153	339	65	95	19	6	11	38	15

255

ARIEL PRIETO

Position: Pitcher
Team: Oakland Athletics
Born: Oct. 22, 1969 Havana, Cuba
Height: 6'3" **Weight:** 225 lbs.
Bats: right **Throws:** right
Acquired: First-round pick in 6/95 free-agent draft

PLAYER SUMMARY	
Fantasy Value	$8 to $10
Card Value	5¢ to 8¢
Will	work the corners
Can't	dominate with heat
Expect	30 starts
Don't Expect	20 wins

The former Cuban star did not especially enjoy the beginning of his first full season in the major leagues. Prieto allowed three home runs in his fourth start and spent most of April with an ERA well over 6.00. On May 19, he was disabled with a strained right elbow and did not return to duty until late July. However, once he came back, Prieto improved tremendously. He allowed only nine home runs on the season and lowered his ERA with several outstanding late-season starts. Prieto features an excellent changeup and spots his fastball well; this allows him to thrive despite a lack of overpowering velocity. He still needs to work on getting ahead in the count consistently, and he could stand to improve against right-handers, who batted .296 against him in 1996. He is by far the most promising starting pitcher on the Athletics staff, and his overall numbers are fantastic considering both his injury problems and the staggering level of offense displayed in the AL last season.

BILL PULSIPHER

Position: Pitcher
Team: New York Mets
Born: Oct. 9, 1973 Fort Benning, GA
Height: 6'3" **Weight:** 200 lbs.
Bats: left **Throws:** left
Acquired: Second-round pick in 6/91 free-agent draft

PLAYER SUMMARY	
Fantasy Value	$4 to $6
Card Value	7¢ to 10¢
Will	be a starter
Can't	count on elbow
Expect	steady recovery
Don't Expect	perfect control

In the grand designs of New York's fans and media, the gritty, eccentric Pulsipher was supposed to team with Jason Isringhausen and Paul Wilson to lead the Mets to the postseason for the first time in years. Pulsipher has arguably the best stuff of the three young guns, but an elbow injury that cropped up in spring training shelved him for the entire 1996 season. He first sprained a ligament in his left elbow in September 1995 and sat out the last two weeks of the season. Everybody seemed to think that would solve his problems, but "Pulse" reinjured the elbow in Florida and had to undergo surgery. He rehabilitated during the summer and is supposed to be ready to throw this spring. Pulsipher had shown great promise in the second half of 1995, going 5-7 with a 3.98 ERA in 17 starts for New York. He started slowly, but ended up allowing less than one runner an inning. There is never any guarantee for a pitcher coming back from elbow surgery, but if Pulsipher can come close to where he was before the injury, he will have a very productive career.

Major League Pitching Register

	W	L	ERA	G	CG	IP	H	ER	BB	SO
95 AL	2	6	4.97	14	1	58.0	57	32	32	37
96 AL	6	7	4.15	21	2	125.2	130	58	54	75
Life	8	13	4.41	35	3	183.2	187	90	86	112

Major League Pitching Register

	W	L	ERA	G	CG	IP	H	ER	BB	SO
95 NL	5	7	3.98	17	2	126.2	122	56	45	81
Life	5	7	3.98	17	2	126.2	122	56	45	81

PAUL QUANTRILL

Position: Pitcher
Team: Toronto Blue Jays
Born: Nov. 3, 1968 London, Ontario
Height: 6'1" **Weight:** 185 lbs.
Bats: left **Throws:** right
Acquired: Traded by Phillies for Howard Battle and Rico Jordan, 12/95

PLAYER SUMMARY	
Fantasy Value	$0
Card Value	4¢ to 7¢
Will	improve in '97
Can't	afford control lapse
Expect	crack at rotation
Don't Expect	many strikeouts

Quantrill, acquired from the Phillies last winter to be the Jays' No. 4 starter, bombed out in the rotation. He dropped his first four decisions and did not win his first AL game until his seventh start, which came on May 9. Bombed for 27 home runs and 172 hits by AL hitters, Quantrill had trouble locating his sinking fastball all season; his ERA hung around the 5.50 mark from start to finish. Moved into middle relief in May, he worked in that role and made occasional spot starts the rest of the season. Junk innings may now be Quantrill's role for the remainder of his career. Both left-handed and right-handed hitters batted well over .300 against Quantrill, who had held righties to a .253 average in 1995. A pitcher who allows opponents to put the ball in play as often as Quantrill must have something on his pitches to induce ground balls; unfortunately for Quantrill and the Jays, that "something" was missing all season in 1996.

Major League Pitching Register

	W	L	ERA	G	S	IP	H	ER	BB	SO
92 AL	2	3	2.19	27	1	49.1	55	12	15	24
93 AL	6	12	3.91	49	1	138.0	151	60	44	66
94 AL	1	1	3.52	17	0	23.0	25	9	5	15
94 NL	2	2	6.00	18	1	30.0	39	20	10	13
95 NL	11	12	4.67	33	0	179.1	212	93	44	103
96 AL	5	14	5.43	38	0	134.1	172	81	51	86
Life	27	44	4.47	182	3	554.0	654	275	169	307
2 Ave	9	14	4.97	38	0	168.0	205	93	50	101

SCOTT RADINSKY

Position: Pitcher
Team: Los Angeles Dodgers
Born: March 3, 1968 Glendale, CA
Height: 6'3" **Weight:** 204 lbs.
Bats: left **Throws:** left
Acquired: Signed as a minor-league free agent, 1/96

PLAYER SUMMARY	
Fantasy Value	$3 to $5
Card Value	4¢ to 7¢
Will	work frequently
Can't	be a closer
Expect	struggles with righties
Don't Expect	many homers

Making a brave comeback from Hodgkin's disease, Radinsky pitched valiantly but poorly for the White Sox in 1995 and earned a ticket to free agency. The Dodgers, who have been desperate for left-handed relief since Steve Howe left town in 1985, came calling and brought Radinsky to spring training. The well-liked Radinsky showed he still had some mustard on his fastball and, after missing some time at the start of the year due to tendinitis in his left middle finger, joined the Dodger bullpen on April 12. Throwing more sinking fastballs and sliders than he had previously, Radinsky allowed just two homers all season, fanned close to a man per inning, and held opposing lefties to a tiny batting average. However, Radinsky continued to struggle with right-handers and had some late-season problems. Used in tandem with fellow southpaw Mark Guthrie, Radinsky was a useful member of the Dodger staff and is almost certain to reprise his role next year.

Major League Pitching Register

	W	L	ERA	G	S	IP	H	ER	BB	SO
90 AL	6	1	4.82	62	4	52.1	47	28	36	46
91 AL	5	5	2.02	67	8	71.1	53	16	23	49
92 AL	3	7	2.73	68	15	59.1	54	18	34	48
93 AL	8	2	4.28	73	4	54.2	61	26	19	44
95 AL	2	1	5.45	46	1	38.0	46	23	17	14
96 NL	5	1	2.41	58	1	52.1	52	14	17	48
Life	29	17	3.43	374	33	328.0	313	125	146	249
2 Ave	4	1	3.77	55	1	48.1	52	20	18	32

257

BRAD RADKE

Position: Pitcher
Team: Minnesota Twins
Born: Oct. 27, 1972 Eau Claire, WI
Height: 6'2" **Weight:** 186 lbs.
Bats: right **Throws:** right
Acquired: Eighth-round pick in 6/91 free-agent draft

PLAYER SUMMARY	
Fantasy Value	$9 to $11
Card Value	4¢ to 7¢
Will	make his starts
Can't	afford wildness
Expect	hot and cold streaks
Don't Expect	an ERA crown

Radke was the AL's surprise pitcher during the season's first few weeks, winning his first three decisions and striking out 20 men in his first 19 innings. Talk of a Cy Young Award ceased, however, when Radke returned to earth by allowing ten runs in his next two starts and losing five games in a row. After this low period, Radke settled down around the All-Star break and pitched well for the Twins in the second half. Improving his ability to throw low strikes, he showed tenacity and a willingness to fight his way out of trouble. However, Radke continued to pay for his mistakes, allowing 40 home runs, which ranked tied for first in the AL. While Radke sees himself as rotation anchor material and has the necessary poise and durability to fill that role, he is not going to carry a contending team unless he improves his command significantly. He is not a true strikeout pitcher, and he will have to induce ground balls more consistently to survive. In his corner, however, are youth, skill, and attitude.

Major League Pitching Register

	W	L	ERA	G	CG	IP	H	ER	BB	SO
95 AL	11	14	5.32	29	2	181.0	195	107	47	75
96 AL	11	16	4.46	35	3	232.0	231	115	57	148
Life	22	30	4.84	64	5	413.0	426	222	104	223
2 Ave	12	16	4.86	34	3	218.1	225	118	55	116

TIM RAINES

Position: Outfield
Team: New York Yankees
Born: Sept. 16, 1959 Sanford, FL
Height: 5'8" **Weight:** 186 lbs.
Bats: both **Throws:** right
Acquired: Traded by White Sox for Blaise Kozeniewski, 12/95

PLAYER SUMMARY	
Fantasy Value	$7 to $9
Card Value	7¢ to 10¢
Will	play if healthy
Can't	show defensive wizardry
Expect	platoon duty
Don't Expect	blazing speed

"The Rock" was chipped a little bit in 1996. Raines suffered a fracture in his left thumb on March 18. The injury bothered him when he tried to swing left-handed, and as a result, the veteran outfielder did not play until mid-April. Soon afterward, Raines's right hamstring began to ache, and he was dropped from the leadoff spot to sixth in the order. Raines was disabled from May 23 to August 11. Meanwhile, the Yanks acquired Darryl Strawberry, forcing Raines to platoon in left. While Raines did not play often, he showed good leadoff skills and stole ten bases. Age has slowed him down, but Raines remains a smart baserunner and a brainy hitter with a good eye.

Major League Batting Register

	BA	G	AB	R	H	2B	3B	HR	RBI	SB
79 NL	.000	6	0	3	0	0	0	0	0	2
80 NL	.050	15	20	5	1	0	0	0	0	5
81 NL	.304	88	313	61	95	13	7	5	37	71
82 NL	.277	156	647	90	179	32	8	4	43	78
83 NL	.298	156	615	133	183	32	8	11	71	90
84 NL	.309	160	622	106	192	38	9	8	60	75
85 NL	.320	150	575	115	184	30	13	11	41	70
86 NL	.334	151	580	91	194	35	10	9	62	70
87 NL	.330	139	530	123	175	34	8	18	68	50
88 NL	.270	109	429	66	116	19	7	12	48	33
89 NL	.286	145	517	76	148	29	6	9	60	41
90 NL	.287	130	457	65	131	11	5	9	62	49
91 AL	.268	155	609	102	163	20	6	5	50	51
92 AL	.294	144	551	102	162	22	9	7	54	45
93 AL	.306	115	415	75	127	16	4	16	54	21
94 AL	.266	101	384	80	102	15	5	10	52	13
95 AL	.285	133	502	81	143	25	4	12	67	13
96 AL	.284	59	201	45	57	10	0	9	33	10
Life	.295	2112	7967	1419	2352	381	109	155	862	787
3 Ave	.277	117	436	83	121	20	4	12	61	14

MANNY RAMIREZ

Position: Outfield
Team: Cleveland Indians
Born: May 30, 1972 Santo Domingo, Dominican Republic
Height: 6′ **Weight:** 190 lbs.
Bats: right **Throws:** right
Acquired: First-round pick in 6/91 free-agent draft

PLAYER SUMMARY	
Fantasy Value	$30 to $35
Card Value	50¢ to $1.25
Will	continue to improve
Can't	carry a team
Expect	big power
Don't Expect	a slump

Ramirez is both a breathtaking and a frustrating player. He can amaze fans with his raw power, improving hitting skills, and powerful arm. He batted over .300 at home and on the road, .322 against lefties, and .304 against righties in '96. He walked nearly as often as he struck out and compiled an excellent .399 on-base percentage along with his tremendous .582 slugging mark. However, Ramirez is still far from perfect. He is a poor baserunner, makes tons of mistakes in the outfield, and seems to miss the cutoff man as often as he hits him. Ramirez did pile up a league-leading 19 outfield assists, showing not only that he is capable of strong and accurate throws, but also that runners are willing to take the chance on forcing him to make a mistake. In addition to his running and fielding foibles, Ramirez is said to possess one of the bigger egos in a clubhouse packed with high-strung stars. Just 24 years old, Ramirez has plenty of time to improve his game and carry himself better.

Major League Batting Register

	BA	G	AB	R	H	2B	3B	HR	RBI	SB
93 AL	.170	22	53	5	9	1	0	2	5	0
94 AL	.269	91	290	51	78	22	0	17	60	4
95 AL	.308	137	484	85	149	26	1	31	107	6
96 AL	.309	152	550	94	170	45	3	33	112	8
Life	.295	402	1377	235	406	94	4	83	284	18
3 Ave	.298	145	501	87	149	35	1	31	106	7

JOE RANDA

Position: Third base
Team: Pittsburgh Pirates
Born: Dec. 18, 1969 Milwaukee, WI
Height: 5′11″ **Weight:** 190 lbs.
Bats: right **Throws:** right
Acquired: Traded by Royals with Jeff Granger, Jeff Martin, and Jeff Wallace for Jay Bell and Jeff King, 12/96

PLAYER SUMMARY	
Fantasy Value	$8 to $10
Card Value	5¢ to 8¢
Will	hit left-handers
Can't	nail down a job
Expect	steady defense
Don't Expect	20 homers

In 1995, most of Randa's playing time for the Royals came off the bench. However, last year he increased his playing time dramatically and tied with Jose Offerman for top batting average on the team. Despite missing 22 days of action in May due to torn cartilage in his left knee, Randa racked up a .303 average that was spiked with line-drive power, 13 stolen bases in 17 tries, and 26 walks. He batted an excellent .340 against southpaws. Randa appeared 92 times at third base, but, like most every other player on Kansas City's roster, was shuffled around in the field. He wound up playing 15 games at second, seven games at first, and one at DH. While versatility is important for most players who lack star quality, being able to play several positions hurts Randa, who is a better-than-average fielder who can also hit. If left alone in Pittsburgh, he could probably bat .300 consistently and provide good defense at the hot corner.

Major League Batting Register

	BA	G	AB	R	H	2B	3B	HR	RBI	SB
95 AL	.171	34	70	6	12	2	0	1	5	0
96 AL	.303	110	337	36	102	24	1	6	47	13
Life	.280	144	407	42	114	26	1	7	52	13

PAT RAPP

Position: Pitcher
Team: Florida Marlins
Born: July 13, 1967 Jennings, LA
Height: 6'3" **Weight:** 205 lbs.
Bats: right **Throws:** right
Acquired: First-round pick from Giants in 11/92 expansion draft

PLAYER SUMMARY	
Fantasy Value	$2 to $4
Card Value	4¢ to 7¢
Will	try to be consistent
Can't	get many strikeouts
Expect	control struggles
Don't Expect	many homers

There was no better pitcher in the NL during the last six weeks of 1995 than Rapp, who was 11-2 after that season's All-Star break and won his last nine decisions. However, Rapp had a poor season for the Marlins in '96 and made a trip to the minor leagues to regroup. He allowed five runs in his first start of 1996 but got stronger later in April and May. Rapp worked into the seventh inning in 11 of his first 13 starts but soon was hammered with alarming regularity. After a disastrous August 21 start when he allowed the Cubs eight runs in four innings, Rapp was sent to Triple-A for two weeks before being recalled in early September. Control, as always, was a problem; Rapp walked at least three men in 17 of his starts and had to pitch behind in the count often. A sinker-slider pitcher, Rapp does not allow many home runs, but he cannot afford to put so many men on base when he does not have a consistent strikeout pitch. His future with Florida is in question.

Major League Pitching Register

	W	L	ERA	G	CG	IP	H	ER	BB	SO
92 NL	0	2	7.20	3	0	10.0	8	8	6	3
93 NL	4	6	4.02	16	1	94.0	101	42	39	57
94 NL	7	8	3.85	24	2	133.1	132	57	69	75
95 NL	14	7	3.44	28	3	167.1	158	64	76	102
96 NL	8	16	5.10	30	0	162.1	184	92	91	86
Life	33	39	4.17	101	6	567.0	583	263	281	323
3 Ave	11	12	4.08	32	2	179.1	183	81	91	102

JEFF REBOULET

Position: Infield
Team: Minnesota Twins
Born: April 30, 1964 Dayton, OH
Height: 6' **Weight:** 169 lbs.
Bats: right **Throws:** right
Acquired: Tenth-round pick in 6/86 free-agent draft

PLAYER SUMMARY	
Fantasy Value	$0
Card Value	4¢ to 7¢
Will	fill in everywhere
Can't	show power or speed
Expect	on-base ability
Don't Expect	regular duty

In his fifth season as Tom Kelly's all-purpose utility man, Reboulet had a rough time at the plate. He reverted to his earlier powerless ways and did little for the Twins but draw walks. He took 25 free passes but still had a poor .298 on-base percentage because he didn't hit much. His good bat in past seasons had always been viewed as gravy; Reboulet's primary value has always been on defense. Last summer, he once again showed his mettle as a jack-of-all-trades by playing six positions—all four infield spots plus left field and right field. (He even served as a DH eight times.) Reboulet is an excellent shortstop, with good range and a strong throwing arm, but does not embarrass Minnesota at any spot. He is not fast but is a smart baserunner and, in previous years, showed unexpected pop at the plate. One of Kelly's personal favorites, "The Inspector" should have some job security this spring despite his poor offensive performance of 1996. He is one of the better utility men in the AL.

Major League Batting Register

	BA	G	AB	R	H	2B	3B	HR	RBI	SB
92 AL	.190	73	137	15	26	7	1	1	16	3
93 AL	.258	109	240	33	62	8	0	1	15	5
94 AL	.259	74	189	28	49	11	1	3	23	0
95 AL	.292	87	216	39	63	11	0	4	23	1
96 AL	.222	107	234	20	52	9	0	0	23	4
Life	.248	450	1016	135	252	46	2	9	100	13
3 Ave	.258	103	248	34	64	12	0	3	27	2

JEFF REED

Position: Catcher
Team: Colorado Rockies
Born: Nov. 12, 1962 Joliet, IL
Height: 6'2" **Weight:** 190 lbs.
Bats: left **Throws:** right
Acquired: Signed as a free agent, 12/95

PLAYER SUMMARY	
Fantasy Value	$1 to $3
Card Value	4¢ to 7¢
Will	be happy at Coors
Can't	excel as a regular
Expect	decent defense
Don't Expect	marquee numbers

Colorado signed Reed as insurance in case the club could not find a regular receiver for 1996. The Rockies could not find another catcher to fit their budget, and therefore decided to use Reed and young Jayhawk Owens behind the plate. Reed set career highs in most categories while seeing the majority of backstop duty. He was quite content to swing away at friendly Coors Field, hitting .307 with seven home runs at home in contrast to just .259 with one four-bagger on the road. He took 43 free passes last year and notched a .365 on-base percentage. Behind the plate, Reed is a fair handler of pitchers but threw out only about 25 percent of potential basestealers. In truth, Reed is a marginal regular who is best suited for backup duty. However, his inflated offensive totals may keep him fully employed for another season.

Major League Batting Register

	BA	G	AB	R	H	2B	3B	HR	RBI	SB
84 AL	.143	18	21	3	3	3	0	0	1	0
85 AL	.200	7	10	2	2	0	0	0	0	0
86 AL	.236	68	165	13	39	6	1	2	9	1
87 AL	.213	75	207	15	44	11	0	1	21	0
88 NL	.226	92	265	20	60	9	2	1	16	1
89 NL	.223	102	287	16	64	11	0	3	23	0
90 NL	.251	72	175	12	44	8	1	3	16	0
91 NL	.267	91	270	20	72	15	2	3	31	0
92 NL	.160	15	25	2	4	0	0	0	2	0
93 NL	.261	66	119	10	31	3	0	6	12	0
94 NL	.175	50	103	11	18	3	0	1	7	0
95 NL	.265	66	113	12	30	2	0	0	9	0
96 NL	.284	116	341	34	97	20	1	8	37	2
Life	.242	838	2101	170	508	91	7	28	184	4

JODY REED

Position: Second base
Team: San Diego Padres
Born: July 26, 1962 Tampa, FL
Height: 5'9" **Weight:** 165 lbs.
Bats: right **Throws:** right
Acquired: Signed as a free agent, 4/95

PLAYER SUMMARY	
Fantasy Value	$1
Card Value	4¢ to 7¢
Will	hit singles
Can't	hold on forever
Expect	reliable glovework
Don't Expect	speed

In his second year with San Diego, Reed provided his usual fine glovework but had a poor year overall at the plate despite showing some strengths. He is patient and will take the walk, drawing 59 in 1996 with a .325 on-base average. Reed is also a good hit-and-run man and does not often strike out. However, he does not hit for power, rarely has a high average, and does not run well. He is best used as an eighth-place hitter, which is where he batted in 1996. Defense is how Reed earns his salary; he is one of the better defensive second sackers in the game today. Showing his usual good range, Reed helped San Diego's ground-ball-pitching staff do their jobs with confidence. He made just nine errors on the season. However, mediocre batwork may relegate Reed to reserve status soon. He may not have much left in his bat, but he would be an excellent bench player due to his fielding prowess.

Major League Batting Register

	BA	G	AB	R	H	2B	3B	HR	RBI	SB
87 AL	.300	9	30	4	9	1	1	0	8	1
88 AL	.293	109	338	60	99	23	1	1	28	1
89 AL	.288	146	524	76	151	42	2	3	40	4
90 AL	.289	155	598	70	173	45	0	5	51	4
91 AL	.283	153	618	87	175	42	2	5	60	6
92 AL	.247	143	550	64	136	27	1	3	40	7
93 NL	.276	132	445	48	123	21	2	2	31	1
94 AL	.271	108	399	48	108	22	0	2	37	5
95 NL	.256	131	445	58	114	18	1	4	40	6
96 NL	.244	146	495	45	121	20	0	2	49	2
Life	.2721232	4442	560	1209	261	10	27	384	37
3 Ave	.258	149	519	59	134	24	0	3	49	5

STEVE REED

Position: Pitcher
Team: Colorado Rockies
Born: March 11, 1966 Los Angeles, CA
Height: 6'2" **Weight:** 202 lbs.
Bats: right **Throws:** right
Acquired: Third-round pick from Giants in
11/92 expansion draft

PLAYER SUMMARY	
Fantasy Value	$2 to $4
Card Value	4¢ to 7¢
Will	pitch effectively
Can't	escape injuries
Expect	some homers
Don't Expect	marquee role

Reed's consistently good performance has
saved Colorado manager Don Baylor
plenty of headaches in the past four years.
Formerly a long-time Giants farmhand,
Reed got his chance with the expansion
Rockies and quickly proved himself a valuable reliever. With his submarining delivery
and effective sinker and sweeping curve,
Reed murders right-handers. In each of the
last three years, his ERA has been under
2.00 in road games, suffering only in the
cozy confines of Denver's Coors Field.
However, Reed had some trouble in 1996.
Occasionally, his pitches will flatten out
against left-handers, who are capable of
doing damage against him; Reed allowed
11 homers last season. He also had some
shoulder problems that sidelined him at
times during the year. There is talk that frequent use is burning Reed's arm out, but
since he has never depended on velocity to
pitch well, the underrated right-hander
should continue to do his job effectively—
even if far removed from the spotlight.

Major League Pitching Register

	W	L	ERA	G	S	IP	H	ER	BB	SO
92 NL	1	0	2.30	18	0	15.2	13	4	3	11
93 NL	9	5	4.48	64	3	84.1	80	42	30	51
94 NL	3	2	3.94	61	3	64.0	79	28	26	51
95 NL	5	2	2.14	71	3	84.0	61	20	21	79
96 NL	4	3	3.96	70	0	75.0	66	33	19	51
Life	22	12	3.54	284	9	323.0	299	127	99	243
3 Ave	5	3	3.29	79	3	87.1	82	32	26	71

BRYAN REKAR

Position: Pitcher
Team: Colorado Rockies
Born: June 3, 1972 Oak Lawn, IL
Height: 6'3" **Weight:** 210 lbs.
Bats: right **Throws:** right
Acquired: Second-round pick in 6/93 free-
agent draft

PLAYER SUMMARY	
Fantasy Value	$0
Card Value	5¢ to 8¢
Will	show good arsenal
Can't	carry a staff
Expect	eventual success
Don't Expect	many strikeouts

After an encouraging rookie season with
the Rockies in 1995, Rekar took a step
back last year. He began the campaign in
the club's starting rotation but was hammered all the way back to Triple-A after a
series of poor starts. He was sent down on
April 28 after allowing 11 earned runs at
home against the Expos. Colorado management felt Rekar was not aggressive
enough and needed a crash course on
pitching inside. He returned to Colorado on
June 11 but was sent down again July 1
and did not return until September. All in all,
it was a dismal season for Rekar, who—
most agree—was brought along far too
quickly. Even manager Don Baylor said as
much late in the season. Rockies management has learned from Rekar's dismal
showing that pitchers must be brought
along slowly; unfortunately, Rekar's lost
season served as the evidence. The talented but still-inexperienced righty will now
start from scratch. He throws five pitches
with good mechanics and velocity, and he
simply needs to be brought along with the
patience and time every young pitcher deserves.

Major League Pitching Register

	W	L	ERA	G	CG	IP	H	ER	BB	SO
95 NL	4	6	4.98	15	1	85.0	95	47	24	60
96 NL	2	4	8.95	14	0	58.1	87	58	26	25
Life	6	10	6.59	29	1	143.1	182	105	50	85

EDGAR RENTERIA

Position: Shortstop
Team: Florida Marlins
Born: Aug. 7, 1975 Barranquilla, Columbia
Height: 6'1" **Weight:** 172 lbs.
Bats: right **Throws:** right
Acquired: Signed as a nondrafted free agent, 2/92

PLAYER SUMMARY	
Fantasy Value.	$7 to $9
Card Value	15¢ to 20¢
Will.	be a star
Can't	be stopped
Expect	flashy defense
Don't Expect	big power

Renteria, who didn't turn 21 until he had already been in the majors for nearly two months, bolted quickly through the Marlins system and ended the year as one of the most impressive rookies in baseball; in fact, he finished second in NL Rookie of the Year voting. In just his fifth year in pro ball, he showed he can hit and field in the big leagues. On May 10, Renteria was called up from Triple-A to replace the injured Kurt Abbott. By the time Abbott came off the DL the next month, the veteran had lost his job. Renteria and fellow rookie second baseman Luis Castillo showed terrific range and fine ability in turning the double play. Renteria also showed some stick. He rapped out 26 extra-base hits, stole 16 bases in 18 tries, and finished second on the club in batting average. Renteria will likely improve against left-handers, who held him to a .244 mark in 1996, and he must learn to take more walks; he drew just 33 in his rookie year. However, his performance was simply outstanding for someone so young, and Renteria is likely to be an All-Star in the not-too-distant future.

Major League Batting Register

	BA	G	AB	R	H	2B	3B	HR	RBI	SB
96 NL	.309	106	431	68	133	18	3	5	31	16
Life	.309	106	431	68	133	18	3	5	31	16

CARLOS REYES

Position: Pitcher
Team: Oakland Athletics
Born: April 4, 1969 Miami, FL
Height: 6'1" **Weight:** 190 lbs.
Bats: both **Throws:** right
Acquired: Rule 5 draft pick from Braves, 12/93

PLAYER SUMMARY	
Fantasy Value.	$1 to $3
Card Value	4¢ to 7¢
Will	work in the middle
Can't.	get many strikeouts
Expect	plenty of changeups
Don't Expect	sudden improvement

After two seasons as a middle reliever, Reyes came to camp in spring 1996 with a chance to expand his role—and he did. After an outstanding Arizona performance, Reyes began the season as the No. 1 starter in a clearly undermanned Oakland rotation. Unfortunately, Reyes allowed ten earned runs in his first ten innings and never really got on track. The right-hander scuffled with shoulder problems and lost his next five games. By early June, he had been removed from the rotation and reinserted into the bullpen. It was a tough season all around for Reyes, who survives by changing speeds on his fastball and utilizing an excellent changeup. Unfortunately, he does not always have pinpoint control, and his mistakes tend to be hit a long way. Reyes allowed 19 home runs on the season in addition to yielding 61 walks. Unless he can become more consistent, Reyes will never get out of long relief. If he continues to experience serious control problems, he might not even stick around in the majors.

Major League Pitching Register

	W	L	ERA	G	S	IP	H	ER	BB	SO
94 AL	0	3	4.15	27	1	78.0	71	36	44	57
95 AL	4	6	5.09	40	0	69.0	71	39	28	48
96 AL	7	10	4.78	46	0	122.1	134	65	61	78
Life	11	19	4.68	113	1	269.1	276	140	133	183
3 Ave	4	7	4.64	43	0	103.1	105	53	51	71

SHANE REYNOLDS

Position: Pitcher
Team: Houston Astros
Born: March 26, 1968 Bastrop, LA
Height: 6'3" **Weight:** 210 lbs.
Bats: right **Throws:** right
Acquired: Third-round pick in 6/89 free-agent draft

PLAYER SUMMARY	
Fantasy Value	$16 to $19
Card Value	8¢ to 12¢
Will	retire left-handers
Can't	be replaced
Expect	reliable starts
Don't Expect	many walks

After a fine 1995 season, Reynolds moved into the NL's pitching elite in 1996. Setting career highs in most categories, he paced the Astros staff—and ranked among the league leaders—in wins and innings pitched. Reynolds is truly a manager's dream, putting the ball in play and refusing to be victimized by the things a team can't defend against: homers and walks. As he has done every year, he again showed an aversion to giving up the free pass (just 44 walks allowed), trailing only Atlanta's Greg Maddux as the stingiest pitcher with the base on balls in the league. Reynolds also allowed just 20 home runs. Following the simple formula of throwing his pitches for low strikes and running his fastball in on left-handers, Reynolds managed to help keep an undermanned Astros squad in the pennant hunt. He has come a long way since being left off the roster for the University of Texas in the 1989 College World Series and going just 25-24 in his first three minor-league seasons.

Major League Pitching Register

	W	L	ERA	G	CG	IP	H	ER	BB	SO
92 NL	1	3	7.11	8	0	25.1	42	20	6	10
93 NL	0	0	0.82	5	0	11.0	11	1	6	10
94 NL	8	5	3.05	33	1	124.0	128	42	21	110
95 NL	10	11	3.47	30	3	189.1	196	73	37	175
96 NL	16	10	3.65	35	4	239.0	227	97	44	204
Life	35	29	3.56	111	8	588.2	604	233	114	509
3 Ave	13	10	3.42	38	3	209.0	209	79	38	185

ARMANDO REYNOSO

Position: Pitcher
Team: New York Mets
Born: May 1, 1966 San Luis Potosi, Mexico
Height: 6' **Weight:** 186 lbs.
Bats: right **Throws:** right
Acquired: Traded by Rockies for Jerry DiPoto, 11/96

PLAYER SUMMARY	
Fantasy Value	$1 to $3
Card Value	4¢ to 7¢
Will	mix his pitches
Can't	stay healthy
Expect	good pickoff move
Don't Expect	consistent success

Never blessed with an overpowering fastball, Reynoso gets by with a baffling assortment of pitches, including a sinker, curve, changeup, split-fingered fastball, and changeup curveball. He also has one of the better pickoff moves of any pitcher in baseball and is a good fielder and hitter. Unfortunately, Reynoso ran into elbow problems in May 1994 and is just getting back to his former level of effectiveness. His control has been inconsistent since the elbow injury, and without good location, Reynoso is much less likely to be effective. During 1996, he allowed over ten hits a game and was rocked for 27 home runs. However, he took his regular turn, making 30 starts, and did show some improvement over his poor performance of 1995. Pitchers with elbow injuries often take up to two years to fully recover; New York is hoping Reynoso proves sound this year.

Major League Pitching Register

	W	L	ERA	G	CG	IP	H	ER	BB	SO
91 NL	2	1	6.17	6	0	23.1	26	16	10	10
92 NL	1	0	4.70	3	0	7.2	11	4	2	2
93 NL	12	11	4.00	30	4	189.0	206	84	63	117
94 NL	3	4	4.82	9	1	52.1	54	28	22	25
95 NL	7	7	5.32	20	0	93.0	116	55	36	40
96 NL	8	9	4.96	30	0	168.2	195	93	49	88
Life	33	32	4.72	98	5	534.0	608	280	182	282
2 Ave	8	8	5.10	26	0	137.1	163	77	45	67

ARTHUR RHODES

Position: Pitcher
Team: Baltimore Orioles
Born: Oct. 24, 1969 Waco, TX
Height: 6'2" **Weight:** 206 lbs.
Bats: left **Throws:** left
Acquired: Second-round pick in 6/88 free-agent draft

PLAYER SUMMARY	
Fantasy Value	$5 to $7
Card Value	4¢ to 7¢
Will	work in relief
Can't	expand his role
Expect	slow recuperation
Don't Expect	perfect control

During his major-league career, the promising Rhodes has been tried in several roles, including starting, short relief, and (in 1996) middle relief. From the start of the 1996 season, Orioles manager Davey Johnson used the hard-throwing Rhodes exclusively in middle and set-up roles. Bothered by occasional control problems and untimely home run balls in his previous tries at the starting rotation, Rhodes seemed to take to the critical but often ignored middle-innings job. He ranked near the top of AL pitchers in relief wins for much of the season until coming up with an inflamed pitching shoulder in July. Rhodes sat out two weeks, returned August 2, and was again disabled four days later. He remained sidelined for the rest of the season. The left-hander is expected to return strong this season, but thoughts of projecting him back into the starting rotation are best reserved until Rhodes proves he can stay healthy and stay effective.

Major League Pitching Register

	W	L	ERA	G	S	IP	H	ER	BB	SO
91 AL	0	3	8.00	8	0	36.0	47	32	23	23
92 AL	7	5	3.63	15	0	94.1	87	38	38	77
93 AL	5	6	6.51	17	0	85.2	91	62	49	49
94 AL	3	5	5.81	10	0	52.2	51	34	30	47
95 AL	2	5	6.21	19	0	75.1	68	52	48	77
96 AL	9	1	4.08	28	1	53.0	48	24	23	62
Life	26	25	5.49	97	1	397.0	392	242	211	335
2 Ave	6	3	5.39	25	1	69.0	62	41	39	74

BILL RIPKEN

Position: Infield
Team: Texas Rangers
Born: Dec. 16, 1964 Havre de Grace, MD
Height: 6'1" **Weight:** 190 lbs.
Bats: right **Throws:** right
Acquired: Signed as a free agent, 12/96

PLAYER SUMMARY	
Fantasy Value	$0
Card Value	4¢ to 7¢
Will	fill in capably
Can't	excel with bat
Expect	slick fielding
Don't Expect	regular duty

After several years of duty as Baltimore's regular second baseman in the late 1980s, Ripken the Younger fell on hard times due to poor offensive performance. He spent two years as a utility man in Texas before landing all the way back in Triple-A during 1995 with Cleveland's Buffalo affiliate. There, he spent the season playing shortstop for the Bisons and making baseball people take notice of his hard-nosed, intelligent play. His hard work paid off last spring as he won a utility job with the O's. While he is still not much to speak of at bat, he is a fine fielder who is capable of excellent defense at both shortstop and second base. He made just three errors on the year. Ripken is a smart, if not fast, runner and a good bunter. However, his lack of overall production on offense always keeps him a step or two from having to find new employment.

Major League Batting Register

	BA	G	AB	R	H	2B	3B	HR	RBI	SB
87 AL	.308	58	234	27	72	9	0	2	20	4
88 AL	.207	150	512	52	106	18	1	2	34	8
89 AL	.239	115	318	31	76	11	2	2	26	1
90 AL	.291	129	406	48	118	28	1	3	38	5
91 AL	.216	104	287	24	62	11	1	0	14	0
92 AL	.230	111	330	35	76	15	0	4	36	2
93 AL	.189	50	132	12	25	4	0	0	11	0
94 AL	.309	32	81	9	25	5	0	0	6	2
95 AL	.412	8	17	4	7	0	0	2	3	0
96 AL	.230	57	135	19	31	8	0	2	12	0
Life	.244	814	2452	261	598	109	5	17	200	22

CAL RIPKEN

Position: Shortstop
Team: Baltimore Orioles
Born: Aug. 24, 1960 Havre de Grace, MD
Height: 6'4" **Weight:** 220 lbs.
Bats: right **Throws:** right
Acquired: Second-round pick in 6/78 free-agent draft

PLAYER SUMMARY	
Fantasy Value	$20 to $25
Card Value	$1.25 to $2.75
Will	play reliable defense
Can't	run very well
Expect	offensive production
Don't Expect	a day off

What Cal Ripken means to the fans of Baltimore cannot be overstated. A year after breaking Lou Gehrig's consecutive-games-played record, Ripken continued to play every day and produce. However, the year was not free from controversy. Local reports painted Ripken's relationship with manager Davey Johnson as less than harmonious, likely stemming from Johnson's failed experiment involving young shortstop Manny Alexander. The decision to insert Alexander into the lineup and move Ripken back to third (his original position) lasted only a week and was unsuccessful. Cal topped 20 homers for the twelfth time and once again walked almost as often as he struck out (59 free passes to 78 whiffs).

Major League Batting Register

	BA	G	AB	R	H	2B	3B	HR	RBI	SB
81 AL	.128	23	39	1	5	0	0	0	0	0
82 AL	.264	160	598	90	158	32	5	28	93	3
83 AL	.318	162	663	121	211	47	2	27	102	0
84 AL	.304	162	641	103	195	37	7	27	86	2
85 AL	.282	161	642	116	181	32	5	26	110	2
86 AL	.282	162	627	98	177	35	1	25	81	4
87 AL	.252	162	624	97	157	28	3	27	98	3
88 AL	.264	161	575	87	152	25	1	23	81	2
89 AL	.257	162	646	80	166	30	0	21	93	3
90 AL	.250	161	600	78	150	28	4	21	84	3
91 AL	.323	162	650	99	210	46	5	34	114	6
92 AL	.251	162	637	73	160	29	1	14	72	4
93 AL	.257	162	641	87	165	26	3	24	90	1
94 AL	.315	112	444	71	140	19	3	13	75	1
95 AL	.262	144	550	71	144	33	2	17	88	0
96 AL	.278	163	640	94	178	40	1	26	102	1
Life	.277	2381	9217	1366	2549	487	43	353	1369	35
3 Ave	.285	161	628	91	179	35	2	21	102	1

BILL RISLEY

Position: Pitcher
Team: Toronto Blue Jays
Born: May 29, 1967 Chicago, IL
Height: 6'2" **Weight:** 215 lbs.
Bats: right **Throws:** right
Acquired: Traded by Mariners with Miguel Cairo for Edwin Hurtado and Paul Menhart, 12/95

PLAYER SUMMARY	
Fantasy Value	$0
Card Value	4¢ to 7¢
Will	have a role
Can't	afford control woes
Expect	set-up work
Don't Expect	perfect health

After two impressive seasons with Seattle, Risley was dealt to the Jays last winter. Toronto manager Cito Gaston expected to use Risley in a set-up role for closer Mike Timlin, but 1996 was an ill-fated season for Risley from the start. Struggling due to a weak pitching shoulder, Risley allowed 11 runs in his first 15 innings before going on the disabled list on May 12. He sat for nearly a month before heading to the minor leagues for a rehabilitation assignment, finally returning to the Jays June 11. Risley assumed a bullpen role, but just 17 days later he was shut down again with more soreness in the shoulder. He did not return until July 31. Just a day later, Indians left fielder Albert Belle greeted Risley by smashing a game-winning grand slam in a 4-2 Cleveland victory. As the season wound down, however, Risley began to show signs of his old effectiveness. He will be in the Jays bullpen in 1997 and could play a key part in the team's success if he can stay healthy.

Major League Pitching Register

	W	L	ERA	G	S	IP	H	ER	BB	SO
92 NL	1	0	1.80	1	0	5.0	4	1	1	2
93 NL	0	0	6.00	2	0	3.0	2	2	2	2
94 AL	9	6	3.44	37	0	52.1	31	20	19	61
95 AL	2	1	3.13	45	1	60.1	55	21	18	65
96 AL	0	1	3.89	25	0	41.2	33	18	25	29
Life	12	8	3.44	110	1	162.1	125	62	65	159
3 Ave	5	4	3.43	43	0	61.0	46	23	24	63

KEVIN RITZ

Position: Pitcher
Team: Colorado Rockies
Born: June 8, 1965 Eatontown, NJ
Height: 6'4" **Weight:** 220 lbs.
Bats: right **Throws:** right
Acquired: Second-round pick from Tigers in 11/92 expansion draft

PLAYER SUMMARY	
Fantasy Value	$5 to $7
Card Value	4¢ to 7¢
Will	struggle with control
Can't	hold runners
Expect	a starting job
Don't Expect	an impressive ERA

An up-and-down April nearly landed Ritz a trip to the Rockies bullpen. Fortunately for Ritz and his team, Colorado manager Don Baylor knew that he did not have many other reliable starting pitchers. As a result, Ritz remained in the club's rotation all year, making a team-high 35 starts and setting career highs in wins and innings while other Rockies hurlers struggled with injuries and inconsistency. Ritz also set a Colorado record for victories in a season (17). Despite trouble with walks and baserunners (27 stole against him in 40 tries), Ritz had a good season overall. Pitching in Coors Field certainly fluffed up his ERA (5.28), but Ritz never complained about numbers, focusing instead on keeping the respect of his teammates and NL hitters by taking over as Colorado's staff ace. He probably will never completely wipe out his control problems, but he has shown durability and a willingness to take the ball. That's something every team needs.

Major League Pitching Register

	W	L	ERA	/G	CG	IP	H	ER	BB	SO
89 AL	4	6	4.38	12	1	74.0	75	36	44	56
90 AL	0	4	11.05	4	0	7.1	14	9	14	3
91 AL	0	3	11.74	11	0	15.1	17	20	22	9
92 AL	2	5	5.60	23	0	80.1	88	50	44	57
94 NL	5	6	5.62	15	0	73.2	88	46	35	53
95 NL	11	11	4.21	31	0	173.1	171	81	65	120
96 NL	17	11	5.28	35	2	213.0	236	125	105	105
Life	39	46	5.19	131	3	637.0	689	367	329	403
3 Ave	12	11	4.94	30	1	171.1	184	94	76	105

MARIANO RIVERA

Position: Pitcher
Team: New York Yankees
Born: Nov. 29, 1969 Panama City, Panama
Height: 6'2" **Weight:** 168 lbs.
Bats: right **Throws:** right
Acquired: Signed as a free agent, 2/90

PLAYER SUMMARY	
Fantasy Value	$8 to $10
Card Value	20¢ to 30¢
Will	throw explosive fastball
Can't	be hit
Expect	more saves
Don't Expect	problems with righties

Although he had a rough rookie season in 1995, Rivera was expected to break through in a big way in '96 due to his outstanding stuff. Yankees manager Joe Torre used Rivera exclusively as a reliever, despite the temptation to use the lanky right-hander to prop up a thin starting rotation. Coming out of the bullpen, Rivera immediately became one of baseball's most valuable pitchers, working in a set-up role for closer John Wetteland. Most feel that Rivera will either become a starter or a full-time closer this year. He throws a 95-mph fastball high in the strike zone, something few pitchers can do on a regular basis. Rivera's smooth, fluid delivery is deceptive, and he can sink his fastball as well as throw a very good slider. American League hitters batted just .189 against Rivera, with righties suffering even more at .157. Minnesota manager Tom Kelly summed up the feelings of most opponents when he said that Rivera "needs to be in a higher league, if there is one. Ban him from baseball. He should be illegal."

Major League Pitching Register

	W	L	ERA	G	S	IP	H	ER	BB	SO
95 AL	5	3	5.51	19	0	67.0	71	41	30	51
96 AL	8	3	2.09	61	5	107.2	73	25	34	130
Life	13	6	3.40	80	5	174.2	144	66	64	181
2 Ave	7	3	3.50	41	3	92.1	76	36	34	94

267

RUBEN RIVERA

Position: Outfield
Team: New York Yankees
Born: Nov. 14, 1973 Chorrera, Panama
Height: 6'3" **Weight:** 200 lbs.
Bats: right **Throws:** right
Acquired: Signed as a free agent, 11/90

PLAYER SUMMARY	
Fantasy Value.................	$6 to $8
Card Value	15¢ to 25¢
Will	get his shot
Can't	afford tantrums
Expect	power and strikeouts
Don't Expect	slowness afoot

The highly rated rookie took one step forward and two steps back in 1996. He spent some time at the major-league level, showing a good bat and speed, and actually would have been on the Yankees postseason roster had he not been injured late in September. Rivera drew 13 walks in 46 games and had a very good .381 on-base percentage. He did strike out 28 times, which is cause for concern. A greater cause for concern was a series of attitude problems. Rivera apparently felt he should be playing every day in the majors, and pouted when the Yankees sent him down in midseason. He was suspended for his insubordination while in Triple-A, and only late in the season was said to have improved his outlook. Rivera is still one of the best position-player prospects in the game, and he could get his chance at 130 games in the majors this year. Rivera, who has a very strong throwing arm and possesses great speed, can play all three outfield positions, appearing at least 13 times in left, center, and right for the Yankees last year.

Major League Batting Register

	BA	G	AB	R	H	2B	3B	HR	RBI	SB
95 AL	.000	5	1	0	0	0	0	0	0	0
96 AL	.284	46	88	17	25	6	1	2	16	6
Life	.281	51	89	17	25	6	1	2	16	6

BIP ROBERTS

Position: Second base
Team: Kansas City Royals
Born: Oct. 27, 1963 Berkeley, CA
Height: 5'7" **Weight:** 165 lbs.
Bats: both **Throws:** right
Acquired: Traded by Padres with Bryan Wolff for Wally Joyner and Aaron Dolarque, 12/95

PLAYER SUMMARY	
Fantasy Value...............	$8 to $10
Card Value	5¢ to 8¢
Will..........	play everywhere if asked
Can't.................	show old speed
Expect	good batting average
Don't Expect	any power

Roberts, never a power machine, holds the current major-league mark for most games played without hitting a home run. His last tater came on August 31, 1995. Despite this utter lack of punch, Roberts spent several games batting cleanup for the Royals, who searched all season for an effective lineup. Roberts hit well while he was in there; unfortunately, he was bothered by injuries for the fourth straight year. He missed nearly a month of action due to a torn hamstring, sat out in August with a strained side muscle, and was also bothered by a sore leg and a bad case of the flu. The leg problems clearly affected Roberts's baserunning; he was successful in just 12 of his 21 steal attempts. He played 63 games at second base but also saw action at DH and at all three outfield spots. Due to his speed and versatility, Roberts might be best utilized as an all-purpose utility player.

Major League Batting Register

	BA	G	AB	R	H	2B	3B	HR	RBI	SB
86 NL	.253	101	241	34	61	5	2	1	12	14
88 NL	.333	5	9	1	3	0	0	0	0	0
89 NL	.301	117	329	81	99	15	8	3	25	21
90 NL	.309	149	556	104	172	36	3	9	44	46
91 NL	.281	117	424	66	119	13	3	3	32	26
92 NL	.323	147	532	92	172	34	6	4	45	44
93 NL	.240	83	292	46	70	13	0	1	18	26
94 NL	.320	105	403	52	129	15	5	2	31	21
95 NL	.304	73	296	40	90	14	0	2	25	20
96 AL	.283	90	339	39	96	21	2	0	52	12
Life	.296	987	3421	555	1011	166	29	25	284	230
3 Ave	.306	107	413	52	126	19	3	2	41	21

Rich Robertson

Position: Pitcher
Team: Minnesota Twins
Born: Sept. 15, 1968 Nacogdoches, TX
Height: 6'4" **Weight:** 175 lbs.
Bats: left **Throws:** left
Acquired: Claimed from Pirates on waivers, 12/94

PLAYER SUMMARY	
Fantasy Value	$0
Card Value	5¢ to 8¢
Will	freeze left-handers
Can't	impress with fastball
Expect	funky delivery
Don't Expect	perfect control

The gawky, cross-body-throwing left-hander finally got his chance at regular rotation duty in 1996 and turned in a reasonable, if flawed, performance. At times, Robertson would get into an unhittable groove; on other occasions, he literally couldn't get the ball over the plate at all. He walked more men than any other pitcher in the American League and was one of just four pitchers in the loop to pass more than 100 hitters. Robertson also allowed 15 of 23 potential basestealers to advance safely, a high total and poor rate indeed for a southpaw. However, Robertson did show he can get left-handers out consistently, holding them to a puny .226 average and little power. Because he does not throw especially hard, he cannot afford lapses in his control. His curve and changeup are hard to hit but even harder for him to control. However, he did finish third in ERA among Twins starters in 1996 and will probably get another shot at rotation duty. Robertson may end up as a southpaw situational reliever, which is something the Twins need anyway.

Major League Pitching Register

	W	L	ERA	G	CG	IP	H	ER	BB	SO
93 NL	0	1	6.00	9	0	9.0	15	6	4	5
94 NL	0	0	6.89	8	0	15.2	20	12	10	8
95 AL	2	0	3.83	25	1	51.2	48	22	31	38
96 AL	7	17	5.12	36	5	186.1	197	106	116	114
Life	9	18	5.00	78	6	262.2	280	146	161	165
2 Ave	5	9	4.81	32	3	122.1	126	65	75	78

Alex Rodriguez

Position: Shortstop
Team: Seattle Mariners
Born: July 27, 1975 New York, NY
Height: 6'3" **Weight:** 195 lbs.
Bats: right **Throws:** right
Acquired: First-round pick in 6/93 free-agent draft

PLAYER SUMMARY	
Fantasy Value	$35 to $40
Card Value	75¢ to $1.25
Will	hit and field
Can't	find a weakness
Expect	All-Star status
Don't Expect	many errors

Baseball got a shot in the arm in 1996 from this 21-year-old shortstop phenom. Starting the season batting eighth and ninth, Rodriguez quickly moved up in the order and was hitting second by midseason. He lashed hits to all fields and all distances, becoming the second-youngest player ever to win a batting crown. He led the AL in runs and doubles, finished fifth in slugging percentage, and was second in hits. While he continued to swing at bad pitches (fanning 104 times with just 59 walks), "A-Rod" showed exceptional bat speed and power. He also showed an outstanding glove at shortstop, combining excellent range and a very strong throwing arm. It will be interesting to see how AL pitchers adjust to Rodriguez in 1997; whatever they're doing now just isn't working. Although he narrowly missed out on MVP honors last year, finishing second in voting to Juan Gonzalez, the handsome young shortstop is already knocking on the door of destiny. Some people feel he will be one of the greatest shortstops ever to play the game.

Major League Batting Register

	BA	G	AB	R	H	2B	3B	HR	RBI	SB
94 AL	.204	17	54	4	11	0	0	0	2	3
95 AL	.232	48	142	15	33	6	2	5	19	4
96 AL	.358	146	601	141	215	54	1	36	123	15
Life	.325	211	797	160	259	60	3	41	144	22

269

FRANK RODRIGUEZ

Position: Pitcher
Team: Minnesota Twins
Born: Dec. 11, 1972 Brooklyn, NY
Height: 6' **Weight:** 175 lbs.
Bats: right **Throws:** right
Acquired: Traded by Red Sox with J.J. Johnson for Rick Aguilera, 7/95

PLAYER SUMMARY	
Fantasy Value	$7 to $9
Card Value	5¢ to 8¢
Will	hold runners effectively
Can't	show perfect control
Expect	good skills
Don't Expect	a Cy Young

Continuing his maturation from thrower to pitcher, the still-raw Rodriguez moved closer to claiming the role of Minnesota's staff ace. Earning the call as Opening Day starter, he led the Twins in victories while finishing second in starts and innings. He even spent some midseason time as a reliever, chalking up two saves in five bullpen appearances when regular closer Dave Stevens was sidelined by injury. Rodriguez pitched his first career complete game on May 15, shutting down Toronto 2-1, and added two more complete games before the season was done. When he is on, Rodriguez has an excellent moving fastball and a promising curve. However, he has not yet learned how to pitch when he doesn't have his good stuff, and at times he seemed unable to rein in his emotions and pace himself when he did have the good fastball and breaking pitch. That kind of learning will come with experience. Rodriguez is already one of the top fielding pitchers in baseball, and he is growing in stature among his teammates, who voted him the Twins' alternate player representative last summer.

Major League Pitching Register

	W	L	ERA	G	CG	IP	H	ER	BB	SO
95 AL	5	8	6.13	25	0	105.2	114	72	57	59
96 AL	13	14	5.05	38	3	206.2	218	116	78	110
Life	18	22	5.42	63	3	312.1	332	188	135	169
2 Ave	9	12	5.45	33	2	163.1	173	99	71	88

HENRY RODRIGUEZ

Position: Outfield
Team: Montreal Expos
Born: Nov. 8, 1967 Santo Domingo, Dominican Republic
Height: 6'1" **Weight:** 210 lbs.
Bats: left **Throws:** left
Acquired: Traded by Dodgers with Jeff Treadway for Joey Eischen and Roberto Kelly, 5/95

PLAYER SUMMARY	
Fantasy Value	$25 to $30
Card Value	15¢ to 20¢
Will	show speed
Can't	play great defense
Expect	success vs. righties
Don't Expect	a homer crown

Rodriguez's breakthrough season helped propel the Expos into the playoff hunt. Hitting .320 in April with nine homers, he won the favor of right-field bleacher fans in Montreal, who showered him with "Oh! Henry" candy bars in what was seemingly a daily ritual. Rodriguez had never before shown he could provide consistent pop, but he had 25 long balls at the All-Star break to rank among NL leaders. However, he saw a steady diet of breaking balls in the second half and was able to muster up only 11 more homers, finishing well out of the league's top ten. He also charged the mound after a beaning from Houston's Danny Darwin in August, leading to a 15-minute brawl and a four-game suspension for Rodriguez. Despite his power, Rodriguez is far from a complete player; he hit just .218 against lefties, fanned a league-leading 160 times, and took only 37 walks. His on-base percentage was a lowly .325.

Major League Batting Register

	BA	G	AB	R	H	2B	3B	HR	RBI	SB
92 NL	.219	53	146	11	32	7	0	3	14	0
93 NL	.222	76	176	20	39	10	0	8	23	1
94 NL	.268	104	306	33	82	14	2	8	49	0
95 NL	.239	45	138	13	33	4	1	2	15	0
96 NL	.276	145	532	81	147	42	1	36	103	2
Life	.257	423	1298	158	333	77	4	57	204	3
2 Ave	.273	146	482	64	131	31	2	24	86	1

IVAN RODRIGUEZ

Position: Catcher
Team: Texas Rangers
Born: Nov. 30, 1971 Vega Baja, Puerto Rico
Height: 5'9" **Weight:** 205 lbs.
Bats: right **Throws:** right
Acquired: Signed as a free agent, 7/88

PLAYER SUMMARY	
Fantasy Value	$19 to $22
Card Value	10¢ to 15¢
Will	be an All-Star
Can't	find his weakness
Expect	strong throwing
Don't Expect	a slump

Continuing to cement his reputation as one of the finest young players in the game, Rodriguez hit .300 for the second straight year and tagged 47 doubles to rank third in the AL and propel the Rangers to the play-offs for the first time ever. He set career highs in games, at bats, runs, hits, doubles, homers, and RBI. Adjusting to the second spot in the Texas lineup, "Pudge" cut down his swing and worked on taking the ball the other way, drawing a career-high 38 walks while fanning just 55 times. While that hardly places him in Wade Boggs realm, it was well over twice the number of bases on balls he had totaled the year before. Behind the dish, Rodriguez continued to show why most AL baserunners fear taking off when he is behind the plate. He threw out 46 of the 94 baserunners who dared to steal against him—a nearly unheard of 49 percent success rate. While Rodriguez still needs to improve his game-calling, time will improve his performance in handling the pitching staff.

Major League Batting Register

	BA	G	AB	R	H	2B	3B	HR	RBI	SB
91 AL	.264	88	280	24	74	16	0	3	27	0
92 AL	.260	123	420	39	109	16	1	8	37	0
93 AL	.273	137	473	56	129	28	4	10	66	8
94 AL	.298	99	363	56	108	19	1	16	57	6
95 AL	.303	130	492	56	149	32	2	12	67	0
96 AL	.300	153	639	116	192	47	3	19	86	5
Life	.285	730	2667	347	761	158	11	68	340	19
3 Ave	.300	146	568	86	171	37	2	18	81	4

KENNY ROGERS

Position: Pitcher
Team: New York Yankees
Born: Nov. 10, 1964 Savannah, GA
Height: 6'1" **Weight:** 205 lbs.
Bats: left **Throws:** left
Acquired: Signed as a free agent, 1/96

PLAYER SUMMARY	
Fantasy Value	$7 to $9
Card Value	5¢ to 8¢
Will	pitch wherever asked
Can't	show blazing heat
Expect	a comeback
Don't Expect	perfect control

When the Yankees signed Rogers—who had spent his entire career in Texas—to a huge contract last winter, many questioned whether the reserved, intense Rogers could adjust to the pressures of pitching in New York. For a time, Rogers was ticketed for the bullpen, but an early shoulder injury forced a stay in extended spring training. Despite the injury (which he tried to hide from manager Joe Torre because he wanted to contribute), Rogers stayed a starter the entire year due to other pitchers' injuries and poor performance. He notched several key wins down the stretch to help New York reach the playoffs. In addition to his sore shoulder, Rogers experienced control problems in 1996, which contributed to his mediocre ERA (4.68) and win-loss record. However, he held lefties to a puny .209 average and gave up just 16 home runs. While not a superstar, Rogers is a decent starting pitcher who will be around for years.

Major League Pitching Register

	W	L	ERA	G	CG	IP	H	ER	BB	SO
89 AL	3	4	2.93	73	0	73.2	60	24	42	63
90 AL	10	6	3.13	69	0	97.2	93	34	42	74
91 AL	10	10	5.42	63	0	109.2	121	66	61	73
92 AL	3	6	3.09	81	0	78.2	80	27	26	70
93 AL	16	10	4.10	35	5	208.1	210	95	71	140
94 AL	11	8	4.46	24	6	167.1	169	83	52	120
95 AL	17	7	3.38	31	3	208.0	192	78	76	140
96 AL	12	8	4.68	30	2	179.0	179	93	83	92
Life	82	59	4.01	406	16	1122.1	1104	500	453	772
3 Ave	16	9	4.13	33	5	216.1	211	99	81	140

MEL ROJAS

Position: Pitcher
Team: Chicago Cubs
Born: Dec. 10, 1966 Haina, Dominican Republic
Height: 5'11" **Weight:** 185 lbs.
Bats: right **Throws:** right
Acquired: Signed as a free agent, 12/96

PLAYER SUMMARY	
Fantasy Value	$30 to $35
Card Value	5¢ to 8¢
Will	get his strikeouts
Can't	carry the load alone
Expect	saves
Don't Expect	consistency

Rojas is an extremely gifted but inconsistent pitcher. As the 1996 season progressed, his control improved. All in all, he threw just three wild pitches and didn't get himself into too much trouble with walks. In August, when the Expos' playoff drive heated up, Rojas was 2-0 with eight saves in 13 games, allowing just one earned run. He blew only four saves on the season and fanned more than one man an inning. He has a terrific moving fastball, a devastating split-fingered pitch, and a good slider. Rojas remains relatively easy to run on due to his protracted delivery, and he loses effectiveness when used for more than one inning per game. The Expos have a deep bullpen, however, and are able to keep Rojas from burning out. With 109 career saves, Rojas is second on the Expos all-time list, just 43 behind Jeff Reardon. The Cubs look to Rojas to shore up their pitching staff for '97.

Major League Pitching Register

	W	L	ERA	G	S	IP	H	ER	BB	SO
90 NL	3	1	3.60	23	1	40.0	34	16	24	26
91 NL	3	3	3.75	37	6	48.0	42	20	13	37
92 NL	7	1	1.43	68	10	100.2	71	16	34	70
93 NL	5	8	2.95	66	10	88.1	80	29	30	48
94 NL	3	2	3.32	58	16	84.0	71	31	21	84
95 NL	1	4	4.12	59	30	67.2	69	31	29	61
96 NL	7	4	3.22	74	36	81.0	56	29	28	92
Life	29	23	3.04	385	109	509.2	423	172	179	418
3 Ave	4	4	3.51	74	31	92.1	78	36	30	93

KIRK RUETER

Position: Pitcher
Team: San Francisco Giants
Born: Dec. 1, 1970 Centralia, IL
Height: 6'3" **Weight:** 195 lbs.
Bats: left **Throws:** left
Acquired: Traded by Expos with Tim Scott for Mark Leiter, 7/96

PLAYER SUMMARY	
Fantasy Value	$5 to $7
Card Value	4¢ to 7¢
Will	get chances
Can't	throw hard
Expect	ground balls
Don't Expect	many strikeouts

Rueter began the 1996 season in the Expos rotation and continued, at least for a while, to receive the kind of spectacular offensive support that had helped him to a 20-6 major-league record. However, he couldn't capitalize; despite 51 runs scored for him in his first five starts, Rueter could only manage a 2-2 record. In a game on April 23, he was ejected after a brushback war with St. Louis' Todd Stottlemyre. He was placed on the disabled list May 10 with an inflamed left knee, and when he returned two weeks later, Rueter simply was not effective. The Expos sent him to Triple-A on July 16 and dealt him to the Giants two weeks later amidst reports that the speed on his fastball had declined to 84 mph. He has never thrown hard, but he can get into a solid groove with his sinker and curve. The Giants had Rueter work at Triple-A Phoenix for most of August and September, but saw enough of him in a trial with the big club to pencil him into the rotation this spring.

Major League Pitching Register

	W	L	ERA	G	CG	IP	H	ER	BB	SO
93 NL	8	0	2.73	14	1	85.2	85	26	18	31
94 NL	7	3	5.17	20	0	92.1	106	53	23	50
95 NL	5	3	3.23	9	1	47.1	38	17	9	28
96 NL	6	8	3.97	20	0	102.0	109	45	27	46
Life	26	14	3.88	63	2	327.1	338	141	77	155
2 Ave	8	6	4.64	24	0	116.0	129	60	30	58

BRUCE RUFFIN

Position: Pitcher
Team: Colorado Rockies
Born: Oct. 4, 1963 Lubbock, TX
Height: 6'2" **Weight:** 213 lbs.
Bats: both **Throws:** left
Acquired: Signed as a free agent, 12/92

PLAYER SUMMARY	
Fantasy Value	$12 to $15
Card Value	4¢ to 7¢
Will	throw hard
Can't	afford wildness
Expect	sinking fastballs
Don't Expect	a slump

Ruffin entered 1996 as the Rockies' top lefty reliever. Although he had been effective for several years, injury and wildness had prevented Ruffin from winning the closer's job. However, Curtis Leskanic—expected to get most of the save opportunities for Colorado in '96—stumbled out of the gate, and Ruffin ended up as the only Rockies pitcher with more than six saves. He throws harder than most left-handers and has good sink on his fastball, making him ideal for the thin air of Coors Field. However, all was not perfect for Ruffin. Although he cut down his walks and allowed just five homers on the year, he did fling ten wild pitches and, oddly, allowed lefties to hit .286 against him. Even if he does not continue as the Rockies closer for 1997, Ruffin is a good man to have around; he can work set-up duty, fill in as a long reliever, and even start if necessary.

Major League Pitching Register

	W	L	ERA	G	S	IP	H	ER	BB	SO
86 NL	9	4	2.46	21	0	146.1	138	40	44	70
87 NL	11	14	4.35	35	0	204.2	236	99	73	93
88 NL	6	10	4.43	55	3	144.1	151	71	80	82
89 NL	6	10	4.44	24	0	125.2	152	62	62	70
90 NL	6	13	5.38	32	0	149.0	178	89	62	79
91 NL	4	7	3.78	31	0	119.0	125	50	38	85
92 AL	1	6	6.67	25	0	58.0	66	43	41	45
93 NL	6	5	3.87	59	2	139.2	145	60	69	126
94 NL	4	5	4.04	56	16	55.2	55	25	30	65
95 NL	0	1	2.12	37	11	34.0	26	8	19	23
96 NL	7	5	4.00	71	24	69.2	55	31	29	74
Life	60	80	4.17	446	56	1246.0	1327	578	547	812
3 Ave	4	4	3.63	64	20	62.0	54	25	31	64

JOHNNY RUFFIN

Position: Pitcher
Team: Cincinnati Reds
Born: July 29, 1971 Butler, AL
Height: 6'3" **Weight:** 170 lbs.
Bats: right **Throws:** right
Acquired: Traded by White Sox with Jeff Pierce for Tim Belcher, 7/93

PLAYER SUMMARY	
Fantasy Value	$1
Card Value	5¢ to 8¢
Will	work in middle
Can't	control fastball
Expect	some improvement
Don't Expect	many saves

Ruffin, once a prized prospect in the Chicago White Sox organization before he was obtained by the Reds in a trade several years ago, seems to have pitched himself completely out of the Reds' plans. At the start of the season, the Reds were counting on him to be a set-up man for closer Jeff Brantley, but Ruffin was bad from Opening Day and got worse. Soon, manager Ray Knight banished Ruffin to the furthest reaches of the Reds bullpen. Ruffin pitched only 24⅓ innings between August 1 and the end of the season despite being on the active roster the entire time—a testament to just how little the Reds trusted him. They would have sent Ruffin to Triple-A, but he was out of options and the club was afraid another team would claim him. In his defense, Ruffin did have a knee injury that wiped out most of his 1995 season. Many knowledgeable medical people think it takes a full year to get back to full strength after surgery; since Ruffin is young and still throws hard, it is possible he can come back and be a decent set-up guy.

Major League Pitching Register

	W	L	ERA	G	S	IP	H	ER	BB	SO
93 NL	2	1	3.58	21	2	37.2	36	15	11	30
94 NL	7	2	3.09	51	1	70.0	57	24	27	44
95 NL	0	0	1.35	10	0	13.1	4	2	11	11
96 NL	1	3	5.49	49	0	62.1	71	38	37	69
Life	10	6	3.88	131	3	183.1	168	79	86	154
2 Ave	5	3	4.02	60	1	80.1	76	36	38	65

JEFF RUSSELL

Position: Pitcher
Team: Texas Rangers
Born: Sept. 2, 1961 Cincinnati, OH
Height: 6'3" **Weight:** 205 lbs.
Bats: right **Throws:** right
Acquired: Signed as a free agent, 4/95

PLAYER SUMMARY	
Fantasy Value	$3 to $5
Card Value	4¢ to 7¢
Will	pitch when asked
Can't	be a closer
Expect	smart pitching
Don't Expect	much velocity

Russell, who had considered retirement after the 1995 campaign, was lured back by the Rangers. Texas management knew they had a thin bullpen and welcomed the experience Russell could bring. He began the season in the minors but came up in early May. Russell is no longer capable of throwing balls past hitters, but he has become a serviceable seventh- and eighth-inning set-up man who keeps opponents at bay before handing the ball to the closer. After several years of piling up successful save totals, his glamour stats have declined three straight years. Russell must be used judiciously these days; he is no longer effective against left-handed batters. Once upon a time, Russell was a workhorse, but age, injury, and decreased velocity have taken their toll. His career is winding down.

Major League Pitching Register

	W	L	ERA	G	S	IP	H	ER	BB	SO
83 NL	4	5	3.03	10	0	68.1	58	23	22	40
84 NL	6	18	4.26	33	0	181.2	186	86	65	101
85 AL	3	6	7.55	13	0	62.0	85	52	27	44
86 AL	5	2	3.40	37	2	82.0	74	31	31	54
87 AL	5	4	4.44	52	3	97.1	109	48	52	56
88 AL	10	9	3.82	34	0	188.2	183	80	66	88
89 AL	6	4	1.98	71	38	72.2	45	16	24	77
90 AL	1	5	4.26	27	10	25.1	23	12	16	16
91 AL	6	4	3.29	68	30	79.1	71	29	26	52
92 AL	4	3	1.63	59	30	66.1	55	12	25	48
93 AL	1	4	2.70	51	33	46.2	39	14	14	45
94 AL	1	6	5.09	42	17	40.2	43	23	16	28
95 AL	1	0	3.03	37	20	32.2	36	11	9	21
96 AL	3	3	3.38	55	3	56.0	58	21	22	23
Life	56	73	3.75	589	186	1099.2	1065	458	415	693
3 Ave	2	4	3.95	52	16	50.0	53	22	18	29

KEN RYAN

Position: Pitcher
Team: Philadelphia Phillies
Born: Oct. 24, 1968 Pawtucket, RI
Height: 6'3" **Weight:** 200 lbs.
Bats: right **Throws:** right
Acquired: Traded by Red Sox with Glenn Murray and Lee Tinsley for Heathcliff Slocumb, Rick Holifield, and Larry Wimberly, 1/96

PLAYER SUMMARY	
Fantasy Value	$5 to $7
Card Value	4¢ to 7¢
Will	struggle with control
Can't	get save chances
Expect	plenty of Ks
Don't Expect	trouble with righties

Ryan got his chance to start a new career this year in Philadelphia, and he showed a strong, durable arm. The onetime Red Sox hope of the future was very effective at times for the Phillies, holding opponents to a .223 batting average and allowing just four home runs all year. Unfortunately, Ryan's curve and slider moved so well that they often missed the strike zone entirely. Ryan walked far too many men for comfort and got hurt if he had to come in with straight fastballs when behind in the count. His control problems kept him from getting a significant amount of save chances, and he blew six of the 14 opportunities he did receive. Ryan may not be a closer (since Philadelphia already has All-Star short man Ricky Bottalico), but he is still an effective reliever who just needs help with location. Perhaps the new Phillies staff can help him turn his talent into results. Philadelphia certainly can't afford to throw away the meager amount of talent they do have.

Major League Pitching Register

	W	L	ERA	G	S	IP	H	ER	BB	SO
92 AL	0	0	6.43	7	1	7.0	4	5	5	5
93 AL	7	2	3.60	47	1	50.0	43	20	29	49
94 AL	2	3	2.44	42	13	48.0	46	13	17	32
95 AL	0	4	4.96	28	7	32.2	34	18	24	34
96 NL	3	5	2.43	62	8	89.0	71	24	45	70
Life	12	14	3.18	186	30	226.2	198	80	120	190
3 Ave	2	5	2.91	51	11	64.1	58	21	32	51

BRET SABERHAGEN

Position: Pitcher
Team: Boston Red Sox
Born: April 11, 1964 Chicago Heights, IL
Height: 6'1" **Weight:** 190 lbs.
Bats: right **Throws:** right
Acquired: Signed as a minor-league free agent, 12/96

PLAYER SUMMARY	
Fantasy Value	$1
Card Value	5¢ to 8¢
Will	try again
Can't	show old fastball
Expect	starts if healthy
Don't Expect	control troubles

Saberhagen, one of baseball's best moundsmen when healthy, has struggled with injuries his entire career. However, 1996 was the first time medical miseries wiped out a whole season. Shoulder woes suffered in 1995 caused him to lose effectiveness as the season went on, and Saberhagen underwent surgery to repair the damage. As expected, he missed all of 1996 to recovery and rehab. Unfortunately, neither doctors nor Saberhagen himself have been able to predict whether he will be physically able to contribute. The Red Sox are hoping he'll make a full recovery. When he's on, Saberhagen's deadly slider and outstanding fastball make him nearly unhittable. It is unlikely he will ever again reach the heights he scaled in 1989, '93, or '94, but he may still be effective.

Major League Pitching Register

	W	L	ERA	G	CG	IP	H	ER	BB	SO
84 AL	10	11	3.48	38	2	157.2	138	61	36	73
85 AL	20	6	2.87	32	10	235.1	211	75	38	158
86 AL	7	12	4.15	30	4	156.0	165	72	29	112
87 AL	18	10	3.36	33	15	257.0	246	96	53	163
88 AL	14	16	3.80	35	9	260.2	271	110	59	171
89 AL	23	6	2.16	36	12	262.1	209	63	43	193
90 AL	5	9	3.27	20	5	135.0	146	49	28	87
91 AL	13	8	3.07	28	7	196.1	165	67	45	136
92 AL	3	5	3.50	17	1	97.2	84	38	27	81
93 NL	7	7	3.29	19	4	139.1	131	51	17	93
94 NL	14	4	2.74	24	4	177.1	169	54	13	143
95 NL	7	6	4.18	25	3	153.0	165	71	33	100
Life	141	100	3.26	337	76	2227.2	2100	807	421	1510

ROGER SALKELD

Position: Pitcher
Team: Cincinnati Reds
Born: March 6, 1971 Burbank, CA
Height: 6'5" **Weight:** 215 lbs.
Bats: right **Throws:** right
Acquired: Traded by Mariners for Tim Belcher, 5/95

PLAYER SUMMARY	
Fantasy Value	$1
Card Value	4¢ to 7¢
Will	allow homers
Can't	throw hard
Expect	swingman duty
Don't Expect	20 wins

Salkeld won a spot in the Reds starting rotation out of spring training, but it didn't take him long to be demoted to the bullpen. The former Mariners righty actually pitched fairly well in long relief for a stretch in the first half, which was good enough to get him a few more starts; however, he never became the pitcher the Reds hoped. His troubles usually stemmed from too many walks (he passed about four men per nine innings), despite his assuring manager Ray Knight repeatedly that he could throw strikes at will. After getting in a jam, Salkeld would have to groove fastballs, 18 of which landed in the outfield bleachers. His home run total was the second highest of any pitcher on the Reds staff, although he pitched far fewer innings (116) than any other starter. Salkeld once featured a tremendous fastball but now throws in the mid-80s after major shoulder surgery in 1993. He will probably continue to work in a swing role, but the Reds don't project him to be a member of their starting rotation next year.

Major League Pitching Register

	W	L	ERA	G	CG	IP	H	ER	BB	SO
93 AL	0	0	2.51	3	0	14.1	13	4	4	13
94 AL	2	5	7.17	13	0	59.0	76	47	45	46
96 NL	8	5	5.20	29	1	116.0	114	67	54	82
Life	10	10	5.61	45	1	189.1	203	118	103	141

TIM SALMON

Position: Outfield
Team: Anaheim Angels
Born: Aug. 24, 1968 Long Beach, CA
Height: 6'3" **Weight:** 220 lbs.
Bats: right **Throws:** right
Acquired: Third-round pick in 6/89 free-agent draft

PLAYER SUMMARY	
Fantasy Value	$30 to $35
Card Value	20¢ to 40¢
Will	hit the ball hard
Can't	carry the team
Expect	premier play
Don't Expect	much speed

Salmon, the Angels' best player, enjoyed another All-Star-caliber season in '96. With the exception of stolen bases, there isn't an offensive category in which he doesn't excel. Salmon actually hits right-handers better than he hits left-handers, which is an unusual feat for a right-handed power hitter. Salmon's hitting zone is out over the plate, but he's a good enough hitter to fight off opponents who try to pitch him inside. Defensively, he has decent range in the field (especially for a big man), sure hands, and a strong, accurate arm, but he lacks great speed. Rarely do runners attempt to move from first to third on Salmon; his 13 outfield assists ranked behind only Manny Ramirez among American League right fielders last year. Salmon's 1996 offensive numbers were not as impressive as 1995's, but he was forced to try to carry a heavier offensive load as Angels batters faltered across the board. Expect more of the same—offensively and defensively—for Salmon in 1997 and years to come.

Major League Batting Register

	BA	G	AB	R	H	2B	3B	HR	RBI	SB
92 AL	.177	23	79	8	14	1	0	2	6	1
93 AL	.283	142	515	93	146	35	1	31	95	5
94 AL	.287	100	373	67	107	18	2	23	70	1
95 AL	.330	143	537	111	177	34	3	34	105	5
96 AL	.286	156	581	90	166	27	4	30	98	4
Life	.293	564	2085	369	610	115	10	120	374	16
3 Ave	.302	153	570	103	172	30	3	34	105	4

REY SANCHEZ

Position: Shortstop
Team: Chicago Cubs
Born: Oct. 15, 1967 Rio Piedras, Puerto Rico
Height: 5'9" **Weight:** 170 lbs.
Bats: right **Throws:** right
Acquired: Traded by Rangers for Bryan House, 1/90

PLAYER SUMMARY	
Fantasy Value	$1
Card Value	4¢ to 7¢
Will	get another shot
Can't	stay healthy
Expect	good defense
Don't Expect	any power

Sanchez was given the opportunity to be the Cubs' everyday shortstop after the club let Shawon Dunston go, but he never did claim the position for good due to his woeful offensive performance. Sanchez managed only one home run, ten total extra-base hits, 12 RBI, and 12 walks—not nearly good enough. Sanchez again missed several weeks with a broken hamate bone in his left hand (the same injury he suffered in 1995) and was placed on the DL in early June, but it's doubtful the Cubs would have stuck with him for the entire season even if he hadn't been hurt. He came off the DL for the last eight weeks of the season and hit exactly the same (.211) as before he was hurt. Sanchez is an excellent defender, but his poor offensive skills keep him from being a good everyday player. With Shawon Dunston back for '97, Sanchez's playing time will be significantly decreased.

Major League Batting Register

	BA	G	AB	R	H	2B	3B	HR	RBI	SB
91 NL	.261	13	23	1	6	0	0	0	2	0
92 NL	.251	74	255	24	64	14	3	1	19	2
93 NL	.282	105	344	35	97	11	2	0	28	1
94 NL	.285	96	291	26	83	13	1	0	24	2
95 NL	.278	114	428	57	119	22	2	3	27	6
96 NL	.211	95	289	28	61	9	0	1	12	7
Life	.264	497	1630	171	430	69	8	5	112	18
3 Ave	.264	119	393	43	104	17	1	1	25	6

RYNE SANDBERG

Position: Second base
Team: Chicago Cubs
Born: Sept. 18, 1959 Spokane, WA
Height: 6'2" **Weight:** 190 lbs.
Bats: right **Throws:** right
Acquired: Traded by Phillies with Larry Bowa for Ivan DeJesus, 1/82

PLAYER SUMMARY	
Fantasy Value	$13 to $16
Card Value	30¢ to 60¢
Will	hit for power
Can't	carry a team
Expect	another season
Don't Expect	All-Star showing

Sandberg returned to baseball after a year and a half off, but 25 home runs and memories of old days have clouded the view of some Cub fans. Sandberg was second on the team with 25 long balls and 92 RBI, but in the year of the home run, all that showed was that he can still hit mistake pitches out of the ballpark. Sandberg often appeared lost at the plate and wound up hitting only .244. Manager Jim Riggleman moved Sandberg all over the lineup, hitting him anywhere from second to seventh, and wound up using him in the cleanup spot for the last six weeks due to Sammy Sosa's injury. Sandberg is still a solid defensive player, but it's obvious he's lost a couple of steps. His arm also isn't what it once was.

Major League Batting Register

	BA	G	AB	R	H	2B	3B	HR	RBI	SB
81 NL	.167	13	6	2	1	0	0	0	0	0
82 NL	.271	156	635	103	172	33	5	7	54	32
83 NL	.261	158	633	94	165	25	4	8	48	37
84 NL	.314	156	636	114	200	36	19	19	84	32
85 NL	.305	153	609	113	186	31	6	26	83	54
86 NL	.284	154	627	68	178	28	5	14	76	34
87 NL	.294	132	523	81	154	25	2	16	59	21
88 NL	.264	155	618	77	163	23	8	19	69	25
89 NL	.290	157	606	104	176	25	5	30	76	15
90 NL	.306	155	615	116	188	30	3	40	100	25
91 NL	.291	158	585	104	170	32	2	26	100	22
92 NL	.304	158	612	100	186	32	8	26	87	17
93 NL	.309	117	456	67	141	20	0	9	45	9
94 NL	.238	57	223	36	53	9	5	5	24	2
96 NL	.244	150	554	85	135	28	4	25	92	12
Life	.286	2029	7938	1264	2268	377	76	270	997	337
2 Ave	.242	115	434	68	105	20	6	16	63	7

REGGIE SANDERS

Position: Outfield
Team: Cincinnati Reds
Born: Dec. 1, 1967 Florence, SC
Height: 6'1" **Weight:** 180 lbs.
Bats: right **Throws:** right
Acquired: Seventh-round pick in 6/87 free-agent draft

PLAYER SUMMARY	
Fantasy Value	$25 to $30
Card Value	12¢ to 20¢
Will	show power
Can't	hit a curve
Expect	strikeouts and walks
Don't Expect	consistency

After the Reds lost Ron Gant to the Cardinals, Sanders was expected to step up and be the main power threat in the lineup. However, he ended up one of the major disappointments in the National League in 1996. Largely due to injuries, Sanders never came close to approaching the form that made him an MVP candidate in 1995. He started out the season hitting poorly and then hurt his back diving for a ball in the outfield. The injury shelved him for two months. He hit well after coming off the DL and had his batting average near .300 in early July, but he struggled badly the rest of the season. While Sanders took enough walks (44) to post a .353 on-base percentage, he also fanned 86 times. Sanders will try to readjust his batting stance because Reds management believes the adjustments he made to his swing late in 1995 caused his poor performance during most of 1996. Sanders is still the best pure power hitter the Reds have, and the club is counting on him to rebound in 1997.

Major League Batting Register

	BA	G	AB	R	H	2B	3B	HR	RBI	SB
91 NL	.200	9	40	6	8	0	0	1	3	1
92 NL	.270	116	385	62	104	26	6	12	36	16
93 NL	.274	138	496	90	136	16	4	20	83	27
94 NL	.262	107	400	66	105	20	8	17	62	21
95 NL	.306	133	484	91	148	36	6	28	99	36
96 NL	.251	81	287	49	72	17	1	14	33	24
Life	.274	584	2092	364	573	115	25	92	316	125
3 Ave	.277	127	465	81	129	29	6	23	77	31

SCOTT SANDERS

Position: Pitcher
Team: Seattle Mariners
Born: March 25, 1969 Hannibal, MO
Height: 6'4" **Weight:** 220 lbs.
Bats: right **Throws:** right
Acquired: Traded by Padres for Sterling Hitchcock, 12/96

PLAYER SUMMARY	
Fantasy Value	$9 to $11
Card Value	5¢ to 8¢
Will	show strong arm
Can't	win starting job
Expect	strikeouts
Don't Expect	closing duty

Sanders was a real bright spot on a fine San Diego pitching staff. After a nightmarish 1995 season (he was plagued by elbow problems that kept him on the disabled list for most of the second half), Sanders rebounded in a big way in 1996, making 30 relief appearances and 16 starts. Most of his starts came in the second half. He allowed fewer hits than innings pitched, fanned over one batter an inning, and walked only one per three innings. One key improvement Sanders made in 1996 was keeping the ball in the park; he allowed only ten home runs. Sanders, who has a biting curve and excellent velocity on his fastball, could very easily wind up in a starting rotation. Sanders has the potential to be very, very good. The Mariners traded for him over the off-season and are looking forward to seeing what Sanders can do.

BENITO SANTIAGO

Position: Catcher
Team: Toronto Blue Jays
Born: March 9, 1965 Ponce, Puerto Rico
Height: 6'1" **Weight:** 185 lbs.
Bats: right **Throws:** right
Acquired: Signed as a free agent, 12/96

PLAYER SUMMARY	
Fantasy Value	$17 to $20
Card Value	5¢ to 8¢
Will	hit for power
Can't	run like before
Expect	strong throws
Don't Expect	many walks

Santiago has been on the rebound for a while, but 1996 was clearly the best season he's had in a long time. In fact, it may have been the best performance of his career. Santiago had seen his stock plummet before improving in 1994 and '95, but the veteran receiver outdid himself in 1996. He crushed a career-high 30 home runs, slugged over .500, and scored 71 runs for a Philadelphia team that was pretty horrible offensively. His 49 walks were by far a career high. He also was given credit for helping out a starting staff that was besieged with injuries the entire season, although he threw out just 30 percent of enemy basestealers. While Santiago may never live up to the potential he showed in his rookie season ten years ago, he has enjoyed three good years in a row and again proved himself to be one of the top catchers in the National League.

Major League Pitching Register

	W	L	ERA	G	S	IP	H	ER	BB	SO
93 NL	3	3	4.13	9	0	52.1	54	24	23	37
94 NL	4	8	4.78	23	1	111.0	103	59	48	109
95 NL	5	5	4.30	17	0	90.0	79	43	31	88
96 NL	9	5	3.38	46	0	144.0	117	54	48	157
Life	21	21	4.08	95	1	397.1	353	180	150	391
3 Ave	7	7	4.16	33	0	134.0	117	62	50	137

Major League Batting Register

	BA	G	AB	R	H	2B	3B	HR	RBI	SB
86 NL	.290	17	62	10	18	2	0	3	6	0
87 NL	.300	146	546	64	164	33	2	18	79	21
88 NL	.248	139	492	49	122	22	2	10	46	15
89 NL	.236	129	462	50	109	16	3	16	62	11
90 NL	.270	100	344	42	93	8	5	11	53	5
91 NL	.267	152	580	60	155	22	3	17	87	8
92 NL	.251	106	386	37	97	21	0	10	42	2
93 NL	.230	139	469	49	108	19	6	13	50	10
94 NL	.273	101	337	35	92	14	2	11	41	1
95 NL	.286	81	266	40	76	20	0	11	44	2
96 NL	.264	136	481	71	127	21	2	30	85	2
Life	.262	1246	4425	507	1161	198	25	150	595	77
3 Ave	.273	123	418	55	114	21	2	19	64	2

STEVE SCARSONE

Position: Infield
Team: San Francisco Giants
Born: April 11, 1966 Anaheim, CA
Height: 6'2" **Weight:** 195 lbs.
Bats: right **Throws:** right
Acquired: Traded by Orioles for Mark Leonard, 3/93

PLAYER SUMMARY	
Fantasy Value	$0
Card Value	4¢ to 7¢
Will	look for work
Can't	learn the strike zone
Expect	some pop
Don't Expect	many at bats

Scarsone came back to earth after a fairly productive season in 1995. Inserted at second base after veteran Robby Thompson went down with yet another injury, the ineffective Scarsone was replaced by rookie Jay Canizaro near the end of the season. Scarsone produced career highs in several offensive categories in 1995, including RBI and home runs, but couldn't come close to matching those totals when given the chance in 1996. Scarsone again feasted on left-handed pitching (.303 average) but hit just .194 against righties. He has always shown poor strike-zone command, and fanned a whopping 91 times in 1996 while taking just 25 walks. Scarsone seems sure to be pushed out in favor of a younger player at the start of the 1997 season. The Giants plan to make Canizaro or Bill Mueller their regular second baseman. It will be hard for Scarsone to hang on, even as a bench player, given his lack of speed, inability to play shortstop, and lack of success against right-handed pitching.

Major League Batting Register

	BA	G	AB	R	H	2B	3B	HR	RBI	SB
92 NL	.154	7	13	1	2	0	0	0	0	0
92 AL	.176	11	17	2	3	0	0	0	0	0
93 NL	.252	44	103	16	26	9	0	2	15	0
94 NL	.272	52	103	21	28	8	0	2	13	0
95 NL	.266	80	233	33	62	10	3	11	29	3
96 NL	.219	105	283	28	62	12	1	5	23	2
Life	.243	299	752	101	183	39	4	20	80	5
2 Ave	.242	98	273	33	66	12	2	9	28	3

CURT SCHILLING

Position: Pitcher
Team: Philadelphia Phillies
Born: Nov. 14, 1966 Anchorage, AK
Height: 6'4" **Weight:** 215 lbs.
Bats: right **Throws:** right
Acquired: Traded by Astros for Jason Grimsley, 4/92

PLAYER SUMMARY	
Fantasy Value	$15 to $18
Card Value	5¢ to 8¢
Will	throw hard
Can't	count on support
Expect	quality innings
Don't Expect	pain-free season

Schilling underwent surgery to repair a torn labrum in his pitching shoulder in August 1995. He was expected to miss up to a year of action. However, Schilling surprised everyone by showing up for spring training, throwing hard and apparently without pain, and going to extended spring training to work his arm into shape. A short Triple-A assignment followed, and on May 14, Schilling joined the Phillies. He shut out the Giants for seven innings, fanning ten, in what was the beginning of an outstanding season. While Schilling's win-loss record was under .500, he was often a dominating pitcher. He completed eight games—two of them shutouts—and held opponents to a measly .223 batting average. When healthy, the competitive, hard-throwing Schilling is one of the five best starting pitchers in the NL. He'll be the Phillies' ace again in 1997, provided he stays healthy.

Major League Pitching Register

	W	L	ERA	G	CG	IP	H	ER	BB	SO
88 AL	0	3	9.82	4	0	14.2	22	16	10	4
89 AL	0	1	6.23	5	0	8.2	10	6	3	6
90 AL	1	2	2.54	35	0	46.0	38	13	19	32
91 NL	3	5	3.81	56	0	75.2	79	32	39	71
92 NL	14	11	2.35	42	10	226.1	165	59	59	147
93 NL	16	7	4.02	34	7	235.1	234	105	57	186
94 NL	2	8	4.48	13	1	82.1	87	41	28	58
95 NL	7	5	3.57	17	1	116.0	96	46	26	114
96 NL	9	10	3.19	26	8	183.1	149	65	50	182
Life	52	52	3.49	232	27	988.1	880	383	291	800
3 Ave	7	9	3.65	21	4	143.1	127	58	40	131

JASON SCHMIDT

Position: Pitcher
Team: Pittsburgh Pirates
Born: Jan. 29, 1973 Kelso, WA
Height: 6'5" **Weight:** 185 lbs.
Bats: right **Throws:** right
Acquired: Traded by Braves with Ron Wright for Denny Neagle, 7/96

PLAYER SUMMARY	
Fantasy Value	$3 to $5
Card Value	8¢ to 12¢
Will	improve
Can't	be an ace yet
Expect	strikeouts
Don't Expect	perfect control

With the pennant-winning Braves, Schmidt had few opportunities to pitch six or seven innings a game and learn from his mistakes. Now that he's with the Pirates, he'll have a chance to start every fifth day for an entire season without the pressures he had in Atlanta. Although he will be key to the Bucs' rebuilding process, he won't be expected to win a Cy Young Award next season. Schmidt has everything a manager looks for in a pitcher. He throws in the mid-90s, is durable, and keeps the ball down. Atlanta fans soured on Schmidt last season as he allowed left-handers to hit .333; however, he has a fine minor-league pedigree, winning the 1995 International League ERA title as well as finishing fourth in the league in strikeouts. It's often forgotten that current stars Greg Maddux, John Smoltz, and Tom Glavine all had ERAs around 5.00 in their first full seasons, and there is little reason to think that Schmidt won't improve dramatically over the next few years. The Pirates may even wind up winning the trade in the long run, thanks to Schmidt.

Major League Pitching Register

	W	L	ERA	G	CG	IP	H	ER	BB	SO
95 NL	2	2	5.76	9	0	25.0	27	16	18	19
96 NL	5	6	5.70	19	1	96.1	108	61	53	74
Life	7	8	5.71	28	1	121.1	135	77	71	93

PETE SCHOUREK

Position: Pitcher
Team: Cincinnati Reds
Born: May 10, 1969 Austin, TX
Height: 6'5" **Weight:** 205 lbs.
Bats: left **Throws:** left
Acquired: Claimed from Mets on waivers, 4/94

PLAYER SUMMARY	
Fantasy Value	$4 to $6
Card Value	7¢ to 10¢
Will	throw changeups
Can't	blow hitters away
Expect	success if healthy
Don't Expect	a fast start

Schourek may have been the Reds' gutsiest player in 1996. It was obvious early in the season that he was not healthy, but the left-hander ignored the pain in his shoulder and took the mound every fifth day until Reds doctors told him not to. Schourek, who finished near the top of the Cy Young voting following his outstanding 1995 season, struggled badly all year because none of his pitches were effective. He had no zip on his fastball, and his breaking balls didn't break. When he's healthy, Schourek is among the best left-handers in the league. He throws fairly hard and his out pitch is an outstanding changeup. Schourek was finally shut down for good in mid-July and underwent surgery on his elbow. It is difficult to know what to expect from a pitcher coming off elbow surgery, but the Reds need their key lefty to bounce back in 1997. A healthy Pete Schourek would go a long way toward putting the Reds over the top in the competitive National League Central Division.

Major League Pitching Register

	W	L	ERA	G	CG	IP	H	ER	BB	SO
91 NL	5	4	4.27	35	1	86.1	82	41	43	67
92 NL	6	8	3.64	22	0	136.0	137	55	44	60
93 NL	5	12	5.96	41	0	128.1	168	85	45	72
94 NL	7	2	4.09	22	0	81.1	90	37	29	69
95 NL	18	7	3.22	29	2	190.1	158	68	45	160
96 NL	4	5	6.01	12	0	67.1	79	45	24	54
Life	45	38	4.32	161	3	689.2	714	331	230	482
3 Ave	11	5	3.95	25	1	132.0	128	58	38	110

DAVID SEGUI

Position: First base
Team: Montreal Expos
Born: July 19, 1966 Kansas City, KS
Height: 6'1" **Weight:** 202 lbs.
Bats: both **Throws:** left
Acquired: Traded by Mets for Reid Cornelius, 6/95

PLAYER SUMMARY	
Fantasy Value	$5 to $7
Card Value	5¢ to 8¢
Will	make contact
Can't	add speed
Expect	everyday duty
Don't Expect	many homers

Segui was consistent in 1996, posting similar numbers in both the first and second halves of the season. He was never outstanding but proved himself—once again—to be a solid player. Segui does not hit as many home runs as most teams like to get from their first basemen, but he shows line-drive power and hit a career-high 30 doubles last year. He also has good discipline at the plate and finished 1996 with more walks (60) than strikeouts (54), which is a sure sign of a crafty hitter. Segui is also a very fine defensive first baseman with a sure glove. He missed six weeks of action from early July until mid-August with a broken thumb, but he came back and hit well over the last month of the season. Segui is a very capable hitter who could probably do well batting third in the order for an entire season. Some baseball pundits feel that Segui may be capable of eventually winning a batting championship.

Major League Batting Register

	BA	G	AB	R	H	2B	3B	HR	RBI	SB
90 AL	.244	40	123	14	30	7	0	2	15	0
91 AL	.278	86	212	15	59	7	0	2	22	1
92 AL	.233	115	189	21	44	9	0	1	17	1
93 AL	.273	146	450	54	123	27	0	10	60	2
94 NL	.241	92	336	46	81	17	1	10	43	0
95 NL	.309	130	456	68	141	25	4	12	68	2
96 NL	.286	115	416	69	119	30	1	11	58	4
Life	.274	724	2182	287	597	122	6	48	283	10
3 Ave	.279	130	467	70	131	27	2	13	65	2

KEVIN SEITZER

Position: First base; designated hitter
Team: Cleveland Indians
Born: March 26, 1962 Springfield, IL
Height: 5'11" **Weight:** 190 lbs.
Bats: right **Throws:** right
Acquired: Traded by Brewers for Jeromy Burnitz, 8/96

PLAYER SUMMARY	
Fantasy Value	$8 to $10
Card Value	5¢ to 8¢
Will	play hard-nosed ball
Can't	play key position
Expect	high average
Don't Expect	much speed

Seitzer began the year with the Brewers and was the subject of trade rumors almost immediately. Milwaukee loved Seitzer's hard-nosed play but wanted to dump his salary. A bidding war developed, and he was shipped off to the first-place Cleveland Indians just before the September 1 trading deadline. Seitzer enjoyed another solid offensive year, with fine numbers in all key offensive categories. He's a smart, "professional" hitter. Seitzer had an outstanding .416 on-base percentage in 1996 and hit .368 against left-handers. No longer a particularly good third baseman, Kevin split his time between first base and DH duties. He provided a fiery clubhouse presence down the stretch. Seitzer has stated that 1997 will be his last year and has expressed interest in returning to Kansas City, where he began his career.

Major League Batting Register

	BA	G	AB	R	H	2B	3B	HR	RBI	SB
86 AL	.323	28	96	16	31	4	1	2	11	0
87 AL	.323	161	641	105	207	33	8	15	83	12
88 AL	.304	149	559	90	170	32	5	5	60	10
89 AL	.281	160	597	78	168	17	2	4	48	17
90 AL	.275	158	622	91	171	31	5	6	38	7
91 AL	.265	85	234	28	62	11	3	1	25	4
92 AL	.270	148	540	74	146	35	1	5	71	13
93 AL	.269	120	417	45	112	16	2	11	57	7
94 AL	.314	80	309	44	97	24	2	5	49	2
95 AL	.311	132	492	56	153	33	3	5	69	2
96 AL	.326	154	573	85	187	35	3	13	78	6
Life	.296	1375	5080	712	1504	271	35	72	589	80
3 Ave	.317	138	521	70	165	35	3	9	75	4

AARON SELE

Position: Pitcher
Team: Boston Red Sox
Born: June 25, 1970 Golden Valley, MN
Height: 6'5" **Weight:** 205 lbs.
Bats: right **Throws:** right
Acquired: First-round pick in 6/91 free-agent draft

PLAYER SUMMARY	
Fantasy Value	$3 to $5
Card Value	5¢ to 8¢
Will	continue rehab
Can't	show perfect control
Expect	frequent starts
Don't Expect	a Cy Young Award

Shoulder injuries kept Sele from full effectiveness for most of 1995, and the resulting rehabilitation and rust carried over into 1996. He was hit hard early in the season, sporting only a high ERA and few wins for his trouble. He won his first game April 22 and did not capture another until May 19. His third victory did not come until July. On May 9, Sele allowed six runs in just ⅔ of an inning to lift his ERA well over 7.00, and it remained high all year. Although Sele showed good velocity, control was a serious problem for him in 1996. He could not locate his off-speed pitches or good fastball against left-handers, who teed off on him at a .322 clip. Unlike the other Red Sox starters, Sele seldom finished what he started, completing just one game. There are better days ahead; even having the trouble he did in 1996, Sele gave up just 14 homers, threw only two wild pitches, and showed a good pickoff move. He will be an improved pitcher this season, provided he can stay healthy.

Major League Pitching Register

	W	L	ERA	G	CG	IP	H	ER	BB	SO
93 AL	7	2	2.74	18	0	111.2	100	34	48	93
94 AL	8	7	3.83	22	2	143.1	140	61	60	105
95 AL	3	1	3.06	6	0	32.1	32	11	14	21
96 AL	7	11	5.32	29	1	157.1	192	93	67	137
Life	25	21	4.03	75	3	444.2	464	199	189	356
2 Ave	9	10	4.48	30	2	180.1	195	89	76	142

SCOTT SERVAIS

Position: Catcher
Team: Chicago Cubs
Born: June 4, 1967 LaCrosse, WI
Height: 6'2" **Weight:** 205 lbs.
Bats: right **Throws:** right
Acquired: Traded by Astros with Luis Gonzalez for Rick Wilkins, 6/95

PLAYER SUMMARY	
Fantasy Value	$7 to $9
Card Value	4¢ to 7¢
Will	play hard-nosed ball
Can't	outrun a snail
Expect	regular duty
Don't Expect	great throwing

Servais had a solid season in 1996, although overall he ranks only slightly above average. He is fearless and solid behind the plate, although he has problems throwing out runners; he caught only 29 percent of basestealers last year. Servais managed 20 doubles and 11 home runs in hitter-friendly Wrigley Field and hit just .252 away from the Friendly Confines. Servais has impressed Cub pitchers with his ability to call a game and his knowledge of opposing hitters, but he needs to do more for a team that doesn't have much offense anywhere on the diamond. Servais will start out as the Cubs' everyday catcher in '97, but if he slumps, he could wind up in a platoon with Tyler Houston, who was impressive in limited duty in '96. Servais will certainly play less in 1997 than he has in the recent past, as nagging injuries from several home-plate collisions and 14 hit-by-pitches sapped his strength last season. The Cubs will do all they can to keep him healthy.

Major League Batting Register

	BA	G	AB	R	H	2B	3B	HR	RBI	SB
91 NL	.162	16	37	0	6	3	0	0	6	0
92 NL	.239	77	205	12	49	9	0	0	15	0
93 NL	.244	85	258	24	63	11	0	11	32	0
94 NL	.195	78	251	27	49	15	1	9	41	0
95 NL	.265	80	264	38	70	22	0	13	47	2
96 NL	.265	129	445	42	118	20	0	11	63	0
Life	.243	465	1460	143	355	80	1	44	204	2
3 Ave	.243	110	365	41	89	22	0	13	58	1

JEFF SHAW

Position: Pitcher
Team: Cincinnati Reds
Born: July 7, 1966 Washington Courthouse, OH
Height: 6'2" **Weight:** 200 lbs.
Bats: right **Throws:** right
Acquired: Signed as a free agent, 1/96

PLAYER SUMMARY	
Fantasy Value	$4 to $6
Card Value	4¢ to 7¢
Will	work often
Can't	overpower hitters
Expect	sinking fastballs
Don't Expect	many saves

The Reds, desperate for pitching, picked Shaw up in the hope he would return to the form he had showed in 1993 and '94. He was ineffective over the first month of the season, giving up three homers and ten runs in his first 15 innings. However, Shaw turned it around after that and finished the season so well he wound up as the primary set-up man for closer Jeff Brantley. He claimed this role despite the presence of veteran Lee Smith and the younger, harder-throwing Hector Carrasco and Johnny Ruffin. The Reds, who apparently think he can continue to be their primary set-up man, signed Shaw to a two-year contract near the end of the 1996 season. Caution is in order, though; relief pitchers who throw more than 100 innings in one season often have arm problems the next year. Shaw should get his innings, though, because he, Carrasco, and Brantley are the only quality relievers the Reds have.

Major League Pitching Register

	W	L	ERA	G	S	IP	H	ER	BB	SO
90 AL	3	4	6.66	12	0	48.2	73	36	20	25
91 AL	0	5	3.36	29	1	72.1	72	27	27	31
92 AL	0	1	8.22	2	0	7.2	7	7	4	3
93 NL	2	7	4.14	55	0	95.2	91	44	32	50
94 NL	5	2	3.88	46	1	67.1	67	29	15	47
95 NL	1	6	4.62	50	3	62.1	58	32	26	45
95 AL	0	0	6.52	9	0	9.2	12	7	1	6
96 NL	8	6	2.49	78	4	104.2	99	29	29	69
Life	19	31	4.05	281	9	468.1	479	211	154	276
3 Ave	5	5	3.53	66	3	90.0	86	35	26	62

DANNY SHEAFFER

Position: Catcher
Team: St. Louis Cardinals
Born: Aug. 21, 1961 Jacksonville, FL
Height: 6' **Weight:** 190 lbs.
Bats: right **Throws:** right
Acquired: Signed as a free agent, 12/94

PLAYER SUMMARY	
Fantasy Value	$0
Card Value	4¢ to 7¢
Will	show versatility
Can't	win regular job
Expect	good throwing
Don't Expect	much offense

After playing just 32 big-league games in his first 12 professional seasons, Sheaffer has had four straight years of uninterrupted service in the majors. He's been lucky; in 1993, he landed with the expansion Colorado Rockies, who needed anyone with experience behind the plate. Last season, he was the designated catcher/pinch hitter/all-purpose utility man on the Cardinals. Tony LaRussa loves to have a catcher who also plays other positions, so Sheaffer—who beat out veteran Pat Borders for the backup job—saw action at first base, third base, and left field in addition to appearing 47 times behind the plate. He's no great shakes as an offensive player, with a .271 on-base percentage, below-average speed, and only occasional punch, but Sheaffer calls a good game and tossed out 30 percent of enemy basestealers for the Cardinals. He's a hard-nosed, gritty player who will do whatever his manager asks. Players like that usually seem to get lucky.

Major League Batting Register

	BA	G	AB	R	H	2B	3B	HR	RBI	SB
87 AL	.121	25	66	5	8	1	0	1	5	0
89 AL	.063	7	16	1	1	0	0	0	0	0
93 NL	.278	82	216	26	60	9	1	4	32	2
94 NL	.218	44	110	11	24	4	0	1	12	0
95 NL	.231	76	208	24	48	10	1	5	30	0
96 NL	.227	79	198	10	45	9	3	2	20	3
Life	.229	313	814	77	186	33	5	13	99	5
2 Ave	.229	82	216	19	50	10	2	4	27	2

GARY SHEFFIELD

Position: Outfield
Team: Florida Marlins
Born: Nov. 18, 1968 Tampa, FL
Height: 5'11" **Weight:** 190 lbs.
Bats: right **Throws:** right
Acquired: Traded by Padres with Rich
  Rodriguez for Trevor Hoffman, Andres
  Berumen, and Jose Martinez, 6/93

PLAYER SUMMARY	
Fantasy Value	$40 to $45
Card Value	20¢ to 40¢
Will	hit for power
Can't	keep his mouth shut
Expect	volatile personality
Don't Expect	a full season of play

The oft-injured Sheffield saw action a career-high 161 times in 1996. What his name on the lineup card means to the Marlins is almost incalculable; he is simply a devastating hitter. Sheffield battered opposing pitchers all year, not discriminating between right-handers or lefties. His offensive stats were the best of any non-Coors Field hitter, and he was clearly the most potent day-in, day-out threat in the NL. As usual, however, off-the-field controversy plagued Sheffield. He feuded with doomed manager Rene Lachemann, tolerated interim manager John Boles, ripped GM Dave Dombrowski, and more than once asked for a trade. However, the Marlins turned down several interesting offers in order to give Sheffield the chance to work with new Florida manager Jim Leyland, who will have his hands full.

Major League Batting Register

	BA	G	AB	R	H	2B	3B	HR	RBI	SB
88 AL	.237	24	80	12	19	1	0	4	12	3
89 AL	.247	95	368	34	91	18	0	5	32	10
90 AL	.294	125	487	67	143	30	1	10	67	25
91 AL	.194	50	175	25	34	12	2	2	22	5
92 NL	.330	146	557	87	184	34	3	33	100	5
93 NL	.294	140	494	67	145	20	5	20	73	17
94 NL	.276	87	322	61	89	16	1	27	78	12
95 NL	.324	63	213	46	69	8	0	16	46	19
96 NL	.314	161	519	118	163	33	1	42	120	16
Life	.291	891	3215	517	937	172	13	159	550	112
3 Ave	.302	118	404	85	122	22	1	33	94	18

CRAIG SHIPLEY

Position: Infield
Team: San Diego Padres
Born: Jan. 7, 1963 New South Wales,
  Australia
Height: 5'11" **Weight:** 190 lbs.
Bats: right **Throws:** right
Acquired: Signed as a free agent, 1/96

PLAYER SUMMARY	
Fantasy Value	$0
Card Value	4¢ to 7¢
Will	fill in
Can't	be an everyday player
Expect	a good effort
Don't Expect	much flash

A nagging left hamstring injury kept Shipley on the DL for much of 1996. However, luckily for the division-winning Padres, his services as a utility infielder were not required as often as they had been in the recent past. Shipley's career has been spent filling the role of solid interim infielder—sometimes for a day, sometimes for a week. At one time, Shipley had been considered an offensive liability with a solid glove, but over the years he has improved his hitting. Last season, he hit over .300. He also swiped seven bases without being caught and hit .338 against right-handers. However, Shipley still doesn't hit enough to project as an everyday player. He took only two walks last season and added little power. In the field, he spent most of his time at third base but also filled in at second, shortstop, and even right field. Shipley will be somebody's key infield reserve in 1997.

Major League Batting Register

	BA	G	AB	R	H	2B	3B	HR	RBI	SB
86 NL	.111	12	27	3	3	1	0	0	4	0
87 NL	.257	26	35	3	9	1	0	0	2	0
89 NL	.143	4	7	3	1	0	0	0	0	0
91 NL	.275	37	91	6	25	3	0	1	6	0
92 NL	.248	52	105	7	26	6	0	0	7	1
93 NL	.235	105	230	25	54	9	0	4	22	12
94 NL	.333	81	240	32	80	14	4	4	30	6
95 NL	.263	92	232	23	61	8	1	3	24	6
96 NL	.315	33	92	13	29	5	0	1	7	7
Life	.272	442	1059	115	288	47	5	13	102	32
2 Ave	.303	109	300	35	91	14	3	5	35	8

PAUL SHUEY

Position: Pitcher
Team: Cleveland Indians
Born: Sept. 16, 1970 Lima, OH
Height: 6'3" **Weight:** 215 lbs.
Bats: right **Throws:** right
Acquired: First-round pick in 6/92 free-agent draft

PLAYER SUMMARY	
Fantasy Value	$4 to $6
Card Value	4¢ to 7¢
Will	throw hard
Can't	count on control
Expect	set-up duty
Don't Expect	righties to hit him

Shuey had not impressed in his previous attempts to carve out a niche for himself in the majors. Control problems had kept him from using his effective arsenal—until 1996. After a short stint with the Indians in April, Shuey got down to the serious business of destroying Triple-A hitters. This he did, fashioning an 0.81 ERA in 19 games for Buffalo and fanning 57 men in just 33.1 innings. The Indians recalled him in June and made him part of the team's excellent bullpen corps. Shuey responded with by far his best major-league performance, holding AL right-handers to a .225 average and keeping lefties to just .237. The Indians need Shuey to continue improving his control, as he walked far too many hitters and gave up six homers in his 53⅔ innings. The big, strong Shuey has come a long way toward improving his mechanics; despite a very high leg kick, only seven men tried to steal on him in 1996, three successfully. The Tribe has a very deep bullpen, but Shuey has a better chance than anybody to be the Indians closer by the year 2000.

Major League Pitching Register

	W	L	ERA	G	S	IP	H	ER	BB	SO
94 AL	0	1	8.49	14	5	11.2	14	11	12	16
95 AL	0	2	4.26	7	0	6.1	5	3	5	5
96 AL	5	2	2.85	42	4	53.2	45	17	26	44
Life	5	5	3.89	63	9	71.2	64	31	43	65

RUBEN SIERRA

Position: Outfield
Team: Cincinnati Reds
Born: Oct. 6, 1965 Rio Piedras, Puerto Rico
Height: 6'1" **Weight:** 200 lbs.
Bats: both **Throws:** right
Acquired: Traded by Tigers for Decomba Conner and Ben Bailey, 10/96

PLAYER SUMMARY	
Fantasy Value	$10 to $13
Card Value	5¢ to 8¢
Will	cause trouble
Can't	escape his reputation
Expect	occasional long ball
Don't Expect	solid team play

In August, the onetime All-Star was jettisoned by the New York Yankees, who were so desperate to get rid of him they were willing to take on Cecil Fielder's hefty contract. Sierra had long ago worn out his welcome in New York; his diminished offensive skills, seeming lack of hustle, poor defense, and public-relations disasters sealed his fate. Sierra has completely lost what were once impressive offensive skills, and has been in decline since 1992. He was not well liked by his Yankees teammates, and unless he turns it around with the Tigers, his career may be over. The reasons for Sierra's decline have been debated for years. Weight lifting is often cited, while others claim that his poor strike-zone command made Sierra vulnerable to good pitching. What is clear is that Sierra presently has little to offer except trouble.

Major League Batting Register

	BA	G	AB	R	H	2B	3B	HR	RBI	SB
86 AL	.264	113	382	50	101	13	10	16	55	7
87 AL	.263	158	643	97	169	35	4	30	109	16
88 AL	.254	156	615	77	156	32	2	23	91	18
89 AL	.306	162	634	101	194	35	14	29	119	8
90 AL	.280	159	608	70	170	37	2	16	96	9
91 AL	.307	161	661	110	203	44	5	25	116	16
92 AL	.278	151	601	83	167	34	7	17	87	14
93 AL	.233	158	630	77	147	23	5	22	101	25
94 AL	.268	110	426	71	114	21	1	23	92	8
95 AL	.263	126	479	73	126	32	0	19	86	5
96 AL	.247	142	518	61	128	26	2	12	72	4
Life	.270	1596	6197	870	1675	332	52	232	1024	130
3 Ave	.260	146	552	81	143	31	1	22	99	7

BILL SIMAS

Position: Pitcher
Team: Chicago White Sox
Born: Nov. 28, 1971 Hanford, CA
Height: 6'3" **Weight:** 220 lbs.
Bats: left **Throws:** right
Acquired: Traded by Angels with Andrew Lorraine, Paul Snyder, and McKay Christensen for Jim Abbott, 7/95

PLAYER SUMMARY	
Fantasy Value	$2 to $4
Card Value	7¢ to 10¢
Will	show good arm
Can't	afford wildness
Expect	improved performance
Don't Expect	many saves

The hard-throwing Simas spent the entire season with the White Sox, but experienced the type of problems most young pitchers with control troubles encounter. Used as a set-up man, Simas allowed far too many Sox leads to fritter away and, by the end of the year, appeared to have completely lost his confidence. He has the classic closer's pitches—a good hard fastball and a devastating slider—but too often could not get the ball where he wanted it. Mechanical problems plagued him all year: His delivery appeared different every game, and he missed high in the strike zone consistently. Simas blew six of eight save chances, allowed left-handed batters to hit .271 against him, and walked more men than any other Chicago reliever. However, unlike most members of the club's mediocre bullpen staff, Simas has the potential to be far better than he was in 1996. Whether the Sox send him to Triple-A for more seasoning or keep him around this year remains to be seen, but Chicago clearly thinks highly of Simas and will give him several more chances.

Major League Pitching Register

	W	L	ERA	G	S	IP	H	ER	BB	SO
95 AL	1	1	2.57	14	0	14.0	15	4	10	16
96 AL	2	8	4.58	64	2	72.2	75	37	39	65
Life	3	9	4.26	78	2	86.2	90	41	49	81

MIKE SIMMS

Position: Outfield; first base
Team: Houston Astros
Born: Jan. 12, 1967 Orange, CA
Height: 6'4" **Weight:** 200 lbs.
Bats: right **Throws:** right
Acquired: Signed as a minor-league free agent, 4/94

PLAYER SUMMARY	
Fantasy Value	$0
Card Value	4¢ to 7¢
Will	face left-handers
Can't	claim everyday job
Expect	another chance
Don't Expect	sterling glovework

Simms, who had an impressive final two months of the 1995 season after several disappointing tryouts the previous few years, reverted to his old form in 1996. He didn't get much of a chance in 1996 and did not do anything with the opportunities he did receive. Simms, who is not a fast runner or a defensive-minded player, didn't do what he needs to do to hang around; that is, hit for average and power. He walked only four times and struck out 16 times (which would put him on a pace for well over 100 for a full season), while neither his on-base percentage nor slugging percentage made it above .279. He appeared in 49 games, playing just five times at first base and 12 times in the outfield. He was used as a pinch hitter 35 times. Simms will be 30 on Opening Day and has fewer than 400 career at bats. He is clearly going nowhere in Houston, as several young outfielders are ahead of him. If Simms doesn't sign with a new organization, he might not even get 70 at bats this coming season.

Major League Batting Register

	BA	G	AB	R	H	2B	3B	HR	RBI	SB
90 NL	.308	12	13	3	4	1	0	1	2	0
91 NL	.203	49	123	18	25	5	0	3	16	1
92 NL	.250	15	24	1	6	1	0	1	3	0
94 NL	.083	6	12	1	1	1	0	0	0	1
95 NL	.256	50	121	14	31	4	0	9	24	1
96 NL	.176	49	68	6	12	2	1	1	8	1
Life	.219	181	361	43	79	14	1	15	53	4

DON SLAUGHT

Position: Catcher
Team: Chicago White Sox
Born: Sept. 11, 1958 Long Beach, CA
Height: 6'1" **Weight:** 190 lbs.
Bats: right **Throws:** right
Acquired: Traded by Angels for Scott Vollmer, 8/96

PLAYER SUMMARY	
Fantasy Value	$0
Card Value	4¢ to 7¢
Will	hit left-handers
Can't	throw out runners
Expect	part-time duty
Don't Expect	much power

Slaught started the year with the Angels, racking up a fine batting average against left-handers (.359), putting the ball in play (he walked just 15 times and fanned only 22), and experiencing some problems behind the plate. Slaught hasn't been any everyday player for years; the wear and tear of catching took its toll. He has made ten career trips to the DL and in July missed two weeks due to back spasms. After being traded to the Sox, things didn't get better; he was flattened in a home-plate collision with Detroit's Mel Nieves in his Chicago debut. By the end of the year, Slaught could barely run. That said, Slaught is a gutsy player who is productive, adaptable, and popular with his teammates.

Major League Batting Register

	BA	G	AB	R	H	2B	3B	HR	RBI	SB
82 AL	.278	43	115	14	32	6	0	3	8	0
83 AL	.312	83	276	21	86	13	4	0	28	3
84 AL	.264	124	409	48	108	27	4	4	42	0
85 AL	.280	102	343	34	96	17	4	8	35	5
86 AL	.264	95	314	39	83	17	1	13	46	3
87 AL	.224	95	237	25	53	15	2	8	16	0
88 AL	.283	97	322	33	91	25	1	9	43	1
89 AL	.251	117	350	34	88	21	3	5	38	1
90 NL	.300	84	230	27	69	18	3	4	29	0
91 NL	.295	77	220	19	65	17	1	1	29	1
92 NL	.345	87	255	26	88	17	3	4	37	2
93 NL	.300	116	377	34	113	19	2	10	55	2
94 NL	.287	76	240	21	69	7	0	2	21	0
95 NL	.304	35	112	13	34	6	0	0	13	0
96 AL	.313	76	243	25	76	10	0	6	36	0
Life	.285	1307	4043	413	1151	235	28	77	476	18
2 Ave	.298	92	291	27	87	10	0	4	33	0

HEATHCLIFF SLOCUMB

Position: Pitcher
Team: Boston Red Sox
Born: June 7, 1966 Jamaica, NY
Height: 6'3" **Weight:** 220 lbs.
Bats: right **Throws:** right
Acquired: Traded by Phillies with Rick Holifield and Larry Wimberly for Ken Ryan, Lee Tinsley, and Glenn Murray, 1/96

PLAYER SUMMARY	
Fantasy Value	$25 to $30
Card Value	5¢ to 8¢
Will	bounce back
Can't	afford slow start
Expect	closing duties
Don't Expect	consistency

Acquired from the Phillies to stabilize Boston's bullpen, Slocumb came to the Hub amidst high hopes of another stellar late-inning performance. However, Slocumb could not find a groove early in the season, as the entire Red Sox team floundered throughout April. Though Slocumb wound up with decent save numbers, he was inconsistent. He walked a huge amount of hitters and tossed ten wild pitches. At various points, Slocumb was bypassed by Boston manager Kevin Kennedy in key situations. The year wasn't all bad, however; Slocumb, throwing his excellent hard sinking fastball, allowed just two homers all year and held right-handers to a .158 average. However, his poor season caused many in New England to think Slocumb's overpowering 1995 performance with the Phillies may have been a one-year fluke. Due to a lack of alternatives, Slocumb will remain Boston's closer.

Major League Pitching Register

	W	L	ERA	G	S	IP	H	ER	BB	SO
91 NL	2	1	3.45	52	1	62.2	53	24	30	34
92 NL	0	3	6.50	30	1	36.0	52	26	21	27
93 NL	1	0	3.38	10	0	10.2	7	4	4	4
93 AL	3	1	4.28	20	0	27.1	28	13	16	18
94 NL	5	1	2.86	52	0	72.1	75	23	28	58
95 NL	5	6	2.89	61	32	65.1	64	21	35	63
96 AL	5	5	3.02	75	31	83.1	68	28	55	88
Life	21	17	3.50	300	65	357.2	347	139	189	292
3 Ave	6	4	2.92	72	22	86.1	82	28	45	80

JOHN SMILEY

Position: Pitcher
Team: Cincinnati Reds
Born: March 17, 1965 Phoenixville, PA
Height: 6'4" **Weight:** 215 lbs.
Bats: left **Throws:** left
Acquired: Signed as a free agent, 11/92

PLAYER SUMMARY	
Fantasy Value	$16 to $19
Card Value	5¢ to 8¢
Will	throw strikes
Can't	catch a break
Expect	another good year
Don't Expect	overpowering heat

Because of injuries to Jose Rijo and Pete Schourek, Smiley wound up the Reds' top starter in 1996. Things didn't look good early in the season when Smiley had to take a cortisone shot in his left shoulder (the third straight season he had to endure the shot), but the medication seemed to work. Smiley had a much better season than his 13-14 record would indicate. He allowed less than a hit an inning, did not walk many, led the team in strikeouts, and was the team's best big-game pitcher late in the season. After season-long rumors of a possible trade, the Reds signed Smiley to a three-year contract late in the season, preventing the veteran lefty from becoming a free agent. The Reds love Smiley and are happy to have him signed. It's not likely that he can be a rotation anchor—and he won't have to be if Rijo or Schourek can rebound from their arm problems.

Major League Pitching Register

	W	L	ERA	G	CG	IP	H	ER	BB	SO
86 NL	1	0	3.86	12	0	11.2	4	5	4	9
87 NL	5	5	5.76	63	0	75.0	69	48	50	58
88 NL	13	11	3.25	34	5	205.0	185	74	46	129
89 NL	12	8	2.81	28	8	205.1	174	64	49	123
90 NL	9	10	4.64	26	2	149.1	161	77	36	86
91 NL	20	8	3.08	33	2	207.2	194	71	44	129
92 AL	16	9	3.21	34	5	241.0	205	86	65	163
93 NL	3	9	5.62	18	2	105.2	117	66	31	60
94 NL	11	10	3.86	24	1	158.2	169	68	37	112
95 NL	12	5	3.46	28	1	176.2	173	68	39	124
96 NL	13	14	3.64	35	2	217.1	207	88	54	171
Life	115	89	3.67	335	28	1753.1	1658	715	455	1164
3 Ave	14	11	3.66	33	2	213.1	213	87	50	156

DWIGHT SMITH

Position: Outfield
Team: Atlanta Braves
Born: Nov. 8, 1963 Tallahassee, FL
Height: 5'11" **Weight:** 175 lbs.
Bats: left **Throws:** right
Acquired: Signed as a free agent, 4/95

PLAYER SUMMARY	
Fantasy Value	$0
Card Value	4¢ to 7¢
Will	pinch hit
Can't	add defense
Expect	good attitude
Don't Expect	much speed

For Smith, 1996 was a lost season. As is the case with many longtime pinch hitters, Smith simply had an off year. One of the hardest things to do in baseball is come off the bench cold and face a tough reliever, even though the loose and pleasant Smith seems to have the right temperament for the job. He collected just eight extra-base hits last season, walked only 17 times, and fanned on 42 occasions. However, all three of his home runs came in pinch-hitting roles, and manager Bobby Cox stuck with Smith all season long as his top bat off the bench. In his earlier days, Smith had excellent speed and even played center field regularly for the Cubs in 1993, but he no longer runs particularly well and is rarely used for his glove or arm. If Smith can augment his outstanding clubhouse presence with a few more timely hits this season, he will reassume his place as one of the game's best pinch hitters.

Major League Batting Register

	BA	G	AB	R	H	2B	3B	HR	RBI	SB
89 NL	.324	109	343	52	111	19	6	9	52	9
90 NL	.262	117	290	34	76	15	0	6	27	11
91 NL	.228	90	167	16	38	7	2	3	21	2
92 NL	.276	109	217	28	60	10	3	3	24	9
93 NL	.300	111	310	51	93	17	5	11	35	8
94 AL	.281	73	196	31	55	7	2	8	30	2
95 NL	.252	103	131	16	33	8	2	3	21	0
96 NL	.203	101	153	16	31	5	0	3	16	1
Life	.275	813	1807	244	497	88	20	46	226	42
2 Ave	.253	102	215	30	54	7	1	7	29	2

LEE SMITH

Position: Pitcher
Team: Cincinnati Reds
Born: Dec. 4, 1957 Jamestown, LA
Height: 6'6" **Weight:** 269 lbs.
Bats: right **Throws:** right
Acquired: Traded by Angels for Chuck McElroy, 5/96

PLAYER SUMMARY	
Fantasy Value	$6 to $8
Card Value	5¢ to 8¢
Will	try to hang on
Can't	show old fastball
Expect	middle relief
Don't Expect	many saves

Smith started out the season with the Angels—on the DL. While he was out, he lost the closer's job to Troy Percival. When Smith complained, he was sent to the Reds. Unfortunately for him, Smith needed only a couple of weeks to pitch himself into middle relief. To his credit, he didn't make the same kind of noise about not being the Reds' closer as he had with the Angels. Smith was still clocked in the 90s on the radar gun, but he had problems getting hitters out due to a lack of movement on his fastball. He blew four of six save chances for Cincinnati.

Major League Pitching Register

	W	L	ERA	G	S	IP	H	ER	BB	SO
80 NL	2	0	2.91	18	0	21.2	21	7	14	17
81 NL	3	6	3.51	40	1	66.2	57	26	31	50
82 NL	2	5	2.69	72	17	117.0	105	35	37	99
83 NL	4	10	1.65	66	29	103.1	70	19	41	91
84 NL	9	7	3.65	69	33	101.0	98	41	35	86
85 NL	7	4	3.04	65	33	97.2	87	33	32	112
86 NL	9	9	3.09	66	31	90.1	69	31	42	93
87 NL	4	10	3.12	62	36	83.2	84	29	32	96
88 AL	4	5	2.80	64	29	83.2	72	26	37	96
89 AL	6	1	3.57	64	25	70.2	53	28	33	96
90 AL	2	1	1.88	11	4	14.1	13	3	9	17
90 NL	3	4	2.10	53	27	68.2	58	16	20	70
91 NL	6	3	2.34	67	47	73.0	70	19	13	67
92 NL	4	9	3.12	70	43	75.0	62	26	26	60
93 NL	2	4	4.50	55	43	50.0	49	25	9	49
93 AL	0	0	0.00	8	3	8.0	4	0	5	11
94 AL	1	4	3.29	41	33	38.1	34	14	11	42
95 AL	0	5	3.47	52	37	49.1	42	19	25	43
96 AL	0	0	2.45	11	0	11.0	8	3	3	6
96 NL	3	4	4.06	43	2	44.1	49	20	23	35
Life	71	91	2.98	997	473	1267.2	1105	420	478	1236
3 Ave	1	5	3.57	53	30	51.1	48	20	22	48

MARK SMITH

Position: Outfield
Team: Baltimore Orioles
Born: May 7, 1970 Pasadena, CA
Height: 6'4" **Weight:** 195 lbs.
Bats: right **Throws:** right
Acquired: First-round pick in 6/91 free-agent draft

PLAYER SUMMARY	
Fantasy Value	$0
Card Value	4¢ to 7¢
Will	show decent stick
Can't	fulfill expectations
Expect	trade talk
Don't Expect	starting duty

Smith is just another victim of the Orioles' historic dependence on veteran ballplayers over homegrown youngsters. In most organizations, a first-round draft choice would have gotten a season's worth of at bats to prove whether he could be a regular or not—especially coming off a decent performance such as the one Smith turned in during 1995. However, Smith has not been so lucky. Even with a shortage of production from Baltimore left fielders in '96, Smith could not get many at bats. He did not do much with the playing time he had, but certainly deserves a shot. Unfortunately, when Jeffrey Hammonds was disabled in August with a strained knee, opening up an opportunity for someone to step in, Smith himself went to the DL with a badly bruised shin suffered from fouling a ball off his leg. The injury was serious enough to keep him out for the rest of the season. The outlook for 1997 is not bright for Smith if he remains in Baltimore. He is not likely to start and could probably benefit from a deal sending him to another organization.

Major League Batting Register

	BA	G	AB	R	H	2B	3B	HR	RBI	SB
94 AL	.143	3	7	0	1	0	0	0	2	0
95 AL	.231	37	104	11	24	5	0	3	15	3
96 AL	.244	27	78	9	19	2	0	4	10	0
Life	.233	67	189	20	44	7	0	7	27	3

JOHN SMOLTZ

Position: Pitcher
Team: Atlanta Braves
Born: May 15, 1967 Detroit, MI
Height: 6'3" **Weight:** 183 lbs.
Bats: right **Throws:** right
Acquired: Traded by Tigers for Doyle Alexander, 8/87

PLAYER SUMMARY	
Fantasy Value	$25 to $30
Card Value	15¢ to 25¢
Will	dominate hitters
Can't	hit very well
Expect	strikeouts
Don't Expect	change of address

Smoltz finally had the type of season many had predicted for several years, and easily was the best pitcher on a team sporting a terrific staff. Smoltz, a dominant power pitcher, had 14 wins by the first of July and never really let up. His 24 wins tied him for the most NL wins in any season since 1972. He kept his game up through the postseason, dominating all comers in the playoffs. A key part of Smoltz's success was improved control. In 1996, he walked fewer than two per nine innings, a rate almost unheard of among power pitchers. All season long, Smoltz consistently got ahead with his fastball, then got strikeouts by throwing his fierce-dropping slider. Smoltz, who had elbow surgery immediately after the work stoppage in 1994, has showed no indications of any recurring problems. The Braves extended the 1996 Cy Young Award winner's contract over the off-season.

Major League Pitching Register

	W	L	ERA	G	CG	IP	H	ER	BB	SO
88 NL	2	7	5.48	12	0	64.0	74	39	33	37
89 NL	12	11	2.94	29	5	208.0	160	68	72	168
90 NL	14	11	3.85	34	6	231.1	206	99	90	170
91 NL	14	13	3.80	36	5	229.2	206	97	77	148
92 NL	15	12	2.85	35	9	246.2	206	78	80	215
93 NL	15	11	3.62	35	3	243.2	208	98	100	208
94 NL	6	10	4.14	21	1	134.2	120	62	48	113
95 NL	12	7	3.18	29	2	192.2	166	68	72	193
96 NL	24	8	2.94	35	6	253.2	199	83	55	276
Life	114	90	3.45	266	37	1804.1	1545	692	627	1528
3 Ave	15	10	3.37	32	3	220.0	185	82	68	217

CHRIS SNOPEK

Position: Infield
Team: Chicago White Sox
Born: Sept. 20, 1970 Cynthiana, KY
Height: 6'1" **Weight:** 185 lbs.
Bats: right **Throws:** right
Acquired: Sixth-round pick in 6/92 free-agent draft

PLAYER SUMMARY	
Fantasy Value	$4 to $6
Card Value	12¢ to 20¢
Will	get more at bats
Can't	show great speed
Expect	balanced offense
Don't Expect	a starting shortstop

Snopek was not highly regarded early in his professional career, but he performed well enough to progress quickly through the White Sox minor-league system. He became a prospect by showing a good glove and bat at Double-A and Triple-A. Snopek will take the walk, hits left-handers well, has line-drive power, and is viewed as a smart player who knows the percentages and how to play them. His defense at third base is already above average despite his brief major-league experience, and he can also play a creditable shortstop—as he did on several occasions last year while subbing for Ozzie Guillen. Snopek spent time in the majors and minors in 1996 as Chicago tried to find ways to fit him into their picture. The Sox are deep in third basemen with Robin Ventura, Snopek, and fellow prospect Greg Norton. If Snopek cannot land an everyday job in 1997, he will at least serve as a top-flight utility man. He is not fast and will not hit 30 homers a year, but Snopek does everything else well.

Major League Batting Register

	BA	G	AB	R	H	2B	3B	HR	RBI	SB
95 AL	.324	22	68	12	22	4	0	1	7	1
96 AL	.260	46	104	18	27	6	1	6	18	0
Life	.285	68	172	30	49	10	1	7	25	1

J.T. SNOW

Position: First base
Team: San Francisco Giants
Born: Feb. 26, 1968 Long Beach, CA
Height: 6′2″ **Weight:** 202 lbs.
Bats: both **Throws:** left
Acquired: Traded by Angels for Allen Watson and Fausto Macey, 11/96

PLAYER SUMMARY

Fantasy Value	$9 to $11
Card Value	10¢ to 15¢
Will	play solid defense
Can't	hit left-handers
Expect	an offensive rebound
Don't Expect	a star season

1996 was a thoroughly frustrating year for Snow, as well as for team management and fans. Some drop-off was to be expected from Snow's fine 1995 performance, but his performance last season was baffling to say the least. Offensively, he fell apart and couldn't hit left-handers at all. It got so bad that he considered dropping switch-hitting, batting left-handed exclusively. Snow didn't get on base, didn't hit for power, showed no speed, and generally clogged the middle of the Angels lineup with untimely hitting. While overrated as a defensive player, he did not let his offensive woes affect his defense. He remained solid around first base. His future with the Angels is cloudy at the moment, as trade rumors flare up often. As they did after Snow's 1994 season, the Angels have begun to look to their surplus of outfielders for a possible first baseman. This would free up Snow for a trade, although it would be difficult to acquire anything of value in exchange at this point.

Major League Batting Register

	BA	G	AB	R	H	2B	3B	HR	RBI	SB
92 AL	.143	7	14	1	2	1	0	0	2	0
93 AL	.241	129	419	60	101	18	2	16	57	3
94 AL	.220	61	223	22	49	4	0	8	30	0
95 AL	.289	143	544	80	157	22	1	24	102	2
96 AL	.257	155	575	69	148	20	1	17	67	1
Life	.257	495	1775	232	457	65	4	65	258	6
3 Ave	.262	134	500	63	131	17	1	18	75	1

PAUL SORRENTO

Position: First base
Team: Seattle Mariners
Born: Nov. 17, 1965 Somerville, MA
Height: 6′2″ **Weight:** 220 lbs.
Bats: left **Throws:** right
Acquired: Signed as a free agent, 1/96

PLAYER SUMMARY

Fantasy Value	$14 to $17
Card Value	7¢ to 10¢
Will	add power
Can't	connect consistently
Expect	decent glovework
Don't Expect	speed

A change in scenery seemed to do wonders for Sorrento, who was let go by Cleveland following a disappointing 1995 season. He signed with Seattle over the winter and helped make up for the loss of Tino Martinez. Although Sorrento was hardly a great hitter, he wasn't bad. His only real drawbacks were 103 strikeouts and a .167 average against left-handed pitchers. Sorrento hit a welcome .307 against righties. The big first baseman slugged over .500 and posted an impressive .370 on-base percentage. Sorrento has hit left-handers fairly well in the past and will have to improve on his 1996 performance if he wants to avoid being a platoon player. He has only average hands in the field, making 11 errors last year, but has good range. With a good up-the-middle defense, the Mariners can afford to have him in the lineup. Sorrento is a good, if not outstanding, player who is capable of putting up solid numbers.

Major League Batting Register

	BA	G	AB	R	H	2B	3B	HR	RBI	SB
89 AL	.238	14	21	2	5	0	0	0	1	0
90 AL	.207	41	121	11	25	4	1	5	13	1
91 AL	.255	26	47	6	12	2	0	4	13	0
92 AL	.269	140	458	52	123	24	1	18	60	0
93 AL	.257	148	463	75	119	26	1	18	65	3
94 AL	.280	95	322	43	90	14	0	14	62	0
95 AL	.235	104	323	50	76	14	0	25	79	1
96 AL	.289	143	471	67	136	32	1	23	93	0
Life	.263	711	2226	306	586	116	4	107	386	5
3 Ave	.270	131	429	61	116	22	0	24	90	0

SAMMY SOSA

Position: Outfield
Team: Chicago Cubs
Born: Oct. 10, 1968 San Pedro de Macoris, Dominican Republic
Height: 6′ **Weight:** 175 lbs.
Bats: right **Throws:** right
Acquired: Traded by White Sox with Ken Patterson for George Bell, 3/92

PLAYER SUMMARY	
Fantasy Value.	$35 to $40
Card Value	20¢ to 30¢
Will	impress with skill
Can't	stay consistent
Expect	35 homers
Don't Expect	many walks

Even with the return of Ryne Sandberg, Sosa is probably still the most popular Cub. He is personable, loves the game, always smiles, and hits plenty of home runs. He had 40 of them when he was forced to the disabled list August 21 with a broken bone in his hand. Had Sosa played the final six weeks of the season, he would have put up numbers to rival anyone in the league—or he could have gone into the tank; one never knows with the streaky Sosa. To his credit, Sosa has slowly started to correct some of the flaws in his game. He's still no Gold Glover, but he plays better defense than he used to and is a little less of an "all-or-nothing" player. It wasn't that long ago that Sosa hit fewer than 20 doubles a season, but he had 21 two-baggers when he got hurt. He still swings for the fences too much, fanning 134 times and taking just 34 walks in 1996.

Major League Batting Register

	BA	G	AB	R	H	2B	3B	HR	RBI	SB
89 AL	.257	58	183	27	47	8	0	4	13	7
90 AL	.233	153	532	72	124	26	10	15	70	32
91 AL	.203	116	316	39	64	10	1	10	33	13
92 NL	.260	67	262	41	68	7	2	8	25	15
93 NL	.261	159	598	92	156	25	5	33	93	36
94 NL	.300	105	426	59	128	17	6	25	70	22
95 NL	.268	144	564	89	151	17	3	36	119	34
96 NL	.273	124	498	84	136	21	2	40	100	18
Life	.259	926	3379	503	874	131	29	171	523	177
3 Ave	.281	145	578	89	162	21	5	39	111	29

STEVE SPARKS

Position: Pitcher
Team: Milwaukee Brewers
Born: July 2, 1965 Tulsa, OK
Height: 6′ **Weight:** 187 lbs.
Bats: right **Throws:** right
Acquired: Fifth-round pick in 6/87 free-agent draft

PLAYER SUMMARY	
Fantasy Value	$1
Card Value	4¢ to 7¢
Will	be durable
Can't	show command
Expect	knuckleballs
Don't Expect	good control

Sparks has in his history one of the game's more unusual injuries. He missed all of the 1993 season with a shoulder injury suffered when he tried to rip a phone book in half after hearing a motivational speech. Partially as a result of the injury, he did not make his major-league debut until he was 30. An undistinguished pitcher for most of his career, he developed a knuckleball to stand out from the crowd, pitched well with it in Triple-A, and graduated to the Brewers rotation in 1995. Unfortunately, Sparks lost his touch last season and ended up back at Triple-A. Injuries to other pitchers prompted his recall in July, and he promptly threw a shutout in a spot start. He spent the rest of the season swinging between long relief and an occasional starting appearance, but he could not find any sort of consistency. Sparks allowed 19 homers in 1996, and right-handers hit .316 against him. He throws a harder fastball than most other pitchers who use the knuckler but has spotty control and lacks a third pitch. Sparks appears fated to go through good periods and bad.

Major League Pitching Register

	W	L	ERA	G	CG	IP	H	ER	BB	SO
95 AL	9	11	4.63	33	3	202.0	210	104	86	96
96 AL	4	7	6.60	20	1	88.2	103	65	52	21
Life	13	18	5.23	53	4	290.2	313	169	138	117
2 Ave	7	10	5.18	29	2	158.0	170	91	74	65

ED SPRAGUE

Position: Third base
Team: Toronto Blue Jays
Born: July 25, 1967 Castro Valley, CA
Height: 6'2" **Weight:** 215 lbs.
Bats: right **Throws:** right
Acquired: First-round pick in 6/88 free-agent
  draft

PLAYER SUMMARY	
Fantasy Value	$16 to $19
Card Value	8¢ to 12¢
Will	play hard
Can't	show flashy glove
Expect	good power
Don't Expect	a batting title

Sprague enjoyed his finest offensive season in 1996. He set career highs in several categories, including home runs, hits, doubles, runs, and RBI. Playing 148 games at third base and ten more at DH, he saw more action than any other Blue Jay and had several game-breaking hits. However, he also had his share of tough times last season. Sprague fanned 146 times to rank fourth in the league and took just 60 walks, totaling a mediocre .325 on-base percentage. A poor .225 average against right-handers kept his batting average under .250 for the third straight season. He also took his share of local abuse for poor defense, although he played with grit and drive. If Sprague can hit with power, he is a valuable player. However, he is not capable of batting cleanup on a contending team. Since the Jays aren't going anywhere in the near future, and they have young infielders coming out of their ears, this would be a heck of a time to trade Sprague for some pitching help.

Major League Batting Register

	BA	G	AB	R	H	2B	3B	HR	RBI	SB
91 AL	.275	61	160	17	44	7	0	4	20	0
92 AL	.234	22	47	6	11	2	0	1	7	0
93 AL	.260	150	546	50	142	31	1	12	73	1
94 AL	.240	109	405	38	97	19	1	11	44	1
95 AL	.244	144	521	77	127	27	2	18	74	0
96 AL	.247	159	591	88	146	35	2	36	101	0
Life	.250	645	2270	276	567	121	6	82	319	2
3 Ave	.243	158	583	76	142	31	2	24	82	0

SCOTT STAHOVIAK

Position: First base
Team: Minnesota Twins
Born: March 6, 1970 Waukegan, IL
Height: 6'5" **Weight:** 222 lbs.
Bats: right **Throws:** right
Acquired: First-round pick in 6/91 free-agent
  draft

PLAYER SUMMARY	
Fantasy Value	$7 to $9
Card Value	5¢ to 8¢
Will	keep improving
Can't	show speed
Expect	decent defense
Don't Expect	30 homers

After splitting the 1995 season between Minnesota and Triple-A, Stahoviak put together a solid spring training last year. As a result, Twins manager Tom Kelly decided to let him sink or swim on the major-league level. Kelly was rewarded with a consistent offensive and defensive performance from Stahoviak, who was better than anyone could have expected. His glovework was much improved in 1996. Settling in at first base helped; Stahoviak had been used at both first and third in his previous stints with the Twins. At bat, he hit for a solid average and took 59 walks, reaching base at a fine .376 clip. Unfortunately, Stahoviak does not run often or successfully (three steals in six tries) and does not make contact well enough to be a No. 2 hitter despite his other skills. He is not really blessed with a traditional first baseman's power, although his 114 strikeouts are in line with the totals of big home run producers. He did show occasional bursts of pop and may even grow into a 20-homer man. The Twins will give him every chance to do so.

Major League Batting Register

	BA	G	AB	R	H	2B	3B	HR	RBI	SB
93 AL	.193	20	57	1	11	4	0	0	1	0
95 AL	.266	94	263	28	70	19	0	3	23	5
96 AL	.284	130	405	72	115	30	3	13	61	3
Life	.270	244	725	101	196	53	3	16	85	8
2 Ave	.276	118	350	52	97	26	2	8	43	4

ANDY STANKIEWICZ

Position: Infield
Team: Montreal Expos
Born: Aug. 10, 1964 Inglewood, CA
Height: 5'9" **Weight:** 165 lbs.
Bats: right **Throws:** right
Acquired: Signed as a free agent, 12/95

PLAYER SUMMARY	
Fantasy Value	$0
Card Value	4¢ to 7¢
Will	get on base
Can't	hit for power
Expect	good glovework
Don't Expect	a regular job

The gritty Stankiewicz, a diminutive utility infielder, played for his third team in three years during 1996. After coming up slowly and steadily through the Yankees organization (eventually making the majors despite being labeled a nonprospect), he spent a year with Houston and then moved to the Expos last season. While he is able to play three infield spots and is regarded as a smart player with good strike-zone judgment, Stankiewicz has several things stacked up against him: He is not young, he does not have much of a bat, and he has missed significant playing time in each of the last two seasons due to injuries. In 1996, a broken nose suffered while trying to lay down a bunt put him on the shelf for three weeks. Whether he can stick around with Montreal—or any other club—this year depends on whether his particular virtues are needed by his manager. Many clubs will not carry a weak-hitting spare infielder who does not hit left-handed or possess blinding speed. Stanky does neither, which limits his effectiveness.

Major League Batting Register

	BA	G	AB	R	H	2B	3B	HR	RBI	SB
92 AL	.268	116	400	52	107	22	2	2	25	9
93 AL	.000	16	9	5	0	0	0	0	0	0
94 NL	.259	37	54	10	14	3	0	1	5	1
95 NL	.115	43	52	6	6	1	0	0	7	4
96 NL	.286	64	77	12	22	5	1	0	9	1
Life	.252	276	592	85	149	31	3	3	46	15

MIKE STANLEY

Position: Catcher
Team: Boston Red Sox
Born: June 25, 1963 Fort Lauderdale, FL
Height: 6' **Weight:** 190 lbs.
Bats: right **Throws:** right
Acquired: Signed as a free agent, 12/95

PLAYER SUMMARY	
Fantasy Value	$15 to $18
Card Value	5¢ to 8¢
Will	provide power
Can't	win acclaim
Expect	defensive struggles
Don't Expect	stolen bases

Stanley has shown he can hit major-league pitching as well as most players at his position. However, he didn't make many friends in his first season in Boston. Though productive offensively, with plenty of homers, a .383 on-base percentage, and a .302 average against lefties, he let the Red Sox down defensively and didn't seem to fit in well with his new team. There was much carping behind his back and in the media about Stanley's defensive abilities, which led many observers to believe he would not return in 1997. Astoundingly—even though he came to Boston with a solid record of poor throwing—Stanley threw out just 20 of 114 runners attempting to steal. However, he remained a hard-working receiver who still has a reputation for calling a good game. Stanley might be moved to DH to take advantage of his bat while minimizing his problems behind the plate.

Major League Batting Register

	BA	G	AB	R	H	2B	3B	HR	RBI	SB
86 AL	.333	15	30	4	10	3	0	1	1	1
87 AL	.273	78	216	34	59	8	1	6	37	3
88 AL	.229	94	249	21	57	8	0	3	27	0
89 AL	.246	67	122	9	30	3	1	1	11	1
90 AL	.249	103	189	21	47	8	1	2	19	1
91 AL	.249	95	181	25	45	13	1	3	25	0
92 AL	.249	68	173	24	43	7	0	8	27	0
93 AL	.305	130	423	70	129	17	1	26	84	1
94 AL	.300	82	290	54	87	20	0	17	57	0
95 AL	.268	118	399	63	107	29	1	18	83	1
96 AL	.270	121	397	73	107	20	1	24	69	2
Life	.270	971	2669	398	721	136	7	109	440	10
3 Ave	.279	123	418	73	117	27	1	23	81	1

MIKE STANTON

Position: Pitcher
Team: New York Yankees
Born: June 2, 1967 Houston, TX
Height: 6'1" **Weight:** 190 lbs.
Bats: left **Throws:** left
Acquired: Signed as a free agent, 12/96

PLAYER SUMMARY	
Fantasy Value	$4 to $6
Card Value	4¢ to 7¢
Will	shut down lefties
Can't	show old velocity
Expect	frequent appearances
Don't Expect	immediate success

Stanton was acquired by Boston in mid-1995 and pitched well in 22 games down the stretch. Beginning last year as the top lefty in the bullpen, he racked up a 4-3 record in 59 games through the end of July before being packed off to the Rangers. Stanton has always had trouble with control, and 1996 was no exception; he cut down his walks total but allowed 11 home runs—many as a result of having to throw center-cut fastballs when behind in the count. While Stanton still throws a hard slider, his fastball does not have the velocity it once did. This may be due in part to struggles with weight gain. Although he still has strikeout ability, there are questions as to whether Stanton will ever again get the chance to be a closer. He blew five of his six save opportunities in 1996 and allowed both lefties and righties to bat over .260. He signed a free-agent deal with the Yankees over the winter.

Major League Pitching Register

	W	L	ERA	G	S	IP	H	ER	BB	SO
89 NL	0	1	1.50	20	7	24.0	17	4	8	27
90 NL	0	3	18.00	7	2	7.0	16	14	4	7
91 NL	5	5	2.88	74	7	78.0	62	25	21	54
92 NL	5	4	4.10	65	8	63.2	59	29	20	44
93 NL	4	6	4.67	63	27	52.0	51	27	29	43
94 NL	3	1	3.55	49	3	45.2	41	18	26	35
95 NL	1	1	5.59	26	1	19.1	31	12	8	13
95 AL	1	0	3.00	22	0	21.0	17	7	8	10
96 AL	4	4	3.66	81	1	78.2	78	32	27	60
Life	23	25	3.88	407	56	389.1	372	168	149	293
2 Ave	4	3	3.61	75	3	71.1	68	29	32	55

TERRY STEINBACH

Position: Catcher
Team: Minnesota Twins
Born: March 2, 1962 New Ulm, MN
Height: 6'1" **Weight:** 200 lbs.
Acquired: Signed as a free agent, 12/96

PLAYER SUMMARY	
Fantasy Value	$19 to $22
Card Value	5¢ to 8¢
Will	give his all
Can't	show much speed
Expect	regular duty
Don't Expect	another 35 homers

Steinbach had his best offensive year to date in '96. His 35th homer and 100th RBI came on the second-to-last day of the season. He had been the subject of constant trade rumors, but Oakland decided to keep him in order to develop their young pitching staff. However, working with those green pitchers created some defensive problems for Steinbach. Opponents ran on him at will, stealing safely in 83 of 117 attempts. How much of that running can be attributed to the pitching staff's inexperience and how much reflects a decline in Steinbach's throwing ability is up for debate, but his caught-stealing percentage has worsened in the past few years. Although fans and teammates alike made it known they wanted Steinbach to finish his career in Oakland, the Twins were able to scoop him up as a free agent over the off-season.

Major League Batting Register

	BA	G	AB	R	H	2B	3B	HR	RBI	SB
86 AL	.333	6	15	3	5	0	0	2	4	0
87 AL	.284	122	391	66	111	16	3	16	56	1
88 AL	.265	104	351	42	93	19	1	9	51	3
89 AL	.273	130	454	37	124	13	1	7	42	1
90 AL	.251	114	379	32	95	15	2	9	57	0
91 AL	.274	129	456	50	125	31	1	6	67	2
92 AL	.279	128	438	48	122	20	1	12	53	2
93 AL	.285	104	389	47	111	19	1	10	43	3
94 AL	.285	103	369	51	105	21	2	11	57	2
95 AL	.278	114	406	43	113	26	1	15	65	1
96 AL	.272	145	514	79	140	25	1	35	100	0
Life	.275	1199	4162	498	1144	205	14	132	595	15
3 Ave	.278	139	497	66	138	28	2	22	84	1

DAVE STEVENS

Position: Pitcher
Team: Minnesota Twins
Born: March 4, 1970 Fullerton, CA
Height: 6'3" **Weight:** 210 lbs.
Bats: right **Throws:** right
Acquired: Traded by Cubs with Matt Walbeck for Willie Banks, 11/93

PLAYER SUMMARY	
Fantasy Value	$8 to $10
Card Value	4¢ to 7¢
Will	register strikeouts
Can't	control his temper
Expect	save opportunities
Don't Expect	ground balls

By moving Rick Aguilera to the starting rotation last spring, manager Tom Kelly gave Stevens a shot at the regular closer's job. However, Stevens showed he lacks the "shrug-it-off" mentality of a closer. In July, he cut his finger smashing a telephone in a dugout tantrum and missed nearly a month. Stevens's tantrum forced Kelly into a closer-by-committee situation, even though it was clear at most times that Stevens was the best closer for the Twins. Stevens has a decent fastball but cannot set it up with other pitches, so he doesn't strike out a lot of batters. Lefties hit .319 against him last year. On the other hand, he holds runners very well and has cut down his walk total. Stevens, a clear fly-ball pitcher, is durable, can pitch on a fairly frequent basis, and can throw more than an inning at a time. It's quite possible that if Stevens spent an uninterrupted year as a closer, he could blossom into a very effective reliever. It appears that as Kelly's confidence in him grows, Stevens becomes a better pitcher.

Major League Pitching Register

	W	L	ERA	G	S	IP	H	ER	BB	SO
94 AL	5	2	6.80	24	0	45.0	55	34	23	24
95 AL	5	4	5.07	56	10	65.2	74	37	32	47
96 AL	3	3	4.66	49	11	58.0	58	30	25	29
Life	13	9	5.39	129	21	168.2	187	101	80	100
3 Ave	5	3	5.51	49	7	65.0	73	40	31	39

KEVIN STOCKER

Position: Shortstop
Team: Philadelphia Phillies
Born: Feb. 13, 1970 Spokane, WA
Height: 6'1" **Weight:** 178 lbs.
Bats: both **Throws:** right
Acquired: Second-round pick in 6/91 free-agent draft

PLAYER SUMMARY	
Fantasy Value	$4 to $6
Card Value	4¢ to 7¢
Will	get another shot
Can't	afford to slide
Expect	some walks and steals
Don't Expect	Gold Glove defense

Since enjoying an outstanding rookie season in 1993, Stocker has been in a steady decline. Only the lack of alternatives at shortstop in the Philadelphia system has kept him employed, and last summer he finally paid the price for more than two years of poor overall performance. Batting just .186 on June 3 and convincing manager Jim Fregosi that he wasn't all that bothered by it, Stocker was shipped out to Triple-A Scranton. He didn't come back until July 1. When he returned from exile, Stocker was a different hitter. He steadily lifted his average (setting a season-ending goal of .250) and made a late push to raise his average 12 points in the last two weeks of the season. Of course, a .254 average is no great shakes, especially since he strikes out often, has little power, shows mediocre on-base ability, and is shaky on defense. Stocker simply needs to do everything better and more consistently in 1997, or else the Phillies will have to look for another answer.

Major League Batting Register

	BA	G	AB	R	H	2B	3B	HR	RBI	SB
93 NL	.324	70	259	46	84	12	3	2	31	5
94 NL	.273	82	271	38	74	11	2	2	28	2
95 NL	.218	125	412	42	90	14	3	1	32	6
96 NL	.254	119	394	46	100	22	6	5	41	6
Life	.260	396	1336	172	348	59	14	10	132	19
3 Ave	.247	125	413	49	102	18	4	3	39	5

TODD STOTTLEMYRE

Position: Pitcher
Team: St. Louis Cardinals
Born: May 20, 1965 Yakima, WA
Height: 6'3" **Weight:** 200 lbs.
Bats: left **Throws:** right
Acquired: Traded by Athletics for Allen Battle, Bret Wagner, Jay Witasick, and Carl Dale, 1/96

PLAYER SUMMARY
Fantasy Value	$13 to $16
Card Value	7¢ to 10¢
Will	throw hard
Can't	hold baserunners
Expect	competitive attitude
Don't Expect	great control

When ex-Oakland manager Tony LaRussa and pitching coach Dave Duncan migrated to St. Louis, they brought Stottlemyre with them. He was the Cardinals' most consistent starter throughout the regular season, was a bulldog in the playoffs, and overall was a major reason why St. Louis nearly made it to the World Series. There had been some worries about Stottlemyre, who had an ERA over 5.00 in the second half of 1995. However, he silenced all doubters by tossing a career-high 223⅓ innings, five complete games, and two shutouts in '96. Opposing hitters batted only .231 against him, and he was even better against right-handed hitters, holding them to a puny .198 average. He still is easy to run on; 30 of 39 men were successful trying to steal against him in 1996. Despite that, Stottlemyre is a big reason why the Cards have one of the best starting staffs in the NL.

Major League Pitching Register
	W	L	ERA	G	CG	IP	H	ER	BB	SO
88 AL	4	8	5.69	28	0	98.0	109	62	46	67
89 AL	7	7	3.88	27	0	127.2	137	55	44	63
90 AL	13	17	4.34	33	4	203.0	214	98	69	115
91 AL	15	8	3.78	34	1	219.0	194	92	75	116
92 AL	12	11	4.50	28	6	174.0	175	87	63	98
93 AL	11	12	4.84	30	1	176.2	204	95	69	98
94 AL	7	7	4.22	26	3	140.2	149	66	48	105
95 AL	14	7	4.55	31	2	209.2	228	106	80	205
96 NL	14	11	3.87	34	5	223.1	191	96	93	194
Life	97	88	4.33	271	22	1572.0	1601	757	587	1061
3 Ave	13	10	4.22	35	4	219.0	219	103	84	191

DOUG STRANGE

Position: Third base
Team: Seattle Mariners
Born: April 13, 1964 Greenville, SC
Height: 6'1" **Weight:** 185 lbs.
Bats: both **Throws:** right
Acquired: Signed as a minor-league free agent, 4/95

PLAYER SUMMARY
Fantasy Value	$0
Card Value	4¢ to 7¢
Will	fill in everywhere
Can't	hit left-handers
Expect	throwing problems
Don't Expect	much pop

Strange's career has been, well, strange. After completely washing out as a midseason third-base replacement with the 1988 Tigers, he worked his way back through the minor leagues as a spare infielder and outfielder and has played well. Strange is a good defensive player and still runs faster than average. However, 1996 was not a red-letter campaign for him. The Mariners hoped Strange could help fill the hot-corner vacancy created when regular third baseman Russ Davis suffered a season-ending broken leg in June. Unfortunately, Strange once again failed in his assignment. He didn't hit a lick, even when used only against right-handed pitching. Things got worse for him late in the year when his elbow began to bother him; after the season ended, he underwent arthroscopic surgery. Serious elbow injuries are bad news to utility infielders, and Strange could well find himself back in the minors in 1997 if his arm (and bat) don't recover quickly.

Major League Batting Register
	BA	G	AB	R	H	2B	3B	HR	RBI	SB
89 AL	.214	64	196	16	42	4	1	1	14	3
91 NL	.444	3	9	0	4	1	0	0	1	1
92 NL	.160	52	94	7	15	1	0	1	5	1
93 AL	.256	145	484	58	124	29	0	7	60	6
94 AL	.212	73	226	26	48	12	1	5	26	1
95 AL	.271	74	155	19	42	9	2	2	21	0
96 NL	.235	88	183	19	43	7	1	3	23	1
Life	.236	499	1347	145	318	63	5	19	150	13
3 Ave	.234	91	225	26	53	11	2	4	28	1

DARRYL STRAWBERRY

Position: Outfield
Team: New York Yankees
Born: March 12, 1962 Los Angeles, CA
Height: 6'6" **Weight:** 215 lbs.
Bats: left **Throws:** left
Acquired: Signed as a free agent, 6/96

PLAYER SUMMARY	
Fantasy Value	$9 to $11
Card Value	10¢ to 15¢
Will	hit long balls
Can't	play strong defense
Expect	the unexpected
Don't Expect	many more years

Strawberry was out of baseball and very close to seeing his career end as he began his odd 1996 saga as a member of the Class-A independent St. Paul Saints. After he battered around young prospects, a bidding war developed for his services. The Yankees signed Strawberry despite the indifference of manager Joe Torre, and with New York injuries enabling Darryl to play more than expected, he performed respectably. He has some pop left in his bat and is still capable of exciting a crowd, but at this point he's just an average player. He struggles against lefties, has lost some speed, and lacks defensive prowess. He shared DH duties with Cecil Fielder last year, played some left field, and—most important for the Yankees—neither self-destructed nor brought unneeded attention onto himself.

Major League Batting Register

	BA	G	AB	R	H	2B	3B	HR	RBI	SB
83 NL	.257	122	420	63	108	15	7	26	74	19
84 NL	.251	147	522	75	131	27	4	26	97	27
85 NL	.277	111	393	78	109	15	4	29	79	26
86 NL	.259	136	475	76	123	27	5	27	93	28
87 NL	.284	154	532	108	151	32	5	39	104	36
88 NL	.269	153	543	101	146	27	3	39	101	29
89 NL	.225	134	476	69	107	26	1	29	77	11
90 NL	.277	152	542	92	150	18	1	37	108	15
91 NL	.265	139	505	86	134	22	4	28	99	10
92 NL	.237	43	156	20	37	8	0	5	25	3
93 NL	.140	32	100	12	14	2	0	5	12	1
94 NL	.239	29	92	13	22	3	1	4	17	0
95 AL	.276	32	87	15	24	4	1	3	13	0
96 AL	.262	63	202	35	53	13	0	11	36	6
Life	.259	1447	5045	843	1309	239	36	308	935	211

B.J. SURHOFF

Position: Third base; outfield
Team: Baltimore Orioles
Born: Aug. 4, 1964 Bronx, NY
Height: 6'1" **Weight:** 200 lbs.
Bats: left **Throws:** right
Acquired: Signed as a free agent, 12/95

PLAYER SUMMARY	
Fantasy Value	$14 to $17
Card Value	7¢ to 10¢
Will	provide some power
Can't	run well
Expect	consistent offense
Don't Expect	a Gold Glove

The Brewers felt that if Surhoff could pull the ball, he'd be able to hit for more power. Unfortunately for Milwaukee, he did so only after coming to Baltimore. Surhoff met all of the Orioles' expectations for him in 1996: He played decent third base, showed he could play left field in a pinch, and hit solidly. While far from spectacular defensively, Surhoff filled the third base hole that has existed in Baltimore for years. His range is limited, but as long as Cal Ripken can still roam into the hole between short and third, Surhoff is adequate. While his batting average dipped slightly from that of 1995, he did hit over .290. His 21 homers were by far his highest yearly total. It will be interesting to find out if Surhoff's power is a one-year fluke or a sign of things to come. Certainly Camden Yards is a more hitter-friendly stadium than County Stadium in Milwaukee.

Major League Batting Register

	BA	G	AB	R	H	2B	3B	HR	RBI	SB
87 AL	.299	115	395	50	118	22	3	7	68	11
88 AL	.245	139	493	47	121	21	0	5	38	21
89 AL	.248	126	436	42	108	17	4	5	55	14
90 AL	.276	135	474	55	131	21	4	6	59	18
91 AL	.289	143	505	57	146	19	4	5	68	5
92 AL	.252	139	480	63	121	19	1	4	62	14
93 AL	.274	148	552	66	151	38	3	7	79	12
94 AL	.261	40	134	20	35	11	2	5	22	0
95 AL	.320	117	415	72	133	26	3	13	73	7
96 AL	.292	143	537	74	157	27	6	21	82	0
Life	.276	1245	4421	546	1221	221	30	78	606	102
2 Ave	.305	137	502	78	153	28	5	18	82	4

298

MARK SWEENEY

Position: First base; outfield
Team: St. Louis Cardinals
Born: Oct. 26, 1969 Framingham, MA
Height: 6'1" **Weight:** 195 lbs.
Bats: left **Throws:** left
Acquired: Traded by Angels with Rod Correia for John Habyan, 7/95

PLAYER SUMMARY	
Fantasy Value	$1
Card Value	5¢ to 8¢
Will	get on base
Can't	impress with power
Expect	part-time play
Don't Expect	much speed

Sweeney finally got a shot at the majors in 1996 after making a long trek through the Angels and then the Cards farm systems. He batted just .265 in '96, mostly in a reserve role, but proved to be an on-base machine by walking 33 times in slightly more than 200 plate appearances. One of the most patient Cardinals, his 33 walks approached the totals of everyday players John Mabry (37), Gary Gaetti (35), and Royce Clayton (35), and at times manager Tony LaRussa even used the not-too-speedy Sweeney as a leadoff hitter. Unfortunately, there is no place for him to play regularly in St. Louis right now while Ron Gant, Brian Jordan, and Ray Lankford roam the new Busch Stadium grass. The one thing in Sweeney's favor is there always seems to be a need for left-handed pinch hitters who get on base, so he could easily stick around as a reserve if he continues to perform at his current pace. He'll need to add significant power to his repertoire to be considered for an everyday role.

Major League Batting Register

	BA	G	AB	R	H	2B	3B	HR	RBI	SB
95 NL	.273	37	77	5	21	2	0	2	13	1
96 NL	.265	98	170	32	45	9	0	3	22	3
Life	.267	135	247	37	66	11	0	5	35	4

BILL SWIFT

Position: Pitcher
Team: Colorado Rockies
Born: Oct. 27, 1961 South Portland, ME
Height: 6' **Weight:** 180 lbs.
Bats: right **Throws:** right
Acquired: Signed as a free agent, 4/95

PLAYER SUMMARY	
Fantasy Value	$1 to $3
Card Value	4¢ to 7¢
Will	throw sinkers
Can't	count on health
Expect	some starts
Don't Expect	many innings

Right shoulder surgery wiped out most of 1996 for Swift. It is a credit to the veteran that he tried to come back at all last season, as many pitchers would have just packed it in once they had been paid. He threw two rehab games at Class-A, and when he finally returned to Denver in September, Swift was relatively ineffective—like most Rockies pitchers. Never a hard thrower, Swift appeared to have lost even more velocity. Opposing batters hit .300 against him, and by all rights Swift's ERA could have been much higher. Should he be able to rehabilitate this winter and get some strength back, Swift will return to Colorado in 1997. He is still a smart pitcher and can get out of jams, but his effectiveness remains to be seen. He hasn't had a full season of work since 1993, and he certainly hasn't approached the form the Rockies hoped for when they signed him.

Major League Pitching Register

	W	L	ERA	G	S	IP	H	ER	BB	SO
85 AL	6	10	4.77	23	0	120.2	131	64	48	55
86 AL	2	9	5.46	29	0	115.1	148	70	55	55
88 AL	8	12	4.59	38	0	174.2	199	89	65	47
89 AL	7	3	4.43	37	1	130.0	140	64	38	45
90 AL	6	4	2.39	55	6	128.0	135	34	21	42
91 AL	1	2	1.99	71	17	90.1	74	20	26	48
92 NL	10	4	2.08	30	1	164.2	144	38	43	77
93 NL	21	8	2.82	34	0	232.2	195	73	55	157
94 NL	8	7	3.38	17	0	109.1	109	41	31	62
95 NL	9	3	4.94	19	0	105.2	122	58	43	68
96 NL	1	1	5.40	7	2	18.1	23	11	5	5
Life	79	63	3.64	360	27	1389.2	1420	562	430	661
2 Ave	11	7	4.06	23	0	136.1	145	62	46	82

GREG SWINDELL

Position: Pitcher
Team: Minnesota Twins
Born: Jan. 2, 1965 Fort Worth, TX
Height: 6'3" **Weight:** 225 lbs.
Bats: right **Throws:** left
Acquired: Signed as a minor-league free
agent, 12/96

PLAYER SUMMARY	
Fantasy Value	$1
Card Value	4¢ to 7¢
Will	search for answers
Can't	waste another chance
Expect	good control
Don't Expect	return to glory

The Astros signing of Swindell to a four-year, $17-million deal before the 1993 season turned out to be an almost total bust. He benefited unduly from the offense-suppressing tendencies of the Astrodome and did not pitch well on the road. The Astros finally cut him loose last June, placing him on waivers and choosing to eat the remainder of his contract. Hoping that perhaps a change of scenery would help, the Indians quickly signed the veteran lefty (who had spent the first part of his career in Cleveland). Unfortunately, Swindell did not pitch well for his new club, either. The former power pitcher has lost much of the bite on his curve and much of the velocity on his fastball. He also suffered a groin injury last year that shelved him for over a month. Unless Swindell can regain his strength, he will have a hard time sticking around.

Major League Pitching Register

	W	L	ERA	G	S	IP	H	ER	BB	SO
86 AL	5	2	4.23	9	0	61.2	57	29	15	46
87 AL	3	8	5.10	16	0	102.1	112	58	37	97
88 AL	18	14	3.20	33	0	242.0	234	86	45	180
89 AL	13	6	3.37	28	0	184.1	170	69	51	129
90 AL	12	9	4.40	34	0	214.2	245	105	47	135
91 AL	9	16	3.48	33	0	238.0	241	92	31	169
92 NL	12	8	2.70	31	0	213.2	210	64	41	138
93 NL	12	13	4.16	31	0	190.1	215	88	40	124
94 NL	8	9	4.37	24	0	148.1	175	72	26	74
95 NL	10	9	4.47	33	0	153.0	180	76	39	96
96 NL	0	3	7.83	8	0	23.0	35	20	11	15
96 AL	1	1	6.59	13	0	28.2	31	21	8	21
Life	103	98	3.90	293	0	1800.0	1905	780	391	1224
2 Ave	11	11	4.41	35	0	191.1	225	93	40	106

JEFF TABAKA

Position: Pitcher
Team: Houston Astros
Born: Jan. 17, 1964 Barberton, OH
Height: 6'2" **Weight:** 195 lbs.
Bats: right **Throws:** left
Acquired: Traded by Padres with Rich Loiselle
for Phil Plantier, 7/95

PLAYER SUMMARY	
Fantasy Value	$0
Card Value	5¢ to 8¢
Will	get more chances
Can't	get righties out
Expect	ups and downs
Don't Expect	marquee duty

Tabaka is one of the many undistinguished left-handed relief pitchers constantly bouncing between the major leagues and Triple-A. He spent several years toiling in the Milwaukee and Philadelphia farm systems without getting close to the majors, but was picked by the Marlins in the 1992 expansion draft and has pitched for three big-league clubs since then. While he sports a confusing delivery and has a fastball better than that of most other garden-variety southpaw relievers, Tabaka has serious problems with control that have kept him from advancing into a permanent role in somebody's bullpen. He saw scant action for the Astros in 1996 even though Houston struggled all season to find veteran left-handed relief. He does have the ability to get left-handed hitters out consistently, but Tabaka must learn to get righties out as well. Houston is likely to go with younger pitchers as their southpaw relievers in 1997. This will leave Tabaka out in the cold unless he can prove he has gotten his game together.

Major League Pitching Register

	W	L	ERA	G	S	IP	H	ER	BB	SO
94 NL	3	1	5.27	39	1	41.0	32	24	27	32
95 NL	1	0	3.23	34	0	30.2	27	11	17	25
96 NL	0	2	6.64	18	1	20.1	28	15	14	18
Life	4	3	4.89	91	2	92.0	87	50	58	75

KEVIN TAPANI

Position: Pitcher
Team: Chicago Cubs
Born: Feb. 18, 1964 Des Moines, IA
Height: 6′ **Weight:** 188 lbs.
Bats: right **Throws:** right
Acquired: Signed as a free agent, 12/96

PLAYER SUMMARY
Fantasy Value. . . . . $10 to $13
Card Value . . . . 5¢ to 8¢
Will . . . . allow home runs
Can't . . . . carry a staff
Expect . . . . ground balls
Don't Expect . . . . a breakdown

The White Sox were not counting on any miracles from Tapani in 1996, and they did not get any. What they did get when they signed the veteran righty, however, was a quality starting pitcher who gave the club good innings and kept them in a lot of games. Throwing his usual combination of curves, changeups, and sinking fastballs, Tapani did his best to keep the ball in the park (he allowed plenty of extra-base hits, as usual, serving up 34 homers) and was stingy enough with walks (76). A control artist, Tapani is a sinker-slider pitcher who also throws a forkball. Serving as the club's third starter, he compiled a decent ERA. He is not spectacular, but he has helped teams win pennants. All in all, Tapani did exactly what he was supposed to do in 1996, and he is likely to do the same for the crosstown Cubs in 1997.

Major League Pitching Register

	W	L	ERA	G	CG	IP	H	ER	BB	SO
89 NL	0	0	3.68	3	0	7.1	5	3	4	2
89 AL	2	2	3.86	5	0	32.2	34	14	8	21
90 AL	12	8	4.07	28	1	159.1	164	72	29	101
91 AL	16	9	2.99	34	4	244.0	225	81	40	135
92 AL	16	11	3.97	34	4	220.0	226	97	48	138
93 AL	12	15	4.43	36	3	225.2	243	111	57	150
94 AL	11	7	4.62	24	4	156.0	181	80	39	91
95 AL	6	11	4.92	20	3	133.2	155	73	34	88
95 NL	4	2	5.05	13	0	57.0	72	32	14	43
96 AL	13	10	4.59	34	1	225.1	236	115	76	150
Life	92	75	4.18	231	20	1461.0	1541	678	349	919
3 Ave	12	11	4.68	30	3	198.1	222	103	56	126

TONY TARASCO

Position: Outfield
Team: Baltimore Orioles
Born: Dec. 9, 1970 New York, NY
Height: 6′1″ **Weight:** 205 lbs.
Bats: left **Throws:** right
Acquired: Traded by Expos for Sherman Obando, 3/94

PLAYER SUMMARY
Fantasy Value. . . . . $4 to $6
Card Value . . . . 5¢ to 8¢
Will . . . . look for a job
Can't. . . . . show patience
Expect . . . . good defense
Don't Expect . . . . 30 homers

For Tarasco, 1996 was a lost year. It became clear in spring training that there was no room for him on the Expos roster, so he was shipped to Baltimore. However, he did not hit well for the Orioles and was sent down to Triple-A. Even though the Orioles' left field situation was muddy for most of the season, Tarasco could not take advantage of the opportunity and failed to impress manager Davey Johnson. To make matters worse, Tarasco missed most of September because of a bad right shoulder. He made the O's playoff roster, largely because of the injury to Jeffrey Hammonds, but was used only as a substitute. Perhaps the icing on the cake to Tarasco's nightmarish 1996 was the incident in which a 12-year-old Yankee fan interfered with the right fielder's attempt to catch a fly ball on a controversial play in the ALCS. While Tarasco has some speed and some power and is relatively young, he will not have many more chances to prove himself. Despite this, however, things almost have to be better for him in 1997.

Major League Batting Register

	BA	G	AB	R	H	2B	3B	HR	RBI	SB
93 NL	.229	24	35	6	8	2	0	0	2	0
94 NL	.273	87	132	16	36	6	0	5	19	5
95 NL	.249	126	438	64	109	18	4	14	40	24
96 AL	.238	31	84	14	20	3	0	1	9	5
Life	.251	268	689	100	173	29	4	20	70	34

DANNY TARTABULL

Position: Outfield
Team: Chicago White Sox
Born: Oct. 30, 1962 Miami, FL
Height: 6'1" **Weight:** 204 lbs.
Bats: right **Throws:** right
Acquired: Traded by Athletics for Andrew Lorraine and Charles Poe, 1/96

PLAYER SUMMARY	
Fantasy Value	$14 to $17
Card Value	7¢ to 10¢
Will	hit left-handers
Can't	play great "D"
Expect	DH duty
Don't Expect	30 homers

The White Sox seem to have a different right fielder every year, and 1996 proved to be no exception. The club took a chance on Tartabull—always reputed to be a problem in the clubhouse—after the veteran had a dismal 1995 that saw him traded from New York to Oakland in midseason. While Tartabull wasn't nearly as bad as he had been the year before, his 1996 numbers were merely average. He hit just .248 against right-handers and finished second on the Sox by whiffing 128 times. Tartabull, who has been hurt frequently in the past, played in only 132 games for the White Sox. Although Tartabull will be just 34 at the start of the season, most feel that his best years are far behind him. The White Sox showed no interest in re-signing the veteran slugger.

Major League Batting Register

	BA	G	AB	R	H	2B	3B	HR	RBI	SB
84 AL	.300	10	20	3	6	1	0	2	7	0
85 AL	.328	19	61	8	20	7	1	1	7	1
86 AL	.270	137	511	76	138	25	6	25	96	4
87 AL	.309	158	582	95	180	27	3	34	101	9
88 AL	.274	146	507	80	139	38	3	26	102	8
89 AL	.268	133	441	54	118	22	0	18	62	4
90 AL	.268	88	313	41	84	19	0	15	60	1
91 AL	.316	132	484	78	153	35	3	31	100	6
92 AL	.266	123	421	72	112	19	0	25	85	2
93 AL	.250	138	513	87	128	33	2	31	102	0
94 AL	.256	104	399	68	102	24	1	19	67	1
95 AL	.236	83	280	34	66	16	0	8	35	0
96 AL	.254	132	472	58	120	23	3	27	101	1
Life	.273	1403	5004	754	1366	289	22	262	925	37
3 Ave	.250	124	450	64	113	25	1	21	78	1

ED TAUBENSEE

Position: Catcher
Team: Cincinnati Reds
Born: Oct. 31, 1966 Beeville, TX
Height: 6'4" **Weight:** 205 lbs.
Bats: right **Throws:** right
Acquired: Traded by Astros for Ross Powell and Marty Lister, 4/94

PLAYER SUMMARY	
Fantasy Value	$6 to $8
Card Value	4¢ to 7¢
Will	play regularly
Can't	outrun a snail
Expect	good offense
Don't Expect	great throwing

It seems the only thing keeping Taubensee from being one of the top catchers in the league is defense. He saw a lot of playing time early in the 1996 season, but he wound up splitting at bats almost evenly with Joe Oliver later on because the Reds felt Oliver called a better game. Taubensee, never an outstanding defender, spent a day in the middle of the season working with Hall-of-Famer Johnny Bench, but the tutelage may not have helped much as Taubensee threw out only 23 percent of runners trying to steal and committed 11 errors. Taubensee was as good as ever at the plate, however, and even hit left-handers well, stinging them at a .333 clip. One of these days—possibly this year—Taubensee is going to get a chance to become the full-time catcher. Oliver has said publicly that he wants to play every day, and the Reds are high on minor-league receiver Brook Fordyce as a backup. It is not out of the question for Taubensee to get 400 at bats in 1997.

Major League Batting Register

	BA	G	AB	R	H	2B	3B	HR	RBI	SB
91 AL	.242	26	66	5	16	2	1	0	8	0
92 NL	.222	104	297	23	66	15	0	5	28	2
93 NL	.250	94	288	26	72	11	1	9	42	1
94 NL	.283	66	187	29	53	8	2	8	21	2
95 NL	.284	80	218	32	62	14	2	9	44	2
96 NL	.291	108	327	46	95	20	0	12	48	3
Life	.263	478	1383	161	364	70	6	43	191	10
3 Ave	.286	97	279	41	80	16	2	11	42	3

JULIAN TAVAREZ

Position: Pitcher
Team: San Francisco Giants
Born: May 22, 1973 Santiago, Dominican Republic
Height: 6'2" **Weight:** 165 lbs.
Bats: right **Throws:** right
Acquired: Traded by Indians with Jeff Kent and Jose Vizcaino for Matt Williams, 11/96

PLAYER SUMMARY	
Fantasy Value	$5 to $7
Card Value	4¢ to 7¢
Will	throw sliders
Can't	get lefties out
Expect	an improvement
Don't Expect	a starting role

The wiry Tavarez had a miserable 1996 season. After his outstanding performance the year before, most observers felt Tavarez was on his way either into the starting rotation or into set-up duty. Unfortunately, Tavarez mucked up the plans by losing his ability to throw his pitches over the plate. His sinker didn't sink, and his slider flattened out. Left-handers tattooed him at a .371 pace, and Tavarez allowed 24 doubles and nine homers in his 81 innings. The Indians tried everything to get him straightened out, even shipping him to Triple-A Buffalo at midseason, but nothing seemed to work. He ended the year pitching middle relief. By that time, nobody was talking about him as a future starter. However, all is not lost. He still has his good pickoff move, stayed injury-free, and never gave up. The Indians did not want to give him up in the trade for Matt Williams, but the Giants insisted and so Tavarez takes his good arm and promising stuff to the National League.

Major League Pitching Register

	W	L	ERA	G	S	IP	H	ER	BB	SO
93 AL	2	2	6.57	8	0	37.0	53	27	13	19
94 AL	0	1	21.60	1	0	1.2	6	4	1	0
95 AL	10	2	2.44	57	0	85.0	76	23	21	68
96 AL	4	7	5.36	51	0	80.2	101	48	22	46
Life	16	12	4.49	117	0	204.1	236	102	57	133
2 Ave	8	5	3.77	58	0	88.0	93	37	23	61

BILL TAYLOR

Position: Pitcher
Team: Oakland Athletics
Born: Oct. 16, 1961 Monticello, FL
Height: 6'8" **Weight:** 200 lbs.
Bats: right **Throws:** right
Acquired: Signed as a minor-league free agent, 12/93

PLAYER SUMMARY	
Fantasy Value	$10 to $13
Card Value	5¢ to 8¢
Will	work often
Can't	throw that hard
Expect	ground balls
Don't Expect	home runs

A career minor-leaguer who spent ten years with six organizations before finally arriving in the majors with the Athletics in 1994, Taylor bounced back last year from a serious knee injury that had disabled him for all of 1995. Taking over as the club's closer when several other options bombed out, he was the best right-hander that Oakland could bring out of the bullpen. He saved 17 games in 19 chances, a 90-percent success rate, and would have gotten more save opportunities if the A's had been any good. The tall and rangy righty throws sidearm by way of third base and, as a result, owns right-handed batters, who he held to just a .225 average in 1996. A sinkerball pitcher with a good curve, he allowed only five home runs on the season and did not beat himself with walks. It is easy to root for Taylor; he has paid his dues but hung in for his big chance. When it came, he pitched well, then came back strong from an injury to again pitch effectively. He also plays the game with joy and energy.

Major League Pitching Register

	W	L	ERA	G	S	IP	H	ER	BB	SO
94 AL	1	3	3.50	41	1	46.1	38	18	18	48
96 AL	6	3	4.33	55	17	60.1	52	29	25	67
Life	7	6	3.97	96	18	106.2	90	47	43	115
2 Ave	4	4	3.89	56	9	63.1	53	27	25	67

303

AMAURY TELEMACO

Position: Pitcher
Team: Chicago Cubs
Born: Jan. 19, 1974 Higuey, Dominican
  Republic
Height: 6'3" **Weight:** 210 lbs.
Bats: right **Throws:** right
Acquired: Signed as a free agent, 5/91

PLAYER SUMMARY	
Fantasy Value.	$3 to $5
Card Value	10¢ to 15¢
Will.	mix pitches
Can't	overpower with heat
Expect	starting berth
Don't Expect.	instant domination

Telemaco, Chicago's best pitching prospect, showed plenty of promise during 1996 but wasn't quite ready to lead the Cubs to the playoffs. Telemaco, who had never pitched above Double-A before 1996, started out the season at Triple-A Iowa and was promoted to Chicago with a 3-0 record in seven starts. He debuted May 16 against Houston and allowed just one hit over eight innings in a 13-1 Cub victory. However, he soon cooled off and ended up making a trip to the DL with minor arm problems. Telemaco did pitch without trouble in relief at the end of the season. When he's on, he has excellent command (he walked hitters once every three innings in his brief minor-league career), a very good changeup, and good movement on his fastball. The Cubs are excited about Telemaco, who will be just 23 years old this year and has been outstanding at every level he has pitched. Like any young pitcher, he will have to adjust to the majors, but if the Cubs (and Cub fans) are patient, there no is reason why he shouldn't be a solid contributor to the rotation for many years.

Major League Pitching Register

	W	L	ERA	G	CG	IP	H	ER	BB	SO
96 NL	5	7	5.46	25	0	97.1	108	59	31	64
Life	5	7	5.46	25	0	97.1	108	59	31	64

MICKEY TETTLETON

Position: Designated hitter
Team: Texas Rangers
Born: Sept. 19, 1960 Oklahoma City, OK
Height: 6'2" **Weight:** 212 lbs.
Bats: both **Throws:** right
Acquired: Signed as a free agent, 4/95

PLAYER SUMMARY	
Fantasy Value.	$10 to $13
Card Value	5¢ to 8¢
Will.	hit for power
Can't	run at all
Expect	DH duty
Don't Expect	low on-base percentage

Tettleton is a fascinating, if flawed, offensive player. He has good eyesight and quick wrists and, as a result, can hit for power despite an odd batting stance. As usual, he walked a ton in 1996, drawing 95 free passes, and totaled a .366 on-base percentage. However, he also strikes out a lot, and when he gets on base he clogs up the basepaths, as he is one of the slower players in the majors. Tettleton's knees, which have been torn up by years of catching duty, can no longer take daily wear and tear. Another concern is that his power from the right has diminished. Due to his inability to catch, play the outfield, or fill in often at first base, time is running out on Tettleton as an everyday player. He can probably stick around for years as a bench player or platoon DH, but he probably won't be getting 500 at bats for much longer.

Major League Batting Register

	BA	G	AB	R	H	2B	3B	HR	RBI	SB
84 AL	.263	33	76	10	20	2	1	1	5	0
85 AL	.251	78	211	23	53	12	0	3	15	2
86 AL	.204	90	211	26	43	9	0	10	35	7
87 AL	.194	82	211	19	41	3	0	8	26	1
88 AL	.261	86	283	31	74	11	1	11	37	0
89 AL	.258	117	411	72	106	21	2	26	65	3
90 AL	.223	135	444	68	99	21	2	15	51	2
91 AL	.263	154	501	85	132	17	2	31	89	3
92 AL	.238	157	525	82	125	25	0	32	83	0
93 AL	.245	152	522	79	128	25	4	32	110	3
94 AL	.248	107	339	57	84	18	2	17	51	0
95 AL	.238	134	429	76	102	19	1	32	78	0
96 AL	.246	143	491	78	121	26	1	24	83	2
Life	.242	1468	4654	706	1128	209	16	242	728	23
3 Ave	.244	148	484	81	118	24	2	28	81	1

BOB TEWKSBURY

Position: Pitcher
Team: Minnesota Twins
Born: Nov. 30, 1960 Concord, NH
Height: 6'4" **Weight:** 205 lbs.
Bats: right **Throws:** right
Acquired: Signed as a free agent, 12/96

PLAYER SUMMARY	
Fantasy Value	$9 to $11
Card Value	5¢ to 8¢
Will	throw softly
Can't	afford control woes
Expect	decent innings
Don't Expect	strikeouts or walks

Even in his prime, Tewksbury never threw hard, relying instead on pinpoint control and the ability to change speeds—from slow to slower to slowest—to get hitters to beat the ball into the ground. While he still doesn't walk very many (fewer than two a game in 1996), he leaves far more pitches over the plate than he did five years ago, and opposing hitters make him pay. Opposing batters hit .275 and slugged .402 against Tewksbury last year, with right-handed hitters pelting him at a .282 clip. There were times when Tewksbury pitched well, however, and his performance was consistent. While his 4.31 ERA was not horrible, it was not overly encouraging, either, considering he is 36 and on the backside of his career. Tewksbury joins the Twins for 1997.

Major League Pitching Register

	W	L	ERA	G	CG	IP	H	ER	BB	SO
86 AL	9	5	3.31	23	2	130.1	144	48	31	49
87 AL	1	4	6.75	8	0	33.1	47	25	7	12
87 NL	0	4	6.50	7	0	18.0	32	13	13	10
88 NL	0	0	8.10	1	0	3.1	6	3	2	1
89 NL	1	0	3.30	7	1	30.0	25	11	10	17
90 NL	10	9	3.47	28	3	145.1	151	56	15	50
91 NL	11	12	3.25	30	3	191.0	206	69	38	75
92 NL	16	5	2.16	33	5	233.0	217	56	20	91
93 NL	17	10	3.83	32	2	213.2	258	91	20	97
94 NL	12	10	5.32	24	4	155.2	190	92	22	79
95 AL	8	7	4.58	21	4	129.2	169	66	20	53
96 NL	10	10	4.31	36	1	206.2	224	99	43	126
Life	95	76	3.80	250	25	1490.0	1669	629	241	660
3 Ave	12	11	4.77	31	4	191.1	227	101	32	99

FRANK THOMAS

Position: First base
Team: Chicago White Sox
Born: May 27, 1968 Columbus, GA
Height: 6'5" **Weight:** 257 lbs.
Bats: right **Throws:** right
Acquired: First-round pick in 6/89 free-agent draft

PLAYER SUMMARY	
Fantasy Value	$40 to $45
Card Value	$1.50 to $3
Will	hit, hit, hit
Can't	carry the team
Expect	defensive struggles
Don't Expect	a slump

Thomas may be the best all-around offensive player in baseball. "The Big Hurt" is a devastating hitter, especially against left-handed pitchers, against whom he batted .403 in 1996. Even having (for him) a rough season in which he freely admitted he was not comfortable at the plate, the intimidating Thomas remained a joy for White Sox fans to watch in '96. He walked over 100 times for the sixth straight year and continued to crush mistakes as well as good pitches. He does not seem to have a batting weakness and is surprisingly quick on inside pitches, with tremendous pull power as well as the ability to spray the ball the other way. He is only an average defensive player, having serious problems with throwing and footwork around first base. The White Sox aren't all that worried about what Thomas does on defense, as long as he continues to slug home runs, bat near .350, and walk 100 times a season.

Major League Batting Register

	BA	G	AB	R	H	2B	3B	HR	RBI	SB
90 AL	.330	60	191	39	63	11	3	7	31	0
91 AL	.318	158	559	104	178	31	2	32	109	1
92 AL	.323	160	573	108	185	46	2	24	115	6
93 AL	.317	153	549	106	174	36	0	41	128	4
94 AL	.353	113	399	106	141	34	1	38	101	2
95 AL	.308	145	493	102	152	27	0	40	111	3
96 AL	.349	141	527	110	184	26	0	40	134	1
Life	.327	930	3291	675	1077	211	8	222	729	17
3 Ave	.337	154	548	125	185	35	0	46	134	2

LARRY THOMAS

Position: Pitcher
Team: Chicago White Sox
Born: Oct. 25, 1969 Miami, FL
Height: 6'1" **Weight:** 195 lbs.
Bats: right **Throws:** left
Acquired: Second-round pick in 6/91 free-agent draft

PLAYER SUMMARY

Fantasy Value	$2 to $4
Card Value	5¢ to 8¢
Will	get tough lefties
Can't	depend on heat
Expect	numerous outings
Don't Expect	pinpoint control

Middle relievers rarely get the credit they deserve. Almost unknown outside of Chicago, Thomas turned in a fine job as a 1996 rookie in the White Sox bullpen. Often facing just one or two left-handed hitters per stint, he made 57 appearances but finished with only 30⅔ innings pitched. Thomas blends his fastball, slider, and changeup so well that he threw only one home run ball last season. His willingness to pitch inside intimidated batters who entertained thoughts of moving closer to the plate against him. Thomas yields one hit per inning and six strikeouts per nine innings but has occasional problems with control (4.11 walks per game). Like Bill Swift, he's a University of Maine product who made good in the majors. Thomas strands most of the runners he inherits (65.6 percent last year) and keeps a close check on the running game (four steals allowed). He helps his own cause with fine fielding. Thomas turned pro after the White Sox made him a second-round draft choice in 1991. One year later, he led the Southern League with a 1.94 ERA. He became a full-time reliever in 1995.

Major League Pitching Register

	W	L	ERA	G	S	IP	H	ER	BB	SO
95 AL	0	0	1.32	17	0	13.2	8	2	6	12
96 AL	2	3	3.23	57	0	30.2	32	11	14	20
Life	2	3	2.64	74	0	44.1	40	13	20	32

JIM THOME

Position: Third base
Team: Cleveland Indians
Born: Aug. 27, 1970 Peoria, IL
Height: 6'4" **Weight:** 220 lbs.
Bats: left **Throws:** right
Acquired: 13th-round pick in 6/89 free-agent draft

PLAYER SUMMARY

Fantasy Value	$30 to $35
Card Value	25¢ to 35¢
Will	provide offense
Can't	avoid errors
Expect	strikeouts and walks
Don't Expect	a trade

It's quite possible that despite Albert Belle's 48 home runs, Jim Thome was the most valuable member of the Cleveland Indians in 1996. Both Belle and Thome batted .311, with Thome ranking just percentage points behind in slugging average. In addition, Thome's 123 walks (third in the AL) helped boost his on-base percentage to .450 (good for fourth in the AL) and a full 50 points better than Belle's. His patience at bat, combined with his home run swing, also resulted in 141 strikeouts. Thome crushed right-handers in 1996, batting .339 with 31 home runs. At various points in the season, Thome was nearly impossible to get out. His worth was all the more obvious in the playoffs, when he suffered a broken wrist in Game 3 against the Orioles and the Indians were left without his bat. Throwing errors have plagued Thome, who has decent range at the hot corner. If he gets his arm under control, he will be considered one of the best third basemen in baseball.

Major League Batting Register

	BA	G	AB	R	H	2B	3B	HR	RBI	SB
91 AL	.255	27	98	7	25	4	2	1	9	1
92 AL	.205	40	117	8	24	3	1	2	12	2
93 AL	.266	47	154	28	41	11	0	7	22	2
94 AL	.268	98	321	58	86	20	1	20	52	3
95 AL	.314	137	452	92	142	29	3	25	73	4
96 AL	.311	151	505	122	157	28	5	38	116	2
Life	.288	500	1647	315	475	95	12	93	284	14
3 Ave	.299	148	489	102	146	30	3	31	90	4

MARK THOMPSON

Position: Pitcher
Team: Colorado Rockies
Born: April 7, 1971 Russellville, KY
Height: 6'2" **Weight:** 205 lbs.
Bats: right **Throws:** right
Acquired: Second-round pick in 6/92 free-agent draft

PLAYER SUMMARY

Fantasy Value	$3 to $5
Card Value	4¢ to 7¢
Will	show good arm
Can't	carry the rotation
Expect	30 starts
Don't Expect	pinpoint control

The Rockies nearly gave up on Thompson following his disappointing 1995 season but gave him another chance last year. They're glad they did; he wound up the Rockies second-best starter in 1996. Thompson rose quickly through Colorado's minor league system, but like many other young Rockies pitchers, he struggled with the thin air of Coors Field. He bounced back after the initial shock and had a decent overall season. Only Kevin Ritz was better for the Rockies, with Thompson's numbers about equal to fellow starters Armando Reynoso and Jamey Wright. Thompson improved as the season went on, going 6-4 in the second half while lowering his ERA from 6.61 to 5.30. He also threw three complete games and one shutout in the second half. The second half of 1996 might have proved that Thompson is no longer letting the park he pitches in intimidate him. If he can continue to improve his control and not dwell on the possibility of giving up a few runs every time he starts at home, Thompson could turn out to be the top-flight starter the Rockies desperately need him to be.

Major League Pitching Register

	W	L	ERA	G	CG	IP	H	ER	BB	SO
94 NL	1	1	9.00	2	0	9.0	16	9	8	5
95 NL	2	3	6.53	21	0	51.0	73	37	22	30
96 NL	9	11	5.30	34	3	169.2	189	100	74	99
Life	12	15	5.72	57	3	229.2	278	146	104	134
2 Ave	6	7	5.61	29	2	114.1	136	71	49	66

MILT THOMPSON

Position: Outfield
Team: Colorado Rockies
Born: Jan. 5, 1959 Washington, DC
Height: 5'11" **Weight:** 203 lbs.
Bats: left **Throws:** right
Acquired: Claimed from Dodgers on waivers, 6/96

PLAYER SUMMARY

Fantasy Value	$0
Card Value	4¢ to 7¢
Will	face right-handers
Can't	run like he once did
Expect	reserve duty
Don't Expect	many more years

A consistent .270-.290 hitter for many seasons in a semiregular role, Thompson has now had two straight poor years as a pinch hitter and fifth outfielder. He began 1996 with the Dodgers being asked to do something he had never really done before: pinch-hit almost exclusively. Not surprisingly, Thompson did not do this job well, garnering just six hits in 51 at bats for L.A. before being waived in late June. The Rockies picked him up, but he collected just one hit in 16 tries for Colorado. Thompson, at one time a fleet center fielder, has seen almost all of his skills deteriorate. He did not face a single left-handed pitcher all season, stole just one base in two tries, showed no power, and reached base at an intolerable .192 rate.

Major League Batting Register

	BA	G	AB	R	H	2B	3B	HR	RBI	SB
84 NL	.303	25	99	16	30	1	0	2	4	14
85 NL	.302	73	182	17	55	7	2	0	6	9
86 NL	.251	96	299	38	75	7	1	6	23	19
87 NL	.302	150	527	86	159	26	9	7	43	46
88 NL	.288	122	378	53	109	16	2	2	33	17
89 NL	.290	155	545	60	158	28	8	4	68	27
90 NL	.218	135	418	42	91	14	7	6	30	25
91 NL	.307	115	326	55	100	16	5	6	34	16
92 NL	.293	109	208	31	61	9	1	4	17	18
93 NL	.262	129	340	42	89	14	2	4	44	9
94 NL	.274	96	241	34	66	7	0	4	33	9
95 NL	.220	92	132	14	29	9	0	2	19	4
96 NL	.106	62	66	3	7	2	0	0	3	1
Life	.274	1359	3761	491	1029	156	37	47	357	214

ROBBY THOMPSON

Position: Second base
Team: San Francisco Giants
Born: May 10, 1962 West Palm Beach, FL
Height: 5'11" **Weight:** 173 lbs.
Bats: right **Throws:** right
Acquired: First-round pick in secondary phase of 6/83 free-agent draft

PLAYER SUMMARY	
Fantasy Value	$1
Card Value	4¢ to 7¢
Will	show some pop
Can't	hit all righties
Expect	solid defense
Don't Expect	injury-free year

Injuries have interfered with Thompson's career for the last three seasons. Never a model of durability, the University of Florida product has had problems with his shoulder, back, rib cage, groin, and quadriceps. As a result, he hasn't had a 100-game season since 1993. That history, plus his advancing athletic age, could mean Thompson's days as a major-league regular are numbered. Not many teams want a 34-year-old with a big salary and history of injuries—even if the healthy Thompson is a fine-fielding second baseman who can hit the ball out of the park. He can bunt, work the hit-and-run, and draw a walk when necessary. His career on-base percentage is nearly 70 points higher than his lifetime batting average. Although he can run, he's not a good No. 2 hitter because of his penchant for striking out.

Major League Batting Register

	BA	G	AB	R	H	2B	3B	HR	RBI	SB
86 NL	.271	149	549	73	149	27	3	7	47	12
87 NL	.262	132	420	62	110	26	5	10	44	16
88 NL	.264	138	477	66	126	24	6	7	48	14
89 NL	.241	148	547	91	132	26	11	13	50	12
90 NL	.245	144	498	67	122	22	3	15	56	14
91 NL	.262	144	492	74	129	24	5	19	48	14
92 NL	.260	128	443	54	115	25	1	14	49	5
93 NL	.312	128	494	85	154	30	2	19	65	10
94 NL	.209	35	129	13	27	8	2	2	7	3
95 NL	.223	95	336	51	75	15	0	8	23	1
96 NL	.211	63	227	35	48	11	1	5	21	2
Life	.257	1304	4612	671	1187	238	39	119	458	103
2 Ave	.219	85	303	46	66	14	1	7	23	2

MIKE TIMLIN

Position: Pitcher
Team: Toronto Blue Jays
Born: March 10, 1966 Midland, TX
Height: 6'4" **Weight:** 210 lbs.
Bats: right **Throws:** right
Acquired: Fifth-round pick in 6/87 free-agent draft

PLAYER SUMMARY	
Fantasy Value	$20 to $25
Card Value	5¢ to 8¢
Will	top 30 saves
Can't	stop all lefties
Expect	fine control
Don't Expect	gopher plague

A professional reliever, Timlin has made only three starts in six big-league seasons. A closer for the first time last summer, he converted 31 of 38 save chances. A control artist who dominates right-handed hitters, Timlin is a power pitcher who blends a mid-90s fastball with a slower slider. In 1996, he fanned 8.26 batters per nine innings and yielded 7.46 hits over the same span. Timlin held righties to a .191 opposing batting average and yielded just 2.86 walks per nine-inning game. The tall right-hander, who survived the surgical removal of elbow bone chips in 1995, stranded 62.5 percent of the runners he inherited and threw only four gopher balls in 56⅔ innings (59 games). He threw three wild pitches and allowed three stolen bases. Although Timlin's follow-through puts him in awkward fielding position, he handles everything he can reach. His pickoff move isn't perfect, but it's good enough to keep runners close. A quick delivery helps.

Major League Pitching Register

	W	L	ERA	G	S	IP	H	ER	BB	SO
91 AL	11	6	3.16	63	3	108.1	94	38	50	85
92 AL	0	2	4.12	26	1	43.2	45	20	20	35
93 AL	4	2	4.69	54	1	55.2	63	29	27	49
94 AL	0	1	5.17	34	2	40.0	41	23	20	38
95 AL	4	3	2.14	31	5	42.0	38	10	17	36
96 AL	1	6	3.65	59	31	56.2	47	23	18	52
Life	20	20	3.72	267	43	346.1	328	143	152	295
3 Ave	2	4	3.74	47	13	53.1	49	22	22	49

LEE TINSLEY

Position: Outfield
Team: Seatle Mariners
Born: March 4, 1969 Shelbyville, KY
Height: 5'10" **Weight:** 185 lbs.
Bats: both **Throws:** right
Acquired: Traded by Red Sox for a player to be named later, 11/96

PLAYER SUMMARY	
Fantasy Value	$3 to $5
Card Value	4¢ to 7¢
Will	use speed better
Can't	solve southpaws
Expect	singles, steals
Don't Expect	the long ball

After four major-league seasons, Tinsley—once dubbed "little Rickey"—has shown he is hardly Rickey Henderson or anything resembling the basestealing champion. Although he's a leadoff type who can run, Tinsley does not hit with Henderson's power or authority. In fact, he hardly hits well enough to keep a job. Tinsley started and finished last year with the Red Sox but had a 31-game stint with the Phillies in between. A better hitter left-handed, he failed to clear the Mendoza Line against left-handed pitching last year. Tinsley can bunt, beat out infield hits, and work the hit-and-run but fans far too frequently for a leadoff man. He also doesn't seem to be the same guy who had four 30-steal seasons in the minors; he was nailed eight times in 14 tries with the Red Sox last year. Tinsley's speed gives him great range in center field, but his arm is weak and his judgment is sometimes questionable. Oakland's former first-round draft choice (1987) has battled back, rib cage, and hamstring problems.

Major League Batting Register

	BA	G	AB	R	H	2B	3B	HR	RBI	SB
93 AL	.158	11	19	2	3	1	0	1	2	0
94 AL	.222	78	144	27	32	4	0	2	14	13
95 AL	.284	100	341	61	97	17	1	7	41	18
96 NL	.135	31	52	1	7	0	0	0	2	2
96 AL	.245	92	192	28	47	6	1	3	14	6
Life	.249	312	748	119	186	28	2	13	73	39
2 Ave	.271	102	288	48	78	13	1	5	30	13

STEVE TRACHSEL

Position: Pitcher
Team: Chicago Cubs
Born: Oct. 31, 1970 Oxnard, CA
Height: 6'4" **Weight:** 205 lbs.
Bats: right **Throws:** right
Acquired: Eighth-round pick in 6/91 free-agent draft

PLAYER SUMMARY	
Fantasy Value	$11 to $14
Card Value	7¢ to 10¢
Will	work aggressively
Can't	afford walks
Expect	solo home runs
Don't Expect	strikeout crown

Will the real Steve Trachsel please stand up? In 1994 and 1996 he was the Cubs' top starter, and in 1995 he was their worst. Trachsel was so bad in 1995 he nearly pitched himself out of the starting rotation, but he was one of the top three or four pitchers in the league last season and even became an All-Star for the first time. The difference between the two seasons is clear to see: Although Trachsel gave up 30 home runs in 1996, he walked far fewer batters (2.7 per nine innings compared to 4.32 in 1995) and gave up far fewer hits per appearance, limiting opponents to just a .235 batting average. Stinginess with hits and walks makes those 30 home runs worth far less. Trachsel went after hitters with much more speed and confidence than he did the previous year. Although Trachsel's 13 wins were second on the staff to Jaime Navarro's 15, he had the best winning percentage of Cub starters. If he can enjoy another season like 1996, Trachsel will cement his position as one of the top starters in the league.

Major League Pitching Register

	W	L	ERA	G	CG	IP	H	ER	BB	SO
93 NL	0	2	4.58	3	0	19.2	16	10	3	14
94 NL	9	7	3.21	22	1	146.0	133	52	54	108
95 NL	7	13	5.15	30	2	160.2	174	92	76	117
96 NL	13	9	3.03	31	3	205.0	181	69	62	132
Life	29	31	3.78	86	6	531.1	504	223	195	371
3 Ave	11	11	3.74	32	2	197.0	188	82	75	139

MIKE TROMBLEY

Position: Pitcher
Team: Minnesota Twins
Born: April 14, 1967 Springfield, MA
Height: 6'4" **Weight:** 208 lbs.
Bats: right **Throws:** right
Acquired: 14th-round pick in 6/89 free-agent draft

PLAYER SUMMARY	
Fantasy Value	$4 to $6
Card Value	4¢ to 7¢
Will	work in middle
Can't	impress with heat
Expect	mix of pitches
Don't Expect	many headlines

Last season, Trombley shared relief duties with many different Twins and was the best in the bullpen many times. After a disappointing 1995 season in which he failed as a starting pitcher, Trombley was outrighted to the minors, where he learned to throw the split-fingered fastball and became an effective reliever. His impressive PCL totals (including a 2.45 ERA and ten saves) could not be ignored by the pitching-desperate Twins, and Trombley was promoted at midseason. He fared very well in what was called his last chance at duty with Minnesota, holding right-handers to a puny .189 mark and giving up just two homers overall in his 68⅔ innings. Although he has probably run out of chances to be a starter for the Twins and lacks the pure fastball to be a closer, he filled in while Dave Stevens was injured and converted six of nine save opportunities. Even though Stevens is likely to reassume his late-inning role in 1996, Trombley has the pitches, durability, and mentality to be a decent middle reliever.

Major League Pitching Register

	W	L	ERA	G	S	IP	H	ER	BB	SO
92 AL	3	2	3.30	10	0	46.1	43	17	17	38
93 AL	6	6	4.88	44	2	114.1	131	62	41	85
94 AL	2	0	6.33	24	0	48.1	56	34	18	32
95 AL	4	8	5.62	20	0	97.2	107	61	42	68
96 AL	5	1	3.01	43	6	68.2	61	23	25	57
Life	20	17	4.72	141	8	375.1	398	197	143	280
3 Ave	4	3	5.09	33	2	82.1	87	47	33	60

MICHAEL TUCKER

Position: Outfield
Team: Kansas City Royals
Born: June 25, 1971 South Boston, VA
Height: 6'2" **Weight:** 185 lbs.
Bats: left **Throws:** right
Acquired: First-round pick in 6/92 free-agent draft

PLAYER SUMMARY	
Fantasy Value	$8 to $10
Card Value	12¢ to 15¢
Will	play somewhere
Can't	carry the team
Expect	medium-range power
Don't Expect	a batting title

Because the Royals have decided in the last year to go to a youth movement, Tucker—who was talented but not quite ready for the major leagues—made the jump to Kansas City in 1995 after just three years of professional baseball. Despite his obvious skills, he was clearly rushed to the big time and had to make a temporary return trip to the minors. In 1996, he was the Royals' starting right fielder for most of the season before landing on the disabled list in late August with a fractured finger. He hit for decent average (.260) and provided some pop, finishing third on the power-short Royals in homers (12). However, Tucker is hardly a classic power-hitting right fielder and may be destined for left field in the future. He struggled against left-handed pitching (.236), but has decent speed, some power, and a good eye for the strike zone. Tucker is definitely in the Royals' future plans, although his exact role and use are yet to be determined.

Major League Batting Register

	BA	G	AB	R	H	2B	3B	HR	RBI	SB
95 AL	.260	62	177	23	46	10	0	4	17	2
96 AL	.260	108	339	55	88	18	4	12	53	10
Life	.260	170	516	78	134	28	4	16	70	12
2 Ave	.260	89	269	40	70	15	2	8	36	6

TOM URBANI

Position: Pitcher
Team: Detroit Tigers
Born: Jan. 21, 1968 Santa Cruz, CA
Height: 6'1" **Weight:** 190 lbs.
Bats: left **Throws:** left
Acquired: Traded by Cardinals with Miguel Inunza for Micah Franklin and Brian Maxcy, 6/96

PLAYER SUMMARY	
Fantasy Value	$0
Card Value	4¢ to 7¢
Will	need location
Can't	throw strikes
Expect	bullpen spot
Don't Expect	men to steal

Urbani made 16 appearances, all but two in relief, after joining the Tigers last June 7. Although he allowed one run and six hits during a six-game stretch from June 30 to July 13 and fanned eight in 4⅔ scoreless innings from July 11 to 13, Urbani was the odd man out when Detroit signed Todd Van Poppel August 6. He spent the rest of the year in Toledo, where he made three starts. Urbani has never had a full season in the big leagues. He spent parts of four years with the Cardinals but always found his way back to Triple-A. The Long Beach State product, a 13th-round St. Louis draft choice in 1990, throws a variety of sinkerballs, sliders, and changeups. He gets hammered when his location is off. Urbani's nine-inning averages last year included 7½ strikeouts but five walks and 12 hits. Much more effective against left-handed hitters, Urbani helps himself by coaxing double-play grounders, playing defense like a fifth infielder, and keeping close tabs on the running game.

Major League Pitching Register

	W	L	ERA	G	S	IP	H	ER	BB	SO
93 NL	1	3	4.65	18	0	62.0	73	32	26	33
94 NL	3	7	5.15	20	0	80.1	98	46	21	43
95 NL	3	5	3.70	24	0	82.2	99	34	21	52
96 NL	1	0	7.71	3	0	11.2	15	10	4	1
96 AL	2	2	8.37	16	0	23.2	31	22	14	20
Life	10	17	4.98	81	0	260.1	316	144	86	149
2 Ave	4	8	4.50	28	0	103.0	125	52	27	60

UGUETH URBINA

Position: Pitcher
Team: Montreal Expos
Born: Feb. 15, 1974 Caracas, Venezuela
Height: 6'2" **Weight:** 184 lbs.
Bats: right **Throws:** right
Acquired: Signed as a free agent, 7/90

PLAYER SUMMARY	
Fantasy Value	$6 to $8
Card Value	5¢ to 8¢
Will	throw hard
Can't	carry the staff
Expect	swing duty
Don't Expect	many saves

Ugueth Urtain Urbina, a starter throughout his minor-league career, was moved to the bullpen after coming off the disabled list late in the 1996 season. Urbina had been forced to the sidelines for the second straight year due to shoulder problems, so the Expos are thinking about using the 23-year-old as a reliever to relieve some of the stress on his arm. The Expos feel his mechanics, which resemble those of Luis Tiant, make him much better suited to relief work than to starting duty. He is being considered as a possible replacement for ex-Expos closer Mel Rojas, who left as a free agent after the 1996 season. Urbina made 16 relief appearances late in the season and thrived in that role, bringing his ERA from over 5.00 at midseason to 3.71 at the end of the year. Urbina certainly has the stuff to be a big-league closer, sporting a fastball in the mid-90s that made him close to unhittable against right-handers last season. Lefties hit .317 against him in 1996, but there's no reason to think Ugie won't find a way to get them out in time.

Major League Pitching Register

	W	L	ERA	G	S	IP	H	ER	BB	SO
95 NL	2	2	6.17	7	0	23.1	26	16	14	15
96 NL	10	5	3.71	33	0	114.0	102	47	44	108
Life	12	7	4.13	40	0	137.1	128	63	58	123

ISMAEL VALDES

Position: Pitcher
Team: Los Angeles Dodgers
Born: Aug. 21, 1973 Victoria, Mexico
Height: 6'3" **Weight:** 183 lbs.
Bats: right **Throws:** right
Acquired: Signed as a free agent, 6/91

PLAYER SUMMARY	
Fantasy Value	$14 to $17
Card Value	7¢ to 10¢
Will	get his strikeouts
Can't	afford overwork
Expect	good control
Don't Expect	many homers

Already one of the best pitchers in the National League, Valdes really came into his own in 1996, just his second full season. Putting together quality start after quality start, Valdes was the anchor of the Dodger pitching staff. He doesn't come from Japan, whirl around while pitching, dazzle with an arms-and-legs delivery, throw a knuckleball, or do any of the fancy things other Los Angeles starters do: He just wins. He is not technically a strikeout pitcher, but his stuff is so good he can blow batters away or get them swinging at sinkers. He has good command of his off-speed pitches, which sink monstrously. Valdes is going to be a long-term mainstay of the Dodger staff, and he is still getting better. Holding runners is a problem: 23 of 27 potential basestealers succeeded against him in 1996. Valdes also has problems when he falls behind in the count—which fortunately for him is not often. Given a solid four days rest, he should spend the next few years competing for Cy Young Awards and is just as likely as not to actually win one or two.

JOHN VALENTIN

Position: Shortstop
Team: Boston Red Sox
Born: Feb. 18, 1967 Mineola, NY
Height: 6' **Weight:** 170 lbs.
Bats: right **Throws:** right
Acquired: Fifth-round pick in 6/88 free-agent draft

PLAYER SUMMARY	
Fantasy Value	$11 to $14
Card Value	8¢ to 12¢
Will	swing good bat
Can't	show speed
Expect	hustle
Don't Expect	perfect attitude

The Red Sox mainstay had another quality offensive season, although it was a bit of a drop-off from his performance of previous years. Valentin was bothered by nagging injuries much of the year, but some of the decline may have been caused by not always knowing where he would play. For much of the year, the Red Sox discussed moving long-time shortstop Valentin to third base and shifting Tim Naehring to second in order to make room for slick-fielding rookie shortstop Nomar Garciaparra. Valentin initially balked at the move, which is an indication of the stress in the clubhouse between many Boston players and now-deposed manager Kevin Kennedy. Valentin did move to third base late in the year, playing 12 games there and performing admirably. He is likely to remain at the hot corner. However, there is a perception that Valentin has put his interests ahead of those of the team, and he could still be dealt.

Major League Pitching Register

	W	L	ERA	G	CG	IP	H	ER	BB	SO
94 NL	3	1	3.18	21	0	28.1	21	10	10	28
95 NL	13	11	3.05	33	6	197.2	168	67	51	150
96 NL	15	7	3.32	33	0	225.0	219	83	54	173
Life	31	19	3.19	87	6	451.0	408	160	115	351
2 Ave	15	10	3.19	35	3	224.1	204	79	56	171

Major League Batting Register

	BA	G	AB	R	H	2B	3B	HR	RBI	SB
92 AL	.276	58	185	21	51	13	0	5	25	1
93 AL	.278	144	468	50	130	40	3	11	66	3
94 AL	.316	84	301	53	95	26	2	9	49	3
95 AL	.298	135	520	108	155	37	2	27	102	20
96 AL	.296	131	527	84	156	29	3	13	59	9
Life	.293	552	2001	316	587	145	10	65	301	36
3 Ave	.302	134	512	93	155	36	3	19	81	12

JOSE VALENTIN

Position: Shortstop
Team: Milwaukee Brewers
Born: Oct. 12, 1969 Manati, Puerto Rico
Height: 5'10" **Weight:** 175 lbs.
Bats: both **Throws:** right
Acquired: Traded by Padres with Ricky Bones and Matt Mieske for Gary Sheffield and Geoff Kellogg, 3/92

PLAYER SUMMARY

Fantasy Value	$14 to $17
Card Value	8¢ to 12¢
Will	supply good pop
Can't	stop striking out
Expect	speed, range, arm
Don't Expect	high fielding pct.

Once confused with the Boston shortstop who shares his surname, the Milwaukee Valentin drew a sharp line of distinction last summer. He collected 64 extra-base hits, 24 of them home runs, and stole 17 bases while giving the Brewers strong defense at a key position. Valentin's biggest weakness is a penchant for striking out. He whiffed 145 times last year, fifth in the league, but showed enough patience to draw 66 walks and improve his on-base percentage. A switch-hitter with more power left-handed, Valentin is fast enough to fatten his average with bunts and infield hits. He also helps his team by working the hit-and-run and picking the right moments to run. His exceptional range at shortstop enables him to reach balls others can't—but also runs up his total of errors. He's led AL shortstops in errors twice in the last three years but has also led several leagues in chances, putouts, assists, and double plays. Valentin has quick reactions, soft hands, a strong arm, and a quick release.

Major League Batting Register

	BA	G	AB	R	H	2B	3B	HR	RBI	SB
92 AL	.000	4	3	1	0	0	0	0	1	0
93 AL	.245	19	53	10	13	1	2	1	7	1
94 AL	.239	97	285	47	68	19	0	11	46	12
95 AL	.219	112	338	62	74	23	3	11	49	16
96 AL	.259	154	552	90	143	33	7	24	95	17
Life	.242	386	1231	210	298	76	12	47	198	46
3 Ave	.241	139	445	75	107	29	3	17	72	17

FERNANDO VALENZUELA

Position: Pitcher
Team: San Diego Padres
Born: Nov. 1, 1960 Navojoa, Mexico
Height: 5'11" **Weight:** 202 lbs.
Bats: left **Throws:** left
Acquired: Signed as a free agent, 4/95

PLAYER SUMMARY

Fantasy Value	$6 to $8
Card Value	5¢ to 8¢
Will	confound opponents
Can't	win with fastball
Expect	starting duty
Don't Expect	retirement

The well-traveled Valenzuela is as close to a modern miracle of pitching as one can get. He has been able to surprise doubters by reaching back for something more. At 35 (or whatever age he really is), he provided the Padres with some clutch pitching down the stretch and was the team's best pitcher late in the year. He can no longer throw an impressive fastball and gets hit hard at times, but considering his age and skills, Fernando could be the smartest pitcher in baseball. His presence was a great boon to his team's attempts to bring the Mexican community into the fold. In fact, he pitched the first-ever regular-season game held in Mexico, a contest between the Padres and Mets in Monterrey. Of course, Fernando won, to the delight of millions of fans.

Major League Pitching Register

	W	L	ERA	G	CG	IP	H	ER	BB	SO
80 NL	2	0	0.00	10	0	17.2	8	0	5	16
81 NL	13	7	2.48	25	11	192.1	140	53	61	180
82 NL	19	13	2.87	37	18	285.0	247	91	83	199
83 NL	15	10	3.75	35	9	257.0	245	107	99	189
84 NL	12	17	3.03	34	12	261.0	218	88	106	240
85 NL	17	10	2.45	35	14	272.1	211	74	101	208
86 NL	21	11	3.14	34	20	269.1	226	94	85	242
87 NL	14	14	3.98	34	12	251.0	254	111	124	190
88 NL	5	8	4.24	23	3	142.1	142	67	76	64
89 NL	10	13	3.43	31	3	196.2	185	75	98	116
90 NL	13	13	4.59	33	5	204.0	223	104	77	115
91 AL	0	2	12.15	2	0	6.2	14	9	3	5
93 AL	8	10	4.94	32	5	178.2	179	98	79	78
94 NL	1	2	3.00	8	0	45.0	42	15	7	19
95 NL	8	3	4.98	29	0	90.1	101	50	34	57
96 NL	13	8	3.62	33	0	171.2	177	69	67	95
Life	171	141	3.50	435	112	2841.0	2612	1105	1105	2013
2 Ave	11	6	4.12	33	0	137.1	145	63	53	80

DAVE VALLE

Position: Catcher
Team: Texas Rangers
Born: Oct. 30, 1960 Bayside, NY
Height: 6'2″ **Weight:** 220 lbs.
Bats: right **Throws:** right
Acquired: Signed as a free agent, 12/94

PLAYER SUMMARY	
Fantasy Value	$0
Card Value	4¢ to 7¢
Will	play good defense
Can't	supply any speed
Expect	strong throwing arm
Don't Expect	another .300 year

Playing behind Ivan Rodriguez, a perennial All-Star, is a thankless job. But Valle made the most of it last year, finishing with a career-best .302 average after entering the season with a 12-year mark of .235. In fact, Seattle fans once had a standing wager that Valle would not hit his weight—an event that once occurred in consecutive seasons. Known primarily for his defense, Valle has led the AL in putouts, fielding percentage, and double plays by a catcher. Valle has twice nailed more than 40 percent of potential basestealers. He calls a good game and handles pitchers well. Valle is also adept at shifting his weight to prevent wild pitches and guarding the plate against runners trying to score. At the plate, Valle has power, patience, and the ability to deliver in the clutch. He hit .480 with men in scoring position last year.

Major League Batting Register

	BA	G	AB	R	H	2B	3B	HR	RBI	SB
84 AL	.296	13	27	4	8	1	0	1	4	0
85 AL	.157	31	70	2	11	1	0	0	4	0
86 AL	.340	22	53	10	18	3	0	5	15	0
87 AL	.256	95	324	40	83	16	3	12	53	2
88 AL	.231	93	290	29	67	15	2	10	50	0
89 AL	.237	94	316	32	75	10	3	7	34	0
90 AL	.214	107	308	37	66	15	0	7	33	1
91 AL	.194	132	324	38	63	8	1	8	32	0
92 AL	.240	124	367	39	88	16	1	9	30	0
93 AL	.258	135	423	48	109	19	0	13	63	1
94 AL	.232	46	112	14	26	8	1	2	10	0
95 AL	.240	36	75	7	18	3	0	0	5	1
96 AL	.302	42	86	14	26	6	1	3	17	0
Life	.237	970	2775	314	658	121	12	77	350	5

JOHN VANDER WAL

Position: Outfield
Team: Colorado Rockies
Born: April 29, 1966 Grand Rapids, MI
Height: 6'2″ **Weight:** 198 lbs.
Bats: left **Throws:** left
Acquired: Purchased from Expos, 3/94

PLAYER SUMMARY	
Fantasy Value	$1
Card Value	4¢ to 7¢
Will	deliver key hits
Can't	play every day
Expect	some power
Don't Expect	complaints

As can be said of other Colorado players, Vander Wal's offensive statistics are inflated due to the thin air of Coors Field. However, that doesn't negate his value to a team. Vander Wal is not upset at being a bench player and relishes the chance to pinch-hit late in games when the pressure is on. In fact, Vander Wal set the major-league record for pinch hits in a season in 1995. Last year, he again was manager Don Baylor's best option off the bench. He appeared in 104 games, pinch-hitting in 72 of them. When he did play defense it was mostly as a left fielder, but he saw action in ten games at first base and made only one error in his appearances in the field. It's doubtful that Vander Wal would be as productive in an everyday role as he is coming off the pine, but he is the type of player a team needs in order to win. He knows what his role is, accepts it, and does not complain. He has hit .335 or better as a pinch hitter for two consecutive years, and there's no reason to think he can't do it again.

Major League Batting Register

	BA	G	AB	R	H	2B	3B	HR	RBI	SB
91 NL	.213	21	61	4	13	4	1	1	8	0
92 NL	.239	105	213	21	51	8	2	4	20	3
93 NL	.233	106	215	34	50	7	4	5	30	6
94 NL	.245	91	110	12	27	3	1	5	15	2
95 NL	.347	105	101	15	35	8	1	5	21	1
96 NL	.252	104	151	20	38	6	2	5	31	2
Life	.251	532	851	106	214	36	11	25	125	14

WILLIAM VANLANDINGHAM

Position: Pitcher
Team: San Francisco Giants
Born: July 16, 1970 Columbia, TN
Height: 6'2" **Weight:** 210 lbs.
Bats: right **Throws:** right
Acquired: Fifth-round selection in 6/91 free-agent draft

PLAYER SUMMARY	
Fantasy Value	$6 to $8
Card Value	4¢ to 7¢
Will	show improvement
Can't	hold runners
Expect	control troubles
Don't Expect	a trade

The big right-hander took a giant step backward in his third season in the big leagues. VanLandingham, 6-3 with a 3.67 ERA in 1995, was supposed to be the anchor of the Giants rotation in 1996, but instead was one of their worst starters. His 14 losses ranked second in the NL, but VanLandingham was still San Francisco's second-winningest pitcher, which says something about the team he played for. Although VanLandingham throws hard and has a good curve, he isn't a strikeout pitcher, fanning just one hitter every other inning. Unfortunately, the third-year player walked almost four hitters per nine innings. Due to a poor pickoff move and a long delivery, an amazing 38 runners tried to steal against VanLandingham in 1996, and 24 were successful. Pitching is something the Giants don't have much of, but VanLandingham must improve if he expects to have a long career. Before the 1996 season, he was 14-5 with a 3.61 ERA in the major leagues, so it is possible to write off last year as a fluke. He should bounce back.

Major League Pitching Register

	W	L	ERA	G	CG	IP	H	ER	BB	SO
94 NL	8	2	3.54	16	0	84.0	70	33	43	56
95 NL	6	3	3.67	18	1	122.2	124	50	40	95
96 NL	9	14	5.40	32	0	181.2	196	109	78	97
Life	23	19	4.45	66	1	388.1	390	192	161	248
3 Ave	9	7	4.35	25	0	146.0	145	71	61	94

TODD VAN POPPEL

Position: Pitcher
Team: Anaheim Angels
Born: Dec. 9, 1971 Hinsdale, IL
Height: 6'5" **Weight:** 210 lbs.
Bats: right **Throws:** right
Acquired: Claimed from Tigers on waivers, 8/96

PLAYER SUMMARY	
Fantasy Value	$0
Card Value	4¢ to 7¢
Will	seek rotation slot
Can't	prevent gopher balls
Expect	flashes of promise
Don't Expect	reliable control

The jury is still out on Van Poppel. The former No. 1 draft choice compiled an abysmal 6.22 ERA over his first five seasons but last year showed flashes of the potential that made him Oakland's first-round draft choice in 1990. After struggling in his final five starts, however, Van Poppel was sent to the Florida Instructional League. The lanky right-hander throws a fastball, changeup, and curve but has trouble throwing strikes. He had more walks than Ks last year, averaging more than 5½ walks per nine innings. Van Poppel also yielded too many hits and too many home runs—an amazing 24 long balls in 99⅓ innings. Van Poppel has done his best work out of the bullpen. In 1995, he led the A's with a 3.54 relief ERA, ranked sixth in the AL in fewest runners allowed per nine frames of relief (9.9), and seventh in lowest average allowed in relief (.209). But he couldn't approach those numbers last year. Van Poppel fields his position well but is an easy target for prospective basestealers.

Major League Pitching Register

	W	L	ERA	G	S	IP	H	ER	BB	SO
91 AL	0	0	9.64	1	0	4.2	7	5	2	6
93 AL	6	6	5.04	16	0	84.0	76	47	62	47
94 AL	7	10	6.09	23	0	116.2	108	79	89	83
95 AL	4	8	4.88	36	0	138.1	125	75	56	122
96 AL	3	9	9.06	37	1	99.1	139	100	62	53
Life	20	33	6.22	113	1	443.0	455	306	271	311
3 Ave	6	11	6.35	37	0	140.1	144	99	83	102

GREG VAUGHN

Position: Outfield
Team: San Diego Padres
Born: July 3, 1965 Sacramento, CA
Height: 6' **Weight:** 205 lbs.
Bats: right **Throws:** right
Acquired: Traded by Brewers for Bryce Florie, Marc Newfield, and Ron Villone, 7/96

PLAYER SUMMARY	
Fantasy Value. . . . . $25 to $30
Card Value . . . . 10¢ to 15¢
Will . . . . drive the ball
Can't. . . . . show old arm
Expect . . . . 25 homers
Don't Expect . . . . high batting average

After two consecutive disappointing years, the Brewers tried to trade Vaughn (and his contract) after the 1995 season. The club found no takers and hoped he would make it easier for the team by playing well in 1996. Vaughn did exactly that and consequently was shipped to the pennant-contending Padres. He started 1996 fast, with 31 homers for Milwaukee. However, after being dealt, Vaughn appeared completely confused against NL pitching. He hit barely over .200 for San Diego, although, almost unbelievably, he finished third overall on the club with ten home runs. Vaughn, a fair outfielder still bothered by lingering shoulder problems, never saw full-time duty for the Padres, sharing at bats with Rickey Henderson and Tony Gwynn. While San Diego would like him back for this year, they will not pay top dollar to keep him. His fine season means Vaughn undoubtedly will find regular work somewhere, however.

Major League Batting Register

	BA	G	AB	R	H	2B	3B	HR	RBI	SB
89 AL	.265	38	113	18	30	3	0	5	23	4
90 AL	.220	120	382	51	84	26	2	17	61	7
91 AL	.244	145	542	81	132	24	5	27	98	2
92 AL	.228	141	501	77	114	18	2	23	78	15
93 AL	.267	154	569	97	152	28	2	30	97	10
94 AL	.254	95	370	59	94	24	1	19	55	9
95 AL	.224	108	392	67	88	19	1	17	59	10
96 AL	.280	102	375	78	105	16	0	31	95	5
96 NL	.206	43	141	20	29	3	1	10	22	4
Life	.245	946	3385	548	828	161	14	179	588	66
3 Ave	.252	119	446	79	112	24	1	26	80	10

MO VAUGHN

Position: First base
Team: Boston Red Sox
Born: Dec. 15, 1957 Norwalk, CT
Height: 6'1" **Weight:** 230 lbs.
Bats: left **Throws:** right
Acquired: First-round pick in 6/89 free-agent draft

PLAYER SUMMARY	
Fantasy Value. . . . . $40 to $45
Card Value . . . . 25¢ to 40¢
Will . . . . show big uppercut
Can't. . . . . win a Gold Glove
Expect. . . . . power and average
Don't Expect . . . . speed

Mo enjoyed yet another wonderful offensive year in 1996, nearly carrying the Red Sox to a playoff spot. Yes, Vaughn is slow, but when one hits the ball as hard as he does, baserunning skills rarely figure into the equation. He uses a fierce uppercut swing to lash line drives to right field, and he can also take the ball the other way. He fanned 154 times—the third-highest total in the AL—but batted .430 when he put the ball in play. He finished in the AL's top ten in several offensive categories, including batting average, on-base percentage, hits, home runs, runs, and RBI. After experiencing trouble against southpaws early in his career, Vaughn has turned things around; now, he doesn't discriminate, hitting over .300 against everyone in 1996. On defense, he is no bargain, but for a big man, Vaughn is not that bad around first base. He prefers to play a position rather than just act as a DH, but he probably won't be able to do so for more than a couple of years.

Major League Batting Register

	BA	G	AB	R	H	2B	3B	HR	RBI	SB
91 AL	.260	74	219	21	57	12	0	4	32	2
92 AL	.234	113	355	42	83	16	2	13	57	3
93 AL	.297	152	539	86	160	34	1	29	101	4
94 AL	.310	111	394	65	122	25	1	26	82	4
95 AL	.300	140	550	98	165	28	3	39	126	11
96 AL	.326	161	635	118	207	29	1	44	143	2
Life	.295	751	2692	430	794	144	8	155	541	26
3 Ave	.312	158	603	107	188	32	2	42	133	7

Randy Velarde

Position: Second base
Team: Anaheim Angels
Born: Nov. 24, 1962 Midland, TX
Height: 6′ **Weight:** 192 lbs.
Bats: right **Throws:** right
Acquired: Signed as a free agent, 11/95

PLAYER SUMMARY
Fantasy Value	$6 to $8
Card Value	4¢ to 7¢
Will	show good bat
Can't	win a Gold Glove
Expect	high batting average
Don't Expect	stolen bases

Velarde filled a huge hole in the Angels middle infield, providing solid defense and a decent bat at a position the team has had problems filling. The Angels asked Velarde to be a leadoff hitter, and although he is not ideally suited for the role, he walked 70 times and compiled a fine .372 on-base percentage. Velarde stole seven bases but was also cut down seven times. He is a better No. 2 hitter, and he also does a good job when used in the seventh or eighth spot. He batted .285 with some pop last season. On defense, Velarde doesn't have much range, but he can turn the double play adequately and always hustles. He did a good job as an emergency regular, but his ability to play several infield and outfield positions makes him even more valuable to a team. Unfortunately, the talent-thin Angels cannot afford not to use their good players in key roles.

Major League Batting Register
	BA	G	AB	R	H	2B	3B	HR	RBI	SB
87 AL	.182	8	22	1	4	0	0	0	1	0
88 AL	.174	48	115	18	20	6	0	5	12	1
89 AL	.340	33	100	12	34	4	2	2	11	0
90 AL	.210	95	229	21	48	6	2	5	19	0
91 AL	.245	80	184	19	45	11	1	1	15	3
92 AL	.272	121	412	57	112	24	1	7	46	7
93 AL	.301	85	226	28	68	13	2	7	24	2
94 AL	.279	77	280	47	78	16	1	9	34	4
95 AL	.278	111	367	60	102	19	1	7	46	5
96 AL	.285	136	530	82	151	27	3	14	54	7
Life	.269	794	2465	345	662	126	13	57	262	29
3 Ave	.281	123	446	72	125	24	2	12	51	6

Robin Ventura

Position: Third Base
Team: Chicago White Sox
Born: July 14, 1967 Santa Maria, CA
Height: 6′1″ **Weight:** 198 lbs.
Bats: left **Throws:** right
Acquired: First-round pick in 6/88 free-agent draft

PLAYER SUMMARY
Fantasy Value	$20 to $25
Card Value	10¢ to 15¢
Will	show power
Can't	steal bases
Expect	fine glovework
Don't Expect	a slump

Ventura puts up such consistently good numbers that many seem to take his outstanding talents for granted. Trade rumors circulated through the second half of the 1996 season, but Ventura remained in Chicago and ended up as the Sox's second-best offensive player. Only Frank Thomas outperformed Ventura, who played hard every day and gave the club strong defense. He was also third on the team, behind Thomas and leadoff hitter Tony Phillips, in runs and walks (78). Once nearly helpless against left-handed pitchers, Ventura has steadily improved and last year batted .265 against them. The former Oklahoma State All-American, Golden Spikes Award winner, and U.S. Olympian played in a team-high 158 games last season. If the Sox plan on making a run at the Central Division title, they are going to need the veteran workhorse at the hot corner.

Major League Batting Register
	BA	G	AB	R	H	2B	3B	HR	RBI	SB
89 AL	.178	16	45	5	8	3	0	0	7	0
90 AL	.249	150	493	48	123	17	1	5	54	1
91 AL	.284	157	606	92	172	25	1	23	100	2
92 AL	.282	157	592	85	167	38	1	16	93	2
93 AL	.262	157	554	85	145	27	1	22	94	1
94 AL	.282	109	401	57	113	15	1	18	78	3
95 AL	.295	135	492	79	145	22	0	26	93	4
96 AL	.287	158	586	96	168	31	2	34	105	1
Life	.276	1039	3769	547	1041	178	7	144	624	14
3 Ave	.288	154	568	88	163	26	1	30	107	3

QUILVIO VERAS

Position: Second base
Team: San Diego Padres
Born: April 3, 1971 Santo Domingo, Dominican Republic
Height: 5'9" **Weight:** 166 lbs.
Bats: both **Throws:** right
Acquired: Traded by Marlins for Dustin Hermanson, 11/96

PLAYER SUMMARY

Fantasy Value	$2 to $4
Card Value	5¢ to 8¢
Will	burn up basepaths
Can't	provide much punch
Expect	great batting eye
Don't Expect	dazzling defense

A little switch-hitter with big-time speed, Veras was a Rookie of the Year contender in 1995, when he led the NL in steals and the Marlins in walks, runs, and triples. He fell behind 1996 rookies Ralph Milliard and Luis Castillo last year but still showed the selective batting eye that makes him a valuable leadoff man. A contact hitter who walks more often than he fans, Veras posted a 1996 on-base percentage of .381, a whopping 128 points above his batting average. He's a singles hitter who uses all fields and is capable of stretching singles into doubles or doubles into triples. He can also drop a bunt. Veras still needs to master the art of stealing. He was nailed 21 times, tops in the majors, two years ago, and went only 8-for-16 in limited playing time last year. Lapses of concentration have also hampered his progress. In the field, Veras has quick reactions, great range, and the ability to turn two, but his defense is sometimes erratic. He still has the potential to become a second Eric Young, whose bat and speed are so good that his few flaws can be overlooked.

Major League Batting Register

	BA	G	AB	R	H	2B	3B	HR	RBI	SB
95 NL	.261	124	440	86	115	20	7	5	32	56
96 NL	.253	73	253	40	64	8	1	4	14	8
Life	.258	197	693	126	179	28	8	9	46	64
2 Ave	.259	106	374	68	97	15	4	5	25	36

DAVE VERES

Position: Pitcher
Team: Montreal Expos
Born: Oct. 19, 1966 Montgomery, AL
Height: 6'2" **Weight:** 195 lbs.
Bats: right **Throws:** right
Acquired: Traded by Astros with Raul Chavez for Sean Berry, 12/95

PLAYER SUMMARY

Fantasy Value	$3 to $5
Card Value	4¢ to 7¢
Will	throw hard
Can't	afford mistakes
Expect	frequent duty
Don't Expect	20 saves

Veres was expected to be the Expos' top set-up man in 1996, but he never performed quite the way Montreal had hoped he could. Coming off a fine 1995 campaign, he struggled badly in the first half of last season. Veres did most of the damage to his 1996 stats in the first half, when he posted a 5.82 ERA, but he got things back in order in the second half. He allowed only eight earned runs after the first of July and posted a 3.07 ERA the rest of the way, which was much more in line with his previous 2.31 career ERA. Veres has never had great control, but in the first portion of the year he fell behind in the count consistently. A hard thrower with good movement on his fastball, Veres made some unwelcome mistakes high in the strike zone and allowed a surprising ten homers in 1996. This year, Veres will be counted on by the Expos to provide quality relief work, especially since closer Mel Rojas is gone. Veres should plan on being used often in 1997, as Montreal manager Felipe Alou goes to his bullpen as much as any manager in the major leagues.

Major League Pitching Register

	W	L	ERA	G	S	IP	H	ER	BB	SO
94 NL	3	3	2.41	32	1	41.0	39	11	7	28
95 NL	5	1	2.26	72	1	103.1	89	26	30	94
96 NL	6	3	4.17	68	4	77.2	85	36	32	81
Life	14	7	2.96	172	6	222.0	213	73	69	203
3 Ave	5	3	2.89	65	2	84.0	80	27	25	75

Ron Villone

Position: Pitcher
Team: Milwaukee Brewers
Born: Jan. 16, 1970 Englewood, NJ
Height: 6'3" **Weight:** 235 lbs.
Bats: left **Throws:** left
Acquired: Traded by Padres with Marc Newfield and Bryce Florie for Greg Vaughn, 7/96

PLAYER SUMMARY	
Fantasy Value.	$4 to $6
Card Value	4¢ to 7¢
Will	throw late heat
Can't	stop gopher balls
Expect	strong, live arm
Don't Expect	rotation berth

For a first-round draft choice, Villone has had a surprising number of address changes in recent seasons. The 14th man selected in the 1992 amateur draft, Villone made just 19 relief outings for Seattle, his original team, before spending parts of two years in San Diego. Last summer, he moved to the Brewers, a team that may finally give him a chance to realize his immense potential. A power pitcher with a perfected changeup, Villone averaged more than one strikeout per inning for the Padres last year, then held AL hitters to a collective batting average of .175. He struggled with his control, however, and also had trouble stranding inherited runners. Villone's other problem is fielding his position: His follow-through leaves him in awkward position. On the other hand, he keeps a close eye on the running game. A 1992 U.S. Olympian who attended the University of Massachusetts, Villone was an unsuccessful minor-league starter who began to show promise after switching to relief work as a second-year pro.

Major League Pitching Register

	W	L	ERA	G	S	IP	H	ER	BB	SO
95 AL	0	2	7.91	19	0	19.1	20	17	23	26
95 NL	2	1	4.21	19	1	25.2	24	12	11	37
96 NL	1	1	2.95	21	0	18.1	17	6	7	19
96 AL	0	0	3.28	23	2	24.2	14	9	18	19
Life	3	4	4.50	82	3	88.0	75	44	59	101

Fernando Vina

Position: Second base
Team: Milwaukee Brewers
Born: April 16, 1969 Sacramento, CA
Height: 5'9" **Weight:** 170 lbs.
Bats: left **Throws:** right
Acquired: Traded by Mets with Javier Gonzalez for Doug Henry, 12/94

PLAYER SUMMARY	
Fantasy Value.	$7 to $9
Card Value	7¢ to 10¢
Will	make great contact
Can't	handle left-handers
Expect	defensive excellence
Don't Expect	double-digit homers

If Vina could hit lefties as well as he hits righties, he'd make the All-Star Team. A .300 hitter against right-handers last year, Vina managed just an anemic .218 mark against lefties. Despite that statistic, he is valuable at the top of the lineup because of his ability to make contact. He fanned only 35 times in 554 at bats for a ratio of 17.6 at bats per strikeout, fourth in the AL. He also slugged 36 extra-base hits, seven of them home runs. Vina not only walks more than he fans but defies the defense with swinging bunts and hit-and-run plays. The Arizona State product is also a threat to steal; he went 16-for-23 in stolen bases last season. Vina's speed helps him in the field, where he has good range and soft hands. He's not afraid of charging baserunners—as he proved last year when he took an Albert Belle elbow in the head. Vina made 16 errors last year, but only because of his propensity to attack ground balls. The one-time utility man has blossomed into a fine defensive second baseman.

Major League Batting Register

	BA	G	AB	R	H	2B	3B	HR	RBI	SB
93 AL	.222	24	45	5	10	2	0	0	2	6
94 NL	.250	79	124	20	31	6	0	0	6	3
95 AL	.257	113	288	46	74	7	7	3	29	6
96 AL	.283	140	554	94	157	19	10	7	46	16
Life	.269	356	1011	165	272	34	17	10	83	31
2 Ave	.274	134	439	73	120	13	9	5	39	11

JOE VITIELLO

Position: Designated hitter; first base
Team: Kansas City Royals
Born: April 11, 1970 Cambridge, MA
Height: 6'2" **Weight:** 215 lbs.
Bats: right **Throws:** right
Acquired: First-round pick in 6/91 free-agent draft

PLAYER SUMMARY
Fantasy Value	$5 to $7
Card Value	5¢ to 8¢
Will	hit to all fields
Can't	find old patience
Expect	improved contact
Don't Expect	great glovework

After hitting .344 to win the American Association batting crown in 1994, Vitiello came to Kansas City with high hopes. But he hasn't been the same kind of hitter in his first two big-league seasons. The University of Alabama product, whose Triple-A batting crown was accompanied by a .440 on-base percentage, has not been as patient at the plate in the AL. He fanned nearly twice per walk last year but still drew enough free passes to push his on-base percentage 101 points higher than his batting average. A line-drive hitter who sends singles to all fields, Vitiello served as K.C.'s primary DH in 1996. He has the size and compact swing of a slugger without the statistics to match. Vitiello had only 24 extra-base hits for the '96 Royals and has never hit more than 15 homers in a pro career that began in 1991. Because he lacks speed, he can't fatten his average by beating out infield hits. Nor does he have much range in the outfield. Vitiello spent most of last year playing his best positions: first base (nine games) and designated hitter (70).

Major League Batting Register
	BA	G	AB	R	H	2B	3B	HR	RBI	SB
95 AL	.254	53	130	13	33	4	0	7	21	0
96 AL	.241	85	257	29	62	15	1	8	40	2
Life	.245	138	387	42	95	19	1	15	61	2

JOSE VIZCAINO

Position: Infield
Team: San Francisco Giants
Born: March 26, 1968 San Cristobal, Dominican Republic
Height: 6'1" **Weight:** 180 lbs.
Bats: both **Throws:** right
Acquired: Traded by Indians with Jeff Kent and Julian Tavarez for Matt Williams, 11/96

PLAYER SUMMARY
Fantasy Value	$1
Card Value	4¢ to 7¢
Will	show slick glove
Can't	add power
Expect	regular duty
Don't Expect	much offense

Swapped to the Indians in the controversial Carlos Baerga trade in July, Vizcaino provided what was expected of him when he got to Cleveland: strong defense at second base and shortstop and a high batting average. He has excellent range and hands at both positions and is clearly a much better second baseman than Baerga. However, one wonders if the trade—and its clubhouse fallout and on-field consequences—ultimately doomed the Indians' chances to repeat as AL champs. Vizcaino simply does not provide much offense. He usually hits around .280, but he rarely walks, doesn't steal many bases, and has almost no power. He does hit for average from both sides of the plate, but after coming to Cleveland, his on-base percentage was a poor .310. His versatility makes him valuable, although it seems odd that he is now on his fifth team in eight seasons.

Major League Batting Register
	BA	G	AB	R	H	2B	3B	HR	RBI	SB
89 NL	.200	7	10	2	2	0	0	0	0	0
90 NL	.275	37	51	3	14	1	1	0	2	1
91 NL	.262	93	145	7	38	5	0	0	10	2
92 NL	.225	86	285	25	64	10	4	1	17	3
93 NL	.287	151	551	74	158	19	4	4	54	12
94 NL	.256	103	410	47	105	13	3	3	33	1
95 NL	.287	135	509	66	146	21	5	3	56	8
96 NL	.303	96	363	47	110	12	6	1	32	9
96 AL	.285	48	179	23	51	5	2	0	13	6
Life	.275	756	2503	294	688	86	25	12	217	42
3 Ave	.280	147	564	70	158	20	6	3	51	8

OMAR VIZQUEL

Position: Shortstop
Team: Cleveland Indians
Born: April 24, 1967 Caracas, Venezuela
Height: 5'9" **Weight:** 165 lbs.
Bats: both **Throws:** right
Acquired: Traded by Mariners for Felix Fermin, Reggie Jefferson, and cash, 12/93

PLAYER SUMMARY	
Fantasy Value.	$15 to $18
Card Value	7¢ to 10¢
Will	play "little ball"
Can't	count on elbow
Expect.	good speed
Don't Expect	many homers

Although Vizquel was a key contributor to the Tribe's AL Central Championship, 1996 was not altogether a happy season for him. His defensive performance was severely hampered by a painful shoulder injury that reduced his arm strength. He underwent surgery during the off-season and was expected to spend most of the winter rehabilitating. Vizquel has excellent range and would have cut down his high error total had his arm been sound. Despite his throwing problem, he again provided exceptional play at shortstop. Considered weak offensively in the past, Vizquel is now a productive part of the lineup. Bunting, running, and getting on base are among his many strengths. Batting .274 against lefties and .307 versus righties, he's a good enough hitter that manager Mike Hargrove used him in the No. 2 hole often. Vizquel set career highs in most offensive categories in 1996 and might even improve a little more.

Major League Batting Register

	BA	G	AB	R	H	2B	3B	HR	RBI	SB
89 AL	.220	143	387	45	85	7	3	1	20	1
90 AL	.247	81	255	19	63	3	2	2	18	4
91 AL	.230	142	426	42	98	16	4	1	41	7
92 AL	.294	136	483	49	142	20	4	0	21	15
93 AL	.255	158	560	68	143	14	2	2	31	12
94 AL	.273	69	286	39	78	10	1	1	33	13
95 AL	.266	136	542	87	144	28	0	6	56	29
96 AL	.297	151	542	98	161	36	1	9	64	35
Life	.263	1016	3481	447	914	134	17	22	284	116
3 Ave	.278	134	518	84	144	27	1	6	58	29

ED VOSBERG

Position: Pitcher
Team: Texas Rangers
Born: Sept. 28, 1961 Tucson, AZ
Height: 6'1" **Weight:** 190 lbs.
Bats: left **Throws:** left
Acquired: Signed as a free agent, 4/95

PLAYER SUMMARY	
Fantasy Value.	$2 to $4
Card Value	4¢ to 7¢
Will	count on curve
Can't.	retire all righties
Expect	great pickoff move
Don't Expect	closer service

Vosberg spent more than ten seasons in the minors—including one in Italy—before finally spending consecutive campaigns in the majors in 1995 and '96. Vosberg became a fixture in the Texas bullpen two years ago. He repeated his success last season, working a career-best 52 games. The University of Arizona product ranked second among the Rangers in games finished (20) and third in appearances. He also had more saves (eight) than any Texas southpaw since Kenny Rogers saved 19 in 1990. A curveball specialist who's much more effective against left-handed hitters, Vosberg averages 6 1/2 strikeouts per nine innings. But he sometimes struggles with his control and yields more hits than innings pitched. Vosberg helps his own cause by keeping the ball in the park, fielding his position well, and controlling the running game. Preceded by his reputation as a pickoff specialist, Vosberg did not allow a stolen base last year. The only two runners who challenged him failed. His ERA at home last year was just 1.75.

Major League Pitching Register

	W	L	ERA	G	S	IP	H	ER	BB	SO
86 NL	0	1	6.59	5	0	13.2	17	10	9	8
90 NL	1	1	5.55	18	0	24.1	21	15	12	12
94 AL	0	2	3.95	16	0	13.2	16	6	5	12
95 AL	5	5	3.00	44	4	36.0	32	12	16	36
96 AL	1	1	3.27	52	8	44.0	51	16	21	32
Life	7	10	4.03	135	12	131.2	137	59	63	100
2 Ave	3	3	3.14	51	6	42.1	44	15	20	36

TERRELL WADE

Position: Pitcher
Team: Atlanta Braves
Born: Jan. 25, 1973 Rembert, SC
Height: 6'3" **Weight:** 205 lbs.
Bats: left **Throws:** left
Acquired: Signed as a free agent, 7/91

PLAYER SUMMARY	
Fantasy Value	$3 to $5
Card Value	4¢ to 7¢
Will	show fine arm
Can't	save games
Expect	strikeouts
Don't Expect	perfect control

Wade was a phenom as a starter while coming up through the Atlanta system, but he made the 1996 Opening Day roster as a middle reliever. He wore several hats in his rookie campaign, taking a turn as the top left-hander in the pen when Pedro Borbon blew out his elbow, and then getting a chance in the starting rotation due to injuries to Jason Schmidt and Steve Avery. While Wade got plenty of opportunities to stay in the rotation, he was far more effective out of the pen because he threw strikes far more often. His control struggles as a starter were evident in an early September appearance in Cincinnati, where he walked four straight batters with a 5-0 lead to let the Reds back into a game they eventually won. Wade will be just 24 years old when the season begins and has an outstanding arm. He fanned well over one man an inning and, oddly, held right-handers to a .210 average while struggling some (.286) with lefties. Wade should have a shot at making the rotation in spring training, but he needs to work on improving his control in order to fully realize his tremendous potential.

BILLY WAGNER

Position: Pitcher
Team: Houston Astros
Born: June 25, 1971 Tannersville, VA
Height: 5'11" **Weight:** 180 lbs.
Bats: left **Throws:** left
Acquired: First-round pick in 6/93 free-agent draft

PLAYER SUMMARY	
Fantasy Value	$10 to $13
Card Value	8¢ to 12¢
Will	show impressive stuff
Can't	find the plate
Expect	strikeouts
Don't Expect	too much too soon

The former NCAA All-American did not get the call until midseason, but his performance in the second half alone warranted Rookie of the Year consideration. Wagner, a starter throughout his short minor-league career, became Houston's closer after injuries to incumbents John Hudek and Todd Jones. The Astros were wary of bringing up Wagner, who already throws as hard as any left-hander in the NL, too soon. However, he racked up save after save in his first few weeks as the closer, converting nine of 13 attempts. Right-handers batted just .178 against Wagner, while lefties hit a meager .083. The only things that troubled Wagner were untimely walks and a leg problem that forced him to the DL for a couple of weeks. However, he returned from injury to pitch well for the last portion of the season. The Astros aren't sure what Wagner's role will be in the future. If Hudek and Jones can't come back from injuries, it's likely he'll be the closer again, but there's also a chance he could be in the starting rotation soon. Wherever he winds up, Wagner has a bright future ahead of him.

Major League Pitching Register

	W	L	ERA	G	S	IP	H	ER	BB	SO
95 NL	0	1	4.50	3	0	4.0	3	2	4	3
96 NL	5	0	2.97	44	1	69.2	57	23	47	79
Life	5	1	3.05	47	1	73.2	60	25	51	82

Major League Pitching Register

	W	L	ERA	G	S	IP	H	ER	BB	SO
95 NL	0	0	0.00	1	0	0.1	0	0	0	0
96 NL	2	2	2.44	37	9	51.2	28	14	30	67
Life	2	2	2.42	38	9	52.0	28	14	30	67

PAUL WAGNER

Position: Pitcher
Team: Pittsburgh Pirates
Born: Nov. 14, 1967 Milwaukee, WI
Height: 6'1" **Weight:** 209 lbs.
Bats: right **Throws:** right
Acquired: Signed as a free agent, 11/96

PLAYER SUMMARY	
Fantasy Value	$0
Card Value	7¢ to 10¢
Will	have to rehab
Can't	find consistency
Expect	starting berth
Don't Expect	15 wins

Wagner began the season in Pittsburgh's starting rotation but was largely ineffective after the first few weeks due to an arm injury that eventually cut short his season. Wagner went on the disabled list in early June with what doctors believed to be tendon problems in his triceps, and he was permanently shelved a month later when he underwent surgery to repair a torn tendon in his elbow. It is doubtful he will be ready for the start of 1997. Wagner is a decent pitcher when he is healthy and has good stuff, but he hasn't figured out how to put everything together yet. He started off strong last year, going 4-2 with a 2.86 ERA in the first five weeks, but quickly went downhill. If Wagner can make it back from elbow surgery, he will be welcomed by the Pirates. He might even get back into the starting rotation before the season is over. However, it is always a big "if" for any pitcher to come back from elbow surgery—particularly one who hadn't proven himself yet.

Major League Pitching Register

	W	L	ERA	G	CG	IP	H	ER	BB	SO
92 NL	2	0	0.69	6	0	13.0	9	1	5	5
93 NL	8	8	4.27	44	1	141.1	143	67	42	114
94 NL	7	8	4.59	29	1	119.2	136	61	50	86
95 NL	5	16	4.80	33	3	165.0	174	88	72	120
96 NL	4	8	5.40	16	1	81.2	86	49	39	81
Life	26	40	4.60	128	6	520.2	548	266	208	406
3 Ave	6	12	4.83	31	2	145.1	158	78	63	112

TIM WAKEFIELD

Position: Pitcher
Team: Boston Red Sox
Born: Aug. 2, 1966 Melbourne, FL
Height: 6'2" **Weight:** 204 lbs.
Bats: right **Throws:** right
Acquired: Signed as a free agent, 4/95

PLAYER SUMMARY	
Fantasy Value	$5 to $7
Card Value	5¢ to 8¢
Will	bamboozle batters
Can't	keep ball in park
Expect	improved location
Don't Expect	runners to freeze

Willie Stargell once said that trying to hit a knuckleball pitcher is like trying to drink coffee with a fork. When Wakefield is on, that description is right on the money. But Wakefield's career has been a rollercoaster ride. A sensation as a 1992 rookie, he went 8-1 with a 2.15 ERA before pitching two complete-game victories in the NLCS. A year later, he lost his confidence, control, and job. After two poor years in the Pittsburgh farm system, the Red Sox, desperate for pitching help, signed both Wakefield and special tutor Phil Niekro, who won 318 games with the unorthodox pitch. The result was a 14-1 record and 1.65 ERA in Wakefield's first 17 Boston starts. He has struggled since but showed flashes of his old form last year, when his 14 wins led the club. The Florida Tech product depends upon location rather than velocity. His nine-inning average of 3.83 walks wasn't bad, but he followed too many of them with gopher balls (only two AL pitchers yielded more than Wakefield's 38).

Major League Pitching Register

	W	L	ERA	G	CG	IP	H	ER	BB	SO
92 NL	8	1	2.15	13	4	92.0	76	22	35	51
93 NL	6	11	5.61	24	3	128.1	145	80	75	59
95 AL	16	8	2.95	27	6	195.1	163	64	68	119
96 AL	14	13	5.14	32	6	211.2	238	121	90	140
Life	44	33	4.12	96	19	627.1	622	287	268	369
2 Ave	16	11	4.03	31	6	216.1	211	97	83	137

MATT WALBECK

Position: Catcher
Team: Detroit Tigers
Born: Oct. 2, 1969 Sacramento, CA
Height: 5'11" **Weight:** 190 lbs.
Bats: both **Throws:** right
Acquired: Traded by Twins for Brent Stentz, 12/96

PLAYER SUMMARY

Fantasy Value	$1
Card Value	4¢ to 7¢
Will	struggle for job
Can't	hit much
Expect	decent defense
Don't Expect	everyday duty

How long Walbeck stays in the majors will ultimately depend on his defensive skills; and in 1996 they weren't good. He has good game-calling skills and blocks pitches enthusiastically and capably, but he has to do a better job throwing out baserunners. Walbeck tossed out just 30 percent of 46 potential runners last year. Offensively, he provides very little. He's never going to be much of a major-league hitter, as he proved again with his poor 1996 showing. Like just about every other catcher, he is very slow. He can't hit right-handers (.191), has negligible power, and took just nine walks last year. His slugging percentage was a flimsy .298, while his on-base percentage was a scarcely believable .252. Last season, Walbeck missed some time with a broken bone in his hand, an injury that could be blamed in some part for his poor plate performance. Whatever the reason, Walbeck took a major step backward in 1996, and his future in the majors could be determined in spring training.

Major League Batting Register

	BA	G	AB	R	H	2B	3B	HR	RBI	SB
93 NL	.200	11	30	2	6	2	0	1	6	0
94 AL	.204	97	338	31	69	12	0	5	35	1
95 AL	.257	115	393	40	101	18	1	1	44	3
96 AL	.223	63	215	25	48	10	0	2	24	3
Life	.230	286	976	98	224	42	1	9	109	7
3 Ave	.228	110	378	38	86	16	0	3	41	3

LARRY WALKER

Position: Outfield
Team: Colorado Rockies
Born: Dec. 1, 1966 Maple Ridge, British Columbia
Height: 6'3" **Weight:** 225 lbs.
Bats: right **Throws:** right
Acquired: Signed as a free agent, 4/95

PLAYER SUMMARY

Fantasy Value	$35 to $40
Card Value	20¢ to 30¢
Will	hit for power
Can't	show old speed
Expect	success at Coors
Don't Expect	perfect health

Walker was expected to take off in his second season in the thin air of Colorado but played only 83 games due to a broken collarbone suffered when he crashed into the Coors Field outfield fence. Walker was hitting .283 with 14 home runs at the time of the injury. He started the year playing center field but was moved back to right after the injury because manager Don Baylor felt that position would be less hazardous to his health. Unfortunately, Baylor couldn't prevent Walker from separating his shoulder in a freak fishing accident just after the season ended. There was much great disparity between Walker's home and road numbers. He batted .393 at home but hit a flimsy .142 on the road. He is certainly a better hitter than that. Walker and Ellis Burks are easily Colorado's best players based on their performances with other teams, and the Rockies are hoping Walker will come around in 1997.

Major League Batting Register

	BA	G	AB	R	H	2B	3B	HR	RBI	SB
89 NL	.170	20	47	4	8	0	0	0	4	1
90 NL	.241	133	419	59	101	18	3	19	51	21
91 NL	.290	137	487	59	141	30	2	16	64	14
92 NL	.301	143	528	85	159	31	4	23	93	18
93 NL	.265	138	490	85	130	24	5	22	86	29
94 NL	.322	103	395	76	127	44	2	19	86	15
95 NL	.306	131	494	96	151	31	5	36	101	16
96 NL	.276	83	272	58	75	18	4	18	58	18
Life	.285	888	3132	522	892	196	25	153	543	132
3 Ave	.306	125	461	91	141	38	4	28	98	19

DONNE WALL

Position: Pitcher
Team: Houston Astros
Born: July 11, 1967 Potosi, MO
Height: 6'1" **Weight:** 180 lbs.
Bats: right **Throws:** right
Acquired: 18th-round pick in 6/89 free-agent draft

PLAYER SUMMARY	
Fantasy Value	$1 to $3
Card Value	5¢ to 8¢
Will	get his shot
Can't	overpower anybody
Expect	ground balls
Don't Expect	many walks

Wall started the season at Triple-A Tucson but was promoted to Houston after the first month. He made a quick impression by going 6-0 in his first nine starts with the Astros. However, he faltered in the second half, going just 2-8 after the break and seeing his ERA rise from 3.36 at midseason to 4.56 by the end of the year. Wall spent three full seasons at Tucson, and even won the Pacific Coast League pitching Triple Crown in 1995, but he hasn't shown that he can get major-league outs consistently. In 1996, Wall allowed a whopping ten hits per nine innings, with opposing hitters batting .286 and slugging .451 against him. The only thing that saved him from a disastrous season was his control, as he walked only two men per game. It is doubtful that Wall, who turned 29 in July, has much of a future in the majors. He doesn't throw hard, and although he walks only a handful of batters, he gets hit mercilessly if his control is off even a little. Luckily for Wall, the Astros are not blessed with many starting pitchers, so he may catch a break in '97.

Major League Pitching Register

	W	L	ERA	G	CG	IP	H	ER	BB	SO
95 NL	3	1	5.55	6	0	24.1	33	15	5	16
96 NL	9	8	4.56	26	2	150.0	170	76	34	99
Life	12	9	4.70	32	2	174.1	203	91	39	115

JEROME WALTON

Position: Outfield
Team: Baltimore Orioles
Born: July 8, 1965 Newnan, GA
Height: 6'1" **Weight:** 175 lbs.
Bats: right **Throws:** right
Acquired: Signed as a minor-league free agent, 12/96

PLAYER SUMMARY	
Fantasy Value	$0
Card Value	4¢ to 7¢
Will	hit lefties hard
Can't	show good arm
Expect	seat on bench
Don't Expect	lots of steals

When healthy, Walton is one of the best fourth outfielders and right-handed pinch hitters in the game. Walton came home to Georgia when the Braves sought him as veteran insurance on the bench. He got off to a great start, hitting .340 in 37 games (and .440 against left-handed pitchers), but went on the shelf with a right hip strain May 30 and did not play again. An aggressive fastball hitter with some power and speed, Walton was named NL Rookie of the Year with the 1989 Chicago Cubs. But he faded fast, even drifting back to the minors before the Reds rescued him in 1994. Walton can play anywhere in the outfield, where his speed gives him good range though his arm is not strong. Walton, who turns 32 in July, could get another shot as a regular with a 1998 expansion club looking for experience. He's not the same guy who twice topped 40 steals in the minors, but he still knows how to swing the bat—especially in clutch situations.

Major League Batting Register

	BA	G	AB	R	H	2B	3B	HR	RBI	SB
89 NL	.293	116	475	64	139	23	3	5	46	24
90 NL	.263	101	392	63	103	16	2	2	21	14
91 NL	.219	123	270	42	59	13	1	5	17	7
92 NL	.127	30	55	7	7	0	1	0	1	1
93 AL	.000	5	2	2	0	0	0	0	0	1
94 NL	.309	46	68	10	21	4	0	1	9	1
95 NL	.290	102	162	32	47	12	1	8	22	10
96 NL	.340	37	47	9	16	5	0	1	4	0
Life	.266	560	1471	229	392	73	8	22	120	58

JEFF WARE

Position: Pitcher
Team: Toronto Blue Jays
Born: Nov. 11, 1970 Norfolk, VA
Height: 6'3" **Weight:** 195 lbs.
Bats: right **Throws:** right
Acquired: Second-round pick in 6/91 free-agent draft

PLAYER SUMMARY	
Fantasy Value	$0
Card Value	5¢ to 8¢
Will	throw hard
Can't	harness fastball
Expect	time in minors
Don't Expect	instant success

The highly rated prospect came into the 1996 season with only 43 professional games under his belt and a 14-11 career record. Despite his lack of polish and experience, Ware spent a good portion of last season with the Jays and had the kind of problems one would expect from such a raw talent. The Jays used him like they would use a 37-year-old swingman: Ware made four starts, pitched long relief, and even was used once as a mid-inning situational reliever. Ware missed all of the 1993 season due to elbow problems and, as a result of the injury, he is still having trouble controlling his pitches. He throws a good fastball but lacks the other pitches to set it up effectively. It is clear from Ware's horrid control that he is not close to being ready to wear a Toronto uniform, and he certainly needs time to learn how to pitch in the majors. It should not have taken Blue Jays management 32 innings to see that, but then again, the club has always had trouble bringing around young pitchers. Ware would best benefit from at least a full season at Double-A or Triple-A.

Major League Pitching Register

	W	L	ERA	G	S	IP	H	ER	BB	SO
95 AL	2	1	5.47	5	0	26.1	28	16	21	18
96 AL	1	5	9.09	13	0	32.2	35	33	31	11
Life	3	6	7.47	18	0	59.0	63	49	52	29

JOHN WASDIN

Position: Pitcher
Team: Oakland Athletics
Born: Aug. 5, 1972 Fort Belvoir, VA
Height: 6'2" **Weight:** 190 lbs.
Bats: right **Throws:** right
Acquired: First-round pick in 6/93 free-agent draft

PLAYER SUMMARY	
Fantasy Value	$0
Card Value	5¢ to 8¢
Will	show good control
Can't	be an instant star
Expect	durability
Don't Expect	blazing fastballs

Like fellow A's pitcher Steve Wojciechowski, Wasdin spent 1996 shuttling between Oakland and Triple-A Edmonton. Wasdin, who pitched just 19 times in Class-A ball, began the year in the PCL but moved up once the Athletics' pitching woes became apparent. Wasdin was the only Oakland starter to end the season with a winning record, and he could usually be counted on for six solid, if unspectacular, innings. He only completed one game, however, and had the second-highest ERA among the club's rotation pitchers. Not a hard thrower, the still-raw Wasdin will occasionally surprise hitters with his fastball but generally looks to get ground balls. He does not strike out or walk many batters. Pitching in Oakland Coliseum, which was a hitters' park in 1996, was not easy for young Wasdin, who allowed 24 homers and was tagged by left-handers at a .312 clip. He also had troubles keeping runners close. Despite his problems in 1996 and even though he is just four years removed from being drafted, Wasdin should open this year as the A's top starter. He is strong and has never suffered an injury.

Major League Pitching Register

	W	L	ERA	G	CG	IP	H	ER	BB	SO
95 AL	1	1	4.67	5	0	17.1	14	9	3	6
96 AL	8	7	5.96	25	1	131.1	145	87	50	75
Life	9	8	5.81	30	1	148.2	159	96	53	81

ALLEN WATSON

Position: Pitcher
Team: San Francisco Giants
Born: Nov. 18, 1970 Jamaica, NY
Height: 6'3" **Weight:** 190 lbs.
Bats: left **Throws:** left
Acquired: Traded by Cardinals with Rich DeLucia and Doug Creek for Royce Clayton and Chris Wimmer, 1/96

PLAYER SUMMARY	
Fantasy Value	$3 to $5
Card Value	5¢ to 8¢
Will	cut off running game
Can't	master control
Expect	an impressive arm
Don't Expect	15 wins

Watson, who became expendable in St. Louis after the Cardinals picked up Todd Stottlemyre and Andy Benes, began the 1996 season slowly and never recovered. His ERA was in the upper 4.00s for the entire season, and he never put together a strong stretch. Watson allowed about one hit per inning, which was a slight improvement over what he'd done in previous years, but again was victimized by the long ball. He allowed 28 homers (although he gave up only eight after the end of June). However, Watson again proved to be one of the toughest pitchers to run against, as 11 of 25 runners who tried to steal on him were thrown out. Watson is still fairly young—he'll be just 26 on Opening Day. More important, he has good stuff, throws with his left arm, and plays for a team desperate for pitching. All of those points indicate that Watson will remain in the Giants rotation. This will be his fifth year in the league, however, so he'll have to show improvement if he wants to stick around.

Major League Pitching Register

	W	L	ERA	G	CG	IP	H	ER	BB	SO
93 NL	6	7	4.60	16	0	86.0	90	44	28	49
94 NL	6	5	5.52	22	0	115.2	130	71	53	74
95 NL	7	9	4.96	21	0	114.1	126	63	41	49
96 NL	8	12	4.61	29	2	185.2	169	95	69	128
Life	27	33	4.90	88	2	501.2	535	273	191	300
3 Ave	8	10	5.01	28	1	159.0	171	89	63	96

DAVID WEATHERS

Position: Pitcher
Team: New York Yankees
Born: Sept. 25, 1969 Lawrenceburg, TN
Height: 6'3" **Weight:** 205 lbs.
Bats: right **Throws:** right
Acquired: Traded by Marlins for Mark Hutton, 7/96

PLAYER SUMMARY	
Fantasy Value	$0
Card Value	4¢ to 7¢
Will	bank on sinker
Can't	quiet lefty bats
Expect	bullpen berth
Don't Expect	pinpoint control

When the Yankees acquired Weathers last July, they viewed him as a starting pitcher. But he landed a berth on the postseason roster only after showing he could be a valuable bullpen hand. Weathers did not work out of the bullpen until September 16, when he worked a scoreless ninth inning at Toronto. From that point on, he was a formidable force, often called on to get a key strikeout or grounder in a critical late-inning situation. A sinker-slider pitcher who also throws a changeup, Weathers may have found his niche as a reliever. In previous years, he had trouble with his control and struggled against left-handed hitters. He also sabotaged his own cause with poor fielding and an inability to control the running game. Weathers was a double-digit winner in four minor-league seasons but never made a smooth transition to the big leagues as a starter. If he shows more success out of the pen this season, a 1998 expansion club could take a long look at him.

Major League Pitching Register

	W	L	ERA	G	S	IP	H	ER	BB	SO
91 AL	1	0	4.91	15	0	14.2	15	8	17	13
92 AL	0	0	8.10	2	0	3.1	5	3	2	3
93 NL	2	3	5.12	14	0	45.2	57	26	13	34
94 NL	8	12	5.27	24	0	135.0	166	79	59	72
95 NL	4	5	5.98	28	0	90.1	104	60	52	60
96 NL	2	2	4.54	31	0	71.1	85	36	28	40
96 AL	0	2	9.35	11	0	17.1	23	18	14	13
Life	17	24	5.48	125	0	377.2	455	230	185	235
3 Ave	6	8	5.32	32	0	121.0	145	72	57	70

LENNY WEBSTER

Position: Catcher
Team: Baltimore Orioles
Born: Feb. 10, 1965 New Orleans, LA
Height: 5'9" **Weight:** 195 lbs.
Bats: right **Throws:** right
Acquired: Signed as a minor-league free agent, 12/96

PLAYER SUMMARY
Fantasy Value	$0
Card Value	4¢ to 7¢
Will	show keen eye
Can't	hit with power
Expect	good defense
Don't Expect	everyday job

Because of his defensive skills, Webster is a valuable backup catcher. He nailed 38 percent of the runners who tried to steal against him last year—overcoming a previous reputation as a receiver with a weak arm and slow release. The Grambling State product was also one of the few players in the majors last year who walked more often than he struck out (25 walks, 21 Ks). A fastball hitter who murders mistake pitches, Webster is willing to walk if it's important to his team. Because he makes contact but doesn't run well, Webster bangs into a lot of double plays. He's no threat to steal (one career stolen base in eight seasons) but will hit an infrequent homer. Webster is regarded as a good game-caller who handles pitchers well. Jeff Fassero, Montreal's ace last year, requested Webster as his personal catcher. The burly backstop is good at preventing wild pitches and blocking the plate.

Major League Batting Register
	BA	G	AB	R	H	2B	3B	HR	RBI	SB
89 AL	.300	14	20	3	6	2	0	0	1	0
90 AL	.333	2	6	1	2	1	0	0	0	0
91 AL	.294	18	34	7	10	1	0	3	8	0
92 AL	.280	53	118	10	33	10	1	1	13	0
93 AL	.198	49	106	14	21	2	0	1	8	1
94 NL	.273	57	143	13	39	10	0	5	23	0
95 NL	.267	49	150	18	40	9	0	4	14	0
96 NL	.230	78	174	18	40	10	0	2	17	0
Life	.254	320	751	84	191	45	1	16	84	1
2 Ave	.248	67	171	19	43	10	0	3	16	0

WALT WEISS

Position: Shortstop
Team: Colorado Rockies
Born: Nov. 28, 1963 Tuxedo, NY
Height: 6' **Weight:** 178 lbs.
Bats: right **Throws:** right
Acquired: Signed as a free agent, 1/94

PLAYER SUMMARY
Fantasy Value	$5 to $7
Card Value	5¢ to 8¢
Will	play steady defense
Can't	add speed
Expect	good on-base pct.
Don't Expect	much pop

On the surface, Weiss appears to be another in the long line of Colorado Rockies players whose stats look decent only because of the park in which they play. Like many of his fellow Rockies, Weiss hit better at home than he did on the road (.337 at Coors vs. .227 on the road). However, the thing that Weiss does—and what most of his teammates haven't yet figured out how to do—is take a walk. His 80 walks in 1996 gave him 178 free passes in the last two seasons. Weiss also showed decent line-drive power, connecting for 20 doubles and eight homers. He is not fast, but he swiped ten bases in 12 tries. Weiss also gives the Rockies decent defense at shortstop. He made 30 errors in 155 games, but turned the double play well and got to a lot of ground balls. Weiss has remained injury-free for the past few seasons, and the Rockies will be looking to him to keep the infield together.

Major League Batting Register
	BA	G	AB	R	H	2B	3B	HR	RBI	SB
87 AL	.462	16	26	3	12	4	0	0	1	1
88 AL	.250	147	452	44	113	17	3	3	39	4
89 AL	.233	84	236	30	55	11	0	3	21	6
90 AL	.265	138	445	50	118	17	1	2	35	9
91 AL	.226	40	133	15	30	6	1	0	13	6
92 AL	.212	103	316	36	67	5	2	0	21	6
93 NL	.266	158	500	50	133	14	2	1	39	7
94 NL	.251	110	423	58	106	11	4	1	32	12
95 NL	.260	137	427	65	111	17	3	1	25	15
96 NL	.282	155	517	89	146	20	2	8	48	10
Life	.256	1088	3475	440	891	122	18	19	274	76
3 Ave	.264	155	531	81	140	18	4	4	40	15

Bob Wells

Position: Pitcher
Team: Seattle Mariners
Born: Nov. 1, 1966 Yakima, WA
Height: 6' **Weight:** 180 lbs.
Bats: right **Throws:** right
Acquired: Claimed from Phillies on waivers, 6/94

PLAYER SUMMARY	
Fantasy Value	$1 to $3
Card Value	5¢ to 8¢
Will	start or relieve
Can't	avoid gophers
Expect	good control
Don't Expect	frequent Ks

A control artist who spots three pitches in the strike zone (fastball, changeup, and slider), Wells was a pleasant surprise for the 1996 Mariners. He made 16 starts and 20 relief outings but still managed to win a dozen games, just one less than team leader Sterling Hitchcock. Much more effective against right-handed hitters, Wells relies on location rather than velocity. He averages three walks per nine innings but yields a lot of home runs (a team-worst 25 in 130⅔ innings last year) because he's always around the strike zone. When he doesn't hit a precise spot, he gets hammered. Lefties also light him up (.300 opposing average last year). Wells fans 6½ hitters per nine innings and averages just over one hit per inning. He helps his own cause with fine fielding and a solid pickoff move. Wells spent nearly six seasons in the minors before getting his first taste of the big leagues. He's entering his third big-league campaign at age 30.

Major League Pitching Register

	W	L	ERA	G	CG	IP	H	ER	BB	SO
94 NL	1	0	1.80	6	0	5.0	4	1	3	3
94 AL	1	0	2.25	1	0	4.0	4	1	1	3
95 AL	4	3	5.75	30	0	76.2	88	49	39	38
96 AL	12	7	5.30	36	1	130.2	141	77	46	94
Life	18	10	5.33	73	1	216.1	237	128	89	138
2 Ave	8	5	5.48	35	1	108.1	120	66	45	68

David Wells

Position: Pitcher
Team: New York Yankees
Born: May 20, 1963 Torrance, CA
Height: 6'4" **Weight:** 225 lbs.
Bats: left **Throws:** left
Acquired: Signed as a free agent, 12/96

PLAYER SUMMARY	
Fantasy Value	$8 to $10
Card Value	5¢ to 8¢
Will	surprise hitters
Can't	keeps lbs. off
Expect	10 to 15 wins
Don't Expect	perfect health

Wells has always been on the verge of a breakout season as a starting pitcher. 1996 wasn't his year, however; in fact, it was a step back (11-14, 5.14 ERA). Weight struggles throughout his career have affected his back, which directly affects his pitching style. He is usually "sneaky fast" with his pitches and at times can blow hitters away. He relies on savvy, skill, and a fine curve. Unfortunately, Wells endured back pain much of last season, especially during the cool opening months. He angered manager Davey Johnson by reporting to spring camp overweight and didn't get in shape until June. Wells's 34 starts were a career high, and Johnson kept sending him to the mound as if pitching him enough would get him into form. The inconsistent Wells has frustrated his managers in the past and is likely to continue doing so in New York.

Major League Pitching Register

	W	L	ERA	G	CG	IP	H	ER	BB	SO
87 AL	4	3	3.99	18	0	29.1	37	13	12	32
88 AL	3	5	4.62	41	0	64.1	65	33	31	56
89 AL	7	4	2.40	54	0	86.1	66	23	28	78
90 AL	11	6	3.14	43	0	189.0	165	66	45	115
91 AL	15	10	3.72	40	2	198.1	188	82	49	106
92 AL	7	9	5.40	41	0	120.0	138	72	36	62
93 AL	11	9	4.19	32	0	187.0	183	87	42	139
94 AL	5	7	3.96	16	5	111.1	113	49	24	71
95 AL	10	3	3.04	18	3	130.1	120	44	37	83
95 NL	6	5	3.59	11	3	72.2	74	29	16	50
96 AL	11	14	5.14	34	3	224.1	247	128	51	130
Life	90	75	3.99	348	16	1413.0	1396	626	371	922
3 Ave	12	11	4.12	30	6	203.1	208	93	48	127

DON WENGERT

Position: Pitcher
Team: Oakland Athletics
Born: Nov. 6, 1969 Sioux City, IA
Height: 6'2" **Weight:** 205 lbs.
Bats: right **Throws:** right
Acquired: Fourth-round pick in 6/92 free-agent draft

PLAYER SUMMARY	
Fantasy Value	$0
Card Value	5¢ to 8¢
Will	be a starter
Can't	set up fastball
Expect	solid innings
Don't Expect	perfect control

Wengert was one of many promising but raw Athletics pitchers who were hit hard through the year. Coming to Oakland with just 16 Triple-A appearances under his belt, he ended 1996 with more starts and more innings pitched than any other member of the staff. When Wengert was given the ball, he took it and did the best he could without complaining. Despite a power fastball and slider, Wengert is not yet a strikeout pitcher and needs to cut down on his walks. Control problems led to a .300 average from both right-handed and left-handed opposing hitters, and Wengert allowed 29 homers on the season. Despite his problems, however, Oakland management likes his arm very much. 1996 was his first full season spent at one level, and he has a lot of learning to do. Thanks to his youth and talent—and a shortage of other qualified starting candidates on the club—he stands a good chance of pitching 200 innings for the A's in 1997. Development of a curve or changeup will improve his chances of becoming a quality major-league starter.

Major League Pitching Register

	W	L	ERA	G	CG	IP	H	ER	BB	SO
95 AL	1	1	3.34	19	0	29.2	30	11	12	16
96 AL	7	11	5.58	36	1	161.1	200	100	60	75
Life	8	12	5.23	55	1	191.0	230	111	72	91

DAVID WEST

Position: Pitcher
Team: Philadelphia Phillies
Born: Sept. 1, 1964 Memphis, TN
Height: 6'6" **Weight:** 230 lbs.
Bats: left **Throws:** left
Acquired: Traded by Twins for Mike Hartley, 12/92

PLAYER SUMMARY	
Fantasy Value	$0
Card Value	4¢ to 7¢
Will	still lefty bats
Can't	avoid injuries
Expect	good velocity
Don't Expect	bullpen duty

A victim of shoulder and elbow woes throughout his career, West began last season on the DL while recovering from July 1995 surgery on his left shoulder. He finally got his first win of the season August 14, when he beat the Braves. Later disabled again with a strained left groin, West worked only seven games (28⅓ innings) for the season. A power pitcher who dominates left-handed hitters, West limited lefties to a .179 batting average from 1993 to '96. When not suffering from physical injuries or weight problems, West is a sinker-slider pitcher who also throws a good curve and changeup—usually from a tough, three-quarters delivery. The sinker has been timed in the low-90s. Although he led three minor leagues in walks, West has learned to throw strikes. West doesn't help himself with his defense or pickoff move but knows how to swing the bat.

Major League Pitching Register

	W	L	ERA	G	CG	IP	H	ER	BB	SO
88 NL	1	0	3.00	2	0	6.0	6	2	3	3
89 NL	0	2	7.40	11	0	24.1	25	20	14	19
89 AL	3	2	6.41	10	0	39.1	48	28	19	31
90 AL	7	9	5.10	29	2	146.1	142	83	78	92
91 AL	4	4	4.54	15	0	71.1	66	36	28	52
92 AL	1	3	6.99	9	0	28.1	32	22	20	19
93 NL	6	4	2.92	76	0	86.1	60	28	51	87
94 NL	4	10	3.55	31	0	99.0	74	39	61	83
95 NL	3	2	3.79	8	0	38.0	34	16	19	25
96 NL	2	2	4.76	7	0	28.1	31	15	11	22
Life	31	38	4.58	198	2	567.1	518	289	304	433

JOHN WETTELAND

Position: Pitcher
Team: New York Yankees
Born: Aug. 21, 1966 San Mateo, CA
Height: 6'2" **Weight:** 215 lbs.
Bats: right **Throws:** right
Acquired: Traded by Expos for Fernando Seguignol and a player to be named later, 4/95

PLAYER SUMMARY
Fantasy Value	$35 to $40
Card Value	8¢ to 12¢
Will	get his saves
Can't	hold runners
Expect	success vs. righties
Don't Expect	many problems

Wetteland had another fine season in 1996. He converted 43 saves in 47 chances to lead the AL and showed his mettle in post-season play by saving all four Yankee World Series wins, earning World Series MVP honors. Working in tandem with outstanding set-up man Mariano Rivera, Wetteland served as one of baseball's most reliable closers. He is prone to the occasional slump but most of the time is overpowering. Wetteland did allow left-handers to bat .283 against him last year, but held righties to a pitiful .133 mark. He had some problems with the long ball, serving up nine of them, and allowed eight runners to steal. However, his stinginess with walks tended to limit any potential damage. Wetteland pitched through pain for most of the season, bothered by a painful right groin pull that eventually forced him out of action for nearly a month.

Major League Pitching Register

	W	L	ERA	G	S	IP	H	ER	BB	SO
89 NL	5	8	3.77	31	1	102.2	81	43	34	96
90 NL	2	4	4.81	22	0	43.0	44	23	17	36
91 NL	1	0	0.00	6	0	9.0	5	0	3	9
92 NL	4	4	2.92	67	37	83.1	64	27	36	99
93 NL	9	3	1.37	70	43	85.1	58	13	28	113
94 NL	4	6	2.83	52	25	63.2	46	20	21	68
95 AL	1	5	2.93	60	31	61.1	40	20	14	66
96 AL	2	3	2.83	62	43	63.2	54	20	21	69
Life	28	33	2.92	370	180	512.0	392	166	174	556
3 Ave	3	6	2.86	68	38	74.0	55	24	22	80

DEVON WHITE

Position: Outfield
Team: Florida Marlins
Born: Dec. 29, 1962 Kingston, Jamaica
Height: 6'2" **Weight:** 190 lbs.
Bats: both **Throws:** right
Acquired: Signed as a free agent, 11/95

PLAYER SUMMARY
Fantasy Value	$13 to $16
Card Value	7¢ to 10¢
Will	show speed
Can't	connect consistently
Expect	stellar defense
Don't Expect	high on-base pct.

White made the jump from the American League to the National League and gave the Florida Marlins everything they thought they were getting when they signed him—outstanding defense and good offense. White made diving catch after diving catch in the outfield. He also held up his end in the batting order, showing surprising power and proving he could still steal a base. White hit 17 home runs and 37 doubles in 1996, improving his performance despite moving to a league with bigger ballparks and less overall offense. However, he remained a poor top-of-the-order man, walking just 38 times, fanning 99 times, and posting a subpar .325 on-base percentage. He will get a push from rookie outfielder Billy McMillon this spring, but new manager Jim Leyland should stick with the veteran for at least another season or two.

Major League Batting Register

	BA	G	AB	R	H	2B	3B	HR	RBI	SB
85 AL	.143	21	7	7	1	0	0	0	0	3
86 AL	.235	29	51	8	12	1	1	1	3	6
87 AL	.263	159	639	103	168	33	5	24	87	32
88 AL	.259	122	455	76	118	22	2	11	51	17
89 AL	.245	156	636	86	156	18	13	12	56	44
90 AL	.217	125	443	57	96	17	3	11	44	21
91 AL	.282	156	642	110	181	40	10	17	60	33
92 AL	.248	153	641	98	159	26	7	17	60	37
93 AL	.273	146	598	116	163	42	6	15	52	34
94 AL	.270	100	403	67	109	24	6	13	49	11
95 AL	.283	101	427	61	121	23	5	10	53	11
96 AL	.274	146	552	77	151	37	6	17	84	22
Life	.261	1414	5494	866	1435	283	64	148	599	271
3 Ave	.275	133	533	80	147	32	7	16	71	17

RONDELL WHITE

Position: Outfield
Team: Montreal Expos
Born: Feb. 23, 1972 Milledgeville, GA
Height: 6'1" **Weight:** 205 lbs.
Bats: right **Throws:** right
Acquired: First-round pick in 6/90 free-agent draft

PLAYER SUMMARY	
Fantasy Value	$13 to $16
Card Value	10¢ to 15¢
Will	play center well
Can't	show great arm
Expect	improved offense
Don't Expect	many walks

The Expos expected big things out of the young White during 1996, but the impressive young center fielder's season never really jelled. He missed 68 games because of kidney and spleen injuries after running into the outfield fence in April. It took White some time to get back in the swing of things, but he wound up hitting in the .290s for the second straight year. However, he did not hit for much power and only drew 22 walks. He did show more discipline and maturity at the plate, though, and cut his strikeout total to 56. The Expos still love White and have not given up on him, although they know he does not have a great throwing arm and is injury prone. His throwing arm is only mediocre. Despite the presence of other fine young players on the team, White will be a regular in the Expos lineup next season. He is still so young and has so much talent that all he needs to do to become a star is stay healthy for an entire season.

Major League Batting Register

	BA	G	AB	R	H	2B	3B	HR	RBI	SB
93 NL	.260	23	73	9	19	3	1	2	15	1
94 NL	.278	40	97	16	27	10	1	2	13	1
95 NL	.295	130	474	87	140	33	4	13	57	25
96 NL	.293	88	334	35	98	19	4	6	41	14
Life	.290	281	978	147	284	65	10	23	126	41
2 Ave	.295	117	434	66	128	28	4	10	53	21

MARK WHITEN

Position: Outfield
Team: Seattle Mariners
Born: Nov. 25, 1966 Pensacola, FL
Height: 6'3" **Weight:** 235 lbs.
Bats: both **Throws:** right
Acquired: Traded by Braves for Roger Blanco, 8/96

PLAYER SUMMARY	
Fantasy Value	$12 to $15
Card Value	5¢ to 8¢
Will	show power and speed
Can't	stay consistent
Expect	a strong arm
Don't Expect	perfect defense

Whiten might have finally found a home in Seattle after bouncing around both leagues for much of two seasons. He became one of the few players in recent history to play for three teams in one season when he was acquired by the Mariners in '96. He started the season in Philadelphia but was cut after a poor start. He then joined the Braves, who were looking for a right fielder. Despite becoming Atlanta's best outfield arm and top basestealer the minute he was signed, Whiten didn't fit into the club's plans. After the Braves dealt him, Whiten exploded for Seattle, hitting .300 with 12 home runs in only 40 games. Although he has put together streaks like that before, he has never enjoyed a stellar full season. Due to inconsistency and frequent deals, Whiten has not played an entire season with one club since 1993. In a hitter-friendly stadium like the Kingdome, Whiten could finally fulfill his tremendous promise.

Major League Batting Register

	BA	G	AB	R	H	2B	3B	HR	RBI	SB
90 AL	.273	33	88	12	24	1	1	2	7	2
91 AL	.243	116	407	46	99	18	7	9	45	4
92 AL	.254	148	508	73	129	19	4	9	43	16
93 NL	.253	152	562	81	142	13	4	25	99	15
94 NL	.293	92	334	57	98	18	2	14	53	10
95 AL	.185	32	108	13	20	3	0	1	10	1
95 NL	.269	60	212	38	57	10	1	11	37	7
96 NL	.243	96	272	45	66	13	1	10	38	15
96 AL	.300	40	140	31	42	7	0	12	33	2
Life	.257	769	2631	396	677	102	20	93	365	72
3 Ave	.273	98	327	56	89	17	2	14	51	12

BOB WICKMAN

Position: Pitcher
Team: Milwaukee Brewers
Born: Feb. 6, 1969 Green Bay, WI
Height: 6'1" **Weight:** 212 lbs.
Bats: right **Throws:** right
Acquired: Traded by Yankees with Gerald Williams for Pat Listach, Graeme Lloyd, and Ricky Bones, 7/96

PLAYER SUMMARY	
Fantasy Value	$4 to $6
Card Value	5¢ to 8¢
Will	work frequently
Can't	keep lefties quiet
Expect	ground-ball outs
Don't Expect	perfect control

After spending most of his first four pro seasons as a starter, Wickman has worked almost exclusively out of the bullpen for the last three. In fact, he's made only one start since 1993. Working a career-high 70 times last year, he averaged seven strikeouts, four walks, and ten hits per nine innings. A set-up man who's more effective against right-handed hitters, Wickman is a sinker-slider specialist who also throws a cut fastball. When he's on, he gets a lot of ground-ball outs and few gopher balls. He's usually good at stranding runners (though not last year) but not at holding them close to the base. Twelve of the 14 basestealers who challenged him last year succeeded. Blessed with a rubber arm that responds to short rest, Wickman often works multiple-inning stints in his role as a set-up man. A Wisconsin native who attended the University of Wisconsin's Whitewater campus, Wickman returned to his roots last year when the Brewers obtained him from the Yankees.

Major League Pitching Register

	W	L	ERA	G	S	IP	H	ER	BB	SO
92 AL	6	1	4.11	8	0	50.1	51	23	20	21
93 AL	14	4	4.63	41	4	140.0	156	72	69	70
94 AL	5	4	3.09	53	6	70.0	54	24	27	56
95 AL	2	4	4.05	63	1	80.0	77	36	33	51
96 AL	7	1	4.42	70	0	95.2	106	47	44	75
Life	34	14	4.17	235	11	436.0	444	202	193	273
3 Ave	5	4	3.84	72	3	95.1	90	40	40	70

RICK WILKINS

Position: Catcher
Team: San Francisco Giants
Born: June 4, 1967 Jacksonville, FL
Height: 6'2" **Weight:** 215 lbs.
Bats: left **Throws:** right
Acquired: Traded by Astros for Kirt Manwaring and cash, 7/96

PLAYER SUMMARY	
Fantasy Value	$7 to $9
Card Value	4¢ to 7¢
Will	hit some homers
Can't	bat .300 again
Expect	trouble with lefties
Don't Expect	lazy play

Wilkins joined San Francisco in mid-1996, making the Giants his third team in three seasons—which is hard to believe, considering he hit 30 home runs only four years ago. Since that banner 1993 season, Wilkins has not been able to even approach those numbers. He sagged to a lowly .203 in 1995 and only raised his average to .243 last season. One reason for Wilkins's decline is his inability to hit left-handed pitching. He batted only .172 against them in 1996. Wilkins did show good patience at the plate, with 67 walks boosting his on-base percentage to a very respectable .344. Wilkins seems destined for platoon duty at best and might be down to his last opportunity. He might not get many chances to even stick with the last-place Giants, who have young catchers Marcus Jensen and Ramon Castro on the way. However, Wilkins's power, good work ethic, and strong arm (he threw out 32 percent of enemy basestealers last year) are valuable.

Major League Batting Register

	BA	G	AB	R	H	2B	3B	HR	RBI	SB
91 NL	.222	86	203	21	45	9	0	6	22	3
92 NL	.270	83	244	20	66	9	1	8	22	0
93 NL	.303	136	446	78	135	23	1	30	73	2
94 NL	.227	100	313	44	71	25	2	7	39	4
95 NL	.203	65	202	30	41	3	0	7	19	0
96 NL	.243	136	411	53	100	18	2	14	59	0
Life	.252	606	1819	246	458	87	6	72	234	9
3 Ave	.228	117	360	50	82	19	2	11	45	2

BERNIE WILLIAMS

Position: Outfield
Team: New York Yankees
Born: Sept. 13, 1968 San Juan, Puerto Rico
Height: 6'2" **Weight:** 200 lbs.
Bats: both **Throws:** right
Acquired: Signed as a free agent, 9/85

PLAYER SUMMARY	
Fantasy Value	$25 to $30
Card Value	12¢ to 20¢
Will	slug from both sides
Can't	show great arm
Expect	good attitude
Don't Expect	on-field problems

Williams was arguably the best center fielder in baseball in 1996, putting up impressive offensive numbers as well as anchoring the Yankee outfield. Even in New York, where every little thing can be overblown, Williams's 1996 was understated. Despite all the turmoil inside and outside the Yankee clubhouse, Williams stayed clear of craziness and went about his business with a notable lack of histrionics. Off the diamond, he is a devoted family man who excels at playing the classical guitar. Williams tends to stay in the background everywhere except on the field, where he shines. He is still young, although it seems he's been hanging around the Yankees for longer than six years. Last year, Williams combined speed (17 steals in 21 tries), punch (.376 against left-handers), and defense (ten assists and outstanding range). He is a skilled player who could prevail at any one of several lineup spots but will probably continue to hit third for New York.

BRIAN WILLIAMS

Position: Pitcher
Team: Detroit Tigers
Born: Feb. 15, 1969 Lancaster, SC
Height: 6'2" **Weight:** 195 lbs.
Bats: right **Throws:** right
Acquired: Signed as a free agent, 1/96

PLAYER SUMMARY	
Fantasy Value	$0
Card Value	4¢ to 7¢
Will	feature good arm
Can't	show command
Expect	walks and strikeouts
Don't Expect	attempted steals

The hard-throwing right-hander was signed by the Tigers after the 1995 season. He had worn out his welcome in San Diego, as he had in Houston before that, due to poor control. Like many of his fellow Detroit pitchers, Williams was battered around pretty well and could not find a role; manager Buddy Bell shifted Williams between rotation and bullpen assignments. He was used as a starter (17 starts), middle reliever, and closer, but nothing seemed to work. Williams walked more batters than he fanned, served up 21 homers, and allowed left-handed batters to tattoo him for a .369 average. Williams's future might be in short relief, as indicated by his ability to hold runners close and his success against right-handed hitters. However, he has to improve overall; even on a pitching-thin team like Detroit, Williams cannot hang around forever pitching the way he did in 1996. The promise he once showed is fading, and a trip back to the minors may be in the offing.

Major League Batting Register

	BA	G	AB	R	H	2B	3B	HR	RBI	SB
91 AL	.237	85	320	43	76	19	4	3	34	10
92 AL	.280	62	261	39	73	14	2	5	26	7
93 AL	.268	139	567	67	152	31	4	12	68	9
94 AL	.289	108	408	80	118	29	1	12	57	16
95 AL	.307	144	563	93	173	29	9	18	82	8
96 AL	.305	143	551	108	168	26	7	29	102	17
Life	.285	681	2670	430	760	148	27	79	369	67
3 Ave	.301	152	586	108	176	33	6	22	92	16

Major League Pitching Register

	W	L	ERA	G	S	IP	H	ER	BB	SO
91 NL	0	1	3.75	2	0	12.0	11	5	4	4
92 NL	7	6	3.92	16	0	96.1	92	42	42	54
93 NL	4	4	4.83	42	3	82.0	76	44	38	56
94 NL	6	5	5.74	20	0	78.1	112	50	41	49
95 NL	3	10	6.00	44	0	72.0	79	48	38	75
96 AL	3	10	6.77	40	2	121.0	145	91	85	72
Life	23	36	5.46	164	5	461.2	515	280	248	310
3 Ave	5	9	6.21	39	1	104.0	131	72	62	75

GEORGE WILLIAMS

Position: Catcher
Team: Oakland Athletics
Born: April 22, 1969 LaCrosse, WI
Height: 5'10" **Weight:** 190 lbs.
Bats: right **Throws:** right
Acquired: 24th-round pick in 6/91 free-agent draft

PLAYER SUMMARY	
Fantasy Value	$1
Card Value	5¢ to 8¢
Will	show some power
Can't	steal any bases
Expect	good batting eye
Don't Expect	dazzling defense

Switch-hitting catchers with power don't grow on trees. That's why Williams is a valuable property. After twice topping a dozen homers in the minors, he made a smash debut with Oakland during three separate stints in 1995. He hit three homers—one with the bases loaded—while hitting .291 with 14 RBI in 79 at bats. A better right-handed hitter, Williams feasts on fastballs but struggles against breaking stuff. He's a selective hitter who walked more than he fanned in his first three years as a pro, starting in 1991. That sharp batting eye helped Williams last year, when his on-base percentage was 159 points better than his anemic batting average. A product of Pan American campus at the University of Texas, Williams isn't a threat to steal. Nor is he adept at stopping others. He nailed only 22 percent of the basestealers who challenged him last year. Because his throwing and defense are suspect behind the plate, Williams has tried his hand at third base and the outfield. His best spot is DH, but he'll have to hike his batting average, which sank below the Mendoza Line last year.

Major League Batting Register

	BA	G	AB	R	H	2B	3B	HR	RBI	SB
95 AL	.291	29	79	13	23	5	1	3	14	0
96 AL	.152	56	132	17	20	5	0	3	10	0
Life	.204	85	211	30	43	10	1	6	24	0

GERALD WILLIAMS

Position: Outfield
Team: Milwaukee Brewers
Born: Aug. 10, 1966 New Orleans, LA
Height: 6'2" **Weight:** 190 lbs.
Bats: right **Throws:** right
Acquired: Traded by Yankees with Bob Wickman for Pat Listach, Graeme Lloyd, and Ricky Bones, 7/96

PLAYER SUMMARY	
Fantasy Value	$3 to $5
Card Value	5¢ to 8¢
Will	hit lefties
Can't	show much pop
Expect	good defense
Don't Expect	everyday duty

Acquired from the Yankees in a confusing and controversial deal, Williams did not play often or impressively with his new team. After starting off 0-for-12 with Milwaukee, he sat out for most of September with an infected shoulder. Williams always seemed on the verge of breaking through in New York, but the Yankees finally gave up on him with the emergence of star center fielder Bernie Williams. Gerald is a fine defender who is capable of playing all three outfield positions, but his bat lags behind his glove. He did hit .290 against left-handers in 1996, which is close to his usual mark, but he was caught stealing nine times in 19 tries and took just 19 walks. His on-base percentage was an anemic .299. The Brewers want to try Williams in center field, and he'll get first shot at the job in the spring. However, judging from his past record, it seems unlikely that Williams can hit enough to stay in the regular lineup. Nonetheless, he is a valuable fourth outfielder and can be platooned effectively.

Major League Batting Register

	BA	G	AB	R	H	2B	3B	HR	RBI	SB
92 AL	.296	15	27	7	8	2	0	3	6	2
93 AL	.149	42	67	11	10	2	3	0	6	2
94 AL	.291	57	86	19	25	8	0	4	13	1
95 AL	.247	100	182	33	45	18	2	6	28	4
96 AL	.252	125	325	43	82	19	4	5	34	10
Life	.247	339	687	113	170	49	9	18	87	19
2 Ave	.250	119	265	40	66	20	3	6	33	7

MATT WILLIAMS

Position: Third base
Team: Cleveland Indians
Born: Nov. 28, 1965 Bishop, CA
Height: 6'2" **Weight:** 216 lbs.
Bats: right **Throws:** right
Acquired: Traded by Giants for Jeff Kent, Julian Tavarez, and Jose Vizcaino, 11/96

PLAYER SUMMARY	
Fantasy Value	$35 to $40
Card Value	15¢ to 25¢
Will	play great defense
Can't	afford injury
Expect	home runs
Don't Expect	much speed

The blockbuster deal sending Williams to Cleveland indicates that the slugging third baseman's standing remains high—even though he has not played a full season since 1993. Williams was having another typically outstanding year in 1996 when he jammed his right shoulder diving for a ball in July. He tried to play through the injury but just couldn't, even after being moved to first base for his final games. Williams's swing was off because he couldn't lift his arm without severe pain. He underwent season-ending surgery August 5. After receiving a clean bill of health in November, he was dealt to the Tribe and is likely to assume the cleanup spot. His arrival forces former third-sacker Jim Thome over to first, a move that will improve the Indians defense. Jacobs Field is a friendly park for hitters. If Williams can avoid injury, he could pile up monstrous numbers.

Major League Batting Register

	BA	G	AB	R	H	2B	3B	HR	RBI	SB
87 NL	.188	84	245	28	46	9	2	8	21	4
88 NL	.205	52	156	17	32	6	1	8	19	0
89 NL	.202	84	292	31	59	18	1	18	50	1
90 NL	.277	159	617	87	171	27	2	33	122	7
91 NL	.268	157	589	72	158	24	5	34	98	5
92 NL	.227	146	529	58	120	13	5	20	66	7
93 NL	.294	145	579	105	170	33	4	38	110	1
94 NL	.267	112	445	74	119	16	3	43	96	1
95 NL	.336	76	283	53	95	17	1	23	65	2
96 NL	.302	105	404	69	122	16	1	22	85	1
Life	.264	1120	4139	594	1092	179	25	247	732	29
3 Ave	.294	116	450	78	132	19	2	36	98	2

WOODY WILLIAMS

Position: Pitcher
Team: Toronto Blue Jays
Born: Aug. 19, 1966 Houston, TX
Height: 6' **Weight:** 190 lbs.
Bats: right **Throws:** right
Acquired: 28th-round pick in 6/88 free-agent draft

PLAYER SUMMARY	
Fantasy Value	$0
Card Value	4¢ to 7¢
Will	rely on location
Can't	hold men close
Expect	decent control
Don't Expect	high K count

Williams opened his professional career as a starter in 1988, then spent most of his time as a reliever before returning to rotation work with the Blue Jays during the second half of the '96 campaign. Relying on location instead of velocity, Williams changes speeds off his fastball and blends a quality curve into the mix. He yields about one hit per inning and fans 6½ batters per nine innings. The University of Houston product, more effective against right-handed hitters, succeeds by throwing strikes. He allowed only 3.2 walks per nine innings last year and also did a reasonably good job of keeping the ball in the park. A good pitcher under pressure, Williams helps his own cause with fine defense but has trouble holding runners close. The right-hander reported no problems last year from the sore shoulder that disabled him in 1995.

Major League Pitching Register

	W	L	ERA	G	CG	IP	H	ER	BB	SO
93 AL	3	1	4.38	30	0	37.0	40	18	22	24
94 AL	1	3	3.64	38	0	59.1	44	24	33	56
95 AL	1	2	3.69	23	0	53.2	44	22	28	41
96 AL	4	5	4.73	12	1	59.0	64	31	21	43
Life	9	11	4.09	103	1	209.0	192	95	104	164
2 Ave	1	3	3.66	40	0	72.0	56	29	39	63

DAN WILSON

Position: Catcher
Team: Seattle Mariners
Born: March 25, 1969 Arlington Heights, IL
Height: 6'3" **Weight:** 190 lbs.
Bats: right **Throws:** right
Acquired: Traded by Reds with Bobby Ayala
for Bret Boone and Erik Hanson, 11/93

PLAYER SUMMARY	
Fantasy Value	$9 to $11
Card Value	5¢ to 8¢
Will	play defense
Can't	run a lick
Expect	a decent year
Don't Expect	Johnny Bench

Wilson put up power numbers in 1996 that nobody had expected of him. Coming into the season, he had just 21 career home runs, but he put a career-high 18 on the board. Wilson was highly thought of while coming up in the Cincinnati Reds organization, but one of the main reasons the Reds traded him to Seattle was that they didn't feel he would hit for much power. They may have felt a little foolish watching Wilson set career highs in doubles and RBI as well as four-baggers last year. Wilson, best known for his defense, threw out 39 percent of runners attempting to steal and committed only four errors in 138 games. He tired considerably late in the season as he had also done in 1995—he had only six doubles and four home runs after July 28—so it will be important for the Mariners to find a quality backup. Nonetheless, the past couple of years have convinced the club that Wilson is their catcher for the foreseeable future, even if his offensive explosion turns out to be a one-year wonder.

Major League Batting Register

	BA	G	AB	R	H	2B	3B	HR	RBI	SB
92 NL	.360	12	25	2	9	1	0	0	3	0
93 NL	.224	36	76	6	17	3	0	0	8	0
94 AL	.216	91	282	24	61	14	2	3	27	1
95 AL	.278	119	399	40	111	22	3	9	51	2
96 AL	.285	138	491	51	140	24	0	18	83	1
Life	.266	396	1273	123	338	64	5	30	172	4
3 Ave	.262	133	446	43	117	23	2	11	59	2

PAUL WILSON

Position: Pitcher
Team: New York Mets
Born: March 28, 1973 Orlando, FL
Height: 6'5" **Weight:** 235 lbs.
Bats: right **Throws:** right
Acquired: First-round pick in 6/94 free-agent
draft

PLAYER SUMMARY	
Fantasy Value	$7 to $9
Card Value	20¢ to 25¢
Will	be a starter
Can't	hold runners
Expect	much improvement
Don't Expect	perfect control

Looking back, there was no way Wilson and the rest of the Mets young starting pitchers could have possibly lived up to the high expectations pushed onto them by club management and the media. Wilson, the brightest prospect in an organization loaded with fine young pitchers, made the big-league team and was supposed to help lead the Mets to the playoffs. Even more pressure fell on him when Bill Pulsipher was hurt in spring training. Wilson started slowly and never fully recovered, although he managed an outstanding start every couple of weeks. He had his share of control problems, and 24 of 28 runners stole successfully against him. Despite having a rough season, Wilson stayed healthy and took the ball every fifth day. Some fans, media figures, and baseball executives often forget that it takes time for young pitchers to figure out how to get experienced big-league hitters out; the experience Wilson gained in '96 should only help him in the future. Wilson has shown he has what it takes with his performance in the minors, and he will soon prove it at the big-league level.

Major League Pitching Register

	W	L	ERA	G	CG	IP	H	ER	BB	SO
96 NL	5	12	5.38	26	1	149.0	157	89	71	109
Life	5	12	5.38	26	1	149.0	157	89	71	109

BOBBY WITT

Position: Pitcher
Team: Texas Rangers
Born: May 11, 1964 Arlington, VA
Height: 6'2" **Weight:** 205 lbs.
Bats: right **Throws:** right
Acquired: Traded by Marlins for Wilson Heredia and Scott Podsednik, 8/95

PLAYER SUMMARY	
Fantasy Value	$5 to $7
Card Value	5¢ to 8¢
Will	provide innings
Can't	fulfill old promise
Expect	starting duty
Don't Expect	great command

Though not spectacular at any point during the 1996 season, Witt was quite solid and supplied plenty of innings for the Rangers' thin rotation. His ERA was higher than it should have been and he gave up a lot of hits, but Witt averaged six innings each start, saving wear and tear on the bullpen. As his stat line from last season shows, Witt didn't fool many hitters, but he ended up with 16 victories thanks to more than five runs per game of support from his teammates and some strong outings. Witt can no longer hurl the ball past hitters like he once did, so he gets by on guile, smarts, and the occasional 90-mph fastball. Although batters hit over .290 against Witt last year, his K total (157) indicates he will be valuable for a couple more years. Control has always been a problem for Witt.

Major League Pitching Register

	W	L	ERA	G	CG	IP	H	ER	BB	SO
86 AL	11	9	5.48	31	0	157.2	130	96	143	174
87 AL	8	10	4.91	26	1	143.0	114	78	140	160
88 AL	8	10	3.92	22	13	174.1	134	76	101	148
89 AL	12	13	5.14	31	5	194.1	182	111	114	166
90 AL	17	10	3.36	33	7	222.0	197	83	110	221
91 AL	3	7	6.09	17	1	88.2	84	60	74	82
92 AL	10	14	4.29	31	0	193.0	183	92	114	125
93 AL	14	13	4.21	35	5	220.0	226	103	91	131
94 AL	8	10	5.04	24	5	135.2	151	76	70	111
95 AL	2	7	3.90	19	1	110.2	104	48	47	95
95 AL	3	4	4.55	10	1	61.1	81	31	21	46
96 AL	16	12	5.41	33	2	199.2	235	120	96	157
Life	112	119	4.61	312	41	1900.1	1821	974	1121	1616
3 Ave	11	13	4.87	33	4	195.1	219	105	90	157

MARK WOHLERS

Position: Pitcher
Team: Atlanta Braves
Born: Jan. 23, 1970 Holyoke, MA
Height: 6'4" **Weight:** 207 lbs.
Bats: right **Throws:** right
Acquired: Eighth-round pick in 6/88 free-agent draft

PLAYER SUMMARY	
Fantasy Value	$35 to $40
Card Value	8¢ to 12¢
Will	get his Ks
Can't	afford walks
Expect	99-mph heat
Don't Expect	a demotion

Wohlers was as dominating as any closer in baseball, saving 39 games in 44 chances last year. He never reached the kind of unhittable stretch he had in the second half of 1995, but he was consistent from Opening Day through the end of the season. He threw 77⅓ innings, the most he had ever thrown in the majors, but showed no signs of wearing down at the end of the season. When Wohlers gets in trouble, it's because he gets behind in the count and has to throw his hard, but relatively straight, fastball over the plate. When he stays ahead of hitters, however, he can get them out with any of three pitches—a fastball, slider, or his devastating forkball. He is just entering his prime (he'll be 27 years old on Opening Day) and is easily the best reliever in the National League. He throws as hard as anybody. Wohlers would benefit even more if the Braves could improve their middle relief so he doesn't have to pitch in the eighth inning.

Major League Pitching Register

	W	L	ERA	G	S	IP	H	ER	BB	SO
91 NL	3	1	3.20	17	2	19.2	17	7	13	13
92 NL	1	2	2.55	32	4	35.1	28	10	14	17
93 NL	6	2	4.50	46	0	48.0	37	24	22	45
94 NL	7	2	4.59	51	1	51.0	51	26	33	58
95 NL	7	3	2.09	65	25	64.2	51	15	24	90
96 NL	2	4	3.03	77	39	77.1	71	26	21	100
Life	26	14	3.26	288	71	296.0	255	108	127	323
3 Ave	7	3	3.22	74	23	74.0	67	27	31	94

STEVE WOJCIECHOWSKI

Position: Pitcher
Team: Oakland Athletics
Born: July 29, 1970 Blue Island, IL
Height: 6'2" **Weight:** 195 lbs.
Bats: left **Throws:** left
Acquired: Fourth-round pick in 6/91 free-agent draft

PLAYER SUMMARY
Fantasy Value	$0
Card Value	5¢ to 8¢
Will	have his good days
Can't	be consistent
Expect	runners to take off
Don't Expect	a smooth ride

Wojciechowski was maddeningly inconsistent in 1996. At times he was very effective, but he often infuriated manager Art Howe with his lack of concentration. After months of wondering which pitcher would show up—the one paying attention or the one giving up buckets of hits—the A's sent them both back to Triple-A. "Wojo" then proceeded to help the Trappers reach the Pacific Coast League playoffs, fashioning a 3.73 ERA in 11 starts. This, in a nutshell, is the problem facing the Oakland staff: Most of their starters have proven they can pitch in the minors, but they are having a tough adjustment to the majors. With the Athletics in '96, Wojciechowski held left-handers to just a .234 average but had plenty of trouble with righties. He also allowed 15 stolen bases, highest on the staff and a poor total for a left-hander. Wojciechowski will be given every chance to make the team in spring training due to his occasional success in 1995 and his ability to get left-handers out, but the A's will not hesitate to ship him out again if he doesn't provide quality innings.

Major League Pitching Register
	W	L	ERA	G	CG	IP	H	ER	BB	SO
95 AL	2	3	5.18	14	0	48.2	51	28	28	13
96 AL	5	5	5.65	16	0	79.2	97	50	28	30
Life	7	8	5.47	30	0	128.1	148	78	56	43
2 Ave	4	4	5.46	16	0	67.1	77	41	30	22

BOB WOLCOTT

Position: Pitcher
Team: Seattle Mariners
Born: Sept. 8, 1973 Huntington Beach, CA
Height: 6' **Weight:** 190 lbs.
Bats: right **Throws:** right
Acquired: Second-round pick in 6/92 free-agent draft

PLAYER SUMMARY
Fantasy Value	$1 to $3
Card Value	4¢ to 7¢
Will	keep rotation spot
Can't	prevent gopher balls
Expect	great pickoff move
Don't Expect	hits by righties

For the rest of his career, Wolcott will be remembered as the scared rookie who started the first ALCS game in Seattle's history. He walked the first three Indians, then settled down to pitch seven innings and pick up the win. Wolcott's inability to maintain that pace was one of the reasons Seattle couldn't defend its AL West title last summer. The club's top right-hander in starts and innings pitched managed only a 7-10 record—even though his teammates supported him with an average of 5.89 runs per start. Despite good control (3.25 walks per nine innings), Wolcott yielded too many hits (11 per game), too many homers (26 in 149⅓ innings), and too lofty an average to lefties (.351). He's fine against righties (.241) but Wolcott's overall average of 4.7 Ks per nine innings was horrible for a pitcher who depends upon power. He mixes a fastball—his top pitch—with a curveball, slider, and changeup. Wolcott's best asset is a pickoff move that is the closest thing to perfection by a right-hander: The only man to try stealing against him last year was caught in the act.

Major League Pitching Register
	W	L	ERA	G	CG	IP	H	ER	BB	SO
95 AL	3	2	4.42	7	0	36.2	43	18	14	19
96 AL	7	10	5.73	30	1	149.1	179	95	54	78
Life	10	12	5.47	37	1	186.0	222	113	68	97

TIM WORRELL

Position: Pitcher
Team: San Diego Padres
Born: July 5, 1967 Pasadena, CA
Height: 6'4" **Weight:** 220 lbs.
Bats: right **Throws:** right
Acquired: 20th-round pick in 6/89 free-agent draft

PLAYER SUMMARY	
Fantasy Value	$4 to $6
Card Value	4¢ to 7¢
Will	work often
Can't	nail down starting job
Expect	strikeouts
Don't Expect	many homers

Like his older brother Todd, Tim graduated from small Biola University in La Mirada, California. Unlike his older brother Todd, the Dodgers' relief ace, Tim has shown himself to be capable of both starting and relieving in the majors. This versatility is a boon for Padres manager Bruce Bochy, but occasionally it gave Tim some headaches. He began the year in the bullpen, filled in as a starter when Andy Ashby went down with a shoulder injury, then returned to the bullpen down the stretch. Worrell prefers starting and made his displeasure at relief work known throughout the season. He is a hard thrower but has not yet shown the consistent stamina required to go six or more innings. As a result, he may begin 1997 back in the bullpen. Wherever he pitches, Worrell is valuable; right-handers batted just .218 against him last year and opponents hit just nine homers on the season. Control improvements made him extremely valuable as a middle-of-the-inning pitcher, and he did a good job cutting off opponents' running ability with an impressive pickoff move.

Major League Pitching Register

	W	L	ERA	G	S	IP	H	ER	BB	SO
93 NL	2	7	4.92	21	0	100.2	104	55	43	52
94 NL	0	1	3.68	3	0	14.2	9	6	5	14
95 NL	1	0	4.72	9	0	13.1	16	7	6	13
96 NL	9	7	3.05	50	1	121.0	109	41	39	99
Life	12	15	3.93	83	1	249.2	238	109	93	178

TODD WORRELL

Position: Pitcher
Team: Los Angeles Dodgers
Born: Sept. 28, 1959 Arcadia, CA
Height: 6'5" **Weight:** 222 lbs.
Bats: right **Throws:** right
Acquired: Signed as a free agent, 12/92

PLAYER SUMMARY	
Fantasy Value	$25 to $30
Card Value	5¢ to 8¢
Will	get 30 saves
Can't	throw old fastball
Expect	streaky performance
Don't Expect	long-term closer duty

Worrell was used frequently and was effective just as frequently in the closer role for the Dodgers in 1996. His 44 saves were the most ever for a Dodger reliever, and Worrell seems to be completely healed from his past arm woes. He was able to come back without rest on many occasions, and his 72 appearances were his highest total since 1987. He still strikes out one batter an inning and is an imposing presence on the mound. Worrell allowed more hits than innings pitched, but that can be attributed to a couple of really poor outings rather than general ineffectiveness through the season. On a team lacking in offense and unable to generate come-from-behind victories, that Worrell could continually close down opponents when needed was especially important. Many fans believe that with the exception of catcher Mike Piazza, Worrell was the most valuable Dodger in 1996.

Major League Pitching Register

	W	L	ERA	G	S	IP	H	ER	BB	SO
85 NL	3	0	2.91	17	5	21.2	17	7	7	17
86 NL	9	10	2.08	74	36	103.2	86	24	41	73
87 NL	8	6	2.66	75	33	94.2	86	28	34	92
88 NL	5	9	3.00	68	32	90.0	69	30	34	78
89 NL	3	5	2.96	47	20	51.2	42	17	26	41
92 NL	5	3	2.11	67	3	64.0	45	15	25	64
93 NL	1	1	6.05	35	5	38.2	46	26	11	31
94 NL	6	5	4.29	38	11	42.0	37	20	12	44
95 NL	4	1	2.02	59	32	62.1	50	14	19	61
96 NL	4	6	3.03	72	44	65.1	70	22	15	66
Life	48	46	2.88	552	221	634.0	548	203	224	567
3 Ave	6	5	3.05	64	32	65.0	59	22	18	66

ANTHONY YOUNG

Position: Pitcher
Team: Houston Astros
Born: Jan. 19, 1966 Houston, TX
Height: 6'2" **Weight:** 220 lbs.
Bats: right **Throws:** right
Acquired: Signed as a minor-league free agent, 1/96

PLAYER SUMMARY	
Fantasy Value	$0
Card Value	4¢ to 7¢
Will	throw sinkers
Can't	overcome injury
Expect	another chance
Don't Expect	significant role

For Young, 1996 was far from a dream homecoming. Coming into the year with a fine 1.89 career ERA as a reliever, he was inked to bolster the Astros weak middle relief corps. Although he made the club out of spring training, he did not enjoy much of a comeback season. In fact, Young only added to his reputation as a pitcher who simply can't get anyone out despite his gifts. Young underwent serious elbow surgery in 1994, and since then has not been able to find the plate consistently. When healthy, he throws a good sinking fastball that induces ground balls. Unfortunately, without control, Young has very little to bank on and was hit very hard in 1996. He allowed left-handers a sky-high .357 mark and—since he does not throw very hard or have another "out pitch"—could not get a strikeout when he needed one. By season's end, he was pitching at Triple-A Tucson, where he suffered a recurrence of his elbow troubles. Young's future is uncertain at best.

Major League Pitching Register

	W	L	ERA	G	S	IP	H	ER	BB	SO
91 NL	2	5	3.10	10	0	49.1	48	17	12	20
92 NL	2	14	4.17	52	15	121.0	134	56	31	64
93 NL	1	16	3.77	39	3	100.1	103	42	42	62
94 NL	4	6	3.92	20	0	114.2	103	50	46	65
95 NL	3	4	3.70	32	2	41.1	47	17	14	15
96 NL	3	3	4.59	28	0	33.1	36	17	22	19
Life	15	48	3.89	181	20	460.0	471	199	167	245
3 Ave	4	5	3.97	31	1	80.1	78	36	34	42

ERIC YOUNG

Position: Second base
Team: Colorado Rockies
Born: May 18, 1967 New Brunswick, NJ
Height: 5'9" **Weight:** 170 lbs.
Bats: right **Throws:** right
Acquired: First-round pick from Dodgers in 11/92 expansion draft

PLAYER SUMMARY	
Fantasy Value	$20 to $25
Card Value	12¢ to 20¢
Will	run often
Can't	add much pop
Expect	regular duty
Don't Expect	Gold Glove defense

Young missed the first few weeks of 1996 with a broken right hand, but he hit well once he returned. The Colorado spark plug was able to keep his performance up all season and proved he is one of the better pure leadoff hitters in the NL. He led the league with 53 stolen bases, ranked in the top ten in batting average, and was also near the top in on-base percentage. Perhaps the most amazing thing about Young's season was his discipline at the plate. He walked 47 times, not an overly impressive total for a leadoff hitter, but fanned only 31 times in 568 at bats, ranking him among the hardest to strike out in the entire league. Young started his career as a second baseman, switched to the outfield, and then switched back to second in 1995. Although he made just 12 errors in 1996, he has a poor throwing arm and is not good on the double play. Young's home and road stats were miles apart (he hit .412 in Coors Field and a poor .219 on the road), but he can eventually overcome that.

Major League Batting Register

	BA	G	AB	R	H	2B	3B	HR	RBI	SB
92 NL	.258	49	132	9	34	1	0	1	11	6
93 NL	.269	144	490	82	132	16	8	3	42	42
94 NL	.272	90	228	37	62	13	1	7	30	18
95 NL	.317	120	366	68	116	21	9	6	36	35
96 NL	.324	141	568	113	184	23	4	8	74	53
Life	.296	544	1784	309	528	74	22	25	193	154
3 Ave	.309	134	434	81	134	22	5	8	52	39

KEVIN YOUNG

Position: First base; third base
Team: Kansas City Royals
Born: June 16, 1969 Alpena, MI
Height: 6'2" **Weight:** 219 lbs.
Bats: right **Throws:** right
Acquired: Signed as a minor-league free agent, 3/96

PLAYER SUMMARY	
Fantasy Value	$0
Card Value	4¢ to 7¢
Will	rip lefty pitching
Can't	avoid strikeouts
Expect	occasional power
Don't Expect	accurate throws

Rescued from the Pittsburgh farm system last season, Young began to realize the potential the Pirates had long predicted for him. Used primarily against left-handed pitchers, he hit a robust .322 vs. southpaws and had eight home runs and 23 RBI in 132 at bats. He hit only .089 against right-handers but was seldom used against them. An aggressive hitter who fans three times per walk, Young needs to shorten his long swing. He runs well enough to fatten his average with bunts and infield hits and could also become a double-digit basestealer. Young's best assets are his youth and his versatility. He played the infield and outfield corners last year in addition to serving as a DH. Young has quick reactions, good range, and soft hands but sometimes has trouble with throws. He led American Association third basemen in chances, assists, and double plays in 1992 and NL first basemen with a .998 fielding percentage a year later. Because of the minimum amount of throwing involved, first base is probably his best position.

Major League Batting Register

	BA	G	AB	R	H	2B	3B	HR	RBI	SB
92 NL	.571	10	7	2	4	0	0	0	4	1
93 NL	.236	141	449	38	106	24	3	6	47	2
94 NL	.205	59	122	15	25	7	2	1	11	0
95 NL	.232	56	181	13	42	9	0	6	22	1
96 AL	.242	55	132	20	32	6	0	8	23	3
Life	.235	321	891	88	209	46	5	21	107	7

TODD ZEILE

Position: Third base
Team: Los Angeles Dodgers
Born: Sept. 9, 1965 Van Nuys, CA
Height: 6'1" **Weight:** 200 lbs.
Bats: right **Throws:** right
Acquired: Signed as a free agent, 12/96

PLAYER SUMMARY	
Fantasy Value	$10 to $13
Card Value	8¢ to 12¢
Will	hit homers
Can't	run well
Expect	fair glovework
Don't Expect	star status

Zeile was a disappointment for Baltimore after coming over late in the year. He was Philadelphia's top hitter for most of the season but became expendable when the woeful Phils decided to go with rookie phenom Scott Rolen at third. Zeile started fast for the Birds, but overall he hit only .239 with five homers. Baltimore had been hoping he could provide more punch during the playoff drive. Shortly after the World Series ended, Zeile told reporters he had been informed the club would not offer him a contract because they intended to move Cal Ripken to third base. This turn of events didn't surprise Zeile, since a shift of Ripken to third had been discussed for most of last year. In addition, 1996 was Zeile's second straight subpar season. Zeile, who can play both third and first, hits left-handers well and will be valuable to the Dodgers, a team looking to shore up its infield.

Major League Batting Register

	BA	G	AB	R	H	2B	3B	HR	RBI	SB
89 NL	.256	28	82	7	21	3	1	1	8	0
90 NL	.244	144	495	62	121	25	3	15	57	2
91 NL	.280	155	565	76	158	36	3	11	81	17
92 NL	.257	126	439	51	113	18	4	7	48	7
93 NL	.277	157	571	82	158	36	1	17	103	5
94 NL	.267	113	415	62	111	25	1	19	75	1
95 NL	.246	113	426	50	105	22	0	14	52	1
96 NL	.268	134	500	61	134	24	0	20	80	1
96 AL	.239	29	117	17	28	8	0	5	19	0
Life	.263	999	3610	468	949	197	13	109	523	34
3 Ave	.261	140	521	68	136	28	0	21	81	1

CHUCK ABBOTT

Position: Shortstop
Team: Anaheim Angels
Born: Jan. 6, 1975 Chicago, IL
Height: 6'1" **Weight:** 180 lbs.
Bats: right **Throws:** right
Acquired: Second-round pick in 6/96 free-agent draft

PLAYER SUMMARY	
Fantasy Value	$0
Card Value	15¢ to 20¢
Will	steal bases
Can't	provide much power
Expect	infield hits
Don't Expect	another Erstad

Abbott owns the distinction of being the Angels' first selection in the 1996 draft, but it would be unrealistic to expect him to arrive as quickly as Darin Erstad, who was the Angels' initial pick a year earlier. Whereas Erstad came as the top pick in the entire '95 draft, Abbott went untabbed until the 55th overall selection in '96. California had lost its first-round pick in exchange for signing free agent Randy Velarde in the previous off-season, and thus had to watch almost two full rounds before participating in the draft. When the Angels finally got to call out a name, however, it belonged to Abbott. Abbott went to school at Austin Peay in Tennessee, where he piled up some impressive offensive credentials. A shortstop, he builds his game on speed. Upon signing, he reported to Boise of the Northwest League, where he had some trouble with his first look at pro pitching. But he did get quite a few at bats, and that experience should help him this year.

Professional Batting Register

	BA	G	AB	R	H	2B	3B	HR	RBI	SB
96 A	.198	70	268	41	53	9	2	0	20	11

JEFF ABBOTT

Position: Outfield
Team: Chicago White Sox
Born: Aug. 17, 1972 Atlanta, GA
Height: 6'2" **Weight:** 190 lbs.
Bats: right **Throws:** left
Acquired: Fourth-round pick in 6/96 free-agent draft

PLAYER SUMMARY	
Fantasy Value	$0
Card Value	10¢ to 15¢
Will	reward persistence
Can't	run
Expect	few whiffs
Don't Expect	big power numbers

A little bit of persistence has given the White Sox one of their top hitting prospects. They first picked Abbott in the 32nd round of the 1993 draft, but he declined to sign. They went after him again a year later, and this time they got him. Ever since, he has blasted his way through minor-league pitching, and he appears on the verge of giving major-leaguers the same treatment. Last year, he compiled a successful season with Chicago's Triple-A club in Nashville, hitting for average and putting the ball in play. He batted in the leadoff spot and played left field for the American League squad in the Triple-A All-Star Game. Abbott attended the University of Kentucky, where he set a school record with 182 runs scored even though he missed most of the 1993 campaign due to a bout with mononucleosis. He has not demonstrated exceptional power so far in the pro ranks, but that aspect may develop with a little experience. Right now, his style seems to have served him very well.

Professional Batting Register

	BA	G	AB	R	H	2B	3B	HR	RBI	SB
94 R	.467	4	15	4	7	1	0	1	3	2
94 A	.393	63	224	47	88	16	6	6	48	2
95 A	.348	70	264	41	92	16	0	4	47	7
95 AA	.320	55	197	25	63	11	1	3	28	1
96 AAA	.325	113	440	64	143	27	1	14	60	12

BOB ABREU

Position: Outfield
Team: Houston Astros
Born: March 11, 1974 Aragua, Venezuela
Height: 6' **Weight:** 160 lbs.
Bats: left **Throws:** right
Acquired: Signed as a nondrafted free agent, 8/90

PLAYER SUMMARY

Fantasy Value	. . . . $1
Card Value	. . . . 10¢ to 15¢
Will	. . . . find a job somewhere
Can't	. . . . let strikeouts climb
Expect	. . . . stolen bases
Don't Expect	. . . . singles hitter

Abreu has ranked with the top prospects for a few years now, ever since he hit at or near .300 three times before reaching his 20th birthday. Now, after six years of pro ball, he should be ready to make an impact somewhere. Last season, in his second year at Triple-A, Abreu did all that anyone could ask of him. Not only did he deliver his usual solid batting average, but he also set a career high in stolen bases (24). He also cut down his strikeout total, which had reached disturbing proportions. He piled up double digits in doubles, triples, and homers, giving him a healthy slugging percentage. That's not unusual for him; he led the Texas League with a .530 slugging mark in 1994. In 1995, he led all professional players with 17 triples. He'll hit some homers, but he's really an extra-base man. Despite Abreu's lengthy minor-league experience, he's only 23 years old. With his bat, it's hard to imagine him not fitting in somewhere.

Professional Batting Register

	BA	G	AB	R	H	2B	3B	HR	RBI	SB
91 R	.301	56	183	21	55	7	3	0	20	10
92 A	.292	135	480	81	140	21	4	8	48	15
93 A	.283	129	474	62	134	21	17	5	55	10
94 AA	.303	118	400	61	121	25	9	16	73	12
95 AAA	.304	114	415	72	126	24	17	10	75	16
96 AAA	.283	132	484	86	137	14	16	13	68	24
96 NL	.227	15	22	1	5	1	0	0	1	0

JERMAINE ALLENSWORTH

Position: Outfield
Team: Pittsburgh Pirates
Born: Jan. 11, 1972 Anderson, IN
Height: 6' **Weight:** 190 lbs.
Bats: right **Throws:** right
Acquired: Supplemental pick in 6/93 free-agent draft

PLAYER SUMMARY

Fantasy Value	. . . . $4 to $6
Card Value	. . . . 10¢ to 15¢
Will	. . . . lead off
Can't	. . . . rule out power
Expect	. . . . top skills
Don't Expect	. . . . consistent contact

Doug Drabek has long since left the Pittsburgh organization, but his presence is still being felt in the person of Allensworth. Allensworth arrived via a pick awarded when Drabek left as a free agent, and now that he has reached the majors, he could be there a long time. Allensworth is a product of Madison Heights High School in Anderson, Indiana, and he went on to play three years of baseball for Purdue. Upon signing with the Pirates, he rose quickly through the system, completing his trip to the majors in his fourth pro season. He broke in with Welland of the New York-Penn League and made the All-Star Team. He also was named the team's Most Valuable Player. Promoted all the way to Double-A in 1994, he collected 26 doubles. He split 1995 between Double- and Triple-A. As a leadoff man for the Pirates, Allensworth will have to draw more walks and improve his contact. When he first joined the Bucs, lefties gave him trouble, but he has since learned to face them.

Professional Batting Register

	BA	G	AB	R	H	2B	3B	HR	RBI	SB
93 A	.308	67	263	44	81	16	4	1	32	18
94 AA	.241	118	452	63	109	26	8	1	34	16
95 AA	.269	56	219	37	59	14	2	1	14	13
95 AAA	.316	51	190	46	60	13	4	3	11	13
96 AAA	.330	95	352	77	116	23	6	8	43	25
96 NL	.262	61	229	32	60	9	3	4	31	11

Richard Almanzar

Position: Second base
Team: Detroit Tigers
Born: April 3, 1976 San Francisco de Macoris, Dominican Republic
Height: 5'10" **Weight:** 155 lbs.
Bats: right **Throws:** right
Acquired: Signed as a nondrafted free agent, 5/93

Player Summary	
Fantasy Value	$0
Card Value	10¢ to 15¢
Will	run
Can't	be a slugger
Expect	a tough out
Don't Expect	Detroit this year

In Almanzar's four years of pro ball, he has never stolen fewer than 43 bases in a season. His first campaign came in the Dominican Summer League when Almanzar was just 17 years old. In his second season, Almanzar stole 105 bases (a DSL record) in only 238 at bats. More important, Almanzar thrived when promoted to the Florida State League last year. He responded by finishing second in the Tiger chain in both steals and batting average. Almanzar maintained his career pattern of fashioning a healthy ratio of strikeouts to walks. That's significant because given his ability to run and his lack of power, Almanzar wants to be getting on base any way he can. He loves to put the ball in play to give him a chance for infield hits. He plays second base, a position handled by Mark Lewis last year. Within a year or two, Almanzar could challenge for a job at second and a spot at the top of the Tiger lineup.

Gabe Alvarez

Position: Infield
Team: San Diego Padres
Born: March 6, 1974 Navojoa, Mexico
Height: 6'1" **Weight:** 185 lbs.
Bats: right **Throws:** right
Acquired: Second-round pick in 6/95 free-agent draft

Player Summary	
Fantasy Value	$0
Card Value	15¢ to 20¢
Will	be solid at plate
Can't	duplicate Fernando
Expect	medium power
Don't Expect	a shortstop

Alvarez comes from the same Mexican town that produced Fernando Valenzuela, and the Padres would be ecstatic if Alvarez could enjoy that degree of success. Right now, the chance definitely exists. Alvarez played for Memphis in the Double-A Southern League last year and delivered a solid, if not spectacular, season. Keep in mind it was only his first full season of pro ball. Alvarez comes out of the University of Southern California, where he was named a third-team All-American as a shortstop and led the Trojans to the College World Series title game. After being drafted, he played in the California League. In only his third pro game, Alvarez turned an unassisted triple play, catching a line drive, stepping on second, and tagging out the runner coming from first. He received a late-season promotion to Double-A, where he collected five hits in nine at bats. After seeing action at both shortstop and second base in 1995, Alvarez was moved to third base last year.

Professional Batting Register

	BA	G	AB	R	H	2B	3B	HR	RBI	SB
94 R	.000	65	238	72	76	10	3	1	37	105
95 A	.247	80	308	47	76	12	1	0	16	32
95 A	.307	42	140	29	43	9	0	1	14	11
96 A	.306	124	471	81	144	22	2	1	36	53

Professional Batting Register

	BA	G	AB	R	H	2B	3B	HR	RBI	SB
95 A	.344	59	212	41	73	17	2	6	36	1
95 AA	.556	2	9	0	5	1	0	0	4	0
96 AA	.247	104	368	58	91	23	1	8	40	2

JIMMY ANDERSON

Position: Pitcher
Team: Pittsburgh Pirates
Born: Jan. 22, 1976 Portsmouth, VA
Height: 6'1" **Weight:** 180 lbs.
Bats: left **Throws:** left
Acquired: Ninth-round pick in 6/95 free-agent draft

PLAYER SUMMARY	
Fantasy Value	$0
Card Value	12¢ to 20¢
Will	compete for job
Can't	rush him
Expect	No. 2 or 3 starter
Don't Expect	poor record

Look at Anderson's career record and one statistic stands out like a smudge on a painting. In 1995, he went 1-5 in his first look at the Class-A Carolina League. Those are hardly the numbers you want to see from a minor-leaguer. But the fact is, Anderson didn't pitch all that badly; he allowed only slightly more hits (56) than innings pitched (52⅓). Still, a 1-5 record gets your attention, which is why Anderson and the Pirates had to be particularly pleased with the way things went last season. Anderson ranked among the most dominant pitchers in the organization, beginning the season back in the Carolina League before earning a promotion to Double-A. Anderson finished the season among the farm system's leaders in ERA, victories, and strikeouts. During one stretch, he allowed only eight earned runs over six starts. He might get a long look from the Bucs this year in spring training, but keep in mind Anderson still is just 21 years old. There's plenty of time to let him develop at his own pace.

Professional Pitching Register

	W	L	ERA	G	CG	IP	H	ER	B	SO
94 R	5	1	1.60	10	0	56.1	35	10	27	66
95 A	4	2	1.53	14	0	76.2	51	13	31	75
95 A	1	5	4.13	10	0	52.1	56	24	21	32
96 A	5	3	1.93	11	1	65.1	51	14	21	56
96 AA	8	3	3.34	17	0	97.0	92	36	44	79

MARLON ANDERSON

Position: Infield
Team: Philadelphia Phillies
Born: Jan. 6, 1974 Montgomery, AL
Height: 5'11" **Weight:** 190 lbs.
Bats: left **Throws:** right
Acquired: Second-round pick in 6/95 free-agent draft

PLAYER SUMMARY	
Fantasy Value	$0
Card Value	15¢ to 20¢
Will	put bat on ball
Can't	play short
Expect	doubles
Don't Expect	limited range

Anderson accumulated his share of honors in 1995, being named the top player in the Sun Belt Conference, getting picked for *Baseball America*'s 1995 College All-America squad, and finally getting drafted in the second round. If Anderson's first two seasons of professional ball are any indication, the laurels won't stop there. He has shown an ability to run, field, and hit. He is alert on the field and simply has the look of a big-time player. After being drafted, Anderson signed quickly and spent the summer with Batavia of the New York-Penn League, making the All-Star squad and posting a .965 fielding percentage. Last year, he climbed rapidly, beginning the season with Class-A Clearwater, then forcing a move to Double-A. He can steal a base and get wood on the ball, making him an ideal candidate to eventually lead off for the Phils. A product of the University of South Alabama, Anderson could soon find himself in the majors.

Professional Batting Register

	BA	G	AB	R	H	2B	3B	HR	RBI	SB
95 A	.295	74	312	52	92	13	4	3	40	22
96 A	.272	60	257	37	70	10	3	2	22	26
96 AA	.274	75	314	38	86	14	3	3	28	17

DAVID ARIAS

Position: First base
Team: Seattle Mariners
Born: Feb. 18, 1975 Santo Domingo, Dominican Republic
Height: 6'4" **Weight:** 190 lbs.
Bats: left **Throws:** left
Acquired: Signed as a nondrafted free agent, 11/92

PLAYER SUMMARY

Fantasy Value	$0
Card Value	15¢ to 25¢
Will	score runs
Can't	rush him
Expect	extra-base pop
Don't Expect	great contact

Named in the Seattle media guide as David Americo Arias Ortiz, this young man was registered under the name Arias in various statistical accounts. No matter what you call him, the guy can hit. He enjoyed a dominating season in the Midwest League last year, ranking among the top hitters and run-producers in the Mariners farm system. He showed a tendency to strike out, hardly uncommon for a young slugger, but he compensated with plenty of extra-base power. Arias, a first baseman, hit .560 over one seven-game span from the end of July through the first week of August. Signed as a free agent by scout Ramon de los Santos, Arias began his professional career in Santo Domingo. He moved to the Arizona short-season league for two campaigns, where he was selected as the Mariners' Most Valuable Player by the organization's player development personnel. This year, Arias will likely advance a level, but he must work on his contact.

GEORGE ARIAS

Position: Infield
Team: Anaheim Angels
Born: March 12, 1972 Tucson, AZ
Height: 5'11" **Weight:** 190 lbs.
Bats: right **Throws:** right
Acquired: Seventh-round pick in 6/93 free-agent draft

PLAYER SUMMARY

Fantasy Value	$4 to $6
Card Value	10¢ to 15¢
Will	get another chance
Can't	play short or second
Expect	runs batted in
Don't Expect	another demotion

Last year, Arias made an unsuccessful attempt to complete a leap from Double-A to the majors. Coming off a monster season with Midland of the Texas League, he made the Angels out of spring training and played several weeks with them before falling into a slump. That meant more time in the minors, this time in Triple-A, but Arias made the best of the demotion and began working his way back to Anaheim. Playing for Vancouver of the Pacific Coast League, Arias hit for the highest average (.337) of his four pro seasons. His game is home runs, doubles, and RBI, with virtually no triples or stolen bases. His defensive work around third base is considered superior. Arias attended Pima Community College in Tucson, where he hit three grand slams in Junior College World Series play. He later transferred to the University of Arizona, where he also hit with great power. This year he'll get another shot at the Angels third base job.

Professional Batting Register

	BA	G	AB	R	H	2B	3B	HR	RBI	SB
94 R	.246	53	167	14	41	10	1	2	20	1
95 R	.332	48	184	30	61	18	4	4	37	2
96 A	.322	129	485	89	156	34	2	18	93	3

Professional Batting Register

	BA	G	AB	R	H	2B	3B	HR	RBI	SB
93 A	.217	74	253	31	55	13	3	9	41	6
94 A	.280	134	514	89	144	28	3	23	80	6
95 AA	.279	134	520	91	145	19	10	30	104	3
96 AAA	.337	59	243	49	82	24	0	9	55	2
96 AL	.238	84	252	19	60	8	1	6	28	2

347

PAUL BAKO

Position: Catcher
Team: Cincinnati Reds
Born: June 20, 1972 Lafayette, LA
Height: 6'2" **Weight:** 195 lbs.
Bats: left **Throws:** right
Acquired: Fifth-round pick in 6/93 free-agent draft

PLAYER SUMMARY	
Fantasy Value	$0
Card Value	15¢ to 20¢
Will	meet challenges
Can't	reduce Ks
Expect	progress
Don't Expect	return to Class-A

Judging by Bako's 1994 statistics, it's unlikely anyone would have spotted him great odds of reaching the majors. After all, a .204 average in Class-A ball doesn't exactly put someone on the fast track, no matter what his defensive skills. But Bako wouldn't settle for an early end to his career. He worked to make himself a hitter and succeeded to the point where he soon could be competing for a job in Cincinnati. Last year, while playing for Chattanooga of the Double-A Southern League, Bako enjoyed his best season in four years as a pro. Bako was selected as a Double-A All-Star but did not get to play in the game. As of July 31, he ranked third among all Reds farmhands in batting average and already had set career bests in runs, doubles, and RBI. He will have to cut down on his strikeouts while continuing his solid work around the plate. Considering Bako's ability to handle challenges, it's easy to believe he'll be in the majors soon.

LARRY BARNES

Position: Infield
Team: Anaheim Angels
Born: July 23, 1974 Bakersfield, CA
Height: 6'1" **Weight:** 195 lbs.
Bats: left **Throws:** left
Acquired: Signed as a nondrafted free agent, 6/95

PLAYER SUMMARY	
Fantasy Value	$0
Card Value	10¢ to 15¢
Will	overcome draft status
Can't	stop working
Expect	extra bases
Don't Expect	a nobody

A player who somehow doesn't get drafted but winds up signing on as a free agent must do something special if he's going to get noticed. And so far, in two professional seasons, Barnes has been nothing but special. He has topped the .300 mark twice, and last year in the Midwest League he registered an exceptional performance. He collected 68 extra-base hits, made the All-Star Team at first base, and was named the league MVP. Barnes comes out of Fresno State University and reported to the Mesa Angels of the rookie Arizona State League, where he led the club in RBI and batting average. Last year he was even better. No one else in the California minor-league system came close to him in terms of offensive production. Now the Angels face a decision on this year's assignment. They can either move Barnes to their High A club or give him a chance at the Double-A level. Either way, he could be challenging for a job in the bigs by 1998.

Professional Batting Register

	BA	G	AB	R	H	2B	3B	HR	RBI	SB
93 R	.314	57	194	34	61	11	0	4	30	5
94 A	.204	90	289	29	59	9	1	3	26	2
95 A	.285	82	249	29	71	11	2	7	27	3
96 AA	.294	110	360	53	106	27	0	8	48	1

Professional Batting Register

	BA	G	AB	R	H	2B	3B	HR	RBI	SB
95 R	.310	56	197	42	61	8	3	3	37	12
96 A	.317	131	489	84	155	36	5	27	112	9

MICHAEL BARRETT

Position: Catcher
Team: Montreal Expos
Born: Oct. 22, 1976 Atlanta, GA
Height: 6'3" **Weight:** 185 lbs.
Bats: right **Throws:** right
Acquired: First-round pick in 6/95 free-agent draft

PLAYER SUMMARY	
Fantasy Value	$0
Card Value	15¢ to 20¢
Will	throw runners out
Can't	play short
Expect	steady progress
Don't Expect	expert defense

The Expos had to wait until the 28th pick to make their first selection in the 1995 draft. When their turn finally came, though, they virtually got two players in one. It appears that Barrett, who was a shortstop in high school, will advance through the pro ranks as a catcher. Not only has Barrett made this very difficult switch, but he's managed to keep his offense together while doing so. So now the Expos have a versatile prospect they believe can make an impact with his bat. The move to catcher made sense, because when the Expos drafted Barrett, there was a good deal of enthusiasm over his arm strength. Then there's the matter of his frame, which is large enough to handle the tough work behind the plate. It's still too early to predict if Barrett can be the prototypical power-hitting catcher, but he collected his share of doubles (29) with Delmarva of the Class-A South Atlantic League last year, playing at the tender age of just 19.

Professional Batting Register

	BA	G	AB	R	H	2B	3B	HR	RBI	SB
95 R	.311	50	183	22	57	13	4	0	19	7
95 A	.100	3	10	0	1	0	0	0	1	0
96 A	.238	129	474	57	113	29	4	4	62	5

TREY BEAMON

Position: Outfield
Team: Pittsburgh Pirates
Born: Feb. 11, 1974 Dallas, TX
Height: 6'3" **Weight:** 195 lbs.
Bats: left **Throws:** right
Acquired: Supplemental pick in 6/92 free-agent draft

PLAYER SUMMARY	
Fantasy Value	$0
Card Value	12¢ to 20¢
Will	fit in somewhere
Can't	ignore him on bases
Expect	good left bat
Don't Expect	power

Beamon was part of a productive 1992 draft that also included catcher Jason Kendall. It took Beamon a little longer than Kendall to get to the big leagues, but now that he has arrived, he could make an impact. Beamon can hit, as shown by the fact that in 1994 he became the youngest player ever to win a Southern League batting title (.323). He kept right on hitting when promoted to Calgary in 1995, finishing third in the Pacific Coast League batting race. Last year, Beamon was right around the .300 mark when summoned to Pittsburgh. One curious side of Beamon is a mysterious lack of power, despite his size and his obvious hitting skills. To hit only five homers in 452 Pacific Coast League at bats, as Beamon did in 1995, raises questions about power potential. Beamon's full name is Clifford Beamon III, and he was nicknamed "Trey" because he was the third Clifford. He was an All-American in his senior year at William T. White High School in Dallas.

Professional Batting Register

	BA	G	AB	R	H	2B	3B	HR	RBI	SB
92 R	.308	13	39	9	12	1	0	1	6	0
92 A	.290	19	69	15	20	5	0	3	9	4
93 A	.271	104	373	64	101	18	6	0	45	19
94 AA	.323	112	434	69	140	18	9	5	47	24
95 AAA	.334	118	452	74	151	29	5	5	62	18
96 AAA	.288	111	378	62	109	15	3	5	52	16
96 NL	.216	24	51	7	11	2	0	0	6	1

JASON BELL

Position: Pitcher
Team: Minnesota Twins
Born: Sept. 30, 1974 Ocala, FL
Height: 6'3" **Weight:** 208 lbs.
Bats: right **Throws:** right
Acquired: Second-round pick in 6/95 free-agent draft

PLAYER SUMMARY	
Fantasy Value	$0
Card Value	15¢ to 20¢
Will	throw it over
Can't	avoid occasional bump
Expect	more Double-A
Don't Expect	first-round hype

Sometimes being taken in the second round instead of the first can bring great advantages. Instead of having to worry about all the expectations that come with first-round status, a player can go about his business. Such seems to be the case with Bell, the 43rd overall pick in 1995. Out of Oklahoma State University, Bell enjoyed a superb first season as a pro, going 3-1 with a 1.31 ERA for Fort Wayne of the Class-A Midwest League. His strikeout-to-walk ratio of 40-to-6 in 34⅓ innings could not fail to impress. Last year, he advanced to high Class-A ball with Fort Myers of the Florida State League. Once again showing his ability to throw the ball over the plate with something on it, Bell went 6-1 in 13 starts and ranked among the league's ERA leaders. Boosted to Double-A ball, Bell didn't enjoy the same level of success, but it's only natural to expect some adjustments along the way. He'll probably see more Double-A this year, and he'll take it from there.

RONNIE BELLIARD

Position: Second base
Team: Milwaukee Brewers
Born: July 4, 1976 Bronx, NY
Height: 5'8" **Weight:** 180 lbs.
Bats: right **Throws:** right
Acquired: Eighth-round pick in 6/94 free-agent draft

PLAYER SUMMARY	
Fantasy Value	$0
Card Value	15¢ to 20¢
Will	help the lineup
Can't	neglect shoulder
Expect	good fielding
Don't Expect	power numbers

Considering the circumstances, Belliard assembled quite a season last year. Not only did he make the jump from low Class-A ball to Double-A, but he did so after suffering a shoulder injury that delayed the start of his season. Despite all that, Belliard was a regular at second base for El Paso, hitting for average and enjoying success on the basepaths. And he's still only 20 years old. Belliard offers a solid offensive game based on mixing in some extra-base hits, making consistent contact, drawing the occasional walk, stealing bases, and scoring runs. He didn't hit the ball out of the park very often last year, but he had 13 homers in 1995 to help Beloit to a first-place finish. As for his glovework, *Baseball America* named Belliard the Texas League's best defensive second baseman. The same speed that enables him to steal bases also gives him good range around second sack. All indications are that Belliard will move to Triple-A before long, provided, of course, that his shoulder cooperates.

Professional Pitching Register

	W	L	ERA	G	CG	IP	H	ER	BB	SO
95 A	3	1	1.31	9	0	34.1	26	5	6	40
96 A	6	3	1.69	16	0	90.1	61	17	22	83
96 AA	2	6	4.40	13	2	94.0	93	46	38	94

Professional Batting Register

	BA	G	AB	R	H	2B	3B	HR	RBI	SB
94 R	.294	39	143	32	42	7	3	0	27	7
95 A	.297	130	461	76	137	28	5	13	76	16
96 AA	.279	109	416	73	116	20	8	3	57	26

ADRIAN BELTRE

Position: Third base
Team: Los Angeles Dodgers
Born: April 7, 1978 Santo Domingo,
Dominican Republic
Height: 5'11" **Weight:** 165 lbs.
Bats: right **Throws:** right
Acquired: Signed as a nondrafted free agent,
7/94

PLAYER SUMMARY	
Fantasy Value	$0
Card Value	12¢ to 20¢
Will	provide power
Can't	steal many bases
Expect	ROTY candidate
Don't Expect	big build

The Dodgers, who already have won the
Rookie of the Year Award far more than
any other franchise, own still another top
prospect. Last year, Beltre tore up two
leagues, the South Atlantic and the California, in his first experience among North American ball. He ranked among the top five
Dodger farmhands in home runs, and also
led all Dodger minor-leaguers in RBI. Beltre opened the season at 17 years of age
as the starting third baseman for Savannah
of the Sally League. He performed well
enough to play in the league's All-Star
Game, where he went 2-for-2. *Baseball
America* tabbed Beltre as the league's best
hitting prospect, best power prospect, and
most exciting player. When promoted to the
California League, Beltre started off in a
slump and had to battle against much more
experienced players. Out of Liceo Maximo
Gomez High School, Beltre signed a pro
contract on his 16th birthday, and it's quite
possible he'll play in the big leagues by the
time he's 20 years old.

KRIS BENSON

Position: Pitcher
Team: Pittsburgh Pirates
Born: Nov. 7, 1974 Duluth, MN
Height: 6'4" **Weight:** 182 lbs.
Bats: right **Throws:** right
Acquired: First-round pick in 6/96 free-agent
draft

PLAYER SUMMARY	
Fantasy Value	$0
Card Value	30¢ to 40¢
Will	fit in quickly
Can't	let hype get to him
Expect	big game worries
Don't Expect	a bust

Now comes the hard part for Benson. He
enjoyed an honor-filled year in 1996, taking
Clemson to the College World Series,
being named *Baseball America*'s College
Player of the Year, making the U.S.
Olympic team, and becoming the first overall selection in the draft. Now he must cope
with the expectations and scrutiny that
come with being a top selection. Already,
his performance in the spotlight of the
Olympics and College World Series has
drawn some attention. He allowed nine
runs in seven innings against Miami in a
key College World Series game. And he
permitted three homers in an Olympic stint
against Japan. Despite these setbacks,
Benson brings a lot of potential to the Pirates. He's got a fastball that can blow past
hitters, and he looks like a pitcher who
could step into the majors quickly and
make an impact. With the Olympics having
occupied his focus, Benson was still un-
signed as of early August. But watch out for
him this season.

Professional Batting Register

	BA	G	AB	R	H	2B	3B	HR	RBI	SB
95 R	.307	62	218	56	67	15	3	8	40	2
96 A	.261	63	238	40	62	13	1	10	40	3
96 A	.307	68	244	48	75	14	3	16	59	4

BRIAN BEVIL

Position: Pitcher
Team: Kansas City Royals
Born: Sept. 5, 1971 Houston, TX
Height: 6'3" **Weight:** 190 lbs.
Bats: right **Throws:** right
Acquired: 30th-round pick in 6/90 free-agent
draft

PLAYER SUMMARY	
Fantasy Value	$0
Card Value	8¢ to 12¢
Will	field position well
Can't	get over hump
Expect	a journeyman
Don't Expect	No. 1 starter

Bevil is hoping he has finally seen the last
of Double-A ball after spending at least
some time there for the fourth straight season. And maybe he has. Last year, Bevil finally made it to the big leagues, making his
debut on June 17. Even though that appearance was far from auspicious—he allowed three runs in three relief innings—it
had to beat the treadmill of Double-A. Bevil
began the season by putting up fine numbers for Wichita, even being named to the
Texas League All-Star Team. Then again,
when he broke in, Bevil had the look of an
All-Star. In 1992, he led the Kansas City organization with 168 strikeouts while pitching in the Midwest League. A year later,
Bevil compiled a 7-1 mark with Wilmington
of the Carolina League. Then came lots of
time in Double-A, with plenty of discour-
agement. Now that he's reached the majors, he'll have to show whether he's truly
over the hump, or if he has merely peaked.

Professional Pitching Register

	W	L	ERA	G	CG	IP	H	ER	BB	SO
91 R	5	3	1.93	13	2	65.1	56	14	19	70
92 A	9	7	3.40	26	4	156.0	129	59	63	168
93 A	7	1	2.30	12	2	74.1	46	19	23	61
93 AA	3	3	4.36	6	0	33.0	36	16	14	26
94 AA	5	4	3.51	17	0	100.0	75	39	40	78
95 AA	5	7	5.84	15	0	74.0	85	48	35	57
95 AAA	1	3	9.41	6	0	22.0	40	23	14	10
96 AA	9	2	2.02	13	2	75.2	56	17	26	74
96 AAA	7	5	4.12	12	0	67.2	62	31	19	73
96 AL	1	0	5.73	3	0	11.0	9	7	5	7

NICK BIERBRODT

Position: Pitcher
Team: Arizona Diamondbacks
Born: May 16, 1978 Tarzana, CA
Height: 6'5" **Weight:** 185 lbs.
Bats: left **Throws:** left
Acquired: First-round pick in 6/96 free-agent
draft

PLAYER SUMMARY	
Fantasy Value	$0
Card Value	20¢ to 35¢
Will	throw strikes
Can't	be distracted by hype
Expect	90-mph fastball
Don't Expect	quick ascent

Bierbrodt made history before he threw
even one pitch as a professional. That's because he was the first player taken in the
amateur draft by the expansion Diamondbacks, who are scheduled to begin play in
1998. Bierbrodt was the last man selected
in the first round, though the Diamondbacks
say they had their eye on him long before
their turn—the 30th—came. Bierbrodt
comes out of Millikan High School in Long
Beach, California, where he turned in an
eye-opening season in his junior year, posting an ERA well under 1.00 and averaging
about 1.5 strikeouts per inning. An injury
slowed him a bit in his senior year, but the
Snakes liked him anyway. Bierbrodt signed
and thrived as the 'Backs eased him into
pro ball. He allowed only nine hits over his
first four appearances with Phoenix of the
Arizona League. After eight games, he was
promoted to Lethbridge of the Pioneer
League. This year, expect to see him in a
low Class-A league.

Professional Pitching Register

	W	L	ERA	G	CG	IP	H	ER	BB	SO
96 R	1	1	1.66	8	0	38.0	25	7	13	46
96 R	2	0	0.50	3	0	18.0	12	1	5	23

DARIN BLOOD

Position: Pitcher
Team: San Francisco Giants
Born: Aug. 31, 1974 Spokane, WA
Height: 6'2" **Weight:** 200 lbs.
Bats: right **Throws:** right
Acquired: Third-round pick in 6/95 free-agent draft

PLAYER SUMMARY

Fantasy Value	$0
Card Value	12¢ to 20¢
Will	strike men out
Can't	do more in A ball
Expect	big repertoire
Don't Expect	many hits

In his two years as a pro, Blood has done nothing but justify the Giants' judgment in making him a high-round pick. Not only has he registered two dominating seasons, but he handled the jump from rookie ball to high Class-A in virtually seamless fashion. In fact, Blood emerged as one of San Francisco's top farmhands while pitching for San Jose in the California League. He led the entire chain in victories and strikeouts by a wide margin, and his hits-to-innings ratio was superb. Among his outings was a two-hit, 1-0 victory over Lancaster on July 27. He made the Cal League All-Star Team and pitched two scoreless innings against the Carolina League standouts. One of Blood's teammates at San Jose was Joe Fontenot, who was drafted two rounds ahead of him in 1995. Blood certainly didn't suffer by comparison. Out of Central Valley High School in Veradale, Washington, Blood attended Gonzaga University, once fanning 18 batters in a game.

HIRAM BOCACHICA

Position: Infield
Team: Montreal Expos
Born: March 4, 1976 Ponce, Puerto Rico
Height: 5'11" **Weight:** 170 lbs.
Bats: right **Throws:** right
Acquired: First-round pick in 6/94 free-agent draft

PLAYER SUMMARY

Fantasy Value	$0
Card Value	15¢ to 20¢
Will	steal bases
Can't	stay healthy
Expect	great offense
Don't Expect	great defense

Bocachica's chances of making an impact in the big leagues are hard to figure, not due to any lack of talent, but because of injuries. Last year, Bocachica seemed headed for a monster year in the Florida State League only to be sidelined with an elbow problem. This happened one season after an ankle injury kept him from playing a full South Atlantic League schedule. Then there's the matter of defense, an area in which Bocachica needs some work. A perfect example came on July 30, when he committed three errors in a game against Brevard County but helped atone for it with a three-run homer. He made an error in every game from August 18 to August 25. As Bocachica approaches the majors, he'll find it harder and harder to make up for his defensive lapses. His bat will take him only so far. Nevertheless, if he can stay healthy, he should get some time in Double-A ball this year. Whether he'll wind up as a shortstop, a bench player, or the designated hitter is another question.

Professional Pitching Register

	W	L	ERA	G	CG	IP	H	ER	BB	SO
95 A	6	3	2.54	14	0	74.1	63	21	32	78
96 A	17	6	2.65	27	2	170.0	140	50	71	193

Professional Batting Register

	BA	G	AB	R	H	2B	3B	HR	RBI	SB
94 R	.280	43	168	31	47	9	0	5	16	11
95 A	.284	96	380	65	108	20	10	2	30	47
96 R	.250	9	32	11	8	3	0	0	2	2
96 A	.337	71	267	50	90	17	5	2	26	21

AARON BOONE

Position: Third base
Team: Cincinnati Reds
Born: March 9, 1973 La Mesa, CA
Height: 6'2" **Weight:** 190 lbs.
Bats: right **Throws:** right
Acquired: Third-round pick in 6/94 free-agent
draft

PLAYER SUMMARY	
Fantasy Value	$0
Card Value	20¢ to 30¢
Will	play third
Can't	escape scrutiny
Expect	eventual job in bigs
Don't Expect	a flop

Boone should soon be in the majors, joining his brother Bret, who plays second base for Cincinnati, and father Bob, the Kansas City Royals manager. Aaron performed for Chattanooga of the Southern League last year, showing no ill effects from a slump and a demotion the previous year. He showed both power and speed at third base for the Lookouts, indicating he could eventually challenge Willie Greene for the same spot with the Reds. Boone graduated from Villa Park High School in California, where he played three sports. He attended the University of Southern California, batting .308 over three seasons. He began his pro career with Billings of the Pioneer League, leading all third basemen in chances, putouts, and assists. Promoted all the way to Double-A in 1995, Boone wasn't ready for the jump and was reassigned to the Carolina League after just 23 games. There he prospered, making the All-Star Team and laying the groundwork for a triumphant return to Double-A.

RUSS BRANYAN

Position: Infield
Team: Cleveland Indians
Born: Dec. 19, 1975 Warner Robins, GA
Height: 6'3" **Weight:** 195 lbs.
Bats: left **Throws:** right
Acquired: Seventh-round pick in 6/94 free-agent draft

PLAYER SUMMARY	
Fantasy Value	$0
Card Value	15¢ to 20¢
Will	swing for fences
Can't	forget contact
Expect	homers in bunches
Don't Expect	Belle-type hitting

Even as they dominate on the major-league level, the Cleveland Indians are working hard to ensure the future. If 1996 was any indication, Branyan could well be part of those plans. Playing for Columbus of the South Atlantic League, Branyan ranked as one of the top sluggers in the entire chain. No one in the Cleveland farm system came close to hitting as many homers as Branyan did. Out of Stratford Academy High School in Georgia, Branyan broke into pro ball with Burlington of the Appalachian League in 1994, where 15 of his 36 hits went for extra bases. He began to blossom in 1995 in the Sally League, where he led Columbus with 19 homers and a .534 slugging percentage despite a strained back. Branyan will definitely have to upgrade his contact in order to have a chance. In 1995, he fanned 120 times in just 277 official at bats. He improved the ratio last year but still soared over 150 whiffs. Look for him in High A ball in '97.

Professional Batting Register

	BA	G	AB	R	H	2B	3B	HR	RBI	SB
94 R	.273	67	256	48	70	15	5	7	55	6
95 A	.261	108	395	61	103	19	1	14	50	11
95 AA	.227	23	66	6	15	3	0	0	3	2
96 AA	.288	136	548	86	158	44	7	17	95	21

Professional Batting Register

	BA	G	AB	R	H	2B	3B	HR	RBI	SB
94 R	.211	55	171	21	36	10	0	5	13	4
95 A	.256	76	277	46	71	8	6	19	55	1
96 A	.268	130	482	102	129	20	4	40	106	7

DERMAL BROWN

Position: Outfield
Team: Kansas City Royals
Born: March 27, 1978 Bronx, NY
Height: 6' **Weight:** 205 lbs.
Bats: left **Throws:** right
Acquired: First-round pick in 6/96 free-agent draft

PLAYER SUMMARY	
Fantasy Value	$0
Card Value	25¢ to 35¢
Will	provide speed
Can't	play center
Expect	multitool man
Don't Expect	quick arrival

One doesn't typically think of New York State as an abundant source of baseball talent, because its winters are too long and cold to let the players get the necessary work. But Brown, out of Marlboro Central High School in a community about 50 miles north of New York City, owns the talent to become the exception. Selected 14th overall by the Royals in last year's draft, Brown was only the third high school position player taken. He offers speed, a hefty build, and a demonstrated ability to hit—at least at the high school level. His running ability helps account for his status as a top college football candidate. *Baseball America* ranked him as the top draft-eligible player in the state of New York. When Brown signed, he experienced pro shock in the Gulf Coast League and quickly found himself on the interstate (under .200). Expect him to start slowly, either in a rookie or low Class-A league. Then it's just a matter of whether he can translate his physical gifts into success.

Professional Batting Register

	BA	G	AB	R	H	2B	3B	HR	RBI	SB
96 R	.050	7	20	1	1	1	0	0	1	0

KEVIN BROWN

Position: Catcher
Team: Texas Rangers
Born: April 21, 1973 Valparaiso, IN
Height: 6'2" **Weight:** 200 lbs.
Bats: right **Throws:** right
Acquired: Second-round pick in 6/94 free-agent draft

PLAYER SUMMARY	
Fantasy Value	$0
Card Value	10¢ to 15¢
Will	whiff often
Can't	throw out runners
Expect	great power
Don't Expect	Rodriguez's arm

Not only do the Rangers offer one of the top major-league catchers in Ivan Rodriguez, but they also boast a blue-chip receiver prospect in Brown. Last year, Brown tore through the Texas League, showing every indication he can be that highly sought-after commodity, a power-hitting catcher. He ranked among the top Texas farmhands in home runs, one of which came in the 14th inning to provide a 4-3 victory over Wichita on July 26. The downside of his hitting is a tendency to strike out. Also, in his first two pro seasons, Brown did not show an overwhelming ability to control baserunners. In 1994, he caught 30 percent of those trying to steal. In 1995, it was 29 percent. Out of Pike Central High School in Petersburg, Indiana, Brown played three seasons at the University of Southern Indiana. He set school records with a .442 batting average, 14 homers, and 62 RBI in 1994 while becoming the Great Lakes Valley Conference Player of the Year.

Professional Batting Register

	BA	G	AB	R	H	2B	3B	HR	RBI	SB
94 A	.246	68	232	33	57	19	1	6	32	0
95 A	.265	107	355	48	94	25	1	11	57	2
95 AAA	.400	3	10	1	4	1	0	0	0	0
96 AA	.263	128	460	77	121	27	1	26	86	0
96 AL	.000	3	4	1	0	0	0	0	1	0

ROB BURGER

Position: Pitcher
Team: Philadelphia Phillies
Born: March 25, 1976 Lancaster, PA
Height: 6'1" **Weight:** 175 lbs.
Bats: right **Throws:** right
Acquired: Tenth-round pick in 6/94 free-agent draft

PLAYER SUMMARY

Fantasy Value	. . . . $0
Card Value	. . . . 15¢ to 20¢
Will	. . . . strike people out
Can't	. . . . expect run support
Expect	. . . . advancement
Don't Expect	. . . . many no-decisions

After two lackluster seasons, Burger emerged as a prospect with his work in the South Atlantic League last year. He was one of the workhorses on an impressive Piedmont staff, collecting decisions in 16 of his first 20 starts. He appeared in the Sally League All-Star Game, going one inning and allowing one base on balls. He ranked among Philadelphia's top farmhands in victories and ERA, and he battled Randy Knoll for the strikeout title in the entire organization. Burger's hits-to-innings ratio and his strikeout rate marked him as special. His win-loss mark is not exactly impressive until you realize he went 0-3 in four starts from June 22 to July 7 despite allowing two or less earned runs. Of course, support gets thin for all pitchers now and then, and the best ones find a way to win. Also, keep in mind the Sally League is a Low A circuit, and Burger must succeed at higher levels. But he has made a good start and appears to have promise.

ADAM BUTLER

Position: Pitcher
Team: Atlanta Braves
Born: Aug. 17, 1973 Fairfax, VA
Height: 6'2" **Weight:** 225 lbs.
Bats: left **Throws:** left
Acquired: Signed as a free agent, 6/95

PLAYER SUMMARY

Fantasy Value	. . . . $0
Card Value	. . . . 12¢ to 20¢
Will	. . . . make adjustments
Can't	. . . . be fazed
Expect	. . . . success vs. lefties
Don't Expect	. . . . instant fame

Credit scout Roy Clark for coming up with one of the most interesting arms in an Atlanta system already loaded with pitching. Clark signed Butler as a nondrafted free agent, and the pitcher has done nothing but impress ever since. Butler emerged as the closer with short-season Eugene in 1995 after being named the team's Pitcher of the Month for July. His average of nearly two strikeouts per inning is impressive, no matter what the league. Butler continued the pattern last year, starting with Macon of the South Atlantic League and quickly climbing through the organization. Through most of the season, Butler owned ten more saves than any other Atlanta farmhand, and the promotions did not seem to faze him in the least. *Baseball Weekly* tabbed him as an emerging prospect in its midseason look at farm systems. Judging by how quickly Butler has come along, no one should be surprised if he arrives in the bigs this season.

Professional Pitching Register

	W	L	ERA	G	CG	IP	H	ER	BB	SO
94 R	1	1	5.68	7	0	19.0	20	12	8	30
95 R	2	4	4.65	9	0	40.2	47	21	23	54
96 A	10	12	3.38	27	2	160.0	129	60	61	171

Professional Pitching Register

	W	L	ERA	G	S	IP	H	ER	BB	SO
95 A	4	1	2.49	23	8	25.1	15	7	12	50
96 A	0	0	0.00	9	5	11.0	2	0	7	14
96 A	0	1	1.23	12	8	14.2	5	2	3	23
96 AA	1	4	5.09	38	17	35.1	36	20	16	31

MIKE CAMERON

Position: Outfield
Team: Chicago White Sox
Born: Jan. 8, 1973 LaGrange, GA
Height: 6'2" **Weight:** 190 lbs.
Bats: right **Throws:** right
Acquired: 18th-round pick in 6/91 free-agent draft

PLAYER SUMMARY	
Fantasy Value	$0
Card Value	10¢ to 15¢
Will	be 20-20 man
Can't	go 30-30 in majors
Expect	versatile outfielder
Don't Expect	another Big Hurt

If Cameron keeps developing at the pace he has established over the last four years, it would almost seem unfair for the White Sox to add him to a lineup that already includes Frank Thomas and Albert Belle. But that's exactly what's likely to happen sometime this year. Cameron, who has increased his double and RBI totals for five straight seasons, emerged as a monster prospect with Birmingham of the Southern League in 1996. He passed the 20-homer, 20-steal mark early in the campaign, then pursued the 30-30 plateau. He also reached double digits in triples and hit for average, giving him impressive stats across the board. He is prone to striking out and also needs to work on his basestealing percentage. Able to play any outfield position, Cameron should find a spot with the White Sox soon. Right now it seems virtually certain that he will compete for a major-league job during spring training.

Professional Batting Register

	BA	G	AB	R	H	2B	3B	HR	RBI	SB
91 R	.221	44	136	20	30	3	0	0	11	13
92 A	.276	28	87	15	24	1	4	2	12	3
92 A	.228	35	114	19	26	8	1	1	9	2
93 A	.238	122	411	52	98	14	5	0	30	19
94 A	.248	131	468	86	116	15	17	6	48	22
95 AA	.249	107	350	64	87	20	5	11	60	21
95 AL	.184	28	38	4	7	2	0	1	2	0
96 AA	.300	123	473	120	142	34	12	28	77	39
96 AL	.091	11	11	1	1	0	0	0	0	0

JAY CANIZARO

Position: Infield
Team: San Francisco Giants
Born: July 4, 1973 Beaumont, TX
Height: 5'9" **Weight:** 170 lbs.
Bats: right **Throws:** right
Acquired: Sixth-round pick in 6/93 free-agent draft

PLAYER SUMMARY	
Fantasy Value	$0
Card Value	15¢ to 20¢
Will	be big-leaguer
Can't	hit .300
Expect	versatility in field
Don't Expect	a shortstop

Canizaro has a chance to spend a lot more time in San Francisco than he took to get there. He rocketed through the farm system, reaching the big leagues in only his fourth pro season. Now, at the age of 23, his package of speed, pop, and durability could make him the favorite that Robby Thompson became. Though he has played shortstop, third base, and the outfield in his pro career, Canizaro can figure on playing a lot of second base. He comes out of West Orange High School in Texas and attended Oklahoma State University and Blinn Junior College in Texas. In 1995, only his third pro season, he led Shreveport to the Texas League title and was selected to the All-Star Team as a utility man. So far, he has shown an ability to hit in the .250-.275 range, throwing in a few long balls now and then and showing some speed on the basepaths. Canizaro experienced some problems at the plate upon his arrival in San Francisco, but nothing that he can't master.

Professional Batting Register

	BA	G	AB	R	H	2B	3B	HR	RBI	SB
93 R	.261	49	180	34	47	10	6	3	41	12
94 A	.252	126	464	77	117	16	2	15	69	12
95 AA	.293	126	440	83	129	25	7	12	60	16
96 AAA	.262	102	363	50	95	21	2	7	64	14
96 NL	.200	43	120	11	24	4	1	2	8	0

357

CHRIS CARPENTER

Position: Pitcher
Team: Toronto Blue Jays
Born: April 27, 1975 Exeter, NH
Height: 6'6" **Weight:** 215 lbs.
Bats: right **Throws:** right
Acquired: First-round pick in 6/93 free-agent draft

PLAYER SUMMARY	
Fantasy Value	$0
Card Value	15¢ to 25¢
Will	provide innings
Can't	fall behind in count
Expect	.500 record
Don't Expect	gopher balls

This Carpenter appears to be building himself a career. Last year, his third as a pro, Carpenter put in his busiest campaign to date, serving as one of the workhorses for Knoxville of the Southern League. Showing the stuff that made him the 15th overall draft pick in 1993, he ranked high among Toronto's minor-leaguers in strikeouts. Unfortunately, he also continued a pattern of imprecise control, something he'll need to correct if he wants to advance. Carpenter comes out of Trinity High School in Manchester, New Hampshire, where he played both hockey and baseball and was a member of the Globe All-Scholastic team as a senior. Carpenter made his pro debut with Medicine Hat of the Pioneer League, finishing third in ERA. He opened the 1995 season with Dunedin of the Florida State League, compiling a 2.17 ERA in 15 starts. He found things a little tougher when promoted to Double-A. This year should find him within a phone call of the majors.

SEAN CASEY

Position: First base
Team: Cleveland Indians
Born: July 2, 1974 Willingsboro, NJ
Height: 6'4" **Weight:** 215 lbs.
Bats: left **Throws:** right
Acquired: Second-round pick in 6/95 free-agent draft

PLAYER SUMMARY	
Fantasy Value	$0
Card Value	15¢ to 25¢
Will	put ball in play
Can't	steal bases
Expect	power
Don't Expect	wild swings

Cleveland management showed what it thought of Casey at the beginning of last season by starting him in the High A Carolina League, jumping him from short-season rookie ball. He could not have responded more favorably than he did, making the All-Star Team and going 2-for-4 with a run scored in the showcase game against the California League. Casey was leading the league with a .331 average when he went on the disabled list with an ankle injury in late July. At that point, he had also collected 12 round-trippers with 57 RBI. A first baseman, Casey comes out of the University of Richmond, where he was a second-team All-American. He also captured an ECAC Player of the Year Award and won an NCAA Division I batting title. In his first year of pro ball, Casey played in the New York-Penn League and struck out only 21 times in 207 at bats. His .329 average tied for second in the league. He'll likely play Double-A ball this season.

Professional Pitching Register

	W	L	ERA	G	CG	IP	H	ER	BB	SO
94 R	6	3	2.76	15	0	84.2	76	26	39	80
95 A	3	5	2.17	15	0	99.1	83	24	50	56
95 AA	3	7	5.18	12	0	64.1	71	37	31	53
96 AA	7	9	3.94	28	1	171.1	161	75	91	150

Professional Batting Register

	BA	G	AB	R	H	2B	3B	HR	RBI	SB
95 A	.329	55	207	26	68	18	0	2	37	3
96 A	.331	92	344	62	114	31	3	12	57	1

LUIS CASTILLO

Position: Second base
Team: Florida Marlins
Born: Sept. 12, 1975 San Pedro de Macoris, Dominican Republic
Height: 5'11" **Weight:** 155 lbs.
Bats: both **Throws:** right
Acquired: Signed as a nondrafted free agent, 8/92

PLAYER SUMMARY

Fantasy Value	$0
Card Value	15¢ to 20¢
Will	team with Renteria
Can't	reinjure shoulder
Expect	wizard on bases
Don't Expect	power

A city that is renowned for producing shortstops has given the Marlins a second baseman. Castillo came to the big leagues last summer, joining Edgar Renteria to form a double-play combination that could last for years. Castillo went to the leadoff spot, where his job was to make things happen in a Florida lineup that had trouble producing runs. At the time of his promotion, Castillo was fighting for top average among Florida farmhands, and he was leading them in stolen bases by a wide margin. Castillo enjoyed his breakthrough season in 1995 with Kane County of the Midwest League. He made the All-Star Team, finishing fourth in batting and third in on-base percentage. He was named to the HOWE SportsData All-Teenager Team and was leading the league in runs and steals when he went on the disabled list with a shoulder injury. A year later, Castillo was in the big leagues, probably to stay.

JOSE CEPEDA

Position: Infield
Team: Kansas City Royals
Born: Aug. 1, 1974 Fajardo, Puerto Rico
Height: 6' **Weight:** 185 lbs.
Bats: right **Throws:** right
Acquired: Signed as a nondrafted free agent, 6/95

PLAYER SUMMARY

Fantasy Value	$0
Card Value	12¢ to 20¢
Will	get his hits
Can't	strike him out
Expect	a third baseman
Don't Expect	big slugging pct.

No pitcher is ever going to want to face Cepeda with a runner on third and less than two outs. That's because with Cepeda at the plate, the man on the mound can pretty much forget about getting a strikeout. Cepeda is going to get a piece of the ball. For example, in his first year as a pro, Cepeda fanned only five times in 187 official at bats in the Gulf Coast League, leading the short-season leagues in lowest strikeout percentage. Last year—while in the Midwest League—Cepeda tended to strike out at a higher rate, but he still established himself as a man who can handle the wood. He attended Western Oregon State College, where he was named first-team All-Western Cascade Conference. The nephew of former major-league star Orlando Cepeda, Jose so far has not shown his uncle's power, but he might add some pop. Plus, if he keeps putting the bat on the ball, good things will happen. Cepeda is likely to be promoted to High A ball this year.

Professional Batting Register

	BA	G	AB	R	H	2B	3B	HR	RBI	SB
94 R	.264	57	216	49	57	8	0	0	16	31
95 A	.326	89	340	71	111	4	4	0	23	41
96 AA	.317	109	420	83	133	15	7	1	35	51
96 NL	.262	41	164	26	43	2	1	1	8	17

Professional Batting Register

	BA	G	AB	R	H	2B	3B	HR	RBI	SB
95 R	.348	54	187	32	65	6	4	0	21	2
96 A	.289	135	558	87	161	29	3	3	81	10

ERIC CHAVEZ

Position: Infield
Team: Oakland Athletics
Born: Sept. 7, 1970 Montebello, CA
Height: 6'1" **Weight:** 190 lbs.
Bats: left **Throws:** right
Acquired: First-round pick in 6/96 free-agent draft

PLAYER SUMMARY	
Fantasy Value	$0
Card Value	20¢ to 30¢
Will	deliver long ball
Can't	challenge Giambi
Expect	natural hitter
Don't Expect	middle infield

The A's know a little bit about power hitters, having brought the likes of Mark McGwire and Jose Canseco to the majors. They just finished developing another rising slugger in the person of Jason Giambi. So when this organization thinks enough of a player to make him its first pick in the draft, people sit up and pay attention. Oakland made Chavez the tenth overall selection and only the fourth position player tabbed in last year's free-agent draft. The reason for all the fuss is Chavez's bat. A member of *Baseball America*'s preseason high school All-America team, Chavez justified the hype by hitting over .450 in his senior year at Mount Carmel High in San Diego. He added enough long balls to make Oakland believe in his power potential. With his build, he could become a power-hitting corner man, first base being an option if the hot corner does not work out. Chavez likely will begin his career in a short-season or Low A league.

PAT CLINE

Position: Catcher
Team: Chicago Cubs
Born: Oct. 9, 1974 Bradenton, FL
Height: 6'3" **Weight:** 225 lbs.
Bats: right **Throws:** right
Acquired: Sixth-round pick in 6/93 free-agent draft

PLAYER SUMMARY	
Fantasy Value	$0
Card Value	12¢ to 20¢
Will	hit it out
Can't	afford 17 errors
Expect	Double-A in '97
Don't Expect	lumbering giant

Given the Florida State League's reputation as a graveyard for power hitters, people take notice when they see someone knocking the ball out of its parks. Such is the case with Cline, who regularly left the yard for Daytona last year. Granted, the Daytona park is a little on the cozy side, but that can't take all the luster from Cline's performance. And when his hefty build is considered, his power production should come as no surprise. Cline looks every bit the prototypical power-hitting receiver. He's no lumbering giant, however; he showed enough quickness to steal some bases. Cline graduated from Manatee High School in Bradenton in 1993 and got his feet wet in rookie ball. A wrist injury knocked him out for virtually the entire 1994 season, but he returned in 1995 to make the Midwest League's midseason All-Star Team. As his 17 errors in 1995 suggest, Cline still needs to improve his defense in order to get to Wrigley Field.

Professional Batting Register

	BA	G	AB	R	H	2B	3B	HR	RBI	SB
93 R	.188	33	96	17	18	6	0	2	13	0
95 A	.272	112	390	65	106	27	0	13	77	6
96 A	.279	124	434	75	121	30	2	17	76	10

KEN CLOUDE

Position: Pitcher
Team: Seattle Mariners
Born: Jan. 9, 1975 Baltimore, MD
Height: 6'1" **Weight:** 180 lbs.
Bats: left **Throws:** right
Acquired: Sixth-round pick in 6/93 free-agent draft

PLAYER SUMMARY	
Fantasy Value	$0
Card Value	10¢ to 15¢
Will	start
Can't	let control slip
Expect	spot in rotation
Don't Expect	complete games

If Cloude had been a little closer to the majors, he might have been able to keep the Mariners from spiraling out of the race last summer. Instead, he had to content himself with an impressive season with Lancaster of the Class-A California League. Cloude was named to start for the Cal League in its All-Star match against the Carolina League: an honor that speaks for itself, even though he gave up two runs in two innings. Cloude didn't rest on his laurels, either. Right down to the end of the season he battled Greg Wooten for most victories in the Seattle farm system. Cloude graduated from McDonogh High School in Baltimore and was named Player of the Year by *The Sun.* Offered a full scholarship to the University of Richmond, he instead signed with the Mariners. In his first year of pro ball, Cloude held opponents to a .200 batting average. He did a good job of improving his walks-to-innings ratio in '96.

DAVE COGGIN

Position: Pitcher
Team: Philadelphia Phillies
Born: Oct. 30, 1976 Covina, CA
Height: 6'4" **Weight:** 195 lbs.
Bats: right **Throws:** right
Acquired: Sandwich pick in 6/95 free-agent draft

PLAYER SUMMARY	
Fantasy Value	$0
Card Value	15¢ to 20¢
Will	take the ball
Can't	win without control
Expect	good fastball
Don't Expect	consistency

The Phillies tabbed Coggin with the 30th overall selection in the 1995 draft, a sandwich pick between the first and second rounds that Philadelphia had earned from the loss of free agent Danny Jackson. Taking Coggin involved some risk, because his football ability gave him other options. However, he signed with the club and is now part of a group of prospects who offer hope to a Phillies team that can certainly use some young arms. Coggin pitched in the South Atlantic League last year and, even though his win-loss record wasn't the best, showed talent and durability as one of Piedmont's three workhorse starters. He showed great improvement in his control over the previous season, indicating that he grasps the importance of throwing strikes. Owner of an impressive fastball, Coggin must add some refinements in order to advance through the farm system. Expect him to be doing exactly that in a high Class-A setting this season.

Professional Pitching Register

	W	L	ERA	G	CG	IP	H	ER	BB	SO
94 R	3	4	2.06	12	0	52.1	36	12	19	61
95 A	9	8	3.24	25	4	161.0	137	58	63	140
96 A	15	4	4.22	28	1	168.1	167	79	60	161

Professional Pitching Register

	W	L	ERA	G	CG	IP	H	ER	BB	SO
95 R	5	3	3.00	11	0	48.0	45	16	31	37
96 A	9	12	4.31	28	3	169.1	156	81	46	129

LOU COLLIER

Position: Shortstop
Team: Pittsburgh Pirates
Born: Aug. 21, 1973 Chicago, IL
Height: 5'10" **Weight:** 176 lbs.
Bats: right **Throws:** right
Acquired: 31st-round pick in 6/92 free-agent draft

PLAYER SUMMARY	
Fantasy Value	$0
Card Value	12¢ to 20¢
Will	do the job
Can't	challenge Bell
Expect	stolen bases
Don't Expect	much pop

The good news for Collier is that he is a legitimate shortstop prospect. The bad news is that he is getting squeezed by talent in the Pittsburgh organization. Above him on the major-league level is Jay Bell, and pursuing close behind is top prospect Chad Hermansen. That leaves Collier precious little room for error, especially considering that he's already 23 and that, as a 31st-round pick, he's not exactly a priority investment. Yet performance often finds a way. Collier has put up some numbers in his four-year pro career. Last season he played at Double-A Carolina, where he hit for average and amassed an impressive total of stolen bases (29). It was the third straight year that he abused opposing batteries with his speed. At the plate, Collier shows only a little pop, so in order to prosper he'll have to hit the ball on the ground and use his wheels. Expect to see him at Triple-A this year. Or it's possible he could end up a utility player in Pittsburgh.

BART COLON

Position: Pitcher
Team: Cleveland Indians
Born: May 24, 1975 Altamira, Dominican Republic
Height: 6' **Weight:** 185 lbs.
Bats: right **Throws:** right
Acquired: Signed as a nondrafted free agent 6/93

PLAYER SUMMARY	
Fantasy Value	$0
Card Value	10¢ to 15¢
Will	shut teams down
Can't	pitch with bad elbow
Expect	crucial '97 season
Don't Expect	150 innings

Colon is one of the top prospects in the Cleveland chain, but elbow problems have marred his last two seasons. Last year he missed most of the season at Canton-Akron of the Eastern League, and still he was tabbed as the circuit's top pitching prospect. However, that won't mean much until he's healthy, so 1997 will be a season to watch. Colon, signed by Dominican scout Winston Llenas, has dazzled almost from the moment he put on a pro uniform. In the Dominican League in 1993, he ranked second in the Cibao Division with a 2.59 ERA. Boosted by short-season Burlington in 1994, Colon finished fifth among Appy League starters with a .192 opponents' batting average. Colon earned another promotion in 1995 and led the Carolina League in strikeouts. He pitched in the league's All-Star Game and was 3-0 in five July starts. But on August 1 he went on the disabled list with a bruised right elbow and was knocked out for the season.

Professional Batting Register

	BA	G	AB	R	H	2B	3B	HR	RBI	SB
93 A	.303	50	201	35	61	6	2	1	19	8
94 A	.280	85	318	48	89	17	4	7	40	32
94 A	.266	43	158	25	42	4	1	6	16	5
95 A	.276	114	399	68	110	19	3	4	38	31
96 AA	.280	119	443	76	124	20	3	3	49	29

Professional Pitching Register

	W	L	ERA	G	CG	IP	H	ER	BB	SO
94 R	7	4	3.14	12	0	66.0	46	23	44	84
95 A	13	3	1.96	21	0	128.2	91	28	39	152
96 AA	2	2	1.74	13	0	62.0	44	12	25	56
96 AAA	0	0	6.00	8	0	15.0	16	10	8	19

STEVE COX

Position: First base
Team: Oakland Athletics
Born: Oct. 31, 1974 Delano, CA
Height: 6'4" **Weight:** 200 lbs.
Bats: left **Throws:** left
Acquired: Fifth-round pick in 6/92 free-agent draft

PLAYER SUMMARY	
Fantasy Value	$0
Card Value	15¢ to 20¢
Will	have to adjust
Can't	repeat '95 season
Expect	power
Don't Expect	challenge to McGwire

Cox found out about the burden of expectations last year when he made the jump to Double-A ball. While his power numbers were nothing to be ashamed of, they certainly did not match what he had amassed in the California League one year earlier. Then again, seasons like that don't come along very often. Cox led the league in homers and runs batted in, was named to the California League's postseason All-Star squad, was tabbed Oakland's Organizational Player of the Year by *Baseball America,* and was selected Oakland's Minor League Player of the Year by the front office. All of this may have helped make him a target when he got to Double-A last year, but top players find a way to deal with that kind of attention. Another challenge for Cox is where exactly he might play when he gets to Oakland, since Mark McGwire is signed through 1997. But that's out of his control, and a good look at Triple-A ball awaits him this summer.

JOSE CRUZ, JR.

Position: Outfield
Team: Seattle Mariners
Born: April 19, 1974 Arroyo, Puerto Rico
Height: 6' **Weight:** 190 lbs.
Bats: both **Throws:** right
Acquired: First-round pick in 6/95 free-agent draft

PLAYER SUMMARY	
Fantasy Value	$1 to $3
Card Value	40¢ to 60¢
Will	drive in runs
Can't	play center
Expect	bloodlines
Don't Expect	big homer man

The Mariners can only hope that this young man can hit the way his father did. Jose Cruz, Sr., was a high-average, line-drive hitter who made quite a name for himself with the Houston Astros. Cruz Jr. so far has shown indications that the apple has landed right next to the tree. Cruz was the third player taken overall in the 1995 draft, and he was sent to short-season Everett, where he singled in his first professional at bat. After only three games, he was boosted to Riverside of the Cal League, where he drove in 29 runs in only 35 games. Cruz attended Rice University and set 15 career records, including average and slugging percentage. A three-time All-American, he also played for Team USA in 1994. Last year, his first full one in pro ball, he began the season with Lancaster of the California League and pounded the ball until he received a promotion to Port City of the Southern League. He needs to cut down on his strikeouts.

Professional Batting Register

	BA	G	AB	R	H	2B	3B	HR	RBI	SB
92 R	.234	52	184	30	43	4	1	1	35	2
93 A	.316	15	57	10	18	4	1	2	16	0
94 A	.241	99	311	37	75	19	2	6	32	2
95 A	.298	132	483	95	144	29	3	30	110	5
96 AA	.281	104	381	59	107	21	1	12	61	2

Professional Batting Register

	BA	G	AB	R	H	2B	3B	HR	RBI	SB
95 A	.455	3	11	6	5	0	0	0	2	1
95 A	.257	35	144	34	37	7	1	7	29	3
96 A	.325	53	203	38	66	17	1	6	43	7
96 AA	.282	47	181	39	51	10	2	3	31	5
96 AAA	.237	22	76	15	18	1	2	6	15	1

TOMMY DAVIS

Position: First base
Team: Baltimore Orioles
Born: May 21, 1973 Mobile, AL
Height: 6'1" **Weight:** 195 lbs.
Bats: right **Throws:** right
Acquired: Second-round pick in 6/94 free-agent draft

PLAYER SUMMARY	
Fantasy Value	. . . . $0
Card Value	. . . . 15¢ to 25¢
Will	. . . . play first
Can't	. . . . play third
Expect	. . . . solid bat
Don't Expect	. . . . challenge to Palmeiro

Davis was actually the Orioles' first pick in the 1994 draft because they had lost their first-round selection to the Mets by signing free agent Sid Fernandez. Nevertheless, the Orioles hope Davis can join an impressive list of first selections who made it to the majors, including Ben McDonald, Mike Mussina, and Jeffrey Hammonds. If Davis's first three years are any indication, it's not out of the question. Last year he played in the Eastern League, a challenging circuit for hitters, and did not seem out of place. His power numbers were respectable, though not overwhelming. Davis has moved from third base to first, a move that should help him in the field but also places him squarely behind Rafael Palmeiro at the major-league level. Palmeiro is signed through 1998, and Davis shouldn't be arriving too much before then. He can't control what Palmeiro does, but he can work on making contact, a project he'll probably get a chance to undertake this year in Triple-A ball.

VALERIO DE LOS SANTOS

Position: Pitcher
Team: Milwaukee Brewers
Born: Oct. 6, 1975 Las Matas, Dominican Republic
Height: 6'2" **Weight:** 180 lbs.
Bats: left **Throws:** left
Acquired: Signed as a nondrafted free agent, 1/93

PLAYER SUMMARY	
Fantasy Value	. . . . $0
Card Value	. . . . 10¢ to 15¢
Will	. . . . advance
Can't	. . . . win ERA title
Expect	. . . . more All-Star outings
Don't Expect	. . . . wild lefty

You hate to lose any game, but if you have to lose one, let it be the All-Star Game. Losing that game means you got there in the first place. Such was the case for de los Santos last season, when he appeared for the West squad in the Midwest League showcase. He went one inning and allowed three runs on three hits to wind up the losing pitcher. But such moments were the minority for the Dominican lefty, who has turned into quite a prospect. Last year he was one of the top winners in the entire Milwaukee organization. His strikeout totals were of top quality, and he even completed a few games. He throws the ball over the plate, something you like to see in every young pitcher but particularly in a left-hander. De los Santos first pitched professionally in the Dominican Republic at the age of 17. Now he definitely seems to have left the days of the 1-7 record behind him. Expect the Brewers to boost him to a high Class-A team this summer.

Professional Batting Register

	BA	G	AB	R	H	2B	3B	HR	RBI	SB
94 A	.273	61	216	35	59	10	1	5	35	2
95 A	.268	130	496	62	133	26	3	15	57	7
95 AA	.313	9	32	5	10	3	0	3	10	0
96 AA	.261	137	524	75	137	32	2	14	54	5

Professional Pitching Register

	W	L	ERA	G	CG	IP	H	ER	BB	SO
94 R	7	6	3.70	17	1	90.1	90	37	35	50
95 R	4	6	2.20	14	0	82.0	81	20	12	57
96 A	10	8	3.55	33	5	164.2	164	65	59	137

KRIS DETMERS

Position: Pitcher
Team: St. Louis Cardinals
Born: June 22, 1974 Decatur, IL
Height: 6'5" **Weight:** 200 lbs.
Bats: both **Throws:** left
Acquired: 22nd-round pick in 6/93 free-agent draft

PLAYER SUMMARY

Fantasy Value	$0
Card Value	15¢ to 20¢
Will	throw a curve
Can't	walk too many
Expect	quality starts
Don't Expect	overpowering heat

There was no mistaking what the Cardinals thought of Detmers when he was named the Opening Day pitcher for their Double-A club in the Texas League last year. He certainly did not disappoint anyone, turning in a season that would seem to place him within consideration for a job with the Cardinals this year. *USA TODAY Baseball Weekly* gave him mention as an emerging prospect in its midseason look at the top farmhands. Highlights give an idea of what Detmers can do. He allowed only five earned runs over four starts stretching from May 24 to June 11. He got hot again in late July and through most of August, winning five of six appearances. Detmers can use some work improving his somewhat shaky control, which is not unusual for a young lefty. Also, expect the bullpen to work when he's pitching, because complete games are not a big item on his resume. You'll probably find Detmers in major-league camp this year, and he could open with the Cardinals or get a midseason call-up.

EDWIN DIAZ

Position: Second base
Team: Texas Rangers
Born: Jan. 15, 1975 Vega Baja, Puerto Rico
Height: 5'11" **Weight:** 172 lbs.
Bats: right **Throws:** right
Acquired: Second-round pick in 6/93 free-agent draft

PLAYER SUMMARY

Fantasy Value	$0
Card Value	12¢ to 15¢
Will	pile up doubles
Can't	steal bases well
Expect	a shot at Rangers
Don't Expect	productive outs

After turning in the best of his four pro seasons in 1996, Diaz could very well find himself in the Texas lineup sometime this year. He is a second baseman with pop, as indicated by his impressive doubles total that he has increased for three straight years. Diaz also will steal an occasional base, though when he takes off he's just as likely to get caught as he is to make it. He also pays for his power with a strong tendency to strike out. Last year, he played for Tulsa of the Texas League and piled up nice numbers for a middle infielder, soaring past 50 extra-base hits by early August. Diaz broke into pro ball in 1993, finishing third in the Gulf Coast League in hitting. In 1994, he was promoted to full-season A ball, where he led Charleston in batting average and triples. A year later, the Rangers sent Diaz to a high Class-A circuit, where he was twice named Florida State League Player of the Week. He batted .358 in May to earn the Rangers' Player of the Month Award.

Professional Pitching Register

	W	L	ERA	G	CG	IP	H	ER	BB	SO
94 A	5	7	3.39	16	0	90.1	88	34	31	74
95 A	10	9	3.25	25	1	146.2	120	53	57	150
96 AA	12	8	3.35	27	0	163.2	154	61	70	97

Professional Batting Register

	BA	G	AB	R	H	2B	3B	HR	RBI	SB
93 R	.305	43	154	27	47	10	5	1	23	12
94 A	.264	122	413	52	109	22	7	11	60	11
95 A	.284	115	450	48	128	26	5	8	56	8
96 AA	.265	121	499	70	132	33	6	16	65	8

EINAR DIAZ

Position: Catcher
Team: Cleveland Indians
Born: Dec. 28, 1972 Chiriqui, Panama
Height: 5'10" **Weight:** 165 lbs.
Bats: right **Throws:** right
Acquired: Signed as a nondrafted free agent, 10/90

PLAYER SUMMARY	
Fantasy Value	$0
Card Value	12¢ to 15¢
Will	control the bases
Can't	supplant Alomar
Expect	job with Cleveland
Don't Expect	16 homers

Diaz may be ready to step in as the backup to Sandy Alomar, a job that has possibilities because of Alomar's unfortunate history of injuries. Diaz, a converted third baseman, is nothing like the strapping Alomar in terms of physique, but he has managed to get the job done. In 1995, while playing in the Class-A Carolina League, Diaz threw out 47.5 percent of the runners who tried to steal against him. He also led the league's catchers with 107 assists, even though he missed a week while sidelined with a jammed left shoulder. In 1994, Diaz was named to the South Atlantic League's post-season All-Star Team after tossing out 43.7 percent of the runners who tested him. He led the league in total chances and in assists. Diaz also showed some power that year with career-high totals in homers and RBI, but whether he could duplicate that in the majors remains a question. Right now his strength seems to be his glove, but he won't hurt you at the plate, either.

R.A. DICKEY

Position: Pitcher
Team: Texas Rangers
Born: Oct. 29, 1974 Nashville, TN
Height: 6'2" **Weight:** 185 lbs.
Bats: right **Throws:** right
Acquired: First-round pick in 6/96 free-agent draft

PLAYER SUMMARY	
Fantasy Value	$0
Card Value	25¢ to 30¢
Will	bring experience
Can't	relax now
Expect	a bulldog
Don't Expect	much time in minors

The Rangers certainly won't have to worry about the experience factor with the player they made the 18th overall selection in last year's draft. Dickey has spent plenty of high-quality, high-pressure time between the white lines in both the college and international ranks. He spent last spring and summer with the U.S. Olympic team, in what was his third season with the national squad. He also starred at the University of Tennessee, setting the career record for victories. *Baseball America* named him a third-team All-American for two straight years. Last year, Dickey was a force on the Olympic team, winning both of his starts, compiling a 3.00 ERA, and averaging a strikeout per inning. With a resume like that, Dickey shouldn't need a whole lot of development time in the minors. Drafted by the Tigers in the tenth round in 1993, Dickey elected not to sign. But last year, after the whirlwind of the Olympics was over, Texas got his name on the dotted line.

Professional Batting Register

	BA	G	AB	R	H	2B	3B	HR	RBI	SB
92 R	.208	52	178	19	37	3	0	1	14	2
93 R	.299	60	231	40	69	15	3	5	33	7
93 A	.000	1	5	0	0	0	0	0	0	0
94 A	.279	120	491	67	137	23	2	16	71	4
95 A	.263	104	373	46	98	21	0	6	43	3
96 AA	.281	104	395	47	111	26	2	3	35	3
96 AL	.000	4	1	0	0	0	0	0	0	0

JASON DICKSON

Position: Pitcher
Team: Anaheim Angels
Born: March 30, 1973 London, Canada
Height: 6' **Weight:** 190 lbs.
Bats: left **Throws:** right
Acquired: Sixth-round pick in 6/94 free-agent draft

PLAYER SUMMARY	
Fantasy Value	$1
Card Value	10¢ to 15¢
Will	seize the game
Can't	take him out
Expect	innings eater
Don't Expect	staff ace

Managers love a starting pitcher who would prefer not to leave the outcome of the game to the bullpen. Such is the case with Dickson, who often finishes what he starts. And even when he doesn't, he still manages to get a decision. Consider the remarkable stat in Dickson's first ten starts at Triple-A last year—he collected a decision in all ten, winning five and losing five. One year earlier, Dickson displayed his endurance by completing nine starts for Cedar Rapids of the Midwest League. Dickson, who attended Northeastern Oklahoma A&M, got his professional start in low Class-A ball in 1994. He blossomed quickly in 1995, leading his team in victories (14) and allowing opponents to hit only .233 against him. Last year, Dickson began the season in Double-A ball but was soon promoted to Triple-A. He eventually made it to the Angels, and he could be in the picture for their rotation this year.

MATT DREWS

Position: Pitcher
Team: Detroit Tigers
Born: Aug. 29, 1974 Sarasota, FL
Height: 6'8" **Weight:** 230 lbs.
Bats: right **Throws:** right
Acquired: Traded by Yankees with Ruben Sierra for Cecil Fielder, 7/96

PLAYER SUMMARY	
Fantasy Value	$0
Card Value	15¢ to 20¢
Will	get a chance
Can't	be intimidated
Expect	a look in '97
Don't Expect	another disaster

Drews was the key player in the deal that sent Cecil Fielder to the Yankees at the trading deadline last summer. If all goes well for the Tigers, he will be pitching long after Fielder has retired. But keep in mind that all did not go well for Drews last year. The Yankees tried to skip him a rung and place him at Triple-A, but he had problems at that level and had to take a couple of steps back. Such a setback is not an unusual event in the development of a young player. One thing is for sure—Drews should get every opportunity in his new setting, because the Tigers desperately needed pitching last year. Drews was the 13th overall pick in the 1993 draft after starring in three sports in high school. He was captain of the football, baseball, and basketball teams and was recruited by colleges for all three sports. He chose baseball as a career, possibly because his grandfather, Karl, played eight years with the Yankees. It looks like Matt may make his mark with another franchise.

Professional Pitching Register

	W	L	ERA	G	CG	IP	H	ER	BB	SO
94 A	3	1	3.86	9	0	44.1	40	19	18	37
95 A	14	6	2.86	25	9	173.0	151	55	45	134
96 AA	5	2	3.58	8	3	55.1	55	22	10	40
96 AAA	7	11	3.80	18	7	130.1	134	55	40	70
96 AL	1	4	4.57	7	0	43.1	52	22	18	20

Professional Pitching Register

	W	L	ERA	G	CG	IP	H	ER	BB	SO
94 A	7	6	2.10	14	1	90.0	76	21	19	69
95 A	15	7	2.27	28	3	182.0	142	46	58	140
96 A	0	3	7.13	4	0	17.2	26	14	12	12
96 AA	1	3	4.50	9	0	46.0	40	23	33	37
96 AA	0	4	4.35	6	1	31.0	26	15	19	40
96 AAA	0	4	8.41	7	0	20.1	18	19	27	7

MIKE DRUMRIGHT

Position: Pitcher
Team: Detroit Tigers
Born: March 19, 1974 Salina, KS
Height: 6'4" **Weight:** 210 lbs.
Bats: left **Throws:** right
Acquired: First-round pick in 6/95 free-agent draft

PLAYER SUMMARY	
Fantasy Value	.... $0
Card Value	.... 15¢ to 20¢
Will	.... need his health
Can't	.... do it alone
Expect	.... breaking ball
Don't Expect	.... long apprenticeship

Maybe things are looking up for the Tigers. Not only did they improve in the second half last year, but the presence of two pitching prospects so close together in this book indicates that even more help might be coming. Drumright was the 11th overall selection in the 1995 draft and has lived up to that status since then. *Baseball America* tabbed him the Southern League's best pitching prospect and also rated his breaking ball as the best in the circuit. He was off to a nice start last year—leading the Detroit farm system in strikeouts—when shoulder problems sidetracked him onto the disabled list. He still showed the ups and downs typical of a young player, as shown by an outing last May 26: He went only 4⅔ innings, allowing ten hits and seven runs. But of the 14 outs he got, ten came on strikeouts. With Matt Drews now in Detroit's farm system and Justin Thompson near the bigs, Drumright need not feel like he carries the whole future on his shoulders.

TODD DUNWOODY

Position: Outfield
Team: Florida Marlins
Born: April 11, 1975 Lafayette, IN
Height: 6'1" **Weight:** 185 lbs.
Bats: left **Throws:** left
Acquired: Seventh-round pick in 6/93 free-agent draft

PLAYER SUMMARY	
Fantasy Value	.... $0
Card Value	.... 15¢ to 20¢
Will	.... bring many tools
Can't	.... let Ks pile up
Expect	.... power plus speed
Don't Expect	.... full year of Triple-A

The Florida farm system has been producing like a fertile orchard, with the likes of Edgar Renteria, Luis Castillo, Billy McMillon, and Marc Valdes all making it to the big club. Now it appears Dunwoody may be on the verge of arriving, too. He played in the Eastern League last year and pretty well had things his way there. He started and played center field for the National League farmhands in the Double-A All-Star Game, going 2-for-5 with a home run. His success in the Eastern League is all the more significant because an assumption exists that if you can hit in that league, you can hit, period. It was Dunwoody's second straight outstanding year; he made the Midwest League All-Star squad a year earlier. He was the Marlins' Minor League Player of the Month for June with a .320 average, and his 89 RBI in '95 ranked him 13th among all Class-A players. The Marlins have shown they are not bashful about promotions, so watch for Dunwoody in '97.

Professional Pitching Register

	W	L	ERA	G	CG	IP	H	ER	BB	SO
95 A	1	1	4.29	5	0	21.0	19	10	9	19
95 AA	0	1	3.69	5	0	31.2	30	13	15	34
96 AA	6	4	3.97	18	1	99.2	80	44	48	109

Professional Batting Register

	BA	G	AB	R	H	2B	3B	HR	RBI	SB
93 R	.193	31	109	13	21	2	2	0	7	5
94 A	.111	15	45	7	5	0	0	1	1	1
94 R	.260	46	169	32	44	6	6	1	25	11
95 A	.283	132	494	89	140	20	8	14	89	39
96 AA	.277	138	552	88	153	30	6	24	93	24

ADAM EATON

Position: Pitcher
Team: Philadelphia Phillies
Born: Nov. 23, 1977 Seattle, WA
Height: 6'1" **Weight:** 180 lbs.
Bats: right **Throws:** right
Acquired: First-round pick in 6/96 free-agent draft

PLAYER SUMMARY	
Fantasy Value	$0
Card Value	15¢ to 20¢
Will	throw well
Can't	help yet
Expect	front end of rotation
Don't Expect	full-season ball

So near, and yet so far. By taking Eaton with the 11th overall selection in last year's draft, the Phillies got themselves some pitching. However, given Eaton's age and stage of development, he won't be able to make a difference to the big club until close to the turn of the century. Eaton became the first high school pitcher taken in the first round by the Phillies in years. With recent picks, they had gone for outfielders and college pitchers. Eaton attended Snohomish High School, where he was rated by *Baseball America* as the top draft-eligible player in the state of Washington. He dominated in his scholastic season, averaging around 1.5 strikeouts per inning. Then again, you wouldn't really expect anything less than that from a first-rounder. The most important issue now is what he does with all that stuff. In most cases, the road for a high school draftee is a long one. Look for Eaton in short-season ball next year, and keep his name in mind for the future.

SCOTT ELARTON

Position: Pitcher
Team: Houston Astros
Born: Feb. 23, 1976 Lamar, CO
Height: 6'7" **Weight:** 225 lbs.
Bats: right **Throws:** right
Acquired: First-round pick in 6/94 free-agent draft

PLAYER SUMMARY	
Fantasy Value	$0
Card Value	15¢ to 20¢
Will	get your attention
Can't	pitch behind
Expect	intelligence
Don't Expect	missed starts

The valedictorian of his high school, Elarton is marching smartly through the Houston farm system, and it doesn't take much intelligence to surmise that he may soon be in the majors. Last year, he posted his third consecutive strong season of pro ball, making a jump to the high Class-A Florida State League. He was one of the jewels of the Houston farm system, ranking among the organizational leaders in wins, ERA, and strikeouts. Elarton has been a workhorse ever since turning pro, making 14 starts in 1994 after becoming the 25th overall pick in the draft. He has topped the 20-start plateau in each of the past two seasons. With his tremendous size, Elarton will certainly get your attention on the mound. On the downside, his walk totals are higher than you'd wish. And remember, it's not just walks, but pitching behind in the count that can also hurt a pitcher. Still, expect Elarton to make a smooth transition to the next level.

Professional Pitching Register

	W	L	ERA	G	CG	IP	H	ER	BB	SO
94 R	4	0	0.00	5	0	28.0	9	0	5	28
94 A	4	1	3.29	9	0	54.2	42	20	18	42
95 A	13	7	4.45	26	0	149.2	149	74	71	112
96 A	12	7	2.92	27	3	172.1	154	56	54	130

JUAN ENCARNACION

Position: Outfield
Team: Detroit Tigers
Born: March 8, 1976 Las Matas de Faran, Dominican Republic
Height: 6'2" **Weight:** 160 lbs.
Bats: right **Throws:** right
Acquired: Signed as a nondrafted free agent, 12/92

PLAYER SUMMARY	
Fantasy Value	$0
Card Value	10¢ to 15¢
Will	put on weight
Can't	lead league in walks
Expect	Double-A this year
Don't Expect	a contact hitter

Encarnacion is a classic example of a young player who bears watching, even if he is not producing big numbers right now. His long and lean frame, along with its potential for carrying additional muscle once he matures and takes advantage of top training methods, is quite appealing to scouts. However, Encarnacion's poor strikeout-to-walk ratio bears watching. During one stretch spanning May and June last year, Encarnacion went 20 games without drawing a walk. If he could combine the potential for muscle with increased selectivity at the plate, he could be something very special. As it is, he isn't bad. Playing in the Florida State League at the age of 20, Encarnacion hit for some power, which is not easy to do in that circuit. His high doubles total testifies to his capacity for power. But keep in mind that improving a batting eye is not easy, and Encarnacion's progress will depend on how well he adjusts to pitchers who can put the ball in specific spots.

KELVIM ESCOBAR

Position: Pitcher
Team: Toronto Blue Jays
Born: April 11, 1976 La Guaira, Venezuela
Height: 6'1" **Weight:** 205 lbs.
Bats: right **Throws:** right
Acquired: Signed as a nondrafted free agent, 7/92

PLAYER SUMMARY	
Fantasy Value	$0
Card Value	15¢ to 20¢
Will	keep climbing
Can't	succeed immediately
Expect	a starter
Don't Expect	Toronto in '97

The Blue Jays are looking for another starter to help them regain the glory they enjoyed earlier this decade, and if Escobar continues to progress at his current rate, he could be filling such a role soon. Escobar pitched in the fast-company Class-A Florida State League last year, making an extremely sharp jump from short-season rookie ball. *USA TODAY Baseball Weekly* termed him an emerging prospect in its midseason overview of baseball's farm systems. He hurled a scoreless inning in the FSL All-Star Game. All in all, Escobar pitched so well that he earned a late-season call-up to Knoxville of the Southern League. To keep things in perspective, remember that the FSL tends to favor pitchers, and that its parks don't easily give up home runs. We'll get a better reading on Escobar this season, when he could well receive some attention at a major-league camp before being sent to an assignment in Double-A ball.

Professional Batting Register

	BA	G	AB	R	H	2B	3B	HR	RBI	SB
94 A	.193	24	83	6	16	1	1	1	4	1
94 R	.249	54	197	16	49	7	1	4	31	9
94 A	.333	3	6	1	2	0	0	0	0	0
95 A	.282	124	457	62	129	31	7	16	72	5
96 A	.240	131	499	54	120	31	2	15	58	11

Professional Pitching Register

	W	L	ERA	G	CG	IP	H	ER	BB	SO
94 R	4	4	2.35	11	1	65.0	56	17	18	64
95 R	3	3	5.71	14	1	69.1	66	44	33	75
96 A	9	5	2.69	18	1	110.1	101	33	33	113
96 AA	3	4	5.33	10	0	54.0	61	32	24	44

BOBBY ESTALELLA

Position: Catcher
Team: Philadelphia Phillies
Born: Aug. 23, 1974 Hialeah, FL
Height: 6'1" **Weight:** 195 lbs.
Bats: right **Throws:** right
Acquired: 22nd-round pick in 6/92 free-agent draft

PLAYER SUMMARY	
Fantasy Value	$0
Card Value	15¢ to 20¢
Will	reach the fences
Can't	win many races
Expect	nice size
Don't Expect	22nd-round results

Last year, the Phillies said farewell to one power-hitting catcher when Darren Daulton decided to retire. If things keep going well, however, Estalella may be able to compensate for Daulton's departure. Estalella surely looked like a power hitter last year when he slapped around Eastern League pitchers to achieve career highs in home runs and RBI. He appeared in the Double-A All-Star Game, going 0-for-2. He assembled a double-digit consecutive-games hitting streak that spanned July and August—not bad for a guy who sat around until the Phillies chose him in 1992. Estalella graduated from Cooper City High School in Florida, then attended Miami Dade South Junior College. His grandfather, Roberto, was an outfielder-first baseman for the Washington Senators, St. Louis Browns, and Philadelphia Athletics. The younger Estalella should move to Triple-A this year.

Professional Batting Register

	BA	G	AB	R	H	2B	3B	HR	RBI	SB
93 R	.295	35	122	14	36	11	0	3	19	0
93 A	.229	11	35	4	8	0	0	0	4	0
94 A	.217	86	299	34	65	19	1	9	41	0
94 A	.261	13	46	3	12	1	0	2	9	0
95 A	.260	117	404	61	105	24	1	15	58	0
95 AA	.235	10	34	5	8	1	0	2	9	0
96 AA	.244	111	365	48	89	14	2	23	72	2
96 AAA	.250	11	36	7	9	3	0	3	8	0
96 NL	.353	7	17	5	6	0	0	2	4	1

BRIAN FALKENBORG

Position: Pitcher
Team: Baltimore Orioles
Born: Jan. 18, 1978 Newport Beach, CA
Height: 6'6" **Weight:** 180 lbs.
Bats: right **Throws:** right
Acquired: Second-round pick in 6/96 free-agent draft

PLAYER SUMMARY	
Fantasy Value	$0
Card Value	15¢ to 20¢
Will	be noticed on hill
Can't	advance quickly
Expect	good delivery
Don't Expect	walks

The Orioles entered the 1996 draft without a first-round pick, having lost it as compensation for their signing of free-agent second baseman Roberto Alomar. They did not get to make a pick until the 51st overall selection, and that's when they went for Falkenborg. *Baseball America* had ranked him as only the 71st-best draft-eligible prospect, so either his stock climbed or the Orioles liked him a little better than others did. Out of Redmond High School in the state of Washington, Falkenborg earned attention for his commanding size and his ability to throw the ball over the plate; he averaged just one walk per five innings. After signing with the O's, Falkenborg quickly learned about the realities of professional life: He reported to Sarasota of the rookie Gulf Coast League, just about as far as he could go from his home. He made the adjustment look easy as Sarasota eased him into duty. Over his first eight outings, he averaged more than a K per inning.

Professional Pitching Register

	W	L	ERA	G	CG	IP	H	ER	BB	SO
96 R	0	3	2.57	8	0	28.0	21	8	8	36
96 A	0	0	0.00	1	0	1.0	1	0	0	1

NELSON FIGUEROA

Position: Pitcher
Team: New York Mets
Born: May 18, 1974 Brooklyn, NY
Height: 6'1" **Weight:** 165 lbs.
Bats: both **Throws:** right
Acquired: 30th-round pick in 6/95 free-agent draft

PLAYER SUMMARY

Fantasy Value	. . . . $0
Card Value	. . . . 12¢ to 15¢
Will	. . . . get a promotion
Can't	. . . . ease up now
Expect	. . . . few hits
Don't Expect	. . . . big buildup

As a native-born New Yorker, Figueroa will just about own the town if he makes it big with the Mets. Unfortunately for him, that's a bit down the road. True, he did dominate with Columbia of the South Atlantic League last year, but the Sally League is a long way from New York, and Figueroa is a low-round pick. Furthermore, the Mets received a refresher course last year in what can happen to highly touted pitchers as they watched Jason Isringhausen, Bill Pulsipher, and Paul Wilson confront a series of misfortunes. None of that should deter Figueroa. What he must do is keep getting batters out, which he did well enough to get a mention as an emerging prospect in *USA TODAY Baseball Weekly*'s midseason overview of farm systems. Figueroa started for the National League farmhands in the Sally League All-Star Game and went two scoreless innings. This year he will likely be assigned to either high Class-A or Double-A as the Mets watch his progress.

JOE FONTENOT

Position: Pitcher
Team: San Francisco Giants
Born: March 20, 1977 Lafayette, LA
Height: 6'2" **Weight:** 185 lbs.
Bats: right **Throws:** right
Acquired: First-round pick in 6/95 free-agent draft

PLAYER SUMMARY

Fantasy Value	. . . . $0
Card Value	. . . . 12¢ to 15¢
Will	. . . . have control lapses
Can't	. . . . make Giants yet
Expect	. . . . scary curve
Don't Expect	. . . . overpowering heat

Fontenot came to the Giants via the 16th overall pick in the 1995 draft, and he immediately began justifying the team's faith in him. Though he lost all three decisions in his initial exposure to pro ball, Fontenot pitched well enough to earn a nod from *Baseball America* as the tenth-best prospect in the Northwest League. San Francisco thought so much of his progress that the front office assigned him to the fast-paced Class-A California League, where he began the season as the youngest pitcher for San Jose. Despite his tender age, he assembled an impressive streak over a span of 13 starts, going 6-0 and allowing just 73 hits over 79⅓ innings. The streak ended abruptly when he was pounded for nine runs in 1⅔ innings on July 9. Fontenot attended Acadiana High School in Lafayette and graduated as the top pitching prospect in Louisiana. Considering his age, Fontenot might be better served by another year of Class-A competition.

Professional Pitching Register

	W	L	ERA	G	CG	IP	H	ER	BB	SO
95 R	7	3	3.07	12	2	76.1	57	26	22	79
96 A	14	7	2.04	26	8	185.1	119	42	58	200

Professional Pitching Register

	W	L	ERA	G	CG	IP	H	ER	BB	SO
95 A	0	3	1.93	6	0	18.2	14	4	10	14
96 A	9	4	4.44	26	0	144.0	137	71	74	124

BRAD FULLMER

Position: Outfield
Team: Montreal Expos
Born: Jan. 17, 1975 Los Angeles, CA
Height: 6'1" **Weight:** 190 lbs.
Bats: left **Throws:** right
Acquired: Second-round pick in 6/93 free-agent draft

PLAYER SUMMARY	
Fantasy Value	$0
Card Value	12¢ to 20¢
Will	hit for average
Can't	sacrifice contact
Expect	doubles
Don't Expect	a third baseman

Fullmer's career has taken some twists and turns since the day he was drafted in 1993. First, he held out while negotiating a contract. Then he underwent shoulder surgery. Finally, last year he changed positions, moving from the infield to the outfield. Fullmer was the starting left fielder for West Palm Beach of the Florida State League, and his shoulder history makes a return to third base very unlikely. Finding the right defensive position for Fullmer is paramount, because the overwhelming impression is that this young man can flat-out hit. He demonstrated some of his hitting ability last year, batting over .300 before his promotion to Double-A and reaching the 30-double plateau for the second time in as many pro seasons. So far he has not shown much in the way of home runs, but that may come with experience. To leave the yard more often, however, Fullmer might have to risk his impressive strikeout-to-walk ratio. Look for him in the Eastern League this year.

CHRIS FUSSELL

Position: Pitcher
Team: Baltimore Orioles
Born: May 19, 1976 Oregon, OH
Height: 6'2" **Weight:** 180 lbs.
Bats: right **Throws:** right
Acquired: Ninth-round pick in 6/94 free-agent draft

PLAYER SUMMARY	
Fantasy Value	$0
Card Value	12¢ to 15¢
Will	be stingy with hits
Can't	succumb to injury
Expect	No. 1 starter
Don't Expect	rookie-league stats

Fussell made it to the Little League World Series in 1988, and the Orioles would like nothing better than to have him reach the fall classic as a member of their organization. While he still has a way to go before that can happen, Fussell has shown an ability to pitch in the lower minors, and he would have built even better stats had he not been sidelined by injury last year. Pitching for Frederick of the Carolina League, Fussell was leading the circuit in strikeouts when injury struck. He had even started the All-Star Game against the California League, going two innings and allowing no runs. *USA TODAY Baseball Weekly* named him one of its prospects to watch. Fussell broke into professional ball in 1994 in the Gulf Coast League, averaging ten strikeouts per nine innings. In 1995, he was named to the postseason All-Star squad in the Appalachian League. If healthy, he should move out of Class-A competition quickly this summer.

Professional Batting Register

	BA	G	AB	R	H	2B	3B	HR	RBI	SB
95 A	.323	123	468	69	151	38	4	8	67	10
96 A	.303	102	380	52	115	29	1	5	63	4
96 AA	.276	24	98	11	27	4	1	4	14	0

Professional Pitching Register

	W	L	ERA	G	CG	IP	H	ER	BB	SO
94 R	2	3	4.15	14	0	56.1	53	26	24	65
95 R	9	1	2.19	12	1	65.2	37	16	32	96
96 A	5	2	2.81	15	1	86.1	71	27	44	94

KARIM GARCIA

Position: Outfield
Team: Los Angeles Dodgers
Born: Oct. 29, 1975 Cuidad Obregon, Mexico
Height: 6′ **Weight:** 172 lbs.
Bats: left **Throws:** left
Acquired: Signed as a nondrafted free agent, 7/92

PLAYER SUMMARY	
Fantasy Value	$1
Card Value	20¢ to 30¢
Will	hit with authority
Can't	step backwards
Expect	an All-Star
Don't Expect	another demotion

Garcia is another in what seems to be an endless supply of talent in the Dodger farm system. He made his first trip to the major leagues late in 1995, arriving at the age of 19. Garcia needed only three years from the time he signed his first contract to the time he made his debut in the majors. Last year, however, he took one—or perhaps two—steps backward After beginning the season as the starting right fielder for the Dodgers Triple-A team in Albuquerque, Garcia suffered an injury that sent him to the disabled list. Upon being reactivated, he was demoted to Double-A San Antonio. He apparently considered that a wake-up call, because he hit .385 over a ten-game span in late July and early August. It's hard to describe a limit for Garcia. He runs well, can hit with power, and throws well enough to play right field. It would be surprising if he did not land a full-time job with the Dodgers sometime this year.

Professional Batting Register

	BA	G	AB	R	H	2B	3B	HR	RBI	SB
93 A	.241	123	460	61	111	20	9	19	54	5
94 A	.265	121	452	72	120	28	10	21	84	8
95 AAA	.319	124	474	88	151	26	10	20	91	12
95 NL	.200	13	20	1	4	0	0	0	0	0
96 AA	.248	35	129	21	32	6	1	5	22	1
96 AAA	.297	84	327	54	97	17	10	13	58	6
96 NL	.000	1	1	0	0	0	0	0	0	0

NOMAR GARCIAPARRA

Position: Shortstop
Team: Boston Red Sox
Born: July 23, 1973 Whittier, CA
Height: 6′ **Weight:** 165 lbs.
Bats: right **Throws:** right
Acquired: First-round pick in 6/94 free-agent draft

PLAYER SUMMARY	
Fantasy Value	$6 to $8
Card Value	20¢ to 30¢
Will	show great range
Can't	play when injured
Expect	challenge to Valentin
Don't Expect	raw recruit

Last year, Garciaparra made his major-league debut and needed little time to prove he belongs at that level. However, things aren't quite that simple, since the Red Sox have an extremely capable shortstop in John Valentin. Garciaparra might have stepped in when Valentin was hurt last year, but Garciaparra himself suffered injury problems that left him with precious few at bats. Even so, he homered twice in an August 7 game at Ottawa, and he also assembled a 15-game hitting streak. Talented as Garciaparra might be at the plate, however, much of his game revolves around great range in the field. In 1995, he led all Eastern League shortstops in total chances and assists. At one point, he played 28 consecutive games without an error. Garciaparra majored in management at Georgia Tech, where he hit .372 over three years. He also played in the 1992 Olympics. Garciaparra played soccer in high school and was a wide receiver in football. The Red Sox are anxious to utilize this enormous all-around talent.

Professional Batting Register

	BA	G	AB	R	H	2B	3B	HR	RBI	SB
94 A	.295	28	105	20	31	8	1	1	16	5
95 AA	.267	125	513	77	137	20	8	8	47	35
96 R	.286	5	14	4	4	2	1	0	5	0
96 AAA	.343	43	172	40	59	15	2	16	46	3
96 AL	.241	24	87	11	21	2	3	4	16	5

JOSH GARRETT

Position: Pitcher
Team: Boston Red Sox
Born: Jan. 12, 1978 Owensboro, KY
Height: 6'4" **Weight:** 210 lbs.
Bats: right **Throws:** right
Acquired: First-round pick in 6/96 free-agent draft

PLAYER SUMMARY

Fantasy Value	$0
Card Value	20¢ to 35¢
Will	rise slowly
Can't	replace Hanson yet
Expect	intelligent athlete
Don't Expect	blazing fastball

The departure of free agent Erik Hanson provided the Red Sox with two extra picks in the 1996 free-agent draft, giving them the opportunity to load up on prospects with a total of four selections in the first two rounds of the draft. Three of those four picks were used on righty pitchers, the first among them being Garrett. Taken with the 26th overall pick, Garrett was the 16th pitcher—and the ninth out of high school—to go in the grab bag. He comes out of South Spencer High School in Richland, Indiana, where he put up big numbers. Quickly signing a contract worth a reported $670,000, he was assigned to Fort Myers of the rookie Gulf Coast League. He made his pro debut there on July 22, allowing one run in two innings. Later, he assembled three straight outings in which he permitted no runs. Red Sox fans should not expect any immediate help from Garrett, though his quick signing and the experience he gained could mean he'll see some full-season Class-A action this summer.

Professional Pitching Register

	W	L	ERA	G	CG	IP	H	ER	BB	SO
96 R	1	1	1.67	7	0	27.0	22	5	5	17

STEVE GIBRALTER

Position: Outfield
Team: Cincinnati Reds
Born: Oct. 9, 1972 Dallas, TX
Height: 6' **Weight:** 190 lbs.
Bats: right **Throws:** right
Acquired: Sixth-round pick in 6/90 free-agent draft

PLAYER SUMMARY

Fantasy Value	$0
Card Value	12¢ to 20¢
Will	hustle
Can't	hit with bad thumb
Expect	crossroads season
Don't Expect	big power numbers

Until quite recently, Gibralter was clearly one of the Reds' top prospects, but now it's not so easy to tell. He has suffered some injuries, and last year his numbers slipped a little. Also, he spent most of the season at Triple-A, even though injuries at the big-league level seemed to have opened up some opportunity in the majors. Thus, 1997 looms as a big one for Gibralter. He came into prominence in 1992 while in the Midwest League, earning MVP honors and leading the circuit in home runs and RBI. A year later, he slumped when assigned to Double-A ball, and he was playing in the Arizona Fall League when he was sidelined by a shoulder problem. He fought his way back by 1995, when he starred for the Reds Triple-A club in Indianapolis. He looked ready for a second call-up to the majors when he tore ligaments in his left thumb. Whether that injury has robbed Gibralter of some much-needed pop may be seen a little more clearly this year.

Professional Batting Register

	BA	G	AB	R	H	2B	3B	HR	RBI	SB
90 R	.259	52	174	26	45	11	3	4	27	9
91 A	.267	140	544	72	145	36	7	6	71	11
92 A	.306	137	529	92	162	32	3	19	99	12
93 AA	.237	132	477	65	113	25	3	11	47	7
94 AA	.270	133	460	71	124	28	3	14	63	10
95 AAA	.316	79	263	49	83	19	3	18	63	0
95 NL	.333	4	3	0	1	0	0	0	0	0
96 AAA	.255	126	447	58	114	29	2	11	54	2
96 NL	.000	2	2	0	0	0	0	0	0	0

DERRICK GIBSON

Position: Outfield
Team: Colorado Rockies
Born: Feb. 5, 1975 Winter Haven, FL
Height: 6'2" **Weight:** 228 lbs.
Bats: right **Throws:** right
Acquired: 13th-round pick in 6/93 free-agent draft

PLAYER SUMMARY	
Fantasy Value $0
Card Value . . . . 15¢ to 25¢
Will . . . . bring tools
Can't. . . . . make steady contact
Expect . . . . left fielder
Don't Expect . . . . a low ceiling

The last thing the Rockies would seem to need is another slugger who can take advantage of the hitter's paradise in Denver. Yet if Gibson progresses the way the Rockies think he can, the rest of the National League can brace for some more long balls. Last year, Gibson played with Colorado's Double-A affiliate in New Haven, where he posted acceptable power numbers. They were nothing like the ones he had hung up a year earlier in Asheville, but that was probably because in '96 he had to adjust to making the jump from a low Class-A league. Gibson comes out of Haines City High School in Florida, where he earned letters in baseball, football, basketball, and track. He had signed a letter of intent to play football at Auburn but wound up signing with the Rockies instead. He is a tools player, offering power and speed. But he needs to refine his approach to hitting and put the ball in play more often. He might get more seasoning at Double-A, with a shot at the big leagues in '97.

ARNOLD GOOCH

Position: Pitcher
Team: New York Mets
Born: Nov. 12, 1976 Levittown, PA
Height: 6'2" **Weight:** 195 lbs.
Bats: right **Throws:** right
Acquired: Traded by Rockies with Juan Acevedo for Bret Saberhagen and David Swanson, 7/95

PLAYER SUMMARY	
Fantasy Value $0
Card Value . . . . 15¢ to 25¢
Will . . . . limit hits
Can't. . . . . seem to win
Expect . . . . good stuff
Don't Expect . . . . a Saberhagen

Almost by default, Gooch has emerged as the key player in the deal that sent Bret Saberhagen from the Mets to Colorado at the 1995 trading deadline. Saberhagen's season was devastated by injury, and Juan Acevedo, another pitcher acquired by the Mets, has not pitched well. Still, Gooch would rate as a factor even if the other pitchers were doing well. He pitched for Port St. Lucie of the Florida State League last year, and, even though his win-loss record won't knock anyone over, all his other stats reflect just what you want in a pitcher. His hits-to-innings ratio was excellent. So was his rate of strikeouts per nine innings. He averaged more than six innings per start over his first 19 outings, and he yielded just one walk per three innings. Gooch was Colorado's ninth pick in the 1994 draft, and he spent his first pro season in the Arizona League. He finished with the Sally League's tenth-best ERA (2.94) in 1995. This season, he might get a chance in Double-A.

Professional Batting Register

	BA	G	AB	R	H	2B	3B	HR	RBI	SB
93 R	.151	34	119	13	18	2	2	0	10	3
94 A	.264	73	284	47	75	19	5	12	57	14
95 A	.292	135	506	91	148	16	10	32	115	31
96 AA	.256	122	449	58	115	21	4	15	62	3

Professional Pitching Register

	W	L	ERA	G	CG	IP	H	ER	BB	SO
94 R	2	4	2.64	15	0	58.0	45	17	16	66
95 A	2	3	4.46	6	0	38.1	39	19	15	34
95 A	5	8	2.94	21	1	128.2	111	42	57	117
96 A	12	12	2.58	26	2	167.2	131	48	51	141

JEREMI GONZALEZ

Position: Pitcher
Team: Chicago Cubs
Born: Jan. 8, 1975 Maracaibo, Venezuela
Height: 6'11" **Weight:** 180 lbs.
Bats: right **Throws:** right
Acquired: Signed as a nondrafted free agent,
10/91

PLAYER SUMMARY	
Fantasy Value	$0
Card Value	15¢ to 25¢
Will	allow few baserunners
Can't	predict next stop
Expect	uncertainty
Don't Expect	form of old

There's no telling where Gonzalez might be today had injury not intruded on his 1996 campaign. Pitching for Orlando of the Double-A Southern League, Gonzalez seemed headed for a breakthrough year in his fifth season as a pro. He collected six wins in his first 12 appearances and had allowed only 19 walks in 71 innings when he was forced to the disabled list. In one sample of his work, Gonzalez struck out 12 in a victory over Carolina on May 24, winning his fifth straight start. At that point, he owned six victories, giving him a piece of the lead in the Cub farm system. Unfortunately for Gonzalez, that would prove to be his last victory for the year. Gonzalez comes out of Colegro La Chinita School in Maracaibo. He signed with the Cubbies when he was about 2½ months shy of his 17th birthday, and he spent his first pro season in Mesa, Arizona. He gave little hint of an emergence until 1995, when he won five of six decisions in a 19-game stint in high Class-A ball.

Professional Pitching Register

	W	L	ERA	G	CG	IP	H	ER	BB	SO
92 R	0	5	7.80	14	0	45.0	65	39	22	39
93 R	3	9	6.25	12	1	67.2	82	47	38	42
94 A	1	7	5.55	13	1	71.1	86	44	32	39
94 A	4	6	4.24	16	1	80.2	83	38	29	64
95 A	4	4	5.10	12	1	65.1	63	37	28	36
95 A	5	1	1.22	19	0	44.1	34	6	13	30
96 AA	6	3	3.34	17	0	97.0	95	36	28	85

DANNY GRAVES

Position: Pitcher
Team: Cleveland Indians
Born: Aug. 7, 1973 Saigon, Vietnam
Height: 5'11" **Weight:** 200 lbs.
Bats: right **Throws:** right
Acquired: Fourth-round pick in 6/94 free-agent
draft

PLAYER SUMMARY	
Fantasy Value	$1
Card Value	15¢ to 25¢
Will	stick around
Can't	rely on his size
Expect	middle reliever
Don't Expect	lingering knee woes

To say the least, not many people born in Saigon ever get to the majors. Not many right-handers who stand under six feet tall ever prosper once they get there. Graves accomplished the first feat last year when he was promoted to Cleveland. Now, only time will tell if he can achieve the second as well. Graves needed only about two years between draft day and his call to the majors, and he might have made it even sooner if not for a torn anterior cruciate ligament in his right knee suffered in the 1994 College World Series. Needless to say, it finished him for the season, but he bounced back with a dominant performance a year later. Graves collected 31 saves and earned recognition as the organization's top pitcher in the minors. He made the Carolina League's postseason All-Star Team and allowed opposing hitters only a .183 average. Though Graves has been a closer in the minors, he'll probably work middle relief or setup in the majors.

Professional Pitching Register

	W	L	ERA	G	S	IP	H	ER	BB	SO
95 A	3	1	0.82	38	21	44.0	30	4	12	46
95 AA	1	0	0.00	17	10	23.1	10	0	2	11
95 AAA	0	0	3.00	3	0	3.0	5	1	1	2
96 AAA	4	3	1.48	43	19	79.0	57	13	24	46
96 AL	2	0	4.55	15	0	29.2	29	15	10	22

CHAD GREEN

Position: Outfield
Team: Milwaukee Brewers
Born: June 28, 1975 Dunkirk, NY
Height: 5'10" **Weight:** 185 lbs.
Bats: both **Throws:** right
Acquired: First-round pick in 6/96 free-agent draft

PLAYER SUMMARY	
Fantasy Value	$0
Card Value	15¢ to 25¢
Will	blaze on bases
Can't	waste speed
Expect	good range
Don't Expect	slap hitter

Green would seem to have all the tools and background needed for a good run at a major-league career. He is a switch-hitter who can run. He also has a wealth of experience, both at the University of Kentucky and with the U.S. Olympic team. Green was the eighth player taken overall—and just the second position player selected—in the 1996 draft. Green was a sensation on the bases in college, and he has shown the ability to hit home runs. Still, he'll have to be careful in his approach to hitting. With speed like his, he doesn't want the ball in the air too often. Upon signing, Green spent time with Ogden of the Pioneer League, where he immediately flashed some of his ability. Over the second half of August, he assembled a double-digit hitting streak and also demonstrated a knack for stealing bases and scoring runs. That brief audition should mean a trip to a full-season Class-A league this season, where the Brewers will watch him closely to see if he can get something going.

SCARBOROUGH GREEN

Position: Outfield
Team: St. Louis Cardinals
Born: June 9, 1974 Creve Coeur, MO
Height: 5'10" **Weight:** 170 lbs.
Bats: right **Throws:** right
Acquired: Tenth-round pick in 6/92 free-agent draft

PLAYER SUMMARY	
Fantasy Value	$0
Card Value	15¢ to 25¢
Will	steal bases
Can't	avoid errors
Expect	speed
Don't Expect	a shortstop

Green was the starting center fielder for the Cardinals club in the Class-A Florida State League last year. That fact alone is worth noting because one year earlier, in the South Atlantic League, Green had played shortstop. There he committed the astonishing total of 51 errors, most of anyone in the organization. That stat, combined with the fact that Green hit only .228, hardly suggested that he was a prospect. But, in an inspired player development decision, the Cardinals decided not only to switch his position, but also to promote him up a notch. So far the switch has seemed to work beautifully. In his new position, Green needed only about two months to play his way through the FSL and advance to Double-A Arkansas. There he had some real problems at the plate, though he did finish among the top basestealers in the St. Louis chain. Green may have had a better chance in the 1980s, when Busch Stadium offered artificial turf, but he might make it anyway.

Professional Batting Register

	BA	G	AB	R	H	2B	3B	HR	RBI	SB
96 R	.358	21	81	22	29	4	1	3	8	12

Professional Batting Register

	BA	G	AB	R	H	2B	3B	HR	RBI	SB
93 R	.221	33	95	16	21	3	1	0	11	3
94 R	.241	54	199	32	48	5	0	0	11	22
95 A	.228	132	429	48	98	7	6	1	25	26
96 A	.293	36	140	26	41	4	1	1	11	13
96 AA	.200	92	300	45	60	6	3	3	24	21

TODD GREENE

Position: Catcher
Team: Anaheim Angels
Born: May 8, 1971 Augusta, GA
Height: 5'10" **Weight:** 200 lbs.
Bats: right **Throws:** right
Acquired: 12th-round pick in 6/93 free-agent draft

PLAYER SUMMARY	
Fantasy Value	$2 to $4
Card Value	10¢ to 15¢
Will	slug home runs
Can't	play center
Expect	bona fide slugger
Don't Expect	a utility man

Now that he has arrived, Greene could be part of California's lineup for years to come. He is a bona fide power hitter who led his league in home runs in his first two pro seasons. Then, in his third campaign, he was promoted in midseason and still managed to hit a total of 40 homers. He was called to the majors last year, where he joined Jorge Fabregas, another catcher developed by the Angels. Greene comes out of Georgia Southern, where he set school records in hits, homers, total bases, RBI, and slugging percentage. A three-time All-American, he also earned a bronze medal as a member of the United States squad in the 1991 Pan Am Games. He began his career as an outfielder, then was switched to catcher in 1994. He also has spent time at first base, which gives the Angels several options for finding room in the lineup for Greene's bat. Chances are he could get 500 at bats this season and use them to become an impact player.

SETH GREISINGER

Position: Pitcher
Team: Detroit Tigers
Born: July 29, 1975 Falls Church, VA
Height: 6'3" **Weight:** 200 lbs.
Bats: right **Throws:** right
Acquired: First-round pick in 6/96 free-agent draft

PLAYER SUMMARY	
Fantasy Value	$0
Card Value	20¢ to 30¢
Will	throw breaking pitch
Can't	rule him out as ace
Expect	buckled knees
Don't Expect	long internship

In the span of only a few months, Greisinger went from barely making *Baseball America*'s list of the top 100 college prospects to becoming the sixth overall pick in the draft. And that's not all. Somewhere along the way, he also made the United States national team and appeared in the Olympics as part of an acclaimed pitching staff. If nothing else, all that progress says a lot about Greisinger's ability to learn and to make adjustments. As for his stuff, it's more than adequate. He throws a fastball that can poke its way into the 90s, and he complements it with a curve that can buckle knees when he has command of it. His size and durability should allow him to deliver plenty of innings. Originally drafted by the Reds in 1993, Greisinger comes out of the University of Virginia, where he dominated with a 12-2 mark in his junior year. He will probably get a high-level assignment this year, with quick advancement likely.

Professional Batting Register

	BA	G	AB	R	H	2B	3B	HR	RBI	SB
93 A	.269	76	305	55	82	15	3	15	71	4
94 A	.302	133	524	98	158	39	2	35	124	10
95 AA	.327	82	318	59	104	19	1	26	57	3
95 AAA	.250	43	168	28	42	3	1	14	35	1
96 AAA	.305	60	223	27	68	18	0	5	33	0
96 AL	.190	29	79	9	15	1	0	2	9	2

BEN GRIEVE

Position: Outfield
Team: Oakland Athletics
Born: May 4, 1976 Arlington, TX
Height: 6'4" **Weight:** 200 lbs.
Bats: left **Throws:** right
Acquired: First-round pick in 6/94 free agent draft

PLAYER SUMMARY	
Fantasy Value	$0
Card Value	20¢ to 30¢
Will	hit for average
Can't	play center
Expect	help for lineup
Don't Expect	move to first yet

Grieve offers the possibility that the A's, who presented one of the most awesome lineups in history last year, could soon be adding still another bat. Grieve really began to blossom last season in the California League, and—if he continues his current pace—will likely arrive in the majors sometime late this year or early in 1998. He has established that he can hit for average, and the power numbers may come as he fills out and gains experience. Son of former major-leaguer Tom Grieve, Ben was taken with the second overall pick in the 1994 draft, making the Grieves the first father-son combo to be selected in the initial round. Ben quickly established himself in pro ball and was named to the postseason All-Star Team in the Northwest League. He split the 1995 season between low and high Class-A ball. Grieve has spent a lot of time in left field, and that's probably where he'll remain, though his being left-handed makes first base an option at some point.

VLAD GUERRERO

Position: Outfield
Team: Montreal Expos
Born: Feb. 9, 1976 Nizao Bani, Dominican Republic
Height: 6'2" **Weight:** 170 lbs.
Bats: right **Throws:** right
Acquired: Signed as a nondrafted free agent, 3/93

PLAYER SUMMARY	
Fantasy Value	$7 to $9
Card Value	30¢ to 40¢
Will	show off cannon
Can't	be ignored
Expect	nice stick
Don't Expect	Andruw Jones

Though overshadowed to some extent by Atlanta's Andruw Jones, Guerrero is one of baseball's top prospects. He brings the same kind of multitool, high-ceiling package that Jones does. Last year, Guerrero won the Triple Crown in the Montreal organization, even though he received an early-season promotion that required some inevitable adjustments. Like Jones, Guerrero began the season in the Class-A Carolina League but soon made it obvious that he had outgrown that level. A promotion to Harrisburg—an outpost in the challenging Double-A Eastern League—merely seemed to bring out the best in Guerrero. He hit the ball hard and consistently, and he utilized his speed on the bases. His throwing arm in the outfield is strong enough to help make a difference in games. Guerrero could join the Expos to begin the 1997 season. After that, it will be Montreal's job to try to hold onto one of the game's most exciting performers.

Professional Batting Register

	BA	G	AB	R	H	2B	3B	HR	RBI	SB
94 A	.329	72	252	44	83	13	0	7	50	2
95 A	.261	102	371	53	97	16	1	4	62	11
95 A	.262	28	107	17	28	5	0	2	14	2
96 A	.356	72	281	61	100	20	1	11	51	8
96 AA	.237	63	232	34	55	8	1	8	32	0

Professional Batting Register

	BA	G	AB	R	H	2B	3B	HR	RBI	SB
94 R	.424	25	92	34	39	11	0	12	35	5
94 R	.314	37	137	24	43	13	3	5	25	0
95 A	.333	110	421	77	140	21	10	16	63	12
96 A	.363	20	80	16	29	8	0	5	18	2
96 AA	.360	118	417	84	150	32	8	19	78	17
96 NL	.185	9	27	2	5	0	0	1	1	0

WILTON GUERRRO

Position: Second base
Team: Los Angeles Dodgers
Born: Oct. 24, 1974 Don Gregorio, Dominican Republic
Height: 5'11" **Weight:** 155 lbs.
Bats: right **Throws:** right
Acquired: Signed as a nondrafted free agent, 10/91

PLAYER SUMMARY	
Fantasy Value	$0
Card Value	20¢ to 25¢
Will	vie for batting title
Can't	win slugging title
Expect	hitting streaks
Don't Expect	return to shortstop

Guerrero might bring a great deal to a team that has lacked chemistry in its lineup despite the presence of several individual bats. With his ability to get on base, steal bases, and score runs, he could find himself stationed at second base for the Dodgers for the next decade. Guerrero posted another fine season at the plate last year, this time at Triple-A Albuquerque. A season earlier, he won the Texas League batting title. In addition, he was named to the Texas League All-Star Team and played in the Double-A All-Star Game. Hitting streaks seem to be a specialty of Guerrero's. In 1995, he assembled a 23-game streak, and last year he put together a 17-game stretch over which he raised his average to .338, third-best in the league. Guerrero came out of the Dominican Republic as a shortstop but was switched to second base. He won the Minor League Sprint Championship in spring training in 1995. His speed is a tool that should serve him well throughout his pro career.

Professional Batting Register

	BA	G	AB	R	H	2B	3B	HR	RBI	SB
93 R	.297	66	256	44	76	5	1	0	21	20
94 A	.294	110	402	55	118	11	4	1	32	23
95 AA	.348	95	382	53	133	13	6	0	26	21
95 AAA	.327	14	49	10	16	1	1	0	2	2
96 AAA	.344	98	425	79	146	17	12	2	38	26
96 NL	.000	5	2	1	0	0	0	0	0	0

JOSE GUILLEN

Position: Outfield
Team: Pittsburgh Pirates
Born: May 17, 1976 San Cristobal, Dominican Republic
Height: 5'11" **Weight:** 165 lbs.
Bats: right **Throws:** right
Acquired: Signed as a nondrafted free agent, 8/92

PLAYER SUMMARY	
Fantasy Value	$0
Card Value	15¢ to 20¢
Will	hit with power
Can't	bulk up
Expect	strong arm
Don't Expect	Pirates in '97

When you look at Guillen's slight physique, his power potential doesn't leap out at you. But when he swings, the ball leaps off his bat often enough to have projected him into the picture as a future Pirate. In his fourth pro season, Guillen turned in a fine year in the Carolina League, making the All-Star Team and going 1-for-5 in the game against the California League All-Stars. He also played right field for that entire game, giving you an idea of what baseball people think about his arm. *USA TODAY Baseball Weekly* gave Guillen a mention as an emerging prospect in its annual check of farm systems. Guillen ranked among the leaders in the Triple Crown categories in the Pittsburgh system last year. His batting average (.322) and RBI totals (94) were especially strong. Over one stretch from July 3 to July 19, he hit .448 with seven homers and 21 RBI. Guillen will probably get an extended look at Double-A ball this year, and if he handles that he could be a Pirate in '98.

Professional Batting Register

	BA	G	AB	R	H	2B	3B	HR	RBI	SB
94 R	.264	30	110	17	29	4	1	4	11	2
95 A	.314	66	258	41	81	17	1	12	46	1
95 A	.235	10	34	6	8	1	1	2	6	0
96 A	.322	136	528	78	170	30	0	21	94	24

ROY HALLADAY

Position: Pitcher
Team: Toronto Blue Jays
Born: May 14, 1977 Denver, CO
Height: 6'5" **Weight:** 200 lbs.
Bats: right **Throws:** right
Acquired: First-round pick in 6/95 free-agent
draft

PLAYER SUMMARY	
Fantasy Value	$0
Card Value	10¢ to 15¢
Will	get a promotion
Can't	skip Double-A
Expect	strikeouts
Don't Expect	lots of hits

Halladay is one of the hottest prospects in
the Toronto organization. He enjoyed a fine
season in Single-A ball last year in what
was only his second professional season.
The Blue Jays named him the MVP of their
Florida State League club in Dunedin. He
led the Jays farm system with victories and
finished second in ERA, even though he
endured a disastrous late-season start in
which he allowed nine runs while getting
only four outs. Halladay comes out of West
High School near Denver, where he allowed only one hit per three innings.
Signed as the 17th overall pick in 1995, he
went to the Gulf Coast League, where he
proceeded to record just under one strikeout per inning. He also held opposing hitters to a .190 batting average. Considering
the speed with which he has moved so far,
it's not impossible that Halladay could get a
peek at the majors soon. But first he must
see if he can handle Double-A hitters as
well as he has handled those at lower levels.

MATT HALLORAN

Position: Infield
Team: San Diego Padres
Born: March 3, 1978 Milton, FL
Height: 6'1" **Weight:** 175 lbs.
Bats: right **Throws:** right
Acquired: First-round pick in 6/96 free-agent
draft

PLAYER SUMMARY	
Fantasy Value	$0
Card Value	25¢ to 35¢
Will	need time to adjust
Can't	challenge for job yet
Expect	.240 hitter
Don't Expect	shortstop in majors

Halloran came to the Padres as the 15th
overall pick in last year's draft, the seventh
position player taken and only the second
high school infielder. Out of Fredericksburg,
Virginia, where he attended Chancellor
High School, Halloran was a highly coveted
player in the state that also produced Seth
Greisinger, a college pitcher and a member
of the U.S. Olympic team. Upon signing,
Halloran went to Peoria of the Arizona
League, where he played shortstop and
was hitting only a shade above .200 after
his first week or so. However, he picked up
the pace as he gained experience. On August 15, he smacked two triples in a victory
against Arizona's farm team. The immediate results don't matter as much as the fact
that Halloran was getting the feel of pro
ball. This year Halloran will probably go to a
short-season league, and the San Diego
organization shouldn't expect to see him in
the big leagues much before the turn of the
century.

Professional Pitching Register

	W	L	ERA	G	CG	IP	H	ER	BB	SO
95 R	3	5	3.40	10	0	50.1	35	19	16	48
96 A	15	7	2.73	27	2	164.2	158	50	46	109

Professional Batting Register

	BA	G	AB	R	H	2B	3B	HR	RBI	SB
96 R	.261	39	134	22	35	7	4	0	15	2

JED HANSEN

Position: Infield
Team: Kansas City Royals
Born: Aug. 19, 1972 Olympia, WA
Height: 6'1" **Weight:** 180 lbs.
Bats: right **Throws:** right
Acquired: Second-round pick in 6/94 free-agent draft

PLAYER SUMMARY	
Fantasy Value	$0
Card Value	15¢ to 25¢
Will	hit in .250 range
Can't	play short
Expect	smarts
Don't Expect	consistent contact

Hansen could be Kansas City's second baseman in 1997 if he can sustain what he accomplished at Double- and Triple-A last season. Beginning the campaign with Wichita of the Double-A Texas League, Hansen worked his way up to Omaha, just a phone call away from the majors. He has shown himself to be a useful offensive player, with an ability to hit for average, steal some bases, and put the ball into the gaps or over the fence. He pays a price for his pop with a very large number of strikeouts, but as a former Stanford Scholar Athlete he should have the intelligence to make the necessary adjustments to prosper in the majors. Hansen was a standout athlete at Capital High School in Olympia, Washington, and he was selected by Cleveland in the 21st round of the 1991 draft. Instead, he attended Stanford, where he studied psychology. With this background, Hansen is also likely to bring a strong mental approach to his game.

WES HELMS

Position: Third base
Team: Atlanta Braves
Born: May 12, 1976 Gastonia, NC
Height: 6'4" **Weight:** 210 lbs.
Bats: right **Throws:** right
Acquired: Tenth-round pick in 6/94 free-agent draft

PLAYER SUMMARY	
Fantasy Value	$0
Card Value	20¢ to 25¢
Will	bring size
Can't	thrive in Triple-A yet
Expect	power hitting
Don't Expect	a utility man

Teams are always looking for a third baseman with pop in his bat, and the Braves, who over the years have had good luck in that regard, may be welcoming another such player. In just three years, Helms has battled his way within shouting distance of the major leagues, having received a couple of midseason promotions. Last year, *USA TODAY Baseball Weekly* tabbed Helms as an emerging prospect. He began his season with Durham of the Carolina League, where he played third base and went 1-for-5 in the All-Star Game against the California League. Shortly thereafter, Helms moved up a notch to Atlanta's Double-A club in Greenville of the Southern League. He found the challenge a little stiffer there, being one of the youngest players in the league. The Braves figure to leave Helms in Double-A for most of the 1997 campaign, with a late-season call-up to the big leagues a likely possibility. He could compete for a spot in the majors by spring training of 1998.

Professional Batting Register

	BA	G	AB	R	H	2B	3B	HR	RBI	SB
94 A	.243	66	235	26	57	8	2	3	17	6
95 A	.258	122	414	86	107	27	7	9	50	44
96 AA	.286	99	405	60	116	27	4	12	50	14
96 AAA	.232	29	99	14	23	4	0	3	9	2

Professional Batting Register

	BA	G	AB	R	H	2B	3B	HR	RBI	SB
94 R	.266	56	184	22	49	15	1	4	29	6
95 A	.276	136	539	89	149	32	1	11	85	2
96 A	.322	67	258	40	83	19	2	13	54	1
96 AA	.255	64	231	24	59	13	2	4	22	2

TODD HELTON

Position: First base
Team: Colorado Rockies
Born: Aug. 20, 1973 Knoxville, TN
Height: 6'2" **Weight:** 190 lbs.
Bats: left **Throws:** left
Acquired: First-round pick in 6/95 free-agent draft

PLAYER SUMMARY	
Fantasy Value	$0
Card Value	25¢ to 40¢
Will	hit for average
Can't	start thinking HR
Expect	good power in Denver
Don't Expect	return to pitching

At least three factors make Helton a very intriguing prospect. First, if he can hit in the tough Eastern League, one can only imagine what will happen when he reaches the thin air of Coors Field. Second, Helton walks as often as he strikes out, which signals an exceptional eye—especially for a man in just his second season of pro ball. Finally, the expectations that come with being a first-round pick don't seem to have bothered Helton at all. He was the first non-pitcher ever taken by the Rockies in the first round of the draft, and he has certainly made their decision seem a wise one. Last year, Helton enjoyed a successful year with Colorado's Double-A team in New Haven. He didn't show much long-ball power, unless you count the Double-A All-Star Game, in which he slugged a home run in his 2-for-2 outing. Helton starred at the University of Tennessee as both a hitter and a pitcher. If he continues as expected, he will play a solid first base in the majors for many years.

FELIX HEREDIA

Position: Pitcher
Team: Florida Marlins
Born: June 18, 1976 Barahona, Dominican Republic
Height: 6' **Weight:** 165 lbs.
Bats: left **Throws:** left
Acquired: Signed as a nondrafted free agent, 11/92

PLAYER SUMMARY	
Fantasy Value	$0
Card Value	12¢ to 20¢
Will	have a future
Can't	start games
Expect	situation pitcher
Don't Expect	a closer

At first glance, you wouldn't say that a minor-league middle reliever rates as a prospect. After all, a middle reliever is often a pitcher who is good enough neither to start nor to close. But Heredia is a left-hander who can throw strikes, and that can lead to a long career in the majors. It's not the most glamorous role on a club, but it can pay the bills. Heredia pitched in the Double-A Eastern League last year, compiling a remarkable record. Used in short stints, Heredia posted excellent ratios of innings-to-hits and innings-to-walks. The Marlins took notice and brought him to the majors. Out of Escuela Dominical, Heredia broke in with the 1993 Gulf Coast Marlins. He was named the Marlins' Organizational Player of the Month for July after posting a 2-1 record and holding opponents to a .196 batting average. Even though that success came as a starter, Heredia has made a productive move to the bullpen.

Professional Batting Register

	BA	G	AB	R	H	2B	3B	HR	RBI	SB
95 A	.254	54	201	24	51	11	1	1	15	1
96 AA	.332	93	319	46	106	24	2	7	51	2
96 AAA	.352	21	71	13	25	4	1	2	13	0

Professional Pitching Register

	W	L	ERA	G	CG	IP	H	ER	BB	SO
93 R	5	1	2.47	12	0	62.0	50	17	11	53
94 A	4	5	5.69	24	1	68.0	86	43	14	65
95 A	6	4	3.57	34	0	95.2	101	38	36	76
96 AA	8	1	1.50	55	0	60.0	48	10	15	42
96 NL	1	1	4.32	21	0	16.2	21	8	10	10

CHAD HERMANSEN

Position: Shortstop
Team: Pittsburgh Pirates
Born: Sept. 10, 1977 Salt Lake City, UT
Height: 6'2" **Weight:** 185 lbs.
Bats: right **Throws:** right
Acquired: First-round pick in 6/95 free-agent draft

PLAYER SUMMARY	
Fantasy Value	$0
Card Value	20¢ to 30¢
Will	hit with power
Can't	vie for bigs yet
Expect	nice build
Don't Expect	a scared kid

The Pirates apparently made a spectacular pick with the tenth overall selection in the 1995 draft. Hermansen has quickly developed into a power-hitting shortstop, and he could soon be in the mix for a job in the Pittsburgh infield. Last year, he was one of the top power hitters in the entire Pirates organization, and that includes the major-league club. Hermanson began the season with Augusta of the low Class-A South Atlantic League. He not only made the All-Star Team, but played shortstop and went 1-for-2 with a stolen base. He needed only about 225 Sally League at bats to reach double digits in doubles, home runs, and stolen bases before being promoted. Hermansen made himself right at home when he got to Lynchburg of the Carolina League, hitting .387 over an eight-game span from July 16 to July 23. This was quite a performance for a young man just one year removed from Green Valley High School in Nevada. Double-A is likely this year.

ELVIN HERNANDEZ

Position: Pitcher
Team: Pittsburgh Pirates
Born: Aug. 20, 1977 Ranchete, Dominican Republic
Height: 6'1" **Weight:** 165 lbs.
Bats: right **Throws:** right
Acquired: Signed as a nondrafted free agent, 6/93

PLAYER SUMMARY	
Fantasy Value	$0
Card Value	12¢ to 20¢
Will	throw strikes
Can't	stop now
Expect	top starter
Don't Expect	deep counts

Success in the South Atlantic League does not necessarily guarantee a continued rise toward the majors. To that extent, you have to keep in perspective what Hernandez accomplished last year. However, you can't blame the young man for excelling at the level where he finds himself, and Hernandez did that. He also did it while pitching most of the season at the age of 18. No one in Pittsburgh's minor-league system won as many games as Hernandez did (17). No one came close to striking out as many batters (171). And, remarkably, he issued only 16 walks in 157⅔ innings. Hernandez went 4-0 in five starts spanning June and July. He fanned ten in a 4-3 victory on August 8, then followed that outing with a three-hitter. Hernandez's success last year seems to have been no fluke. In his previous campaign, he went 6-1 in 14 starts. With this record of achievement, Hernandez will no doubt get a look at a higher level this year.

Professional Batting Register

	BA	G	AB	R	H	2B	3B	HR	RBI	SB
95 R	.304	24	92	14	28	10	1	3	17	0
95 A	.273	44	165	30	45	8	3	6	25	4
96 A	.275	66	251	40	69	11	3	10	46	5
96 A	.252	62	226	41	57	11	3	14	41	11

Professional Pitching Register

	W	L	ERA	G	CG	IP	H	ER	BB	SO
94 R	4	5	0.00	11	2	70.0	62	21	13	68
95 A	6	1	2.89	14	2	90.1	82	29	22	54
96 A	17	5	3.14	27	2	157.2	140	55	16	171

LIVAN HERNANDEZ

Position: Pitcher
Team: Florida Marlins
Born: Feb. 20, 1975 Villa Clara, Cuba
Height: 6'2" **Weight:** 220 lbs.
Bats: right **Throws:** right
Acquired: Signed as a nondrafted free agent, 1/96

PLAYER SUMMARY	
Fantasy Value	$1
Card Value	15¢ to 20¢
Will	need time
Can't	learn it all at once
Expect	a world of talent
Don't Expect	return to Cuba

Hernandez came out of the gold medal-winning Cuban baseball program with so much talent that the Marlins paid in the millions when they had a chance to get him. He represented a challenge in player development because no matter how much ability an international player brings, he must still face the adjustments of playing pro ball. The Marlins tried starting Hernandez at Triple-A, then were forced to change their thinking and placed him in the Double-A Eastern League. He even had a one-game tryout with the major-league ballclub (no decision). Hernandez's early troubles in Triple-A should in no way reflect upon his chances of giving the Marlins a return on their investment. He is still just a 22-year-old pitcher who has been placed in a fishbowl. Hernandez played two years on the Cuban Junior National Team and two years on the national squad. He went 2-0 with a 0.00 ERA during the 1992 Junior World Championships. He left the national team in 1995, defecting from Cuba while in Monterrey, Mexico, preparing for a World Cup.

RICHARD HIDALGO

Position: Outfield
Team: Houston Astros
Born: July 2, 1975 Caracas, Venezuela
Height: 6'2" **Weight:** 175 lbs.
Bats: right **Throws:** right
Acquired: Signed as a nondrafted free agent, 7/91

PLAYER SUMMARY	
Fantasy Value	$0
Card Value	12¢ to 15¢
Will	reach second base
Can't	rule out 20-20
Expect	high slugging pct.
Don't Expect	dearth of power

Even though Hidalgo plays the outfield, he spends more time near second base than many infielders do. That's because during his five-year pro career, Hidalgo has shown a knack for hitting doubles. In 1994, he set a Midwest League record with 47 two-baggers, earning both midseason and postseason All-Star laurels. Last year, he zoomed past 30 doubles with weeks to go. He also has reached double digits in home runs for four consecutive years and stolen ten or more bases in four of five years. He accomplished all of this even though he only turned 21 last season. It's because of his young age, in fact, that he spent a second straight year in Double-A when, by many indications, he could have played at a higher level. Hidalgo was signed to his first contract on his 16th birthday, and he was playing in the Gulf Coast League the following summer. Now he's just about ready to compete for a job with the Astros.

Professional Pitching Register

	W	L	ERA	G	CG	IP	H	ER	BB	SO
96 AAA	2	4	5.14	10	0	49.0	61	28	34	45
96 AA	9	2	4.34	15	0	93.1	81	45	34	95
96 NL	0	0	0.00	1	0	3.0	3	0	2	2

Professional Batting Register

	BA	G	AB	R	H	2B	3B	HR	RBI	SB
92 R	.310	51	184	20	57	7	3	1	27	14
93 A	.270	111	403	49	109	23	3	10	55	21
94 A	.292	124	476	68	139	47	6	12	76	12
95 AA	.266	133	489	59	130	28	6	14	59	8
96 AA	.294	130	513	66	151	34	2	14	78	11

VICTOR HURTADO

Position: Pitcher
Team: Florida Marlins
Born: June 14, 1977 Salcedo, Dominican Republic
Height: 6'2" **Weight:** 170 lbs.
Bats: right **Throws:** right
Acquired: Signed as nondrafted free agent, 7/93

PLAYER SUMMARY	
Fantasy Value	$0
Card Value	12¢ to 15¢
Will	anchor a rotation
Can't	top his workload
Expect	quality starts
Don't Expect	worn-out bullpen

Hurtado is yet another product of Florida's extensive scouting network in the Caribbean. He emerged as one of the top winners in the Florida farm system last year, even though he began the season at just 18 years of age. Working for Kane County of the Midwest League, Hurtado ranked among the top Marlin minor-leaguers in strikeouts (126) and ERA (3.27) as well as wins (15). USA TODAY Baseball Weekly noted his progress in its midseason overview of farm systems. From July 15 to August 11, Hurtado went 5-0 over six starts. One of those outings resulted in a complete-game four-hitter against South Bend. Among other things, last year tested Hurtado's endurance, as he made more starts than he had in his first two seasons of professional ball combined. It's also worth noting that five of his first 19 starts resulted in route-going performances. Look for Hurtado in the Florida State League in '97.

RAUL IBANEZ

Position: Outfield
Team: Seattle Mariners
Born: June 2, 1972 New York, NY
Height: 6' **Weight:** 172 lbs.
Bats: left **Throws:** right
Acquired: 36th-round pick in 6/92 free-agent draft

PLAYER SUMMARY	
Fantasy Value	$0
Card Value	15¢ to 20¢
Will	contribute with bat
Can't	surpass Martinez
Expect	a role player
Don't Expect	Buhner or Griffey

Despite Ibanez's impressive statistics in the minors, it's difficult to see where he might fit into the picture in Seattle. A one-time catcher in a system that has its share of receiver prospects, he might also play the outfield, but with Ken Griffey and Jay Buhner out there, the opportunities are limited. And he certainly won't see much time at DH with Edgar Martinez on the team. Despite all that, Ibanez got a call to the majors last year and picked up a few at bats. At this point, he may challenge for the third outfield spot or be a lefty bat off the bench. Ibanez put up standout years in 1994 and '95, hitting over .300 both times. In '94, he was picked for the Midwest League All-Star Game, but missed it with a sore shoulder. Even so, he finished the season with 30 doubles. In '95, he made the California League All-Star Team and was named the Mariners' Minor League Player of the Year. He'll need good stats—and a break—to find a regular spot in Seattle.

Professional Pitching Register

	W	L	ERA	G	CG	IP	H	ER	BB	SO
94 R	6	2	0.00	11	1	62.2	71	26	14	26
95 R	3	1	0.81	7	1	33.1	14	3	16	28
96 A	15	7	3.27	27	5	176.0	167	64	56	126

Professional Batting Register

	BA	G	AB	R	H	2B	3B	HR	RBI	SB
92 R	.308	33	120	25	37	8	2	1	16	1
93 A	.274	52	157	26	43	9	0	5	21	0
93 A	.284	43	134	16	38	5	2	0	15	0
94 A	.312	91	327	55	102	30	3	7	59	10
95 A	.332	95	361	59	120	23	9	20	108	4
96 AA	.368	19	76	12	28	8	1	1	13	3
96 AAA	.284	111	405	59	115	20	3	11	47	7
96 AL	.000	4	5	0	0	0	0	0	0	0

JOHNNY ISOM

Position: Outfield
Team: Baltimore Orioles
Born: Aug. 9, 1973 Urbana, IL
Height: 5'11" **Weight:** 210 lbs.
Bats: right **Throws:** right
Acquired: 28th-round pick in 6/95 free-agent draft

PLAYER SUMMARY	
Fantasy Value	$0
Card Value	20¢ to 25¢
Will	drive in runs
Can't	miss
Expect	shot at higher level
Don't Expect	a disappointment

Isom is a husky specimen who simply punishes the ball when he hits it. His healthy swing definitely got results last year in the Carolina League, where he piled up RBI for the second time in as many pro seasons. Isom played left field for the Carolina League in its All-Star Game against the California League, the second straight year he has made an All-Star Team. In 1996, he was selected to the postseason squad in the Appalachian League after finishing second in the circuit in RBI (104). This was quite a performance for someone who was still hanging around in the 28th round of the draft in 1995. He comes out of Texas Wesleyan, where he played baseball for three years. Before that, Isom attended Crowley High School in Fort Worth, Texas, where he was an all-county punter. A computer maven who likes to collect baseball cards, Isom worked in the front office of the Texas Rangers over the off-season. He may be an opponent of theirs before long.

Professional Batting Register

	BA	G	AB	R	H	2B	3B	HR	RBI	SB
95 R	.344	59	212	47	73	14	4	6	56	9
96 A	.290	124	486	69	141	27	3	18	104	8

GEOFF JENKINS

Position: Outfield
Team: Milwaukee Brewers
Born: July 21, 1974 Olympia, WA
Height: 6'1" **Weight:** 200 lbs.
Bats: left **Throws:** right
Acquired: First-round pick in 6/95 free-agent draft

PLAYER SUMMARY	
Fantasy Value	$0
Card Value	20¢ to 30¢
Will	get back on track
Can't	intimidate runners
Expect	strong hitter
Don't Expect	perfect shoulder

Jenkins hit a snag last year just as quickly as he had progressed one year earlier. A shoulder injury caused him to miss most of the season, delaying what seemed to be a fast rise to the majors. Jenkins began the season with El Paso of the Texas League and was settling in with some extra-base pop when his shoulder forced him to the sidelines. Now there's the question of how healthy he will be in 1997, and where he'll play if able. The injury is all the more frustrating because of the promise Jenkins showed in his first year of pro ball. After becoming the ninth overall pick in the 1995 draft, he began his career in the Pioneer League and needed only seven games to graduate. Promoted to Stockton of the California League, he impressed there as well, and soon received a boost to Double-A ball. All this came after he capped his college career by taking the University of Southern California to the College World Series.

Professional Batting Register

	BA	G	AB	R	H	2B	3B	HR	RBI	SB
95 R	.321	7	28	2	9	0	1	0	9	0
95 A	.255	13	47	13	12	2	0	3	12	2
95 AA	.278	22	79	12	22	4	2	1	13	3
96 A	.348	37	138	27	48	8	4	3	25	3
96 AA	.286	22	77	17	22	5	4	1	11	1

JONATHAN JOHNSON

Position: Pitcher
Team: Texas Rangers
Born: July 16, 1974 Ocala, FL
Height: 6′ **Weight:** 180 lbs.
Bats: right **Throws:** right
Acquired: First-round pick in 6/95 free-agent
  draft

PLAYER SUMMARY	
Fantasy Value	$0
Card Value	15¢ to 20¢
Will	post good ratios
Can't	break ankle again
Expect	All-Star selection
Don't Expect	another 1-5 record

Based on what Johnson showed last year
in the Texas League, he could soon be a
member of the Ranger starting rotation. He
has pitched in two tough professional
leagues, and he should begin this season
no lower than Triple-A. That's quite a run
for someone who missed the early part of
preseason 1995 workouts with a fractured
left ankle. But things have pretty much
gone Johnson's way since then. He finished his third season at Florida State University with a 12-3 mark, giving him a
career record of 34-5. He was a first-team
All-American and a second-team All-
Atlantic Coast Conference selection. He
picked up wins in the ACC Tournament, the
Atlantic 1 Regionals, and the College World
Series. After signing with the Rangers, he
pitched well in the Florida State League,
though he somehow managed to go 1-5
despite posting a 2.70 ERA. Last year he
appeared in the Double-A All-Star Game
and allowed two runs to take the loss.

MARK JOHNSON

Position: Pitcher
Team: Houston Astros
Born: May 2, 1975 Dayton, OH
Height: 6′3″ **Weight:** 215 lbs.
Bats: right **Throws:** right
Acquired: First-round pick in 6/96 free-agent
  draft

PLAYER SUMMARY	
Fantasy Value	$0
Card Value	20¢ to 25¢
Will	throw breaking ball
Can't	waste much time
Expect	ninth man on staff
Don't Expect	20-game winner

Johnson's potential is much more attractive
than his statistics in college last season. At
least the Astros must have thought so, because they made him the 19th overall pick
in the draft. Pitching for the University of
Hawaii, Johnson finished barely above
.500, allowed nearly a hit per inning, and
sported an ERA well above 4.00. Those
numbers can make you a lot of money
when you're already in the major leagues,
but coming from a college player they
hardly suggest a first-round pick. Still, the
Astros made Johnson the 11th pitcher
taken in the draft, and only the sixth from a
college program. Trouble is, his uninspired
statistics extended to his performance with
the national team, and he wound up not
even making the final cut for the Olympic
squad. As of mid-summer, Johnson had not
yet signed. Because of his past experience,
Johnson probably will go to the mid-minors.
There he will have to affirm that he has
major-league ability.

Professional Pitching Register

	W	L	ERA	G	CG	IP	H	ER	BB	SO
95 A	1	5	2.70	8	1	43.1	34	13	16	25
96 AA	13	10	3.56	26	6	174.1	176	69	41	97
96 AAA	1	0	0.00	1	1	9.0	2	0	1	6

389

ANDRUW JONES

Position: Outfield
Team: Atlanta Braves
Born: April 23, 1977 Curacao
Height: 6'1" **Weight:** 185 lbs.
Bats: right **Throws:** right
Acquired: Signed as a nondrafted free agent, 7/93

PLAYER SUMMARY	
Fantasy Value	$8 to $10
Card Value	60¢ to $1
Will	bring tools
Can't	get caught up in hype
Expect	a smart player
Don't Expect	everything at once

Jones is one of the best young players in the game. He joined the Braves last year in midseason and, barring injury or some unforeseen circumstance, should be a fixture in Atlanta's outfield well into the next century. Jones began the '96 season in the Carolina League and kept producing as Atlanta moved him ever higher through the system. He made his major-league debut on August 15, playing right field and batting second. His arrival came only a little more than three years after he signed as a 16-year-old. Jones brings a multifaceted game. He can run well enough to play center field and steal 30 bases and can hit for average as well as power. He throws well and gets high marks for intangibles. In the 1996 fall classic, Jones became the youngest player ever to hit a home run in the World Series. It would be unfair to place too many statistical expectations on Jones at this point; it's sufficient to say he does not show any glaring weakness even at this tender age.

Professional Batting Register

	BA	G	AB	R	H	2B	3B	HR	RBI	SB
94 R	.221	27	95	22	21	5	1	2	10	5
94 R	.336	36	143	20	48	9	2	1	16	16
95 A	.277	139	537	104	149	41	5	25	100	56
96 A	.313	66	243	65	76	14	3	17	43	16
96 AA	.369	38	157	39	58	10	1	12	37	12
96 AAA	.378	12	45	11	17	3	1	5	12	2
96 NL	.217	31	106	11	23	7	1	5	13	3

JAIME JONES

Position: Outfield
Team: Florida Marlins
Born: Aug. 2, 1976 San Diego, CA
Height: 6'4" **Weight:** 195 lbs.
Bats: left **Throws:** left
Acquired: First-round pick in 6/95 free-agent draft

PLAYER SUMMARY	
Fantasy Value	$0
Card Value	25¢ to 35¢
Will	whiff batters
Can't	learn with bad wrist
Expect	more time in Class-A
Don't Expect	pitcher in majors

Teams never know what's going to happen when they draft a player. One can never predict, for example, what role injury might have in a player's career. James Paul (Jaime) Jones, taken with the sixth overall pick in the 1995 draft, was finding his way with Kane County of the Midwest League last year when he suffered a wrist injury. At the time, he had begun to show a little of the batting skill that had made him a high school All-America choice of both *Baseball America* and *USA TODAY Baseball Weekly*. However, he also had demonstrated a need to learn the strike zone and make more contact. Jones went to Rancho Bernardo High School and led them to the San Diego County championship game, which was played in Jack Murphy Stadium. He went 4-0 as a pitcher, including a three-hit shutout that put his team into the title game. The Marlins prefer him as a batter, however. His older brother, Donny, was picked by the Red Sox in 1991, but it's Jaime who has the high ceiling.

Professional Batting Register

	BA	G	AB	R	H	2B	3B	HR	RBI	SB
95 R	.222	5	18	2	4	0	0	0	3	0
95 A	.284	31	116	21	33	6	2	4	11	5
96 A	.249	62	237	29	59	17	1	8	45	7

GABE KAPLER

Position: Outfield
Team: Detroit Tigers
Born: Aug. 31, 1975 Hollywood, CA
Height: 6'2" **Weight:** 190 lbs.
Bats: left **Throws:** right
Acquired: 57th-round pick in 6/95 free-agent draft

PLAYER SUMMARY	
Fantasy Value	$0
Card Value	12¢ to 20¢
Will	bring promise
Can't	play with bad wrist
Expect	great power
Don't Expect	immediate stardom

Keep this young man's name in mind. The odds are probably against him because of his low draft status, but another year like last year will mark him as a top prospect to watch. Playing in the South Atlantic League, Kapler hit for power and average and even managed to steal some bases. He finished fifth in the league in batting and tied Bubba Trammell for second in the Detroit organization in RBI. He collected the astonishing total of 45 doubles, more than twice as many as league-MVP Russell Branyan, and 12 more than anyone else in the Sally League. Out of Moorepark College in California, Kapler broke into pro ball with a respectable season in the New York-Penn League in 1995. But nothing in that season could have prepared anyone for what he did last season. Among last year's stats were almost as many extra-base hits (71) as strikeouts (73), indicating unusual selectivity and discipline in a power hitter.

Professional Batting Register

	BA	G	AB	R	H	2B	3B	HR	RBI	SB
95 A	.288	63	236	38	68	19	4	4	34	1
96 A	.300	138	524	81	157	45	0	26	99	14

BROOKS KIESCHNICK

Position: Outfield
Team: Chicago Cubs
Born: June 6, 1972 Robstown, TX
Height: 6'4" **Weight:** 225 lbs.
Bats: left **Throws:** right
Acquired: First-round pick in 6/93 free-agent draft

PLAYER SUMMARY	
Fantasy Value	$1 to $3
Card Value	10¢ to 15¢
Will	hit homers
Can't	play center
Expect	a role player
Don't Expect	defensive help

Kieschnick must act quickly or lose his status as a prospect. He entered the Chicago organization with a reputation as a big hitter, but he has now played two years of Triple-A ball. It's difficult to imagine a better time for him to help the big club than last year, when the Cubs endured a mediocre season and Sammy Sosa was lost to injury, creating some opportunity. Kieschnick can hit home runs and drive in runs, but he's never inspired much confidence as a defensive player. He can't run very well, and his strikeout-to-walk ratio last year (almost 3-to-1) wasn't all that impressive. He comes out of the University of Texas, where he majored in sports management and starred as a hitter and pitcher. He was a three-time All-American, a three-time choice as Southwest Conference Player of the Year, and a two-time winner of the Dick Howser Award as the nation's top player. If Kieschnick opens this season at Triple-A, his star has truly lost its luster.

Professional Batting Register

	BA	G	AB	R	H	2B	3B	HR	RBI	SB
93 R	.222	3	9	0	2	1	0	0	0	0
93 A	.182	6	22	1	4	2	0	0	2	0
93 AA	.341	25	91	12	31	8	0	2	10	1
94 AA	.282	126	468	57	132	25	3	14	55	3
95 AAA	.295	138	505	61	149	30	1	23	73	2
96 AAA	.259	117	441	47	114	20	1	18	64	0
96 NL	.345	25	29	6	10	2	0	1	6	0

GENE KINGSALE

Position: Outfield
Team: Baltimore Orioles
Born: Aug. 20, 1976 Aruba
Height: 6'3" **Weight:** 170 lbs.
Bats: both **Throws:** right
Acquired: Signed as a nondrafted free agent, 6/93

PLAYER SUMMARY

Fantasy Value	$0
Card Value	15¢ to 20¢
Will	use speed
Can't	stay in majors yet
Expect	high on-base pct.
Don't Expect	power

Kingsale made his major-league debut in the heat of a pennant race last year, and he did so at the tender age of 20. Kingsale is a speedy player who eventually may have a big impact on a lineup. He can reach base with either a hit or a walk, and once he's on first, he's a good bet to reach second and score a run. Kingsale comes from Aruba, where he was a member of the Antillean Babe Ruth Championship team. He played baseball, softball, basketball, and soccer while attending John F. Kennedy Technical High School. Signed to his first pro contract at age 16, he was assigned to the Gulf Coast League but did not play. He made his debut in 1994 and stole 15 bases in 23 tries. Promoted to Bluefield in 1995, Kingsale finished third in the Appalachian League in on-base percentage and made the postseason All-Star squad. Despite his boost to Baltimore last year, Kingsale will still need seasoning so he'll likely get some time in Double-A this summer.

RANDY KNOLL

Position: Pitcher
Team: Philadelphia Phillies
Born: March 21, 1977 Corona, CA
Height: 6'4" **Weight:** 190 lbs.
Bats: right **Throws:** right
Acquired: Third-round pick in 6/95 free-agent draft

PLAYER SUMMARY

Fantasy Value	$0
Card Value	12¢ to 15¢
Will	be in rotation
Can't	revert to '95 form
Expect	clean game
Don't Expect	many baserunners

In only his second season of pro ball, Knoll enjoyed a fine year in Class-A, leading the Philadelphia farm system in ERA and showing the ability to throw strikes with something on them. He opened the season with Piedmont of the South Atlantic League and graduated to Clearwater of the Florida State League. Through it all, Knoll averaged nearly one strikeout per inning while allowing only one walk for every five innings. In an early-season masterpiece, Knoll fired a four-hit shutout on May 26, striking out ten and walking only two. He shut out Asheville on July 26, and at that point was on a roll in which he permitted only two earned runs in a 21-inning span. Knoll's emergence is somewhat surprising, considering the problems he had upon breaking into pro ball just one year earlier. He went 0-3 with an 8.83 ERA, but some of that may have been due to rookie nerves. This year, Knoll could start in high Class-A or Double-A.

Professional Batting Register

	BA	G	AB	R	H	2B	3B	HR	RBI	SB
94 R	.310	50	168	26	52	2	3	0	9	15
95 R	.316	47	171	45	54	11	2	0	16	20
96 A	.271	49	166	26	45	6	4	0	9	23
96 AL	.000	3	0	0	0	0	0	0	0	0

Professional Pitching Register

	W	L	ERA	G	CG	IP	H	ER	BB	SO
95 R	0	3	8.83	6	0	17.1	21	17	9	22
96 A	1	0	3.05	4	0	20.2	17	7	2	19
96 A	10	7	2.09	22	3	151.0	111	35	31	144

BILLY KOCH

Position: Pitcher
Team: Toronto Blue Jays
Born: Dec. 14, 1971 West Babylon, NY
Height: 6'3" **Weight:** 200 lbs.
Bats: right **Throws:** right
Acquired: First-round pick in 6/96 free-agent draft

PLAYER SUMMARY	
Fantasy Value	$0
Card Value	25¢ to 35¢
Will	light up gun
Can't	stop working
Expect	starter or closer
Don't Expect	just another arm

Koch has the kind of arm strength that can produce that magic three-digit reading on speed guns—100 mph. It was enough to make him a big part of the Clemson staff and get him a spot on the U.S. Olympic team. Whether it can give him success in the major leagues remains to be seen, but Toronto is betting that it can. The Blue Jays made Koch the fourth overall pick of the 1996 draft after a campaign in which he helped pitch Clemson into the College World Series. But there's still lots of work to be done. For one thing, Koch did not enjoy an exceptional Olympics, losing his only decision and compiling an ERA above 6.00 over three games. His control isn't yet where it will need to be, either. However, his arm strength is something you can't teach. The Blue Jays, who have always been in love with raw tools, should have fun with the challenge of developing Koch. He might get his pro start in a high Class-A or Double-A league this year.

DAN KOLB

Position: Pitcher
Team: Texas Rangers
Born: March 29, 1975 Sterling, IL
Height: 6'4" **Weight:** 185 lbs.
Bats: right **Throws:** right
Acquired: Sixth-round pick in 6/95 free-agent draft

PLAYER SUMMARY	
Fantasy Value	$0
Card Value	12¢ to 20¢
Will	pitch at Double-A
Can't	discount success
Expect	90-mph fastball
Don't Expect	short outings

Kolb has needed just two pro seasons to stamp himself as one of the top prospects in the Texas organization. He has pitched well in two consecutive seasons, though the two campaigns yielded vastly different results. In 1995, Kolb somehow managed to tie for second in losses (seven) in the Gulf Coast League, even though he finished eighth in earned run average (2.21). Last year he posted another fine ERA but managed to get some wins, too. Kolb came out of Sauk Valley Community College in Illinois and signed quickly enough so that he could make 11 starts in rookie ball in '95. He was a workhorse last year, ranking among the Texas farm system's leaders in innings pitched. It's important to note that Kolb experienced his success last year against South Atlantic League hitters, a few notches below the majors. As he climbs higher, some of his excess walks will catch up with him. But for now, he merits a very close watch.

Professional Pitching Register

	W	L	ERA	G	CG	IP	H	ER	BB	SO
95 R	1	7	2.21	12	0	53.0	38	13	28	46
96 AA	1	0	0.77	2	0	11.2	5	1	8	7
96 A	2	2	4.26	6	0	38.0	38	18	14	28
96 A	8	6	2.57	20	4	126.0	80	36	60	127

PAUL KONERKO

Position: Catcher
Team: Los Angeles Dodgers
Born: March 5, 1976 Providence, RI
Height: 6'3" **Weight:** 205 lbs.
Bats: right **Throws:** right
Acquired: First-round pick in 6/94 free agent draft

PLAYER SUMMARY	
Fantasy Value	$0
Card Value	10¢ to 15¢
Will	keep hitting
Can't	keep him down
Expect	power
Don't Expect	catcher in majors

Konerko seems determined to make the Dodger ballclub, no matter who is blocking his way. Drafted as a catcher, Konerko was looking up at All-Star Mike Piazza. Switched to first base, Konerko suddenly found himself behind Eric Karros. However, if he keeps hitting the way he has in his three years in the minors, Konerko will find a way into a major-league lineup. Konerko broke into professional ball with Yakima in the Northwest League in 1994, made the All-Star Team, and was named one of the circuit's top prospects. Boosted to San Bernardino in the California League in 1995, Konerko kept developing nicely. Last year was his most successful yet, and that's saying something. He tore up the Texas League, leading Double-A San Antonio in home runs (29) and RBI (86) by a wide margin. He served as a DH in the Double-A All-Star Game. He'll have to keep producing while he waits to see how things work out in the majors.

CLINT KOPPE

Position: Pitcher
Team: Cincinnati Reds
Born: Aug. 14, 1973 Webster, TX
Height: 6'4" **Weight:** 225 lbs.
Bats: right **Throws:** right
Acquired: Sixth-round pick in 6/94 free-agent draft

PLAYER SUMMARY	
Fantasy Value	$0
Card Value	12¢ to 15¢
Will	take the ball
Can't	figure 7-13 record
Expect	strength
Don't Expect	runners galore

Koppe is a big, strong specimen who has produced three straight effective seasons as a pro, putting him into position to compete for a big-league job before too long. A starting pitcher who can deliver a ton of innings, Koppe also produced nice victory totals in two of those three campaigns. The exception was 1995 at Charleston of the South Atlantic League, where his 7-13 record cannot be considered entirely Koppe's fault—not when he allowed only 144 hits in 157⅔ innings. Last year, Koppe began with Winston-Salem of the Carolina League. He led the circuit with five victories in May. The last one—a seven-inning three-hitter in which he walked two and struck out eight—came on May 28. Before long, it was on to Chattanooga of the Double-A Southern League, where Koppe won three of his first four decisions. Koppe will likely open 1997 in Double-A ball, but if he pitches the way he did last year, he could soon get the call to Cincinnati.

Professional Batting Register

	BA	G	AB	R	H	2B	3B	HR	RBI	SB
94 A	.288	67	257	25	74	15	2	6	58	1
95 A	.277	118	448	77	124	21	1	19	77	3
96 AA	.300	133	470	78	141	23	2	29	86	1
96 AAA	.429	4	14	2	6	0	0	1	2	0

Professional Pitching Register

	W	L	ERA	G	CG	IP	H	ER	BB	SO
94 R	9	2	4.23	14	1	89.1	85	42	23	61
95 A	7	13	3.37	30	2	157.2	144	59	47	119
96 A	8	2	3.30	16	3	95.1	87	35	25	46
96 AA	4	2	3.49	10	1	56.2	54	22	18	30

MARK KOTSAY

Position: Outfield
Team: Florida Marlins
Born: Dec. 2, 1975 Woodier, CA
Height: 6' **Weight:** 180 lbs.
Bats: left **Throws:** left
Acquired: First-round pick in 6/96 free-agent draft

PLAYER SUMMARY	
Fantasy Value	$0
Card Value	35¢ to 60¢
Will	come to play
Can't	be out-hustled
Expect	clutch performance
Don't Expect	top tools

If Kotsay keeps winning laurels at the rate he did in college, he'll have to build an extension on his trophy area. And—more important to the Marlins—they may have to make room for some hardware—perhaps even a championship trophy. Kotsay, taken ninth overall in the draft last year, simply delivers results. A two-time member of *Baseball America*'s college All-America team, Kotsay always seems to be at his best in big games. He was the MVP of the 1995 College World Series and was named to the All-Midwest Regional squad in 1996, though Cal State-Fullerton failed to advance to Omaha. He won the Golden Spikes Award in 1995 as the nation's top college baseball player. In 1996, he hit over .300 while playing for the U.S. Olympic team. Those who have seen him play agree that his intangibles grade out high. Whether that can help him offset unexceptional tools is what the Marlins will find out.

MARC KROON

Position: Pitcher
Team: San Diego Padres
Born: April 2, 1973 Bronx, NY
Height: 6'2" **Weight:** 195 lbs.
Bats: right **Throws:** right
Acquired: Traded by Mets with Randy Curtis for Frank Seminara, Tracy Sanders, and Pablo Martinez, 12/93

PLAYER SUMMARY	
Fantasy Value	$0
Card Value	8¢ to 12¢
Will	blow hitters away
Can't	always find plate
Expect	inconsistency
Don't Expect	return to starting

After five seasons spent mostly as a starter, Kroon may finally have found a role that suits him. Pitching in the Southern League last season, Kroon served as the closer for Memphis. He zoomed past the 20-save mark after compiling just four saves in his career to that point. Just as he was coming into his own, however, his season ended in injury. It's easy to understand how Kroon could nail down a game. He has the kind of stuff that can bury a hitter. Through 1995, he owned 497 strikeouts in 498⅔ innings of pro ball. In his brief stop in the majors in 1995, Kroon achieved two of his four outs on whiffs. Unfortunately for him, he also walked two, allowed one hit, and was charged with two runs. Kroon came to the Padres as part of the 1993 deal that sent Frank Seminara to New York. Perhaps the Padres have harnessed his talent.

Professional Batting Register

	BA	G	AB	R	H	2B	3B	HR	RBI	SB
96 A	.283	17	60	16	17	5	0	2	8	3

Professional Pitching Register

	W	L	ERA	G	S	IP	H	ER	BB	SO
91 R	2	3	4.53	12	0	47.2	39	24	22	39
92 R	3	5	4.10	12	0	68.0	52	31	57	60
93 A	2	11	3.47	29	2	124.1	123	48	70	122
94 A	11	6	4.83	26	0	143.1	143	77	81	153
95 AA	7	5	3.51	22	2	115.1	90	45	61	123
96 AA	2	4	2.89	44	22	46.2	33	15	28	56
96 NL	0	1	10.80	2	0	1.2	1	2	2	2

RICKY LEDEE

Position: Outfield
Team: New York Yankees
Born: Nov. 22, 1973 Ponce, Puerto Rico
Height: 6'1" **Weight:** 160 lbs.
Bats: left **Throws:** left
Acquired: 16th-round pick in 6/90 free-agent draft

PLAYER SUMMARY	
Fantasy Value	$0
Card Value	20¢ to 25¢
Will	hit with punch
Can't	explain his power
Expect	utility role
Don't Expect	return to Class-A

Just when it seemed that Ledee was hopelessly stuck in Class-A ball, he put together a breakthrough season. Operating on the high end of the Yankee farm system, Ledee delivered power and average. That kind of season could not fail to impress the Yankees—or anyone else who was watching. Actually, Ledee had enjoyed one other year of note, with Greensboro of the South Atlantic League in 1994. But along with his 22 homers and 71 RBI came 126 strikeouts, and that was probably a factor in his return to the Sally League in 1995. Last year, Ledee opened as the starting right fielder for New York's Double-A club in the Eastern League. With a .365 average, he made the jump to Triple-A and did not seem to mind the tougher competition one bit. Despite having spent seven years in the minors, Ledee is still only 23 years old, and his long apprenticeship may serve him well. All he needs at this stage is a chance at the bigs.

Professional Batting Register

	BA	G	AB	R	H	2B	3B	HR	RBI	SB
90 R	.108	19	37	5	4	2	0	0	1	2
91 R	.267	47	165	22	44	6	2	0	18	3
92 R	.229	52	179	25	41	9	2	2	23	1
93 A	.255	52	192	32	49	7	6	8	20	7
94 A	.250	134	484	87	121	23	9	22	71	10
95 A	.269	89	335	65	90	16	6	14	49	10
96 AA	.365	39	137	27	50	11	1	8	37	2
96 AAA	.282	96	358	79	101	22	6	21	64	6

DERREK LEE

Position: Infield
Team: San Diego Padres
Born: Sept. 6, 1975 Sacramento, CA
Height: 6'5" **Weight:** 205 lbs.
Bats: right **Throws:** right
Acquired: First-round pick in 6/93 free-agent draft

PLAYER SUMMARY	
Fantasy Value	$0
Card Value	20¢ to 30¢
Will	hit for extra bases
Can't	play the outfield
Expect	strikeouts
Don't Expect	majors this year

The Padres have taken their time with Lee, being careful not to rush him, and he now appears on the verge of rewarding their patience. Lee has grown into one of the top power prospects in all of baseball, as evidenced by his output with Memphis of the Double-A Southern League last year. He reached career highs in home runs (34) and RBI (104). It was the fourth consecutive time his RBI total has risen, and the third time his homer output has increased. Lee, drafted 14th overall in 1993, had spent part of three years with Rancho Cucamonga of the Class-A California League before finally receiving his promotion. Lee is the son of Leon Lee, who was drafted by the Cardinals and made it to Triple-A before moving to Japan and enjoying a ten-year career there. Lee's uncle Leron played with the Padres from 1971 to 1973. Lee will likely get a year at Triple-A, putting him on track to succeed first baseman Wally Joyner, who is signed with the Padres through 1997.

Professional Batting Register

	BA	G	AB	R	H	2B	3B	HR	RBI	SB
93 R	.327	15	52	11	17	1	1	2	5	4
93 A	.274	20	73	13	20	5	1	1	10	0
94 A	.267	126	442	66	118	19	2	8	53	18
95 A	.301	128	502	82	151	25	2	23	95	14
95 AA	.111	2	9	0	1	0	0	0	1	0
96 AA	.280	134	500	98	140	39	2	34	104	13

TRAVIS LEE

Position: First base
Team: Minnesota Twins
Born: May 26, 1975 San Diego, CA
Height: 6'3" **Weight:** 205 lbs.
Bats: left **Throws:** left
Acquired: First-round pick in 6/96 free-agent draft

PLAYER SUMMARY	
Fantasy Value	$0
Card Value	20¢ to 30¢
Will	bring work ethic
Can't	be another Hrbek
Expect	smart hitter
Don't Expect	dead pull hitter

Not too long ago, the Twins won a couple of World Series with Kent Hrbek, a slugging first baseman who was also a hit with the fans. Now comes Lee, and the Twins can only hope that history repeats itself. Lee was the second player (and the first position player) taken in last year's draft. He had gone undrafted out of high school before embarking on a successful career at San Diego State. Last year's preseason hype made him out to be one of the top prospects, and he did not disappoint. He hit in the .350 range, stole over 30 bases, wound up on *Baseball America*'s College All-America squad, and hit .382 for the United States in the Olympics. He has earned respect for his work around first base, and favorable conditions at the Metrodome would magnify his power. However, a contract dispute in which Lee's father petitioned the commissioner's office to make him a free agent raised questions about where Lee will be performing.

JEFF LIEFER

Position: Infield
Team: Chicago White Sox
Born: Aug. 17, 1974 Upland, CA
Height: 6'3" **Weight:** 195 lbs.
Bats: left **Throws:** right
Acquired: First-round pick in 6/95 free-agent draft

PLAYER SUMMARY	
Fantasy Value	$0
Card Value	15¢ to 20¢
Will	rebound in '97
Can't	win Gold Glove
Expect	third, first, or DH
Don't Expect	slick fielder

The White Sox seem to have found themselves a bat when they tabbed Liefer as the 25th selection in the 1995 draft. Or did they? It depends on which half of last season you wish to consider. In his first season in pro ball, Liefer played for South Bend of the Midwest League and hit well enough to earn a midseason promotion. At Prince William of the Carolina League, however, Liefer ran into all kinds of problems. Until they see otherwise, the White Sox would prefer to believe in the first half, when Liefer performed as he did in college. He set school records in home runs, RBI, hits, and doubles at Long Beach State after he graduated from Upland High School in California, where he lettered three times in baseball. In 1995, Liefer was named a second-team All-American by *Baseball America*. He was selected by Cleveland in the sixth round of the 1992 free-agent draft but did not sign. The White Sox hope Cleveland's loss will be their gain.

Professional Batting Register

	BA	G	AB	R	H	2B	3B	HR	RBI	SB
96 A	.325	74	277	60	90	14	0	15	58	6
96 A	.224	37	147	17	33	6	0	1	13	0

MARK LITTLE

Position: Outfield
Team: Texas Rangers
Born: July 11, 1972 Edwardsville, IL
Height: 6′ **Weight:** 195 lbs.
Bats: right **Throws:** right
Acquired: Eighth-round pick in 6/94 free-agent draft

PLAYER SUMMARY	
Fantasy Value	$0
Card Value	15¢ to 20¢
Will	blend speed with pop
Can't	steal every base
Expect	center fielder
Don't Expect	a Texas slugger

Every club can use a little extra speed, and that's one of the things that Little brings with him. He has stolen in double digits in each of his three pro seasons, increasing the total each time. His success rate has not always been optimum—he was caught 14 times in 34 attempts in 1995—but at least he brings aggressiveness and raw tools. Little comes out of Memphis University, where he was a second-team All-America outfielder. After signing with the Rangers, he led Hudson Valley of the short-season New York-Penn League with a .457 on-base percentage. He ranked second on the club in batting, and at one point went on an 11-game hitting streak. Boosted to high Class-A ball in 1995, Little ranked third in the Florida State League in triples and fifth in extra-base hits. Last year, he thrived after a promotion to Double-A, where he played center field for Tulsa. Expect him at Triple-A this year, where he may even get an emergency call-up.

TERRENCE LONG

Position: Outfield
Team: New York Mets
Born: Feb. 29, 1976 Montgomery, AL
Height: 6′1″ **Weight:** 180 lbs.
Bats: left **Throws:** left
Acquired: First-round pick in 6/94 free-agent draft

PLAYER SUMMARY	
Fantasy Value	$0
Card Value	20¢ to 25¢
Will	bring tools
Can't	match Wilson's pace
Expect	more development
Don't Expect	another setback

Long has finally begun taking giant steps toward fulfilling the potential the Mets predicted when they made him the 20th pick in the 1994 draft. Last year was the best of his three pro seasons, as he wound up among New York's leaders in stolen bases and RBI. He has not yet hit homers with the frequency the Mets had hoped, but he's still only 21 years old, gaining experience, and filling out a bit. Long was drafted without any of the hype that accompanied New York's first pick that year, right-hander Paul Wilson. Unlike Wilson, Long has not taken the fast track to the bigs. In fact, he had to take a step back in 1995, when he began the season in the Sally League but had so many problems he had to go down to short-season Pittsfield to regain his bearings. He reestablished himself in '96 and will likely head to the challenging Florida State League in '97, where his response will tell a lot about his prospects.

Professional Batting Register

	BA	G	AB	R	H	2B	3B	HR	RBI	SB
94 A	.293	54	208	33	61	15	5	3	27	14
95 A	.256	115	438	75	112	31	8	9	50	20
96 AA	.291	101	409	69	119	24	2	13	50	22

Professional Batting Register

	BA	G	AB	R	H	2B	3B	HR	RBI	SB
94 R	.233	60	215	39	50	9	2	12	39	9
95 A	.197	55	178	27	35	1	2	2	13	8
95 A	.257	51	187	24	48	9	4	4	31	11
96 A	.288	123	473	66	136	26	9	12	78	32

BRADEN LOOPER

Position: Pitcher
Team: St. Louis Cardinals
Born: Oct. 28, 1974 Weatherford, OK
Height: 6'4" **Weight:** 210 lbs.
Bats: right **Throws:** right
Acquired: First-round pick in 6/96 free-agent
   draft

PLAYER SUMMARY	
Fantasy Value $0
Card Value . . . . 20¢ to 30¢
Will . . . . throw hard
Can't . . . . dwell on failures
Expect . . . . role to be defined
Don't Expect . . . . long stay in minors

The Cardinals reached across the prairies
to grab a right-hander who brings a strong
arm and a healthy amount of experience as
he begins his pro career. Looper collected
a variety of honors last year, leading Wichita State to the College World Series, making *Baseball America*'s collegiate
All-America team, and playing for the U.S.
Olympic squad. He made four appearances
in the Olympics, allowing no earned runs
over six innings. His two scoreless innings
against Nicaragua put the finishing touches
on the bronze medal. Looper's College
World Series experience did not turn out
quite as well, however. He was on the
mound when Florida State rallied to elimi-
nate Wichita State, a development he took
very hard. Looper throws with all the power
that his substantial size might indicate, and
he offers a slider, too. Looper will likely
need some time in the minors, but don't be
surprised if he gets the call to St. Louis in a
hurry.

JOSE LOPEZ

Position: Third base
Team: New York Mets
Born: Aug. 4, 1975 Santiago, Puerto Rico
Height: 6' **Weight:** 175 lbs.
Bats: right **Throws:** right
Acquired: Signed as a nondrafted free agent,
   9/93

PLAYER SUMMARY	
Fantasy Value $0
Card Value . . . . 15¢ to 25¢
Will . . . . make progress
Can't . . . . let contact slip
Expect . . . . moderate power
Don't Expect . . . . another HoJo

Throughout their 35-year history, no position has bedeviled the Mets the way third
base has. They have used more than 100
men at that spot, only occasionally finding
someone like Howard Johnson to be a fixture there. Into this situation comes Lopez,
who showed some pop at the hot corner for
Port St. Lucie of the Florida State League
last year. He went on a tear from mid-May
to early June, hitting .379, and then heated
up again over the last half of July and into
August, when he hit .385. *USA TODAY
Baseball Weekly* took note of his progress
in its midseason look at the farm systems,
and Lopez was selected to the FSL All-Star
Game, where he failed to collect a hit.
Lopez originally broke into pro ball in 1994
and was the Mets' Gulf Coast League Doubleday Award winner, finishing ninth in the
league in hitting. He slipped a bit in 1995,
piling up the strikeouts in low Class-A ball.
That's something he'll have to work on this
year, when he'll probably be at Double-A
Binghamton.

Professional Batting Register

	BA	G	AB	R	H	2B	3B	HR	RBI	SB
94 R	.323	45	164	34	53	10	1	2	31	2
94 R	.267	4	15	1	4	3	0	1	1	0
95 A	.232	82	280	37	65	17	4	5	38	7
95 A	1.000	1	2	0	2	0	0	0	1	0
96 A	.291	121	419	63	122	17	5	11	60	18

CURT LYONS

Position: Pitcher
Team: Cincinnati Reds
Born: Oct. 17, 1974 Greencastle, IN
Height: 6'5" **Weight:** 240 lbs.
Bats: right **Throws:** right
Acquired: Sixth-round pick in 6/92 free-agent draft

PLAYER SUMMARY

Fantasy Value	$1
Card Value	10¢ to 20¢
Will	be No. 1 or 2 starter
Can't	do more in Double-A
Expect	some gopher balls
Don't Expect	men on bases

Lyons has spent five years in pro ball, and only once has he posted an ERA over 3.00 in the minors. Last year was by far his best, when he was one of the top pitchers in Double-A ball. Working for the Reds' Southern League club in Chattanooga, Lyons looked like a man among boys, averaging well over one strikeout per inning. Through 141⅔ innings, he allowed only 113 hits. Over one stretch, he fanned nine, ten, and 13 batters. In one game, he fanned six men in a row but lost his chance at a win when he permitted three homers in one inning. In one period spanning June and July, he went four straight starts without allowing more than two earned runs in a game. Lyons's stats were not all that surprising after what he accomplished in high Class-A ball in 1995. Though he only went 9-9, his 2.41 ERA and ratio of less than one hit per inning indicated quality. Lyons will likely need some seasoning this year, but don't be surprised if he shows up in the majors.

Professional Pitching Register

	W	L	ERA	G	CG	IP	H	ER	BB	SO
92 R	5	3	2.77	11	0	55.1	61	17	17	33
93 R	7	3	3.00	15	2	84.0	89	28	20	64
94 A	3	6	3.86	12	0	65.1	64	28	22	55
94 R	1	1	1.98	4	0	27.1	16	6	2	28
95 A	9	9	2.98	26	0	160.1	139	53	67	122
96 AA	13	4	2.41	24	1	141.2	113	38	52	176
96 NL	2	0	4.50	3	0	16.0	17	8	7	14

CALVIN MADURO

Position: Pitcher
Team: Philadelphia Phillies
Born: Sept. 5, 1974 Santa Cruz, Aruba
Height: 6' **Weight:** 175 lbs.
Bats: right **Throws:** right
Acquired: Traded by Orioles with Don Florence for Pete Incaviglia and Todd Zeile, 7/96

PLAYER SUMMARY

Fantasy Value	$0
Card Value	12¢ to 20¢
Will	be a trivia answer
Can't	rule out bigs in '97
Expect	ups and downs
Don't Expect	a savior

Maduro was one of two players Philadelphia received in the August 29 trade that sent Pete Incaviglia and Todd Zeile to the Orioles for last year's stretch drive. Shortly thereafter, Maduro became the first native of Aruba ever to play in the major leagues. Clearly, Baltimore preferred a couple of experienced bats over Maduro's young arm, and the Phillies hope to reap the benefits. Pitching for the Double-A Bowie Baysox and the Triple-A Rochester Red Wings in '96, Maduro led Baltimore's farm system with 12 victories and three shutouts. He also finished second in strikeouts with 127 and pitched a no-hitter. Maduro attended Tourist Economy School in Aruba, where he played volleyball, soccer, and baseball. In 1994, he pitched the entire season in the high Class-A Carolina League at the age of 19. With the Phils' pitching staff in shambles, Maduro should get a chance to contribute. If anything, there's a danger he'll be viewed too much as a savior.

Professional Pitching Register

	W	L	ERA	G	CG	IP	H	ER	BB	SO
92 R	1	4	2.27	13	1	71.1	56	18	26	66
93 R	9	4	3.96	14	3	91.0	90	40	17	83
94 A	9	8	4.25	27	0	152.1	132	72	59	137
95 A	8	5	2.94	20	2	122.1	109	40	34	120
95 AA	0	6	5.09	7	0	35.1	39	20	27	26
96 AA	9	7	3.26	19	4	124.1	116	45	36	87
96 AAA	3	5	4.74	8	0	43.2	49	23	18	40
96 NL	0	1	3.52	4	0	15.1	13	6	3	11

KATSUHIRO MAEDA

Position: Pitcher
Team: New York Yankees
Born: June 23, 1971 Kobe-Shi Hyogo, Japan
Height: 6'2" **Weight:** 220 lbs.
Bats: right **Throws:** right
Acquired: Purchased from Seibu Lions, 5/96

PLAYER SUMMARY	
Fantasy Value	$0
Card Value	20¢ to 30¢
Will	bring good fastball
Can't	let media get to him
Expect	adjustment period
Don't Expect	another Nomo

Baseball pundits knew the minute Hideo Nomo came over from Japan and became a sensation that signings of other Japanese players would follow. Maeda is a product of that reality, with the Yanks having the big-market wherewithal to make a deal. They paid a reported bonus of over a million dollars to get his signature, plus what they gave the Seibu Lions of Japan's Pacific League for compensation. Maeda broke in with the Gulf Coast League, making two starts. One of them was a 3-0 one-hitter on June 28. He received a promotion to the Class-A Florida State League, where he made two more appearances before being shipped to Norwich of the Eastern League. On July 19, he went 6⅓ innings in a 1-0 win. He still must work on his control. He's not as experienced as Nomo was when he got to North America, and Maeda must prove himself in the minors. While he won't face the same scrutiny as Nomo, there will be attention.

DIEGOMAR MARKWELL

Position: Pitcher
Team: Toronto Blue Jays
Born: Aug. 8, 1980 Schelpwyk, Curacao
Height: 6'1" **Weight:** 175 lbs.
Bats: left **Throws:** left
Acquired: Signed as a nondrafted free agent, 8/96

PLAYER SUMMARY	
Fantasy Value	$0
Card Value	12¢ to 20¢
Will	throw good curve
Can't	match hard throwers
Expect	prized prospect
Don't Expect	meteoric rise

Markwell is the most recent high-profile result of Toronto's aggressive efforts in the international arena. The Blue Jays had been tracking him for two years and finally decided to move after they saw him in a July youth tournament in the U.S. Virgin Islands. They gave Markwell—scouted by at least four other teams—a bonus reportedly worth about $750,000, more than what they lavished on Brazilian prospect Jose Pett when they signed him as a 16-year-old four years earlier. Markwell is described as having an average fastball, with plenty of room for development. The Blue Jays like the rotation on his curveball and believe he has the potential to be a power pitcher. The Jays will be taking a closer look at Markwell this year in spring training and likely will assign him to a rookie league. Expect Markwell to travel a very deliberate path, with an arrival in the majors sometime after the turn of the century.

Professional Pitching Register

	W	L	ERA	G	CG	IP	H	ER	BB	SO
96 R	1	1	3.00	2	1	9.0	4	3	2	7
96 A	0	0	4.22	2	0	10.2	11	5	6	8
96 AA	3	2	4.05	9	1	53.1	49	24	21	30

ELI MARRERO

Position: Catcher
Team: St. Louis Cardinals
Born: Nov. 17, 1973 Havana, Cuba
Height: 6'1" **Weight:** 180 lbs.
Bats: right **Throws:** right
Acquired: Third-round pick in 6/93 free-agent draft

PLAYER SUMMARY	
Fantasy Value	$0
Card Value	12¢ to 20¢
Will	control the basepaths
Can't	swing for fences
Expect	high-quality defense
Don't Expect	strong second half

Marrero is one of the fine catching prospects in the game. *Baseball America* tabbed him as the top defensive receiver in the Texas League last year, and he has shown more than a hint of power. He has reached double digits in home runs for three straight years and has hit for a respectable average in three of his four pro campaigns. Marrero graduated from Coral Gables High School in Miami, where he made All-State. He debuted with Johnson City of the Appalachian League in 1994, batting .393 as a catcher and only .200 as a DH. Promoted in 1995, he made the South Atlantic League All-Star Team and led that circuit's catchers in games played and putouts. Marrero experienced an inconsistent season in 1995, hitting all ten of his homers and producing all but 14 of his RBI before June 27. He played for West Oahu in the Hawaiian Winter League. This year you can expect to see him as a regular in Triple-A ball.

Professional Batting Register

	BA	G	AB	R	H	2B	3B	HR	RBI	SB
93 R	.361	18	61	10	22	8	0	2	14	2
94 A	.261	116	421	71	110	16	3	21	79	5
95 A	.211	107	383	43	81	16	1	10	55	9
96 AA	.270	116	374	65	101	17	3	19	65	9

RUBEN MATEO

Position: Outfield
Team: Texas Rangers
Born: Feb. 10, 1978 San Cristobal, Dominican Republic
Height: 6' **Weight:** 170 lbs.
Bats: right **Throws:** right
Acquired: Signed as a nondrafted free agent, 10/94

PLAYER SUMMARY	
Fantasy Value	$0
Card Value	10¢ to 20¢
Will	offer speed and pop
Can't	move up too fast
Expect	good arm
Don't Expect	25-homer man

Mateo spent his first season in North American pro ball last year and certainly made a good impression. He wound up among the top basestealers in the entire Texas organization, earning recognition as one of the best prospects in the South Atlantic League. Playing for Charleston, Mateo led the club in doubles (30) and RBI (58), and tied for the lead in homers (eight). This blend of power and pop could prove extremely intriguing as Mateo moves up the ladder. He went 4-for-4 with two home runs on August 18 as part of a nine-game hitting streak. Earlier, he had fashioned a 12-game streak that pulled his average from .249 to .266. Such spirited hitting in the second half of the season was especially impressive for a player still learning his way around the pro game. Mateo has earned plaudits for his arm strength, too. All of this adds up to the promise of a productive season in 1997, when Mateo can expect a trip to a high Class-A league.

Professional Batting Register

	BA	G	AB	R	H	2B	3B	HR	RBI	SB
96 A	.260	134	496	65	129	30	8	8	58	30

BILLY MCMILLON

Position: Outfield
Team: Florida Marlins
Born: Nov. 17, 1971 Otero, NM
Height: 5'11" **Weight:** 172 lbs.
Bats: left **Throws:** left
Acquired: Eighth-round pick in 6/93 free-agent draft

PLAYER SUMMARY	
Fantasy Value	$0
Card Value	15¢ to 20¢
Will	hit for average
Can't	learn more in Triple-A
Expect	left fielder
Don't Expect	Conine to surrender job

McMillon received a call to the majors last year, capping a swift and sure rise through the farm system. He posted impressive numbers for four consecutive years, never blinking when the time came for a promotion. He looks like a player who can hit for average while adding more than occasional home run power. Last year, as the starting left fielder for Charlotte, he virtually tore through the International League. He played right field in the Triple-A All-Star Game. McMillon attended Clemson University, where he set a school record with a .382 career average. As a first-year professional, he showed that things wouldn't change, hitting .305 in the short-season New York-Penn League. Upon his promotion to the Midwest League, McMillon led the circuit in RBI (101). In 1995, he paced the Eastern League in hits (162). Now he faces a challenge with Jeff Conine ahead of him, so he'll have to fight for a job.

GIL MECHE

Position: Pitcher
Team: Seattle Mariners
Born: Sept. 8, 1978 Lafayette, LA
Height: 6'3" **Weight:** 185 lbs.
Bats: right **Throws:** right
Acquired: First-round pick in 6/96 free-agent draft

PLAYER SUMMARY	
Fantasy Value	$0
Card Value	20¢ to 30¢
Will	move slowly
Can't	pitch when sick
Expect	90-mph fastball
Don't Expect	complete games

It may be some time before anyone knows if this particular selection will work out for the Mariners, because Meche endured physical problems both before and after the draft. They weren't of the serious variety, but they were enough to leave Meche below his best in his scholastic season, and enough to shut him down after only two appearances at his first pro stop. Meche, who was rated the tenth-best high school prospect in the nation in *Baseball America*'s preseason rankings, did not pitch up to that level last year at Acadiana High School in Lafayette, Louisiana. He fell to 81st place in *Baseball America*'s ratings by the end of the season. Nevertheless, the Mariners made him the 22nd overall pick, with only six high school pitchers selected ahead of him. Upon signing, Meche reported to Seattle's team in the Arizona League. The Mariners have no choice but to take things slowly with Meche, and they'll probably send him to short-season ball this summer.

Professional Batting Register

	BA	G	AB	R	H	2B	3B	HR	RBI	SB
93 A	.305	57	226	38	69	14	2	6	35	5
94 A	.252	137	496	88	125	25	3	17	101	7
95 AA	.313	141	518	92	162	29	3	14	93	15
96 AAA	.352	97	347	72	122	32	2	17	70	5
96 NL	.216	28	51	4	11	0	0	0	4	0

Professional Pitching Register

	W	L	ERA	G	CG	IP	H	ER	BB	SO
96 R	0	1	6.00	2	0	3.0	4	2	1	4

JACKSON MELIAN

Position: Outfield
Team: New York Yankees
Born: Jan. 7, 1980 Porta La Cruz, Venezuela
Height: 6'1" **Weight:** 185 lbs.
Bats: right **Throws:** right
Acquired: Signed as a nondrafted free agent, 7/96

PLAYER SUMMARY	
Fantasy Value	$0
Card Value	15¢ to 25¢
Will	impress with tools
Can't	zoom to top
Expect	strong speed
Don't Expect	great stats yet

This has become the era of the high-priced international free agent, with major-league teams bidding for talent from such varied outposts as Japan, Brazil, Australia, and Cuba. The Yankees were busy in this arena last summer, shelling out big bucks to acquire two players they believe will have an impact. First it was pitcher Katsuhiro Maeda of Japan, who quickly began playing in the farm system. Then came Melian, a native of Venezuela who could not play professionally last summer because he was only 16. But the Yankees are willing to wait for Melian because he appears to have all the tools needed for a rise to the majors: power, speed, and a strong throwing arm. As can well be imagined, those gifts will not be refined overnight. For that reason, expect Melian to make his debut in a rookie league and then make a move to a short-season league. The Yankees will be careful not to have him overmatched early on, which would hurt his growth and confidence.

JUAN MELO

Position: Shortstop
Team: San Diego Padres
Born: May 11, 1976 Bani, Dominican Republic
Height: 6'1" **Weight:** 160 lbs.
Bats: both **Throws:** right
Acquired: Signed as a nondrafted free agent, 6/93

PLAYER SUMMARY	
Fantasy Value	$0
Card Value	10¢ to 15¢
Will	hold own in field
Can't	stop swinging
Expect	some power
Don't Expect	high on-base pct.

Melo played shortstop in the California League All-Star Game last year, getting one hit in three at bats. His appearance in such a showcase game, at the age of 20, added another line to what has become an impressive resume. He was cowinner of the Arizona League MVP Award in 1994, and also was selected to the 1994 All-Star squad. A year later, he tied for first among Midwest League shortstops in games and double plays. Last year, he played for Rancho Cucamonga, where he raised his home run and RBI totals for the second consecutive year. He could conceivably hit ten to 15 homers in the big leagues and drive in 70 runs. One potential weakness made itself evident in mid-summer, when Melo went 22 straight games without drawing a walk. If he does not practice some kind of selectivity at the plate, pitchers at the higher levels will cut him to pieces. Melo's next stop is Double-A.

Professional Batting Register

	BA	G	AB	R	H	2B	3B	HR	RBI	SB
94 A	.364	3	11	4	4	1	0	1	2	0
94 R	.283	37	145	20	41	3	3	0	15	3
95 A	.282	134	479	65	135	32	1	5	46	12
96 A	.304	128	503	75	153	27	6	8	75	6

ERIC MILTON

Position: Pitcher
Team: New York Yankees
Born: Aug. 5, 1975 State College, PA
Height: 6'3" **Weight:** 195 lbs.
Bats: left **Throws:** left
Acquired: First-round pick in 6/96 free-agent draft

PLAYER SUMMARY	
Fantasy Value	. . . . $0
Card Value	. . . . 20¢ to 30¢
Will	. . . . make them hit it
Can't	. . . . throw like Rivera
Expect	. . . . refined lefty
Don't Expect	. . . . another Pettitte

When an organization likes free agents the way the Yankees do, homegrown prospects often face a challenge in trying to climb to the big club. But the Yankees would not have achieved what they did last year without farm-system products like Andy Pettitte and Mariano Rivera, and so the message for Milton is that the opportunity is there. He is a bit of a diamond in the rough, coming out of a lackluster University of Maryland program where his record didn't impress anyone. But the Yankees thought enough of him to make him the 20th overall pick in the 1996 draft, and only the seventh college pitcher taken. He's a young lefty who has proven he can throw strikes: a relatively rare breed that always has a chance to succeed, especially in Yankee Stadium. His size certainly won't hurt him. There doesn't seem to be much to be gained by starting Milton in a rookie league, so he'll probably make his professional debut in a Class-A circuit this year. The Yanks will be watching him.

SHANE MONAHAN

Position: Outfield
Team: Seattle Mariners
Born: Aug. 12, 1974 Syosset, NY
Height: 6' **Weight:** 195 lbs.
Bats: left **Throws:** right
Acquired: Second-round pick in 6/95 free-agent draft

PLAYER SUMMARY	
Fantasy Value	. . . . $0
Card Value	. . . . 15¢ to 20¢
Will	. . . . hit for power
Can't	. . . . ignore him
Expect	. . . . extra-base hits
Don't Expect	. . . . lots of walks

It didn't take the Mariners long to realize what they had found in the second round of the 1995 draft. After seeing Monahan in the Midwest League for a year, they invited him to spring training for a closer look in '96. You can't blame them. Monahan made the adjustment to pro ball appear routine. After going hitless in his debut in '95, he hit .295 in July. After cooling off a bit in August, Monahan finished the season with a nine-game hitting streak. A graduate of Wheeler High School in Georgia, Monahan attended Clemson and became a two-time NCAA All-America selection. He played for Team USA in 1994, leading the squad in hits. He was also one of nine finalists for the 1994 Golden Spikes Award. Last year, Monahan played for Seattle's team in the California League, where he ranked among the top RBI producers in the entire Mariner system. He also reached double digits in doubles, triples, homers, and stolen bases. He'll jump at least one notch in '97.

Professional Batting Register

	BA	G	AB	R	H	2B	3B	HR	RBI	SB
95 A	.283	59	233	34	66	9	6	1	32	9
96 A	.281	132	584	107	164	31	12	14	97	19

SCOTT MORGAN

Position: Outfield
Team: Cleveland Indians
Born: July 19, 1973 Westlake, CA
Height: 6'7" **Weight:** 230 lbs.
Bats: right **Throws:** right
Acquired: Seventh-round pick in 6/95 free-agent draft

PLAYER SUMMARY	
Fantasy Value	$0
Card Value	10¢ to 20¢
Will	run a little
Can't	be missed on field
Expect	hit by pitches
Don't Expect	wild swinger

When you look at the talent Cleveland has assembled in its system, you wonder how this could be the same organization that produced such futility for so many decades. Morgan is just another indication of the fact those days are over. He made a big impression in the Sally League last year, ranking among the top hitters in the farm system and finishing on the fringe of the home run and RBI leaders. Then again, you'd expect a big impression from someone Morgan's size. He has good body control for a big man, with strikeout totals that are well within range for a young slugger. Out of Allan Hancock College in Santa Monica, California, Morgan broke into pro ball with short-season Watertown and tied for fifth in the New York-Penn League in doubles in 1995. He was hit by a pitch eight times, giving him a share of the club lead in that category. If Morgan can maintain his rate of putting the ball in play, then nothing but good things should await him on his trip.

MATT MORRIS

Position: Pitcher
Team: St. Louis Cardinals
Born: Aug. 9, 1974 Middletown, NY
Height: 6'5" **Weight:** 210 lbs.
Bats: right **Throws:** right
Acquired: First-round pick in 6/95 free-agent draft

PLAYER SUMMARY	
Fantasy Value	$0
Card Value	20¢ to 30¢
Will	work innings
Can't	whiff one per frame
Expect	No. 2 or 3 starter
Don't Expect	slow stuff

Morris is advancing quickly through the St. Louis farm system, and it's not out of the question that he could play a role in the Cards' season in 1997. He was the 12th overall pick in the 1995 draft, capping a college career in which he played for Team USA in 1994 and became a first-team All-American at Seton Hall University in '95. Upon signing, Morris reported to New Jersey of the New York-Penn League and debuted with five shutout innings against Pittsfield. After winning his first two starts there, Morris received a promotion to high Class-A ball. He scarcely could have improved on his Florida State League debut, facing the minimum 21 batters in a seven-inning victory in which he gave up only one hit. He was named the league's Pitcher of the Week for August 21-27. Morris was a workhorse last year in the Texas League, leading Arkansas in decisions (24). This year, he'll probably start in Triple-A and work toward that phone call to the majors.

Professional Batting Register

	BA	G	AB	R	H	2B	3B	HR	RBI	SB
95 A	.262	66	244	42	64	18	0	2	33	6
96 A	.311	87	305	62	95	25	1	22	80	9

Professional Pitching Register

	W	L	ERA	G	CG	IP	H	ER	BB	SO
95 A	2	0	1.64	2	0	11.0	12	2	3	13
95 A	3	2	2.38	6	1	34.0	22	9	11	31
96 AA	12	12	3.88	27	4	167.0	178	72	48	120
96 AAA	0	1	3.38	1	0	8.0	8	3	1	9

DAMIAN MOSS

Position: Pitcher
Team: Atlanta Braves
Born: Nov. 24, 1976 Darlinghurst, Australia
Height: 6′ **Weight:** 187 lbs.
Bats: right **Throws:** left
Acquired: Signed as a nondrafted free agent, 7/93

PLAYER SUMMARY

Fantasy Value	$0
Card Value	15¢ to 25¢
Will	be stingy with hits
Can't	fall behind hitters
Expect	quality arm
Don't Expect	one-pitch outs

Atlanta has found a man from down under who could soon be helping the team stay on top. Moss, signed out of Australia at the age of 16, was one of the gems of the Braves' farm system last year, and found himself pitching in Double-A before his 20th birthday. He opened the season with Durham of the Class-A Carolina League, and pitched two shutout innings in the All-Star Game against the California League. Moss didn't remain long in Class-A, winning nine of 14 starts to earn a trip to Greenville. The jump to Double-A proved to be a big one for Moss, but even with his problems there he still managed to finish among the victory, strikeout, and ERA leaders in the Atlanta system. So far in his pro career, an unsatisfactory ratio of innings and walks has not caught up to Moss. But it will as he gets closer to the majors and starts throwing a lot of 3-1 fastballs. However, his quality arm, combined with the coaching that Atlanta can provide, could promise a bright future.

HEATH MURRAY

Position: Pitcher
Team: San Diego Padres
Born: April 19, 1973 Troy, OH
Height: 6′4″ **Weight:** 205 lbs.
Bats: left **Throws:** left
Acquired: Third-round pick in 6/94 free-agent draft

PLAYER SUMMARY

Fantasy Value	$0
Card Value	15¢ to 20¢
Will	dominate at times
Can't	win without runs
Expect	control lapses
Don't Expect	high ERA

Murray was the starting pitcher for the National League farmhands in the Double-A All-Star Game last year, and it may not be the last time he starts in a showcase game. Only three years into his pro career, Murray has climbed to the point where he could soon get a chance at the San Diego rotation. His work in the farm system has ranged from solid to superb, and there's no reason to think he'll falter now. Murray comes out of the University of Michigan, where he played baseball and led the Wolverines to the 1994 Big Ten title. Drafted shortly thereafter, he finished with the ninth-best ERA in the Northwest League in his professional debut. Of his six losses, three came when he allowed two or less earned runs. Murray split the 1995 season between Class-A and Double-A, leading all San Diego minor-leaguers with 14 victories. He allowed one earned run or less in six of his last seven starts. This year, Murray is on target to open at Triple-A, with an in-season call to San Diego a possibility.

Professional Pitching Register

	W	L	ERA	G	CG	IP	H	ER	BB	SO
94 R	2	5	3.58	12	1	60.1	30	24	55	77
95 A	9	10	4.74	27	0	149.1	134	59	70	177
96 A	9	1	2.25	14	0	84.0	52	21	40	89
96 AA	2	5	4.97	11	0	58.0	57	32	35	48

Professional Pitching Register

	W	L	ERA	G	CG	IP	H	ER	BB	SO
94 A	5	6	2.90	15	2	99.1	101	32	18	78
95 A	9	4	3.12	14	4	92.1	80	32	38	81
95 AA	5	4	3.38	14	0	77.1	83	29	42	71
96 AA	13	9	3.21	27	1	174.0	154	62	60	156

TODD NOEL

Position: Pitcher
Team: Chicago Cubs
Born: Sept. 28, 1978 Abbeville, LA
Height: 6'4" **Weight:** 185 lbs.
Bats: right **Throws:** right
Acquired: First-round pick in 6/96 free-agent draft

PLAYER SUMMARY

Fantasy Value	$0
Card Value	20¢ to 30¢
Will	start or relieve
Can't	soar to majors
Expect	velocity
Don't Expect	refined pitcher

Noel became the third straight high school right-hander taken by the Cubs with their first pick, following Jay Peterson in 1994 and Kerry Wood in '95. Now the Cubs can only hope that Noel rises to the big leagues as quickly as he appeared on their board. When last year began, Noel was not even included in *Baseball America*'s list of the top 100 high school prospects. By virtue of a superb season, however, he became the 17th player drafted overall, and only the ninth pitcher. He comes out of Vermillion High School in Maurice, Louisiana, where he struck out almost two batters per inning. After signing, Noel began his career with Chicago's affiliate in the rookie Gulf Coast League. There he eased his way into pro ball, working out of the bullpen. In three appearances, Noel pitched a total of four innings, allowing four hits and striking out four. It's unlikely he'll jump to the majors as quickly as he jumped to Chicago's attention. Look for him in short-season ball in 1997.

VLADIMIR NUNEZ

Position: Pitcher
Team: Arizona Diamondbacks
Born: March 15, 1975 Havana, Cuba
Height: 6'5" **Weight:** 220 lbs.
Bats: right **Throws:** right
Acquired: Signed as a nondrafted free agent, 2/96

PLAYER SUMMARY

Fantasy Value	$0
Card Value	15¢ to 25¢
Will	reach 91 to 92 mph
Can't	reach bigs before '98
Expect	nice breaking pitch
Don't Expect	another struggle

The Diamondbacks made an aggressive move in February '96, signing this promising international free agent a full two years before they ever play their first game. It cost them nearly $2 million, but their purchase could pay off well. If nothing else, the acquisition signals that the Diamondbacks are going to be strong players in the free-agent market. Nunez left the Cuban squad in October 1995 while on a trip to Venezuela. The 'Backs assigned him to Visalia, a co-op team in the California League, where he absorbed some early bumps. They then moved Nunez to their rookie league club in Lethbridge, where he helped win a second-half championship in the Pioneer League. He led the league in ERA, strikeouts, and victories, indicating he's ready for some full-season ball. The Diamondbacks view Nunez as a strong prospect who can throw in the 90-mph range and complement his fastball with a slider. He could arrive in three years.

Professional Pitching Register

	W	L	ERA	G	S	IP	H	ER	BB	SO
96 R	0	0	6.75	3	0	4.0	4	3	2	4

Professional Pitching Register

	W	L	ERA	G	CG	IP	H	ER	BB	SO
96 R	10	0	2.22	14	0	85.0	78	21	10	93
96 A	1	6	5.43	12	0	53.0	64	32	17	37

RYAN NYE

Position: Pitcher
Team: Philadelphia Phillies
Born: June 24, 1973 Biloxi, MS
Height: 6'2" **Weight:** 195 lbs.
Bats: right **Throws:** right
Acquired: Second-round pick in 6/94 free-agent draft

PLAYER SUMMARY	
Fantasy Value	$0
Card Value	20¢ to 30¢
Will	complete some games
Can't	win ERA title
Expect	step up to bigs
Don't Expect	staff ace

Nye won 13 games last season, more than any member of the Philadelphia staff. Of course, Nye's victories came in Double- and Triple-A, but he did show an ability to get the job done, even if his ERA was sometimes on the inelegant side. Actually, a step up to the majors would only seem logical, since Nye has moved very smartly and surely through the farm system since being drafted. He broke into pro ball with Batavia of the New York-Penn League in 1994 and averaged almost exactly one strikeout per inning. Promoted to the Florida State League in '95, Nye completed five of 27 starts, while walking only one man every five innings. Pitching for Reading in the Double-A Eastern League last year, Nye owned an 8-2 mark with a 3.84 ERA, winning his last three starts in impressive fashion. Upon being boosted to Triple-A, Nye kept winning. Originally drafted by the Seattle Mariners in both 1991 and 1992, he declined to sign with them.

Professional Pitching Register

	W	L	ERA	G	CG	IP	H	ER	BB	SO
94 A	7	2	2.64	13	1	71.2	64	21	15	71
95 A	12	7	3.40	27	5	167.0	164	63	33	116
96 AA	8	2	3.84	14	0	86.2	76	37	30	90
96 AAA	5	2	5.02	14	0	80.2	97	45	30	51

JOHN OLIVER

Position: Outfield
Team: Cincinnati Reds
Born: May 14, 1978 Wilkes Barre, PA
Height: 6'3" **Weight:** 180 lbs.
Bats: right **Throws:** right
Acquired: First-round pick in 6/96 free agent draft

PLAYER SUMMARY	
Fantasy Value	$0
Card Value	20¢ to 35¢
Will	cover ground
Can't	forget contact
Expect	extra-base potential
Don't Expect	high on-base pct.

The Reds have a little extra reason to hope that Oliver turns out well, because their first-round draft selections have not exactly yielded dividends in recent years. In two of the three drafts before last season's, the Reds did not even own a first-round selection. And the one player they did draft in the first round, pitcher C.J. Nitkowski in 1994, is no longer with the organization. Amid this piece of history, the Reds made Oliver the 25th overall pick last year. He was only the tenth position player taken, and only the third high school outfielder. Oliver comes out of Lake-Lehman High School in Pennsylvania, where he hit over .600 in his last season. His biggest gift is the speed that enables him to steal bases and cover ground in center field. After signing, Oliver went to the Reds farm club in the Appalachian League, where he didn't get much going on the basepaths in his first weeks as a pro. But this year will be a truer test of his potential, with a possible trip to low Class-A ball in the picture.

Professional Batting Register

	BA	G	AB	R	H	2B	3B	HR	RBI	SB
96 R	.203	41	143	20	29	5	0	2	13	3

RAFAEL ORELLANO

Position: Pitcher
Team: Boston Red Sox
Born: April 28, 1973 Humacao, Puerto Rico
Height: 6'2" **Weight:** 160 lbs.
Bats: left **Throws:** left
Acquired: Signed as a nondrafted free agent, 11/92

PLAYER SUMMARY	
Fantasy Value $0
Card Value . . . . 15¢ to 20¢
Will . . . . get another chance
Can't . . . . explain the nosedive
Expect . . . . better things
Don't Expect . . . . another disaster

Nothing could have prepared the Red Sox for what happened to Orellano last year. Seemingly on a path that would inevitably take him to the majors, he slumped badly at the Triple-A level last year. This collapse came after Orellano had distinguished himself at two different stops in the Boston farm system. It seems hard to believe that Orellano didn't have the stuff to handle Triple-A hitters, because he had dominated at Double-A, even leading the Eastern League in strikeouts. He finished third in the league in batting average against and was promoted to Boston's 40-man roster in November. From there, the Red Sox would have loved to have sent him to Pawtucket for some Triple-A experience before bringing him to Boston, but he never made it that far. Orellano's 1996 numbers tell the story of a disastrous season. Still, it's too early to write him off as a prospect. Many players go into prolonged slumps that require adjustments. Keep an eye on him this year.

KEVIN ORIE

Position: Third base
Team: Chicago Cubs
Born: Sept. 1, 1972 West Chester, PA
Height: 6'4" **Weight:** 210 lbs.
Bats: right **Throws:** right
Acquired: Supplemental pick in 6/92 free-agent draft

PLAYER SUMMARY	
Fantasy Value $0
Card Value . . . . 20¢ to 25¢
Will . . . . bring promise
Can't . . . . play with bad wrist
Expect . . . . Wrigley Field power
Don't Expect . . . . immediate stardom

Not too long ago, the Cubs allowed themselves great expectations regarding a third-base prospect. But Gary Scott never made it. Now along comes Orie, who has shown some offensive ability throughout his quick rise through the farm system. Whether he has enough to win the major-league job this season is something to be observed in spring training. Last year he did all he could at Double-A, where he was named the best batting prospect in the Southern League by *Baseball America*. He did not fare all that well in a brief appearance in Triple-A, but that sample is too small to tell much about Orie's chances. He was a member of the Pennsylvania state championship football team at Upper St. Clair High School in Pittsburgh in 1990. He attended Indiana University, where he was a two-time All-Big Ten Conference selection. After a wrist injury wrecked virtually all of his 1994 season, he bounced back well in 1995 at Class-A Daytona. He should get his shot at the big-league third base job in '97.

Professional Pitching Register

	W	L	ERA	G	CG	IP	H	ER	BB	SO
93 A	1	2	5.79	11	0	18.2	22	12	7	13
94 R	1	0	2.03	4	0	13.1	6	3	4	10
94 A	11	3	2.40	16	2	97.1	68	26	25	103
95 AA	11	7	3.09	27	2	186.2	146	64	72	160
96 AAA	4	11	7.88	22	0	99.1	124	87	62	66

Professional Batting Register

	BA	G	AB	R	H	2B	3B	HR	RBI	SB
93 A	.269	65	238	28	64	17	1	7	45	3
94 A	.412	6	17	4	7	3	1	1	5	0
95 A	.244	119	409	54	100	17	4	9	51	5
96 AA	.314	82	296	42	93	25	0	8	58	2
96 AAA	.208	14	48	5	10	1	0	2	6	0

RUSS ORTIZ

Position: Pitcher
Team: San Francisco Giants
Born: June 5, 1974 Encino, CA
Height: 6'1" **Weight:** 190 lbs.
Bats: right **Throws:** right
Acquired: Fourth-round pick in 6/95 free-agent draft

PLAYER SUMMARY	
Fantasy Value	$0
Card Value	12¢ to 20¢
Will	see more time in minors
Can't	save 35 every year
Expect	middle reliever
Don't Expect	sure thing

Minor-league bullpen aces often present a problem for fans trying to predict how much success lies in their future. Being a closer in the lower minors is no guarantee a player will hold the same job in the majors. But sometimes a player's stats are just too good to ignore. Such is the case with Ortiz, who blazed through the Class-A California League last year, earning a promotion to Double-A. When the minor-league season ended on the first weekend in September, Ortiz owned more saves than the Giants' closer, Rod Beck. Ortiz's dominance can be measured by a look at one of his few failures; when he failed to hold a lead against Jackson on August 20, it marked the first time in ten outings he had allowed an earned run. Ortiz graduated from Montclair Prep in Van Nuys, California, and went on to the University of Oklahoma. He earned Rolaids Relief Man of the Year honors in the Northwest League while pitching for Bellingham in 1995.

ROY PADILLA

Position: Outfield
Team: Boston Red Sox
Born: Aug. 4, 1975 Panama City, Panama
Height: 6'5" **Weight:** 227 lbs.
Bats: left **Throws:** left
Acquired: Signed as a nondrafted free agent, 9/92

PLAYER SUMMARY	
Fantasy Value	$0
Card Value	15¢ to 20¢
Will	bring size, speed
Can't	learn overnight
Expect	more punch
Don't Expect	return to pitching

Padilla enjoyed reasonable success in the Midwest League last year, but nothing that would mark him as spectacular. It's only when you understand his background that you appreciate his potential. You see, last year was Padilla's first as an outfielder and batter. Until then, he had worked as a pitcher. Another thing to notice about Padilla is his size. He is tall, solid, and well built, and when you factor in his more than 20 stolen bases in '96, you get a better idea of the kind of talent the Red Sox have found. Signed in 1992, Padilla tasted success in the Gulf Coast League in 1994, finishing first in wins for his team. But after the 1995 campaign, in which he went a combined 2-8, Padilla attended the Florida Instructional League as a position player. He handled his new assignment well and did not strike out more often than any other prospect. He still hasn't hit for power, but this year he may give a better indication of his potential in that area.

Professional Pitching Register

	W	L	ERA	G	S	IP	H	ER	BB	SO
95 A	2	0	0.52	25	11	34.1	19	2	13	55
95 A	0	1	1.50	5	0	6.0	4	1	2	7
96 A	0	0	0.25	34	23	36.2	16	1	20	63
96 AA	1	2	4.05	26	13	26.2	22	12	21	29

Professional Batting Register

	BA	G	AB	R	H	2B	3B	HR	RBI	SB
95 R	.000	16	1	0	0	0	0	0	0	0
96 A	.296	8	27	2	8	2	0	0	2	4
96 A	.280	103	386	58	108	20	6	2	40	21

JOHN PATTERSON

Position: Pitcher
Team: Montreal Expos
Born: Jan. 30, 1978
Height: 6'5" **Weight:** 185 lbs.
Bats: right **Throws:** right
Acquired: First-round pick in 6/96 free-agent draft

PLAYER SUMMARY	
Fantasy Value	$0
Card Value	20¢ to 25¢
Will	bring bloodlines
Can't	skyrocket to majors
Expect	bit of a breaking ball
Don't Expect	raw prospect

You won't see Patterson's name on any minor-league stat sheets from last year. And, as of late last summer, you didn't see his name on a signed contract, either. That's because Patterson was one of a group of top draft picks who cited a technical violation in the way their contract was tendered. All this was bad news for the Expos because Patterson is a player with baseball in his blood and background. Patterson, a high school standout in Texas, is the son of Doug Patterson, a one-time Baltimore farmhand. With his experience, the elder Patterson can provide loads of baseball wisdom. Of course, none of this wisdom would help if the son lacked talent, but that's not the case. John, who can hurl the ball at 90 mph, was the first high school pitcher taken in last year's draft, and only the fifth pitcher taken overall. He comes out of West Orange Stark High School, and was the state's top-rated prospect in 1996, averaging nearly two strikeouts per inning.

CARL PAVANO

Position: Pitcher
Team: Boston Red Sox
Born: Jan. 8, 1976 New Britain, CT
Height: 6'5" **Weight:** 228 lbs.
Bats: right **Throws:** right
Acquired: 13th-round pick in 6/94 free-agent draft

PLAYER SUMMARY	
Fantasy Value	$0
Card Value	12¢ to 15¢
Will	play in New England
Can't	be distracted
Expect	bona fide starter
Don't Expect	repeat of '96

This New England native took huge strides last year toward pitching for the Red Sox very soon. He starred for Trenton of the Double-A Eastern League last year, leading his team in victories (16) and strikeouts (146). As a result, he'll likely get a long look in spring training and wind up pitching either in Pawtucket or in Fenway. Pavano graduated from Southington High School in 1994. He twice won All-State honors and was a member of the state championship team his senior year. Upon signing with the BoSox, Pavano got his feet wet in the Gulf Coast League, then attended the Florida Instructional League. In 1995, Pavano advanced to the Class-A Midwest League, where he ranked third in strikeouts per nine innings. In 1996, he was the starting pitcher for the American League farmhands in the Double-A All-Star Game, allowing one run in two innings. It will be interesting to see how Pavano likes playing in his home region. Sometimes that brings too much pressure for a youngster to handle gracefully.

Professional Pitching Register

	W	L	ERA	G	CG	IP	H	ER	BB	SO
94 R	4	3	1.84	9	0	44.0	31	9	7	47
95 A	6	6	3.44	22	1	141.1	118	54	52	138
96 AA	16	5	2.63	27	6	185.0	154	54	47	146

JAY PAYTON

Position: Outfield
Team: New York Mets
Born: Nov. 22, 1972 Zanesville, OH
Height: 5'10" **Weight:** 185 lbs.
Bats: right **Throws:** right
Acquired: Supplemental pick in 6/94 free-agent draft

PLAYER SUMMARY

Fantasy Value	$1
Card Value	60¢ to $1
Will	hit line drives
Can't	excel when hurt
Expect	strong slugging pct.
Don't Expect	perfect elbow

Payton is one of the top hitters in the New York organization, but a major elbow injury sidelined him just as he was about to take the final steps toward the majors. He finally got back into the lineup last year in Triple-A Norfolk and resumed hitting the ball. But how well Payton's elbow will hold up, as well as where he might fit into the New York lineup this year, are still questions to be answered. An All-American in baseball and academics at Georgia Tech, Payton starred from the moment he turned pro. In 1994, he hit .365 in short-season ball before being summoned to Binghamton, where he enjoyed a late-season run with the Double-A team. Payton spent the early part of 1995 in Double-A, becoming an Eastern League All-Star and at one point getting a hit in 25 straight games. A contact hitter who can really punish the ball, Payton will pile up extra-base hits. Expect him to play in the majors sometime this year if he stays healthy.

Professional Batting Register

	BA	G	AB	R	H	2B	3B	HR	RBI	SB
94 A	.365	58	219	47	80	16	2	3	37	10
94 AA	.280	8	25	3	7	1	0	0	1	1
95 A	.345	85	357	59	123	20	3	14	54	16
95 AAA	.240	50	196	33	47	11	4	4	30	11
96 R	.385	3	13	3	5	1	0	1	2	1
96 A	.308	9	26	4	8	2	0	0	1	2
96 AA	.200	4	10	0	2	0	0	0	2	0
96 AAA	.307	55	153	30	47	6	3	6	26	10

JUAN PENA

Position: Pitcher
Team: Boston Red Sox
Born: June 27, 1977 Santo Domingo, Dominican Republic
Height: 6'5" **Weight:** 211 lbs.
Bats: right **Throws:** right
Acquired: 27th-round pick in 6/95 free-agent draft

PLAYER SUMMARY

Fantasy Value	$0
Card Value	10¢ to 15¢
Will	stay in rotation
Can't	miss him on mound
Expect	good control
Don't Expect	27th-round results

Considering what Pena has accomplished in his first two years of pro ball, one has to wonder why he remained on the sidelines until the 27th round of the 1995 draft. His size certainly would not seem to be a problem. And judging by his strikeout-to-innings ratio in pro ball, his stuff would seem to be decent enough. In the end, however, it doesn't matter where a player was drafted, but only how he performs. And Pena has performed well enough that a boost to high Class-A would seem to be in order this year. He appeared in the Midwest League All-Star Game last summer, going one inning and allowing one run. Over one stretch of four starts, he permitted no more than two earned runs per game. By the end of the season, Pena ranked among the top Red Sox minor-leaguers in victories, strikeouts, and ERA. He began his pro career in the rookie Gulf Coast League in 1995, appearing mostly in relief, and got a brief look in the Florida State League as well.

Professional Pitching Register

	W	L	ERA	G	CG	IP	H	ER	BB	SO
95 R	3	2	1.95	13	2	55.1	41	12	6	47
95 A	1	1	4.91	2	0	7.1	8	4	3	5
96 A	12	10	2.97	26	4	187.2	149	62	34	156

DANNY PEOPLES

Position: First base
Team: Cleveland Indians
Born: Jan. 20, 1975 Austin, TX
Height: 6'1" **Weight:** 210 lbs.
Bats: right **Throws:** right
Acquired: First-round pick in 6/96 free-agent draft

PLAYER SUMMARY

Fantasy Value	$0
Card Value	20¢ to 30¢
Will	hit homers
Can't	vault past others
Expect	possible DH
Don't Expect	Gold Glove

When executives have made as many correct moves as Cleveland's have recently, you've got to grant them the benefit of the doubt when they depart from conventional wisdom. Such seems to have been the case when the ballclub selected Peoples with the 28th overall pick last year. Cleveland appears to have valued Peoples far more than others did; *Baseball America* ranked him only the 88th-best pick entering the draft. Peoples comes out of the University of Texas, where he homered roughly once every 13 official trips to the plate. A first baseman, Peoples faces a considerable challenge in an organization that features Richie Sexson and Sean Casey ahead of him in the minors. His quick signing enabled him to collect quite a few at bats last summer. He served as a designated hitter for Watertown of the New York-Penn League, at one point hitting .308 over an 11-game stretch spanning late June and early July.

Professional Batting Register

	BA	G	AB	R	H	2B	3B	HR	RBI	SB
96 A	.239	35	117	20	28	7	0	3	26	3

NEIFI PEREZ

Position: Shortstop
Team: Colorado Rockies
Born: Feb. 2, 1975 Villa Mella, Dominican Republic
Height: 6' **Weight:** 173 lbs.
Bats: both **Throws:** right
Acquired: Signed as a nondrafted free agent, 11/92

PLAYER SUMMARY

Fantasy Value	$0
Card Value	10¢ to 15¢
Will	thrive in Colorado
Can't	swing for fences
Expect	spectacular fielding
Don't Expect	second baseman

Described as spectacular in the field, Perez also has offensive gifts that will only be enhanced by the playing conditions in Colorado. That makes for quite a powerful package in a young man of 22 who has already received a taste of the majors. The only question might be what position he'll play. When he came up last year, he made his debut at second base. But he is a shortstop by training, and that's probably where he'll land in the long run. Perez broke into pro ball in 1993 and was quickly recognized as a prospect to watch. In 1994, he led the California League in chances, putouts, and double plays. His 19 sacrifices also led the league. In 1995, Perez paced the Eastern League's shortstops in fielding percentage and tied for the lead in double plays. At the plate, Perez can be counted on for a solid average, with his annual home run potential somewhere between ten and 20. Expect to see a lot of Perez in the next several years.

Professional Batting Register

	BA	G	AB	R	H	2B	3B	HR	RBI	SB
93 A	.260	75	296	35	77	11	4	3	32	19
94 A	.239	134	506	64	121	16	7	1	35	9
95 AA	.253	116	427	59	108	28	3	5	43	5
95 AAA	.278	11	36	4	10	4	0	0	2	1
96 AAA	.316	133	570	77	180	28	12	7	72	16
96 NL	.156	17	45	4	7	2	0	0	3	2

CHARLES PETERSON

Position: Outfield
Team: Pittsburgh Pirates
Born: May 8, 1974 Laurens, SC
Height: 6'3" **Weight:** 203 lbs.
Bats: right **Throws:** right
Acquired: First-round pick in 6/93 free-agent draft

PLAYER SUMMARY	
Fantasy Value	$0
Card Value	15¢ to 20¢
Will	pile up numbers
Can't	stay off DL
Expect	outs on bases
Don't Expect	a home run hitter

Peterson put in a full season in the Double-A Southern League last year, leading Carolina in RBI and stolen bases, tying for the lead in doubles, and finishing third in runs. It was the kind of performance that would seem to ensure some kind of promotion this season. Peterson is a fine all-around athlete who was a *Parade* All-American as a quarterback at Laurens High School. He made an impact as soon as he arrived in pro ball, being named to the Gulf Coast League's All-Star squad. Boosted to the Class-A South Atlantic League in 1994, Peterson led his team in runs, hits, and triples even though he suffered from a strained left quadriceps muscle. Injury struck again in 1995 when he was playing for Lynchburg of the Carolina League, with a sprained ankle forcing a stretch on the disabled list. Peterson so far hasn't shown much home run power for someone his size. He has also had trouble with his stolen-base percentage.

BEN PETRICK

Position: Catcher
Team: Colorado Rockies
Born: April 7, 1977 Salem, OR
Height: 6' **Weight:** 190 lbs.
Bats: right **Throws:** right
Acquired: Second-round pick in 6/95 free-agent draft

PLAYER SUMMARY	
Fantasy Value	$0
Card Value	10¢ to 15¢
Will	only get better
Can't	neglect contact
Expect	a good athlete
Don't Expect	quick rise

For a player experiencing his first look at pro ball, Petrick handled himself extremely well last year. Not only did he handle a full-season schedule with no prior professional experience, he also did it at the age of 19, and he did so while playing a position that requires leadership. Petrick played for Asheville of the South Atlantic League and was one of the top run-producers on the team, ranking among the leaders in homers, RBI, and doubles. Showing great athletic ability, he was also one of his team's biggest threats on the bases. Not surprisingly, he also was among the team's strikeout leaders, but that's something his coaches will address at further stops along the way. Petrick played football, baseball, and basketball in high school, winning the state rushing title in 1994. He played in the U.S. Olympic Festival in Colorado Springs, getting acquainted with the Rocky Mountain region. He also played in the Florida Instructional League in September 1995.

Professional Batting Register

	BA	G	AB	R	H	2B	3B	HR	RBI	SB
93 R	.303	49	188	26	57	11	3	1	23	8
94 A	.255	108	415	55	106	14	6	4	40	27
95 A	.274	107	391	61	107	9	4	7	51	31
95 AA	.329	20	70	13	23	3	1	0	7	2
96 AA	.275	125	462	71	127	24	2	7	63	33

Professional Batting Register

	BA	G	AB	R	H	2B	3B	HR	RBI	SB
96 A	.235	122	446	74	105	24	2	14	52	19

JOSE PETT

Position: Pitcher
Team: Pittsburgh Pirates
Born: Jan. 8, 1976 Sao Paulo, Brazil
Height: 6'6" **Weight:** 210 lbs.
Bats: right **Throws:** right
Acquired: Traded by Blue Jays with Jose
Silva, Brandon Cromer, and three players to
be named later for Orlando Merced, Carlos
Garcia, and Dan Plesac, 11/96

PLAYER SUMMARY	
Fantasy Value	$0
Card Value	12¢ to 20¢
Will	bounce back
Can't	make adjustment
Expect	good stuff
Don't Expect	another poor showing

If it seems that Pett has been around for years, that's because he has. The Blue Jays signed him when he was just 16 years old, winning a bidding war that attracted plenty of competition. After watching last year's debacle at Triple-A, one might be tempted to write off Pett as an eternal prospect. Remember, however, that Pett is just 21 years old and still has plenty of time to come up with the refinements that can translate potential into performance. In his first look at Triple-A ball, Pett had his worst year as a pro, giving up far more hits than innings and posting an ERA near 6.00. His ERA and hit totals have both gone up every year of his pro career. But again, keep in mind that even to pitch in Triple-A at his age is unusual. Before turning pro, Pett was a member of the Brazilian team that played in the World Junior Championships in Mexico. Look for him in Pittsburgh's training camp this spring, where he'll get some attention.

A.J. PIERZYNSKI

Position: Catcher
Team: Minnesota Twins
Born: Dec. 30, 1976 Bridgehampton, NY
Height: 6'3" **Weight:** 202 lbs.
Bats: left **Throws:** right
Acquired: Third-round pick in 6/94 free-agent
draft

PLAYER SUMMARY	
Fantasy Value	$0
Card Value	12¢ to 20¢
Will	earn promotions
Can't	worry about Valentin
Expect	all-around game
Don't Expect	25-homer man

The Twins can only salivate at the potential Pierzynski brings: a big, strong, lefty-hitting catcher with defensive skills and youth on his side. Pierzynski played in the Midwest League last year and did so with enough distinction to wind up as the youngest player on *Baseball America*'s list of top prospects in the circuit. He led Fort Wayne in RBI (70) and tied for first in doubles (30). He also had 17 more RBI than strikeouts, a tidy accomplishment for such a young player. Pierzynski was born near the eastern tip of Long Island—an unusual history for a young ballplayer. He now resides in Orlando, Florida, and this year he could find himself playing much closer to home, as a berth on a Florida State League club is a possibility. Down the road, Pierzynski may have to confront the presence of catching prospect Jose Valentin, who is a couple of rungs ahead of him in the farm system, but right now the job for Pierzynski is to keep improving.

Professional Pitching Register

	W	L	ERA	G	CG	IP	H	ER	BB	SO
93 R	1	1	3.60	4	0	10.0	10	4	3	7
94 A	4	8	3.77	15	1	90.2	103	38	20	49
95 AA	8	9	4.26	26	1	141.2	132	67	48	89
96 AA	4	2	4.09	7	1	44.0	37	20	10	38
96 AAA	2	9	5.83	20	1	109.2	134	71	42	50

Professional Batting Register

	BA	G	AB	R	H	2B	3B	HR	RBI	SB
94 R	.289	43	152	21	44	8	1	1	19	0
95 A	.310	22	84	10	26	5	1	2	14	0
95 R	.332	56	205	29	68	13	1	7	45	0
96 A	.274	114	431	48	118	30	3	7	70	0

JIM PITTSLEY

Position: Pitcher
Team: Kansas City Royals
Born: April 3, 1974 DuBois, PA
Height: 6'1" **Weight:** 175 lbs.
Bats: right **Throws:** right
Acquired: First-round pick in 6/92 free-agent draft

PLAYER SUMMARY	
Fantasy Value	$0
Card Value	15¢ to 20¢
Will	contend for job
Can't	carry big load
Expect	lots of strikeouts
Don't Expect	pinpoint control

Pittsley turned in a strong season last year, bouncing back from elbow surgery to reclaim a place in Kansas City's plans. Pitching for Omaha of the Triple-A American Association, he made the most of his 13 appearances and likely will be in the running for a spot on the Royals staff this season. That was by no means a certainty during the 1995 campaign, when Pittsley went from a high point to a low one in the span of days. He got the call to the majors on May 21, made his debut two days later, was returned to Omaha after making just one appearance, then hurt his elbow. He underwent surgery on August 4 and was lost for the year. In 1994, Pittsley was named cowinner of the Royals' Minor League Pitcher of the Year Award after making the Carolina League All-Star Team and winning the league strikeout title with 171. Pittsley was the 17th overall selection in the 1992 draft out of DuBois (Pennsylvania) High School.

Professional Pitching Register

	W	L	ERA	G	CG	IP	H	ER	BB	SO
92 R	4	1	3.32	9	0	43.1	27	16	15	47
92 A	0	0	0.00	1	0	3.0	2	0	1	4
93 A	5	5	4.26	15	2	80.1	76	38	32	87
94 A	11	5	3.17	27	1	161.2	154	57	42	171
95 AAA	4	1	3.21	8	0	47.2	38	17	16	39
95 AL	0	0	13.50	1	0	3.1	7	5	1	0
96 A	0	1	11.00	2	0	9.0	13	11	5	10
96 AA	3	0	0.41	3	0	22.0	9	1	5	7
96 AAA	7	1	3.97	13	0	70.1	74	31	39	53

CLIFF POLITTE

Position: Pitcher
Team: St. Louis Cardinals
Born: Feb. 24, 1974 Kirkwood, MO
Height: 5'11" **Weight:** 180 lbs.
Bats: right **Throws:** right
Acquired: 54th-round pick in 6/95 free-agent draft

PLAYER SUMMARY	
Fantasy Value	$0
Card Value	10¢ to 20¢
Will	advance
Can't	relax now
Expect	90-mph fastball
Don't Expect	54th-round talent

On paper, Politte seems to have about as much chance of getting to the majors as the St. Louis Arch has of getting moved to Hoboken, New Jersey. After all, not only was he drafted in the nether rounds of the draft in 1995, but he also stands less than six feet tall, and scouts generally don't like right-handers who come in that size. But Politte certainly pitched big in the Midwest League last year, looking more like a high-level draft choice. He finished among the victory, strikeout, and ERA leaders in the St. Louis organization. He did not get the publicity that went to his Peoria teammate Britt Reames, but the Cardinals won't mind as long as Politte keeps putting up the numbers. Of course, whether or not he can do so remains to be seen, and a promotion often has a way of separating prospects from suspects. But if Politte keeps throwing the ball over the plate with something on it, he can survive in the Florida State League, his probable assignment for this summer.

Professional Pitching Register

	W	L	ERA	G	CG	IP	H	ER	BB	SO
96 A	14	6	2.59	25	0	149.2	108	43	47	151

DANTE POWELL

Position: Outfield
Team: San Francisco Giants
Born: Aug. 25, 1973 Long Beach, CA
Height: 6'2" **Weight:** 185 lbs.
Bats: right **Throws:** right
Acquired: First-round pick in 6/94 free-agent draft

PLAYER SUMMARY	
Fantasy Value	$0
Card Value	25¢ to 35¢
Will	be a force
Can't	do more in Double-A
Expect	a bit of Triple-A
Don't Expect	much time in minors

Powell's talent is so abundant and obvious that teams made him a first-round selection in two separate drafts. In 1991, Toronto took him with a supplemental selection. Three years later, the Giants made him the 22nd overall pick. Now it's easy to see why. Powell spent most of last season in the Double-A Texas League and added some spectacular feats to his resume. He hit for a strong average, produced runs, and wound up second in the San Francisco farm system in stolen bases. Powell comes out of Cal State-Fullerton, where he hit .315 with 26 homers and 141 RBI over three seasons. In 1994, he led his team into the College World Series and also played for the U.S. Olympic squad. Upon turning pro, he led the Northwest League in stolen bases (27) and made the All-Star Team. In 1995, Powell moved up to the Cal League, making the All-Star squad again. He seems very close to the majors, though he may need some fine-tuning at Triple-A.

Professional Batting Register

	BA	G	AB	R	H	2B	3B	HR	RBI	SB
94 A	.309	41	165	31	51	15	1	5	25	27
94 A	.500	1	4	0	2	0	1	0	0	0
95 A	.248	135	505	74	125	23	8	10	70	12
96 AA	.280	135	508	92	142	27	2	21	78	43
96 AAA	.250	2	8	0	2	0	1	0	0	0

ARQUIMEDEZ POZO

Position: Infield
Team: Boston Red Sox
Born: Aug. 24, 1973 Santo Domingo, Dominican Republic
Height: 5'10" **Weight:** 160 lbs.
Bats: right **Throws:** right
Acquired: Traded by Mariners for Jeff Manto, 7/96

PLAYER SUMMARY	
Fantasy Value	$0
Card Value	15¢ to 20¢
Will	homer in Fenway
Can't	steal bases
Expect	250 at bats
Don't Expect	a shortstop

Pozo had a cup of coffee in Boston last summer and could be a contender for a job with the Red Sox this year. It could be at second base, where the Red Sox may have an opening, or it could be in a utility role. Pozo played 21 games for the Red Sox upon being acquired by the team, including ten apiece at second and third. Unfortunately for him, he did not hit a great deal, certainly not up to the standard he set in Triple-A last year, when he popped 15 homers in only 365 at bats. Originally signed by Seattle as a nondrafted free agent in 1990, Pozo began his North American career in 1992. A year later, he emerged as a force in the Class-A California League, leading all minor-leaguers with 44 doubles. Upon his promotion to Double-A in 1994, Pozo compiled the fourth-lowest strikeout ratio in the Southern League. He spent 1995 in Triple-A, leading Tacoma in hits and RBI.

Professional Batting Register

	BA	G	AB	R	H	2B	3B	HR	RBI	SB
92 A	.261	54	199	33	52	8	4	3	19	13
92 A	.322	39	149	37	48	12	0	7	21	9
93 A	.342	127	515	98	176	44	6	13	83	10
94 A	.289	119	447	70	129	31	1	14	54	11
95 AAA	.300	122	450	57	135	19	6	10	62	3
95 AL	.000	1	1	0	0	0	0	0	0	0
96 AAA	.243	11	37	6	9	1	0	1	3	0
96 AAA	.279	95	365	55	102	12	5	15	64	3
96 AL	.172	21	58	4	10	3	1	1	11	1

ALEJANDRO PRIETO

Position: Shortstop
Team: Kansas City Royals
Born: June 19, 1976 Caracas, Venezuela
Height: 5'11" **Weight:** 150 lbs.
Bats: both **Throws:** right
Acquired: Signed as a nondrafted free agent, 11/92

PLAYER SUMMARY	
Fantasy Value	$0
Card Value	12¢ to 20¢
Will	cover ground
Can't	hit for power
Expect	flexibility
Don't Expect	big slugging pct.

Had he not suffered a shoulder injury in 1994, Prieto might be competing for a job in Kansas City already. As it is, he's not all that far away. Prieto performed in the high Class-A Carolina League last year, making the jump from the Midwest League with ease. He hit the 25-steal plateau and scored his share of runs. He doesn't look like he'll be a power player, but with his ability to switch-hit, he should add speed and flexibility to any lineup. He and keystone partner Sergio Nunez combined to steal well over 60 bases in Class-A ball, forming a tandem with interesting possibilities if it remains together up the ladder. Prieto signed at the age of 16 and broke into pro ball with the Gulf Coast League in 1993. The injury to his left shoulder knocked him out for most of 1994, but he looked as good as new in 1995, leading Midwest League shortstops in putouts and tying for first in double plays. This year, Prieto will probably see how things go in Double-A.

STEVE RAIN

Position: Pitcher
Team: Chicago Cubs
Born: June 2, 1975 Los Angeles, CA
Height: 6'6" **Weight:** 245 lbs.
Bats: right **Throws:** right
Acquired: 11th-round pick in 6/93 free-agent draft

PLAYER SUMMARY	
Fantasy Value	$0
Card Value	10¢ to 20¢
Will	push for majors
Can't	rule out set-up work
Expect	size on mound
Don't Expect	return to starting

It's not that Rain was a flop as a starting pitcher. He didn't do all that badly in his first two years of pro ball, when 16 of his 24 appearances came in a starting role. It's just that the decision to make him a closer may have been a truly inspired one. Rain has excelled in that assignment for the last two years, and he may soon be getting a chance to work in Chicago's bullpen. Rain got a chance to close while with Rockford of the Midwest League in 1995, and he wound up being named to the Midwest League's midseason All-Star Team. Last year, he began at Double-A Orlando and pitched himself into a promotion to Chicago's Triple-A team in Iowa. By the time the season was over, Rain ranked among the save leaders in the Chicago system, and no other minor-leaguer in the chain had done it at a higher level. With his great size, he looks formidable walking out to the mound. He should get a shot at the big-league team in '97.

Professional Batting Register

	BA	G	AB	R	H	2B	3B	HR	RBI	SB
93 R	.246	43	114	14	28	3	0	0	6	4
94 R	.300	18	60	15	18	5	0	2	17	1
95 A	.251	124	431	61	108	9	3	2	44	11
96 A	.284	119	447	65	127	19	6	1	40	26

Professional Pitching Register

	W	L	ERA	G	S	IP	H	ER	BB	SO
93 R	1	3	3.89	10	0	37.0	37	16	17	29
94 R	3	3	2.65	14	0	68.0	55	20	19	55
95 A	5	2	1.21	53	23	59.1	38	8	23	66
96 AA	1	0	2.56	35	10	38.2	32	11	12	48
96 AAA	2	1	3.12	10	0	26.0	17	9	8	23

ARAMIS RAMIREZ

Position: Third base
Team: Pittsburgh Pirates
Born: June 25, 1978 Santo Domingo,
Dominican Republic
Height: 6'1" **Weight:** 176 lbs.
Bats: right **Throws:** right
Acquired: Signed as a nondrafted free agent,
11/94

PLAYER SUMMARY	
Fantasy Value $0
Card Value . . . . 20¢ to 25¢
Will . . . . hit long ones
Can't . . . . play short or second
Expect . . . . strong offense
Don't Expect . . . . speed on bases

Ramirez shows the potential to be a third
baseman with real power. He hit nine home
runs in only 223 at bats for Erie of the New
York-Penn League last year, and some of
them were really tagged. He finished seventh in the league batting race, only 14
points off the lead, and made the All-Star
Team. He opened the season with a three-
RBI game and got hot during the middle of
August, driving in 14 runs in a span of 12
games. By the end of the year, Ramirez led
Erie in hits, doubles, and RBI as well as in
homers. His performance is all the more interesting because he played most of the
season having just turned 18 years old. A
year earlier, Ramirez had shown power potential with his play in the Dominican Summer League, and the fact that he backed it
up with a successful transition to North
American ball marks him as special. With
only two stolen bases in his two pro seasons, Ramirez will make it as a slugger or
not at all.

BRITT REAMES

Position: Pitcher
Team: St. Louis Cardinals
Born: Aug. 19, 1973 Seneca, SC
Height: 5'11" **Weight:** 175 lbs.
Bats: right **Throws:** right
Acquired: 18th-round pick in 6/95 free-agent
draft

PLAYER SUMMARY	
Fantasy Value $0
Card Value . . . . 12¢ to 20¢
Will . . . . be a winner
Can't . . . . get to St. Louis yet
Expect . . . . decent bat
Don't Expect . . . . return to catching

Reames is one of three Peoria starters who
had big seasons last year (Cliff Politte and
Jose Jimenez are the others). But Reames
had the best stats of the three. In fact, he
had better stats than most pitchers in
Class-A, in or out of the St. Louis organization. His ERA led the Cards' chain by a
wide margin, and he battled Blake Stein of
St. Petersburg for the strikeout and victory
titles. In a *Baseball America* poll, Reames
was termed the best pitching prospect and
owner of the best breaking pitch and control in the Midwest League. During one
span in late July and early August, Reames
won four straight outings, permitting only
one run. A catcher in high school, Reames
made the conversion to the mound while at
The Citadel. He owns a basic repertoire in
which a breaking ball and changeup complement his fastball. Due to his background
as an everyday player, he may be able to
help himself at the plate in the National
League.

Professional Batting Register

	BA	G	AB	R	H	2B	3B	HR	RBI	SB
95 R	.294	64	214	41	63	13	0	11	54	2
96 A	.200	6	20	3	4	1	0	1	2	0
96 A	.305	61	223	37	68	14	4	9	42	0

Professional Pitching Register

	W	L	ERA	G	CG	IP	H	ER	BB	SO
95 A	2	1	1.52	5	0	29.2	19	5	12	42
95 A	3	5	3.46	10	1	54.2	41	21	15	63
96 A	15	7	1.90	25	2	161.0	97	34	41	167

MARK REDMAN

Position: Pitcher
Team: Minnesota Twins
Born: Jan. 5, 1974 San Diego, CA
Height: 6'5" **Weight:** 220 lbs.
Bats: left **Throws:** left
Acquired: First-round pick in 6/95 free-agent draft

PLAYER SUMMARY	
Fantasy Value	$0
Card Value	10¢ to 15¢
Will	win big games
Can't	fall behind hitters
Expect	lots of pitches
Don't Expect	lack of effort

Redman is a prospect to watch this year. He is big, has extensive college experience, and moved quickly through the farm system last year. Like many other young lefties, he doesn't have pinpoint control. Originally taken by Detroit in the 41st round of the 1992 draft, Redman passed up the Tigers in favor of Masters College in Santa Clarinda, which he attended for one year before transferring to Oklahoma. He pitched the Sooners to the College World Series title in 1994 with a 5-0 mark in postseason play. During the regular season, Redman set school records for strikeouts and innings. He once pitched a no-hitter in the Alaska Baseball League. Redman came to Minnesota as the 12th overall selection in 1995. He made his pro debut in the Florida State League, earning a victory in relief. He seemed to fare better in relief than as a starter, but as of now, the plan is to groom him to join the Twins rotation, perhaps as early as this year.

Professional Pitching Register

	W	L	ERA	G	CG	IP	H	ER	BB	SO
95 A	2	1	2.76	8	0	32.2	28	10	13	26
96 A	3	4	1.85	13	1	82.2	63	17	34	75
96 AA	7	7	3.81	16	3	106.1	101	45	50	96
96 AAA	0	0	9.00	1	0	4.0	7	4	2	4

CHRIS REED

Position: Pitcher
Team: Cincinnati Reds
Born: Aug. 25, 1973 Orange, CA
Height: 6'2" **Weight:** 220 lbs.
Bats: right **Throws:** right
Acquired: Seventh-round pick in 6/91 free-agent draft

PLAYER SUMMARY	
Fantasy Value	$0
Card Value	10¢ to 15¢
Will	eat innings
Can't	drop ERA under 4.00
Expect	busy bullpen
Don't Expect	spectacular stuff

After five years in the lower minors, Reed finally broke through last season, winning 13 games in the Double-A Southern League. He didn't compile the prettiest pitching line you've ever seen; in fact, for the fifth time in six seasons his ERA was over 4.00. However, Reed has established a track record of taking the ball. He has made 20 or more starts in four consecutive seasons. His innings total has increased four times in a row. So even if he's not spectacular, Reed could help a staff as an innings eater who could be a third or fourth starter, or perhaps a middle reliever. He has never shown exceptional control, and that's the one factor that kept him in the low minors for so long. You can get an indication of his stuff by considering his eight-inning, 14-strikeout performance against Carolina last August 15. Now that Reed has shown he can compete in Double-A, he may get a look in camp, with a possible trip to the bigs in '97.

Professional Pitching Register

	W	L	ERA	G	CG	IP	H	ER	BB	SO
91 R	3	6	4.86	13	0	63.0	68	34	30	51
92 R	6	3	5.06	10	0	48.0	46	27	32	39
93 A	7	9	4.09	21	0	112.1	99	51	58	84
94 A	11	7	4.82	26	1	145.2	156	78	72	99
95 A	10	7	3.32	24	3	149.0	116	55	68	104
96 AA	13	10	4.09	28	2	176.0	157	80	91	135

CHRIS RICHARD

Position: First base
Team: St. Louis Cardinals
Born: June 7, 1974 San Diego, CA
Height: 6'2" **Weight:** 190 lbs.
Bats: left **Throws:** left
Acquired: 19th-round pick in 6/95 free-agent draft

PLAYER SUMMARY	
Fantasy Value	$0
Card Value	15¢ to 20¢
Will	hit some homers
Can't	worry about Young
Expect	good fielding
Don't Expect	impact before 1999

Because Busch Stadium's artificial surface dictated a speed game, the Cardinals developed very few power hitters for several years. Now that the grass is back, power becomes part of the plan, and that's where Richard may come in. Out of Oklahoma State, he made a very modest beginning in his first year as a pro. But last year he hit for power in the pitcher-friendly Florida State League, something that will always catch your eye. Last August, Richard was one of the league's top all-around players, hitting for average and playing a very impressive first base. He finished as one of the top RBI men in the farm system and wound up just below the leaders in home runs. He appeared in the FSL All-Star Game, going 1-for-4. Right now, Richard has prospect Dmitri Young ahead of him at first base, but Richard also has two years in which to produce and let other factors sort themselves out. This year should find him in the Texas League.

Professional Batting Register

	BA	G	AB	R	H	2B	3B	HR	RBI	SB
95 A	.282	75	284	36	80	14	3	3	43	6
96 A	.283	129	460	65	130	28	6	14	82	7

BRIAN RICHARDSON

Position: Third base
Team: Los Angeles Dodgers
Born: Aug. 31, 1975 Los Angeles, CA
Height: 6'2" **Weight:** 198 lbs.
Bats: right **Throws:** right
Acquired: Seventh-round pick in 6/91 free-agent draft

PLAYER SUMMARY	
Fantasy Value	$0
Card Value	15¢ to 25¢
Will	compete for job
Can't	steal bases
Expect	youthful mistakes
Don't Expect	consistent contact

Only 21 years old, Richardson may nevertheless be a candidate for third base in Los Angeles soon. He showed his aptitude by climbing all the way to Triple-A last season. He has shown some significant flaws on the way up, including a poor stolen-base percentage and a tendency to strike out, but the rate at which the Dodgers have moved him speaks eloquently about what they think of him. Richardson, drafted out of local St. Bernard High School, spent two undistinguished years in the minors. He finally began putting something together in 1994, when he drove in 44 runs for Yakima of the Northwest League. He built on that success in 1995, when he led California League third basemen in putouts and assists. Richardson was named the league's Player of the Week for June 11-17. He opened last year in the Texas League and was hitting well when he got the call to Triple-A. He may need more seasoning in the Pacific Coast League in '97. Then again, maybe not.

Professional Batting Register

	BA	G	AB	R	H	2B	3B	HR	RBI	SB
92 R	.213	37	122	8	26	6	2	0	15	3
93 R	.225	54	178	16	40	11	0	0	13	1
94 A	.231	19	52	3	12	0	1	0	3	3
94 A	.233	70	266	35	62	15	0	5	44	12
95 A	.284	127	462	68	131	18	1	12	58	17
96 AA	.323	19	62	10	20	1	1	0	7	0
96 AAA	.245	105	355	52	87	17	2	9	43	4

LUIS RIVAS

Position: Shortstop
Team: Minnesota Twins
Born: Aug. 30, 1979 La Guaira, Venezuela
Height: 5'10" **Weight:** 155 lbs.
Bats: right **Throws:** right
Acquired: Signed as a nondrafted free agent, 10/95

PLAYER SUMMARY	
Fantasy Value	$0
Card Value	12¢ to 20¢
Will	run when he can
Can't	project his physique
Expect	good shortstop
Don't Expect	rapid advancement

Rivas's batting statistics in the Gulf Coast League last year were not awe-inspiring. However, when the fact he played virtually the entire season at the age of 16 is taken into account, suddenly these stats are impressive. His stolen-base total in particular is promising. Rivas came to the Twins out of Ricenciado Arauda High School. He looked like anything but a schoolboy in his first look at professional ball, leading Fort Myers in doubles as well as steals and finishing second on the club in runs and hits. Despite playing only a short-season schedule, Rivas tied for most steals in Minnesota's minor-league system. He swiped three in a single game on July 24. Rivas can expect to do at least a little bit of growing over the next two or three years, so it's not out of the question he could have some punch one day. If it's anything like his speed, the Twins will have something special in their system.

Professional Batting Register

	BA	G	AB	R	H	2B	3B	HR	RBI	SB
96 R	.259	53	201	29	52	12	1	1	13	35

LONELL ROBERTS

Position: Outfield
Team: Texas Rangers
Born: June 7, 1971 Bloomington, CA
Height: 6' **Weight:** 177 lbs.
Bats: both **Throws:** right
Acquired: Traded by Blue Jays for a player to be named later, 11/96

PLAYER SUMMARY	
Fantasy Value	$0
Card Value	15¢ to 25¢
Will	burn on bases
Can't	ignore injury
Expect	leadoff man
Don't Expect	anything but speed

Roberts kicked around the Toronto farm system for nine years before the Rangers dealt for him over the off-season. Under usual circumstances, such a length of time in the minors would mean death to aspirations of playing in the majors. But Roberts remains a prospect because of his great speed, which makes him a threat on the bases and a factor in center field. Roberts led the Toronto farm system in steals in four of the last five years, and he might have made it five straight last year except for a hamstring problem that limited his participation. That injury now looms as crucial because Roberts has little to commend him except his speed and an ability to switch-hit. He hits with virtually no power, and last year marked the first time he has shown a healthy batting average. If his hamstring balks, he can forget about the majors. If it remains healthy, he could find a home at the top of a major-league lineup.

Professional Batting Register

	BA	G	AB	R	H	2B	3B	HR	RBI	SB
89 R	.141	29	78	2	11	1	0	0	6	3
90 R	.212	38	118	14	25	2	0	0	8	8
91 A	.222	110	388	39	86	7	2	2	27	35
92 A	.205	62	244	37	50	3	1	0	11	33
92 AA	.000	5	14	1	0	0	0	0	0	1
93 A	.240	131	501	78	120	21	4	3	46	54
94 A	.269	118	490	74	132	18	3	3	31	61
95 AA	.236	116	454	66	107	12	3	1	29	57
96 AA	.291	58	237	35	69	1	0	1	12	24

LARRY RODRIGUEZ

Position: Pitcher
Team: Arizona Diamondbacks
Born: Sept. 9, 1974 Guanajay, Cuba
Height: 6'2" **Weight:** 195 lbs.
Bats: right **Throws:** right
Acquired: Seventh-round pick in 6/95 free-
agent draft

PLAYER SUMMARY	
Fantasy Value	$0
Card Value	15¢ to 20¢
Will	gain attention
Can't	handle majors yet
Expect	90-mph fastball
Don't Expect	raw prospect

When resources meet opportunity, exciting things can happen. And that's how the 'Backs acquired one of the more interesting names on the international market. Rodriguez, along with Vladimir Nunez, left a Cuban squad while it was in Venezuela late in 1995. Not long after that, Arizona, an aggressive franchise that is shaping up as a big-market player, laid out money for both Cuban defectors. Like Nunez, Rodriguez began last season with Visalia, a co-op club in the California League. He was not quite ready for that level, and when Arizona's affiliate in the Pioneer League opened its season, Rodriguez went there and prospered. He throws a fastball with plenty of movement that reaches into the 90s. He's also got a curveball the Diamondbacks describe as being above average. They give him high marks for the way he handles himself on the mound. The next step would seem to be a full-season club, with arrival in the big leagues possible in 1999.

SCOTT ROLEN

Position: Third base
Team: Philadelphia Phillies
Born: April 4, 1975 Evansville, IN
Height: 6'4" **Weight:** 195 lbs.
Bats: right **Throws:** right
Acquired: Second-round pick in 6/93 free-
agent draft

PLAYER SUMMARY	
Fantasy Value	$6 to $8
Card Value	25¢ to 35¢
Will	play third for Phils
Can't	steal bases
Expect	power
Don't Expect	162 games

Rolen's season came to an abrupt end last year when a pitch fractured his right forearm. It marked the second straight year that an injury cut into his season, a sobering occurrence that could cloud an otherwise promising picture. Rolen is a top-notch prospect, maybe the best one the Phillies have had at third base since Mike Schmidt arrived. He brings the promise of power and should be more than adequate in the field as well. A fine all-around athlete, Rolen received basketball scholarship offers from many schools, including Oklahoma State and Georgia. Instead, he embarked on a baseball career. After hitting over .300 in his debut season, Rolen made the South Atlantic League's postseason All-Star squad. He led the league's third basemen in double plays. In 1995, playing in only 86 games, he hit 13 homers and drove in 54 runs while splitting the season between Single- and Double-A. It's more than likely Rolen will be Philadelphia's third baseman this year.

Professional Batting Register

	BA	G	AB	R	H	2B	3B	HR	RBI	SB
93 R	.313	25	80	8	25	5	0	0	12	3
94 A	.294	138	513	83	151	34	5	14	72	6
95 A	.290	66	238	45	69	13	2	10	39	4
95 AA	.289	20	76	16	22	3	0	3	15	1
96 AA	.361	61	230	44	83	22	2	9	42	8
96 AAA	.274	45	168	23	46	17	0	2	19	4
96 NL	.254	37	130	10	33	7	0	4	18	0

Professional Pitching Register

	W	L	ERA	G	CG	IP	H	ER	BB	SO
96 R	7	1	3.83	10	1	54.0	56	23	9	46
96 A	2	5	5.24	13	0	56.2	72	33	19	37

DAMIAN ROLLS

Position: Third base
Team: Los Angeles Dodgers
Born: Sept. 15, 1977 Manhattan, KS
Height: 6'3" **Weight:** 205 lbs.
Bats: right **Throws:** right
Acquired: First-round pick in 6/96 free-agent draft

PLAYER SUMMARY

Fantasy Value	$0
Card Value	25¢ to 35¢
Will	need time to adjust
Can't	worry about history
Expect	power potential
Don't Expect	big impact yet

The most astonishing thing about the Dodgers' domination of the Rookie of the Year Award is that they have done it largely without first-round picks. It has been more than a decade since they've selected an impact player in the first round, though Darren Dreifort (1993) has reached the majors and Paul Konerko (1994) is knocking on the door. Into this history comes Rolls, a third baseman out of Schlagel High School in Kansas City, Kansas. *Baseball America* rated him as the 46th-best prospect entering the 1996 draft, but his stock seemed to rise, at least in the Dodgers' eyes. They took him with the 23rd overall pick. He was the ninth position player drafted, and only the fourth high school infielder. Upon signing, he reported to Yakima of the Pioneer League, where he made only a modest impact. At least he got his first pro season in the books. This year he'll likely go to low Class-A, where we'll learn more about the Dodgers' latest first-rounder.

Professional Batting Register

	BA	G	AB	R	H	2B	3B	HR	RBI	SB
96 A	.265	66	257	31	68	11	1	4	27	8

MELVIN ROSARIO

Position: Catcher
Team: Baltimore Orioles
Born: May 25, 1973 Santo Domingo, Dominican Republic
Height: 6' **Weight:** 190 lbs.
Bats: both **Throws:** right
Acquired: Traded by Padres for Keith Eaddy, 4/96

PLAYER SUMMARY

Fantasy Value	$0
Card Value	12¢ to 15¢
Will	keep pushing
Can't	slump or else
Expect	more Double-A
Don't Expect	overwhelming talent

Anything Rosario accomplishes from this point on is a bonus. That doesn't necessarily mean he won't get to the majors. It's just that he already has surpassed some expectations just by getting to Double-A. The White Sox didn't think enough of him to protect him in the 1995 Rule 5 draft. San Diego picked him up and then traded him to the Orioles. Suddenly, Rosario began to play the best ball of a pro career that began in 1992. Assigned to High Desert of the California League, Rosario hit for power and average. He was the starting catcher for the Cal League's All-Star Game against the Carolina League, going 2-for-3 with a run scored. When promoted to Double-A Bowie, Rosario ranked among the home run and RBI leaders in the Baltimore organization. Unfortunately for him, he hit a huge slump when he got to the Eastern League. Does that mean he's reached his peak, or can he make the adjustment? That's something for the Orioles to watch.

Professional Batting Register

	BA	G	AB	R	H	2B	3B	HR	RBI	SB
92 A	.228	66	237	38	54	13	1	10	40	5
93 AA	.210	32	105	15	22	6	2	5	15	5
93 A	.229	41	140	17	32	5	0	4	19	2
95 A	.273	118	450	58	123	30	6	15	57	1
96 A	.273	10	33	7	9	3	0	3	10	1
96 A	.319	42	163	35	52	93	9	1	10	45
96 AA	.210	47	162	14	34	10	0	2	17	3
96 AAA	.000	3	2	0	0	0	0	0	0	0

BRIAN ROSE

Position: Pitcher
Team: Boston Red Sox
Born: Feb. 13, 1976 New Bedford, MA
Height: 6'3" **Weight:** 212 lbs.
Bats: right **Throws:** right
Acquired: Third-round pick in 6/94 free-agent draft

PLAYER SUMMARY	
Fantasy Value	$0
Card Value	15¢ to 20¢
Will	be a starter
Can't	avoid spotlight now
Expect	name recognition
Don't Expect	hockey career

Massachusetts fans have known about Rose for a number of years, and if he keeps pitching the way he has, they'll get to know him even better. Operating for Dartmouth High School, Rose went 26-2 in three seasons on the varsity squad. He twice earned recognition on *The Boston Globe* All-Scholastic team. He was named the New England Player of the Year. He also played four years of high school hockey. All this athletic ability has been very much in evidence during Rose's two years of pro ball. After participating in the Florida Instructional League in 1994, Rose made his debut in the Midwest League in 1995, finishing second on the Michigan club in wins and strikeouts. Last year, Rose was one of two standout pitchers for Boston's Double-A club. He finished second to Carl Pavano for the club lead in wins and strikeouts. This year Rose should be back in his home region, either in Pawtucket or Boston.

Professional Pitching Register

	W	L	ERA	G	CG	IP	H	ER	BB	SO
95 A	8	5	3.44	21	2	136.0	127	52	31	105
96 AA	12	7	4.01	27	4	163.2	157	73	45	115

SCOTT RUFFCORN

Position: Pitcher
Team: Chicago White Sox
Born: Dec. 29, 1969 New Braunfels, TX
Height: 6'4" **Weight:** 210 lbs.
Bats: right **Throws:** right
Acquired: First-round pick in 6/91 free-agent draft

PLAYER SUMMARY	
Fantasy Value	$0
Card Value	8¢ to 12¢
Will	get another chance
Can't	solve major leagues
Expect	good stuff
Don't Expect	major-league impact

Time is rapidly running out on Ruffcorn's prospect status. He is already 26 years old and does not have a win in the majors. In four separate seasons in which Ruffcorn has peeked his head into the majors, he has never emerged with an ERA lower than 7.88. Still, with his outstanding record at Triple-A last year, he may merit one final look. Ruffcorn comes out of Baylor, where he was the team's MVP as a sophomore. Picked 25th overall in 1991, Ruffcorn fanned 60 batters in only 55 innings in his first pro season. In 1992, the White Sox showed what they thought of his potential by naming him to start in the Hall of Fame exhibition game in Cooperstown. After six years of pro ball, Ruffcorn owns a 54-23 minor-league mark but is 0-5 in the majors. That may reflect the need to bulk up his confidence.

Professional Pitching Register

	W	L	ERA	G	CG	IP	H	ER	BB	SO
91 R	0	0	3.18	4	0	11.1	8	4	5	15
91 A	1	3	3.92	9	0	43.2	35	19	25	45
92 A	14	5	2.19	25	2	160.1	122	39	39	140
93 AA	9	4	2.73	20	3	135.0	108	41	52	141
93 AAA	2	2	2.80	7	1	45.0	30	14	8	44
93 AL	0	2	8.10	3	0	10.0	9	9	10	2
94 AAA	15	3	2.72	24	3	165.2	139	50	40	144
94 AL	0	2	12.79	2	0	6.1	15	9	5	3
95 R	0	0	0.90	3	0	10.0	7	1	5	7
95 AA	0	2	5.63	3	0	16.0	17	10	10	13
95 AAA	0	0	108.00	2	0	0.1	3	4	3	0
95 AL	0	0	7.88	4	0	8.0	10	7	13	5
96 AAA	13	4	3.87	24	2	149.0	142	64	61	129
96 AL	0	1	11.37	3	0	6.1	10	8	6	3

GLENDON RUSCH

Position: Pitcher
Team: Kansas City Royals
Born: Nov. 7, 1974 Seattle, WA
Height: 6'2" **Weight:** 170 lbs.
Bats: left **Throws:** left
Acquired: 17th-round pick in 6/93 free-agent draft

PLAYER SUMMARY	
Fantasy Value	$0
Card Value	15¢ to 20¢
Will	be a starter
Can't	beat him with walks
Expect	good fielder
Don't Expect	a thrower

Rusch figures to be a strong candidate for a spot in the Kansas City rotation this year. He's only 22, but he's got four years of pro experience behind him, and he held his own in the Triple-A American Association last year. He's just what managers love—a lefty who can throw the ball over the plate. He allowed more hits than innings last year and finished only two games over .500 at Omaha, but a lefty with control will always have a job. Rusch has been a starter for most of his pro career, the one exception coming with Rockford of the Midwest League in 1994, when he made 11 relief appearances and picked up a save. He returned to starting exclusively in 1995 in the Carolina League and was named to the Topps/National Association Class-A All-Star Team. He led the minors in batting average against at .188. Last year, the Royals liked him enough to skip him all the way to Triple-A. Now his song should be: "I'm going to Kansas City."

DONNIE SADLER

Position: Shortstop
Team: Boston Red Sox
Born: June 17, 1975 Golshon, TX
Height: 5'6" **Weight:** 165 lbs.
Bats: right **Throws:** right
Acquired: 11th-round pick in 6/94 free-agent draft

PLAYER SUMMARY	
Fantasy Value	$0
Card Value	15¢ to 20¢
Will	need a position
Can't	beat out Garciaparra
Expect	speed
Don't Expect	many walks

Sadler tried some center field while playing for Boston's affiliate in the Double-A Eastern League last year. The move did not work out well, which may be unfortunate for Sadler because he is a shortstop by trade, and that position may belong to Nomar Garciaparra for a long time. That would seem to leave few options for a player who otherwise has lots to offer the Red Sox. He stole 34 bases for Trenton last year, bringing a dimension of speed that the Red Sox have often lacked. He does not seem to have made the best of his small strike zone, as he struck out roughly twice as many times as he walked last year. Sadler attended Valley Mills High School in Texas, where he was a running back and point guard. He broke into pro ball with 32 steals in only 53 games in the Gulf Coast League. Promoted in 1995, Sadler made the Midwest League All-Star Team. His next stop should be one of Boston's more interesting decisions.

Professional Pitching Register

	W	L	ERA	G	CG	IP	H	ER	BB	SO
93 R	4	2	1.60	11	0	62.0	43	11	11	48
93 A	0	1	3.38	2	0	8.0	10	3	7	8
94 A	8	5	4.66	28	1	114.0	111	59	34	122
95 A	14	6	1.74	26	1	165.2	110	32	34	147
96 AAA	11	9	3.98	28	1	169.2	177	75	40	117

Professional Batting Register

	BA	G	AB	R	H	2B	3B	HR	RBI	SB
94 R	.272	53	206	52	56	8	6	1	16	32
95 A	.283	118	438	103	124	25	8	9	55	41
96 AA	.267	115	454	68	121	20	8	6	46	34

427

JULIO SANTANA

Position: Pitcher
Team: Texas Rangers
Born: Jan. 20, 1973 San Pedro de Macoris, Dominican Republic
Height: 6′ **Weight:** 175 lbs.
Bats: right **Throws:** right
Acquired: Signed as a nondrafted free agent, 2/90

PLAYER SUMMARY	
Fantasy Value	$0
Card Value	12¢ to 20¢
Will	fill in somewhere
Can't	lead a staff
Expect	few hits per inning
Don't Expect	return to short

This is the year we can start judging how well the Rangers did when they switched Santana from a light-hitting position player to a pitcher in 1992. His minor-league stats have been just fine, but the experiment can only be considered a success if Santana begins to contribute in the majors. Last year, Santana did his work for the Rangers' Triple-A affiliate in the American Association, proving to be Oklahoma City's second-biggest winner. Despite a fine ratio of hits to innings, Santana finished with an ERA above 4.00. This year should find him a candidate for a spot on the Texas staff, either as a starter or in middle relief. Santana spent two full years of professional ball at shortstop, not surprising since he comes from that legendary home of shortstops in the Dominican Republic. He began the transition to pitcher after showing little with the bat in the Dominican Summer League. In his first full year of pitching, he made the Gulf Coast League All-Star Team.

BOBBY SEAY

Position: Pitcher
Team: Tampa Bay Devil Rays
Born: June 20, 1978 Sarasota, FL
Height: 6′2″ **Weight:** 185 lbs.
Bats: left **Throws:** left
Acquired: Signed as a free agent, 11/96

PLAYER SUMMARY	
Fantasy Value	$0
Card Value	15¢ to 20¢
Will	have place in history
Can't	escape scrutiny
Expect	talent
Don't Expect	consistent control

Without ever throwing a pitch in pro ball, Seay may have taken his place in history among those who have changed the shape of the relationship between player and management. Seay, a high school left-hander out of Sarasota, Florida, was taken 12th overall by the White Sox in last year's draft. He was the eighth pitcher taken, and only the fourth from high school. But he challenged his ties with the White Sox, contending the club had not tendered him a contract in time. The White Sox wound up relinquishing their rights to him, and Seay became a free agent. Because the dispute caught the attention of other high draft picks, it's safe to say that in the future, clubs will be more vigilant in following the letter of the law when it comes to dealing with recently drafted players. As for Seay, he is a talented lefty who has a promising future in Tampa Bay. The question is, will he have as big an impact on the mound as he did at the negotiating table?

Professional Pitching Register

	W	L	ERA	G	CG	IP	H	ER	BB	SO
93 R	4	1	1.38	26	0	39.0	31	6	7	50
94 A	6	7	2.46	16	0	91.1	65	25	44	103
94 AA	7	2	2.90	11	2	71.1	50	23	41	45
95 AAA	0	2	39.00	2	0	3.0	9	13	7	6
95 A	0	3	3.73	5	1	31.1	32	13	16	27
95 AA	6	4	3.15	15	3	103.0	91	36	52	71
96 AAA	11	12	4.02	29	4	185.2	171	83	66	113

Dan Serafini

Position: Pitcher
Team: Minnesota Twins
Born: Jan. 25, 1974 San Francisco, CA
Height: 6'1" **Weight:** 180 lbs.
Bats: both **Throws:** left
Acquired: First-round pick in 6/92 free-agent draft

Player Summary

Fantasy Value	$0
Card Value	15¢ to 20¢
Will	get a shot
Can't	flirt with walks
Expect	major-league starter
Don't Expect	No. 1 starter

This one-time high school water polo player struggled to stay afloat in Triple-A ball last year, putting up stats that would alarm anyone watching his progress. But remember that Serafini was only 22 years old last year while he pitched in the batter-friendly Pacific Coast League. In fact, the Salt Lake City staff was filled with inflated ERAs, so Serafini's stats may not be as bad as they look. Besides, the ERAs at the major-league level weren't all that spectacular for Minnesota last year, so there's no reason to think Serafini won't get a long look in spring training. Serafini comes out of Serra High School in Bruno, California, where he played football and basketball as well as baseball and water polo. His best year thus far as a pro came in 1995, when he tied for third in the Eastern League in wins with 12. But even then he walked 72 batters in only 162⅔ innings, and he will have to sharpen that control if his ERA is ever to fall.

Richie Sexson

Position: First base
Team: Cleveland Indians
Born: Dec. 29, 1974 Portland, OR
Height: 6'6" **Weight:** 206 lbs.
Bats: right **Throws:** right
Acquired: 24th-round pick in 6/93 free-agent draft

Player Summary

Fantasy Value	$0
Card Value	15¢ to 20¢
Will	sparkle in field
Can't	limit his whiffs
Expect	high slugging pct.
Don't Expect	under 75 runs

For the third straight year, Richmond Lockwood Sexson advanced in the Cleveland farm system and responded to the higher level of competition. His numbers in Double-A last year fell off a bit from the previous season's in the Carolina League, but they still marked Sexson as a factor in Cleveland's future. Playing for Canton-Akron of the Eastern League, Sexson led his team in doubles and runs. It was the third straight time he scored 80 or more runs. On the negative side, Sexson soared past the 100-strikeout mark for the second consecutive year. He started putting up numbers in 1994, when he led South Atlantic League first basemen in assists and led all Cleveland minor-leaguers in runs. In 1995, Sexson made the Carolina League All-Star Team and was named the circuit's MVP. He also led the league's first basemen in chances, putouts, assists, and double plays. If he keeps it up, he could be in Cleveland very soon.

Professional Pitching Register

	W	L	ERA	G	CG	IP	H	ER	BB	SO
92 R	1	0	3.64	8	0	29.2	27	12	15	33
93 A	10	8	3.65	27	1	140.2	117	57	83	147
94 A	9	9	4.61	23	2	136.2	149	70	57	130
95 AA	12	9	3.38	27	1	162.2	155	61	72	123
95 AAA	0	0	6.75	1	0	4.0	4	3	1	4
96 AAA	7	7	5.58	25	1	130.2	164	81	58	109
96 AL	0	1	10.38	1	0	4.1	7	5	2	1

Professional Batting Register

	BA	G	AB	R	H	2B	3B	HR	RBI	SB
93 R	.186	40	97	11	18	3	0	1	5	1
94 A	.273	130	488	88	133	25	2	14	77	7
95 A	.306	131	494	80	151	34	0	22	85	4
96 AA	.276	133	518	85	143	33	3	16	76	2

MARK SIEVERT

Position: Pitcher
Team: Toronto Blue Jays
Born: Feb. 16, 1973 Janesville, WI
Height: 6'4" **Weight:** 195 lbs.
Bats: left **Throws:** right
Acquired: Signed as a free agent, 8/91

PLAYER SUMMARY	
Fantasy Value	$0
Card Value	12¢ to 20¢
Will	vie for rotation spot
Can't	have worse year
Expect	strikes
Don't Expect	another no-hitter

Sievert signed with the Blue Jays in late 1991 but did not throw a pitch in their system until early 1993. That's because he underwent surgery to his right elbow before the 1992 season, knocking him out for the duration. He has made up for it ever since, being one of the top starters in the Toronto organization. He has climbed steadily through one level after another and last year pitched in both Double-A and Triple-A. His experience at Triple-A was not something to write home about, because he won only two of ten appearances and had an ERA that nearly reached the 6.00 mark. But that can't offset all the good he's done. In 1995, he was named to the South Atlantic League All-Star Team and finished fifth among league starters with just 9.75 runners per nine innings. In 1994, while pitching in the New York-Penn League, he hurled a no-hitter in the second game of a doubleheader, allowing only one runner to reach first base.

Professional Pitching Register

	W	L	ERA	G	CG	IP	H	ER	BB	SO
93 R	6	3	5.00	15	0	63.0	63	35	30	52
94 A	7	4	3.09	14	1	81.2	59	28	28	82
95 A	12	6	2.91	27	3	160.2	126	52	46	140
96 AA	9	2	2.58	17	0	101.1	79	29	51	75
96 AAA	2	5	5.93	10	1	54.2	62	36	33	46

JOSE SILVA

Position: Pitcher
Team: Pittsburgh Pirates
Born: Dec. 19, 1973 Tijuana, Mexico
Height: 6'5" **Weight:** 210 lbs.
Bats: right **Throws:** right
Acquired: Traded by Blue Jays with Jose Pett, Brandon Cromer, and three players to be named later for Orlando Merced, Carlos Garcia, and Dan Plesac, 11/96

PLAYER SUMMARY	
Fantasy Value	$0
Card Value	12¢ to 20¢
Will	start or relieve
Can't	redo '94 and '95
Expect	stories of his accident
Don't Expect	Sally League form

The days of 1993, when Silva won 12 games and appeared to be one of Toronto's fastest-rising stars, seem very far away. Since then, Silva has endured two trips to the disabled list, an auto accident, and two seasons in which his combined record was 4-10. It was the auto accident, which produced a broken jaw, nose, and two eye orbits, that raised the gravest questions. Yet there was Silva late last year, making his major-league debut. Even though he allowed two runs in his first outing, his very presence was a triumph. Before the accident, Silva was a starter. Last year, with Knoxville of the Southern League, he appeared mostly in relief. It's quite possible that when Silva has regained his form he will return to the rotation. The Pirates, who acquired Silva over the winter, can only hope he will be the pitcher he was in 1993, when he limited South Atlantic League hitters to a .202 average and finished fifth in the league with a 2.52 ERA.

Professional Pitching Register

	W	L	ERA	G	CG	IP	H	ER	BB	SO
92 R	6	4	2.28	12	0	59.1	42	15	18	78
93 A	12	5	2.52	24	0	142.2	103	40	62	161
94 A	0	2	3.77	8	0	43.0	41	18	24	41
94 AA	4	8	4.14	16	1	91.1	89	42	31	71
95 AA	0	0	9.00	3	0	2.0	3	2	6	2
96 AA	2	3	4.91	22	0	44.0	45	24	22	26
96 AL	0	0	13.50	2	0	2.0	5	3	0	0

BRIAN SIMMONS

Position: Outfield
Team: Chicago White Sox
Born: Sept. 4, 1973 Lebanon, PA
Height: 6'2" **Weight:** 185 lbs.
Bats: both **Throws:** right
Acquired: Second-round pick in 6/95 free-agent draft

PLAYER SUMMARY	
Fantasy Value	$0
Card Value	10¢ to 15¢
Will	show tools
Can't	afford another slump
Expect	taste of Double-A
Don't Expect	easy adjustment

At 23, Simmons is a little old for someone who has never stepped out of Class-A ball, but he looks like a player to watch, nonetheless. The White Sox themselves have shown what they think of him, first by taking him in the second round in 1995, then by inviting him to spring training in 1996. Simmons enjoyed a fine season with Chicago's Midwest League affiliate in South Bend last year, hitting nearly .300 and showing speed and power. He slumped upon a late-season promotion to Prince William of the Carolina League, and indeed has hit under .200 in three of his four pro stops. That fact, combined with the age factor, means that 1997 looms as an especially crucial season for him. Originally taken by Baltimore in the 35th round in 1992, Simmons instead attended the University of Michigan and earned Academic All-Big Ten honors. He led Michigan with 13 homers and 45 RBI as a junior in 1995.

RANDALL SIMON

Position: First base; outfield
Team: Atlanta Braves
Born: May 26, 1975 Willemstad, Netherlands
Height: 6' **Weight:** 180 lbs.
Bats: left **Throws:** left
Acquired: Signed as a nondrafted free agent, 7/92

PLAYER SUMMARY	
Fantasy Value	$0
Card Value	15¢ to 25¢
Will	bring discipline to plate
Can't	unseat McGriff
Expect	extra-base power
Don't Expect	outfielder in Atlanta

A late-season trade that sent first baseman Ron Wright to Pittsburgh has created an opportunity for Simon. Now the question is whether he can take advantage of it and, based on what he has done in his four years of pro ball, whether he has the skill. Simon played in the Double-A Southern League last year and fell just short of raising his power numbers for the third straight season. He tied his career high in homers and was only two RBI short of his previous best. He also set career highs in doubles and runs. Best of all, he's not a wild swinger who will strike out 100 times year. His ability to adjust to a new level each year and his discipline at the plate make him an especially intriguing power hitter. On the downside, Simon doesn't figure to break into the very deep Atlanta outfield, and first baseman Fred McGriff is signed through 1999. So all Simon can do is take the next step, which figures to be Triple-A.

Professional Batting Register

	BA	G	AB	R	H	2B	3B	HR	RBI	SB
95 R	.176	5	17	5	3	1	0	1	5	0
95 A	.190	41	163	13	31	6	1	2	11	4
96 A	.298	92	356	73	106	29	6	17	58	14
96 A	.198	33	131	17	26	4	3	4	14	2

Professional Batting Register

	BA	G	AB	R	H	2B	3B	HR	RBI	SB
93 R	.254	61	232	28	59	17	1	3	31	1
94 A	.293	106	358	45	105	23	1	10	54	7
95 A	.264	122	420	56	111	18	1	18	79	6
96 AA	.279	134	498	74	139	26	2	18	77	4

CHRIS SINGLETON

Position: Outfield
Team: San Francisco Giants
Born: Aug. 15, 1972 Martinez, CA
Height: 6'2" **Weight:** 195 lbs.
Bats: left **Throws:** left
Acquired: Second-round pick in 6/93 free-agent draft

PLAYER SUMMARY	
Fantasy Value	$0
Card Value	20¢ to 30¢
Will	play center
Can't	rule out power
Expect	extra bases
Don't Expect	high on-base pct.

Singleton now seems to be only one Triple-A season away from reaching the majors. Depending on how he does early in the season, he could receive a call-up sometime this year. He confirmed his readiness with a more-than-competent showing at Double-A Shreveport last year, when he hit for average, drove in runs, and stole bases. He also reached a career high in home runs, a hint that this part of his game is still developing. A gifted athlete, Singleton was originally drafted by Houston in the 30th round in 1990 but instead chose to attend the University of Nevada at Reno. There he played wide receiver for the football team, an indication of the kind of speed he owns. Drafted again in 1993, he showed his speed game in the Northwest League. In 1994, Singleton received an invitation to attend major-league spring training. He spent the season with San Jose of the California League, playing center field. He repeated the Cal League in 1995, topping the 30-steal mark.

J.D. SMART

Position: Pitcher
Team: Montreal Expos
Born: Nov. 12, 1973 San Saba, TX
Height: 6'2" **Weight:** 180 lbs.
Bats: right **Throws:** right
Acquired: Fourth-round pick in 6/95 free-agent draft

PLAYER SUMMARY	
Fantasy Value	$0
Card Value	15¢ to 20¢
Will	top 90 mph
Can't	match stuff of others
Expect	a craftsman
Don't Expect	a dominating record

Smart was the first pitcher taken by Montreal in the 1995 draft, and the choice shapes up as a promising one. He has now spent two years in pro ball, showing an ability to get hitters out without needing to overpower them. Smart, out of the University of Texas, began last season with Delmarva of the South Atlantic League and was one of five pitchers to make at least 23 starts for the club. He also owned the best ratio of walks to innings among Delmarva's starting pitchers. He claimed ten strikeout victims in a 3-0 win over Piedmont on August 13, then ten days later hurled a shutout against Greensboro. It's curious that someone of Smart's age with his level of college experience remained in a low Class-A league all year long. It probably has something to do with his limited number of outings in 1995. But he still bears watching, if only because of the quality of his control. The next step for Smart is the Florida State League, a circuit that tends to favor pitchers.

Professional Batting Register

	BA	G	AB	R	H	2B	3B	HR	RBI	SB
93 A	.265	58	219	39	58	14	4	3	18	14
94 A	.249	113	425	51	106	17	5	2	49	19
95 A	.277	94	405	55	112	13	5	2	31	33
96 AA	.298	129	500	68	149	31	9	5	72	27
96 AAA	.125	9	32	3	4	0	0	0	0	0

Professional Pitching Register

	W	L	ERA	G	CG	IP	H	ER	BB	SO
95 R	2	0	1.69	2	0	10.2	10	2	1	6
95 A	0	1	2.28	5	0	27.2	29	7	7	21
96 A	9	8	3.39	25	3	156.2	155	59	31	109

ROBERT SMITH

Position: Infield
Team: Atlanta Braves
Born: May 10, 1974 Oakland, CA
Height: 6'3" **Weight:** 190 lbs.
Bats: right **Throws:** right
Acquired: 11th-round pick in 6/92 free-agent draft

PLAYER SUMMARY	
Fantasy Value	$0
Card Value	15¢ to 25¢
Will	have a chance
Can't	limit strikeouts
Expect	some pop
Don't Expect	big buildup

Smith has played a lot of third base, and could probably contend for the job in Atlanta this year. However, don't be surprised if he shows up at shortstop. It could be a logical move, especially with phenom Wes Helms just about ready to arrive to play third. While not a prospect on the level of Helms, Smith—just 22 years old—held his own in Triple-A last year. Playing for Richmond of the International League, Smith led his team in stolen bases, was second in RBI, tied for second in doubles, and finished third in home runs. Unfortunately for him, he has also struck out at least 100 times in three straight seasons, and major-league pitchers will carve him to pieces unless he shows more discipline at the plate. Smith graduated from Fremont High School in Oakland, earning Athlete of the Year honors his senior year. He has moved steadily through the Atlanta farm system. In 1995, he was named MVP for Greenville of the Southern League.

Professional Batting Register

	BA	G	AB	R	H	2B	3B	HR	RBI	SB
92 R	.235	57	217	31	51	9	1	3	28	5
93 A	.245	108	384	53	94	16	7	4	38	12
94 A	.266	127	478	49	127	27	2	12	71	18
95 AA	.261	127	444	75	116	27	3	14	58	12
96 AAA	.256	124	445	49	114	27	0	8	58	15

SHANNON STEWART

Position: Outfield
Team: Toronto Blue Jays
Born: Feb. 25, 1974 Cincinnati, OH
Height: 6'1" **Weight:** 190 lbs.
Bats: right **Throws:** right
Acquired: First-round pick in 6/92 free-agent draft

PLAYER SUMMARY	
Fantasy Value	$2 to $4
Card Value	10¢ to 15¢
Will	bring speed
Can't	predict power peak
Expect	majors this year
Don't Expect	bad shoulder

Stewart should be ready to step in and win a regular job in Toronto this year, culminating a five-year climb after being taken with the 19th overall pick in 1992. Although he already has experienced brief trips to the majors, Stewart might have arrived even sooner had it not been for a dislocated shoulder suffered on June 13, 1994, ending his season in the Class-A South Atlantic League. Stewart is a very intriguing prospect whose chief gift might be his speed. But last year in the International League, he posted career highs in doubles, triples, and home runs, suggesting that he has not yet peaked in the power department. He cracked the 30-steal mark for the third time in five pro seasons, but there have been times when his percentage was not as strong as it could have been. Stewart was the team MVP in 1995 while playing for Knoxville of the Southern League. He received his first call to the majors that season, playing 12 games.

Professional Batting Register

	BA	G	AB	R	H	2B	3B	HR	RBI	SB
92 R	.233	50	172	44	40	1	0	1	11	32
93 A	.279	75	301	53	84	15	2	3	29	25
94 A	.324	56	225	39	73	10	5	4	25	15
95 AA	.287	138	498	89	143	24	6	5	55	42
95 AL	.211	12	38	2	8	0	0	0	1	2
96 AAA	.298	112	420	77	125	26	8	6	42	35
96 AL	.176	7	17	2	3	1	0	0	2	1

ROBERT STRATTON

Position: Outfield
Team: New York Mets
Born: Oct. 7, 1977 Santa Barbara, CA
Height: 6'3" **Weight:** 220 lbs.
Bats: right **Throws:** right
Acquired: First-round pick in 6/96 free-agent draft

PLAYER SUMMARY	
Fantasy Value	$0
Card Value	20¢ to 30¢
Will	run well
Can't	hit for average
Expect	raw talent
Don't Expect	selective hitter

The Mets went for power potential with the 13th overall pick in the 1996 draft, selecting this big, strong specimen out of San Marcos High School in Santa Barbara, California. Stratton was the first high school outfielder taken in the entire draft, and only the fifth position player overall. Not since 1991, when they took Al Shirley, had the Mets taken a high school outfielder with their first pick in a draft. Shirley had trouble making contact and is no longer with the organization. As for Stratton, he reported to the Mets' team in the rookie Gulf Coast League last year and got a rough initiation into pro ball. He struck out approximately once every three trips to the plate but did flash signs of his potential. In an early August game, he went 4-for-4 with a double, a home run, and four RBI. Stratton will probably be on a slow timetable, because the Mets don't want this young slugger to lose his confidence. Expect to see him in a short-season league or low Class-A this year.

Professional Batting Register

	BA	G	AB	R	H	2B	3B	HR	RBI	SB
96 R	.254	17	59	5	15	2	0	2	9	3

MARCUS STURDIVANT

Position: Outfield
Team: Seattle Mariners
Born: Oct. 29, 1973 Albemarie, NC
Height: 5'10" **Weight:** 150 lbs.
Bats: left **Throws:** left
Acquired: 28th-round pick in 6/92 free-agent draft

PLAYER SUMMARY	
Fantasy Value	$0
Card Value	15¢ to 20¢
Will	play speed game
Can't	hit ball out of park
Expect	ball to be in play
Don't Expect	Seattle outfield

Sturdivant brings some intriguing qualifications, and he has steadily improved through a five-year apprenticeship in the minors, but none of that will matter very much as long as Ken Griffey, Jr., and Jay Buhner form the core of the Seattle outfield. Sturdivant, who plays a game built on speed, won't be dislodging either of those two power hitters, leaving him very few options in the Seattle system. Unless something changes drastically, his best bet would be to continue stealing bases and hope another club notices. Last year, Sturdivant raised his stolen base total for the fourth straight year, even though he had to handle his first jump to Double-A ball. He has never been the type to strike out much, but he doesn't tend to walk a whole lot, either. As a left-handed batter, he gets that extra step closer to first base, giving him a chance to beat out infield hits. He eventually may find a spot as a leadoff hitter or a pesky No. 9 hitter somewhere.

Professional Batting Register

	BA	G	AB	R	H	2B	3B	HR	RBI	SB
92 R	.312	42	141	27	44	6	1	0	14	7
93 A	.256	64	238	34	61	8	3	4	32	8
94 A	.252	113	413	50	104	12	7	2	36	20
95 A	.274	99	347	60	95	13	5	1	34	31
96 A	.284	68	292	54	83	19	6	0	31	23
96 AA	.284	63	243	34	69	11	4	2	23	13

JEFF SUPPAN

Position: Pitcher
Team: Boston Red Sox
Born: Jan. 2, 1975 Oklahoma City, OK
Height: 6'2" **Weight:** 210 lbs.
Bats: right **Throws:** right
Acquired: Second-round pick in 6/93 free-agent draft

PLAYER SUMMARY	
Fantasy Value	$0
Card Value	10¢ to 15¢
Will	stay in majors
Can't	pitch with injury
Expect	grit in big games
Don't Expect	omens to stick

For the second straight year, Suppan received a rude greeting upon his arrival in the majors. In 1995, he gave up a home run to the first batter he faced. And last year, shortly after rejoining the Red Sox, he went on the disabled list. But unless these are omens, 1997 should be the year Suppan starts the season with the Red Sox and does what he has done throughout a four-year career in the minors—pitch well. Out of Crespi High School in Encino, California, Suppan arrived via the 49th overall pick in 1993 and began his career in the rookie Gulf Coast League. A year later, he tied for the lead in victories in the Florida State League, going 10-1 from May 11 to early August. He won 13 of his last 15 decisions and pitched eight scoreless innings in Game 1 of the Western Division playoffs. In 1995, Suppan began in Double-A and enjoyed a brief cup of coffee in the majors, becoming the youngest Red Sox pitcher to make his debut since Mike Garman in 1969.

Professional Pitching Register

	W	L	ERA	G	CG	IP	H	ER	BB	SO
93 R	4	3	2.18	10	2	57.2	52	14	16	64
94 A	13	7	3.26	27	4	174.0	153	63	50	173
95 AA	6	2	2.36	15	1	99.0	86	26	26	88
95 AAA	2	3	5.32	7	0	45.2	50	27	9	32
95 AL	1	2	5.96	8	0	22.2	29	15	5	19
96 AAA	10	6	3.22	22	7	145.1	130	52	25	142
96 AL	1	1	7.54	8	0	22.2	29	19	13	13

MIKE SWEENEY

Position: Catcher
Team: Kansas City Royals
Born: July 22, 1973 Orange, CA
Height: 6'1" **Weight:** 195 lbs.
Bats: right **Throws:** right
Acquired: Tenth-round pick in 6/91 free-agent draft

PLAYER SUMMARY	
Fantasy Value	$5 to $7
Card Value	20¢ to 30¢
Will	hit with punch
Can't	pass Macfarlane yet
Expect	big role this year
Don't Expect	a quitter

Sweeney figures to do a lot of catching for Kansas City this season. Then again, he spent 50 games with the Royals last year, capping a strong season in which he started at Double-A and made it all the way to the show. Sweeney's arrival in the majors is a tribute to hard work, as he showed little offensive promise in his first two professional seasons. But he began to pick up the pace a bit in 1993 while playing for Eugene, and his efforts landed him on the Northwest League All-Star squad. Sweeney improved his average four consecutive years, beginning in 1992, and was rewarded with his first trip to the majors in 1995. Now he looks like he might be one of the major league's better hitting catchers, with the ability to hit 15 to 20 homers and drive in 75 runs while maintaining a solid average. Whether he can push Mike Macfarlane out of the way this year is a question, but Sweeney looms as the heir apparent when Macfarlane's contract is up.

Professional Batting Register

	BA	G	AB	R	H	2B	3B	HR	RBI	SB
91 R	.216	38	102	8	22	3	0	1	11	1
92 A	.221	59	199	17	44	12	1	4	28	3
93 A	.240	53	175	32	42	10	2	6	29	1
94 A	.301	86	276	47	83	20	3	10	52	0
95 A	.310	99	332	61	103	23	1	18	53	6
95 AL	.250	4	4	1	1	0	0	0	0	0
96 AA	.319	66	235	45	75	18	1	14	51	3
96 AAA	.257	25	101	14	26	9	0	3	16	0
96 AL	.279	50	165	23	46	10	0	4	24	1

435

MIGUEL TEJADA

Position: Shortstop
Team: Oakland Athletics
Born: May 25, 1976 Bani, Dominican Republic
Height: 5'10" **Weight:** 150 lbs.
Bats: right **Throws:** right
Acquired: Signed as a nondrafted free agent, 7/93

PLAYER SUMMARY

Fantasy Value	$0
Card Value	10¢ to 15¢
Will	find ways to win
Can't	blend in with crowd
Expect	surprising power
Don't Expect	a dull performance

What do you call a young shortstop who hits 20 homers a year and can steal more than 25 bases? You can start by calling Miguel Odalis Tejada a prospect. You can call him a Northwest League All-Star for the 1995 season. Or you can listen to *Baseball America* when it said, in its 1996 tools ratings, that he was the most exciting player in the California League. Suffice to say that Tejada, signed by Juan Marichal, better get used to hearing people sing his praises. In just three years of pro ball, he has managed to generate attention and, at the age of 20, should be reporting to Double-A ball this season. He is coming off a year in which he ranked among the top Oakland farmhands in steals and homers despite missing time with a thumb injury. Tejada played in the All-Star Game against the Carolina League, and *USA TODAY Baseball Weekly* labeled him an emerging prospect in its midseason look at farm systems.

JAY TESSMER

Position: Pitcher
Team: New York Yankees
Born: Dec. 26, 1971 Meadville, PA
Height: 6'3" **Weight:** 190 lbs.
Bats: right **Throws:** right
Acquired: 19th-round pick in 6/95 free-agent draft

PLAYER SUMMARY

Fantasy Value	$0
Card Value	12¢ to 15¢
Will	get a look
Can't	be Wetteland
Expect	sidearm delivery
Don't Expect	another MVP year

It's tempting to predict a great future for Tessmer based on what he accomplished last year. Not only did he lead the Florida State League in saves, but he was named the circuit's MVP and was also tabbed as the Rolaids Relief Man of the Year. But history shows that pitchers with large save totals in the minors often stall before they reach the show. Each case is a different one, however, and Tessmer's performance in two pro seasons will guarantee him at least a promotion to Double-A this year. Unfortunately for him, he's already 25 years old, which doesn't leave him much room for error. A 19th-round draft choice, Tessmer uses a sidearm-submarine delivery that gets him a lot of ground balls and strikeouts. Dan Quisenberry used something like it with great effectiveness during a career in the Kansas City bullpen. Tessmer attended the University of Miami and majored in chemistry. Will he become an addition to a big-league club?

Professional Batting Register

	BA	G	AB	R	H	2B	3B	HR	RBI	SB
94 R	.000	74	218	51	64	9	1	18	62	13
95 A	.245	74	269	45	66	15	5	8	44	19
96 A	.279	114	458	97	128	12	5	20	72	27

Professional Pitching Register

	W	L	ERA	G	S	IP	H	ER	BB	SO
95 A	2	0	0.95	34	20	38.0	27	4	12	52
96 A	*12	4	1.48	68	25	97.1	68	16	19	104

ANDY THOMPSON

Position: Third base
Team: Toronto Blue Jays
Born: Oct. 8, 1975 Oconomowoc, WI
Height: 6'3" **Weight:** 210 lbs.
Bats: right **Throws:** right
Acquired: 25th-round pick in 6/94 free-agent draft

PLAYER SUMMARY	
Fantasy Value	$0
Card Value	20¢ to 25¢
Will	offer some pop
Can't	make plays in field
Expect	trip to Double-A
Don't Expect	a Gold Glove

Thompson entered last season as a marginal prospect, but he enjoyed a respectable season in the Class-A Florida State League. In fact, third baseman Thompson and shortstop Kevin Witt played the left side of Dunedin's infield, raising the intriguing possibility of those two someday advancing to the majors together. Thompson gave some hints of his talent in 1995 with Hagerstown of the South Atlantic League, producing some runs despite his modest batting average. In '96, he led Dunedin in games played and narrowly missed the team lead in several other categories. He stole 16 bases in 20 tries and posted a .445 slugging average. With an 18-game hitting streak from late July through mid-August, Thompson landed among the top hitters in the Toronto system. On the downside, Thompson showed himself to be error-prone, and no amount of batting skill will get him to the majors if he fails to correct that.

Professional Batting Register

	BA	G	AB	R	H	2B	3B	HR	RBI	SB
95 A	.239	124	461	48	110	19	2	6	57	2
96 A	.282	129	425	64	120	26	5	11	50	16

JOHN THOMPSON

Position: Pitcher
Team: Colorado Rockies
Born: Oct. 1, 1973 Vicksburg, MS
Height: 6'3" **Weight:** 175 lbs.
Bats: right **Throws:** right
Acquired: Seventh-round pick in 6/93 free-agent draft

PLAYER SUMMARY	
Fantasy Value	$0
Card Value	15¢ to 20¢
Will	need more seasoning
Can't	judge him yet
Expect	big-game pitcher
Don't Expect	home-away quirk

Thompson attended Blinn Junior College in Brenham, Texas, the same school at which big-league manager Don Baylor once studied. If all goes well this year, the two will soon be sharing the same clubhouse in the major leagues. For that to happen, however, Thompson must iron out whatever went wrong at Triple-A Colorado Springs last season. After a superb stint in Double-A New Haven, Thompson received a call to Triple-A. He started well, winning two of his first three appearances with a good ratio of walks and hits per innings. After that, things began to fall apart. Still, he wound up among the top winners in Colorado's minor-league system. In 1995, Thompson might have been a big winner had he been able to pitch only in home games. He went 6-2 at Yale Field, but only 1-6 on the road. He pitched well in the league championship series against Reading, hurling 6⅓ scoreless innings. Thompson will be in the mix for a job with the Rockies this season.

Major League Pitching Register

	W	L	ERA	G	CG	IP	H	ER	BB	SO
93 R	3	5	4.62	11	0	50.2	43	26	31	36
94 A	6	6	2.85	19	1	88.1	70	28	33	79
94 A	3	1	3.28	9	0	49.1	43	18	18	41
95 AA	7	8	4.18	26	0	131.1	132	61	56	82
96 AA	9	4	2.86	16	1	97.2	82	31	27	86
96 AAA	4	7	5.04	11	0	69.2	76	39	26	62

BRETT TOMKO

Position: Pitcher
Team: Cincinnati Reds
Born: April 7, 1973 Cincinnati, OH
Height: 6'4" **Weight:** 205 lbs.
Bats: right **Throws:** right
Acquired: Second-round pick in 6/95 free-agent draft

PLAYER SUMMARY	
Fantasy Value	$0
Card Value	15¢ to 20¢
Will	make his starts
Can't	complete games
Expect	good control
Don't Expect	shoulder problems

The Reds had no first-round pick in 1995, so their second-round selection was a crucial one. Tomko has made the pick look like an act of genius by pitching as well as, or better than, most first-rounders. He also gets credit for his progress, having made a rapid and successful jump from low Class-A to Double-A. Working for Cincinnati's team in Chattanooga of the Southern League last season, he tied for the team lead in starts. He finished second in the Reds minor-league system in strikeouts, with only teammate Curt Lyons ahead of him. Tomko comes out of Florida Southern, where he went 15-2 with a 1.35 ERA and was named Division II National Player of the Year in his only season. Upon turning pro, Tomko reported to Charleston of the Sally League only to have his season cut short by a shoulder strain. The injury came shortly after he was named the league's Player of the Week. He'll probably get a look in Triple-A in '97.

BUBBA TRAMMELL

Position: Infield
Team: Detroit Tigers
Born: Nov. 6, 1971 Knoxville, TN
Height: 6'3" **Weight:** 205 lbs.
Bats: right **Throws:** right
Acquired: 11th-round pick in 6/94 free-agent draft

PLAYER SUMMARY	
Fantasy Value	$0
Card Value	15¢ to 20¢
Will	be crowd-pleaser
Can't	waste much time
Expect	doubles
Don't Expect	a speedster

Just as one Trammell era ends in Detroit, another one may soon be starting. Bubba Trammell is one of those rare and enjoyable baseball figures who exudes personality and can back it up with talent. He was one of the top hitters in the Double-A Southern League last year, leading Jacksonville in home runs and RBI while hitting .328. Upon his promotion to Triple-A, Trammell kept up the hitting. Of particular note was his season total of 37 doubles. In all, Trammell finished second in home runs in the Detroit minor-league system, and wound up tied for second with Fayetteville's Gabe Kapler in RBI. Trammell comes out of the University of Tennessee and has shown some punch in all three years as a pro. At Jamestown in the New York-Penn League in 1994, Trammell collected 18 doubles in only 235 at bats. On the downside, he is already 25 years old, so he doesn't have much room for error as he takes the last couple of steps to Detroit.

Professional Pitching Register

	W	L	ERA	G	CG	IP	H	ER	BB	SO
95 A	4	2	1.84	9	0	49.0	41	10	9	46
96 AA	11	7	3.88	27	0	157.2	131	68	54	164

Professional Batting Register

	BA	G	AB	R	H	2B	3B	HR	RBI	SB
94 A	.298	65	235	37	70	18	6	5	41	9
95 A	.284	122	454	61	129	32	3	16	72	13
96 AA	.328	83	311	63	102	23	2	27	75	3
96 AAA	.294	51	180	32	53	14	1	6	24	5

JOSE VALENTIN

Position: Catcher
Team: Minnesota Twins
Born: Sept. 19, 1975 Manati, Puerto Rico
Height: 5'10" **Weight:** 191 lbs.
Bats: both **Throws:** right
Acquired: Third-round pick in 6/93 free-agent draft

PLAYER SUMMARY	
Fantasy Value	$0
Card Value	10¢ to 15¢
Will	throw out runners
Can't	steal bases
Expect	impact big-leaguer
Don't Expect	thieves to succeed

Brother of the shortstop for the Milwaukee Brewers, Jose Valentin prefers to do his work behind the plate. Judging by the pace at which the Twins have moved him along, he's done it quite well. Valentin played at both the Class-A and Double-A levels last year, amassing 34 doubles on the season. He hits with decent power, and his ability to switch-hit should make him even more valuable to a major-league lineup. But it's his defensive ability that has intrigued the brass. For instance, in 1995 Valentin was a standout in the Midwest League, being named to the All-Star squad. He led all league catchers by throwing out 43 percent of runners attempting to steal. He also led the circuit in putouts, assists, and double plays. Valentin comes out of Fernando Callejo High School in Puerto Rico, where he won the RBI title in his last three years. Valentin can no doubt benefit from some more time in Double-A, but it's not impossible he'll see action in the bigs this summer.

JASON VARITEK

Position: Catcher
Team: Seattle Mariners
Born: April 11, 1972 Rochester, MN
Height: 6'2" **Weight:** 210 lbs.
Bats: both **Throws:** right
Acquired: First-round pick in 6/94 free-agent draft

PLAYER SUMMARY	
Fantasy Value	$0
Card Value	20¢ to 30¢
Will	be a standout
Can't	neglect contact
Expect	strong will
Don't Expect	productive outs

It wasn't an easy thing getting Varitek's signature on a major-league contract. The Minnesota Twins tried in 1993 when they made him a first-round pick, but Varitek balked. The Mariners took a shot in 1994, but they didn't get him into uniform until a year later. Now it's just a matter of time until they see if all the trouble was worth it. Last year, Varitek played his second straight season of Double-A ball. Performing for Port City of the Southern League, Varitek led his team in at bats, doubles, home runs, and walks. Varitek comes out of Georgia Tech, where he was a three-time All-American. He played for Team USA in 1992, taking part in the Olympic Games in Barcelona. Upon turning pro, Varitek had problems at the plate. He finished the season with 126 strikeouts, fifth most in the league. He'll have to work on that, obviously, but last year's power numbers suggest he's already made the adjustment.

Professional Batting Register

	BA	G	AB	R	H	2B	3B	HR	RBI	SB
93 R	.262	32	103	18	27	6	1	1	19	0
93 R	.208	9	24	3	5	1	0	0	3	0
94 R	.210	54	210	23	44	5	0	9	27	0
95 A	.321	112	383	59	123	26	5	19	65	0
96 A	.263	87	338	34	89	26	1	7	54	1
96 AA	.236	48	165	22	39	8	0	3	14	0

Professional Batting Register

	BA	G	AB	R	H	2B	3B	HR	RBI	SB
95 AA	.224	104	352	42	79	14	2	10	44	0
96 AA	.262	134	503	63	132	34	1	12	67	7

JAVIER VAZQUEZ

Position: Pitcher
Team: Montreal Expos
Born: June 25, 1976 Ponce, Puerto Rico
Height: 6'2" **Weight:** 175 lbs.
Bats: right **Throws:** right
Acquired: Seventh-round pick in 6/94 free-agent draft

PLAYER SUMMARY	
Fantasy Value	$0
Card Value	15¢ to 20¢
Will	dominate
Can't	win without runs
Expect	quality starts
Don't Expect	complete games

Vazquez was one of the most dominating pitchers in the South Atlantic League last year. He began the season as one of two 19-year-olds on the Delmarva pitching staff, then went out and blew away the league. Vazquez led the Montreal farm system in victories and strikeouts, and he finished with the ninth-best ERA in the Sally League. In one stretch spanning July and August, Vazquez went 4-0 with a 1.88 ERA over eight starts. He didn't allow a single run in his first three August starts, but picked up only one victory over that stretch, suggesting that with some run support his win-loss record could have been even more spectacular than it was. His only complete game of the season came on July 20, a four-hit victory over Hagerstown. He was the winning pitcher in the Sally League All-Star Game, going two innings and allowing only two hits. Vazquez will have to prove he can do it at a higher level, but he is on a fast track.

EDGARD VELAZQUEZ

Position: Outfield
Team: Colorado Rockies
Born: Dec. 15, 1975 Santurce, Puerto Rico
Height: 5'11" **Weight:** 175 lbs.
Bats: right **Throws:** right
Acquired: Tenth-round pick in 6/93 free-agent draft

PLAYER SUMMARY	
Fantasy Value	$0
Card Value	15¢ to 20¢
Will	pick up assists
Can't	eclipse uncle's star
Expect	strikeouts
Don't Expect	weak arm

If bloodlines mean anything in baseball—and they often do—then watch out for Velazquez. He is the nephew of Hall of Famer Roberto Clemente, who was killed in a plane crash three years before Edgard was born. At the age of 21, he just finished his fourth pro season, and his stats keep getting better and better. Playing in the Double-A Eastern League, a proving ground for hitters, Velazquez set career highs in doubles, homers, and walks. He led his team in extra-base hits and scored 14 more runs than any of his mates. Tempering the good news is the fact that Velazquez struck out 114 times, the third straight year he has passed the century mark in whiffs. Besides offering a promising bat, Velazquez, like his late uncle, owns a strong throwing arm. At Salem in 1995, he tied for the league lead with 16 outfield assists, one reason he made the Carolina League All-Star Team. He should have a ball playing Triple-A in Colorado Springs.

Professional Pitching Register

	W	L	ERA	G	CG	IP	H	ER	BB	SO
94 R	5	2	2.53	15	1	67.2	37	19	15	56
95 A	6	6	5.08	21	1	102.2	109	58	47	87
96 A	14	3	2.68	27	1	164.1	138	49	57	173

Professional Batting Register

	BA	G	AB	R	H	2B	3B	HR	RBI	SB
93 R	.245	39	147	20	36	4	2	2	20	7
94 A	.237	119	447	50	106	22	3	11	39	9
95 A	.300	131	497	74	149	25	6	13	69	7
96 AA	.290	132	486	72	141	29	4	19	62	6

BRET WAGNER

Position: Pitcher
Team: Oakland Athletics
Born: April 18, 1973 Harrisburg, PA
Height: 6′ **Weight:** 205 lbs.
Bats: left **Throws:** left
Acquired: Traded by Cardinals with Allen Battle, Carl Dale, and Jay Witasick for Todd Stottlemyre, 1/96

PLAYER SUMMARY	
Fantasy Value	$0
Card Value	10¢ to 15¢
Will	be third starter
Can't	finish games
Expect	majors this year
Don't Expect	.500 record

Wagner was originally picked by the Cardinals as the 19th selection in the 1994 free-agent draft. He rose quickly through the lower levels of their farm system until January 9, 1996, when he was packaged with Allen Battle, Carl Dale, and Jay Witasick in a deal that sent pitcher Todd Stottlemyre to the Cardinals. Last year Wagner got a full season of Double-A ball, leading Huntsville of the Southern League in starts. Of possible concern is the fact that in five minor-league stops, Wagner only once has posted a record of more than one game over .500. In fact, he owns a career record of 18-16. Wagner never has allowed as many hits as innings pitched in a season, which is a stat far more telling of his abilities. In fact, last year he was the only one of Huntsville's four main starters to sport a tidy hits-to-innings ratio. This year he'll probably work in the Pacific Coast League, a hitter's paradise where his abilities will get a stern test. If he succeeds, expect the A's to take a long look at him.

TODD WALKER

Position: Infield
Team: Minnesota Twins
Born: May 25, 1973 Bakersfield, CA
Height: 6′ **Weight:** 170 lbs.
Bats: left **Throws:** right
Acquired: First-round pick in 6/94 free-agent draft

PLAYER SUMMARY	
Fantasy Value	$0
Card Value	25¢ to 30¢
Will	hit for power
Can't	win Gold Glove
Expect	offensive force
Don't Expect	middle infielder

Walker is one of the top prospects in the game, someone who could win a job this season and keep it for a long time. Though listed as a second baseman-third baseman in the Minnesota press guide, Walker played mostly third when he got a late-season look with the Twins last year. He showed some weakness against left-handed pitching and tended to hit better in the Metrodome than on the road, but neither one of those tendencies is unusual. Originally drafted by Texas in the 51st round in 1991, Walker came to the Twins as the eighth overall selection in 1994. It was a winning pick from the start, as Walker hit over .300 with power in the Florida State League. In 1995, he played in the Eastern League and wound up as the second baseman on the Double-A All-Star Team. He also played in the Arizona Fall League, being named an All-Star. Walker could be a bona fide power hitter, especially playing his games in the Metrodome.

Professional Pitching Register

	W	L	ERA	G	CG	IP	H	ER	BB	SO
94 A	0	1	5.11	3	0	12.1	10	7	4	10
94 A	4	1	1.23	7	0	44.0	27	6	6	43
95 A	5	4	2.12	17	1	93.1	77	22	26	59
95 AA	1	2	3.19	6	0	36.2	34	13	18	31
96 AA	8	8	4.23	27	0	134.0	125	63	77	98

Professional Batting Register

	BA	G	AB	R	H	2B	3B	HR	RBI	SB
94 A	.304	46	171	29	52	5	2	10	34	6
95 AA	.290	137	513	83	149	27	3	21	85	23
96 AAA	.339	135	551	94	187	41	9	28	111	13
96 AL	.256	25	82	8	21	6	0	0	6	2

DEREK WALLACE

Position: Pitcher
Team: New York Mets
Born: Sept. 1, 1971 Van Nuys, CA
Height: 6'3" **Weight:** 185 lbs.
Bats: right **Throws:** right
Acquired: Traded by Royals with John Carter for Jason Jacome and Allen McDill, 7/95

PLAYER SUMMARY	
Fantasy Value	$1
Card Value	15¢ to 25¢
Will	get a chance
Can't	close
Expect	middle relief
Don't Expect	return to Cubs or Royals

Wallace has an excellent opportunity to find a job because the Mets figure to make many changes after a season in which their bullpen cost them a lot of games. The problem for Wallace is that he did not look all that good in a fairly long audition in New York. He didn't show any particular ability to handle either lefty or righty wingers, and the slugging and on-base percentages against him were both in the unsightly range. Perhaps it was just a case of Wallace needing some time to adjust to the majors after never having been there in his five-year pro career. Originally drafted by the Cubs, Wallace went to Kansas City as part of the deal that sent Brian McRae to Chicago. Then the Royals packaged Wallace to New York in a trade that brought Jason Jacome and a minor-leaguer to Kansas City. Wallace did not impress during his first season in the Mets organization, but last year he did a nice job with Tidewater of the Triple-A level.

Professional Pitching Register

	W	L	ERA	G	CG	IP	H	ER	BB	SO
92 A	0	1	4.91	2	0	3.2	3	2	1	2
93 A	5	6	4.20	14	0	79.1	85	37	23	34
93 AA	5	7	5.03	15	2	96.2	105	54	28	69
93 AAA	0	0	11.25	1	0	4.0	8	5	1	2
94 AA	2	9	5.74	33	1	89.1	95	57	31	49
94 AAA	0	1	4.15	5	0	4.1	4	2	4	3
95 AA	4	3	4.40	26	0	43.0	51	21	13	24
95 AA	0	1	5.28	15	0	15.1	11	9	9	8
96 AAA	5	2	1.72	49	0	57.2	37	11	17	52
96 NL	2	3	4.01	19	0	24.2	29	11	14	15

DARYLE WARD

Position: Infield
Team: Houston Astros
Born: June 27, 1975 Lynwood, CA
Height: 6'2" **Weight:** 240 lbs.
Bats: left **Throws:** left
Acquired: Traded by Tigers with Brad Ausmus, Trever Miller, C.J. Nitkowski, Jose Lima, and a player to be named later for Todd Jones, Doug Brocail, Orlando Miller, and Brian Hunter, 12/96

PLAYER SUMMARY	
Fantasy Value	$0
Card Value	15¢ to 20¢
Will	drive in runs
Can't	lead league in homers
Expect	good student
Don't Expect	huge leaps

This young man is the son of Gary Ward, who hit .276 with 130 homers over a 12-year career in the major leagues. No one knows yet whether his son can have that kind of career, but Daryle hasn't made a bad start. He burst into prominence with a huge 1995 season, when he made the South Atlantic League All-Star Team as a reward for a 106-RBI season. He led Fayetteville in doubles, runs, and RBI. Ward advanced to the Florida State League in 1996 where, even though he did not dominate to the same extent, he played well enough to get a brief look at Triple-A ball. Playing for Lakeland of the FSL, Ward raised his batting average, cut down on his strikeouts, and led the team in doubles and RBI. He does not look like a prodigy who can take huge leaps. Instead, he will go one level at a time, learning at each step. That's why he will probably go to Double-A ball this year. If he comes through the Southern League intact, he could get the call.

Professional Batting Register

	BA	G	AB	R	H	2B	3B	HR	RBI	SB
94 R	.267	48	161	17	43	6	0	5	30	4
95 A	.284	137	524	75	149	32	0	14	106	1
96 A	.291	128	464	65	135	29	4	10	68	1
96 AAA	.174	6	23	1	4	0	0	0	1	0

JARROD WASHBURN

Position: Pitcher
Team: Anaheim Angels
Born: Aug. 13, 1974 La Crosse, WI
Height: 6'1" **Weight:** 190 lbs.
Bats: left **Throws:** left
Acquired: Second-round pick in 6/95 free-agent draft

PLAYER SUMMARY	
Fantasy Value	$0
Card Value	15¢ to 20¢
Will	be in rotation
Can't	be rushed
Expect	strikeouts
Don't Expect	Angels this year

You couldn't blame Washburn if his head was spinning by the end of last season. Not only did he make a swift ascent through three levels of the Anaheim farm system, but he did so in only his second pro season. Even though his numbers don't look all that impressive, the rapid promotions tell you what the Angels think of this left-hander out of the University of Wisconsin-Oshkosh. Washburn began last year in the rotation at Lake Elsinore of the California League and quickly pitched himself into a promotion. By the end of the season, Washburn also appeared in Double- and Triple-A ball and ranked among the top Angel farmhands in strikeouts and victories. Washburn made an impression almost from the moment he came out of the draft, making 11 starts in the lower minors and emerging with a solid ratio of strikeouts to innings. He could probably use more time in the minors, and the Angels should guard against rushing him.

NEIL WEBER

Position: Pitcher
Team: Montreal Expos
Born: Dec. 6, 1972 Newport Beach, CA
Height: 6'5" **Weight:** 215 lbs.
Bats: right **Throws:** right
Acquired: Eighth-round pick in 6/93 free-agent draft

PLAYER SUMMARY	
Fantasy Value	$0
Card Value	15¢ to 20¢
Will	get attention
Can't	overwork shoulder
Expect	caution
Don't Expect	big winner this year

A season that began with much promise ended in doubt for Weber last year. Pitching for Harrisburg of the Eastern League, Weber made the Double-A All-Star Team. But shortly thereafter, he was shut down with problems in his shoulder. He was slated to go to winter ball, pending the health of his shoulder, of course. The Expos are holding their breath on this one because Weber would seem to have a future. A onetime member of the California Stars (a Connie Mack team managed by former major-leaguer Doug DeCinces), Weber owned 333 strikeouts in his first three pro seasons. In 1995, he made 28 starts for Harrisburg, and his league-high 90 walks certified that he threw a lot of pitches. Whether that led to last year's shoulder problems is anyone's guess, but the fact is that walking that many men in just 152⅔ innings isn't a good idea, period. This season looms as a big one for Weber, both in terms of his health and where he gets assigned.

Professional Pitching Register

	W	L	ERA	G	CG	IP	H	ER	BB	SO
95 A	3	2	3.33	8	0	46.0	35	17	14	54
95 A	0	1	3.44	3	0	18.1	17	7	7	20
96 A	6	3	3.30	14	3	92.2	79	34	33	93
96 AA	5	6	4.40	13	1	88.0	77	43	25	58
96 AAA	0	2	10.80	2	0	8.1	12	10	12	5

Professional Pitching Register

	W	L	ERA	G	CG	IP	H	ER	BB	SO
93 A	6	5	2.77	16	2	94.1	84	29	36	80
94 A	9	7	3.20	25	1	135.0	113	48	62	134
95 AA	6	11	5.01	28	0	152.2	157	85	90	119
96 AA	7	4	3.03	18	1	107.0	90	36	44	74

JAKE WESTBROOK

Position: Pitcher
Team: Colorado Rockies
Born: Sept. 29, 1977 Athens, GA
Height: 6'4" **Weight:** 210 lbs.
Bats: right **Throws:** right
Acquired: First-round pick in 6/96 free-agent draft

PLAYER SUMMARY	
Fantasy Value	$0
Card Value	15¢ to 20¢
Will	be a starter
Can't	fear Coors Field
Expect	basic repertoire
Don't Expect	huge leap this year

The formula seldom varies for the Rockies. They will draft pitching and try to develop it within their own organization, believing that free-agent pitchers won't want to work in Coors Field. Thus, for the fourth time in five drafting seasons, the Rockies used their top pick on a pitcher. Exercising the 21st overall pick in 1996, the Rockies took Westbrook out of Madison County High School in Danielsville, Georgia. He was the 13th pitcher taken, and only the sixth from high school. So far the Rockies have to be happy with the way things have turned out. Reporting to Mesa of the Arizona League, Westbrook tied for the team lead in starts and wins. He kept up the good work upon a promotion to Portland of the Northwest League, where he walked only five in 24⅔ innings. Just out of high school, Westbrook will probably go to a low Class-A circuit this year. The Sally League fits the bill and has the added advantage of keeping him fairly close to home.

MATT WHITE

Position: Pitcher
Team: Tampa Bay Devil Rays
Height: 6'5" **Weight:** 230 lbs.
Bats: right **Throws:** right
Acquired: Signed as a free agent, 11/96

PLAYER SUMMARY	
Fantasy Value	$0
Card Value	15¢ to 20¢
Will	light up radar gun
Can't	pitch without scrutiny
Expect	great tools
Don't Expect	easy terms

Before the draft, White loomed as a tough sign because he was being represented by hard-line agent Scott Boras. Those concerns appeared to have been justified. White, out of Waynesboro Area High School in Pennsylvania, waited until November to sign with the Devil Rays, jilting the San Francisco Giants. The picture was further muddled by some of the historic developments that made free agents of some first-round picks. Boras also represents Bobby Seay, a highly touted pitching prospect who gained free agency when the White Sox relinquished rights to him rather than fight a technical contract point. Legal issues aside, White may be one of the top pitching prospects in the country. *Baseball America* tabbed him as having the best fastball, best breaking ball, and the fastest timetable to the majors of any high school pitcher. The Giants took him with the seventh pick in last year's draft, and John Patterson was the only high school pitcher taken ahead of him.

Professional Pitching Register

	W	L	ERA	G	CG	IP	H	ER	BB	SO
96 R	4	2	2.87	11	0	62.2	66	20	14	57
96 A	1	1	2.55	4	0	24.2	22	7	5	19

GREG WHITEMAN

Position: Pitcher
Team: Detroit Tigers
Born: June 12, 1973 Cumberland, MD
Height: 6'2" **Weight:** 180 lbs.
Bats: left **Throws:** left
Acquired: Third-round pick in 6/94 free-agent draft

PLAYER SUMMARY	
Fantasy Value	$0
Card Value	15¢ to 20¢
Will	strike men out
Can't	fall behind in count
Expect	trip to Double-A
Don't Expect	seven-pitch innings

The Tigers hope this young man from Cumberland can help fill one of the gaps in their pitching staff before too long. Just three years into his pro career, Whiteman has made steady progress and has allowed fewer hits than innings in all four of his minor-league stops. He pitched for Lakeland of the Florida State League last year, tying for the team lead in starts and pacing the staff in victories. Of the six Lakeland pitchers who reached double digits in starts, only Willis Roberts owned a lower ERA than Whiteman did. Whiteman finished the season among the victory and strikeout leaders in the Detroit farm system. Out of James Madison University, Whiteman broke into pro ball with Jamestown of the short-season New York-Penn League in 1994. A year later, while working at Fayetteville of the South Atlantic League, Whiteman compiled a modest win-loss record but got attention by averaging more than one strikeout per inning.

CASEY WHITTEN

Position: Pitcher
Team: Cleveland Indians
Born: May 23, 1972 Evansville, IN
Height: 6' **Weight:** 175 lbs.
Bats: left **Throws:** left
Acquired: Second-round pick in 6/93 free-agent draft

PLAYER SUMMARY	
Fantasy Value	$0
Card Value	20¢ to 25¢
Will	get his chance
Can't	develop while hurt
Expect	toughness with men on
Don't Expect	25 starts

Cleveland hopes Whitten is ready to make a bid for a spot in the starting rotation after two seasons marred by injury. Last year he suffered vascular problems, and the year before that it was tendinitis in the left elbow. As a result, Whitten has not made more than 20 starts since 1994. Charles Kenneth Whitten comes out of Gibson Southern High School in Ft. Branch, Indiana, where he was named the state's Amateur Player of the Year in 1990. He attended Indiana State and became a third-team All-American. He broke into pro ball in 1993 and made the postseason All-Star Team in the New York-Penn League. A year later, Whitten finished third in the Class-A Carolina League in strikeouts and ranked fifth among league starters in batting average against. Promoted to Double-A in 1995, Whitten finished sixth in the Eastern League in ERA and held hitters to a .217 average with men on base. If he's healthy, he's a candidate for a major-league job.

Professional Pitching Register

	W	L	ERA	G	CG	IP	H	ER	BB	SO
94 A	6	5	4.04	15	1	75.2	72	34	35	67
95 A	1	2	6.05	4	0	19.1	18	13	15	20
95 A	6	8	4.23	23	1	125.2	108	59	58	145
96 A	11	10	3.71	27	1	150.1	134	62	89	122

Professional Pitching Register

	W	L	ERA	G	CG	IP	H	ER	BB	SO
93 A	6	3	2.42	14	0	81.2	75	22	18	81
94 A	9	10	4.28	27	0	153.1	127	73	64	148
95 AA	9	8	3.31	20	2	114.1	100	42	38	91
96 AA	3	1	1.67	8	0	37.2	23	7	13	44
96 AAA	3	4	8.04	12	0	43.2	54	39	24	35

PAUL WILDER

Position: Outfield
Team: Tampa Bay Devil Rays
Born: Jan. 9, 1978
Height: 6'5" **Weight:** 230 lbs.
Bats: left **Throws:** right
Acquired: First-round pick in 6/96 free-agent draft

PLAYER SUMMARY	
Fantasy Value	$0
Card Value	20¢ to 30¢
Will	strike out
Can't	play center
Expect	long homers
Don't Expect	rapid advancement

Olympic gymnastics coach Bela Karolyi says that the surest way to finish second is to copy someone else. If their first-ever draft pick is any indication, the Devil Rays share that philosophy. Exercising the 29th overall selection in last year's grab bag, they pulled a surprise. They went for Wilder, a player who did not even appear on *Baseball America*'s list of the nation's top 100 picks. Only time will tell if the Devil Rays have gained by daring to be different, but for now they have acquired someone with power. Out of Cary High School in North Carolina, Wilder brings some size to go along with some impressive stats, having hit ten homers in his scholastic season. Upon signing, Wilder went to the Devil Rays' team in the Gulf Coast League, where he struck out in more than one-third of his official at bats. But 15 of his 38 hits went for extra bases. He will be interesting to watch, particularly as a barometer of the Devil Rays' judgment and drafting style.

Professional Batting Register

	BA	G	AB	R	H	2B	3B	HR	RBI	SB
96 R	.207	53	184	31	38	10	2	3	20	7

ANTONE WILLIAMSON

Position: Infield
Team: Milwaukee Brewers
Born: July 18, 1973 Harbor City, CA
Height: 6'1" **Weight:** 195 lbs.
Bats: left **Throws:** right
Acquired: First-round pick in 6/94 free-agent draft

PLAYER SUMMARY	
Fantasy Value	$0
Card Value	25¢ to 30¢
Will	play first or DH
Can't	play third
Expect	a role player
Don't Expect	lots of bunts

Williamson is not the hot prospect he was a year ago. Injuries, plus the emergence of Jeff Cirillo at third and the presence of John Jaha at first, have conspired to leave Williamson with a challenge. But the memory of a .309 batting average and 90 RBI in Double-A ball two years ago should tell everyone that this young man may still have something to offer. This year should be an important one for Williamson, one in which he must show he can collect 400 at bats (something he has not yet done in three minor-league seasons). He must also show the ability to DH or play first, since his shoulder problems would seem to preclude a job at third base. Williamson attended Arizona State and led the Sun Devils to a trip to the College World Series. He was the fourth overall pick in the 1994 draft, the Brewers' highest selection since they tabbed B.J. Surhoff first in 1985. In 1994, Williamson hit his first professional grand slam and squeezed home a run in a two-week span.

Professional Batting Register

	BA	G	AB	R	H	2B	3B	HR	RBI	SB
94 R	.423	6	26	5	11	2	1	0	4	0
94 A	.224	23	85	6	19	4	0	3	13	0
94 AA	.250	14	48	8	12	3	0	1	9	0
95 AA	.309	104	392	62	121	30	6	7	90	3
96 AAA	.261	55	199	23	52	10	1	5	23	1

ENRIQUE WILSON

Position: Shortstop
Team: Cleveland Indians
Born: July 27, 1975 Santo Domingo, Dominican Republic
Height: 5'11" **Weight:** 160 lbs.
Bats: both **Throws:** right
Acquired: Traded by Twins for Shawn Bryant, 2/94

PLAYER SUMMARY

Fantasy Value	$0
Card Value	10¢ to 15¢
Will	contribute at plate
Can't	unseat Vizquel yet
Expect	a job somewhere
Don't Expect	strikeouts

Wilson came to Cleveland for left-handed pitcher Shawn Bryant and has quickly climbed through the farm system to the point where he should be ready for the majors either this year or next. Trouble is, where does he play? Wilson is a shortstop, putting him squarely behind Omar Vizquel, who is signed into the next century. Maybe a hint came last year when Wilson got a brief look at Triple-A and played some third base. Anyway, one suspects Cleveland will try to find somewhere for Wilson to contribute, because he brings several intriguing dimensions to the field. Named the best defensive shortstop in the Carolina League by *Baseball America* in 1995, Wilson also was the second-hardest player in the league to strike out. He has topped 20 stolen bases in two of the last three years, though his percentage is not always tops. He provides a bit of power and draws a few walks. With tremendous abilities on both sides of the ball, he should make it soon.

Professional Batting Register

	BA	G	AB	R	H	2B	3B	HR	RBI	SB
92 R	.341	13	44	12	15	1	0	0	8	3
93 R	.289	58	197	42	57	8	4	13	50	5
94 A	.279	133	512	82	143	28	12	10	72	21
95 A	.267	117	464	55	124	24	7	6	52	18
96 AA	.304	117	484	70	147	17	5	5	50	23
96 AAA	.500	3	8	1	4	1	0	0	0	0

KEVIN WITT

Position: Shortstop
Team: Toronto Blue Jays
Born: Jan. 5, 1976 High Point, NC
Height: 6'4" **Weight:** 185 lbs.
Bats: left **Throws:** right
Acquired: First-round pick in 6/94 free-agent draft

PLAYER SUMMARY

Fantasy Value	$0
Card Value	12¢ to 20¢
Will	play Double-A in '97
Can't	overtake Gonzalez
Expect	strikeouts
Don't Expect	light hitting

Witt rebounded with a solid year in his third pro season, putting him squarely in Toronto's plans for sometime before the turn of the 21st century. By hitting 13 round-trippers in the Florida State League (one of the toughest circuits to clout a long ball), he showed himself to have legitimate power for a shortstop. He isn't Alex Rodriguez, but it would not be impossible to see Witt collect 20 dingers a year in the majors. His display at the plate was all the more pleasing after the .232 season—with 148 strikeouts—he registered the previous year at a lower level of ball. Witt also shows keen ability with the leather. He came to the Toronto organization as the Blue Jays 28th overall pick in the 1994 free-agent draft. Witt's emergence seems to give Toronto a little depth at shortstop, especially with Alex Gonzalez having shown some ability at the plate. Whether Witt can eventually challenge for that spot is a pleasant question that the Blue Jays will mull as they watch his 1997 season.

Professional Batting Register

	BA	G	AB	R	H	2B	3B	HR	RBI	SB
94 R	.255	60	243	37	62	10	4	7	36	4
95 A	.232	119	479	58	111	35	1	14	50	1
96 A	.271	124	446	63	121	18	6	13	70	9

447

KERRY WOOD

Position: Pitcher
Team: Chicago Cubs
Born: June 6, 1977 Irving, TX
Height: 6'5" **Weight:** 195 lbs.
Bats: right **Throws:** right
Acquired: First-round pick in 6/95 free-agent draft

PLAYER SUMMARY	
Fantasy Value	$0
Card Value	12¢ to 15¢
Will	bury hitters
Can't	throw strikes
Expect	heat in high 90s
Don't Expect	150-pitch days

Wood owns the potential to be one of the top power pitchers in the game. Just look at what he accomplished last year for the Cubs' Class-A team in the Florida State League. Making 22 starts for Daytona, Wood fanned 136 batters in only 114⅓ innings while giving up only 72 hits. If he hadn't walked 70 hitters, his win-loss record and ERA would have been even more impressive. You couldn't really ask for more from a player in his first full year of pro ball. Wood graduated from Grand Prairie High School in Texas in 1995, after being named Texas 5-A Player of the Year. The end of his high school career involved controversy when he threw more than 150 pitches two days after being drafted. He made his pro debut later that year, appearing in three games. He seems none the worse for wear, and only injury or his high walk total can keep Wood from being an impact pitcher. Look for him in Double-A this year, and in the friendly confines of Wrigley Field in 1998.

Professional Pitching Register

	W	L	ERA	G	CG	IP	H	ER	BB	SO
95 R	0	0	0.00	1	0	3.0	0	0	1	2
95 A	0	0	10.38	2	0	4.1	5	5	5	5
96 A	10	2	2.91	22	0	114.1	72	37	70	136

JAMIE WRIGHT

Position: Pitcher
Team: Colorado Rockies
Born: Dec. 24, 1974 Oklahoma City, OK
Height: 6'5" **Weight:** 203 lbs.
Bats: right **Throws:** right
Acquired: First-round pick in 6/93 free-agent draft

PLAYER SUMMARY	
Fantasy Value	$1 to $3
Card Value	10¢ to 15¢
Will	be in rotation
Can't	get away with walks
Expect	large mound presence
Don't Expect	big win totals

Wright looks like one of the more successful draft picks by a franchise that knows it must build its pitching through the farm system. He joined the major-league rotation in the second half of last season and did well enough for someone just three years out of the draft. Of all the Rockies starters who were in the rotation at the end of the season, however, only Kevin Ritz had a higher rate of walks per nine innings than Wright did. That must change, or the long ball will really hurt. An exceptional athlete, Wright could have attended the University of Oklahoma on a basketball scholarship but passed it up when the Rockies made him the 28th overall pick in the 1993 free-agent draft. Wright progressed quickly even though he had trouble picking up wins in the Sally League in 1994. A year later, he spent most of the season in high Class-A, then got a late-season promotion to New Haven, where he won the first game of the playoffs. He's a candidate for Colorado's staff this year.

Professional Pitching Register

	W	L	ERA	G	CG	IP	H	ER	BB	SO
93 R	1	3	4.00	8	0	36.0	35	16	9	26
94 A	7	14	5.97	28	2	143.1	188	95	59	103
95 A	10	8	2.47	26	2	171.0	160	47	72	95
95 AA	0	1	9.00	1	0	3.0	6	3	3	0
96 AA	5	1	0.81	7	1	44.2	27	4	12	54
96 AAA	4	2	2.72	9	0	59.2	53	18	22	40
96 NL	4	4	4.93	16	0	91.1	105	50	41	45

JARET WRIGHT

Position: Pitcher
Team: Cleveland Indians
Born: Dec. 29, 1975 Anaheim, CA
Height: 6'2" **Weight:** 220 lbs.
Bats: right **Throws:** right
Acquired: First-round pick in 6/94 free-agent draft

PLAYER SUMMARY	
Fantasy Value	$0
Card Value	15¢ to 20¢
Will	dominate
Can't	pitch behind hitters
Expect	No. 1 or 2 starter
Don't Expect	comfortable hitters

Cleveland's pitching looked old and worn-out late last year, especially in the playoffs. Wright could be part of the group that will come along as replenishment. He worked in the Class-A Carolina League last year, averaging more than one strikeout per inning and allowing only 65 hits in 19 starts. The son of former major-leaguer Clyde Wright, Jaret was the tenth overall pick in 1994, out of Katella High School in Anaheim. After a year of getting his feet wet in rookie ball, Wright went to the South Atlantic League, showing a little of what makes him special. He held opposing hitters to a .205 average, fifth lowest in the league and seventh lowest among all Class-A pitchers. He also tied for the club lead with 13 hit batsmen, something that will be sure to make hitters a little uncomfortable. He was even more dominant last year, pushing his professional career win-loss mark over .500. Wright should start this season in Double-A ball.

RON WRIGHT

Position: First base
Team: Pittsburgh Pirates
Born: Jan. 21, 1976 Delta, UT
Height: 6' **Weight:** 210 lbs.
Bats: right **Throws:** right
Acquired: Traded by Braves with Jason Schmidt and Corey Pointer for Denny Neagle, 8/96

PLAYER SUMMARY	
Fantasy Value	$1
Card Value	25¢ to 35¢
Will	make an impact
Can't	steal bases
Expect	power prospect
Don't Expect	regrets over Neagle

Wright came to the Pirates as part of the deal that sent Denny Neagle to Atlanta late last year. The trade was part of a salary dump that left Jim Leyland so discouraged he resigned as Pirates' manager. But if Wright hits the way some of the brass in the Bucs' front office think he can, Pittsburgh could benefit long after Neagle is a footnote. Last year, Wright played in the Class-A Carolina League and the Double-A Southern League, leading the Atlanta farm system in home runs and RBI. He has an undeniable tendency to strike out, but he has time to develop into a more selective hitter. A first baseman, he was stuck behind Fred McGriff and then Ryan Klesko in Atlanta. But now that he is in the Pirate organization, Wright could challenge for a job in Steel Town soon—maybe even this season. Wright was Atlanta's seventh pick in the 1994 June draft and endured a rough debut in pro ball. But he blossomed in 1995 in the Class-A South Atlantic League, hitting a home run once in every 16.5 at bats, and tied for the lead in homers.

Professional Pitching Register

	W	L	ERA	G	CG	IP	H	ER	BB	SO
94 R	0	1	5.40	4	0	13.1	13	8	9	16
95 A	5	6	3.00	24	0	129.0	93	43	79	113
96 A	7	4	2.50	19	0	101.0	65	28	55	109

Professional Batting Register

	BA	G	AB	R	H	2B	3B	HR	RBI	SB
94 R	.172	45	169	10	29	9	0	1	16	1
95 A	.271	135	527	93	143	23	1	32	104	2
96 A	.275	66	240	47	66	15	2	20	62	1
96 AA	.143	4	14	1	2	0	0	0	0	0
96 AA	.254	63	232	39	59	11	1	16	52	1

DMITRI YOUNG

Position: First base
Team: St. Louis Cardinals
Born: Oct. 11, 1973 Vicksburg, MS
Height: 6'2" **Weight:** 240 lbs.
Bats: both **Throws:** right
Acquired: First-round pick in 6/91 free-agent draft

PLAYER SUMMARY	
Fantasy Value	$1
Card Value	10¢ to 15¢
Will	contend for job
Can't	play outfield
Expect	first baseman
Don't Expect	home run hitter

Young's case illustrates the patience a ballclub needs when developing a player. After being drafted fourth overall in 1991, Young spent six years in the St. Louis system, and only last year did he blossom into a bona fide contender for a job. Playing in the Triple-A American Association, Young led Louisville in batting average, runs, triples, and doubles while posting career highs in home runs and stolen bases. Young comes out of Rio Mesa High School in California, and made the *USA Today* High School All-America team in his senior year. He made the Cardinals' choice look like a wise one when he homered in his pro debut. A year later, playing in the Class-A Midwest League at age 18, Young made the All-Star squad. In 1993, Young got a midseason promotion to Double-A Arkansas but stalled there for parts of three seasons. As for this year, St. Louis may give him a look at first base. Despite impressive size, Young doesn't figure as a huge home run hitter.

Professional Batting Register

	BA	G	AB	R	H	2B	3B	HR	RBI	SB
91 R	.256	37	129	22	33	10	0	2	22	2
92 A	.310	135	493	74	153	36	6	14	72	14
93 A	.315	69	270	31	85	13	3	5	43	3
93 AA	.247	45	166	13	41	11	2	3	21	4
94 AA	.272	125	453	53	123	33	2	8	54	0
95 AA	.292	97	367	54	107	18	6	10	62	2
95 AAA	.286	2	7	3	2	0	0	0	0	0
96 AAA	.333	122	459	90	153	31	8	15	64	16
96 NL	.241	16	29	3	7	0	0	0	2	0

A.J. ZAPP

Position: First base
Team: Atlanta Braves
Born: April 24, 1978 Indianapolis, IN
Height: 6'2" **Weight:** 190 lbs.
Bats: left **Throws:** right
Acquired: Supplemental pick in 6/92 free-agent draft

PLAYER SUMMARY	
Fantasy Value	$0
Card Value	25¢ to 35¢
Will	slump occasionally
Can't	play the outfield
Expect	power potential
Don't Expect	a quick arrival

Atlanta traded a top first base prospect in Ron Wright last year, but the franchise remains well stocked at the position. First of all, Fred McGriff remains at the major-league level, and Randall Simon is pushing his way into Triple-A. Plus, Atlanta took Zapp with the 27th pick in the 1996 draft, giving them the potential for even more power. Zapp was one of only three first basemen selected in the initial round. He comes out of Center Grove High School in Greenwood, Indiana, where he hit roughly one home run in every five at bats. He signed a contract in time to collect 161 professional at bats and learned exactly how challenging his career will be. Playing for West Palm Beach of the Gulf Coast League, Zapp struck out more than once every three trips to the plate. He also finished the season in an 0-for-31 slump. By no means should that lead anyone to give up on him. Atlanta will probably let him establish something in a short-season league this year.

Professional Batting Register

	BA	G	AB	R	H	2B	3B	HR	RBI	SB
96 R	.149	47	161	9	24	9	0	0	5	0

TEAM OVERVIEWS

You'll find an overview of the 28 major-league organizations in this section. This section is arranged alphabetically, starting with the AL East, followed by the AL Central, the AL West, the NL East, the NL Central, and the NL West.

The teams are ordered as follows: Baltimore Orioles, Boston Red Sox, Detroit Tigers, New York Yankees, and Toronto Blue Jays in the AL East; Chicago White Sox, Cleveland Indians, Kansas City Royals, Milwaukee Brewers, and Minnesota Twins in the AL Central; Anaheim Angels, Oakland Athletics, Seattle Mariners, and Texas Rangers in the AL West; Atlanta Braves, Florida Marlins, Montreal Expos, New York Mets, and Philadelphia Phillies in the NL East; Chicago Cubs, Cincinnati Reds, Houston Astros, Pittsburgh Pirates, and St. Louis Cardinals in the NL Central; and Colorado Rockies, Los Angeles Dodgers, San Diego Padres, and San Francisco Giants in the NL West.

Each team overview includes a listing of the team's manager (including his record in the majors and with the team) and coaches as well as a description of the ballparks that the franchise has occupied, plus the years that the organization was there. If more than one ballpark is listed for a given year, the franchise occupied both parks during that season. The seating capacity and the dimensions of the present ballpark are included, as is the team's address. A brief history of each organization is also presented, as well as an analysis of the 1996 season.

The "1996 Season" box includes last year's manager, the team's wins (W), losses (L), winning percentage (PCT), and the number of games the team finished behind the league or division winner (GB). It also includes the team's record and winning percentage over the last five years as well as the team's "Five-Year Rank," which compares its five-year record against the other 27 major-league organizations.

BALTIMORE ORIOLES

Oriole Park at Camden Yards ● 333 West Camden Street ● Baltimore, MD 21201

Managing General Partner: Peter Angelos ● **Vice Chairman:** Joseph E. Foss ●
General Manager: Pat Gillick ● **Director of Player Development:** Syd Thrift ●
Assistant Director of Player Development: Don Buford ● **Scouting Director:** Gary Nickels

Manager: Davey Johnson
ML record: 887-643 (.580)
with Orioles: 88-74 (.543)

Coaches: Pat Dobson, Rick Down,
Andy Etchebarren, Elrod Hendricks,
Sam Perlozzo, John Stearns

BALLPARKS

Milwaukee: Lloyd Street Grounds 1901	**Capacity:** 48,876
St. Louis: Sportsman's Park 1902-1953	**1996 Attendance:** 3,646,950
Baltimore: Memorial Stadium 1954-1991; Oriole Park at Camden Yards 1992-present	**Surface:** natural grass
	Left field fence: 333 feet
	Center field fence: 400 feet
	Right field fence: 318 feet
	Left-center fence: 410 feet
	Right-center fence: 373 feet

ORIOLES HISTORY

For nearly 45 years, futility in American League baseball had a home in St. Louis. The Browns, founded in 1902, wallowed at the bottom of the standings until 1944. Winning the pennant in 1944, they lost the Series to the crosstown Cardinals. The franchise began anew in 1954, moving to Baltimore. By developing a very productive farm system, the Orioles became pennant contenders by the 1960s. A first-ever World Series win came to the franchise in 1966, and the Orioles went on to become a force to be dealt with, challenging for the top honors for three consecutive years (1969 to '71). Boasting the talents of such players as Brooks and Frank Robinson, Boog Powell, Jim Palmer, and Cal Ripken, Jr., as well as manager Earl Weaver, the franchise is noted for its unity and strong fundamentals. The Orioles have won seven division titles, six pennants, and three world titles (1966, 1970, and 1983). They stumbled out of the blocks in 1984, but by 1989 they had recovered, going from last place to one game out of first.

1996 SEASON
Manager: Davey Johnson

W	L	PCT	GB
88	74	.543	4

Last Five Years: 396-346; .534
Five-Year Rank: 4th in AL; 6th in ML

1996 ANALYSIS

Even though the Orioles pulled off the shocker of the 1996 season by whipping Cleveland in the first round of the American League playoffs, it was still a rough year in Baltimore. The club didn't get out of the blocks too fast, and there was midseason talk of gutting the team's veterans and starting anew. Acrimony sprung up between GM Pat Gillick and owner Peter Angelos, and then there was Roberto Alomar. The gifted second baseman, clearly an inspired free-agent pickup before the year, turned into public enemy No. 1 in late September when he spit on an umpire during a dispute. By the time the Yankees eliminated the O's in the ALCS, Alomar was a pariah throughout the nation, with talk about his punishment superseding consideration of his excellent season (.328, 22, 94).

Through it all, first-year manager Davey Johnson kept his cool and directed Baltimore to a fine season. Of course, it wasn't all that hard, considering the big years turned in by guys like Brady Anderson (.297, 50, 110), Rafael Palmeiro (.289, 39, 142), Bobby Bonilla (.287, 28, 116), Cal Ripken (.278, 26, 102) and Chris Hoiles (.258, 25, 73). What made things difficult was the usually reliable Orioles pitching staff, which faltered. Even though Mike Mussina came close to winning 20 games (19-11), his ERA was uncharacteristically high (4.81). Scott Erickson (13-12, 5.02) was his usual erratic self, and David Wells (11-14, 5.14) disappointed. Randy Myers (31 saves) was a bullpen stalwart, as was veteran Jesse Orosco.

BOSTON RED SOX

Fenway Park • 4 Yawkey Way • Boston, MA 02215

CEO: John L. Harrington • **Executive VP & GM:** Daniel F. Duquette • **Assistant GM:** Michael D. Port • **Assistant GM:** Elaine W. Steward • **Director of Baseball Operations:** Steven W. August • **Director of Field Operations:** Robert W. Schaefer • **Director of Scouting:** W. Wayne Britton

Manager: Jimy Williams
ML record: 281-241 (.534)
with Red Sox: 0-0 (.000)

Coaches: Dave Jauss, Joe Kerrigan, Wendall Kim, Grady Little, Jim Rice, Herm Starrette

BALLPARKS

Huntington Avenue Grounds 1901-1911; Fenway Park 1912-present

Capacity: 33,871
1996 Attendance: 2,315,233
Surface: natural grass
Left field fence: 315 feet
Center field fence: 390 feet
Right field fence: 302 feet
Left-center fence: 379 feet
Right-center fence: 380 feet

RED SOX HISTORY

Long-suffering Beantown fans wish they could be transported back to the early 1900s, when the BoSox were winners—five pennants, four world titles. But after selling Babe Ruth to the Yankees in 1920, the franchise fell fast. The Sox rebounded in the 1940s and 1950s, but didn't bounce back quite enough, save a pennant in '46. The arrival of young blood in the 1960s helped elevate the team to a pennant in '67. Not until 1975, and the appearance of more youngsters, did the sagging Sox get another lift. They stretched out a run at a world championship in '75, only to lose to the Reds in Game 7. Again in 1986, exceptional talent brought the BoSox a pennant, but not even the likes of Wade Boggs and Roger Clemens could overcome what seems to be the perpetual close-but-no-cigar syndrome. The Red Sox also won division championships in 1988 and '90, but failed to move past the Athletics in the LCS each time. They also won the division championship in 1995.

1996 SEASON

Manager: Kevin Kennedy

W	L	PCT	GB
85	77	.525	7

Last Five Years: 378-367; .507
Five-Year Rank: 7th in AL; 11th in ML

1996 ANALYSIS

Despite a strong 38-18 finish and much talk about the team's pride and fight, Boston couldn't overcome a wretched start. By beginning the '96 campaign 6-19, the BoSox effectively eliminated themselves from any chance of contention and doomed manager Kevin Kennedy to a swift post-season appointment with the guillotine. Despite its usual dose of heavy hitting, Boston was unable to overcome spotty starting pitching, erratic bullpen work, and some weak fielding. And even though the Red Sox rallied to finish eight games over the .500 mark, they were fooling themselves if they didn't think a lot more work needed to be done.

As expected, there were plenty of offensive highlights, beginning with first baseman Mo Vaughn (.326, 44, 143), who was more relaxed thanks to his contract extension. Jose Canseco (.289, 28, 82) had his moments, but he was unhappy at the end of the year with Kennedy's pending firing. John Valentin (.296, 13, 59), Tim Naehring (.288, 17, 65), Mike Stanley (.270, 24, 69), and surprising Reggie Jefferson (.347, 19, 74) comprised the heart of the remaining lineup. The pitching situation wasn't quite so stable, unfortunately. Roger Clemens (10-13, 3.63, 257 Ks) rarely approached his dominant self. Knuckleballer Tim Wakefield (14-13, 5.14) mixed brilliance with batting-practice offerings, and Tom Gordon (12-9, 5.59) needed plenty of run support. Heathcliff Slocumb (5-5, 3.02, 31 saves) was a bullpen workhorse.

DETROIT TIGERS

Tiger Stadium • 2121 Trumbull • Detroit, MI 48216

Chairman: Michael Ilitch • **President & CEO:** John McHale, Jr. • **Vice President of Baseball Operations:** Randy Smith • **Assistant General Manager:** Steve Lubratich • **Director of Scouting:** Jeff Scott • **Director of Minor League Operations:** Dave Miller • **Director of Baseball Administration:** Darrell Rodgers

Manager: Buddy Bell
ML record: 53-109 (.329)
with Tigers: 53-109 (.329)

Coaches: Rick Adair, Larry Herndon, Perry Hill, Fred Kendall, Jon Matlack, Jerry White

BALLPARKS

Bennett Park 1901-1911; Tiger Stadium 1912-present

Capacity: 52,416
1996 Attendance: 1,168,610
Surface: natural grass
Left field fence: 340 feet
Center field fence: 440 feet
Right field fence: 325 feet
Left-center fence: 365 feet
Right-center fence: 375 feet

TIGERS HISTORY

With a winning percentage of over .500, the Tigers have been perennial contenders since their inception in 1901. They have finished last only six times (including 1996's dismal 53-109 finish) and have never had more than four consecutive losing seasons. The franchise has won 11 titles and brought world championships to the Motor City in 1935, 1945, 1968, and 1984. The Tigers brought a feisty manager on board in mid-1979. Sparky Anderson provided a mature, seasoned presence, shaping the Detroit club into a formidable force in less than five years. The Tigers were a mighty power in '84, boasting big arms on offense and defense. The next two years, however, they dipped down to third in their division. In 1987, they roared back to win the AL pennant, but could not grab the grand prize. In 1989, they bottomed out, finishing last in their division. The Tigers have found offense, but are still looking for pitching in the 1990s.

1996 ANALYSIS

About the best thing to be said about Buddy Bell's debut in Detroit was that the Tigers didn't set the major-league record for fewest wins. After a dreadful start, the Tigers appeared a cinch to outdo the 1962 New York Mets, who won only 40 games, but a 29-28 stretch saved the Tigers from ignominy and rendered 1996 merely awful, not record-setting. Still, no team in the 1980s or '90s lost more games in a season than the Tigers, who were outscored by more runs (1,103-783) than any team since the '62 Mets. The statistical evidence generated by the Tigers' collapse into the AL East basement was as thorough as one could imagine. The team ERA of 6.38 was easily the worst in the majors, and the Tigers hit just .256 in the weak-pitching American League. No Detroit pitcher won more than seven games, and only a few players had what could be considered a successful year at the plate.

Among the bright spots was the play of rookie outfielder Bobby Higginson (.320, 26, 81), Travis Fryman's 100 RBI, Curtis Pride's production (.300, 10, 31) as a part-time outfielder, and the performance of rookie infielder Tony Clark (.250, 27, 72). Don't even ask about pitching. Only Omar Olivares (7-11, 4.89 ERA) could be considered reasonably successful. The Tigers didn't win a home game during the month of September, but late in the year fans rallied around Alan Trammell, who retired following his 20th big-league season.

1996 SEASON
Manager: Buddy Bell

W	L	PCT	GB
53	109	.329	39

Last Five Years: 326-419; .438
Five-Year Rank: 14th in AL; 27th in ML

NEW YORK YANKEES

Yankee Stadium • Bronx, NY 10451

Principal Owner: George M. Steinbrenner • **Managing General Partner:** Joseph A. Molloy •
Vice President, GM: Bob Watson • **Director of Player Development & Scouting:** Jack Hubbard •
Director of Scouting: Lin Garrett

Manager: Joe Torre
ML record: 986-1073 (.479)
with Yankees: 92-70 (.568)

Coaches: Jose Cardenal, Chris
Chambliss, Tony Cloninger, Willie
Randolph, Mel Stottlemyre, Don
Zimmer

BALLPARKS

American League Park 1901-
1902; Hilltop Park 1903-1912;
Polo Grounds 1913-1922; Shea
Stadium 1974-1975; Yankee
Stadium 1923-1973, 1976-
present

Capacity: 57,545
1996 Attendance: 2,250,839
Surface: natural grass
Left field fence: 318 feet
Center field fence: 408 feet
Right field fence: 314 feet
Left-center fence: 399 feet
Right-center fence: 385 feet

YANKEES HISTORY

Easily baseball's showcase franchise, the Yankees have won a record 23 world championships and have fielded some of the game's greatest teams, players, and managers. The 1927 "Murderer's Row" unit featured immortals Babe Ruth and Lou Gehrig, while Hall of Famers like Joe DiMaggio, Yogi Berra, Whitey Ford, and Mickey Mantle dotted the rosters in the 1930s, 1940s, and 1950s. The 1977 and '78 championship squads boasted Reggie Jackson and Catfish Hunter. The 1980s saw the Yankees twist in the wind. Owner George Steinbrenner had Billy Martin in a revolving door when it came to the skipper position. During Steinbrenner's 17 years as an owner, there were 17 different managers. By 1990, the Yankees were at the bottom of their division. In 1991 and '92, they had stepped up to fifth, and they finished second in 1993. In 1994, the Bombers had the best record in the AL, and they were the first wild-card team in the AL in 1995. In 1996, the Yanks added another world championship to their repertoire.

1996 SEASON
Manager: Joe Torre

W	L	PCT	GB
92	70	.568	—

Last Five Years: 405-338; .544
Five-Year Rank: 2nd in AL; 4th in ML

1996 ANALYSIS

The 1996 Bronx Bombers won the World Series with a team largely devoid of big egos and pretension. The Yanks were a direct representation of their manager—quiet, unassuming Joe Torre, who led the team through a tough beginning to the AL East crown and, ultimately, the Series title over Atlanta. It was an improbable championship, since the Yankees were hardly a dominant club. And when they fell behind 2-0 in the World Series, many expected a quick fold. But New York, instead of surrendering, took the next four straight to stun the Braves and the world.

Despite hitting just .217 in the Series, the Yankees won with excellent fundamentals and superior pitching, especially in the bullpen. Series MVP John Wetteland saved four games on top of the 43 he nailed down during the regular season. Reliever Mariano Rivera (8-3, 2.09), was all but unhittable all year long, and Graeme Lloyd was an unsung relief hero. Andy Pettitte (21-8, 3.87) assumed the ace role when David Cone had arm problems, and Jimmy Key (12-11, 4.68), and Doc Gooden (11-7, 5.01), who authored a stirring comeback story, were solid rotation components. Bernie Williams (.305, 29, 102) led the way with the bat, with support from Paul O'Neill (.302, 19, 91), Wade Boggs (.311), late-season acquisition Cecil Fielder (.252, 39, 117), Tino Martinez (.292, 25, 117), AL Rookie of the Year shortstop Derek Jeter (.314), and Darryl Strawberry, another reclamation project.

TORONTO BLUE JAYS

SkyDome • 1 Blue Jays Way, Suite 3200 • Toronto, Ontario M5V 1J1

Chairman: Sam Pollock • **President & CEO:** Paul Beeston • **VP, GM:** Gord Ash •
VP, Baseball: Bob Mattick • **VP, Baseball:** Al LaMacchia • **Assistant GM:** Bob Engle •
Assistant GM: Tim McCleary

Manager: Cito Gaston
ML record: 603-545 (.525)
with Blue Jays: 603-545 (.525)

Coaches: Alfredo Griffin, Nick
Leyva, Mel Queen, Gene Tenace,
Willie Upshaw

BALLPARKS

Exhibition Stadium 1977-1989;
SkyDome 1989-present

Capacity: 50,516
1996 Attendance: 2,559,563
Surface: artificial turf
Retractable Dome
Left field fence: 328 feet
Center field fence: 400 feet
Right field fence: 328 feet
Left-center fence: 375 feet
Right-center fence: 380 feet

BLUE JAYS HISTORY

Unlike their 1977 expansion siblings, Seattle, the Blue Jays have enjoyed growing success over the years. Toronto asserted itself in the early 1980s and became a contender. The Jays won the 1985 AL East crown but choked away the '87 title, losing their last seven games. In 1989, the Blue Jays moved from Exhibition Stadium to SkyDome. It was that same year that Cito Gaston took over as skipper. They rebounded to a division title again in '89, but that was as far as the Blue Jays progressed. The following season was disappointing for the Jays. After much effort, they failed to sew up their division in '90 on the final day of regular-season play. The team, developing a reputation for choking, put an end to that in 1992 by becoming world champions by winning in six games over Atlanta. The Blue Jays again took a trophy through customs in 1993 by beating the Phillies in six. The mid-1990s have featured mediocrity for the franchise.

1996 SEASON
Manager: Cito Gaston

W	L	PCT	GB
74	88	.457	18

Last Five Years: 376-369; .505
Five-Year Rank: 8th in AL; 12th in ML

1996 ANALYSIS

Even though the Blue Jays began the long climb back to contention from the depths of their '95 finish, the 1996 season didn't bring much happiness to Toronto fans, who no longer packed SkyDome the way they had when the Jays were winning pennants and World Series titles. In fact, attendance tumbled 35 percent in 1996, Canadian TV rights were expected to bring much less revenue, and the team was up for sale throughout the season. And with three strong teams ahead of it in the AL East, Toronto faces a long road back.

While the Jays did generate some offense, their pitching was largely erratic—aside from Cy Young winner Pat Hentgen and Juan Guzman. Hentgen (20-10, 3.22, 177 Ks) finished strongly, capturing his 20th win on the last day of the season. Guzman (11-8, 2.93, 165), meanwhile, captured the AL ERA title. Erik Hanson (13-17, 5.41) had his moments, but the rest of the rotation was weak. Mike Timlin (31 saves) was a strong closer, and rookie Tim Crabtree (5-3, 2.54) was another bullpen stalwart. There were mixed blessings on offense. Toronto had three players with 25 or more homers but four with 100 or more strikeouts. Carlos Delgado (.270, 25, 92), Joe Carter (.253, 30, 107), and Ed Sprague (.247, 36, 101) provided power, while outfielder Otis Nixon (.286, 54 steals) supplied speed. John Olerud (.274, 18, 61) didn't approach his former greatness, but youngsters Shawn Green (.280) and Alex Gonzalez (14 HR, 64 RBI) showed some promise.

CHICAGO WHITE SOX

Comiskey Park • 333 W. 35th Street • Chicago, IL 60616

Chairman: Jerry Reinsdorf • **Vice Chairman:** Eddie Einhorn •
Executive Vice President: Howard Pizer • **Senior VP, Major League Operations:** Ron Schueler •
Senior VP, Baseball: Jack Gould • **Director of Baseball Operations:** Daniel Evans •
Director of Scouting: Duane Shaffer

Manager: Terry Bevington
ML record: 142-133 (.516)
with White Sox: 142-133 (.516)

Coaches: Bill Buckner, Roly de
Armas, Ron Jackson, Joe Nossek,
Mike Pazik, Mark Salas

BALLPARKS

South Side Park 1901-1910;
Comiskey Park 1910-1990;
Comiskey Park II 1991-present

Capacity: 44,321
1996 Attendance: 1,676,416
Surface: natural grass
Left field fence: 347 feet
Center field fence: 400 feet
Right field fence: 347 feet
Left-center fence: 375 feet
Right-center fence: 375 feet

WHITE SOX HISTORY

Although the Sox's 91-year history has been a roller coaster ride, no one could ever call it boring. They won the AL pennant in their first year (1901) and captured world championships in 1906 and 1917. Baseball got a black eye when the infamous "Black Sox" scandal hit after the 1919 World Series, and the Sox found themselves stripped of their stars. A drought began after this unfortunate event, and the ChiSox didn't win another pennant for 40 years. In 1959, under the ownership of Bill Veeck, the Sox experienced a resurgence and won their division title. The Sox also claimed AL West titles in 1983 and 1993. They finished second in their division in 1990 and 1991, and they had the best record in the new AL Central in 1994. The Sox got a new home in 1991, the new Comiskey Park, located just across the street from where the old Comiskey stood.

1996 ANALYSIS

For a while there, it looked as if the Sox were going to mount a serious challenge to Cleveland's primacy in the AL Central. Chicago started the year quickly and jockeyed with the Indians for the top spot in the division. But the year ended with considerably less fanfare than it began. The ChiSox were booed at home by fans who had become disenchanted with the franchise, owner Jerry Reinsdorf, and Comiskey Park, which pales in comparison to some of the other ballparks recently opened. That's hardly the reception expected by a team that finished only three games out of the playoff hunt.

Of course, the fans couldn't find much reason to get down on first baseman Frank Thomas (.349, 40, 134), who had another superior year at the plate. And he had some help. Ageless Harold Baines (.311, 22, 95), third baseman Robin Ventura (.287, 34, 105), and Danny Tartabull (.254, 27, 101) handled the run production, while Dave Martinez (.318) hit well. The Sox pitching staff was one of the league's deepest and most balanced, although it lacked a fifth starter. Alex Fernandez (16-10, 3.45, 200 Ks) took a big step toward becoming one of baseball's best, while Wilson Alvarez (15-10, 4.22) was excellent. Kevin Tapani (13-10, 4.59) and James Baldwin (11-6, 4.42) were also productive. Roberto Hernandez (6-5, 1.91, 38 saves) anchored a bullpen that faltered despite strong performances from rookie Larry Thomas and Tony Castillo. It wasn't a bad year, but it wasn't the one fans expected.

1996 SEASON
Manager: Terry Bevington

W	L	PCT	GB
85	77	.525	14½

Last Five Years: 400-342; .537
Five-Year Rank: 3rd in AL; 5th in ML

CLEVELAND INDIANS

Jacobs Field • 2401 Ontario • Cleveland, OH 44115

Chairman & CEO: Richard E. Jacobs • **Executive Vice President, GM:** John Hart •
Director of Baseball Operations/Asst. GM: Dan O'Dowd • **Director, Scouting:** Jay Robertson •
Director, Minor League Operations: Mark Shapiro

Manager: Mike Hargrove
ML record: 449-378 (.543)
with Indians: 449-378 (.543)

Coaches: Johnny Goryl, Luis Isaac,
Charlie Manuel, Dave Nelson, Jeff
Newman, Mark Wiley

BALLPARKS

League Park 1901-1946;
Cleveland Stadium 1932-1993;
Jacobs Field 1994-present

Capacity: 42,865
1996 Attendance: 3,318,174
Surface: natural grass
Left field fence: 325 feet
Center field fence: 405 feet
Right field fence: 325 feet
Left-center fence: 370 feet
Right-center fence: 375 feet

INDIANS HISTORY

Fans of the Indians finally got something to cheer about. In their earlier days, the Tribe was an AL power. Cleveland won the AL pennant in 1920 and again in '48, taking the world championship trophy both times. Six years later, they set a league record for wins (111), en route to the 1954 pennant. But from 1969 to 1992, the Tribe finished in last place in the AL East eight times and second to last ten times. In 1990, Cleveland finished fourth in the AL East. Reality set in again in 1991, and the Indians plummeted to 105 losses. But a new regime took over, signing young stars to long-term contracts. The Indians moved into Jacobs Field in 1994 and finished second in the new AL Central. The Tribe almost realized its dream in 1995, winning 100 games and the AL pennant but losing the Series to the Braves.

1996 ANALYSIS

That resounding thud you heard was the collective heart of the city of Cleveland dropping after the Indians' unexpected first-round playoff collapse against Baltimore. After fashioning the finest regular-season record in baseball in '96, the Tribe fell into a quick, 2-0 hole against the Orioles and was finally subdued in a thrilling fourth-game showdown. It was an improbable, unbelievable ending for the team many thought could capture the world title that had eluded it in '95. The Indians had heroes at nearly every position and perhaps the AL's finest collection of pitchers. But it wasn't enough come playoff time. Perhaps the Tribe would have had more success if it hadn't let go of second baseman Carlos Baerga or veteran leader Eddie Murray.

The usual heroes stepped up at the plate, including brooding Albert Belle (.311, 48, 148), speedy Kenny Lofton (.317, 75 stolen bases), Jim Thome (.311, 38, 116), and Manny Ramirez (.309, 33, 112). Some new faces contributed, too, such as Kevin Seitzer (.326, 13, 78) and Julio Franco (.322, 14, 76). On the mound, Charles Nagy (17-5, 3.41, 167 Ks) blossomed into the ace everyone expected. Orel Hershiser (15-9, 4.24) and Jack McDowell (13-9, 5.11) benefited from the Indians' husky offense, while young Chad Ogea (10-6, 4.79) showed potential. Jose Mesa (39 saves) was again overpowering out of the bullpen, and Eric Plunk (3-2, 2.43), Paul Shuey (5-2, 2.85), Jim Poole (4-0, 3.04), and Paul Assenmacher (4-2, 3.09) were all strong in long relief.

1996 SEASON
Manager: Mike Hargrove

W	L	PCT	GB
99	62	.615	—

Last Five Years: 417-325; .560
Five-Year Rank: 1st in AL; 2nd in ML

KANSAS CITY ROYALS

P.O. Box 419969 • Kansas City, MO 64141-6969

Chairman, CEO: David Glass • **President:** Mike Herman • **Executive VP & GM:** Herk Robinson •
VP, Baseball Operations: George Brett • **Assistant GM:** Jay Hinrichs •
Director Player Personnel: Larry Doughty • **Director, Scouting:** Art Stewart

Manager: Bob Boone
ML record: 145-160 (.475)
with Royals: 145-160 (.475)

Coaches: Tim Foli, Guy Hansen,
Bruce Kison, Greg Luzinski, Mitchell
Page, Jamie Quirk

BALLPARKS

Municipal Stadium 1969-1972; Kauffman Stadium 1973- present	Capacity: 40,625 1996 Attendance: 1,436,007 Surface: natural grass Left field fence: 330 feet Center field fence: 400 feet Right field fence: 330 feet Left-center fence: 375 feet Right-center fence: 375 feet

ROYALS HISTORY

The Kansas City Royals came into existence in 1968 to fill a void left by the departed A's. In no time at all, the Royals began to make themselves known. Moving quickly to the top of the AL West, they won divisional titles from 1976 through '78, led by George Brett. The team took its first pennant in 1980. In 1984, they took another AL West crown. They went on to win a world championship in 1985, overcoming 3-1 deficits in the playoffs and World Series. The Royals continued to show their strength from 1986 through '89 by remaining in second or third place in their division. In 1990, however, they plummeted to the sixth spot in the AL West. This fast, hard tumble came as a surprise to all, and the drought lasted a few years. For the most part, the Royals have turned in solid seasons in recent years.

1996 ANAYSIS

Even though the Royals completed the first last-place finish in team history, they were only 11 games below .500 and didn't play all that poorly. But the team concluded 1996 in need of a big-time run-producer capable of carrying the team offensively and filling seats in Kauffman Stadium. With only 123 homers and a league-low 746 runs scored, it's little wonder the Royals struggled so much at times last year. Had their pitching staff not been much improved, there's no telling how far they would have fallen. K.C. had three pitchers with double-digit wins, but the story of the season may well have been rookie left-hander Jose Rosado (8-6, 3.21), who surprised everybody with a fabulous second half and actually led the team in ERA.

Kevin Appier (14-11, 3.62, 207 Ks) and Tim Belcher (15-11, 3.92) were strong all season long, while Chris Haney (10-14, 4.70) proved dependable. While the starters were solid, the bullpen was not. Jeff Montgomery (24 saves) was the leader of a shaky group. The success of the starters was magnified by K.C.'s unimpressive .267 team batting average. Shortstop Jose Offerman (.303) and third sacker Joe Randa (.303) hit for average but little else, while Mike Macfarlane (.274, 19, 54) and Craig Paquette (.259, 22, 67) were the team's two main power plants. Outfielder Tom Goodwin (.282) stole 66 bases—second-best in the league—while rookie Johnny Damon (.271, 25 swipes) showed signs of being a future stalwart.

1996 SEASON
Manager: Bob Boone

W	L	PCT	GB
75	86	.466	24

Last Five Years: 365-379; .490
Five-Year Rank: 9th in AL; 15th in ML

MILWAUKEE BREWERS

P.O. Box 3099 • Milwaukee, WI 53201-3099

President, CEO: Allan H. (Bud) Selig • **Senior VP-Baseball Operations:** Sal Bando •
Scouting Director: Ken Califano • **Director of Baseball Administration:** Brian Small

Manager: Phil Garner
ML record: 359-386 (.482)
with Brewers: 359-386 (.482)

Coaches: Chris Bando, Bill Castro,
Jim Gantner, Lamar Johnson, Don
Rowe

BALLPARKS	
Seattle: Sicks Stadium 1969	**Capacity:** 53,192
Milwaukee: County Stadium 1970-present	**1996 Attendance:** 1,327,155
	Surface: natural grass
	Left field fence: 362 feet
	Center field fence: 402 feet
	Right field fence: 362 feet
	Left-center fence: 392 feet
	Right-center fence: 392 feet

BREWERS HISTORY

After a one-year stint as the last-place, first-year Seattle Pilots, this franchise brought baseball back to Milwaukee in 1970. The Brewers floundered in the AL East for much of the next decade. By 1978, however, they posted their first winning season, finishing third. The Brew Crew really came alive in the early 1980s, due largely to the multitalented Robin Yount. The Brewers won the second-half crown in strike-shortened 1981. In 1982, they took their only AL pennant, not coincidentally during Yount's MVP, All-Star, and Gold Glove season, and took the Cardinals all the way to seven games in a futile bid for the world championship. The brightest moment for the franchise was its sprint out of the gate in 1987. The Brewers got off to a record-tying start of 13 consecutive wins. They hit the skids shortly thereafter, losing 12 games in a row. This decline has continued through much of the 1990s.

1996 ANALYSIS

The magic wasn't completely back in Milwaukee, but the 1996 Brew Crew played exciting baseball and came within one win of finishing the year at .500—quite an improvement from its '95 performance. Although the franchise remained under the direction of president Bud Selig, arguably public enemy No. 1 in all of baseball, it managed to stage a spirited chase for a wild-card spot, despite some glaring weaknesses on the mound. Milwaukee's 5.14 team ERA was high, even by American League standards, and Brewer pitchers gave up 213 home runs throughout the year. Final team stats showed just how even a year it was in Milwaukee. The Brewers scored five fewer runs than their opposition, had but eight more hits, and out-hit their rivals .279 to .278. Sounds like a .500 year, doesn't it?

It could have been better, but other than Ben McDonald (12-10, 3.90, 146 Ks) and Scott Karl (13-9, 4.86), the Brewers had big problems among their starting pitchers. No other Milwaukee hurler started more than 17 games, and none won more than seven. The bullpen was helped by strong performances by Mike Fetters (3-3, 3.38, 32 saves) and Bob Wickman (7-1, 70 appearances). The Brewers did generate some pop at the plate. John Jaha (.300, 34, 118) led the way with the best season of his career. Catcher Dave Nilsson (.331, 17, 84), Jeff Cirillo (.325, 15, 83), Greg Vaughn (.280, 31, 95), and Jose Valentin (.259, 24, 95) were productive, too.

1996 SEASON			
Manager: Phil Garner			
W	L	PCT	GB
80	82	.481	19½
Last Five Years: 359-386; .482			
Five-Year Rank: 12th in AL; 20th in ML			

MINNESOTA TWINS

501 Chicago Avenue South • Hubert H. Humphrey Metrodome • Minneapolis, MN 55415

Owner: Carl R. Pohlad • **Chairman:** Howart T. Fox, Jr. • **President:** T. Geron Bell •
VP, GM: Terry Ryan • **VP, Assistant GM:** Bill Smith • **Director of Minor Leagues:** Jim Rantz •
Director of Scouting: Mike Radcliff

Manager: Tom Kelly
ML record: 785-791 (.498)
with Twins: 785-791 (.498)

Coaches: Terry Crowley, Ron Gardenhire, Rick Stelmaszek, Dick Such, Scott Ullger

BALLPARKS	
Washington: American League Park 1901-1910; Griffith Stadium 1911-1960 **Minnesota:** Metropolitan Stadium 1961-1981; Hubert H. Humphrey Metrodome 1982-present	**Capacity:** 56,783 **1996 Attendance:** 1,437,352 **Surface:** artificial turf Stationary Dome **Left field fence:** 343 feet **Center field fence:** 408 feet **Right field fence:** 327 feet **Left-center fence:** 385 feet **Right-center fence:** 367 feet

TWINS HISTORY

As the Washington Senators, this franchise mixed a few highs—three pennants and a 1924 world championship—with years of deep lows. After a move to the Twin Cities in 1960, the team won the 1965 pennant but slid out of contention for most of the next two decades. Perhaps all they needed was to be sheltered from the elements. The team moved indoors in '82 and captured the World Series in '87 with a young team of sluggers. In 1990, they finished last in their division. Then, as if a magic wand had been waved over the Metrodome, the Twins came back with a vengeance in '91. They posted a regular-season record of 95-67, won the pennant, and went seven games in the World Series, overcoming Atlanta for all the marbles. The Twins finished second in their division in 1992, then endured a decline for the next few years.

1996 ANALYSIS

Believe it or not, the 1996 Twins weren't awful. While that is hardly a glowing endorsement of the club's performance, it certainly is an apt description for a club that had sunk from 1991 World Series champion to American League patsy. Minnesota never challenged for any postseason honors, but it did threaten the .500 mark and actually appeared to be building for the future. Of course, there was still plenty of work to be done when '96 concluded. Having lost fan-favorite and team star Kirby Puckett to retirement at the start of the season, the Twins hit only 118 homers all year and had nobody with more than 16. And the team's 5.28 ERA didn't exactly attract the attention of too many Cy Young Award voters.

The most interesting pitching story of the year was Rick Aguilera (8-6, 5.42), who returned to the starting rotation after years as a closer. By season's end, however, it appeared that the experiment was less than successful, and Aguilera was expected to return to the bullpen in '97. That doesn't mean the starting group will be awful. Youngsters Brad Radke (11-16, 4.46), Frank Rodriguez (13-14, 5.05), and Rich Robertson (7-17, 5.12) all had their moments. The offense was keyed by ageless Paul Molitor (.341, 9, 113), who made it into the 3,000-hit club. Second baseman Chuck Knoblauch (.341, 13, 72), youngster Marty Cordova (.309, 16, 111), Rich Becker (.291, 12, 71), and Scott Stahoviak (.284, 13, 61) comprised the heart of a pretty good lineup.

1996 SEASON			
Manager: Tom Kelly			
W	L	PCT	GB
78	84	.481	21½
Last Five Years: 347-397; .533			
Five-Year Rank: 5th in AL; 7th in ML			

461

ANAHEIM ANGELS

Anaheim Stadium • 2000 Gene Autry Way • Anaheim, CA 92806

Chairman of the Board: Gene Autry • **President & CEO:** Richard M. Brown •
Executive VP: Jackie Autry • **Vice President & GM:** W.J. Bavasi •
Assistant GM: Tim Mead • **Director, Player Development:** Ken Forsch

Manager: Terry Collins
ML record: 224-197 (.532)
with Angels: 0-0 (.000)

Coaches: Larry Bowa, Rod Carew,
Joe Coleman, Marcel Lachemann,
Joe Maddon, Dave Parker

BALLPARKS

Los Angeles: Wrigley Field 1961; Dodger Stadium 1962-1965	**Capacity:** 64,593
Anaheim: Anaheim Stadium 1966-present	**1996 Attendance:** 1,820,532
	Surface: natural grass
	Left field fence: 333 feet
	Center field fence: 404 feet
	Right field fence: 333 feet
	Left-center fence: 386 feet
	Right-center fence: 386 feet

ANGELS HISTORY

Cowboy singer Gene Autry gave birth to the Angels in Los Angeles in 1961. His Halos, however, have yet to ride off into the sunset with an AL pennant. Although they managed to finish third in 1964, they faltered for the next 14 years. They spent freely when the era of free agency began in the mid-1970s. This strategy seemed to pay off for them a few years later. In 1979, they won a divisional title, using veteran free agents. The Angels did manage to repeat the feat in 1982 and '86. The loss in 1986 was perhaps the most painful of all as the California team was only one pitch away from clinching the pennant when fate stepped in. The Halos once again walked off empty handed, losing this time to Boston. In 1995, the Angels had a ten-game lead in the AL West in mid-August. They fell apart, ending up tied with the Mariners with a 78-66 record the last day of the season, and lost the one-game playoff. Management renamed the California Angels the Anaheim Angels over the 1996 off-season.

1996 ANALYSIS

The Angels' colossal 1995 collapse had to have had some effect on the '96 campaign. One year after coming within a whisper of the AL West title, California slid into the division cellar and finished last for just the fourth time in its 36-year history. The fall cost manager Marcel Lachemann his job and forced the Angels to recycle John McNamara as an interim skipper. That wasn't the only turmoil that characterized the year. Angels owner Gene Autry spent much of the season in negotiations with the Disney people about selling the team. All in all, it wasn't a great year to be an Angel.

The Angels' aggregate ERA was a poor 5.30 despite a strong performance from Chuck Finley (15-16, 4.16, 215 Ks), who became the first Angels lefty to fan 200 since Frank Tanana in 1977. The rest of the rotation was shaky. Shawn Boskie (12-11, 5.32) needed big-time run support, while Jim Abbott suffered through an awful 2-18 season that included a trip to the minors. Troy Percival (2.31, 36 saves) led an overworked bullpen. The Angels weren't a juggernaut on offense, but they did have some highlights, most notably Chili Davis (.292, 28, 95), who set a team record for homers by a DH. Jim Edmonds (.304, 27, 66) and Tim Salmon (.286, 30, 98) were sturdy contributors, but Garret Anderson (.285, 12, 72) slipped, as did J.T. Snow (.257, 17, 67). The Angels were also hurt by poor team speed. They stole only 53 bases all season.

1996 SEASON
Manager: Marcel Lachemann; John McNamara

W	L	PCT	GB
70	91	.435	19½

Last Five Years: 338-407; .454
Five-Year Rank: 13th in AL; 25th in ML

OAKLAND ATHLETICS

7677 Oakport Street, 2nd Floor • Oakland, CA 94621

President/Owner: Steve Schott • **Partner/Owner:** Ken Hofmann •
Executive VP & GM: Sandy Alderson • **Assistant GM:** Billy Beane •
Director of Player Development: Keith Lieppman • **Director of Scouting:** Grady Fuson

Manager: Art Howe
ML record: 470-502 (.484)
with Athletics: 78-84 (.485)

Coaches: Bob Cluck, Duffy Dyer,
Brad Fischer, Denny Walling, Ron
Washington

BALLPARKS

Philadelphia: Columbia Park 1901-1908; Shibe Park 1909-1954	**Capacity:** 42,313
	1996 Attendance: 1,148,380
	Surface: natural grass
Kansas City: Municipal Stadium 1955-1967	**Left field fence:** 330 feet
Oakland: Oakland-Alameda County Coliseum 1968-present	**Center field fence:** 400 feet
	Right field fence: 330 feet
	Left-center fence: 375 feet
	Right-center fence: 375 feet

ATHLETICS HISTORY

The Athletics have had a colorful existence. Formed in 1901 in Philadelphia, the A's captured world championships in 1910, 1911, '13, '29, and '30, before embarking on a dismal period that saw the franchise move to Kansas City. Then in 1968, Charlie Finley had a plan. He wanted to move his team to Oakland, make them a success, and sell lots of tickets. His Oakland team became a reality and the winning began—just not in front of as large an audience as had been anticipated. Three straight world titles came from 1972 to '74. After the franchise captured the division championship in the strike-affected '81 season, area businesses took over the reins. Packing the team with power and talent, the A's won pennants from 1988 to '90, with a world championship in 1989. Topping their division again in '92, Oakland went from first to worst in 1993.

1996 SEASON
Manager: Art Howe

W	L	PCT	GB
78	84	.485	12

Last Five Years: 360-384; .483
Five-Year Rank: 11th in AL; 19th in ML

1996 ANALYSIS

The A's began the season as something of a big-league joke, playing their early home games in a minor-league park in Las Vegas while the Coliseum underwent renovations. But by the time the season ended, nobody was laughing at Oakland, which fielded one of the most dangerous collections of sluggers in recent history. The A's bashed 243 homers and even stayed alive in the wild-card hunt until September, when their awful pitching could no longer be hidden by superior offensive firepower.

Leading the way was first baseman Mark McGwire (.312, 52, 113), who had a career year and even threatened Roger Maris's home run record despite playing in only 130 games. Terry Steinbach (.272, 35, 100) set a major-league record for homers by a catcher, while Geronimo Berroa (.290, 36, 106), Scott Brosius (.304, 22, 71), Jason Giambi (.291, 20, 79), and Ernie Young (.242, 19, 64) pounded the fences without mercy. The pitching situation was another story. The A's had a wretched 5.20 team ERA, and no Oakland starter won more than seven games. The A's gave up 1,638 hits—a club record. John Wasdin (8-7, 5.96) and Ariel Prieto (6-7, 4.15) came closest to what could be called a decent year, and neither of them were too good. The bullpen was overworked. Mike Mohler (6-3, 3.67) appeared in 72 games, while Jim Corsi (6-0, 4.03) somehow managed to escape the year without a loss. Bill Taylor (6-3) saved 17 games.

SEATTLE MARINERS

83 South King Street, Suite 300 • Seattle, WA 98104

Chairman & CEO: John Ellis • **President & COO:** Chuck Armstrong • **VP, Baseball Operations:**
Woody Woodward • **VP, Scouting & Player Development:** Roger Jongewaard •
Director, Baseball Administration: Lee Pelekoudas

Manager: Lou Piniella
ML record: 774-709 (.522)
with Mariners: 295-285 (.509)

Coaches: Nardi Contreras, Lee Elia,
John McLaren, Sam Mejias, Steve
Smith, Matt Sinatro

BALLPARK

Kingdome 1977-present

Capacity: 59,166
1996 Attendance: 2,722,392
Surface: artificial turf
Stationary Dome
Left field fence: 331 feet
Center field fence: 405 feet
Right field fence: 312 feet
Left-center fence: 389 feet
Right-center fence: 380 feet

MARINERS HISTORY

When the Seattle Pilots flew out of the Pacific Northwest, Seattle was a little more than miffed to be stranded. Demanding a team to call its own, the city was awarded the 1977 expansion team, the Seattle Mariners. Before 1995, the Mariners were dismal, only placing fourth in the AL West three times—1982, 1987, and 1993. In 1989, they claimed their first All-Star selection, Ken Griffey, Jr. The Mariners posted their first winning season in 1991. But in 1993, manager Sweet Lou Piniella arrived to much fanfare, and he delivered in 1995. The "Refuse to Lose" Mariners came back from a ten-game deficit in mid-August to tie the Angels on the last day of the season. The Mariners beat the Halos in a one-game playoff, then Seattle dropped two to the Yankees before winning three to win the divisional playoffs. The Mariners' dream season was stopped by the Indians in the ALCS.

1996 ANALYSIS

Well, the Mariners almost did it again. After spotting the Texas Rangers a huge lead in the AL West, Seattle stormed back into contention in September and almost replicated its improbable pennant rally of 1995—almost. The '96 Mariners fell four games short of the division crown and three away from a wild-card berth. But one can't blame the Mariners' shortfall completely on procrastination. Had pitcher Randy Johnson not succumbed to back trouble early, and had Ken Griffey, Jr., not missed 21 games due to injury, it's possible the M's would have taken the division with ease.

Seattle was arguably the most exciting offensive team in the majors. Griffey (.303, 49, 140) was again amazing. But young Alex Rodriguez (.358, 36, 123) was even more remarkable. The 21-year-old shortstop became the third-youngest player ever to win a batting title and established himself as one of the game's top young stars. Edgar Martinez (.327, 26, 103), Jay Buhner (.271, 44, 138), Paul Sorrento (.289, 23, 89), and Dan Wilson (.285, 18, 83) comprised the rest of the potent Seattle attack. Johnson (5-0, 3.67, 70 Ks) was enjoying a superior year before his back surgery, and the Mariners' rotation relied on castaways after that—with pretty good success. Jamie Moyer (13-3, 3.98) and Sterling Hitchcock (13-9, 5.35) were dependable, and Terry Mulholland (5-4) was steady after coming over in a late trade. Mike Jackson and Norm Charlton (20 saves) anchored the bullpen.

1996 SEASON
Manager: Lou Piniella

W	L	PCT	GB
85	76	.528	4

Last Five Years: 361-383; .485
Five-Year Rank: 10th in AL; 17th in ML

TEXAS RANGERS
1000 Ballpark Way • Arlington, TX 76011

President: J. Thomas Schieffer • **Vice President, GM:** R. Douglas Melvin •
Director, Player Development: Reid Nichols • **Director of Scouting:** Lenny Strelitz

Manager: Johnny Oates
ML record: 455-412 (.525)
with Rangers: 164-142 (.536)

Coaches: Dick Bosnan, Bucky
Dent, Larry Hardy, Rudy Jaramillo,
Ed Napoleon, Jerry Narron

BALLPARKS

Washington: Griffith Stadium 1961; Robert F. Kennedy Stadium 1962-1971	**Capacity:** 49,178
	1996 Attendance: 2,888,920
	Surface: natural grass
Texas: Arlington Stadium 1972-1993; The Ballpark in Arlington 1994-present	**Left field fence:** 332 feet
	Center field fence: 400 feet
	Right field fence: 325 feet
	Left-center fence: 390 feet
	Right-center fence: 379 feet

RANGERS HISTORY

What can you expect from a team that began as the reincarnation of the Washington Senators? In the three decades since its inception in 1961 in the nation's capital, this franchise has won no titles and has rarely managed to sneak above .500. The team circled the wagons in 1972 and headed west for Arlington. Racked by instability, the Rangers have become an exercise in futility. Billy Martin, taking a stab at making something happen, took the team as far as second place in 1974. The team had been worked so hard, though, that by mid-1975 they fizzled out. In 1977, four different managers attempted to take over the helm. The fourth one, Billy Hunter, drove the team to a club-record 94 wins. Since the move in '72 through 1993, the team reached second place in the AL West six times. Looking to build a strong tradition in their new stadium, the Rangers had the best record in the AL West in 1994. They also had the best record in the AL West in '96, when they made it to the playoffs for the first time in franchise history.

1996 ANALYSIS

After spending 25 years as the American League's perennial punch line, the Rangers finally won a championship in 1996, capturing the AL West Division title. It sure was fun to watch Texas bang out homers and win games 10-7, and even though the Yankees dispatched the Rangers in the first round of the playoffs and Seattle almost caught them from behind during September, it was a great year.

Texas clubbed 221 homers during '96, third in the American League, and AL MVP Juan Gonzalez (.314, 47, 144) led the way. He had plenty of help. Dean Palmer (.280, 38, 107), Kevin Elster (.252, 24, 99), and Mickey Tettleton (.246, 24, 83) joined Gonzalez in a formidable lineup. As usual, Ivan Rodriguez (.300, 19, 86) was one of the best catchers in baseball, while Rusty Greer (.332, 18, 100) had a breakout year in only his second full major-league season. What was possibly even more impressive was the Texas pitching staff, annually one of the worst in baseball. Although the Rangers' 4.65 aggregate ERA wasn't reminiscent of the 1969 Orioles, it was better than usual, and Texas was the only team in baseball with five starters with double-digit victories. Leading the way was Ken Hill (16-10, 3.63, 170 Ks), with Darren Oliver (14-6, 4.66), Roger Pavlik (15-8, 5.19), Kevin Gross (11-8, 5.22), and Bobby Witt (16-12, 5.41) behind him. Mike Henneman saved 31 games, while bullpen mates Ed Vosberg and Jeff Russell handled the long stuff well.

1996 SEASON
Manager: Johnny Oates

W	L	PCT	GB
90	72	.556	—

Last Five Years: 379-365; .509
Five-Year Rank: 6th in AL; in 10th ML

ATLANTA BRAVES

P.O. Box 4064 • Atlanta, GA 30302

Owner: R.E. Turner III • **Chairman of the Board:** William C. Bartholomay •
President: Stanley H. Kasten • **Executive VP & GM:** John Schuerholz •
Senior VP & Assistant to the President: Henry L. Aaron • **Assistant GM:** Dean Taylor •
Director of Scouting and Player Development: Paul Snyder

Manager: Bobby Cox
ML record: 1211-1028 (.541)
with Braves: 856-736, (.538)

Coaches: Jim Beauchamp, Pat
Corrales, Clarence Jones, Leo
Mazzone, Ned Yost

BALLPARKS

Boston: South End Grounds 1871-1914; Braves Field 1914-1952	**Capacity:** 49,831
	1996 Attendance: 2,901,242
	Surface: natural grass
Milwaukee: County Stadium 1953-1965	**Left field fence:** 335 feet
	Center field fence: 400 feet
Atlanta: Fulton County Stadium 1966-1996; Turner Stadium 1997	**Right field fence:** 330 feet
	Left-center fence: 380 feet
	Right-center fence: 385 feet

BRAVES HISTORY

The Braves began in the National Association in 1871 as the Boston Red Stockings. After winning four NA pennants and joining the National League in 1876, the Braves flourished and dominated the NL in the 1890s (winning five pennants). Money woes caused five decades of misery to follow, broken only by the "Miracle Braves" of 1914 and the pennant winners of 1948. Boston loved the Red Sox, so the Braves moved to Milwaukee in 1953. The Spahn- and Aaron-led clubs won a world championship in '57 and a pennant in '58. The Braves were the first club to shift twice, moving to Atlanta in 1966. The Braves won NL West titles in 1969 and 1982. The worst club in the league in 1990, the Braves then won three straight NL West pennants. The team won the NLCS in 1991 and 1992 but lost in the Series. Finally, in 1995, the Braves took the title.

1996 SEASON

Manager: Bobby Cox

W	L	PCT	GB
96	66	.593	—

Last Five Years: 456-288; .612
Five-Year Rank: 1st in NL; 1st in ML

1996 ANALYSIS

Although the Braves put together a season that would have thrilled nearly every other franchise in the majors, their stunning collapse against the Yankees in the World Series after building a 2-0 lead on the road was a crushing blow. It left a tremendous team worrying about its legacy. The self-proclaimed "Team of the '90s" blew its shot at back-to-back Series titles and a spot in the history books when its offense deserted it against New York. Atlanta stormed to the NL East title, buried the Dodgers in the first round of the playoffs, and raged out of a 3-1 hole against St. Louis in the NLCS before meeting its Waterloo in the Bronx.

As usual, the Braves had superior starting pitching, with NL Cy Young Award winner John Smoltz (24-8, 2.94, 276 Ks) taking the lead. Greg Maddux (15-11, 2.72) and Tom Glavine (15-10, 2.98) were also dominant, while Mark Wohlers (39 saves) was a fire-breathing closer. Atlanta's offense underwent something of a transition in 1996. After Dave Justice was lost for the year, youth asserted itself. Shortstop Chipper Jones (.309, 30, 110) moved to the brink of true stardom, as did catcher Javier Lopez (.282, 23, 69) and slugger Ryan Klesko (.282, 34, 93). Youngsters Andruw Jones, who slugged a pair of homers in the Series opener, and Jermaine Dye also flashed signs of future success. Of course, the vets did their share. Marquis Grissom (.308, 23, 74) and Fred McGriff (.295, 28, 107) weren't exactly ready to cede leadership status to the kids.

FLORIDA MARLINS

Pro Player Stadium • 2267 NW 199th Street • Miami, FL 33056

Chairman: H. Wayne Huizenga • **President:** Donald A. Smiley •
Executive VP & GM: David Dombrowski • **VP & Assistant GM:** Frank Wren •
VP of Player Personnel: Garry Hughes • **VP of Player Development:** John Boles

Manager: Jim Leyland
ML record: 854-863 (.497)
with Marlins: 0-0 (.000)

Coaches: Rich Donnelly, Bruce
Kimm, Jerry Manuel, Milt May, Larry
Rothschild, Tommy Sandt

BALLPARK

Pro Player Stadium 1993-present	**Capacity:** 47,226
	1996 Attendance: 1,746,767
	Surface: natural grass
	Left field fence: 335 feet
	Center field fence: 410 feet
	Right field fence: 345 feet
	Left-center fence: 380 feet
	Right-center fence: 380 feet

MARLINS HISTORY

In 1989, the NL started a search for two teams to increase the loop's number of franchises from 12 to 14, matching the AL. The next year, Blockbuster Video owner Wayne Huizenga purchased half of Joe Robbie Stadium, intending to fill the stadium with 82 baseball games a year. His ownership group was chosen over several others in the South Florida area, and on June 10, 1990, the Marlins and the Rockies were chosen as the two new NL franchises to play in the 1993 year. Carl Berger and Dave Dombrowski were initially hired to start the organization, with Rene Lachemann as the first manager. By signing such high-priced veterans as Gary Sheffield, the Marlins have shown that they are not afraid to spend money. There is a natural rivalry with the Rockies, and it was with consternation that the Marlins watched playoff baseball in Colorado in 1995, just three short years after expansion.

1996 SEASON
Manager: Rene Lachemann; John Boles

W	L	PCT	GB
80	82	.494	16

Last Four Years: 262-320; .450
Four-Year Rank: 13th in NL; 26th in ML

1996 ANALYSIS

Even though the Marlins continued their gradual climb toward contention, the best news of their 1996 season came about a week after it was completed. That was when owner Wayne Huizenga shelled out millions to sign former Pirates manager Jim Leyland—one of the game's best strategists—to a fat multiyear deal. Although Leyland didn't shine during his last few years in Pittsburgh (a result of a roster filled with painfully inexperienced players), he should be much better right away with the Marlins. Though the Marlins slipped from their early flirtation with playoff possibilities, they boasted some strong pitching and a few first-rate offensive performers and finished 1996 with the best record in their short history.

Leading the way was starter Kevin Brown (17-11, 1.89, 159 Ks), who led the league in ERA and might have won the Cy Young Award had Atlanta pitcher John Smoltz not won 24 games. Joining Brown as a dominant starter was Al Leiter (16-12, 2.93, 200 Ks), who enjoyed his best season. Things were a little shaky after that, but the bullpen was pretty good. Closer Robb Nen (5-1, 1.95, 35 saves) dominated, while Terry Mathews and Jay Powell showed promise in the middle innings. Gary Sheffield (.314, 42, 120) enjoyed good health for the first time in a couple of years and celebrated with a monstrous year. Jeff Conine (.293, 26, 95) was pretty good, too. Greg Colbrunn (.286, 16, 69) continued his development into a solid first baseman, and veteran Devon White (.274, 17, 84) produced steadily.

MONTREAL EXPOS

P.O. Box 500, Station M • Montreal, Quebec H1V 3P2

President and General Partner: Claude R. Brochu •
Chairman of the Partnership Committee: L. Jacques Menard •
VP, Baseball Operations: Bill Stoneman • **VP & GM:** Jim Beattie •
Director, Scouting: Ed Creech • **Director, Player Development:** Bill Geivett

Manager: Felipe Alou
ML record: 392-335 (.539)
with Expos: 392-335 (.539)

Coaches: Pierre Arsenault, Bobby
Cuellar, Tommy Harper, Pete
Mackanin, Luis Pujols, Jim Tracy

BALLPARKS	
Jarry Park 1969-1976; Stade Olympique 1977-present	**Capacity:** 46,500
	1996 Attendance: 1,618,573
	Surface: artificial turf
	Retractable Dome
	Left field fence: 325 feet
	Center field fence: 404 feet
	Right field fence: 325 feet
	Left-center fence: 375 feet
	Right-center fence: 375 feet

EXPOS HISTORY

Named for the city's world exposition in the late 1960s, the Expos had given fans few highlights until recently. Their humble beginnings in tiny Jarry Park were matched by modest performances. The Expos did not contend for the NL East title until 1973, when their fourth-place finish belied the fact that they were only 3½ games out of first. The franchise did not come close again until 1979, finishing second by two games to the eventual world champion Pirates. The Expos captured the division crown in 1981. From 1982 through 1989, the Expos never went above the third rung in their division. By 1991, the Expos were last in the division. Montreal built a fine farm system and has leaned on youngsters to provide talent. In 1992 and '93, the team finished second in the NL East. In 1994, the Expos had the best record in baseball but were denied a shot at the world championship due to the strike.

1996 ANALYSIS

Given the Expos' commitment to cost-cutting and attention to the bottom line, it's amazing they were able to battle the Atlanta Braves for much of the year and fall just two games short of a wild-card berth. Like many other "small market" clubs, the Expos waged the difficult battle to produce a winner under tight budget constraints. A large share of the credit for the Expos' strong season goes to manager Felipe Alou, who remains one of the game's most underrated minds. He directed an offense which generated just enough pop (Montreal tied the NL record for grand slams in a season with nine) and one of the game's best pitching staffs (team ERA of 3.78). That combination kept the Expos close until mid-September, when four straight losses to the Braves all but eliminated them.

Leading the offensive charge was surprising shortstop Mark Grudzielanek (.306), who became only the second player in club history to collect 200 hits. Henry Rodriguez (.276, 36, 103) was the chief power source, although Moises Alou (.281, 21, 96) and third baseman Shane Andrews (.227, 19, 64) also provided pop. Catcher Darrin Fletcher and first baseman David Segui were also steady contributors. Jeff Fassero (15-11, 3.30, 220 Ks) had a big year, and Pedro Martinez (13-10, 3.70, 222 Ks) and rookie Ugueth Urbina (10-5, 3.71) also contributed. Mel Rojas (7-4, 3.22, 36 saves) was among the best closers in all of baseball, and Barry Manuel (4-1, 3.24) was a strong set-up man.

1996 SEASON			
Manager: Felipe Alou			
W	L	PCT	GB
88	74	.543	8

Last Five Years: 409-335; .549
Five-Year Rank: 2nd in NL; 3rd in ML

NEW YORK METS

Shea Stadium • Flushing, NY 11368

Chairman of the Board: Nelson Doubleday • **President & CEO:** Fred Wilpon •
Executive VP, Baseball Operations: Joe McIlvaine • **Assistant GM:** Steve Phillips •
VP & Consultant: Frank Cashen • **Director of Scouting:** John Barr •
Director of Minor League Operations: Jack Zduriencik

Manager: Bobby Valentine
ML record: 593-624 (.487)
with Mets: 12-19 (.387)

Coaches: Bob Apodaca, Bruce
Benedict, Randy Niemann, Cookie
Rojas, Tom Robson, Mookie Wilson

BALLPARKS

Polo Grounds 1962-63; Shea Stadium 1964-present	**Capacity:** 55,777
	1996 Attendance: 1,588,323
	Surface: natural grass
	Left field fence: 338 feet
	Center field fence: 410 feet
	Right field fence: 338 feet
	Left-center fence: 371 feet
	Right-center fence: 371 feet

METS HISTORY

The 30-year history of the Big Apple's "other" franchise has been filled with meteoric highs and laughable lows. New York debuted in 1962 and lost 120 games, but the Miracle Mets stunned the baseball world in 1969 with a storybook World Series title. New York won another pennant in 1973 but was inept until a mid-1980s renaissance. The Mets struggled through the first four years of the decade, finishing last or next to last. They became contenders in '84 under new manager Davey Johnson. Another second-place finish was in order in 1985, as they closed the gap, finishing only three games out of first. Adding clutch-hitting and a fine offensive lineup to their sterling pitching staff, the Mets won it all in '86, bringing home their second world championship trophy. Although they took another division title in 1988, they have yet to duplicate the success enjoyed in the mid-1980s.

1996 SEASON
Managers: Dallas Green; Bobby Valentine

W	L	PCT	GB
71	91	.438	25

Last Five Years: 326-417; .438
Five-Year Rank: 14th in NL; 28th in ML

1996 ANALYSIS

Believe it or not, the Mets entered the 1996 season with a pretty bright outlook—or so they thought. A young pitching staff was expected to continue blossoming, and the offense looked to have some more pop. So much for expectations. By the time '96 was over, crusty manager Dallas Green was gone, replaced by Bobby Valentine, and the Mets were in fourth place, well behind the NL East leaders. New York never came close to contention and had to endure a season in which its sister team, the Yankees, won the World Series. The Mets weren't awful, but they remained several players away from any real success.

It didn't help that promising left-hander Bill Pulsipher tore his elbow tendon in early April and didn't pitch all season, or that Carlos Baerga played only 26 games due to injury after coming over from Cleveland in a midseason deal. The offense was keyed by newcomer Lance Johnson (.333, 50 stolen bases), Bernard Gilkey (.317, 30, 117), and catcher Todd Hundley (.259, 41, 112). First baseman Butch Huskey (.278, 15, 60) had his moments, and Rey Ordonez made some spectacular plays (and plenty of errors) at shortstop. But the Mets were hardly an offensive juggernaut. Even if Pulsipher had pitched, the Mets wouldn't have had much of a rotation, other than Mark Clark (14-11, 3.43). Pete Harnisch (8-12, 4.21) was a disappointment, as was young Jason Isringhausen (6-14, 4.77). And the bullpen was worthless, with the exception of veteran John Franco (4-3, 1.83, 28 saves).

PHILADELPHIA PHILLIES

P.O. Box 7575 • Philadelphia, PA 19101

President, CEO & Managing General Partner, Bill Giles •
Executive VP, COO, & Co-General Partner: David Montgomery •
Senior VP & General Manager: Lee Thomas • **Assistant General Manager:** Ed Wade •
Director, Player Development: Del Unser • **Director, Scouting:** Mike Arbuckle

Manager: Terry Francona
ML record: 0-0 (.000)
with Phillies: 0-0 (.000)

Coaches: Galen Cisco, Chuck Cottier, Hal McRae, Brad Mills, John Vukovich

BALLPARKS

Philadelphia Base Ball Grounds 1887-1894; Baker Bowl 1895-1938; Shibe Park/Connie Mack Stadium 1938-1970; Veterans Stadium 1971-present	**Capacity:** 62,136 **1996 Attendance:** 1,801,677 **Surface:** artificial turf **Left field fence:** 330 feet **Center field fence:** 408 feet **Right field fence:** 330 feet **Left-center fence:** 371 feet **Right-center fence:** 371 feet

PHILLIES HISTORY

The Phillies waited a record 97 years as a franchise to gain their first world championship. The 1915 pennant winners lost in the Series to Boston, while the 1950 NL champion "Whiz Kids" were dropped by the Yankees. The Phils won the NL East from 1976 to '78 but didn't reach the Series again until 1980, when they finally won. They won the 1983 NL flag but took only one game against the Orioles in the Series. Only once in the 1980s did the Phils grab second place in the NL East (1986), and that year they were more than 20 games behind the first-place Mets. Winding up the decade with two successive last-place finishes, the outlook was grim. In 1992, they finished in last place, but they turned it around and won the NL pennant in 1993 with a bunch of gruff, fun-loving ballplayers, only to lose to Toronto in the World Series. The team's fortunes have plummeted since.

1996 SEASON

Manager: Jim Fregosi

W	L	PCT	GB
67	95	.414	29

Last Five Years: 357-388; .480
Five-Year Rank: 9th in NL; 21st in ML

1996 ANALYSIS

It would be easy to look at the Phillies' club-record 23 uses of the disabled list and blame their awful 1996 season on injuries, but that would not be at all accurate. The Phils were putrid in '96 because of an overwhelming lack of talent, and they wouldn't have challenged for a playoff spot even if all their players were healthy. Last year was the final, resounding thud in the Phillies' fall from '93 World Series participant to NL pauper. And for the first time in the past decade, the Philadelphia fans finally let owner Bill Giles know what they thought of his product by staying away in droves. The Phillies were easily the worst team in the NL and managed to fail on just about every level.

The team's offense featured few highlights other than catcher Benito Santiago (.264, 30, 85), Gregg Jefferies (.292), and classy outfielder Jim Eisenreich (.361), who challenged for the batting title much of the year before a late injury ruined his chances. Philadelphia hit just .256 as a team and finished the year with no power outlets other than Santiago. The pitching was even worse. Fortunately, Curt Schilling rebounded from arm trouble to post a 9-10 record (no mean feat on that team), a 3.19 ERA, and eight complete games, but injuries to Sid Fernandez, Mike Grace, and David West sabotaged the starting rotation. Ricky Bottalico's emergence as a genuine closer (34 saves) was about the only bright spot in the bullpen.

CHICAGO CUBS

1060 West Addison Street • Chicago, IL 60613-4397

President & CEO: Andrew B. MacPhail • **General Manager:** Ed Lynch •
Director, Scouting: Jim Hendry • **Director, Baseball Administration:** Scott Nelson •
Director, Minor Leagues: David Wilder

Manager: Jim Riggleman
ML record: 261-336 (.437)
with Cubs: 149-157 (.487)

Coaches: Dave Bialas, Tony Muser, Mako Oliveras, Dan Radison, Phil Regan, Billy Williams

BALLPARKS

Union Base-Ball Grounds, 23rd Street Grounds, LakeFront Park, South Side Park pre-1916; Wrigley Field 1916-present	**Capacity:** 38,765
	1996 Attendance: 2,219,110
	Surface: natural grass
	Left field fence: 355 feet
	Center field fence: 400 feet
	Right field fence: 353 feet
	Left-center fence: 368 feet
	Right-center fence: 368 feet

CUBS HISTORY

The Cubs are notorious for having baseball's longest championship drought. Born the White Stockings in 1870, the franchise dominated NL play during the late 1800s. Chicago won the 1906 pennant and featured the likes of double-play combo Joe Tinker, Johnny Evers, and Frank Chance, as well as pitcher Three Finger Brown. The franchise captured world championships in 1907 and 1908, beating the Tigers both times. Despite seven NL pennants from 1910 to '45, the Cubs couldn't win another Series. It was about this time that the Cubs began to acquire their reputation for being perpetual also-rans. There were only three seasons from 1940 through 1966 that were winning ones, and the Cubs finished dead last six times. Chicago never won another pennant, though they did take the NL East in 1984 and 1989. In the 1990s, the Cubs have been mostly mediocre.

1996 SEASON

Manager: Jim Riggleman

W	L	PCT	GB
76	86	.489	12

Last Five Years: 360-383; .483

Five-Year Rank: 8th in NL; 18th in ML

1996 ANALYSIS

Thanks to the overall mediocrity of the NL Central, the Cubs actually remained in the hunt for a division title until early September, when an eight-game losing streak torpedoed their hopes. Chicago wasn't an awful team in 1996, but Jim Riggleman's second edition wasn't exactly stout, either. The Cubs were just 33-48 on the road—their worst record away from the Friendly Confines since 1986—and had holes in their starting rotation and in the lineup, which hit only .251 as a group.

One can't fault Sammy Sosa for that light output. The outfielder had another big year, clubbing 40 homers and knocking in 100 in just 124 games. Ryne Sandberg (.244, 25, 92) made the most of the first year of his comeback by pulling within one homer of the all-time record for second basemen. Mark Grace (.331, 75 RBI) was his usual sweet-swinging self at first base, while Brian McRae (.276, 17, 66) and Luis Gonzalez (.271, 15, 79) were steady in the outfield, and Scott Servais (.265, 11, 63) provided occasional pop behind the plate. Nobody nominated Steve Trachsel (13-9, 3.03) or Jamie Navarro (15-11, 3.92) for the Cy Young Award, but each gave a good accounting every fifth day. The rest of the rotation was the problem. Neither Frank Castillo (7-16, 5.28) nor Jim Bullinger (6-10, 6.54) came close to their solid 1995 performances. The bullpen was dependable. Turk Wendell (4-5, 2.84, 18 saves) was a reliable closer, while Larry Casian (1-1, 1.88) led the set-up contingent.

CINCINNATI REDS

100 Riverfront Stadium • Cincinnati, OH 45202

President & CEO: Marge Schott • **General Manager:** James G. Bowden •
Director of Scouting: Julian Mock • **Director of Player Development:** Sheldon Bender

Manager: Ray Knight
ML record: 81-81 (.500)
with Reds: 81-81 (.500)

Coaches: Ken Griffey, Don Gullett,
Tom Hume, Ron Oester, Denis
Menke, Joel Youngblood

BALLPARKS

Lincoln Park Grounds 1876;	**Capacity:** 52,952
Avenue Grounds 1876-1879;	**1996 Attendance:** 1,861,428
Bank Street Grounds 1880;	**Surface:** artificial turf
League Park 1890-1901;	**Left field fence:** 330 feet
Palace of the Fans 1902-1911;	**Center field fence:** 404 feet
Crosley Field 1912-1970; River-	**Right field fence:** 330 feet
front Stadium 1970-present	**Left-center fence:** 375 feet
	Right-center fence: 375 feet

REDS HISTORY

Baseball's first professional team has enjoyed recent history much more than its earlier decades. The Reds won the tainted 1919 World Series but didn't top the baseball world again until 1939. A 1961 pennant was followed by the emergence of the "Big Red Machine." During the 1970s, this powerhouse organization finished in first place six times, won four National League pennants, and won the 1975 and '76 World Series, with stars such as Pete Rose, Johnny Bench, and Joe Morgan. But the 1980s were not as kind to the franchise. To add to Cincy's woes, manager Pete Rose was shrouded in controversy over alleged gambling. In 1990, the Reds put the scandal behind and bolted all the way to first. The Reds then swept the favored Oakland A's in the Series and brought another world championship crown to Cincinnati. The Reds finished first in the NL Central in 1994 and 1995.

1996 SEASON
Manager: Ray Knight

W	L	PCT	GB
81	81	.500	7

Last Five Years: 395-349; .530
Five-Year Rank: 3rd in NL; 8th in ML

1996 ANALYSIS

With all the nonsense about Marge Schott and her big mouth, the Reds' fall from first place was almost secondary. After two seasons on top, Cincinnati slid to third place in the Central Division, and the irony was delicious. Schott, who had been publicly at odds with former manager Davey Johnson and had favored Ray Knight as the skipper, saw the exiled Johnson lead Baltimore into the ALCS while she and Knight sat at home and watched. When the media wasn't chronicling Schott's slide from power, it concentrated on the Reds, who faded from contention late in the season after looking pretty strong early on.

Injuries certainly played a role. Pete Schourek, the 1995 Cy Young Award runner-up, pitched only 67⅓ innings and stumbled to a 4-5 record, thanks to elbow problems. Jose Rijo, whom the Reds had hoped would come back and contribute some quality innings, didn't pitch at all. That left John Smiley (13-14, 3.64), Dave Burba (11-13, 3.83) and Mike Morgan (6-11, 4.63) as three solid, but not spectacular, starters. There was nothing wrong with Jeff Brantley, who led the majors with 44 saves. The Reds offense was productive, thanks mostly to the usual suspects. Shortstop Barry Larkin (.298, 33, 89) had another big year, as did Hal Morris (.313, 16, 80). Eric Davis returned to the site of his greatest accomplishments and fashioned an excellent (.287, 26, 83) season, while young Willie Greene flashed signs of big-time power with 19 home runs.

HOUSTON ASTROS

The Astrodome • P.O. Box 288 • Houston, TX 77001-9500

Chairman & CEO: Drayton McLane, Jr. • **President:** Tal Smith •
General Manager: Gerry Hunsicker • **Director of Player Development & Scouting:** Dan O'Brien •
Director of Baseball Administration: Barry Waters

Manager: Larry Dierker
ML record: 0-0 (.000)
with Astros: 0-0 (.000)

Coaches: Alan Ashby, Jose Cruz,
Mike Cubbage, Tom McGraw, Vern
Ruhle, Bill Virdon

BALLPARKS

Colt Stadium 1962-1964; The Astrodome 1965-present	**Capacity:** 54,370
	1996 Attendance: 1,975,888
	Surface: artificial turf
	Stationary Dome
	Left field fence: 325 feet
	Center field fence: 400 feet
	Right field fence: 325 feet
	Left-center fence: 375 feet
	Right-center fence: 375 feet

ASTROS HISTORY

Baseball purists may curse the arrival of baseball in Texas. After three years outdoors as the Colt .45s, the franchise became the first to play indoors. In an attempt to beat the heat, the Astrodome was built in 1965. However, growing real grass indoors presented a problem. AstroTurf arrived the next year. Houston's play, however, hasn't been nearly so innovative. Although they contended for most of the 1970s, the Astros did not win their first division title until 1980. In strike-split '81, Houston won the second half of the season, but lost to the Dodgers in postseason play. The Astros didn't see another division title until 1986, and failed in the attempt for a pennant when the Mets prevailed four games to two. After finishing dead last in 1991, the Astros depended on such young players as Jeff Bagwell to rebound, contending during much of the 1990s.

1996 SEASON
Manager: Terry Collins

W	L	PCT	GB
82	80	.506	6

Last Five Years: 390-355; .523
Five-Year Rank: 4th in NL; 9th in ML

1996 ANALYSIS

After entering the season with high hopes, Houston completed 1996 with a disheartening September fade that removed it from playoff contention and failed to divert interest from the same old questions about the team's future. It also cost intense manager Terry Collins his job. Despite the fourth-best attendance figure in club history, the Astros continued to threaten a move to Virginia if they didn't get a new stadium. Houston certainly wasn't a bad team in '96, but it lacked the pitching pop to win consistently in big games. The offense couldn't be faulted. Houston set a club record by scoring 752 runs, thanks mainly to several standouts at the plate.

As usual, Jeff Bagwell (.315, 31, 120) led the way and actually played a full season—his first in three years. Second baseman Craig Biggio (.288, 15, 75) continued his steady play with the bat and glove, while outfielder Derek Bell's average was down a little (.263), but his RBI production was way up (113). Third baseman Sean Berry (.281, 17, 95) had one of the best seasons of his career. Even though four starters won in double digits, only two—Shane Reynolds and Darryl Kile—were completely dependable. Reynolds (16-10, 3.65, 204 Ks) had a breakthrough year, while Kile (12-11, 4.19, 219) rebounded nicely from a dismal '95 campaign. Mike Hampton (10-10, 3.59) had the lowest ERA of the starting contingent, but his shoulder problems were worrisome. The bullpen was an even greater area of concern, with Todd Jones's club-leading 17 saves hardly enough.

PITTSBURGH PIRATES

P.O. Box 7000 • Pittsburgh, PA 15212

CEO: Kevin McClatchy • **President:** Mark Sauer • **Senior VP & GM:** Cam Bonifay •
Director of Major League Baseball Administration: John Sirignano •
Director of Scouting: Paul Tinnell

Manager: Gene Lamont
ML record: 258-210 (.551)
with Pirates: 0-0 (.000)

Coaches: Joe Jones, Jack Lind,
Lloyd McLendon, Rick Renick, Pete
Vuckovich, Spin Williams

BALLPARKS	
Exposition Park 1891-1909; Forbes Field 1909-1970; Three Rivers Stadium 1970-present	**Capacity:** 47,972
	1996 Attendance: 1,326,640
	Surface: artificial turf
	Left field fence: 335 feet
	Center field fence: 400 feet
	Right field fence: 335 feet
	Left-center fence: 375 feet
	Right-center fence: 375 feet

PIRATES HISTORY

Pittsburgh won five pennants from 1900 through '30 and two World Series (1909 and '25). After sagging throughout the 1940s and 1950s, the Bucs stunned the Yankees in the 1960 fall classic. The Pirates also captured the 1971 and 1979 world championships. The 1970s were a joyous time to be a Pirate fan. The Bucs finished first or second in the NL East nine out of ten years. As the 1980s unfolded, that joy turned to pain. Instead of being a perennial contender, the highest level of success the Pirates attained was two trips to second in the division along with three consecutive years (1984 through '86) in dead last. The early 1990s were good, however. From 1990 through 1992, the Pirates won the division title every year, though they didn't win the NL pennant. By 1993, they experienced a talent drain, losing Barry Bonds, Bobby Bonilla, and others because of their high salary demands.

1996 ANALYSIS

Although Pittsburgh fans have become somewhat used to watching a losing team stumble around Three Rivers Stadium, the 1996 season was poignant, since long-time manager Jim Leyland, easily one of the classiest men in baseball—not to mention one of the finest skippers—announced his resignation late in the year. Pirates faithful paid tribute to him during the emotional home finale, while the front office went about its now-customary efforts to find money for a new stadium and discover ways to keep costs down. Even though Pittsburgh duplicated 1995 by finishing last in the NL Central with the same record as the year before, one can't blame Leyland. The team had few stars, precious little starting pitching, and a dearth of experience. Considering all that, it's amazing the Bucs approached 75 wins.

The top offensive guns were outfielder Al Martin (.300, 18, 72, 38 stolen bases), who continued to blossom, third baseman Jeff King (.271, 30, 111), and outfielder Orlando Merced (.287, 17, 80). The rest of the lineup was shaky. Mark Johnson (.274, 13, 47) showed signs of promise at first base, as did catcher Jason Kendall (.300), while Jay Bell (.250, 13, 71) was solid at short. As for the pitching, it's a wonder Leyland was able to remember the names of all 23 guys who took the mound for Pittsburgh. Jon Lieber (9-5, 3.99) bounced between the bullpen and the starting rotation, leading the Bucs in wins, but no other starter won more than five games.

1996 SEASON
Manager: Jim Leyland

W	L	PCT	GB
73	89	.451	15

Last Five Years: 355-389; .477
Five-Year Rank: 11th in NL; 23rd in ML

St. Louis Cardinals

250 Stadium Plaza • St. Louis, MO 63102

Chairman of the Board: August A. Busch, III • **Vice Chairman:** Fred Kuhlmann •
President/CEO: Mark Lamping • **Vice President, GM:** Walt Jocketty •
Director, Player Development: Mike Jorgensen • **Director, Scouting:** Marty Maier

Manager: Tony LaRussa
ML record: 1428-1257 (.532)
with Cardinals: 88-74 (.543)

Coaches: Mark DeJohn, Dave Duncan, Ron Hassey, George Hendrick, Dave McKay, Tommie Reynolds

BALLPARKS

Robison Field 1893-1920;	**Capacity:** 57,673
Sportsman's Park 1920-1966;	**1996 Attendance:** 2,659,239
Busch Stadium 1966-present	**Surface:** natural grass
	Left field fence: 330 feet
	Center field fence: 402 feet
	Right field fence: 330 feet
	Left-center fence: 375 feet
	Right-center fence: 375 feet

CARDINALS HISTORY

Born the Browns in 1884, the St. Louis Cardinals won six world championships from 1926 through '46, thanks mostly to Branch Rickey's fine farm system. St. Louis was back on top in 1964 and '67. The 1970s were thin on excitement for Cardinal fans, but then the tide turned. In strike-split '81, the Cards had the best winning percentage overall, but did not get to progress into postseason play due to the method of determining regular-season winners. They continued on in earnest in '82, winning the division, the pennant, and then the World Series after emerging victorious over Milwaukee. The St. Louis team migrated to the lower half of the standings for the next few years, but got right back in the thick of things in '85. They won pennants in 1985 and again in 1987. The 1990s featured a decline in performance until the '96 season, when new manager Tony LaRussa brought his veteran crew to the Mound City. The Cards won the NL Central division title under his savvy leadership.

1996 ANALYSIS

Try to keep in mind that the Cardinals played 170 games before their colossal collapse against Atlanta in the NLCS. During that time, St. Louis won the NL Central Division and swept San Diego in the first round of the playoffs. That's what should be remembered from the 1996 season, not just how the Cards, up 3-1 on the Braves and closing in on a World Series berth, suffered as ugly a three-game beating as can be imagined as Atlanta outscored St. Louis 32-1 in the final three contests to take the pennant. But St. Louis still had a good year. New manager Tony LaRussa immediately put to rest speculation about whether a career AL manager could hack it in the senior circuit.

The Cards' success was largely due to pitching. St. Louis had an aggregate 3.97 ERA, among the best in baseball. Andy Benes (18-10, 3.83, 160 Ks), Todd Stottlemyre (14-11, 3.87, 194) and rookie Alan Benes (13-10, 4.90) anchored the rotation, while ageless Dennis Eckersley (30 saves) was again a highly effective closer. The Cards weren't packed with sluggers on offense (they hit only 142 long balls all season), but they did have some threats. Brian Jordan (.310, 17, 104), John Mabry (.297, 13, 74), Ray Lankford (.275, 21, 86), Gary Gaetti (.274, 23, 80), and Ron Gant (.246, 30, 82) formed a sturdy heart of the order, while veterans Willie McGee (.307) and Ozzie Smith (.282), who retired after the season, were their usual steady selves.

1996 SEASON
Manager: Tony LaRussa

W	L	PCT	GB
88	74	.543	—

Last Five Years: 373-370; .501
Five-Year Rank: 5th in NL; 13th in ML

COLORADO ROCKIES

2001 Blake St. • Denver, CO 80205

Chairman, President & CEO: Jerry McMorris • **Executive VP/GM:** Bob Gebhard •
VP, Player Personnel: Dick Balderson • **Assistant General Manager:** Tony Siegle •
Director, Scouting: Pat Daugherty

Manager: Don Baylor
ML record: 280-305 (.479)
with Rockies: 280-305 (.479)

Coaches: Frank Funk, Gene Glynn, Jackie Moore, Paul Zuvella

BALLPARKS

Mile High Stadium 1993-1994;
Coors Field 1995-present

Capacity: 50,200
1996 Attendance: 3,891,014
Surface: natural grass
Left field fence: 347 feet
Center field fence: 415 feet
Right field fence: 350 feet
Left-center fence: 390 feet
Right-center fence: 375 feet

ROCKIES HISTORY

It took the Colorado Rockies only three years to taste postseason action; free agency and four million fans can make a team grow up in a hurry. In 1990, the NL chose the Rockies (along with the Marlins) as the latest franchises. Before beginning play in 1993, the Rockies chose Bob Gebhard as their GM. He in turn chose former slugger and batting coach Don Baylor as the team's first manager. First baseman Andres Galarraga in 1993 became the first player in expansion history to win a batting title by hitting .370. While the owners figured baseball would go over big, they had no idea how hungry area fans were. A record 4,483,270 patrons watched the Rockies in their initial season. The Rockies improved substantially in 1994, and by 1995 they finished just one game behind the Dodgers in the race for the NL West crown and became the league's first wild-card entry.

1996 ANALYSIS

One year after slugging their way into the playoffs, the Rockies faded from contention in September and fell into third place in the West, thanks to some truly miserable pitching and a road record that tied Florida's for the worst in the NL. Colorado was unbeatable when its bats were going, but when the altitude dropped and the Rockies had to play baseball, instead of home run derby, trouble started. The Rocks were a formidable 55-26 at Coors Field but a simpering 28-53 away from their cozy park. And the Colorado pitchers weren't very good anywhere, as the team's aggregate 5.59 ERA proved. As usual, however, there was no shortage of offense.

Ellis Burks (.344, 40, 128), Dante Bichette (.313, 31, 141), Vinny Castilla (.304, 40, 113), and Andres Galarraga (.304, 47, 150) helped the Rockies become only the second team in major-league history to have three players with 40 or more dingers. Eric Young (.324) didn't hit many homers, but he stole 53 bases, while Walt Weiss (.282) balanced admirable offense with some awful fielding (30 errors) at shortstop. Despite his 5.28 ERA, Kevin Ritz led the pitching staff with a 17-11 record. After that, it was a crapshoot. Mark Thompson (9-11, 5.30), Armando Reynoso (8-9, 4.26), and Marvin Freeman (7-9, 6.04) won only when their teammates scored lots of runs. Bruce Ruffin continued to be a steady closer (24 saves), while Steve Reed (4-3, 3.96) and Darren Holmes (5-4, 3.97) weren't awful in long relief.

1996 SEASON
Manager: Don Baylor

W	L	PCT	GB
83	79	.512	8

Last Four Years: 280-305; .479
Four-Year Rank: 10th in NL; 22nd in ML

LOS ANGELES DODGERS

1000 Elysian Park Avenue • Los Angeles, CA 90012

President: Peter O'Malley • **Executive Vice President:** Fred Claire •
Vice President, Minor League Operations: Charlie Blaney • **Director, Scouting:** Terry Reynolds

Manager: Bill Russell
ML record: 49-37 (.570)
with Dodgers: 49-37 (.570)

Coaches: Joe Amalfitano, Mark Cresse, Reggie Smith, Dave Wallace

BALLPARKS

Brooklyn: Union Grounds 1976; Washington Park 1891-1897; Ebbets Field 1913-1957
Los Angeles: Memorial Coliseum 1958-1961; Dodger Stadium 1962-present

Capacity: 56,000
1996 Attendance: 3,188,454
Surface: natural grass
Left field fence: 330 feet
Center field fence: 395 feet
Right field fence: 330 feet
Left-center fence: 385 feet
Right-center fence: 385 feet

DODGERS HISTORY

The National League's most successful franchise got its start in Brooklyn in 1884, named after the borough's Trolley Dodgers. Flatbush fans suffered until "next year" finally brought a world championship in 1955. They cried two years later when Walter O'Malley moved the team to Los Angeles, where the Dodgers won world championships in 1959, 1963, 1965, 1977, and 1988. In 1989, the team from tinseltown finished fourth in their division. They took some steps in the right direction during 1990, regaining second place in the division but finishing five games behind the eventual world champion Reds that season. Spirits were high in '91, but the mighty Dodgers fell apart down the stretch. L.A. finished the '91 season only one game behind the Braves. After coming so close, the '92 season was an extra-painful reality, though the Dodgers rebounded in 1993. The Dodgers finished first in the NL West in both 1994 and 1995.

1996 SEASON

Managers: Tommy Lasorda; Bill Russell

W	L	PCT	GB
90	72	.556	1

Last Five Years: 370-374; .497
Five-Year Rank: 6th in NL; 14th in ML

1996 ANALYSIS

It was a year of change but also more of the same for the Dodgers in 1996, with long-time manager and team symbol Tommy Lasorda retiring because of his failing health and L.A. again losing a first-round playoff series with nary a whimper. Lasorda, who had hoped to continue managing the club after heart surgery, was unable to continue, and longtime coach and onetime Dodger shortstop Bill Russell took over. Although he led L.A. to an impressive 49-37 record during his halfseason of work, Russell couldn't nail down the NL West title (losing to San Diego on the season's last day). He then managed the Dodgers to a quiet, three-game loss to Atlanta in the playoffs.

As usual, L.A. won with great pitching and some big bats. The starting rotation was excellent, with Hideo Nomo (16-11, 3.19, 234 Ks), Ismael Valdes (15-7, 3.32), and Ramon Martinez (15-6, 3.42) leading the way and Pedro Astacio (9-8, 3.44) not far behind. And if teams couldn't get to those guys, they had little hope after that, thanks to a bullpen led by Todd Worrell (44 saves), Mark Guthrie (2-3, 2.22), and Scott Radinsky (5-1, 2.41). Catcher Mike Piazza (.336, 36, 105) had another big year, while Raul Mondesi (.297, 24, 88), Eric Karros (.260, 34, 111), and NL Rookie of the Year Todd Hollandsworth (.291, 12, 59) were solid lineup components as well. The Dodgers could have used a little more speed, however. Second baseman Delino DeShields (48 steals) was about the only real threat on the basepaths.

SAN DIEGO PADRES

P.O. Box 2000 • San Diego, CA 92112-2000

Chairman: John Moores • **President & CEO:** Larry Lucchino •
Executive Vice President: Bill Adams • **VP/Baseball Operations & GM:** Kevin Towers •
Assistant GM: Fred Uhlman, Jr. • **Director, Baseball Operations:** Eddie Epstein

Manager: Bruce Bochy
ML record: 161-145 (.526)
with Padres: 161-145 (.526)

Coaches: Tim Flannery, Grady
Little, Davey Lopes, Rob Picciolo,
Merv Rettenmund, Dan Warthen

BALLPARK	
Jack Murphy Stadium 1969-present	**Capacity:** 46,510
	1996 Attendance: 2,187,886
	Surface: natural grass
	Left field fence: 327 feet
	Center field fence: 405 feet
	Right field fence: 327 feet
	Left-center fence: 370 feet
	Right-center fence: 370 feet

PADRES HISTORY

A product of the 1969 expansion with Montreal, the Padres struggled below .500 for their first 15 seasons. Their first winning year—1984—also brought home a pennant. Taking three out of five games in the NLCS, the Padres put away the Cubs and faced the formidable force that was the Tigers. Unfortunately for San Diego fans, the dream season ended in short order with the Tigers snuffing out any championship hopes the Padres had in only five games. The rest of the 1980s featured middle-division finishes. One little glimmer came in 1989, when the Padres finished second in their division, just three games behind the eventual pennant-winning Giants. Injuries hit the San Diego team hard in 1990, and it was evidenced in their next-to-last-place finish. The Pads rebounded somewhat in 1991 and '92, but in 1993 fell to the bottom as the team unloaded its high-priced veterans. The Padres enjoyed a rebirth in '96 as they claimed the NL West title.

1996 ANALYSIS

All those people who lit into the Padres for their 1993 fire sale that resulted in a seventh-place finish and considerable misery for the San Diego faithful were made to offer copious apologies during the 1996 season. The Padres completed a stunning turnaround from that doormat team of '93, winning the NL West title in dramatic fashion—by sweeping the Dodgers in Chavez Ravine on the last weekend of the season. Even though the Padres went down rather meekly to St. Louis in the first round of the playoffs, they had a truly remarkable year and appear well armed for the future.

The clear star of the team—and the NL—was MVP third baseman Ken Caminiti (.326, 40, 130), whose tremendous hustle and clutch production were the cornerstones of the team. Of course, Tony Gwynn (.353) wasn't too far behind him, despite missing nearly 50 games. He won his seventh batting title, which tied him for third on the all-time list. Outfielder Steve Finley (.298, 30, 95) joined Caminiti in the power department, while Wally Joyner (.277) was another tough out in the top half of the Padres lineup. San Diego's starting rotation was one of the deepest and finest in all of baseball, led by Joey Hamilton (15-9, 4.17), who enjoyed a breakout year. Ageless Fernando Valenzuela (13-8, 3.62), Bob Tewksbury (10-10), Andy Ashby (9-5, 3.23), and Scott Sanders (9-5, 3.38) rounded out a group with no visible weak spot. As usual, closer Trevor Hoffman (9-5, 2.25, 42 saves) slammed the door with regularity.

1996 SEASON
Manager: Bruce Bochy

W	L	PCT	GB
91	71	.562	—

Last Five Years: 351-396; .471
Five-Year Rank: 12th in NL; 24th in ML

SAN FRANCISCO GIANTS

3Com Park • San Francisco, CA 94124

Managing General Partner: Peter A. Magowan • **Senior General Partner:** Harmon E. Burns •
Executive Vice President: Laurence M. Baer • **Senior VP & GM:** Robert E. Quinn •
General Manager: Brian Sabean • **Director of Player Development:** Jack Hiatt •
Coordinator of Scouting: Bob Hartsfield

Manager: Dusty Baker
ML record: 293-290 (.503)
with Giants: 293-290 (.503)

Coaches: Carlos Alphonso, Gene
Clines, Sonny Jackson, Ron
Perranoski, Dick Pole

BALLPARKS

New York: Polo Grounds 1883-1888, 1891-1957; St. George Cricket Grounds 1889-1890 **San Francisco:** Seals Stadium 1958-1959; 3Com Park 1960-present

Capacity: 63,000
1996 Attendance: 1,413,687
Surface: natural grass
Left field fence: 335 feet
Center field fence: 400 feet
Right field fence: 328 feet
Left-center fence: 365 feet
Right-center fence: 365 feet

GIANTS HISTORY

Few dispute the economic reasons for moving this proud franchise west from New York, but many believe the Giants were never the same after coming to San Francisco. The Giants dominated the NL before 1900, and they won 15 pennants and five world championships from 1904 to '54. Led by Willie Mays, Willie McCovey, and Juan Marichal, the Giants enjoyed 14 consecutive winning seasons after their 1958 move, but won only two more pennants—1962 and 1989. In the latter World Series, they lost to the world-shaking Athletics. The Giants also won their division in 1987, but lost the pennant to the Cardinals. When the 1990s began, San Francisco fans had little to cheer about. After almost moving out of the Bay Area, the Giants in 1993 returned to lose by one game against the Braves in one of the greatest pennant battles of all time.

1996 ANALYSIS

It was an ugly year in San Francisco, beginning with the team's decision to sell out to corporate interests and change the name of Candlestick Park—one of the truly great ballpark monikers—to 3Com Park. It helped take away any remaining identity the Giants had. San Francisco made an early break for the NL West basement and settled in there, hardly making a ripple on the playoff race. What looked like a budding contender as recently as two years ago resembled a disaster area in '96.

Some things, however, remained the same. For instance, Barry Bonds (.308, 42, 129, 40 stolen bases) became only the second player in big-league history to hit 40 homers and steal 40 bases. Matt Williams (.302, 22, 85) played in only 105 games due to injury, an all-too common occurrence in recent years. The rest of the offense was extremely sporadic. Some highlights included Glenallen Hill (.280, 19, 67), who posted great numbers despite missing 61 games with a broken wrist. Rookie Marvin Benard (25 steals) added a little speed in the outfield, and Rick Wilkins was steady behind the plate. Only one pitcher reached double digits in wins—journeyman Mark Gardner (12-7, 4.42 ERA), who hardly qualified as an ace. Allen Watson (8-12, 4.61), rookie Osvaldo Fernandez (7-13, 4.61), and William VanLandingham (9-14, 5.40) had their moments but were largely disappointing. Rod Beck saved 35 games, and Jim Poole (2-1, 2.66) was solid in relief, too.

1996 SEASON
Manager: Dusty Baker

W	L	PCT	GB
68	94	.420	23

Last Five Years: 365-380; .490
Five-Year Rank: 7th in NL; 16th in ML

HALL OF FAME

Profiles of the players, managers, umpires, and executives who have been inducted into the National Baseball Hall of Fame and Museum in Cooperstown, New York, comprise this section. The profiles are presented in alphabetical order. At the end of each profile is a date in parentheses; this is the year the member was enshrined into the Hall.

In preparation for baseball's centennial in 1939, a National Baseball Museum was proposed, first as a matter of civic pride, and later as a memorial for the greatest of those who have ever played the game.

While the rules governing election to the Hall of Fame have varied in specifics over the years, in general the criteria have remained the same. One must be named on 75 percent of ballots cast by members of the Baseball Writers' Association of America. To be eligible, players must have played for at least ten years. The players have to be retired for at least five years but not more than 20 years. A player is eligible for 15 years in the BBWAA vote.

If the player is not named on 75 percent of the ballots in 15 years, his name becomes eligible for consideration by the Committee on Baseball Veterans. This committee also considers managers, umpires, and executives for induction to Cooperstown. The same 75 percent rule applies. Anyone on baseball's permanently ineligible list is excluded from consideration.

The Committee on the Negro Leagues was added to the selection process in 1971. This board considered players who had ten years of service in the pre-1946 Negro Leagues, and also those who made the major leagues. The Negro League board dissolved into the Veterans' Committee in 1977.

HANK AARON

Outfielder (1954-1976) Aaron is baseball's all-time leader in home runs with 755 and in RBI with 2,297. During a 23-year career with the Braves and the Brewers, "Hammerin' Hank" stood out as one of the game's most complete and consistent performers. He was the NL MVP in 1957 when he hit .322 with 44 home runs and 132 RBI. Aaron hit 40 home runs or more eight times and totaled over 100 RBI 11 times. (1982)

GROVER ALEXANDER

Pitcher (1911-1930) Despite his battles with alcohol and epilepsy, Alexander's 373 wins are tied for the NL record. With Philadelphia in 1916, he recorded a major-league-record 16 shutouts on his way to a 33-12 record. "Pete" led the senior loop in wins six times, ERA five times, and shutouts seven times. His 90 shutouts are second on the all-time list. (1938)

WALTER ALSTON

Manager (1954-1976) In 23 years as manager of the Dodgers, all under one-year contracts, Alston led the club to seven pennants and four world championships. Under his patient leadership, the Dodgers made pitching and defense a winning combination. His career record is 2,040-1,613—a .558 winning percentage. (1983)

CAP ANSON

First baseman (1871-1897); manager (1879-1898) A baseball pioneer, as player, manager, and part-owner of NL Chicago, "Pop" Anson was the game's most influential figure in the 19th century. He hit .300 or better in 20 consecutive seasons and won five pennants. However, in 1887, his racist views led him to intimidate organized baseball into banning blacks. (1939)

LUIS APARICIO
Shortstop (1956-1973) No man played more games at shortstop—2,581—than Aparicio. The swift, sure-handed infielder played a vital role in championship seasons for the White Sox in 1959 and the Orioles in 1966. The winner of nine Gold Gloves, Aparicio led the AL in stolen bases nine times en route to 506 career thefts. (1984)

RICHIE ASHBURN
Outfielder (1948-1962) A classic leadoff hitter for the Phillies, Ashburn led the NL in batting twice (.338 in 1955 and .350 in 1958), runs three times, and walks four times. He batted .308 for his career and was even more impressive in center field, where he recorded 6,089 putouts (fifth all time). Ashburn finished his career with the Cubs and Mets. (1995)

LUKE APPLING
Shortstop (1930-1943; 1945-1950) Known better for his bat than his glove, Appling nonetheless played shortstop for the White Sox for 20 seasons. "Old Aches and Pains" led the AL in batting twice, finishing with a .310 career average, 1,116 RBI, and 1,319 runs scored. In 1936, he hit .388 with 128 RBI, despite hitting only six home runs. (1964)

EARL AVERILL
Outfielder (1929-1941) The only outfielder selected to the first six All-Star Games, Averill didn't turn pro until age 23, and didn't make the major leagues, with Cleveland, until age 26. In his first ten seasons he was one of the game's best sluggers. In a 1933 doubleheader, he hit four home runs, three consecutively. Averill had more

than 90 RBI in nine seasons. A congenital back condition cut his career short. (1975)

FRANK BAKER
Third baseman (1908-1922) Despite never hitting more than 12 home runs in a season, Baker was a slugger supreme during baseball's dead-ball era. He led the AL in home runs from 1911 to 1914. Two 1911 World Series home runs earned him his "Home Run" nickname. In six World Series with the A's and Yanks, he hit .363. (1955)

DAVE BANCROFT
Shortstop (1915-1930) One of the best fielding shortstops of all time, Bancroft set a major-league record in 1922 when he handled 984 chances. A heady ballplayer, "Beauty" was named captain of the Giants in 1920 and led them to three straight pennants. He batted over .300 five times. (1971)

ERNIE BANKS
Shortstop; first baseman (1953-1971) Banks combined unbridled enthusiasm with remarkable talent to become one of the most popular players of his era. As a shortstop he won back-to-back NL MVP Awards in 1958 and 1959 and a Gold Glove in 1960, before switching to first base. Despite his 512 career home runs, the Cubs did not win a pennant during his tenure. "Mr. Cub" had 2,583 lifetime hits and 1,636 RBI. (1977)

AL BARLICK
Umpire (1940-1971) A respected arbiter, Barlick worked in Jackie Robinson's first game. Barlick umpired in seven All-Star contests and in seven World Series. (1989)

ED BARROW
Executive In 1918, BoSox manager Barrow transferred Babe Ruth from the mound to the outfield. Barrow followed Ruth to the Yankees. "Cousin Ed" was in charge of the Bronx Bombers from 1920 to 1947. (1953)

JAKE BECKLEY

First baseman (1888-1907) Beckley played more games at first base than anyone else. He had 2,930 hits, 1,600 runs, and 1,575 RBI. His handlebar mustache made him a fan favorite. "St. Jacob's" 243 career triples are fourth all time. (1971)

COOL PAPA BELL

Outfielder (1922-1946) Perhaps the fastest man to ever play the game, Bell starred as an outfielder in the Negro Leagues for more than two decades. Satchel Paige claimed Bell was so fast he could switch off the light and leap into bed before the room got dark. Often credited with scoring from second on a sacrifice fly, Bell hit .392 against organized major-league competition. (1974)

JOHNNY BENCH

Catcher (1967-1983) Upon his arrival in the big leagues in 1967, Bench was heralded as baseball's best defensive catcher. After his NL MVP year in 1970 at age 22, with 45 home runs and 148 RBI, he was baseball's best catcher, period. He won his second MVP in 1972. With Bench behind the plate, the Reds won four pennants and two World Series. In the 1976 World Series, he hit .533. He had 389 homers and 1,376 RBI. (1989)

CHIEF BENDER

Pitcher (1903-1917; 1925) An alumnus of the Carlisle Indian School, the half-Chippewa Bender overcame bigotry to become one of the Philadelphia A's most valued members. He had a career 212-127 record, and he won six World Series games. He led the AL in winning percentage three times, including a 17-3 mark in 1914. (1953)

YOGI BERRA

Catcher (1946-1965) If championships are the best measure of success, then Berra stands second to no one. His 14 World Series appearances, 75 Series games played, and 71 Series hits are all records. A three-time MVP, the Yankee hit 20 homers in ten consecutive seasons. Known as well for his way with words, Berra will be remembered for the oft-quoted "It's never over till it's over." He had 1,430 lifetime RBI to go with his 358 home runs. (1972)

JIM BOTTOMLEY

First baseman (1922-1937) One of the first products of the famous Cardinals farm system, Bottomley was named NL MVP in 1928 for hitting .325 with 31 homers and driving in 136 runs. On September 16, 1924, "Sunny Jim" knocked in 12 runs with six hits against Brooklyn. He batted .310 lifetime with 1,422 RBI. (1974)

LOU BOUDREAU

Shortstop (1938-1952); manager (1942-1950; 1952-1957; 1960) Boudreau was one of the game's great shortstops. He was named Cleveland's player-manager at age 24. In 1948, he led the club to the AL pennant, hitting .355, scoring 116 runs and driving in 106, and capturing the AL MVP Award. He led AL shortstops in fielding eight times. As a manager, he won 1,162 games. (1970)

ROGER BRESNAHAN

Catcher (1897; 1900-1915) The first catcher elected to the Hall of Fame, Bresnahan is most famous for pioneering the use of shin guards and batting helmets. Bresnahan hit .350 and stole 34 bases with the Giants in 1903. (1945)

LOU BROCK

Outfielder (1961-1979) Brock's career totals of 938 stolen bases and 3,023 hits, coupled with a .293 batting average, gained him admittance to the Hall. In 1974, at age 35, he stole 118 bases. He excelled in three World Series for the Cardinals, hitting .391 and scoring 16 runs. Brock reached 200 hits four times. (1985)

DAN BROUTHERS

First baseman (1879-1896; 1904) Baseball's premier 19th-century slugger, Brouthers toiled for 11 different clubs, in three major leagues, for 19 seasons. He was the first man to win back-to-back batting titles, in 1882 and 1883. He batted over .300 in 16 consecutive seasons, reaching .374 in 1883. (1945)

THREE FINGER BROWN

Pitcher (1903-1916) A farm accident in a corn grinder mutilated Brown's right hand, severing most of his index finger, mangling his middle finger, and paralyzing his little finger. The injuries, however, gave his pitches a natural sink and curve. Pitching with the Cubs, between 1904 and 1910 Brown's highest ERA was 1.86, helping Chicago to four pennants. He had a career 239-129 record, with a 2.06 ERA and 55 shutouts. (1948)

MORGAN BULKELEY

NL President (1876) In 1876, Bulkeley was named the first president of the new National League. He served one year without distinction and resigned. (1937)

JIM BUNNING

Pitcher (1955-1971) A hard-working sidearmer, Bunning (224-184, 3.27 ERA) pitched primarily for the Tigers and Phillies. The eight-time All-Star won 100 games in both the American and National Leagues—the first player since Cy Young to do so. "The Lizard" pitched one of baseball's 14 perfect games. Bunning ranked second in career strikeouts when he retired in 1971. (1996)

JESSE BURKETT

Outfielder (1890-1905) In the 1890s, the left-handed-hitting Burkett hit over .400 two times. A fine baserunner and bunter, the third-strike foul-bunt rule was created due to Burkett's prowess at the art. "Crab" won three batting titles. He scored 1,720 runs, drew 1,029 walks, and notched 2,850 base hits in his 16-year career. (1946)

ROY CAMPANELLA

Catcher (1948-1957) Campanella, one of the great athletes of his time, had a .312 average, 41 homers, 103 runs scored, and 142 RBI in 1953—amazing marks for a backstop. In 1951, 1953, and 1955, the Dodger catcher was named the National League's MVP. He led his team to five pennants in ten years. A 1958 automobile accident left Campanella paralyzed, and his struggle to remain active served as an inspiration to baseball fans everywhere. (1969)

ROD CAREW

First baseman; second baseman (1967-1985) An infielder with Minnesota and California, Carew was one of baseball's premier singles hitters, notching 3,053 hits and a lifetime .328 batting average. He topped .300 in 15 consecutive seasons on his way to seven batting titles, a mark surpassed only by Ty Cobb's ten. Carew's 1977 Most Valuble Player year consisted of a .388 batting average, 239 hits, 128 runs scored, and 100 runs batted in. (1991)

MAX CAREY

Outfielder (1910-1929) A tremendous defensive center fielder, primarily with Pittsburgh, Carey swiped 738 bases. In 1925, despite two broken ribs, "Scoops" batted .458 in the World Series as the Pirates defeated Washington. In game seven, his four hits and three runs scored beat the great Walter Johnson. Carey scored 1,545 runs and had 2,665 base hits in his 20-year career. (1961)

STEVE CARLTON

Pitcher (1965-1988) "Lefty" set a major-league record with four Cy Young Awards (1972, '77, '80, and '82), won 329 games with a career 3.22 ERA, and finished second to Nolan Ryan on the all-time strikeout list with 4,136. In 1972, Carlton went 27-10 for a Phillies team that won just 59 games, accounting for a modern record 45.8 percent of his club's wins. He was devout in his work habits and in his refusal to speak to the press. (1994)

ALEXANDER CARTWRIGHT

Executive On September 23, 1845, Alexander Cartwright formed the Knickerbocker Base Ball Club and formalized a set of 20 rules that gave baseball its basic shape. While Cartwright's involvement with the game lasted only a few years, he is the man most responsible for the game that is played today. (1938)

HENRY CHADWICK

Writer-Statistician While Alexander Cartwright is baseball's inventor, Chadwick is the first man to chronicle the game. The only sportswriter enshrined in the Hall itself, Chadwick published guides and instructional booklets that helped popularize the game, and his method of scoring led to the game's wealth of statistics. (1938)

FRANK CHANCE

First baseman (1898-1914) Anchor of the Cubs' "Tinker-to-Evers-to-Chance" double-play combo, Chance helped Chicago win four pennants. While he was hardly a dominant player, he nevertheless hit .296 during his career and hit .310 in Series play. Chance's career was cut short by repeated beanings that eventually left him deaf in one ear. "The Peerless Leader" managed the Cubs for seven years. (1946)

HAPPY CHANDLER

Commissioner (1945-1951) The former governor and U.S. senator from Kentucky, Chandler succeeded Judge Kenesaw Mountain Landis as the second commissioner of baseball. Despite the opposition of most baseball owners, Chandler backed

Branch Rickey's signing of Jackie Robinson and prevented a player strike by threatening to ban any striking player for life. Preferring a "yes-man," the owners voted Chandler out in 1951. (1982)

OSCAR CHARLESTON

Outfielder (1915-1941) Blessed with speed and power in abundance, center fielder Charleston is thought by many to be the greatest of all Negro League players. Superb defensively, on offense he could both steal a base and hit a home run. In 1932, he became player-manager of the Pittsburgh Crawfords, whose lineup, including Charleston, featured five Hall of Famers. The team went 99-36 that year, and Charleston hit .363. (1976)

JACK CHESBRO

Pitcher (1899-1909) Chesbro's 41 victories in 454⅔ innings in 1904 stand as one of the game's most remarkable single-season achievements. A master of the spitball, Chesbro's wild pitch in the next to the last game of the 1904 season against Boston, however, cost New York the AL pennant. "Happy Jack" led his league in winning percentage in three seasons. (1946)

FRED CLARKE

Outfielder (1894-1911; 1913-1915); manager (1897-1915) For 19 of his 21 big-league seasons, Clarke was a manager as well as a player for the NL Louisville-Pittsburgh franchise. As a player, he hit .312 with 2,672 base hits and 1,619 runs scored. As manager, he won one World Series, in 1909, and four pennants, including three in a row from 1901 to 1903. "Cap" was 1,602-1,881 as a manager. (1945)

JOHN CLARKSON

Pitcher (1882-1894) Clarkson excelled during the years when the pitching distance was 50 feet. Six times he hurled more than 400 innings, twice more than 600. In 1885 with the White Stockings, he went 53-16. With the Beaneaters in 1889, Clarkson's record was 49-19 in 73 appearances. Winner of 328 career games, he had 485 complete games and led the NL in strikeouts three times. (1963)

ROBERTO CLEMENTE

Outfielder (1955-1972) Clemente won four NL batting titles and also possessed one of the strongest outfield arms in baseball history. Intensely proud of his Puerto Rican heritage, it was not until the 1971 World Series, when Clemente led Pittsburgh to victory with a .414 average, that he began to receive his due. In 13 of his 18 seasons he hit .300 or better, topping the .350 mark three times. On New Year's Eve, 1972, Clemente died in a plane crash bringing supplies to earthquake-ravaged Nicaragua. Clemente was the first Hispanic elected to the Hall of Fame. (1973)

TY COBB

Outfielder (1905-1928) The first man elected to the Hall of Fame, Cobb received more votes than any of his counterparts. Intense beyond belief, the daring Cobb epitomized the "scientific" style of play that dominated baseball in the first quarter of the 20th century. In 22 of his 24 seasons Cobb hit over .320, and his lifetime .366 average is still the all-time best. He led the AL in batting average ten seasons. The "Georgia Peach's" 2,246 runs scored are the most in history, while his 4,189 hits and 891 stolen bases rank second and fourth, respectively. (1936)

MICKEY COCHRANE

Catcher (1925-1937) An exceptional defensive catcher and dangerous hitter, Cochrane led the Athletics and Tigers to five pennants, including two as Detroit manager. "Black Mike" cracked the .300 mark in eight seasons, and his lifetime .320 batting average is the highest of any catcher. Mickey was twice AL MVP. In 1937, Cochrane was beaned by Yankee pitcher Bump Hadley and

suffered a fractured skull, ending his career at the age of 34. (1947)

EDDIE COLLINS

Second baseman (1906-1930) As Connie Mack's on-field manager, Collins led the Athletics to four pennants in five years. Traded to the White Sox, he helped that club to two more. An accomplished all-around ballplayer, Collins smacked 3,312 hits for a career average of .333, yet led the AL in batting only once. A consummate basestealer, he ranks sixth on the all-time list with 744 career swipes. "Cocky" scored 1,821 runs and drove in 1,300 runs in his 25-year career. (1939)

JIMMY COLLINS

Third baseman (1895-1908) Collins revolutionized the third base position by moving around, charging in, and fielding bunts bare-handed. Playing primarily for both the Boston Beaneaters in the National League and the Boston Pilgrims in the AL, Collins hit a robust .294, topping the .300 mark five times and the 100 RBI mark twice. (1945)

EARLE COMBS

Outfielder (1924-1935) While Babe Ruth and Lou Gehrig cleaned up at the plate, Combs set the table. As the leadoff man and center fielder for the Yankees, Combs scored 100 or more runs in eight straight seasons. "The Kentucky Colonel" had a lifetime .325 average and scored 1,186 runs. A collision with an outfield fence in 1934 forced his retirement a year later. (1970)

CHARLES COMISKEY

Executive Comiskey parlayed modest field success into managerial brilliance, later becoming the first former player to be sole owner of a major-league franchise, the White Sox. The "Old Roman" assisted Ban Johnson in the formation of the American League. Some historians feel that his parsimonious spending habits indirectly led to the 1919 "Black Sox" scandal. (1939)

JOCKO CONLAN

Umpire (1941-1964) Conlan started umpiring by accident. In a 1935 minor-league game, when one of the regular umpires was overcome by the heat, Conlan was rushed in to pinch-ump. He umpired in six World Series and six All-Star Games. (1974)

TOMMY CONNOLLY

Umpire (1898-1931) Connolly became an NL umpire in 1898. Frustrated with the circuit, he signed with the AL in 1901. Thirty years later he was named chief of AL umpires. Connolly and Bill Klem became the first umpires named to the Hall of Fame. Connolly umpired in eight World Series, including the first, in 1903. (1953)

ROGER CONNOR

First baseman (1880-1897) Until Babe Ruth broke the mark in 1921, Connor held the lifetime record for home runs with 138. A career .317 hitter, the Giant first baseman was a bona fide dead-ball era slugger, smacking 233 triples, fifth all time. In his first game (1883), he hit such an impressive shot that the fans passed the hat and bought him a gold watch. He scored 1,620 runs and had 1,322 RBI in his career. (1976)

STAN COVELESKI

Pitcher (1912; 1916-1928) A coal miner at age 13, Coveleski didn't reach the majors to stay until 1916, at age 27. The spitball artist had his best years with Cleveland from 1918 to 1921, winning 20 games or more each season. Coveleski won 215 games, while his brother Harry won 81. Stan lost only 142 games and retired with a lifetime 2.89 ERA. (1969)

SAM CRAWFORD

Outfielder (1899-1917) Crawford played outfield for Detroit alongside Ty Cobb. The powerful Crawford is baseball's all-time leader in triples with 309, having smashed at least ten in every full season he played. A native of Wahoo, Nebraska, "Wahoo Sam" retired only 39 hits shy of 3,000. He hit .309 lifetime, with 1,391 runs scored and 1,525 RBI. He later returned to baseball as an umpire in the Pacific Coast League. (1957)

JOE CRONIN

Shortstop (1926-1945); manager (1933-1947); AL President (1959-1973) For 50 years, Cronin excelled as a player, manager, and executive. In 1934 the Red Sox purchased the hard-hitting shortstop from Washington for a record $225,000. Cronin was a .301 career batter, and he had 1,233 runs scored and 1,424 RBI to go with his 515 doubles. As a manager, Cronin led the Senators to a pennant in 1933 and the Red Sox to one in 1946. From 1959 to 1973, he served as AL president. (1956)

CANDY CUMMINGS

Pitcher (1872-1877) Baseball's legendary inventor of the curveball, Cummings allegedly discovered the pitch while tossing clam shells as a youngster. Despite standing 5'9" and never weighing more than 120 pounds, he won 146 games from 1872 to 1877. (1939)

KIKI CUYLER

Outfielder (1921-1938) Pronounced "Cuy-Cuy," Kiki Cuyler hit a robust .354 as a Pirate rookie in 1924 and was heralded as "the next Ty Cobb." Kiki hit over .300 ten times and topped the .350 mark four times. He accumulated 2,299 hits for a lifetime mark of .321. He had 1,295 runs, 1,065 RBI, and 328 stolen bases during his career. (1968)

RAY DANDRIDGE

Third baseman (1933-1950) Dandridge excelled at third base in the Negro and Mexican Leagues, hitting for power and average while fielding with precision. He accumulated a .347 average against white big-league pitching. In 1949, he signed with the Giants and tore apart the American Association for Minneapolis, but at age 36 never received a call to the majors. (1987)

LEON DAY
Pitcher; second baseman; outfielder (1934-1949) Using a no-windup delivery, Day was a star pitcher in the Negro Leagues. He defeated the legendary Satchel Paige three out of four times and once struck out 19 men in one game. Day also played the field and posted an unofficial lifetime mark of .288. He was named to the Hall of Fame a week before he died. (1995)

DIZZY DEAN
Pitcher (1930-1941; 1947) Baseball's most colorful pitcher, Dean threw smoke, spoke in homespun hyperbole, and by age 26 had won 134 games for the Cardinals. After breaking his toe in the 1937 All-Star Game, Dean altered his pitching motion, hurt his arm, and never approached his previous record. He had a 150-83 career record with a 3.02 ERA. Dizzy was the last NL pitcher to notch 30 wins in a season (30-7 in 1934). (1953)

ED DELAHANTY
Outfielder (1888-1903) One of five brothers to play in the majors, Delahanty was perhaps baseball's premier hitter of the 1890s. He hit .400 three times, and his .346 career mark is fourth all time. He lived as hard as he played. In 1903, Delahanty was suspended for drinking. En route to his home, "Big Ed" (age 35) was kicked off a train, fell into the Niagara River, and was swept over the falls to his death. (1945)

BILL DICKEY
Catcher (1928-1943; 1946) Catcher of 100 or more games for 13 consecutive seasons, Dickey hit .362 in 1936, still a record for the position. He also accumulated a .313 batting average and 1,209 RBI in his career. During his 17 years, the Yankees won nine pennants and captured eight world championships. Dickey is also credited with developing the receiving skills of Yogi Berra. (1954)

MARTIN DIHIGO
Pitcher; infielder; outfielder (1923-1945) The first Cuban elected to the Hall of Fame, Dihigo starred as a pitcher, infielder, and outfielder in Negro and Caribbean baseball. Winner of more than 250 games from the mound, he hit over .400 three times. He was one of the most versatile players in the game's history; he was able to play all of the infield positions, as well as being one of the best hurlers in history. (1977)

JOE DIMAGGIO
Outfielder (1936-1942; 1946-1951) "Joltin' Joe" led the Yankees to nine pennants while making 13 All-Star Teams in 13 seasons. A three-time MVP, the quiet, graceful center fielder is often credited with being the best player of his generation. In 1941, "The Yankee Clipper" hit in a record 56 consecutive games. He led the AL in batting average twice, slugging average twice, triples once, home runs twice, runs scored once, and RBI twice. He retired with a .325 batting average, 361 home runs, 1,390 runs scored, and 1,537 RBI. (1955)

BOBBY DOERR
Second baseman (1937-1944; 1946-1951) Doerr was known for his reliable defensive play and potent bat. For 14 seasons he was one of the best second basemen in baseball, spending his entire career with the Red Sox, and never playing a game at another position. In 1944, Doerr led the AL in slugging at .528. He had a career .288 average, 223 homers, and 1,247 RBI. (1986)

DON DRYSDALE

Pitcher (1956-1969) In the early 1960s, Drysdale and teammate Sandy Koufax gave the Dodgers baseball's best pitching tandem. The intimidating Drysdale led the NL in Ks three times. He won the Cy Young Award in 1962, going 25-9 with a 2.83 ERA and a league-best 232 strikeouts. In 1968, "Big D" hurled six shutouts in a row on his way to 58 consecutive scoreless innings. He was 209-166 with a 2.95 ERA and 2,486 strikeouts. (1984)

HUGH DUFFY

Outfielder (1888-1906) In 1894, the diminutive Duffy hit .440 for NL Boston, the highest mark ever recorded under current rules. He also captured the Triple Crown that year, with 18 homers and 145 RBI. He compiled a career .324 average, 1,551 runs, and 1,299 RBI. After his retirement, Duffy continued in baseball another 48 seasons. (1945)

LEO DUROCHER

Manager (1939-1946; 1948-1955; 1966-1973) A shortstop for 17 years in the bigs, "Leo the Lip" as manager compiled a 2,008-1,709 record—a .540 winning percentage. In 1951, he piloted the Giants to the "Miracle at Coogan's Bluff" and reached three World Series overall, winning the championship in 1954. In 1947, he was suspended for one year for conduct detrimental to baseball. (1994)

BILLY EVANS

Umpire (1906-1927) Evans was a sportswriter and then did what many writers thought they could do better—be an umpire. He was one of the best, working six World Series. (1973)

JOHNNY EVERS

Second baseman (1902-1917; 1922; 1929) Perhaps the best of the "Tinker-to-Evers-to-Chance" double-play combination, second baseman Evers relied on a steady glove and just enough hitting to help lead his club to five pennants in 16 seasons. Although he played most of his career with the Cubs, in 1914 he was the NL MVP with the "Miracle" Boston Braves. "The Trojan" had 919 runs and 324 stolen bases. (1946)

BUCK EWING

Catcher (1880-1897) Connie Mack called Ewing "the greatest catcher of all time." He eclipsed the .300 mark in ten seasons, including a string of eight straight times. Ewing had a lifetime .303 batting average and scored 1,129 runs. (1939)

RED FABER

Pitcher (1914-1933) One of the last spitball pitchers, Faber spent his entire 20-year career with the White Sox, posting a 254-213 record. An illness and injury in 1919 left him untouched by the "Black Sox" scandal. He led the AL in ERA and in complete games twice. Faber posted a career 3.15 ERA in 4,086⅔ innings, with 273 complete games. (1964)

BOB FELLER

Pitcher (1936-1941; 1945-1956) Phenom Feller left the farm at age 17 and struck out 15 in his first official big-league appearance. Amazingly, he was signed by a Cleveland scout for one dollar and an autographed baseball. Feller's fastball, once timed at over 98 mph, may have been the fastest of all time. "Rapid Robert" led the American League seven times in strikeouts, six seasons in wins, and four times in shutouts. Feller won 266 games, all for Cleveland, with three no-hitters. (1962)

RICK FERRELL

Catcher (1929-1947) One of the few players inducted primarily for his defense, Ferrell nonetheless hit .300 four times. He was a career .281 hitter and drew 931 walks. For four seasons with the Red Sox, Ferrell teamed with brother Wes. (1984)

ROLLIE FINGERS

Pitcher (1968-1985) The earliest to be used in a "closer" role, Fingers was the first pitcher to reach 300 saves. He was the fireman for the champion Athletics in the early 1970s, then led the NL in saves with San Diego. In 1981 with the Brewers, he won the MVP and Cy Young awards. He had 341 career saves. (1992)

ELMER FLICK

Outfielder (1898-1910) A speedy outfielder for the Phillies and Indians, in 1905 Flick won the AL batting crown with an average of .308. In the spring of 1907, Detroit thought so much of Flick it offered Ty Cobb in trade but was turned down. That season Flick hit .302 in his last full season, while Cobb hit .350 in his first. Flick had a .313 career batting average. (1963)

WHITEY FORD

Pitcher (1950; 1953-1967) Ford's winning percentage of .690 is the best of any 20th-century pitcher. The Yankee pitcher led the American League in wins three times and ERA twice. Ford holds eight World Series pitching records, including wins (ten) and strikeouts (94). His 25-4 record in 1961 earned him the Cy Young Award. "The Chairman of the Board" was 236-106 lifetime with a 2.75 ERA and 156 complete games. (1974)

BILL FOSTER

Pitcher (1923-1937) One of the best left-handed pitchers in Negro League history, Foster won more games (137) than anyone, including Satchel Paige. He was only 29 years old in 1933, his last full season. (1996)

RUBE FOSTER

Executive; pitcher As a star pitcher for a number of early black teams, and later as the first president of the Negro National League, Foster earned the title "Father of Black Baseball." Foster's efforts in organizing the NNL gave black baseball stability. He in effect saved the Negro League and made it popular. (1981)

JIMMIE FOXX

First baseman (1925-1942; 1944-1945) For 12 consecutive seasons with the Athletics and Red Sox, Foxx slammed 30 or more home runs and knocked in more than 100 runs. In 1933, Foxx hit .356, swatted 48 homers, and knocked in 163 runs to win the Triple Crown. Winner of three MVP Awards, "Double X" had a lifetime slugging average of .609, fourth all time. Foxx had 534 career homers, 1,922 RBI, and a .325 batting average. (1951)

FORD FRICK

NL President (1934-1951); Commissioner (1951-1965) Frick was named NL president in 1934. In 1951, he was elected commissioner. He helped establish the Hall of Fame, supported Branch Rickey's signing of Jackie Robinson, and presided over baseball's busiest period of expansion. (1970)

FRANKIE FRISCH

Second baseman (1919-1937) A member of more NL pennant winners than any other player, Frisch played in four fall classics with the Giants and four with the Cardinals. He cracked the .300 mark 13 times, scored 100 runs seven times, and was the 1931 NL MVP. As player-manager, "The Fordham Flash" led the "Gashouse Gang" to the title in 1934. He scored 1,532 career runs and hit .316. (1947)

PUD GALVIN

Pitcher (1875; 1879-1892) Nicknamed "Pud" because he made pudding out of hitters, Galvin was pitcher supreme for NL Buffalo in the 1880s. On his way to 364 career victories, Galvin pitched more than 400 innings nine times and won 46 games in 1883 and '84. "Gentle Jeems" is tied for tenth on the all-time list with 58 shutouts and is second all time with 646 complete games in his career and 6,000⅓ innings. (1965)

LOU GEHRIG

First baseman (1923-1939) "The Iron Horse," Gehrig played in 2,130 consecutive games for the Yankees. Gehrig knocked 46 home runs and set the AL record for RBI with 184 in 1931. He had more than 40 home runs in five seasons, more than 150 RBI in seven seasons, and a .600 slugging percentage in nine seasons. "Columbia Lou" had a .632 career slugging percentage, a .340 batting average, 493 home runs, 1,995 RBI, and 1,888 runs scored. Although fatally ill with amyotrophic lateral sclerosis, he bid farewell to 61,000 fans at Yankee Stadium in 1939 by saying, "Today I consider myself the luckiest man on the face of the Earth." The waiting period for the Hall was waived, and Gehrig was admitted. (1939)

CHARLIE GEHRINGER

Second baseman (1924-1942) His efficient play at second base for the Tigers earned Gehringer the appellation "The Mechanical Man." He regularly led the league in fielding and hit over .300 in 13 of 16 seasons. He logged over 100 RBI and had 200 or more hits in seven seasons. In 1937, his loop-high .371 average made him AL MVP. He had a career .320 batting average, 2,839 hits, 1,774 runs scored, and 1,427 RBI. (1949)

BOB GIBSON

Pitcher (1959-1975) In 1968, Gibson had the second-lowest ERA in modern NL history, a stingy 1.12, while winning both Cy Young and MVP honors. He also won the Cy Young Award in 1970. In the 1967 World Series, he led St. Louis to victory over Boston, winning three times while giving up only 14 hits. Gibson's speed and control resulted in 251 career wins. "Hoot" had a career 2.91 ERA, 3,117 Ks, and 255 complete games. (1981)

JOSH GIBSON

Catcher (1930-1946) For 16 seasons Gibson reigned as the Negro Leagues' supreme slugger, perhaps smacking nearly 1,000 home runs and as many as 90 in a single season. The powerful catcher was often called the black Babe Ruth; in another time, Ruth may have been referred to as the poor man's Josh Gibson. One of the most dedicated players ever, Gibson would play 200 games over a single year. In 1947, with Jackie Robinson on the verge of breaking the big-league color line, Gibson, only age 36, died of a brain hemorrhage. (1972)

WARREN GILES

NL President (1951-1969) Giles started as president of minor-league Moline in 1919 and ended 50 years later as president of the National League. During his tenure, he oversaw the transfer of the Giants and Dodgers to California, and he approved the addition of four expansion franchises. (1979)

LEFTY GOMEZ

Pitcher (1930-1943) Gomez's sense of humor was matched only by his skill on the mound. A 20-game winner four times for the Yankees, Gomez went undefeated in six World Series decisions. He led the American League in strikeouts three times and in ERA twice. His secret to success? Quipped Lefty, "Clean living and a fast outfield." "Goofy" was 189-102 with a 3.34 ERA. (1972)

GOOSE GOSLIN

Outfielder (1921-1938) The best hitter ever to play for the Senators, Goslin led Washington to its only three appearances in the World Series. He slugged three home runs in both the 1924 and 1925 fall classics. Goose had 100 RBI or more and batted over .300 in 11 seasons. He had 1,609 RBI, 2,735 hits, and a .316 average. (1968)

HANK GREENBERG

First baseman (1930; 1933-1941; 1945-1947) Despite playing only nine full seasons, Greenberg smacked 331 home runs and captured AL MVP honors in 1935 and 1940 for the Tigers. He lost three years to World War II but came back in 1946 to lead the AL in homers and RBI. He had league- and career-high totals of 58 dingers (1938) and 183 RBI (1937). "Hammerin' Hank" had a career .313 batting average, a .605 slugging percentage, and 1,276 RBI. (1956)

CLARK GRIFFITH

Manager (1901-1920) A leading pitcher of the 1890s, Griffith won 20 games in six straight seasons. Over a 20-year period, the cagey "Old Fox" managed the White Sox, Yankees, Reds, and Senators. He had a 1,491-1,367 career record and won only one pennant. He also served as president of the Senators from 1920 to 1955. (1946)

BURLEIGH GRIMES

Pitcher (1916-1934) In 1934, Grimes threw the last legal spitter in baseball history. Over the preceding 19 seasons, he won 270 games with seven teams. One of a handful of pitchers allowed to throw the spitter after its ban in 1920, Grimes was the most successful. "Ol' Stubblebeard" won more than 20 games five times. (1964)

LEFTY GROVE

Pitcher (1925-1941) In an era dominated by hitting, the left-handed Grove was almost unhittable, winning 20 games or more seven straight seasons with Connie Mack's Philadelphia A's, including a remarkable 31-4 mark in 1931. That year, "Mose" was the AL MVP. On his way to 300 wins, he led the AL in strikeouts seven times, ERA nine times, complete games three times, and winning percentage five times. (1947)

CHICK HAFEY

Outfielder (1924-1937) Hafey's misfortune was to play before the advent of the batting helmet. Several beanings and a chronic sinus condition affected his vision, forcing him to wear glasses in an effort to correct the damage. Nevertheless, Chick hit over .300 in nine seasons and captured the NL title in 1931 with a .349 mark. He was known for his rifle arm and his line drives. Ill health and vision problems, however, forced the career .317 batter to retire. (1971)

JESSE HAINES

Pitcher (1918; 1920-1937) Knuckleballer Haines didn't make the big leagues for good until he was 26 years old. However, he stuck around until he was 45, winning 20 games three times and finishing with 210 victories for the Cardinals, including a no-hitter against the Braves in 1924. In 1927, he racked up a 24-10 record, leading the NL with 25 complete games and six shutouts. "Pop" had 209 complete games. (1970)

BILLY HAMILTON

Outfielder (1888-1901) While playing with Philadelphia and Boston in the NL, "Sliding Billy" ran into the record books. He was credited with 912 stolen bases, although for most of his career a runner received credit for a base theft by advancing an extra base on a hit. He had a lifetime .344 batting average. In 1894, his ability on the bases let him score a record 196 times. (1961)

NED HANLON

Manager (1889-1907) Hanlon had a career 1,315-1,164 record as a manager, achieving his greatest success in Baltimore, where he won three pennants. The savvy skipper also brought two pennants to Brooklyn. Hanlon was noted for helping to introduce the game of baseball around the world with a global tour in 1888. (1996)

WILL HARRIDGE
AL President (1931-1959) Harridge stayed out of the limelight and quietly led the league. An early supporter of the All-Star Game and night baseball, Harridge insisted on order. (1972)

BUCKY HARRIS
Manager (1924-1943; 1947-1948; 1950-1956) An above-average second baseman for the Senators, Harris was a natural leader who had his greatest success as manager. In his first season as player-manager in 1924, he led the Senators to their only world championship. He went on to manage another 28 seasons with five other clubs, going 2,157-2,218. Harris was a respected strategist. (1975)

GABBY HARTNETT
Catcher (1922-1941) In his time, Hartnett was likely the NL's best catcher. A fine defensive catcher, his best season was 1930, when he hit .339 with 37 home runs and 122 RBI. He was an All-Star from 1933 through 1938. In the 1934 game, he was the backstop when Ruth, Gehrig, Foxx, Simmons, and Cronin were struck out in order. He hit .344 as the NL MVP in 1935. His late-season, ninth-inning "homer in the gloaming" against Pittsburgh won the 1938 pennant for the Cubs. He had a .297 career batting average, with 236 homers and 1,179 RBI. (1955)

HARRY HEILMANN
Outfielder (1914; 1916-1930; 1932) In the four seasons that Heilmann won the AL batting crown, his lowest average was .393. He batted over .300 in 12 seasons and hit an amazing .403 in 1923. Playing mostly for Detroit, the slow-footed outfielder (nicknamed "Slug") wielded a line-drive bat that resulted in 2,660 hits, including 542 doubles, for a .342 average. (1952)

BILLY HERMAN
Second baseman (1931-1943; 1946-1947) A ten-time All-Star, Herman's 227 hits and 57 doubles in 1935 were tops in the NL. The best defensive second baseman in the loop, he hit .300 or better eight times in his career. After playing most of his career for the Cubs, in 1941 he was traded to Brooklyn. Herman had a career .304 batting average and 486 doubles. (1975)

HARRY HOOPER
Outfielder (1909-1925) A right field star, Hooper's arm was legendary (he averaged 20 assists a year). He teamed with Duffy Lewis and Tris Speaker to give the BoSox the best outfield of the era. A lifetime .281 hitter, Hooper scored 1,429 runs. (1971)

ROGERS HORNSBY
Second baseman (1915-1937) Perhaps the greatest right-handed hitter of all time, Hornsby's career .358 average is second only to Ty Cobb's .366. "Rajah's" .424 mark in 1924 is the best of the 20th century. His greatest success came with the Cardinals; from 1920 to 1925 he collected six straight batting titles, as well as two Triple Crowns. Hornsby's fierce demeanor and competitive nature made him one of the most disliked players of his time. (1942)

WAITE HOYT
Pitcher (1918-1938) The Yankee pitching ace of the 1920s, Hoyt won 20 games only twice but compiled a 6-4 record in the World Series with a 1.83 ERA. In 1927, "Schoolboy" led the American League in wins (22) and ERA (2.63). He won in double digits 12 seasons and had a career 237-182 record. Hoyt was one of the first ex-ballplayers to work in broadcasting. (1969)

CAL HUBBARD

Umpire (1936-1951; 1954-1962) Hubbard is the only man in the baseball, college football, and pro football Halls of Fame. When he retired from football he became an AL umpire. (1976)

CARL HUBBELL

Pitcher (1928-1943) Hubbell used the screwball to notch 253 career wins and a 2.98 ERA, all for the Giants. From 1933 to 1937, he posted five straight 20-win seasons, and was NL MVP in '33 and '36. "King Carl" led the NL in wins three times, ERA three times, and strikeouts once. In the 1934 All-Star Game, the left-handed "Meal Ticket" struck out five straight Hall of Famers—Babe Ruth, Lou Gehrig, Jimmie Foxx, Al Simmons, and Joe Cronin. (1947)

MILLER HUGGINS

Manager (1913-1929) Huggins was the Yankee manager of the 1920s. Standing only 5'6", he was the one man able to temper the boisterous Babe Ruth. "The Mighty Mite's" 1927 Yankees team is widely considered the best of all time. "Hug" was 1,413-1,134 in his career, including five seasons with mediocre Cardinal clubs. He won six pennants and three Series in his 12 years with the Yankees. (1964)

WILLIAM HULBERT

Executive Hulbert, an official in the poorly run National Association during the 1870s, spearheaded the formation of the National League in 1876. Becoming NL president in 1877, Hulbert successfully dealt with such league problems as gambling and loose organization and kept the league alive. He also owned the Chicago White Stockings, an NL dynasty in the 1880s. (1995)

CATFISH HUNTER

Pitcher (1965-1979) Given his nickname by A's owner Charlie Finley, Hunter went directly from high school to the major leagues. Beginning in 1971, Catfish won more than 20 games five straight seasons and earned the Cy Young Award in 1974 with a 25-12 record. After three A's world championships (1972 to 1974), Hunter signed with the Yankees for $3.75 million in 1975, then the biggest contract in baseball history. He had a 224-166 career record with a 3.26 ERA and 2,012 strikeouts. (1987)

MONTE IRVIN

Outfielder (Negro Leagues 1939-1943; 1945-1948; NL 1949-1956) Despite twice leading the Negro National League in hitting, the 30-year-old Irvin was not signed by the Giants until 1949. He began his Negro League career in 1939, and he also played in the Mexican League, where he won a Triple Crown in 1940. In eight NL seasons, he hit .293, leading the league in RBI with 121 in 1951. (1973)

REGGIE JACKSON

Outfielder (1967-1987) "The Straw that Stirs the Drink," Jackson was a publicity hog, a prolific slugger, a superior outfielder, and most of all, a big winner. He played on 11 division winners and five world champions. "Mr. October's" finest moment came in game six of the 1977 Series, when he smacked three homers. The four-time home run king had 563 homers and 1,702 RBI, but he also compiled more strikeouts (2,597) than any other player. (1993)

TRAVIS JACKSON

Shortstop (1922-1936) A solid defensive shortstop for the Giants of the 1920s and 1930s, Jackson helped the club to four pennants. "Stonewall" also batted over .300 in six seasons. He accumulated a career average of .291. (1982)

FERGUSON JENKINS

Pitcher (1965-1983) After being traded from the Phillies to the Cubs in early 1966, Jenkins embarked on a string of six consecutive 20-plus win seasons. He won only

493

14 games in 1973 and was traded to Texas, where he won the 1974 Cy Young Award with a 25-12 record. One of the game's most durable pitchers, Jenkins had a career 284-226 record, with a 3.34 ERA and 3,192 Ks. (1991)

HUGHIE JENNINGS

Shortstop (1891-1903; 1907; 1909; 1912; 1918); manager (1907-1920; 1924) From 1894 to 1897 as shortstop of NL Baltimore, Jennings led the club to pennants. In his five years with Baltimore, he never hit below .328 and was a lifetime .311 hitter. He was 1,163-984 as a manager. (1945)

BAN JOHNSON

AL President (1901-1927) The founder of the American League, Johnson was arguably the most powerful man in baseball during the first quarter of the 20th century. When the minor Western League folded in 1893, Johnson revived it. He put it on solid footing and made it a major league in 1901. The "Black Sox" scandal of 1920 undermined his power, however, and led to the commissioner system, ultimately leading to Johnson's retirement in 1927. (1937)

JUDY JOHNSON

Third baseman (1919-1936) The greatest third baseman in Negro League history, Johnson combined steady defensive play with stellar batting performances. A line-drive hitter, Johnson hit .390 and .406 in two of his seasons with the Philadelphia Hilldales, leading them to two black World Series appearances. In later years, Judy scouted for the A's and Phillies. (1975)

WALTER JOHNSON

Pitcher (1907-1927) One of the first five men elected to the Hall, Johnson's legendary fastball and pinpoint control enabled him to win 417 games (second on the all-time list) with the usually inferior Senators. In his 20-year career, "The Big Train" led the AL in strikeouts 12 times,

shutouts seven times, and victories six times. Johnson's 110 shutouts are the most in history. "Barney's" 2.17 career ERA is eighth lowest, his 531 complete games rank fourth, and his 5,915 innings pitched are the third most in baseball. (1936)

ADDIE JOSS

Pitcher (1902-1910) In only nine seasons with Cleveland, Joss won 160 games with a winning percentage of .623 and an ERA of 1.89 (second all time). He struck out 920 batters and walked only 364 in 2,327 innings pitched. In 1911, he died of tubercular meningitis at age 31. The Hall's usual ten-year career requirement was waived for Joss. (1978)

AL KALINE

Outfielder (1953-1974) As a 20-year-old outfielder with Detroit in 1955, Kaline won the batting title, with a .340 average, to become the youngest batting champion ever. Although he never duplicated that figure, he played in 18 All-Star Games, won 11 Gold Gloves, and accumulated 3,007 hits. He also belted 498 doubles, 399 home runs, and 1,583 RBI, with 1,622 runs scored and 1,277 walks. (1980)

TIM KEEFE

Pitcher (1880-1893) In only 14 seasons, Keefe won 342 games, one of six 19th-century pitchers to top the 300 mark. Remarkably, after overhand pitching was legalized in 1884, Keefe continued to pitch—and win—underhanded. "Sir Timothy" pioneered the use of the changeup to notch a career 2.62 ERA with 554 complete games. (1964)

WEE WILLIE KEELER

Outfielder (1892-1910) Keeler said, "I hit 'em where they ain't." Utilizing his good speed and batting skills, he developed the "Baltimore chop" to bounce the ball over and between infielders. From 1894 to

1901, he collected a major-league-record 200 hits each season. He had 2,932 career hits, 1,719 runs, and a .341 batting average. In 1897, he hit in 44 consecutive games. That same year he notched a personal best .424 batting average. (1939)

GEORGE KELL

Third baseman (1943-1957) An excellent third baseman and career .306 hitter, Kell excelled for five different clubs in the 1940s and 1950s. In 1949, he edged out Ted Williams for his only batting crown, hitting .3429 to Williams's .3427. Kell scored a lifetime 881 runs and drove in 870 runs. (1983)

JOE KELLEY

Outfielder (1891-1906; 1908) Kelley played for the great Baltimore teams of the 1890s and later went on to star with Brooklyn and Cincinnati. He batted over .300 for 11 straight years. In 1894, he hit .393 and went 9-for-9 in a doubleheader. Kelley had a lifetime .317 batting average, with 194 triples, and 1,424 runs scored. (1971)

GEORGE KELLY

First baseman (1915-1917; 1919-1930; 1932) After failing in his first three seasons in the bigs, Kelly came into his own for the Giants in 1919. From 1921 to '26, Kelly hit over .300 and averaged 108 RBI, helping the Giants capture four pennants. He was a .297 hitter and totaled 1,020 RBI. (1973)

KING KELLY

Outfielder; catcher (1878-1893) Baseball's first celebrity, Kelly was the subject of the popular song, "Slide, Kelly, Slide" and recited "Casey At The Bat" on stage. On the field, he perfected the hit-and-run and developed the hook and head-first slides. He hit .308 lifetime and scored 1,357 runs. (1945)

HARMON KILLEBREW

First baseman; third baseman (1954-1975) Killebrew hit 573 home runs;

only Babe Ruth hit more in AL history. Killebrew led the league in homers six times, each time hitting more than 40. "Killer" had 40 or more homers in eight different seasons. The 1969 AL MVP also drove in more than 100 RBI in nine years, pacing the AL three times. He hit only .256 lifetime but had 1,559 bases on balls. (1984)

RALPH KINER

Outfielder (1946-1955) Joining Pittsburgh after World War II, Kiner led or tied for the National League lead in homers in his first seven seasons. He had 369 lifetime dingers, 1,015 RBI, and 1,011 bases on balls in ten years. Kiner has enjoyed a second career as a broadcaster for the Mets. (1975)

CHUCK KLEIN

Outfielder (1928-1944) Playing five and one-half seasons in Philadelphia's cozy Baker Bowl, Klein led the NL in homers four times and never hit below .337. He was the 1932 NL MVP and won the Triple Crown in 1933 (.368 average, 28 homers, 120 RBI). Klein set an all-time record for outfield assists with 44 in 1930. He had a lifetime .320 batting average, 300 homers, and 1,201 RBI. (1980)

BILL KLEM

Umpire (1905-1941) Baseball's best known umpire, Klem revolutionized the position and is credited with being the first to employ hand signals and don a chest protector. He worked a record 18 World Series, and he was the umpire at the first All-Star Game in 1933. (1953)

SANDY KOUFAX

Pitcher (1955-1966) Koufax had two careers. His best record in his first six years was an 11-11 mark. But between 1961 and 1966, the lefty led the NL in wins and shutouts three times each and Ks four times. Koufax paced the Dodgers to pennants in 1963, '65, and '66 while winning the Cy Young Award each year. His 25-5 record in 1963 earned him the National League MVP Award. Pitching in excruciating pain due to arthritis, Koufax led the NL in ERA his final five seasons, culminating with a 1.73 mark while going 27-9 in '66. He had a 165-87 record with a 2.76 career ERA, 2,396 Ks, and only 817 walks. (1972)

NAP LAJOIE

Second baseman (1896-1916) One of the best righty batters in history, Lajoie was the best second baseman of his era and became the first man at his position to be elected to the Hall. A graceful fielder, he hit over .300 16 times in his career. He won the Triple Crown in 1901, the American League's debut season; he batted .426 with 14 homers and 125 RBI. His presence gave the AL respect. Lajoie had a career .338 average, 3,242 hits, and 657 doubles. (1937)

KENESAW MOUNTAIN LANDIS

Commissioner (1920-1944) Baseball's first commissioner, Landis left his job as a federal judge in 1920 to take complete control of the major leagues. In cleaning up the "Black Sox" scandal, he restored the public's confidence in the integrity of baseball. His rule was law, and nobody dared challenge his authority. A champion of player rights, he unsuccessfully tried to halt the farm system—one of the few battles he ever lost. (1944)

TONY LAZZERI

Second baseman (1926-1939) The second baseman on the "Murderer's Row" Yankee teams of the 1920s and '30s, Lazzeri combined power, high average, and slick fielding. A career .292 hitter who socked 178 homers, "Poosh 'Em Up" topped the .300 mark five times and hit .354 in 1929. (1991)

BOB LEMON

Pitcher (1941-1942; 1946-1958) Lemon made the big leagues as a third baseman, but he made the Hall of Fame as a pitcher. Switched to pitching during World War II, Lemon won 20 games for the Indians seven times from 1948 to 1956. He led the AL in wins three times and in complete games five times. He had a career 207-128 record for a .618 winning percentage. As manager, he led the Yankees to a championship in 1978. (1976)

BUCK LEONARD

First baseman (1934-1948) In the Negro Leagues, Walter Leonard played Lou Gehrig to teammate Josh Gibson's Babe Ruth. Leonard played for the Homestead Grays and helped lead them to nine consecutive pennants. He was a left-handed power hitter and clutch RBI man who hit for a high average. He twice led the NNL in hitting, peaking at .410 in 1947. In 1952, at age 45, Leonard turned down an offer from Bill Veeck to play for the St. Louis Browns. (1972)

FREDDIE LINDSTROM

Third baseman (1924-1936) Lindstrom survived two bad-hop grounders in the '24 World Series and went on to top the .300 mark seven times, including a .379 average in 1930. A year later an injury led to a switch to the outfield. He batted .311 lifetime, with 301 doubles and 895 runs scored. (1976)

POP LLOYD

Shortstop (1905-1932) The finest shortstop in Negro baseball, Lloyd's stellar performance in a 1909 exhibition series against Ty Cobb's Tigers so embarrassed Cobb he vowed never to play blacks again. In 1928, despite being age 44, Lloyd led the Negro National League in batting with an eye-popping .564 average. From his time in Cuba, his nickname was *"El Cuchara,"* which means "scoop" in Spanish. (1977)

ERNIE LOMBARDI

Catcher (1931-1947) Called "Schnozz" because of his enormous nose, Lombardi was a slow, awkward-looking catcher who could hit a ton. He surpassed the .300 mark ten times. In 1938, his league-leading .342 average with Cincinnati earned him the NL MVP Award. Five years later with the Braves, Lombardi again led the league with a .330 average, becoming the only catcher to do so twice. He hit .306 lifetime, with 990 RBI. (1986)

AL LOPEZ

Catcher (1928; 1930-1947); manager (1951-1965; 1968-1969) A workhorse behind the plate, Lopez held the major-league record for games caught until 1987. He turned manager in 1951, and in 1954 led Cleveland to 111 wins. In 1959, he won another pennant with the White Sox. He drove his 17 teams to a 1,410-1,004 record for a .584 winning percentage. Usually losing the pennant to the Yankees, Lopez's clubs finished second in the AL ten times. (1977)

TED LYONS

Pitcher (1923-1942; 1946) Lyons had the misfortune of pitching for some bad White Sox teams. He won 260 games, with 356 complete games. He led the AL in shutouts twice and wins twice. In 1942, he led the AL with a 2.10 ERA. At age 42, he served three years in World War II, then returned to baseball for one last season. (1955)

CONNIE MACK

Manager (1894-1896; 1901-1950) As player, manager, and owner, Mack had a career that spanned an incredible eight decades. Manager of the Athletics from 1901 to 1950, Mack built then tore apart several championship clubs. His first dynasty was from 1910 to 1914, when the Athletics won four pennants and three world championships. He sold off many of those players and finished in last place

from 1915 to 1921. His second dynasty was the 1929 to 1931 clubs—three pennants and two world champs. He compiled a 3,731-3,948 record in his 53 years as a manager. (1937)

LARRY MACPHAIL

Executive As an executive with the Reds, Dodgers, and Yankees, MacPhail played a part in virtually every baseball development between the wars. He brought air travel and lights to the major leagues in 1935, and radio broadcasts to Brooklyn in 1938. (1978)

MICKEY MANTLE

Outfielder (1951-1968) Named after Mickey Cochrane, Mantle was taught to switch hit and became baseball's leading switch-hitter. Succeeding Joe DiMaggio as Yankee center fielder, all Mantle did was match Joe's three MVP Awards (1956, 1957, 1962). "The Commerce Comet" hit .353 with 52 homers and 130 RBI to win the Triple Crown in 1956. He led the AL in home runs four times, RBI once, runs scored six times, and walks five times. If not for a series of knee injuries, Mantle may have been the best of all time. He had the most all-time World Series homers, RBI, and runs. He possessed a .298 batting average, 536 homers, 1,509 RBI, 1,677 runs scored, and 1,733 walks. (1974)

HEINIE MANUSH

Outfielder (1923-1939) Often overlooked, Manush was one of the best hitters during his era. Topping the .300 mark 11 times, he compiled a career average of .330. Playing for the Tigers, Browns, Senators, Braves, Pirates, and Dodgers, he led his league in hits twice. Manush notched 1,183 career RBI and 1,287 runs. (1964)

RABBIT MARANVILLE

Shortstop (1912-1933; 1935) A top defensive shortstop and consummate showman, Maranville was the kind of

497

player that did the little things to make his team better. A superior fielder, he ranks first among all shortstops in putouts (5,139). Maranville collected 2,605 hits and scored 1,255 runs. (1954)

JUAN MARICHAL

Pitcher (1960-1975) In the mid-1960s, the Giants' Marichal was one of the best and most consistent pitchers in the game. His patented high leg kick masked a multitude of pitches. A six-time 20-game winner, Marichal somehow failed to win the Cy Young Award. His 243 career wins more than made up for that omission. He led the league in shutouts and in complete games twice. "The Dominican Dandy" had a career 243-142 record, a 2.89 ERA, 2,303 Ks, and 52 shutouts. (1983)

RUBE MARQUARD

Pitcher (1908-1925) In 1912, Marquard won his first 19 decisions for the Giants on his way to a 26-11 record. Although he won 23 games the following season, he never again matched his earlier play. Marquard had a 201-177 career record with 197 complete games. (1971)

EDDIE MATHEWS

Third baseman (1952-1968) Mathews combined with Hank Aaron to form one of the best power combos ever. For 14 consecutive years, Mathews hit 23 or more home runs, hitting 40 or more four times. A steady defensive player, he was an All-Star nine times. He led the NL in bases on balls in four seasons to retire with a total of 1,444. He also tallied 512 career homers, 1,453 RBI, and 1,509 runs scored. (1978)

CHRISTY MATHEWSON

Pitcher (1900-1916) As the most popular player in his day, Mathewson dispelled the notion at the time that ballplayers need be crude and uneducated. "Big Six" was also perhaps the game's best pitcher. For 12 consecutive seasons he won 20 or more

games for the Giants, as his trademark "fadeaway," a screwball, baffled a generation of batters. In the 1905 World Series, he hurled three shutouts in six days. He led the NL in ERA in five seasons, in Ks five times, and in shutouts four times. "Matty" had a 373-188 career record, with a 2.13 ERA and 79 shutouts. (1936)

WILLIE MAYS

Outfielder (1951-1952; 1954-1973) Mays could do everything: hit, field, and run. While the Giant center fielder's 660 home runs rank third all time, his magnificent over-the-shoulder catch of Vic Wertz's blast to center field in the 1954 World Series has become the standard against which all other catches are compared. "The Say Hey Kid" led the NL in slugging percentage five times, homers and stolen bases four times, triples three times, and runs scored twice. He had 3,283 career hits, a .302 batting average, a .557 slugging percentage, 1,903 RBI, and 2,062 runs scored. (1979)

JOE MCCARTHY

Manager (1926-1946; 1948-1950) In 24 years as manager, McCarthy collected seven world championships and nine pennants. His 2,125-1,333 record gives him an all-time-best .615 winning percentage. Most of his success came with the Yankees, where he won four straight World Series from 1936 to 1939. After winning the National League pennant with the Cubs in 1929, McCarthy piloted the Yankees to a pennant in 1932 to become the first manager to win a pennant in both leagues. (1957)

TOMMY MCCARTHY

Outfielder (1884-1896) McCarthy made a lasting mark by perfecting the fly-ball trap in order to throw out the lead runner of a double play, leading to the infield fly rule. Although known for his defense, in 1890 he hit a robust .350. He was a career .292 hitter and topped .300 four times. (1946)

WILLIE McCOVEY

First baseman (1959-1980) Willie McCovey joined Giants teammate Willie Mays to give NL pitchers the willies. McCovey smashed 30 or more home runs seven times, leading the NL in dingers three times and in RBI twice. In 1969, "Stretch" was NL MVP with a .320 average, 45 homers, and 126 RBI. That same year he drew a record 45 intentional walks. In 1970, McCovey homered in all 12 parks, a rare feat. "Big Mac" notched 521 homers, 1,555 RBI, 1,229 runs scored, and 1,345 walks. (1986)

JOE McGINNITY

Pitcher (1899-1908) While McGinnity's nickname "Iron Man" was derived from his off-season occupation in a foundry, it well described his mound efforts. For nine consecutive years he pitched 300-plus innings, topping 400 innings twice and leading the league four times. He had a career 246-142 record with a 2.66 ERA and 314 complete games. He then went on to pitch another 17 seasons in the minors. (1946)

BILL McGOWAN

Umpire (1925-1954) McGowan earned his "No. 1" nickname in the AL because of his renown for accuracy. Chosen to work in eight World Series, he also worked four All-Star Games, including the first in 1933. (1992)

JOHN McGRAW

Manager (1899; 1901-1932) As third baseman for Baltimore in the 1890s, McGraw was talented enough to make the Hall on his merits as a player. As the Giants manager from 1902 to 1932, he dominated baseball during its "scientific" era, and successfully made the transition to the power game of the 1920s. Despite capturing ten pennants, "Little Napoleon" won the World Series only three times. A manager for 33 years, McGraw racked up 2,784 victories in

4,801 games, both second on the all-time list to Connie Mack. (1937)

BILL McKECHNIE

Manager (1915; 1922-1926; 1928-1946) McKechnie may have been the best-liked manager ever while winning pennants with three different teams. "The Deacon's" best effort, though, might have been with the fifth-place 1937 Braves, enough to win the Manager of the Year award. He won two world championships and was 1,896-1,723 in 25 years. (1962)

JOE MEDWICK

Outfielder (1932-1948) Medwick provided the power to light up the 1930s Cardinals' "Gashouse Gang." He led the NL in RBI three consecutive years and in hits twice. In 1937, "Ducky" (a nickname he loathed) batted .374 with 31 homers and 154 RBI to capture the Triple Crown. "Muscles" was a brawler who had a career .324 average, 1,383 RBI, and 540 doubles. In the 1934 World Series against Detroit, he was ordered from the field for his own safety. (1968)

JOHNNY MIZE

First baseman (1936-1942; 1946-1953) Despite losing three prime years to World War II, Mize still connected for 359 home runs, primarily with the Cardinals and Giants. He led the NL in homers four times and RBI three times. Sold to the Yankees in 1949, Mize played in five World Series, hitting three home runs in the 1952 classic. "The Big Cat" batted .312 lifetime, slugged .562, and drove in 1,337 runs. (1981)

JOE MORGAN

Second baseman (1963-1984) Where Morgan played, championships followed. After leading Cincinnati's "Big Red Machine" of the mid-1970s to two World Series victories, Morgan led the 1980 Astros to a division title. He then helped Philadelphia capture the pennant in 1983. "Little Joe" won back-to-back NL MVP Awards in 1975 and '76. Only 5'7", he had 268 career homers, 689 stolen bases, 1,133 RBI, 1,650 runs, and 1,865 walks. (1990)

STAN MUSIAL

Outfielder; first baseman (1941-1944; 1946-1963) Originally signed as a pitcher, Musial hurt his arm and transferred to the outfield. Joining the Cardinals in 1941, Musial batted .426 in 12 games, and he went on to lead the NL seven times in batting average. NL MVP in 1943, '46, and '48, he used his "corkscrew" batting stance to hit over .310 for 16 seasons in a row. When he retired in 1963, "Stan the Man" held more than 50 major-league and NL records. He had a career .331 batting average, 3,630 base hits (fourth all time), 725 doubles (third), 475 home runs, 1,951 RBI, and 1,949 runs scored. (1969)

HAL NEWHOUSER

Pitcher (1939-1955) The only pitcher to win back-to-back MVP Awards (in 1944 and '45), Newhouser was a Detroit native who pitched 15 seasons for the Tigers. Slighted by some as a wartime wonder, he had 275 Ks and a 26-9 record in 1946, and a 21-12 record in 1948. He had 207 career wins. (1992)

KID NICHOLS

Pitcher (1890-1901; 1904-1906) Ranked sixth all time in wins with 361, Nichols starred in the 1890s for Boston, leading them to five NL pennants. Winner of 30 games seven times, Nichols finished what he started: In his 501 starts, he was relieved only 25 times. He had a lifetime 361-208 record and a 2.95 ERA. (1949)

JIM O'ROURKE

Outfielder (1872-1893; 1904) In 1876, O'Rourke collected the first base hit in NL

history, one of 2,304 he'd gather for his career. A lifetime .310 hitter, O'Rourke's manner of speaking earned him the nickname "Orator Jim." (1945)

MEL OTT

Outfielder (1926-1947) Despite his small stature (5'9", 170 pounds), this Giant outfielder stands as a colossus among the game's sluggers. Ott's unique leg kick enabled him to generate the power for 511 home runs, the first man in NL history to hit 500. He led the NL in homers six times, but in RBI only once. When he retired in 1947, he held the NL career mark for homers, runs scored (1,859), RBI (1,860), and walks (1,708). "Master Melvin" retired with a .304 batting average. (1951)

SATCHEL PAIGE

Pitcher (Negro Leagues 1926-1947; 1950; AL 1948-1949; 1951-1953; 1965) The first African American ever elected to the Hall of Fame, Paige was the Negro Leagues' greatest drawing card. He began pitching for the Birmingham Black Barons in 1926 at age 20. His blazing fastball and effervescent personality made him a legend by age 30. He made his greatest mark on the game by pitching for the Kansas City Monarchs in the 1940s. In 1948, at age 42, he made his major-league debut and helped Cleveland to the AL pennant. (1971)

JIM PALMER

Pitcher (1965-1967; 1969-1984) Ace of Baltimore's powerful teams of the 1970s, Palmer won 20 games eight times on his way to three Cy Young Awards and 268 career wins. He led the AL in ERA twice and in innings pitched four times. He had a career 2.86 ERA, 2,212 Ks, and 1,311 walks in 3,948 innings pitched. (1990)

HERB PENNOCK
Pitcher (1912-1917; 1919-1934) Pennock finessed his way through 22 seasons to earn 240 wins. He had his greatest success with the Yankees of the 1920s, for whom he went 5-0 in World Series play. "The Knight of Kennett Square" won in double figures for 13 seasons and completed 247 of his 420 career starts. (1948)

GAYLORD PERRY
Pitcher (1962-1983) Though he won 314 games, struck out 3,534 batters, and registered a 3.11 ERA during a 22-year career, Perry was best known for throwing—or not throwing—a spitball. He won 20 games five times in his career. He won the AL Cy Young in 1972 and the NL Cy Young in 1978, making him the only pitcher in history to have won the award in both leagues. (1991)

EDDIE PLANK
Pitcher (1901-1917) A late bloomer, Plank didn't reach Connie Mack's A's until age 26. No matter, the left-hander blossomed to win 326 games. He won at least 20 games in eight seasons, with four in a row from 1902 to 1905. "Gettysburg Eddie" compiled 69 career shutouts (fifth all time) and a 2.35 ERA. (1946)

OLD HOSS RADBOURN
Pitcher (1880-1891) In 1884, Radbourn won 59 games for NL Providence, still an all-time record, notching a 1.38 ERA and 679 innings pitched. In only 12 seasons he chalked up 309 wins and a 2.67 ERA. Old Hoss's 489 career complete games are eighth on the all-time list. (1939)

PEE WEE REESE
Shortstop (1940-1942; 1946-1958) Reese led the Dodgers to seven pennants between 1941 and 1956. One of the top fielding shortstops during the 1940s and 1950s, Pee Wee was an All-Star from 1947 to 1954. He scored 1,338 runs in his career, leading the NL in 1947 with 132. When Branch Rickey signed Jackie Robinson, it was Reese, a Southerner, who led the Dodgers to accept Robinson as a teammate. (1984)

SAM RICE
Outfielder (1915-1934) Rice, a fleet 150-pounder, smacked 2,987 hits on his way to a .322 career average for Washington. He led the AL in hits twice and had 200 or more base hits six times. He scored 1,514 career runs and stole 351 bases. A master of bat control, Rice struck out only nine times in 616 at bats in 1929. (1963)

BRANCH RICKEY
Executive Rickey invented the farm system and built NL dynasties in St. Louis and Brooklyn. When he joined the Cardinals in 1919 as president and field manager, the franchise could not compete with richer clubs. "The Mahatma" began to buy minor-league clubs from which the Cards could obtain talent. By 1941, St. Louis had 32 minor-league affiliates. Rickey moved to Brooklyn in 1942 and integrated the major leagues in 1947, winning his biggest fight when he signed Jackie Robinson. (1967)

EPPA RIXEY
Pitcher (1912-1917; 1919-1933) Rixey was a very good pitcher for some not very good teams, winning 266 games while losing 251. A master of control, Rixey won in double digits in 14 seasons and won 20 games four times. In 1922, he went a league-leading 25-13 for Cincinnati. (1963)

PHIL RIZZUTO
Shortstop (1941-1942; 1946-1956) "Scooter" played Yankee shortstop for 13 years and went to the World Series in nine of them. Just 5'6", he won the AL MVP Award in 1950 with a .324 average, 200 hits, and 125 runs scored. He was selected for the All-Star Game five times. He

embarked on a long broadcasting career after his playing days. (1994)

ROBIN ROBERTS

Pitcher (1948-1966) Despite a penchant for throwing the gopher ball, Roberts won 20 games for six consecutive seasons from 1950 to 1955. He topped the NL in wins four straight years, and in innings and complete games five times each. He also led the NL two years in a row in Ks. In 1952, he went 28-7 for the Phillies. Roberts was 286-245 with a 3.41 ERA. (1976)

BROOKS ROBINSON

Third baseman (1955-1977) One of the greatest fielding third basemen ever, Robinson won the Gold Glove 16 times in 23 seasons. The American League MVP in 1964, Brooks turned in a .317 average, 28 homers, and a league-leading 118 RBI. He sparkled in postseason play, posting a .348 average in 18 ALCS games. In the 1970 World Series, he led the Orioles over the Reds, hitting .429 and turning in one spectacular fielding play after another, earning him MVP honors for the Series. "Hoover" had 268 career homers, 1,357 RBI, and 1,232 runs. (1983)

FRANK ROBINSON

Outfielder (1956-1976) Robinson was the first player to be selected MVP in both leagues. He was named NL Rookie of the Year in 1956 and the loop's MVP in 1961, when he paced the NL with a .611 slugging average and led the Reds to a pennant. Traded to Baltimore after the '65 season, Frank responded in '66 by hitting .316, slugging 49 home runs, and knocking in 122 runs to win the Triple Crown. He hit 30 homers in 11 seasons, and his 586 career homers rank fourth on the all-time list. He also had 1,812 career RBI and 1,829 runs scored. Named manager of the Indians in 1975, Robinson was the first African American to manage a major-league team. (1982)

JACKIE ROBINSON

Second baseman (1947-1956) The first African American to play major-league baseball since 1884, Robinson succeeded under almost unbearable pressure to secure the black player a permanent place in the game. He endured numerous racial slights, even from his own teammates, without yielding his dignity, while leading the Dodgers to six pennants. A tremendous athlete, Robinson was a four-sport star at UCLA and also served in the Army during World War II. As a 28-year-old rookie for Brooklyn in 1947, Robinson's aggressive base-running and hitting earned him Rookie of the Year honors. Two years later, in 1949, he led the NL with a .342 average and was named NL MVP. He had a career .311 batting average. (1962)

WILBERT ROBINSON

Manager (1902; 1914-1931) A catching star for Baltimore in the 1890s, Robinson coached under the Giants' John McGraw before becoming Brooklyn's manager in 1914. "Uncle Robbie" won pennants in 1916 and 1920 but never won a World Series. He had a career 1,399-1,398 record. (1945)

EDD ROUSH

Outfielder (1913-1929; 1931) One of the great defensive outfielders, Roush swung his 48-ounce bat with enough authority to attain two NL batting titles and a .323 lifetime average. In his ten years in Cincinnati, he never hit lower than .321. He had 1,099 career runs and 981 RBI. Roush habitually held out of spring training. (1962)

RED RUFFING

Pitcher (1924-1942; 1945-1947) In six seasons with the Red Sox, Ruffing couldn't win, going 39-96 from 1924 to 1930 and leading the AL in losses twice. After he was traded to the Yankees, he couldn't lose, with a career 273-225 record and a 7-2 mark in ten World Series games. He won

20 games each season from 1936 to 1939. (1967)

AMOS RUSIE

Pitcher (1889-1895; 1897-1898; 1901)
Rusie's fastball forced the rule makers to move the mound from 45 feet to 60 feet 6 inches. From 1890 to 1895, the Giants pitcher led the NL in strikeouts five times, yet he had about one walk for every K. "The Hoosier Thunderbolt" had eight 20-win seasons and 245 career victories. (1977)

BABE RUTH

Outfielder; pitcher (1914-1935) George Herman Ruth is arguably the greatest player of all time. A man of gargantuan appetites and ability, the Babe's mystique has transcended the sport of baseball and has become ingrained in American mythology. Starting his career as a pitcher with Boston, he was one of the best in the AL. In 1916, the Babe led the AL with a 1.75 ERA while going 23-12. He had 24 wins in '17 with a loop-high 35 complete games. Converted to the outfield part-time in 1918, he led the AL in homers with 11. After he was sold to the Yankees in 1920, he became a full-time flycatcher, and all but invented the home run, slugging 714 for his career, including a then-record 60 in 1927. He led the AL in homers 12 seasons, RBI six seasons, slugging percentage 12 times, and bases on balls 11 times. He had a career .342 batting average, .690 slugging average (first all time), 506 doubles, 2,213 RBI (second all time), 2,174 runs (second all time), and 2,056 walks (first all time). (1936)

RAY SCHALK

Catcher (1912-1929) Although Schalk's career average was .253, few complained when he was elected to the Hall. A superb catcher, Ray's game was defense. In 1920, he caught four 20-game winners for the White Sox, and he caught four no-hitters, more than any other catcher. He holds the AL record for assists by a catcher (1,811). (1955)

MIKE SCHMIDT

Third baseman (1972-1989) The leader of a Phillies team that finally won its first world championship in 1980, Schmidt is credited with being the greatest all-around third baseman in history. A fine power hitter, he was an eight-time NL home run leader, had more than 100 RBI in a season nine times, and retired with 548 homers and 1,595 RBI. Schmidt was the NL MVP in 1980, '81, and '86 and won ten Gold Gloves. (1995)

RED SCHOENDIENST

Second baseman (1945-1963) Schoendienst teamed with shortstop Marty Marion to form one of baseball's best-ever double-play combinations. Red could also hit, reaching a career-high .342 average in 1953. He had 2,449 career hits and 1,223 runs scored. (1989)

TOM SEAVER

Pitcher (1967-1986) In 1992, Seaver was named on a record 98.8 percent of the ballots for enshrinement, indicating his stature among fans. A three-time Cy Young winner (1969, '73, and '75), he also finished second twice and third once. "Tom Terrific" led the Mets to a miracle world championship in 1969. He won 311 games and struck out 3,640 batters, and his .603 winning percentage was the best of any 300-game winner since Lefty Grove retired in 1941. (1992)

JOE SEWELL

Shortstop (1920-1933) Sewell replaced Ray Chapman in the Cleveland lineup following Chapman's tragic death in 1920. One of the game's best shortstops, Sewell struck out only 114 times in 7,132 at bats. He had 1,141 runs and 1,051 RBI. (1977)

AL SIMMONS

Outfielder (1924-1941; 1943-1944) An unlikely looking hitter due to his "foot in the bucket" batting stance, Simmons was a leading slugger of his era. From 1929 to 1931, he helped the Athletics to three consecutive pennants, winning batting titles in both 1930 and 1931 with averages of .381 and .390. "Bucketfoot Al" batted over .300 in the first 11 seasons of his career, racking up 2,927 hits and a career .334 batting average. (1953)

GEORGE SISLER

First baseman (1915-1922; 1924-1930) Like Babe Ruth, Sisler's hitting was too good to be on a pitcher's schedule. He was switched to first base full-time in 1916 for the Browns and became one of the best, defensively. At bat he was simply unbelievable, hitting .407, .371, and .420 from 1920 to 1922. In 1920, "Gorgeous George" collected 257 base hits, still the all-time record. A sinus infection that affected his vision sidelined him in 1923. He returned to play seven more seasons. (1939)

ENOS SLAUGHTER

Outfielder (1938-1942; 1946-1959) Slaughter would do anything in order to win, using hustle to make up for any shortcomings in talent. His mad dash from first to home on a double won the 1946 World Series for the Cardinals. "Country" led the NL in base hits in 1942 before going to war; he led the league in RBI when he came back. (1985)

DUKE SNIDER

Outfielder (1947-1964) Known as the "Duke of Flatbush" to his Brooklyn fans, Snider was one of a trio of Hall of Fame center fielders in New York during the 1950s. The others were named Willie Mays and Mickey Mantle. Snider hit 40 homers from 1953 to 1957. He had 407 career homers, 1,333 RBI, and 1,259 runs scored. (1980)

WARREN SPAHN

Pitcher (1942; 1946-1965) Baseball's winningest left-hander, Spahn didn't even stick in the majors until age 25. With the Braves, he won 20 games or more 13 times, tying the major-league record. He led the league in wins eight times, complete games nine times, and Ks four times. He won the Cy Young Award in 1957. Spahn retired with 363 wins (fifth all time), 245 losses, a 3.09 ERA, 382 complete games, and 63 shutouts (sixth all time). (1973)

AL SPALDING

Pitcher (1871-1878); executive A star pitcher in the 1870s, Spalding started a sporting goods company and took over NL Chicago. As a pitcher, he had a .796 career winning percentage. He helped write the new NL's constitution and was inducted as an executive. (1939)

TRIS SPEAKER

Outfielder (1907-1928) The best center fielder of his time, Speaker played close enough to the infield to take pickoff throws at second. "The Grey Eagle" hit over .300 in 18 seasons and topped .375 six times on his way to a career .345 mark (fifth all time). Traded from Boston to Cleveland in 1916, he won his only batting title, at .386. "Spoke" had a record 792 career doubles and 3,514 hits (fifth all time). (1937)

WILLIE STARGELL

Outfielder; first baseman (1962-1982) One of the strongest players ever, Stargell made tape-measure homers common. He had 13 consecutive years of 20 or more home runs, pacing the NL in 1971 and 1973. He was named season, NLCS, and World Series MVP in 1979, when he led the world champion Bucs. He had 475 career homers and 1,540 RBI. (1988)

CASEY STENGEL

Manager (1934-1936; 1938-1943; 1949-1960; 1962-1965) As manager of Brooklyn and Boston, Stengel earned a reputation as an entertaining, if not very effective, skipper. His creative use of the language, dubbed "Stengelese," made him a fan favorite. Named Yankee manager in 1949, "The Old Professor" won ten pennants in 12 years, plus seven world championships. He had a career 1,905-1,842 record. (1966)

BILL TERRY

First baseman (1923-1936) A career .341 hitter, Terry was the last National Leaguer to hit over .400, batting .401 in 1930 with 254 hits. "Memphis Bill" had more than 100 RBI from 1927 to 1932. Showing long-ball power when he wanted, Terry smashed 28 homers in 1932. Generally, though, his strengths were doubles and triples. He took over as Giant manager in 1932 and led the team to three pennants. (1954)

SAM THOMPSON

Outfielder (1885-1898; 1906) Thompson was a home run hitter in an era when the talent was not appreciated. He had his greatest success with the Phillies in the 1890s, where he hit .407 in 1894. "Big Sam" led the NL in hits three times, and in homers and RBI twice each. He had 127 career homers, with a .331 average and 1,299 RBI. (1974)

JOE TINKER

Shortstop (1902-1916) Interestingly, Tinker, Johnny Evers, and Frank Chance were all elected to the Hall in the same year. Shortstop Tinker was a fielding whiz who keyed the success of that double-play combo. Although not a great hitter, he stole 336 career bases to augment his .263 average. (1946)

PIE TRAYNOR

Third baseman (1920-1935; 1937) Traynor earned his way into the Hall of Fame as the best fielding third baseman of his era. A career .320 hitter for Pittsburgh,

he hit .300 or better ten times and slugged more than 100 RBI seven times. Pie racked up 1,273 career RBI and 1,183 runs. (1948)

DAZZY VANCE

Pitcher (1915; 1918; 1922-1935) As a 31-year-old rookie with Brooklyn in 1922, Vance won 18 games. Two years later his mark of 28-6 earned him league MVP honors. Armed with an incredible fastball, he led the major leagues in Ks in each of his first seven seasons and paced the NL in ERA three times. Dazzy had a career 197-140 record. (1955)

ARKY VAUGHAN

Shortstop (1932-1943; 1947-1948) One of the game's best hitting shortstops, only twice in 14 seasons did Vaughan fail to hit .300. In 1935, his .385 average for Pittsburgh led the NL. Arky notched a career .406 on-base percentage, .318 batting average, 1,173 runs, and 926 RBI. He eventually became a top fielder, leading the NL in putouts and assists three times. (1985)

BILL VEECK

Executive One of baseball's most colorful showmen, Veeck integrated the AL by signing Larry Doby with the Indians. He owned three AL teams—Cleveland, St. Louis, and Chicago. He sent the 3'7" Eddie Gaedel up to bat for the Browns, and as the chief of the White Sox, introduced baseball's first exploding scoreboard. (1991)

RUBE WADDELL

Pitcher (1897; 1899-1910) Waddell threw hard and lived even harder. In the AL's first six seasons, Rube was the circuit's best left-hander, under the watchful eye of Connie Mack, winning 20 games four straight years and leading the league in Ks six consecutive years. The eccentric Waddell had a career 193-143 record with 2,316 Ks. (1946)

HONUS WAGNER

Shortstop (1897-1917) One of the game's first five inductees to the Hall of Fame, Wagner hit over .300 15 consecutive seasons. Bowlegged and awkward looking, Wagner possessed tremendous speed and range afield. For his 21-year career, he had 722 stolen bases and a .327 batting average, highest of any shortstop. Honus led the NL in batting eight times, slugging six times, RBI five times, runs scored twice, and doubles seven times. "The Flying Dutchman" had 3,415 career hits, 640 doubles, 252 triples, 1,732 RBI, 1,736 runs scored, and 963 walks. Some consider Wagner the greatest player of all time. (1936)

BOBBY WALLACE

Shortstop (1894-1918) The first AL shortstop elected to the Hall, Wallace made his mark with the glove, leading the league in putouts three times and assists four times. He had 6.1 chances per game lifetime. (1953)

ED WALSH

Pitcher (1904-1917) Perhaps no other pitcher threw the spitball as successfully as Walsh. While his arm gave out after only seven full seasons as a starter, he recorded nearly 170 of his career 195 wins during that span. In 1908, he pitched 464 innings for the White Sox on his way to 40 victories. He led the AL in games pitched five times, innings pitched four times, and strikeouts twice. "Big Ed" had a career 195-126 record with a 1.82 ERA, the lowest of all time. (1946)

LLOYD WANER

Outfielder (1927-1942; 1944-1945) "Little Poison," to older brother Paul's "Big Poison," Lloyd Waner used his speed to cover the vast Forbes Field outfield, leading the NL in putouts four times. In 1927, Waner's rookie year, the little leadoff man hit 198 one-baggers. Waner had a .316 career batting average, 2,459 hits, and 1,201 runs scored. (1967)

PAUL WANER

Outfielder (1926-1945) "Big Poison" didn't settle for hitting singles like his little brother; 905 of Paul Waner's 3,152 career hits were for extra bases. He led the NL in hitting four times, peaking at .380 in 1927, when he led Pittsburgh to the pennant and was named league MVP. Waner retired with a .333 batting average, 605 doubles, 1,627 runs scored, and 1,309 RBI. (1952)

MONTE WARD

Pitcher; shortstop (1878-1894) Perhaps no figure in baseball had distinguished himself in so many areas as did Ward. As a pitcher for Providence, he led the NL in ERA in 1878 and in wins in 1879. Switched to shortstop in 1885, he became the best in the league for New York. Unhappy with the reserve clause, in 1890 he helped form the Players' League. Becoming a manager, he led the Giants to a championship in 1894. (1964)

EARL WEAVER

Manager (1968-1985) "The Earl of Baltimore," a manager far ahead of his time, spent 17 seasons with the Orioles, winning six AL East titles, four pennants, and one world championship. He won 100-plus games five times and wrapped up his career with a .583 winning percentage (1,480-1,060). Weaver was known for his energetic disputes with umpires and was ejected from 91 games. (1996)

GEORGE WEISS

Executive As farm director and general manager of the Yankees from 1932 to 1960, Weiss deserves much of the credit for creating the Yankee dynasty. He built the farm system to 21 teams, then became general manager and dealt from strength, constantly picking up precisely the player the Yankees needed in exchange for

MICKEY WELCH

Pitcher (1880-1892) The third man to win 300 games, Welch starred in the 1880s for Troy and New York of the NL. In 1885 he won 17 consecutive decisions on his way to 44 victories for the year. "Smiling Mickey" won at least 20 games nine times, with four seasons of more than 30. He had a career 307-210 record with a 2.71 ERA. (1973)

ZACK WHEAT

Outfielder (1909-1927) The Dodgers' first star, Wheat played left field in Ebbets Field for 18 seasons. A line-drive hitter, he topped the .300 mark in 14 seasons, including an NL-best .335 in 1918. He had a career .317 average, 2,884 hits, 1,248 RBI, 1,289 runs scored, and 205 stolen bases. (1959)

HOYT WILHELM

Pitcher (1952-1972) Wilhelm was the first pitcher elected to the Hall solely on his merits as a reliever. A knuckleballer, he toiled for nine teams, pitching in a record 1,070 games and winning 124 in relief. He started only 52 games in his 21-year career, compiling 227 saves and a 2.52 ERA. "Snacks" pitched five consecutive seasons (1964 to 1968) with an ERA under 2.00. (1985)

BILLY WILLIAMS

Outfielder (1959-1976) Williams's much admired swing produced 426 career homers and a .290 batting average. The NL Rookie of the Year in 1961, he had at least 20 home runs and 84 RBI in 13 consecutive seasons. His two best seasons were in 1970 and 1972. In 1970, Billy hit .322 with 42 homers, a league-best 137 runs scored, and 129 RBI. He led the NL with a .333 batting average and a .606 slugging average, with 37 homers and 122 RBI in 1972. Play-ing most of his career for the Cubs, between 1963 and 1970 Williams played in an NL-record 1,117 consecutive games. (1987)

TED WILLIAMS

Outfielder (1939-1942; 1946-1960) Williams's one desire was to walk down the street and have people say, "There goes the greatest hitter that ever lived." Arguably, he was. Despite missing nearly five years to the military, the Red Sox left fielder won two MVP Awards, six batting and four home run titles, and two Triple Crowns. "The Splendid Splinter" batted over .316 in each of his 19 seasons except one. In 1941, "The Kid" hit a .406 mark. He's the last player to attain that plateau. He had 30 or more homers in eight seasons, 20 or more in 16 seasons. "Teddy Ballgame" has the sixth-highest career batting average (.344), the second-highest slugging average (.634), the second-most bases on balls (2,019), the tenth-most home runs (521), and the 11th-most RBI (1,839). (1966)

VIC WILLIS

Pitcher (1898-1910) A big right-hander with a wicked curveball, Willis gained a reputation for durability, winning at least 20 games eight times. He pitched for the Boston Beaneaters, Pittsburgh Pirates, and St. Louis Cardinals, fashioning a 249-205 record and a 2.63 ERA. (1995)

HACK WILSON

Outfielder (1923-1934) From 1926 to 1930, the muscular, squat Wilson was one of the game's greatest sluggers. In 1930, the Cub outfielder hit an NL-record 56 homers and knocked in a major-league-record 190 runs. He led the NL in homers four times and in RBI twice. Liquor, however, was Wilson's downfall, and by the end of 1934, he was out of baseball. (1979)

GEORGE WRIGHT

Shortstop (1869-1882) The star shortstop for the original Cincinnati Red Stockings team that went undefeated for the entire 1869 season, Wright played through the 1882 season. He then helped start the Union Association in 1884. Later in life he served on baseball's Centennial Commission, and was instrumental in the creation of the National Baseball Hall of Fame. (1937)

HARRY WRIGHT

Manager (1871-1893) Harry Wright, the older brother of George, was player-manager of the Cincinnati Red Stockings (the first overtly all-professional team), which Harry led to some 130 consecutive victories. He helped start the National Association in 1871, and later managed a number of NL teams, going 225-60 in the National Association and 1,000-825 in the National League. (1953)

EARLY WYNN

Pitcher (1939; 1941-1944; 1946-1963) Wynn was traded to Cleveland in 1949 and became a big winner. He won 20 games for the Indians four times and had eight consecutive winning seasons. Traded to the White Sox after the '57 season, "Gus" led Chicago to the pennant in 1959 by winning 22 games, plus the Cy Young Award. He had a 300-244 career record and a 3.54 ERA. (1972)

CARL YASTRZEMSKI

Outfielder (1961-1983) Spending his entire 23-year career with the Red Sox, Yastrzemski was the first AL player to collect over 3,000 hits and 400 home runs. "Yaz" will always be remembered for one remarkable season—1967, the year of The Impossible Dream. He won the Triple Crown, and during a most remarkable September that season, he single-handedly won the pennant for Boston. Taking over left field for Ted Williams, "Captain Carl" won batting titles in 1963, '67, and '68. He had 3,419 career hits, a .285 average, 646 doubles, 452 home runs, 1,844 RBI, 1,816 runs scored, and 1,845 walks. (1989)

508

TOM YAWKEY

Executive Yawkey is one of the few inducted to the Hall who neither played, coached, umpired, nor served as a general manager. In 1933, at age 30, he received his inheritance and bought the Red Sox for $1.5 million. Boston at that time was a doormat and Fenway Park was falling apart. Over the next 44 seasons he spent lavishly on the club and the stadium, doling out another $1.5 million for renovations alone. (1980)

CY YOUNG

Pitcher (1890-1911) Young won 511 games, which is 94 victories more than runner-up Walter Johnson. In a career that bridged three decades and several eras of play, Cy was consistently superb. Blessed with speed, control, stamina, and just about every quality a successful pitcher needs, Young won 20 or more games 15 times, including nine seasons in a row from 1891 to 1899. He led his league in victories four times, and in ERA, winning percentage, and strikeouts twice each. Cy is also first on the complete-game list with 749 and innings pitched list with 7,356⅔. When they decided to give an award to the season's top pitcher, they named it after Young. (1937)

ROSS YOUNGS

Outfielder (1917-1926) Youngs was a star on four straight pennant winners for John McGraw's Giants in the early 1920s. On the verge of greatness, Youngs's skills deserted him in 1925. Diagnosed with Bright's disease, a terminal kidney disorder, Youngs gamely played one more season and died in 1927. He had a .322 career batting average with 1,491 hits and 812 runs scored. (1972)

AWARDS AND HIGHLIGHTS

Baseball's top achievements and tributes are listed in this section. The all-time career leaders in batting and pitching categories are included (with players active in 1996 in **bold**), as well as the leaders among active players. The all-time single-season leaders are next. The Most Valuable Players, the Cy Young Award winners, and the Rookies of the Year follow. Fielding excellence is acknowledged with the Gold Glove Award winners. Finally, the winners and losers of the World Series, the National League and American League Championship Series, and the Division Series are listed.

ALL-TIME LEADERS

BATTING AVERAGE
1. Ty Cobb .... .366
2. Rogers Hornsby .... .358
3. Joe Jackson .... .356
4. Ed Delahanty .... .346
5. Tris Speaker .... .345
6. Ted Williams .... .344
7. Billy Hamilton .... .344
8. Dan Brouthers .... .342
9. Babe Ruth .... .342
10. Harry Heilmann .... .342
11. Pete Browning .... .341
12. Willie Keeler .... .341
13. Bill Terry .... .341
14. George Sisler .... .340
15. Lou Gehrig .... .340
16. Jesse Burkett .... .338
17. Nap Lajoie .... .338
18. **Tony Gwynn** .... .337
19. Riggs Stephenson ..... .336
20. Al Simmons .... .334

HITS
1. Pete Rose 4,256
2. Ty Cobb 4,189
3. Hank Aaron 3,771
4. Stan Musial 3,630
5. Tris Speaker 3,514
6. Carl Yastrzemski 3,419
7. Cap Anson 3,418
8. Honus Wagner 3,415
9. Eddie Collins 3,315
10. Willie Mays 3,283
11. Nap Lajoie 3,242
12. **Eddie Murray** 3,218
13. George Brett 3,154
14. Paul Waner 3,152
15. Robin Yount 3,142
16. Dave Winfield 3,110
17. Rod Carew 3,053

18. Lou Brock 3,023
19. **Paul Molitor** 3,014
20. Al Kaline 3,007

DOUBLES
1. Tris Speaker 792
2. Pete Rose 746
3. Stan Musial 725
4. Ty Cobb 724
5. George Brett 665
6. Nap Lajoie 657
7. Carl Yastrzemski 646
8. Honus Wagner 640
9. Hank Aaron 624
10. Paul Waner 605
11. Robin Yount 583
12. Cap Anson 581
13. Charlie Gehringer 574
14. **Eddie Murray** 553
15. **Paul Molitor** 544
16. Harry Heilmann 542
17. Rogers Hornsby 541
18. Dave Winfield 540
    Joe Medwick 540
20. Al Simmons 539

TRIPLES
1. Sam Crawford 309
2. Ty Cobb 295
3. Honus Wagner 252
4. Jake Beckley 243
5. Roger Connor 233
6. Tris Speaker 222
7. Fred Clarke 220
8. Dan Brouthers 205
9. Joe Kelley 194
10. Paul Waner 191
11. Bid McPhee 188
12. Eddie Collins 187
13. Ed Delahanty 185

14. Sam Rice 184
15. Edd Roush 182
    Jesse Burkett 182
17. Ed Konetchy 181
18. Buck Ewing 178
19. Stan Musial 177
    Rabbit Maranville 177

HOME RUNS
1. Hank Aaron 755
2. Babe Ruth 714
3. Willie Mays 660
4. Frank Robinson 586
5. Harmon Killebrew 573
6. Reggie Jackson 563
7. Mike Schmidt 548
8. Mickey Mantle 536
9. Jimmie Foxx 534
10. Ted Williams 521
    Willie McCovey 521
12. Eddie Mathews 512
    Ernie Banks 512
14. Mel Ott 511
15. **Eddie Murray** 501
16. Lou Gehrig 493
17. Willie Stargell 475
    Stan Musial 475
19. Dave Winfield 465
20. Carl Yastrzemski 452

RUNS BATTED IN
1. Hank Aaron 2,297
2. Babe Ruth 2,213
3. Cap Anson 2,076
4. Lou Gehrig 1,995
5. Stan Musial 1,951
6. Ty Cobb 1,937
7. Jimmie Foxx 1,922
8. Willie Mays 1,903
9. **Eddie Murray** 1,899

509

10. Mel Ott.....................1,860
11. Carl Yastrzemski 1,844
12. Ted Williams..............1,839
13. Dave Winfield............1,833
14. Al Simmons...............1,827
15. Frank Robinson.........1,812
16. Honus Wagner...........1,732
17. Reggie Jackson.........1,702
18. Tony Perez................1,652
19. Ernie Banks..............1,636
20. Goose Goslin.............1,609

SLUGGING AVERAGE

1. Babe Ruth 690
2. Ted Williams...............634
3. Lou Gehrig..................632
4. Jimmie Foxx 609
5. Hank Greenberg..........605
6. Joe DiMaggio..............579
7. Rogers Hornsby 577
8. Johnny Mize...............562
9. Stan Musial................559
10. Willie Mays................557
11. Mickey Mantle............557
12. Hank Aaron...............555
13. Ken Griffey Jr...........549
14. Ralph Kiner...............548
15. Barry Bonds.............548
16. Hack Wilson..............545
17. Mark McGwire..........544
18. Chuck Klein..............543
19. Duke Snider.............540
20. Frank Robinson 537

ON-BASE PERCENTAGE

1. Ted Williams...............483
2. Babe Ruth..................474
3. John McGraw..............466
4. Billy Hamilton.............455
5. Lou Gehrig..................447
6. Rogers Hornsby..........434
7. Ty Cobb.....................433
8. Jimmie Foxx 428
9. Tris Speaker..............428
10. Wade Boggs.............425
11. Ferris Fain 425
12. Eddie Collins 424
13. Dan Brouthers...........423
14. Joe Jackson 423
15. Max Bishop...............423
16. Mickey Mantle...........423
17. Mickey Cochrane.......419
18. Stan Musial...............418
19. Cupid Childs..............416
20. Jesse Burkett............415

STOLEN BASES

1. Rickey Henderson..1,186
2. Lou Brock..................938
3. Billy Hamilton.............912
4. Ty Cobb.....................892
5. Tim Raines.................787
6. Vince Coleman...........752
7. Eddie Collins 744
8. Arlie Latham...............739
9. Max Carey.................738
10. Honus Wagner 722
11. Joe Morgan 689
12. Willie Wilson..............668
13. Tom Brown................657
14. Bert Campaneris.........649
15. George Davis.............616
16. Dummy Hoy...............594
17. Maury Wills...............586
18. George VanHaltren 583
19. Ozzie Smith..............580
20. Hugh Duffy 574

RUNS SCORED

1. Ty Cobb..................2,246
2. Babe Ruth...............2,174
   Hank Aaron 2,174
4. Pete Rose...............2,165
5. Willie Mays..............2,062
6. Cap Anson...............1,996
7. Stan Musial..............1,949
8. Lou Gehrig...............1,888
9. Tris Speaker............1,882
10. Mel Ott...................1,859
11. Frank Robinson........1,829
    Rickey Henderson..1,829
13. Eddie Collins 1,821
14. Carl Yastrzemski 1,816
15. Ted Williams............1,798
16. Charlie Gehringer......1,774
17. Jimmie Foxx 1,751
18. Honus Wagner..........1,736
19. Jim O'Rourke 1,729
20. Jesse Burkett 1,720

BASES ON BALLS

1. Babe Ruth................2,056
2. Ted Williams............2,019
3. Joe Morgan 1,865
4. Carl Yastrzemski 1,845
5. Mickey Mantle 1,733
6. Mel Ott...................1,708
7. Rickey Henderson..1,675
8. Eddie Yost...............1,614
9. Darrell Evans...........1,605
10. Stan Musial.............1,599

11. Pete Rose................1,566
12. Harmon Killebrew 1,559
13. Lou Gehrig...............1,508
14. Mike Schmidt............1,507
15. Eddie Collins 1,499
16. Willie Mays..............1,464
17. Jimmie Foxx 1,452
18. Eddie Mathews..........1,444
19. Frank Robinson.........1,420
20. Hank Aaron..............1,402

GAMES PLAYED

1. Pete Rose................3,562
2. Carl Yastrzemski 3,308
3. Hank Aaron..............3,298
4. Ty Cobb...................3,035
5. Stan Musial..............3,026
6. Willie Mays..............2,992
7. Dave Winfield 2,973
8. Eddie Murray...........2,971
9. Rusty Staub..............2,951
10. Brooks Robinson.......2,896
11. Robin Yount..............2,856
12. Al Kaline..................2,834
13. Eddie Collins 2,826
14. Reggie Jackson.........2,820
15. Frank Robinson.........2,808
16. Honus Wagner..........2,792
17. Tris Speaker.............2,789
18. Tony Perez...............2,777
19. Mel Ott...................2,730
20. George Brett.............2,707

WINS

1. Cy Young..................511
2. Walter Johnson..........417
3. Christy Mathewson.....373
   Pete Alexander...........373
5. Pud Galvin................364
6. Warren Spahn 363
7. Kid Nichols...............361
8. Tim Keefe.................342
9. Steve Carlton.............329
10. John Clarkson 328
11. Eddie Plank..............326
12. Don Sutton...............324
    Nolan Ryan..............324
14. Phil Niekro...............318
15. Gaylord Perry 314
16. Tom Seaver..............311
17. Charley Radbourn 309
18. Mickey Welch...........307
19. Early Wynn...............300
    Lefty Grove...............300

510

WINNING PERCENTAGE

1. Al Spalding .... .795
2. Dave Foutz .... .690
3. Whitey Ford .... .690
4. Bob Caruthers .... .688
5. Lefty Grove .... .680
6. Vic Raschi .... .667
7. Larry Corcoran .... .665
8. Christy Mathewson ..... .665
9. Sam Leever .... .660
10. Sal Maglie .... .657
11. Dick McBride .... .656
12. Sandy Koufax .... .655
13. Johnny Allen .... .654
14. Ron Guidry .... .651
15. Lefty Gomez .... .649
16. John Clarkson .... .648
17. Mordecai Brown .... .648
18. **Dwight Gooden .... .646**
19. Dizzy Dean .... .644
20. Pete Alexander .... .642

EARNED RUN AVERAGE

1. Ed Walsh 1.82
2. Addie Joss 1.89
3. Al Spalding 2.04
4. Mordecai Brown 2.06
5. John Ward 2.10
6. Christy Mathewson 2.13
7. Tommy Bond 2.14
8. Rube Waddell 2.16
9. Walter Johnson 2.17
10. Orval Overall 2.23
11. Will White 2.28
12. Ed Reulbach 2.28
13. Jim Scott 2.30
14. Eddie Plank 2.35
15. Larry Corcoran 2.36
16. George McQuillan 2.38
17. Ed Killian 2.38
18. Eddie Cicotte 2.38
19. Candy Cummings 2.39
20. Doc White 2.39

STRIKEOUTS

1. Nolan Ryan 5,714
2. Steve Carlton 4,136
3. Bert Blyleven 3,701
4. Tom Seaver 3,640
5. Don Sutton 3,574
6. Gaylord Perry 3,534
7. Walter Johnson 3,509
8. Phil Niekro 3,342
9. Fergie Jenkins 3,192
10. Bob Gibson 3,117

11. Jim Bunning 2,855
12. Mickey Lolich 2,832
13. Cy Young 2,803
14. Frank Tanana 2,773
15. **Roger Clemens 2,590**
16. Warren Spahn 2,583
17. Bob Feller 2,581
18. Tim Keefe 2,560
19. Jerry Koosman 2,556
20. Christy Mathewson ...2,502

SAVES

1. **Lee Smith 473**
2. Jeff Reardon 367
3. **Dennis Eckersley 353**
4. Rollie Fingers 341
5. John Franco 323
6. Tom Henke 311
7. Rich Gossage 310
8. Bruce Sutter 300
9. **Randy Myers 274**
10. Dave Righetti 252
11. Dan Quisenberry 244
12. Jeff Montgomery 242
    Doug Jones 242
14. Sparky Lyle 238
15. Hoyt Wilhelm 227
16. **Todd Worrell 221**
17. Gene Garber 218
18. Dave Smith 216
19. **Rick Aguilera 211**
20. **Bobby Thigpen 201**

COMPLETE GAMES

1. Cy Young 749
2. Pud Galvin 646
3. Tim Keefe 554
4. Kid Nichols 531
   Walter Johnson 531
6. Mickey Welch 525
   Bobby Mathews 525
8. Charley Radbourn 489
9. John Clarkson 485
10. Tony Mullane 468
11. Jim McCormick 466
12. Gus Weyhing 448
13. Pete Alexander 437
14. Christy Mathewson 434
15. Jack Powell 422
16. Eddie Plank 410
17. Will White 394
18. Amos Rusie 393
19. Vic Willis 388
20. Tommy Bond 386

SHUTOUTS

1. Walter Johnson 110
2. Pete Alexander 90
3. Christy Mathewson 79
4. Cy Young 76
5. Eddie Plank 69
6. Warren Spahn 63
7. Tom Seaver 61
   Nolan Ryan 61
9. Bert Blyleven 60
10. Don Sutton 58
11. Ed Walsh 57
    Pud Galvin 57
13. Bob Gibson 56
14. Steve Carlton 55
    Mordecai Brown 55
16. Gaylord Perry 53
    Jim Palmer 53
18. Juan Marichal 52
19. Vic Willis 50
    Rube Waddell 50

GAMES PITCHED

1. Hoyt Wilhelm 1,070
2. Kent Tekulve 1,050
3. Rich Gossage 1,002
4. **Lee Smith 997**
5. Lindy McDaniel 987
6. **Dennis Eckersley 964**
7. Rollie Fingers 944
8. Gene Garber 931
9. Cy Young 906
10. Sparky Lyle 899
11. Jim Kaat 898
12. Jesse Orosco 885
13. Jeff Reardon 880
14. Don McMahon 874
15. Phil Niekro 864

INNINGS PITCHED

1. Cy Young 7,356.0
2. Pud Galvin 6,003.1
3. Walter Johnson 5,914.2
4. Phil Niekro 5,404.1
5. Nolan Ryan 5,386.0
6. Gaylord Perry 5,350.1
7. Don Sutton 5,282.1
8. Warren Spahn 5,243.2
9. Steve Carlton 5,217.1
10. Pete Alexander 5,190.0
11. Kid Nichols 5,056.1
12. Tim Keefe 5,047.2
13. Bert Blyleven 4,970.0
14. Bobby Mathews 4,956.0
15. Mickey Welch 4,802.0

GAMES STARTED
1. Cy Young.....................815
2. Nolan Ryan..................773
3. Don Sutton..................756
4. Phil Niekro..................716
5. Steve Carlton...............709
6. Tommy John.................700
7. Gaylord Perry...............690
8. Pud Galvin...................688
9. Bert Blyleven 685
10. Walter Johnson 666

11. Warren Spahn 665
12. Tom Seaver..................647
13. Jim Kaat 625
14. Frank Tanana 616
15. Early Wynn 612

RATIO OF BASERUNNERS
1. Addie Joss....................8.71
2. Ed Walsh.....................9.00
3. John Ward....................9.40
4. Christy Mathewson.....9.53

5. Walter Johnson 9.55
6. Mordecai Brown 9.59
7. George Bradley 9.81
8. Tommy Bond...............9.82
9. Babe Adams...............9.83
10. Juan Marichal.............9.91
11. Rube Waddell..............9.92
12. Larry Corcoran 9.94
13. Deacon Phillippe 9.95
14. Sandy Koufax 9.96
15. Ed Morris....................9.97

ACTIVE LEADERS

HITS
1. Eddie Murray 3,218
2. Paul Molitor 3,014
3. Andre Dawson 2,774
4. Wade Boggs 2,697
5. Tony Gwynn 2,560
6. Cal Ripken 2,549
7. Ozzie Smith 2,460
8. Rickey Henderson 2,450
9. Harold Baines 2,425
10. Alan Trammell 2,365

HOME RUNS
1. Eddie Murray 501
2. Andre Dawson 438
3. Joe Carter...................357
4. Cal Ripken 353
5. Barry Bonds................334
6. Mark McGwire 329
7. Jose Canseco..............328
8. Harold Baines 323
9. Fred McGriff 317
10. Gary Gaetti 315

RUNS BATTED IN
1. Eddie Murray 1,899
2. Andre Dawson..........1,591
3. Cal Ripken 1,369
4. Harold Baines 1,356
5. Joe Carter.................1,280
6. Chili Davis 1,195
7. Gary Gaetti 1,155

8. Paul Molitor 1,149
9. Tim Wallach...............1,125
10. Jose Canseco...........1,033

GAMES PLAYED
1. Eddie Murray 2,971
2. Andre Dawson 2,627
3. Ozzie Smith 2,573
4. Paul Molitor 2,422
5. Cal Ripken 2,381
6. Rickey Henderson 2,340
7. Harold Baines 2,326
8. Alan Trammell 2,293
9. Tim Wallach...............2,212
10. Wade Boggs.............2,123

WINS
1. Dennis Martinez.........240
2. Dennis Eckersley........192
   Roger Clemens 192
4. Frank Viola 176
5. Mark Langston............172
6. Fernando Valenzuela ..171
7. Dwight Gooden............168
8. Greg Maddux...............165
   Orel Hershiser 165
10. Jimmy Key..................164

GAMES PITCHED
1. Lee Smith 997
2. Dennis Eckersley.........964
3. Jesse Orosco 885

4. Rick Honeycutt 795
5. Roger McDowell 723
6. John Franco 712
7. Paul Assenmacher 685
8. Danny Darwin..............652
9. Dennis Martinez..........630
10. Mike Jackson.............623

STRIKEOUTS
1. Roger Clemens 2,590
2. Mark Langston..........2,335
3. Dennis Eckersley......2,334
4. Dennis Martinez........2,070
5. F. Valenzuela 2,013
6. Dwight Gooden..........2,001
7. Frank Viola 1,844
8. David Cone...............1,812
9. Danny Darwin...........1,769
10. Sid Fernandez.........1,740

SAVES
1. Lee Smith 473
2. Dennis Eckersley........353
3. John Franco 323
4. Randy Myers 274
5. Jeff Montgomery.........242
   Doug Jones 242
7. Todd Worrell................221
8. Rick Aguilera 211
9. Mike Henneman 193
10. Jeff Russell.................186

SINGLE-SEASON LEADERS (SINCE 1900)

BATTING AVERAGE	BA	YEAR
1. Nap Lajoie PHI (AL)	.426	1901
2. Rogers Hornsby STL (NL)	.424	1924
3. George Sisler STL (AL)	.420	1922
4. Ty Cobb DET	.420	1911
5. Ty Cobb DET	.410	1912
6. Joe Jackson CLE	.408	1911
7. George Sisler STL (AL)	.407	1920
8. Ted Williams BOS (AL)	.406	1941
9. Rogers Hornsby STL (NL)	.403	1925
10. Harry Heilmann DET	.403	1923
11. Rogers Hornsby STL (NL)	.401	1922
12. Bill Terry NY (NL)	.401	1930
13. Ty Cobb DET	.401	1922

	AVG	YEAR
14. Lefty O'Doul PHI (NL)	.398	1929
15. Harry Heilmann DET	.398	1927
16. Rogers Hornsby STL (NL)	.397	1921
17. Joe Jackson CLE	.395	1912
18. Tony Gwynn SD	.394	1994
19. Harry Heilmann DET	.394	1921
20. Babe Ruth NY (AL)	.393	1923

HITS	H	YEAR
1. George Sisler STL (AL)	257	1920
2. Lefty O'Doul PHI (NL)	254	1929
Bill Terry NY (NL)	254	1930
4. Al Simmons PHI (AL)	253	1925
5. Rogers Hornsby STL (NL)	250	1922
Chuck Klein PHI (NL)	250	1930
7. Ty Cobb DET	248	1911
8. George Sisler STL (AL)	246	1922
9. Heinie Manush STL (AL)	241	1928
Babe Herman BKN	241	1930
11. Wade Boggs BOS	240	1985
12. Rod Carew MIN	239	1977
13. Don Mattingly NY (AL)	238	1986
14. Harry Heilmann DET	237	1921
Paul Waner PIT	237	1927
Joe Medwick STL (NL)	237	1937
17. Jack Tobin STL (AL)	236	1921
18. Rogers Hornsby STL (NL)	235	1921
19. Lloyd Waner PIT	234	1929
Kirby Puckett MIN	234	1988

DOUBLES	2B	YEAR
1. Earl Webb BOS (AL)	67	1931
2. George Burns CLE	64	1926
Joe Medwick STL (NL)	64	1936
4. Hank Greenberg DET	63	1934
5. Paul Waner PIT	62	1932
6. Charlie Gehringer DET	60	1936
7. Tris Speaker CLE	59	1923
Chuck Klein PHI (NL)	59	1930
9. Billy Herman CHI (NL)	57	1935
Billy Herman CHI (NL)	57	1936

TRIPLES	3B	YEAR
1. Owen Wilson PIT	36	1912
2. Joe Jackson CLE	26	1912
Sam Crawford DET	26	1914
Kiki Cuyler PIT	26	1925
5. Sam Crawford DET	25	1903
Larry Doyle NY (NL)	25	1911
Tommy Long STL (NL)	25	1915
8. Ty Cobb DET	24	1911
Ty Cobb DET	24	1917
10. Ty Cobb DET	23	1912
Sam Crawford DET	23	1913
Earle Combs NY (AL)	23	1927
Adam Comorosky PIT	23	1930
Dale Mitchell CLE	23	1949

HOME RUNS	HR	YEAR
1. Roger Maris NY (AL)	61	1961
2. Babe Ruth NY (AL)	60	1927
3. Babe Ruth NY (AL)	59	1921
4. Jimmie Foxx PHI (AL)	58	1932
Hank Greenberg DET	58	1938
6. Hack Wilson CHI (NL)	56	1930
7. Babe Ruth NY (AL)	54	1920
Babe Ruth NY (AL)	54	1928
Ralph Kiner PIT	54	1949
Mickey Mantle NY (AL)	54	1961
11. Mickey Mantle NY (AL)	52	1956
Willie Mays SF	52	1965
George Foster CIN	52	1977
Mark McGwire OAK	52	1996
15. Ralph Kiner PIT	51	1947
Johnny Mize NY (NL)	51	1947
Willie Mays NY (NL)	51	1955
Cecil Fielder DET	51	1990
19. Jimmie Foxx BOS (AL)	50	1938
Albert Belle CLE	50	1995
Brady Anderson BAL	50	1996

HOME RUN PERCENTAGE	HR%	YEAR
1. Mark McGwire OAK	12.3	1996
2. Babe Ruth NY (AL)	11.8	1920
3. Babe Ruth NY (AL)	11.1	1927
4. Babe Ruth NY (AL)	10.9	1921
5. Mickey Mantle NY (AL)	10.5	1961
6. Hank Greenberg DET	10.4	1938
7. Roger Maris NY (AL)	10.3	1961
8. Babe Ruth NY (AL)	10.1	1928
9. Jimmie Foxx PHI (AL)	9.9	1932
10. Ralph Kiner PIT	9.8	1949
11. Mickey Mantle NY (AL)	9.8	1956
12. Jeff Bagwell HOU	9.8	1994
13. Kevin Mitchell CIN	9.7	1994
14. Matt Williams SF	9.7	1994
15. Hack Wilson CHI (NL)	9.6	1930

RUNS BATTED IN	RBI	YEAR
1. Hack Wilson CHI (NL)	190	1930
2. Lou Gehrig NY (AL)	184	1931
3. Hank Greenberg DET	183	1937
4. Lou Gehrig NY (AL)	175	1927
Jimmie Foxx BOS (AL)	175	1938
6. Lou Gehrig NY (AL)	174	1930
7. Babe Ruth NY (AL)	171	1921
8. Chuck Klein PHI (NL)	170	1930
Hank Greenberg DET	170	1935
10. Jimmie Foxx PHI (AL)	169	1932
11. Joe DiMaggio NY (AL)	167	1937
12. Al Simmons PHI (AL)	165	1930
Lou Gehrig NY (AL)	165	1934
14. Babe Ruth NY (AL)	164	1927
15. Babe Ruth NY (AL)	163	1931

Jimmie Foxx PHI (AL)	163	1933
17. Hal Trosky CLE	162	1936
18. Hack Wilson CHI (NL)	159	1929
Lou Gehrig NY (AL)	159	1937
Vern Stephens BOS (AL)	159	1949
Ted Williams BOS (AL)	159	1949

SLUGGING AVERAGE	SA	YEAR
1. Babe Ruth NY (AL)	.847	1920
2. Babe Ruth NY (AL)	.846	1921
3. Babe Ruth NY (AL)	.772	1927
4. Lou Gehrig NY (AL)	.765	1927
5. Babe Ruth NY (AL)	.764	1923
6. Rogers Hornsby STL (NL)	.756	1925
7. Jeff Bagwell HOU	.750	1994
8. Jimmie Foxx PHI (AL)	.749	1932
9. Babe Ruth NY (AL)	.739	1924
10. Babe Ruth NY (AL)	.737	1926
11. Ted Williams BOS (AL)	.735	1941
12. Babe Ruth NY (AL)	.732	1930
13. Ted Williams BOS	.731	1957
14. Mark McGwire OAK	.730	1996
15. Frank Thomas CHI (AL)	.729	1994
16. Hack Wilson CHI (NL)	.723	1930
17. Rogers Hornsby STL (NL)	.722	1922
18. Lou Gehrig NY (AL)	.721	1930
19. Albert Belle CLE	.714	1994
20. Babe Ruth NY (AL)	.709	1928

ON-BASE PERCENTAGE	OBP	YEAR
1. Ted Williams BOS (AL)	.551	1941
2. Babe Ruth NY (AL)	.545	1923
3. Babe Ruth NY (AL)	.530	1920
4. Ted Williams BOS (AL)	.528	1957
5. Ted Williams BOS (AL)	.516	1954
6. Babe Ruth NY (AL)	.516	1926
7. Mickey Mantle NY (AL)	.515	1957
8. Babe Ruth NY (AL)	.513	1924
9. Babe Ruth NY (AL)	.512	1921
10. Rogers Hornsby STL (NL)	.507	1924
11. John McGraw STL (NL)	.505	1900
12. Ted Williams BOS (AL)	.499	1942
13. Ted Williams BOS (AL)	.499	1947
14. Rogers Hornsby BOS (NL)	.498	1928
15. Ted Williams BOS (AL)	.497	1946
16. Ted Williams BOS (AL)	.497	1948
17. Babe Ruth NY (AL)	.495	1931
18. Frank Thomas CHI (AL)	.494	1994
19. Babe Ruth NY (AL)	.493	1930
20. Arky Vaughan PIT (NL)	.491	1935

TOTAL BASES	TB	YEAR
1. Babe Ruth NY (AL)	457	1921
2. Rogers Hornsby STL (NL)	450	1922
3. Lou Gehrig NY (AL)	447	1927
4. Chuck Klein PHI (NL)	445	1930
5. Jimmie Foxx PHI (AL)	438	1932

6. Stan Musial STL (NL)	429	1948
7. Hack Wilson CHI (NL)	423	1930
8. Chuck Klein PHI (NL)	420	1932
9. Lou Gehrig NY (AL)	419	1930
10. Joe DiMaggio NY (AL)	418	1937
11. Babe Ruth NY (AL)	417	1927
12. Babe Herman BKN	416	1930
13. Lou Gehrig NY (AL)	410	1931
14. Rogers Hornsby CHI (NL)	409	1929
Lou Gehrig NY (AL)	409	1934

BASES ON BALLS	BB	YEAR
1. Babe Ruth NY (AL)	170	1923
2. Ted Williams BOS (AL)	162	1947
Ted Williams BOS (AL)	162	1949
4. Ted Williams BOS (AL)	156	1946
5. Eddie Yost WAS	151	1956
Barry Bonds SF	151	1996
7. Eddie Joost PHI (AL)	149	1949
8. Babe Ruth NY (AL)	148	1920
Eddie Stanky BKN	148	1945
Jimmy Wynn HOU	148	1969
11. Jimmy Sheckard CHI (AL)	147	1911
12. Mickey Mantle NY (AL)	146	1957

RUNS SCORED	RS	YEAR
1. Babe Ruth NY (AL)	177	1921
2. Lou Gehrig NY (AL)	167	1936
3. Babe Ruth NY (AL)	163	1928
Lou Gehrig NY (AL)	163	1931
5. Babe Ruth NY (AL)	158	1920
Babe Ruth NY (AL)	158	1927
Chuck Klein PHI (NL)	158	1930
8. Rogers Hornsby CHI (NL)	156	1929
9. Kiki Cuyler CHI (NL)	155	1930
10. Lefty O'Doul PHI (NL)	152	1929
Woody English CHI (NL)	152	1930
Al Simmons PHI (AL)	152	1930
Chuck Klein PHI (NL)	152	1932
14. Babe Ruth NY (AL)	151	1923
Jimmie Foxx PHI (AL)	151	1932
Joe DiMaggio NY (AL)	151	1937
17. Babe Ruth NY (AL)	150	1930
Ted Williams BOS (AL)	150	1949
19. Lou Gehrig NY (AL)	149	1927
Babe Ruth NY (AL)	149	1931

STOLEN BASES	SB	YEAR
1. Rickey Henderson OAK	130	1982
2. Lou Brock STL	118	1974
3. Vince Coleman STL	110	1985
4. Vince Coleman STL	109	1987
5. Rickey Henderson OAK	108	1983
6. Vince Coleman STL	107	1986
7. Maury Wills LA	104	1962
8. Rickey Henderson OAK	100	1980

9. Ron LeFlore MON	97	1980
10. Ty Cobb DET	96	1915
Omar Moreno PIT	96	1980
12. Maury Wills LA	94	1965
13. Rickey Henderson NY (AL)	93	1988
14. Tim Raines MON	90	1983
15. Clyde Milan WAS	88	1912
16. Rickey Henderson NY (AL)	87	1986
17. Ty Cobb DET	83	1911
Willie Wilson KC	83	1979
19. Eddie Collins PHI (AL)	81	1910
Bob Bescher CIN	81	1911
Vince Coleman STL	81	1988

WINS	W	YEAR
1. Jack Chesbro NY (NL)	41	1904
2. Ed Walsh CHI (AL)	40	1908
3. Christy Mathewson NY (NL)	37	1908
4. Walter Johnson WAS	36	1913
5. Joe McGinnity NY (NL)	35	1904
6. Smoky Joe Wood BOS (AL)	34	1912
7. Cy Young BOS (AL)	33	1901
Christy Mathewson NY (NL)	33	1904
Walter Johnson WAS	33	1912
Grover Alexander PHI (NL)	33	1916
11. Cy Young BOS (AL)	32	1902
12. Joe McGinnity NY (NL)	31	1903
Christy Mathewson NY (NL)	31	1905
Jack Coombs PHI (AL)	31	1910
Grover Alexander PHI (NL)	31	1915
Jim Bagby CLE	31	1920
Lefty Grove PHI (AL)	31	1931
Denny McLain DET	31	1968
19. Christy Mathewson NY (NL)	30	1903
Grover Alexander PHI (NL)	30	1917
Dizzy Dean STL (NL)	30	1934

WINNING PERCENTAGE	W%	YEAR
1. Roy Face PIT	.947	1959
2. Rick Sutcliffe CHI (NL)	.941	1984
3. Johnny Allen CLE	.938	1937
4. Greg Maddux ATL	.905	1995
5. Randy Johnson SEA	.900	1995
6. Ron Guidry NY (AL)	.893	1978
7. Freddie Fitzsimmons BKN	.889	1940
8. Lefty Grove PHI (AL)	.886	1931
9. Bob Stanley BOS	.882	1978
10. Preacher Roe BKN	.880	1951
11. Tom Seaver CIN	.875	1981
12. Smoky Joe Wood BOS (AL)	.872	1912
13. David Cone NY (NL)	.870	1988
14. Orel Hershiser LA	.864	1985
15. Wild Bill Donovan DET	.862	1907
Whitey Ford NY (AL)	.862	1961

EARNED RUN AVERAGE	ERA	YEAR
1. Dutch Leonard BOS (AL)	0.96	1914
2. Three Finger Brown CHI (NL)	1.04	1906
3. Bob Gibson STL	1.12	1968
4. Christy Mathewson NY (NL)	1.14	1909
5. Walter Johnson WAS	1.14	1913
6. Jack Pfiester CHI (NL)	1.15	1907
7. Addie Joss CLE	1.16	1908
8. Carl Lundgren CHI (NL)	1.17	1907
9. Grover Alexander PHI (NL)	1.22	1915
10. Cy Young BOS (AL)	1.26	1908
11. Ed Walsh CHI (AL)	1.27	1910
12. Walter Johnson WAS	1.27	1918
13. Christy Mathewson NY (NL)	1.28	1905
14. Jack Coombs PHI (AL)	1.30	1910
15. Three Finger Brown CHI (NL)	1.31	1909

STRIKEOUTS	SO	YEAR
1. Nolan Ryan CAL	383	1973
2. Sandy Koufax LA	382	1965
3. Nolan Ryan CAL	367	1974
4. Rube Waddell PHI (AL)	349	1904
5. Bob Feller CLE	348	1946
6. Nolan Ryan CAL	341	1977
7. Nolan Ryan CAL	329	1972
8. Nolan Ryan CAL	327	1976
9. Sam McDowell CLE	325	1965
10. Sandy Koufax LA	317	1966
11. Walter Johnson WAS	313	1910
J.R. Richard HOU	313	1979
13. Steve Carlton PHI	310	1972
14. Mickey Lolich DET	308	1971
Randy Johnson SEA	308	1993

SAVES	SV	YEAR
1. Bobby Thigpen CHI (AL)	57	1990
2. Randy Myers CHI (NL)	53	1993
3. Dennis Eckersley OAK	51	1992
4. Dennis Eckersley OAK	48	1990
Rod Beck SF	48	1993
6. Lee Smith STL	47	1991
7. Dave Righetti NY (AL)	46	1986
Bryan Harvey CAL	46	1991
Jose Mesa CLE	46	1995
10. Dan Quisenberry KC	45	1983
Bruce Sutter STL	45	1984
Dennis Eckersley OAK	45	1988
Bryan Harvey FLA	45	1993
Jeff Montgomery KC	45	1993
Duane Ward TOR	45	1993

SHUTOUTS	ShO	YEAR
1. Pete Alexander PHI (NL)	16	1916
2. Jack Coombs PHI (AL)	13	1910
Bob Gibson STL (NL)	13	1968
4. Pete Alexander PHI (NL)	12	1915

515

5.	Christy Mathewson NY (NL)	11	1908
	Ed Walsh CHI (AL)	11	1908
	Walter Johnson WAS	11	1913
	Sandy Koufax LA (NL)	11	1963
	Dean Chance LA (AL)	11	1964
10.	Cy Young BOS (AL)	10	1904
	Ed Walsh CHI (AL)	10	1906
	Smoky Joe Wood BOS (AL)	10	1912
	Dave Davenport STL (FL)	10	1915
	Carl Hubbell NY (NL)	10	1933
	Mort Cooper STL (NL)	10	1942
	Bob Feller CLE	10	1946
	Bob Lemon CLE	10	1948
	Juan Marichal SF	10	1965
	Jim Palmer BAL	10	1975
	John Tudor STL	10	1985

COMPLETE GAMES		CG	YEAR
1.	Jack Chesbro NY (NL)	48	1904
2.	Vic Willis BOS (NL)	45	1902
3.	Joe McGinnity NY (NL)	44	1903
4.	George Mullin DET	42	1904
	Ed Walsh CHI (AL)	42	1908
6.	Noodles Hahn CIN	41	1901
	Cy Young BOS (AL)	41	1902
	Irv Young BOS (NL)	41	1905
9.	Cy Young BOS (AL)	40	1904
10.	Joe McGinnity BAL	39	1901

	Bill Dinneen BOS (AL)	39	1902
	Jack Taylor STL (NL)	39	1904
	Vic Willis BOS (NL)	39	1904
	Rube Waddell PHI (AL)	39	1904

GAMES PITCHED		GP	YEAR
1.	Mike Marshall LA	106	1974
2.	Kent Tekulve PIT	94	1979
3.	Mike Marshall MON	92	1973
4.	Kent Tekulve PIT	91	1978
5.	Wayne Granger CIN	90	1969
	Mike Marshall MIN	90	1979
	Kent Tekulve PHI	90	1987
8.	Mark Eichhorn TOR	89	1987
9.	Wilbur Wood CHI (AL)	88	1968
10.	Rob Murphy CIN	87	1987

INNINGS PITCHED		IP	YEAR
1.	Ed Walsh CHI (AL)	464.0	1908
2.	Jack Chesbro NY (NL)	454.2	1904
3.	Joe McGinnity NY (NL)	434.0	1903
4.	Ed Walsh CHI (AL)	422.1	1907
5.	Vic Willis BOS (NL)	410.0	1902
6.	Joe McGinnity NY (NL)	408.0	1904
7.	Ed Walsh CHI (AL)	393.0	1912
8.	Dave Davenport STL (FL)	392.2	1915
9.	Christy Mathewson NY (NL)	390.2	1908
10.	Jack Powell NY (NL)	390.1	1904

Most Valuable Players

NATIONAL LEAGUE

CHALMERS
1911 Wildfire Schulte CHI (OF)
1912 Larry Doyle NY (2B)
1913 Jake Daubert BKN (1B)
1914 Johnny Evers BOS (2B)
1915-21 No Selection

LEAGUE
1922-23 No Selection
1924 Dazzy Vance BKN (P)
1925 Rogers Hornsby STL (2B)
1926 Bob O'Farrell STL (C)
1927 Paul Waner PIT (OF)
1928 Jim Bottomley STL (1B)
1929 Rogers Hornsby CHI (2B)
1930 No Selection

**BASEBALL WRITERS
ASSOCIATION OF AMERICA**
1931 Frankie Frisch STL (2B)
1932 Chuck Klein CHI (OF)
1933 Carl Hubbell NY (P)
1934 Dizzy Dean STL (P)
1935 Gabby Hartnett CHI (C)

1936 Carl Hubbell NY (P)
1937 Joe Medwick STL (OF)
1938 Ernie Lombardi CIN (C)
1939 Bucky Walters CIN (P)
1940 Frank McCormick
    CIN (1B)
1941 Dolph Camilli BKN (1B)
1942 Mort Cooper STL (P)
1943 Stan Musial STL (OF)
1944 Marty Marion STL (SS)
1945 Phil Cavarretta CHI (1B)
1946 Stan Musial STL (1B)
1947 Bob Elliott BOS (3B)
1948 Stan Musial STL (OF)
1949 Jackie Robinson
    BKN (2B)
1950 Jim Konstanty PHI (P)
1951 Roy Campanella BKN (C)
1952 Hank Sauer CHI (OF)
1953 Roy Campanella BKN (C)
1954 Willie Mays NY (OF)
1955 Roy Campanella BKN (C)
1956 Don Newcombe BKN (P)
1957 Hank Aaron MIL (OF)
1958 Ernie Banks CHI (SS)

1959 Ernie Banks CHI (SS)
1960 Dick Groat PIT (SS)
1961 Frank Robinson CIN (OF)
1962 Maury Wills LA (SS)
1963 Sandy Koufax LA (P)
1964 Ken Boyer STL (3B)
1965 Willie Mays SF (OF)
1966 Roberto Clemente
    PIT (OF)
1967 Orlando Cepeda STL (1B)
1968 Bob Gibson STL (P)
1969 Willie McCovey SF (1B)
1970 Johnny Bench CIN (C)
1971 Joe Torre STL (3B)
1972 Johnny Bench CIN (C)
1973 Pete Rose CIN (OF)
1974 Steve Garvey LA (1B)
1975 Joe Morgan CIN (2B)
1976 Joe Morgan CIN (2B)
1977 George Foster CIN (OF)
1978 Dave Parker PIT (OF)
1979 Keith Hernandez
    STL (1B)
    Willie Stargell PIT (1B)
1980 Mike Schmidt PHI (3B)

1981 Mike Schmidt PHI (3B)
1982 Dale Murphy ATL (OF)
1983 Dale Murphy ATL (OF)
1984 Ryne Sandberg CHI (2B)
1985 Willie McGee STL (OF)
1986 Mike Schmidt PHI (3B)
1987 Andre Dawson CHI (OF)
1988 Kirk Gibson LA (OF)
1989 Kevin Mitchell SF (OF)
1990 Barry Bonds PIT (OF)
1991 Terry Pendleton ATL (3B)
1992 Barry Bonds PIT (OF)
1993 Barry Bonds SF (OF)
1994 Jeff Bagwell HOU (1B)
1995 Barry Larkin CIN (SS)
1996 Ken Caminiti SD (3B)

AMERICAN LEAGUE

CHALMERS
1911 Ty Cobb DET (OF)
1912 Tris Speaker BOS (OF)
1913 Walter Johnson WAS (P)
1914 Eddie Collins PHI (2B)
1915-21 No Selection

LEAGUE
1922 George Sisler STL (1B)
1923 Babe Ruth NY (OF)
1924 Walter Johnson WAS (P)
1925 Roger Peckinpaugh
    WAS (SS)
1926 George Burns CLE (1B)
1927 Lou Gehrig NY (1B)
1928 Mickey Cochrane PHI (C)
1929-30 No Selection

**BASEBALL WRITERS
ASSOCIATION OF AMERICA**
1931 Lefty Grove PHI (P)

1932 Jimmie Foxx PHI (1B)
1933 Jimmie Foxx PHI (1B)
1934 Mickey Cochrane
    DET (C)
1935 Hank Greenberg
    DET (1B)
1936 Lou Gehrig NY (1B)
1937 Charlie Gehringer
    DET (2B)
1938 Jimmie Foxx BOS (1B)
1939 Joe DiMaggio NY (OF)
1940 Hank Greenberg
    DET (1B)
1941 Joe DiMaggio NY (OF)
1942 Joe Gordon NY (2B)
1943 Spud Chandler NY (P)
1944 Hal Newhouser DET (P)
1945 Hal Newhouser DET (P)
1946 Ted Williams BOS (OF)
1947 Joe DiMaggio NY (OF)
1948 Lou Boudreau CLE (SS)
1949 Ted Williams BOS (OF)
1950 Phil Rizzuto NY (SS)
1951 Yogi Berra NY (C)
1952 Bobby Shantz PHI (P)
1953 Al Rosen CLE (3B)
1954 Yogi Berra NY (C)
1955 Yogi Berra NY (C)
1956 Mickey Mantle NY (OF)
1957 Mickey Mantle NY (OF)
1958 Jackie Jensen BOS (OF)
1959 Nellie Fox CHI (2B)
1960 Roger Maris NY (OF)
1961 Roger Maris NY (OF)
1962 Mickey Mantle NY (OF)
1963 Elston Howard NY (C)
1964 Brooks Robinson
    BAL (3B)

1965 Zoilo Versalles MIN (SS)
1966 Frank Robinson
    BAL (OF)
1967 Carl Yastrzemski
    BOS (OF)
1968 Denny McLain DET (P)
1969 Harmon Killebrew
    MIN (3B)
1970 Boog Powell BAL (1B)
1971 Vida Blue OAK (P)
1972 Richie Allen CHI (1B)
1973 Reggie Jackson OAK (OF)
1974 Jeff Burroughs TEX (OF)
1975 Fred Lynn BOS (OF)
1976 Thurman Munson NY (C)
1977 Rod Carew MIN (1B)
1978 Jim Rice BOS (OF)
1979 Don Baylor CAL (DH)
1980 George Brett KC (3B)
1981 Rollie Fingers MIL (P)
1982 Robin Yount MIL (SS)
1983 Cal Ripken BAL (SS)
1984 Willie Hernandez DET (P)
1985 Don Mattingly NY (1B)
1986 Roger Clemens BOS (P)
1987 George Bell TOR (OF)
1988 Jose Canseco OAK (OF)
1989 Robin Yount MIL (OF)
1990 Rickey Henderson
    OAK (OF)
1991 Cal Ripken BAL (SS)
1992 Dennis Eckersley
    OAK (P)
1993 Frank Thomas CHI (1B)
1994 Frank Thomas CHI (1B)
1995 Mo Vaughn BOS (1B)
1996 Juan Gonzalez TEX (DH)

Cy Young Award Winners (one selection 1956-66)

NATIONAL LEAGUE
1956 Don Newcombe BKN (RH)
1957 Warren Spahn MIL (LH)
1960 Vern Law PIT (RH)
1962 Don Drysdale LA (RH)
1963 Sandy Koufax LA (LH)
1965 Sandy Koufax LA (LH)
1966 Sandy Koufax LA (LH)
1967 Mike McCormick SF (LH)
1968 Bob Gibson STL (RH)
1969 Tom Seaver NY (RH)
1970 Bob Gibson STL (RH)
1971 Ferguson Jenkins
    CHI (RH)

1972 Steve Carlton PHI (LH)
1973 Tom Seaver NY (RH)
1974 Mike Marshall LA (RH)
1975 Tom Seaver NY (RH)
1976 Randy Jones SD (LH)
1977 Steve Carlton PHI (LH)
1978 Gaylord Perry SD (RH)
1979 Bruce Sutter CHI (RH)
1980 Steve Carlton PHI (LH)
1981 Fernando Valenzuela
    LA (LH)
1982 Steve Carlton PHI (LH)
1983 John Denny PHI (RH)
1984 Rick Sutcliffe CHI (RH)

1985 Dwight Gooden NY (RH)
1986 Mike Scott HOU (RH)
1987 Steve Bedrosian
    PHI (RH)
1988 Orel Hershiser LA (RH)
1989 Mark Davis SD (LH)
1990 Doug Drabek PIT (RH)
1991 Tom Glavine ATL (LH)
1992 Greg Maddux CHI (RH)
1993 Greg Maddux ATL (RH)
1994 Greg Maddux ATL (RH)
1995 Greg Maddux ATL (RH)
1996 John Smoltz ATL (RH)

AMERICAN LEAGUE

1958 Bob Turley NY (RH)
1959 Early Wynn CHI (RH)
1961 Whitey Ford NY (LH)
1964 Dean Chance LA (RH)
1967 Jim Lonborg BOS (RH)
1968 Denny McLain DET (RH)
1969 Mike Cuellar BAL (LH)
    Denny McLain DET (RH)
1970 Jim Perry MIN (RH)
1971 Vida Blue OAK (LH)
1972 Gaylord Perry CLE (RH)
1973 Jim Palmer BAL (RH)

1974 Jim (Catfish) Hunter
    OAK (RH)
1975 Jim Palmer BAL (RH)
1976 Jim Palmer BAL (RH)
1977 Sparky Lyle NY (LH)
1978 Ron Guidry NY (LH)
1979 Mike Flanagan BAL (LH)
1980 Steve Stone BAL (RH)
1981 Rollie Fingers MIL (RH)
1982 Pete Vuckovich MIL (RH)
1983 LaMarr Hoyt CHI (RH)
1984 Willie Hernandez
    DET (LH)
1985 Bret Saberhagen KC (RH)

1986 Roger Clemens BOS (RH)
1987 Roger Clemens
    BOS (RH)
1988 Frank Viola MIN (LH)
1989 Bret Saberhagen
    KC (RH)
1990 Bob Welch OAK (RH)
1991 Roger Clemens BOS (RH)
1992 Dennis Eckersley
    OAK (RH)
1993 Jack McDowell CHI (RH)
1994 David Cone KC (RH)
1995 Randy Johnson SEA (LH)
1996 Pat Hentgen TOR (RH)

ROOKIES OF THE YEAR (ONE SELECTION 1947-48)

NATIONAL LEAGUE

1947 Jackie Robinson
    BKN (1B)
1948 Alvin Dark BOS (SS)
1949 Don Newcombe BKN (P)
1950 Sam Jethroe BOS (OF)
1951 Willie Mays NY (OF)
1952 Joe Black BKN (P)
1953 Junior Gilliam BKN (2B)
1954 Wally Moon STL (OF)
1955 Bill Virdon STL (OF)
1956 Frank Robinson CIN (OF)
1957 Jack Sanford PHI (P)
1958 Orlando Cepeda SF (1B)
1959 Willie McCovey SF (1B)
1960 Frank Howard LA (OF)
1961 Billy Williams CHI (OF)
1962 Ken Hubbs CHI (2B)
1963 Pete Rose CIN (2B)
1964 Richie Allen PHI (3B)
1965 Jim Lefebvre LA (2B)
1966 Tommy Helms CIN (2B)
1967 Tom Seaver NY (P)
1968 Johnny Bench CIN (C)
1969 Ted Sizemore LA (2B)
1970 Carl Morton MON (P)
1971 Earl Williams ATL (C)
1972 Jon Matlack NY (P)
1973 Gary Matthews SF (OF)
1974 Bake McBride STL (OF)
1975 Jon Montefusco SF (P)
1976 Pat Zachry CIN (P)
    Butch Metzger SD (P)
1977 Andre Dawson MON (OF)
1978 Bob Horner ATL (3B)
1979 Rick Sutcliffe LA (P)
1980 Steve Howe LA (P)
1981 Fernando Valenzuela
    LA (P)

1982 Steve Sax LA (2B)
1983 Darryl Strawberry NY (OF)
1984 Dwight Gooden NY (P)
1985 Vince Coleman STL (OF)
1986 Todd Worrell STL (P)
1987 Benito Santiago SD (C)
1988 Chris Sabo CIN (3B)
1989 Jerome Walton CHI (OF)
1990 Dave Justice ATL (OF)
1991 Jeff Bagwell HOU (1B)
1992 Eric Karros LA (1B)
1993 Mike Piazza LA (C)
1994 Raul Mondesi LA (OF)
1995 Hideo Nomo LA (P)
1996 Todd Hollandsworth
    LA (OF)

AMERICAN LEAGUE

1949 Roy Sievers STL (OF)
1950 Walt Dropo BOS (1B)
1951 Gil McDougald NY (3B)
1952 Harry Byrd PHI (P)
1953 Harvey Kuenn DET (SS)
1954 Bob Grim NY (P)
1955 Herb Score CLE (P)
1956 Luis Aparicio CHI (SS)
1957 Tony Kubek NY (SS)
1958 Albie Pearson WAS (OF)
1959 Bob Allison WAS (OF)
1960 Ron Hansen BAL (SS)
1961 Don Schwall BOS (P)
1962 Tom Tresh NY (SS)
1963 Gary Peters CHI (P)
1964 Tony Oliva MIN (OF)
1965 Curt Blefary BAL (OF)
1966 Tommie Agee CHI (OF)
1967 Rod Carew MIN (2B)
1968 Stan Bahnsen NY (P)
1969 Lou Piniella KC (OF)

1970 Thurman Munson NY (C)
1971 Chris Chambliss
    CLE (1B)
1972 Carlton Fisk BOS (C)
1973 Al Bumbry BAL (OF)
1974 Mike Hargrove TEX (1B)
1975 Fred Lynn BOS (OF)
1976 Mark Fidrych DET (P)
1977 Eddie Murray BAL (DH)
1978 Lou Whitaker DET (2B)
1979 Alfredo Griffin TOR (SS)
    John Castino MIN (3B)
1980 Joe Charboneau
    CLE (OF)
1981 Dave Righetti NY (P)
1982 Cal Ripken BAL (SS)
1983 Ron Kittle CHI (OF)
1984 Alvin Davis SEA (1B)
1985 Ozzie Guillen CHI (SS)
1986 Jose Canseco OAK (OF)
1987 Mark McGwire OAK (1B)
1988 Walt Weiss OAK (SS)
1989 Gregg Olson BAL (P)
1990 Sandy Alomar CLE (C)
1991 Chuck Knoblauch MIN (2B)
1992 Pat Listach MIL (SS)
1993 Tim Salmon CAL (OF)
1994 Bob Hamelin KC (DH)
1995 Marty Cordova MIN (OF)
1996 Derek Jeter NY (SS)

GOLD GLOVE AWARD WINNERS

COMBINED SELECTION-1957

P	Bobby Shantz	NY (AL)
C	Sherm Lollar	CHI (AL)
1B	Gil Hodges	BKN
2B	Nellie Fox	CHI (AL)
3B	Frank Malzone	BOS
SS	Roy McMillan	CIN
LF	Minnie Minoso	CHI (AL)
CF	Willie Mays	NY (NL)
RF	Al Kaline	DET

Pitchers/NL

1958 Harvey Haddix CIN
1959-60 Harvey Haddix PIT
1961 Bobby Shantz PIT
1962-63 Bobby Shantz STL
1964 Bobby Shantz PHI
1965-73 Bob Gibson STL
1974-75 Andy Messersmith LA
1976-77 Jim Kaat PHI
1978-80 Phil Niekro ATL
1981 Steve Carlton PHI
1982-83 Phil Niekro ATL
1984 Joaquin Andujar STL
1985 Rick Reuschel PIT
1986 Fernando Valenzuela LA
1987 Rick Reuschel SF
1988 Orel Hershiser LA
1989 Ron Darling NY
1990-92 Greg Maddux CHI
1993-96 Greg Maddux ATL

Pitchers/AL

1958-60 Bobby Shantz NY
1961 Frank Lary DET
1962-72 Jim Kaat MIN
1973 Jim Kaat MIN, CHI
1974-75 Jim Kaat CHI
1976-79 Jim Palmer BAL
1980-81 Mike Norris OAK
1982-86 Ron Guidry NY
1987-88 Mark Langston SEA
1989 Bret Saberhagen KC
1990 Mike Boddicker BOS
1991-95 Mark Langston CAL
1996 Mike Mussina BAL

Catchers/NL

1958-60 Del Crandall MIL
1961 Johnny Roseboro LA
1962 Del Crandall MIL
1963-64 Johnny Edwards CIN
1965 Joe Torre MIL
1966 Johnny Roseboro LA

1967 Randy Hundley CHI
1968-77 Johnny Bench CIN
1978-79 Bob Boone PHI
1980-82 Gary Carter MON
1983-85 Tony Pena PIT
1986 Jody Davis CHI
1987 Mike LaValliere PIT
1988-90 Benito Santiago SD
1991-92 Tom Pagnozzi STL
1993 Kurt Manwaring SF
1994 Tom Pagnozzi STL
1995-96 Charles Johnson FLA

Catchers/AL

1958-59 Sherm Lollar CHI
1960 Earl Battey WAS
1961-62 Earl Battey MIN
1963-64 Elston Howard NY
1965-69 Bill Freehan DET
1970-71 Ray Fosse CLE
1972 Carlton Fisk BOS
1973-75 Thurman Munson NY
1976-81 Jim Sundberg TEX
1982 Bob Boone CAL
1983-85 Lance Parrish DET
1986-88 Bob Boone CAL
1989 Bob Boone KC
1990 Sandy Alomar CLE
1991 Tony Pena BOS
1992-96 Ivan Rodriguez TEX

First Basemen/NL

1958-59 Gil Hodges LA
1960-65 Bill White STL
1966 Bill White PHI
1967-72 Wes Parker LA
1973 Mike Jorgenson MON
1974-77 Steve Garvey LA
1978-82 Keith Hernandez STL
1983 Keith Hernandez STL, NY
1984-88 Keith Hernandez NY
1989-90 Andres Galarraga MON
1991 Will Clark SF
1992-93 Mark Grace CHI
1994 Jeff Bagwell HOU
1995-96 Mark Grace CHI

First Basemen/AL

1958-61 Vic Power CLE
1962-63 Vic Power MIN
1964 Vic Power LA
1965-66 Joe Pepitone NY
1967-68 George Scott BOS
1969 Joe Pepitone NY
1970 Jim Spencer CAL

1971 George Scott BOS
1972-76 George Scott MIL
1977 Jim Spencer CHI
1978 Chris Chambliss NY
1979-80 Cecil Cooper MIL
1981 Mike Squires CHI
1982-84 Eddie Murray BAL
1985-89 Don Mattingly NY
1990 Mark McGwire OAK
1991-94 Don Mattingly NY
1995-96 J.T. Snow CAL

Second Basemen/NL

1958 Bill Mazeroski PIT
1959 Charlie Neal LA
1960-61 Bill Mazeroski PIT
1962 Ken Hubbs CHI
1963-67 Bill Mazeroski PIT
1968 Glenn Beckert CHI
1969 Felix Millan ATL
1970-71 Tommy Helms CIN
1972 Felix Millan ATL
1973-77 Joe Morgan CIN
1978 Davey Lopes LA
1979 Manny Trillo PHI
1980 Doug Flynn NY
1981-82 Manny Trillo PHI
1983-91 Ryne Sandberg CHI
1992 Jose Lind PIT
1993 Robby Thompson SF
1994-96 Craig Biggio HOU

Second Basemen/AL

1958 Frank Bolling DET
1959-60 Nellie Fox CHI
1961-65 Bobby Richardson NY
1966-68 Bobby Knoop CAL
1969-71 Dave Johnson BAL
1972 Doug Griffin BOS
1973-76 Bobby Grich BAL
1977-82 Frank White KC
1983-85 Lou Whitaker DET
1986-87 Frank White KC
1988-90 Harold Reynolds SEA
1991-96 Roberto Alomar TOR

Third Basemen/NL

1958-61 Ken Boyer STL
1962 Jim Davenport SF
1963 Ken Boyer STL
1964-68 Ron Santo CHI
1969 Clete Boyer ATL
1970-74 Doug Rader HOU
1975 Ken Reitz STL
1976-84 Mike Schmidt PHI

519

1985 Tim Wallach MON
1986 Mike Schmidt PHI
1987 Terry Pendleton STL
1988 Tim Wallach MON
1989 Terry Pendleton STL
1990 Tim Wallach MON
1991 Matt Williams SF
1992 Terry Pendleton ATL
1993-94 Matt Williams SF
1995-96 Ken Caminiti SD

Third Basemen/AL
1958-59 Frank Malzone BOS
1960-75 Brooks Robinson BAL
1976 Aurelio Rodriguez DET
1977-78 Graig Nettles NY
1979-84 Buddy Bell TEX
1985 George Brett KC
1986-89 Gary Gaetti MIN
1990 Kelly Gruber TOR
1991-93 Robin Ventura CHI
1994-95 Wade Boggs NY
1996 Robin Ventura CHI

Shortstops/NL
1958-59 Roy McMillan CIN
1960 Ernie Banks CHI
1961-62 Maury Wills LA
1963 Bobby Wine PHI
1964 Ruben Amaro PHI
1965 Leo Cardenas CIN
1966-67 Gene Alley PIT
1968 Dal Maxvill STL
1969-70 Don Kessinger CHI
1971 Bud Harrelson NY
1972 Larry Bowa PHI
1973 Roger Metzger HOU
1974-77 Dave Concepcion CIN
1978 Larry Bowa PHI
1979 Dave Concepcion CIN
1980-81 Ozzie Smith SD
1982-92 Ozzie Smith STL
1993 Jay Bell PIT
1994-96 Barry Larkin CIN

Shortstops/AL
1958-62 Luis Aparicio CHI
1963 Zoilo Versalles MIN
1964 Luis Aparicio BAL
1965 Zoilo Versalles MIN
1966 Luis Aparicio BAL
1967 Jim Fregosi CAL
1968 Luis Aparicio CHI
1969 Mark Belanger BAL
1970 Luis Aparicio CHI
1971 Mark Belanger BAL
1972 Eddie Brinkman DET
520

1973-78 Mark Belanger BAL
1979 Rick Burleson BOS
1980-81 Alan Trammell DET
1982 Robin Yount MIL
1983-84 Alan Trammell DET
1985 Alfredo Griffin OAK
1986-89 Tony Fernandez TOR
1990 Ozzie Guillen CHI
1991-92 Cal Ripken BAL
1993 Omar Vizquel SEA
1994-96 Omar Vizquel CLE

Outfielders/NL
1958
Frank Robinson CIN (LF)
Willie Mays SF (CF)
Hank Aaron MIL (RF)

1959
Jackie Brant SF (LF)
Willie Mays SF (CF)
Hank Aaron MIL (RF)

1960
Wally Moon LA (LF)
Willie Mays SF (CF)
Hank Aaron MIL (RF)

1961
Willie Mays SF
Roberto Clemente PIT
Vada Pinson CIN

1962
Willie Mays SF
Roberto Clemente PIT
Bill Virdon PIT

1963-68
Willie Mays SF
Roberto Clemente PIT
Curt Flood STL

1969
Roberto Clemente PIT
Curt Flood STL
Pete Rose CIN

1970
Roberto Clemente PIT
Tommy Agee NY
Pete Rose CIN

1971
Roberto Clemente PIT
Bobby Bonds SF
Willie Davis LA

1972
Roberto Clemente PIT
Cesar Cedeno HOU

Willie Davis LA

1973
Bobby Bonds SF
Cesar Cedeno HOU
Willie Davis LA

1974
Cesar Cedeno HOU
Cesar Geronimo CIN
Bobby Bonds SF

1975-76
Cesar Cedeno HOU
Cesar Geronimo CIN
Garry Maddox PHI

1977
Cesar Geronimo CIN
Garry Maddox PHI
Dave Parker PIT

1978
Garry Maddox PHI
Dave Parker PIT
Ellis Valentine MON

1979
Garry Maddox PHI
Dave Parker PIT
Dave Winfield SD

1980
Andre Dawson MON
Garry Maddox PHI
Dave Winfield SD

1981
Andre Dawson MON
Garry Maddox PHI
Dusty Baker LA

1982
Andre Dawson MON
Dale Murphy ATL
Garry Maddox PHI

1983
Andre Dawson MON
Dale Murphy ATL
Willie McGee STL

1984
Dale Murphy ATL
Bob Dernier CHI
Andre Dawson MON

1985
Willie McGee STL
Andre Dawson MON
Dale Murphy ATL

1986
Dale Murphy ATL
Willie McGee STL
Tony Gwynn SD

1987
Eric Davis CIN
Tony Gwynn SD
Andre Dawson CHI

1988
Andre Dawson CHI
Eric Davis CIN
Andy Van Slyke PIT

1989
Eric Davis CIN
Tony Gwynn SD
Andy Van Slyke PIT

1990-91
Barry Bonds PIT
Tony Gwynn SD
Andy Van Slyke PIT

1992
Barry Bonds PIT
Larry Walker MON
Andy Van Slyke PIT

1993
Barry Bonds SF
Marquis Grissom MON
Larry Walker MON

1994
Barry Bonds SF
Marquis Grissom MON
Darren Lewis SF

1995-96
Steve Finley SD
Marquis Grissom ATL
Raul Mondesi LA

Outfielders/AL
1958
Norm Siebern NY (LF)
Jimmy Piersall BOS (CF)
Al Kaline DET (RF)

1959
Minnie Minoso CLE (LF)
Al Kaline DET (CF)
Jackie Jenson BOS (RF)

1960
Minnie Minoso CHI (LF)
Jim Landis CHI (CF)
Roger Maris NY (RF)

1961
Al Kaline DET
Jimmy Piersall CLE
Jim Landis CHI

1962
Jim Landis CHI
Mickey Mantle NY
Al Kaline DET

1963
Al Kaline DET
Carl Yastrzemski BOS
Jim Landis CHI

1964
Al Kaline DET
Jim Landis CHI
Vic Davalillo CLE

1965
Al Kaline DET
Tom Tresh NY
Carl Yastrzemski BOS

1966
Al Kaline DET
Tommy Agee CHI
Tony Oliva MIN

1967
Carl Yastrzemski BOS
Paul Blair BAL
Al Kaline DET

1968
Mickey Stanley DET
Carl Yastrzemski BOS
Reggie Smith BOS

1969
Paul Blair BAL
Mickey Stanley DET
Carl Yastrzemski BOS

1970
Mickey Stanley DET
Paul Blair BAL
Ken Berry CHI

1971
Paul Blair BAL
Amos Otis KC
Carl Yastrzemski BOS

1972
Paul Blair BAL
Bobby Murcer NY
Ken Berry CAL

1973
Paul Blair BAL
Amos Otis KC
Mickey Stanley DET

1974
Paul Blair BAL
Amos Otis KC
Joe Rudi OAK

1975
Paul Blair BAL
Joe Rudi OAK
Fred Lynn BOS

1976
Joe Rudi OAK
Dwight Evans BOS
Rick Manning CLE

1977
Juan Beniquez TEX
Carl Yastrzemski BOS
Al Cowens KC

1978
Fred Lynn BOS
Dwight Evans BOS
Rick Miller CAL

1979
Dwight Evans BOS
Sixto Lezcano MIL
Fred Lynn BOS

1980
Fred Lynn BOS
Dwayne Murphy OAK
Willie Wilson KC

1981
Dwayne Murphy OAK
Dwight Evans BOS
Rickey Henderson OAK

1982-84
Dwight Evans BOS
Dave Winfield NY
Dwayne Murphy OAK

1985
Gary Pettis CAL
Dave Winfield NY
Dwight Evans BOS
Dwayne Murphy OAK

1986
Jesse Barfield TOR
Kirby Puckett MIN
Gary Pettis CAL

1987
Jesse Barfield TOR
Kirby Puckett MIN
Dave Winfield NY

1988
Devon White CAL
Gary Pettis CAL
Kirby Puckett MIN

1989
Devon White CAL
Gary Pettis DET
Kirby Puckett MIN

1990
Ken Griffey Jr. SEA
Ellis Burks BOS
Gary Pettis TEX

1991-92
Ken Griffey Jr. SEA
Devon White TOR
Kirby Puckett MIN

1993-95
Ken Griffey Jr. SEA
Kenny Lofton CLE
Devon White TOR

1996
Jay Buhner SEA
Ken Griffey Jr. SEA
Kenny Lofton CLE

WORLD SERIES 1903-96

YEAR	WINNER	SERIES	LOSER	YEAR	WINNER	SERIES	LOSER
1903	BOS Pilgrims	5-3	PIT Pirates (NL)	1947	NY Yankees (AL)	4-3	BKN Dodgers (NL)
1904	NO SERIES			1948	CLE Indians (AL)	4-2	BOS Braves (NL)
1905	NY Giants (NL)	4-1	PHI Athletics (AL)	1949	NY Yankees (AL)	4-1	BKN Dodgers (NL)
1906	CHI White Sox (AL)	4-2	CHI Cubs (NL)	1950	NY Yankees (AL)	4-0	PHI Phillies (NL)
1907	CHI Cubs (NL)	4-0	DET Tigers (AL)	1951	NY Yankees (AL)	4-2	NY Giants (NL)
1908	CHI Cubs (NL)	4-1	DET Tigers (AL)	1952	NY Yankees (AL)	4-3	BKN Dodgers (NL)
1909	PIT Pirates (NL)	4-3	DET Tigers (AL)	1953	NY Yankees (AL)	4-2	BKN Dodgers (NL)
1910	PHI Athletics (AL)	4-1	CHI Cubs (NL)	1954	NY Giants (NL)	4-0	CLE Indians (AL)
1911	PHI Athletics (AL)	4-2	NY Giants (NL)	1955	BKN Dodgers (NL)	4-3	NY Yankees (AL)
1912	BOS Red Sox (AL)	4-3	NY Giants (NL)	1956	NY Yankees (AL)	4-3	BKN Dodgers (NL)
1913	PHI Athletics (AL)	4-1	NY Giants (NL)	1957	MIL Braves (NL)	4-3	NY Yankees (AL)
1914	BOS Braves (NL)	4-0	PHI Athletics (AL)	1958	NY Yankees (AL)	4-3	MIL Braves (NL)
1915	BOS Red Sox (AL)	4-1	PHI Phillies (NL)	1959	LA Dodgers (NL)	4-2	CHI White Sox (AL)
1916	BOS Red Sox (AL)	4-1	BKN Robins (NL)	1960	PIT Pirates (NL)	4-3	NY Yankees (AL)
1917	CHI White Sox (AL)	4-2	NY Giants (NL)	1961	NY Yankees (AL)	4-1	CIN Reds (NL)
1918	BOS Red Sox (AL)	4-2	CHI Cubs (NL)	1962	NY Yankees (AL)	4-3	SF Giants (NL)
1919	CIN Reds (NL)	5-3	CHI White Sox (AL)	1963	LA Dodgers (NL)	4-0	NY Yankees (AL)
1920	CLE Indians (AL)	5-2	BKN Robins (NL)	1964	STL Cardinals (NL)	4-3	NY Yankees (AL)
1921	NY Giants (NL)	5-3	NY Yankees (AL)	1965	LA Dodgers (NL)	4-3	MIN Twins (AL)
1922	NY Giants (NL)	4-0	NY Yankees (AL)	1966	BAL Orioles (AL)	4-0	LA Dodgers (NL)
1923	NY Yankees (AL)	4-2	NY Giants (NL)	1967	STL Cardinals (NL)	4-3	BOS Red Sox (AL)
1924	WAS Senators (AL)	4-3	NY Giants (NL)	1968	DET Tigers (AL)	4-3	STL Cardinals (NL)
1925	PIT Pirates (NL)	4-3	WAS Senators (AL)	1969	NY Mets (NL)	4-1	BAL Orioles (AL)
1926	STL Cardinals (NL)	4-3	NY Yankees (AL)	1970	BAL Orioles (AL)	4-1	CIN Reds (NL)
1927	NY Yankees (AL)	4-0	PIT Pirates (NL)	1971	PIT Pirates (NL)	4-3	BAL Orioles (AL)
1928	NY Yankees (AL)	4-0	STL Cardinals (NL)	1972	OAK Athletics (AL)	4-3	CIN Reds (NL)
1929	PHI Athletics (AL)	4-1	CHI Cubs (NL)	1973	OAK Athletics (AL)	4-3	NY Mets (NL)
1930	PHI Athletics (AL)	4-2	STL Cardinals (NL)	1974	OAK Athletics (AL)	4-1	LA Dodgers (NL)
1931	STL Cardinals (NL)	4-3	PHI Athletics (AL)	1975	CIN Reds (NL)	4-3	BOS Red Sox (AL)
1932	NY Yankees (AL)	4-0	CHI Cubs (NL)	1976	CIN Reds (NL)	4-0	NY Yankees (AL)
1933	NY Giants (NL)	4-1	WAS Senators (AL)	1977	NY Yankees (AL)	4-2	LA Dodgers (NL)
1934	STL Cardinals (NL)	4-3	DET Tigers (AL)	1978	NY Yankees (AL)	4-2	LA Dodgers (NL)
1935	DET Tigers (AL)	4-2	CHI Cubs (NL)	1979	PIT Pirates (NL)	4-3	BAL Orioles (AL)
1936	NY Yankees (AL)	4-2	NY Giants (NL)	1980	PHI Phillies (NL)	4-2	KC Royals (AL)
1937	NY Yankees (AL)	4-1	NY Giants (NL)	1981	LA Dodgers (NL)	4-2	NY Yankees (AL)
1938	NY Yankees (AL)	4-0	CHI Cubs (NL)	1982	STL Cardinals (NL)	4-3	MIL Brewers (AL)
1939	NY Yankees (AL)	4-0	CIN Reds (NL)	1983	BAL Orioles (AL)	4-1	PHI Phillies (NL)
1940	CIN Reds (NL)	4-3	DET Tigers (AL)	1984	DET Tigers (AL)	4-1	SD Padres (NL)
1941	NY Yankees (AL)	4-1	BKN Dodgers (NL)	1985	KC Royals (AL)	4-3	STL Cardinals (NL)
1942	STL Cardinals (NL)	4-1	NY Yankees (AL)	1986	NY Mets (NL)	4-3	BOS Red Sox (AL)
1943	NY Yankees (AL)	4-1	STL Cardinals (NL)	1987	MIN Twins (AL)	4-3	STL Cardinals (NL)
1944	STL Cardinals (NL)	4-2	STL Browns (AL)	1988	LA Dodgers (NL)	4-1	OAK Athletics (AL)
1945	DET Tigers (AL)	4-3	CHI Cubs (NL)	1989	OAK Athletics (AL)	4-0	SF Giants (NL)
1946	STL Cardinals (NL)	4-3	BOS Red Sox (AL)	1990	CIN Reds (NL)	4-0	OAK Athletics (AL)

1991	MIN Twins (AL)	4-3	ATL Braves (NL)	1994	NO SERIES		
1992	TOR Blue Jays (AL)	4-2	ATL Braves (NL)	1995	ATL Braves (NL)	4-2	CLE Indians (AL)
1993	TOR Blue Jays (AL)	4-2	PHI Phillies (NL)	1996	NY Yankees (AL)	4-2	ATL Braves (NL)

LEAGUE CHAMPIONSHIP SERIES 1969-96

		NLCS				ALCS	
YEAR	WINNER	SERIES	LOSER	YEAR	WINNER	SERIES	LOSER
1969	NY Mets (E)	3-0	ATL Braves (W)	1969	BAL Orioles (E)	3-0	MIN Twins (W)
1970	CIN Reds (W)	3-0	PIT Pirates (E)	1970	BAL Orioles (E)	3-0	MIN Twins (W)
1971	PIT Pirates (E)	3-1	SF Giants (W)	1971	BAL Orioles (E)	3-0	OAK Athletics (W)
1972	CIN Reds (W)	3-2	PIT Pirates (E)	1972	OAK Athletics (W)	3-2	DET Tigers (E)
1973	NY Mets (E)	3-2	CIN Reds (W)	1973	OAK Athletics (W)	3-2	BAL Orioles (E)
1974	LA Dodgers (W)	3-1	PIT Pirates (E)	1974	OAK Athletics (W)	3-1	BAL Orioles (E)
1975	CIN Reds (W)	3-0	PIT Pirates (E)	1975	BOS Red Sox (E)	3-0	OAK Athletics (W)
1976	CIN Reds (W)	3-0	PHI Phillies (E)	1976	NY Yankees (E)	3-2	KC Royals (W)
1977	LA Dodgers (W)	3-1	PHI Phillies (E)	1977	NY Yankees (E)	3-2	KC Royals (W)
1978	LA Dodgers (W)	3-1	PHI Phillies (E)	1978	NY Yankees (E)	3-1	KC Royals (W)
1979	PIT Pirates (W)	3-0	CIN Reds (W)	1979	BAL Orioles (E)	3-1	CAL Angels (W)
1980	PHI Phillies (E)	3-2	HOU Astros (W)	1980	KC Royals (W)	3-0	NY Yankees (E)
1981	NL EAST PLAYOFF			1981	AL EAST PLAYOFF		
	MON Expos	3-2	PHI Phillies		NY Yankees	3-2	MIL Brewers
	NL WEST PLAYOFF				AL WEST PLAYOFF		
	LA Dodgers	3-2	HOU Astros		OAK Athletics	3-0	KC Royals
	LCS				LCS		
	LA Dodgers (W)	3-2	MON Expos (E)		NY Yankees (E)	3-0	OAK Athletics (W)
1982	STL Cardinals (E)	3-0	ATL Braves (W)	1982	MIL Brewers (E)	3-2	CAL Angels (W)
1983	PHI Phillies (E)	3-1	LA Dodgers (W)	1983	BAL Orioles (E)	3-1	CHI White Sox (W)
1984	SD Padres (W)	3-2	CHI Cubs (E)	1984	DET Tigers (E)	3-0	KC Royals (W)
1985	STL Cardinals (E)	4-2	LA Dodgers (W)	1985	KC Royals (W)	4-3	TOR Blue Jays (E)
1986	NY Mets (E)	4-2	HOU Astros (W)	1986	BOS Red Sox (E)	4-3	CAL Angels (W)
1987	STL Cardinals (E)	4-3	SF Giants (W)	1987	MIN Twins (W)	4-1	DET Tigers (E)
1988	LA Dodgers (W)	4-3	NY Mets (E)	1988	OAK Athletics (W)	4-0	BOS Red Sox (E)
1989	SF Giants (W)	4-1	CHI Cubs (E)	1989	OAK Athletics (W)	4-1	TOR Blue Jays (E)
1990	CIN Reds (W)	4-2	PIT Pirates (E)	1990	OAK Athletics (W)	4-0	BOS Red Sox (E)
1991	ATL Braves (W)	4-3	PIT Pirates (E)	1991	MIN Twins (W)	4-2	TOR Blue Jays (E)
1992	ATL Braves (W)	4-3	PIT Pirates (E)	1992	TOR Blue Jays (E)	4-2	OAK Athletics (W)
1993	PHI Phillies (E)	4-2	ATL Braves (W)	1993	TOR Blue Jays (E)	4-2	CHI White Sox (W)
1994	NO SERIES			1994	NO SERIES		
1995	ATL Braves (E)	4-0	CIN Reds (C)	1995	CLE Indians (C)	4-2	SEA Mariners (W)
1996	ATL Braves (E)	4-3	STL Cardinals (C)	1996	NY Yankees (E)	4-1	BAL Orioles (E)

DIVISION SERIES 1995-96

	NATIONAL LEAGUE				AMERICAN LEAGUE		
YEAR	WINNER	SERIES	LOSER	YEAR	WINNER	SERIES	LOSER
1995	ATL Braves (E)	3-1	COL Rockies (W)	1995	CLE Indians (C)	3-0	BOS Red Sox (E)
	CIN Reds (C)	3-0	LA Dodgers (W)		SEA Mariners (W)	3-2	NY Yankees (E)
1996	ATL Braves (E)	3-0	LA Dodgers (W)	1996	NY Yankees (E)	3-1	TEX Rangers (W)
	STL Cardinals (C)	3-0	SD Padres (W)		BAL Orioles (E)	3-1	CLE Indians (C)

YEARLY TEAM AND INDIVIDUAL LEADERS

In this section, you will find how each National League and American League organization did in each season since 1900. Included also are each league's individual leaders in batting and pitching for each year.

W = wins; **L** = losses; **PCT** = winning percentage; **GB** = games the team finished behind the league winner or the division winner; **R** = runs scored by the team; **OR** = runs scored by the team's opponents; **BA** = team batting average; **FA** = team fielding average; **ERA** = team earned run average. The league's total runs, opponents' runs, batting average, fielding average, and earned run average are shown totaled below the columns. The team that won the World Series receives a star (★), the team that won the LCS but not the fall classic receives a bullet (•).

The year's individual leaders in each league follow, beginning with hitters' categories—batting average, hits, doubles, triples, home runs, runs batted in, slugging average (post 1946), stolen bases, and runs scored. Pitchers' categories follow—wins, winning percentage, earned run average, strikeouts, saves, complete games, shutouts, games pitched, and innings pitched. Most of these categories will have the top three leaders in the league. When two or more players tied for a position, it is indicated. If there are two who were far and away the leaders in any one category, and many who either tied or were among the ordinary, only two players are listed.

1900 NATIONAL LEAGUE STANDINGS

	W	L	PCT	GB	R	OR
BKN	82	54	.603	—	816	722
PIT	79	60	.568	4.5	733	612
PHI	75	63	.543	8	810	792
BOS	66	72	.478	17	778	739
CHI	65	75	.464	19	635	751
STL	65	75	.464	19	744	748
CIN	62	77	.446	21.5	703	745
NY	60	78	.435	23	713	823
					5932	5932

BATTING AVERAGE
Honus Wagner PIT .... .381
Elmer Flick PHI .... .367
Jesse Burkett STL .... .363

HITS
Willie Keeler BKN 204
Jesse Burkett STL 203
Honus Wagner PIT 201

DOUBLES
Honus Wagner PIT 45
Nap Lajoie PHI 33
two tied at 32

TRIPLES
Honus Wagner PIT 22

C. Hickman NY 17
Joe Kelley BKN................... 17

HOME RUNS
Herman Long BOS 12
Elmer Flick PHI................... 11
Mike Donlin STL 10

RUNS BATTED IN
Elmer Flick PHI 110
Ed Delahanty PHI 109
Honus Wagner PIT 100

STOLEN BASES
Patsy Donovan STL............ 45
Van Haltren NY................... 45
Jimmy Barrett CIN 44

RUNS SCORED
Roy Thomas PHI 132
Jimmy Slagle PHI 115
two tied at 114

WINS
Joe McGinnity BKN 28
four tied at 20

EARNED RUN AVERAGE
Rube Waddell PIT 2.37
Ned Garvin CHI 2.41
Jack Taylor CHI 2.55

STRIKEOUTS
Rube Waddell PIT 130
Noodles Hahn CIN............ 132
Cy Young STL 115

SAVES
Frank Kitson BKN 4

COMPLETE GAMES
Pink Hawley NY 34

SHUTOUTS
four tied at............................. 4

INNINGS PITCHED
Joe McGinnity BKN 343

	W	L	PCT	GB	R	OR
PHI	83	53	.610	—	775	636
STL	78	58	.574	5	619	607
BOS	77	60	.562	6.5	664	600
CHI	74	60	.552	8	675	602
CLE	69	67	.507	14	686	667
WAS	61	75	.449	22	707	790
DET	52	83	.385	30.5	566	657
BAL	50	88	.362	34	715	848
					5407	5407

BATTING AVERAGE
N. Lajoie PHI, CLE .... .378
Ed Delahanty WAS .... .376
C. Hickman BOS, CLE .... .361

HITS
C. Hickman BOS, CLE 193
Lave Cross PHI 191
Bill Bradley CLE................ 187

DOUBLES
Ed Delahanty WAS 43
Harry Davis PHI................. 43
two tied at 39

TRIPLES
Jimmy Williams BAL 21

Buck Freeman BOS............ 19
two tied at 14

HOME RUNS
Socks Seybold PHI............ 16
three tied at........................ 11

RUNS BATTED IN
Buck Freeman BOS........... 121
C. Hickman BOS, CLE 110
Lave Cross PHI 108

STOLEN BASES
Topsy Hartsel PHI 47
Sam Mertes CHI 46
Dave Fultz PHI 44

RUNS SCORED
Topsy Hartsel PHI 109
Dave Fultz PHI 109
Sammy Strang CHI........... 108

WINS
Cy Young BOS 32
Rube Waddell PHI 24
two tied at 22

EARNED RUN AVERAGE
Ed Siever DET................. 1.91
Rube Waddell PHI 2.05
B. Bernhard PHI, CLE 2.15

STRIKEOUTS
Rube Waddell PHI 210
Cy Young BOS 160
Jack Powell STL 137

SAVES
Jack Powell STL 2

COMPLETE GAMES
Cy Young BOS 41

SHUTOUTS
Addie Joss CLE 5

INNINGS PITCHED
Cy Young BOS 385

	W	L	PCT	GB	R	OR
PIT	90	49	.647	—	776	534
PHI	83	57	.593	7.5	668	543
BKN	79	57	.581	9.5	744	600
STL	76	64	.543	14.5	792	689
BOS	69	69	.500	20.5	531	556
CHI	53	86	.381	37	578	699
NY	52	85	.380	37	544	755
CIN	52	87	.374	38	561	818
					5194	5194

BATTING AVERAGE
Jesse Burkett STL .... .382
Ed Delahanty PHI .... .357
J. Sheckard BKN .... .354

HITS
Jesse Burkett STL 226
W. Keeler BKN 202
J. Sheckard BKN 196

DOUBLES
Ed Delahanty PHI 39
Tom Daly BKN................... 38
Honus Wagner PIT 37

TRIPLES
Jimmy Sheckard BKN......... 19

Elmer Flick PHI 17

HOME RUNS
Sam Crawford CIN 16
Jimmy Sheckard BKN........ 11
Jesse Burkett STL 10

RUNS BATTED IN
Honus Wagner PIT 126
Ed Delahanty PHI 108
two tied at 104

STOLEN BASES
Honus Wagner PIT 49
Topsy Hartsel CHI 41
Sammy Strang NY 40

RUNS SCORED
Jesse Burkett STL 142
W. Keeler BKN 123
G. Beaumont PIT.............. 120

WINS
B. Donovan BKN 25
Jack Harper STL................ 23
two tied at 22

EARNED RUN AVERAGE
Jesse Tannehill PIT 2.18
D. Phillippe PIT 2.22
Al Orth PHI 2.27

STRIKEOUTS
Noodles Hahn CIN............ 239
B. Donovan BKN 226
T. Hughes CHI.................. 225

SAVES
Jack Powell STL 3

COMPLETE GAMES
Noodles Hahn CIN 41

SHUTOUTS
three tied at.......................... 6

INNINGS PITCHED
Noodles Hahn CIN 375

	W	L	PCT	GB	R	OR
PHI	83	53	.610	—	775	636
STL	78	58	.574	5	619	607
BOS	77	60	.562	6.5	664	600
CHI	74	60	.552	8	675	602
CLE	69	67	.507	14	686	667
WAS	61	75	.449	22	707	790
DET	52	83	.385	30.5	566	657
BAL	50	88	.362	34	715	848
					5407	5407

BATTING AVERAGE
N. Lajoie PHI, CLE .... .378
Ed Delahanty WAS........... .376
C. Hickman BOS, CLE .... .361

HITS
C. Hickman BOS, CLE 193
Lave Cross PHI 191
Bill Bradley CLE................ 187

DOUBLES
Ed Delahanty WAS............. 43
Harry Davis PHI.................. 43
two tied at 39

TRIPLES
Jimmy Williams BAL 21

HOME RUNS
Socks Seybold PHI............. 16
three tied at........................ 11

RUNS BATTED IN
Buck Freeman BOS.......... 121
C. Hickman BOS, CLE 110
Lave Cross PHI 108

STOLEN BASES
Topsy Hartsel PHI 47
Sam Mertes CHI 46
Dave Fultz PHI 44

Buck Freeman BOS............. 19
two tied at 14

RUNS SCORED
Topsy Hartsel PHI 109
Dave Fultz PHI 109
Sammy Strang CHI........... 108

WINS
Cy Young BOS 32
Rube Waddell PHI.............. 24
two tied at 22

EARNED RUN AVERAGE
Ed Siever DET................. 1.91
Rube Waddell PHI 2.05
Bill Bernhard PHI, CLE 2.15

STRIKEOUTS
Rube Waddell PHI 210
Cy Young BOS 160
Jack Powell STL 137

SAVES
Jack Powell STL 2

COMPLETE GAMES
Cy Young BOS 41

SHUTOUTS
Addie Joss CLE 5

INNINGS PITCHED
Cy Young BOS 385

	W	L	PCT	GB	R	OR
PIT	103	36	.741	—	775	440
BKN	75	63	.543	27.5	564	519
BOS	73	64	.533	29	572	516
CIN	70	70	.500	33.5	633	566
CHI	68	69	.496	34	530	501
STL	56	78	.418	44.5	517	695
PHI	56	81	.409	46	484	649
NY	48	88	.353	53.5	401	590
					4476	4476

BATTING AVERAGE
G. Beaumont PIT............. .357
Sam Crawford CIN .... .333
W. Keeler BKN .... .333

HITS
G. Beaumont PIT............. 193
W. Keeler BKN 186
Sam Crawford CIN 185

DOUBLES
Honus Wagner PIT 33
Fred Clarke PIT 27
Duff Cooley BOS 26

TRIPLES
Sam Crawford CIN 22

Tommy Leach PIT 22
Honus Wagner PIT 16

HOME RUNS
Tommy Leach PIT 6
Jake Beckley CIN 5
two tied at 4

RUNS BATTED IN
Honus Wagner PIT 91
Tommy Leach PIT 85
Sam Crawford CIN 78

STOLEN BASES
Honus Wagner PIT 42
Jimmy Slagle CHI 40
Patsy Donovan STL............ 34

RUNS SCORED
Honus Wagner PIT........... 105
Fred Clarke PIT 103
G. Beaumont PIT............. 100

WINS
Jack Chesbro PIT 28
Togie Pittinger BOS............ 27
Vic Willis BOS.................... 27

EARNED RUN AVERAGE
Jack Taylor CHI 1.33
Noodles Hahn CIN............ 1.77
Jesse Tannehill PIT 1.95

STRIKEOUTS
Vic Willis BOS.................. 225
Doc White PHI 185

SAVES
Vic Willis BOS...................... 3

COMPLETE GAMES
Vic Willis BOS.................... 45

SHUTOUTS
Christy Mathewson NY 8
Jack Chesbro PIT 8

INNINGS PITCHED
Vic Willis BOS.................. 410

	W	L	PCT	GB	R	OR
★ BOS	91	47	.659	—	708	504
PHI	75	60	.556	14.5	597	519
CLE	77	63	.550	15	639	579
NY	72	62	.537	17	579	573
DET	65	71	.478	25	567	539
STL	65	74	.468	26.5	500	525
CHI	60	77	.438	30.5	516	613
WAS	43	94	.314	47.5	437	691
					4543	4543

BATTING AVERAGE
Nap Lajoie CLE .... .344
Sam Crawford DET .... .335
P. Dougherty BOS .... .331

HITS
P. Dougherty BOS 195
Sam Crawford DET 184
Freddie Parent BOS 170

DOUBLES
Socks Seybold PHI............. 45
Nap Lajoie CLE 41
Buck Freeman BOS............ 39

TRIPLES
Sam Crawford DET 25

Bill Bradley CLE.................. 22
Buck Freeman BOS............ 20

HOME RUNS
Buck Freeman BOS............ 13
C. Hickman CLE................. 12
Hobe Ferris BOS 9

RUNS BATTED IN
Buck Freeman BOS............ 104
C. Hickman CLE.................. 97
Nap Lajoie CLE 93

STOLEN BASES
Harry Bay CLE.................... 45
Ollie Pickering PHI.............. 40
two tied at 35

RUNS SCORED
P. Dougherty BOS 107
Bill Bradley CLE................. 101
two tied at 95

WINS
Cy Young BOS 28
Eddie Plank PHI 23
four tied at.......................... 21

EARNED RUN AVERAGE
Earl Moore CLE 1.77
Cy Young BOS 2.08
Bill Bernhard CLE 2.12

STRIKEOUTS
Rube Waddell PHI 302
Bill Donovan DET 187
two tied at 176

SAVES
five tied at 2

COMPLETE GAMES
three tied at........................ 34

SHUTOUTS
Cy Young BOS 7

INNINGS PITCHED
Cy Young BOS 342

	W	L	PCT	GB	R	OR
PIT	91	49	.650	—	793	613
NY	84	55	.604	6.5	729	567
CHI	82	56	.594	8	695	599
CIN	74	65	.532	16.5	765	656
BKN	70	66	.515	19	667	682
BOS	58	80	.420	32	578	699
PHI	49	86	.363	39.5	617	738
STL	43	94	.314	46.5	505	795
					5349	5349

BATTING AVERAGE
Honus Wagner PIT .... .355
Fred Clarke PIT .... .351
Mike Donlin CIN................ .351

HITS
G. Beaumont PIT 209
Cy Seymour CIN................ 191
George Browne NY 185

DOUBLES
Sam Mertes NY 32
Harry Steinfeldt CIN............ 32
Fred Clarke PIT 32

TRIPLES
Honus Wagner PIT.............. 19

Mike Donlin CIN.................. 18
Tommy Leach PIT 17

HOME RUNS
Jimmy Sheckard BKN.......... 9
six tied at 7

RUNS BATTED IN
Sam Mertes NY 104
Honus Wagner PIT 101
Jack Doyle BKN.................. 91

STOLEN BASES
Jimmy Sheckard BKN.......... 67
Frank Chance CHI............... 67
two tied at 46

RUNS SCORED
G. Beaumont PIT.............. 137
Mike Donlin CIN................ 110
George Browne NY 105

WINS
Joe McGinnity NY.............. 31
C. Mathewson NY.............. 30
two tied at 25

EARNED RUN AVERAGE
Sam Leever PIT................ 2.06
C. Mathewson NY.............. 2.26
Jake Weimer CHI 2.30

STRIKEOUTS
C. Mathewson NY.............. 267
Joe McGinnity NY.............. 171

SAVES
Carl Lundgren CHI................ 3
Roscoe Miller NY 3

COMPLETE GAMES
Joe McGinnity NY.............. 44

SHUTOUTS
Sam Leever PIT 7

INNINGS PITCHED
Joe McGinnity NY.............. 434

	W	L	PCT	GB	R	OR
BOS	95	59	.617	—	608	466
NY	92	59	.609	1.5	598	526
CHI	89	65	.578	6	600	482
CLE	86	65	.570	7.5	647	482
PHI	81	70	.536	12.5	557	503
STL	65	87	.428	29	481	604
DET	62	90	.408	32	505	627
WAS	38	113	.252	55.5	437	743
					4433	4433

BATTING AVERAGE
Nap Lajoie CLE .... .376
W. Keeler NY .... .343
Harry Davis PHI .... .309

HITS
Nap Lajoie CLE 208
W. Keeler NY 186
Bill Bradley CLE 183

DOUBLES
Nap Lajoie CLE 49
Jimmy Collins BOS 33
Bill Bradley CLE 32

TRIPLES
Joe Cassidy WAS 19

Buck Freeman BOS 19
Chick Stahl BOS 19

HOME RUNS
Harry Davis PHI 10
Buck Freeman BOS 7
Danny Murphy PHI 7

RUNS BATTED IN
Nap Lajoie CLE 102
Buck Freeman BOS 84
Bill Bradley CLE 83

STOLEN BASES
Elmer Flick CLE 38
Harry Bay CLE 38
Emmet Heidrick STL 35

RUNS SCORED
Dougherty BOS, NY 113
Elmer Flick CLE 97
Bill Bradley CLE 94

WINS
Jack Chesbro NY 41
Eddie Plank PHI 26
Cy Young BOS 26

EARNED RUN AVERAGE
Addie Joss CLE 1.59
Rube Waddell PHI 1.62
Doc White CHI 1.78

STRIKEOUTS
Rube Waddell PHI 349
Jack Chesbro NY 239
Jack Powell NY 202

SAVES
Casey Patten WAS 3

COMPLETE GAMES
Jack Chesbro NY 48

SHUTOUTS
Cy Young BOS 10

INNINGS PITCHED
Jack Chesbro NY 455

	W	L	PCT	GB	R	OR
NY	106	47	.693	—	744	476
CHI	93	60	.608	13	599	517
CIN	88	65	.575	18	695	547
PIT	87	66	.569	19	675	592
STL	75	79	.487	31.5	602	595
BKN	56	97	.366	50	497	614
BOS	55	98	.359	51	491	749
PHI	52	100	.342	53.5	571	784
					4874	4874

BATTING AVERAGE
Honus Wagner PIT .... .349
M. Donlin CIN, NY .... .329
Jake Beckley STL .... .325

HITS
G. Beaumont PIT 185
Jake Beckley STL 179
Honus Wagner PIT 171

DOUBLES
Honus Wagner PIT 44
Sam Mertes NY 28
Joe Delahanty BOS 27

TRIPLES
Harry Lumley BKN 18

Honus Wagner PIT 14
three tied at 13

HOME RUNS
Harry Lumley BKN 9
Dave Brain STL 7
four tied at 6

RUNS BATTED IN
Bill Dahlen NY 80
Sam Mertes NY 78
Harry Lumley BKN 78

STOLEN BASES
Honus Wagner PIT 53
Bill Dahlen NY 47
Sam Mertes NY 47

RUNS SCORED
George Browne NY 99
Honus Wagner PIT 97
Ginger Beaumont PIT 97

WINS
Joe McGinnity NY 35
C. Mathewson NY 33
Jack Harper CIN 23

EARNED RUN AVERAGE
Joe McGinnity NY 1.61
Ned Garvin BKN 1.68
T. Brown CHI 1.86

STRIKEOUTS
C. Mathewson NY 212
Vic Willis BOS 196

SAVES
Joe McGinnity NY 5

COMPLETE GAMES
Jack Taylor STL 39
Vic Willis BOS 39

SHUTOUTS
Joe McGinnity NY 9

INNINGS PITCHED
Joe McGinnity NY 408

	W	L	PCT	GB	R	OR
PHI	92	56	.622	—	623	492
CHI	92	60	.605	2	612	451
DET	79	74	.516	15.5	512	602
BOS	78	74	.513	16	579	564
CLE	76	78	.494	19	567	587
NY	71	78	.477	21.5	586	622
WAS	64	87	.424	29.5	559	623
STL	54	99	.353	40.5	511	608
					4549	4549

BATTING AVERAGE
Elmer Flick CLE .... .306
W. Keeler NY .... .302
Harry Bay CLE .... .301

HITS
George Stone STL 187
Harry Davis PHI 173
Sam Crawford DET 171

DOUBLES
Harry Davis PHI 47
Sam Crawford DET 38
two tied at 37

TRIPLES
Elmer Flick CLE 18

Hobe Ferris BOS 16
Terry Turner CLE 14

HOME RUNS
Harry Davis PHI 8
George Stone STL 7
five tied at 6

RUNS BATTED IN
Harry Davis PHI 83
Lave Cross PHI 77
Jiggs Donahue CHI 76

STOLEN BASES
Danny Hoffman PHI 46
Dave Fultz NY 44
Jake Stahl WAS 41

RUNS SCORED
Harry Davis PHI 93
Fielder Jones CHI 91
Harry Bay CLE 90

WINS
Rube Waddell PHI 27
Eddie Plank PHI 24
two tied at 23

EARNED RUN AVERAGE
Rube Waddell PHI 1.48
Doc White CHI 1.76
Cy Young BOS 1.82

STRIKEOUTS
Rube Waddell PHI 287
Eddie Plank PHI 210
Cy Young BOS 210

SAVES
Jim Buchanan STL 2

COMPLETE GAMES
three tied at 35

SHUTOUTS
Ed Killian DET 8

INNINGS PITCHED
George Mullin DET 348

	W	L	PCT	GB	R	OR
★ NY	105	48	.686	—	780	505
PIT	96	57	.627	9	692	570
CHI	92	61	.601	13	667	442
PHI	83	69	.546	21.5	708	602
CIN	79	74	.516	26	735	698
STL	58	96	.377	47.5	535	734
BOS	51	103	.331	54.5	468	733
BKN	48	104	.316	56.5	506	807
					5091	5091

BATTING AVERAGE
Cy Seymour CIN .... .377
Honus Wagner PIT .... .363
Mike Donlin NY .... .356

HITS
Cy Seymour CIN 219
Mike Donlin NY 216
Honus Wagner PIT 199

DOUBLES
Cy Seymour CIN 40
John Titus PHI 36
Honus Wagner PIT 32

TRIPLES
Cy Seymour CIN 21

Sam Mertes NY 17
Sherry Magee PHI 17

HOME RUNS
Fred Odwell CIN 9
Cy Seymour CIN 8
three tied at 7

RUNS BATTED IN
Cy Seymour CIN 121
Sam Mertes NY 108
Honus Wagner PIT 101

STOLEN BASES
Billy Maloney CHI 59
Art Devlin NY 59
Honus Wagner PIT 57

RUNS SCORED
Mike Donlin NY 124
Roy Thomas PHI 118
Miller Huggins CIN 117

WINS
C. Mathewson NY 31
Togie Pittinger PHI 23
Red Ames NY 22

EARNED RUN AVERAGE
C. Mathewson NY 1.28
Ed Reulbach CHI 1.42
Bob Wicker CHI 2.02

STRIKEOUTS
C. Mathewson NY 206
Red Ames NY 198
Orval Overall CIN 173

SAVES
Claude Elliott NY 6

COMPLETE GAMES
Irv Young BOS 41

SHUTOUTS
C. Mathewson NY 8

INNINGS PITCHED
Irv Young BOS 378

	W	L	PCT	GB	R	OR
★ CHI	93	58	.616	—	570	460
NY	90	61	.596	3	644	543
CLE	89	64	.582	5	663	482
PHI	78	67	.538	12	561	543
STL	76	73	.510	16	558	498
DET	71	78	.477	21	518	599
WAS	55	95	.367	37.5	518	664
BOS	49	105	.318	45.5	463	706
					4495	4495

BATTING AVERAGE
George Stone STL............ .358
Nap Lajoie CLE .... .355
Hal Chase NY .... .323

HITS
Nap Lajoie CLE 214
George Stone STL 208
Elmer Flick CLE 194

DOUBLES
Nap Lajoie CLE 48
Harry Davis PHI 42
Elmer Flick CLE 34

TRIPLES
Elmer Flick CLE................. 22

George Stone STL.............. 20
Sam Crawford DET 16

HOME RUNS
Harry Davis PHI 12
C. Hickman WAS 9
George Stone STL............... 6

RUNS BATTED IN
Harry Davis PHI 96
Nap Lajoie CLE 91
George Davis CHI 80

STOLEN BASES
Elmer Flick CLE 39
John Anderson WAS 39
two tied at 37

RUNS SCORED
Elmer Flick CLE................. 98
Topsy Hartsel PHI 96
Wee Willie Keeler NY 96

WINS
Al Orth NY 27
Jack Chesbro NY................ 23
two tied at 22

EARNED RUN AVERAGE
Doc White CHI.................. 1.52
Barney Pelty STL.............. 1.59
Addie Joss CLE 1.72

STRIKEOUTS
Rube Waddell PHI 196
Cy Falkenberg WAS 178

SAVES
Otto Hess CLE..................... 3
Chief Bender PHI 3

COMPLETE GAMES
Al Orth NY 36

SHUTOUTS
Ed Walsh CHI 10

INNINGS PITCHED
Al Orth NY 339

	W	L	PCT	GB	R	OR
CHI	116	36	.763	—	705	381
NY	96	56	.632	20	625	510
PIT	93	60	.608	23.5	623	470
PHI	71	82	.464	45.5	528	564
BKN	66	86	.434	50	496	625
CIN	64	87	.424	51.5	533	582
STL	52	98	.347	63	470	607
BOS	49	102	.325	66.5	408	649
					4388	4388

BATTING AVERAGE
Honus Wagner PIT .... .339
Harry Steinfeldt CHI........ .327
Harry Lumley BKN............ .324

HITS
Harry Steinfeldt CHI.......... 176
Honus Wagner PIT 175
Cy Seymour CIN, NY........ 165

DOUBLES
Honus Wagner PIT 38
Sherry Magee PHI 36
Kitty Bransfield PHI 28

TRIPLES
Wildfire Schulte CHI 13

Fred Clarke PIT 13
two tied at 12

HOME RUNS
Tim Jordan BKN................. 12
Harry Lumley BKN................ 9
Cy Seymour CIN, NY............ 8

RUNS BATTED IN
Jim Nealon PIT 83
Harry Steinfeldt CHI........... 83
Cy Seymour CIN, NY.......... 80

STOLEN BASES
Frank Chance CHI 57
Sherry Magee PHI 55
Art Devlin NY 54

RUNS SCORED
Frank Chance CHI............. 103
Honus Wagner PIT........... 103
Jimmy Sheckard CHI.......... 90

WINS
Joe McGinnity NY................ 27
T. Brown CHI 26
Vic Willis PIT 23

EARNED RUN AVERAGE
T. Brown CHI 1.04
Jack Pfiester CHI 1.51
Ed Reulbach CHI.............. 1.65

STRIKEOUTS
F. Beebe CHI, STL 171
Big Jeff Pfeffer BOS 158
Red Ames NY 156

SAVES
George Ferguson NY 7

COMPLETE GAMES
Irv Young BOS.................... 37

SHUTOUTS
T. Brown CHI 9

INNINGS PITCHED
Irv Young BOS.................. 358

	W	L	PCT	GB	R	OR
DET	92	58	.613	—	694	532
PHI	88	57	.607	1.5	582	511
CHI	87	64	.576	5.5	588	474
CLE	85	67	.559	8	530	525
NY	70	78	.473	21	605	665
STL	69	83	.454	24	542	555
BOS	59	90	.396	32.5	464	558
WAS	49	102	.325	43.5	506	691
					4511	4511

BATTING AVERAGE
Ty Cobb DET 350
Sam Crawford DET 323
George Stone STL 320

HITS
Ty Cobb DET 212
George Stone STL............ 191
Sam Crawford DET 188

DOUBLES
Harry Davis PHI 37
Sam Crawford DET 34
two tied at 30

TRIPLES
Elmer Flick CLE 18

Sam Crawford DET 17
Ty Cobb DET 14

HOME RUNS
Harry Davis PHI.................... 8
three tied at............................ 5

RUNS BATTED IN
Ty Cobb DET 119
Socks Seybold PHI............. 92
Harry Davis PHI................... 87

STOLEN BASES
Ty Cobb DET 49
Wid Conroy NY 41
Elmer Flick CLE.................. 41

RUNS SCORED
Sam Crawford DET 102
Davy Jones DET................ 101
Ty Cobb DET 97

WINS
Addie Joss CLE 27
Doc White CHI.................... 27
two tied at 25

EARNED RUN AVERAGE
Ed Walsh CHI 1.60
Ed Killian CHI 1.78
Addie Joss CLE 1.83

STRIKEOUTS
Rube Waddell PHI 232
Ed Walsh CHI 206
Eddie Plank PHI 183

SAVES
three tied at............................ 4

COMPLETE GAMES
Ed Walsh CHI 37

SHUTOUTS
Eddie Plank PHI 8

INNINGS PITCHED
Ed Walsh CHI 422

	W	L	PCT	GB	R	OR
★ CHI	107	45	.704	—	574	390
PIT	91	63	.591	17	634	510
PHI	83	64	.565	21.5	512	476
NY	82	71	.536	25.5	574	5102
BKN	65	83	.439	40	446	522
CIN	66	87	.431	41.5	526	519
BOS	58	90	.392	47	502	652
STL	52	101	.340	55.5	419	608
					4187	4187

BATTING AVERAGE
Honus Wagner PIT 350
Sherry Magee PHI 328
G. Beaumont BOS........... 322

HITS
G. Beaumont BOS........... 187
Honus Wagner PIT 180
Tommy Leach PIT 166

DOUBLES
Honus Wagner PIT 38
Sherry Magee PHI 28
two tied at 25

TRIPLES
W. Alperman BKN 16

John Ganzel CIN 16
two tied at 14

HOME RUNS
Dave Brain BOS 10
Harry Lumley BKN................ 9
Red Murray STL 7

RUNS BATTED IN
Sherry Magee PHI 85
Honus Wagner PIT 82
Ed Abbaticchio PIT 82

STOLEN BASES
Honus Wagner PIT 61
Johnny Evers CHI............... 46
Sherry Magee PHI 46

RUNS SCORED
Spike Shannon NY 104
Tommy Leach PIT 102
Honus Wagner PIT............. 98

WINS
C. Mathewson NY.............. 24
Orval Overall CHI 23
Tully Sparks PHI 22

EARNED RUN AVERAGE
Jack Pfiester CHI............. 1.15
Carl Lundgren CHI.......... 1.17
T. Brown CHI 1.39

STRIKEOUTS
C. Mathewson NY............. 178
Buck Ewing CIN................ 147

SAVES
Joe McGinnity NY................ 4

COMPLETE GAMES
Stoney McGlynn STL.......... 33

SHUTOUTS
Christy Mathewson NY 8
Orval Overall CHI 8

INNINGS PITCHED
S. McGlynn STL 352

	W	L	PCT	GB	R	OR
DET	90	63	.588	—	647	547
CLE	90	64	.584	.5	568	457
CHI	88	64	.579	1.5	537	470
STL	83	69	.546	6.5	544	483
BOS	75	79	.487	15.5	564	513
PHI	68	85	.444	22	486	562
WAS	67	85	.441	22.5	479	539
NY	51	103	.331	39.5	459	713
					4284	4284

BATTING AVERAGE
Ty Cobb DET .... .324
Sam Crawford DET .... .311
Doc Gessler BOS .... .308

HITS
Ty Cobb DET 188
Sam Crawford DET 184
two tied at 168

DOUBLES
Ty Cobb DET 36
Sam Crawford DET 33
C. Rossman DET................ 33

TRIPLES
Ty Cobb DET 20
Sam Crawford DET 16
Jake Stahl BOS, NY 16

HOME RUNS
Sam Crawford DET 7
Bill Hinchman CLE................ 6
three tied at........................... 5

RUNS BATTED IN
Ty Cobb DET 108
Sam Crawford DET 80
two tied at........................... 74

STOLEN BASES
Patsy Dougherty CHI.......... 47
Charlie Hemphill NY 42
G. Schaefer DET 40

RUNS SCORED
Matty McIntyre DET 105
Sam Crawford DET 102
G. Schaefer DET 96

WINS
Ed Walsh CHI 40
Addie Joss CLE.................. 24
Ed Summers DET............... 24

EARNED RUN AVERAGE
Addie Joss CLE 1.16
Cy Young BOS 1.26
Ed Walsh CHI 1.42

STRIKEOUTS
Ed Walsh CHI 269
Rube Waddell STL 232
Tom Hughes WAS 165

SAVES
Ed Walsh CHI 6

COMPLETE GAMES
Ed Walsh CHI 42

SHUTOUTS
Ed Walsh CHI 11

INNINGS PITCHED
Ed Walsh CHI 464

	W	L	PCT	GB	R	OR
★ CHI	99	55	.643	—	624	461
NY	98	56	.636	1	652	456
PIT	98	56	.636	1	585	469
PHI	83	71	.539	16	504	445
CIN	73	81	.474	26	489	544
BOS	63	91	.409	36	537	622
BKN	53	101	.344	46	377	516
STL	49	105	.318	50	371	626
					4139	4139

BATTING AVERAGE
Honus Wagner PIT .... .354
Mike Donlin NY .... .334
Larry Doyle NY .... .308

HITS
Honus Wagner PIT 201
Mike Donlin NY 198
two tied at 167

DOUBLES
Honus Wagner PIT 39
Sherry Magee PHI 30
Frank Chance CHI 27

TRIPLES
Honus Wagner PIT 19

Hans Lobert CIN................ 18
two tied at 16

HOME RUNS
Tim Jordan BKN 12
Honus Wagner PIT 10
Red Murray STL 7

RUNS BATTED IN
Honus Wagner PIT 109
Mike Donlin NY 106
Cy Seymour NY 92

STOLEN BASES
Honus Wagner PIT 53
Red Murray STL 48
Hans Lobert CIN................ 47

RUNS SCORED
Fred Tenney NY 101
Honus Wagner PIT 100
Tommy Leach PIT 93

WINS
C. Mathewson NY.............. 37
T. Brown CHI 29
Ed Reulbach CHI 24

EARNED RUN AVERAGE
C. Mathewson NY............ 1.43
T. Brown CHI 1.47
G. McQuillan PHI 1.53

STRIKEOUTS
C. Mathewson NY............. 259
Nap Rucker BKN 199
Orval Overall CHI 167

SAVES
three tied at........................... 5

COMPLETE GAMES
C. Mathewson NY.............. 34

SHUTOUTS
C. Mathewson NY.............. 11

INNINGS PITCHED
C. Mathewson NY............ 391

	W	L	PCT	GB	R	OR
DET	98	54	.645	—	666	493
PHI	95	58	.621	3.5	605	408
BOS	88	63	.583	9.5	597	550
CHI	78	74	.513	20	492	463
NY	74	77	.490	23.5	590	587
CLE	71	82	.464	27.5	493	532
STL	61	89	.407	36	441	575
WAS	42	110	.276	56	380	656
					4264	4264

BATTING AVERAGE
Ty Cobb DET .... .377
Eddie Collins PHI .... .346
Nap Lajoie CLE .... .324

HITS
Ty Cobb DET 216
Eddie Collins PHI 198
Sam Crawford DET 185

DOUBLES
Sam Crawford DET 35
Nap Lajoie CLE 33
Ty Cobb DET 33

TRIPLES
Frank Baker PHI 19

Danny Murphy PHI 14
Sam Crawford DET 14

HOME RUNS
Ty Cobb DET 9
Tris Speaker BOS................ 7
two tied at 6

RUNS BATTED IN
Ty Cobb DET 107
Sam Crawford DET 97
Frank Baker PHI 85

STOLEN BASES
Ty Cobb DET 76
Eddie Collins PHI............... 67
Donie Bush DET 53

RUNS SCORED
Ty Cobb DET..................... 116
Donie Bush DET............... 114
Eddie Collins PHI.............. 104

WINS
George Mullin DET 29
Frank Smith CHI 25
Ed Willett DET 21

EARNED RUN AVERAGE
Harry Krause PHI 1.39
Ed Walsh CHI 1.41
Chief Bender PHI............. 1.66

STRIKEOUTS
Frank Smith CHI 177
W. Johnson WAS 164
Heinie Berger CLE............ 162

SAVES
Frank Arellanes BOS............ 8

COMPLETE GAMES
Frank Smith CHI 37

SHUTOUTS
Ed Walsh CHI....................... 8

INNINGS PITCHED
Frank Smith CHI 365

	W	L	PCT	GB	R	OR
★ PIT	110	42	.724	—	699	447
CHI	104	49	.680	6.5	635	390
NY	92	61	.601	18.5	623	546
CIN	77	76	.503	33.5	606	599
PHI	74	79	.484	36.5	516	518
BKN	55	98	.359	55.5	444	627
STL	54	98	.355	56	583	731
BOS	45	108	.294	65.5	435	683
					4541	4541

BATTING AVERAGE
Honus Wagner PIT .... .339
Mike Mitchell CIN............. .310
Dick Hoblitzell CIN............ .308

HITS
Larry Doyle NY 172
Eddie Grant PHI 170
Honus Wagner PIT 168

DOUBLES
Honus Wagner PIT 39
Sherry Magee PHI 33
Dots Miller PIT 31

TRIPLES
Mike Mitchell CIN............... 17

Sherry Magee PHI 14
Ed Konetchy STL................ 14

HOME RUNS
Red Murray NY 7
three tied at.......................... 6

RUNS BATTED IN
Honus Wagner PIT 100
Red Murray NY.................. 91
Dots Miller PIT 87

STOLEN BASES
Bob Bescher CIN.............. 54
Red Murray NY.................. 48
Dick Egan CIN................... 39

RUNS SCORED
Tommy Leach PIT 126
Fred Clarke PIT 97
two tied at 92

WINS
T. Brown CHI 27
Howie Camnitz PIT 25
C. Mathewson NY.............. 25

EARNED RUN AVERAGE
C. Mathewson NY............ 1.14
T. Brown CHI 1.31
Orval Overall CHI 1.42

STRIKEOUTS
Orval Overall CHI 205
Nap Rucker BKN 201
Earl Moore PHI 173

SAVES
T. Brown CHI 7

COMPLETE GAMES
T. Brown CHI 32

SHUTOUTS
Orval Overall CHI 9

INNINGS PITCHED
T. Brown CHI..................... 343

	W	L	PCT	GB	R	OR
★ PHI	102	48	.680	—	673	441
NY	88	63	.583	14.5	626	557
DET	86	68	.558	18	679	582
BOS	81	72	.529	22.5	638	564
CLE	71	81	.467	32	548	657
CHI	68	85	.444	35.5	457	479
WAS	66	85	.437	36.5	501	550
STL	47	107	.305	57	451	743
					4573	4573

BATTING AVERAGE
Nap Lajoie CLE .... .384
Ty Cobb DET .... .383
Tris Speaker BOS............. .340

HITS
Nap Lajoie CLE 227
Ty Cobb DET 194
Eddie Collins PHI 188

DOUBLES
Nap Lajoie CLE 51
Ty Cobb DET........................ 35
Duffy Lewis BOS 29

TRIPLES
Sam Crawford DET 19

Danny Murphy PHI 18
Bris Lord CLE, PHI 18

HOME RUNS
Jake Stahl BOS 10
Ty Cobb DET........................ 8
Duffy Lewis BOS 8

RUNS BATTED IN
Sam Crawford DET 120
Ty Cobb DET........................ 91
Eddie Collins PHI 81

STOLEN BASES
Eddie Collins PHI 81
Ty Cobb DET........................ 65
two tied at........................ 49

RUNS SCORED
Ty Cobb DET.................... 106
Nap Lajoie CLE 94
Tris Speaker BOS............. 92

WINS
Jack Coombs PHI.............. 31
Russ Ford NY 26
Walter Johnson WAS 25

EARNED RUN AVERAGE
Ed Walsh CHI 1.27
Jack Coombs PHI............. 1.30
W. Johnson WAS 1.36

STRIKEOUTS
W. Johnson WAS 313
Ed Walsh CHI 258
Jack Coombs PHI............. 224

SAVES
Ed Walsh CHI 5

COMPLETE GAMES
Walter Johnson WAS 38

SHUTOUTS
Jack Coombs PHI.............. 13

INNINGS PITCHED
W. Johnson WAS 370

	W	L	PCT	GB	R	OR
CHI	104	50	.675	—	712	499
NY	91	63	.591	13	715	567
PIT	86	67	.562	17.5	655	576
PHI	78	75	.510	25.5	674	639
CIN	75	79	.487	29	620	684
BKN	64	90	.416	40	497	623
STL	63	90	.412	40.5	639	718
BOS	53	100	.346	50.5	495	701
					5007	5007

BATTING AVERAGE
Sherry Magee PHI .... .331
Vin Campbell PIT............. .326
Solly Hofman CHI .... .325

HITS
Bobby Byrne PIT 178
Honus Wagner PIT 178
two tied at 172

DOUBLES
Bobby Byrne PIT 43
Sherry Magee PHI 39
Zack Wheat BKN 36

TRIPLES
Mike Mitchell CIN................ 18

Sherry Magee PHI 17
two tied at 16

HOME RUNS
Fred Beck BOS.................... 10
Wildfire Schulte CHI 10
two tied at 8

RUNS BATTED IN
Sherry Magee PHI 123
Mike Mitchell CIN................ 88
Red Murray NY 87

STOLEN BASES
Bob Bescher CIN................ 70
Red Murray NY 57
Dode Paskert CIN................ 51

RUNS SCORED
Sherry Magee PHI 110
Miller Huggins STL 101
Bobby Byrne PIT 101

WINS
C. Mathewson NY.............. 27
T. Brown CHI 25
Earl Moore PHI 22

EARNED RUN AVERAGE
King Cole CHI.................. 1.80
T. Brown CHI 1.86
C. Mathewson NY............. 1.89

STRIKEOUTS
Earl Moore PHI 185
C. Mathewson NY............. 184

SAVES
T. Brown CHI 7
Harry Gaspar CIN................ 7

COMPLETE GAMES
three tied at.......................... 27

SHUTOUTS
four tied at............................. 6

INNINGS PITCHED
Nap Rucker BKN 320

	W	L	PCT	GB	R	OR
★ PHI	101	50	.669	—	861	601
DET	89	65	.578	13.5	831	776
CLE	80	73	.523	22	691	712
CHI	77	74	.510	24	719	624
BOS	78	75	.510	24	680	643
NY	76	76	.500	25.5	684	724
WAS	64	90	.416	38.5	625	766
STL	45	107	.296	56.5	567	812
					5658	5658

BATTING AVERAGE
Ty Cobb DET .... .420
Joe Jackson CLE .... .408
Sam Crawford DET .... .378

HITS
Ty Cobb DET 248
Joe Jackson CLE 233
Sam Crawford DET 217

DOUBLES
Ty Cobb DET 47
Joe Jackson CLE 45
Frank Baker PHI 42

TRIPLES
Ty Cobb DET 24

Birdie Cree NY 22
Joe Jackson CLE 19

HOME RUNS
Frank Baker PHI 11
Ty Cobb DET 8
Tris Speaker BOS 8

RUNS BATTED IN
Ty Cobb DET 127
Frank Baker PHI 115
Sam Crawford DET 115

STOLEN BASES
Ty Cobb DET 83
Clyde Milan WAS 58
Birdie Cree NY 48

RUNS SCORED
Ty Cobb DET 147
Joe Jackson CLE 126
Donie Bush DET 126

WINS
Jack Coombs PHI 28
Ed Walsh CHI 27
Walter Johnson WAS 25

EARNED RUN AVERAGE
Vean Gregg CLE 1.80
W. Johnson WAS 1.90
Joe Wood BOS 2.02

STRIKEOUTS
Ed Walsh CHI 255
Joe Wood BOS 231

SAVES
three tied at 4

COMPLETE GAMES
Walter Johnson WAS 36

SHUTOUTS
Eddie Plank PHI 6
Walter Johnson WAS 6

INNINGS PITCHED
Ed Walsh CHI 369

	W	L	PCT	GB	R	OR
NY	99	54	.647	—	756	542
CHI	92	62	.597	7.5	757	607
PIT	85	69	.552	14.5	744	557
PHI	79	73	.520	19.5	658	669
STL	75	74	.503	22	671	745
CIN	70	83	.458	29	682	706
BKN	64	86	.427	33.5	539	659
BOS	44	107	.291	54	699	1021
					5506	5506

BATTING AVERAGE
Honus Wagner PIT .... .334
Dots Miller BOS .... .333
Chief Meyers NY .... .332

HITS
Dots Miller BOS 192
Dick Hoblitzell CIN 180
Jake Daubert BKN 176

DOUBLES
Ed Konetchy STL 38
Dots Miller BOS 36
Owen Wilson PIT 34

TRIPLES
Larry Doyle NY 25

Mike Mitchell CIN 22
Wildfire Schulte CHI 21

HOME RUNS
Wildfire Schulte CHI 21
Fred Luderus PHI 16
Sherry Magee PHI 15

RUNS BATTED IN
Wildfire Schulte CHI 107
Owen Wilson PIT 107
Fred Luderus PHI 99

STOLEN BASES
Bob Bescher CIN 80
Josh Devore NY 61
Fred Snodgrass NY 51

RUNS SCORED
J. Sheckard CHI 121
Miller Huggins STL 106
Bob Bescher CIN 106

WINS
Grover Alexander PHI 28
C. Mathewson NY 26
Rube Marquard NY 24

EARNED RUN AVERAGE
C. Mathewson NY 1.99
Lew Richie CHI 2.31
Babe Adams PIT 2.33

STRIKEOUTS
Rube Marquard NY 237
G. Alexander PHI 227
Nap Rucker BKN 190

SAVES
T. Brown CHI 13

COMPLETE GAMES
Grover Alexander PHI 31

SHUTOUTS
Grover Alexander PHI 7

INNINGS PITCHED
G. Alexander PHI 367

	W	L	PCT	GB	R	OR
★ BOS	105	47	.691	—	799	544
WAS	91	61	.599	14	699	581
PHI	90	62	.592	15	779	658
CHI	78	76	.506	28	639	648
CLE	75	78	.490	30.5	677	681
DET	69	84	.451	36.5	720	777
STL	53	101	.344	53	552	764
NY	50	102	.329	55	630	842
					5495	5495

BATTING AVERAGE
Ty Cobb DET...............409
Joe Jackson CLE...........395
Tris Speaker BOS..........383

HITS
Ty Cobb DET............. 226
Joe Jackson CLE......... 226
Tris Speaker BOS........ 222

DOUBLES
Tris Speaker BOS........ 53
Joe Jackson CLE......... 44
Frank Baker PHI.......... 40

TRIPLES
Joe Jackson CLE.......... 26

Ty Cobb DET.................. 23
two tied at 21

HOME RUNS
Frank Baker PHI.............. 10
Tris Speaker BOS............ 10
Ty Cobb DET.................... 7

RUNS BATTED IN
Frank Baker PHI.............. 130
Duffy Lewis BOS 109
Sam Crawford DET 109

STOLEN BASES
Clyde Milan WAS.............. 88
Eddie Collins PHI............. 63
Ty Cobb DET................... 61

RUNS SCORED
Eddie Collins PHI.............. 137
Tris Speaker BOS.............. 136
Joe Jackson CLE.............. 121

WINS
Joe Wood BOS.................... 34
Walter Johnson WAS 33
Ed Walsh CHI 27

EARNED RUN AVERAGE
W. Johnson WAS 1.39
Joe Wood BOS................ 1.91
Ed Walsh CHI 2.15

STRIKEOUTS
W. Johnson WAS 303
Joe Wood BOS 258
Ed Walsh CHI 254

SAVES
Ed Walsh CHI 10

COMPLETE GAMES
Joe Wood BOS.................... 35

SHUTOUTS
Joe Wood BOS.................... 10

INNINGS PITCHED
Ed Walsh CHI..................... 393

	W	L	PCT	GB	R	OR
NY	103	48	.682	—	823	571
PIT	93	58	.616	10	751	565
CHI	91	59	.607	11.5	756	668
CIN	75	78	.490	29	656	722
PHI	73	79	.480	30.5	670	688
STL	63	90	.412	41	659	830
BKN	58	95	.379	46	651	754
BOS	52	101	.340	52	693	861
					5659	5659

BATTING AVERAGE
H. Zimmerman CHI .... .372
Chief Meyers NY .... .358
Bill Sweeney BOS .... .344

HITS
H. Zimmerman CHI 207
Bill Sweeney BOS 204
Vin Campbell BOS 185

DOUBLES
H. Zimmerman CHI 41
Dode Paskert PHI 37
Honus Wagner PIT............ 35

TRIPLES
Owen Wilson PIT 36

Honus Wagner PIT............ 20
Red Murray NY 20

HOME RUNS
H. Zimmerman CHI 14
Wildfire Schulte CHI 12
three tied at 11

RUNS BATTED IN
Honus Wagner PIT........... 102
Bill Sweeney BOS 100
H. Zimmerman CHI 99

STOLEN BASES
Bob Bescher CIN 67
Max Carey PIT 45
Fred Snodgrass NY 43

RUNS SCORED
Bob Bescher CIN 120
Max Carey PIT 114
two tied at........................ 102

WINS
Larry Cheney CHI 26
Rube Marquard NY 26
Claude Hendrix PIT............ 24

EARNED RUN AVERAGE
Jeff Tesreau NY 1.96
C. Mathewson NY 2.12
Nap Rucker BKN............... 2.21

STRIKEOUTS
G. Alexander PHI 195
Claude Hendrix PIT........... 176
Rube Marquard NY 175

SAVES
Slim Sallee STL.................... 6

COMPLETE GAMES
Larry Cheney CHI 28

SHUTOUTS
Nap Rucker BKN.................... 6

INNINGS PITCHED
G. Alexander PHI 310

	W	L	PCT	GB	R	OR
★ PHI	96	57	.627	—	794	592
WAS	90	64	.584	6.5	596	561
CLE	86	66	.566	9.5	633	536
BOS	79	71	.527	15.5	631	610
CHI	78	74	.513	17.5	488	498
DET	66	87	.431	30	624	716
NY	57	94	.377	38	529	668
STL	57	96	.373	39	528	642
					4823	4823

BATTING AVERAGE
Ty Cobb DET .... .390
Joe Jackson CLE .... .373
Tris Speaker BOS .... .363

HITS
Joe Jackson CLE 197
Sam Crawford DET 193
Frank Baker PHI 190

DOUBLES
Joe Jackson CLE 39
Tris Speaker BOS 35
Frank Baker PHI 34

TRIPLES
Sam Crawford DET 23

Tris Speaker BOS 22
Joe Jackson CLE 17

HOME RUNS
Frank Baker PHI 12
Sam Crawford DET 9
Ping Bodie CHI 8

RUNS BATTED IN
Frank Baker PHI 117
Duffy Lewis BOS 90
Stuffy McInnis PHI 90

STOLEN BASES
Clyde Milan WAS................ 75
Danny Moeller WAS 62
Eddie Collins PHI................ 55

RUNS SCORED
Eddie Collins PHI.............. 125
Frank Baker PHI 116
Joe Jackson CLE.............. 109

WINS
Walter Johnson WAS 36
Cy Falkenberg CLE 23
Reb Russell CHI 22

EARNED RUN AVERAGE
W. Johnson WAS 1.14
Eddie Cicotte CHI 1.58
Jim Scott CHI................... 1.90

STRIKEOUTS
W. Johnson WAS 243
Vean Gregg CLE 166
Cy Falkenberg CLE 166

SAVES
Chief Bender PHI................ 13

COMPLETE GAMES
W. Johnson WAS 29

SHUTOUTS
Walter Johnson WAS 11

INNINGS PITCHED
W. Johnson WAS 346

	W	L	PCT	GB	R	OR
NY	101	51	.664	—	684	515
PHI	88	63	.583	12.5	693	636
CHI	88	65	.575	13.5	720	630
PIT	78	71	.523	21.5	673	585
BOS	69	82	.457	31.5	641	690
BKN	65	84	.436	34.5	595	613
CIN	64	89	.418	37.5	607	717
STL	51	99	.340	49	528	755
					5141	5141

BATTING AVERAGE
Jake Daubert BKN............ .350
Gavvy Cravath PHI........... .341
Jim Viox PIT .... .317

HITS
Gavvy Cravath PHI........... 179
Jake Daubert BKN............ 178
George Burns NY 173

DOUBLES
Red Smith BKN 40
George Burns NY 37
Sherry Magee PHI 36

TRIPLES
Vic Saier CHI 21

Dots Miller PIT 20
Ed Konetchy STL................ 17

HOME RUNS
Gavvy Cravath PHI............ 19
Fred Luderus PHI 18
Vic Saier CHI 14

RUNS BATTED IN
Gavvy Cravath PHI............ 128
H. Zimmerman CHI............. 95
Vic Saier CHI 92

STOLEN BASES
Max Carey PIT.................... 61
Hy Myers BOS.................... 57
Hans Lobert PHI 41

RUNS SCORED
Max Carey PIT..................... 99
Tommy Leach CHI................ 99
Hans Lobert PHI 98

WINS
Tom Seaton PHI 27
C. Mathewson NY................ 25
Rube Marquard NY.............. 23

EARNED RUN AVERAGE
C. Mathewson NY.............. 2.06
Babe Adams PIT 2.15
Jeff Tesreau NY................. 2.17

STRIKEOUTS
Tom Seaton PHI 168
Jeff Tesreau NY................. 167
G. Alexander PHI 159

SAVES
Larry Cheney CHI................ 11

COMPLETE GAMES
Lefty Tyler BOS 28

SHUTOUTS
Grover Alexander PHI 9

INNINGS PITCHED
Tom Seaton PHI 322

	W	L	PCT	GB	R	OR
PHI	99	53	.651	—	749	529
BOS	91	62	.595	8.5	589	510
WAS	81	73	.526	19	572	519
DET	80	73	.523	19.5	615	618
STL	71	82	.464	28.5	523	615
CHI	70	84	.455	30	487	560
NY	70	84	.455	30	537	550
CLE	51	102	.333	48.5	538	709
					4610	4610

BATTING AVERAGE
Ty Cobb DET .... .368
Eddie Collins PHI .... .344
Tris Speaker BOS .... .338

HITS
Tris Speaker BOS 193
Sam Crawford DET 183
Frank Baker PHI 182

DOUBLES
Tris Speaker BOS 46
Duffy Lewis BOS 37
two tied at 34

TRIPLES
Sam Crawford DET 26

Larry Gardner BOS............. 19
Tris Speaker BOS.............. 18

HOME RUNS
Frank Baker PHI 9
Sam Crawford DET 8
two tied at 6

RUNS BATTED IN
Sam Crawford DET 104
Stuffy McInnis PHI 95
Tris Speaker BOS.............. 90

STOLEN BASES
Fritz Maisel NY 74
Eddie Collins PHI............... 58
Tris Speaker BOS.............. 42

RUNS SCORED
Eddie Collins PHI.............. 122
Eddie Murphy PHI 101
Tris Speaker BOS............. 101

WINS
Walter Johnson WAS 28
Harry Coveleski DET 22
Ray Collins BOS................. 20

EARNED RUN AVERAGE
Dutch Leonard BOS 0.96
Rube Foster BOS 1.70
W. Johnson WAS 1.72

STRIKEOUTS
W. Johnson WAS 225
Willie Mitchell CLE 179
Dutch Leonard BOS 176

SAVES
five tied at 4

COMPLETE GAMES
W. Johnson WAS 33

SHUTOUTS
Walter Johnson WAS 9

INNINGS PITCHED
W. Johnson WAS 372

	W	L	PCT	GB	R	OR
★ BOS	94	59	.614	—	657	548
NY	84	70	.545	10.5	672	576
STL	81	72	.529	13	558	540
CHI	78	76	.506	16.5	605	638
BKN	75	79	.487	19.5	622	618
PHI	74	80	.481	20.5	651	687
PIT	69	85	.448	25.5	503	540
CIN	60	94	.390	34.5	530	651
					4798	4798

BATTING AVERAGE
Jake Daubert BKN........... .329
Beals Becker PHI .... .325
Jack Dalton BKN .... .319

HITS
Sherry Magee PHI 171
George Burns NY 170
Zack Wheat BKN 170

DOUBLES
Sherry Magee PHI 39
H. Zimmerman CHI............ 36
George Burns NY 35

TRIPLES
Max Carey PIT.................... 17

three tied at........................ 12

HOME RUNS
Gavvy Cravath PHI 19
Vic Saier CHI 18
Sherry Magee PHI 15

RUNS BATTED IN
Sherry Magee PHI 103
Gavvy Cravath PHI........... 100
Zack Wheat BKN 89

STOLEN BASES
George Burns NY 62
Buck Herzog CIN................ 46
Cozy Dolan STL 42

RUNS SCORED
George Burns NY 100
Sherry Magee PHI 96
Jake Daubert BKN.............. 89

WINS
Dick Rudolph BOS.............. 27
three tied at........................ 26

EARNED RUN AVERAGE
Bill Doak STL..................... 1.72
Bill James BOS.................. 1.90
Jeff Pfeffer BKN................. 1.97

STRIKEOUTS
G. Alexander PHI............... 214
Jeff Tesreau NY 189
Hippo Vaughn CHI............. 165

SAVES
Red Ames CIN..................... 6
Slim Sallee STL 6

COMPLETE GAMES
Grover Alexander PHI 32

SHUTOUTS
Jeff Tesreau NY 8

INNINGS PITCHED
G. Alexander PHI............... 355

	W	L	PCT	GB	R	OR
★ BOS	101	50	.669	—	669	499
DET	100	54	.649	2.5	778	597
CHI	93	61	.604	9.5	717	509
WAS	85	68	.556	17	569	491
NY	69	83	.454	32.5	584	588
STL	63	91	.409	39.5	521	680
CLE	57	95	.375	44.5	539	670
PHI	43	109	.283	58.5	545	888
					4922	4922

BATTING AVERAGE
Ty Cobb DET .... .369
Eddie Collins CHI .... .332
Jack Fournier CHI .... .322

HITS
Ty Cobb DET 208
Sam Crawford DET 183
Bobby Veach DET 178

DOUBLES
Bobby Veach DET 40
four tied at.......................... 31

TRIPLES
Sam Crawford DET 19
Jack Fournier CHI.............. 18

three tied at........................ 17

HOME RUNS
Braggo Roth CHI, CLE 7
Rube Oldring PHI 6
five tied at 5

RUNS BATTED IN
Bobby Veach DET 112
Sam Crawford DET 112
Ty Cobb DET 99

STOLEN BASES
Ty Cobb DET 96
Fritz Maisel NY 51
Eddie Collins CHI 46

RUNS SCORED
Ty Cobb DET 144
Eddie Collins CHI 118
Ossie Vitt DET 116

WINS
Walter Johnson WAS 28
three tied at...................... 24

EARNED RUN AVERAGE
Joe Wood BOS................. 1.49
W. Johnson WAS 1.55
Ernie Shore BOS 1.64

STRIKEOUTS
W. Johnson WAS 203
Red Faber CHI 182
John Wyckoff PHI 157

SAVES
Carl Mays BOS 7

COMPLETE GAMES
W. Johnson WAS 35

SHUTOUTS
Walter Johnson WAS 7
Jim Scott CHI....................... 7

INNINGS PITCHED
W. Johnson WAS 337

	W	L	PCT	GB	R	OR
PHI	90	62	.592	—	589	463
BOS	83	69	.546	7	582	545
BKN	80	72	.526	10	536	560
CHI	73	80	.477	17.5	570	620
PIT	73	81	.474	18	557	520
STL	72	81	.471	18.5	590	601
CIN	71	83	.461	20	516	585
NY	69	83	.454	21	582	628
					4522	4522

BATTING AVERAGE
Larry Doyle NY .... .320
Fred Luderus PHI .... .315
Tommy Griffith CIN .... .307

HITS
Larry Doyle NY 189
Tommy Griffith CIN 179
Bill Hinchman PIT 177

DOUBLES
Larry Doyle NY 40
Fred Luderus PHI 36
Vic Saier CHI 35

TRIPLES
Tommy Long STL................ 25

Honus Wagner PIT 17
Tommy Griffith CIN 16

HOME RUNS
Gavvy Cravath PHI............. 24
Cy Williams CHI................. 13
Wildfire Schulte CHI 12

RUNS BATTED IN
Gavvy Cravath PHI........... 115
Sherry Magee BOS 87
Tommy Griffith CIN 85

STOLEN BASES
Max Carey PIT.................... 36
Buck Herzog CIN 35
two tied at 29

RUNS SCORED
Gavvy Cravath PHI............. 89
Larry Doyle NY 86
Dave Bancroft PHI............. 85

WINS
G. Alexander PHI............... 31
Dick Rudolph BOS............. 22
two tied at 21

EARNED RUN AVERAGE
G. Alexander PHI.............. 1.22
Fred Toney CIN 1.58
Al Mamaux PIT 2.04

STRIKEOUTS
G. Alexander PHI............. 241
Jeff Tesreau NY................ 176
Tom Hughes BOS 171

SAVES
Tom Hughes BOS 9

COMPLETE GAMES
Grover Alexander PHI 36

SHUTOUTS
Grover Alexander PHI 12

INNINGS PITCHED
G. Alexander PHI............. 376

	W	L	PCT	GB	R	OR
★ BOS	91	63	.591	—	550	480
CHI	89	65	.578	2	601	497
DET	87	67	.565	4	670	595
NY	80	74	.519	11	577	561
STL	79	75	.513	12	588	545
CLE	77	77	.500	14	630	602
WAS	76	77	.497	14.5	536	543
PHI	36	117	.235	54.5	447	776
					4599	4599

BATTING AVERAGE
Tris Speaker CLE .... .386
Ty Cobb DET .... .371
Joe Jackson CHI .... .341

HITS
Tris Speaker CLE 211
Joe Jackson CHI 202
Ty Cobb DET 201

DOUBLES
Jack Graney CLE 41
Tris Speaker CLE 41
Joe Jackson CHI 40

TRIPLES
Joe Jackson CHI 21

Eddie Collins CHI 17
two tied at 15

HOME RUNS
Wally Pipp NY 12
Frank Baker NY 10
two tied at 7

RUNS BATTED IN
Del Pratt STL 103
Wally Pipp NY 93
Bobby Veach DET 91

STOLEN BASES
Ty Cobb DET 68
A. Marsans STL 46
Burt Shotton STL 41

RUNS SCORED
Ty Cobb DET 113
Jack Graney CLE 106
Tris Speaker CLE 102

WINS
Walter Johnson WAS 25
Bob Shawkey NY 24
Babe Ruth BOS 23

EARNED RUN AVERAGE
Babe Ruth BOS 1.75
Eddie Cicotte CHI 1.78
W. Johnson WAS 1.90

STRIKEOUTS
W. Johnson WAS 228
Elmer Myers PHI 182
Babe Ruth BOS 170

SAVES
Bob Shawkey NY 8

COMPLETE GAMES
W. Johnson WAS 36

SHUTOUTS
Babe Ruth BOS 9

INNINGS PITCHED
W. Johnson WAS 370

	W	L	PCT	GB	R	OR
BKN	94	60	.610	—	585	471
PHI	91	62	.595	2.5	581	489
BOS	89	63	.586	4	542	453
NY	86	66	.566	7	597	504
CHI	67	86	.438	26.5	520	541
PIT	65	89	.422	29	484	586
CIN	60	93	.392	33.5	505	617
STL	60	93	.392	33.5	476	629
					4290	4290

BATTING AVERAGE
Hal Chase CIN .... .339
Jake Daubert BKN .... .316
Bill Hinchman PIT .... .315

HITS
Hal Chase CIN 184
Dave Robertson NY 180
Zack Wheat BKN 177

DOUBLES
Bert Niehoff PHI 42
Zack Wheat BKN 32
Dode Paskert PHI 30

TRIPLES
Bill Hinchman PIT 16

three tied at 15

HOME RUNS
Dave Robertson NY 12
Cy Williams CHI 12
Gavvy Cravath PHI 11

RUNS BATTED IN
H. Zimmerman CHI, NY 83
Hal Chase CIN 82
Bill Hinchman PIT 76

STOLEN BASES
Max Carey PIT 63
Benny Kauff NY 40
Bob Bescher STL 39

RUNS SCORED
George Burns NY 105
Max Carey PIT 90
Dave Robertson NY 88

WINS
Grover Alexander PHI 33
Jeff Pfeffer BKN 25
Eppa Rixey PHI 22

EARNED RUN AVERAGE
G. Alexander PHI 1.55
R. Marquard BKN 1.58
Eppa Rixey PHI 1.85

STRIKEOUTS
G. Alexander PHI 167
Larry Cheney BKN 166
Al Mamaux PIT 163

SAVES
Red Ames STL 8

COMPLETE GAMES
G. Alexander PHI 38

SHUTOUTS
Grover Alexander PHI 16

INNINGS PITCHED
G. Alexander PHI 389

	W	L	PCT	GB	R	OR
★ CHI	100	54	.649	—	656	464
BOS	90	62	.592	9	555	454
CLE	88	66	.571	12	584	543
DET	78	75	.510	21.5	639	577
WAS	74	79	.484	25.5	543	566
NY	71	82	.464	28.5	524	558
STL	57	97	.370	43	510	687
PHI	55	98	.359	44.5	529	691
					4540	4540

BATTING AVERAGE
Ty Cobb DET .... .383
George Sisler STL .... .353
Tris Speaker CLE .... .352

HITS
Ty Cobb DET 225
George Sisler STL 190
Tris Speaker CLE 184

DOUBLES
Ty Cobb DET 44
Tris Speaker CLE 42
Bobby Veach DET 31

TRIPLES
Ty Cobb DET 24

Joe Jackson CHI 17
Joe Judge WAS 15

HOME RUNS
Wally Pipp NY 9
Bobby Veach DET 8
Ping Bodie PHI 7

RUNS BATTED IN
Bobby Veach DET 103
Ty Cobb DET 102
Happy Felsch CHI 102

STOLEN BASES
Ty Cobb DET 55
Eddie Collins CHI 53
Ray Chapman CLE............. 52

RUNS SCORED
Donie Bush DET 112
Ty Cobb DET 107
Ray Chapman CLE............. 98

WINS
Eddie Cicotte CHI 28
Babe Ruth BOS 24
two tied at 23

EARNED RUN AVERAGE
Eddie Cicotte CHI 1.53
Carl Mays BOS................. 1.74
Stan Coveleski CLE........... 1.81

STRIKEOUTS
W. Johnson WAS 188
Eddie Cicotte CHI 150
Dutch Leonard BOS 144

SAVES
Dave Danforth CHI 9

COMPLETE GAMES
Babe Ruth BOS 35

SHUTOUTS
Stan Coveleski CLE............. 9

INNINGS PITCHED
Eddie Cicotte CHI 347

	W	L	PCT	GB	R	OR
NY	98	56	.636	—	635	457
PHI	87	65	.572	10	578	500
STL	82	70	.539	15	531	567
CIN	78	76	.506	20	601	611
CHI	74	80	.481	24	552	567
BOS	72	81	.471	25.5	536	552
BKN	70	81	.464	26.5	511	559
PIT	51	103	.331	47	464	595
					4408	4408

BATTING AVERAGE
Edd Roush CIN................. .341
R. Hornsby STL .... .327
Zack Wheat BKN .... .312

HITS
Heinie Groh CIN 182
George Burns NY 180
Edd Roush CIN 178

DOUBLES
Heinie Groh CIN 39
F. Merkle BKN, CHI 31
Red Smith BOS 31

TRIPLES
Rogers Hornsby STL 17

Gavvy Cravath PHI............. 16
Hal Chase CIN.................... 15

HOME RUNS
Dave Robertson NY 12
Gavvy Cravath PHI............. 12
Rogers Hornsby STL........... 8

RUNS BATTED IN
H. Zimmerman NY 102
Hal Chase CIN.................... 86
Gavvy Cravath PHI............. 83

STOLEN BASES
Max Carey PIT.................... 46
George Burns NY 40
Benny Kauff NY 30

RUNS SCORED
George Burns NY 103
Heinie Groh CIN 91
Benny Kauff NY 89

WINS
Grover Alexander PHI 30
Fred Toney CIN 24
Hippo Vaughn CHI............. 23

EARNED RUN AVERAGE
F. Anderson NY 1.44
G. Alexander PHI............... 1.83
Pol Perritt NY 1.88

STRIKEOUTS
G. Alexander PHI............... 200
Hippo Vaughn CHI............. 195
Phil Douglas CHI 151

SAVES
Slim Sallee NY...................... 4

COMPLETE GAMES
Grover Alexander PHI 34

SHUTOUTS
Grover Alexander PHI 8

INNINGS PITCHED
G. Alexander PHI............... 388

	W	L	PCT	GB	R	OR
★ BOS	75	51	.595	—	474	380
CLE	73	54	.575	2.5	504	447
WAS	72	56	.563	4	461	412
NY	60	63	.488	13.5	493	475
STL	58	64	.475	15	426	448
CHI	57	67	.460	17	457	446
DET	55	71	.437	20	476	557
PHI	52	76	.406	24	412	538
					3703	3703

BATTING AVERAGE
Ty Cobb DET .... .382
George Burns PHI .... .352
George Sisler STL .... .341

HITS
George Burns PHI 178
Ty Cobb DET 161
two tied at 154

DOUBLES
Tris Speaker CLE 33
Harry Hooper BOS 26
Babe Ruth BOS 26

TRIPLES
Ty Cobb DET 14

Harry Hooper BOS 13
Bobby Veach DET 13

HOME RUNS
Tilly Walker PHI 11
Babe Ruth BOS 11
two tied at 6

RUNS BATTED IN
Bobby Veach DET 78
George Burns PHI 70
two tied at 66

STOLEN BASES
George Sisler STL 45
Braggo Roth CLE 35
Ty Cobb DET 34

RUNS SCORED
Ray Chapman CLE............. 84
Ty Cobb DET 83
Harry Hooper BOS 81

WINS
Walter Johnson WAS 23
Stan Coveleski CLE............ 22
Carl Mays BOS................... 21

EARNED RUN AVERAGE
W. Johnson WAS 1.27
Stan Coveleski CLE 1.82

STRIKEOUTS
W. Johnson WAS 162
Jim Shaw WAS.................. 129

SAVES
George Mogridge NY........... 7

COMPLETE GAMES
Carl Mays BOS................... 30
Scott Perry PHI 30

SHUTOUTS
Carl Mays BOS..................... 8
Walter Johnson WAS 8

INNINGS PITCHED
Scott Perry PHI 332

	W	L	PCT	GB	R	OR
CHI	84	45	.651	—	538	393
NY	71	53	.573	10.5	480	415
CIN	68	60	.531	15.5	530	496
PIT	65	60	.520	17	466	412
BKN	57	69	.452	25.5	360	463
PHI	55	68	.447	26	430	507
BOS	53	71	.427	28.5	424	469
STL	51	78	.395	33	454	527
					3682	3682

BATTING AVERAGE
Zack Wheat BKN .... .335
Edd Roush CIN................. .333
Heinie Groh CIN .... .320

HITS
C. Hollocher CHI............... 161
Heinie Groh CIN 158
Edd Roush CIN................. 145

DOUBLES
Heinie Groh CIN 28
Les Mann CHI 27
Gavvy Cravath PHI............. 27

TRIPLES
Jake Daubert BKN.............. 15

three tied at......................... 13

HOME RUNS
Gavvy Cravath PHI............... 8
Walt Cruise STL 6
Cy Williams PHI 6

RUNS BATTED IN
Sherry Magee CIN.............. 76
George Cutshaw PIT 68
Fred Luderus PHI 67

STOLEN BASES
Max Carey PIT 58
George Burns NY 40
Charlie Hollocher CHI......... 26

RUNS SCORED
Heinie Groh CIN 88
George Burns NY 80
Max Flack CHI 74

WINS
Hippo Vaughn CHI.............. 22
Claude Hendrix CHI............ 20
three tied at........................ 19

EARNED RUN AVERAGE
Hippo Vaughn CHI............ 1.74
Lefty Tyler CHI................. 2.00
Wilbur Cooper PIT 2.11

STRIKEOUTS
Hippo Vaughn CHI............ 148
Wilbur Cooper PIT 117
B. Grimes BKN.................. 113

SAVES
four tied at............................ 3

COMPLETE GAMES
Art Nehf BOS 28

SHUTOUTS
Hippo Vaughn CHI............... 8

INNINGS PITCHED
Hippo Vaughn CHI............ 290

	W	L	PCT	GB	R	OR
CHI	88	52	.629	—	667	534
CLE	84	55	.604	3.5	636	537
NY	80	59	.576	7.5	578	506
DET	80	60	.571	8	618	578
STL	67	72	.482	20.5	533	567
BOS	66	71	.482	20.5	564	552
WAS	56	84	.400	32	533	570
PHI	36	104	.257	52	457	742
					4586	4586

BATTING AVERAGE
Ty Cobb DET .... .384
Bobby Veach DET .... .355
George Sisler STL .... .352

HITS
Bobby Veach DET 191
Ty Cobb DET 191
Joe Jackson CHI 181

DOUBLES
Bobby Veach DET 45
Tris Speaker CLE 38
Ty Cobb DET 36

TRIPLES
Bobby Veach DET 17

George Sisler STL 15
Harry Heilmann DET 15

HOME RUNS
Babe Ruth BOS 29
three tied at 10

RUNS BATTED IN
Babe Ruth BOS 114
Bobby Veach DET 101
Joe Jackson CHI 96

STOLEN BASES
Eddie Collins CHI 33
George Sisler STL 28
Ty Cobb DET 28

RUNS SCORED
Babe Ruth BOS 103
George Sisler STL 96
Ty Cobb DET 92

WINS
Eddie Cicotte CHI 29
Stan Coveleski CLE............ 24
Lefty Williams CHI 23

EARNED RUN AVERAGE
W. Johnson WAS 1.49
Eddie Cicotte CHI 1.82
Carl Weilman STL 2.07

STRIKEOUTS
W. Johnson WAS 147
Jim Shaw WAS.................. 128

SAVES
three tied at............................ 5

COMPLETE GAMES
Eddie Cicotte CHI 30

SHUTOUTS
Walter Johnson WAS 7

INNINGS PITCHED
Eddie Cicotte CHI 307
Jim Shaw WAS................. 307

	W	L	PCT	GB	R	OR
★ CIN	96	44	.686	—	577	401
NY	87	53	.621	9	605	470
CHI	75	65	.536	21	454	407
PIT	71	68	.511	24.5	472	466
BKN	69	71	.493	27	525	513
BOS	57	82	.410	38.5	465	563
STL	54	83	.394	40.5	463	552
PHI	47	90	.343	47.5	510	699
					4071	4071

BATTING AVERAGE
Gavvy Cravath PHI .... .341
Edd Roush CIN................. .321
R. Hornsby STL .... .318

HITS
Ivy Olsen BKN 164
R. Hornsby STL 163
two tied at 162

DOUBLES
Ross Youngs NY 31
George Burns NY 30
Fred Luderus PHI 30

TRIPLES
Billy Southworth PIT 14

Hy Myers BKN 14

HOME RUNS
Gavvy Cravath PHI 12
Benny Kauff NY 10
Cy Williams PHI 9

RUNS BATTED IN
Hy Myers BKN 73
Edd Roush CIN................... 71
Rogers Hornsby STL 71

STOLEN BASES
George Burns NY 40
George Cutshaw PIT 36
Carson Bigbee PIT 31

RUNS SCORED
George Burns NY 86
Jake Daubert CIN 79
Heinie Groh CIN 79

WINS
Jesse Barnes NY............... 25
Slim Sallee CIN 21
Hippo Vaughn CHI............. 21

EARNED RUN AVERAGE
G. Alexander CHI 1.72
Hippo Vaughn CHI........... 1.79
Dutch Ruether CIN 1.82

STRIKEOUTS
Hippo Vaughn CHI 141
Hod Eller CIN.................... 137
G. Alexander CHI 121

SAVES
Oscar Tuero STL 4

COMPLETE GAMES
Wilbur Cooper PIT.............. 27

SHUTOUTS
Grover Alexander CHI 9

INNINGS PITCHED
Hippo Vaughn CHI............ 307

1920 AMERICAN LEAGUE STANDINGS

	W	L	PCT	GB	R	OR
★ CLE	98	56	.636	—	857	642
CHI	96	58	.623	2	794	665
NY	95	59	.617	3	838	629
STL	76	77	.497	21.5	797	766
BOS	72	81	.471	25.5	650	698
WAS	68	84	.447	29	723	802
DET	61	93	.396	37	652	833
PHI	48	106	.312	50	558	834
					5869	5869

BATTING AVERAGE
George Sisler STL .... .407
Tris Speaker CLE .... .388
Joe Jackson CHI .... .382

HITS
George Sisler STL 257
Eddie Collins CHI 224
Joe Jackson CHI 218

DOUBLES
Tris Speaker CLE 50
George Sisler STL 49
Joe Jackson CHI 42

TRIPLES
Joe Jackson CHI 20

George Sisler STL 18
Harry Hooper BOS 17

HOME RUNS
Babe Ruth NY 54
George Sisler STL 19
Tilly Walker PHI 17

RUNS BATTED IN
Babe Ruth NY 137
B. Jacobson STL 122
George Sisler STL 122

STOLEN BASES
Sam Rice WAS 63
George Sisler STL 42
Braggo Roth WAS 24

RUNS SCORED
Babe Ruth NY 158
George Sisler STL 137
Tris Speaker CLE 137

WINS
Jim Bagby CLE 31
Carl Mays NY 26
Stan Coveleski CLE 24

EARNED RUN AVERAGE
Bob Shawkey NY 2.45
Stan Coveleski CLE 2.49
Urban Shocker STL 2.71

STRIKEOUTS
Stan Coveleski CLE 133
Lefty Williams CHI 128

SAVES
Dickie Kerr CHI 5
Urban Shocker STL 5

COMPLETE GAMES
Jim Bagby CLE 30

SHUTOUTS
Carl Mays NY 6

INNINGS PITCHED
Jim Bagby CLE 340

1920 NATIONAL LEAGUE STANDINGS

	W	L	PCT	GB	R	OR
BKN	93	61	.604	—	660	528
NY	86	68	.558	7	682	543
CIN	82	71	.536	10.5	639	569
PIT	79	75	.513	14	530	552
CHI	75	79	.487	18	619	635
STL	75	79	.487	18	675	682
BOS	62	90	.408	30	523	670
PHI	62	91	.405	30.5	565	714
					4893	4893

BATTING AVERAGE
R. Hornsby STL .... .370
Fred Nicholson PIT .... .360
Ross Youngs NY .... .351

HITS
R. Hornsby STL 218
Milt Stock STL 204
Ross Youngs NY 204

DOUBLES
Rogers Hornsby STL 44
three tied at 36

TRIPLES
Hy Myers BKN 22
Rogers Hornsby STL 20

Edd Roush CIN 16

HOME RUNS
Cy Williams PHI 15
Irish Meusel PHI 14
George Kelly NY 11

RUNS BATTED IN
George Kelly NY 94
Rogers Hornsby STL 94
Edd Roush CIN 90

STOLEN BASES
Max Carey PIT 52
Edd Roush CIN 36
Frankie Frisch NY 34

RUNS SCORED
George Burns NY 115
D. Bancroft PHI, NY 102
Jake Daubert CIN 97

WINS
G. Alexander CHI 27
Wilbur Cooper PIT 24
Burleigh Grimes BKN 23

EARNED RUN AVERAGE
G. Alexander CHI 1.91
Babe Adams PIT 2.16
B. Grimes BKN 2.22

STRIKEOUTS
G. Alexander CHI 173
Hippo Vaughn CHI 131
B. Grimes BKN 131

SAVES
Bill Sherdel STL 6

COMPLETE GAMES
G. Alexander CHI 33

SHUTOUTS
Babe Adams PIT 8

INNINGS PITCHED
G. Alexander CHI 363

	W	L	PCT	GB	R	OR
NY	98	55	.641	—	948	708
CLE	94	60	.610	4.5	925	712
STL	81	73	.526	17.5	835	845
WAS	80	73	.523	18	704	738
BOS	75	79	.487	23.5	668	696
DET	71	82	.464	27	883	852
CHI	62	92	.403	36.5	683	858
PHI	53	100	.346	45	657	894
					6303	6303

BATTING AVERAGE
Harry Heilmann DET .... .394
Ty Cobb DET .... .389
Babe Ruth NY .... .378

HITS
Harry Heilmann DET 237
Jack Tobin STL 236
George Sisler STL 216

DOUBLES
Tris Speaker CLE 52
Babe Ruth NY 44
two tied at 43

TRIPLES
Howard Shanks WAS 18

Jack Tobin STL 18
George Sisler STL 18

HOME RUNS
Babe Ruth NY 59
Ken Williams STL 24
Bob Meusel NY 24

RUNS BATTED IN
Babe Ruth NY 171
Harry Heilmann DET 139
Bob Meusel NY 135

STOLEN BASES
George Sisler STL 35
Bucky Harris WAS 29
Sam Rice WAS 26

RUNS SCORED
Babe Ruth NY 177
Jack Tobin STL 132
R. Peckinpaugh NY 128

WINS
Carl Mays NY 27
Urban Shocker STL 27
Red Faber CHI 25

EARNED RUN AVERAGE
Red Faber CHI 2.48
G. Mogridge WAS........... 3.00
Carl Mays NY 3.05

STRIKEOUTS
W. Johnson WAS 143
Urban Shocker STL 132

SAVES
Jim Middleton DET 7
Carl Mays NY 7

COMPLETE GAMES
Red Faber CHI 32

SHUTOUTS
Sad Sam Jones BOS............ 5

INNINGS PITCHED
Carl Mays NY 337

	W	L	PCT	GB	R	OR
★ NY	94	59	.614	—	840	637
PIT	90	63	.588	4	692	595
STL	87	66	.569	7	809	681
BOS	79	74	.516	15	721	697
BKN	77	75	.507	16.5	667	681
CIN	70	83	.458	24	618	649
CHI	64	89	.418	30	668	773
PHI	51	103	.331	43.5	617	919
					5632	5632

BATTING AVERAGE
R. Hornsby STL .... .397
Edd Roush CIN.................. .352
Austin McHenry STL......... .350

HITS
R. Hornsby STL 235
Frankie Frisch NY 211
Carson Bigbee PIT 204

DOUBLES
Rogers Hornsby STL 44
George Kelly NY 42
Jimmy Johnston BKN 41

TRIPLES
Rogers Hornsby STL.......... 18

Ray Powell BOS 18
three tied at........................ 17

HOME RUNS
George Kelly NY 23
Rogers Hornsby STL.......... 21
Cy Williams PHI 18

RUNS BATTED IN
R. Hornsby STL 126
George Kelly NY 122
two tied at 102

STOLEN BASES
Frankie Frisch NY 49
Max Carey PIT................... 37
Jimmy Johnston BKN 28

RUNS SCORED
R. Hornsby STL 131
Frankie Frisch NY 121
Dave Bancroft NY............. 121

WINS
Burleigh Grimes BKN 22
Wilbur Cooper PIT 22
two tied at 20

EARNED RUN AVERAGE
Bill Doak STL.................... 2.59
Babe Adams PIT 2.64
Whitey Glazner PIT 2.77

STRIKEOUTS
B. Grimes BKN 136
Wilbur Cooper PIT 134
Dolf Luque CIN 102

SAVES
Lou North STL 7

COMPLETE GAMES
Burleigh Grimes BKN 30

SHUTOUTS
eight tied at............................ 3

INNINGS PITCHED
Wilbur Cooper PIT 327

	W	L	PCT	GB	R	OR
NY	94	60	.610	—	758	618
STL	93	61	.604	1	867	643
DET	79	75	.513	15	828	791
CLE	78	76	.506	16	768	817
CHI	77	77	.500	17	691	691
WAS	69	85	.448	25	650	706
PHI	65	89	.422	29	705	830
BOS	61	93	.396	33	598	769
					5865	5865

BATTING AVERAGE
George Sisler STL .... .420
Ty Cobb DET .... .401
Tris Speaker CLE .... .378

HITS
George Sisler STL 246
Ty Cobb DET 211
Jack Tobin STL................. 207

DOUBLES
Tris Speaker CLE 48
Del Pratt BOS 44
two tied at 42

TRIPLES
George Sisler STL 18

Ty Cobb DET 16
B. Jacobson STL 16

HOME RUNS
Ken Williams STL 39
Tilly Walker PHI 37
Babe Ruth NY 35

RUNS BATTED IN
Ken Williams STL 155
Bobby Veach DET 126
Marty McManus STL 109

STOLEN BASES
George Sisler STL 51
Ken Williams STL 37
Bucky Harris WAS 25

RUNS SCORED
George Sisler STL 134
Lu Blue DET 131
Ken Williams STL 128

WINS
Eddie Rommel PHI 27
Joe Bush NY 26
Urban Shocker STL 24

EARNED RUN AVERAGE
Red Faber CHI 2.81
H. Philette DET 2.85
Bob Shawkey NY 2.91

STRIKEOUTS
Urban Shocker STL 149
Red Faber CHI 148
Bob Shawkey NY 130

SAVES
Sad Sam Jones NY 8

COMPLETE GAMES
Red Faber CHI 31

SHUTOUTS
George Uhle CLE 5

INNINGS PITCHED
Red Faber CHI 352

	W	L	PCT	GB	R	OR
★ NY	93	61	.604	—	852	658
CIN	86	68	.558	7	766	677
PIT	85	69	.552	8	865	736
STL	85	69	.552	8	863	819
CHI	80	74	.519	13	771	808
BKN	76	78	.494	17	743	754
PHI	57	96	.373	35.5	738	920
BOS	53	100	.346	39.5	596	822
					6194	6194

BATTING AVERAGE
R. Hornsby STL .... .401
Ray Grimes CHI .... .354
Hack Miller CHI................ .352

HITS
R. Hornsby STL 250
Carson Bigbee PIT 215
Dave Bancroft NY 209

DOUBLES
Rogers Hornsby STL 46
Ray Grimes CHI 45
Pat Duncan CIN................. 44

TRIPLES
Jake Daubert CIN 22

Irish Meusel NY 17
two tied at 15

HOME RUNS
R. Hornsby STL 42
Cy Williams PHI ,.............. 26
two tied at 17

RUNS BATTED IN
R. Hornsby STL 152
Irish Meusel NY 132
Zack Wheat BKN 112

STOLEN BASES
Max Carey PIT 51
Frankie Frisch NY 31
George Burns CIN 30

RUNS SCORED
R. Hornsby STL 141
Max Carey PIT.................. 140
two tied at 117

WINS
Eppa Rixey CIN 25
Wilbur Cooper PIT 23
Dutch Ruether BKN 21

EARNED RUN AVERAGE
P. Douglas NY 2.63
Rosy Ryan NY 3.01
Pete Donohue CIN 3.12

STRIKEOUTS
Dazzy Vance BKN 134
Wilbur Cooper PIT 129
Jimmy Ring PHI................ 116

SAVES
Claude Jonnard NY 5

COMPLETE GAMES
Wilbur Cooper PIT 27

SHUTOUTS
two tied at 5

INNINGS PITCHED
Eppa Rixey CIN 313

	W	L	PCT	GB	R	OR
★ NY	98	54	.645	—	823	622
DET	83	71	.539	16	831	741
CLE	82	71	.536	16.5	888	746
WAS	75	78	.490	23.5	720	747
STL	74	78	.487	24	688	720
PHI	69	83	.454	29	661	761
CHI	69	85	.448	30	692	741
BOS	61	91	.401	37	584	809
					5887	5887

RUNS SCORED
Babe Ruth NY 151
Tris Speaker CLE 133
C. Jamieson CLE.............. 130

WINS
George Uhle CLE 26
Sad Sam Jones NY 21
Hooks Dauss DET 21

EARNED RUN AVERAGE
Stan Coveleski CLE........ 2.76
Waite Hoyt NY 3.02
Allan Russell WAS........... 3.03

STRIKEOUTS
W. Johnson WAS 130
Joe Bush NY 125
Bob Shawkey NY 125

SAVES
Allan Russell WAS 9

COMPLETE GAMES
George Uhle CLE 29

SHUTOUTS
Stan Coveleski CLE............. 5

INNINGS PITCHED
George Uhle CLE 358

BATTING AVERAGE
H. Heilmann DET............. .403
Babe Ruth NY .... .393
Tris Speaker CLE .... .380

HITS
C. Jamieson CLE............. 222
Tris Speaker CLE 218
Harry Heilmann DET 211

DOUBLES
Tris Speaker CLE 59
George Burns BOS............. 47
Babe Ruth NY..................... 45

TRIPLES
Goose Goslin WAS............. 18

Sam Rice WAS 18
two tied at 15

HOME RUNS
Babe Ruth NY 41
Ken Williams STL 29
Harry Heilmann DET 18

RUNS BATTED IN
Babe Ruth NY 131
Tris Speaker CLE 130
Harry Heilmann DET 115

STOLEN BASES
Eddie Collins CHI 47
Johnny Mostil STL 41
Bucky Harris WAS 23

	W	L	PCT	GB	R	OR
NY	95	58	.621	—	854	679
CIN	91	63	.591	4.5	708	629
PIT	87	67	.565	8.5	786	696
CHI	83	71	.539	12.5	756	704
STL	79	74	.516	16	746	732
BKN	76	78	.494	19.5	753	741
BOS	54	100	.351	41.5	636	798
PHI	50	104	.325	45.5	748	1008
					5987	5987

RUNS SCORED
Ross Youngs NY 121
Max Carey PIT.................. 120
Frankie Frisch NY 116

WINS
Dolf Luque CIN 27
Johnny Morrison PIT 25
G. Alexander CHI 22

EARNED RUN AVERAGE
Dolf Luque CIN 1.93
Eppa Rixey CIN 2.80
Vic Keen CHI 3.00

STRIKEOUTS
Dazzy Vance BKN 197
Dolf Luque CIN 151
B. Grimes BKN 119

SAVES
Claude Jonnard NY 5

COMPLETE GAMES
Burleigh Grimes BKN 33

SHUTOUTS
Dolf Luque CIN 6

INNINGS PITCHED
B. Grimes BKN 327

BATTING AVERAGE
R. Hornsby STL .... .384
Zack Wheat BKN .... .375
Jim Bottomley STL .... .371

HITS
Frankie Frisch NY 223
Jigger Statz CHI 209
Pie Traynor PIT 208

DOUBLES
Edd Roush CIN 41
G. Grantham CHI............... 36
C. Tierney PIT, PHI 36

TRIPLES
Pie Traynor PIT 19

Max Carey PIT.................. 19
Edd Roush CIN 18

HOME RUNS
Cy Williams PHI................. 41
Jack Fournier BKN 22
Hack Miller CHI 20

RUNS BATTED IN
Irish Meusel NY 125
Cy Williams PHI 114
Frankie Frisch NY 111

STOLEN BASES
Max Carey PIT.................. 51
G. Grantham CHI............... 43
two tied at 32

	W	L	PCT	GB	R	OR
★ WAS	92	62	.597	—	755	613
NY	89	63	.586	2	798	667
DET	86	68	.558	6	849	796
STL	74	78	.487	17	769	809
PHI	71	81	.467	20	685	778
CLE	67	86	.438	24.5	755	814
BOS	67	87	.435	25	737	806
CHI	66	87	.431	25.5	793	858
					6141	6141

BATTING AVERAGE
Babe Ruth NY .... .378
C. Jamieson CLE .... .359
Bibb Falk CHI .... .352

HITS
Sam Rice WAS 216
C. Jamieson CLE 213
Ty Cobb DET 211

DOUBLES
Harry Heilmann DET 45
Joe Sewell CLE 45
two tied at 41

TRIPLES
Wally Pipp NY 19

Goose Goslin WAS 17
Harry Heilmann DET 16

HOME RUNS
Babe Ruth NY 46
Joe Hauser PHI 27
B. Jacobson STL 19

RUNS BATTED IN
Goose Goslin WAS 129
Babe Ruth NY 121
Bob Meusel NY 120

STOLEN BASES
Eddie Collins CHI 42
Bob Meusel NY 26
Sam Rice WAS 24

RUNS SCORED
Babe Ruth NY 143
Ty Cobb DET 115
Eddie Collins CHI 108

WINS
Walter Johnson WAS 23
Herb Pennock NY 21
two tied at 20

EARNED RUN AVERAGE
W. Johnson WAS 2.72
Tom Zachary WAS 2.75
Herb Pennock NY 2.83

STRIKEOUTS
W. Johnson WAS 158
Howard Ehmke BOS 119
Bob Shawkey NY 114

SAVES
Firpo Marberry WAS 15

COMPLETE GAMES
Sloppy Thurston CHI 28

SHUTOUTS
Walter Johnson WAS 6

INNINGS PITCHED
Howard Ehmke BOS 315

	W	L	PCT	GB	R	OR
NY	93	60	.608	—	857	641
BKN	92	62	.597	1.5	717	675
PIT	90	63	.588	3	724	588
CIN	83	70	.542	10	649	579
CHI	81	72	.529	12	698	699
STL	65	89	.422	28.5	740	750
PHI	55	96	.364	37	676	849
BOS	53	100	.346	40	520	800
					5581	5581

BATTING AVERAGE
R. Hornsby STL .... .424
Zack Wheat BKN .... .375
Ross Youngs NY .... .356

HITS
R. Hornsby STL 227
Zack Wheat BKN 212
Frankie Frisch NY 198

DOUBLES
R. Hornsby STL 43
Zack Wheat BKN 41
George Kelly NY 37

TRIPLES
Edd Roush CIN 21

Rabbit Maranville PIT 20
Glenn Wright PIT 18

HOME RUNS
Jack Fournier BKN 27
Rogers Hornsby STL 25
Cy Williams PHI 24

RUNS BATTED IN
George Kelly NY 136
Jack Fournier BKN 116
two tied at 111

STOLEN BASES
Max Carey PIT 49
Kiki Cuyler PIT 32
Cliff Heathcote CHI 26

RUNS SCORED
Frankie Frisch NY 121
R. Hornsby STL 121
Max Carey PIT 113

WINS
Dazzy Vance BKN 28
Burleigh Grimes BKN 22
two tied at 20

EARNED RUN AVERAGE
Dazzy Vance BKN 2.16
Hugh McQuillan NY 2.69
Eppa Rixey CIN 2.76

STRIKEOUTS
Dazzy Vance BKN 262
Burleigh Grimes BKN 135

SAVES
Jackie May CIN 6

COMPLETE GAMES
Dazzy Vance BKN 30
Burleigh Grimes BKN 30

SHUTOUTS
six tied at 4

INNINGS PITCHED
Burleigh Grimes BKN 311

	W	L	PCT	GB	R	OR
WAS	96	55	.636	—	829	670
PHI	88	64	.579	8.5	831	713
STL	82	71	.536	15	900	906
DET	81	73	.526	16.5	903	829
CHI	79	75	.513	18.5	811	770
CLE	70	84	.455	27.5	782	817
NY	69	85	.448	28.5	706	774
BOS	47	105	.309	49.5	639	922
					6401	6401

BATTING AVERAGE
H. Heilmann DET .... .393
Tris Speaker CLE .... .389
Al Simmons PHI .... .387

HITS
Al Simmons PHI 253
Sam Rice WAS................. 227
Harry Heilmann DET 225

DOUBLES
Marty McManus STL 44
Earl Sheely CHI 43
Al Simmons PHI 43

TRIPLES
Goose Goslin WAS............. 20

Johnny Mostil CHI 16
George Sisler STL 15

HOME RUNS
Bob Meusel NY................... 33
Ken Williams STL 25
Babe Ruth NY.................... 25

RUNS BATTED IN
Bob Meusel NY................. 138
Harry Heilmann DET 134
Al Simmons PHI 129

STOLEN BASES
Johnny Mostil CHI 43
Goose Goslin WAS............. 27
Sam Rice WAS.................. 26

RUNS SCORED
Johnny Mostil CHI 135
Al Simmons PHI 122
Earle Combs NY............... 117

WINS
Eddie Rommel PHI............. 21
Ted Lyons CHI.................... 21
two tied at 20

EARNED RUN AVERAGE
S. Coveleski WAS 2.84
Herb Pennock NY 2.96
Ted Blankenship CHI........ 3.03

STRIKEOUTS
Lefty Grove PHI 116
W. Johnson WAS 108

SAVES
Firpo Marberry WAS........... 15

COMPLETE GAMES
Sherry Smith CLE............... 22
Howard Ehmke BOS 22

SHUTOUTS
Ted Lyons CHI....................... 5

INNINGS PITCHED
Herb Pennock NY 277

	W	L	PCT	GB	R	OR
★ PIT	95	58	.621	—	912	715
NY	86	66	.566	8.5	736	702
CIN	80	73	.523	15	690	643
STL	77	76	.503	18	828	764
BOS	70	83	.458	25	708	802
BKN	68	85	.444	27	786	866
PHI	68	85	.444	27	812	930
CHI	68	86	.442	27.5	723	773
					6195	6195

BATTING AVERAGE
R. Hornsby STL .... .403
Jim Bottomley STL .... .367
Zack Wheat BKN .... .359

HITS
Jim Bottomley STL 227
Zack Wheat BKN 221
Kiki Cuyler PIT 220

DOUBLES
Jim Bottomley STL 44
Kiki Cuyler PIT 43
Zack Wheat BKN 42

TRIPLES
Kiki Cuyler PIT 26

three tied at.......................... 16

HOME RUNS
Rogers Hornsby STL 39
Gabby Hartnett CHI 24
Jack Fournier BKN 22

RUNS BATTED IN
R. Hornsby STL 143
Jack Fournier BKN 130
Jim Bottomley STL 128

STOLEN BASES
Max Carey PIT.................... 46
Kiki Cuyler PIT 41
Sparky Adams CHI............. 26

RUNS SCORED
Kiki Cuyler PIT................... 144
R. Hornsby STL 133
Zack Wheat BKN 125

WINS
Dazzy Vance BKN.............. 22
Eppa Rixey CIN 21
Pete Donohue CIN 21

EARNED RUN AVERAGE
Dolf Luque CIN 2.63
Eppa Rixey CIN 2.88
Pete Donohue CIN 3.08

STRIKEOUTS
Dazzy Vance BKN 221
Dolf Luque CIN 140

SAVES
Johnny Morrison PIT 4
Guy Bush CHI....................... 4

COMPLETE GAMES
Pete Donohue CIN 27

SHUTOUTS
three tied at............................ 4

INNINGS PITCHED
Pete Donohue CIN 301

	W	L	PCT	GB	R	OR
NY	91	63	.591	—	847	713
CLE	88	66	.571	3	738	612
PHI	83	67	.553	6	677	570
WAS	81	69	.540	8	802	761
CHI	81	72	.529	9.5	730	665
DET	79	75	.513	12	793	830
STL	62	92	.403	29	682	845
BOS	46	107	.301	44.5	562	835
					5831	5831

BATTING AVERAGE
Heinie Manush DET .... .378
Babe Ruth NY .... .372
two tied at .... .367

HITS
Sam Rice WAS 216
George Burns CLE 216
Goose Goslin WAS 201

DOUBLES
George Burns CLE 64
Al Simmons PHI 53
Tris Speaker CLE 52

TRIPLES
Lou Gehrig NY 20

C. Gehringer DET 17
two tied at 15

HOME RUNS
Babe Ruth NY 47
Al Simmons PHI 19
Tony Lazzeri NY 18

RUNS BATTED IN
Babe Ruth NY 146
George Burns CLE 114
Tony Lazzeri NY 114

STOLEN BASES
Johnny Mostil CHI 35
Sam Rice WAS 24
Bill Hunnefield CHI 24

RUNS SCORED
Babe Ruth NY 139
Lou Gehrig NY 135
Johnny Mostil CHI 120

WINS
George Uhle CLE 27
Herb Pennock NY 23
Urban Shocker NY 19

EARNED RUN AVERAGE
Lefty Grove PHI 2.51
George Uhle CLE 2.83
Ted Lyons CHI 3.01

STRIKEOUTS
Lefty Grove PHI 194
George Uhle CLE 159

SAVES
Firpo Marberry WAS 22

COMPLETE GAMES
George Uhle CLE 32

SHUTOUTS
Ed Wells DET 4

INNINGS PITCHED
George Uhle CLE 318

	W	L	PCT	GB	R	OR
★ STL	89	65	.578	—	817	678
CIN	87	67	.565	2	747	651
PIT	84	69	.549	4.5	769	689
CHI	82	72	.532	7	682	602
NY	74	77	.490	13.5	663	668
BKN	71	82	.464	17.5	623	705
BOS	66	86	.434	22	624	719
PHI	58	93	.384	29.5	687	900
					5612	5612

BATTING AVERAGE
B. Hargrave CIN .... .353
C. Christenson CIN .... .350
Earl Smith PIT .... .346

HITS
Eddie Brown BOS 201
Kiki Cuyler PIT 197
Sparky Adams CHI 193

DOUBLES
Jim Bottomley STL 40
Edd Roush CIN 37
Hack Wilson CHI 36

TRIPLES
Paul Waner PIT 22

Curt Walker CIN 20
Pie Traynor PIT 17

HOME RUNS
Hack Wilson CHI 21
Jim Bottomley STL 19
Cy Williams PHI 18

RUNS BATTED IN
Jim Bottomley STL 120
Hack Wilson CHI 109
Les Bell STL 100

STOLEN BASES
Kiki Cuyler PIT 35
Sparky Adams CHI 27
two tied at 23

RUNS SCORED
Kiki Cuyler PIT 113
Paul Waner PIT 101
two tied at 99

WINS
four tied at 20

EARNED RUN AVERAGE
Ray Kremer PIT 2.61
Charlie Root CHI 2.82
Jesse Petty BKN 2.84

STRIKEOUTS
Dazzy Vance BKN 140
Charlie Root CHI 127
two tied at 103

SAVES
Chick Davies NY 6

COMPLETE GAMES
Carl Mays CIN 24

SHUTOUTS
Pete Donohue CIN 5

INNINGS PITCHED
Pete Donohue CIN 286

	W	L	PCT	GB	R	OR
★ NY	110	44	.714	—	975	599
PHI	91	63	.591	19	841	726
WAS	85	69	.552	25	782	730
DET	82	71	.536	27.5	845	805
CHI	70	83	.458	39.5	662	708
CLE	66	87	.431	43.5	668	766
STL	59	94	.386	50.5	724	904
BOS	51	103	.331	59	597	856
					6094	6094

BATTING AVERAGE
H. Heilmann DET .... .398
Al Simmons PHI .... .392
Lou Gehrig NY .... .373

HITS
Earle Combs NY 231
Lou Gehrig NY 218
two tied at 201

DOUBLES
Lou Gehrig NY 52
George Burns CLE 51
Harry Heilmann DET 50

TRIPLES
Earle Combs NY 23

Heinie Manush DET 18
Lou Gehrig NY 18

HOME RUNS
Babe Ruth NY 60
Lou Gehrig NY 47
Tony Lazzeri NY 18

RUNS BATTED IN
Lou Gehrig NY 175
Babe Ruth NY 164
two tied at 120

STOLEN BASES
George Sisler STL 27
Bob Meusel NY 24
three tied at 22

RUNS SCORED
Babe Ruth NY 158
Lou Gehrig NY 149
Earle Combs NY 137

WINS
Waite Hoyt NY 22
Ted Lyons CHI 22
Lefty Grove PHI 20

EARNED RUN AVERAGE
Wilcy Moore NY 2.28
Waite Hoyt NY 2.63

STRIKEOUTS
Lefty Grove PHI 174
Rube Walberg PHI 136

SAVES
G. Braxton WAS 13
Wilcy Moore NY 13

COMPLETE GAMES
Ted Lyons CHI 30

SHUTOUTS
Hod Lisenbee WAS 4

INNINGS PITCHED
Tommy Thomas CHI 308
Ted Lyons CHI 308

	W	L	PCT	GB	R	OR
PIT	94	60	.610	—	817	659
STL	92	61	.601	1.5	754	665
NY	92	62	.597	2	817	720
CHI	85	68	.556	8.5	750	661
CIN	75	78	.490	18.5	643	653
BKN	65	88	.425	28.5	541	619
BOS	60	94	.390	34	651	771
PHI	51	103	.331	43	678	903
					5651	5651

BATTING AVERAGE
Paul Waner PIT .... .380
Rogers Hornsby NY .... .361
Lloyd Waner PIT .... .355

HITS
Paul Waner PIT 237
Lloyd Waner PIT 223
Frankie Frisch STL 208

DOUBLES
R. Stephenson CHI 46
Paul Waner PIT 42
two tied at 36

TRIPLES
Paul Waner PIT 18

Jim Bottomley STL 15
F. Thompson PHI 14

HOME RUNS
Hack Wilson CHI 30
Cy Williams PHI 30
Rogers Hornsby NY 26

RUNS BATTED IN
Paul Waner PIT 131
Hack Wilson CHI 129
Rogers Hornsby NY 125

STOLEN BASES
Frankie Frisch STL 48
Max Carey BKN 32
Harvey Hendrick BKN........ 29

RUNS SCORED
Lloyd Waner PIT 133
Rogers Hornsby NY 133
Hack Wilson CHI 119

WINS
Charlie Root CHI 26
Jesse Haines STL 24
Carmen Hill PIT 22

EARNED RUN AVERAGE
Ray Kremer PIT 2.47
G. Alexander STL 2.52
Dazzy Vance BKN 2.70

STRIKEOUTS
Dazzy Vance BKN 184
Charlie Root CHI 145
Jackie May CIN 121

SAVES
Bill Sherdel STL 6

COMPLETE GAMES
three tied at........................ 25

SHUTOUTS
Jesse Haines STL 6

INNINGS PITCHED
Charlie Root CHI 309

	W	L	PCT	GB	R	OR
★ NY	101	53	.656	—	894	685
PHI	98	55	.641	2.5	829	615
STL	82	72	.532	19	772	742
WAS	75	79	.487	26	718	705
CHI	72	82	.468	29	656	725
DET	68	86	.442	33	744	804
CLE	62	92	.403	39	674	830
BOS	57	96	.373	43.5	589	770
					5876	5876

BATTING AVERAGE
Goose Goslin WAS.......... .379
Heinie Manush STL .... .378
Lou Gehrig NY .... .374

HITS
Heinie Manush STL 241
Lou Gehrig NY 210
Sam Rice WAS 202

DOUBLES
Lou Gehrig NY 47
Heinie Manush STL 47
Bob Meusel NY 45

TRIPLES
Earle Combs NY 21

Heinie Manush STL 20
C. Gehringer DET 16

HOME RUNS
Babe Ruth NY 54
Lou Gehrig NY 27
Goose Goslin WAS............ 17

RUNS BATTED IN
Lou Gehrig NY 142
Babe Ruth NY 142
Bob Meusel NY................. 113

STOLEN BASES
Buddy Myer BOS............... 30
Johnny Mostil CHI 23
Harry Rice DET 20

RUNS SCORED
Babe Ruth NY.................... 163
Lou Gehrig NY 139
Earle Combs NY............... 118

WINS
Lefty Grove PHI 24
George Pipgras NY 24
Waite Hoyt NY 23

EARNED RUN AVERAGE
G. Braxton WAS 2.51
Herb Pennock NY 2.56
Lefty Grove PHI 2.58

STRIKEOUTS
Lefty Grove PHI 183
George Pipgras NY 139
Tommy Thomas CHI 129

SAVES
Waite Hoyt NY 8

COMPLETE GAMES
Red Ruffing BOS 25

SHUTOUTS
Herb Pennock NY 5

INNINGS PITCHED
George Pipgras NY 301

	W	L	PCT	GB	R	OR
STL	95	59	.617	—	807	636
NY	93	61	.604	2	807	653
CHI	91	63	.591	4	714	615
PIT	85	67	.559	9	837	704
CIN	78	74	.513	16	648	686
BKN	77	76	.503	17.5	665	640
BOS	50	103	.327	44.5	631	878
PHI	43	109	.283	51	660	957
					5769	5769

BATTING AVERAGE
R. Hornsby BOS .... .387
Paul Waner PIT .... .370
F. Lindstrom NY............... .358

HITS
F. Lindstrom NY................ 231
Paul Waner PIT 223
Lloyd Waner PIT 221

DOUBLES
Paul Waner PIT 50
Chick Hafey STL............... 46
two tied at 42

TRIPLES
Jim Bottomley STL 20

Paul Waner PIT 19
Lloyd Waner PIT................ 14

HOME RUNS
Hack Wilson CHI 31
Jim Bottomley STL 31
Chick Hafey STL................ 27

RUNS BATTED IN
Jim Bottomley STL 136
Pie Traynor PIT 124
Hack Wilson CHI 120

STOLEN BASES
Kiki Cuyler CHI 37
Frankie Frisch STL 29
two tied at 19

RUNS SCORED
Paul Waner PIT 142
Jim Bottomley STL 123
Lloyd Waner PIT............... 121

WINS
Larry Benton NY 25
Burleigh Grimes PIT 25
Dazzy Vance BKN 22

EARNED RUN AVERAGE
Dazzy Vance BKN 2.09
Sheriff Blake CHI 2.47

STRIKEOUTS
Dazzy Vance BKN 200
Pat Malone CHI 155

SAVES
Bill Sherdel STL.................. 5
Hal Haid STL 5

COMPLETE GAMES
Burleigh Grimes PIT 28
Larry Benton NY 28

SHUTOUTS
five tied at 4

INNINGS PITCHED
Burleigh Grimes PIT 331

	W	L	PCT	GB	R	OR
★ PHI	104	46	.693	—	901	615
NY	88	66	.571	18	899	775
CLE	81	71	.533	24	717	736
STL	79	73	.520	26	733	713
WAS	71	81	.467	34	730	776
DET	70	84	.455	36	926	928
CHI	59	93	.388	46	627	792
BOS	58	96	.377	48	605	803
					6138	6138

BATTING AVERAGE
Lew Fonseca CLE .... .369
Al Simmons PHI .... .365
Heinie Manush STL .... .355

HITS
Dale Alexander DET 215
C. Gehringer DET 215
Al Simmons PHI 212

DOUBLES
Roy Johnson DET 45
C. Gehringer DET 45
Heinie Manush STL 45

TRIPLES
C. Gehringer DET 19

Russ Scarritt BOS 17
Bing Miller PHI 16

HOME RUNS
Babe Ruth NY 46
Lou Gehrig NY 35
Al Simmons PHI 34

RUNS BATTED IN
Al Simmons PHI 157
Babe Ruth NY 154
Dale Alexander DET 137

STOLEN BASES
C. Gehringer DET 27
Bill Cissell CHI 25
Bing Miller PHI 24

RUNS SCORED
C. Gehringer DET 131
Roy Johnson DET 128
Lou Gehrig NY 127

WINS
G. Earnshaw PHI 24
Wes Ferrell CLE 21
Lefty Grove PHI 20

EARNED RUN AVERAGE
Lefty Grove PHI 2.81
Firpo Marberry WAS 3.06
T. Thomas CHI 3.19

STRIKEOUTS
Lefty Grove PHI 170
G. Earnshaw PHI 149
George Pipgras NY 125

SAVES
Firpo Marberry WAS........... 11

COMPLETE GAMES
Tommy Thomas CHI 24

SHUTOUTS
four tied at............................. 4

INNINGS PITCHED
Sam Gray STL 305

	W	L	PCT	GB	R	OR
CHI	98	54	.645	—	982	758
PIT	88	65	.575	10.5	904	780
NY	84	67	.556	13.5	897	709
STL	78	74	.513	20	831	806
PHI	71	82	.464	27.5	897	1032
BKN	70	83	.458	28.5	755	888
CIN	66	88	.429	33	686	760
BOS	56	98	.364	43	657	876
					6609	6609

BATTING AVERAGE
Lefty O'Doul PHI .... .398
Babe Herman BKN .... .381
R. Hornsby CHI .... .380

HITS
Lefty O'Doul PHI 254
Lloyd Waner PIT 234
Rogers Hornsby CHI 229

DOUBLES
J. Frederick BKN 52
Rogers Hornsby CHI 47
Chick Hafey STL................ 47

TRIPLES
Lloyd Waner PIT 20

Curt Walker CIN 15
Paul Waner PIT 15

HOME RUNS
Chuck Klein PHI 43
Mel Ott NY 42
two tied at 39

RUNS BATTED IN
Hack Wilson CHI 159
Mel Ott NY 151
Rogers Hornsby CHI 149

STOLEN BASES
Kiki Cuyler CHI 43
Evar Swanson CIN 33
Frankie Frisch STL 24

RUNS SCORED
Rogers Hornsby CHI 156
Lefty O'Doul PHI 152
Mel Ott NY 138

WINS
Pat Malone CHI 22
Red Lucas CIN 19
Charlie Root CHI 19

EARNED RUN AVERAGE
Bill Walker NY 3.09
B. Grimes PIT 3.13
Charlie Root CHI 3.47

STRIKEOUTS
Pat Malone CHI 166
Watty Clark BKN 140

SAVES
Johnny Morrison BKN........... 8
Guy Bush CHI....................... 8

COMPLETE GAMES
Red Lucas CIN 28

SHUTOUTS
Pat Malone CHI 5

INNINGS PITCHED
Watty Clark BKN 279

	W	L	PCT	GB	R	OR
★ PHI	102	52	.662	—	951	751
WAS	94	60	.610	8	892	689
NY	86	68	.558	16	1062	898
CLE	81	73	.526	21	890	915
DET	75	79	.487	27	783	833
STL	64	90	.416	38	751	886
CHI	62	92	.403	40	729	884
BOS	52	102	.338	50	612	814
					6670	6670

BATTING AVERAGE
Al Simmons PHI .... .381
Lou Gehrig NY .... .379
Babe Ruth NY .... .359

HITS
Johnny Hodapp CLE 225
Lou Gehrig NY 220
Al Simmons PHI 211

DOUBLES
Johnny Hodapp CLE 51
H. Manush STL/WAS 49
two tied at 47

TRIPLES
Earle Combs NY 22

Carl Reynolds CHI 18
Lou Gehrig NY 17

HOME RUNS
Babe Ruth NY 49
Lou Gehrig NY 41
two tied at 37

RUNS BATTED IN
Lou Gehrig NY 174
Al Simmons PHI 165
Jimmie Foxx PHI 156

STOLEN BASES
Marty McManus DET 23
C. Gehringer DET 19
three tied at 17

RUNS SCORED
Al Simmons PHI 152
Babe Ruth NY 150
C. Gehringer DET 144

WINS
Lefty Grove PHI 28
Wes Ferrell CLE 25
two tied at 22

EARNED RUN AVERAGE
Lefty Grove PHI 2.54
Wes Ferrell CLE 3.31
Lefty Stewart STL 3.45

STRIKEOUTS
Lefty Grove PHI 209
G. Earnshaw PHI 193
Bump Hadley WAS 162

SAVES
Lefty Grove PHI 9

COMPLETE GAMES
Ted Lyons CHI 29

SHUTOUTS
three tied at 3

INNINGS PITCHED
Ted Lyons CHI 298

	W	L	PCT	GB	R	OR
STL	92	62	.597	—	1004	784
CHI	90	64	.584	2	998	870
NY	87	67	.565	5	959	814
BKN	86	68	.558	6	871	738
PIT	80	74	.519	12	891	928
BOS	70	84	.455	22	693	835
CIN	59	95	.383	33	665	857
PHI	52	102	.338	40	944	1199
					7025	7025

BATTING AVERAGE
Bill Terry NY .... .401
Babe Herman BKN .... .393
Chuck Klein PHI .... .386

HITS
Bill Terry NY 254
Chuck Klein PHI 250
Babe Herman BKN 241

DOUBLES
Chuck Klein PHI 59
Kiki Cuyler CHI 50
Babe Herman BKN 48

TRIPLES
Adam Comorosky PIT 23

Paul Waner PIT 18
two tied at 17

HOME RUNS
Hack Wilson CHI 56
Chuck Klein PHI 40
Wally Berger BOS 38

RUNS BATTED IN
Hack Wilson CHI 190
Chuck Klein PHI 170
Kiki Cuyler CHI 134

STOLEN BASES
Kiki Cuyler CHI 37
Babe Herman BKN 18
Paul Waner PIT 18

RUNS SCORED
Chuck Klein PHI 158
Kiki Cuyler CHI 155
Woody English CHI 152

WINS
Ray Kremer PIT 20
Pat Malone CHI 20
F. Fitzsimmons NY 19

EARNED RUN AVERAGE
Dazzy Vance BKN 2.61
Carl Hubbell NY 3.87

STRIKEOUTS
Bill Hallahan STL 177
Dazzy Vance BKN 173

SAVES
Hi Bell STL 8

COMPLETE GAMES
Erv Brame PIT 22
Pat Malone CHI 22

SHUTOUTS
Charlie Root CHI 4
Dazzy Vance BKN 4

INNINGS PITCHED
Ray Kremer PIT 276

	W	L	PCT	GB	R	OR
PHI	107	45	.704	—	858	626
NY	94	59	.614	13.5	1067	760
WAS	92	62	.597	16	843	691
CLE	78	76	.506	30	885	833
STL	63	91	.409	45	722	870
BOS	62	90	.408	45	625	800
DET	61	93	.396	47	651	836
CHI	56	97	.366	51.5	704	939
					6355	6355

BATTING AVERAGE
Al Simmons PHI .... .390
Babe Ruth NY .... .373
Ed Morgan CLE .... .351

HITS
Lou Gehrig NY 211
Earl Averill CLE 209
Al Simmons PHI 200

DOUBLES
Earl Webb BOS 67
Dale Alexander DET 47
Red Kress STL 46

TRIPLES
Roy Johnson DET 19

Lou Gehrig NY 15
Lu Blue CHI 15

HOME RUNS
Lou Gehrig NY 46
Babe Ruth NY 46
Earl Averill CLE 32

RUNS BATTED IN
Lou Gehrig NY 184
Babe Ruth NY 163
Earl Averill CLE 143

STOLEN BASES
Ben Chapman NY 61
Roy Johnson DET 33
Jack Burns STL 19

RUNS SCORED
Lou Gehrig NY 163
Babe Ruth NY 149
Earl Averill CLE 140

WINS
Lefty Grove PHI 31
Wes Ferrell CLE 22
two tied at 21

EARNED RUN AVERAGE
Lefty Grove PHI 2.06
Lefty Gomez NY 2.67
Bump Hadley WAS 3.06

STRIKEOUTS
Lefty Grove PHI 175
G. Earnshaw PHI 152

SAVES
Wilcy Moore BOS 10

COMPLETE GAMES
Lefty Grove PHI 27
Wes Ferrell CLE 27

SHUTOUTS
Lefty Grove PHI 4

INNINGS PITCHED
Rube Walberg PHI 291

	W	L	PCT	GB	R	OR
★ STL	101	53	.656	—	815	614
NY	87	65	.572	13	768	599
CHI	84	70	.545	17	828	710
BKN	79	73	.520	21	681	673
PIT	75	79	.487	26	636	691
PHI	66	88	.429	35	684	828
BOS	64	90	.416	37	533	680
CIN	58	96	.377	43	592	742
					5537	5537

BATTING AVERAGE
Chick Hafey STL .... .349
Bill Terry NY .... .349
Jim Bottomley STL .... .348

HITS
Lloyd Waner PIT 214
Bill Terry NY 213
two tied at 202

DOUBLES
Sparky Adams STL 46
Wally Berger BOS 44
three tied at 43

TRIPLES
Bill Terry NY 20

Babe Herman BKN 16
Pie Traynor PIT 15

HOME RUNS
Chuck Klein PHI 31
Mel Ott NY 29
Wally Berger BOS 19

RUNS BATTED IN
Chuck Klein PHI 121
Mel Ott NY 115
Bill Terry NY 112

STOLEN BASES
Frankie Frisch STL 28
Babe Herman BKN 17
two tied at 16

RUNS SCORED
Chuck Klein PHI 121
Bill Terry NY 121
Woody English CHI 117

WINS
Bill Hallahan STL 19
Heinie Meine PIT 19
Jumbo Elliott PHI 19

EARNED RUN AVERAGE
Bill Walker NY 2.26
Carl Hubbell NY 2.65
Ed Brandt BOS 2.92

STRIKEOUTS
Bill Hallahan STL 159
Carl Hubbell NY 155
Dazzy Vance BKN 150

SAVES
Jack Quinn BKN 15

COMPLETE GAMES
Red Lucas CIN 24

SHUTOUTS
Bill Walker NY 6

INNINGS PITCHED
Heinie Meine PIT 284

	W	L	PCT	GB	R	OR
★ NY	107	47	.695	—	1002	724
PHI	94	60	.610	13	981	752
WAS	93	61	.604	14	840	716
CLE	87	65	.572	19	845	747
DET	76	75	.503	29.5	799	787
STL	63	91	.409	44	736	898
CHI	49	102	.325	56.5	667	897
BOS	43	111	.279	64	566	915
					6436	6436

BATTING AVERAGE
D. Alexander DET, BOS .. .367
Jimmie Foxx PHI .... .364
Lou Gehrig NY .... .349

HITS
Al Simmons PHI 216
Heinie Manush WAS 214
Jimmie Foxx PHI 213

DOUBLES
Eric McNair PHI 47
C. Gehringer DET 44
Joe Cronin WAS 43

TRIPLES
Joe Cronin WAS 18

Tony Lazzeri NY 16
Buddy Myer WAS 16

HOME RUNS
Jimmie Foxx PHI 58
Babe Ruth NY 41
Al Simmons PHI 35

RUNS BATTED IN
Jimmie Foxx PHI 169
Lou Gehrig NY 151
Al Simmons PHI 151

STOLEN BASES
Ben Chapman NY 38
Gee Walker DET 30
R. Johnson DET, BOS....... 20

RUNS SCORED
Jimmie Foxx PHI 151
Al Simmons PHI 144
Earle Combs NY 143

WINS
G. Crowder WAS 26
Lefty Grove PHI 25
Lefty Gomez NY 24

EARNED RUN AVERAGE
Lefty Grove PHI 2.84
Red Ruffing NY 3.09
Ted Lyons CHI................... 3.28

STRIKEOUTS
Red Ruffing NY 190
Lefty Grove PHI 188

SAVES
Firpo Marberry WAS........... 13

COMPLETE GAMES
Lefty Grove PHI 27

SHUTOUTS
Tommy Bridges DET 4
Lefty Grove PHI 4

INNINGS PITCHED
G. Crowder WAS 327

	W	L	PCT	GB	R	OR
CHI	90	64	.584	—	720	633
PIT	86	68	.558	4	701	711
BKN	81	73	.526	9	752	747
PHI	78	76	.506	12	844	796
BOS	77	77	.500	13	649	655
NY	72	82	.468	18	755	706
STL	72	82	.468	18	684	717
CIN	60	94	.390	30	575	715
					5680	5680

BATTING AVERAGE
Lefty O'Doul BKN .... .368
Bill Terry NY .... .350
Chuck Klein PHI .... .348

HITS
Chuck Klein PHI 226
Bill Terry NY 225
Lefty O'Doul BKN 219

DOUBLES
Paul Waner PIT 62
Chuck Klein PHI 50
R. Stephenson CHI............. 49

TRIPLES
Babe Herman CIN 19

Gus Suhr PIT 16
Chuck Klein PHI 15

HOME RUNS
Chuck Klein PHI 38
Mel Ott NY 38
Bill Terry NY 28

RUNS BATTED IN
Don Hurst PHI 143
Chuck Klein PHI 137
Pinky Whitney PHI............ 124

STOLEN BASES
Chuck Klein PHI 20
Tony Piet PIT...................... 19
two tied at 18

RUNS SCORED
Chuck Klein PHI 152
Bill Terry NY 124
Lefty O'Doul BKN 120

WINS
Lon Warneke CHI 22
Watty Clark BKN................ 20
Guy Bush CHI..................... 19

EARNED RUN AVERAGE
Lon Warneke CHI 2.37
Carl Hubbell NY 2.50
Huck Betts BOS................ 2.80

STRIKEOUTS
Dizzy Dean STL................ 191
Carl Hubbell NY 137
Pat Malone CHI 120

SAVES
Jack Quinn BKN 8

COMPLETE GAMES
Red Lucas CIN 28

SHUTOUTS
three tied at............................ 4

INNINGS PITCHED
Dizzy Dean STL................ 286

	W	L	PCT	GB	R	OR
WAS	99	53	.651	—	850	665
NY	91	59	.607	7	927	768
PHI	79	72	.523	19.5	875	853
CLE	75	76	.497	23.5	654	669
DET	75	79	.487	25	722	733
CHI	67	83	.447	31	683	814
BOS	63	86	.423	34.5	700	758
STL	55	96	.364	43.5	669	820
					6080	6080

BATTING AVERAGE
Jimmie Foxx PHI .... .356
Heinie Manush WAS ...... .336
Lou Gehrig NY .... .334

HITS
Heinie Manush WAS 221
C. Gehringer DET 204
Jimmie Foxx PHI 204

DOUBLES
Joe Cronin WAS 45
Bob Johnson PHI................ 44
Jack Burns STL 43

TRIPLES
Heinie Manush WAS 17

Earl Averill CLE 16
Earle Combs NY 16

HOME RUNS
Jimmie Foxx PHI 48
Babe Ruth NY 34
Lou Gehrig NY 32

RUNS BATTED IN
Jimmie Foxx PHI 163
Lou Gehrig NY 139
Al Simmons CHI 119

STOLEN BASES
Ben Chapman NY.............. 27
Gee Walker DET 26
Evar Swanson CHI 19

RUNS SCORED
Lou Gehrig NY................. 138
Jimmie Foxx PHI 125
Heinie Manush WAS 115

WINS
Lefty Grove PHI 24
G. Crowder WAS................ 24
Earl Whitehill WAS 22

EARNED RUN AVERAGE
Mel Harder CLE 2.95
T. Bridges DET 3.09
Lefty Gomez NY 3.18

STRIKEOUTS
Lefty Gomez NY 163
Bump Hadley STL 149
Red Ruffing NY 122

SAVES
Jack Russell WAS 13

COMPLETE GAMES
Lefty Grove PHI 21

SHUTOUTS
Oral Hildebrand CLE 6

INNINGS PITCHED
Bump Hadley STL 317

	W	L	PCT	GB	R	OR
★ NY	91	61	.599	—	636	515
PIT	87	67	.565	5	667	619
CHI	86	68	.558	6	646	536
BOS	83	71	.539	9	552	531
STL	82	71	.536	9.5	687	609
BKN	65	88	.425	26.5	617	695
PHI	60	92	.395	31	607	760
CIN	58	94	.382	33	496	643
					4908	4908

BATTING AVERAGE
Chuck Klein PHI .... .368
Spud Davis PHI .... .349
R. Stephenson CHI.......... .329

HITS
Chuck Klein PHI 223
Chick Fullis PHI 200
Paul Waner PIT 191

DOUBLES
Chuck Klein PHI 44
Joe Medwick STL 40
F. Lindstrom PIT 39

TRIPLES
Arky Vaughan PIT 19

Paul Waner PIT 16
two tied at 12

HOME RUNS
Chuck Klein PHI 28
Wally Berger BOS 27
Mel Ott NY 23

RUNS BATTED IN
Chuck Klein PHI 120
Wally Berger BOS 106
Mel Ott NY 103

STOLEN BASES
Pepper Martin STL 26
Chick Fullis PHI 18
Frankie Frisch STL 18

RUNS SCORED
Pepper Martin STL 122
Chuck Klein PHI 101
Paul Waner PIT 101

WINS
Carl Hubbell NY 23
three tied at........................ 20

EARNED RUN AVERAGE
Carl Hubbell NY 1.66
Lon Warneke CHI 2.00
H. Schumacher NY.......... 2.16

STRIKEOUTS
Dizzy Dean STL................ 199
Carl Hubbell NY 156
Tex Carleton STL 147

SAVES
Phil Collins PHI 6

COMPLETE GAMES
Dizzy Dean STL................. 26
Lon Warneke CHI.............. 26

SHUTOUTS
Carl Hubbell NY 10

INNINGS PITCHED
Carl Hubbell NY 309

	W	L	PCT	GB	R	OR
DET	101	53	.656	—	958	708
NY	94	60	.610	7	842	669
CLE	85	69	.552	16	814	763
BOS	76	76	.500	24	820	775
PHI	68	82	.453	31	764	838
STL	67	85	.441	33	674	800
WAS	66	86	.434	34	729	806
CHI	53	99	.349	47	704	946
					6305	6305

BATTING AVERAGE
Lou Gehrig NY .... .363
C. Gehringer DET .... .356
Heinie Manush WAS .... .349

HITS
C. Gehringer DET 214
Lou Gehrig NY 210
Hal Trosky CLE 206

DOUBLES
Hank Greenberg DET 63
C. Gehringer DET 50
Earl Averill CLE 48

TRIPLES
Ben Chapman NY 13

Heinie Manush WAS 11

HOME RUNS
Lou Gehrig NY 49
Jimmie Foxx PHI 44
Hal Trosky CLE 35

RUNS BATTED IN
Lou Gehrig NY 165
Hal Trosky CLE 142
H. Greenberg DET 139

STOLEN BASES
Bill Werber BOS 40
Jo-Jo White DET 28
Ben Chapman NY 26

RUNS SCORED
C. Gehringer DET 134
Bill Werber BOS 129
two tied at 128

WINS
Lefty Gomez NY 26
S. Rowe DET 24
Tommy Bridges DET 22

EARNED RUN AVERAGE
Lefty Gomez NY 2.33
Mel Harder CLE 2.61
Johnny Murphy NY 3.12

STRIKEOUTS
Lefty Gomez NY 158
T. Bridges DET 151

SAVES
Jack Russell WAS 7

COMPLETE GAMES
Lefty Gomez NY 25

SHUTOUTS
Mel Harder CLE 6
Lefty Gomez NY 6

INNINGS PITCHED
Lefty Gomez NY 282

	W	L	PCT	GB	R	OR
★ STL	95	58	.621	—	799	656
NY	93	60	.608	2	760	583
CHI	86	65	.570	8	705	639
BOS	78	73	.517	16	683	714
PIT	74	76	.493	19.5	735	713
BKN	71	81	.467	23.5	748	795
PHI	56	93	.376	37	675	794
CIN	52	99	.344	42	590	801
					5695	5695

BATTING AVERAGE
Paul Waner PIT .... .362
Bill Terry NY .... .354
Kiki Cuyler CHI .... .338

HITS
Paul Waner PIT 217
Bill Terry NY 213
Ripper Collins STL 200

DOUBLES
Kiki Cuyler CHI 42
Ethan Allen PHI 42
Arky Vaughan PIT 41

TRIPLES
Joe Medwick STL 18

Paul Waner PIT 16
Gus Suhr PIT 13

HOME RUNS
Mel Ott NY 35
Ripper Collins STL 35
Wally Berger BOS 34

RUNS BATTED IN
Mel Ott NY 135
Ripper Collins STL 128
Wally Berger BOS 121

STOLEN BASES
Pepper Martin STL 23
Kiki Cuyler CHI 15
Dick Bartell PHI 13

RUNS SCORED
Paul Waner PIT 122
Mel Ott NY 119
Ripper Collins STL 116

WINS
Dizzy Dean STL 30
Hal Schumacher NY 23
Lon Warneke CHI 22

EARNED RUN AVERAGE
Carl Hubbell NY 2.30
Dizzy Dean STL 2.66
Waite Hoyt NY 2.93

STRIKEOUTS
Dizzy Dean STL 195
Van Mungo BKN 184
Paul Dean STL 150

SAVES
Carl Hubbell NY 8

COMPLETE GAMES
Carl Hubbell NY 25

SHUTOUTS
Dizzy Dean STL 7

INNINGS PITCHED
Van Mungo BKN 315

	W	L	PCT	GB	R	OR
★ DET	93	58	.616	—	919	665
NY	89	60	.597	3	818	632
CLE	82	71	.536	12	776	739
BOS	78	75	.510	16	718	732
CHI	74	78	.487	19.5	738	750
WAS	67	86	.438	27	823	903
STL	65	87	.428	28.5	718	930
PHI	58	91	.389	34	710	869
					6220	6220

BATTING AVERAGE
Buddy Myer WAS .... .349
Joe Vosmik CLE .... .348
Jimmie Foxx PHI .... .346

HITS
Joe Vosmik CLE 216
Buddy Myer WAS 215
Doc Cramer PHI 214

DOUBLES
Joe Vosmik CLE 47
Hank Greenberg DET 46
M. Solters BOS, STL 45

TRIPLES
Joe Vosmik CLE 20

John Stone WAS 18
Hank Greenberg DET 16

HOME RUNS
Hank Greenberg DET 36
Jimmie Foxx PHI 36
Lou Gehrig NY 30

RUNS BATTED IN
Hank Greenberg DET 170
Lou Gehrig NY 119
Jimmie Foxx PHI 115

STOLEN BASES
Bill Werber BOS 29
Lyn Lary WAS, STL 28
Mel Almada BOS 20

RUNS SCORED
Lou Gehrig NY 125
C. Gehringer DET 123
Hank Greenberg DET 121

WINS
Wes Ferrell BOS................. 25
Mel Harder CLE.................. 22
T. Bridges DET 21

EARNED RUN AVERAGE
Lefty Grove BOS 2.70
Ted Lyons CHI................. 3.02
Red Ruffing NY................ 3.12

STRIKEOUTS
T. Bridges DET 163
S. Rowe DET 140
Lefty Gomez NY 138

SAVES
Jack Knott STL 7

COMPLETE GAMES
Wes Ferrell BOS................. 31

SHUTOUTS
Schoolboy Rowe DET 6

INNINGS PITCHED
Wes Ferrell BOS.............. 322

	W	L	PCT	GB	R	OR
CHI	100	54	.649	—	847	597
STL	96	58	.623	4	829	625
NY	91	62	.595	8.5	770	675
PIT	86	67	.562	13.5	743	647
BKN	70	83	.458	29.5	711	767
CIN	68	85	.444	31.5	646	772
PHI	64	89	.418	35.5	685	871
BOS	38	115	.248	61.5	575	852
					5806	5806

BATTING AVERAGE
Arky Vaughan PIT .... .385
Joe Medwick STL .... .353
Gabby Hartnett CHI .... .344

HITS
Billy Herman CHI 227
Joe Medwick STL 224
four tied at 203

DOUBLES
Billy Herman CHI 57
Ethan Allen PHI 46
Joe Medwick STL 46

TRIPLES
Ival Goodman CIN 18

Lloyd Waner PIT 14
Joe Medwick STL 13

HOME RUNS
Wally Berger BOS 34
Mel Ott NY 31
Dolf Camilli PHI 25

RUNS BATTED IN
Wally Berger BOS 130
Joe Medwick STL 126
Ripper Collins STL............. 122

STOLEN BASES
Augie Galan CHI.................. 22
Pepper Martin STL 20
F. Bordagaray BKN 18

RUNS SCORED
Augie Galan CHI................ 133
Joe Medwick STL 132
Pepper Martin STL 121

WINS
Dizzy Dean STL.................. 28
Carl Hubbell NY 23
Paul Derringer CIN 22

EARNED RUN AVERAGE
Cy Blanton PIT 2.58
Bill Swift PIT 2.70
H. Schumacher NY 2.89

STRIKEOUTS
Dizzy Dean STL................ 190
Carl Hubbell NY 150
two tied at 143

SAVES
Dutch Leonard BKN.............. 8

COMPLETE GAMES
Dizzy Dean STL................. 29

SHUTOUTS
five tied at 4

INNINGS PITCHED
Dizzy Dean STL................ 325

	W	L	PCT	GB	R	OR
★ NY	102	51	.667	—	1065	731
DET	83	71	.539	19.5	921	871
CHI	81	70	.536	20	920	873
WAS	82	71	.536	20	889	799
CLE	80	74	.519	22.5	921	862
BOS	74	80	.481	28.5	775	764
STL	57	95	.375	44.5	804	1064
PHI	53	100	.346	49	714	1045
					7009	7009

BATTING AVERAGE
Luke Appling CHI .388
Earl Averill CLE .378
Bill Dickey NY .362

HITS
Earl Averill CLE 232
C. Gehringer DET 227
Hal Trosky CLE 216

DOUBLES
C. Gehringer DET 60
Gee Walker DET 55
two tied at 50

TRIPLES
Earl Averill CLE 15
Red Rolfe NY 15
Joe DiMaggio NY 15

HOME RUNS
Lou Gehrig NY 49
Hal Trosky CLE 42
Jimmie Foxx BOS 41

RUNS BATTED IN
Hal Trosky CLE 162
Lou Gehrig NY 152
Jimmie Foxx BOS 143

STOLEN BASES
Lyn Lary STL 37
J. Powell WAS, NY 26
Bill Werber BOS 23

RUNS SCORED
Lou Gehrig NY 167
Harlond Clift STL 145
C. Gehringer DET 144

WINS
Tommy Bridges DET 23
Vern Kennedy CHI 21
three tied at 20

EARNED RUN AVERAGE
Lefty Grove BOS 2.81
Johnny Allen CLE 3.44
Pete Appleton WAS 3.53

STRIKEOUTS
T. Bridges DET 175
Johnny Allen CLE 165
Bobo Newsom WAS 156

SAVES
Pat Malone NY 9

COMPLETE GAMES
Wes Ferrell BOS 28

SHUTOUTS
Lefty Grove BOS 6

INNINGS PITCHED
Wes Ferrell BOS 301

	W	L	PCT	GB	R	OR
NY	92	62	.597	—	742	621
CHI	87	67	.565	5	755	603
STL	87	67	.565	5	795	794
PIT	84	70	.545	8	804	718
CIN	74	80	.481	18	722	760
BOS	71	83	.461	21	631	715
BKN	67	87	.435	25	662	752
PHI	54	100	.351	38	726	874
					5837	5837

BATTING AVERAGE
Paul Waner PIT .373
Babe Phelps BKN .367
Joe Medwick STL .351

HITS
Joe Medwick STL 223
Paul Waner PIT 218
Frank Demaree CHI 212

DOUBLES
Joe Medwick STL 64
Billy Herman CHI 57
Paul Waner PIT 53

TRIPLES
Ival Goodman CIN 14

Dolf Camilli PHI 13
Joe Medwick STL 13

HOME RUNS
Mel Ott NY 33
Dolf Camilli PHI 28
two tied at 25

RUNS BATTED IN
Joe Medwick STL 138
Mel Ott NY 135
Gus Suhr PIT 118

STOLEN BASES
Pepper Martin STL 23
three tied at 17

RUNS SCORED
Arky Vaughan PIT 122
Pepper Martin STL 121
Mel Ott NY 120

WINS
Carl Hubbell NY 26
Dizzy Dean STL 24
Paul Derringer CIN 19

EARNED RUN AVERAGE
Carl Hubbell NY 2.31
D. MacFayden BOS 2.87
Frank Gabler NY 3.12

STRIKEOUTS
Van Mungo BKN 238
Dizzy Dean STL 195
Cy Blanton PIT 127

SAVES
Dizzy Dean STL 11

COMPLETE GAMES
Dizzy Dean STL 28

SHUTOUTS
seven tied at 4

INNINGS PITCHED
Dizzy Dean STL 315

	W	L	PCT	GB	R	OR
★ NY	102	52	.662	—	979	671
DET	89	65	.578	13	935	841
CHI	86	68	.558	16	780	730
CLE	83	71	.539	19	817	768
BOS	80	72	.526	21	821	775
WAS	73	80	.477	28.5	757	841
PHI	54	97	.358	46.5	699	854
STL	46	108	.299	56	715	1023
					6503	6503

BATTING AVERAGE
C. Gehringer DET............ .371
Lou Gehrig NY................. .351
Joe DiMaggio NY............. .346

HITS
Beau Bell STL................... 218
Joe DiMaggio NY.............. 215
Gee Walker DET 213

DOUBLES
Beau Bell STL..................... 51
Hank Greenberg DET......... 49
Wally Moses PHI 48

TRIPLES
Dixie Walker CHI 16

Mike Kreevich CHI.............. 16
two tied at 15

HOME RUNS
Joe DiMaggio NY................ 46
Hank Greenberg DET......... 40
Lou Gehrig NY.................... 37

RUNS BATTED IN
Hank Greenberg DET......... 183
Joe DiMaggio NY.............. 167
Lou Gehrig NY................... 159

STOLEN BASES
B. Chapman WAS, BOS..... 35
Bill Werber PHI................... 35
Gee Walker DET 23

RUNS SCORED
Joe DiMaggio NY.............. 151
Red Rolfe NY.................... 143
Lou Gehrig NY 138

WINS
Lefty Gomez NY 21
Red Ruffing NY.................. 20
Roxie Lawson DET............ 18

EARNED RUN AVERAGE
Lefty Gomez NY 2.33
Monty Stratton CHI 2.40
Johnny Allen CLE 2.55

STRIKEOUTS
Lefty Gomez NY 194
Dick Newsom WAS, BOS. 166
Lefty Grove BOS 153

SAVES
Clint Brown CHI 18

COMPLETE GAMES
W. Ferrell BOS, WAS 26

SHUTOUTS
Lefty Gomez NY 6

INNINGS PITCHED
W. Ferrell BOS, WAS 281

	W	L	PCT	GB	R	OR
NY	95	57	.625	—	732	602
CHI	93	61	.604	3	811	682
PIT	86	68	.558	10	704	646
STL	81	73	.526	15	789	733
BOS	79	73	.520	16	579	556
BKN	62	91	.405	33.5	616	772
PHI	61	92	.399	34.5	724	869
CIN	56	98	.364	40	612	707
					5567	5567

BATTING AVERAGE
Joe Medwick STL .... .374
Johnny Mize STL............... .364
Gabby Hartnett CHI .... .354

HITS
Joe Medwick STL 237
Paul Waner PIT 219
Johnny Mize STL............... 204

DOUBLES
Joe Medwick STL 56
Johnny Mize STL................ 40
Dick Bartell NY 38

TRIPLES
Arky Vaughan PIT 17

Gus Suhr PIT 14
two tied at 12

HOME RUNS
Joe Medwick STL 31
Mel Ott NY 31
Dolf Camilli PHI 27

RUNS BATTED IN
Joe Medwick STL 154
Frank Demaree CHI 115
Johnny Mize STL.............. 113

STOLEN BASES
Augie Galan CHI................. 23
Stan Hack CHI.................... 16
four tied at.......................... 13

RUNS SCORED
Joe Medwick STL 111
Stan Hack CHI.................. 106
Billy Herman CHI 106

WINS
Carl Hubbell NY................. 22
three tied at....................... 20

EARNED RUN AVERAGE
Jim Turner BOS............... 2.38
Cliff Melton NY................. 2.61
Dizzy Dean STL............... 2.69

STRIKEOUTS
Carl Hubbell NY................ 159
Lee Grissom CIN.............. 149
Cy Blanton PIT 143

SAVES
Mace Brown PIT 7
Cliff Melton NY..................... 7

COMPLETE GAMES
Jim Turner BOS................. 24

SHUTOUTS
three tied at.......................... 5

INNINGS PITCHED
C. Passeau PHI 292

	W	L	PCT	GB	R	OR
★ NY	99	53	.651	—	966	710
BOS	88	61	.591	9.5	902	751
CLE	86	66	.566	13	847	782
DET	84	70	.545	16	862	795
WAS	75	76	.497	23.5	814	873
CHI	65	83	.439	32	709	752
STL	55	97	.362	44	755	962
PHI	53	99	.349	46	726	956
					6581	6581

BATTING AVERAGE
Jimmie Foxx BOS .... .349
Jeff Heath CLE .... .343
Ben Chapman BOS .... .340

HITS
Joe Vosmik BOS 201
Doc Cramer BOS 198
two tied at 197

DOUBLES
Joe Cronin BOS 51
George McQuinn STL 42
two tied at 40

TRIPLES
Jeff Heath CLE 18

Earl Averill CLE 15
Joe DiMaggio NY 13

HOME RUNS
Hank Greenberg DET 58
Jimmie Foxx BOS 50
Harlond Clift STL 34

RUNS BATTED IN
Jimmie Foxx BOS 175
Hank Greenberg DET 146
Joe DiMaggio NY 140

STOLEN BASES
Frank Crosetti NY 27
Lyn Lary CLE 23
Bill Werber PHI 19

RUNS SCORED
Hank Greenberg DET 144
Jimmie Foxx BOS 139
C. Gehringer DET 133

WINS
Red Ruffing NY 21
Bobo Newsom STL 20
Lefty Gomez NY 18

EARNED RUN AVERAGE
Lefty Grove BOS 3.08
Red Ruffing NY 3.31
Lefty Gomez NY 3.35

STRIKEOUTS
Bob Feller CLE 240
Bobo Newsom STL 226
Lefty Mills STL 134

SAVES
Johnny Murphy NY 11

COMPLETE GAMES
Bobo Newsom STL 31

SHUTOUTS
Lefty Gomez NY 4

INNINGS PITCHED
Bobo Newsom STL 330

	W	L	PCT	GB	R	OR
CHI	89	63	.586	—	713	598
PIT	86	64	.573	2	707	630
NY	83	67	.553	5	705	637
CIN	82	68	.547	6	723	634
BOS	77	75	.507	12	561	618
STL	71	80	.470	17.5	725	721
BKN	69	80	.463	18.5	704	710
PHI	45	105	.300	43	550	840
					5388	5388

BATTING AVERAGE
Ernie Lombardi CIN .... .342
Johnny Mize STL .... .337
F. McCormick CIN .... .327

HITS
F. McCormick CIN 209
Stan Hack CHI 195
Lloyd Waner PIT 194

DOUBLES
Joe Medwick STL 47
F. McCormick CIN 40
two tied at 36

TRIPLES
Johnny Mize STL 16

Don Gutteridge STL 15
Gus Suhr PIT 14

HOME RUNS
Mel Ott NY 36
Ival Goodman CIN 30
Johnny Mize STL 27

RUNS BATTED IN
Joe Medwick STL 122
Mel Ott NY 116
Johnny Rizzo PIT 111

STOLEN BASES
Stan Hack CHI 16
Ernie Koy BKN 15
C. Lavagetto BKN 15

RUNS SCORED
Mel Ott NY 116
Stan Hack CHI 109
Dolf Camilli BKN 106

WINS
Bill Lee CHI 22
Paul Derringer CIN 21
Clay Bryant CHI 19

EARNED RUN AVERAGE
Bill Lee CHI 2.66
Charlie Root CHI 2.86
Paul Derringer CIN 2.93

STRIKEOUTS
Clay Bryant CHI 135
Paul Derringer CIN 132
J. Vander Meer CIN 125

SAVES
Dick Coffman NY 12

COMPLETE GAMES
Paul Derringer CIN 26

SHUTOUTS
Bill Lee CHI 9

INNINGS PITCHED
Paul Derringer CIN 307

	W	L	PCT	GB	R	OR
★ NY	106	45	.702	—	967	556
BOS	89	62	.589	17	890	795
CLE	87	67	.565	20.5	797	700
CHI	85	69	.552	22.5	755	737
DET	81	73	.526	26.5	849	762
WAS	65	87	.428	41.5	702	797
PHI	55	97	.362	51.5	711	1022
STL	43	111	.279	64.5	733	1035
					6404	6404

BATTING AVERAGE
Joe DiMaggio NY............ .381
Jimmie Foxx BOS............ .360
Bob Johnson PHI............ .338

HITS
Red Rolfe NY.................... 213
G. McQuinn STL............... 195
Ken Keltner CLE............... 191

DOUBLES
Red Rolfe NY.................... 46
Ted Williams BOS 44
Hank Greenberg DET........ 42

TRIPLES
Buddy Lewis WAS............. 16

B. McCoskey DET 14
two tied at 13

HOME RUNS
Jimmie Foxx BOS.............. 35
Hank Greenberg DET........ 33
Ted Williams BOS 31

RUNS BATTED IN
Ted Williams BOS 145
Joe DiMaggio NY.............. 126
Bob Johnson PHI.............. 114

STOLEN BASES
George Case WAS............. 51
Mike Kreevich CHI............. 23
Pete Fox DET 23

RUNS SCORED
Red Rolfe NY.................... 139
Ted Williams BOS 131
Jimmie Foxx BOS............. 130

WINS
Bob Feller CLE 24
Red Ruffing NY................. 21
two tied at 20

EARNED RUN AVERAGE
Lefty Grove BOS 2.54
Ted Lyons CHI.................. 2.76
Bob Feller CLE 2.85

STRIKEOUTS
Bob Feller CLE 246
B. Newsom STL, DET 192

SAVES
Johnny Murphy NY 19

COMPLETE GAMES
B. Newsom STL, DET 24
Bob Feller CLE 24

SHUTOUTS
Red Ruffing NY.................... 5

INNINGS PITCHED
Bob Feller CLE 297

	W	L	PCT	GB	R	OR
CIN	97	57	.630	—	767	595
STL	92	61	.601	4.5	779	633
BKN	84	69	.549	12.5	708	645
CHI	84	70	.545	13	724	678
NY	77	74	.510	18.5	703	685
PIT	68	85	.444	28.5	666	721
BOS	63	88	.417	32.5	572	659
PHI	45	106	.298	50.5	553	856
					5472	5472

BATTING AVERAGE
Don Padgett STL.............. .399
Johnny Mize STL.............. .349
F. McCormick CIN .... .332

HITS
F. McCormick CIN 209
Joe Medwick STL 201
Johnny Mize STL.............. 197

DOUBLES
Enos Slaughter STL 52
Joe Medwick STL 48
Johnny Mize STL.............. 44

TRIPLES
Billy Herman CHI 18

Ival Goodman CIN 16
Johnny Mize STL.............. 14

HOME RUNS
Johnny Mize STL.............. 28
Mel Ott NY 27
Dolf Camilli BKN 26

RUNS BATTED IN
F. McCormick CIN 128
Joe Medwick STL 117
Johnny Mize STL.............. 108

STOLEN BASES
Lee Handley PIT................ 17
Stan Hack CHI................... 17
Bill Werber CIN................. 15

RUNS SCORED
Bill Werber CIN................. 115
Stan Hack CHI.................. 112
Billy Herman CHI 111

WINS
Bucky Walters CIN 27
Paul Derringer CIN 25
Curt Davis STL 22

EARNED RUN AVERAGE
Bucky Walters CIN 2.29
Bob Bowman STL............. 2.60
Carl Hubbell NY................ 2.75

STRIKEOUTS
C. Passeau PHI, CHI........ 137
Bucky Walters CIN 137
Mort Cooper STL 130

SAVES
two tied at 9

COMPLETE GAMES
Bucky Walters CIN 31

SHUTOUTS
Lou Fette BOS..................... 6

INNINGS PITCHED
Bucky Walters CIN 319

	W	L	PCT	GB	R	OR
DET	90	64	.584	—	888	717
CLE	89	65	.578	1	710	637
NY	88	66	.571	2	817	671
BOS	82	72	.532	8	872	825
CHI	82	72	.532	8	735	672
STL	67	87	.435	23	757	882
WAS	64	90	.416	26	665	811
PHI	54	100	.351	36	703	932
					6147	6147

BATTING AVERAGE
Joe DiMaggio NY .... .352
Luke Appling CHI .... .348
Ted Williams BOS .... .344

HITS
Rip Radcliff STL 200
Doc Cramer BOS 200
B. McCoskey DET 200

DOUBLES
Hank Greenberg DET 50
Lou Boudreau CLE 46
Rudy York DET 46

TRIPLES
B. McCoskey DET 19

Lou Finney BOS 15
Charlie Keller NY 15

HOME RUNS
Hank Greenberg DET 41
Jimmie Foxx BOS 36
Rudy York DET 33

RUNS BATTED IN
Hank Greenberg DET 150
Rudy York DET 134
Joe DiMaggio NY 133

STOLEN BASES
George Case WAS 35
Gee Walker WAS 21
Joe Gordon NY 18

RUNS SCORED
Ted Williams BOS 134
Hank Greenberg DET 129
B. McCoskey DET 123

WINS
Bob Feller CLE 27
Bobo Newsom DET 21
Al Milnar CLE 18

EARNED RUN AVERAGE
Bob Feller CLE 2.61
Bobo Newsom DET 2.83
Johnny Rigney CHI 3.11

STRIKEOUTS
Bob Feller CLE 261
Bobo Newsom DET 164
Johnny Rigney CHI 141

SAVES
Al Benton DET 17

COMPLETE GAMES
Bob Feller CLE 31

SHUTOUTS
three tied at 4

INNINGS PITCHED
Bob Feller CLE 320

	W	L	PCT	GB	R	OR
★ CIN	100	53	.654	—	707	528
BKN	88	65	.575	12	697	621
STL	84	69	.549	16	747	699
PIT	78	76	.506	22.5	809	783
CHI	75	79	.487	25.5	681	636
NY	72	80	.474	27.5	663	659
BOS	65	87	.428	34.5	623	745
PHI	50	103	.327	50	494	750
					5421	5421

BATTING AVERAGE
Debs Garms PIT .... .355
Spud Davis PIT .... .326
Ernie Lombardi CIN .... .319

HITS
F. McCormick CIN 191
Stan Hack CHI 191
Johnny Mize STL 182

DOUBLES
F. McCormick CIN 44
Arky Vaughan PIT 40
Jim Gleeson CHI 39

TRIPLES
Arky Vaughan PIT 15

Chet Ross BOS 14
three tied at 13

HOME RUNS
Johnny Mize STL 43
Bill Nicholson CHI 25
J. Rizzo PIT, CIN, PHI 24

RUNS BATTED IN
Johnny Mize STL 137
F. McCormick CIN 127
M. Van Robays PIT 116

STOLEN BASES
Lonny Frey CIN 22
Stan Hack CHI 21
Terry Moore STL 18

RUNS SCORED
Arky Vaughan PIT 113
Johnny Mize STL 111
Bill Werber CIN 105

WINS
Bucky Walters CIN 22
Paul Derringer CIN 20
Claude Passeau CHI 20

EARNED RUN AVERAGE
Bucky Walters CIN 2.48
C. Passeau CHI 2.50

STRIKEOUTS
Kirby Higbe PHI 137
Whit Wyatt BKN 124
C. Passeau CHI 124

SAVES
three tied at 7

COMPLETE GAMES
Bucky Walters CIN 29

SHUTOUTS
Manny Salvo BOS 5
Whit Wyatt BKN 5

INNINGS PITCHED
Bucky Walters CIN 305

	W	L	PCT	GB	R	OR
★ NY	101	53	.656	—	830	631
BOS	84	70	.545	17	865	750
CHI	77	77	.500	24	638	649
CLE	75	79	.487	26	677	668
DET	75	79	.487	26	686	743
STL	70	84	.455	31	765	823
WAS	70	84	.455	31	728	798
PHI	64	90	.416	37	713	840
					5902	5902

BATTING AVERAGE
Ted Williams BOS .... .406
Cecil Travis WAS .... .359
Joe DiMaggio NY .... .357

HITS
Cecil Travis WAS 218
Jeff Heath CLE 199
Joe DiMaggio NY 193

DOUBLES
Lou Boudreau CLE 45
Joe DiMaggio NY 43
Walt Judnich STL 40

TRIPLES
Jeff Heath CLE 20

Cecil Travis WAS 19
Ken Keltner CLE 13

HOME RUNS
Ted Williams BOS 37
Charlie Keller NY 33
Tommy Henrich NY 31

RUNS BATTED IN
Joe DiMaggio NY 125
Jeff Heath CLE 123
Charlie Keller NY 122

STOLEN BASES
George Case WAS 33
Joe Kuhel CHI 20
Jeff Heath CLE 18

RUNS SCORED
Ted Williams BOS 135
Joe DiMaggio NY 122
Dom DiMaggio BOS 117

WINS
Bob Feller CLE 25
Thorton Lee CHI 22
Dick Newsome BOS 19

EARNED RUN AVERAGE
Thorton Lee CHI 2.37
Al Benton DET 2.97
C. Wagner BOS 3.07

STRIKEOUTS
Bob Feller CLE 260
Bobo Newsom DET 175
Thorton Lee CHI 130

SAVES
Johnny Murphy NY 15

COMPLETE GAMES
Thonton Lee CHI 30

SHUTOUTS
Bob Feller CLE 6

INNINGS PITCHED
Bob Feller CLE 343

	W	L	PCT	GB	R	OR
BKN	100	54	.649	—	800	581
STL	97	56	.634	2.5	734	589
CIN	88	66	.571	12	616	564
PIT	81	73	.526	19	690	643
NY	74	79	.484	25.5	667	706
CHI	70	84	.455	30	666	670
BOS	62	92	.403	38	592	720
PHI	43	111	.279	57	501	793
					5266	5266

BATTING AVERAGE
Pete Reiser BKN .... .343
J. Cooney BOS .... .319
Joe Medwick BKN .... .318

HITS
Stan Hack CHI 186
Pete Reiser BKN 184
Danny Litwhiler PHI 180

DOUBLES
Pete Reiser BKN 39
Johnny Mize STL 39
Johnny Rucker NY 38

TRIPLES
Pete Reiser BKN 17

Elbie Fletcher PIT 13
Johnny Hopp STL 11

HOME RUNS
Dolf Camilli BKN 34
Mel Ott NY 27
Bill Nicholson CHI 26

RUNS BATTED IN
Dolf Camilli BKN 120
Bobby Young NY 104
two tied at 100

STOLEN BASES
Danny Murtaugh PHI 18
Stan Benjamin PHI 17
two tied at 16

RUNS SCORED
Pete Reiser BKN 117
Stan Hack CHI 111
Joe Medwick BKN 100

WINS
Kirby Higbe BKN 22
Whit Wyatt BKN 22
two tied at 19

EARNED RUN AVERAGE
Elmer Riddle CIN 2.24
Whit Wyatt BKN 2.34
Ernie White STL 2.40

STRIKEOUTS
J. Vander Meer CIN 202
Whit Wyatt BKN 176
Bucky Walters CIN 129

SAVES
Jumbo Brown NY 8

COMPLETE GAMES
Bucky Walters CIN 27

SHUTOUTS
Whit Wyatt BKN 7

INNINGS PITCHED
Bucky Walters CIN 302

	W	L	PCT	GB	R	OR
NY	103	51	.669	—	801	507
BOS	93	59	.612	9	761	594
STL	82	69	.543	19.5	730	637
CLE	75	79	.487	28	590	659
DET	73	81	.474	30	589	587
CHI	66	82	.446	34	538	609
WAS	62	89	.411	39.5	653	817
PHI	55	99	.357	48	549	801
					5211	5211

BATTING AVERAGE
Ted Williams BOS .... .356
Johnny Pesky BOS.......... .331
Stan Spence WAS........... .323

HITS
Johnny Pesky BOS.......... 205
Stan Spence WAS........... 203
two tied at 186

DOUBLES
Don Kolloway CHI 40
Harlond Clift STL 39
Jeff Heath CLE 37

TRIPLES
Stan Spence WAS.............. 15

Jeff Heath CLE 13
Joe DiMaggio NY................ 13

HOME RUNS
Ted Williams BOS 36
Chet Laabs STL.................. 27
Charlie Keller NY 26

RUNS BATTED IN
Ted Williams BOS 137
Joe DiMaggio NY.............. 114
Charlie Keller NY 108

STOLEN BASES
George Case WAS 44
Mickey Vernon WAS........... 25
two tied at 22

RUNS SCORED
Ted Williams BOS 141
Joe DiMaggio NY 123
Dom DiMaggio BOS 110

WINS
Tex Hughson BOS.............. 22
Ernie Bonham NY 21
two tied at 17

EARNED RUN AVERAGE
Ted Lyons CHI 2.10
Ernie Bonham NY 2.27
Spud Chandler NY........... 2.38

STRIKEOUTS
Bobo Newsom WAS 113
Tex Hughson BOS............ 113

SAVES
Johnny Murphy NY 11

COMPLETE GAMES
Ernie Bonham NY............... 22
Tex Hughson BOS............... 22

SHUTOUTS
Ernie Bonham NY................. 6

INNINGS PITCHED
Tex Hughson BOS............ 281

	W	L	PCT	GB	R	OR
★ STL	106	48	.688	—	755	482
BKN	104	50	.675	2	742	510
NY	85	67	.559	20	675	600
CIN	76	76	.500	29	527	545
PIT	66	81	.449	36.5	585	631
CHI	68	86	.442	38	591	665
BOS	59	89	.399	44	515	645
PHI	42	109	.278	62.5	394	706
					4784	4784

BATTING AVERAGE
Ernie Lombardi BOS........ .330
Enos Slaughter STL .... .318
Stan Musial STL .... .315

HITS
Enos Slaughter STL 188
Bill Nicholson CHI 173
three tied at...................... 166

DOUBLES
Marty Marion STL.............. 38
Joe Medwick BKN.............. 37
Stan Hack CHI................... 36

TRIPLES
Enos Slaughter STL 17

Bill Nicholson CHI 11
Stan Musial STL 10

HOME RUNS
Mel Ott NY 30
Johnny Mize NY 26
Dolf Camilli BKN 26

RUNS BATTED IN
Johnny Mize NY 110
Dolf Camilli BKN 109
Enos Slaughter STL 98

STOLEN BASES
Pete Reiser BKN 20
N. Fernandez BOS 15
Pee Wee Reese BKN......... 15

RUNS SCORED
Mel Ott NY 118
Enos Slaughter STL 100
Johnny Mize NY 97

WINS
Mort Cooper STL 22
Johnny Beazley STL........... 21
two tied at 19

EARNED RUN AVERAGE
Mort Cooper STL 1.78
Johnny Beazley STL.......... 2.13
Curt Davis BKN 2.36

STRIKEOUTS
J. Vander Meer CIN.......... 186
Mort Cooper STL 152
Kirby Higbe BKN 115

SAVES
Hugh Casey BKN 13

COMPLETE GAMES
Jim Tobin BOS 28

SHUTOUTS
Mort Cooper STL 10

INNINGS PITCHED
Jim Tobin BOS 288

	W	L	PCT	GB	R	OR
★ NY	98	56	.636	—	669	542
WAS	84	69	.549	13.5	666	595
CLE	82	71	.536	15.5	600	577
CHI	82	72	.532	16	573	594
DET	78	76	.506	20	632	560
STL	72	80	.474	25	596	604
BOS	68	84	.447	29	563	607
PHI	49	105	.318	49	497	717
					4796	4796

BATTING AVERAGE
Luke Appling CHI .... .328
Dick Wakefield DET .... .316
Ralph Hodgin CHI .... .314

HITS
Dick Wakefield DET 200
Luke Appling CHI 192
Doc Cramer DET 182

DOUBLES
Dick Wakefield DET 38
George Case WAS 36
two tied at 35

TRIPLES
Johnny Lindell NY 12

Wally Moses CHI 12
two tied at 11

HOME RUNS
Rudy York DET 34
Charlie Keller NY 31
Vern Stephens STL 22

RUNS BATTED IN
Rudy York DET 118
Nick Etten NY 107
Billy Johnson NY 94

STOLEN BASES
George Case WAS 61
Wally Moses CHI 56
Thurman Tucker CHI 29

RUNS SCORED
George Case WAS 102
Charlie Keller NY 97
Dick Wakefield DET 91

WINS
Spud Chandler NY 20
Dizzy Trout DET 20
Early Wynn WAS 18

EARNED RUN AVERAGE
Spud Chandler NY 1.64
Ernie Bonham NY 2.27

STRIKEOUTS
Allie Reynolds CLE 151
Hal Newhouser DET 144

SAVES
G. Maltzberger CHI 14

COMPLETE GAMES
Spud Chandler NY 20
Tex Hughson BOS 20

SHUTOUTS
Spud Chandler NY 5
Dizzy Trout DET 5

INNINGS PITCHED
Jim Bagby CLE 273

	W	L	PCT	GB	R	OR
STL	105	49	.682	—	679	475
CIN	87	67	.565	18	608	543
BKN	81	72	.529	23.5	716	674
PIT	80	74	.519	25	669	605
CHI	74	79	.484	30.5	632	600
BOS	68	85	.444	36.5	465	612
PHI	64	90	.416	41	571	676
NY	55	98	.359	49.5	558	713
					4898	4898

BATTING AVERAGE
Stan Musial STL .... .357
Billy Herman BKN .... .330
Walker Cooper STL .... .318

HITS
Stan Musial STL 220
Mickey Witek NY 195
Billy Herman BKN 193

DOUBLES
Stan Musial STL 48
Vince DiMaggio PIT 41
Billy Herman BKN 41

TRIPLES
Stan Musial STL 20

Lou Klein STL 14
two tied at 12

HOME RUNS
Bill Nicholson CHI 29
Mel Ott NY 18
Ron Northey PHI 16

RUNS BATTED IN
Bill Nicholson CHI 128
Bob Elliott PIT 101
Billy Herman BKN 100

STOLEN BASES
Arky Vaughan BKN 20
Peanuts Lowrey CHI 13
three tied at 12

RUNS SCORED
Arky Vaughan BKN 112
Stan Musial STL 108
Bill Nicholson CHI 95

WINS
Elmer Riddle CIN 21
Mort Cooper STL 21
Rip Sewell PIT 21

EARNED RUN AVERAGE
Max Lanier STL 1.90
Mort Cooper STL 2.30
Whit Wyatt BKN 2.49

STRIKEOUTS
J. Vander Meer CIN 174
Mort Cooper STL 141
Al Javery BOS 134

SAVES
Les Webber BKN 10

COMPLETE GAMES
Rip Sewell PIT 25

SHUTOUTS
Hi Bithorn CHI 7

INNINGS PITCHED
Al Javery BOS 303

	W	L	PCT	GB	R	OR
STL	89	65	.578	—	684	587
DET	88	66	.571	1	658	581
NY	83	71	.539	6	674	617
BOS	77	77	.500	12	739	676
CLE	72	82	.468	17	643	677
PHI	72	82	.468	17	525	594
CHI	71	83	.461	18	543	662
WAS	64	90	.416	25	592	664
					5058	5058

BATTING AVERAGE
Lou Boudreau CLE .... .327
Bobby Doerr BOS .... .325
Bob Johnson BOS .... .324

HITS
S. Stirnweiss NY 205
Lou Boudreau CLE 191
Stan Spence WAS 187

DOUBLES
Lou Boudreau CLE 45
Ken Keltner CLE 41
Bob Johnson BOS 40

TRIPLES
Johnny Lindell NY.............. 16

Snuffy Stirnweiss NY 16
Don Gutteridge STL............ 11

HOME RUNS
Nick Etten NY 22
Vern Stephens STL 20
three tied at...................... 18

RUNS BATTED IN
Vern Stephens STL 109
Bob Johnson BOS 106
Johnny Lindell NY............ 103

STOLEN BASES
Snuffy Stirnweiss NY 55
George Case WAS 49
Glenn Myatt WAS 26

RUNS SCORED
S. Stirnweiss NY................ 125
Bob Johnson BOS 106
Roy Cullenbine CLE 98

WINS
Hal Newhouser DET.......... 29
Dizzy Trout DET 27
Nels Potter STL 19

EARNED RUN AVERAGE
Dizzy Trout DET 2.12
H. Newhouser DET.......... 2.22
Tex Hughson BOS........... 2.26

STRIKEOUTS
Hal Newhouser DET 187
Dizzy Trout DET 144
Bobo Newsom PHI 142

SAVES
three tied at...................... 12

COMPLETE GAMES
Dizzy Trout DET 33

SHUTOUTS
Dizzy Trout DET 7

INNINGS PITCHED
Dizzy Trout DET 352

	W	L	PCT	GB	R	OR
★ STL	105	49	.682	—	772	490
PIT	90	63	.588	14.5	744	662
CIN	89	65	.578	16	573	537
CHI	75	79	.487	30	702	669
NY	67	87	.435	38	682	773
BOS	65	89	.422	40	593	674
BKN	63	91	.409	42	690	832
PHI	61	92	.399	43.5	539	658
					5295	5295

BATTING AVERAGE
Dixie Walker BKN .... .357
Stan Musial STL .... .347
Joe Medwick NY .... .337

HITS
Phil Cavarretta CHI........... 197
Stan Musial STL 197
T. Holmes BOS................. 195

DOUBLES
Stan Musial STL 51
Augie Galan BKN 43
T. Holmes BOS.................. 42

TRIPLES
Johnny Barrett PIT.............. 19

Bob Elliott PIT.................... 16
Phil Cavarretta CHI............. 15

HOME RUNS
Bill Nicholson CHI.............. 33
Mel Ott NY 26
Ron Northey PHI 22

RUNS BATTED IN
Bill Nicholson CHI............ 122
Bob Elliott PIT.................. 108
Ron Northey PHI 104

STOLEN BASES
Johnny Barrett PIT............. 28
Tony Lupien PHI................. 18
Roy Hughes CHI................ 16

RUNS SCORED
Bill Nicholson CHI............. 116
Stan Musial STL 112
Jim Russell PIT................. 109

WINS
Bucky Walters CIN 23
Mort Cooper STL 22
two tied at 21

EARNED RUN AVERAGE
Ed Heusser CIN 2.38
Bucky Walters CIN 2.40
Mort Cooper STL 2.46

STRIKEOUTS
Bill Voiselle NY 161
Max Lanier STL 141
Al Javery BOS 137

SAVES
Ace Adams NY 13

COMPLETE GAMES
Jim Tobin BOS 28

SHUTOUTS
Mort Cooper STL 7

INNINGS PITCHED
Bill Voiselle NY 313

	W	L	PCT	GB	R	OR
★ DET	88	65	.575	—	633	565
WAS	87	67	.565	1.5	622	562
STL	81	70	.536	6	597	548
NY	81	71	.533	6.5	676	606
CLE	73	72	.503	11	557	548
CHI	71	78	.477	15	596	633
BOS	71	83	.461	17.5	599	674
PHI	52	98	.347	34.5	494	638
					4774	4774

BATTING AVERAGE
S. Stirnweiss NY .... .309
T. Cuccinello CHI.............. .308
J. Dickshot CHI .... .302

HITS
S. Stirnweiss NY 195
Wally Moses CHI 168
Vern Stephens STL 165

DOUBLES
Wally Moses CHI 35
Snuffy Stirnweiss NY 32
George Binks WAS............ 32

TRIPLES
Snuffy Stirnweiss NY 22

Wally Moses CHI 15
Joe Kuhel WAS 13

HOME RUNS
Vern Stephens STL 24
three tied at....................... 18

RUNS BATTED IN
Nick Etten NY 111
Roy Cullenbine CLE, DET .. 93
Vern Stephens STL 89

STOLEN BASES
Snuffy Stirnweiss NY 33
George Case WAS 30
Glenn Myatt WAS 30

RUNS SCORED
S. Stirnweiss NY 107
Vern Stephens STL 90
Roy Cullenbine CLE, DET .. 83

WINS
Hal Newhouser DET 25
Boo Ferriss BOS................ 21
Roger Wolff WAS 20

EARNED RUN AVERAGE
H. Newhouser DET.......... 1.81
Al Benton DET 2.02
Roger Wolff WAS 2.12

STRIKEOUTS
Hal Newhouser DET 212
Nels Potter STL 129
Bobo Newsom PHI 127

SAVES
Jim Turner NY 10

COMPLETE GAMES
Hal Newhouser DET........... 29

SHUTOUTS
Hal Newhouser DET............. 8

INNINGS PITCHED
Hal Newhouser DET........ 313

	W	L	PCT	GB	R	OR
CHI	98	56	.636	—	735	532
STL	95	59	.617	3	756	583
BKN	87	67	.565	11	795	724
PIT	82	72	.532	16	753	686
NY	78	74	.513	19	668	700
BOS	67	85	.441	30	721	728
CIN	61	93	.396	37	536	694
PHI	46	108	.299	52	548	865
					5512	5512

BATTING AVERAGE
Phil Cavarretta CHI.......... .355
Tommy Holmes BOS....... .352
Goody Rosen BKN .... .325

HITS
Tommy Holmes BOS 224
Goody Rosen BKN 197
Stan Hack CHI 193

DOUBLES
Tommy Holmes BOS 47
Dixie Walker BKN 42
two tied at 36

TRIPLES
Luis Olmo BKN 13

Andy Pafko CHI 12
two tied at 11

HOME RUNS
Tommy Holmes BOS.......... 28
Chuck Workman BOS 25
B. Adams PHI, STL 22

RUNS BATTED IN
Dixie Walker BKN 124
Tommy Holmes BOS....... 117
two tied at 110

STOLEN BASES
R. Schoendienst STL......... 26
Johnny Barrett PIT............. 25
Dain Clay CIN..................... 19

RUNS SCORED
Eddie Stanky BKN 128
Goody Rosen BKN 126
Tommy Holmes BOS........ 125

WINS
R. Barrett BOS, STL 23
Hank Wyse CHI 22
two tied at 19

EARNED RUN AVERAGE
Ray Prim CHI................... 2.40
C. Passeau CHI............... 2.46
Harry Brecheen STL........ 2.52

STRIKEOUTS
Preacher Roe PIT............. 148
Hal Gregg BKN 139

SAVES
Ace Adams NY 15
Andy Karl PHI 15

COMPLETE GAMES
R. Barrett BOS, STL.......... 24

SHUTOUTS
Claude Passeau CHI............ 5

INNINGS PITCHED
R. Barrett BOS, STL 285

1946 AL

	W	L	PCT	GB	R	OR	BA	FA	ERA
BOSTON	104	50	.675	—	792	594	.271	.977	3.38
DETROIT	92	62	.597	12	704	567	.258	.974	3.22
NEW YORK	87	67	.565	17	684	547	.248	.975	3.13
WASHINGTON	76	78	.494	28	608	706	.260	.966	3.74
CHICAGO	74	80	.481	30	562	595	.257	.972	3.10
CLEVELAND	68	86	.442	36	537	638	.245	.975	3.62
ST. LOUIS	66	88	.429	38	621	710	.251	.974	3.95
PHILADELPHIA	49	105	.318	55	529	680	.253	.971	3.90
					5037	5037	.256	.973	3.50

BATTING AVERAGE
Mickey Vernon WAS . .353
Ted Williams BOS...... .342
Johnny Pesky BOS.... .335

HITS
Johnny Pesky BOS..... 208
Mickey Vernon WAS... 207
Luke Appling CHI........ 180

DOUBLES
Mickey Vernon WAS..... 51
Stan Spence WAS........ 50
Johnny Pesky BOS....... 43

TRIPLES
Hank Edwards CLE 16
Buddy Lewis WAS 13
three tied at................... 10

HOME RUNS
Hank Greenberg DET ... 44
Ted Williams BOS......... 38
Charlie Keller NY 30

RUNS BATTED IN
Hank Greenberg DET. 127
Ted Williams BOS....... 123
Rudy York BOS 119

SLUGGING AVERAGE
Ted Williams BOS...... .667
Hank Greenberg DET .604
Charlie Keller NY .... .533

STOLEN BASES
George Case CLE 28
Snuffy Stirnweiss NY 18
Eddie Lake DET............ 15

RUNS SCORED
Ted Williams BOS....... 142
Johnny Pesky BOS..... 115
Eddie Lake DET.......... 105

WINS
Hal Newhouser DET 26
Bob Feller CLE 26
Boo Ferriss BOS........... 25

WINNING PERCENTAGE
Boo Ferriss BOS........ .806
Hal Newhouser DET .. .743
Spud Chandler NY...... .714

EARNED RUN AVERAGE
Hal Newhouser DET .. 1.94
Spud Chandler NY..... 2.10
Bob Feller CLE 2.18

STRIKEOUTS
Bob Feller CLE 348
Hal Newhouser DET ... 275
Tex Hughson BOS...... 172

SAVES
Bob Klinger BOS............. 9
Earl Caldwell CHI............ 8
Johnny Murphy NY 7

COMPLETE GAMES
Bob Feller CLE 36
Hal Newhouser DET..... 29
Boo Ferriss BOS........... 26

SHUTOUTS
Bob Feller CLE 10
four tied at....................... 6

GAMES PITCHED
Bob Feller CLE 48
Boo Ferriss BOS........... 40
Bob Savage PHI 40

INNINGS PITCHED
Bob Feller CLE 371
Hal Newhouser DET ... 292
Tex Hughson BOS...... 278

1946 NL

	W	L	PCT	GB	R	OR	BA	FA	ERA
★ ST. LOUIS*	98	58	.628	—	712	545	.265	.980	3.01
BROOKLYN	96	60	.615	2	701	570	.260	.972	3.05
CHICAGO	82	71	.536	14.5	626	581	.254	.976	3.24
BOSTON	81	72	.529	15.5	630	592	.264	.972	3.35
PHILADELPHIA	69	85	.448	28	560	705	.258	.975	3.99
CINCINNATI	67	87	.435	30	523	570	.239	.975	3.08
PITTSBURGH	63	91	.409	34	552	668	.250	.970	3.72
NEW YORK	61	93	.396	36	612	685	.255	.973	3.92
					4916	4916	.256	.974	3.42

*Defeated Brooklyn in a playoff 2 games to 0

BATTING AVERAGE
Stan Musial STL .... .365
Johnny Hopp BOS ..... .333
Dixie Walker BKN .... .319

HITS
Stan Musial STL 228
Dixie Walker BKN 184
Enos Slaughter STL.... 183

DOUBLES
Stan Musial STL 50
Tommy Holmes BOS 35
Whitey Kurowski STL.... 32

TRIPLES
Stan Musial STL 20
Phil Cavarretta CHI...... 10
Pee Wee Reese BKN ... 10

HOME RUNS
Ralph Kiner PIT 23
Johnny Mize NY............ 22
Enos Slaughter STL...... 18

RUNS BATTED IN
Enos Slaughter STL.... 130
Dixie Walker BKN 116
Stan Musial STL 103

SLUGGING AVERAGE
Stan Musial STL .... .587
Del Ennis PHI .... .485
Enos Slaughter STL.... .465

STOLEN BASES
Pete Reiser BKN........... 34
Bert Haas CIN............... 22
Johnny Hopp BOS 21

RUNS SCORED
Stan Musial STL 124
Enos Slaughter STL.... 100
Eddie Stanky BKN 98

WINS
Howie Pollet STL 21
Johnny Sain BOS 20
Kirby Higbe BKN........... 17

WINNING PERCENTAGE
Murry Dickson STL .... .714
Kirby Higbe BKN........ .680
Howie Pollet STL .... .677

EARNED RUN AVERAGE
Howie Pollet STL 2.10
Johnny Sain BOS 2.21
Joe Beggs CIN........... 2.32

STRIKEOUTS
Johnny Schmitz CHI ... 135
Kirby Higbe BKN......... 134
Johnny Sain BOS 129

SAVES
Ken Raffensberger PHI... 6
four tied at...................... 5

COMPLETE GAMES
Johnny Sain BOS 24
Howie Pollet STL 22
Dave Koslo NY 17

SHUTOUTS
Ewell Blackwell CIN........ 6
Harry Brecheen STL....... 5
three tied at..................... 4

GAMES PITCHED
Ken Trinkle NY.............. 48
Murry Dickson STL 47
Hank Behrman BKN 47

INNINGS PITCHED
Howie Pollet STL 266
Dave Koslo NY 265
Johnny Sain BOS 265

1947 AL

	W	L	PCT	GB	R	OR	BA	FA	ERA
★ NEW YORK	97	57	.630	—	794	568	.271	.981	3.39
DETROIT	85	69	.552	12	714	642	.258	.975	3.57
BOSTON	83	71	.539	14	720	669	.265	.977	3.81
CLEVELAND	80	74	.519	17	687	588	.259	.983	3.44
PHILADELPHIA	78	76	.506	19	633	614	.252	.976	3.51
CHICAGO	70	84	.455	27	553	661	.256	.975	3.64
WASHINGTON	64	90	.416	33	496	675	.241	.976	3.97
ST. LOUIS	59	95	.383	38	564	744	.241	.977	4.33
					5161	5161	.256	.977	3.71

BATTING AVERAGE
Ted Williams BOS...... .343
B. McCoskey PHI....... .328
Johnny Pesky BOS.... .324

HITS
Johnny Pesky BOS..... 207
George Kell DET......... 188
Ted Williams BOS....... 181

DOUBLES
Lou Boudreau CLE 45
Ted Williams BOS......... 40
Tommy Henrich NY 35

TRIPLES
Tommy Henrich NY 13
Mickey Vernon WAS..... 12
Dave Philley CHI........... 11

HOME RUNS
Ted Williams BOS......... 32
Joe Gordon CLE 29
Jeff Heath STL.............. 27

RUNS BATTED IN
Ted Williams BOS....... 114
Tommy Henrich NY 98
Joe DiMaggio NY 97

SLUGGING AVERAGE
Ted Williams BOS....... .634
Joe DiMaggio NY ...... .522
Joe Gordon CLE .... .496

STOLEN BASES
Bob Dillinger STL.......... 34
Dave Philley CHI........... 21
two tied at 12

RUNS SCORED
Ted Williams BOS....... 125
Tommy Henrich NY 109
Johnny Pesky BOS..... 106

WINS
Bob Feller CLE 20
Allie Reynolds NY 19
Phil Marchildon PHI 19

WINNING PERCENTAGE
Allie Reynolds NY ...... .704
Joe Dobson BOS .... .692
Phil Marchildon PHI ... .679

EARNED RUN AVERAGE
Joe Haynes CHI......... 2.42
Bob Feller CLE 2.68
Dick Fowler PHI 2.81

STRIKEOUTS
Bob Feller CLE 196
Hal Newhouser DET.... 176
W. Masterson WAS 135

SAVES
Joe Page NY................. 17
Eddie Klieman CLE....... 17
Russ Christopher PHI ... 12

COMPLETE GAMES
Hal Newhouser DET.... 24
Early Wynn WAS 22
Eddie Lopat CHI 22

SHUTOUTS
Bob Feller CLE 5
three tied at.................... 4

GAMES PITCHED
Eddie Klieman CLE....... 58
Joe Page NY................. 56
Earl Johnson BOS 45

INNINGS PITCHED
Bob Feller CLE 299
Hal Newhouser DET ... 285
Phil Marchildon PHI 277

1947 NL

	W	L	PCT	GB	R	OR	BA	FA	ERA
BROOKLYN	94	60	.610	—	774	668	.272	.978	3.82
ST. LOUIS	89	65	.578	5	780	634	.270	.979	3.53
BOSTON	86	68	.558	8	701	622	.275	.974	3.62
NEW YORK	81	73	.526	13	830	761	.271	.974	4.44
CINCINNATI	73	81	.474	21	681	755	.259	.977	4.41
CHICAGO	69	85	.448	25	567	722	.259	.975	4.04
PHILADELPHIA	62	92	.403	32	589	687	.258	.974	3.96
PITTSBURGH	62	92	.403	32	744	817	.261	.975	4.68
					5666	5666	.265	.976	4.06

BATTING AVERAGE
H. Walker STL, PHI ... .363
Bob Elliott BOS .... .317
Phil Cavarretta CHI.... .314

HITS
Tommy Holmes BOS.. 191
H. Walker STL, PHI 186
two tied at 183

DOUBLES
Eddie Miller CIN............ 38
Bob Elliott BOS 35
two tied at 33

TRIPLES
H. Walker STL, PHI 16
Stan Musial STL 13
Enos Slaughter STL...... 13

HOME RUNS
Ralph Kiner PIT 51
Johnny Mize NY............ 51
Willard Marshall NY 36

RUNS BATTED IN
Johnny Mize NY.......... 138
Ralph Kiner PIT 127
Walker Cooper NY 122

SLUGGING AVERAGE
Ralph Kiner PIT .... .639
Johnny Mize NY......... .614
Walker Cooper NY ..... .586

STOLEN BASES
Jackie Robinson BKN ... 29
Pete Reiser BKN........... 14
two tied at 13

RUNS SCORED
Johnny Mize NY.......... 137
J. Robinson BKN 125
Ralph Kiner PIT 118

WINS
Ewell Blackwell CIN 22
four tied at..................... 21

WINNING PERCENTAGE
Larry Jansen NY .... .808
G. Munger STL .... .762
Ewell Blackwell CIN .... .733

EARNED RUN AVERAGE
Warren Spahn BOS..... 2.33
Ewell Blackwell CIN 2.47
Ralph Branca BKN..... 2.67

STRIKEOUTS
Ewell Blackwell CIN 193
Ralph Branca BKN...... 148
Johnny Sain BOS 132

SAVES
Hugh Casey BKN........... 18
Harry Gumbert CIN....... 10
Ken Trinkle NY.............. 10

COMPLETE GAMES
Ewell Blackwell CIN 23
Johnny Sain BOS 22
Warren Spahn BOS...... 22

SHUTOUTS
Warren Spahn BOS........ 7
George Munger STL 6
Ewell Blackwell CIN 6

GAMES PITCHED
Ken Trinkle NY.............. 62
Kirby Higbe BKN, PIT ... 50
H. Behrman PIT, BKN... 50

INNINGS PITCHED
Warren Spahn BOS.... 290
Ralph Branca BKN...... 280
Ewell Blackwell CIN 273

1948 AL

	W	L	PCT	GB	R	OR	BA	FA	ERA
★ CLEVELAND*	97	58	.626	—	840	568	.282	.982	3.22
BOSTON	96	59	.619	1	907	720	.274	.981	4.26
NEW YORK	94	60	.610	2.5	857	633	.278	.979	3.75
PHILADELPHIA	84	70	.545	12.5	729	735	.260	.981	4.43
DETROIT	78	76	.506	18.5	700	726	.267	.974	4.15
ST. LOUIS	59	94	.386	37	671	849	.271	.972	5.01
WASHINGTON	56	97	.366	40	578	796	.244	.974	4.65
CHICAGO	51	101	.336	44.5	559	814	.251	.974	4.89
					5841	5841	.266	.977	4.29

* Defeated Boston in a 1-game playoff

BATTING AVERAGE
Ted Williams BOS...... .369
Lou Boudreau CLE .... .355
Dale Mitchell CLE ...... .336

HITS
Bob Dillinger STL........ 207
Dale Mitchell CLE 204
Lou Boudreau CLE 199

DOUBLES
Ted Williams BOS......... 44
Tommy Henrich NY 42
Hank Majeski PHI 41

TRIPLES
Tommy Henrich NY 14
B. Stewart NY, WAS..... 13
three tied at.................. 11

HOME RUNS
Joe DiMaggio NY.......... 39
Joe Gordon CLE........... 32
Ken Keltner CLE........... 31

RUNS BATTED IN
Joe DiMaggio NY........ 155
Vern Stephens BOS ... 137
Ted Williams BOS....... 127

SLUGGING AVERAGE
Ted Williams BOS...... .615
Joe DiMaggio NY........ .598
Tommy Henrich NY ... .554

STOLEN BASES
Bob Dillinger STL.......... 28
Gill Coan WAS.............. 23
Mickey Vernon WAS..... 15

RUNS SCORED
Tommy Henrich NY 138
Dom DiMaggio BOS ... 127
two tied at 124

WINS
Hal Newhouser DET..... 21
Gene Bearden CLE 20
Bob Lemon CLE 20

WINNING PERCENTAGE
Jack Kramer BOS ...... .783
Gene Bearden CLE ... .741
Vic Raschi NY............ .704

EARNED RUN AVERAGE
Gene Bearden CLE ... 2.43
R. Scarborough WAS. 2.82
Bob Lemon CLE 2.82

STRIKEOUTS
Bob Feller CLE 164
Bob Lemon CLE 147
Hal Newhouser DET... 143

SAVES
R. Christopher CLE....... 17
Joe Page NY................. 16
two tied at 10

COMPLETE GAMES
Bob Lemon CLE 20
Hal Newhouser DET..... 19
two tied at 18

SHUTOUTS
Bob Lemon CLE 10
Gene Bearden CLE 6
Vic Raschi NY................. 6

GAMES PITCHED
Joe Page NY................. 55
Al Widmar STL.............. 49
Frank Biscan STL 47

INNINGS PITCHED
Bob Lemon CLE 294
Bob Feller CLE 280
Hal Newhouser DET... 272

1948 NL

	W	L	PCT	GB	R	OR	BA	FA	ERA
BOSTON	91	62	.595	—	739	584	.275	.976	3.37
ST. LOUIS	85	69	.552	6.5	742	646	.263	.980	3.91
BROOKLYN	84	70	.545	7.5	744	667	.261	.973	3.75
PITTSBURGH	83	71	.539	8.5	706	699	.263	.977	4.15
NEW YORK	78	76	.506	13.5	780	704	.256	.974	3.93
PHILADELPHIA	66	88	.429	25.5	591	729	.259	.964	4.08
CINCINNATI	64	89	.418	27	588	752	.247	.973	4.47
CHICAGO	64	90	.416	27.5	597	706	.262	.972	4.00
					5487	5487	.261	.974	3.95

BATTING AVERAGE
Stan Musial STL .... .376
Richie Ashburn PHI ... .333
Tommy Holmes BOS . .325

HITS
Stan Musial STL 230
Tommy Holmes BOS.. 190
Stan Rojek PIT............ 186

DOUBLES
Stan Musial STL 46
Del Ennis PHI 40
Alvin Dark BOS............. 39

TRIPLES
Stan Musial STL 18
Johnny Hopp PIT.......... 12
Enos Slaughter STL...... 11

HOME RUNS
Johnny Mize NY............ 40
Ralph Kiner PIT 40
Stan Musial STL 39

RUNS BATTED IN
Stan Musial STL 131
Johnny Mize NY.......... 125
Ralph Kiner PIT 123

SLUGGING AVERAGE
Stan Musial STL .... .702
Johnny Mize NY.......... .564
Sid Gordon NY............ .537

STOLEN BASES
Richie Ashburn PHI 32
Pee Wee Reese BKN ... 25
Stan Rojek PIT.............. 24

RUNS SCORED
Stan Musial STL 135
Whitey Lockman NY ... 117
Johnny Mize NY.......... 110

WINS
Johnny Sain BOS 24
Harry Brecheen STL..... 20
two tied at 18

WINNING PERCENTAGE
H. Brecheen STL .... .741
Sheldon Jones NY ..... .667
Johnny Sain BOS ...... .615

EARNED RUN AVERAGE
H. Brecheen STL 2.24
Dutch Leonard PHI 2.51
Johnny Sain BOS 2.60

STRIKEOUTS
Harry Brecheen STL... 149
Rex Barney BKN......... 138
Johnny Sain BOS 137

SAVES
Harry Gumbert CIN....... 17
Ted Wilks STL 13
Kirby Higbe PIT............. 10

COMPLETE GAMES
Johnny Sain BOS 28
Harry Brecheen STL..... 21
Johnny Schmitz CHI 18

SHUTOUTS
Harry Brecheen STL....... 7
four tied at...................... 4

GAMES PITCHED
Harry Gumbert CIN....... 61
Ted Wilks STL 57
Kirby Higbe PIT............. 56

INNINGS PITCHED
Johnny Sain BOS 315
Larry Jansen NY 277
Warren Spahn BOS 257

1949 AL

	W	L	PCT	GB	R	OR	BA	FA	ERA
★ NEW YORK	97	57	.630	—	829	637	.269	.977	3.69
BOSTON	96	58	.623	1	896	667	.282	.980	3.97
CLEVELAND	89	65	.578	8	675	574	.260	.983	3.36
DETROIT	87	67	.565	10	751	655	.267	.978	3.77
PHILADELPHIA	81	73	.526	16	726	725	.260	.976	4.23
CHICAGO	63	91	.409	34	648	737	.257	.977	4.30
ST. LOUIS	53	101	.344	44	667	913	.254	.971	5.21
WASHINGTON	50	104	.325	47	584	868	.254	.973	5.10
					5776	5776	.263	.977	4.20

BATTING AVERAGE
George Kell DET........ .343
Ted Williams BOS...... .343
Bob Dillinger STL........ .324

HITS
Dale Mitchell CLE 203
Ted Williams BOS....... 194
Dom DiMaggio BOS ... 186

DOUBLES
Ted Williams BOS......... 39
George Kell DET........... 38
Dom DiMaggio BOS ... 34

TRIPLES
Dale Mitchell CLE 23
Bob Dillinger STL.......... 13
Elmer Valo PHI 12

HOME RUNS
Ted Williams BOS......... 43
Vern Stephens BOS 39
four tied at..................... 24

RUNS BATTED IN
Vern Stephens BOS ... 159
Ted Williams BOS....... 159
Vic Wertz DET 133

SLUGGING AVERAGE
Ted Williams BOS....... .650
V. Stephens BOS........ .539
Tommy Henrich NY ... .526

STOLEN BASES
Bob Dillinger STL.......... 20
Phil Rizzuto NY............. 18
Elmer Valo PHI 14

RUNS SCORED
Ted Williams BOS....... 150
Eddie Joost PHI 128
Dom DiMaggio BOS ... 126

WINS
Mel Parnell BOS 25
Ellis Kinder BOS 23
Bob Lemon CLE 22

WINNING PERCENTAGE
Ellis Kinder BOS .... .793
Mel Parnell BOS .... .781
Allie Reynolds NY ...... .739

EARNED RUN AVERAGE
Mike Garcia CLE........ 2.36
Mel Parnell BOS 2.77
Virgil Trucks DET....... 2.81

STRIKEOUTS
Virgil Trucks DET........ 153
Hal Newhouser DET ... 144
two tied at 138

SAVES
Joe Page NY................. 27
Al Benton CLE 10
Tom Ferrick STL............. 6

COMPLETE GAMES
Mel Parnell BOS 27
Bob Lemon CLE 22
Hal Newhouser DET 22

SHUTOUTS
Ellis Kinder BOS 6
Virgil Trucks DET............ 6
Mike Garcia CLE............. 5

GAMES PITCHED
Joe Page NY................. 60
Dick Welteroth WAS 52
Tom Ferrick STL............ 50

INNINGS PITCHED
Mel Parnell BOS 295
Hal Newhouser DET ... 292
Bob Lemon CLE 280

1949 NL

	W	L	PCT	GB	R	OR	BA	FA	ERA
BROOKLYN	97	57	.630	—	879	651	.274	.980	3.80
ST. LOUIS	96	58	.623	1	766	616	.277	.976	3.44
PHILADELPHIA	81	73	.526	16	662	668	.254	.974	3.89
BOSTON	75	79	.487	22	706	719	.258	.976	3.99
NEW YORK	73	81	.474	24	736	693	.261	.973	3.82
PITTSBURGH	71	83	.461	26	681	760	.259	.978	4.57
CINCINNATI	62	92	.403	35	627	770	.260	.977	4.34
CHICAGO	61	93	.396	36	593	773	.256	.970	4.50
					5650	5650	.262	.975	4.04

BATTING AVERAGE
J. Robinson BKN .... .342
Stan Musial STL .... .338
Enos Slaughter STL... .336

HITS
Stan Musial STL 207
J. Robinson BKN 203
Bobby Thomson NY.... 198

DOUBLES
Stan Musial STL 41
Del Ennis PHI 39
two tied at 38

TRIPLES
Stan Musial STL 13
Enos Slaughter STL...... 13
Jackie Robinson BKN ... 12

HOME RUNS
Ralph Kiner PIT 54
Stan Musial STL 36
Hank Sauer CIN, CHI ... 31

RUNS BATTED IN
Ralph Kiner PIT 127
J. Robinson BKN 124
Stan Musial STL 123

SLUGGING AVERAGE
Ralph Kiner PIT .... .658
Stan Musial STL .... .624
J. Robinson BKN .... .528

STOLEN BASES
Jackie Robinson BKN ... 37
Pee Wee Reese BKN ... 26
four tied at 12

RUNS SCORED
Pee Wee Reese BKN . 132
Stan Musial STL 128
J. Robinson BKN 122

WINS
Warren Spahn BOS 21
Howie Pollet STL 20
K. Raffensberger CIN ... 18

WINNING PERCENTAGE
Preacher Roe BKN .... .714
Howie Pollet STL .... .690
two tied at .... .680

EARNED RUN AVERAGE
Dave Koslo NY 2.50
Gerry Staley STL 2.73
Howie Pollet STL 2.77

STRIKEOUTS
Warren Spahn BOS.... 151
D. Newcombe BKN..... 149
Larry Jansen NY 113

SAVES
Ted Wilks STL 9
Jim Konstanty PHI 7
Nels Potter BOS 7

COMPLETE GAMES
Warren Spahn BOS...... 25
K. Raffensberger CIN ... 20
Don Newcombe BKN.... 19

SHUTOUTS
four tied at...................... 5

GAMES PITCHED
Ted Wilks STL 59
Jim Konstanty PHI 53
Erv Palica BKN 49

INNINGS PITCHED
Warren Spahn BOS.... 302
K. Raffensberger CIN . 284
Larry Jansen NY 260

1950 AL

	W	L	PCT	GB	R	OR	BA	FA	ERA
★ NEW YORK	98	56	.636	—	914	691	.282	.980	4.15
DETROIT	95	59	.617	3	837	713	.282	.981	4.12
BOSTON	94	60	.610	4	1027	804	.302	.981	4.88
CLEVELAND	92	62	.597	6	806	654	.269	.978	3.75
WASHINGTON	67	87	.435	31	690	813	.260	.972	4.66
CHICAGO	60	94	.390	38	625	749	.260	.977	4.41
ST. LOUIS	58	96	.377	40	684	916	.246	.967	5.20
PHILADELPHIA	52	102	.338	46	670	913	.261	.974	5.49
					6253	6253	.271	.976	4.58

BATTING AVERAGE
Billy Goodman BOS ... .354
George Kell DET .... .340
Dom DiMaggio BOS .. .328

HITS
George Kell DET 218
Phil Rizzuto NY 200
Dom DiMaggio BOS ... 193

DOUBLES
George Kell DET 56
Vic Wertz DET 37
Phil Rizzuto NY 36

TRIPLES
Dom DiMaggio BOS 11
Bobby Doerr BOS 11
Hoot Evers DET 11

HOME RUNS
Al Rosen CLE 37
Walt Dropo BOS 34
Joe DiMaggio NY 32

RUNS BATTED IN
Vern Stephens BOS ... 144
Walt Dropo BOS 144
Yogi Berra NY 124

SLUGGING AVERAGE
Joe DiMaggio NY .... .585
Walt Dropo BOS .... .583
Hoot Evers DET .... .551

STOLEN BASES
Dom DiMaggio BOS 15
Elmer Valo PHI 12
Phil Rizzuto NY 12

RUNS SCORED
Dom DiMaggio BOS ... 131
Vern Stephens BOS ... 125
Phil Rizzuto NY 125

WINS
Bob Lemon CLE 23
Vic Raschi NY 21
Art Houtteman DET 19

WINNING PERCENTAGE
Vic Raschi NY .... .724
Eddie Lopat NY .... .692
Early Wynn CLE .... .692

EARNED RUN AVERAGE
Early Wynn CLE 3.20
Ned Garver STL 3.39
Bob Feller CLE 3.43

STRIKEOUTS
Bob Lemon CLE 170
Allie Reynolds NY 160
Vic Raschi NY 155

SAVES
Mickey Harris WAS 15
Joe Page NY 13
Tom Ferrick STL, NY 11

COMPLETE GAMES
Ned Garver STL 22
Bob Lemon CLE 22
two tied at 21

SHUTOUTS
Art Houtteman DET 4

GAMES PITCHED
Mickey Harris WAS 53
Ellis Kinder BOS 48
three tied at 46

INNINGS PITCHED
Bob Lemon CLE 288
Art Houtteman DET 275
Ned Garver STL 260

1950 NL

	W	L	PCT	GB	R	OR	BA	FA	ERA
PHILADELPHIA	91	63	.591	—	722	624	.265	.975	3.50
BROOKLYN	89	65	.578	2	847	724	.272	.979	4.28
NEW YORK	86	68	.558	5	735	643	.258	.977	3.71
BOSTON	83	71	.539	8	785	736	.263	.970	4.14
ST. LOUIS	78	75	.510	12.5	693	670	.259	.978	3.97
CINCINNATI	66	87	.431	24.5	654	734	.260	.976	4.32
CHICAGO	64	89	.418	26.5	643	772	.248	.968	4.28
PITTSBURGH	57	96	.373	33.5	681	857	.264	.977	4.96
					5760	5760	.261	.975	4.14

BATTING AVERAGE
Stan Musial STL .... .346
J. Robinson BKN .... .328
Duke Snider BKN....... .321

HITS
Duke Snider BKN........ 199
Stan Musial STL 192
Carl Furillo BKN 189

DOUBLES
R. Schoendienst STL.... 43
Stan Musial STL 41
Jackie Robinson BKN ... 39

TRIPLES
Richie Ashburn PHI 14
Gus Bell PIT.................. 11
Duke Snider BKN.......... 10

HOME RUNS
Ralph Kiner PIT 47
Andy Pafko CHI 36
two tied at 32

RUNS BATTED IN
Del Ennis PHI 126
Ralph Kiner PIT 118
Gil Hodges BKN.......... 113

SLUGGING AVERAGE
Stan Musial STL .... .596
Andy Pafko CHI .... .591
Ralph Kiner PIT .... .590

STOLEN BASES
Sam Jethroe BOS......... 35
Pee Wee Reese BKN ... 17
Duke Snider BKN.......... 16

RUNS SCORED
Earl Torgeson BOS..... 120
Eddie Stanky NY......... 115
Ralph Kiner PIT 112

WINS
Warren Spahn BOS 21
Robin Roberts PHI........ 20
Johnny Sain BOS 20

WINNING PERCENTAGE
Sal Maglie NY .... .818
Jim Konstanty PHI ..... .696
Curt Simmons PHI..... .680

EARNED RUN AVERAGE
Sal Maglie NY 2.71
Ewell Blackwell CIN ... 2.97
Larry Jansen NY 3.01

STRIKEOUTS
Warren Spahn BOS.... 191
Ewell Blackwell CIN.... 188
Larry Jansen NY 161

SAVES
Jim Konstanty PHI 22
Bill Werle PIT 8
two tied at 7

COMPLETE GAMES
Vern Bickford BOS........ 27
Warren Spahn BOS...... 25
Johnny Sain BOS 25

SHUTOUTS
four tied at....................... 5

GAMES PITCHED
Jim Konstanty PHI 74
Murry Dickson PIT 51
Bill Werle PIT 48

INNINGS PITCHED
Vern Bickford BOS...... 312
Robin Roberts PHI...... 304
Warren Spahn BOS.... 293

1951 AL

	W	L	PCT	GB	R	OR	BA	FA	ERA
★ NEW YORK	98	56	.636	—	798	621	.269	.975	3.56
CLEVELAND	93	61	.604	5	696	594	.256	.978	3.38
BOSTON	87	67	.565	11	804	725	.266	.977	4.14
CHICAGO	81	73	.526	17	714	644	.270	.975	3.50
DETROIT	73	81	.474	25	685	741	.265	.973	4.29
PHILADELPHIA	70	84	.455	28	736	745	.262	.973	4.47
WASHINGTON	62	92	.403	36	672	764	.263	.973	4.49
ST. LOUIS	52	102	.338	46	611	882	.247	.971	5.18
					5716	5716	.262	.975	4.12

BATTING AVERAGE
Ferris Fain PHI............ .344
M. Minoso CLE, CHI.. .326
George Kell DET........ .319

HITS
George Kell DET......... 191
Dom DiMaggio BOS ... 189
Nellie Fox CHI............. 189

DOUBLES
Sam Mele WAS 36
George Kell DET.......... 36
Eddie Yost WAS 36

TRIPLES
M. Minoso CLE, CHI 14
Nellie Fox CHI............... 12
R. Coleman STL, CHI ... 12

HOME RUNS
Gus Zernial CHI, PHI.... 33
Ted Williams BOS......... 30
Eddie Robinson CHI 29

RUNS BATTED IN
G. Zernial CHI, PHI..... 129
Ted Williams BOS....... 126
Eddie Robinson CHI ... 117

SLUGGING AVERAGE
Ted Williams BOS....... .556
Larry Doby CLE .... .512
Gus Zernial CHI, PHI . .511

STOLEN BASES
M. Minoso CLE, CHI 31
Jim Busby CHI 26
Phil Rizzuto NY............. 18

RUNS SCORED
Dom DiMaggio BOS ... 113
M. Minoso CLE, CHI ... 112
two tied at 109

WINS
Bob Feller CLE 22
Eddie Lopat NY............. 21
Vic Raschi NY 21

WINNING PERCENTAGE
Bob Feller CLE .... .733
Eddie Lopat NY.......... .700
Allie Reynolds NY ...... .680

EARNED RUN AVERAGE
S. Rogovin DET, CHI. 2.78
Eddie Lopat NY.......... 2.91
Early Wynn CLE 3.02

STRIKEOUTS
Vic Raschi NY............. 164
Early Wynn CLE 133
Bob Lemon CLE 132

SAVES
Ellis Kinder BOS 14
Carl Scheib PHI 10
Lou Brissie PHI, CLE...... 9

COMPLETE GAMES
Ned Garver STL............ 24
Early Wynn CLE 21
Eddie Lopat NY............. 20

SHUTOUTS
Allie Reynolds NY 7
three tied at..................... 4

GAMES PITCHED
Ellis Kinder BOS 63
Lou Brissie PHI, CLE.... 56
Mike Garcia CLE........... 47

INNINGS PITCHED
Early Wynn CLE 274
Bob Lemon CLE 263
Vic Raschi NY............. 258

NATIONAL LEAGUE STANDINGS

1951 NL

	W	L	PCT	GB	R	OR	BA	FA	ERA
NEW YORK*	98	59	.624	—	781	641	.260	.972	3.48
BROOKLYN	97	60	.618	1	855	672	.275	.979	3.88
ST. LOUIS	81	73	.526	15.5	683	671	.264	.980	3.95
BOSTON	76	78	.494	20.5	723	662	.262	.976	3.75
PHILADELPHIA	73	81	.474	23.5	648	644	.260	.977	3.81
CINCINNATI	68	86	.442	28.5	559	667	.248	.977	3.70
PITTSBURGH	64	90	.416	32.5	689	845	.258	.972	4.79
CHICAGO	62	92	.403	34.5	614	750	.250	.971	4.34
					5552	5552	.260	.975	3.96

*Defeated Brooklyn in a playoff 2 games to 1

BATTING AVERAGE
Stan Musial STL .... .355
Richie Ashburn PHI ... .344
J. Robinson BKN .... .338

HITS
Richie Ashburn PHI 221
Stan Musial STL 205
Carl Furillo BKN 197

DOUBLES
Alvin Dark NY 41
Ted Kluszewski CIN...... 35
two tied at 33

TRIPLES
Stan Musial STL 12
Gus Bell PIT.................. 12
Monte Irvin NY 11

HOME RUNS
Ralph Kiner PIT 42
Gil Hodges BKN............ 40
Roy Campanella BKN... 33

RUNS BATTED IN
Monte Irvin NY 121
Sid Gordon BOS 109
Ralph Kiner PIT 109

SLUGGING AVERAGE
Ralph Kiner PIT .... .627
Stan Musial STL .... .614
R. Campanella BKN... .590

STOLEN BASES
Sam Jethroe BOS.......... 35
Richie Ashburn PHI 29
Jackie Robinson BKN ... 25

RUNS SCORED
Stan Musial STL 124
Ralph Kiner PIT 124
Gil Hodges BKN.......... 118

WINS
Sal Maglie NY 23
Larry Jansen NY 23
two tied at 22

WINNING PERCENTAGE
Preacher Roe BKN .... .880
Sal Maglie NY .... .793
D. Newcombe BKN.... .690

EARNED RUN AVERAGE
Chet Nichols BOS...... 2.88
Sal Maglie NY 2.93
Warren Spahn BOS ... 2.98

STRIKEOUTS
Warren Spahn BOS.... 164
D. Newcombe BKN..... 164
Sal Maglie NY 146

SAVES
Ted Wilks STL, PIT....... 13
Frank Smith CIN 11
Jim Konstanty PHI 9

COMPLETE GAMES
Warren Spahn BOS...... 26
Robin Roberts PHI........ 22
Sal Maglie NY 22

SHUTOUTS
Warren Spahn BOS........ 7
Robin Roberts PHI.......... 6
K. Raffensberger CIN 5

GAMES PITCHED
Ted Wilks STL, PIT....... 65
Bill Werle PIT................ 59
Jim Konstanty PHI 58

INNINGS PITCHED
Robin Roberts PHI...... 315
Warren Spahn BOS.... 311
Sal Maglie NY 298

1952 AL

	W	L	PCT	GB	R	OR	BA	FA	ERA
★ NEW YORK	95	59	.617	—	727	557	.267	.979	3.14
CLEVELAND	93	61	.604	2	763	606	.262	.975	3.32
CHICAGO	81	73	.526	14	610	568	.252	.980	3.25
PHILADELPHIA	79	75	.513	16	664	723	.253	.977	4.15
WASHINGTON	78	76	.506	17	598	608	.239	.978	3.37
BOSTON	76	78	.494	19	668	658	.255	.976	3.80
ST. LOUIS	64	90	.416	31	604	733	.250	.974	4.12
DETROIT	50	104	.325	45	557	738	.243	.975	4.25
					5191	5191	.253	.977	3.67

BATTING AVERAGE
Ferris Fain PHI............ .327
Dale Mitchell CLE ...... .323
Mickey Mantle NY ...... .311

HITS
Nellie Fox CHI............. 192
Bobby Avila CLE......... 179
two tied at 176

DOUBLES
Ferris Fain PHI.............. 43
Mickey Mantle NY 37
two tied at 33

TRIPLES
Bobby Avila CLE........... 11
three tied at.................. 10

HOME RUNS
Larry Doby CLE 32
Luke Easter CLE........... 31
Yogi Berra NY 30

RUNS BATTED IN
Al Rosen CLE 105
Eddie Robinson CHI ... 104
Larry Doby CLE 104

SLUGGING AVERAGE
Larry Doby CLE .... .541
Mickey Mantle NY ...... .530
Al Rosen CLE .... .524

STOLEN BASES
Minnie Minoso CHI 22
Jim Rivera STL, CHI 21
J. Jensen NY, WAS 18

RUNS SCORED
Larry Doby CLE 104
Bobby Avila CLE......... 102
Al Rosen CLE 101

WINS
Bobby Shantz PHI 24
Early Wynn CLE 23
two tied at 22

WINNING PERCENTAGE
Bobby Shantz PHI ..... .774
Vic Raschi NY............. .727
Allie Reynolds NY ...... .714

EARNED RUN AVERAGE
Allie Reynolds NY 2.06
Mike Garcia CLE........ 2.37
Bobby Shantz PHI 2.48

STRIKEOUTS
Allie Reynolds NY 160
Early Wynn CLE 153
Bobby Shantz PHI 152

SAVES
Harry Dorish CHI 11
Satchel Paige STL........ 10
Johnny Sain NY.............. 7

COMPLETE GAMES
Bob Lemon CLE 28
Bobby Shantz PHI 27
Allie Reynolds NY 24

SHUTOUTS
Allie Reynolds NY 6
Mike Garcia CLE............. 6
two tied at 5

GAMES PITCHED
Bill Kennedy CHI........... 47
Mike Garcia CLE.......... 46
Satchel Paige STL........ 46

INNINGS PITCHED
Bob Lemon CLE 310
Mike Garcia CLE......... 292
Early Wynn CLE 286

1952 NL

	W	L	PCT	GB	R	OR	BA	FA	ERA
BROOKLYN	96	57	.627	—	775	603	.262	.982	3.53
NEW YORK	92	62	.597	4.5	722	639	.256	.974	3.59
ST. LOUIS	88	66	.571	8.5	677	630	.267	.977	3.66
PHILADELPHIA	87	67	.565	9.5	657	552	.260	.975	3.07
CHICAGO	77	77	.500	19.5	628	631	.264	.976	3.58
CINCINNATI	69	85	.448	27.5	615	659	.249	.982	4.01
BOSTON	64	89	.418	32	569	651	.233	.975	3.78
PITTSBURGH	42	112	.273	54.5	515	793	.231	.970	4.65
					5158	5158	.253	.976	3.73

BATTING AVERAGE
Stan Musial STL .... .336
F. Baumholtz CHI ...... .325
Ted Kluszewski CIN... .320

HITS
Stan Musial STL 194
R. Schoendienst STL.. 188
Bobby Adams CIN 180

DOUBLES
Stan Musial STL 42
R. Schoendienst STL.... 40
Roy McMillan CIN 32

TRIPLES
Bobby Thomson NY...... 14
Enos Slaughter STL...... 12
Ted Kluszewski CIN...... 11

HOME RUNS
Hank Sauer CHI............. 37
Ralph Kiner PIT 37
Gil Hodges BKN............ 32

RUNS BATTED IN
Hank Sauer CHI.......... 121
Bobby Thomson NY..... 108
Del Ennis PHI 107

SLUGGING AVERAGE
Stan Musial STL .... .538
Hank Sauer CHI......... .531
Ted Kluszewski CIN... .509

STOLEN BASES
Pee Wee Reese BKN ... 30
Sam Jethroe BOS......... 28
Jackie Robinson BKN ... 24

RUNS SCORED
Stan Musial STL 105
Solly Hemus STL........ 105
J. Robinson BKN 104

WINS
Robin Roberts PHI........ 28
Sal Maglie NY 18
three tied at.................. 17

WINNING PERCENTAGE
Hoyt Wilhelm NY........ .833
Robin Roberts PHI..... .800
Joe Black BKN........... .789

EARNED RUN AVERAGE
Hoyt Wilhelm NY........ 2.43
Warren Hacker CHI ... 2.58
Robin Roberts PHI..... 2.59

STRIKEOUTS
Warren Spahn BOS 183
Bob Rush CHI............. 157
Robin Roberts PHI...... 148

SAVES
Al Brazle STL................ 16
Joe Black BKN.............. 15
two tied at 11

COMPLETE GAMES
Robin Roberts PHI........ 30
Murry Dickson PIT 21
Warren Spahn BOS...... 19

SHUTOUTS
Curt Simmons PHI.......... 6
K. Raffensberger CIN 6

GAMES PITCHED
Hoyt Wilhelm NY........... 71
Joe Black BKN.............. 56
Eddie Yuhas STL.......... 54

INNINGS PITCHED
Robin Roberts PHI...... 330
Warren Spahn BOS.... 290
Murry Dickson PIT 278

1953 AL

	W	L	PCT	GB	R	OR	BA	FA	ERA
★ NEW YORK	99	52	.656	—	801	547	.273	.979	3.20
CLEVELAND	92	62	.597	8.5	770	627	.270	.979	3.64
CHICAGO	89	65	.578	11.5	716	592	.258	.980	3.41
BOSTON	84	69	.549	16	656	632	.264	.975	3.58
WASHINGTON	76	76	.500	23.5	687	614	.263	.979	3.66
DETROIT	60	94	.390	40.5	695	923	.266	.978	5.25
PHILADELPHIA	59	95	.383	41.5	632	799	.256	.977	4.67
ST. LOUIS	54	100	.351	46.5	555	778	.249	.974	4.48
					5512	5512	.262	.978	3.99

BATTING AVERAGE
Mickey Vernon WAS.. .337
Al Rosen CLE .... .336
Billy Goodman BOS.... .313

HITS
Harvey Kuenn DET..... 209
Mickey Vernon WAS... 205
Al Rosen CLE 201

DOUBLES
Mickey Vernon WAS..... 43
George Kell BOS 41
Sammy White BOS....... 34

TRIPLES
Jim Rivera CHI.............. 16
Mickey Vernon WAS..... 11
two tied at 9

HOME RUNS
Al Rosen CLE 43
Gus Zernial PHI 42
Larry Doby CLE 29

RUNS BATTED IN
Al Rosen CLE 145
Mickey Vernon WAS... 115
R. Boone CLE, DET.... 114

SLUGGING AVERAGE
Al Rosen CLE .... .613
Gus Zernial PHI .... .559
Yogi Berra NY............. .523

STOLEN BASES
Minnie Minoso CHI 25
Jim Rivera CHI.............. 22
Jackie Jensen WAS...... 18

RUNS SCORED
Al Rosen CLE 115
Eddie Yost WAS 107
Mickey Mantle NY....... 105

WINS
Bob Porterfield WAS..... 22
Bob Lemon CLE 21
Mel Parnell BOS 21

WINNING PERCENTAGE
Eddie Lopat NY.......... .800
Whitey Ford NY .... .750
Mel Parnell BOS .... .724

EARNED RUN AVERAGE
Eddie Lopat NY.......... 2.42
Billy Pierce CHI........... 2.72
V. Trucks STL, CHI.... 2.93

STRIKEOUTS
Billy Pierce CHI........... 186
V. Trucks STL, CHI..... 149
Early Wynn CLE 138

SAVES
Ellis Kinder BOS 27
Harry Dorish CHI 18
Allie Reynolds NY 13

COMPLETE GAMES
Bob Porterfield WAS..... 24
Bob Lemon CLE 23
Mike Garcia CLE........... 21

SHUTOUTS
Bob Porterfield WAS....... 9
Billy Pierce CHI.............. 7
three tied at..................... 5

GAMES PITCHED
Ellis Kinder BOS 69
Marlan Stuart STL..... 60
Morrie Martin PHI.......... 58

INNINGS PITCHED
Bob Lemon CLE 287
Mike Garcia CLE......... 272
Billy Pierce CHI........... 271

1953 NL

	W	L	PCT	GB	R	OR	BA	FA	ERA
BROOKLYN	105	49	.682	—	955	689	.285	.980	4.10
MILWAUKEE	92	62	.597	13	738	589	.266	.976	3.30
PHILADELPHIA	83	71	.539	22	716	666	.265	.975	3.80
ST. LOUIS	83	71	.539	22	768	713	.273	.977	4.23
NEW YORK	70	84	.455	35	768	747	.271	.975	4.25
CINCINNATI	68	86	.442	37	714	788	.261	.978	4.64
CHICAGO	65	89	.422	40	633	835	.260	.967	4.79
PITTSBURGH	50	104	.325	55	622	887	.247	.973	5.22
					5914	5914	.266	.975	4.29

BATTING AVERAGE
Carl Furillo BKN .... .344
R. Schoendienst STL .. .342
Stan Musial STL .... .337

HITS
Richie Ashburn PHI 205
Stan Musial STL 200
Duke Snider BKN........ 198

DOUBLES
Stan Musial STL 53
Alvin Dark NY 41
two tied at 38

TRIPLES
Jim Gilliam BKN............ 17
Bill Bruton MIL 14
two tied at 11

HOME RUNS
Eddie Mathews MIL 47
Duke Snider BKN.......... 42
Roy Campanella BKN... 41

RUNS BATTED IN
R. Campanella BKN.... 142
Eddie Mathews MIL 135
Duke Snider BKN........ 126

SLUGGING AVERAGE
Duke Snider BKN........ .627
Eddie Mathews MIL .... .627
R. Campanella BKN... .611

STOLEN BASES
Bill Bruton MIL................ 26
Pee Wee Reese BKN ... 22
Jim Gilliam BKN............. 21

RUNS SCORED
Duke Snider BKN........ 132
Stan Musial STL 127
Alvin Dark NY 126

WINS
Warren Spahn MIL........ 23
Robin Roberts PHI........ 23
two tied at 20

WINNING PERCENTAGE
Carl Erskine BKN .... .769
Warren Spahn MIL...... .767
two tied at .... .750

EARNED RUN AVERAGE
Warren Spahn MIL..... 2.10
Robin Roberts PHI..... 2.75
Harvey Haddix STL.... 3.06

STRIKEOUTS
Robin Roberts PHI...... 198
Carl Erskine BKN........ 187
V. Mizell STL................ 173

SAVES
Al Brazle STL................ 18
Hoyt Wilhelm NY........... 15
Jim Hughes BKN 9

COMPLETE GAMES
Robin Roberts PHI........ 33
Warren Spahn MIL........ 24
two tied at 19

SHUTOUTS
Harvey Haddix STL......... 6
Robin Roberts PHI.......... 5
Warren Spahn MIL.......... 5

GAMES PITCHED
Hoyt Wilhelm NY........... 68
Al Brazle STL................ 60
Johnny Hetki PIT 54

INNINGS PITCHED
Robin Roberts PHI...... 347
Warren Spahn MIL...... 266
Harvey Haddix STL..... 253

1954 AL

	W	L	PCT	GB	R	OR	BA	FA	ERA
CLEVELAND	111	43	.721	—	746	504	.262	.979	2.78
NEW YORK	103	51	.669	8	805	563	.268	.979	3.26
CHICAGO	94	60	.610	17	711	521	.267	.982	3.05
BOSTON	69	85	.448	42	700	728	.266	.972	4.01
DETROIT	68	86	.442	43	584	664	.258	.978	3.81
WASHINGTON	66	88	.429	45	632	680	.246	.977	3.84
BALTIMORE	54	100	.351	57	483	668	.251	.975	3.88
PHILADELPHIA	51	103	.331	60	542	875	.236	.972	5.18
					5203	5203	.257	.977	3.72

BATTING AVERAGE
Bobby Avila CLE......... .341
Minnie Minoso CHI .... .320
Irv Noren NY .... .319

HITS
Nellie Fox CHI.............. 201
Harvey Kuenn DET..... 201
Bobby Avila CLE......... 189

DOUBLES
Mickey Vernon WAS..... 33
Minnie Minoso CHI 29
Al Smith CLE 29

TRIPLES
Minnie Minoso CHI 18
Pete Runnels WAS....... 15
Mickey Vernon WAS..... 14

HOME RUNS
Larry Doby CLE 32
Ted Williams BOS......... 29
Mickey Mantle NY 27

RUNS BATTED IN
Larry Doby CLE 126
Yogi Berra NY 125
Jackie Jensen BOS 117

SLUGGING AVERAGE
Minnie Minoso CHI .... .535
Mickey Mantle NY...... .525
Al Rosen CLE .... .506

STOLEN BASES
Jackie Jensen BOS 22
Jim Rivera CHI.............. 18
Minnie Minoso CHI 18

RUNS SCORED
Mickey Mantle NY....... 129
Minnie Minoso CHI 119
Bobby Avila CLE......... 112

WINS
Bob Lemon CLE 23
Early Wynn CLE 23
Bob Grim NY................. 20

WINNING PERCENTAGE
S. Consuegra CHI...... .842
Bob Grim NY.............. .769
Bob Lemon CLE .... .767

EARNED RUN AVERAGE
Mike Garcia CLE........ 2.64
Bob Lemon CLE 2.72
Early Wynn CLE 2.73

STRIKEOUTS
Bob Turley BAL........... 185
Early Wynn CLE 155
Virgil Trucks CHI......... 152

SAVES
Johnny Sain NY 22
Ellis Kinder BOS 15
Ray Narleski CLE 13

COMPLETE GAMES
Bob Porterfield WAS..... 21
Bob Lemon CLE 21
Early Wynn CLE 20

SHUTOUTS
Virgil Trucks CHI.............. 5
Mike Garcia CLE............. 5

GAMES PITCHED
S. Dixon WAS, PHI....... 54
three tied at.................. 48

INNINGS PITCHED
Early Wynn CLE 271
Virgil Trucks CHI......... 265
Mike Garcia CLE......... 259

1954 NL

	W	L	PCT	GB	R	OR	BA	FA	ERA
★ NEW YORK	97	57	.630	—	732	550	.264	.975	3.09
BROOKLYN	92	62	.597	5	778	740	.270	.978	4.31
MILWAUKEE	89	65	.578	8	670	556	.265	.981	3.19
PHILADELPHIA	75	79	.487	22	659	614	.267	.975	3.59
CINCINNATI	74	80	.481	23	729	763	.262	.977	4.50
ST. LOUIS	72	82	.468	25	799	790	.281	.976	4.50
CHICAGO	64	90	.416	33	700	766	.263	.974	4.51
PITTSBURGH	53	101	.344	44	557	845	.248	.971	4.92
					5624	5624	.265	.976	4.07

BATTING AVERAGE
Willie Mays NY .... .345
Don Mueller NY .... .342
Duke Snider BKN .... .341

HITS
Don Mueller NY 212
Duke Snider BKN 199
two tied at 195

DOUBLES
Stan Musial STL 41
three tied at 39

TRIPLES
Willie Mays NY 13
Granny Hamner PHI 11
Duke Snider BKN 10

HOME RUNS
Ted Kluszewski CIN 49
Gil Hodges BKN 42
two tied at 41

RUNS BATTED IN
Ted Kluszewski CIN 141
Gil Hodges BKN 130
Duke Snider BKN 130

SLUGGING AVERAGE
Willie Mays NY .... .667
Duke Snider BKN .... .647
Ted Kluszewski CIN .. .642

STOLEN BASES
Bill Bruton MIL 34
Johnny Temple CIN 21
Dee Fondy CHI 20

RUNS SCORED
Duke Snider BKN 120
Stan Musial STL 120
Willie Mays NY 119

WINS
Robin Roberts PHI 23
Johnny Antonelli NY 21
Warren Spahn MIL 21

WINNING PERCENTAGE
Johnny Antonelli NY ... .750
B. Lawrence STL .... .714
Ruben Gomez NY ...... .654

EARNED RUN AVERAGE
J. Antonelli NY 2.30
Lew Burdette MIL 2.76
Curt Simmons PHI 2.81

STRIKEOUTS
Robin Roberts PHI 185
Harvey Haddix STL 184
Carl Erskine BKN 166

SAVES
Jim Hughes BKN 24
Frank Smith CIN 20
Marv Grissom NY 19

COMPLETE GAMES
Robin Roberts PHI 29
Warren Spahn MIL 23
Curt Simmons PHI 21

SHUTOUTS
Johnny Antonelli NY 6

GAMES PITCHED
Jim Hughes BKN 60
Al Brazle STL 58
Johnny Hetki PIT 58

INNINGS PITCHED
Robin Roberts PHI 337
Warren Spahn MIL 283
two tied at 260

1955 AL

	W	L	PCT	GB	R	OR	BA	FA	ERA
NEW YORK	96	58	.623	—	762	569	.260	.978	3.23
CLEVELAND	93	61	.604	3	698	601	.257	.981	3.39
CHICAGO	91	63	.591	5	725	557	.268	.981	3.37
BOSTON	84	70	.545	12	755	652	.264	.977	3.72
DETROIT	79	75	.513	17	775	658	.266	.976	3.79
KANSAS CITY	63	91	.409	33	638	911	.261	.976	5.35
BALTIMORE	57	97	.370	39	540	754	.240	.972	4.21
WASHINGTON	53	101	.344	43	598	789	.248	.974	4.62
					5491	5491	.258	.977	3.96

BATTING AVERAGE
Al Kaline DET .... .340
Vic Power KC............. .319
George Kell CHI......... .312

HITS
Al Kaline DET 200
Nellie Fox CHI............. 198
two tied at 190

DOUBLES
Harvey Kuenn DET....... 38
Vic Power KC................ 34
Billy Goodman BOS...... 31

TRIPLES
Andy Carey NY............. 11
Mickey Mantle NY......... 11
Vic Power KC................ 10

HOME RUNS
Mickey Mantle NY......... 37
Gus Zernial KC 30
Ted Williams BOS......... 28

RUNS BATTED IN
Ray Boone DET.......... 116
Jackie Jensen BOS 116
Yogi Berra NY............. 108

SLUGGING AVERAGE
Mickey Mantle NY...... .611
Al Kaline DET .... .546
Gus Zernial KC .... .508

STOLEN BASES
Jim Rivera CHI.............. 25
Minnie Minoso CHI 19
Jackie Jensen BOS 16

RUNS SCORED
Al Smith CLE 123
Al Kaline DET 121
Mickey Mantle NY....... 121

WINS
Whitey Ford NY 18
Bob Lemon CLE 18
Frank Sullivan BOS 18

WINNING PERCENTAGE
Tommy Byrne NY .... .762
Whitey Ford NY .... .720
Billy Hoeft DET .... .696

EARNED RUN AVERAGE
Billy Pierce CHI.......... 1.97
Whitey Ford NY 2.63
Early Wynn CLE 2.82

STRIKEOUTS
Herb Score CLE.......... 245
Bob Turley NY 210
Billy Pierce CHI........... 157

SAVES
Ray Narleski CLE 19
Tom Gorman KC........... 18
Ellis Kinder BOS 18

COMPLETE GAMES
Whitey Ford NY 18
Billy Hoeft DET 17

SHUTOUTS
Billy Hoeft DET 7
three tied at..................... 6

GAMES PITCHED
Ray Narleski CLE 60
Don Mossi CLE............. 57
Tom Gorman KC........... 57

INNINGS PITCHED
Frank Sullivan BOS 260
Whitey Ford NY 254
Bob Turley NY 247

1955 NL

	W	L	PCT	GB	R	OR	BA	FA	ERA
★ BROOKLYN	98	55	.641	—	857	650	.271	.978	3.68
MILWAUKEE	85	69	.552	13.5	743	668	.261	.975	3.85
NEW YORK	80	74	.519	18.5	702	673	.260	.976	3.77
PHILADELPHIA	77	77	.500	21.5	675	666	.255	.981	3.93
CINCINNATI	75	79	.487	23.5	761	684	.270	.977	3.95
CHICAGO	72	81	.471	26	626	713	.247	.975	4.17
ST. LOUIS	68	86	.442	30.5	654	757	.261	.975	4.56
PITTSBURGH	60	94	.390	38.5	560	767	.244	.972	4.39
					5578	5578	.259	.976	4.04

BATTING AVERAGE
Richie Ashburn PHI ... .338
Willie Mays NY .... .319
Stan Musial STL .... .319

HITS
Ted Kluszewski CIN.... 192
Hank Aaron MIL.......... 189
Gus Bell CIN 188

DOUBLES
Hank Aaron MIL............ 37
Johnny Logan MIL 37
Duke Snider BKN.......... 34

TRIPLES
Willie Mays NY.............. 13
Dale Long PIT............... 13
Bill Bruton MIL 12

HOME RUNS
Willie Mays NY.............. 51
Ted Kluszewski CIN...... 47
Ernie Banks CHI 44

RUNS BATTED IN
Duke Snider BKN........ 136
Willie Mays NY............ 127
Del Ennis PHI 120

SLUGGING AVERAGE
Willie Mays NY........... .659
Duke Snider BKN........ .628
Eddie Mathews MIL .... .601

STOLEN BASES
Bill Bruton MIL 25
Willie Mays NY.............. 24
Ken Boyer STL 22

RUNS SCORED
Duke Snider BKN........ 126
Willie Mays NY............ 123
two tied at 116

WINS
Robin Roberts PHI........ 23
Don Newcombe BKN.... 20
two tied at 17

WINNING PERCENTAGE
D. Newcombe BKN.... .800
Robin Roberts PHI..... .622
Joe Nuxhall CIN .... .586

EARNED RUN AVERAGE
Bob Friend PIT........... 2.83
D. Newcombe BKN.... 3.20
Bob Buhl MIL 3.21

STRIKEOUTS
Sam Jones CHI........... 198
Robin Roberts PHI...... 160
Harvey Haddix STL..... 150

SAVES
Jack Meyer PHI 16
Ed Roebuck BKN.......... 12
two tied at 11

COMPLETE GAMES
Robin Roberts PHI........ 26
Don Newcombe BKN.... 17
Warren Spahn MIL........ 16

SHUTOUTS
Joe Nuxhall CIN.............. 5
Murry Dickson PHI.......... 4
Sam Jones CHI............... 4

GAMES PITCHED
Clem Labine BKN 60
Hoyt Wilhelm NY........... 59
Paul LaPalme STL........ 56

INNINGS PITCHED
Robin Roberts PHI...... 305
Joe Nuxhall CIN.......... 257
Warren Spahn MIL...... 246

1956 AL

	W	L	PCT	GB	R	OR	BA	FA	ERA
★ NEW YORK	97	57	.630	—	857	631	.270	.977	3.63
CLEVELAND	88	66	.571	9	712	581	.244	.978	3.32
CHICAGO	85	69	.552	12	776	634	.267	.979	3.73
BOSTON	84	70	.545	13	780	751	.275	.972	4.17
DETROIT	82	72	.532	15	789	699	.279	.976	4.06
BALTIMORE	69	85	.448	28	571	705	.244	.977	4.20
WASHINGTON	59	95	.383	38	652	924	.250	.972	5.33
KANSAS CITY	52	102	.338	45	619	831	.252	.973	4.86
					5756	5756	.260	.975	4.16

BATTING AVERAGE
Mickey Mantle NY ...... .353
Ted Williams BOS ...... .345
Harvey Kuenn DET .... .332

HITS
Harvey Kuenn DET 196
Al Kaline DET 194
Nellie Fox CHI 192

DOUBLES
Jimmy Piersall BOS 40
Al Kaline DET 32
Harvey Kuenn DET 32

TRIPLES
four tied at 11

HOME RUNS
Mickey Mantle NY 52
Vic Wertz CLE 32
Yogi Berra NY 30

RUNS BATTED IN
Mickey Mantle NY 130
Al Kaline DET 128
Vic Wertz CLE 106

SLUGGING AVERAGE
Mickey Mantle NY ...... .705
Ted Williams BOS ...... .605
Charlie Maxwell DET . .534

STOLEN BASES
Luis Aparicio CHI 21
Jim Rivera CHI 20
Bobby Avila CLE 17

RUNS SCORED
Mickey Mantle NY 132
Nellie Fox CHI 109
Minnie Minoso CHI 106

WINS
Frank Lary DET 21
five tied at 20

WINNING PERCENTAGE
Whitey Ford NY .... .760
three tied at .... .690

EARNED RUN AVERAGE
Whitey Ford NY 2.47
Herb Score CLE 2.53
Early Wynn CLE 2.72

STRIKEOUTS
Herb Score CLE 263
Billy Pierce CHI 192
Paul Foytack DET 184

SAVES
George Zuverink BAL ... 16
Tom Morgan NY 11
Don Mossi CLE 11

COMPLETE GAMES
Billy Pierce CHI 21
Bob Lemon CLE 21
Frank Lary DET 20

SHUTOUTS
Herb Score CLE 5

GAMES PITCHED
George Zuverink BAL ... 62
Jack Crimian KC 54
Tom Gorman KC 52

INNINGS PITCHED
Frank Lary DET 294
Early Wynn CLE 278
Billy Pierce CHI 276

1956 NL

	W	L	PCT	GB	R	OR	BA	FA	ERA
BROOKLYN	93	61	.604	—	720	601	.258	.981	3.57
MILWAUKEE	92	62	.597	1	709	569	.259	.979	3.11
CINCINNATI	91	63	.591	2	775	658	.266	.981	3.85
ST. LOUIS	76	78	.494	17	678	698	.268	.978	3.97
PHILADELPHIA	71	83	.461	22	668	738	.252	.975	4.20
NEW YORK	67	87	.435	26	540	650	.244	.976	3.78
PITTSBURGH	66	88	.429	27	588	653	.257	.973	3.74
CHICAGO	60	94	.390	33	597	708	.244	.976	3.96
					5275	5275	.256	.977	3.77

BATTING AVERAGE
Hank Aaron MIL......... .328
Bill Virdon STL, PIT ... .319
R. Clemente PIT .... .311

HITS
Hank Aaron MIL.......... 200
Richie Ashburn PHI 190
Bill Virdon STL, PIT 185

DOUBLES
Hank Aaron MIL............ 34
three tied at.................. 33

TRIPLES
Bill Bruton MIL 15
Hank Aaron MIL............ 14
two tied at 11

HOME RUNS
Duke Snider BKN.......... 43
Frank Robinson CIN 38
Joe Adcock MIL 38

RUNS BATTED IN
Stan Musial STL 109
Joe Adcock MIL 103
Ted Kluszewski CIN.... 102

SLUGGING AVERAGE
Duke Snider BKN....... .598
Joe Adcock MIL .... .597
Hank Aaron MIL......... .558

STOLEN BASES
Willie Mays NY.............. 40
Jim Gilliam BKN............. 21
Bill White NY 15

RUNS SCORED
Frank Robinson CIN ... 122
Duke Snider BKN........ 112
Hank Aaron MIL.......... 106

WINS
Don Newcombe BKN.... 27
Warren Spahn MIL 20
Johnny Antonelli NY 20

WINNING PERCENTAGE
Don Newcombe BKN. .794
Bob Buhl MIL .... .692
two tied at .... .655

EARNED RUN AVERAGE
Lew Burdette MIL........ 2.70
Warren Spahn MIL 2.78
Johnny Antonelli NY .. 2.86

STRIKEOUTS
Sam Jones CHI........... 176
H. Haddix STL, PHI 170
Bob Friend PIT............ 166

SAVES
Clem Labine BKN 19
Hersh Freeman CIN...... 18
Turk Lown CHI.............. 13

COMPLETE GAMES
Robin Roberts PHI 22
Warren Spahn MIL....... 20
Bob Friend PIT............. 19

SHUTOUTS
Lew Burdette MIL............ 6
Johnny Antonelli NY 5
Don Newcombe BKN...... 5

GAMES PITCHED
Roy Face PIT................. 68
Hersh Freeman CIN...... 64
Hoyt Wilhelm NY........... 64

INNINGS PITCHED
Bob Friend PIT............ 314
Robin Roberts PHI...... 297
Warren Spahn MIL...... 281

1957 AL

	W	L	PCT	GB	R	OR	BA	FA	ERA
NEW YORK	98	56	.636	—	723	534	.268	.980	3.00
CHICAGO	90	64	.584	8	707	566	.260	.982	3.35
BOSTON	82	72	.532	16	721	668	.262	.976	3.88
DETROIT	78	76	.506	20	614	614	.257	.980	3.56
BALTIMORE	76	76	.500	21	597	588	.252	.981	3.46
CLEVELAND	76	77	.497	21.5	682	722	.252	.974	4.06
KANSAS CITY	59	94	.386	38.5	563	710	.244	.979	4.19
WASHINGTON	55	99	.357	43	603	808	.244	.979	4.85
					5210	5210	.255	.979	3.79

BATTING AVERAGE
Ted Williams BOS....... .388
Mickey Mantle NY....... .365
Gene Woodling CLE.. .321

HITS
Nellie Fox CHI............. 196
Frank Malzone BOS ... 185
Minnie Minoso CHI 176

DOUBLES
Billy Gardner BAL 36
Minnie Minoso CHI 36
Frank Malzone BOS 31

TRIPLES
Harry Simpson KC, NY ... 9
Gil McDougald NY 9
Hank Bauer NY............... 9

HOME RUNS
Roy Sievers WAS 42
Ted Williams BOS......... 38
Mickey Mantle NY......... 34

RUNS BATTED IN
Roy Sievers WAS 114
Vic Wertz CLE 105
three tied at................. 103

SLUGGING AVERAGE
Ted Williams BOS....... .731
Mickey Mantle NY...... .665
Roy Sievers WAS ...... .579

STOLEN BASES
Luis Aparicio CHI 28
Minnie Minoso CHI 18
Jim Rivera CHI.............. 18

RUNS SCORED
Mickey Mantle NY....... 121
Nellie Fox CHI............. 110
Jimmy Piersall BOS.... 103

WINS
Jim Bunning DET.......... 20
Billy Pierce CHI............. 20
three tied at................... 16

WINNING PERCENTAGE
Dick Donovan CHI ..... .727
Tom Sturdivant NY .... .727
Jim Bunning DET....... .714

EARNED RUN AVERAGE
Bobby Shantz NY 2.45
Tom Sturdivant NY 2.54
Jim Bunning DET....... 2.69

STRIKEOUTS
Early Wynn CLE 184
Jim Bunning DET........ 182
C. Johnson BAL........... 177

SAVES
Bob Grim NY................. 19
Ray Narleski CLE 16
Ike Delock BOS 11

COMPLETE GAMES
Dick Donovan CHI 16
Billy Pierce CHI............ 16
Tom Brewer BOS.......... 15

SHUTOUTS
Jim Wilson CHI 5
Billy Pierce CHI............... 4
Bob Turley NY 4

GAMES PITCHED
George Zuverink BAL ... 56
Tex Clevenger WAS 52
Dick Hyde WAS 52

INNINGS PITCHED
Jim Bunning DET........ 267
Early Wynn CLE 263
Billy Pierce CHI........... 257

1957 NL

	W	L	PCT	GB	R	OR	BA	FA	ERA
★ MILWAUKEE	95	59	.617	—	772	613	.269	.981	3.47
ST. LOUIS	87	67	.565	8	737	666	.274	.979	3.78
BROOKLYN	84	70	.545	11	690	591	.253	.979	3.35
CINCINNATI	80	74	.519	15	747	781	.269	.982	4.62
PHILADELPHIA	77	77	.500	18	623	656	.250	.976	3.79
NEW YORK	69	85	.448	26	643	701	.252	.974	4.01
CHICAGO	62	92	.403	33	628	722	.244	.975	4.13
PITTSBURGH	62	92	.403	33	586	696	.268	.972	3.88
					5426	5426	.260	.977	3.88

BATTING AVERAGE
Stan Musial STL .... .351
Willie Mays NY........... .333
Frank Robinson CIN .. .322

HITS
R. Schoendienst NY, MIL.. 200
Hank Aaron MIL.......... 198
Frank Robinson CIN 197

DOUBLES
Don Hoak CIN............... 39
Stan Musial STL 38
Ed Bouchee PHI 35

TRIPLES
Willie Mays NY.............. 20
Bill Virdon PIT 11
two tied at 9

HOME RUNS
Hank Aaron MIL............ 44
Ernie Banks CHI 43
Duke Snider BKN.......... 40

RUNS BATTED IN
Hank Aaron MIL.......... 132
Del Ennis STL............. 105
two tied at 102

SLUGGING AVERAGE
Willie Mays NY........... .626
Stan Musial STL .... .612
Hank Aaron MIL.......... .600

STOLEN BASES
Willie Mays NY.............. 38
Jim Gilliam BKN............ 26
Don Blasingame STL.... 21

RUNS SCORED
Hank Aaron MIL.......... 118
Ernie Banks CHI 113
Willie Mays NY............ 112

WINS
Warren Spahn MIL........ 21
Jack Sanford PHI.......... 19
Bob Buhl MIL 18

WINNING PERCENTAGE
Bob Buhl MIL .... .720
Jack Sanford PHI........ .704
Warren Spahn MIL...... .656

EARNED RUN AVERAGE
Johnny Podres BKN .. 2.66
Don Drysdale BKN..... 2.69
Warren Spahn MIL..... 2.69

STRIKEOUTS
Jack Sanford PHI........ 188
Dick Drott CHI............. 170
Moe Drabowsky CHI... 170

SAVES
Clem Labine BKN 17
Marv Grissom NY 14
Turk Lown CHI.............. 12

COMPLETE GAMES
Warren Spahn MIL........ 18
Bob Friend PIT.............. 17
Ruben Gomez NY......... 16

SHUTOUTS
Johnny Podres BKN 6
three tied at...................... 4

GAMES PITCHED
Turk Lown CHI.............. 67
Roy Face PIT 59
Clem Labine BKN 58

INNINGS PITCHED
Bob Friend PIT............. 277
Warren Spahn MIL....... 271
Lew Burdette MIL........ 257

1958 AL

	W	L	PCT	GB	R	OR	BA	FA	ERA
★ NEW YORK	92	62	.597	—	759	577	.268	.978	3.22
CHICAGO	82	72	.532	10	634	615	.257	.981	3.61
BOSTON	79	75	.513	13	697	691	.256	.976	3.92
CLEVELAND	77	76	.503	14.5	694	635	.258	.974	3.73
DETROIT	77	77	.500	15	659	606	.266	.982	3.59
BALTIMORE	74	79	.484	17.5	521	575	.241	.980	3.40
KANSAS CITY	73	81	.474	19	642	713	.247	.979	4.15
WASHINGTON	61	93	.396	31	553	747	.240	.980	4.53
					5159	5159	.254	.979	3.77

BATTING AVERAGE
Ted Williams BOS...... .328
Pete Runnels BOS..... .322
Harvey Kuenn DET.... .319

HITS
Nellie Fox CHI............. 187
Frank Malzone BOS ... 185
Vic Power KC, CLE..... 184

DOUBLES
Harvey Kuenn DET....... 39
Vic Power KC, CLE....... 37
Al Kaline DET 34

TRIPLES
Vic Power KC, CLE....... 10
three tied at.................... 9

HOME RUNS
Mickey Mantle NY......... 42
Rocky Colavito CLE 41
Roy Sievers WAS 39

RUNS BATTED IN
Jackie Jensen BOS 122
Rocky Colavito CLE..... 113
Roy Sievers WAS 108

SLUGGING AVERAGE
Rocky Colavito CLE.... .620
Bob Cerv KC............... .592
Mickey Mantle NY...... .592

STOLEN BASES
Luis Aparicio CHI 29
Jim Rivera CHI............... 21
Jim Landis CHI 19

RUNS SCORED
Mickey Mantle NY....... 127
Pete Runnels BOS...... 103
Vic Power KC, CLE....... 98

WINS
Bob Turley NY 21
Billy Pierce CHI............. 17
two tied at 16

WINNING PERCENTAGE
Bob Turley NY .... .750
Cal McLish CLE.......... .667
Billy Pierce CHI.......... .607

EARNED RUN AVERAGE
Whitey Ford NY 2.01
Billy Pierce CHI.......... 2.68
J. Harshman BAL....... 2.89

STRIKEOUTS
Early Wynn CHI 179
Jim Bunning DET........ 177
Bob Turley NY 168

SAVES
Ryne Duren NY............. 20
Dick Hyde WAS 18
Leo Kiely BOS 12

COMPLETE GAMES
Bob Turley NY 19
Billy Pierce CHI............. 19
Frank Lary DET 19

SHUTOUTS
Whitey Ford NY 7
Bob Turley NY 6
three tied at..................... 4

GAMES PITCHED
Tex Clevenger WAS 55
D. Tomanek CLE, KC ... 54
Dick Hyde WAS 53

INNINGS PITCHED
Frank Lary DET 260
Pedro Ramos WAS..... 259
Dick Donovan CHI 248

1958 NL

	W	L	PCT	GB	R	OR	BA	FA	ERA
MILWAUKEE	92	62	.597	—	675	541	.266	.980	3.21
PITTSBURGH	84	70	.545	8	662	607	.264	.978	3.56
SAN FRANCISCO	80	74	.519	12	727	698	.263	.975	3.98
CINCINNATI	76	78	.494	16	695	621	.258	.983	3.73
CHICAGO	72	82	.468	20	709	725	.265	.975	4.22
ST. LOUIS	72	82	.468	20	619	704	.261	.974	4.12
LOS ANGELES	71	83	.461	21	668	761	.251	.975	4.47
PHILADELPHIA	69	85	.448	23	664	762	.266	.978	4.32
					5419	5419	.262	.977	3.95

BATTING AVERAGE
Richie Ashburn PHI ... .350
Willie Mays SF .... .347
Stan Musial STL .... .337

HITS
Richie Ashburn PHI 215
Willie Mays SF 208
Hank Aaron MIL.......... 196

DOUBLES
Orlando Cepeda SF...... 38
Dick Groat PIT 36
Stan Musial STL 35

TRIPLES
Richie Ashburn PHI 13
three tied at................... 11

HOME RUNS
Ernie Banks CHI 47
Frank Thomas PIT 35
two tied at 31

RUNS BATTED IN
Ernie Banks CHI 129
Frank Thomas PIT 109
Harry Anderson PHI...... 97

SLUGGING AVERAGE
Ernie Banks CHI .... .614
Willie Mays SF .... .583
Hank Aaron MIL.......... .546

STOLEN BASES
Willie Mays SF 31
Richie Ashburn PHI 30
Tony Taylor CHI............. 21

RUNS SCORED
Willie Mays SF 121
Ernie Banks CHI 119
Hank Aaron MIL.......... 109

WINS
Bob Friend PIT.............. 22
Warren Spahn MIL........ 22
Lew Burdette MIL......... 20

WINNING PERCENTAGE
Warren Spahn MIL....... .667
Lew Burdette MIL........ .667
Bob Friend PIT........... .611

EARNED RUN AVERAGE
Stu Miller SF 2.47
Sam Jones STL 2.88
Lew Burdette MIL....... 2.91

STRIKEOUTS
Sam Jones STL 225
Warren Spahn MIL...... 150
two tied at 143

SAVES
Roy Face PIT................ 20
Clem Labine LA 14
Dick Farrell PHI............. 11

COMPLETE GAMES
Warren Spahn MIL........ 23
Robin Roberts PHI........ 21
Lew Burdette MIL.......... 19

SHUTOUTS
Carl Willey MIL................ 4
four tied at....................... 3

GAMES PITCHED
Don Elston CHI 69
J. Klippstein CIN, LA..... 57
Roy Face PIT................ 57

INNINGS PITCHED
Warren Spahn MIL...... 290
Lew Burdette MIL........ 275
Bob Friend PIT............ 274

1959 AL

	W	L	PCT	GB	R	OR	BA	FA	ERA
CHICAGO	94	60	.610	—	669	588	.250	.979	3.29
CLEVELAND	89	65	.578	5	745	646	.263	.978	3.75
NEW YORK	79	75	.513	15	687	647	.260	.978	3.60
DETROIT	76	78	.494	18	713	732	.258	.978	4.20
BOSTON	75	79	.487	19	726	696	.256	.978	4.17
BALTIMORE	74	80	.481	20	551	621	.238	.976	3.56
KANSAS CITY	66	88	.429	28	681	760	.263	.973	4.35
WASHINGTON	63	91	.409	31	619	701	.237	.973	4.01
					5391	5391	.253	.977	3.86

BATTING AVERAGE
Harvey Kuenn DET.... .353
Al Kaline DET .... .327
Pete Runnels BOS..... .314

HITS
Harvey Kuenn DET..... 198
Nellie Fox CHI............. 191
Pete Runnels BOS...... 176

DOUBLES
Harvey Kuenn DET....... 42
Frank Malzone BOS 34
Nellie Fox CHI............... 34

TRIPLES
Bob Allison WAS............. 9
Gil McDougald NY 8

HOME RUNS
Rocky Colavito CLE...... 42
H. Killebrew WAS 42
Jim Lemon WAS 33

RUNS BATTED IN
Jackie Jensen BOS 112
Rocky Colavito CLE.... 111
H. Killebrew WAS 105

SLUGGING AVERAGE
Al Kaline DET .... .530
H. Killebrew WAS ...... .516
Mickey Mantle NY ...... .514

STOLEN BASES
Luis Aparicio CHI.......... 56
Mickey Mantle NY 21
two tied at 20

RUNS SCORED
Eddie Yost DET 115
Mickey Mantle NY 104
Vic Power CLE............ 102

WINS
Early Wynn CHI 22
Cal McLish CLE 19
Bob Shaw CHI 18

WINNING PERCENTAGE
Bob Shaw CHI .... .750
Cal McLish CLE .... .704
Early Wynn CHI .... .688

EARNED RUN AVERAGE
Hoyt Wilhelm BAL....... 2.19
Camilo Pascual WAS. 2.64
Bob Shaw CHI 2.69

STRIKEOUTS
Jim Bunning DET........ 201
Camilo Pascual WAS.. 185
Early Wynn CHI 179

SAVES
Turk Lown CHI.............. 15
three tied at................... 14

COMPLETE GAMES
Camilo Pascual WAS.... 17
Don Mossi DET............. 15
Milt Pappas BAL 15

SHUTOUTS
Camilo Pascual WAS...... 6
Early Wynn CHI 5
Milt Pappas BAL 4

GAMES PITCHED
George Staley CHI........ 67
Turk Lown CHI.............. 60
Tex Clevenger WAS 50

INNINGS PITCHED
Early Wynn CHI 256
Jim Bunning DET........ 250
Paul Foytack DET....... 240

1959 NL

	W	L	PCT	GB	R	OR	BA	FA	ERA
★ LOS ANGELES*	88	68	.564	—	705	670	.257	.981	3.79
MILWAUKEE	86	70	.551	2	724	623	.265	.979	3.51
SAN FRANCISCO	83	71	.539	4	705	613	.261	.974	3.47
PITTSBURGH	78	76	.506	9	651	680	.263	.975	3.90
CHICAGO	74	80	.481	13	673	688	.249	.977	4.01
CINCINNATI	74	80	.481	13	764	738	.274	.978	4.31
ST. LOUIS	71	83	.461	16	641	725	.269	.975	4.34
PHILADELPHIA	64	90	.416	23	599	725	.242	.973	4.27
					5462	5462	.260	.977	3.95

* Defeated Milwaukee in a playoff 2 games to 0

BATTING AVERAGE
Hank Aaron MIL......... .355
J. Cunningham STL.... .345
Orlando Cepeda SF... .317

HITS
Hank Aaron MIL.......... 223
Vada Pinson CIN 205
Orlando Cepeda SF.... 192

DOUBLES
Vada Pinson CIN 47
Hank Aaron MIL............ 46
Willie Mays SF 43

TRIPLES
Charlie Neal LA............. 11
Wally Moon LA.............. 11
three tied at...................... 9

HOME RUNS
Eddie Mathews MIL 46
Ernie Banks CHI 45
Hank Aaron MIL............. 39

RUNS BATTED IN
Ernie Banks CHI 143
Frank Robinson CIN ... 125
Hank Aaron MIL.......... 123

SLUGGING AVERAGE
Hank Aaron MIL.......... .636
Ernie Banks CHI .... .596
Eddie Mathews MIL ... .593

STOLEN BASES
Willie Mays SF 27
three tied at................... 23

RUNS SCORED
Vada Pinson CIN 131
Willie Mays SF 125
Eddie Mathews MIL 118

WINS
Lew Burdette MIL.......... 21
Sam Jones SF 21
Warren Spahn MIL........ 21

WINNING PERCENTAGE
Roy Face PIT.............. .947
Vern Law PIT .... .667
Johnny Antonelli SF... .655

EARNED RUN AVERAGE
Sam Jones SF 2.83
Stu Miller SF 2.84
Bill Buhl MIL................ 2.86

STRIKEOUTS
Don Drysdale LA......... 242
Sam Jones SF 209
Sandy Koufax LA........ 173

SAVES
Lindy McDaniel STL...... 15
Don McMahon MIL 15
Don Elston CHI............. 13

COMPLETE GAMES
Warren Spahn MIL........ 21
Vern Law PIT................ 20
Lew Burdette MIL.......... 20

SHUTOUTS
seven tied at 4

GAMES PITCHED
Bill Henry CHI 65
Don Elston CHI 65
Lindy McDaniel STL...... 62

INNINGS PITCHED
Warren Spahn MIL........ 292
Lew Burdette MIL........ 290
Johnny Antonelli SF.... 282

1960 AL

	W	L	PCT	GB	R	OR	BA	FA	ERA
NEW YORK	97	57	.630	—	746	627	.260	.979	3.52
BALTIMORE	89	65	.578	8	682	606	.253	.982	3.52
CHICAGO	87	67	.565	10	741	617	.270	.982	3.60
CLEVELAND	76	78	.494	21	667	693	.267	.978	3.95
WASHINGTON	73	81	.474	24	672	696	.244	.973	3.77
DETROIT	71	83	.461	26	633	644	.239	.977	3.64
BOSTON	65	89	.422	32	658	775	.261	.976	4.62
KANSAS CITY	58	96	.377	39	615	756	.249	.979	4.38
					5414	5414	.255	.978	3.87

BATTING AVERAGE
Pete Runnels BOS..... .320
Al Smith CHI .... .315
Minnie Minoso CHI .... .311

HITS
Minnie Minoso CHI 184
Nellie Fox CHI............. 175
Brooks Robinson BAL. 175

DOUBLES
Tito Francona CLE........ 36
Bill Skowron NY 34
two tied at 32

TRIPLES
Nellie Fox CHI.............. 10
Brooks Robinson BAL..... 9

HOME RUNS
Mickey Mantle NY......... 40
Roger Maris NY 39
Jim Lemon WAS 38

RUNS BATTED IN
Roger Maris NY 112
Minnie Minoso CHI 105
Vic Wertz BOS............ 103

SLUGGING AVERAGE
Roger Maris NY .... .581
Mickey Mantle NY...... .558
H. Killebrew WAS ...... .534

STOLEN BASES
Luis Aparicio CHI 51
Jim Landis CHI 23
Lenny Green WAS........ 21

RUNS SCORED
Mickey Mantle NY....... 119
Roger Maris NY 98
two tied at 89

WINS
Jim Perry CLE.............. 18
Chuck Estrada BAL 18
Buddy Daley KC 16

WINNING PERCENTAGE
Jim Perry CLE............. .643
Art Ditmar NY.............. .625
Chuck Estrada BAL ... .621

EARNED RUN AVERAGE
F. Baumann CHI........ 2.67
Jim Bunning DET....... 2.79
Hal Brown BAL 3.06

STRIKEOUTS
Jim Bunning DET........ 201
Pedro Ramos WAS..... 160
Early Wynn CHI 158

SAVES
Mike Fornieles BOS...... 14
J. Klippstein CLE 14
Ray Moore CHI, WAS... 13

COMPLETE GAMES
Frank Lary DET 15
Pedro Ramos WAS....... 14
Ray Herbert KC 14

SHUTOUTS
Jim Perry CLE.................. 4
Whitey Ford NY 4
Early Wynn CHI 4

GAMES PITCHED
Mike Fornieles BOS 70
Gerry Staley CHI........... 64
Tex Clevenger WAS 53

INNINGS PITCHED
Frank Lary DET 274
Pedro Ramos WAS..... 274
Jim Perry CLE............. 261

1960 NL

	W	L	PCT	GB	R	OR	BA	FA	ERA
★ PITTSBURGH	95	59	.617	—	734	593	.276	.979	3.49
MILWAUKEE	88	66	.571	7	724	658	.265	.976	3.76
ST. LOUIS	86	68	.558	9	639	616	.254	.976	3.64
LOS ANGELES	82	72	.532	13	662	593	.255	.979	3.40
SAN FRANCISCO	79	75	.513	16	671	631	.255	.972	3.44
CINCINNATI	67	87	.435	28	640	692	.250	.979	4.00
CHICAGO	60	94	.390	35	634	776	.243	.977	4.35
PHILADELPHIA	59	95	.383	36	546	691	.239	.974	4.01
					5250	5250	.255	.977	3.76

BATTING AVERAGE
Dick Groat PIT .... .325
Norm Larker LA .... .323
Willie Mays SF .... .319

HITS
Willie Mays SF 190
Vada Pinson CIN 187
Dick Groat PIT 186

DOUBLES
Vada Pinson CIN 37
Orlando Cepeda SF 36
two tied at 33

TRIPLES
Bill Bruton MIL 13
Willie Mays SF 12
Vada Pinson CIN 12

HOME RUNS
Ernie Banks CHI 41
Hank Aaron MIL 40
Eddie Mathews MIL 39

RUNS BATTED IN
Hank Aaron MIL 126
Eddie Mathews MIL 124
Ernie Banks CHI 117

SLUGGING AVERAGE
Frank Robinson CIN .. .595
Hank Aaron MIL .... .566
Ken Boyer STL .... .562

STOLEN BASES
Maury Wills LA 50
Vada Pinson CIN 32
Tony Taylor CHI, PHI.... 26

RUNS SCORED
Bill Bruton MIL 112
Eddie Mathews MIL 108
two tied at 107

WINS
Ernie Broglio STL.......... 21
Warren Spahn MIL........ 21
Vern Law PIT 20

WINNING PERCENTAGE
Ernie Broglio STL........ .700
Vern Law PIT .... .690
Warren Spahn MIL...... .677

EARNED RUN AVERAGE
Mike McCormick SF... 2.70
Ernie Broglio STL....... 2.74
Don Drysdale LA........ 2.84

STRIKEOUTS
Don Drysdale LA......... 246
Sandy Koufax LA........ 197
Sam Jones SF 190

SAVES
Lindy McDaniel STL...... 26
Roy Face PIT................ 24
Bill Henry CIN 17

COMPLETE GAMES
Warren Spahn MIL....... 18
Vern Law PIT 18
Lew Burdette MIL.......... 18

SHUTOUTS
Jack Sanford SF 6
Don Drysdale LA............. 5

GAMES PITCHED
Roy Face PIT................ 68
Lindy McDaniel STL...... 65
Don Elston CHI 60

INNINGS PITCHED
Larry Jackson STL...... 282
Lew Burdette MIL....:.... 276
Bob Friend PIT............. 276

1961 AL

	W	L	PCT	GB	R	OR	BA	FA	ERA
★ NEW YORK	109	53	.673	—	827	612	.263	.980	3.46
DETROIT	101	61	.623	8	841	671	.266	.976	3.55
BALTIMORE	95	67	.586	14	691	588	.254	.980	3.22
CHICAGO	86	76	.531	23	765	726	.265	.980	4.06
CLEVELAND	78	83	.484	30.5	737	752	.266	.977	4.15
BOSTON	76	86	.469	33	729	792	.254	.977	4.29
MINNESOTA	70	90	.438	38	707	778	.250	.972	4.28
LOS ANGELES	70	91	.435	38.5	744	784	.245	.969	4.31
KANSAS CITY	61	100	.379	47.5	683	863	.247	.972	4.74
WASHINGTON	61	100	.379	47.5	618	776	.244	.975	4.23
					7342	7342	.256	.976	4.02

BATTING AVERAGE
Norm Cash DET .... .361
Al Kaline DET .... .324
Jimmy Piersall CLE.... .322

HITS
Norm Cash DET 193
Brooks Robinson BAL. 192
Al Kaline DET 190

DOUBLES
Al Kaline DET 41
Tony Kubek NY............. 38
Brooks Robinson BAL... 38

TRIPLES
Jake Wood DET............ 14
Marty Keough WAS 9
Jerry Lumpe KC.............. 9

HOME RUNS
Roger Maris NY 61
Mickey Mantle NY 54
two tied at 46

RUNS BATTED IN
Roger Maris NY 142
Jim Gentile BAL 141
Rocky Colavito DET.... 140

SLUGGING AVERAGE
Mickey Mantle NY...... .687
Norm Cash DET .... .662
Jim Gentile BAL .... .646

STOLEN BASES
Luis Aparicio CHI.......... 53
Dick Howser KC............ 37
Jake Wood DET............ 30

RUNS SCORED
Roger Maris NY 132
Mickey Mantle NY....... 132
Rocky Colavito DET.... 129

WINS
Whitey Ford NY 25
Frank Lary DET 23
Steve Barber BAL 18

WINNING PERCENTAGE
Whitey Ford NY .... .862
Ralph Terry NY .... .842
Luis Arroyo NY........... .750

EARNED RUN AVERAGE
Dick Donovan WAS ... 2.40
Bill Stafford NY 2.68
Don Mossi DET.......... 2.96

STRIKEOUTS
Camilo Pascual MIN ... 221
Whitey Ford NY 209
Jim Bunning DET........ 194

SAVES
Luis Arroyo NY.............. 29
Hoyt Wilhelm BAL.......... 18
Mike Fornieles BOS...... 15

COMPLETE GAMES
Frank Lary DET 22
Camilo Pascual MIN 15
Steve Barber BAL......... 14

SHUTOUTS
Camilo Pascual MIN 8
Steve Barber BAL........... 8
three tied at..................... 4

GAMES PITCHED
Luis Arroyo NY.............. 65
Tom Morgan LA............. 59
Turk Lown CHI.............. 59

INNINGS PITCHED
Whitey Ford NY 283
Frank Lary DET 275
Jim Bunning DET........ 268

1961 NL

	W	L	PCT	GB	R	OR	BA	FA	ERA
CINCINNATI	93	61	.604	—	710	653	.270	.977	3.78
LOS ANGELES	89	65	.578	4	735	697	.262	.975	4.04
SAN FRANCISCO	85	69	.552	8	773	655	.264	.977	3.77
MILWAUKEE	83	71	.539	10	712	656	.258	.982	3.89
ST. LOUIS	80	74	.519	13	703	668	.271	.972	3.74
PITTSBURGH	75	79	.487	18	694	675	.273	.975	3.92
CHICAGO	64	90	.416	29	689	800	.255	.970	4.48
PHILADELPHIA	47	107	.305	46	584	796	.243	.976	4.61
					5600	5600	.262	.976	4.03

BATTING AVERAGE
R. Clemente PIT .... .351
Vada Pinson CIN .... .343
Ken Boyer STL .... .329

HITS
Vada Pinson CIN 208
R. Clemente PIT 201
Hank Aaron MIL.......... 197

DOUBLES
Hank Aaron MIL............ 39
Vada Pinson CIN 34
three tied at.................. 32

TRIPLES
George Altman CHI 12
three tied at.................. 11

HOME RUNS
Orlando Cepeda SF...... 46
Willie Mays SF 40
Frank Robinson CIN 37

RUNS BATTED IN
Orlando Cepeda SF.... 142
Frank Robinson CIN ... 124
Willie Mays SF 123

SLUGGING AVERAGE
Frank Robinson CIN .. .611
Orlando Cepeda SF... .609
Hank Aaron MIL.......... .594

STOLEN BASES
Maury Wills LA.............. 35
Vada Pinson CIN 23
Frank Robinson CIN 22

RUNS SCORED
Willie Mays SF 129
Frank Robinson CIN ... 117
Hank Aaron MIL.......... 115

WINS
Joey Jay CIN 21
Warren Spahn MIL........ 21
Jim O'Toole CIN 19

WINNING PERCENTAGE
Johnny Podres LA ..... .783
Jim O'Toole CIN .... .679
Joey Jay CIN .... .677

EARNED RUN AVERAGE
Warren Spahn MIL..... 3.02
Jim O'Toole CIN 3.10
Curt Simmons STL 3.13

STRIKEOUTS
Sandy Koufax LA........ 269
Stan Williams LA......... 205
Don Drysdale LA......... 182

SAVES
Stu Miller SF 17
Roy Face PIT................ 17
two tied at 16

COMPLETE GAMES
Warren Spahn MIL....... 21
Sandy Koufax LA.......... 15
two tied at 14

SHUTOUTS
Joey Jay CIN 4
Warren Spahn MIL.......... 4

GAMES PITCHED
Jack Baldschun PHI...... 65
Stu Miller SF 63
Roy Face PIT................ 62

INNINGS PITCHED
Lew Burdette MIL........ 272
Warren Spahn MIL...... 263
Don Cardwell CHI 259

1962 AL

	W	L	PCT	GB	R	OR	BA	FA	ERA
★ NEW YORK	96	66	.593	—	817	680	.267	.979	3.70
MINNESOTA	91	71	.562	5	798	713	.260	.979	3.89
LOS ANGELES	86	76	.531	10	718	706	.250	.973	3.70
DETROIT	85	76	.528	10.5	758	692	.248	.974	3.81
CHICAGO	85	77	.525	11	707	658	.257	.982	3.73
CLEVELAND	80	82	.494	16	682	745	.245	.978	4.14
BALTIMORE	77	85	.475	19	652	680	.248	.980	3.69
BOSTON	76	84	.475	19	707	756	.258	.979	4.22
KANSAS CITY	72	90	.444	24	745	837	.263	.979	4.79
WASHINGTON	60	101	.373	35.5	599	716	.250	.978	4.04
					7183	7183	.255	.978	3.97

BATTING AVERAGE
Pete Runnels BOS...... .326
Mickey Mantle NY ...... .321
Floyd Robinson CHI.... .312

HITS
B. Richardson NY 209
Jerry Lumpe KC.......... 193
B. Robinson BAL 192

DOUBLES
Floyd Robinson CHI...... 45
C. Yastrzemski BOS..... 43
Ed Bressoud BOS......... 40

TRIPLES
Gino Cimoli KC 15
three tied at................... 10

HOME RUNS
H. Killebrew MIN 48
Norm Cash DET 39
two tied at 37

RUNS BATTED IN
H. Killebrew MIN 126
Norm Siebern KC........ 117
Rocky Colavito DET.... 112

SLUGGING AVERAGE
Mickey Mantle NY ...... .605
H. Killebrew MIN .... .545
Rocky Colavito DET... .514

STOLEN BASES
Luis Aparicio CHI 31
Chuck Hinton WAS....... 28
Jake Wood DET............ 24

RUNS SCORED
Albie Pearson LA 115
Norm Siebern KC........ 114
Bob Allison MIN 102

WINS
Ralph Terry NY 23
three tied at.................. 20

WINNING PERCENTAGE
Ray Herbert CHI .... .690
Whitey Ford NY .... .680
two tied at .... .667

EARNED RUN AVERAGE
Hank Aguirre DET...... 2.21
Robin Roberts BAL.... 2.78
Whitey Ford NY 2.90

STRIKEOUTS
Camilo Pascual MIN ... 206
Jim Bunning DET........ 184
Ralph Terry NY 176

SAVES
Dick Radatz BOS.......... 24
Marshall Bridges NY 18
Terry Fox DET 16

COMPLETE GAMES
Camilo Pascual MIN ... 18
Jim Kaat MIN 16
Dick Donovan CLE 16

SHUTOUTS
Camilo Pascual MIN 5
Dick Donovan CLE 5
Jim Kaat MIN 5

GAMES PITCHED
Dick Radatz BOS.......... 62
John Wyatt KC.............. 59

INNINGS PITCHED
Ralph Terry NY 299
Jim Kaat MIN 269
Jim Bunning DET....... 258

1962 NL

	W	L	PCT	GB	R	OR	BA	FA	ERA
SAN FRANCISCO*	103	62	.624	—	878	690	.278	.977	3.79
LOS ANGELES	102	63	.618	1	842	697	.268	.970	3.62
CINCINNATI	98	64	.605	3.5	802	685	.270	.977	3.75
PITTSBURGH	93	68	.578	8	706	626	.268	.976	3.37
MILWAUKEE	86	76	.531	15.5	730	665	.252	.980	3.68
ST. LOUIS	84	78	.519	17.5	774	664	.271	.979	3.55
PHILADELPHIA	81	80	.503	20	705	759	.260	.977	4.28
HOUSTON	64	96	.400	36.5	592	717	.246	.973	3.83
CHICAGO	59	103	.364	42.5	632	827	.253	.977	4.54
NEW YORK	40	120	.250	60.5	617	948	.240	.967	5.04
*Defeated Los Angeles in a playoff 2 games to 1					7278	7278	.261	.975	3.94

BATTING AVERAGE
Tommy Davis LA .... .346
Frank Robinson CIN .. .342
Stan Musial STL .... .330

HITS
Tommy Davis LA 230
Frank Robinson CIN ... 208
Maury Wills LA............. 208

DOUBLES
Frank Robinson CIN 51
Willie Mays SF 36
Dick Groat PIT 34

TRIPLES
four tied at..................... 10

HOME RUNS
Willie Mays SF 49
Hank Aaron MIL 45
Frank Robinson CIN 39

RUNS BATTED IN
Tommy Davis LA 153
Willie Mays SF 141
Frank Robinson CIN ... 136

SLUGGING AVERAGE
Frank Robinson CIN .. .624
Hank Aaron MIL.......... .618
Willie Mays SF .... .615

STOLEN BASES
Maury Wills LA............ 104
Willie Davis LA.............. 32
two tied at 26

RUNS SCORED
Frank Robinson CIN ... 134
Maury Wills LA............ 130
Willie Mays SF 130

WINS
Don Drysdale LA........... 25
Jack Sanford SF 24
Bob Purkey CIN............ 23

WINNING PERCENTAGE
Bob Purkey CIN .... .821
Jack Sanford SF .... .774
Don Drysdale LA........ .735

EARNED RUN AVERAGE
Sandy Koufax LA 2.54
Bob Shaw MIL 2.80
Bob Purkey CIN 2.81

STRIKEOUTS
Don Drysdale LA......... 232
Sandy Koufax LA........ 216
Bob Gibson STL 208

SAVES
Roy Face PIT................ 28
Ron Perranoski LA........ 20
Stu Miller SF 19

COMPLETE GAMES
Warren Spahn MIL........ 22
Art Mahaffey PHI 20
Billy O'Dell SF.............. 20

SHUTOUTS
Bob Gibson STL 5
Bob Friend PIT................ 5

GAMES PITCHED
Ron Perranoski LA........ 70
Jack Baldshun PHI 67
Ed Roebuck LA............. 64

INNINGS PITCHED
Don Drysdale LA......... 314
Bob Purkey CIN 288
Billy O'Dell SF............. 281

1963 AL

	W	L	PCT	GB	R	OR	BA	FA	ERA
NEW YORK	104	57	.646	—	714	547	.252	.982	3.07
CHICAGO	94	68	.580	10.5	683	544	.250	.979	2.97
MINNESOTA	91	70	.565	13	767	602	.255	.976	3.28
BALTIMORE	86	76	.531	18.5	644	621	.249	.984	3.45
CLEVELAND	79	83	.488	25.5	635	702	.239	.977	3.79
DETROIT	79	83	.488	25.5	700	703	.252	.981	3.90
BOSTON	76	85	.472	28	666	704	.252	.978	3.97
KANSAS CITY	73	89	.451	31.5	615	704	.247	.980	3.92
LOS ANGELES	70	91	.435	34	597	660	.250	.974	3.52
WASHINGTON	56	106	.346	48.5	578	812	.227	.971	4.42
					6599	6599	.247	.978	3.63

BATTING AVERAGE
C. Yastrzemski BOS .. .321
Al Kaline DET .... .312
Rich Rollins MIN .... .307

HITS
C. Yastrzemski BOS ... 183
Pete Ward CHI............ 177
Albie Pearson LA 176

DOUBLES
C. Yastrzemski BOS..... 40
Pete Ward CHI.............. 34
three tied at.................... 32

TRIPLES
Zoilo Versalles MIN..... 13
Jim Fregosi LA.............. 12
Chuck Hinton WAS....... 12

HOME RUNS
H. Killebrew MIN........... 45
Dick Stuart BOS............ 42
Bob Allison MIN 35

RUNS BATTED IN
Dick Stuart BOS.......... 118
Al Kaline DET 101
H. Killebrew MIN 96

SLUGGING AVERAGE
H. Killebrew MIN .... .555
Bob Allison MIN .... .533
Elston Howard NY .... .528

STOLEN BASES
Luis Aparicio BAL 40
Chuck Hinton WAS....... 25
two tied at 18

RUNS SCORED
Bob Allison MIN 99
Albie Pearson LA 92
three tied at................... 91

WINS
Whitey Ford NY 24
Jim Bouton NY.............. 21
Camilo Pascual MIN 21

WINNING PERCENTAGE
Whitey Ford NY .... .774
Jim Bouton NY .... .750
Dick Radatz BOS........ .714

EARNED RUN AVERAGE
Gary Peters CHI 2.33
Juan Pizarro CHI 2.39
Camilo Pascual MIN .. 2.46

STRIKEOUTS
Camilo Pascual MIN ... 202
Jim Bunning DET........ 196
Dick Stigman MIN....... 193

SAVES
Stu Miller BAL............... 27
Dick Radatz BOS.......... 25
three tied at.................... 21

COMPLETE GAMES
Ralph Terry NY 18
Camilo Pascual MIN 18
Dick Stigman MIN......... 15

SHUTOUTS
Ray Herbert CHI 7
Jim Bouton NY................ 6

GAMES PITCHED
Stu Miller BAL............... 71
Dick Radatz BOS.......... 66
Bill Dailey MIN 66

INNINGS PITCHED
Whitey Ford NY 269
Ralph Terry NY 268
B. Monbouquette BOS. 267

1963 NL

	W	L	PCT	GB	R	OR	BA	FA	ERA
★ LOS ANGELES	99	63	.611	—	640	550	.251	.975	2.85
ST. LOUIS	93	69	.574	6	747	628	.271	.976	3.32
SAN FRANCISCO	88	74	.543	11	725	641	.258	.975	3.35
PHILADELPHIA	87	75	.537	12	642	578	.252	.978	3.09
CINCINNATI	86	76	.531	13	648	594	.246	.978	3.29
MILWAUKEE	84	78	.519	15	677	603	.244	.980	3.27
CHICAGO	82	80	.506	17	570	578	.238	.976	3.08
PITTSBURGH	74	88	.457	25	567	595	.250	.972	3.10
HOUSTON	66	96	.407	33	464	640	.220	.974	3.44
NEW YORK	51	111	.315	48	501	774	.219	.967	4.12
					6181	6181	.245	.975	3.29

BATTING AVERAGE
Tommy Davis LA .... .326
R. Clemente PIT .... .320
two tied at .... .319

HITS
Vada Pinson CIN 204
Hank Aaron MIL 201
Dick Groat STL 201

DOUBLES
Dick Groat STL 43
Vada Pinson CIN 37
three tied at 36

TRIPLES
Vada Pinson CIN 14
Tony Gonzalez PHI 12
three tied at 11

HOME RUNS
Willie McCovey SF 44
Hank Aaron MIL 44
Willie Mays SF 38

RUNS BATTED IN
Hank Aaron MIL 130
Ken Boyer STL 111
Bill White STL 109

SLUGGING AVERAGE
Hank Aaron MIL .... .586
Willie Mays SF .... .582
Willie McCovey SF ..... .566

STOLEN BASES
Maury Wills LA 40
Hank Aaron MIL 31
Vada Pinson CIN 27

RUNS SCORED
Hank Aaron MIL 121
Willie Mays SF 115
Curt Flood STL 112

WINS
Sandy Koufax LA 25
Juan Marichal SF 25
two tied at 23

WINNING PERCENTAGE
Ron Perranoski LA ..... .842
Sandy Koufax LA .... .833
two tied at .... .767

EARNED RUN AVERAGE
Sandy Koufax LA 1.88
Dick Ellsworth CHI 2.11
Bob Friend PIT 2.34

STRIKEOUTS
Sandy Koufax LA 306
Jim Maloney CIN 265
Don Drysdale LA 251

SAVES
Lindy McDaniel CHI 22
Ron Perranoski LA 21
two tied at 16

COMPLETE GAMES
Warren Spahn MIL 22
Sandy Koufax LA 20
Dick Ellsworth CHI 19

SHUTOUTS
Sandy Koufax LA 11
Warren Spahn MIL 7
two tied at 6

GAMES PITCHED
Ron Perranoski LA 69
Jack Baldschun PHI 65
Larry Bearnarth NY 58

INNINGS PITCHED
Juan Marichal SF 321
Don Drysdale LA 315
Sandy Koufax LA 311

1964 AL

	W	L	PCT	GB	R	OR	BA	FA	ERA
NEW YORK	99	63	.611	—	730	577	.253	.983	3.15
CHICAGO	98	64	.605	1	642	501	.247	.981	2.72
BALTIMORE	97	65	.599	2	679	567	.248	.985	3.16
DETROIT	85	77	.525	14	699	678	.253	.982	3.84
LOS ANGELES	82	80	.506	17	544	551	.242	.978	2.91
CLEVELAND	79	83	.488	20	689	693	.247	.981	3.75
MINNESOTA	79	83	.488	20	737	678	.252	.977	3.58
BOSTON	72	90	.444	27	688	793	.258	.977	4.50
WASHINGTON	62	100	.383	37	578	733	.231	.979	3.98
KANSAS CITY	57	105	.352	42	621	836	.239	.975	4.71
					6607	6607	.247	.980	3.63

BATTING AVERAGE
Tony Oliva MIN .... .323
Brooks Robinson BAL .317
Elston Howard NY ..... .313

HITS
Tony Oliva MIN 217
Brooks Robinson BAL. 194
B. Richardson NY 181

DOUBLES
Tony Oliva MIN 43
Ed Bressoud BOS......... 41
Brooks Robinson BAL... 35

TRIPLES
Rich Rollins MIN 10
Zoilo Versalles MIN....... 10
three tied at...................... 9

HOME RUNS
H. Killebrew MIN 49
Boog Powell BAL 39
Mickey Mantle NY......... 35

RUNS BATTED IN
Brooks Robinson BAL. 118
Dick Stuart BOS.......... 114
two tied at 111

SLUGGING AVERAGE
Boog Powell BAL....... .606
Mickey Mantle NY...... .591
Tony Oliva MIN .... .557

STOLEN BASES
Luis Aparicio BAL 57
Al Weis CHI 22
Vic Davalillo CLE 21

RUNS SCORED
Tony Oliva MIN 109
Dick Howser CLE........ 101
H. Killebrew MIN........... 95

WINS
Gary Peters CHI 20
Dean Chance LA 20
three tied at.................. 19

WINNING PERCENTAGE
Wally Bunker BAL....... .792
Whitey Ford NY .... .739
Gary Peters CHI .... .714

EARNED RUN AVERAGE
Dean Chance LA 1.65
Joe Horlen CHI 1.88
Whitey Ford NY 2.13

STRIKEOUTS
Al Downing NY............ 217
Camilo Pascual MIN ... 213
Dean Chance LA 207

SAVES
Dick Radatz BOS.......... 29
Hoyt Wilhelm CHI 27
Stu Miller BAL............... 23

COMPLETE GAMES
Dean Chance LA 15
Camilo Pascual MIN 14
three tied at................... 13

SHUTOUTS
Dean Chance LA 11
Whitey Ford NY 8
Milt Pappas BAL 7

GAMES PITCHED
John Wyatt KC.............. 81
Dick Radatz BOS.......... 79
Hoyt Wilhelm CHI 73

INNINGS PITCHED
Dean Chance LA 278
Gary Peters CHI 274
Jim Bouton NY............ 271

1964 NL

	W	L	PCT	GB	R	OR	BA	FA	ERA
★ ST. LOUIS	93	69	.574	—	715	652	.272	.973	3.43
CINCINNATI	92	70	.568	1	660	566	.249	.979	3.07
PHILADELPHIA	92	70	.568	1	693	632	.258	.975	3.36
SAN FRANCISCO	90	72	.556	3	656	587	.246	.975	3.19
MILWAUKEE	88	74	.543	5	803	744	.272	.977	4.12
LOS ANGELES	80	82	.494	13	614	572	.250	.973	2.95
PITTSBURGH	80	82	.494	13	663	636	.264	.972	3.52
CHICAGO	76	86	.469	17	649	724	.251	.975	4.08
HOUSTON	66	96	.407	27	495	628	.229	.976	3.41
NEW YORK	53	109	.327	40	569	776	.246	.974	4.25
					6517	6517	.254	.975	3.54

BATTING AVERAGE
R. Clemente PIT .... .339
Rico Carty MIL .... .330
Hank Aaron MIL .... .328

HITS
Curt Flood STL 211
R. Clemente PIT 211
two tied at 201

DOUBLES
Lee Maye MIL 44
R. Clemente PIT 40
Billy Williams CHI 39

TRIPLES
Dick Allen PHI 13
Ron Santo CHI 13
two tied at 11

HOME RUNS
Willie Mays SF 47
Billy Williams CHI 33
three tied at 31

RUNS BATTED IN
Ken Boyer STL 119
Ron Santo CHI 114
Willie Mays SF 111

SLUGGING AVERAGE
Willie Mays SF .... .607
Ron Santo CHI .... .564
Dick Allen PHI .... .557

STOLEN BASES
Maury Wills LA 53
Lou Brock CHI, STL 43
Willie Davis LA 42

RUNS SCORED
Dick Allen PHI 125
Willie Mays SF 121
Lou Brock CHI, STL 111

WINS
Larry Jackson CHI 24
Juan Marichal SF 21
Ray Sadecki STL 20

WINNING PERCENTAGE
Sandy Koufax LA .... .792
Juan Marichal SF .... .724
Jim O'Toole CIN .... .708

EARNED RUN AVERAGE
Sandy Koufax LA 1.74
Don Drysdale LA 2.18
Chris Short PHI 2.20

STRIKEOUTS
Bob Veale PIT 250
Bob Gibson STL 245
Don Drysdale LA 237

SAVES
Hal Woodeshick HOU ... 23
Al McBean PIT 22
Jack Baldschun PHI 21

COMPLETE GAMES
Juan Marichal SF 22
Don Drysdale LA 21
Larry Jackson CHI 19

SHUTOUTS
Sandy Koufax LA 7
four tied at 5

GAMES PITCHED
Bob Miller LA 74
Ron Perranoski LA 72
Jack Baldschun PHI 71

INNINGS PITCHED
Don Drysdale LA 321
Larry Jackson CHI 298
Bob Gibson STL 287

1965 AL

	W	L	PCT	GB	R	OR	BA	FA	ERA
MINNESOTA	102	60	.630	—	774	600	.254	.973	3.14
CHICAGO	95	67	.586	7	647	555	.246	.980	2.99
BALTIMORE	94	68	.580	8	641	578	.238	.980	2.98
DETROIT	89	73	.549	13	680	602	.238	.981	3.35
CLEVELAND	87	75	.537	15	663	613	.250	.981	3.30
NEW YORK	77	85	.475	25	611	604	.235	.978	3.28
CALIFORNIA	75	87	.463	27	527	569	.239	.981	3.17
WASHINGTON	70	92	.432	32	591	721	.228	.977	3.93
BOSTON	62	100	.383	40	669	791	.251	.974	4.24
KANSAS CITY	59	103	.364	43	585	755	.240	.977	4.24
					6388	6388	.242	.978	3.46

BATTING AVERAGE
Tony Oliva MIN .... .321
C. Yastrzemski BOS .. .312
Vic Davalillo CLE .... .301

HITS
Tony Oliva MIN 185
Zoilo Versalles MIN... 182
Rocky Colavito CLE... 170

DOUBLES
C. Yastrzemski BOS..... 45
Zoilo Versalles MIN....... 45
Tony Oliva MIN 40

TRIPLES
Bert Campaneris KC..... 12
Zoilo Versalles MIN...... 12
Luis Aparicio BAL 10

HOME RUNS
Tony Conigliaro BOS.... 32
Norm Cash DET 30
Willie Horton DET 29

RUNS BATTED IN
Rocky Colavito CLE.... 108
Willie Horton DET 104
Tony Oliva MIN 98

SLUGGING AVERAGE
C. Yastrzemski BOS.. .536
T. Conigliaro BOS...... .512
Norm Cash DET .... .512

STOLEN BASES
Bert Campaneris KC..... 51
Jose Cardenal CAL....... 37
Zoilo Versalles MIN....... 27

RUNS SCORED
Zoilo Versalles MIN.... 126
Tony Oliva MIN 107
Tom Tresh NY 94

WINS
Mudcat Grant MIN 21
Mel Stottlemyre NY....... 20
Jim Kaat MIN 18

WINNING PERCENTAGE
Mudcat Grant MIN ..... .750
Denny McLain DET.... .727
Mel Stottlemyre NY.... .690

EARNED RUN AVERAGE
Sam McDowell CLE.... 2.18
Eddie Fisher CHI 2.40
Sonny Siebert CLE.... 2.43

STRIKEOUTS
Sam McDowell CLE.... 325
Mickey Lolich DET...... 226
Denny McLain DET..... 192

SAVES
Ron Kline WAS............. 29
Eddie Fisher CHI 24
Stu Miller BAL 24

COMPLETE GAMES
Mel Stottlemyre NY....... 18
Mudcat Grant MIN 14
Sam McDowell CLE...... 14

SHUTOUTS
Mudcat Grant MIN 6
four tied at....................... 4

GAMES PITCHED
Eddie Fisher CHI 82
Ron Kline WAS.............. 74
Bob Lee CAL 69

INNINGS PITCHED
Mel Stottlemyre NY..... 291
Sam McDowell CLE.... 273
Mudcat Grant MIN 270

1965 NL

	W	L	PCT	GB	R	OR	BA	FA	ERA
★ LOS ANGELES	97	65	.599	—	608	521	.245	.979	2.81
SAN FRANCISCO	95	67	.586	2	682	593	.252	.976	3.20
PITTSBURGH	90	72	.556	7	675	580	.265	.977	3.01
CINCINNATI	89	73	.549	8	825	704	.273	.981	3.88
MILWAUKEE	86	76	.531	11	708	633	.256	.978	3.52
PHILADELPHIA	85	76	.528	11.5	654	667	.250	.975	3.53
ST. LOUIS	80	81	.497	16.5	707	674	.254	.979	3.77
CHICAGO	72	90	.444	25	635	723	.238	.974	3.78
HOUSTON	65	97	.401	32	596	711	.237	.974	3.84
NEW YORK	50	112	.309	47	495	752	.221	.974	4.06
					6558	6558	.249	.977	3.54

BATTING AVERAGE
R. Clemente PIT .... .329
Hank Aaron MIL......... .318
Willie Mays SF .... .317

HITS
Pete Rose CIN............ 209
Vada Pinson CIN 204
Billy Williams CHI........ 203

DOUBLES
Hank Aaron MIL............ 40
Billy Williams CHI.......... 39
two tied at 35

TRIPLES
Johnny Callison PHI 16
three tied at................... 14

HOME RUNS
Willie Mays SF 52
Willie McCovey SF........ 39
Billy Williams CHI.......... 34

RUNS BATTED IN
Deron Johnson CIN 130
Frank Robinson CIN ... 113
Willie Mays SF 112

SLUGGING AVERAGE
Willie Mays SF .... .645
Hank Aaron MIL......... .560
Billy Williams CHI....... .552

STOLEN BASES
Maury Wills LA.............. 94
Lou Brock STL............... 63
Jimmy Wynn HOU 43

RUNS SCORED
Tommy Harper CIN..... 126
Willie Mays SF 118
Pete Rose CIN............ 117

WINS
Sandy Koufax LA.......... 26
Tony Cloninger MIL 24
Don Drysdale LA........... 23

WINNING PERCENTAGE
Sandy Koufax LA .... .765
Jim Maloney CIN .... .690
Sammy Ellis CIN......... .688

EARNED RUN AVERAGE
Sandy Koufax LA 2.04
Juan Marichal SF 2.13
Vern Law PIT 2.15

STRIKEOUTS
Sandy Koufax LA 382
Bob Veale PIT............. 276
Bob Gibson STL 270

SAVES
Ted Abernathy CHI....... 31
Billy McCool CIN........... 21
Frank Linzy SF.............. 21

COMPLETE GAMES
Sandy Koufax LA 27
Juan Marichal SF.......... 24
two tied at 20

SHUTOUTS
Juan Marichal SF.......... 10
Sandy Koufax LA 8
three tied at..................... 7

GAMES PITCHED
Ted Abernathy CHI....... 84
H. Woodeshick HOU, STL. 78
Lindy McDaniel CHI...... 71

INNINGS PITCHED
Sandy Koufax LA 336
Don Drysdale LA......... 308
Bob Gibson STL 299

1966 AL

	W	L	PCT	GB	R	OR	BA	FA	ERA
★ BALTIMORE	97	63	.606	—	755	601	.258	.981	3.32
MINNESOTA	89	73	.549	9	663	581	.249	.977	3.13
DETROIT	88	74	.543	10	719	698	.251	.980	3.85
CHICAGO	83	79	.512	15	574	517	.231	.976	2.68
CLEVELAND	81	81	.500	17	574	586	.237	.978	3.23
CALIFORNIA	80	82	.494	18	604	643	.232	.979	3.56
KANSAS CITY	74	86	.463	23	564	648	.236	.977	3.56
WASHINGTON	71	88	.447	25.5	557	659	.234	.977	3.70
BOSTON	72	90	.444	26	655	731	.240	.975	3.92
NEW YORK	70	89	.440	26.5	611	612	.235	.977	3.41
					6276	6276	.240	.978	3.44

BATTING AVERAGE
Frank Robinson BAL.. .316
Tony Oliva MIN .... .307
Al Kaline DET .... .288

HITS
Tony Oliva MIN 191
Frank Robinson BAL.... 182
Luis Aparicio BAL 182

DOUBLES
C. Yastrzemski BOS 39
Brooks Robinson BAL... 35
Frank Robinson BAL..... 34

TRIPLES
Bobby Knoop CAL 11
Bert Campaneris KC 10
Ed Brinkman WAS 9

HOME RUNS
Frank Robinson BAL..... 49
H. Killebrew MIN 39
Boog Powell BAL 34

RUNS BATTED IN
Frank Robinson BAL... 122
H. Killebrew MIN 110
Boog Powell BAL 109

SLUGGING AVERAGE
Frank Robinson BAL.. .637
H. Killebrew MIN .... .538
Al Kaline DET .... .534

STOLEN BASES
Bert Campaneris KC..... 52
Don Buford CHI 51
Tommy Agee CHI 44

RUNS SCORED
Frank Robinson BAL... 122
Tony Oliva MIN 99
two tied at 98

WINS
Jim Kaat MIN 25
Denny McLain DET....... 20
E. Wilson BOS, DET..... 18

WINNING PERCENTAGE
Sonny Siebert CLE .... .667
Jim Kaat MIN .... .658
E. Wilson BOS, DET... .621

EARNED RUN AVERAGE
Gary Peters CHI 1.98
Joe Horlen CHI 2.43
Steve Hargan CLE...... 2.48

STRIKEOUTS
Sam McDowell CLE.... 225
Jim Kaat MIN 205
E. Wilson BOS, DET ... 200

SAVES
Jack Aker KC 32
Ron Kline WAS 23
Larry Sherry DET.......... 20

COMPLETE GAMES
Jim Kaat MIN 19
Denny McLain DET....... 14
E. Wilson BOS, DET..... 13

SHUTOUTS
Luis Tiant CLE 5
Sam McDowell CLE........ 5
Tommy John CHI............ 5

GAMES PITCHED
E. Fisher CHI, BAL 67
Casey Cox WAS........... 66
Jack Aker KC 66

INNINGS PITCHED
Jim Kaat MIN 305
Denny McLain DET..... 264
E. Wilson BOS, DET... 264

1966 NL

	W	L	PCT	GB	R	OR	BA	FA	ERA
LOS ANGELES	95	67	.586	—	606	490	.256	.979	2.62
SAN FRANCISCO	93	68	.578	1.5	675	626	.248	.974	3.24
PITTSBURGH	92	70	.568	3	759	641	.279	.978	3.52
PHILADELPHIA	87	75	.537	8	696	640	.258	.982	3.57
ATLANTA	85	77	.525	10	782	683	.263	.976	3.68
ST. LOUIS	83	79	.512	12	571	577	.251	.977	3.11
CINCINNATI	76	84	.475	18	692	702	.260	.980	4.08
HOUSTON	72	90	.444	23	612	695	.255	.972	3.76
NEW YORK	66	95	.410	28.5	587	761	.239	.975	4.17
CHICAGO	59	103	.364	36	644	809	.254	.974	4.33
					6624	6624	.256	.977	3.61

BATTING AVERAGE
Matty Alou PIT .... .342
Felipe Alou ATL .... .327
Rico Carty ATL .... .326

HITS
Felipe Alou ATL 218
Pete Rose CIN 205
R. Clemente PIT 202

DOUBLES
Johnny Callison PHI 40
Pete Rose CIN 38
Vada Pinson CIN 35

TRIPLES
Tim McCarver STL 13
Lou Brock STL 12
R. Clemente PIT 11

HOME RUNS
Hank Aaron ATL 44
Dick Allen PHI 40
Willie Mays SF 37

RUNS BATTED IN
Hank Aaron ATL 127
R. Clemente PIT 119
Dick Allen PHI 110

SLUGGING AVERAGE
Dick Allen PHI .... .632
Willie McCovey SF ..... .586
Willie Stargell PIT ...... .581

STOLEN BASES
Lou Brock STL 74
Sonny Jackson HOU 49
Maury Wills LA 38

RUNS SCORED
Felipe Alou ATL 122
Hank Aaron ATL 117
Dick Allen PHI 112

WINS
Sandy Koufax LA 27
Juan Marichal SF 25
two tied at 21

WINNING PERCENTAGE
Juan Marichal SF .... .806
Sandy Koufax LA .... .750
Gaylord Perry SF .... .724

EARNED RUN AVERAGE
Sandy Koufax LA 1.73
Mike Cuellar HOU 2.22
Juan Marichal SF 2.23

STRIKEOUTS
Sandy Koufax LA 317
Jim Bunning PHI 252
Bob Veale PIT 229

SAVES
Phil Regan LA 21
Billy McCool CIN 18
Roy Face PIT 18

COMPLETE GAMES
Sandy Koufax LA 27
Juan Marichal SF 25
Bob Gibson STL 20

SHUTOUTS
six tied at 5

GAMES PITCHED
Clay Carroll ATL 73
Pete Mikkelsen PIT 71
Darold Knowles PHI...... 69

INNINGS PITCHED
Sandy Koufax LA 323
Jim Bunning PHI 314
Juan Marichal SF 307

1967 AL

	W	L	PCT	GB	R	OR	BA	FA	ERA
BOSTON	92	70	.568	—	722	614	.255	.977	3.36
DETROIT	91	71	.562	1	683	587	.243	.978	3.32
MINNESOTA	91	71	.562	1	671	590	.240	.978	3.14
CHICAGO	89	73	.549	3	531	491	.225	.979	2.45
CALIFORNIA	84	77	.522	7.5	567	587	.238	.982	3.19
BALTIMORE	76	85	.472	15.5	654	592	.240	.980	3.32
WASHINGTON	76	85	.472	15.5	550	637	.223	.978	3.38
CLEVELAND	75	87	.463	17	559	613	.235	.981	3.25
NEW YORK	72	90	.444	20	522	621	.225	.976	3.24
KANSAS CITY	62	99	.385	29.5	533	660	.233	.978	3.68
					5992	5992	.236	.979	3.23

BATTING AVERAGE
C. Yastrzemski BOS .. .326
Frank Robinson BAL.. .311
Al Kaline DET .... .308

HITS
C. Yastrzemski BOS ... 189
Cesar Tovar MIN 173
two tied at 171

DOUBLES
Tony Oliva MIN 34
Cesar Tovar MIN 32
C. Yastrzemski BOS 31

TRIPLES
Paul Blair BAL............... 12
Don Buford CHI 9

HOME RUNS
H. Killebrew MIN 44
C. Yastrzemski BOS 44
Frank Howard WAS 36

RUNS BATTED IN
C. Yastrzemski BOS ... 121
H. Killebrew MIN 113
Frank Robinson BAL..... 94

SLUGGING AVERAGE
C. Yastrzemski BOS .. .622
Frank Robinson BAL.. .576
H. Killebrew MIL......... .558

STOLEN BASES
Bert Campaneris KC..... 55
Don Buford CHI 34
Tommy Agee CHI 28

RUNS SCORED
C. Yastrzemski BOS ... 112
H. Killebrew MIN 105
Cesar Tovar MIN 98

WINS
Jim Lonborg BOS 22
Earl Wilson DET 22
Dean Chance MIN 20

WINNING PERCENTAGE
Joe Horlen CHI .... .731
Jim Lonborg BOS ...... .710
Earl Wilson DET .... .667

EARNED RUN AVERAGE
Joe Horlen CHI 2.06
Gary Peters CHI 2.28
Sonny Siebert CLE 2.38

STRIKEOUTS
Jim Lonborg BOS 246
Sam McDowell CLE.... 236
Dean Chance MIN 220

SAVES
Minnie Rojas CAL......... 27
John Wyatt BOS 20
Bob Locker CHI 20

COMPLETE GAMES
Dean Chance MIN 18
Jim Lonborg BOS 15
Steve Hargan CLE........ 15

SHUTOUTS
five tied at 6

GAMES PITCHED
Bob Locker CHI 77
Minnie Rojas CAL......... 72
Bill Kelso CAL............... 69

INNINGS PITCHED
Dean Chance MIN 284
Jim Lonborg BOS 273
Earl Wilson DET 264

1967 NL

	W	L	PCT	GB	R	OR	BA	FA	ERA
★ ST. LOUIS	101	60	.627	—	695	557	.263	.978	3.05
SAN FRANCISCO	91	71	.562	10.5	652	551	.245	.979	2.92
CHICAGO	87	74	.540	14	702	624	.251	.981	3.48
CINCINNATI	87	75	.537	14.5	604	563	.248	.980	3.05
PHILADELPHIA	82	80	.506	19.5	612	581	.242	.978	3.10
PITTSBURGH	81	81	.500	20.5	679	693	.277	.978	3.74
ATLANTA	77	85	.475	24.5	631	640	.240	.978	3.47
LOS ANGELES	73	89	.451	28.5	519	595	.236	.975	3.21
HOUSTON	69	93	.426	32.5	626	742	.249	.974	4.03
NEW YORK	61	101	.377	40.5	498	672	.238	.975	3.73
					6218	6218	.249	.978	3.38

BATTING AVERAGE
R. Clemente PIT .... .357
Tony Gonzalez PHI.... .339
Matty Alou PIT .... .338

HITS
R. Clemente PIT 209
Lou Brock STL............. 206
Vada Pinson CIN 187

DOUBLES
Rusty Staub HOU 44
Orlando Cepeda STL.... 37
Hank Aaron ATL 37

TRIPLES
Vada Pinson CIN 13
Lou Brock STL.............. 12
Billy Williams CHI.......... 12

HOME RUNS
Hank Aaron ATL 39
Jimmy Wynn HOU 37
two tied at 31

RUNS BATTED IN
O. Cepeda STL............ 111
R. Clemente PIT 110
Hank Aaron ATL 109

SLUGGING AVERAGE
Hank Aaron ATL .... .573
Dick Allen PHI............ .566
R. Clemente PIT .... .554

STOLEN BASES
Lou Brock STL.............. 52
Maury Wills PIT............. 29
Joe Morgan HOU.......... 29

RUNS SCORED
Lou Brock STL............. 113
Hank Aaron ATL 113
Ron Santo CHI............ 107

WINS
Mike McCormick SF...... 22
Fergie Jenkins CHI 20
two tied at 17

WINNING PERCENTAGE
Dick Hughes STL........ .727
Mike McCormick SF... .688
Bob Veale PIT............ .667

EARNED RUN AVERAGE
Phil Niekro ATL.......... 1.87
Jim Bunning PHI........ 2.29
Chris Short PHI.......... 2.39

STRIKEOUTS
Jim Bunning PHI 253
Fergie Jenkins CHI 236
Gaylord Perry SF 230

SAVES
Ted Abernathy CIN 28
Frank Linzy SF.............. 17
Roy Face PIT................ 17

COMPLETE GAMES
Fergie Jenkins CHI 20
three tied at................... 18

SHUTOUTS
Jim Bunning PHI 6
three tied at..................... 5

GAMES PITCHED
Ron Perranoski LA........ 70
Ted Abernathy CIN 70
Ron Willis STL 65

INNINGS PITCHED
Jim Bunning PHI 302
Gaylord Perry SF 293
Fergie Jenkins CHI 289

1968 AL

	W	L	PCT	GB	R	OR	BA	FA	ERA
★ DETROIT	103	59	.636	—	671	492	.235	.983	2.71
BALTIMORE	91	71	.562	12	579	497	.225	.981	2.66
CLEVELAND	86	75	.534	16.5	516	504	.234	.979	2.66
BOSTON	86	76	.531	17	614	611	.236	.979	3.33
NEW YORK	83	79	.512	20	536	531	.214	.979	2.79
OAKLAND	82	80	.506	21	569	544	.240	.977	2.94
MINNESOTA	79	83	.488	24	562	546	.237	.973	2.89
CALIFORNIA	67	95	.414	36	498	615	.227	.977	3.43
CHICAGO	67	95	.414	36	463	527	.228	.977	2.75
WASHINGTON	65	96	.404	37.5	524	665	.224	.976	3.64
					5532	5532	.230	.978	2.98

BATTING AVERAGE
C. Yastrzemski BOS .. .301
Danny Cater OAK ...... .290
Tony Oliva MIN .... .289

HITS
B. Campaneris OAK ... 177
Cesar Tovar MIN 167
two tied at 164

DOUBLES
Reggie Smith BOS........ 37
Brooks Robinson BAL... 36
C. Yastrzemski BOS 32

TRIPLES
Jim Fregosi CAL 13
Tom McCraw CHI 12
two tied at 10

HOME RUNS
Frank Howard WAS 44
Willie Horton DET 36
Ken Harrelson BOS 35

RUNS BATTED IN
Ken Harrelson BOS 109
Frank Howard WAS 106
Jim Northrup DET 90

SLUGGING AVERAGE
Frank Howard WAS .... .552
Willie Horton DET .... .543
Ken Harrelson BOS ... .518

STOLEN BASES
B. Campaneris OAK 62
Jose Cardenal CLE...... 40
Cesar Tovar MIN 35

RUNS SCORED
Dick McAuliffe DET....... 95
C. Yastrzemski BOS 90
two tied at 89

WINS
Denny McLain DET....... 31
Dave McNally BAL........ 22
two tied at 21

WINNING PERCENTAGE
Denny McLain DET.... .838
Ray Culp BOS .... .727
Luis Tiant CLE .... .700

EARNED RUN AVERAGE
Luis Tiant CLE 1.60
Sam McDowell CLE..... 1.81
Dave McNally BAL..... 1.95

STRIKEOUTS
Sam McDowell CLE.... 283
Denny McLain DET..... 280
Luis Tiant CLE 264

SAVES
Al Worthington MIN....... 18
Wilbur Wood CHI 16
Dennis Higgins WAS 13

COMPLETE GAMES
Denny McLain DET....... 28
Luis Tiant CLE 19
Mel Stottlemyre NY....... 19

SHUTOUTS
Luis Tiant CLE 9

GAMES PITCHED
Wilbur Wood CHI 88
Hoyt Wilhelm CHI 72
Bob Locker CHI 70

INNINGS PITCHED
Denny McLain DET..... 336
Dean Chance MIN 292
Mel Stottlemyre NY..... 279

1968 NL

	W	L	PCT	GB	R	OR	BA	FA	ERA
ST. LOUIS	97	65	.599	—	583	472	.249	.978	2.49
SAN FRANCISCO	88	74	.543	9	599	529	.239	.975	2.71
CHICAGO	84	78	.519	13	612	611	.242	.981	3.41
CINCINNATI	83	79	.512	14	690	673	.273	.978	3.56
ATLANTA	81	81	.500	16	514	549	.252	.980	2.92
PITTSBURGH	80	82	.494	17	583	532	.252	.979	2.74
LOS ANGELES	76	86	.469	21	470	509	.230	.977	2.69
PHILADELPHIA	76	86	.469	21	543	615	.233	.980	3.36
NEW YORK	73	89	.451	24	473	499	.228	.979	2.72
HOUSTON	72	90	.444	25	510	588	.231	.975	3.26
					5577	5577	.243	.978	2.99

BATTING AVERAGE
Pete Rose CIN............ .335
Matty Alou PIT .... .332
Felipe Alou ATL .... .317

HITS
Pete Rose CIN............ 210
Felipe Alou ATL 210
Glenn Beckert CHI...... 189

DOUBLES
Lou Brock STL.............. 46
Pete Rose CIN.............. 42
Johnny Bench CIN........ 40

TRIPLES
Lou Brock STL.............. 14
R. Clemente PIT 12
Willie Davis LA.............. 10

HOME RUNS
Willie McCovey SF........ 36
Dick Allen PHI.............. 33
Ernie Banks CHI 32

RUNS BATTED IN
Willie McCovey SF...... 105
Billy Williams CHI......... 98
Ron Santo CHI.............. 98

SLUGGING AVERAGE
Willie McCovey SF..... .545
Dick Allen PHI............. .520
Billy Williams CHI....... .500

STOLEN BASES
Lou Brock STL.............. 62
Maury Wills PIT............. 52
Willie Davis LA.............. 36

RUNS SCORED
Glenn Beckert CHI........ 98
Pete Rose CIN.............. 94
Tony Perez CIN 93

WINS
Juan Marichal SF.......... 26
Bob Gibson STL 22
Fergie Jenkins CHI 20

WINNING PERCENTAGE
Steve Blass PIT .... .750
Juan Marichal SF......... .743
Bob Gibson STL .... .710

EARNED RUN AVERAGE
Bob Gibson STL 1.12
Bobby Bolin SF 1.99
Bob Veale PIT............. 2.05

STRIKEOUTS
Bob Gibson STL 268
Fergie Jenkins CHI 260
Bill Singer LA 227

SAVES
Phil Regan LA, CHI....... 25
Joe Hoerner STL 17
Clay Carroll ATL, CIN ... 17

COMPLETE GAMES
Juan Marichal SF.......... 30
Bob Gibson STL 28
Fergie Jenkins CHI 20

SHUTOUTS
Bob Gibson STL 13
Don Drysdale LA............. 8
two tied at 7

GAMES PITCHED
Ted Abernathy CIN....... 78
Phil Regan LA, CHI....... 73
Clay Carroll ATL, CIN ... 68

INNINGS PITCHED
Juan Marichal SF........ 326
Fergie Jenkins CHI 308
Bob Gibson STL 305

1969 AL

EAST	W	L	PCT	GB	R	OR	BA	FA	ERA
• BALTIMORE	109	53	.673	—	779	517	.265	.984	2.83
DETROIT	90	72	.556	19	701	601	.242	.979	3.31
BOSTON	87	75	.537	22	743	736	.251	.975	3.92
WASHINGTON	86	76	.531	23	694	644	.251	.978	3.49
NEW YORK	80	81	.497	28.5	562	587	.235	.979	3.23
CLEVELAND	62	99	.385	46.5	573	717	.237	.976	3.94

WEST	W	L	PCT	GB	R	OR	BA	FA	ERA
MINNESOTA	97	65	.599	—	790	618	.268	.977	3.24
OAKLAND	88	74	.543	9	740	678	.249	.979	3.71
CALIFORNIA	71	91	.438	26	528	652	.230	.978	3.54
KANSAS CITY	69	93	.426	28	586	688	.240	.975	3.72
CHICAGO	68	94	.420	29	625	723	.247	.981	4.21
SEATTLE	64	98	.395	33	639	799	.234	.974	4.35
					7960	7960	.246	.978	3.62

BATTING AVERAGE
Rod Carew MIN............... .332
Reggie Smith BOS .... .309
Tony Oliva MIN................ .309

HITS
Tony Oliva MIN................ 197
Horace Clarke NY 183
Paul Blair BAL 178

DOUBLES
Tony Oliva MIN.................... 39
Reggie Jackson OAK......... 36
Davey Johnson BAL............ 34

TRIPLES
Del Unser WAS 8
Horace Clarke NY 7
Reggie Smith BOS 7

HOME RUNS
Harmon Killebrew MIN 49
Frank Howard WAS............ 48
Reggie Jackson OAK......... 47

RUNS BATTED IN
Harmon Killebrew MIN 140
Boog Powell BAL 121
Reggie Jackson OAK 118

SLUGGING AVERAGE
Reggie Jackson OAK...... .608
Rico Petrocelli BOS......... .589
Harmon Killebrew MIN .... .584

STOLEN BASES
Tommy Harper SEA ... 73
Bert Campaneris OAK...... 62
Cesar Tovar MIN 45

RUNS SCORED
Reggie Jackson OAK....... 123
Frank Howard WAS.......... 111
Frank Robinson BAL........ 111

WINS
Denny McLain DET 24
Mike Cuellar BAL 23
four tied at 20

WINNING PERCENTAGE
Jim Palmer BAL .... .800
Jim Perry MIN .... .769
Dave McNally BAL .... .741

EARNED RUN AVERAGE
Dick Bosman WAS.......... 2.19
Jim Palmer BAL 2.34
Mike Cuellar BAL 2.38

STRIKEOUTS
Sam McDowell CLE 279
Mickey Lolich DET 271
Andy Messersmith CAL.... 211

SAVES
Ron Perranoski MIN........... 31
Ken Tatum CAL.................. 22
Sparky Lyle BOS................ 17

COMPLETE GAMES
Mel Stottlemyre NY 24
Denny McLain DET............ 23
two tied at............................ 18

SHUTOUTS
Denny McLain DET 9
Jim Palmer BAL 6
Mike Cuellar BAL 5

GAMES PITCHED
Wilbur Wood CHI 76
Ron Perranoski MIN........... 75
Sparky Lyle BOS................ 71

INNINGS PITCHED
Denny McLain DET 325
Mel Stottlemyre NY 303
Mike Cuellar BAL 291

1969 NL

EAST	W	L	PCT	GB	R	OR	BA	FA	ERA
★ NEW YORK	100	62	.617	—	632	541	.242	.980	2.99
CHICAGO	92	70	.568	8	720	611	.253	.979	3.34
PITTSBURGH	88	74	.543	12	725	652	.277	.975	3.61
ST. LOUIS	87	75	.537	13	595	540	.253	.978	2.94
PHILADELPHIA	63	99	.389	37	645	745	.241	.978	4.14
MONTREAL	52	110	.321	48	582	791	.240	.971	4.33

WEST	W	L	PCT	GB	R	OR	BA	FA	ERA
ATLANTA	93	69	.574	—	691	631	.258	.981	3.53
SAN FRANCISCO	90	72	.556	3	713	636	.242	.974	3.26
CINCINNATI	89	73	.549	4	798	768	.277	.974	4.11
LOS ANGELES	85	77	.525	8	645	561	.254	.980	3.08
HOUSTON	81	81	.500	12	676	668	.240	.975	3.60
SAN DIEGO	52	110	.321	41	468	746	.225	.975	4.24
					7890	7890	.250	.977	3.59

BATTING AVERAGE
Pete Rose CIN .... .348
Roberto Clemente PIT .... .345
Cleon Jones NY .... .340

HITS
Matty Alou PIT.................. 231
Pete Rose CIN 218
Lou Brock STL 195

DOUBLES
Matty Alou PIT.................... 41
Don Kessinger CHI 38
three tied at 33

TRIPLES
Roberto Clemente PIT 12
Pete Rose CIN 11
three tied at 10

HOME RUNS
Willie McCovey SF............. 45
Hank Aaron ATL................. 44
Lee May CIN 38

RUNS BATTED IN
Willie McCovey SF........... 126
Ron Santo CHI 123
Tony Perez CIN 122

SLUGGING AVERAGE
Willie McCovey SF .... .656
Hank Aaron ATL................ .607
Dick Allen PHI .... .573

STOLEN BASES
Lou Brock STL 53
Joe Morgan HOU 49
Bobby Bonds SF 45

RUNS SCORED
Pete Rose CIN 120
Bobby Bonds SF 120
Jimmy Wynn HOU 113

WINS
Tom Seaver NY 25
Phil Niekro ATL 23
two tied at............................ 21

WINNING PERCENTAGE
Tom Seaver NY .... .781
Juan Marichal SF .... .656
two tied at.......................... .654

EARNED RUN AVERAGE
Juan Marichal SF 2.10
Steve Carlton STL........... 2.17
Bob Gibson STL.............. 2.18

STRIKEOUTS
Ferguson Jenkins CHI...... 273
Bob Gibson STL............... 269
Bill Singer LA.................... 247

SAVES
Fred Gladding HOU 29
Wayne Granger CIN........... 27
Cecil Upshaw ATL.............. 27

COMPLETE GAMES
Bob Gibson STL................. 28
Juan Marichal SF 27
Gaylord Perry SF 26

SHUTOUTS
Juan Marichal SF 8
Ferguson Jenkins CHI.......... 7
Claude Osteen LA................ 7

GAMES PITCHED
Wayne Granger CIN............ 90
Dan McGinn MON.............. 74
two tied at........................... 71

INNINGS PITCHED
Gaylord Perry SF 325
Claude Osteen LA............. 321
Bill Singer LA.................... 316

1970 AL

EAST	W	L	PCT	GB	R	OR	BA	FA	ERA
★ BALTIMORE	108	54	.667	—	792	574	.257	.981	3.15
NEW YORK	93	69	.574	15	680	612	.251	.980	3.24
BOSTON	87	75	.537	21	786	722	.262	.974	3.87
DETROIT	79	83	.488	29	666	731	.238	.978	4.09
CLEVELAND	76	86	.469	32	649	675	.249	.979	3.91
WASHINGTON	70	92	.432	38	626	689	.238	.982	3.80

WEST	W	L	PCT	GB	R	OR	BA	FA	ERA
MINNESOTA	98	64	.605	—	744	605	.262	.980	3.23
OAKLAND	89	73	.549	9	678	593	.249	.977	3.30
CALIFORNIA	86	76	.531	12	631	630	.251	.980	3.48
KANSAS CITY	65	97	.401	33	611	705	.244	.976	3.78
MILWAUKEE	65	97	.401	33	613	751	.242	.978	4.21
CHICAGO	56	106	.346	42	633	822	.253	.975	4.54
					8109	8109	.250	.978	3.71

BATTING AVERAGE
Alex Johnson CAL............ .329
Carl Yastrzemski BOS..... .329
Tony Oliva MIN................. .325

HITS
Tony Oliva MIN.................. 204
Alex Johnson CAL............ 202
Cesar Tovar MIN 195

DOUBLES
Cesar Tovar MIN 36
Tony Oliva MIN................... 36
Amos Otis KC...................... 36

TRIPLES
Cesar Tovar MIN 13
Mickey Stanley DET 11
Amos Otis KC....................... 9

HOME RUNS
Frank Howard WAS............ 44
Harmon Killebrew MIN 41
Carl Yastrzemski BOS........ 40

RUNS BATTED IN
Frank Howard WAS.......... 126
Tony Conigliaro BOS 116
Boog Powell BAL.............. 114

SLUGGING AVERAGE
Carl Yastrzemski BOS..... .592
Boog Powell BAL .... .549
Harmon Killebrew MIN .... .546

STOLEN BASES
Bert Campaneris OAK........ 42
Tommy Harper MIL............. 38
Sandy Alomar CAL............. 35

RUNS SCORED
Carl Yastrzemski BOS...... 125
Cesar Tovar MIN 120
two tied at......................... 109

WINS
Dave McNally BAL 24
Jim Perry MIN 24
Mike Cuellar BAL 24

WINNING PERCENTAGE
Mike Cuellar BAL .... .750
Dave McNally BAL .... .727
two tied at........................ .667

EARNED RUN AVERAGE
Diego Segui OAK............ 2.56
Jim Palmer BAL 2.71
Clyde Wright CAL............ 2.83

STRIKEOUTS
Sam McDowell CLE 304
Mickey Lolich DET 230
Bob Johnson KC 206

SAVES
Ron Perranoski MIN........... 34
Lindy McDaniel NY............. 29
two tied at........................... 27

COMPLETE GAMES
Mike Cuellar BAL 21
Sam McDowell CLE 19
Jim Palmer BAL 17

SHUTOUTS
Jim Palmer BAL 5
Chuck Dobson OAK............. 5
three tied at 4

GAMES PITCHED
Wilbur Wood CHI 77
Mudcat Grant OAK............. 72
Darold Knowles WAS 71

INNINGS PITCHED
Sam McDowell CLE 305
Jim Palmer BAL 305
Mike Cuellar BAL 298

1970 NL

EAST	W	L	PCT	GB	R	OR	BA	FA	ERA
PITTSBURGH	89	73	.549	—	729	664	.270	.979	3.70
CHICAGO	84	78	.519	5	806	679	.259	.978	3.76
NEW YORK	83	79	.512	6	695	630	.249	.979	3.45
ST. LOUIS	76	86	.469	13	744	747	.263	.977	4.06
PHILADELPHIA	73	88	.453	15.5	594	730	.238	.981	4.17
MONTREAL	73	89	.451	16	687	807	.237	.977	4.50

WEST	W	L	PCT	GB	R	OR	BA	FA	ERA
● CINCINNATI	102	60	.630	—	775	681	.270	.976	3.69
LOS ANGELES	87	74	.540	14.5	749	684	.270	.978	3.82
SAN FRANCISCO	86	76	.531	16	831	826	.262	.973	4.50
HOUSTON	79	83	.488	23	744	763	.259	.978	4.23
ATLANTA	76	86	.469	26	736	772	.270	.977	4.33
SAN DIEGO	63	99	.389	39	681	788	.246	.975	4.36
					8771	8771	.258	.977	4.05

BATTING AVERAGE
Rico Carty ATL .... .366
Joe Torre STL.................... .325
Manny Sanguillen PIT ..... .325

HITS
Billy Williams CHI 205
Pete Rose CIN 205
Joe Torre STL.................... 203

DOUBLES
Wes Parker LA 47
Willie McCovey SF 39
Pete Rose CIN 37

TRIPLES
Willie Davis LA 16
Don Kessinger CHI 14
two tied at............................ 10

HOME RUNS
Johnny Bench CIN 45
Billy Williams CHI 42
Tony Perez CIN 40

RUNS BATTED IN
Johnny Bench CIN 148
Billy Williams CHI 129
Tony Perez CIN 129

SLUGGING AVERAGE
Willie McCovey SF .... .612
Tony Perez CIN .... .589
Johnny Bench CIN .... .587

STOLEN BASES
Bobby Tolan CIN 57
Lou Brock STL 51
Bobby Bonds SF 48

RUNS SCORED
Billy Williams CHI 137
Bobby Bonds SF 134
Pete Rose CIN 120

WINS
Gaylord Perry SF 23
Bob Gibson STL................. 23
Ferguson Jenkins CHI........ 22

WINNING PERCENTAGE
Bob Gibson STL............... .767
Gary Nolan CIN .... .720
Luke Walker PIT.............. .714

EARNED RUN AVERAGE
Tom Seaver NY 2.82
Wayne Simpson CIN 3.02
Luke Walker PIT.............. 3.04

STRIKEOUTS
Tom Seaver NY 283
Bob Gibson STL................ 274
Ferguson Jenkins CHI...... 274

SAVES
Wayne Granger CIN........... 35
Dave Giusti PIT.................. 26
Jim Brewer LA 24

COMPLETE GAMES
Ferguson Jenkins CHI........ 24
Gaylord Perry SF 23
Bob Gibson STL................. 23

SHUTOUTS
Gaylord Perry SF 5
four tied at 4

GAMES PITCHED
Ron Herbel SD, NY............ 76
Dick Selma PHI 73
two tied at........................... 67

INNINGS PITCHED
Gaylord Perry SF 329
Ferguson Jenkins CHI...... 313
Bob Gibson STL............... 294

1971 AL

EAST	W	L	PCT	GB	R	OR	BA	FA	ERA
● BALTIMORE	101	57	.639	—	742	530	.261	.981	2.99
DETROIT	91	71	.562	12	701	645	.254	.983	3.63
BOSTON	85	77	.525	18	691	667	.252	.981	3.80
NEW YORK	82	80	.506	21	648	641	.254	.981	3.43
WASHINGTON	63	96	.396	38.5	537	660	.230	.977	3.70
CLEVELAND	60	102	.370	43	543	747	.238	.981	4.28

WEST	W	L	PCT	GB	R	OR	BA	FA	ERA
OAKLAND	101	60	.627	—	691	564	.252	.981	3.05
KANSAS CITY	85	76	.528	16	603	566	.250	.979	3.25
CHICAGO	79	83	.488	22.5	617	597	.250	.975	3.12
CALIFORNIA	76	86	.469	25.5	511	576	.231	.980	3.10
MINNESOTA	74	86	.463	26.5	654	670	.260	.980	3.81
MILWAUKEE	69	92	.429	32	534	609	.229	.977	3.38
					7472	7472	.247	.980	3.46

BATTING AVERAGE
Tony Oliva MIN .... .337
Bobby Murcer NY .... .331
Merv Rettenmund BAL .... .318

HITS
Cesar Tovar MIN 204
Sandy Alomar CAL........... 179
Rod Carew MIN................ 177

DOUBLES
Reggie Smith BOS 33
Paul Schaal KC 31
two tied at............................ 30

TRIPLES
Freddie Patek KC 11
Rod Carew MIN 10
Paul Blair BAL 8

HOME RUNS
Bill Melton CHI 33
Norm Cash DET 32
Reggie Jackson OAK 32

RUNS BATTED IN
Harmon Killebrew MIN 119
Frank Robinson BAL 99
Reggie Smith BOS 96

SLUGGING AVERAGE
Tony Oliva MIN .... .546
Bobby Murcer NY .... .543
Norm Cash DET .... .531

STOLEN BASES
Amos Otis KC..................... 52
Freddie Patek KC 49
Sandy Alomar CAL............ 39

RUNS SCORED
Don Buford BAL 99
Bobby Murcer NY.............. 94
Cesar Tovar MIN 94

WINS
Mickey Lolich DET 25
Vida Blue OAK 24
Wilbur Wood CHI 22

WINNING PERCENTAGE
Dave McNally BAL .... .808
Vida Blue OAK .... .750
Chuck Dobson OAK........ .750

EARNED RUN AVERAGE
Vida Blue OAK 1.82
Wilbur Wood CHI 1.91
Jim Palmer BAL 2.68

STRIKEOUTS
Mickey Lolich DET 308
Vida Blue OAK 301
Joe Coleman DET............ 236

SAVES
Ken Sanders MIL 31
Ted Abernathy KC............. 23
Fred Scherman DET 20

COMPLETE GAMES
Mickey Lolich DET 29
Vida Blue OAK 24
Wilbur Wood CHI 22

SHUTOUTS
Vida Blue OAK 8
Mel Stottlemyre NY 7
Wilbur Wood CHI 7

GAMES PITCHED
Ken Sanders MIL 83
Fred Scherman DET 69
Tom Burgmeier KC............. 67

INNINGS PITCHED
Mickey Lolich DET 376
Wilbur Wood CHI 334
Vida Blue OAK 312

1971 NL

EAST	W	L	PCT	GB	R	OR	BA	FA	ERA
★ PITTSBURGH	97	65	.599	—	788	599	.274	.979	3.31
ST. LOUIS	90	72	.556	7	739	699	.275	.978	3.85
CHICAGO	83	79	.512	14	637	648	.258	.980	3.61
NEW YORK	83	79	.512	14	588	550	.249	.981	2.99
MONTREAL	71	90	.441	25.5	622	729	.246	.976	4.12
PHILADELPHIA	67	95	.414	30	558	688	.233	.981	3.71

WEST	W	L	PCT	GB	R	OR	BA	FA	ERA
SAN FRANCISCO	90	72	.556	—	706	644	.247	.972	3.32
LOS ANGELES	89	73	.549	1	663	587	.266	.979	3.23
ATLANTA	82	80	.506	8	643	699	.257	.977	3.75
CINCINNATI	79	83	.488	11	586	581	.241	.984	3.35
HOUSTON	79	83	.488	11	567	567	.240	.983	3.13
SAN DIEGO	61	100	.379	28.5	486	610	.233	.974	3.22
					7601	7601	.252	.979	3.47

BATTING AVERAGE
Joe Torre STL.................. .363
Ralph Garr ATL .... .343
Glenn Beckert CHI .... .342

HITS
Joe Torre STL.................. 230
Ralph Garr ATL 219
Lou Brock STL 200

DOUBLES
Cesar Cedeno HOU 40
Lou Brock STL 37
two tied at............................ 34

TRIPLES
Joe Morgan HOU 11
Roger Metzger HOU........... 11
Willie Davis LA 10

HOME RUNS
Willie Stargell PIT.............. 48
Hank Aaron ATL................. 47
Lee May CIN 39

RUNS BATTED IN
Joe Torre STL.................... 137
Willie Stargell PIT 125
Hank Aaron ATL 118

SLUGGING AVERAGE
Hank Aaron ATL.............. .669
Willie Stargell PIT............. .628
Joe Torre STL.................... .555

STOLEN BASES
Lou Brock STL 64
Joe Morgan HOU 40
Ralph Garr ATL 30

RUNS SCORED
Lou Brock STL 126
Bobby Bonds SF 110
Willie Stargell PIT.............. 104

WINS
Ferguson Jenkins CHI........ 24
three tied at 20

WINNING PERCENTAGE
Don Gullett CIN................ .727
Steve Carlton STL............ .690
Al Downing LA.................. .690

EARNED RUN AVERAGE
Tom Seaver NY 1.76
Dave Roberts SD 2.10
Don Wilson HOU............. 2.45

STRIKEOUTS
Tom Seaver NY 289
Ferguson Jenkins CHI...... 263
Bill Stoneman MON.......... 251

SAVES
Dave Giusti PIT.................. 30
Mike Marshall MON............ 23
Jim Brewer LA.................... 22

COMPLETE GAMES
Ferguson Jenkins CHI........ 30
Tom Seaver NY 21
two tied at............................ 20

SHUTOUTS
four tied at 5

GAMES PITCHED
Wayne Granger CIN........... 70
Jerry Johnson SF 67
Mike Marshall MON........... 66

INNINGS PITCHED
Ferguson Jenkins CHI...... 325
Bill Stoneman MON.......... 295
Tom Seaver NY 286

1972 AL

EAST	W	L	PCT	GB	R	OR	BA	FA	ERA
DETROIT	86	70	.551	—	558	514	.237	.984	2.96
BOSTON	85	70	.548	.5	640	620	.248	.978	3.47
BALTIMORE	80	74	.519	5	519	430	.229	.983	2.53
NEW YORK	79	76	.510	6.5	557	527	.249	.978	3.05
CLEVELAND	72	84	.462	14	472	519	.234	.981	2.92
MILWAUKEE	65	91	.417	21	493	595	.235	.977	3.45

WEST	W	L	PCT	GB	R	OR	BA	FA	ERA
★ OAKLAND	93	62	.600	—	604	457	.240	.979	2.58
CHICAGO	87	67	.565	5.5	566	538	.238	.977	3.12
MINNESOTA	77	77	.500	15.5	537	535	.244	.974	2.84
KANSAS CITY	76	78	.494	16.5	580	545	.255	.981	3.24
CALIFORNIA	75	80	.484	18	454	533	.242	.981	3.06
TEXAS	54	100	.351	38.5	461	628	.217	.972	3.53
					6441	6441	.239	.979	3.06

BATTING AVERAGE
Rod Carew MIN............... .318
Lou Piniella KC................ .312
Dick Allen CHI................. .308

HITS
Joe Rudi OAK 181
Lou Piniella KC............... 179
Bobby Murcer NY............ 171

DOUBLES
Lou Piniella KC................... 33
Joe Rudi OAK 32
Bobby Murcer NY............... 30

TRIPLES
Joe Rudi OAK 9
Carlton Fisk BOS 9
Paul Blair BAL...................... 8

HOME RUNS
Dick Allen CHI..................... 37
Bobby Murcer NY............... 33
two tied at............................ 26

RUNS BATTED IN
Dick Allen CHI................... 113
John Mayberry KC 100
Bobby Murcer NY............... 96

SLUGGING AVERAGE
Dick Allen CHI................. .603
Carlton Fisk BOS .... .538
Bobby Murcer NY............ .537

STOLEN BASES
Bert Campaneris OAK........ 52
Dave Nelson TEX............... 51
Freddie Patek KC............... 33

RUNS SCORED
Bobby Murcer NY............. 102
Joe Rudi OAK 94
Tommy Harper BOS 92

WINS
Wilbur Wood CHI 24
Gaylord Perry CLE............. 24
Mickey Lolich DET 22

WINNING PERCENTAGE
Catfish Hunter OAK......... .750
Blue Moon Odom OAK.... .714
Luis Tiant BOS .... .714

EARNED RUN AVERAGE
Luis Tiant BOS 1.91
Gaylord Perry CLE........... 1.92
Catfish Hunter OAK......... 2.04

STRIKEOUTS
Nolan Ryan CAL 329
Mickey Lolich DET 250
Gaylord Perry CLE........... 234

SAVES
Sparky Lyle NY................... 35
Terry Forster CHI............... 29
Rollie Fingers OAK............. 21

COMPLETE GAMES
Gaylord Perry CLE............. 29
Mickey Lolich DET 23
two tied at............................ 20

SHUTOUTS
Nolan Ryan CAL 9
Wilbur Wood CHI 8
Mel Stottlemyre NY 7

GAMES PITCHED
Paul Lindblad TEX 66
Rollie Fingers OAK............. 65
Wayne Granger MIN 63

INNINGS PITCHED
Wilbur Wood CHI 377
Gaylord Perry CLE........... 343
Mickey Lolich DET 327

1972 NL

EAST	W	L	PCT	GB	R	OR	BA	FA	ERA
PITTSBURGH	96	59	.619	—	691	512	.274	.978	2.81
CHICAGO	85	70	.548	11	685	567	.257	.979	3.22
NEW YORK	83	73	.532	13.5	528	578	.225	.980	3.26
ST. LOUIS	75	81	.481	21.5	568	600	.260	.977	3.42
MONTREAL	70	86	.449	26.5	513	609	.234	.978	3.59
PHILADELPHIA	59	97	.378	37.5	503	635	.236	.981	3.66

WEST	W	L	PCT	GB	R	OR	BA	FA	ERA
● CINCINNATI	95	59	.617	—	707	557	.251	.982	3.21
HOUSTON	84	69	.549	10.5	708	636	.258	.977	3.77
LOS ANGELES	85	70	.548	10.5	584	527	.256	.974	2.78
ATLANTA	70	84	.455	25	628	730	.258	.974	4.27
SAN FRANCISCO	69	86	.445	26.5	662	649	.244	.974	3.69
SAN DIEGO	58	95	.379	36.5	488	665	.227	.976	3.78
					7265	7265	.248	.978	3.45

BATTING AVERAGE
Billy Williams CHI .... .333
Ralph Garr ATL .... .325
Dusty Baker ATL .... .321

HITS
Pete Rose CIN 198
Lou Brock STL 193
Billy Williams CHI 191

DOUBLES
Cesar Cedeno HOU 39
Willie Montanez PHI........... 39
Ted Simmons STL.............. 36

TRIPLES
Larry Bowa PHI 13
Pete Rose CIN 11
three tied at 8

HOME RUNS
Johnny Bench CIN 40
Nate Colbert SD 38
Billy Williams CHI 37

RUNS BATTED IN
Johnny Bench CIN 125
Billy Williams CHI 122
Willie Stargell PIT 112

SLUGGING AVERAGE
Billy Williams CHI .... .606
Willie Stargell PIT .... .558
Johnny Bench CIN .... .541

STOLEN BASES
Lou Brock STL 63
Joe Morgan CIN 58
Cesar Cedeno HOU 55

RUNS SCORED
Joe Morgan CIN 122
Bobby Bonds SF 118
Jimmy Wynn HOU 117

WINS
Steve Carlton PHI 27
Tom Seaver NY 21
two tied at 20

WINNING PERCENTAGE
Gary Nolan CIN............... .750
Steve Carlton PHI .... .730
Milt Pappas CHI .... .708

EARNED RUN AVERAGE
Steve Carlton PHI 1.97
Gary Nolan CIN............... 1.99
Don Sutton LA.................. 2.08

STRIKEOUTS
Steve Carlton PHI 310
Tom Seaver NY 249
Bob Gibson STL................ 208

SAVES
Clay Carroll CIN 37
Tug McGraw NY 27
Dave Giusti PIT 22

COMPLETE GAMES
Steve Carlton PHI 30
Ferguson Jenkins CHI........ 23
Bob Gibson STL................ 23

SHUTOUTS
Don Sutton LA...................... 9
Steve Carlton PHI 8
Fred Norman SD 6

GAMES PITCHED
Mike Marshall MON............ 65
Clay Carroll CIN 65
Pedro Borbon CIN.............. 62

INNINGS PITCHED
Steve Carlton PHI 346
Ferguson Jenkins CHI...... 289
Phil Niekro ATL 282

1973 AL

EAST	W	L	PCT	GB	R	OR	BA	FA	ERA
BALTIMORE	97	65	.599	—	754	561	.266	.981	3.07
BOSTON	89	73	.549	8	738	647	.267	.979	3.65
DETROIT	85	77	.525	12	642	674	.254	.982	3.90
NEW YORK	80	82	.494	17	641	610	.261	.976	3.34
MILWAUKEE	74	88	.457	23	708	731	.253	.977	3.98
CLEVELAND	71	91	.438	26	680	826	.256	.978	4.58

WEST	W	L	PCT	GB	R	OR	BA	FA	ERA
★ OAKLAND	94	68	.580	—	758	615	.260	.978	3.29
KANSAS CITY	88	74	.543	6	755	752	.261	.974	4.19
MINNESOTA	81	81	.500	13	738	692	.270	.978	3.77
CALIFORNIA	79	83	.488	15	629	657	.253	.975	3.53
CHICAGO	77	85	.475	17	652	705	.256	.977	3.86
TEXAS	57	105	.352	37	619	844	.255	.974	4.64
					8314	8314	.259	.977	3.82

BATTING AVERAGE
Rod Carew MIN .350
George Scott MIL .306
Tommy Davis BAL .306

HITS
Rod Carew MIN 203
Dave May MIL 189
Bobby Murcer NY 187

DOUBLES
Sal Bando OAK 32
Pedro Garcia MIL 32
three tied at 30

TRIPLES
Rod Carew MIN 11
Al Bumbry BAL 11
Jorge Orta CHI 10

HOME RUNS
Reggie Jackson OAK 32
Frank Robinson CAL 30
Jeff Burroughs TEX 30

RUNS BATTED IN
Reggie Jackson OAK 117
George Scott MIL 107
John Mayberry KC 100

SLUGGING AVERAGE
Reggie Jackson OAK .531
Sal Bando OAK .498
Frank Robinson CAL .489

STOLEN BASES
Tommy Harper BOS 54
Billy North OAK 53
Dave Nelson TEX 43

RUNS SCORED
Reggie Jackson OAK 99
three tied at 98

WINS
Wilbur Wood CHI 24
Joe Coleman DET 23
Jim Palmer BAL 22

WINNING PERCENTAGE
Catfish Hunter OAK .808
Jim Palmer BAL .710
Vida Blue OAK .690

EARNED RUN AVERAGE
Jim Palmer BAL 2.40
Bert Blyleven MIN 2.52
Bill Lee BOS 2.75

STRIKEOUTS
Nolan Ryan CAL 383
Bert Blyleven MIN 258
Bill Singer CAL 241

SAVES
John Hiller DET 38
Sparky Lyle NY 27
Rollie Fingers OAK 22

COMPLETE GAMES
Gaylord Perry CLE 29
Nolan Ryan CAL 26
Bert Blyleven MIN 25

SHUTOUTS
Bert Blyleven MIN 9
Gaylord Perry CLE 7
Jim Palmer BAL 6

GAMES PITCHED
John Hiller DET 65
Rollie Fingers OAK 62
Doug Bird KC 54

INNINGS PITCHED
Wilbur Wood CHI 359
Gaylord Perry CLE 344
Nolan Ryan CAL 326

1973 NL

EAST	W	L	PCT	GB	R	OR	BA	FA	ERA
● NEW YORK	82	79	.509	—	608	588	.246	.980	3.26
ST. LOUIS	81	81	.500	1.5	643	603	.259	.975	3.25
PITTSBURGH	80	82	.494	2.5	704	693	.261	.976	3.73
MONTREAL	79	83	.488	3.5	668	702	.251	.974	3.71
CHICAGO	77	84	.478	5	614	655	.247	.975	3.66
PHILADELPHIA	71	91	.438	11.5	642	717	.249	.979	3.99

WEST	W	L	PCT	GB	R	OR	BA	FA	ERA
CINCINNATI	99	63	.611	—	741	621	.254	.982	3.40
LOS ANGELES	95	66	.590	3.5	675	565	.263	.981	3.00
SAN FRANCISCO	88	74	.543	11	739	702	.262	.974	3.79
HOUSTON	82	80	.506	17	681	672	.251	.981	3.75
ATLANTA	76	85	.472	22.5	799	774	.266	.974	4.25
SAN DIEGO	60	102	.370	39	548	770	.244	.973	4.16
					8062	8062	.254	.977	3.66

BATTING AVERAGE
Pete Rose CIN .... .338
Cesar Cedeno HOU .... .320
Garry Maddox SF .... .319

HITS
Pete Rose CIN 230
Ralph Garr ATL 200
Lou Brock STL 193

DOUBLES
Willie Stargell PIT 43
Al Oliver PIT 38
three tied at 36

TRIPLES
Roger Metzger HOU 14
Garry Maddox SF 10
Gary Matthews SF 10

HOME RUNS
Willie Stargell PIT 44
Davey Johnson ATL 43
Darrell Evans ATL 41

RUNS BATTED IN
Willie Stargell PIT 119
Lee May HOU 105
two tied at 104

SLUGGING AVERAGE
Willie Stargell PIT .... .646
Darrell Evans ATL .... .556
Davey Johnson ATL .... .546

STOLEN BASES
Lou Brock STL 70
Joe Morgan CIN 67
Cesar Cedeno HOU 56

RUNS SCORED
Bobby Bonds SF 131
Joe Morgan CIN 116
Pete Rose CIN 115

WINS
Ron Bryant SF 24
Tom Seaver NY 19
Jack Billingham CIN 19

WINNING PERCENTAGE
Tommy John LA .... .696
Don Gullett CIN .... .692
Ron Bryant SF .... .667

EARNED RUN AVERAGE
Tom Seaver NY 2.08
Don Sutton LA 2.42
Wayne Twitchell PHI 2.50

STRIKEOUTS
Tom Seaver NY 251
Steve Carlton PHI 223
Jon Matlack NY 205

SAVES
Mike Marshall MON 31
Tug McGraw NY 25
two tied at 20

COMPLETE GAMES
Tom Seaver NY 18
Steve Carlton PHI 18
Jack Billingham CIN 16

SHUTOUTS
Jack Billingham CIN 7
Dave Roberts HOU 6
two tied at 5

GAMES PITCHED
Mike Marshall MON 92
Pedro Borbon CIN 80
Elias Sosa SF 71

INNINGS PITCHED
Steve Carlton PHI 293
Jack Billingham CIN 293
Tom Seaver NY 290

1974 AL

EAST	W	L	PCT	GB	R	OR	BA	FA	ERA
BALTIMORE	91	71	.562	—	659	612	.256	.980	3.27
NEW YORK	89	73	.549	2	671	623	.263	.977	3.31
BOSTON	84	78	.519	7	696	661	.264	.977	3.72
CLEVELAND	77	85	.475	14	662	694	.255	.977	3.80
MILWAUKEE	76	86	.469	15	647	660	.244	.980	3.76
DETROIT	72	90	.444	19	620	768	.247	.975	4.16

WEST	W	L	PCT	GB	R	OR	BA	FA	ERA
★ OAKLAND	90	72	.556	—	689	551	.247	.977	2.95
TEXAS	84	76	.525	5	690	698	.272	.974	3.82
MINNESOTA	82	80	.506	8	673	669	.272	.976	3.64
CHICAGO	80	80	.500	9	684	721	.268	.977	3.94
KANSAS CITY	77	85	.475	13	667	662	.259	.976	3.51
CALIFORNIA	68	94	.420	22	618	657	.254	.977	3.52
					7976	7976	.258	.977	3.62

BATTING AVERAGE
Rod Carew MIN .... .364
Jorge Orta CHI .... .316
Hal McRae KC .... .310

HITS
Rod Carew MIN 218
Tommy Davis BAL 181
Don Money MIL 178

DOUBLES
Joe Rudi OAK 39
George Scott MIL 36
Hal McRae KC 36

TRIPLES
Mickey Rivers CAL 11
Amos Otis KC 9

HOME RUNS
Dick Allen CHI 32
Reggie Jackson OAK 29
Gene Tenace OAK 26

RUNS BATTED IN
Jeff Burroughs TEX 118
Sal Bando OAK 103
Joe Rudi OAK 99

SLUGGING AVERAGE
Dick Allen CHI .... .563
Reggie Jackson OAK ...... .514
Jeff Burroughs TEX .... .504

STOLEN BASES
Billy North OAK 54
Rod Carew MIN 38
John Lowenstein CLE 36

RUNS SCORED
Carl Yastrzemski BOS 93
Bobby Grich BAL 92
Reggie Jackson OAK 90

WINS
Catfish Hunter OAK 25
Ferguson Jenkins TEX 25
four tied at 22

WINNING PERCENTAGE
Mike Cuellar BAL .... .688
Catfish Hunter OAK .... .676
Ferguson Jenkins TEX .... .676

EARNED RUN AVERAGE
Catfish Hunter OAK 2.49
Gaylord Perry CLE 2.51
Andy Hassler CAL 2.61

STRIKEOUTS
Nolan Ryan CAL 367
Bert Blyleven MIN 249
Ferguson Jenkins TEX 225

SAVES
Terry Forster CHI 24
Tom Murphy MIL 20
Bill Campbell MIN 19

COMPLETE GAMES
Ferguson Jenkins TEX 29
Gaylord Perry CLE 28
Mickey Lolich DET 27

SHUTOUTS
Luis Tiant BOS 7
Catfish Hunter OAK 6
Ferguson Jenkins TEX 6

GAMES PITCHED
Rollie Fingers OAK 76
Tom Murphy MIL 70
Steve Foucault TEX 69

INNINGS PITCHED
Nolan Ryan CAL 333
Ferguson Jenkins TEX 328
Gaylord Perry CLE 322

1974 NL

EAST	W	L	PCT	GB	R	OR	BA	FA	ERA
PITTSBURGH	88	74	.543	—	751	657	.274	.975	3.49
ST. LOUIS	86	75	.534	1.5	677	643	.265	.977	3.48
PHILADELPHIA	80	82	.494	8	676	701	.261	.976	3.91
MONTREAL	79	82	.491	8.5	662	657	.254	.976	3.60
NEW YORK	71	91	.438	17	572	646	.235	.975	3.42
CHICAGO	66	96	.407	22	669	826	.251	.969	4.28

WEST	W	L	PCT	GB	R	OR	BA	FA	ERA
• LOS ANGELES	102	60	.630	—	798	561	.272	.975	2.97
CINCINNATI	98	64	.605	4	776	631	.260	.979	3.41
ATLANTA	88	74	.543	14	661	563	.249	.979	3.05
HOUSTON	81	81	.500	21	653	632	.263	.982	3.46
SAN FRANCISCO	72	90	.444	30	634	723	.252	.972	3.78
SAN DIEGO	60	102	.370	42	541	830	.229	.973	4.58
					8070	8070	.255	.976	3.62

BATTING AVERAGE
Ralph Garr ATL .... .353
Al Oliver PIT .... .321
two tied at .... .314

HITS
Ralph Garr ATL 214
Dave Cash PHI 206
Steve Garvey LA 200

DOUBLES
Pete Rose CIN 45
Al Oliver PIT 38
Johnny Bench CIN 38

TRIPLES
Ralph Garr ATL 17
Al Oliver PIT 12
Dave Cash PHI 11

HOME RUNS
Mike Schmidt PHI 36
Johnny Bench CIN 33
Jimmy Wynn LA 32

RUNS BATTED IN
Johnny Bench CIN 129
Mike Schmidt PHI 116
Steve Garvey LA 111

SLUGGING AVERAGE
Mike Schmidt PHI .... .546
Willie Stargell PIT .... .537
Reggie Smith STL .... .528

STOLEN BASES
Lou Brock STL 118
Davey Lopes LA 59
Joe Morgan CIN 58

RUNS SCORED
Pete Rose CIN 110
Mike Schmidt PHI 108
Johnny Bench CIN 108

WINS
Phil Niekro ATL 20
Andy Messersmith LA 20
two tied at 19

WINNING PERCENTAGE
Andy Messersmith LA ..... .769
Don Sutton LA .... .679
Buzz Capra ATL .... .667

EARNED RUN AVERAGE
Buzz Capra ATL 2.28
Phil Niekro ATL 2.38
Jon Matlack NY 2.41

STRIKEOUTS
Steve Carlton PHI 240
Andy Messersmith LA 221
Tom Seaver NY 201

SAVES
Mike Marshall LA 21
Randy Moffitt SF 15
Pedro Borbon CIN 14

COMPLETE GAMES
Phil Niekro ATL 18
Steve Carlton PHI 17
Jim Lonborg PHI 16

SHUTOUTS
Jon Matlack NY 7
Phil Niekro ATL 6

GAMES PITCHED
Mike Marshall LA 106
Larry Hardy SD 76
Pedro Borbon CIN 73

INNINGS PITCHED
Phil Niekro ATL 302
Andy Messersmith LA 292
Steve Carlton PHI 291

1975 AL

EAST	W	L	PCT	GB	R	OR	BA	FA	ERA
● BOSTON	95	65	.594	—	796	709	.275	.977	3.98
BALTIMORE	90	69	.566	4.5	682	553	.252	.983	3.17
NEW YORK	83	77	.519	12	681	588	.264	.978	3.29
CLEVELAND	79	80	.497	15.5	688	703	.261	.978	3.84
MILWAUKEE	68	94	.420	28	675	792	.250	.971	4.34
DETROIT	57	102	.358	37.5	570	786	.249	.972	4.27

WEST	W	L	PCT	GB	R	OR	BA	FA	ERA
OAKLAND	98	64	.605	—	758	606	.254	.977	3.27
KANSAS CITY	91	71	.562	7	710	649	.261	.976	3.47
TEXAS	79	83	.488	19	714	733	.256	.971	3.86
MINNESOTA	76	83	.478	20.5	724	736	.271	.973	4.05
CHICAGO	75	86	.466	22.5	655	703	.255	.978	3.93
CALIFORNIA	72	89	.447	25.5	628	723	.246	.971	3.89
					8281	8281	.258	.975	3.78

BATTING AVERAGE
Rod Carew MIN.............. .359
Fred Lynn BOS................ .331
Thurman Munson NY ...... .318

HITS
George Brett KC.............. 195
Rod Carew MIN............... 192
Thurman Munson NY 190

DOUBLES
Fred Lynn BOS.................. 47
Reggie Jackson OAK......... 39
three tied at 38

TRIPLES
Mickey Rivers CAL............. 13
George Brett KC................ 13
Jorge Orta CHI 10

HOME RUNS
George Scott MIL.............. 36
Reggie Jackson OAK......... 36
John Mayberry KC 34

RUNS BATTED IN
George Scott MIL.............. 109
John Mayberry KC 106
Fred Lynn BOS................. 105

SLUGGING AVERAGE
Fred Lynn BOS................. .566
John Mayberry KC .... .547
Boog Powell CLE .... .524

STOLEN BASES
Mickey Rivers CAL............ 70
C. Washington OAK........... 40
Amos Otis KC..................... 39

RUNS SCORED
Fred Lynn BOS................. 103
John Mayberry KC 95
Bobby Bonds NY................ 93

WINS
Jim Palmer BAL 23
Catfish Hunter NY 23
Vida Blue OAK 22

WINNING PERCENTAGE
Mike Torrez BAL.............. .690
Dennis Leonard KC.......... .682
Jim Palmer BAL .... .676

EARNED RUN AVERAGE
Jim Palmer BAL 2.09
Catfish Hunter NY 2.58
Dennis Eckersley CLE 2.60

STRIKEOUTS
Frank Tanana CAL 269
Bert Blyleven MIN 233
G. Perry CLE, TEX.......... 233

SAVES
Goose Gossage CHI.......... 26
Rollie Fingers OAK........... 24
Tom Murphy MIL 20

COMPLETE GAMES
Catfish Hunter NY 30
Jim Palmer BAL 25
Gaylord Perry CLE, TEX 25

SHUTOUTS
Jim Palmer BAL 10
Catfish Hunter NY 7

GAMES PITCHED
Rollie Fingers OAK............. 75
Paul Lindblad OAK............. 68
Goose Gossage CHI 62

INNINGS PITCHED
Catfish Hunter NY 328
Jim Palmer BAL 323
G. Perry CLE, TEX.......... 306

1975 NL

EAST	W	L	PCT	GB	R	OR	BA	FA	ERA
PITTSBURGH	92	69	.571	—	712	565	.263	.976	3.01
PHILADELPHIA	86	76	.531	6.5	735	694	.269	.976	3.82
NEW YORK	82	80	.506	10.5	646	625	.256	.976	3.39
ST. LOUIS	82	80	.506	10.5	662	689	.273	.973	3.57
CHICAGO	75	87	.463	17.5	712	827	.259	.972	4.49
MONTREAL	75	87	.463	17.5	601	690	.244	.973	3.72

WEST	W	L	PCT	GB	R	OR	BA	FA	ERA
★ CINCINNATI	108	54	.667	—	840	586	.271	.984	3.37
LOS ANGELES	88	74	.543	20	648	534	.248	.979	2.92
SAN FRANCISCO	80	81	.497	27.5	659	671	.259	.976	3.74
SAN DIEGO	71	91	.438	37	552	683	.244	.971	3.48
ATLANTA	67	94	.416	40.5	583	739	.244	.972	3.91
HOUSTON	64	97	.398	43.5	664	711	.254	.979	4.04
					8014	8014	.257	.976	3.62

BATTING AVERAGE
Bill Madlock CHI.............. .354
Ted Simmons STL........... .332
Manny Sanguillen PIT ..... .328

HITS
Dave Cash PHI 213
Steve Garvey LA 210
Pete Rose CIN 210

DOUBLES
Pete Rose CIN 47
Dave Cash PHI 40
two tied at........................... 39

TRIPLES
Ralph Garr ATL.................. 11
four tied at 10

HOME RUNS
Mike Schmidt PHI.............. 38
Dave Kingman NY............. 36
Greg Luzinski PHI 34

RUNS BATTED IN
Greg Luzinski PHI 120
Johnny Bench CIN 110
Tony Perez CIN 109

SLUGGING AVERAGE
Dave Parker PIT.............. .541
Greg Luzinski PHI .... .540
Mike Schmidt PHI............ .523

STOLEN BASES
Davey Lopes LA................. 77
Joe Morgan CIN 67
Lou Brock STL 56

RUNS SCORED
Pete Rose CIN 112
Dave Cash PHI................. 111
Davey Lopes LA............... 108

WINS
Tom Seaver NY 22
Randy Jones SD 20
Andy Messersmith LA 19

WINNING PERCENTAGE
Don Gullet CIN................ .789
Tom Seaver NY .... .710
Burt Hooton CHI, LA .... .667

EARNED RUN AVERAGE
Randy Jones SD 2.24
Andy Messersmith LA 2.29
Tom Seaver NY 2.38

STRIKEOUTS
Tom Seaver NY 243
John Montefusco SF 215
Andy Messersmith LA 213

SAVES
Rawley Eastwick CIN......... 22
Al Hrabosky STL 22
Dave Giusti PIT 17

COMPLETE GAMES
Andy Messersmith LA 19
Randy Jones SD 18
two tied at........................... 15

SHUTOUTS
Andy Messersmith LA 7
Randy Jones SD 6
Jerry Reuss PIT 6

GAMES PITCHED
Gene Garber PHI 71
Will McEnaney CIN 70
two tied at........................... 67

INNINGS PITCHED
Andy Messersmith LA 322
Randy Jones SD 285
Tom Seaver NY 280

1976 AL

EAST	W	L	PCT	GB	R	OR	BA	FA	ERA
● NEW YORK	97	62	.610	—	730	575	.269	.980	3.19
BALTIMORE	88	74	.543	10.5	619	598	.243	.982	3.32
BOSTON	83	79	.512	15.5	716	660	.263	.978	3.52
CLEVELAND	81	78	.509	16	615	615	.263	.980	3.47
DETROIT	74	87	.460	24	609	709	.257	.974	3.87
MILWAUKEE	66	95	.410	32	570	655	.246	.975	3.64

WEST	W	L	PCT	GB	R	OR	BA	FA	ERA
KANSAS CITY	90	72	.556	—	713	611	.269	.978	3.21
OAKLAND	87	74	.540	2.5	686	598	.246	.977	3.26
MINNESOTA	85	77	.525	5	743	704	.274	.973	3.69
CALIFORNIA	76	86	.469	14	550	631	.235	.977	3.36
TEXAS	76	86	.469	14	616	652	.250	.976	3.45
CHICAGO	64	97	.398	25.5	586	745	.255	.979	4.25
					7753	7753	.256	.977	3.52

BATTING AVERAGE
George Brett KC.............. .333
Hal McRae KC .... .332
Rod Carew MIN.............. .331

HITS
George Brett KC.............. 215
Rod Carew MIN.............. 200
Chris Chambliss NY 188

DOUBLES
Amos Otis KC.................... 40
four tied at 34

TRIPLES
George Brett KC................ 14
Phil Garner OAK 12
Rod Carew MIN................. 12

HOME RUNS
Graig Nettles NY 32
Sal Bando OAK................. 27
Reggie Jackson BAL.......... 27

RUNS BATTED IN
Lee May BAL.................... 109
Thurman Munson NY 105
Carl Yastrzemski BOS...... 102

SLUGGING AVERAGE
Reggie Jackson BAL....... .502
Jim Rice BOS.................. .482
Graig Nettles NY .... .475

STOLEN BASES
Billy North OAK 75
Ron LeFlore DET 58
Bert Campaneris OAK....... 54

RUNS SCORED
Roy White NY................... 104
Rod Carew MIN................. 97
Mickey Rivers NY.............. 95

WINS
Jim Palmer BAL 22
Luis Tiant BOS 21
Wayne Garland BAL.......... 20

WINNING PERCENTAGE
Bill Campbell MIN............. .773
Wayne Garland BAL........ .741
Doc Ellis NY .... .680

EARNED RUN AVERAGE
Mark Fidrych DET 2.34
Vida Blue OAK 2.35
Frank Tanana CAL 2.44

STRIKEOUTS
Nolan Ryan CAL 327
Frank Tanana CAL 261
B. Blyleven MIN, TEX....... 219

SAVES
Sparky Lyle NY.................. 23
Dave LaRoche CLE 21
two tied at.......................... 20

COMPLETE GAMES
Mark Fidrych DET 24
Frank Tanana CAL 23
Jim Palmer BAL 23

SHUTOUTS
Nolan Ryan CAL 7
three tied at 6

GAMES PITCHED
Bill Campbell MIN............... 78
Rollie Fingers OAK............. 70
Paul Lindblad OAK............. 65

INNINGS PITCHED
Jim Palmer BAL 315
Catfish Hunter NY 299
Vida Blue OAK 298

1976 NL

EAST	W	L	PCT	GB	R	OR	BA	FA	ERA
PHILADELPHIA	101	61	.623	—	770	557	.272	.981	3.08
PITTSBURGH	92	70	.568	9	708	630	.267	.975	3.36
NEW YORK	86	76	.531	15	615	538	.246	.979	2.94
CHICAGO	75	87	.463	26	611	728	.251	.978	3.93
ST. LOUIS	72	90	.444	29	629	671	.260	.973	3.60
MONTREAL	55	107	.340	46	531	734	.235	.976	3.99

WEST	W	L	PCT	GB	R	OR	BA	FA	ERA
★ CINCINNATI	102	60	.630	—	857	633	.280	.984	3.51
LOS ANGELES	92	70	.568	10	608	543	.251	.980	3.02
HOUSTON	80	82	.494	22	625	657	.256	.978	3.56
SAN FRANCISCO	74	88	.457	28	595	686	.246	.971	3.53
SAN DIEGO	73	89	.451	29	570	662	.247	.978	3.65
ATLANTA	70	92	.432	32	620	700	.245	.973	3.86
					7739	7739	.255	.977	3.50

BATTING AVERAGE
Bill Madlock CHI.............. .339
Ken Griffey CIN .... .336
Garry Maddox PHI .... .330

HITS
Pete Rose CIN 215
W. Montanez SF, ATL....... 206
Steve Garvey LA 200

DOUBLES
Pete Rose CIN 42
Jay Johnstone PHI 38
two tied at.......................... 37

TRIPLES
Dave Cash PHI 12
Cesar Geronimo CIN.......... 11
two tied at.......................... 10

HOME RUNS
Mike Schmidt PHI............... 38
Dave Kingman NY.............. 37
Rick Monday CHI 32

RUNS BATTED IN
George Foster CIN........... 121
Joe Morgan CIN................ 111
Mike Schmidt PHI............. 107

SLUGGING AVERAGE
Joe Morgan CIN .... .576
George Foster CIN.......... .530
Mike Schmidt PHI............ .524

STOLEN BASES
Davey Lopes LA 63
Joe Morgan CIN 60
two tied at........................... 58

RUNS SCORED
Pete Rose CIN 130
Joe Morgan CIN 113
Mike Schmidt PHI............. 112

WINS
Randy Jones SD 22
Jerry Koosman NY 21
Don Sutton LA.................... 21

WINNING PERCENTAGE
Steve Carlton PHI .... .741
John Candelaria PIT .... .696
two tied at.......................... .677

EARNED RUN AVERAGE
John Denny STL 2.52
Doug Rau LA.................... 2.57
Tom Seaver NY................ 2.59

STRIKEOUTS
Tom Seaver NY 235
J.R. Richard HOU 214
Jerry Koosman NY 200

SAVES
Rawley Eastwick CIN......... 26
Skip Lockwood NY............. 19
Ken Forsch HOU................ 19

COMPLETE GAMES
Randy Jones SD 25
Jerry Koosman NY 17
Jon Matlack NY 16

SHUTOUTS
Jon Matlack NY 6
John Montefusco SF 6
two tied at........................... 5

GAMES PITCHED
Dale Murray MON 81
Charlie Hough LA.............. 77
Butch Metzger SD 77

INNINGS PITCHED
Randy Jones SD 315
J.R. Richard HOU 291
two tied at.......................... 271

1977 AL

EAST	W	L	PCT	GB	R	OR	BA	FA	ERA
★ NEW YORK	100	62	.617	—	831	651	.281	.979	3.61
BALTIMORE	97	64	.602	2.5	719	653	.261	.983	3.74
BOSTON	97	64	.602	2.5	859	712	.281	.978	4.11
DETROIT	74	88	.457	26	714	751	.264	.978	4.13
CLEVELAND	71	90	.441	28.5	676	739	.269	.979	4.10
MILWAUKEE	67	95	.414	33	639	765	.258	.978	4.32
TORONTO	54	107	.335	45.5	605	882	.252	.974	4.57

WEST	W	L	PCT	GB	R	OR	BA	FA	ERA
KANSAS CITY	102	60	.630	—	822	651	.277	.978	3.52
TEXAS	94	68	.580	8	767	657	.270	.982	3.56
CHICAGO	90	72	.556	12	844	771	.278	.974	4.25
MINNESOTA	84	77	.522	17.5	867	776	.282	.978	4.36
CALIFORNIA	74	88	.457	28	675	695	.255	.976	3.72
SEATTLE	64	98	.395	38	624	855	.256	.976	4.83
OAKLAND	63	98	.391	38.5	605	749	.240	.970	4.04
					10247	10247	.266	.977	4.06

BATTING AVERAGE
Rod Carew MIN............... .388
Lyman Bostock MIN .... .336
Ken Singleton BAL .... .328

HITS
Rod Carew MIN............... 239
Ron LeFlore DET 212
Jim Rice BOS 206

DOUBLES
Hal McRae KC 54
Reggie Jackson NY........... 39
two tied at........................... 38

TRIPLES
Rod Carew MIN................. 16
Jim Rice BOS.................... 15
Al Cowens KC 14

HOME RUNS
Jim Rice BOS..................... 39
Graig Nettles NY 37
Bobby Bonds CAL.............. 37

RUNS BATTED IN
Larry Hisle MIN................. 119
Bobby Bonds CAL............. 115
Jim Rice BOS 114

SLUGGING AVERAGE
Jim Rice BOS................... .593
Rod Carew MIN............... .570
Reggie Jackson NY......... .550

STOLEN BASES
Freddie Patek KC.............. 53
Mike Page OAK.................. 42
two tied at............................ 41

RUNS SCORED
Rod Carew MIN............... 128
Carlton Fisk BOS 106
George Brett KC.............. 105

WINS
Jim Palmer BAL 20
Dave Goltz MIN.................. 20
Dennis Leonard KC............ 20

WINNING PERCENTAGE
Paul Splittorff KC.............. .727
Ron Guidry NY .... .696
Tom Johnson MIN .... .696

EARNED RUN AVERAGE
Frank Tanana CAL 2.54
Bert Blyleven TEX........... 2.72
Nolan Ryan CAL 2.77

STRIKEOUTS
Nolan Ryan CAL 341
Dennis Leonard KC.......... 244
Frank Tanana CAL 205

SAVES
Bill Campbell BOS............. 31
Sparky Lyle NY.................. 26
Lerrin LaGrow CHI 25

COMPLETE GAMES
Jim Palmer BAL 22
Nolan Ryan CAL 22
two tied at........................... 21

SHUTOUTS
Frank Tanana CAL 7
three tied at 5

GAMES PITCHED
Sparky Lyle NY................... 72
Tom Johnson MIN 71
Bill Campbell BOS............. 69

INNINGS PITCHED
Jim Palmer BAL 319
Dave Goltz MIN................ 303
Nolan Ryan CAL 299

1977 NL

EAST	W	L	PCT	GB	R	OR	BA	FA	ERA
PHILADELPHIA	101	61	.623	—	847	668	.279	.981	3.71
PITTSBURGH	96	66	.593	5	734	665	.274	.977	3.61
ST. LOUIS	83	79	.512	18	737	688	.270	.978	3.81
CHICAGO	81	81	.500	20	692	739	.266	.977	4.01
MONTREAL	75	87	.463	26	665	736	.260	.980	4.01
NEW YORK	64	98	.395	37	587	663	.244	.978	3.77

WEST	W	L	PCT	GB	R	OR	BA	FA	ERA
● LOS ANGELES	98	64	.605	—	769	582	.266	.981	3.22
CINCINNATI	88	74	.543	10	802	725	.274	.984	4.21
HOUSTON	81	81	.500	17	680	650	.254	.978	3.54
SAN FRANCISCO	75	87	.463	23	673	711	.253	.972	3.75
SAN DIEGO	69	93	.426	29	692	834	.249	.971	4.43
ATLANTA	61	101	.377	37	678	895	.254	.972	4.85
					8556	8556	.262	.977	3.91

BATTING AVERAGE
Dave Parker PIT .... .338
Garry Templeton STL .322
George Foster CIN .... .320

HITS
Dave Parker PIT 215
Pete Rose CIN 204
Garry Templeton STL 200

DOUBLES
Dave Parker PIT 44
Dave Cash MON 42
two tied at 41

TRIPLES
Garry Templeton STL 18
three tied at 11

HOME RUNS
George Foster CIN 52
Jeff Burroughs ATL 41
Greg Luzinski PHI 39

RUNS BATTED IN
George Foster CIN 149
Greg Luzinski PHI 130
Steve Garvey LA 115

SLUGGING AVERAGE
George Foster CIN .... .631
Greg Luzinski PHI .... .594
Reggie Smith LA .... .576

STOLEN BASES
Frank Taveras PIT 70
Cesar Cedeno HOU 61
Gene Richards SD 56

RUNS SCORED
George Foster CIN 124
Ken Griffey CIN 117
Mike Schmidt PHI 114

WINS
Steve Carlton PHI 23
Tom Seaver NY, CIN 21
four tied at 20

WINNING PERCENTAGE
John Candelaria PIT .... .800
Tom Seaver NY, CIN .... .778
Larry Christenson PHI ..... .760

EARNED RUN AVERAGE
John Candelaria PIT 2.34
Tom Seaver NY, CIN 2.58
Burt Hooton LA 2.62

STRIKEOUTS
Phil Niekro ATL 262
J.R. Richard HOU 214
Steve Rogers MON 206

SAVES
Rollie Fingers SD 35
Bruce Sutter CHI 31
Goose Gossage PIT 26

COMPLETE GAMES
Phil Niekro ATL 20
Tom Seaver NY, CIN 19
two tied at 17

SHUTOUTS
Tom Seaver NY, CIN 7
Rick Reuschel CHI 4
Steve Rogers MON 4

GAMES PITCHED
Rollie Fingers SD 78
Dan Spillner SD 76
Dave Tomlin SD 76

INNINGS PITCHED
Phil Niekro ATL 330
Steve Rogers MON 302
Steve Carlton PHI 283

1978 AL

EAST	W	L	PCT	GB	R	OR	BA	FA	ERA
★ NEW YORK*	100	63	.613	—	735	582	.267	.982	3.18
BOSTON	99	64	.607	1	796	657	.267	.977	3.54
MILWAUKEE	93	69	.574	6.5	804	650	.276	.977	3.65
BALTIMORE	90	71	.559	9	659	633	.258	.982	3.56
DETROIT	86	76	.531	13.5	714	653	.271	.981	3.64
CLEVELAND	69	90	.434	29	639	694	.261	.980	3.97
TORONTO	59	102	.366	40	590	775	.250	.979	4.54

WEST	W	L	PCT	GB	R	OR	BA	FA	ERA
KANSAS CITY	92	70	.568	—	743	634	.268	.976	3.44
CALIFORNIA	87	75	.537	5	691	666	.259	.978	3.65
TEXAS	87	75	.537	5	692	632	.253	.976	3.36
MINNESOTA	73	89	.451	19	666	678	.267	.977	3.69
CHICAGO	71	90	.441	20.5	634	731	.264	.977	4.21
OAKLAND	69	93	.426	23	532	690	.245	.971	3.62
SEATTLE	56	104	.350	35	614	834	.248	.978	4.67
* Defeated Boston in a 1-game playoff					9509	9509	.261	.978	3.76

BATTING AVERAGE
Rod Carew MIN............... .333
Al Oliver TEX.................... .324
Jim Rice BOS................... .315

HITS
Jim Rice BOS................... 213
Ron LeFlore DET 198
Rod Carew MIN............... 188

DOUBLES
George Brett KC................ 45
Carlton Fisk BOS 39
Hal McRae KC 39

TRIPLES
Jim Rice BOS.................... 15
Rod Carew MIN................. 10
Dan Ford MIN.................... 10

HOME RUNS
Jim Rice BOS.................... 46
Larry Hisle MIL.................. 34
Don Baylor CAL 34

RUNS BATTED IN
Jim Rice BOS................... 139
Rusty Staub DET 121
Larry Hisle MIL 115

SLUGGING AVERAGE
Jim Rice BOS.................. .600
Larry Hisle MIL................ .533
Doug DeCinces BAL .... .526

STOLEN BASES
Ron LeFlore DET 68
Julio Cruz SEA 59
Bump Wills TEX 52

RUNS SCORED
Ron LeFlore DET 126
Jim Rice BOS................... 121
Don Baylor CAL 103

WINS
Ron Guidry NY 25
Mike Caldwell MIL 22
two tied at............................ 21

WINNING PERCENTAGE
Ron Guidry NY .... .893
Bob Stanley BOS .... .882
Larry Gura KC .... .800

EARNED RUN AVERAGE
Ron Guidry NY 1.74
Jon Matlack TEX 2.27
Mike Caldwell MIL 2.36

STRIKEOUTS
Nolan Ryan CAL 260
Ron Guidry NY 248
Dennis Leonard KC.......... 183

SAVES
Goose Gossage NY 27
Dave LaRoche CAL 25
Don Stanhouse BAL........... 24

COMPLETE GAMES
Mike Caldwell MIL.............. 23
Dennis Leonard KC............ 20
Jim Palmer BAL 19

SHUTOUTS
Ron Guidry NY 9
Mike Caldwell MIL 6
Jim Palmer BAL 6

GAMES PITCHED
Bob Lacey OAK.................. 74
Dave Heaverlo OAK........... 69
Elias Sosa OAK................. 68

INNINGS PITCHED
Jim Palmer BAL 296
Dennis Leonard KC........... 295
Mike Caldwell MIL............. 293

1978 NL

EAST	W	L	PCT	GB	R	OR	BA	FA	ERA
PHILADELPHIA	90	72	.556	—	708	586	.258	.983	3.33
PITTSBURGH	88	73	.547	1.5	684	637	.257	.973	3.41
CHICAGO	79	83	.488	11	664	724	.264	.978	4.05
MONTREAL	76	86	.469	14	633	611	.254	.979	3.42
ST. LOUIS	69	93	.426	21	600	657	.249	.978	3.58
NEW YORK	66	96	.407	24	607	690	.245	.979	3.87

WEST	W	L	PCT	GB	R	OR	BA	FA	ERA
● LOS ANGELES	95	67	.586	—	727	573	.264	.978	3.12
CINCINNATI	92	69	.571	2.5	710	688	.256	.978	3.81
SAN FRANCISCO	89	73	.549	6	613	594	.248	.977	3.30
SAN DIEGO	84	78	.519	11	591	598	.252	.975	3.28
HOUSTON	74	88	.457	21	605	634	.258	.978	3.63
ATLANTA	69	93	.426	26	600	750	.244	.975	4.08
					7742	7742	.254	.978	3.57

BATTING AVERAGE
Dave Parker PIT.............. .334
Steve Garvey LA .... .316
Jose Cruz HOU .... .315

HITS
Steve Garvey LA 202
Pete Rose CIN 198
Enos Cabell HOU 195

DOUBLES
Pete Rose CIN 51
Jack Clark SF 46
Ted Simmons STL.............. 40

TRIPLES
Garry Templeton STL......... 13
Dave Parker PIT................. 12
Gene Richards SD 12

HOME RUNS
George Foster CIN............. 40
Greg Luzinski PHI 35
Dave Parker PIT................. 30

RUNS BATTED IN
George Foster CIN........... 120
Dave Parker PIT............... 117
Steve Garvey LA 113

SLUGGING AVERAGE
Dave Parker PIT.............. .585
Reggie Smith LA .... .559
George Foster CIN.......... .546

STOLEN BASES
Omar Moreno PIT 71
Frank Taveras PIT............. 46
Davey Lopes LA................. 45

RUNS SCORED
Ivan DeJesus CHI 104
Pete Rose CIN 103
Dave Parker PIT.............. 102

WINS
Gaylord Perry SD 21
Ross Grimsley MON 20
two tied at............................ 19

WINNING PERCENTAGE
Gaylord Perry SD .... .778
Burt Hooton LA................ .655
Ross Grimsley MON .... .645

EARNED RUN AVERAGE
Craig Swan NY................ 2.43
Steve Rogers MON......... 2.47
Pete Vuckovich STL........ 2.54

STRIKEOUTS
J.R. Richard HOU 303
Phil Niekro ATL 248
Tom Seaver CIN................ 226

SAVES
Rollie Fingers SD 37
Kent Tekulve PIT 31
Doug Bair CIN 28

COMPLETE GAMES
Phil Niekro ATL 22
Ross Grimsley MON 19
two tied at............................ 16

SHUTOUTS
Bob Knepper SF.................... 6
four tied at 4

GAMES PITCHED
Kent Tekulve PIT 91
Mark Littell STL 72
Donnie Moore CHI 71

INNINGS PITCHED
Phil Niekro ATL 334
J.R. Richard HOU 275
Ross Grimsley MON 263

1979 AL

EAST	W	L	PCT	GB	R	OR	BA	FA	ERA
● BALTIMORE	102	57	.642	—	757	582	.261	.980	3.26
MILWAUKEE	95	66	.590	8	807	722	.280	.980	4.03
BOSTON	91	69	.569	11.5	841	711	.283	.977	4.03
NEW YORK	89	71	.556	13.5	734	672	.266	.981	3.83
DETROIT	85	76	.528	18	770	738	.269	.981	4.27
CLEVELAND	81	80	.503	22	760	805	.258	.978	4.57
TORONTO	53	109	.327	50.5	613	862	.251	.975	4.82

WEST	W	L	PCT	GB	R	OR	BA	FA	ERA
CALIFORNIA	88	74	.543	—	866	768	.282	.978	4.34
KANSAS CITY	85	77	.525	3	851	816	.282	.977	4.45
TEXAS	83	79	.512	5	750	698	.278	.979	3.86
MINNESOTA	82	80	.506	6	764	725	.278	.979	4.13
CHICAGO	73	87	.456	14	730	748	.275	.972	4.10
SEATTLE	67	95	.414	21	711	820	.269	.978	4.58
OAKLAND	54	108	.333	34	573	860	.239	.972	4.75
					10527	10527	.270	.978	4.22

BATTING AVERAGE
Fred Lynn BOS .333
George Brett KC .329
Brian Downing CAL .326

HITS
George Brett KC 212
Jim Rice BOS 201
Buddy Bell TEX 200

DOUBLES
Cecil Cooper MIL 44
Chet Lemon CHI 44
three tied at 42

TRIPLES
George Brett KC 20
Paul Molitor MIL 16
two tied at 13

HOME RUNS
Gorman Thomas MIL 45
Fred Lynn BOS 39
Jim Rice BOS 39

RUNS BATTED IN
Don Baylor CAL 139
Jim Rice BOS 130
Gorman Thomas MIL 123

SLUGGING AVERAGE
Fred Lynn BOS .637
Jim Rice BOS .596
Sixto Lezcano MIL .573

STOLEN BASES
Willie Wilson KC 83
Ron LeFlore DET 78
Julio Cruz SEA 49

RUNS SCORED
Don Baylor CAL 120
George Brett KC 119
Jim Rice BOS 117

WINS
Mike Flanagan BAL 23
Tommy John NY 21
Jerry Koosman MIN 20

WINNING PERCENTAGE
Mike Caldwell MIL .727
Mike Flanagan BAL .719
Jack Morris DET .708

EARNED RUN AVERAGE
Ron Guidry NY 2.78
Tommy John NY 2.96
Dennis Eckersley BOS 2.99

STRIKEOUTS
Nolan Ryan CAL 223
Ron Guidry NY 201
Mike Flanagan BAL 190

SAVES
Mike Marshall MIN 32
Jim Kern TEX 29
two tied at 21

COMPLETE GAMES
Dennis Martinez BAL 18
three tied at 17

SHUTOUTS
Dennis Leonard KC 5
Mike Flanagan BAL 5
Nolan Ryan CAL 5

GAMES PITCHED
Mike Marshall MIN 90
Sid Monge CLE 76
Jim Kern TEX 71

INNINGS PITCHED
Dennis Martinez BAL 292
Tommy John NY 276
Mike Flanagan BAL 266

1979 NL

EAST	W	L	PCT	GB	R	OR	BA	FA	ERA
★ PITTSBURGH	98	64	.605	—	775	643	.272	.979	3.41
MONTREAL	95	65	.594	2	701	581	.264	.979	3.14
ST. LOUIS	86	76	.531	12	731	693	.278	.980	3.72
PHILADELPHIA	84	78	.519	14	683	718	.266	.983	4.16
CHICAGO	80	82	.494	18	706	707	.269	.975	3.88
NEW YORK	63	99	.389	35	593	706	.250	.978	3.84

WEST	W	L	PCT	GB	R	OR	BA	FA	ERA
CINCINNATI	90	71	.559	—	731	644	.264	.980	3.58
HOUSTON	89	73	.549	1.5	583	582	.256	.978	3.20
LOS ANGELES	79	83	.488	11.5	739	717	.263	.981	3.83
SAN FRANCISCO	71	91	.438	19.5	672	751	.246	.974	4.16
SAN DIEGO	68	93	.422	22	603	681	.242	.978	3.69
ATLANTA	66	94	.413	23.5	669	763	.256	.970	4.18
					8186	8186	.261	.978	3.73

BATTING AVERAGE
Keith Hernandez STL ...... .344
Pete Rose PHI .... .331
Ray Knight CIN .... .318

HITS
Garry Templeton STL 211
Keith Hernandez STL 210
Pete Rose PHI 208

DOUBLES
Keith Hernandez STL......... 48
Warren Cromartie MON 46
Dave Parker PIT................ 45

TRIPLES
Garry Templeton STL 19
three tied at 12

HOME RUNS
Dave Kingman CHI 48
Mike Schmidt PHI.............. 45
Dave Winfield SD 34

RUNS BATTED IN
Dave Winfield SD 118
Dave Kingman CHI............ 115
Mike Schmidt PHI.............. 114

SLUGGING AVERAGE
Dave Kingman CHI .... .613
Mike Schmidt PHI............. .564
George Foster CIN........... .561

STOLEN BASES
Omar Moreno PIT 77
Billy North SF 58
two tied at 44

RUNS SCORED
Keith Hernandez STL 116
Omar Moreno PIT............. 110
three tied at 109

WINS
Phil Niekro ATL 21
Joe Niekro HOU 21
three tied at 18

WINNING PERCENTAGE
Tom Seaver CIN.............. .727
Joe Niekro HOU .... .656
Silvio Martinez STL .... .652

EARNED RUN AVERAGE
J.R. Richard HOU 2.71
Tom Hume CIN................ 2.76
Dan Schatzeder MON..... 2.83

STRIKEOUTS
J.R. Richard HOU 313
Steve Carlton PHI 213
Phil Niekro ATL 208

SAVES
Bruce Sutter CHI................ 37
Kent Tekulve PIT................ 31
Gene Garber ATL............... 25

COMPLETE GAMES
Phil Niekro ATL 23
J.R. Richard HOU 19
two tied at.......................... 13

SHUTOUTS
Tom Seaver CIN................... 5
Steve Rogers MON.............. 5
Joe Niekro HOU 5

GAMES PITCHED
Kent Tekulve PIT................ 94
Enrique Romo PIT.............. 84
Grant Jackson PIT 72

INNINGS PITCHED
Phil Niekro ATL 342
J.R. Richard HOU 292
Joe Niekro HOU 264

1980 AL

EAST	W	L	PCT	GB	R	OR	BA	FA	ERA
NEW YORK	103	59	.636	—	820	662	.267	.978	3.58
BALTIMORE	100	62	.617	3	805	640	.273	.985	3.64
MILWAUKEE	86	76	.531	17	811	682	.275	.977	3.71
BOSTON	83	77	.519	19	757	767	.283	.977	4.38
DETROIT	84	78	.519	19	830	757	.273	.979	4.25
CLEVELAND	79	81	.494	23	738	807	.277	.983	4.68
TORONTO	67	95	.414	36	624	762	.251	.979	4.19

WEST	W	L	PCT	GB	R	OR	BA	FA	ERA
● KANSAS CITY	97	65	.599	—	809	694	.286	.978	3.83
OAKLAND	83	79	.512	14	686	642	.259	.979	3.46
MINNESOTA	77	84	.478	19.5	670	724	.265	.977	3.93
TEXAS	76	85	.472	20.5	756	752	.284	.977	4.02
CHICAGO	70	90	.438	26	587	722	.259	.973	3.92
CALIFORNIA	65	95	.406	31	698	797	.265	.978	4.52
SEATTLE	59	103	.364	38	610	793	.248	.977	4.38
					10201	10201	.269	.978	4.03

BATTING AVERAGE
George Brett KC.............. .390
Cecil Cooper MIL .... .352
Miguel Dilone CLE .... .341

HITS
Willie Wilson KC.............. 230
Cecil Cooper MIL 219
Mickey Rivers TEX.......... 210

DOUBLES
Robin Yount MIL................ 49
Al Oliver TEX..................... 43
Jim Morrison CHI 40

TRIPLES
Willie Wilson KC................ 15
Alfredo Griffin TOR............ 15
two tied at 11

HOME RUNS
Reggie Jackson NY........... 41
Ben Oglivie MIL 41
Gorman Thomas MIL 38

RUNS BATTED IN
Cecil Cooper MIL 122
George Brett KC............... 118
Ben Oglivie MIL 118

SLUGGING AVERAGE
George Brett KC.............. .664
Reggie Jackson NY......... .597
Ben Oglivie MIL............... .563

STOLEN BASES
R. Henderson OAK 100
Willie Wilson KC................ 79
Miguel Dilone CLE 61

RUNS SCORED
Willie Wilson KC.............. 133
Robin Yount MIL............... 121
Al Bumbry BAL 118

WINS
Steve Stone BAL................ 25
Tommy John NY 22
Mike Norris OAK 22

WINNING PERCENTAGE
Steve Stone BAL.............. .781
Rudy May NY .... .750
Scott McGregor BAL .... .714

EARNED RUN AVERAGE
Rudy May NY 2.46
Mike Norris OAK 2.53
Britt Burns CHI 2.84

STRIKEOUTS
Len Barker CLE................ 187
Mike Norris OAK 180
Ron Guidry NY................. 166

SAVES
Dan Quisenberry KC 33
Goose Gossage NY 33
Ed Farmer CHI 30

COMPLETE GAMES
Rick Langford OAK............ 28
Mike Norris OAK 24
Matt Keough OAK 20

SHUTOUTS
Tommy John NY 6
Geoff Zahn MIN.................... 5
three tied at 4

GAMES PITCHED
Dan Quisenberry KC 75
Doug Corbett MIN 73
two tied at............................ 67

INNINGS PITCHED
Rick Langford OAK.......... 290
Mike Norris OAK 284
Larry Gura KC 283

1980 NL

EAST	W	L	PCT	GB	R	OR	BA	FA	ERA
★ PHILADELPHIA	91	71	.562	—	728	639	.270	.979	3.43
MONTREAL	90	72	.556	1	694	629	.257	.977	3.48
PITTSBURGH	83	79	.512	8	666	646	.266	.978	3.58
ST. LOUIS	74	88	.457	17	738	710	.275	.981	3.93
NEW YORK	67	95	.414	24	611	702	.257	.975	3.85
CHICAGO	64	98	.395	27	614	728	.251	.974	3.89

WEST	W	L	PCT	GB	R	OR	BA	FA	ERA
HOUSTON*	93	70	.571	—	637	589	.261	.978	3.10
LOS ANGELES	92	71	.564	1	663	591	.263	.981	3.25
CINCINNATI	89	73	.549	3.5	707	670	.262	.983	3.85
ATLANTA	81	80	.503	11	630	660	.250	.975	3.77
SAN FRANCISCO	75	86	.466	17	573	634	.244	.975	3.46
SAN DIEGO	73	89	.451	19.5	591	654	.255	.980	3.65
					7852	7852	.259	.978	3.60

*Defeated Los Angeles in a 1-game playoff

BATTING AVERAGE
Bill Buckner CHI .324
Keith Hernandez STL .321
Garry Templeton STL .319

HITS
Steve Garvey LA 200
Gene Richards SD 193
Keith Hernandez STL 191

DOUBLES
Pete Rose PHI 42
Bill Buckner CHI 41
Andre Dawson MON 41

TRIPLES
Rodney Scott MON 13
Omar Moreno PIT 13
two tied at 11

HOME RUNS
Mike Schmidt PHI 48
Bob Horner ATL 35
Dale Murphy ATL 33

RUNS BATTED IN
Mike Schmidt PHI 121
George Hendrick STL 109
Steve Garvey LA 106

SLUGGING AVERAGE
Mike Schmidt PHI .624
Jack Clark SF .517
Dale Murphy ATL .510

STOLEN BASES
Ron LeFlore MON 97
Omar Moreno PIT 96
Dave Collins CIN 79

RUNS SCORED
Keith Hernandez STL 111
Mike Schmidt PHI 104
Dale Murphy ATL 98

WINS
Steve Carlton PHI 24
Joe Niekro HOU 20
Jim Bibby PIT 19

WINNING PERCENTAGE
Jim Bibby PIT .760
Jerry Reuss LA .750
Steve Carlton PHI .727

EARNED RUN AVERAGE
Don Sutton LA 2.20
Steve Carlton PHI 2.34
Jerry Reuss LA 2.51

STRIKEOUTS
Steve Carlton PHI 286
Nolan Ryan HOU 200
Mario Soto CIN 182

SAVES
Bruce Sutter CHI 28
Tom Hume CIN 25
Rollie Fingers SD 23

COMPLETE GAMES
Steve Rogers MON 14
Steve Carlton PHI 13
two tied at 11

SHUTOUTS
Jerry Reuss LA 6
J.R. Richard HOU 4
Steve Rogers MON 4

GAMES PITCHED
Dick Tidrow CHI 84
Tom Hume CIN 78
Kent Tekulve PIT 78

INNINGS PITCHED
Steve Carlton PHI 304
Steve Rogers MON 281
Phil Niekro ATL 275

1981 AL

EAST	W	L	PCT	GB	R	OR	BA	FA	ERA
MILWAUKEE**	62	47	.569	—	493	459	.257	.982	3.91
BALTIMORE	59	46	.562	1	429	437	.251	.983	3.70
● NEW YORK*†	59	48	.551	2	421	343	.252	.982	2.90
DETROIT	60	49	.550	2	427	404	.256	.984	3.53
BOSTON	59	49	.546	2.5	519	481	.275	.979	3.81
CLEVELAND	52	51	.505	7	431	442	.263	.978	3.88
TORONTO	37	69	.349	23.5	329	466	.226	.975	3.81

WEST	W	L	PCT	GB	R	OR	BA	FA	ERA
OAKLAND*†	64	45	.587	—	458	403	.247	.980	3.30
TEXAS	57	48	.543	5	452	389	.270	.984	3.40
CHICAGO	54	52	.509	8.5	476	423	.272	.979	3.47
KANSAS CITY**	50	53	.485	11	397	405	.267	.982	3.56
CALIFORNIA	51	59	.464	13.5	476	453	.256	.977	3.70
SEATTLE	44	65	.404	20	426	521	.251	.979	4.23
MINNESOTA	41	68	.376	23	378	486	.240	.978	3.98
					6112	6112	.256	.980	3.66

BATTING AVERAGE
Carney Lansford BOS ..... .336
Tom Paciorek SEA .... .326
Cecil Cooper MIL .... .320

HITS
R. Henderson OAK 135
Carney Lansford BOS 134
two tied at 133

DOUBLES
Cecil Cooper MIL 35
Al Oliver TEX..................... 29
Tom Paciorek SEA 28

TRIPLES
John Castino MIN.................. 9
four tied at 7

HOME RUNS
four tied at 22

RUNS BATTED IN
Eddie Murray BAL 78
Tony Armas OAK................ 76
Ben Oglivie MIL.................. 72

SLUGGING AVERAGE
Bobby Grich CAL .... .543
Eddie Murray BAL............ .534
Dwight Evans BOS........... .522

STOLEN BASES
Rickey Henderson OAK 56
Julio Cruz SEA 43
Ron LeFlore CHI 36

RUNS SCORED
Rickey Henderson OAK 89
Dwight Evans BOS............. 84
Cecil Cooper MIL 70

WINS
four tied at 14

WINNING PERCENTAGE
Pete Vuckovich MIL......... .778
Dennis Martinez BAL ...... .737
Scott McGregor BAL .... .722

EARNED RUN AVERAGE
Dave Righetti NY............. 2.05
Sammy Stewart BAL 2.32
Steve McCatty OAK 2.33

STRIKEOUTS
Len Barker CLE................ 127
Britt Burns CHI 108
two tied at......................... 107

SAVES
Rollie Fingers MIL 28
Goose Gossage NY 20
Dan Quisenberry KC 18

COMPLETE GAMES
Rick Langford OAK 18
Steve McCatty OAK 16
Jack Morris DET................ 15

SHUTOUTS
four tied at 4

GAMES PITCHED
Doug Corbett MIN 54
Rollie Fingers MIL 47
Shane Rawley SEA............ 46

INNINGS PITCHED
Dennis Leonard KC.......... 202
Jack Morris DET............... 198
Rick Langford OAK 195

1981 NL

EAST	W	L	PCT	GB	R	OR	BA	FA	ERA
ST. LOUIS	59	43	.578	—	464	417	.265	.981	3.63
MONTREAL**†	60	48	.556	2	443	394	.246	.980	3.30
PHILADELPHIA*	59	48	.551	2.5	491	472	.273	.980	4.05
PITTSBURGH	46	56	.451	13	407	425	.257	.979	3.56
NEW YORK	41	62	.398	18.5	348	432	.248	.968	3.55
CHICAGO	38	65	.369	21.5	370	483	.236	.974	4.01

WEST	W	L	PCT	GB	R	OR	BA	FA	ERA
CINCINNATI	66	42	.611	—	464	440	.267	.981	3.73
★ LOS ANGELES*†	63	47	.573	4	450	356	.262	.980	3.01
HOUSTON**	61	49	.555	6	394	331	.257	.980	2.66
SAN FRANCISCO	56	55	.505	11.5	427	414	.250	.977	3.28
ATLANTA	50	56	.472	15	395	416	.243	.976	3.45
SAN DIEGO	41	69	.373	26	382	455	.256	.977	3.72
					5035	5035	.255	.978	3.49

*Winner of first half **Winner of second half †Winner of playoff

BATTING AVERAGE
Bill Madlock PIT .... .341
Pete Rose PHI .... .325
Dusty Baker LA .... .320

HITS
Pete Rose PHI 140
Bill Buckner CHI 131
Dave Concepcion CIN...... 129

DOUBLES
Bill Buckner CHI 35
Ruppert Jones SD 34
Dave Concepcion CIN........ 28

TRIPLES
Craig Reynolds HOU......... 12
Gene Richards SD 12
Tommy Herr STL 9

HOME RUNS
Mike Schmidt PHI............... 31
Andre Dawson MON 24
two tied at........................... 22

RUNS BATTED IN
Mike Schmidt PHI............... 91
George Foster CIN............. 90
Bill Buckner CHI 75

SLUGGING AVERAGE
Mike Schmidt PHI............. .644
Andre Dawson MON .... .553
George Foster CIN............ .519

STOLEN BASES
Tim Raines MON............... 71
Omar Moreno PIT 39
Rodney Scott MON 30

RUNS SCORED
Mike Schmidt PHI............... 78
Pete Rose PHI 73
Andre Dawson MON 71

WINS
Tom Seaver CIN.................. 14
Steve Carlton PHI 13
F. Valenzuela LA 13

WINNING PERCENTAGE
Tom Seaver CIN.................. .875
Steve Carlton PHI .... .765
Nolan Ryan HOU .... .688

EARNED RUN AVERAGE
Nolan Ryan HOU 1.69
Bob Knepper HOU 2.18
Burt Hooton LA................. 2.28

STRIKEOUTS
F. Valenzuela LA 180
Steve Carlton PHI 179
Mario Soto CIN................ 151

SAVES
Bruce Sutter STL............... 25
Greg Minton SF................. 21
Neil Allen NY 18

COMPLETE GAMES
F. Valenzuela LA................ 11
Mario Soto CIN................. 10
Steve Carlton PHI 10

SHUTOUTS
Fernando Valenzuela LA...... 8
Bob Knepper HOU 5
Burt Hooton LA.................... 4

GAMES PITCHED
Gary Lucas SD.................. 57
Greg Minton SF................. 55
two tied at........................... 51

INNINGS PITCHED
F. Valenzuela LA 192
Steve Carlton PHI 190
Mario Soto CIN................. 175

1982 AL

EAST	W	L	PCT	GB	R	OR	BA	FA	ERA
● MILWAUKEE	95	67	.586	—	891	717	.279	.980	3.98
BALTIMORE	94	68	.580	1	774	687	.266	.984	3.99
BOSTON	89	73	.549	6	753	713	.274	.981	4.03
DETROIT	83	79	.512	12	729	685	.266	.981	3.80
NEW YORK	79	83	.488	16	709	716	.256	.979	3.99
CLEVELAND	78	84	.481	17	683	748	.262	.980	4.11
TORONTO	78	84	.481	17	651	701	.262	.978	3.95

WEST	W	L	PCT	GB	R	OR	BA	FA	ERA
CALIFORNIA	93	69	.574	—	814	670	.274	.983	3.82
KANSAS CITY	90	72	.556	3	784	717	.285	.979	4.08
CHICAGO	87	75	.537	6	786	710	.273	.976	3.87
SEATTLE	76	86	.469	17	651	712	.254	.978	3.88
OAKLAND	68	94	.420	25	691	819	.236	.974	4.54
TEXAS	64	98	.395	29	590	749	.249	.981	4.28
MINNESOTA	60	102	.370	33	657	819	.257	.982	4.72
					10163	10163	.264	.980	4.07

BATTING AVERAGE
Willie Wilson KC .... .332
Robin Yount MIL .... .331
Rod Carew CAL .... .319

HITS
Robin Yount MIL 210
Cecil Cooper MIL 205
Paul Molitor MIL 201

DOUBLES
Robin Yount MIL 46
Hal McRae KC 46
Frank White KC 45

TRIPLES
Willie Wilson KC 15
Larry Herndon DET 13
Robin Yount MIL 12

HOME RUNS
Reggie Jackson CAL 39
Gorman Thomas MIL 39
Dave Winfield NY 37

RUNS BATTED IN
Hal McRae KC 133
Cecil Cooper MIL 121
Andre Thornton CLE 116

SLUGGING AVERAGE
Robin Yount MIL .... .578
Dave Winfield NY .... .560
Eddie Murray BAL .... .549

STOLEN BASES
R. Henderson OAK 130
Damaso Garcia TOR 54
Julio Cruz SEA 46

RUNS SCORED
Paul Molitor MIL 136
Robin Yount MIL 129
Dwight Evans BOS 122

WINS
LaMarr Hoyt CHI 19
three tied at 18

WINNING PERCENTAGE
Pete Vuckovich MIL .... .750
Jim Palmer BAL .... .750
Geoff Zahn CAL .... .692

EARNED RUN AVERAGE
Rick Sutcliffe CLE 2.96
Bob Stanley BOS 3.10
Jim Palmer BAL 3.13

STRIKEOUTS
Floyd Bannister SEA 209
Len Barker CLE 187
Dave Righetti NY 163

SAVES
Dan Quisenberry KC 35
Goose Gossage NY 30
Rollie Fingers MIL 29

COMPLETE GAMES
Dave Stieb TOR 19
Jack Morris DET 17
Rick Langford OAK 15

SHUTOUTS
Dave Stieb TOR 5
Geoff Zahn CAL 4
Ken Forsch CAL 4

GAMES PITCHED
Ed Vande Berg SEA 78
Tippy Martinez BAL 76
Dan Quisenberry KC 72

INNINGS PITCHED
Dave Stieb TOR 288
Jim Clancy TOR 267
Jack Morris DET 266

1982 NL

EAST	W	L	PCT	GB	R	OR	BA	FA	ERA
★ ST. LOUIS	92	70	.568	—	685	609	.264	.981	3.37
PHILADELPHIA	89	73	.549	3	664	654	.260	.981	3.61
MONTREAL	86	76	.531	6	697	616	.262	.980	3.31
PITTSBURGH	84	78	.519	8	724	696	.273	.977	3.81
CHICAGO	73	89	.451	19	676	709	.260	.979	3.92
NEW YORK	65	97	.401	27	609	723	.247	.972	3.88

WEST	W	L	PCT	GB	R	OR	BA	FA	ERA
ATLANTA	89	73	.549	—	739	702	.256	.979	3.82
LOS ANGELES	88	74	.543	1	691	612	.264	.979	3.26
SAN FRANCISCO	87	75	.537	2	673	687	.253	.973	3.64
SAN DIEGO	81	81	.500	8	675	658	.257	.976	3.52
HOUSTON	77	85	.475	12	569	620	.247	.978	3.42
CINCINNATI	61	101	.377	28	545	661	.251	.980	3.66
					7947	7947	.258	.978	3.60

BATTING AVERAGE
Al Oliver MON .... .331
Bill Madlock PIT .... .319
Leon Durham CHI .... .312

HITS
Al Oliver MON 204
Bill Buckner CHI 201
Andre Dawson MON 183

DOUBLES
Al Oliver MON 43
Terry Kennedy SD 42
Andre Dawson MON 37

TRIPLES
Dickie Thon HOU 10
three tied at 9

HOME RUNS
Dave Kingman NY.............. 37
Dale Murphy ATL 36
Mike Schmidt PHI............... 35

RUNS BATTED IN
Dale Murphy ATL 109
Al Oliver MON 109
Bill Buckner CHI 105

SLUGGING AVERAGE
Mike Schmidt PHI............ .547
Pedro Guerrero LA........... .536
Leon Durham CHI .... .521

STOLEN BASES
Tim Raines MON................ 78
Lonnie Smith STL.............. 68
Omar Moreno PIT 60

RUNS SCORED
Lonnie Smith STL............. 120
Dale Murphy ATL.............. 113
Mike Schmidt PHI.............. 108

WINS
Steve Carlton PHI 23
Steve Rogers MON............. 19
F. Valenzuela LA 19

WINNING PERCENTAGE
Phil Niekro ATL .... .810
Steve Rogers MON .... .704
Steve Carlton PHI .... .676

EARNED RUN AVERAGE
Steve Rogers MON 2.40
Joe Niekro HOU 2.47
Joaquin Andujar STL....... 2.47

STRIKEOUTS
Steve Carlton PHi 286
Mario Soto CIN................ 274
Nolan Ryan HOU 245

SAVES
Bruce Sutter STL.............. 36
Greg Minton SF................. 30
Gene Garber ATL 30

COMPLETE GAMES
Steve Carlton PHI 19
F. Valenzuela LA 18
Joe Niekro HOU 16

SHUTOUTS
Steve Carlton PHI 6
Joaquin Andujar STL.......... 5
Joe Niekro HOU 5

GAMES PITCHED
Kent Tekulve PIT 85
Greg Minton SF.................. 78
Rod Scurry PIT................... 76

INNINGS PITCHED
Steve Carlton PHI 296
F. Valenzuela LA 285
Steve Rogers MON 277

1983 AL

EAST	W	L	PCT	GB	R	OR	BA	FA	ERA
★ BALTIMORE	98	64	.605	—	799	652	.269	.981	3.63
DETROIT	92	70	.568	6	789	679	.274	.980	3.80
NEW YORK	91	71	.562	7	770	703	.273	.978	3.86
TORONTO	89	73	.549	9	795	726	.277	.981	4.12
MILWAUKEE	87	75	.537	11	764	708	.277	.982	4.02
BOSTON	78	84	.481	20	724	775	.270	.979	4.34
CLEVELAND	70	92	.432	28	704	785	.265	.980	4.43

WEST	W	L	PCT	GB	R	OR	BA	FA	ERA
CHICAGO	99	63	.611	—	800	650	.262	.981	3.67
KANSAS CITY	79	83	.488	20	696	767	.271	.974	4.25
TEXAS	77	85	.475	22	639	609	.255	.982	3.31
OAKLAND	74	88	.457	25	708	782	.262	.974	4.34
CALIFORNIA	70	92	.432	29	722	779	.260	.977	4.31
MINNESOTA	70	92	.432	29	709	822	.261	.980	4.66
SEATTLE	60	102	.370	39	558	740	.240	.978	4.12
					10177	10177	.266	.979	4.06

BATTING AVERAGE
Wade Boggs BOS .... .361
Rod Carew CAL .... .339
Lou Whitaker DET .... .320

HITS
Cal Ripken BAL 211
Wade Boggs BOS 210
Lou Whitaker DET............ 206

DOUBLES
Cal Ripken BAL.................. 47
Wade Boggs BOS 44
two tied at............................ 42

TRIPLES
Robin Yount MIL.................. 10
three tied at 9

HOME RUNS
Jim Rice BOS..................... 39
Tony Armas BOS................ 36
Ron Kittle CHI 35

RUNS BATTED IN
Cecil Cooper MIL 126
Jim Rice BOS..................... 126
Dave Winfield NY 116

SLUGGING AVERAGE
George Brett KC................. .563
Jim Rice BOS.................... .550
Eddie Murray BAL............. .538

STOLEN BASES
R. Henderson OAK 108
Rudy Law CHI 77
Willie Wilson KC................. 59

RUNS SCORED
Cal Ripken BAL................. 121
Eddie Murray BAL 115
Cecil Cooper MIL 106

WINS
LaMarr Hoyt CHI 24
Rich Dotson CHI 22
Ron Guidry NY 21

WINNING PERCENTAGE
Rich Dotson CHI .... .759
Scott McGregor BAL .... .720
LaMarr Hoyt CHI .... .706

EARNED RUN AVERAGE
Rick Honeycutt TEX 2.42
Mike Boddicker BAL........ 2.77
Dave Stieb TOR 3.04

STRIKEOUTS
Jack Morris DET............... 232
Floyd Bannister CHI ... 193
Dave Stieb TOR 187

SAVES
Dan Quisenberry KC.......... 45
Bob Stanley BOS 33
Ron Davis MIN 30

COMPLETE GAMES
Ron Guidry NY 21
Jack Morris DET............... 20
Dave Stieb TOR 14

SHUTOUTS
Mike Boddicker BAL............ 5
Britt Burns CHI 4
Dave Stieb TOR 4

GAMES PITCHED
Dan Quisenberry KC 69
Ed Vande Berg SEA........... 68
Ron Davis MIN 66

INNINGS PITCHED
Jack Morris DET............... 294
Dave Stieb TOR 278
Dan Petry DET.................. 266

1983 NL

EAST	W	L	PCT	GB	R	OR	BA	FA	ERA
● PHILADELPHIA	90	72	.556	—	696	635	.249	.976	3.34
PITTSBURGH	84	78	.519	6	659	648	.264	.982	3.55
MONTREAL	82	80	.506	8	677	646	.264	.981	3.58
ST. LOUIS	79	83	.488	11	679	710	.270	.976	3.79
CHICAGO	71	91	.438	19	701	719	.261	.982	4.08
NEW YORK	68	94	.420	22	575	680	.241	.976	3.68

WEST	W	L	PCT	GB	R	OR	BA	FA	ERA
LOS ANGELES	91	71	.562	—	654	609	.250	.974	3.10
ATLANTA	88	74	.543	3	746	640	.272	.978	3.67
HOUSTON	85	77	.525	6	643	646	.257	.977	3.45
SAN DIEGO	81	81	.500	10	653	653	.250	.979	3.62
SAN FRANCISCO	79	83	.488	12	687	697	.247	.973	3.70
CINCINNATI	74	88	.457	17	623	710	.239	.981	3.98
					7993	7993	.255	.978	3.63

BATTING AVERAGE
Bill Madlock PIT .... .323
Lonnie Smith STL............ .321
Jose Cruz HOU................ .318

HITS
Jose Cruz HOU 189
Andre Dawson MON 189
Rafael Ramirez ATL 185

DOUBLES
Al Oliver MON 38
Johnny Ray PIT 38
Bill Buckner CHI 38

TRIPLES
Brett Butler ATL 13
Omar Moreno HOU 11
two tied at 10

HOME RUNS
Mike Schmidt PHI.............. 40
Dale Murphy ATL 36
two tied at.......................... 32

RUNS BATTED IN
Dale Murphy ATL 121
Andre Dawson MON 113
Mike Schmidt PHI............. 109

SLUGGING AVERAGE
Dale Murphy ATL .... .540
Andre Dawson MON .... .539
Pedro Guerrero LA .... .531

STOLEN BASES
Tim Raines MON................ 90
Alan Wiggins SD 66
Steve Sax LA 56

RUNS SCORED
Tim Raines MON............. 133
Dale Murphy ATL 131
two tied at........................ 104

WINS
John Denny PHI................ 19
three tied at 17

WINNING PERCENTAGE
John Denny PHI.............. .760
three tied at .... .652

EARNED RUN AVERAGE
Atlee Hammaker SF 2.25
John Denny PHI 2.37
Bob Welch LA 2.65

STRIKEOUTS
Steve Carlton PHI 275
Mario Soto CIN................ 242
Larry McWilliams PIT 199

SAVES
Lee Smith CHI................... 29
Al Holland PHI................... 25
Greg Minton SF................. 22

COMPLETE GAMES
Mario Soto CIN................. 18
Steve Rogers MON............ 13
Bill Gullickson MON 10

SHUTOUTS
Steve Rogers MON 5
three tied at 4

GAMES PITCHED
Bill Campbell CHI 82
Kent Tekulve PIT 76
G. Hernandez CHI, PHI...... 74

INNINGS PITCHED
Steve Carlton PHI 284
Mario Soto CIN................ 274
Steve Rogers MON 273

1984 AL

EAST	W	L	PCT	GB	R	OR	BA	FA	ERA
★ DETROIT	104	58	.642	—	829	643	.271	.979	3.49
TORONTO	89	73	.549	15	750	696	.273	.980	3.86
NEW YORK	87	75	.537	17	758	679	.276	.977	3.78
BOSTON	86	76	.531	18	810	764	.283	.977	4.18
BALTIMORE	85	77	.525	19	681	667	.252	.981	3.71
CLEVELAND	75	87	.463	29	761	766	.265	.977	4.26
MILWAUKEE	67	94	.416	36.5	641	734	.262	.978	4.06

WEST	W	L	PCT	GB	R	OR	BA	FA	ERA
KANSAS CITY	84	78	.519	—	673	686	.268	.979	3.92
CALIFORNIA	81	81	.500	3	696	697	.249	.980	3.96
MINNESOTA	81	81	.500	3	673	675	.265	.980	3.85
OAKLAND	77	85	.475	7	738	796	.259	.975	4.48
CHICAGO	74	88	.457	10	679	736	.247	.981	4.13
SEATTLE	74	88	.457	10	682	774	.258	.979	4.31
TEXAS	69	92	.429	14.5	656	714	.261	.977	3.91
					10027	10027	.264	.979	3.99

BATTING AVERAGE
Don Mattingly NY .... .343
Dave Winfield NY .... .340
Wade Boggs BOS .... .325

HITS
Don Mattingly NY 207
Wade Boggs BOS 203
Cal Ripken BAL................ 195

DOUBLES
Don Mattingly NY 44
Larry Parrish TEX 42
George Bell TOR................ 39

TRIPLES
Dave Collins TOR 15
Lloyd Moseby TOR 15
two tied at............................ 10

HOME RUNS
Tony Armas BOS................ 43
Dave Kingman OAK 35
three tied at 33

RUNS BATTED IN
Tony Armas BOS.............. 123
Jim Rice BOS.................... 122
Dave Kingman OAK 118

SLUGGING AVERAGE
Harold Baines CHI .... .541
Don Mattingly NY .... .537
Dwight Evans BOS........... .532

STOLEN BASES
Rickey Henderson OAK 66
Dave Collins TOR 60
Brett Butler CLE 52

RUNS SCORED
Dwight Evans BOS........... 121
R. Henderson OAK............ 113
Wade Boggs BOS 109

WINS
Mike Boddicker BAL........... 20
Bert Blyleven CLE.............. 19
Jack Morris DET................ 19

WINNING PERCENTAGE
Doyle Alexander TOR ..... .739
Bert Blyleven CLE .... .731
Dan Petry DET .... .692

EARNED RUN AVERAGE
Mike Boddicker BAL........ 2.79
Dave Stieb TOR 2.83
Bert Blyleven CLE 2.87

STRIKEOUTS
Mark Langston SEA 204
Dave Stieb TOR 198
Mike Witt CAL 196

SAVES
Dan Quisenberry KC 44
Bill Caudill OAK.................. 36
G. Hernandez DET............. 32

COMPLETE GAMES
Charlie Hough TEX 17
Mike Boddicker BAL........... 16
Rich Dotson CHI 14

SHUTOUTS
Geoff Zahn CAL 5
Bob Ojeda BOS.................... 5
two tied at............................. 4

GAMES PITCHED
G. Hernandez DET............. 80
Dan Quisenberry KC 72
Aurelio Lopez DET 71

INNINGS PITCHED
Dave Stieb TOR 267
Charlie Hough TEX 266
Doyle Alexander TOR 262

1984 NL

EAST	W	L	PCT	GB	R	OR	BA	FA	ERA
CHICAGO	96	65	.596	—	762	658	.260	.981	3.75
NEW YORK	90	72	.556	6.5	652	676	.257	.979	3.60
ST. LOUIS	84	78	.519	12.5	652	645	.252	.982	3.58
PHILADELPHIA	81	81	.500	15.5	720	690	.266	.975	3.62
MONTREAL	78	83	.484	18	593	585	.251	.978	3.31
PITTSBURGH	75	87	.463	21.5	615	567	.255	.980	3.11

WEST	W	L	PCT	GB	R	OR	BA	FA	ERA
● SAN DIEGO	92	70	.568	—	686	634	.259	.978	3.48
ATLANTA	80	82	.494	12	632	655	.247	.978	3.57
HOUSTON	80	82	.494	12	693	630	.264	.979	3.32
LOS ANGELES	79	83	.488	13	580	600	.244	.975	3.17
CINCINNATI	70	92	.432	22	627	747	.244	.977	4.16
SAN FRANCISCO	66	96	.407	26	682	807	.265	.973	4.39
					7894	7894	.255	.978	3.59

BATTING AVERAGE
Tony Gwynn SD .... .351
Lee Lacy PIT .... .321
Chili Davis SF .... .315

HITS
Tony Gwynn SD 213
Ryne Sandberg CHI 200
Tim Raines MON 192

DOUBLES
Johnny Ray PIT 38
Tim Raines MON 38
two tied at 36

TRIPLES
Juan Samuel PHI 19
Ryne Sandberg CHI 19
Jose Cruz HOU 13

HOME RUNS
Dale Murphy ATL 36
Mike Schmidt PHI 36
Gary Carter MON 27

RUNS BATTED IN
Gary Carter MON 106
Mike Schmidt PHI 106
Dale Murphy ATL 100

SLUGGING AVERAGE
Dale Murphy ATL .... .547
Mike Schmidt PHI .... .536
Ryne Sandberg CHI .... .520

STOLEN BASES
Tim Raines MON 75
Juan Samuel PHI 72
Alan Wiggins SD 70

RUNS SCORED
Ryne Sandberg CHI 114
Tim Raines MON 106
Alan Wiggins SD 106

WINS
Joaquin Andujar STL 20
Mario Soto CIN 18
Dwight Gooden NY 17

WINNING PERCENTAGE
Rick Sutcliffe CHI .... .941
Mario Soto CIN .... .720
Dwight Gooden NY .... .654

EARNED RUN AVERAGE
Alejandro Pena LA 2.48
Dwight Gooden NY 2.60
Orel Hershiser LA 2.66

STRIKEOUTS
Dwight Gooden NY 276
F. Valenzuela LA 240
Nolan Ryan HOU 197

SAVES
Bruce Sutter STL 45
Lee Smith CHI 33
Jesse Orosco NY 31

COMPLETE GAMES
Mario Soto CIN 13
F. Valenzuela LA 12
Joaquin Andujar STL 12

SHUTOUTS
Alejandro Pena LA 4
Joaquin Andujar STL 4
Orel Hershiser LA 4

GAMES PITCHED
Ted Power CIN 78
Gary Lavelle SF 77
Greg Minton SF 74

INNINGS PITCHED
Joaquin Andujar STL 261
F. Valenzuela LA 261
Joe Niekro HOU 248

1985 AL

EAST	W	L	PCT	GB	R	OR	BA	FA	ERA
TORONTO	99	62	.615	—	759	588	.269	.980	3.31
NEW YORK	97	64	.602	2	839	660	.267	.979	3.69
DETROIT	84	77	.522	15	729	688	.253	.977	3.78
BALTIMORE	83	78	.516	16	818	764	.263	.979	4.38
BOSTON	81	81	.500	18.5	800	720	.282	.977	4.06
MILWAUKEE	71	90	.441	28	690	802	.263	.977	4.39
CLEVELAND	60	102	.370	39.5	729	861	.265	.977	4.91

WEST	W	L	PCT	GB	R	OR	BA	FA	ERA
★ KANSAS CITY	91	71	.562	—	687	639	.252	.980	3.49
CALIFORNIA	90	72	.556	1	732	703	.251	.982	3.91
CHICAGO	85	77	.525	6	736	720	.253	.982	4.07
MINNESOTA	77	85	.475	14	705	782	.264	.980	4.48
OAKLAND	77	85	.475	14	757	787	.264	.977	4.41
SEATTLE	74	88	.457	17	719	818	.255	.980	4.68
TEXAS	62	99	.385	28.5	617	785	.253	.980	4.56
					10317	10317	.261	.979	4.15

BATTING AVERAGE
Wade Boggs BOS .... .368
George Brett KC .... .335
Don Mattingly NY .... .324

HITS
Wade Boggs BOS 240
Don Mattingly NY 211
Bill Buckner BOS.............. 201

DOUBLES
Don Mattingly NY 48
Bill Buckner BOS............... 46
Wade Boggs BOS 42

TRIPLES
Willie Wilson KC................. 21
Brett Butler CLE 14
Kirby Puckett MIN 13

HOME RUNS
Darrell Evans DET 40
Carlton Fisk CHI................. 37
Steve Balboni KC 36

RUNS BATTED IN
Don Mattingly NY 145
Eddie Murray BAL 124
Dave Winfield NY 114

SLUGGING AVERAGE
George Brett KC.............. .585
Don Mattingly NY .... .567
Jesse Barfield TOR .... .536

STOLEN BASES
Rickey Henderson NY 80
Gary Pettis CAL 56
Brett Butler CLE 47

RUNS SCORED
Rickey Henderson NY 146
Cal Ripken BAL 116
Eddie Murray BAL............. 111

WINS
Ron Guidry NY 22
Bret Saberhagen KC 20
two tied at............................ 18

WINNING PERCENTAGE
Ron Guidry NY .... .786
Bret Saberhagen KC .... .769
Charlie Leibrandt KC....... .654

EARNED RUN AVERAGE
Dave Stieb TOR 2.48
Charlie Leibrandt KC....... 2.69
Bret Saberhagen KC 2.87

STRIKEOUTS
B. Blyleven CLE, MIN....... 206
Floyd Bannister CHI 198
Jack Morris DET............... 191

SAVES
Dan Quisenberry KC 37
Bob James CHI 32
two tied at.......................... 31

COMPLETE GAMES
Bert Blyleven CLE, MIN 24
Charlie Hough TEX 14
Mike Moore SEA 14

SHUTOUTS
Bert Blyleven CLE, MIN 5
Jack Morris DET.................. 4
Britt Burns CHI 4

GAMES PITCHED
Dan Quisenberry KC 84
Ed Vande Berg SEA........... 76
two tied at.......................... 74

INNINGS PITCHED
B. Blyleven CLE, MIN....... 294
Oil Can Boyd BOS 272
Dave Stieb TOR 265

1985 NL

EAST	W	L	PCT	GB	R	OR	BA	FA	ERA
● ST. LOUIS	101	61	.623	—	747	572	.264	.983	3.10
NEW YORK	98	64	.605	3	695	568	.257	.982	3.11
MONTREAL	84	77	.522	16.5	633	636	.247	.981	3.55
CHICAGO	77	84	.478	23.5	686	729	.254	.979	4.16
PHILADELPHIA	75	87	.463	26	667	673	.245	.978	3.68
PITTSBURGH	57	104	.354	43.5	568	708	.247	.979	3.97

WEST	W	L	PCT	GB	R	OR	BA	FA	ERA
LOS ANGELES	95	67	.586	—	682	579	.261	.974	2.96
CINCINNATI	89	72	.553	5.5	677	666	.255	.980	3.71
HOUSTON	83	79	.512	12	706	691	.261	.976	3.66
SAN DIEGO	83	79	.512	12	650	622	.255	.980	3.40
ATLANTA	66	96	.407	29	632	781	.246	.976	4.19
SAN FRANCISCO	62	100	.383	33	556	674	.233	.976	3.61
					7899	7899	.252	.979	3.59

BATTING AVERAGE
Willie McGee STL .... .353
Pedro Guerrero LA.......... .320
Tim Raines MON............. .320

HITS
Willie McGee STL 216
Dave Parker CIN 198
Tony Gwynn SD 197

DOUBLES
Dave Parker CIN 42
Glenn Wilson PHI............... 39
Tommy Herr STL 38

TRIPLES
Willie McGee STL 18
Juan Samuel PHI 13
Tim Raines MON................ 13

HOME RUNS
Dale Murphy ATL 37
Dave Parker CIN 34
two tied at............................ 33

RUNS BATTED IN
Dave Parker CIN 125
Dale Murphy ATL 111
Tommy Herr STL 110

SLUGGING AVERAGE
Pedro Guerrero LA.......... .577
Dave Parker CIN .... .551
Dale Murphy ATL .... .539

STOLEN BASES
Vince Coleman STL.......... 110
Tim Raines MON............... 70
Willie McGee STL 56

RUNS SCORED
Dale Murphy ATL.............. 118
Tim Raines MON 115
Willie McGee STL............. 114

WINS
Dwight Gooden NY 24
John Tudor STL.................. 21
Joaquin Andujar STL.......... 21

WINNING PERCENTAGE
Orel Hershiser LA............. .864
Dwight Gooden NY .... .857
Bryn Smith MON .... .783

EARNED RUN AVERAGE
Dwight Gooden NY 1.53
John Tudor STL................ 1.93
Orel Heshiser LA.............. 2.03

STRIKEOUTS
Dwight Gooden NY 268
Mario Soto CIN................. 214
Nolan Ryan HOU 209

SAVES
Jeff Reardon MON 41
Lee Smith CHI.................... 33
two tied at............................ 27

COMPLETE GAMES
Dwight Gooden NY 16
F. Valenzuela LA 14
John Tudor STL.................. 14

SHUTOUTS
John Tudor STL.................. 10
Dwight Gooden NY 8
two tied at.............................. 5

GAMES PITCHED
Tim Burke MON.................. 78
Mark Davis SF.................... 77
Scott Garrelts SF................ 74

INNINGS PITCHED
Dwight Gooden NY 277
John Tudor STL................. 275
F. Valenzuela LA 272

1986 AL

EAST	W	L	PCT	GB	R	OR	BA	FA	ERA
● BOSTON	95	66	.590	—	794	696	.271	.979	3.93
NEW YORK	90	72	.556	5.5	797	738	.271	.979	4.11
DETROIT	87	75	.537	8.5	798	714	.263	.982	4.02
TORONTO	86	76	.531	9.5	809	733	.269	.984	4.08
CLEVELAND	84	78	.519	11.5	831	841	.284	.975	4.57
MILWAUKEE	77	84	.478	18	667	734	.255	.976	4.01
BALTIMORE	73	89	.451	22.5	708	760	.258	.978	4.30

WEST	W	L	PCT	GB	R	OR	BA	FA	ERA
CALIFORNIA	92	70	.568	—	786	684	.255	.983	3.84
TEXAS	87	75	.537	5	771	743	.267	.980	4.11
KANSAS CITY	76	86	.469	16	654	673	.252	.980	3.82
OAKLAND	76	86	.469	16	731	760	.252	.978	4.31
CHICAGO	72	90	.444	20	644	699	.247	.981	3.93
MINNESOTA	71	91	.438	21	741	839	.261	.980	4.77
SEATTLE	67	95	.414	25	718	835	.253	.975	4.65
					10449	10449	.262	.979	4.18

BATTING AVERAGE
Wade Boggs BOS .... .357
Don Mattingly NY .... .352
Kirby Puckett MIN .... .328

HITS
Don Mattingly NY 238
Kirby Pucket MIN 223
Tony Fernandez TOR 213

DOUBLES
Don Mattingly NY 53
Wade Boggs BOS 47
three tied at 39

TRIPLES
Brett Butler CLE 14
Ruben Sierra TEX 10
two tied at 9

HOME RUNS
Jesse Barfield TOR 40
Dave Kingman OAK 35
Gary Gaetti MIN 34

RUNS BATTED IN
Joe Carter CLE 121
Jose Canseco OAK 117
Don Mattingly NY 113

SLUGGING AVERAGE
Don Mattingly NY .... .573
Jesse Barfield TOR .... .559
Kirby Puckett MIN .... .537

STOLEN BASES
Rickey Henderson NY 87
Gary Pettis CAL 50
John Cangelosi CHI 50

RUNS SCORED
Rickey Henderson NY 130
Kirby Puckett MIN............. 119
Don Mattingly NY 117

WINS
Roger Clemens BOS.......... 24
Jack Morris DET................. 21
Ted Higuera MIL................. 20

WINNING PERCENTAGE
Roger Clemens BOS........ .857
Dennis Rasmussen NY ... .750
Jack Morris DET.............. .724

EARNED RUN AVERAGE
Roger Clemens BOS....... 2.48
Ted Higuera MIL............... 2.79
Mike Witt CAL 2.84

STRIKEOUTS
Mark Langston SEA 245
Roger Clemens BOS........ 238
Jack Morris DET............... 223

SAVES
Dave Righetti NY................ 46
Don Aase BAL.................... 34
Tom Henke TOR 27

COMPLETE GAMES
Tom Candiotti CLE 17
Bert Blyleven MIN 16
two tied at............................ 15

SHUTOUTS
Jack Morris DET................... 6
Bruce Hurst BOS................. 4
Ted Higuera MIL................... 4

GAMES PITCHED
Mitch Williams TEX 80
Dave Righetti NY................ 74
Greg Harris TEX................. 73

INNINGS PITCHED
Bert Blyleven MIN 272
Mike Witt CAL 269
Jack Morris DET............... 267

1986 NL

EAST	W	L	PCT	GB	R	OR	BA	FA	ERA
★ NEW YORK	108	54	.667	—	783	578	.263	.978	3.11
PHILADELPHIA	86	75	.534	21.5	739	713	.253	.978	3.85
ST. LOUIS	79	82	.491	28.5	601	611	.236	.981	3.37
MONTREAL	78	83	.484	29.5	637	688	.254	.979	3.78
CHICAGO	70	90	.438	37	680	781	.256	.980	4.49
PITTSBURGH	64	98	.395	44	663	700	.250	.978	3.90

WEST	W	L	PCT	GB	R	OR	BA	FA	ERA
HOUSTON	96	66	.593	—	654	569	.255	.979	3.15
CINCINNATI	86	76	.531	10	732	717	.254	.978	3.91
SAN FRANCISCO	83	79	.512	13	698	618	.253	.977	3.33
SAN DIEGO	74	88	.457	22	656	723	.261	.978	3.99
LOS ANGELES	73	89	.451	23	638	679	.251	.971	3.76
ATLANTA	72	89	.447	23.5	615	719	.250	.978	3.97
					8096	8096	.253	.978	3.72

BATTING AVERAGE
Tim Raines MON .... .334
Steve Sax LA .... .332
Tony Gwynn SD .... .329

HITS
Tony Gwynn SD 211
Steve Sax LA 210
Tim Raines MON 194

DOUBLES
Von Hayes PHI 46
Steve Sax LA 43
Sid Bream PIT 37

TRIPLES
Mitch Webster MON 13
Juan Samuel PHI 12
Tim Raines MON 10

HOME RUNS
Mike Schmidt PHI 37
Glenn Davis HOU 31
Dave Parker CIN 31

RUNS BATTED IN
Mike Schmidt PHI 119
Dave Parker CIN 116
Gary Carter NY 105

SLUGGING AVERAGE
Mike Schmidt PHI .... .547
Darryl Strawberry NY .... .507
Kevin McReynolds SD .... .504

STOLEN BASES
Vince Coleman STL 107
Eric Davis CIN 80
Tim Raines MON 70

RUNS SCORED
Tony Gwynn SD 107
Von Hayes PHI 107
two tied at 97

WINS
F. Valenzuela LA 21
Mike Krukow SF 20
two tied at 18

WINNING PERCENTAGE
Bob Ojeda NY .... .783
Dwight Gooden NY .... .739
Sid Fernandez NY .... .727

EARNED RUN AVERAGE
Mike Scott HOU 2.22
Bob Ojeda NY 2.57
Ron Darling NY 2.81

STRIKEOUTS
Mike Scott HOU 306
F. Valenzuela LA 242
Floyd Youmans MON 202

SAVES
Todd Worrell STL 36
Jeff Reardon MON 35
Dave Smith HOU 33

COMPLETE GAMES
F. Valenzuela LA 20
Rick Rhoden PIT 12
Dwight Gooden NY 12

SHUTOUTS
Mike Scott HOU 5
Bob Knepper HOU 5
two tied at 3

GAMES PITCHED
Craig Lefferts SD 83
Roger McDowell NY 75
two tied at 74

INNINGS PITCHED
Mike Scott HOU 275
F. Valenzuela LA 269
Bob Knepper HOU 258

1987 AL

EAST	W	L	PCT	GB	R	OR	BA	FA	ERA
DETROIT	98	64	.605	—	896	735	.272	.980	4.02
TORONTO	96	66	.593	2	845	655	.269	.982	3.74
MILWAUKEE	91	71	.562	7	862	817	.276	.976	4.62
NEW YORK	89	73	.549	9	788	758	.262	.983	4.36
BOSTON	78	84	.481	20	842	825	.278	.982	4.77
BALTIMORE	67	95	.414	31	729	880	.258	.982	5.01
CLEVELAND	61	101	.377	37	742	957	.263	.975	5.28

WEST	W	L	PCT	GB	R	OR	BA	FA	ERA
★ MINNESOTA	85	77	.525	—	786	806	.261	.984	4.63
KANSAS CITY	83	79	.512	2	715	691	.262	.979	3.86
OAKLAND	81	81	.500	4	806	789	.260	.977	4.32
SEATTLE	78	84	.481	7	760	801	.272	.980	4.49
CHICAGO	77	85	.475	8	748	746	.258	.981	4.30
CALIFORNIA	75	87	.463	10	770	803	.252	.981	4.38
TEXAS	75	87	.463	10	823	849	.266	.976	4.63
					11112	11112	.265	.980	4.46

BATTING AVERAGE
Wade Boggs BOS .... .363
Paul Molitor MIL .... .353
Alan Trammell DET .... .343

HITS
Kevin Seitzer KC 207
Kirby Puckett MIN 207
Alan Trammell DET 205

DOUBLES
Paul Molitor MIL 41
Wade Boggs BOS 40

TRIPLES
Willie Wilson KC 15
Luis Polonia OAK 10
Phil Bradley SEA 10

HOME RUNS
Mark McGwire OAK 49
George Bell TOR................ 47
four tied at 34

RUNS BATTED IN
George Bell TOR............. 134
Dwight Evans BOS........ 123
Mark McGwire OAK........ 118

SLUGGING AVERAGE
Mark McGwire OAK .... .618
George Bell TOR............. .605
Wade Boggs BOS .... .588

STOLEN BASES
Harold Reynolds SEA 60
Willie Wilson KC................. 59
Gary Redus CHI................. 52

RUNS SCORED
Paul Molitor MIL 114
George Bell TOR 111
two tied at 110

WINS
Roger Clemens BOS.......... 20
Dave Stewart OAK 20
Mark Langston SEA 19

WINNING PERCENTAGE
Roger Clemens BOS....... .690
Jimmy Key TOR .... .680
two tied at........................ .643

EARNED RUN AVERAGE
Jimmy Key TOR 2.76
Frank Viola MIN 2.90
Roger Clemens BOS....... 2.97

STRIKEOUTS
Mark Langston SEA 262
Roger Clemens BOS........ 256
Ted Higuera MIL............... 240

SAVES
Tom Henke TOR 34
Jeff Reardon MIN 31
Dave Righetti NY................ 31

COMPLETE GAMES
Roger Clemens BOS.......... 18
Bruce Hurst BOS............... 15
Bret Saberhagen KC 15

SHUTOUTS
Roger Clemens BOS........... 7
Bret Saberhagen KC 4

GAMES PITCHED
Mark Eichhorn TOR 89
Mitch Williams TEX 85
Dale Mohorcic TEX 74

INNINGS PITCHED
Charlie Hough TEX 285
Roger Clemens BOS........ 282
Mark Langston SEA 272

1987 NL

EAST	W	L	PCT	GB	R	OR	BA	FA	ERA
● ST. LOUIS	95	67	.586	—	798	693	.263	.982	3.91
NEW YORK	92	70	.568	3	823	698	.268	.978	3.84
MONTREAL	91	71	.562	4	741	720	.265	.976	3.92
PHILADELPHIA	80	82	.494	15	702	749	.254	.980	4.18
PITTSBURGH	80	82	.494	15	723	744	.264	.980	4.20
CHICAGO	76	85	.472	18.5	720	801	.264	.979	4.55

WEST	W	L	PCT	GB	R	OR	BA	FA	ERA
SAN FRANCISCO	90	72	.556	—	783	669	.260	.980	3.68
CINCINNATI	84	78	.519	6	783	752	.266	.979	4.24
HOUSTON	76	86	.469	14	648	678	.253	.981	3.84
LOS ANGELES	73	89	.451	17	635	675	.252	.975	3.72
ATLANTA	69	92	.429	20.5	747	829	.258	.982	4.63
SAN DIEGO	65	97	.401	25	668	763	.260	.976	4.27
					8771	8771	.261	.979	4.08

BATTING AVERAGE
Tony Gwynn SD .... .370
Pedro Guerrero LA .... .338
Tim Raines MON .... .330

HITS
Tony Gwynn SD 218
Pedro Guerrero LA 184
Ozzie Smith STL 182

DOUBLES
Tim Wallach MON 42
Ozzie Smith STL 40
Andres Galarraga MON 40

TRIPLES
Juan Samuel PHI 15
Tony Gwynn SD 13
two tied at 11

HOME RUNS
Andre Dawson CHI 49
Dale Murphy ATL 44
Darryl Strawberry NY 39

RUNS BATTED IN
Andre Dawson CHI 137
Tim Wallach MON 123
Mike Schmidt PHI 113

SLUGGING AVERAGE
Jack Clark STL .... .597
Eric Davis CIN .... .593
Darryl Strawberry NY ...... .583

STOLEN BASES
Vince Coleman STL 109
Tony Gwynn SD 56
Billy Hatcher HOU 53

RUNS SCORED
Tim Raines MON 123
Vince Coleman STL 121
Eric Davis CIN 120

WINS
Rick Sutcliffe CHI 18
Shane Rawley PHI 17
two tied at 16

WINNING PERCENTAGE
Dwight Gooden NY .... .682
Rick Sutcliffe CHI .... .643
Bob Welch LA .... .625

EARNED RUN AVERAGE
Nolan Ryan HOU 2.76
Mike Dunne PIT 3.03
Orel Hershiser LA 3.06

STRIKEOUTS
Nolan Ryan HOU 270
Mike Scott HOU 233
Bob Welch LA 196

SAVES
Steve Bedrosian PHI 40
Lee Smith CHI 36
Todd Worrell STL 33

COMPLETE GAMES
Rick Reuschel PIT, SF 12
F. Valenzuela LA 12
Orel Hershiser LA 10

SHUTOUTS
Rick Reuschel PIT, SF 4
Bob Welch LA 4

GAMES PITCHED
Kent Tekulve PHI 90
Rob Murphy CIN 87
Frank Williams CIN 85

INNINGS PITCHED
Orel Hershiser LA 265
Bob Welch LA 252
F. Valenzuela LA 251

1988 AL

EAST	W	L	PCT	GB	R	OR	BA	FA	ERA
BOSTON	89	73	.549	—	813	689	.283	.984	3.97
DETROIT	88	74	.543	1	703	658	.250	.982	3.71
MILWAUKEE	87	75	.537	2	682	616	.257	.981	3.45
TORONTO	87	75	.537	2	763	680	.268	.982	3.80
NEW YORK	85	76	.528	3.5	772	748	.263	.978	4.26
CLEVELAND	78	84	.481	11	666	731	.261	.980	4.16
BALTIMORE	54	107	.335	34.5	550	789	.238	.980	4.54

WEST	W	L	PCT	GB	R	OR	BA	FA	ERA
● OAKLAND	104	58	.642	—	800	620	.263	.983	3.44
MINNESOTA	91	71	.562	13	759	672	.274	.986	3.93
KANSAS CITY	84	77	.522	19.5	704	648	.259	.980	3.65
CALIFORNIA	75	87	.463	29	714	771	.261	.979	4.32
CHICAGO	71	90	.441	32.5	631	757	.244	.976	4.12
TEXAS	70	91	.435	33.5	637	735	.252	.979	4.05
SEATTLE	68	93	.422	35.5	664	744	.257	.980	4.15
					9858	9858	.259	.981	3.97

BATTING AVERAGE
Wade Boggs BOS .... .366
Kirby Puckett MIN .... .356
Mike Greenwell BOS .... .325

HITS
Kirby Puckett MIN 234
Wade Boggs BOS 214
Mike Greenwell BOS 192

DOUBLES
Wade Boggs BOS 45
three tied at 42

TRIPLES
Willie Wilson KC 11
Harold Reynolds SEA 11
Robin Yount MIL 11

HOME RUNS
Jose Canseco OAK 42
Fred McGriff TOR 34
Mark McGwire OAK 32

RUNS BATTED IN
Jose Canseco OAK 124
Kirby Puckett MIN 121
Mike Greenwell BOS 119

SLUGGING AVERAGE
Jose Canseco OAK .... .569
Fred McGriff TOR .... .552
Gary Gaetti MIN .... .551

STOLEN BASES
Rickey Henderson NY 93
Gary Pettis DET 44
Paul Molitor MIL 41

RUNS SCORED
Wade Boggs BOS 128
Jose Canseco OAK 120
Rickey Henderson NY 118

WINS
Frank Viola MIN 24
Dave Stewart OAK 21
Mark Gubicza KC 20

WINNING PERCENTAGE
Frank Viola MIN .... .774
Bruce Hurst BOS .... .750
Mark Gubicza KC .... .714

EARNED RUN AVERAGE
Allan Anderson MIN 2.45
Ted Higuera MIL 2.45
Frank Viola MIN 2.64

STRIKEOUTS
Roger Clemens BOS 291
Mark Langston SEA 235
Frank Viola MIN 193

SAVES
Dennis Eckersley OAK 45
Jeff Reardon MIN 42
Doug Jones CLE 37

COMPLETE GAMES
Roger Clemens BOS 14
Dave Stewart OAK 14
Bobby Witt TEX 13

SHUTOUTS
Roger Clemens BOS 8
three tied at 4

GAMES PITCHED
Chuck Crim MIL 70
Bobby Thigpen CHI 68
Mitch Williams TEX 67

INNINGS PITCHED
Dave Stewart OAK 276
Mark Gubicza KC 270
Roger Clemens BOS 264

1988 NL

EAST	W	L	PCT	GB	R	OR	BA	FA	ERA
NEW YORK	100	60	.625	—	703	532	.256	.981	2.91
PITTSBURGH	85	75	.531	15	651	616	.247	.980	3.47
MONTREAL	81	81	.500	20	628	592	.251	.978	3.08
CHICAGO	77	85	.475	24	660	694	.261	.980	3.84
ST. LOUIS	76	86	.469	25	578	633	.249	.981	3.47
PHILADELPHIA	65	96	.404	35.5	597	734	.239	.976	4.14

WEST	W	L	PCT	GB	R	OR	BA	FA	ERA
★ LOS ANGELES	94	67	.584	—	628	544	.248	.977	2.96
CINCINNATI	87	74	.540	7	641	596	.246	.980	3.35
SAN DIEGO	83	78	.516	11	594	583	.247	.981	3.28
SAN FRANCISCO	83	79	.512	11.5	670	626	.248	.980	3.39
HOUSTON	82	80	.506	12.5	617	631	.244	.978	3.41
ATLANTA	54	106	.338	39.5	555	741	.242	.976	4.09
					7522	7522	.248	.979	3.45

BATTING AVERAGE
Tony Gwynn SD .... .313
Rafael Palmeiro CHI .... .307
Andre Dawson CHI .... .303

HITS
A. Galarraga MON 184
Andre Dawson CHI 179
Rafael Palmeiro CHI 178

DOUBLES
Andres Galarraga MON 42
Rafael Palmeiro CHI 41
Chris Sabo CIN 40

TRIPLES
Andy Van Slyke PIT 15
Vince Coleman STL 10
three tied at 9

HOME RUNS
Darryl Strawberry NY 39
Glenn Davis HOU 30
two tied at 29

RUNS BATTED IN
Will Clark SF 109
Darryl Strawberry NY 101
two tied at 100

SLUGGING AVERAGE
Darryl Strawberry NY ...... .545
A. Galarraga MON .... .540
Will Clark SF .... .508

STOLEN BASES
Vince Coleman STL 81
Gerald Young HOU 65
Ozzie Smith STL 57

RUNS SCORED
Brett Butler SF 109
Kirk Gibson LA 106
Will Clark SF 102

WINS
Orel Hershiser LA 23
Danny Jackson CIN 23
David Cone NY 20

WINNING PERCENTAGE
David Cone NY .... .870
Tom Browning CIN .... .783
two tied at .... .742

EARNED RUN AVERAGE
Joe Magrane STL 2.18
David Cone NY 2.22
Orel Hershiser LA 2.26

STRIKEOUTS
Nolan Ryan HOU 228
David Cone NY 213
Jose DeLeon STL 208

SAVES
John Franco CIN 39
Jim Gott PIT 34
Todd Worrell STL 32

COMPLETE GAMES
Orel Hershiser LA 15
Danny Jackson CIN 15
Eric Show SD 13

SHUTOUTS
Orel Hershiser LA 8
Tim Leary LA 6
Danny Jackson CIN 6

GAMES PITCHED
Rob Murphy CIN 76
Jeff Robinson PIT 75
Juan Agosto HOU 75

INNINGS PITCHED
Orel Hershiser LA 267
Danny Jackson CIN 261
Tom Browning CIN 251

1989 AL

EAST	W	L	PCT	GB	R	OR	BA	FA	ERA
TORONTO	89	73	.549	—	731	651	.260	.980	3.58
BALTIMORE	87	75	.537	2	708	686	.252	.986	4.00
BOSTON	83	79	.512	6	774	735	.277	.980	4.01
MILWAUKEE	81	81	.500	8	707	679	.259	.975	3.80
NEW YORK	74	87	.460	14.5	698	792	.269	.980	4.50
CLEVELAND	73	89	.451	16	604	654	.245	.981	3.65
DETROIT	59	103	.364	30	617	816	.242	.979	4.53

WEST	W	L	PCT	GB	R	OR	BA	FA	ERA
★ OAKLAND	99	63	.611	—	712	576	.261	.979	3.09
KANSAS CITY	92	70	.568	7	690	635	.261	.982	3.55
CALIFORNIA	91	71	.562	8	669	578	.256	.985	3.28
TEXAS	83	79	.512	16	695	714	.263	.978	3.91
MINNESOTA	80	82	.494	19	740	738	.276	.982	4.28
SEATTLE	73	89	.451	26	694	728	.257	.977	4.00
CHICAGO	69	92	.429	29.5	693	750	.271	.975	4.23
					9732	9732	.261	.980	3.88

BATTING AVERAGE
Kirby Puckett MIN .... .339
Carney Lansford OAK ..... .336
Wade Boggs BOS .... .330

HITS
Kirby Puckett MIN 215
Wade Boggs BOS 205
Steve Sax NY 205

DOUBLES
Wade Boggs BOS 51
Kirby Puckett MIN 45
Jody Reed BOS 42

TRIPLES
Ruben Sierra TEX 14
Devon White CAL 13
Phil Bradley BAL 10

HOME RUNS
Fred McGriff TOR 36
Joe Carter CLE 35
Mark McGwire OAK 33

RUNS BATTED IN
Ruben Sierra TEX 119
Don Mattingly NY 113
Nick Esasky BOS 108

SLUGGING AVERAGE
Ruben Sierra TEX .... .543
Fred McGriff TOR .... .525
Robin Yount MIL .... .511

STOLEN BASES
R. Henderson NY, OAK 77
Cecil Espy TEX 45
Devon White CAL 44

RUNS SCORED
R. Henderson NY, OAK 113
Wade Boggs BOS 113
two tied at 101

WINS
Bret Saberhagen KC 23
Dave Stewart OAK 21
two tied at 19

WINNING PERCENTAGE
Bret Saberhagen KC .... .793
Bert Blyleven CAL .... .773
Storm Davis OAK .... .731

EARNED RUN AVERAGE
Bret Saberhagen KC 2.16
Chuck Finley CAL 2.57
Mike Moore OAK 2.61

STRIKEOUTS
Nolan Ryan TEX 301
Roger Clemens BOS 230
Bret Saberhagen KC 193

SAVES
Jeff Russell TEX 38
Bobby Thigpen CHI 34
three tied at 33

COMPLETE GAMES
Bret Saberhagen KC 12
Jack Morris DET 10
Chuck Finley CAL 9

SHUTOUTS
Bert Blyleven CAL 5
Kirk McCaskill CAL 4
Bret Saberhagen KC 4

GAMES PITCHED
Chuck Crim MIL 76
Rob Murphy BOS 74
Kenny Rogers TEX 73

INNINGS PITCHED
Bret Saberhagen KC 262
Dave Stewart OAK 258
Mark Gubicza KC 255

1989 NL

EAST	W	L	PCT	GB	R	OR	BA	FA	ERA
CHICAGO	93	69	.574	—	702	623	.261	.980	3.43
NEW YORK	87	75	.537	6	683	595	.246	.976	3.29
ST. LOUIS	86	76	.531	7	632	608	.258	.982	3.36
MONTREAL	81	81	.500	12	632	630	.247	.979	3.48
PITTSBURGH	74	88	.457	19	637	680	.241	.975	3.64
PHILADELPHIA	67	95	.414	26	629	735	.243	.979	4.04

WEST	W	L	PCT	GB	R	OR	BA	FA	ERA
● SAN FRANCISCO	92	70	.568	—	699	600	.250	.982	3.30
SAN DIEGO	89	73	.549	3	642	626	.251	.976	3.38
HOUSTON	86	76	.531	6	647	669	.239	.977	3.64
LOS ANGELES	77	83	.481	14	554	536	.240	.981	2.95
CINCINNATI	75	87	.463	17	632	691	.247	.980	3.73
ATLANTA	63	97	.394	28	584	680	.234	.976	3.70
					7673	7673	.246	.978	3.49

BATTING AVERAGE
Tony Gwynn SD .... .336
Will Clark SF .... .333
Lonnie Smith ATL .... .315

HITS
Tony Gwynn SD 203
Will Clark SF 196
Roberto Alomar SD 184

DOUBLES
Pedro Guerrero STL.......... 42
Tim Wallach MON 42
Howard Johnson NY 41

TRIPLES
Robby Thompson SF 11
Bobby Bonilla PIT.............. 10
three tied at 9

HOME RUNS
Kevin Mitchell SF 47
Howard Johnson NY 36
two tied at.......................... 34

RUNS BATTED IN
Kevin Mitchell SF 125
Pedro Guerrero STL......... 117
Will Clark SF 111

SLUGGING AVERAGE
Kevin Mitchell SF .... .635
Howard Johnson NY .... .559
Will Clark SF .... .546

STOLEN BASES
Vince Coleman STL 65
Juan Samuel PHI, NY 42
Roberto Alomar SD 42

RUNS SCORED
Howard Johnson NY 104
Will Clark SF 104
Ryne Sandberg CHI 104

WINS
Mike Scott HOU 20
Greg Maddux CHI 19
two tied at......................... 18

WINNING PERCENTAGE
Mike Bielecki CHI .... .720
D. Martinez MON .... .696
Rick Reuschel SF............. .680

EARNED RUN AVERAGE
Scott Garrelts SF............. 2.28
Orel Hershiser LA............ 2.31
Mark Langston MON 2.39

STRIKEOUTS
Jose DeLeon STL 201
Tim Belcher LA................. 200
Sid Fernandez NY............ 198

SAVES
Mark Davis SD 44
Mitch Williams CHI 36
John Franco CIN................ 32

COMPLETE GAMES
Tim Belcher LA.................. 10
Bruce Hurst SD 10
three tied at 9

SHUTOUTS
Tim Belcher LA.................... 8
Doug Drabek PIT 5
three tied at 4

GAMES PITCHED
Mitch Williams CHI 76
Rob Dibble CIN 74
Jeff Parrett PHI................. 72

INNINGS PITCHED
Orel Hershiser LA............. 257
Tom Browning CIN 250
two tied at........................ 245

1990 AL

EAST	W	L	PCT	GB	R	OR	BA	FA	ERA
BOSTON	88	74	.543	—	699	664	.272	.980	3.72
TORONTO	86	76	.531	2	767	661	.265	.986	3.84
DETROIT	79	83	.488	9	750	754	.259	.979	4.39
CLEVELAND	77	85	.475	11	732	737	.267	.981	4.26
BALTIMORE	76	85	.472	11.5	669	698	.245	.985	4.04
MILWAUKEE	74	88	.457	14	732	760	.256	.976	4.08
NEW YORK	67	95	.414	21	603	749	.241	.980	4.21

WEST	W	L	PCT	GB	R	OR	BA	FA	ERA
● OAKLAND	103	59	.636	—	733	570	.254	.986	3.18
CHICAGO	94	68	.580	9	682	633	.258	.980	3.61
TEXAS	83	79	.512	20	676	696	.259	.979	3.83
CALIFORNIA	80	82	.494	23	690	706	.260	.978	3.79
SEATTLE	77	85	.475	26	640	680	.259	.979	3.69
KANSAS CITY	75	86	.466	27.5	707	709	.267	.980	3.93
MINNESOTA	74	88	.457	29	666	729	.265	.983	4.12
					9746	9746	.259	.981	3.91

BATTING AVERAGE
George Brett KC.............. .329
R. Henderson OAK .... .325
Rafael Palmeiro TEX....... .319

HITS
Rafael Palmeiro TEX........ 191
Wade Boggs BOS 187
Roberto Kelly NY............. 183

DOUBLES
George Brett KC................. 45
Jody Reed BOS 45
two tied at............................ 44

TRIPLES
Tony Fernandez TOR......... 17
Sammy Sosa CHI.............. 10
three tied at 9

HOME RUNS
Cecil Fielder DET 51
Mark McGwire OAK 39
Jose Canseco OAK............ 37

RUNS BATTED IN
Cecil Fielder DET 132
Kelly Gruber TOR............. 118
Mark McGwire OAK 108

SLUGGING AVERAGE
Cecil Fielder DET .... .592
R. Henderson OAK .... .577
Jose Canseco OAK.......... .543

STOLEN BASES
R. Henderson OAK 65
Steve Sax NY.................... 43
Roberto Kelly NY............... 42

RUNS SCORED
Rickey Henderson OAK ... 119
Cecil Fielder DET 104
Harold Reynolds SEA 100

WINS
Bob Welch OAK 27
Dave Stewart OAK 22
Roger Clemens BOS.......... 21

WINNING PERCENTAGE
Bob Welch OAK .... .818
Roger Clemens BOS........ .778
Dave Stieb TOR .... .750

EARNED RUN AVERAGE
Roger Clemens BOS 1.93
Chuck Finley CAL 2.40
Dave Stewart OAK 2.56

STRIKEOUTS
Nolan Ryan TEX 232
Bobby Witt TEX................ 221
Erik Hanson SEA............. 211

SAVES
Bobby Thigpen CHI............ 57
Dennis Eckersley OAK....... 48
Doug Jones CLE................ 43

COMPLETE GAMES
Jack Morris DET.................. 11
Dave Stewart OAK 11
five tied at............................. 7

SHUTOUTS
Roger Clemens BOS............ 4
Dave Stewart OAK............... 4
three tied at 3

GAMES PITCHED
Bobby Thigpen CHI............ 77
Jeff Montgomery KC 73
Duane Ward TOR............... 73

INNINGS PITCHED
Dave Stewart OAK 267
Jack Morris DET................ 250
Bob Welch OAK 238

1990 NL

EAST	W	L	PCT	GB	R	OR	BA	FA	ERA
PITTSBURGH	95	67	.586	—	733	619	.259	.979	3.40
NEW YORK	91	71	.562	4	775	613	.256	.978	3.42
MONTREAL	85	77	.525	10	662	598	.250	.982	3.37
CHICAGO	77	85	.475	18	690	774	.263	.980	4.34
PHILADELPHIA	77	85	.475	18	646	729	.255	.981	4.07
ST. LOUIS	70	92	.432	25	599	698	.256	.979	3.87

WEST	W	L	PCT	GB	R	OR	BA	FA	ERA
★ CINCINNATI	91	71	.562	—	693	597	.265	.983	3.39
LOS ANGELES	86	76	.531	5	728	685	.262	.979	3.72
SAN FRANCISCO	85	77	.525	6	719	710	.262	.983	4.08
HOUSTON	75	87	.463	16	573	656	.242	.978	3.61
SAN DIEGO	75	87	.463	16	673	673	.257	.977	3.68
ATLANTA	65	97	.401	26	682	821	.250	.974	4.58
					8173	8173	.256	.980	3.79

BATTING AVERAGE
Willie McGee STL .... .335
Eddie Murray LA .... .330
Dave Magadan NY.......... .328

HITS
Brett Butler SF................. 192
Lenny Dykstra PHI 192
Ryne Sandberg CHI 188

DOUBLES
Gregg Jefferies NY............ 40
Bobby Bonilla PIT.............. 39
Chris Sabo CIN 38

TRIPLES
Mariano Duncan CIN.......... 11
Tony Gwynn SD 10
three tied at 9

HOME RUNS
Ryne Sandberg CHI 40
Darryl Strawberry NY 37
Kevin Mitchell SF 35

RUNS BATTED IN
Matt Williams SF 122
Bobby Bonilla PIT............. 120
Joe Carter SD.................... 115

SLUGGING AVERAGE
Barry Bonds PIT............... .565
Ryne Sandberg CHI .... .559
Kevin Mitchell SF .... .544

STOLEN BASES
Vince Coleman STL 77
Eric Yelding HOU 64
Barry Bonds PIT................. 52

RUNS SCORED
Ryne Sandberg CHI 116
Bobby Bonilla PIT............. 112
Brett Butler SF................. 108

WINS
Doug Drabek PIT 22
Ramon Martinez LA 20
Frank Viola NY 20

WINNING PERCENTAGE
Doug Drabek PIT .... .786
Ramon Martinez LA .... .769
Dwight Gooden NY .... .731

EARNED RUN AVERAGE
Danny Darwin HOU......... 2.21
Zane Smith MON, PIT..... 2.55
Ed Whitson SD................. 2.60

STRIKEOUTS
David Cone NY 233
Dwight Gooden NY 223
Ramon Martinez LA 223

SAVES
John Franco NY 33
Randy Myers CIN.............. 31
Lee Smith STL 27

COMPLETE GAMES
Ramon Martinez LA 12
Doug Drabek PIT 9
Bruce Hurst SD 9

SHUTOUTS
Mike Morgan LA.................... 4
Bruce Hurst SD 4

GAMES PITCHED
Juan Agosto HOU 82
Paul Assenmacher CHI...... 74
Greg Harris SD................... 73

INNINGS PITCHED
Frank Viola NY 250
Greg Maddux CHI 237
Ramon Martinez LA 234

1991 AL

EAST	W	L	PCT	GB	R	OR	BA	FA	ERA
TORONTO	91	71	.562	—	684	622	.257	.980	3.50
BOSTON	84	78	.519	7	731	712	.269	.981	4.01
DETROIT	84	78	.519	7	817	794	.247	.983	4.51
MILWAUKEE	83	79	.512	8	799	744	.271	.981	4.14
NEW YORK	71	91	.438	20	674	777	.256	.979	4.42
BALTIMORE	67	95	.414	24	686	796	.254	.985	4.59
CLEVELAND	57	105	.352	34	576	759	.254	.976	4.23

WEST	W	L	PCT	GB	R	OR	BA	FA	ERA
★ MINNESOTA	95	67	.586	—	776	652	.280	.985	3.69
CHICAGO	87	75	.534	8	758	681	.262	.982	3.79
TEXAS	85	77	.525	10	829	814	.270	.979	4.47
OAKLAND	84	78	.519	11	760	776	.248	.982	4.57
SEATTLE	83	79	.512	12	702	674	.255	.983	3.79
KANSAS CITY	82	80	.506	13	727	722	.264	.980	3.92
CALIFORNIA	81	81	.500	14	653	649	.255	.984	3.69
					10172	10172	.260	.981	4.09

BATTING AVERAGE
Julio Franco TEX............. .341
Wade Boggs BOS .... .332
Willie Randolph MIL .... .327

HITS
Paul Molitor MIL 216
Cal Ripken BAL................. 210
two tied at........................ 203

DOUBLES
Rafael Palmeiro TEX........... 49
Cal Ripken BAL................... 46
Ruben Sierra TEX 44

TRIPLES
Lance Johnson CHI............. 13
Paul Molitor MIL 13
Roberto Alomar TOR.......... 11

HOME RUNS
Cecil Fielder DET 44
Jose Canseco OAK............. 44
Cal Ripken BAL.................. 34

RUNS BATTED IN
Cecil Fielder DET 133
Jose Canseco OAK 122
Ruben Sierra TEX 116

SLUGGING AVERAGE
Danny Tartabull KC .... .593
Cal Ripken BAL................ .566
Jose Canseco OAK......... .556

STOLEN BASES
Rickey Henderson OAK 58
Roberto Alomar TOR 53
Tim Raines CHI.................. 51

RUNS SCORED
Paul Molitor MIL 133
Jose Canseco OAK 115
Rafael Palmeiro TEX........ 115

WINS
Scott Erickson MIN............. 20
Bill Gullickson DET............. 20
Mark Langston CAL 19

WINNING PERCENTAGE
Scott Erickson MIN........ .714
Mark Langston CAL .... .704
Bill Gullickson DET.......... .690

EARNED RUN AVERAGE
Roger Clemens BOS...... 2.62
T. Candiotti CLE,TOR...... 2.65
Bill Wegman MIL 2.84

STRIKEOUTS
Roger Clemens BOS........ 241
Randy Johnson SEA 228
Nolan Ryan TEX 203

SAVES
Bryan Harvey CAL 46
Dennis Eckersley OAK....... 43
Rick Aguilera MIN 42

COMPLETE GAMES
Jack McDowell CHI 15
Roger Clemens BOS........... 13
two tied at........................... 10

SHUTOUTS
Roger Clemens BOS............. 4
four tied at 3

GAMES PITCHED
Duane Ward TOR................ 81
Mike Jackson SEA 72
Gregg Olson BAL................ 72

INNINGS PITCHED
Roger Clemens BOS........ 271
Jack McDowell CHI 254
Jack Morris MIN 247

1991 NL

EAST	W	L	PCT	GB	R	OR	BA	FA	ERA
PITTSBURGH	98	64	.605	—	768	632	.263	.981	3.44
ST. LOUIS	84	78	.519	14	651	648	.255	.982	3.69
PHILADELPHIA	78	84	.481	20	629	680	.241	.981	3.86
CHICAGO	77	83	.481	20	695	734	.253	.982	4.03
NEW YORK	77	84	.478	20.5	640	646	.244	.977	3.56
MONTREAL	71	90	.441	26.5	579	655	.246	.979	3.64

WEST	W	L	PCT	GB	R	OR	BA	FA	ERA
• ATLANTA	94	68	.580	—	749	644	.258	.978	3.49
LOS ANGELES	93	69	.574	1	665	565	.253	.980	3.06
SAN DIEGO	84	78	.519	10	636	646	.244	.982	3.57
SAN FRANCISCO	75	87	.463	19	649	697	.246	.982	4.03
CINCINNATI	74	88	.457	20	689	691	.258	.979	3.83
HOUSTON	65	97	.401	29	605	717	.244	.974	4.00
					7955	7955	.250	.980	3.68

BATTING AVERAGE
Terry Pendleton ATL........ .319
Hal Morris CIN................. .318
Tony Gwynn SD .... .317

HITS
Terry Pendleton ATL......... 187
Brett Butler LA................. 182
Chris Sabo CIN 175

DOUBLES
Bobby Bonilla PIT.............. 44
Felix Jose STL 40
two tied at.......................... 36

TRIPLES
Ray Lankford STL 15
Tony Gwynn SD................. 11
Steve Finley HOU 10

HOME RUNS
Howard Johnson NY 38
Matt Williams SF 34
Ron Gant ATL 32

RUNS BATTED IN
Howard Johnson NY 117
Barry Bonds PIT 116
Will Clark SF..................... 116

SLUGGING AVERAGE
Will Clark SF .... .536
Howard Johnson NY .... .535
Terry Pendleton ATL........ .517

STOLEN BASES
Marquis Grissom MON....... 76
Otis Nixon ATL 72
Delino DeShields MON 56

RUNS SCORED
Brett Butler LA 112
Howard Johnson NY 108
Ryne Sandberg CHI 104

WINS
John Smiley PIT 20
Tom Glavine ATL................ 20
Steve Avery ATL................. 18

WINNING PERCENTAGE
Jose Rijo CIN .... .714
John Smiley PIT .... .714
Steve Avery ATL.............. .692

EARNED RUN AVERAGE
Dennis Martinez MON..... 2.39
Jose Rijo CIN 2.51
Tom Glavine ATL.............. 2.55

STRIKEOUTS
David Cone NY 241
Greg Maddux CHI 198
Tom Glavine ATL.............. 192

SAVES
Lee Smith STL 47
Rob Dibble CIN 31
two tied at........................... 30

COMPLETE GAMES
Tom Glavine ATL.................. 9
Dennis Martinez MON.......... 9
Terry Mulholland PHI............ 8

SHUTOUTS
Dennis Martinez MON.......... 5
Ramon Martinez LA 4
three tied at 3

GAMES PITCHED
Barry Jones MON............... 77
Paul Assenmacher CHI...... 75
Mike Stanton ATL............... 74

INNINGS PITCHED
Greg Maddux CHI 263
Tom Glavine ATL.............. 247
Mike Morgan LA 236

1992 AL

EAST	W	L	PCT	GB	R	OR	BA	FA	ERA
★ TORONTO	96	66	.593	—	780	682	.263	.985	3.91
MILWAUKEE	92	70	.568	4	740	604	.268	.986	3.43
BALTIMORE	89	73	.549	7	705	656	.259	.985	3.79
CLEVELAND	76	86	.469	20	674	746	.266	.978	4.11
NEW YORK	76	86	.469	20	733	746	.261	.982	4.21
DETROIT	75	87	.463	21	791	794	.256	.981	4.60
BOSTON	73	89	.451	23	599	669	.246	.978	3.58

WEST	W	L	PCT	GB	R	OR	BA	FA	ERA
OAKLAND	96	66	.593	—	745	672	.258	.979	3.73
MINNESOTA	90	72	.556	6	747	653	.277	.985	3.70
CHICAGO	86	76	.531	10	738	690	.261	.979	3.82
TEXAS	77	85	.475	19	682	753	.250	.975	4.09
CALIFORNIA	72	90	.444	24	579	671	.243	.979	3.84
KANSAS CITY	72	90	.444	24	610	667	.256	.980	3.81
SEATTLE	64	98	.395	32	679	799	.263	.982	4.55
					9802	9802	.259	.981	3.94

BATTING AVERAGE
Edgar Martinez SEA........ .343
Kirby Puckett MIN .... .329
Frank Thomas CHI.......... .323

HITS
Kirby Puckett MIN 210
Carlos Baerga CLE 205
Paul Molitor MIL 195

DOUBLES
Edgar Martinez SEA........... 46
Frank Thomas CHI............. 46
two tied at 40

TRIPLES
Lance Johnson CHI............ 12
Mike Devereaux BAL.......... 11
Brady Anderson BAL.......... 10

HOME RUNS
Juan Gonzalez TEX 43
Mark McGwire OAK 42
Cecil Fielder DET 35

RUNS BATTED IN
Cecil Fielder DET 124
Joe Carter TOR 119
Frank Thomas CHI 115

SLUGGING AVERAGE
Mark McGwire OAK .... .585
Edgar Martinez SEA........ .544
Frank Thomas CHI.......... .536

STOLEN BASES
Kenny Lofton CLE.............. 66
Pat Listach MIL 54
Brady Anderson BAL.......... 53

RUNS SCORED
Tony Phillips DET 114
Frank Thomas CHI 108
Roberto Alomar TOR 105

WINS
Kevin Brown TEX 21
Jack Morris TOR 21
Jack McDowell CHI 20

WINNING PERCENTAGE
Mike Mussina BAL .... .783
Jack Morris TOR .... .778
Juan Guzman TOR .... .762

EARNED RUN AVERAGE
Roger Clemens BOS........ 2.41
Mike Appier KC............... 2.46
Mike Mussina BAL 2.54

STRIKEOUTS
Randy Johnson SEA........ 241
Melido Perez NY 218
Roger Clemens BOS........ 208

SAVES
Dennis Eckersley OAK....... 51
Rick Aguilera MIN 41
Jeff Montgomery KC 39

COMPLETE GAMES
Jack McDowell CHI 13
Roger Clemens BOS.......... 11
Kevin Brown TEX 11

SHUTOUTS
Roger Clemens BOS............ 5
Mike Mussina BAL 4
Dave Fleming SEA............... 4

GAMES PITCHED
Kevin Rogers TEX.............. 81
Duane Ward TOR 79
Steve Olin CLE 72

INNINGS PITCHED
Kevin Brown TEX 266
Bill Wegman MIL............... 262
Jack McDowell CHI.......... 261

1992 NL

EAST	W	L	PCT	GB	R	OR	BA	FA	ERA
PITTSBURGH	96	66	.593	—	693	595	.255	.984	3.35
MONTREAL	87	75	.537	9	648	581	.252	.980	3.25
ST. LOUIS	83	79	.512	13	631	604	.262	.985	3.38
CHICAGO	78	84	.481	18	593	624	.254	.982	3.39
NEW YORK	72	90	.444	24	599	653	.235	.981	3.66
PHILADELPHIA	70	92	.432	26	686	717	.253	.978	4.11

WEST	W	L	PCT	GB	R	OR	BA	FA	ERA
●ATLANTA	98	64	.605	—	682	569	.254	.982	3.14
CINCINNATI	90	72	.556	8	660	609	.260	.984	3.46
SAN DIEGO	82	80	.506	16	617	636	.255	.982	3.56
HOUSTON	81	81	.500	17	608	668	.246	.981	3.72
SAN FRANCISCO	72	90	.444	26	574	647	.244	.982	3.61
LOS ANGELES	63	99	.389	35	548	636	.248	.972	3.41
					7539	7539	.252	.981	3.50

BATTING AVERAGE
Gary Sheffield SD .... .330
Andy Van Slyke PIT .... .324
John Kruk PHI .... .323

HITS
Terry Pendleton ATL 199
Andy Van Slyke PIT 199
Ryne Sandberg CHI 186

DOUBLES
Andy Van Slyke PIT 45
three tied at 40

TRIPLES
Deion Sanders ATL 14
Steve Finley HOU 13
Andy Van Slyke PIT 12

HOME RUNS
Fred McGriff SD 35
Barry Bonds PIT 34
Gary Sheffield SD 33

RUNS BATTED IN
Darren Daulton PHI.......... 109
Terry Pendleton ATL........ 105
Fred McGriff SD 104

SLUGGING AVERAGE
Barry Bonds PIT............... .624
Gary Sheffield SD .... .580
Fred McGriff SD .... .556

STOLEN BASES
Marquis Grissom MON....... 78
Delino DeShields MON 46
two tied at........................... 44

RUNS SCORED
Barry Bonds PIT............... 109
Dave Hollins PHI.............. 104
Andy Van Slyke PIT 103

WINS
Greg Maddux CHI 20
Tom Glavine ATL............... 20
four tied at 16

WINNING PERCENTAGE
Bob Tewksbury STL .... .762
Tom Glavine ATL.............. .714
Charlie Liebrandt ATL ..... .682

EARNED RUN AVERAGE
Bill Swift SF 2.08
Bob Tewksbury STL 2.16
Greg Maddux CHI 2.18

STRIKEOUTS
John Smoltz ATL 215
David Cone NY 214
Greg Maddux CHI 199

SAVES
Lee Smith STL 43
Randy Myers SD 38
John Wetteland MON........ 37

COMPLETE GAMES
Terry Mulholland PHI......... 12
Doug Drabek PIT 10
Curt Schilling PHI.............. 10

SHUTOUTS
David Cone NY 5
Tom Glavine ATL................. 5

GAMES PITCHED
Joe Boever HOU 81
Doug Jones HOU 80
two tied at........................... 77

INNINGS PITCHED
Greg Maddux CHI 268
Doug Drabek PIT 257
John Smoltz ATL.............. 247

1993 AL

EAST	W	L	PCT	GB	R	OR	BA	FA	ERA
★ TORONTO	95	67	.586	—	847	742	.279	.982	4.21
NEW YORK	88	74	.543	7	821	761	.279	.983	4.35
BALTIMORE	85	77	.525	10	786	745	.267	.984	4.31
DETROIT	85	77	.525	10	899	837	.275	.979	4.65
BOSTON	80	82	.494	15	686	698	.264	.980	3.77
CLEVELAND	76	86	.469	19	790	813	.275	.976	4.58
MILWAUKEE	69	93	.426	26	733	792	.258	.979	4.45

WEST	W	L	PCT	GB	R	OR	BA	FA	ERA
CHICAGO	94	68	.580	—	776	664	.265	.982	3.70
TEXAS	86	76	.531	8	835	751	.267	.979	4.28
KANSAS CITY	84	78	.519	10	675	694	.263	.984	4.04
SEATTLE	82	80	.506	12	734	731	.260	.985	4.20
CALIFORNIA	71	91	.438	23	684	770	.260	.980	4.34
MINNESOTA	71	91	.438	23	693	830	.264	.984	4.71
OAKLAND	68	94	.420	26	715	846	.254	.982	4.90
					10674	10674	.267	.981	4.32

BATTING AVERAGE
John Olerud TOR .... .363
Paul Molitor TOR............ .332
Roberto Alomar TOR ...... .326

HITS
Paul Molitor TOR............ 211
Carlos Baerga CLE 200
John Olerud TOR 200

DOUBLES
John Olerud TOR 54
Devon White TOR 42
two tied at........................ 40

TRIPLES
Lance Johnson CHI............ 14
Joey Cora CHI.................... 13
David Hulse TEX................ 10

HOME RUNS
Juan Gonzalez TEX 46
Ken Griffey SEA 45
Frank Thomas CHI............ 41

RUNS BATTED IN
Albert Belle CLE.............. 129
Frank Thomas CHI.......... 128
Joe Carter TOR................ 121

SLUGGING AVERAGE
Juan Gonzalez TEX .... .632
Ken Griffey SEA .... .617
Frank Thomas CHI .... .607

STOLEN BASES
Kenny Lofton CLE 70
Roberto Alomar TOR 55
Luis Polonia CAL................ 55

RUNS SCORED
Rafael Palmeiro TEX........ 124
Paul Molitor TOR.............. 121
two tied at 116

WINS
Jack McDowell CHI 22
Randy Johnson SEA 19
Pat Hentgen TOR.............. 19

WINNING PERCENTAGE
Jimmy Key NY.................. .750
Randy Johnson SEA .... .704
Kevin Appier KC.............. .692

EARNED RUN AVERAGE
Kevin Appier KC.............. 2.56
Wilson Alvarez CHI 2.95
Jimmy Key NY.................. 3.00

STRIKEOUTS
Randy Johnson SEA 308
Mark Langston CAL 196
Juan Guzman TOR 194

SAVES
Jeff Montgomery KC 45
Duane Ward TOR.............. 45
Tom Henke TEX 40

COMPLETE GAMES
Chuck Finley CAL 13
Kevin Brown TEX.............. 12
two tied at........................... 10

SHUTOUTS
Jack McDowell CHI 4
three tied at 3

GAMES PITCHED
Greg Harris BOS 80
Scott Radinsky CHI 73
three tied at 71

INNINGS PITCHED
Cal Eldred MIL 258
Jack McDowell CHI 257
Mark Langston CAL 256

1993 NL

EAST	W	L	PCT	GB	R	OR	BA	FA	ERA
● PHILADELPHIA	97	65	.599	—	877	740	.274	.977	3.95
MONTREAL	94	68	.580	3	732	682	.257	.975	3.55
ST. LOUIS	87	75	.537	10	758	744	.272	.982	4.09
CHICAGO	84	78	.519	13	738	739	.270	.982	4.18
PITTSBURGH	75	87	.463	22	707	806	.267	.983	4.77
FLORIDA	64	98	.395	33	581	724	.248	.980	4.13
NEW YORK	59	103	.364	38	672	744	.248	.975	4.05

WEST	W	L	PCT	GB	R	OR	BA	FA	ERA
ATLANTA	104	58	.642	—	767	599	.262	.983	3.14
SAN FRANCISCO	103	59	.636	1	808	636	.276	.984	3.61
HOUSTON	85	77	.525	19	716	630	.267	.979	3.49
LOS ANGELES	81	81	.500	23	675	662	.261	.979	3.50
CINCINNATI	73	89	.451	31	722	785	.264	.980	4.51
COLORADO	67	95	.414	37	758	927	.273	.973	5.41
SAN DIEGO	61	101	.377	43	679	772	.252	.974	4.23
					10190	10190	.264	.978	4.04

BATTING AVERAGE
Andres Galarraga COL ... .370
Tony Gwynn SD .... .358
Gregg Jefferies STL .... .342

HITS
Lenny Dykstra PHI 194
Mark Grace CHI 193
Marquis Grissom MON..... 188

DOUBLES
Charlie Hayes COL 45
Lenny Dykstra PHI 44
Dante Bichette COL 43

TRIPLES
Steve Finley HOU 13
Brett Butler LA 10
two tied at 9

HOME RUNS
Barry Bonds SF................. 46
David Justice ATL 40
Matt Williams SF 38

RUNS BATTED IN
Barry Bonds SF............... 123
David Justice ATL 120
Ron Gant ATL................... 117

SLUGGING AVERAGE
Barry Bonds SF .... .677
Andres Galarraga COL ... .602
Matt Williams SF .... .561

STOLEN BASES
Chuck Carr FLA 58
Marquis Grissom MON...... 53
Otis Nixon ATL 47

RUNS SCORED
Lenny Dykstra PHI 143
Barry Bonds SF................ 129
Ron Gant ATL................... 113

WINS
Tom Glavine ATL................ 22
John Burkett SF 22
Billy Swift SF 21

WINNING PERCENTAGE
Mark Portugal HOU .... .818
Tommy Greene PHI.......... .800
Tom Glavine ATL.............. .786

EARNED RUN AVERAGE
Greg Maddux ATL 2.36
Jose Rijo CIN 2.48
Mark Portugal HOU 2.77

STRIKEOUTS
Jose Rijo CIN 227
John Smoltz ATL.............. 208
Greg Maddux ATL............ 197

SAVES
Randy Myers CHI.............. 53
Rod Beck SF 48
Bryan Harvey FLA............. 45

COMPLETE GAMES
Greg Maddux ATL 8
five tied at............................ 7

SHUTOUTS
Pete Harnisch HOU............. 4
Ramon Martinez LA 3

GAMES PITCHED
Mike Jackson SF................ 81
Rod Beck SF 76
David West PHI 76

INNINGS PITCHED
Greg Maddux ATL 267
Jose Rijo CIN 257
John Smoltz ATL............... 244

1994 AL

EAST	W	L	PCT	GB	R	OR	BA	FA	ERA
NEW YORK	70	43	.619	—	670	534	.290	.982	4.34
BALTIMORE	63	49	.563	6.5	589	497	.272	.986	4.31
TORONTO	55	60	.478	16	566	579	.269	.981	4.70
BOSTON	54	61	.470	17	552	621	.263	.981	4.93
DETROIT	53	62	.465	18	652	671	.265	.981	5.38

CENTRAL	W	L	PCT	GB	R	OR	BA	FA	ERA
CHICAGO	67	46	.593	—	633	498	.287	.981	3.96
CLEVELAND	66	47	.584	1	679	562	.290	.980	4.36
KANSAS CITY	64	51	.557	4	574	532	.269	.982	4.23
MINNESOTA	53	60	.469	14	594	688	.276	.982	5.68
MILWAUKEE	53	62	.461	15	547	586	.263	.981	4.62

WEST	W	L	PCT	GB	R	OR	BA	FA	ERA
TEXAS	52	62	.456	—	613	697	.280	.976	5.45
OAKLAND	51	63	.447	1	549	589	.260	.979	4.80
SEATTLE	49	63	.438	2	569	616	.269	.977	4.99
CALIFORNIA	47	68	.409	5.5	543	660	.264	.983	5.42
					8330	8330	.273	.981	4.80

BATTING AVERAGE
Paul O'Neill NY .... .359
Albert Belle CLE .... .357
Frank Thomas CHI .... .353

HITS
Kenny Lofton CLE 160
Paul Molitor TOR 155
Albert Belle CLE 147

DOUBLES
Chuck Knoblauch MIN 45
Albert Belle CLE 35
two tied at 34

TRIPLES
Lance Johnson CHI 14
Vince Coleman KC 12
Kenny Lofton CLE 9

HOME RUNS
Ken Griffey Jr. SEA 40
Frank Thomas CHI 38
Albert Belle CLE 36

RUNS BATTED IN
Kirby Puckett MIN 112
Joe Carter TOR 103
two tied at 101

SLUGGING AVERAGE
Frank Thomas CHI .... .729
Albert Belle CLE .... .714
Ken Griffey Jr. SEA .... .674

STOLEN BASES
Kenny Lofton CLE 60
Vince Coleman KC 50
Otis Nixon BOS 42

RUNS SCORED
Frank Thomas CHI 106
Kenny Lofton CLE 105
Ken Griffey Jr. SEA 94

WINS
Jimmy Key NY 17
David Cone KC 16
Mike Mussina BAL 16

WINNING PERCENTAGE
Jason Bere CHI .... .857
Jimmy Key NY .... .810
Mark Clark CLE .... .786

EARNED RUN AVERAGE
Steve Ontiveros OAK 2.65
Roger Clemens BOS 2.85
David Cone KC 2.94

STRIKEOUTS
Randy Johnson SEA 204
Roger Clemens BOS 168
Chuck Finley CAL 148

SAVES
Lee Smith BAL 33
Jeff Montgomery KC 27
Rick Aguilera MIN 23

COMPLETE GAMES
Randy Johnson SEA 9
Chuck Finley CAL 7
Dennis Martinez CLE 7

SHUTOUTS
Randy Johnson SEA 4
five tied at 3

GAMES PITCHED
Bob Wickman NY 53
Jose Mesa CLE 51
two tied at 50

INNINGS PITCHED
Chuck Finley CAL 183
Jack McDowell CHI 181
Cal Eldred MIL 179

1994 NL

EAST	W	L	PCT	GB	R	OR	BA	FA	ERA
MONTREAL	74	40	.649	—	585	454	.278	.979	3.56
ATLANTA	68	46	.596	6	542	448	.267	.982	3.57
NEW YORK	55	58	.487	18.5	506	526	.250	.980	4.13
PHILADELPHIA	54	61	.470	20.5	521	497	.262	.978	3.85
FLORIDA	51	64	.443	23.5	468	576	.266	.978	4.50

CENTRAL	W	L	PCT	GB	R	OR	BA	FA	ERA
CINCINNATI	66	48	.579	—	609	490	.286	.983	3.78
HOUSTON	66	49	.574	.5	602	503	.278	.983	3.97
PITTSBURGH	53	61	.465	13	466	580	.259	.980	4.64
ST. LOUIS	53	61	.465	13	535	621	.263	.982	5.14
CHICAGO	49	64	.434	16.5	500	549	.259	.982	4.47

WEST	W	L	PCT	GB	R	OR	BA	FA	ERA
LOS ANGELES	58	56	.509	—	532	509	.270	.980	4.17
SAN FRANCISCO	55	60	.478	3.5	504	500	.249	.985	3.99
COLORADO	53	64	.453	6.5	573	638	.274	.981	5.15
SAN DIEGO	47	70	.402	12.5	479	531	.275	.975	4.08
					7422	7422	.267	.980	4.21

BATTING AVERAGE
Tony Gwynn SD .... .394
Jeff Bagwell HOU .... .367
Moises Alou MON .... .339

HITS
Tony Gwynn SD 165
Jeff Bagwell HOU 147
Dante Bichette COL 147

DOUBLES
Craig Biggio HOU................44
Larry Walker MON...............44
two tied at...........................35

TRIPLES
Darren Lewis SF 9
Brett Butler LA......................9
three tied at 8

HOME RUNS
Matt Williams SF 43
Jeff Bagwell HOU 39
Barry Bonds SF...................37

RUNS BATTED IN
Jeff Bagwell HOU 116
Matt Williams SF 96
Dante Bichette COL 95

SLUGGING AVERAGE
Jeff Bagwell HOU............ .750
Kevin Mitchell CIN........... .681
Barry Bonds SF................ .647

STOLEN BASES
Craig Biggio HOU................39
Deion Sanders ATL, CIN......38
Marquis Grissom MON........36

RUNS SCORED
Jeff Bagwell HOU 104
Marquis Grissom MON........96
two tied at............................89

WINS
Ken Hill MON 16
Greg Maddux ATL 16
two tied at............................14

WINNING PERCENTAGE
Marvin Freeman COL...... .833
Bret Saberhagen NY .... .778
Ken Hill MON .... .762

EARNED RUN AVERAGE
Greg Maddux ATL 1.56
Bret Saberhagen NY 2.74
Doug Drabek HOU 2.84

STRIKEOUTS
Andy Benes SD.................189
Jose Rijo CIN 171
Greg Maddux ATL 156

SAVES
John Franco NY 30
Rod Beck SF 28
Doug Jones PHI 27

COMPLETE GAMES
Greg Maddux ATL...............10
Doug Drabek HOU 6
Tom Candiotti LA 5

SHUTOUTS
Ramon Martinez LA 3
Greg Maddux ATL 3
two tied at.............................2

GAMES PITCHED
Steve Reed COL 61
Mel Rojas MON...................58
Jose Bautista CHI 58

INNINGS PITCHED
Greg Maddux ATL 202
Danny Jackson PHI...........179
Bret Saberhagen NY 177

1995 AL

EAST	W	L	PCT	GB	R	OR	BA	FA	ERA
BOSTON	86	58	.597	—	791	698	.280	.978	4.39
NEW YORK	79	65	.549	7	749	688	.276	.986	4.56
BALTIMORE	71	73	.493	15	704	640	.262	.986	4.31
DETROIT	60	84	.417	26	654	844	.247	.981	5.49
TORONTO	56	88	.389	30	642	777	.260	.982	4.88

CENTRAL	W	L	PCT	GB	R	OR	BA	FA	ERA
● CLEVELAND	100	44	.694	—	840	607	.291	.982	3.83
KANSAS CITY	70	74	.486	30	629	691	.260	.984	4.49
CHICAGO	68	76	.472	32	755	758	.280	.980	4.85
MILWAUKEE	65	79	.451	35	740	747	.266	.981	4.82
MINNESOTA	56	88	.389	44	703	889	.279	.981	5.76

WEST	W	L	PCT	GB	R	OR	BA	FA	ERA
SEATTLE*	79	66	.545	—	796	708	.276	.980	4.50
CALIFORNIA	78	67	.538	1	801	697	.277	.982	4.52
TEXAS	74	70	.514	4.5	691	720	.265	.982	4.66
OAKLAND	67	77	.465	11.5	730	761	.264	.981	4.93
					10225	10225	.270	.982	4.71

*Defeated California in a 1-game playoff

BATTING AVERAGE
Edgar Martinez SEA......... .356
Chuck Knoblauch MIN .... .333
Tim Salmon CAL .... .330

HITS
Lance Johnson CHI.......... 186
Edgar Martinez SEA........182
Chuck Knoblauch MIN 179

DOUBLES
Albert Belle CLE..................52
Edgar Martinez SEA......... 52
Kirby Puckett MIN 39

TRIPLES
Kenny Lofton CLE.............. 13
Lance Johnson CHI........... 12
Brady Anderson BAL.......... 10

HOME RUNS
Albert Belle CLE................. 50
Jay Buhner SEA................. 40
Frank Thomas CHI............. 40

RUNS BATTED IN
Albert Belle CLE............... 126
Mo Vaughn BOS 126
Jay Buhner SEA................ 121

SLUGGING AVERAGE
Albert Belle CLE............... .690
Edgar Martinez SEA........ .628
Frank Thomas CHI.......... .606

STOLEN BASES
Kenny Lofton CLE.............. 54
Tom Goodwin KC 50
Otis Nixon TEX.................. 50

RUNS SCORED
Albert Belle CLE............... 121
Edgar Martinez SEA........ 121
Jim Edmonds CAL 120

WINS
Mike Mussina BAL 19
David Cone TOR, NY 18
Randy Johnson SEA 18

WINNING PERCENTAGE
Randy Johnson SEA .... .900
Erik Hanson BOS .... .737
two tied at......................... .727

EARNED RUN AVERAGE
Randy Johnson SEA 2.48
Tim Wakefield BOS 2.95
Dennis Martinez CLE 3.08

STRIKEOUTS
Randy Johnson SEA 294
Todd Stottlemyre OAK...... 205
Chuck Finley CAL 195

SAVES
Jose Mesa CLE................. 46
Lee Smith CAL.................. 37
two tied at.......................... 32

COMPLETE GAMES
Jack McDowell NY 8
Scott Erickson MIN, BAL..... 7
Mike Mussina BAL 7

SHUTOUTS
Mike Mussina BAL 4
Randy Johnson SEA 3
six tied at.............................2

GAMES PITCHED
Jesse Orosco BAL 65
Roger McDowell TEX........ 64
three tied at....................... 63

INNINGS PITCHED
David Cone TOR, NY 229
Mike Mussina BAL 222
Jack McDowell NY 218

1995 NL

EAST	W	L	PCT	GB	R	OR	BA	FA	ERA
★ ATLANTA	90	54	.625	—	645	540	.250	.982	3.44
NEW YORK	69	75	.479	21	657	618	.267	.979	3.88
PHILADELPHIA	69	75	.479	21	615	658	.262	.982	4.21
FLORIDA	67	76	.469	22.5	673	673	.262	.979	4.27
MONTREAL	66	78	.458	24	621	638	.259	.980	4.11

CENTRAL	W	L	PCT	GB	R	OR	BA	FA	ERA
CINCINNATI	85	59	.590	—	747	623	.270	.986	4.03
HOUSTON	76	68	.528	9	747	674	.275	.979	4.06
CHICAGO	73	71	.507	12	693	671	.265	.979	4.13
ST. LOUIS	62	81	.434	22.5	563	658	.247	.980	4.09
PITTSBURGH	58	86	.403	27	629	736	.259	.978	4.70

WEST	W	L	PCT	GB	R	OR	BA	FA	ERA
LOS ANGELES	78	66	.542	—	634	609	.264	.976	3.66
COLORADO	77	67	.535	1	785	783	.282	.981	4.97
SAN DIEGO	70	74	.486	8	668	672	.272	.980	4.13
SAN FRANCISCO	67	77	.465	11	652	776	.253	.980	4.86
					9329	9329	.263	.980	4.18

BATTING AVERAGE
Tony Gwynn SD .... .368
Mike Piazza LA .... .346
Dante Bichette COL .... .340

HITS
Dante Bichette COL 197
Tony Gwynn SD 197
Mark Grace CHI 180

DOUBLES
Mark Grace CHI 51
Dante Bichette COL 38
Brian McRae CHI 38

TRIPLES
Brett Butler NY, LA 9
Eric Young COL.................... 9
three tied at 8

HOME RUNS
Dante Bichette COL 40
Sammy Sosa CHI............... 36
Larry Walker COL............... 36

RUNS BATTED IN
Dante Bichette COL 128
Sammy Sosa CHI............. 119
Andres Galarraga COL 106

SLUGGING AVERAGE
Dante Bichette COL .... .620
Larry Walker COL............ .607
Mike Piazza LA .... .606

STOLEN BASES
Quilvio Veras FLA 56
Barry Larkin CIN................ 51
Delino DeShields LA 39

RUNS SCORED
Craig Biggio HOU............. 123
Barry Bonds SF................ 109
Steve Finley SD 104

WINS
Greg Maddux ATL 19
Pete Schourek CIN 18
Ramon Martinez LA 17

WINNING PERCENTAGE
Greg Maddux ATL .... .905
Pete Schourek CIN .... .720
Ramon Martinez LA .... .708

EARNED RUN AVERAGE
Greg Maddux ATL 1.63
Hideo Nomo LA................ 2.54
Andy Ashby SD 2.94

STRIKEOUTS
Hideo Nomo LA................ 236
John Smoltz ATL.............. 193
Greg Maddux ATL............ 181

SAVES
Randy Myers CHI.............. 38
Tom Henke STL 36
Rod Beck SF 33

COMPLETE GAMES
Greg Maddux ATL 10
Mark Leiter SF.................... 7
Ismael Valdes LA 6

SHUTOUTS
Greg Maddux ATL 3
Hideo Nomo LA.................... 3

GAMES PITCHED
Curt Leskanic COL............. 76
David Veres HOU............... 72
Steve Reed COL................ 71

INNINGS PITCHED
Greg Maddux ATL 210
Denny Neagle PIT............ 210
Ramon Martinez LA 206

1996 AL

EAST	W	L	PCT	GB	R	OR	BA	FA	ERA
★ NEW YORK	92	70	.568	—	871	787	.288	.985	4.65
BALTIMORE	88	74	.543	4	949	903	.274	.984	5.14
BOSTON	85	77	.525	7	928	921	.283	.978	4.98
TORONTO	74	88	.457	18	928	809	.259	.982	4.57
DETROIT	53	109	.327	39	783	1103	.256	.978	5.30

CENTRAL	W	L	PCT	GB	R	OR	BA	FA	ERA
CLEVELAND	99	62	.615	—	952	769	.293	.980	4.34
CHICAGO	85	77	.525	14.5	898	794	.281	.982	4.52
MILWAUKEE	80	82	.494	19.5	894	899	.279	.978	5.14
MINNESOTA	78	84	.481	21.5	877	900	.288	.984	5.28
KANSAS CITY	75	86	.466	24	746	786	.267	.982	4.55

WEST	W	L	PCT	GB	R	OR	BA	FA	ERA
TEXAS	90	72	.556	—	928	799	.284	.986	4.65
SEATTLE	85	76	.528	4	993	895	.287	.981	5.21
OAKLAND	78	84	.485	12	861	900	.265	.984	5.20
CALIFORNIA	70	91	.435	19.5	762	943	.276	.979	5.30

BATTING AVERAGE
Alex Rodriguez SEA .358
Frank Thomas CHI .349
Paul Molitor MIN .341

HITS
Paul Molitor MIN 225
Alex Rodriguez SEA 215
Kenny Lofton CLE 210

DOUBLES
Alex Rodriguez SEA 54
Edgar Martinez SEA 52
Ivan Rodriguez TEX 47

TRIPLES
Chuck Knoblauch MIN 14
Fernando Vina MIL 10

HOME RUNS
Mark McGwire OAK 52
Brady Anderson BAL 50
Ken Griffey Jr. SEA 49

RUNS BATTED IN
Albert Belle CLE 148
Juan Gonzalez TEX 144
Mo Vaughn BOS 143

SLUGGING AVERAGE
Mark McGwire OAK .730
Juan Gonzalez TEX .643
Brady Anderson BAL .637

STOLEN BASES
Kenny Lofton CLE 75
Tom Goodwin KC 66
Otis Nixon TOR 54

RUNS SCORED
Alex Rodriguez SEA 141
Chuck Knoblauch MIN 140
Roberto Alomar BAL 132

WINS
Andy Pettitte NY 21
Pat Hentgen TOR 20
Mike Mussina BAL 19

WINNING PERCENTAGE
Charles Nagy CLE .773
Andy Pettitte NY .724
Pat Hentgen TOR .667

EARNED RUN AVERAGE
Juan Guzman TOR 2.93
Pat Hentgen TOR 3.22
Charles Nagy CLE 3.41

STRIKEOUTS
Roger Clemens BOS 257
Chuck Finley CAL 215
Kevin Appier KC 207

SAVES
John Wetteland NY 43
Jose Mesa CLE 39
Roberto Hernandez CHI 38

COMPLETE GAMES
Pat Hentgen TOR 10
Ken Hill TEX 7
Roger Pavlik TEX 7

SHUTOUTS
Pat Hentgen TOR 3
Ken Hill TEX 3
Rich Robertson MIN 3

GAMES PITCHED
Eddie Guardado MIN 83
Mike Myers DET 83
Mike Stanton BOS/TEX 81

INNINGS PITCHED
Pat Hentgen TOR 265.2
Alex Fernandez CHI 258.0
Ken Hill TEX 250.2

1996 NL

EAST	W	L	PCT	GB	R	OR	BA	FA	ERA
● ATLANTA	96	66	.593	—	773	648	.270	.980	3.52
MONTREAL	88	74	.543	8	741	668	.262	.980	3.78
FLORIDA	80	82	.494	16	688	703	.257	.982	3.95
NEW YORK	71	91	.438	25	746	779	.270	.974	4.22
PHILADELPHIA	67	95	.414	29	650	790	.256	.981	4.48

CENTRAL	W	L	PCT	GB	R	OR	BA	FA	ERA
ST. LOUIS	88	74	.543	—	759	706	.267	.980	3.97
HOUSTON	82	80	.506	6	753	792	.262	.978	4.37
CINCINNATI	81	81	.500	7	778	773	.256	.980	4.32
CHICAGO	76	86	.469	12	772	771	.251	.983	4.36
PITTSBURGH	73	89	.451	15	776	833	.266	.980	4.61

WEST	W	L	PCT	GB	R	OR	BA	FA	ERA
SAN DIEGO	91	71	.562	—	771	682	.265	.981	3.72
LOS ANGELES	90	72	.556	1	703	652	.252	.980	3.46
COLORADO	83	79	.512	8	961	964	.287	.976	5.59
SAN FRANCISCO	68	94	.420	23	752	862	.253	.978	4.71

BATTING AVERAGE
Tony Gwynn SD .... .353
Ellis Burks COL .... .344
Mike Piazza LA .... .336

HITS
Lance Johnson NY 227
Ellis Burks COL 211
Marquis Grissom ATL....... 207

DOUBLES
Jeff Bagwell HOU 48
Ellis Burks COL 45
Steve Finley SD 45

TRIPLES
Lance Johnson NY............. 21
Marquis Grissom ATL......... 10

HOME RUNS
Andres Galarraga COL 47
Barry Bonds SF.................. 42
Gary Sheffield FLA............. 42

RUNS BATTED IN
Andres Galarraga COL 150
Dante Bichette COL 141
Ken Caminiti SD............... 130

SLUGGING AVERAGE
Ellis Burks COL .... .639
Gary Sheffield FLA.......... .624
Ken Caminiti SD............... .621

STOLEN BASES
Eric Young COL.................. 53
Lance Johnson NY............. 50
Delino DeShields LA 48

RUNS SCORED
Ellis Burks COL................ 142
Steve Finley SD 126
Barry Bonds SF................ 122

WINS
John Smoltz ATL 24
Andy Benes StL 18
two tied at........................... 17

WINNING PERCENTAGE
John Smoltz ATL .... .750
Andy Benes StL .... .643
Denny Neagle PIT, ATL... .640

EARNED RUN AVERAGE
Kevin Brown FLA 1.89
Greg Maddux ATL 2.72
Al Leiter FLA 2.93

STRIKEOUTS
John Smoltz ATL.............. 276
Hideo Nomo LA................ 234
Jeff Fassero MTL 222

SAVES
Jeff Brantley CIN 44
Todd Worrell LA................. 44
Trevor Hoffman SD 42

COMPLETE GAMES
Curt Schilling PHI................. 8
John Smoltz ATL 6
Kevin Brown FLA 5

SHUTOUTS
Kevin Brown FLA 3
three tied at 2

GAMES PITCHED
Brad Clontz ATL................. 81
Bob Patterson CHI 79
two tied at........................... 78

INNINGS PITCHED
John Smoltz ATL 253.2
Greg Maddux ATL 245
Shane Reynolds HOU...... 239

AL MOST VALUABLE PLAYER VOTING

PLAYER	1st	2nd	3rd	Tot
Juan Gonzalez TEX	11	7	5	290
Alex Rodriguez SEA	10	10	4	287
Albert Belle CLE	2	8	10	228
Ken Griffey Jr. SEA	4	1	2	188
Mo Vaughn BOS	0	1	3	184
Rafael Palmeiro BAL	0	0	2	104
Mark McGwire OAK	0	0	2	100
Frank Thomas CHI	0	0	0	88
Brady Anderson BAL	0	0	0	53
Ivan Rodriguez TEX	1	0	0	52
Kenny Lofton CLE	0	0	0	34
Mariano Rivera NY	0	1	0	27
Paul Molitor MIN	0	0	0	19
Andy Pettitte NY	0	0	0	11
Jim Thome CLE	0	0	0	9
Chuck Knoblauch MIN	0	0	0	8
Jay Buhner SEA	0	0	0	6
Bernie Williams NY	0	0	0	6
John Wetteland NY	0	0	0	4
Roberto Alomar BAL	0	0	0	3
Terry Steinbach OAK	0	0	0	1

AL CY YOUNG AWARD VOTING

PLAYER	1st	2nd	3rd	Tot
Pat Hentgen TOR	16	9	3	110
Andy Pettitte NY	11	16	1	104
Mariano Rivera NY	1	1	10	18
Charles Nagy CLE	0	1	9	12
Mike Mussina BAL	0	1	2	5
Alex Fernandez CHI	0	0	1	1
Roberto Hernandez CHI	0	0	1	1
Ken Hill TEX	0	0	1	1

AL ROOKIE OF THE YEAR VOTING

PLAYER	1st	2nd	3rd	Tot
Derek Jeter NY	28	0	0	140
James Baldwin CHI	0	19	7	64
Tony Clark DET	0	6	12	30
Rocky Coppinger BAL	0	1	3	6
Jose Rosado KC	0	1	3	6
Darin Erstad CAL	0	1	0	3
Tony Batista OAK	0	0	1	1
Tim Crabtree TOR	0	0	1	1
Jeff D'Amico MIL	0	0	1	1

NL MOST VALUABLE PLAYER VOTING

PLAYER	1st	2nd	3rd	Tot
Ken Caminiti SD	28	0	0	392
Mike Piazza LA	0	18	7	237
Ellis Burks COL	0	5	4	186
Chipper Jones ATL	0	2	7	158
Barry Bonds SF	0	0	4	132
Andres Galarraga COL	0	1	2	112
Gary Sheffield FLA	0	1	2	112
Brian Jordan STL	0	1	1	69
Jeff Bagwell HOU	0	0	0	59
Steve Finley SD	0	0	0	38
John Smoltz ATL	0	0	0	33
Barry Larkin CIN	0	0	0	29
Marquis Grissom ATL	0	0	0	23
Bernard Gilkey NY	0	0	0	13
Sammy Sosa CHI	0	0	0	12
Eric Karros LA	0	0	0	10
Henry Rodriguez MON	0	0	0	9
Todd Hundley NY	0	0	0	7
Lance Johnson NY	0	0	0	7
Dante Bichette COL	0	0	0	6
Todd Worrell LA	0	0	0	3
Kevin Brown FLA	0	0	0	2
Trevor Hoffman SD	0	0	0	2
Moises Alou MON	0	0	0	1

NL CY YOUNG AWARD VOTING

PLAYER	1st	2nd	3rd	Tot
John Smoltz ATL	26	2	0	136
Kevin Brown FLA	2	26	0	88
Andy Benes STL	0	0	9	9
Hideo Nomo LA	0	0	5	5
Trevor Hoffman SD	0	0	3	3
Greg Maddux ATL	0	0	3	3
Todd Worrell LA	0	0	3	3
Denny Neagle PIT, ATL	0	0	2	2
Jeff Fassero MON	0	0	1	1
Al Leiter FLA	0	0	1	1
Shane Reynolds HOU	0	0	1	1

NL ROOKIE OF THE YEAR VOTING

PLAYER	1st	2nd	3rd	Tot
Todd Hollandsworth LA	15	9	3	105
Edgar Rentaria FLA	10	10	4	84
Jason Kendall PIT	1	5	10	30
F.P. Santangelo MON	1	2	4	15
Rey Ordonez NY	1	0	2	7
Jermaine Dye ATL	0	2	0	6
Alan Benes STL	0	0	5	5